An encyclopaedia of London

London, that great sea, whose ebb and flow
At once is deaf and loud, and on the shore
Vomits its wrecks, and still howls on for more,
Yet in its depth what treasures!

SHELLEY

No person can be said to know London. The most that any one can claim is that he knows something of it.

OLIVER WENDELL HOLMES

Books by William Kent

London for Everyman

London Worthies

The Lost Treasures of London

My Lord Mayor

Mine Host London

London for the Literary Pilgrim

London for Americans

London for the Curious

Walks in London

The Testament of a Victorian Youth: An Autobiography

Lift Up Your Heads: An Anthology for Freethinkers

John Burns: Labour's Lost Leader

etc.

An encyclopaedia of London

Edited by William Kent F S A

Revised by Godfrey Thompson

illustrated with 32 pages of photographs

J. M. Dent & Sons Limited

Printed in Great Britain at
Lowe & Brydone *Printers* Limited London
for J. M. Dent & Sons Limited
Aldine House Bedford Street London
First published 1937
Revised and reset 1951
Revised 1970

SBN: 460 03837 0

PREFACE

The great demand for the 1937 and 1951 editions of this book have forced on the publishers the production of a new edition. That the face of London changed between 1937 and 1951 is obvious, but the changes since then have been almost as great. Wartime bombing was of course the chief catalyst but when the last edition of this book was compiled, many hundreds of ruins were still standing. Now they have been restored, cleared away, posted overseas or otherwise altered, so that whole streets have sometimes disappeared. Change on a vast scale is still going on but though much is taken, much abides and a new guide to it all, old and new, is needed.

This does not pretend to be a complete guide to all London. Such a book does not exist, nor will it ever exist: the subject is too large. Suburbs extend interminably, but many had in the past a life of their own and made their contribution to the story. The problem, as always, is where to draw the line.

If there is a single theme to this book it is that of leading the reader from the existing London scene to the roots from which it sprang; many of the roots are still to be seen by those who have the zeal to search amid the bustle of the great modern city.

This is still William Kent's *Encyclopaedia of London* – not mine. He built up this great accumulation of facts and opinions, and their authority lies, not in a multitude of bibliographical references, but in the years of devotion which he gave to the history of London.

GODFREY THOMPSON.

READING LIST

No complete bibliography of London exists: such a vast undertaking may never be attempted. The nearest approach to it is the London Subject Catalogue of Guildhall Library. A useful classified select bibliography of London is to be found in *The Geography of Greater London* edited by R. Clayton, 1964.

Throughout this book, at the end of the appropriate article, reference is made to a book or two on the subject. The list below is only of books readily available for the beginner who would like to know a little more about the greatest of all cities.

Banks, F. R., *Penguin Guide to London*, 4th edn, 1968.

Clunn, Harold, *The Face of London*, 1932; revised edn, 1951.

Eades, George Edward, *Historic London*, 1966.

Hayes, John, *London from the earliest times to the present day*, 1959.

Hobson, Oscar, *How the City works*, 8th edn, 1966.

Corporation of London, *The Living City*, 1968 (mainly illustrations).

Pevsner, Nikolaus, *The Buildings of England: London*, 2 vols, 1952, 1962.

Trent, Christopher, *Greater London*, 1965.

No list of this kind could omit two indispensable works, both long out of print:

Harben, Henry A., *A Dictionary of London*, 1918 (confined to the City).

Wheatley, H. B., *London past and present . . . based upon the 'Handbook of London' by Peter Cunningham*, 1891.

NOTE

THE NAME OF LONDON. *William Maitland, in the second edition of his* London *(1756), advanced the theory that the name was 'a Gaelic compound; "Lon," the first syllable thereof, being a plain; and "Dun" or "Don," the second syllable, the eminence or hill.' Maitland added: 'than which no denomination could better suit London: for the Lon or Plain anciently lay along the Northern side of the River Thames; and the Dun or Hill adjoining to it on the North was by the Anglo-Saxons called Cornhill. Thomas Pennant in the second edition of his* London *(1793) acknowledged indebtedness to William Owen of Barmouth for the suggestion he adopted that the same was derived from Celtic "Llyn Din" or the "City on the Lake." This latter derivation held sway until the 20th century. W. J. Loftie wrote (1883): "The derivation of Londinium from 'Lyn-din,' the lake fort, seems to agree best with the situation and the history," and he quoted in support a "distinguished antiquary," T. G. Godfrey Faussett, of Canterbury. Sir Walter Besant followed in Loftie's train. The late Dr. Henry Bradley, the eminent philologist, declined to do so. He considered that the Roman "Londinium" represents a Celtic "Londinion," and might be derived from a Celtic personal name "Londinos." Dr. Bradley concluded that it was "unwise to go beyond the statement that London was a Celtic place-name." '*

ILLUSTRATIONS

King's Bench Walk
St Paul's from Waterloo Bridge

Photographs copyright The British Travel Association

ABBREVIATIONS

Abp., *Archbishop*
Abp. of C., *Archbishop of Canterbury*
B., *Bridge*
b., *born*
B.C., *Borough Council*
bd., *buried*
bdg., *building*
B.Mus., *British Museum*
bor., *borough*
Bp., *Bishop*
c. (*circa*), about
C.C., *City Corporation*
Ch., *Church*
Chyd., *Churchyard*
Co., *Company*
Coll., *College*
d., *died*
D., *Duke*
E., *Earl*
G.F., *Great Fire* (1666)
G.L.C.,*Greater London Council*
G.Mus., *Guildhall Museum*
Govt., *Government*
H.C., *House of Commons*
Hosp., *Hospital*
K., *King*

L., *London*
L.B., *London Bridge*
L.C.C., *London County Council*
Ld., *Lord*
Ld.M., *Lord Mayor*[1]
L.Mus., *London Museum*
m., *married*
M.B.W., *Metropolitan Board of Works*
Met., *Metropolitan*
Mus., *Museum*
N.G., *National Gallery*
N.P.G., *National Portrait Gallery*
P., *Prince*
p.a., *per annum*
par., *parish*
Q., *Queen*
Sch., *School*
Soc., *Society*
St. P.'s Cath., *St. Paul's Cathedral*
T.L., *Tower of London*
V. & A. Mus., *Victoria and Albert Museum*
W.A., *Westminster Abbey*

[1] The chief magistrate of London was not entitled 'Lord' Mayor in medieval times. The title, however, has never been conferred, and the date of adoption is uncertain (see p. 165). To avoid confusion the same abbreviation is used throughout.

A

Adelphi is the Latinized form of the Greek word for brothers, commemorating the brothers Robert and James Adam, Scottish architects, who were the originators of the building scheme which extended from a point a few yards S. of the Strand down to York House Water Gate, now in the Victoria Embankment Gardens. It consisted 'of a number of small low-lying houses, coal-sheds, and laystalls.' The property was then in possession of the D. of St. Albans, from whom the brothers Adam obtained a 99-years lease dating from 1768. Before the construction of the Victoria Embankment the river came up to the water gate referred to, and, to overcome the difficulty of the muddy foundations, immense arched vaults were constructed. These Adelphi arches, until 1936, could be traversed from Robert St. to Adam St. The youthful Dickens found them very attractive, and later wrote of them as a place where you 'might easily be murdered with the placid reputation of having merely gone down to the seaside.' When they were completed it was expected that the Govt. would take over the arches for the purposes of the Ordnance Dept. They were, however, found to be subject to inundation at high tide, and the proposal was not entertained. This involved the brothers Adam in considerable loss. In 1848 a battery of guns was placed here in preparation for the expected Chartist riots.

The Adams brothers were beset by difficulty. They managed to raise £140,000—half by means of mortgages on the buildings—but this would not suffice. Fanny Burney wrote: 'The undertaking was, I believe, too great for them, and they have suffered much in their fortunes. I cannot but wonder that so noble and elegant a plan should fail of encouragement.' (Miss Burney had met Robt. and Jas. Adam in 1770, and described the latter as a 'well behaved good sort of young man.') David Garrick took the centre house on the Royal Adelphi Terrace, as it was first called, and there Fanny Burney visited him in 1772. Garrick's last days were spent in this house. From it he went on 10th June 1776 to make his last appearance at Drury Lane Theatre as Don Felix in Mrs. Centlivre's comedy, *The Wonder! a Woman keeps a Secret.* In the same year Hannah More took up her residence with the Garricks.

Here Garrick d. in 1779. In 1781 Johnson dined in the house with Mrs. Garrick, Jas. Boswell, Dr. Burney, Sir Joshua Reynolds, and Hannah More. Mrs. Garrick lived on in her husband's house until 1822, when she died in her ninety-ninth year.

At 8 Adelphi Terrace Thos. Hardy studied architecture under (Sir) Arthur Blomfield.

The Savage Club was here until 1936; it is now at Covent Garden.

At 10 Adelphi Terrace, Bernard Shaw lived from 1896 (the yr. of his marriage) to 1927. Here also the L. Sch. of Economics, which originated at 9 John St., found a home. Miss Charlotte Payne-Townshend, who became Mrs. Shaw, took the two top floors, and thereby rendered financial assistance. Sir Jas. Barrie lived opposite, and when he had a visitor he wanted Shaw to see he used to throw a missile across to the other's window, and vice versa. In some versions this was a biscuit, and in others a cherry stone.

In 1936 Adelphi Terrace was demolished, and there were sold by auction ceilings painted by Angelica Kauffmann (one of the thirty-six foundation members of the Royal Academy) and Cipriani, and mantelpieces designed by the Adam brothers.

The new Adelphi bdg. was opened on 31st Oct. 1938. It comprises 323,550 sq. ft. of floor space, covering twelve floors.

Adam St. remains, with houses of the Adam design, and in their original condition for the most part, whereas those on the Terrace had been considerably altered: the latter had also once small iron balconies. At No. 1 *Hood's Magazine* was published in 1844 by Thos. Hood. Vicesimus Knox, the compiler of *Elegant Extracts*, lived in this house for a time, as also for about twenty yrs. did Geo. Blamire, an eccentric hermit barrister mentioned in Timbs's *Curiosities of London*. The now demolished Adelphi Hotel, at the corner of Adam St. and John St., was originally the Adelphi New Tavern and Coffee House. There Gibbon stayed in 1787, when he arrived from Lausanne with the concluding volumes of *The Decline and Fall of the Roman Empire*. Isaac D'Israeli was a resident on his return from his wedding tour in 1802. The poet Geo. Crabbe and his wife were there on their visit to L. in 1813. The rooms they occupied were in 1824 those of King Kamahame and his wife who inspired the popular song, *King of the Cannibal Islands*. The Q. d. there of measles in 1823, the K. a few days later at the Caledonian Hotel in Robert St. In 1827 Thos. Rowlandson the caricaturist (commemorated by a plaque), d. in the Adelphi Hotel. As 'Osborne's Hotel' it figures in one of the later chapters of *Pickwick Papers*. A bridge over Durham House St. was erected in 1799 under a special Act of Parliament by Thos. Coutts, the banker, to connect the bank with his private apartments. Only the supports now remain. In 1904, when the bank moved to the N. side of the Strand—an underground passage was used for the removal of their valuables—the Solicitor's Dept. of the L.C.C. was established in the premises, and used the room over the arch until they removed to the new County Hall in 1922.

John St. is now John Adam St. Both names are inappropriate. John Adam had nothing to do with the bdg. of the Adelphi and it is doubtful if he ever came to L. In 1951 in Robert St. there was placed a L.C.C. plaque commemorating Robert Adam, Thos. Hood, John Galsworthy and Sir James Barrie.

(See *The Literary History of the Adelphi and its Neighbourhood*, by Austin Brereton, 1907, and *The Adelphi*, by Chas. Pendrill, 1934.)

Airports. There are four airports serving L., three of them being the responsibility of the British Airports Authority. The fourth, the Westland Heliport, is privately operated. The traffic carried during 1966 was:

	Aircraft movements	Total passengers handled
London Airport (Heathrow)	224,083	11,955,999
London Airport (Gatwick) .	65,248	1,631,369
Stansted	28,314	8,769
Westland Heliport . .	2,767	1,505
Total . . .	320,412	13,597,642

Albert Hall. This is the short title of what was designed as The Royal Albert Hall of Arts and Sciences and was the result of one of many conceptions of the P. Consort. It is immediately S. of the Albert Memorial, and is on the site of Gore House, of the Countess of Blessington and Count D'Orsay. The foundation stone was laid by Q. Victoria in 1867; it was opened in 1871. It was designed by Capt. Fowke and Major-General Scott, and is in the form of a gigantic ellipse covered by a dome; the external walls are decorated by a frieze. It is 200 ft. in length, 160 ft. in width, and 140 ft. in height. The organ, by Willis, is one of the most powerful in the world with nearly 9,000 pipes. The hall will seat 6,036, and in addition there is standing room for a thousand. The seats are in tiers, and the cost of the bdg., about £200,000, was defrayed by selling the boxes in the first tier, seating ten persons, for £1,000 each, and those in the second tier, seating five persons, for £500 each. This explains why, with other parts of the hall uncomfortably full, these boxes and stalls are sometimes empty.

(See *The Royal Albert Hall*, by R. W. Clark, 1958.)

Aldersgate in its earliest form is 'Ealdredesgate' (10th and 11th centuries). In the 12th century it was 'Aldredesgate'; in 1283 'Aldrichesgate'. The name, H. A. Harben thought, was almost certainly derived from the personal name 'Ealdred' or 'Aldred.' In 1335 it was ordered that the gate should be covered with lead, and a small house made under it for the gatekeeper. Over the gate John Day, a 16th century printer, lived. Here he printed the Folio Bible, dedicated to Edward VI, in 1549; Latimer's Sermons; one of the earliest almanacs, *A Prognostication for the Year of Our Lord 1550*; Roger Ascham's *Scholemaster*, 1570, and Tyndale's *Works*, 1572. In 1564 Foxe, the martyrologist, lived with Day. In 1563 he had published *Actes and Monuments of these latter and perilouse times touching matters of the Church*—familiarly known as 'The Book of Martyrs.' It is said Day used to shout to his apprentices: 'Arise for it is Day.' The gate was taken down and rebuilt in 1617. On the N. side were figures of Jeremiah (underneath, the text: 'Then shall enter into the gates of this city kings and princes sitting upon the throne of David, riding in chariots and on horses, they and their princes, and the men of Judah and the inhabitants of Jerusalem, and this city shall remain for ever') and of Samuel (with the text: 'And Samuel said unto all Israel, Behold, I have hearkened unto your voice in all that you said unto me, and have made a king over you'). These inscriptions had relation to the fact that by this gate, in 1603, James I first entered into L. A small metal representation of the gate is on a pillar of the wall of St. Botolph's Chyd. in Little Britain. On 20th Oct. 1660 Pepys 'saw the limbs of some of our new traitors set upon Aldersgate, which was a sad sight to see.' It sustained some damage in the G.F., but was soon repaired and 'beautified.' It was repaired again in 1739, and in 1750 the apartments over the gate were occupied by the common crier, and the eastern postern, which had been shut up, was reopened. The gate was removed in 1761, the materials being sold for £91.

Aldgate. The derivation is highly speculative. Stow's suggestion that it meant 'old gate' is untenable. Probably it was the 'Æstagate' mentioned in 1052 in the *Anglo-Saxon Chronicle*, and the name was afterwards changed. The earliest form of the present name is 'Alegate' (1108) or 'Allegate.' 'Aldgate' does not occur until 1486-7. Colonel Prideaux suggested that it might have meant the gate of the foreigners from *ael* = foreign, but why this gate more than any other should be associated with aliens is not clear. Stow says it was one of the four original gates of the City. Norman, the first prior of Holy Trinity (1108-47), rebuilt the gate. It was repaired in 1215 by the rebellious barons who, according to Stow, used stones taken from the despoiled houses of the Jews. The dwelling house above the gate was occupied by Chaucer from 1374 to 1385. He was here when, in 1381, the men of Essex, engaged in Wat Tyler's rebellion, had Aldgate opened to them. Sir Wm. Walworth had closed it the day before, but it was unbarred against his orders. In 1553, through the same gate, came Q. Mary, with her sister Elizabeth waiting there affectionately to greet her. It was rebuilt 1607-9. On the E. side was 'a fair golden sphere with a goodly vane on it.' On the upper battlements were

figures of two soldiers each holding a ball 'as denying entrance to any bold enemies.' Beneath, in a large sq., stood the figure of James I in gilt armour. On the W. side was a gilt figure of Fortune. Somewhat lower were female figures representing Peace and Charity. Ben Jonson referred to these in *The Silent Woman*:

'Many things that seem foul in the doing do please done. . . . How long did the canvas hang before Aldgate? Were the people suffered to see the city's Love and Charity, while they were rude stone, before they were painted and burnished?'

In 1750 the rooms over the gate were being used as a charity sch. In 1761 it was pulled down, and the materials brought the sum of £177 10s. 0d. Some of the decorative portions were obtained by Sir. Wm. Blackett of Wallington, Northumberland, for Rothley Castle, which he built. Remains of the foundation of an old gate, probably medieval, were found on the S. side of Aldgate High St., 25 ft. E. from the corner of Jewry St., at a depth of 16 ft. 6 in. in 1907; and on the N. side of the st. under the Post Office in 1908. On the latter site is now a C.C. tablet commemorating the gate. There is a model in the L. Mus.

Aldgate Pump. There was 'Alegate' well adjoining the City wall in the time of K. John. In the 15th century it was called 'St. Michael's Well from a neighbouring chapel of that name occupying nearly the same spot. Probably medicinal or holy virtues were claimed for the water of the well. A pump was erected over the well at about the end of the 16th century. Between 1860 and 1870 the pump was removed several feet farther W., when the frontage of the property at the corner was set back to broaden the thoroughfare. 'Owing partly,' says A. S. Foord, 'to the imaginary medicinal qualities of the water, and perhaps still more to its long continued use, the inhabitants resented, or at least obstructed, any proposals which were made for the removal of the pump.' The continuance of its use by the public was, however, shown by chemical analysis to be attended with such grave risk to the public health that the well was in 1876 filled in, and a cistern below the ground connected with the New River supply substituted. Aldgate Pump therefore still exists, enclosed in an ornamental stone casing, the spout of bronze being in the shape of a dog's head.

Aldwych. The name is probably derived from *eald*=old, and *wic*=town, village, or settlement. It is said that Alfred the Great, after he had finally subdued the Danes, and wrested L. from them, allotted territory for their occupation outside the City. This therefore was the village that clustered round their ch. (see 'Strand'); and the high road, connecting it with the Hosp. of St. Giles, was known up to the beginning of the 17th century as the 'Via de Aldwych,' and is now represented by Drury Lane. In 1398 the name Aldwych is found in a document. There was in Stuart times an 'Oldwyck Close,' an open space S. of Lincoln's Inn Fields, and there was a private way through which James I and his council could pass on their way to Theobalds. According to Sir Walter Besant, at the NE. end of Drury Lane there was once 'Aldewych Cross,' a stone construction. 'Oldwych Close' appears to have changed its name to White Hart Close from an Inn demolished early in the 18th century. The yard or close remained a century longer.

The L.C.C. scheme for constructing Aldwych and Kingsway was devised in 1892 by Frederic Harrison, Chairman of the Improvement Committee. It was not until 1900 that the work was undertaken, it was completed in 1905. Wych St., Holywell St., Clare Market, all disappeared, and thoroughfares 100 ft. wide replaced a number of mean streets which, however, were much more alluring and romantic. It was a clearance covering 28 acres, 12¼ of which were taken up by streets. Percy Harris rightly calls it the greatest st. improvement carried through by the L.C.C. It was largely due to its clerk, the late Sir Geo. Laurence Gomme, a keen antiquary and writer of several books on L., that the historic name Aldwych was adopted.

(See *Old time Aldwych, Kingsway and neighbourhood*, by Charles Gordon, 1903.)

Antiquaries, Society of. It was founded by Abp. Parker in 1572. The members including the celebrated Wm. Camden, assembled at the house of Sir Robt.

Cotton, near W.A., for twenty years. They applied to Q. Elizabeth for a charter, but this had not been granted when she d. James I took offence at some of the soc.'s proceedings, and in 1604 dissolved it. As, however, there is a reference in the diary of Elias Ashmole of 'the Antiquaries' feast' in 1659, there appears to have been some kind of a revival. In 1707 meetings were publicly resumed, and for a time they met at the Young Devil Tavern in Fleet St., which was near to the older 'Devil' associated with Ben Jonson. Peter Le Neve, Norroy King of Arms, was the first president. The minutes start in 1717, and in the same year the soc. resolved to issue the first of the great series of prints which grew up into the work known as the *Vetusta Monumenta*. A magazine called *Archaeologia* was started in 1770, and this was followed by *The Antiquaries' Journal*, of which sixteen volumes were published. In 1751 a Royal Charter of Incorporation was granted to the soc. and in 1776 George III gave orders that, when Somerset House was rebuilt, it should be accommodated with apartments. The whole of the fittings were installed at the expense of the Govt., and in 1781 the soc. took possession of these handsome apartments. Horace Walpole quarrelled with the Antiquaries, and resigned in 1772. 'I dropped my attendance there four or five years ago,' he wrote, 'being sick of their ignorance and stupidity, and have not been three times amongst them since.' The soc. moved to Burlington House in 1866.

It is governed by a council of twenty, and a president, who is also *ex officio* a trustee of the B.Mus. Ld. Stanhope, previously known as Ld. Mahon, occupied the presidential chair for twenty-nine years, 1846 to 1875. The members number about 800, and the limit is 1,000. Membership is by election. Amongst the distinguished members have been almost every well-known antiquary and archaeologist, including John Stow, Dr. Wm. Stukeley, Humphrey Wanley, Samuel Lysons, J. P. Malcolm, Thos. Pennant, Peter Cunningham, Ld. Avebury, H. B. Wheatley, Sir Arthur Evans, Sir Fredk. Kenyon, and W. G. Bell. The proceedings are published now in *The Antiquaries' Journal*. In the library is a bust of Jeremiah Milles by Bacon. Milles was president when Horace Walpole was a member, and it was his criticism of the latter's *Historic Doubts on the Life and Reign of Richard III* that caused the latter to quit the soc. There is also a bust of George III, and there are paintings of a number of past presidents. The lib. contains a magnificent collection of engravings. Three items of particular interest to Londoners are an engraving of the medieval St. P.'s Cath.; a play-bill of the Swan Theatre; and a diptych of St. Paul's Cross.

Architecture in London.

L. as the capital of England and the metropolis of the British Empire was bound to become the greatest city of English architecture. Here stand some of the best bdgs. in the land. The White Tower of the T.L. is the finest Norman keep. W.A. is the noblest Gothic ch.; St. P.'s Cath. is our greatest Renaissance work. The modern palace of the Houses of Parliament is unsurpassed.

The site of L., with winding river and undulating ground, provides an effective setting to the bdgs., whilst the parks and gardens intervene with quiet stretches of green grass and foliage. L. architecture has its most important centres at the Mansion House and St.P.'s Cath. in the City, the Imperial Institute and Museums at Kensington, and Trafalgar Sq. (with the art galleries), the Houses of Parliament, and Buckingham Palace in Westminster.

There is no British city which can compare with L. for the study of general architecture. Remains of ancient Egyptian temples exist at the B.Mus., and these exhibit features which may well have suggested the Greek styles. The Greek galleries at the B.Mus. provide a wealth of material for appreciating the refined beauty of Greek temples and monuments. Early in the 19th century L. bdgs. were copied directly from Athens: these include the arch at Euston Station, now removed, new St. Pancras Ch. in the Euston Rd., and the façade of the B.Mus.

Roman architecture which was developed from Greek and Etruscan art, is reproduced (more or less) in countless L. bdgs. It underlies the design of St.P.'s Cath., the Mansion House, the Royal Exchange, the Bank of England, the N.G., and St. Martin's-in-the-Fields. Modern L. is a finer Roman city than under the Roman Empire. Roman L. extended from Ludgate to the Tower. Portions of the City wall remain (see 'Roman Remains').

Saxon architecture has left no bdg. in L. Elsewhere it is shown to be based upon the Roman style with its semicircular arches.

When Edward the Confessor rebuilt W.A. he was not erecting the last Saxon, but the first Norman ch., for he had lived in Normandy. At the abbey the dark cloisters and the adjoining crypts and chapels are Early Norman of the 11th century. Here the heavy semicircular arches are Norman copies of the Roman style, which entitle both Saxon and Norman work to be classed as Romanesque. The T.L. possesses a unique example of the Early Norman period in the White Tower, begun by William the Conqueror. This Norman keep is remarkable for the exceptionally large character of the Royal Chapel of St. John. The crypt of St. Mary-le-Bow, Cheapside, also belongs to the 11th century. The Middle Norman work of the first half of the 12th century provided the long choir of St. Bartholomew's Priory Ch., Smithfield, with its fine arcade and restored apse. The western crypts of the Ch. of the Knights of St. John of Jerusalem, Clerkenwell, belong to the same period; but the eastern crypt and chapels belong to the second half of the 12th century and show the pointed arch of the Transitional Norman period when Norman architecture was passing into Gothic.

The Round Nave of the Temple Ch. is not only the best Transitional Norman building in L., but one of the best examples in England. It was consecrated in 1185 as the ch. of the great Order of the Knights Templars. The richly carved western doorway is semicircular; but the nave arcade consists of pointed arches, carried upon groups of Purbeck marble shafts with concave capitals.

The Transitional style was influenced by Byzantine architecture, which travelled. The greatest modern example of Byzantine is the vast Roman Catholic Cath. at Westminster; where Greek, Roman, and Eastern art are blended, and where the beauty of marbles, mosaics, and capitals well represent the rich architectural style of the Eastern Empire.

Gothic architecture, which developed the pointed arch to the general exclusion of the semicircular, is well represented in

_. in all its three phases. These may all be seen within the ch. of W.A. Early or 'Early English' Gothic (13th century) is found at the crossing of presbytery, choir, and transepts. Middle or 'Decorated' Gothic (14th century) occurs in three beautiful tombs by the high altar and in the style of the modern choir-screen and choir-stalls. Late or 'Perpendicular' Gothic (15th, 16th centuries, and occasionally later) appears in the W. wall and W. window of the nave, and provides the rich architecture of Henry VII's chapel, with its elaborate fan-vaulting.

If Salisbury Cath. reaches the greatest eminence for its Gothic exterior, certainly W.A. ch. possesses the most exquisitely beautiful interior in England. Viewed from the W. end of the nave, the great height and the fine proportions are most impressive. The graceful dignity of the apse is calm and inspiring. All the eastern part of the ch. belongs to the middle of the 13th century, and represents Early English Gothic at its most perfect development.

On the S. side of the abbey ch. the cloisters form the centre of the domestic quarters of the monks, and provide a remarkably complete record of the bdgs. required by a great Benedictine abbey. The chapter house, in spite of partial rebuilding, represents the lightness and spaciousness of Early English Gothic at its best.

The Decorated Gothic of the 14th century, which is so famous for its loving portrayal of foliage, flowers, and fruit, is to be found at St. Etheldreda's, Ely Place, Holborn, and in the crypt chapel of the H. of C. The Dutch ch. in Austin Friars (q.v.), another fine example, has been destroyed.

Southwark Cath. (q.v.) forms a very complete summary of English architecture, and has an air of quiet simplicity. Norman and Transitional fragments remain on the N. side, the beautiful choir is Early English Gothic, the transepts belong to the Decorated style, and the sq. central tower and the great reredos of the high altar are Perpendicular Gothic. The reredos resembles that at Winchester Cath., and was erected in 1520, when Southwark belonged to the diocese of Winchester.

The 15th and 16th centuries witnessed a great advance in wealth and power in L. Most of the City chs. were enlarged or rebuilt. Palaces, civic buildings, and rich merchants' houses were being erected. The architectural style of this period is known as Perpendicular Gothic in reference to the general vertical lines of windows and wall panelling. Chs. of this period include St. Peter-ad-Vincula, within the precincts of the T.L.; St. Andrew Undershaft, Leadenhall St.; the chs. of St. Ethelburga and St. Helen, Bishopsgate; St. Sepulchre's, Holborn; and St. Margaret's, Westminster.

The civil buildings of the Perpendicular period are numerous in L. The vast Westminster Hall was now transformed, and the Norman Banqueting Hall of the old palace was converted into Perpendicular Gothic by Richard II, who added the magnificent hammer-beam roof with its winged angels on every beam. It is the noblest roof in all England. At the royal palace at Eltham, the great hall, now finely restored, also belongs to this style, and was built in the 15th century. Guildhall was erected in 1411, and was known to Dick Whittington. The walls are original, and the roof, destroyed in 1940, was rebuilt on the pattern of the 15th-century one. This is the most important civic hall in the country. Crosby Hall (q.v.) is now on Chelsea Embankment. The timber roof, with its multitude of pendants, is beautiful work. Picturesque half-timber gabled houses of this period are to be found at Staple Inn, Holborn.

L. possesses several red-brick buildings of Tudor date in Perpendicular Gothic. These include the delightful courtyard of the Bp. of L.'s Palace at Fulham, the fine gateway of the Abp. of Canterbury's Palace facing the river at Lambeth, the Old Hall at Lincoln's Inn (recently rebuilt with much old material), and the gateway of Lincoln's Inn in Chancery Lane. St. James's Palace was erected by Henry VIII in the same style, and the great gateway, chapel, and several state rooms remain.

The Renaissance began with the importation of small works from the Continent, such as tapestries, furniture, and the twelve Italian terra-cotta plaques (with Roman emperors' heads) which Cardinal Wolsey affixed to the towers of his palace at Hampton Court. Henry

VIII's visit to France fostered the Renaissance in England. At Chelsea Old Ch. Sir Thomas More's chapel has a Gothic arch supported on two Renaissance capitals. Although the ch. has been almost entirely destroyed, this has survived. Henry VIII's great hall at Hampton Court, which is Perpendicular Gothic, has Renaissance decoration. The hall of Gray's Inn, Holborn, and the Middle Temple hall are fine examples of the Elizabethan period where the general features are Perpendicular Gothic, but the screens and minstrels' galleries are in the full Renaissance style. The screen at the Middle Temple hall is one of the finest in England, full of vigorous figure carving and other enrichments. Middle Temple hall has been restored since the bomb damage. Gray's Inn hall was practically destroyed. Canonbury Tower, Islington, a Tudor brick residence, has Elizabethan panelling and fireplaces. The monastery of the Carthusian monks at the Charterhouse (q.v.), with the great hall, great staircase, and the master's lodge, presents fine examples of Elizabethan Renaissance carvings and ceilings. The chapel was enlarged in 1611, when the new north aisle was built with an arcade of Roman arches and Tuscan columns. The mantelpieces in the hall and drawing-room belong to this period.

English Renaissance architecture during the 17th and 18th centuries became more and more classic in character, and the Gothic admixture disappeared. The first important Renaissance architect was Inigo Jones, who had studied in Italy. He built the banqueting hall at Whitehall in pure Renaissance style. It was intended as the first instalment of a great Italian palace to extend along Whitehall. Inigo Jones, also built in Renaissance style the Queen's House at Greenwich, York House Water Gate in the Embankment Gardens, and houses in Lincoln's Inn Fields. Lincoln's Inn Chapel, which he designed, has Gothic windows, and Roman columns in the undercroft. St. Katharine Cree Ch., Leadenhall St., which is the ecclesiastical gem of this period, was built in 1631 and has an arcade of Corinthian columns and Perpendicular Gothic windows. The architect is unknown.

English Renaissance reached its height under Sir Christopher Wren after the G.F. Wren had been a professor of astronomy before he became an architect. His ability as a mathematician joined to his sensibility as an artist made him a master of proportion. Wren's mental and spiritual qualities have given to the dome of St.P.'s Cath. its perfection. It is the noblest dome in Christendom. It crowns the metropolis with a sense of dominion— the domination of service through sacrifice. The dome of St. Paul's is the symbol of L., and figures in every symbolic view of the capital.

The W. front of St.P.'s Cath. has a stately façade with its portico in two stories flanked by two lofty towers. The interior of the Cath. is worthy of the commanding exterior. To enter by the N. transept doorway and to encounter the vast space covered by the dome, is to gain a view overpowering in its impressiveness, and to be lost amongst the endless perspectives and altitudes of transepts, aisles, nave and choir. Sir Jas. Thornhill's great paintings cover the majestic canopy of the dome itself. The spandrels of its arches, the quarter domes, and the shallow domes of the choir and the eastern apse are encrusted with mosaics. The delicate carvings of Grinling Gibbons everywhere enrich the Cath. with their exquisite luxuriousness, and stand matchless for their inspired love of nature.

It is difficult to estimate the full value of Wren's work for L. He rebuilt some fifty par. churches, all skilfully planned to fit the surroundings.

Amongst the Renaissance chs., St. Stephen's, Walbrook, is Wren's masterpiece for interior design. The Ch. has a forest of Corinthian columns under an exquisitely proportioned dome and is ornamented with a wealth of wood carving. It is less well known that Wren employed Perpendicular Gothic for the fine spire of St. Dunstan-in-the-E. (it remains, although the body of the ch. has been destroyed), and also for the towers of St. Michael, Cornhill; St. Mary Aldermary (with fan vaulting); and St. Alban, Wood St.

One notable Wren ch. destroyed before the Second World War was All Hallows, Lombard St.

Wren was also employed at the royal palaces. He built the beautiful E. front

at Hampton Court, where the red brickwork is finely set off by the spreading
green lawns. He carried out work at
Windsor Castle, and built most of Kensington Palace. He was the architect of
Marlborough House; Morden Coll., Blackheath; Chelsea Hosp.; part of Greenwich
Hosp. with its magnificent colonnade, its
domes, and the great hall painted by
Thornhill. He also erected Temple Bar
(*q.v.*).

Wren's influence continued after his
death in 1723, and Renaissance continued.
His pupil, Jas. Gibbs, built St. Martin-
in-the-Fields, the very beautiful little ch.
of St. Mary-le-Strand, and St. Clement
Danes, Strand. This restored ch. has a
fine plaster ceiling and rich woodcarvings.
Nicholas Hawksmoor, another pupil, built
St. Mary Woolnoth, Lombard St., and
St. George's, Bloomsbury. The Mansion
House is a very stately pile with a rich
French Renaissance interior erected by
Geo. Dance, and completed in 1753. Sir
Wm. Chambers is praised for Somerset
House, finished in 1789.

In the 18th century L. spread westward
and the streets and squares were full of
the houses of the nobility and wealthy
families. Many have elaborate and
glittering interiors in the French style.
At the V. & A. Mus., S. Kensington,
have been erected many typical rooms
from L. houses of the 17th and 18th
centuries.

A new style was developed in the latter
part of the 18th century by the Adam
brothers, who introduced Greek features
into their delicate decorations. Good
examples of the 'Adam style' include
Ken Wood House, Hampstead Lane,
Highgate; Apsley House, Hyde Park
Corner; the Courtauld Institute, 20
Portland Sq., and houses in the Adelphi.

Early in the 19th century the Greek
revival followed the arrival of the Elgin
Marbles from Athens, and produced the
new St. Pancras Ch. in the Euston Rd.,
and the B.Mus. The Roman style,
however, continued, as may be seen at
Lancaster House (where formerly was the
L.Mus.); University Coll., Gower St.;
the N.G.; and the Royal Exchange—all of
which belong to the Roman Corinthian
style.

The Gothic revival, which also appeared
early in the 19th century, produced important results. Perpendicular Gothic,
which had never quite disappeared, was
the first Gothic style to be revived. The
ch. of St. Luke, Chelsea, was built in
this style in 1820, and St. Dunstan's,
Fleet St., in 1833. The remarkable
Catholic Apostolic Ch. in Gordon Sq.
was erected in Early English Gothic in
1854, and the 'English chapel' of this ch.
contains wonderful carving in the Decorated style which is evidently inspired
by Southwell Cath. Chapter House. The
greatest product of the Gothic revival
is the Houses of Parliament, which were
completed by Sir Chas. Barry in 1860. The
exterior with its clock tower and noble
Victoria tower, together with its innumerable turrets and pinnacles, is amazingly
elaborate. The interior with its corresponding richness rises to its height in the
magnificence of the House of Lords. It is
the greatest Gothic palace ever erected
in England. The Royal Courts of Justice
in the Strand were completed in 1882.
They were designed by Geo. Street,
who did not live to see the end of his
work. They form a noble example of
Early English Gothic, with their vast
and lofty hall, richly carved with masses
of the beautiful conventional foliage of
the period. The extremely beautiful
Middlesex Guildhall in Westminster, set
like a gem within the ring of great
architecture represented by the Abbey,
the Houses of Parliament, and Whitehall,
is designed in the richest possible adaptation of Perpendicular Gothic. It was
completed in 1913. London chs. of the
19th and 20th centuries are mostly
Gothic, but the Brompton Oratory in
Brompton Rd. is rich Renaissance, and
the Greek Cath., Moscow Rd., and the
Roman Catholic Cath., Westminster, are
in the Byzantine style.

Renaissance having been pronounced
as most generally suitable for civic architecture, the Govt. bdgs. in Whitehall
have been erected in that style, such
as the Treasury, India Office, Admiralty,
War Office, and Scotland Yard. Renaissance has been adopted for the
Town Halls of Woolwich, Chelsea, and
Marylebone; for the Port of L. Authority,
near the T.L., the Met. Water Board at
Islington, the Central Criminal Courts
in the Old Bailey, the County Hall of
the G.L.C. (*q.v.*), and the new front of

Buckingham Palace.

Since the First World War L. architecture has struck a new note of severe simplicity and strict utility. The handling of mass and form has been the keynote rather than elaborate detail. Such a work as the Shell-Mex bdg. in the Strand, especially as seen from the Embankment when flood-lit, is typical. The offices of the London Transport Executive in Broadway, Westminster, with their remarkable Epstein carvings, the *Daily Telegraph* Offices in Fleet St., Broadcasting House in Portland Place, and London University building in Bloomsbury, are all varied examples of modern architectural thought.

Buildings of the last fifteen years show an even more striking change, the main features being height, acreage of glass, and, as some will say, ugliness. The skyline of London has changed more in the last fifteen years than in the previous three hundred: on Millbank, on South Bank and in the City itself tall white blocks dominate and dwarf the surrounding buildings. The Barbican project with its line of glass-fronted cliffs along London Wall, the office blocks around the stations alter the perspective to the stranger. Notable single examples of originality are the 'Daily Mirror' building in Holborn Circus, the Stock Exchange Towers and the office development around Charing Cross Road and Tottenham Court Road. The tallest of all is the Post Office Tower, symbol of its age, an age of experiment.

(See *The Vanished City*, by R. Carrier and O. L. Dick, 1957; and *Royal Commission on Historical Monuments, London*, 1924-30, 5 vols.)

Art in London. Few cities in the world can approach L. in wealth of art treasures to delight alike the student and the sightseer.

The National Gallery in Trafalgar Square has an unrivalled collection of European painting; the Tate Gallery, Millbank—the national gallery of British art—contains much of the national collections of British painting and also modern foreign painting and sculpture; the Wallace Collection in Manchester Square is a treasure house of French painting and furniture. Smaller galleries include the Iveagh Bequest, Ken Wood; The Soane Museum, Lincoln's Inn

Fields; the Guildhall Art Gallery; the Dulwich College Art Gallery; the Queen's Gallery in Buckingham Palace Road; and the Courtauld Institute Galleries in Woburn Square, which contain the collections of paintings left by Lord Lee of Fareham and Roger Fry and of drawings left by Sir Robert Witt.

The British Museum has extensive collections of Oriental and early European art, and a large department devoted to prints and drawings; while the Victoria and Albert—the national art museum—contains art in many manifestations—painting, prints, drawings, sculpture, costume, interior decoration and even architecture. Its outlying department at Bethnal Green has among other exhibits a splendid collection of toys of the past four centuries.

The Whitechapel Art Gallery adjoining Aldgate East Underground Station and the South London Art Gallery in Camberwell hold periodical loan exhibitions of different types of painting, originally intended for the benefit of people in their own areas, but now widely visited. The best known commercial galleries are concentrated in the Bond Street, Mayfair, and St. James's districts, and in addition to excellent exhibitions, scholarly advice is frequently available. Among the most famous are Colnaghi's, Agnew's, Tooth's, Leggatt's, the Cooling Galleries, the Parker Galleries, Bernard's and Newman's, but there are many others worthy of a visit.

The main wealth of material in the various classes of artistic development lies in different institutions, which nevertheless, should not be considered as exhausting the resources of L. in any particular field of art.

Ancient Sculpture. Examples of Assyrian, Egyptian, Greek, and Roman sculpture, can be seen at the B.Mus. Among them are the famous Elgin marbles, including the Parthenon frieze brought back by Ld. Elgin from Athens in the early 19th century.

Chinese Art. The B.Mus. shares the Eumorfopoulos Collection with the V. & A. Mus., which also contains the Salting Bequest of Chinese ceramics. The Eumorfopoulos Collection contains a huge T'ang pottery figure of a Lo-han.

Indian Art may be seen in the Indian section, V. & A. Mus. The same mus. contains numerous specimens of Persian and other Oriental art.

Mediæval Sculpture. W.A. contains splendid English mediæval sculpture, while Italian work of this period is to be found in the V. & A. Mus.

Renaissance and Baroque Sculpture. The V. & A. Mus. contains good examples of this period, and examples are to be found all over L. The Guildhall Art Gallery has works by Nicholas Stone and Stephen Colein, the Central Criminal Court has three fine Bushnell statues.

18th-century Sculpture. Apart from the numerous examples of 18th-century monumental sculpture in W.A., St.P.'s Cath., and other places, good portrait work is to be found at the N.P.G., which contains some works by Roubiliac.

19th-century Sculpture. A great deal of outdoor 19th-century sculpture exists in London, particularly in the form of commemorative statues and monuments. Guildhall has monuments to Nelson, Chatham, Pitt and Wellington and statues by Onslow Ford, Frampton and Watts, while the Mansion House contains a representative collection of life-size classical figures by the more popular sculptors of the Victorian age. The Tate Gallery includes work by Ford, Frampton, Calder Marshall and Thornycroft.

Contemporary and Recent Sculpture. The Tate Gallery concerns itself particularly with this branch of art, mainly by British masters, but including some foreign work. Sculptors |of note represented include Jacob Epstein, Sir Alfred Gilbert, Eric Gill, Auguste Rodin, Henry Moore and Barbara Hepworth.

Italian Painting. The N.G. contains examples of all periods of Italian work. At the beginning we have Graeco-Roman encaustic portraits painted in wax. The next stage is marked by the flat hieratic non-representational altar piece by Margaritone. Then the great regional schs. follow: Siena, traditional and decorative, with Duccio and the Lorenzetti: Florence, beginning with Cimabue and passing through the decorative work of Fra Angelico, the 'divine perspective' of Uccello, the sculpturesque Masaccio; the nobility of 'Plein air' Piero della Francesca, the figures of Pollaiuolo, the airiness of Botticelli, finally bringing us to the tremendous figures of Leonardo da Vinci and Michelangelo. The Umbrian Sch. is

there, with Perugino and Raphael, and the Paduan with Mantegna. The glory of Venetian colour is there also, with Titian, Tintoretto, and Paolo Veronese. The Mannerists appear—Pontormo, Bronzino, and Parmegianino. The Naturalists, like Caravaggio, and the Eclectics, like the Caracci brothers, are followed by the Baroque painters and the great 18th-century topographical painters, Canaletto and Guardi.

The Wallace Collection has numerous Italian works of all periods up to the 18th century. The V. & A. Mus. has a set of Raphael cartoons for tapestry. Hampton Court contains Mantegna's 'Triumphs of Julius Cæsar.'

The Dulwich Gallery contains works by Corregio, Raphael, Pietro da Cortona, Parmegianino, Salvator Rosa, all the Caracci brothers, Guido Reni, and many more.

Flemish and Dutch Painting. The N.G. contains the work of Netherlands painters of all periods, beginning with the portrait of a man by Jan Van Eyck, and the famous Arnolfini wedding group. Roger van der Weyden, Mabuse, Breughel, Matsys, lead us to the elegant portraiture of Van Dyck and the Baroque exuberance of Rubens, in his sumptuous allegorical groups and his landscape—the 'Chateau de Steen'—alike. Rembrandt is better represented in the N.G. than in any other gallery outside Holland. The great domestic Dutchmen—Vermeer, Pieter de Hoogh, Metsu, and the like, are well represented, as are the 'open window' landscapists, Hobbema, Cuyp, Konnink, Ruysdael, Van de Velde. Less widely known, but to be seen in the same institution, are examples of the Dutch 19th-century masters, Bosboom, Israels, the Maris Brothers, and their contemporaries.

In the Wallace Collection can be found works by Dutch painters of the 18th and early 19th centuries and Belgian painters of the 19th century, in addition to a representative collection of Flemish and Dutch work of the 15th, 16th, and 17th centuries, notably 'The Laughing Cavalier' by Frans Hals.

The Dulwich Gallery has works by Van Dyck, Rubens and Rembrandt, and an extensive collection of 17th-century masters — Hobbema, Cuyp, Ruysdael, Brouwer, Ostade, Teniers, Douw, Potter,

Both, and others.

German Painting. This sch. is not so well represented as the other national schs., but examples are to be seen in the N.G. of the work of Dürer, Baldung, and Holbein, notably the latter's famous *Ambassadors.* The Wallace Collection has some German works ranging from the 16th to the 19th centuries, and the V. & A. Mus. contains Holbein portraits.

Spanish Painting. In the N.G. can be found examples of the work of El Greco, Ribera, Zurbarán, Velasquez, Murillo, and Goya; and the Wallace Collection has a few works by Velasquez, del Mazo, and Murillo; the Dulwich Gallery has some good Murillos.

French Painting. This can be seen at the N.G., Wallace Collection, and Tate Gallery. Claude and Poussin are shown at the N.G., 'The Embarkation of the Queen of Sheba' and 'Cephalus and Aurora' being respective examples. The Wallace Collection is exceptionally rich in French work, from Clouet and Corneille de Lyon, Philippe de Champaigne, through Poussin and Claude to the great 18th-century masters, Vernet, Lancret, Fragonard, Watteau, Boucher and Greuze, and Meissonier and the 19th-century men. Modern work is to be found at the Tate Gallery—Tissot, Monet, Manet, Cézanne, Van Gogh, Picasso. The V. & A. Mus. contains works by the 16th-century Le Nain and the 19th-century Millet. The Iveagh Bequest has some 18th-century work and Guildhall Art Gallery a few traditional 19th-century pictures, including two fine Tissots. The Wallace Collection is arranged in a setting of French furniture and craftsmanship. Claude and Poussin are well represented in the Dulwich Collection.

English Painting. It is to be expected that an abundance of this work will be accessible in L. The earliest specimens are probably in W.A.—the famous retable of comparatively recent re-discovery. Tudor work can be studied in the miniatures, notably by Nicholas Hilliard, in the V. & A. Mus., and at Windsor Castle. The 17th-century portrait sch. is to be found in the N.P.G. This gallery concerns itself first with history and second with art, but contains good portraits by J. M. Wright, Lely, Kneller, Closterman, and Vanderbank. Reynolds (particularly

'Samuel Johnson' and 'Self-portrait)', Romney, Hoppner, Haydon, Watts, and the Hon. John Collier, bring us to the present century.

Gainsborough, both in portrait and landscape, is well shown in the N.G., and Constable is represented in this gallery, the Tate, the V. & A. Mus., and Guildhall.

Hogarth, that typically English satirist of the 18th century, has 'Marriage à la Mode' in the Tate and 'The Rake's Progress' and 'Election' series in the Soane Mus.

Blake, poet and mystic, is seen in strength at the Tate, as is Turner, whose works occupy a whole gallery there. English landscape is well represented at the N.G., notably with the East Anglian pieces of Crome and Cotman and the work of Cox and Bonington; and the Tate has many fine examples and includes some delicate work by Birket Foster.

Genre or narrative pictures were the predominant feature of 19th-century painting in this country. 'Every picture tells a story,' said our grandfathers, and let the story take charge of the picture. So in the Tate Gallery we may see the highly finished results of this passion for illustration, in the work of Alma-Tadema, Calderon, Frith, Gilbert, Leighton, Maclise, Millais, Orchardson, Poynter, Watts, and many more. English genre includes, of course, the work of Pre-Raphaelite Brotherhood, and here the Tate is very prolific, with Millais, Rossetti, Holman Hunt, Burne-Jones, and their followers, notably W. S. Burton. The Guildhall collection contains numerous examples of 19th-century genre, including a superb Poynter, and the Pre-Raphaelite pictures there include two good Dyce works and a jewel-like Burton.

Modern work is best seen at the Tate, where Grant and Wadsworth, Sickert and Spencer, Lavery and Sargent, John and Kennington, Rushbury and Munnings, are well represented, and the work of many other distinguished present-day artists is shown. Guildhall contains a number of large modern ceremonial canvases by Solomon, Salisbury, Cuneo and Dring, and good portraits by Lavery and Llewellyn, and some paintings by young artists of today, purchased at the annual 'Lord Mayor's Art Award' exhibitions for professional artists. A wider appreciation of modern art can be gained by visiting the current exhibitions of the art societies at the Royal Institute Galleries in Piccadilly, the R.W.S. (Royal Society of Painters in Water Colours) Galleries in Conduit Street, and the long-established R.B.A. (Royal Society of British Artists) in Suffolk Street (the last will move to new galleries on The Mall in 1971); and the Institute of Contemporary Arts at Nash House, The Mall. Other important 'Royal Societies' are the Marine Artists and the Portrait Painters. The R.S.M.A. exhibits annually at the Guildhall Gallery, which also accommodates the exhibition of children's drawings mounted by the Royal Drawing Society. The association between the R.D.S. and Guildhall goes back to 1916.

The National Maritime Mus., Greenwich, has a splendid collection of sea pictures and naval portraits.

Prints and drawings can be seen in the unrivalled collections at the British Museum and there are fine collections of drawings also at the Courtauld Institute Galleries in Woburn Square, and in the Royal Collection, of which selections are exhibited from time to time in the Queen's Gallery in Buckingham Palace Road. The Guildhall Library contains the Willshire Collection of early engravings. Topographical prints and drawings exist in the local collections of many London borough libraries, and Guildhall Library contains some 30,000 London items.

Outdoor sculpture in London is neither profuse nor uniformly good. The oldest outdoor statue is said to be that called King Alfred in Trinity Church Square in Southwark. Among items worthy of note are Watt's 'Physical Energy' and Frampton's 'Peter Pan' in Kensington Gardens, Epstein's 'Rima' in Hyde Park, Eric Gill's group on Broadcasting House in Portland Place, Sir William Reid Dick's George V at Westminster and President Roosevelt in Grosvenor Square, 'Meridian' by Barbara Hepworth, at State House, Holborn, and Henry Moore's screen on the Time-Life building.

The world-famous statue known as Eros in Piccadilly Circus was executed by Sir Alfred Gilbert in aluminium and is a memorial to the 7th Earl of Shaftesbury. Epstein's Field-Marshal Smuts in Parliament Square, Rodin's 'Burghers of Calais' in Victoria Tower Gardens and Thomas

Thornycroft's Boadicea on the Embankment are conservative in comparison with Franta Belsky's fountain across the river by the Shell Centre.

Education of artists is carried out at the Royal Academy Schools, the Slade, St. Martin's and the Royal College of Art, and there are good local art schools in the suburbs, notably the City and Guilds Art School in Kennington and the Wimbledon and Kingston Art Schools. The Sir John Cass College School of Art and Crafts teaches painting, drawing, sculpture, lithography, pottery, silversmithing and metalwork.

It will be readily appreciated, therefore, that L. has a great care for art, and from the most dignified public institution to the most progressive private or commercial gallery caters for the student and lover of all branches of it.

Auction Rooms. They have a place in L. history and some are distinguished too by the sites they occupy in its streets. The premises of Messrs. Christie, Manson & Wood, usually known only by the name of the first partner, in King St., St. James's, are worthy of a fashionable club. The firm was founded in 1766 by Jas. Christie; it first occupied premises in Pall Mall on a site now occupied by the United Service Club. The business was removed in 1770 to 125 Pall Mall (adjoining Schomberg House); and there in 1803 Jas. Christie died. Under his successor, Jas. Christie II, a move was made in 1823 to King Street. These premises were destroyed by bombs in 1941 and the firm moved to Spencer House, St. James's Place but are now back in King St. Pictures take prior place in their sales, but they also dispose of furniture, jewellery, and books. Sotheby's have their premises in New Bond St., the bdg. being one that formerly housed the Doré Gallery. Over the central archway of the entrance is a bust of Sekhet, the Egyptian goddess of War; it came from the Belzoni collection, sold many yrs. ago, and was brought from Wellington St., the previous premises, as a mascot. Hodgson's, in Chancery Lane, have an extensive business in book auctions. Puttick & Simpson's specialize in china, silver, and musical instruments. Books, furniture, and pictures also come under the hammer at their premises in Blenheim St. Until it was demolished in 1937 they occupied Sir Joshua Reynolds's house in Leicester Sq. One of the most memorable of their transactions was the sale of an original manuscript poem of John Keats for £2,800. For landed estates, houses, or businesses the principal auctioneers are L. Auction Mart and Estate Exchange, 155 Q. Victoria St., and Knight, Frank & Rutley, of Hanover Sq. Other important firms in these lines are Hampton & Sons Ltd., 6 Arlington St., S.W.1, and Goddard & Smith, of King St., St. James's.

Austin Friars. The Order which settled in the part of L. so called was the Friars Hermits of the Order of St. Augustine of Hippo. Their ch. was founded in 1253 by Humphrey Bohun E. of Hereford and Essex, Constable of England, and godfather of Edward I, 'to the honour of God, and the Virgin for the health of the soul' of his father, Henry III, and his descendants. The original edifice was a small one, and the area occupied by the priory, ch., domestic bdgs., cloister and gardens, lay between Throgmorton St. on the S. and London Wall on the N. Broad St. formed its eastern limit, and what are now known as Angel Court and Copthall Avenue formed the W. boundary. In 1354 the ch. was rebuilt on a more elaborate scale, by another Humphrey Bohun, grandson of the first founder. The new ch. was a magnificent example of the decorated Gothic style, having a nave 153 ft. long by 83 ft. wide, with ample transepts and choir. At one time it was called 'the Westminster Abbey of the City,' owing to the number and splendour of its monuments. Edwd., eldest son of the Black P., and the Fair Maid of Kent, were buried in the choir (1371), and before the altar Sir Humphrey Bohun, its founder. Others bd. here were Edmund Plantagenet, half-brother of Richard II (1371); Richd. Fitzalan, E. of Arundel (1397); John de Vere, 12th E. of Oxford (1463); and the D. of Buckingham, of Shakespeare's *Henry VIII* (1521). The two last were executed on Tower Hill. One old chronicle says that some of the barons slain at the Battle of Barnet (1471) were bd. here, and this seems to be confirmed by the discovery of skeletons over 6 ft. long. Erasmus lived at Austin Friars in 1513; Stow described the steeple as 'most fine,' and added: 'I have not seen the like.' The Augustinian Friars continued in possession of the ch. until, in 1538, they were disestablished by Henry VIII, and the ch. closed. In 1545 the ch. was used as a warehouse for storing wine seized from the French ships, and subsequently it was used as a naval storehouse. In 1547, on the succession of Edward VI, the Ld. Protector Somerset invited divines from Germany and the Netherlands to this country to assist the Reformation, and in 1548 there were about 5,000 refugees from the latter here. Through the influence of the Duchess of Suffolk, the Privy Council agreed to give them part of the ch. of the Austin Friars, and it was carefully repaired at the expense of the Crown. The grant, with other privileges, was confirmed by letters patent of the K., dated at Leigh, 24th July 1550.

Only the use of the nave had been granted to the strangers. The eastern part, comprising the transept, choir, and tower, as also the whole of the conventual bdgs., had previously been granted under letters patent to Sir Wm. Paulet, Ld. Treasurer, and afterwards Marquis of Winchester, who utilized a part of the bdg. as a storehouse for corn. The choir he turned into a coal-house, the monuments he sold for £100, and the lead was stripped from the roof and disposed of. On the death of Edward VI in 1553, and the accession of Q. Mary, a proclamation was issued ordering all the Netherlanders and other Protestant refugees to leave the kingdom within twenty-four days. The Dutch congregation left England in Sept. 1553. They returned under Elizabeth in 1559. In 1609 the lofty and beautiful spire fell down for want of the necessary repair, although the Marquis of Winchester had been earnestly requested to restore it. He afterwards sold the materials with the portion of the choir on which it stood, and a dwelling-house was subsequently erected on the site. In 1617 the Dutch merchants subscribed £20,000 on security apparently given by members of the Privy Council. In 1618 this sum and the interest due was forfeited by a decision of the Star Chamber as a result of an action having been commenced in which it was alleged that the presence of the strangers was inimical to the interest of the nation on account of their making large sums of money which they sent out of the country. The Dutch community have, however, retained possession of their ch. without serious interference to the time of its destruction by a land mine in Oct. 1940. The tracery of the windows was particularly fine, and it had the largest floor space of any City ch. The plate has survived; also a document bearing the signature of Erasmus and a tablet in memory of Hugo Grotius, father of international law (d. 1645),

which was erected in Feb. 1939.

On 23 July 1950 Princess Irene, the ten-years old daughter of the Queen of the Netherlands, laid the foundation stone of a new Austin Friars Ch. as a part of a service to commemorate the 400th anniversary of the granting of the previous bdg. to Dutch refugees by Edward VI.

Bakewell Hall. The earliest reference to it is 'Bakkewelle' in 1356. It stood on the E. side of Guildhall Yard. It seems to have derived its name from John de Bankewelle who appears in letters in the C.C. records for 1336-9. In 1396 a messuage called 'Bakwellehalle,' and a garden in the pars. of St. Michael de Bassyngeshawe and St. Lawrence in the Jewry were conveyed to the Ld.M. and commonalty, and thenceforth it appears to have been used as a market place for woollen clothes. Foreigners were directed to bring their woollen cloth here for sale. From c. 1465 it is also referred to as 'Blakewele hall.' The C.C. rebuilt the hall in 1588. In Thos. Deloney's story, *Jack of Newberie* (1597), the hero says: 'Then let two honest discreet men bee chosen, and sent out of every towne to meet me at Blackwell Hall in London'— he being a broad cloth weaver. The hall was burned in the G.F., and rebuilt in 1672, the fees from the lettings being handed over to Christ's Hosp. It was removed in 1820 to make way for the Court of Common Pleas. There is a C.C. plaque on the site.

Baltic Exchange. It appears to have had its origin in the 18th century. The *Daily Post*, a newspaper published in 1744, notified the fact that the Baltic Coffee House would be removed to Threadneedle St. The proprietor supplied refreshments of all kinds, and the members had a special room assigned for their business, which was trade with Russia. In 1854-5 the premises in Threadneedle St. known as the South Sea House were vacant. As the membership had greatly increased, it was decided to move there. The Baltic remained in occupation of these premises until 1899, when the owners decided to terminate the tenancy. It happened that about the same time the L. Shipping Exchange, which had been established in Billiter St. since 1892, was anxious to acquire new premises. An arrangement was made to bring about a fusion of interests, and to seek other quarters. A handsome structure was erected in St. Mary Axe, and opened in 1903 by Sir Marcus Samuel, afterwards Ld. Bearsted, then Ld.M. The Exchange Room, which has a central dome, has a superficial floor-space of nearly 20,000 sq. ft. Whilst there is still a considerable amount of business with the Baltic countries, the members now deal with commodities from every part of the world.

There is a 'Ceres' Bell, rung on special occasions, like the Lutine Bell of Lloyd's.

Bank of England. It was established in 1694 by Royal Charter, which was granted by virtue of an Act of Parliament based on the proposals of Wm. Paterson, a Scotsman. The Act provided that subscribers to the capital of £1,200,000 should be granted certain rights and privileges on the condition that the entire capital should be lent to the Govt. at 8 per cent. The money was required by the Govt. for carrying on the war with France. The management of the Corporation was entrusted to a Governor, Deputy Governor, and twenty-four Directors, who were to be chosen annually by the votes of those persons having at least £500 stock.

For a few months the business of the Bank was carried on at Mercers' Hall; but at the end of 1694 a move was made to Grocers' Hall, where it was domiciled until 1734. In 1724 a site in Threadneedle St. was purchased by the Bank. Geo. Sampson erected a public office in 1732-4, and on the 5th June 1734 the Bank took possession of the new premises. Between 1765 and 1788 wings were added to the original bdg. by Sir Robt. Taylor, the extension westward involving the destruction of St. Christopher-le-Stocks Ch. in 1781. The remainder of the present island site, which extends to about 3¾ acres, was acquired during the last decade of the 18th century, and the buildings on the northern portion of the site were erected from the designs of Sir John Soane, who was architect to the Bank from 1788 to 1833. Soane also rebuilt, or remodelled, the greater part of the work of his predecessors; but the Court Room, which was erected by Taylor in 1767, and decorated in the Adam style, remained unaltered.

Except for minor alterations and additions, Soane's bdgs. and the few survivals of the earlier architect's work remained intact until 1925. It was then decided to rebuild the premises in Threadneedle St.

so that the greatly increased staff, which it had been necessary to employ during and after the War of 1914–18, might be accommodated in offices on the site.

The new bdg., from the designs of Sir Herbert Baker, was completed in 1940. Within the old external walls, which have been underpinned and preserved, a series of banking halls has been reconstructed with domes and vaulted ceilings, which were a characteristic of Soane's work, and in these halls some of the ornaments from the old bdgs. have been reinstated. A central block, rising to a height of 100 ft., encloses a garden court, which is flanked by open vaulted colonnades, and from this central bdg. the main portico projects to Threadneedle St. On the pediment of this bdg. has been placed a modern representation of Britannia, executed by Mr. Chas. Wheeler; and below this figure are six buttress figures representing bearers and guardians of wealth, which are the work of the same artist. A projection on the W. side of the central block forms the portico of the Princes St. entrance, and two great wings connect the new high bdgs. with Soane's screen wall in Lothbury. At the NW. corner the architectural feature known as the 'Temple,' which was copied by Soane from the Temple of the Sibyl at Tivoli, has been preserved, but a footway has been constructed beneath it to enable the roadway to be widened at the corner of Princes St. and Lothbury.

The bronze doors of the Threadneedle St. entrance bear various symbolic designs. On the central doors Latin inscriptions, each placed round a lion's head, record the dates of the foundation of the Bank and of its rebuilding, and the symbols on these doors indicate the contrast in methods of communication at the dates mentioned— one showing an argosy, and the other the hand of Zeus grasping the lightning, representing electrical energy. The side entrance doors are decorated with lions guarding mounds of money, after the manner of the old Mycenaean symbolism.

The main entrance hall, with its domed and vaulted ceilings, is built of Hopton Wood stone, except for the twenty large columns of Belgian marble, 18 ft. 6 in. in height, and some smaller monoliths of Italian marble. The floor of this hall, and of all the public halls and corridors on the ground floor, are in mosaic from the designs of Boris Anrep. Those in the hall itself represent: St. George and the Dragon; lions guarding a mound of coins; a puteal, or wellhead, representing that in the Forum at which the bankers in Rome transacted their business; the head of Minerva which appeared on Roman-British and English coinage; and the head of Mercury, patron of bankers, and his caduceus. In the corridors are mosaic representations of British coins of various dates.

Since 1780, when an attack was made on the Bank by those concerned in the Gordon Riots, a military guard has been in attendance at the Bank each night.

Although the Bank of England had exercised many of the functions of a State bank, it remained a private company until 1st March 1946, when it passed into public ownership by Act of Parliament. The management is now in the hands of a Governor, a Deputy Governor and sixteen Directors, all of whom are appointed by the Crown. In addition to acting as banker to the British banks and to most of the overseas central banks, its principal duties are to manage the National Debt, to administer the Exchange Control, act as the Govt's. banker, and to be the Central Reserve Bank of the country.

Its familiar name, 'The Old Lady of Threadneedle Street,' was given to the Bank of England by Sheridan in the H.C. and popularized in a Gilray cartoon; another attribution is to Wm. Cobbett. He compared the Governors to Mrs. Partington, in that they 'endeavoured with their financial broom to stem the Atlantic waves of national progress.'

(See *The Bank of England: a history*, by John Giuseppi, 1966.)

Banks. The majority of the L. banks belong to one or other of the great joint stock companies. Their headquarters are in the neighbourhood of the Bank of England and they include the Midland, National Westminster, and Lloyds banks. The most interesting banks historically are the old banks that originated as goldsmiths' shops in the 16th century and are still in many cases family concerns, like Child's, Coutts', Glyn Mills', and Rothschild's. We have to be grateful to the banks for perpetuating the old L. signs. Even the comparatively modern banks have adopted signs in some way associated with their original premises, like the well-known running horse displayed outside Lloyds in Lombard St. A walk down Lombard St. on a bright day, especially if they are showing the flags as well as the signs, provides a welcome glimpse of old L., for in this one short and once traffic-less thoroughfare leading from the Mansion House to Gracechurch St., practically entirely occupied by banks, a most attractive array of old signs is to be seen. Barclays display their Eagle, the Commercial Bank of Scotland, King Charles (it is questionable whether I or II) and their cat and fiddle; Alexanders display the Artichoke; Lloyds the aforementioned horse; Martin's, the Grasshopper, showing some connection with Sir Thos. Gresham; and Glyn Mills' sign is the Anchor. In the middle of the 18th century Glyn Mills' amalgamated with Child's in Fleet St., having the sign of the Marigold. Another device associated with the Glyn Mills family banking house is the squirrel. The oldest of this group of banks is said to be Martin's which, as a goldsmith's business, was in Lombard St. in 1558. Child's owes its origin to one Wm. Wheeler, who was established as a goldsmith in 'Chepe,' now Cheapside, in 1559, the second year of the reign of Q. Elizabeth. John, Wm.'s son, moved to Fleet St., and his descendants early in the reign of Charles I carried on business at the 'Marygold,' formerly a tavern, next door to Temple Bar. The goldsmith's and banking business passed to the Child family by marriage. Sir Francis Child was Ld. M. of L. in 1698, being the first banker to abandon the goldsmith's craft and devote himself entirely to finance. He has been called the father of the profession, and bought the famous historic seat of Osterley in 1711. Vere and Glyn are two of the leading names in banking in the middle of the 18th century, and later in the same century the name of Mills appears, the Currie family becoming associated with the existing group of partners at the close of this period.

The bdg. known as No. 1 Fleet St. has a romantic history in keeping with that of the bank it houses. At one time part of the premises was actually inside Temple Bar, and great sums of money were stored inside the famous gateway to the City of L.: the more sensational and spectacular objects were deposited outside, in the form of the heads of traitors, a practice still prevailing in the year 1773. Ch. Dickens gives a picturesque account of 'Telson's Bank,' as he calls Child's in his *Tale of Two Cities*. Among the romantic stories of the papers and treasure chests once stored in the lofty chambers over Temple Bar is the following, related in the history of Child's, published by its partners. It concerns a midnight visitor to the bank in the days of the French Revolution. The tale goes that a certain Marquise de Rambouillet left two great chests of plate one winter's night, and the lady and her companion, returning to France, were never heard of again. When the chests were eventually opened one was found to contain nothing but the remains of a store of provisions, but the second box yielded a collection of solid gold plate and diamonds worth nearly £100,000. The ledgers of Child's show that O. Cromwell, the D. and Duchess of Marlborough, Samuel Pepys, John Dryden, Sir Godfrey Kneller, Sir Hans Sloane, and the D. of Bridgewater, whom the Childs financed to enable him to construct the famous canal, were a few of the bank's host of famous clients. The present bdg., erected in 1829, has marigolds sculptured on the façade.

Glyns were instrumental in founding the Clearing House, of which an interesting description is given in an old Guide to L. The practice of clearing, adjusting accounts each day between the various banks, dates back to the 18th century. The banks employed special clerks for this duty, known as clearers, who used to settle their accounts on top of a post, or on one another's backs in Lombard St., and eventually resorted to one banking house which had a large recess in the window they found convenient; but the house in question found just the opposite, and the noise made such a hindrance to business that it is said the clearers were often summarily turned out. Glyns decided to improve on this primitive system of adjusting accounts in the st. under all conditions of weather, and took a room where the clerks could meet. A document of 1773 records a quarterly charge of 19s. 6d. for the use of this clearing-room. In 1810 a suitable house was obtained which is the origin of the Clearing House of to-day.

Coutts' and Rothschild's are two other

private banks with a remarkable history. Rothschild's in New Court, St. Swithin's Lane, dates its influence in the financial world from 1810. The D. of Wellington made drafts that the English Govt. could not meet at the time: they were bought by Rothschild on very advantageous terms, renewed to the Govt. and later redeemed at par. From that period the house was financially associated with the Allies in their great fight with Napoleon, Rothschild's being willing to bank on the final overthrow of the Emperor.

Coutts and Co., with offices at 15 Lombard St. and 440 Strand, perpetuates the name of Thomas Coutts, 1731–1822. A suave, hospitable and benevolent citizen, he was a great figure among the literary men of his day. The romantic story of his m. to a young maidservant and the brilliant m. of his three daughters have fired the imagination of writers of fiction. Thomas Coutts was twice m., and his second wife, Harriett Mellon, the actress who survived him, became the Duchess of St. Albans.

Bankside. The name of a long and straggling riverside thoroughfare in the Bor. of Southwark which recalls the pleasure park of the Elizabethans. It consisted of the liberty of the Clink, and a more westerly area called Paris Garden. The former appertained to the Bp. of Winchester, who had a palace close to the S. side of London Bridge. The liberty extended along the foreshore of the Thames, westward to Paris Garden. (See Prisons.)

Paris Garden apparently took its name from Robt. de Paris, who held the manor in the reign of Richard II (1377–99). Previously it had been in possession of the monks of Bermondsey Abbey; from them it passed to the Knights Templars. In 1312, on the dissolution of that order, it became with other possessions the property of the Knights of St. John of Jerusalem. About 1420 they leased it to John, D. of Bedford, and in 1505 to Robt. Udall, citizen and goldsmith. Being thus private property, it was without the jurisdiction of the City, and so became the common resort of the ranks of Bohemia. The 'Stews' were located here, and the 'Winchester geese' referred to in *1 Henry VI* were the women of ill-fame.

There was a Love Lane to which Sir Walter Besant made reference in *The Bell of St. Paul's* (1889), a novel dealing with

Bankside. Its name was changed to Fletcher Lane in 1938. It has since been destroyed for the erection of the new Power Station.

It is probable that bear-baiting was witnessed there. It is not likely that the players would have gone to a place that was hitherto barren ground so far as entertainment was concerned. In 1539, according to John Foxe, the martyrologist, bear-baiting was there attended by Henry VIII. Ralph Morice, secretary to Cranmer, took a book criticizing the Six Articles in a wherry from Whitehall to St. Paul's Wharf. The K. was 'then in his barge, with a great number of boats about him, for baiting of bears over against the Bank.' The bear broke loose and climbed into the wherry, which upset. The dangerous book fell into the Thames and was discovered. Through the good office of Thos. Cromwell, E. of Essex, Morice escaped trouble. In 1545 Henry VIII, in a proclamation against vagabonds, players, etc., noted their 'fashions commonly used at the Bank and such-like naughty places where they much haunt.' In 1547 Gardiner, Bp. of Winchester, made complaint that when he proposed to hold a solemn dirge and mass for the late, if not dear, departed Henry VIII, the actors in Southwark planned to exhibit a 'solemn play to try who shall have the most resort, they in game or I in earnest.' By the time that the map of L. by Braun and Hogenberg was made (1554–8), there were two amphitheatres labelled respectively 'The Bear Baiting' and 'The Bull Baiting.' John Chamberlain, writing in 1623, said: 'The Spanish Ambassador is much delighted in bear-baiting. He was the last weeke at Paris-Garden, where they showed him all the pleasures they could with bull, bear, and horse, besides jackanapes, and then turned a white bear into the Thames, where the dogs baited him swimming.' It is not surprising that so astute a student of what the public wanted as Philip Henslowe should conceive the idea of something similar for plays, with the result that the Rose, the first of the Bankside theatres, was opened in 1587, followed by the Swan (*c.* 1595), the Globe (1599), and the Hope (1613). The appeal thus made by the Bankside to what now would be called sadism—represented by the animal-baiting—and to the passion for drama, made the Bank a synonym for rowdyism and profanity. 'Do you take the court for Paris Garden?' says the porter, addressing the rabble in *Henry VIII*. The Puritan attitude towards the subtle allurements of the Devil is well put in a dialogue in *The Muses' Looking-Glass* by Thos. Randolph (1605–35):

FLOWERDEW
It was a zealous prayer
I heard a brother make concerning play houses.

BIRD
For charity, what is it?

FLOWERDEW
That the Globe,
'Wherein,' quoth he, 'reigns a whole world of vice,
Had been consum'd; the Phoenix burnt to ashes;
The Fortune whip't for a blind whore. Black Fryers,
He wonders how it scap'd demolishing,
I' th' time of Reformation. Lastly he wish'd
The Bull might cross the Thames to the Bear Garden,
And there be soundly baited.'

The Fortune (in Cripplegate) was built largely on the same lines as the Globe, and its specification, still extant, alludes to the latter several times. It had been burnt, as also the Globe, at the time this play was written. The Red Bull was in Clerkenwell; the Phoenix in Drury Lane. Whatever it was to the Puritan mind, Bankside was to the Elizabethan something like the Crystal Palace to the Victorian. When in 1601 Sir Walter Raleigh undertook to entertain the French ambassador and his train, he took him to view the monuments in W.A. and to the new Bear Garden on Bankside. They seem to have found the latter more enjoyable. There also were the Queen's Pike-ponds, shown in Braun and Hogenberg's map as W. of the bull- and bear-baiting amphitheatres. Until about 1925 there was a cul-de-sac off Bankside that bore the name of Pike Gardens.

There were a number of Bankside taverns. The 'Anchor' still remains, with its door cut in the angle of the wall, at its east end. It once had mysterious cubby-holes, thought to have secreted smuggled goods. It was said that Shakespeare patronized its ale. 'He probably came here. He should have come here. He must have come here. Let us say, definitely and finally, that he did.' So wrote H. E. Popham. Alas for these speculations the L.C.C. Survey Volume (1950) dates the tavern 1770–75.

Another Bankside tavern was the 'Cardinal's Cap.' It is commemorated in the name of a narrow alley at Nos. 49–50. Here in 1613, the watermen, headed by John Taylor, their poet, had a conference with the players over an alarming report that it was proposed to rebuild the Globe, after the fire, on the N. side of the river. The players waxed sarcastic, and suggested that the watermen might like St. P.'s Cath. or the Royal Exchange sent on transpontine travels to suit their purpose. However, the Globe arose once more as 'the glory of the Bank.' (See 'Theatres.')

The Falcon Inn was at the W. end of Bankside, in Paris Garden, and represented to-day only by Falcon Dock. There is a letter extant, dated 21st Feb. 1645, from John Aske 'To Mr. John Smith at Mrs. Austin's the ffalcon on the banke syde.' 'The Falcon on the Stewes, Bankside,' was sold in 1647 to Thos. Rolinson for £484. The unsavoury name was probably derived from the use of the old manor house, which almost abutted on it. In *Holland's Leaguer* (1632), Dona Britannica Hollandia, the proprietress, is represented as being much pleased with the situation:

'Especially, and above all the rest, she was most taken with the report of three famous amphitheatres, which stood so near situated that her eye might take view of them from the lowest turret. One was the Continent of the World [i.e. the Globe], because half the year a world of beauties and brave spirits resorted unto it; the other was a building of excellent Hope, and though wild beasts and gladiators did most possess it, yet the gallants that came to behold those combats, though they were of a mixt society, yet were many noble worthies amongst them: the last, which stood, and as it were shak'd hands with this fortress, being in times past as famous as any of the other, was now fallen to decay, and like a dying Swanne, hanging down her head, seemed to sing her own dirge.'

There is now Holland St., about where this house must have stood. The warehouses Nos. 8–11 Bankside are on the site of the houses once called 'The Oliphant' and 'The Crane.' The former was probably the hostelry called 'The Elephant' in *Twelfth Night*.

Pepys was on Bankside a number of times for bull-baiting, and more questionable pleasures. He usually landed at Falcon Stairs. On 27th Jan. 1665, he took Jane Welsh there, and his proceedings caused H. B. Wheatley to draw a veil—or a row of dots—over them. In 1627, John Marshall of St. Saviour's Southwark, left the sum of £700 to erect a ch. This was not erected until 1671, and the old manor of Paris Garden then became conterminous with the par. of Christ Ch., as the edifice was called.

The inscription on the house next to the Provost's, to the effect that from a bdg. on the site Wren watched the erection of St. P.'s Cath., may be justifiable, but he never resided on Bankside. An old house (*c.* 1712) E. of Cardinal Cap Alley—described in *A Village in Piccadilly* by Mrs. R. Henrey—has been mistakenly associated with him.

Barbican. The first mention is 'Barbekan,' 1294–5. The name was applied to an outer fortification, frequently a tower erected over a gate. Here it was a tower on the N. side of the st. of that name. Stow says it was pulled down by Henry III in 1267, during the war with the barons. During excavations in the chyd. of St. Giles, Cripplegate, there was found a curious oval-shaped passage, running towards Barbican, under the site of the ancient gate. It was remarkably dry, and the air was pure. This probably had been made to connect with the outer fortification 'from whence a man,' wrote Stow, 'might behold and view the whole city towards the south, as also in Kent, Sussex, and Surrey, and likewise every other way, east, north, or west.' The tower must have been rebuilt, as there are references to it being given to Robt., E. of Suffolk, by Edward III in 1336, and in this family it remained until the reign of Q. Mary. It then passed into the keeping of the Baroness Katharine Willoughby d'Eresby, widow of Chas. Brandon, D. of Suffolk, who had a mansion thereby. It is not known when it was demolished, but in Strype's time (1720) there was a house on the site.

In a house in the thoroughfare called Barbican, John Milton lived with his wife, his father, and the nephews he was educating, from 1645–7. Here he wrote a few sonnets, but it was rather an unproductive period.

During the Second World War this area suffered very severely from bombing and a whole sector of the City, previously crowded and largely occupied by the clothing trade, was gutted. The C.C. took the opportunity to plan a complete new area, a 'City within the City', under the name of the Barbican project. This highly imaginative and modern multi-million pound scheme includes not only flats for residents (an endeavour to reverse the trend of the century and bring people back to the City to live), but an Arts Centre with a permanent home for the London Symphony Orchestra, the Royal Shakespeare Theatre, the Guildhall School of Music and Drama, a Library and an Art Gallery. This great scheme has been held up by the cold winds of the economic climate but the C.C. hope to complete it in the early 1970s.

Barnard's Inn is first referred to in 1454 as 'Macworth Inne.' It appears also at about the same time as 'Barnardes Inn.' Macworth was Dean of Lincoln, and it appears that licence was granted to his executor to demise a messuage in Holborn called 'Macworth's Inn' to the dean and chapter of Lincoln for pious purposes. It was then leased to one Lionel Bernard, by whose name it became to be known. Shortly after it came into use as an inn of Chancery, the dean and chapter of Lincoln receiving a yearly rent in respect of the premises. In 1549 a lease was first granted to the inn, which was attached to Gray's Inn. In the reign of Elizabeth there were 112 students in term time, and 24 out of term. During the Civil War members were permitted to bring their wives and children into the inn, but the practice was soon again prohibited. The soc., principal, antients, and students used to march in full robes to service at St. Andrew's Ch., Holborn, where they had their own pews. In 1659, when the rector, Mr. King, was about to take his D.D., the soc. sent him 40s. as 'a remembrance of their loves.' The rector, however, saying that he had 'expected a better remembrance than that,' sent the money back and got nothing. He therefore removed the locks from the doors of the soc.'s pews, and admitted ordinary citizens. He had to give way, however, and have the locks replaced. The govt. of the inn was in the hands of the principal and antients, the principal being elected by the antients from among their number, at first for five years, later for three. 'There is on record,' says R. C. Boulter, 'a pleasant testimonial written in 1604 by George Coppledyke, Principal, whose arms appear on the fourth window in the hall. Addressing the "Right Worshipful the Readers of Greis Inne" he asks them to admit "John Godbold, of Toddington, in the county of Suffolk, Gentleman of this Inn, who has very honestly and orderly used and behaved himself, and shown himself a good student in his exercises of learning." ' The said Godbold afterwards became a judge. Not all the members of Barnard's Inn behaved in so exemplary a manner. In 1601 Mr. Bellamy was fined 3s. 4d. for 'striking the cook in the kitchen,' and 6d. for abusing an antient who reproved him. In 1633, Thos. Marsh proved so refractory that the authorities expelled him and locked his door. He broke off the lock, and was imprisoned in the Marshalsea. Five yrs. later, being 'heartily sorry,' he was 'enlarged.' In 1667, attempts were made by the authorities at Lincoln to eject the inn, but the trouble was peacefully settled, and further periodical leases granted. In 1693 dinners only were provided, suppers being forbidden. In 1706, at the initiation ceremony, two quarts of wine were allowed for each mess of four men, over and above the ordinary allowance. At one time the Ld.M. was entertained at the inn, and the members went to the Mansion House in return. In 1888 the Dean and Chapter of Lincoln refused to renew the lease to an inn that was little more than a dining club and the freehold was bought by Bartle Frere, representing the trustee, by whom in 1892 it was sold to the Mercers' Co., whose sch. was here from 1894 to 1959.

The hall dates from c. 1540. Some of the coloured glass goes back to 1545, that being the date of the armorial bearings of the first principal so represented—Wm. Harvy. Some damage was caused by the 'No Popery' riots of 1780. In 1932 a careful restoration was undertaken to remedy the Victorian disfigurement. This

had led to the timbers of the roof being painted and grained, and to the panelling being crudely patched and ugly fireplaces inserted. The old timbers were scraped, made good, and replaced, the panelling was repaired, and a stone fireplace of Tudor design supplied. Wm. Morris used to lecture to the Art Workers' Guild in this hall in the eighteen-eighties.

In chambers in the inn Wm. Hayley, friend of Cowper and Blake, lived in 1737. He said the inn was 'a cheap, pleasant, and useful residence in Town for literary purposes.' Dickens was far less favourable (see Great Expectations). Festing Jones, Samuel Butler's Boswell, had chambers here from 1881 to 1893. He tells us that there was a night watchman who went round calling out the hours. He and Butler went to concerts in the hall, and when, after Jones had removed to Staple Inn, they found his old chambers being dismantled, Butler's eyes filled with tears. There are no longer any chambers, and in 1908 the Holborn front was rebuilt, and now displays the Mercers' Co.'s Queen. Until then the arms of the Macworth family adopted by Barnard's Inn were displayed.

Bartholomew Fair. It was held regularly every summer from about 1123 to 1855, and had the longest history of any L. fair. Its early yrs. were closely associated with the history of the Ch. of St. Bartholomew the Gt. In the charter of 1133 Henry I said: 'I grant also my firm peace to all persons coming to and returning from the fair which is wont to be celebrated in that place at the Feast of St. Bartholomew; and I forbid any of the royal servants to implead any of their persons, or without the consent of the canons, on those three days, to wit the eve of the feast, the feast itself, and the day following, to levy dues upon those going thither.'

As in the 11th century a fair was held on Mount Calvary, there was nothing incongruous to the medieval mind in this close association of piety with pelf. Before the ch. was erected, there had been held in Smithfield every Friday a market for the sale of horses, cattle, sheep, pigs, and farm implements. The establishment of a fair there was an astute move on the part of Rahere, the founder of St. Bartholomew's Priory and Ch., whom Henry Morley regarded as a cunning man in the old medieval sense—even more than a Christian one. There is no doubt, to begin with, it was held in the chyd., and the merchants who came to barter were sure to lay some offering on the shrine. A fair in the chyd. might be the ancient counterpart of the modern bazaar in the ch. hall. To these traders were probably added jugglers, wrestlers, acrobats, such as are depicted in some delightful sketches in a 13th-century MS. of St. Gregory's Decretals, which is now in the B.Mus., and originally belonged to St. Bartholomew's Priory. The fair was held for three days in Aug., 23rd, 24th (St. Bartholomew's Day), and 25th. All other fairs were prohibited during that period. In addition to the sale of cloths, stuffs, leather, pewter, and cattle, and the entertainments mentioned, there were probably other attractions at times in the form of those miracle plays which were the seed that flowered in Elizabethan drama.

The fair had its court of Pied Poudres. The prior presided, and it sat within the priory gates. It met later close to its original site, in the Hand and Shears Tavern in Cloth Fair. Probably 'Pie Corner'—one place where the G.F. stopped, derived its name from this court. The Court of Pied Poudres (the dusty-footed or travellers) had jurisdiction only in commercial matters. It empanelled a jury of traders formed upon the spot. It could only take cognizance of plaints of offences arising out of the fair, and could try a thief who had been guilty of theft, only if he was captured within its bounds.

Rahere secured a grant of the tolls paid at the fair from the Crown, without whose express sanction no fair could be held. In the first instance there was a stronger ground for this privilege than could be maintained later. In its early yrs., probably all the commerce was carried on in the priory precincts. When, however, it included live-stock and more bulky commodities, it extended to outside, and a claim was made to Edward I (c. 1292) by the City of L. for a half-share of the tolls. The judgment went in favour of the priory. In Edward II's reign (c. 1321) a writ was issued, inquiring by what warrant the priory held its rights over Bartholomew Fair. The production of the royal charters satisfied the Crown, and in Edward III's reign (c. 1334) the old rights were confirmed in another charter. This reassured people travelling to and from the fair in the K.'s peace, and forbade 'any servant of a royal or episcopal court to implead any of their persons' without the consent of the Prior and the Canons on the days of the Fair. The City cos. took cognizance of Bartholomew Fair, and the Merchant Taylors' Co. deputed members to attend to try the measures of the clothiers and drapers with a silver yard 36 oz. in weight. The right was maintained so long as any business was transacted in Cloth Fair. In 1566 a dealer, named Cullen, was committed to prison for using an unlawful yard, which was found in his shop at the time of the search. In 1612 there is record of a dinner at Merchant Taylors' Hall, 'for the search on St. Bartholomew's Eve.'

No doubt the fair, at an early stage, reflected the world of letters as well as of affairs outside. Henry Morley thought that a scriptural play of the Creation, such as was performed at Clerkenwell, 'was the first wild beast show at the Fair; for one of the dramatic effects connected with this play, as we read in an ancient stage direction, was to represent the creation of beasts by unloosing and sending among the excited crowds, as great a variety of strange animals as could be brought together, and to create the birds by sending up a flight of pigeons.' Another sketch by a friar of St. Bartholomew's in Gregory's Decretals, may have been taken from the pegma or platform on which 'Satan has been battering at a door of Heaven which is falling as a result of his attack, but is prostrate at the feet of the Virgin who is threatening him with a club.' In Henry VIII's reign, a hangman named Grotwell or Cartwell was himself hanged with two others for robbery of a booth at Bartholomew Fair. They were executed in a wrestling place at Clerkenwell. In 1547 the suppression of the monasteries affected the fair. Sir Richd. Rich not only came into possession of the priory, but of all the rights of the fair possessed by the priors. It was probably due to his avarice that Stow reported that, 'now, notwithstanding all proclamations of the prince, and also the Act of Parliament, in place of booths within this churchyard, only let out in the fair time, and closed up all the year after, be many large houses built, and the north wall towards Long Lane taken down, a number of tenements are there erected for such as will give great rent.' These were the houses, which, modernized at the fronts, remained in the chyd. until 1917.

In 1598 Paul Hentzner, a German traveller, visited Bartholomew Fair. He reported that it was—

'usual for the mayor, attended by the twelve principal aldermen, to walk in a neighbouring field, dressed in his scarlet gown, and about his neck a gold chain, to which is hung a golden Fleece, and, besides, that particular ornament which distinguishes the most noble order of the Garter. . . . Upon their arrival at a place appointed for that purpose, where a tent is pitched, the mob begin to wrestle before them, two at a time; the conquerors receive rewards from the magistrates. After this is over a parcel of live rabbits are turned loose among the crowd, which are pursued by a number of boys, who endeavour to catch them, with all the noise they can make. While we were at this show, one of our company, Tobias Salander, Doctor of Physic, had his pocket picked of his purse, with nine crowns, which, without doubt, was so cleverly taken from him by an Englishman, who always kept very close to him, that the Doctor did not perceive it.'

Five yrs. before Hentzner's visit the fair was closed by reason of the plague, and this occurred again five yrs. after—in 1603. In 1604 there were issued specific orders for the opening of Bartholomew Fair. The Aldermen were to meet the Ld.M. and the Sheriffs at the Guildhall Chapel 'at two of the clock after dinner, in their violet gowns lined, and their horses without cloaks, and hear Evening Prayer; which being done they take their horses and ride to Newgate, and so forth to the gate entering in at the Cloth Fair and there make a proclamation.' It appears that Sunday trading in fairs was not forbidden, for in the seventh yr. of Q. Elizabeth it was ordained that 'in all Fairs and Common Markets, falling upon the Sunday, there be no showing of any wares before the service be done.'

In 1614 Ben Jonson produced his *Bartholomew Fair.* This must rank with Dekker's *Shoemaker's Holiday* as an excellent transcript of plebeian life in L. Here

Jonson has imparted all the bustle and buffoonery of this Vanity Fair—as it certainly was—to Zeal-of-the-land Busy. Pigs, gingerbread, puppets, ballads, hobbyhorses confront the reader, and the stocks and the Court of Pied Poudres are not forgotten. All the characters buzz in and out of this lively market, and seem to say in effect, 'All the world's a fair—and all the men and women merely buyers.' Charles I's accession was marked by the arrival of another plague, which caused Bartholomew Fair to be closed.

With Cromwell, the reign of Zeal-of-the-land Busy commenced, but the fair was never suppressed. Evelyn was there in 1648, and an undated broadside describes the efforts of a Ld.M. to stop some of the frivolity

'Ile have no puppet-players, quoth he,
The harmless mirth displeaseth me.
Begun on August twenty three,
'tis full twelve howres too early.'

Apparently the objection was overruled, except possibly in the matter of the taking of time by too long a forelock, and, despite the Act of 1647 against theatres, puppet-shows at Bartholomew Fair seem to have been unmolested. When the Restoration came Pepys was often in attendance. In 1665 there was no fair because of the worst visitation of the plague on record, and although it had abated by the following yr., as a precautionary measure, Bartholomew Fair was closed again. Therefore, although the time of the fair had, since the Restoration, been extended to cover the early days of Sept., there was no fair when the G.F. occurred and just missed its venue. Pepys went in 1667 to Bartholomew Fair: 'which I was glad to see again after two years missing it by the Plague.' This yr. there was the following attraction:

'THE WONDER OF NATURE

'Girl, above Sixteen Years of Age, born in Cheshire, and not above Eighteen inches long, having shed the Teeth seven several Times, and not a perfect Bone in any part of her, only the Head; yet she hath all her senses to Admiration, and Discourses, Reads very well, Sings, Whistles, and all very pleasant to hear.

'God Save the King.
'Sept. 4 1667.'

Whether Pepys saw this is not known. He, however, mentions something equally remarkable to his eyes to be seen at the fair, 'my Lady Castlemaine at a puppet-play (*Patient Grisel*), and the street full of people expecting her coming out. I confess I did wonder at her courage to come abroad, thinking the people would abuse her: but they, silly people! do not know the work she makes, and therefore suffered her with great respect to take coach, and she went away without any trouble at all.' In 1668 Pepys took his wife, Mercer, and Deb, and there saw 'a ridiculous obscene little stage play called *Marry Andrey*, a foolish thing, but seen by everybody.' Jacob Hall's 'dancing of the ropes,' however, was 'a thing worth seeing.' Pepys also saw the same yr. 'the mare that tells money, and many things to admiration; and among others, come to me, when she was bid to go to him of the company that most loved a **pretty wench in a corner**. And this did cost me 12*d*. to the horse; which I had flung him before and did give me occasion to baiser a mighty belle fille that was in the house that was exceeding plain but fort belle.' Pepys also saw Ben Jonson's *Bartholomew Fair* performed there. 'An excellent play' was his verdict, 'the more I see it, the more I love the wit of it.' In 1671, in a skit on the Puritans, Richd. Baxter was concerned to hear that he was introduced. This was nothing worse than calling one Presbyterian by his name, and the other by Mr. Calamy's.

'The Fair,' said Henry Morley, 'was as the House of Commons, part of the Representation of the English People; not, indeed, its Lower, but its Lowest House. When Spain threatened us with an Armada, the monkey of the Fair was taught to show defiance of the King of Spain. When Gunpowder Plot was the topic of the day, it was the great show of the Fair, played to eighteen or twenty penny audiences, nine times in an after-noon. When England broke loose from civil and religious despotism, the Puritan was in the Fair preaching down vanity; and the Cavalier was in the Fair with all the puppets on his side, crying down excesses of religious zeal.' In this way anti-Popery plays reflected the sinister influence of Titus Oates, and in William III's time anti-Irish plays heralded the glorious Revolution. In 1695 *Poor Robin's*

Almanac says: 'It also tells farmers what manner of wife they shall choose; not one trickt up with ribbons and knots like a Bartholomew baby, for such an one will prove a holyday wife all play and no work.' These Bartholomew babies were dolls, sometimes called 'poppets'—the fair was famous for the quality of these, and the elegance of their frocks. In 1699 there was a lottery with 200 tickets at a guinea each—and it was drawn in the cloisters of St. Bartholomew's Ch. In 1702 Thos. Doggett kept a booth in the fair, and in 1707 Elkanah Settle, the City poet, adapted *The Siege of Troy*, an opera which he had produced at Drury Lane Theatre in 1701.

In 1708 attempts were made to suppress Bartholomew Fair. These were unsuccess-ful, but in that year a notice appeared in the *Gazette* that henceforth it was to be restricted to three days, 23rd, 24th, and 25th Aug. At this time there was consider-able agitation against the gaming that went on in the cloisters of St. Bartholo-mew's Ch., and in 1708 the *Postman* records: 'A Person did Penance in the Chapter House of St. Paul's, for publicly showing in Bartholomew's Fair a book called a Blow-Book, in which were many filthy obscene pictures. The book was like-wise burnt, and the Person paid costs.' It would be interesting to know what was the nature of the Protestant penance imposed.

In 1729 *The Beggar's Opera* was per-formed at the Black Boy on the Paved Stones near Hosier Lane, Smithfield. Joe Miller, the famous comedian, was on the boards there, and, strange to say, Greene's *Dorastus and Fawnia* (upon which Shakespeare's *Winter's Tale* was founded) was also on the programme. Austin Dobson exploded the idea that Henry Fielding had a booth at Bartholomew Fair, as Henry Morley stated (it was due to a confusion with one Timothy Fielding), and said the only positive evidence of any connexion with the author of *Tom Jones* was that Theophilus Cibber's co. played *The Miser* there in 1733. In 1749 topical L. plays were performed, i.e. *The Blind Beggar of Bethnal Green*, and *The History of Whittington*. Apparently the order limiting the fair to three days was hon-oured in the breach as well as the obser-vance, for in 1750 the Ld.M. made another order as before, and acted on the representation of more than a hundred of the chief graziers, salesmen, and inhabitants of Smithfield, who complained that 'the insolent violation of the law by the fair peoples, not only encouraged profligacy, but also obstructed business for six weeks.'

In 1753 the change in the calendar (which in 1752 had made 3rd Sept. the 14th Sept.) put Bartholomew Fair back to 3rd Sept. Again in 1760 the City Cos. considered the abolition of fairs. Southwark Fair was abolished, as over this the City Cos. had sole control; in the case of Bartholomew Fair, however, the rights of Ld. Kensington, who had some of those originally possessed by Sir Richd. Rich, had to be reckoned with—so it was allowed to continue. In 1762 one Stevens wrote a racy poem on the fair:

'Here's Punch's whole play of the gunpowder plot, sir,
With beasts all alive, and pease-porridge all hot, sir:
Fine sausages fry'd, and the black on the wire,
The whole court of France, and nice pig at the fire.
Here's the ups and downs; who'll take a seat in the chair-o?
Tho' there's more up and downs than at Bartlemew fair-o.

Here's Whittington's cat, and the tall dromedary,
The chaise without horses, and queen of Hungary;
Here's the merry-go-rounds, come who rides, come who rides, sir?
Wine, beer, ale, and cakes, fire-eating besides, sir;
The fam'd learn'd dog that can tell all his letters,
And some men, as scholars, are not much his betters.'

When John Wilkes was Ld.M. in 1774 he distinguished himself by making the entire circuit of the booths in his state coach. It was certainly much to his mind. In 1775 a Turkish artist danced on a rope 38 ft. high; in 1779 a hog 14 ft. long was exhibited; in 1790 a ram with six legs appeared; in 1794 Edmund Kean (about 10 yrs. of age) played Tom Thumb; later he broke his legs in a feat of horsemanship there. In 1814 Madam Giradelli, the 'Fireproof Lady,' performed. In 1815, Daniel Gyngell introduced a Dutch dwarf, 26 yrs. of age and 28 ins. high, as an attraction. The latter was presented to the Ld.M. Patrick Cotter, 8 ft. 7 ins. in height (a plaster cast of his hand is in the Mus. of the Royal Coll. of Surgeons), was often to be seen there about 15 yrs. before. In 1830 *The Red Barn Tragedy (Maria Marten)* could be seen for a penny. In 1832 Clarke from Astley's was there.

In 1830 the City Cos. bought from Ld. Kensington the old priory rights, vested in the heirs of Sir Richd. Rich; and by this acquisition the fair was doomed. In 1839 the L. City Mission petitioned the City Cos. about the polluting influence of Bartholomew Fair, and as a result it was restricted to two days. After 1840 no gilt Ld.M.'s coach came, and the opening was informal and colourless. In 1850 Ld.M. Musgrove found hardly any fair worth proclaiming. After that the Ld.M. came no more, and it was opened by a nondescript personage. In 1855 it was proclaimed for the last time. In 1923 there was a revival for the benefit of St. Bartholomew's Hosp.

(See *Memoirs of Bartholomew Fair*, by Henry Morley, 1859.)

Battersea now part of the L. Bor. of Wandsworth, was a met. and parly. bor. of 2,307 acres.

A document of A.D. 693, now in the Chapter House at W.A., makes mention of a grant of '28 hides of land in Badericesece,' by which the place-name would appear to mean 'the isle of Badric.' Between 693 and the end of the 16th century occur no fewer than seventy variants of this place-name. The earliest settlement grew up in the area now occupied by Falcon Rd., High St., Vicarage Rd., and Bridge Rd., with its trading centre at the ancient 'porta' or landing-place hard by the par. ch.

The ch. is mentioned in the Domesday Survey of 1086, when the manor and the rectory were held by the Abbey of Westminster. ('St. Peter of Westminster holds Patricesy.') The present riverside ch. of St. Mary, erected in 1775, superseded the medieval ch. The registers, which date from 1559, contain some interesting entries, for here, on 4th Feb. 1631, Edwd. Hyde, afterwards E. of Clarendon, m. Anne Ayliffe, and on 18th Aug. 1782 Wm. Blake m. Catherine Sophia

Boucher.

A fine armorial window at the E. end commemorates Battersea's most famous family—the St. Johns—six generations of whom were buried in the ch. Their monuments are in the north gallery, among them a large mural memorial by the famous sculptor Roubiliac to the best-known member of this family, 'Henry St. John, in the reign of Queen Anne Secretary of War, Secretary of State and Viscount Bolingbroke,' who died in 1751. There are finely executed medallion portraits of him and his wife Marie Claire, Marchioness of Villette. Other notable monuments are those to Sir Edward Wynter (d. 1685), an East India merchant whose notable exploits, recorded here in verse, included crushing a tiger to death in his arms and routing 40 mounted Moors single-handed; to Sir John Fleet (d. 1712), Ld.M., 1693; to Sir Thos. Astle, the Antiquary (d. 1803); and, in the churchyard by the portico, to Wm. Curtis, the botanist (d. 1799). In the quaint little vestry at the W. end is preserved a chair in which J. M. W. Turner used to sit and admire the sunsets seen across the river. The crypt has been cleared and a number of the older coffin plates have been set up on the walls.

The honoured name of St. John is not confined to the memorials in the ch., for in 1700 Sir Walter St. John, third baronet, was 'minded to erect and endow a school for the education of twenty free scholars.' This school, for 150 years the only one in Battersea, was rebuilt in 1859 and 1915. At the end of the High St. and over its picturesque gateway are the arms of the founder and his motto, 'Rather Deathe than False of Faythe.'

In Vicarage Rd. still stands Old Battersea House—a beautiful structure built in 1699 by Sir Walter St. John as a golden wedding present for his wife, Lady Joanna. It is said to have been of Wren's design. It contains some fine panelling and a magnificent oak staircase, and houses a wonderful collection of old furniture, pictures by Evelyn de Morgan, and pottery by her more famous husband, Wm. de Morgan. It is owned by the Corporation and may be visited by appointment.

The best-known Battersea resident of late years was John Burns, who d. in 1943. He was its M.P. from 1892–1918.

From 1905–14 he was President of the Local Government Board.

Next to Old Battersea House stands Battersea Vicarage, which bears a plaque stating that 'Edward Adrian Wilson, Antarctic Explorer and Naturalist (1872–1912), lived here.' It was the birthplace of E. M. Forster, the novelist (1879). The fine gates that front Devonshire House (7 Vicarage Rd.) are also worthy of notice.

Battersea Park, opened in 1859, contains nearly 200 acres. It has lakes and sports facilities; an outdoor sculpture exhibition is an annual event. In 1951, to celebrate the Festival of Britain a Funfair and Pleasure Gardens were laid out. The G.L.C. now own these and they have become one of the features of L. from Easter to the end of September.

Baynard's Castle. according to Stow, was originally built by Baynard, a nobleman who came over with William the Conqueror, and died in the reign of William II. Forfeited by Wm. Baynard, Baron of Dunmow, in 1111, it was then given to Robt. Fitz Richard, who was succeeded by Walter. Walter was succeeded by Robt. Fitz Walter, and according to Stow the castle remained in the same family for more than a century. It seems to have been one of the two fortified castles referred to by Fitz Stephen about 1183 as being on the W. In the *Annales Londonienses* it is said to have been destroyed by K. John in 1212. This was in consequence of Robt. Fitz Walter having joined the barons against the K., and been compelled to flee to France. There, according to a pretty story, his valour in a joust earned the admiration of John when, on a visit to that country and, not knowing his identity, the K. cried out: 'By God's sooth, he were a king indeed who had such a knight.' This led to a restoration of Fitz Walter to John's favour, and he was allowed to rebuild his castle. He had, however, lost a favourite daughter who, having preserved her chastity against John's desire, had been shut up in the T.L. and there poisoned by means of powder on a poached egg. She was said to have been bd. at Dunmow. The word 'poached', however, is later in date. In 1275 licence was granted to Robt. Fitz Walter to sell Baynard's Castle with the appurtenances in dykes etc., and in 1278 it was in the hands of the Abp. of C., and granted by him to the K. In the same yr. the friars preachers obtained a grant of the site for the erection of their ch. and priory. The Baynard's Castle Tavern (at the corner of St. Andrew's Hill and Q. Victoria St.) marks the site.

After this time a new Baynard's Castle was erected; exactly when and by whom is not known. A reference to it in 1338 indicates that it had been built in the reign of Edward II (1307–1327). This was destroyed in 1428, and then rebuilt by Humphrey, D. of Gloucester. In a deed of grant in 1453 it is referred to as 'Baynardescastell by Pollesquarfe (Paul's Wharf).' It was here, in 1461, that Edward IV was proclaimed K. In the same yr. it was granted to Ciceley, Duchess of York, the K.'s mother. Here also occurred the incident in *Richard III* (closely following Sir Thos. More's *Life of Edward V*), when the D. of Buckingham offered the crown to Richd., then D. of Gloucester. Henry VII largely rebuilt it in 1487.

In Baynard's Castle P. Arthur, Henry's eldest son, resided for a few days in 1502 with Catherine of Aragon, and later it became the jointure of the latter as Q. of Henry VIII. It passed in this way to Anne Boleyn, but after her execution it was granted to the young D. of Richmond, Henry's illegitimate son by Elizabeth Blount. He, however, d. in the same yr. (1536). In 1540 Anne of Cleves lived here for a time. On the death of Henry VIII Katharine Parr, by letters patent, appointed Sir Wm. Herbert as Keeper, his wife being the late Q.'s sister. He became the E. of Pembroke, father of one of the 'incomparable paire' to whom the First Folio of Shakespeare was dedicated. In 1559 Q. Elizabeth supped with the E. at Baynard's Castle.

It was no longer occupied by the K.'s consort, as Somerset House was allotted to Anne of Denmark, James I's Q. It was garrisoned by parliamentary forces, 1648. Pepys relates that in 1660 Charles II and Edwd. Montagu (afterwards E. of Sandwich) supped there. At the time of the G.F. it was in possession of the E. of Shrewsbury. It was not entirely destroyed in 1666, but the walls were severely damaged, and there was no attempt to rebuild. Two turrets were left, and

repaired for habitation. One survived until 1720. Fragments of the lower part of the old castle were built into dwelling-houses until the site was entirely cleared at the beginning of the 19th century. There is a C.C. plaque on Nos. 12 and 13. Close by is Baynard's Castle Wharf, and this is in Baynard's Castle Ward. There is a model of the castle in the L. Mus.

Belgravia. In the early years of the 18th century strolling out of what are today the gates at Hyde Park Corner, we could have stood and looked across a pleasant and rural scene of green fields to a large country residence on the site of which stands today St. George's Hosp. The owner of the house, Ld. Lanesborough, an eccentric, d. in 1723, and ten yrs. later Lanesborough House, on account of the salubrious air of the neighbourhood, was converted into an infirmary. The old house for many yrs. formed the central portion of the hosp., two wings being added later. It was not, however, until about 1835 that the present edifice was designed and built by Wm. Wilkins, R.A., the architect of the N.G.

Q. Caroline, wife of George II, was a generous patron to the hosp.; in 1736 she granted a charter and donation to the governors of the infirmary at Hyde Park Corner, to establish themselves into a corporation, the same to be called St. George's Hospital.

From old maps of this period it appears that at the SE. corner of St. George's Hosp. stood formerly the entrance to Tattersall's celebrated auction mart, founded in 1766, an establishment renowned through all the breadth and length of horse-loving, horse-breeding, horse-racing Europe. It was not till 1865, when the lease of the premises at Hyde Park Corner expired, that Tattersall's moved further westward to Knightsbridge. It is now finally closed.

The name Belgravia was originally applied as a sobriquet to Belgrave and Eaton Sqs. and the sts. immediately radiating from them. The Belgravia of the twentieth century lies roughly to the S. of Knightsbridge with Grosvenor Place as its eastern, and Sloane St. as its western boundaries. To the S., Buckingham Palace Rd. separates it from the vast mass of Victoria Station, and the northern fringe of Pimlico; its intriguing etymology is referred to later.

Belgravia was first laid out and built upon by Thos. Cubitt under a special Act of Parliament passed in 1826, which empowered Ld. Grosvenor to drain the site and raise the levels. A few yrs. later, in 1831, a writer states: 'During the late reign (that of George IV) Lord Grosvenor has built a new and elegant town on the site of fields of no healthy aspect, thus connecting London and Chelsea, and improving the western entrance to the Metropolis.'

Cubitt, who d. in 1856, belonged to a distinguished family; of his two brothers, one, Alderman Cubitt, became twice Ld.M. of L., and the other, Lewis Cubitt, was the architect of the Great Northern Railway terminus.

Proceeding from Hyde Park Corner, and following Grosvenor Place, built in 1767, overlooking the gardens of Buckingham Palace, one can trace out the development of the houses and sts. which impinge on its western flank. In the early yrs. of the nineteenth century, George III added a portion of the Green Park to the new garden at Buckingham House. Peter Cunningham, quoting from Walpole's *George III*, writes: 'the fields on the opposite side of the road were to be sold at the price of £20,000. This sum Grenville refused to issue from the Treasury. The ground was consequently leased to builders, and a new row of houses, overlooking the King in his private walks, was erected to his great annoyance.' So Grosvenor Place owes its existence to a display of parsimony on the part of a British Prime Minister! Although the houses of Grosvenor Place were small, they were fashionable. One of the early residents here, in 1775, was Horace Walpole's friend, Lady Ossory.

Chapel St. leads into Belgrave Sq., built in 1825, and so named after the Viscountcy of Belgrave, the second title of the E. of Grosvenor. Till recent times, and under changed conditions, Belgrave Sq. was the unchallenged home of the British aristocracy, and of the representatives of all that stood highest in English life of the nineteenth century.

A number of distinguished men and women have resided in this famous sq. Ld. Ellesmere lived here till he built

Bridgewater House. Among other notable residents were the first Ld. Combermere, Sir Roderick Murchison, the geologist, Sir Chas. Wood, afterwards Ld. Halifax, and General Sir Geo. Murray, who acted as Quartermaster General to the British army during the Peninsular War.

Drama as well as comedy has played its share in the history of Hobart Place, for here, one summer day in June 1823, took place a double tragedy. A young man murdered his father and then committed suicide. It was the usual custom at that time to bury a suicide at cross-roads' in the parish concerned, with a stake driven through his body. The site selected on this occasion was at the junction of Hobart Place with Grosvenor Place and Gardens, immediately opposite the grounds of Buckingham Palace. This so annoyed K. George IV, who quite naturally objected to this occurring so close to the Palace, that the custom of burying suicides at cross-roads was abolished by Act of Parliament on 8th July 1823.

Hobart Place leads westward into Eaton Sq., which derives its name, of course, from the ducal seat of the Westminsters in Cheshire. Designed and built by Cubitt in 1827, it has had a long connection with the legal and parliamentary world. Here at No. 83, during the close of his life, lived Ld. Truro, who in 1820 was engaged as one of the counsel for Q. Caroline on her trial in the House of Lords.

Chester Sq., on the S. side of Eaton Sq., and so named after the City of Chester, near which Eaton Hall is situated, was not commenced until 1840. Matthew Arnold was a resident for some yrs. He left in 1867.

Just off Chester Sq., in a large house at the corner of Eccleston St., once resided the eminent sculptor Sir Francis Chantrey. He came here shortly after his marriage in 1809. Originally the house consisted of two separate residences —Nos. 29 and 30 Lower Belgrave Place— but Chantrey, throwing the two houses into one, renamed them as part of Eccleston St. In his studio at the back, his best known works—the bust of Sir Walter Scott, his *Sleeping Children*, and his statue of Watt—were executed.

A few steps southwards and we find ourselves in Ebury St. As we cross the modern thoroughfare it is difficult to connect it with an Elizabethan and rural background—but such was its early state.

Both Ebury St. and Ebury Sq. are so called after Ebury or Eabury Farm, which, in the 16th century, stood on this site and embraced some 400 acres.

According to Strype, Q. Elizabeth let the farm on lease for the sum of £21 per annum to an individual named Whaske, by whom, as Strype tells us, 'the same was let to divers persons, who, for their private commodity, did enclose the same and had made pastures of arable land; thereby not only annoying Her Majesty in her walks and passages, but to the hindrance of her game and great injury to the common, which at Lammas was wont to be laid open.'

The old manor house of the Eabury estate stood approximately between Hobart Place and the bottom of Grosvenor Place.

In a modern map of Belgravia the southern portion of the district merges into what is known today as Pimlico. Some authorities even venture to state, and I think questionably, that Pimlico embraces the whole of Belgravia. In any case, over the origin of this curious name, obviously of foreign derivation, there is still considerable controversy. We have at least a fairly reliable date from which to start, for the district is not mentioned by the name of Pimlico in any existing document prior to the yr. 1628. In a map of that period a small field, near where Buckingham Palace now stands, is marked as PIMLICO. Early 18th century maps show three or four houses here. Sailing up the Thames came barges, with their brown sails, to unload coal and timber at what became designated as the Pimlico wharf, at the termination of the Grosvenor Canal, where now stands Victoria Station. Apparently the wharf derived its name from Pimlico or Pimlicay, a place in Honduras, whence ships obtained mahogany—and so, brought from the Spanish Main, the name Pimlico has become attached to a modern London district. Other writers differ as to the origin of the name—they say it is derived from an ale, 'Ben Pimlico's Nut Browne,' referred to in a tract entitled *Newes from Hogsdon* (1598).

Continuing N. from where the Pimlico

rd. joins Lower Sloane St., we cross Sloane Sq., and pass the western limits of Belgravia—Cadogan Place and Lowndes Sq.

Sloane Sq., Sloane St., and Hans Place, are all dedicated to the memory of that celebrated physician, and collector of antiques, Sir Hans Sloane. In 1712 Sir Hans Sloane bought the manor of Chelsea, and later moved there with his collection, which, after his death in Jan. 1753, formed the nucleus of the B.Mus. In the early yrs. of the 19th century, Sloane Sq. was merely an open space, enclosed with wooden posts connected with iron chains.

On the large scale ordnance survey maps of today, at the NE. corner of the sq., are the words 'Bloody Bridge (site of).' Here, at the commencement of the 19th century, stood a bridge, about twelve or fourteen ft. wide, and which had on either side a wall of sufficient height to protect passengers from falling into the narrow rivulet, the Westbourne, which flowed beneath. In old records this bridge, dating from the time of Charles II, is referred to as 'Blandel Bridge,' and it may be assumed that its more sanguinary title arises not only from the fact that on the site were found relics of the Civil Var, but also that here took place many robberies and murders, committed by the numerous footpads and others who haunted this area in the opening days of Belgravia's history. Duellists also met here to decide points of honour. Later, it became known as Grosvenor Bridge and, in more recent times, owing to the exigencies of modern requirements, it has ceased to exist.

Cadogan Place is connected in name with the family of Ld. Cadogan, into whose hands came the manor of Chelsea, by the marriage of the first Ld. Cadogan with the heiress of Sir Hans Sloane. Dickens, in *Nicholas Nickleby*, describes Cadogan Place as 'the connecting link between the aristocratic pavements of Belgrave Square and the barbarism of Chelsea!' Here lived Mr. and Mrs. Zachary Macaulay from about 1818 to 1823, when they moved to Great Ormond St. From Cadogan Place the young Macaulays used to walk on the *Sabbath*— as it was known in those days—across the Fields, now Belgrave Sq., to the Lock

Hosp., then situated in Grosvenor Place.

Wm. Wilberforce, who devoted his life to the abolition of the Slave Trade, d. here in July 1833, just as the Act which was to bring freedom to the lives of countless human beings throughout the world was being carried through Parliament. Here, too, was the last L. residence of that celebrated actress Mrs. Jordan, the mistress of William IV. Another famous character in history who lived in Cadogan Place was Lady Sarah Napier, better known as the beautiful Lady Sarah Lennox, whom George III wanted to marry, and who became the mother of that remarkable trio, two of whom were destined to make history and one to write it.

Lowndes Sq. itself dates from about the yr. 1838, when it appears to have been built upon a vacant piece of ground, described in Rocque's *Map of London and its Environs*, engraved in 1746, as then the property of Lowndes Esq., and which, according to Peter Cunningham, was so called 'after Mr. Lowndes, of the Bury, near Chesham, in Buckinghamshire, the ground landlord, a descendant of William Lowndes, Secretary to the Treasury in the reign of Queen Anne.'

As one looks at Lowndes Sq. today it is difficult to realise that it was once a coppice which supplied the Abbot and Convent of Westminster with fuel! Many distinguished citizens have resided in Lowndes Sq. Of these, we may mention that eminent engineer Sir John Rennie, the architect of both London Bridge and the bridge which spans the Serpentine in Hyde Park.

Down to about 1831 there was an open and rural expanse where now stands Belgrave Sq.—the heart, as it were, of Belgravia. This rural space was known as the 'Five Fields.' They were intersected by mud banks, occupied by only a few hamlets, and, until the beginning of the 19th century, infested by foot pads and robbers. One of the first, and unsuccessful attempts at ballooning in L. was carried out from these fields. Chambers, in his *Book of Days*, gives us an illuminating account of the event.

In the long distant past Belgravia and other parts of the valley bordering upon London, were a lagoon of the Thames. The clayey swamp in this region retained so much water that no one would build

there until Thos. Cubitt, with considerable foresight and ingenuity, discovered that the strata consisted of gravel and clay to an inconsiderable depth. As an historian tells us: 'The clay he removed and burned into bricks, and by building upon the substratum of gravel, he converted this spot from the most unhealthy to one of the most healthy in the metropolis, in spite of the fact that its surface is but a few feet above the level of the river Thames at high water during spring tides.' The early suburb of Belgravia, as it is today, passed into the possession of the Grosvenor family in 1656, when the daughter and sole heiress of Alexander Davies, Esq., of Ebury Farm, married Sir Thomas Grosvenor, the ancestor of the Dukes of Westminster. This Davies died in 1665, five years after the Restoration, little realising the immense wealth that lay in the future value of his five pasturing fields. (He was a victim of the Great Plague, though this is not mentioned on his tomb, the only one remaining in the chyd. of St. Margaret, Westminster.)

A poem of the period gives a descriptive account of the conditions prevailing in the area of the 'Five Fields' in the early days of the 19th century:

'Time was, when here, where palaces now stand,
Where dwell at ease the magnates of the land,
A barren waste existed, fetid, damp,
Cheered by the ray of no enlivening lamp!
A marshy spot, where not one patch of green,
No stunted shrub, nor sickly flower was seen;
But all things base, the refuse of the town,
Loathsome and rank, in one foul mass were thrown.'

Belgravia's northern limits are well defined, running as they do eastwards from where Sloane St. joins with Knightsbridge, to Hyde Park Corner. Originally this portion of the district, known as St. George's Place or Terrace, consisted of a long row of low-built houses before a more stately series of mansions usurped their place. Here lived John Liston, one of England's most famous comedians, from 1829 until his death in 1846. Leigh Hunt wrote: 'He had long outlived the use of his faculties, and used to stand at his window at the Corner, sadly gazing at the tide of human existence which was going by and which he had once helped to enliven.' Pope tells us that it was in this terrace that he was sent to school at the age of ten or eleven, adding that he forgot nearly all that he had learnt from his first instructor, a worthy priest. Later in life he fell back on reminiscences of his scholastic days in the following lines:

'Soon as I enter at my country door,
My mind resumes the thread it dropt
    before;
Thoughts which at Hyde Park Corner
    I forgot,
Meet and rejoin me in my pensive grot.'

Wilton Place, which was formed in 1827, occupies the site of what was once a cow-yard entered by a narrow passage from Knightsbridge.

In the 18th century, traffic along this great coaching thoroughfare was seriously congested, as it approached the western outskirts of the metropolis, by the old toll gate which stood for many years at Hyde Park Corner, at the junction of the rds. close to St. George's Hosp. It was not until as late as the end of the yr. 1825 that this encumbrance was eventually removed. The old print of the period gives us a graphic illustration of the auctioneer brandishing his hammer at the sale of the turnpike gates, rails and posts, to the infinite satisfaction of the residents in the neighbourhood.

Under modern Belgravia flows one of L.'s hidden rivers, the Westbourne stream, which, rising in the heights of Hampstead, and flowing through the Serpentine, passes under Knightsbridge and thence into the Thames, to the W. of Chelsea Bridge. Continual floods, the growth of houses along its banks, and the consequent unsanitary conditions arising therefrom, compelled the authorities in 1834 to harness this turbulent stream, and to control its future course by converting it into a prosaic sewer! Few Londoners today realise that the erstwhile Westbourne stream, now the Ranelagh sewer, is conducted to the Thames in an iron conduit high above the platforms of the Underground Station at Sloane Sq.

Bermondsey, now part of the L. Bor. of Southwark, was a met. bor., on right bank of Thames below L.B. Formerly in Surrey, it was formed by uniting the pars. of Bermondsey, Rotherhithe, Horselydown, St. Olave, and St. Thomas.

Bermondsey means 'the island of Beormund' (a Saxon personal name): it indicates the former marshy character of the place. Its area, forming the centre of the bor., was about 514 acres. The par. ch. of St. Mary Magdalen, well inland, is in Bermondsey St., near Abbey St., and stands on the site of a conventual ch. In 1082 Aylwin Child, 'citizen of London,' founded here one of the several Cluniac monasteries established in England soon after the Conquest. It was presented with the manor of Bermondsey by William Rufus, and in the 14th century became an abbey. In the abbey d. (1113) Maria, daughter of Malcolm, K. of Scotland; (1437) Katharine of Valois (widow of Henry V and m. to Owen Tudor); and (1492) Elizabeth Woodville (widow of Edward IV). After the dissolution, the manor belonged to Sir Robt. Southwell, Master of the Rolls; and then to Sir Thomas Pope, founder of Trinity Coll., Oxford—who built Bermondsey House (out of the materials of the conventual ch.) on that part of the abbey site now occupied by Bermondsey Sq. The adjacent Crucifix Lane takes its name from the Holy Rood of the abbey. The only parts of the abbey now remaining are a piece of its gatehouse in Grange Walk, and what is believed to be a consecration stone, which was found in excavating for a petrol-filling station in Bermondsey Sq.— it is preserved under glass there. A 14th-century silver salver which came from the abbey is now the offertory plate of the par. ch. St. Mary Magdalen, erected in 1680. The Gothic tower is of much later date—1830.

The treasures of the ch. include a mazer (c. 1400) and a communion cup with a Shakespearean interest. (See 'Theatres'—Swan.) There are two interesting entries in the registers which are fairly complete since 1538. One refers to a re-union between a long-parted couple who thereby renounced bigamy (1604); another mentions, under date 4 Jan. 1624-5 one Jas. Herriott as 'one of the forty children of his father, a

Scotchman.'

Other churches of interest are St. James's built in 1827 by J. Savage, architect, which has a peal of 10 bells cast from cannon captured at Waterloo; the ruined St. John, Horselydown, built 1732 and wrecked in an air-raid; and St. Thomas', built in 1702, which became in 1901 the Chapter House to Southwark Cathedral. It still contains its 'Queen Anne' reredos and pulpit. St. Olave, Tooley St., was demolished in 1926 and its par. divided between St. John Horselydown and St. Paul, Bermondsey.

An inlet called St. Saviour's Dock marks the W. end of ancient Bermondsey's river-front, where it touches Horselydown: the locality S. of it is called Dockhead. Still farther E., Cherry Garden Pier commemorates a pleasure-ground famous in the 17th century.

Rotherhithe, whose name seems to have been derived from 'Aetheredes Hyth,' mentioned in a charter of A.D. 898—though another opinion is that it comes from *rethra* (meaning a mariner), and *hythe* (a haven)—contains 754 acres, chiefly the Surrey Commercial Docks. West Lane marks the division of Rotherhithe's river-front from that of Bermondsey (proper). Rotherhithe was long popularly known as Redriff. Anciently it was a possession of Bermondsey Abbey.

There have been rectors of Rotherhithe since 1282 at latest. The present ch. of St. Mary, on the site of a medieval one, by the riverside, was opened in 1715. It is of brick; there is old stained-glass in the E. window, representing the Assumption; there is carving attributed to Grinling Gibbons in the sanctuary; a tablet, showing a ship in full sail, commemorating Capt. Anthony Wood (d. 1625); and a brass to Peter Hills, founder of the local charity sch.—an old house near the rectory, with figures of charity-children in front. In the churchyard is buried Lee Boo, prince of the Pelew Islands, who died of smallpox in L., 1784, aged twenty. The inscription concludes:

'Stop, reader, stop! let Nature claim a Tear.
A Prince of Mine, Lee Boo, lies bury'd here.'

Christopher Jones, master of the *May-*

flower, was buried here in 1622. The registers date from 1555, and the entry remains.

The Most Holy Trinity Catholic Church, Dockhead, which was totally destroyed by one of the last V2 rockets to fall on London, has now been rebuilt and was consecrated in 1960. The fine Norwegian ch., near Rotherhithe tunnel, was opened in 1927. There is a figure of St. Olaf in the porch and in a window. A model schooner hangs from the roof. When in this country during the Second World War K. Hakon VII regularly worshipped here. Nearby is the Finnish Seamen's Mission.

Bethlehem Hospital is hardly recognised by those who still talk of 'Bedlam,' a name found in the 14th century as well as in Agas's Elizabethan map of L. The founder of the priory was one Simon Fitzmary, and the date of the foundation 1247 (1240 is the erroneous date to be found on the apex of a tavern at the corner of Bishopsgate and Liverpool St. which is very close to the site). It was a child of the monastery of St. Mary, Bethlehem, Palestine, and there is an early reference to 'an oratory of New Bethlehem in London.' Fitzmary was an alderman and a man of wealth and influence. The second half of his surname indicates that he derived his name from his mother; possibly he was illegitimate. The deed poll of his foundation, not surprisingly therefore, stated that he had 'an especial and peculiar devotion to the church of the glorious Virgin Mary of Bethlehem.'

The priory was erected just outside Bishopsgate, on the site of a Roman cemetery. In 1257 Henry III granted 'protection to the brethren of St. Mary of New Bethlehem dwelling or to dwell in London without Bishopsgate.' These brethren wore as badge a red star five-rayed—the mythical star of Bethlehem. In 1329 Edward III granted a 'protection' to the hospice which extended hospitality to the poor and infirm, enabling alms to be solicited, and in 1346 the house and the order were taken under the patronage and protection of the mayor and aldermen of the City of L. In 1361 the Drapers of Cornhill enrolled themselves in the confraternity of St. Mary of Bethlehem and annually met on the Feast of Purification (2 Feb.) to hear mass in the hosp.

chapel. In 1367 the mayor and aldermen urged the Bp. of 'Bedlem' (Bethlehem) not to farm out the L. hosp. as it was rumoured he proposed to do. In the same yr. the hosp. felt the heavy hand of Edward III. He ordered the arrest of the master and proctor for obtaining money by forced indulgences, and in 1375 seized the hosp. as an alien priory, on the ground that it was the daughter house of a foreign convent in France, to which it annually paid 13s. 4d.

A document found in the muniment room of Bridewell Palace in 1632, stated that 1377 was the yr. in which Bethlehem Hosp. began to be used by 'distracted persons,' and about that date there were removed there a number of these who had been confined at the 'Stonehouse,' Charing Cross. From 1380 to 1395 a brotherhood of Skinners met in the ch. on Corpus Christi Day. There was a long procession, and, says Rev. E. G. Donoghue:

'For a space, as they wend their way around the quadrangle, priest and alderman, sister and citizen, pause outside a long low gallery in front of a group of the possessed, some of whom are heavily manacled. They kneel instinctively, or are forced on their knees, as the tabernacle of the most Holy Sacrament under its rich canopy is held up before wild or languid eyes. Then in the solemn hush which has stilled hysterical laughter and unclean tongue, the stern voice of the exorcist is heard, as he traces the cross with the monstrance: "Unclean spirits of evil, I adjure you by the Body of Him Who hath burst the gates of hell, and hath taken away the chains from its captives, that ye cease to torment these servants of Christ," and once again a cry for help rises up to heaven.

'O Saving Victim, opening wide
   The gate of heaven to man below,
Our foes press on from every side.
   Thine aid supply, Thy strength
      bestow.'

Between 1388 and 1403 Peter Taverner, the janitor, was also treasurer of the hosp., and he pocketed all the funds contributed. Amongst other goods he was charged with stealing were: 2 pairs of socks, 4 pairs of iron manacles, 5 other chains of iron and 6 chains of iron with 6 locks.' In 1383 the famous Sir Wm. Walworth

(see 'City Companies: A—Fishmongers') left 20s. to every London hosp., so that the inmates might pray for his soul, and in 1389 Ld. Basset of Drayton left £100 to found two chantries in the ch. In 1408 John Gower, the poet, left 8d. to each of the patients, and in 1441 John Carpenter, former Town Clerk of the City, left 40s. for the 'poor inmates.' Sir John Crosby in 1475 left 20s. to be given among the 'distract people being then within the hospital of Bedlam, in ready money or good wholesome food.' In Sir Thos. More's *Four Last Things* (1520) is apparently a reminiscence of what he had seen at the hosp., so close to Crosby Hall where he may have lived for a time: 'Think not that everything is pleasant that men for madness laugh at. For thou shalt in Bedlam see one laughing at the knocking of his head against a post, and yet there is little pleasure therein. But what will ye say if ye see the sage fool laugh, when he hath done his neighbour wrong, for which he shall weep for ever hereafter?' There is another allusion to the hosp. in *The Hyeway to the Spytel House*, by R. Copland (1536). It is there suggested that it is the last resort, if St. Bartholomew's Hosp. is not available, for the disposal of nagging wives:

'We have chambers purposely for them,
   Or else they should be lodged in
      Bedlem.'

The last word, as Rev. E. G. O'Donoghue points out, was used by Sir Thos. More and Wm. Tyndale 'in their theological battles with a fury worthy of the origin of the epithet.' In 1529 Geo. Boleyn, a brother of Q. Anne Boleyn, was appointed master; in 1536 Viscount Rochford, as he became, was executed on Tower Hill.

In 1546 Henry VIII, by deed of covenant, agreed to grant St. Bartholomew's Hosp. to the City, and further granted that 'the Mayor, commonalty and citizens and their successors should be masters, rulers, governors of the hospital, or house, called Bethlem.' In 1557 the two hosps. were placed under the same management. Thos. Harman, in *A Caveat or Warning for Common Cursitors, vulgarly called Vagabonds* (1566), which deals with the 'detestable behaviour of all these rowsey, ragged, rabblement of rakehells,' exposed one Nicholas Jennings, who professed to have been a yr. and a half in 'Bedlam.' This was found to be a fabrication; and the astute Harman discovering many more, Jennings was placed in the pillory, both in his ordinary and in his professional attire. In a dirty lane he had been seen to daub the latter with fresh blood from a bladder, and his face also. He was also whipped and placed in Bridewell. These beggars sometimes wore tin plates on their arms, engraved with a cross, and professed to have a licence to beg from the hosp. Tom o' Bedlam became a sign for inns, one such existed down to this century in the village of Redbourn (Herts.). Poor Tom of *King Lear* is another reminiscence. In 1563 *Dickon of Bedlam*, one of the earliest English comedies, was composed. Thos. Dekker (1577–1638) placed whole scenes in his plays in the hosp. In 1569 Sir T. Roe, Ld.M., caused an acre of ground in Bethlem to be enclosed as a chyd. for strangers, and in 1575 the old ch., after serving as a foundry, was pulled down and a dozen houses erected in its place. In 1630 the accounts of Bethlem and Bridewell were separated for the first time since Henry VIII's Deed of Covenant. In 1632–3 a Royal Commission investigated scandals in the hosp., and in 1638 Charles I confirmed its charter. In 1656, Daniel, Oliver Cromwell's porter, was admitted as patient. The poet Prior wrote a conversation in the next world between man and master (published for the first time in 1907), and Daniel was there made to say: 'From a porter I raised myself to be a prophet. I was the senior inhabitant of old Bedlam, prince of the planets, and absolute dispenser of everything. I excommunicated, or blest, as I thought proper, and when the palace of Bethlem was on fire, I forbade the people to quench the flames, and told them the day of judgment was come, and, unconcerned, I read on.' The G.F. did not, however, reach Bethlehem Hosp.

In 1674 it was suggested that Bethlehem Hosp. be moved to another site. A lease of lands in Moorfields was granted by the C.C., and in 1675–6 the new bdg. was erected. Over the stone piers of the great gate were placed two figures, carved by Caius Gabriel Cibber, representing Dementia and Acute Mania. It is said they were designed from Cromwell's porter, and there is a facial resemblance. They were greatly admired by Roubiliac. In 1684 Nat Lee, the dramatist, was a patient. In 1714 Dean Swift was elected as a governor. In 1732–3 Hogarth painted Bedlam in the eighth scene of *The Rake's Progress* ('LE' on the wall probably stood for the dramatist mentioned). Up to 1770, when admission was only by ticket, visitors to 'Bedlam' were as welcome as now to the Zoo. In *Westward Ho*, while certain persons are waiting for their horses to be saddled at the 'Dolphin' without Bishopsgate, they go over 'to Bedlam to see what Greeks are within,' satire by way of antithesis. In Ben Jonson's *The Silent Woman* 'Bedlam' is listed with the china-houses and the Exchange as among the sights of L. Oddly enough Wm. Cowper, when a schoolboy and before mental instability had manifested itself, used to go to Bedlam. 'I was not altogether insensitive to the miseries of these poor captives,' he wrote, 'but the madness of them had such a humorous air, and displayed itself in so many whimsical feats, that it was impossible not to be entertained; at the same time I was angry with myself for being so.' A writer in the *World* in 1753 said: 'I saw a hundred spectators making sport of the miserable inhabitants, provoking them into furies of rage.' John Yeoman, coming to L. from Wanstrow, near Frome, in 1774, went to 'Bedlam.' Sophie v. La Roche, a German visitor to L. in 1786, visited 'Bedlam' and wrote a lengthy account of it. She mentioned 'the two statues of the sad and raving lunatic above the entrance, by the sculptor Cibber, regarded as masterpieces for the penetrating truth of their expression, and deservedly.' She described the building as 'very palatial.' It was 540 ft. in length, 'with two large wings either side and fine gardens, where the poor people can enjoy fresh air and recreate themselves amongst trees, flowers, and plants.' She was introduced to 'Mistress Nicholson,' who had attempted to murder George III a short time before.

On two occasions at least, John Wesley visited Bethlehem Hosp. Later this was prohibited. 'So we are forbidden,' he said, 'to go Newgate for fear of making them wicked, and to Bedlam for fear of making them mad!' Horace Walpole went also. Hannah Snell, the female marine, died in Bethlehem Hosp. in 1792 (she was bd. in the graveyard of Chelsea Hosp.). In 1800 the architect reported the hosp. to be in an insecure condition; and a new bdg. was erected in St. George's Fields, Southwark, 1812–15. In 1844, a chapel with a dome was erected by S. Smirke. In 1844, the criminal patients were removed to Broadmoor. Between 1865 and 1870, the estates in Liverpool St.—then still in the possession of Bethlehem Hosp.—were sold to the Gt. Eastern and Met. Railway Cos. In 1863 the N. London Railway had thrown down the brick wall of the old burial ground wherein had been laid: Robt. Greene, the dramatist, in 1592, John Lilburne, victim of the Star Chamber, in 1657, and Lodowick Muggleton, founder of a small and now extinct sect, in 1698. Immense heaps of bones were then carried away. In 1931 the hosp. in St. George's Rd., Southwark, was emptied of its patients, who were taken to a new bdg. at W. Wickham.

(See *The Story of Bethlehem Hospital*, by the Rev. E. G. Donoghue, 1914.)

Bethnal Green now part of the L. Bor. of Tower Hamlets, was a met. bor., an area formerly in Middlesex, about ¼ mile NE. of the City of L., and was one of the Stepney (or Tower) Hamlets. Stow called it Blethenhall Green, and the ballad supposed to have been made in the reign of Q. Elizabeth has another spelling:

'My father, shee said, is soone to be seene,
    The seely blind beggar of Bednall Greene,
    That daily sits begging for charitie,
    He is the good father of pretty Bessee.'

The name may come from the family of Bathon who resided here in the reign of Edward I.

A wide green was formed S. of the Old Ford Rd., the old NE. exit from L.; and about this green the hamlet rose. Bishop's Hall, a one-time residence of the Bps. of L., stood in the NE. on ground now part of Victoria Park, and the remaining portion was pulled down on the formation of the park, opened in 1844. Another notable mansion was Bethnall House or Kirby's Castle, built by John Kirby, a L. citizen, in the time of Elizabeth. It was known as 'the Blind Beggar's House.' In Pepys' time it belonged to Sir Wm. Ryder, Deputy Master of Trinity House, and in

it Pepys deposited most of his valuables at the time of the G.F. It was SE. of the Green, and in its later days was used as an Asylum. The local silk weaving industry was really an overflow from the neighbouring par. of Spitalfields, where the Huguenot refugees had established themselves in 1685. Overcrowding was rife, and some of the weavers lived three or four families in a house. The looms usually occupied a long attic room with large windows to give good light for working, and some of these houses still remain in St. Andrew's St. and elsewhere.

The par. ch., dedicated to St. Matthew, is in Church Row, and was built in 1746. It was gutted by fire in 1859 and re-opened after restoration in 1861 when a peculiar upper storey was added to the tower. There was a handsome choir screen of inlaid polished wood. It was gutted by incendiary bombs in 1940. St. John's, consecrated in 1828, was designed by Sir John Soane, but much altered after a fire in 1870.

The first of the German flying bombs to fall in the L. area hit a bridge in Bethnal Green, 13th June 1944.

Birkbeck College was founded as the L. Mechanics' Institute, at a meeting held at the Crown and Anchor Tavern, Strand, on 2nd Dec. 1823. The promoters were Geo. Birkbeck, M.D., Jas. Clinton Robertson, journalist and patent-agent, and Thos. Hodgskin, ex-officer of the Navy and writer on economics. The last two were Radical agitators, more extreme than Francis Place, who also was associated with the scheme: and their aim, expressed in a new weekly, the *Mechanics' Magazine*, was more upheaval than uplift. Hodgskin was the real inventor of the 'surplus value' theory afterwards elaborated by Karl Marx. Birkbeck was respectable and mild. The other two objected to receiving help from the non-labouring classes: but the scheme would not move until Birkbeck brought in money and upper-class influence, and Hodgskin fell into line. This he was induced to do by being permitted—in spite of Place—to lecture on economics.

The first home of the Institute was an ancient meeting-house, Dr. Lindsey's Chapel in Monkwell St., Cripplegate— apparently the chapel up a gateway, viz. Windsor Court. Temporary offices were taken at 15 Furnival's Inn: and on 2nd Dec. 1824 was laid the foundation stone of permanent premises, 29 Southampton Bdgs., near Chancery Lane. The D. of Sussex opened the lecture-theatre 8th July 1825. In the eighteen-fifties the Institute languished. Changing conditions tended to modify the kind of instruction given, elementary classes were given up, the Institute became a place of preparation for L. University degrees when these were made accessible to outside students in 1858, and in 1866 the name was changed to 'Birkbeck Literary and Scientific Institution.'

In 1885 the Institute migrated to its recent premises in Bream's Bdgs. One old student, Francis Ravenscroft, who had joined in 1848, served on the committee of management till his death in 1902: he gathered the money to build the new premises. An arrangement that never worked was made in 1891, by which the institution became the 'Birkbeck Institute' and one of a group of three establishments (the other two were the City of L. Coll. and the Northampton Institute) called collectively the 'City Polytechnic,' in order to obtain certain grants long withheld because of the Birkbeck aspiration to University status. In 1907 the 'City Polytechnic' idea was buried, and 'Birkbeck Coll.' replaced the 'Birkbeck Institute' as title. In 1920 the coll. became a sch. of L. University for evening and part-time students—retaining all its grants, and a good deal of democracy in its govt.

After the war the college moved to Bloomsbury as part of the Univ. of L. site.

(See *The History of Birkbeck College, University of London*, by C. Delisle Burns, 1924, and *A History of Birkbeck College 1939-45* by E. H. Warmington, 1955.)

Bishopsgate. H. A. Harben says that the first reference is *Ad portam episcopi* in Domesday Book. It is also mentioned in a charter of K. Stephen to the monastery of St. Pancras, Lewes, confirming the grant of land at 'Bissopesgate' which Goder the priest gave. It was probably one of the Roman gates, and Gordon Home assumes that from it went 'the great artery, in mediæval days named Ermin Street, to the great potteries at Durobrivate [Caister, near Peterborough], the Colony of Lindum [Lincoln], and

Eboracum [York].' It is a matter of speculation as to the bp. from whom it derived a name in Saxon times. Erkenwald who d. in 685, has been suggested, but on no known authority. The name may have been due to the liability of the Bp. of L. in mediæval times, to make the hinges of Bishopsgate, in return for which he was allowed to receive one stick from every cart laden with wood as it entered the gate. In 1260 Henry III confirmed the Hanse merchants in their privileges by which, in return for their goods being exempt from toll, they were bound to keep Bishopsgate in repair. In 1470 Faulconbridge, on behalf of Henry VI, attacked this gate. He was repelled with the help of Sir John Crosby. In 1479 the Hanse merchants rebuilt it, and the new gate is said to have been adorned with the figures of two bps., Erkenwald and William the Norman who repaired it. It was repaired in 1648, and rebuilt in 1731—in a plainer form, the only ornamentation being the royal arms surmounting in a pediment over the arch. It was finally demolished in 1760. The site of Bishopsgate was clearly indicated by a mass of masonry found at a depth of 10 ft., and there is a tablet, surmounted by a mitre at the corner of Wormwood St. Over Dirty Dick's Tavern and over the entrance to the National Provincial Bank at the junction of Bishopsgate and Threadneedle St. there are sculptured representations of the gate. There is a model in L. Mus.

Blackfriars. It derives its name from the colour of the habits of the Dominican friars. They first reached L. in 1221, and were there given land by Hubert de Burgh. It was in the par. of St. Andrew, Holborn, and near the NE. corner of Shoe Lane. By 1250 the priory bdgs. must have been of considerable size, for, when a General Chapter was held, four hundred members of the Order were present. In 1262 licence was granted to them for enclosing a lane for the enlargement of their house. In 1278 the friars received a grant of the site of Baynard's Castle for the erection of a ch., cloister, and other bdgs.; and the site in Holborn was sold to Henry de Lacy, E. of Lincoln, for 550 marks. Permission was given to the Friars to pull down a portion of the City wall for the erection of their house, and in 1283 Edward I directed that the wall should be rebuilt by the C.C. The ch. was begun in 1279, and in 1287 a royal grant of 100 marks was secured towards erection.

In the next year the ch. was still in process of building. When finished, it was 220 ft. in length from E. to W., the choir measuring about 95 ft. The division between nave and choir is represented to-day by 'Church Entry.' A wall, revealed by excavations in 1925, was 5 ft. thick. The site of the W. front is now covered by houses in Blackfriars Lane; the E. end is occupied by the houses on the W. side of Friar St. Stow says 'this was a large church and richly furnished with ornaments.' A. W. Clapham, F.S.A., and Walter H. Godfrey (*Some Famous Buildings and Their Story*) quote a long passage from *Piers the Ploughman's Creed* which they thought applied almost certainly to the Blackfriars Priory:

'I thought on that house and long thereon looked,
How the pillars were painted and finely adorned,
And quaintly were carven with curious knots,
With windows well wrought lofty and wide.'

In 1292 the cloisters were being made, and in 1294 a quay on the Thames side was under construction. A number of distinguished burials took place in the ch. Hubert de Burgh's body was removed from the original ch. in Holborn where it was bd. in 1243. The heart of Q. Eleanor was bd. here in 1290; also John of Eltham, brother of Edward III; the E. of Worcester (beheaded 1470) and his wife Margaret, daughter of the K. of Scotland.

In 1382, at the Blackfriars Priory, there was a meeting of the Council of the Province of Canterbury, summoned by Courtenay, the abp., to judge Wycliffe's opinions. G. M. Trevelyan writes:

'A curious incident enabled Wycliffe's friends to boast that, though their master had been condemned by the Bishops, the Bishops had been condemned by God. It was on May 19 that the theses were pronounced to be "heresies and errors." About two o'clock that afternoon, while the churchmen were sitting round the table at the pious work, the house was shaken by a terrible earthquake that struck with panic all present except the stern and zealous Courtenay. He insisted that his subordinates should resume their seats and go on with the business, although the shock appears to have been more violent than is usual in our country, casting down pinnacles and steeples, and shaking stones out of castle walls. It took away from this solemn act of censure some at least of the effect on which the Bishops had calculated, and Wycliffe did not let pass the opportunity to point the moral. Such an omen was no light thing in such an age.'

The castle referred to was doubtless Baynard's Castle (*q.v.*) about a hundred yards away. Parliament met at the priory in 1450, 1523, and 1529. At the Parliament of 1523 Sir Thos. More was made speaker. The Emperor Charles V was lodged in the priory in 1522. Here also, in 1529, met the Legatine Court before which Catherine of Aragon was summoned respecting the proposed divorce from Henry VIII. In 1534 the prior signed submission to the royal supremacy; and three weeks later an order was made for the burial in the cloisters of two Benedictine monks, Edwd. Bocking and John Dearing, who had been hanged and beheaded at Tyburn, with Elizabeth Barton, 'Holy Maid of Kent,' for their share in the denunciation of the K.'s divorce. The priory was surrendered in 1538. There followed the granting of leases, sales, and gifts, by the Crown to favoured persons. In 1547, on the accession of Edward VI, Sir Francis Bryan obtained the hall and the site of the prior's lodging, while three yrs. later Sir Thos. Carwarden, Master of the Revels, received the lion's share in the form of the 'church, cloister, chapterhouse, and part of the guest-house, beside the churchyard and other yards and closes.' Blackfriars became an aristocratic quarter. Here (1601) Ld. Herbert, son of the fourth E. of Worcester, received a visit from Q. Elizabeth on the occasion of his marriage with Anne the daughter and heiress of Ld. John Russell. The latter was the sister of Lady Elizabeth Russell who d. a few days later (see 'Westminster Abbey'). Her Majesty was met by the bride at the waterside, and was borne on a palanquin by six noblemen to the bridegroom's house, where she dined, afterwards supping with Ld. Herbert's neighbour, Ld. Cobham. (There is a modern bdg. called Cobham House in Blackfriars Lane.) The E. and Countess of Somerset were living in Blackfriars when Sir Thos. Overbury was murdered in the T.L. Another of the Blackfriars mansions was Hunsdon House, named after Henry Carey, Baron Hunsdon, Q. Elizabeth's cousin and Ld. Chamberlain. In 1623 it was the scene of a tragic incident. It was in the occupation of Count de Tillier, the French ambassador, and in a long garret on the third story a congregation of about three hundred Roman Catholics assembled to hear a sermon from Father Drury, a famous Jesuit preacher. When Father Drury had been discoursing for about half an hour, the floor gave way and many of the congregation were precipitated to the floor below. This also yielded, and ninety-five persons lost their lives, including Father Drury and another priest who was in the room below the garret. 'The Fatal Vespers,' as the tragedy came to be called, had of course a moral in Protestant minds. Roman Catholics, on the other hand, did not scruple to suggest that the calamity had been deliberately caused. It was the presence of the aristocrats that made it difficult for Burbage to establish his theatre at Blackfriars (see 'Theatres'). Isaac Oliver, the celebrated miniaturist, lived there and was bd. in St. Anne's Ch. in 1617; Van Dyck lived there 1632–41 (he was bd. in St. P.'s Cath. and there is a memorial tablet in the crypt). Another artist, Cornelius Jansen (d. 1665), lived in the neighbourhood also. It was a Puritan quarter and many of them were feather-makers. One of the characters in Ben Jonson's *Bartholomew Fair* asks: 'What say you to your feather-makers in the Friars that are of your faction of faith? Are they not, with their perukes and their puffs, their fans and their huffs, as much pages of Pride, and waiters upon Vanity?' Another industry that flourished here was the manufacture of glass. Up to recent times this was recalled by Glasshouse Yard.

The remains of the priory for the most part perished in the G.F., but during rebuilding on the site many fragments have come to light. In 1856 the plinth and foundation of one of the buttresses of the ch. was uncovered. In 1872, during the rebuilding of the offices of *The Times*, a considerable piece of a wall, probably of the frater, was exposed. According to *Piers the Ploughman*, it was 'wrought as a chirche,' and in this section there were two pointed windows. In 1890 an arcade was discovered, and it was re-erected in Selsdon Park, Surrey. In 1900 there were discovered several pointed arches, capitals, shafts, and bases, all in situ. One of the pillars, with its base and capital, is preserved in the Ch. of St. Dominic's, Haverstock Hill. An arch from the priory was also set up in Selsdon Park, the inscription being as follows: 'This arch originally formed one of the entrances to the monastery of the black friars erected in the city of London in the thirteenth century. Removed and re-erected here in June 1900.' These remains came from Ireland Yard. They were S. of the ch. and were identified as part of a sub-vault of the S. dorter. In 1915 a portion of the W. wall of the ch. and of the S. aisle was laid bare. 'It was then observed,' wrote the late Dr. Wm. Martin, 'that this wall abutted upon the north wall of the Apothecaries' Hall, a Hall which stands upon a guest-house of the Priory.' In 1925, in digging the foundations of a bdg on the E. side. of Ch. Entry, a part of the choir was found in situ. It measured some 7 ft. in length, over 3 ft. in height, and 3 ft. 3 in. in thickness. Immediately to the W. of this, was the base and capital of a clustered column. Some of the stones showed traces of fire, probably the G.F. At the expense of the Brethren of the Dominican Order at Haverstock Hill, many of the fragments were conveyed there. The short length of wall was set up at St. Dominic's Priory, substantially as it was when discovered. 'The sections of the columns of the nave-arcades were also assembled, along with fragments and bases of capitals, to form two dwarf pillars. Isolated fragments of window tracery, stones of arches, etc., were aggregated to form a mass which balanced the walling on the other side of the pillars.'

(See *Transactions of the London and Middlesex Archæological Soc.*, New Series, Vol. 5, Part iv, 1928, and *Some Famous Buildings and Their Story*, by A. W.

Clapham and W. H. Godfrey, 1913.)

Blitz. The first attack upon central L. was on the night of Saturday, 24th Aug. 1940. Then the ch. of St. Giles, Cripplegate, started the long line of City chs. that were fated for destruction. The ch. in which Cromwell—himself a demidictator—was m. was, on this occasion, only slightly damaged. It received more severe blows later. On 12th Sept. St. Thomas's Hosp. had its first hit—one of many. On the same night a delayed action bomb fell outside St. P.'s Cath., and on 14th Sept. Buckingham Palace (*q.v.*) was struck. There were two other 'incidents' in the same month. Also in Sept. the ch. of St. Clement Danes had its first attack, as also Lambeth Palace, Guy's Hosp., and Tate Gallery.

By Oct. 1940 there had come a considerable diminution in the day raids, but attacks continued for fifty-seven consecutive nights. In Oct. the high altar of St. P.'s Cath. was destroyed. There was also damage to St. James's Ch., Piccadilly, and again to Lambeth Palace, the Tate Gallery, and St. Thomas's Hosp. In this month occurred the destruction of the Dutch Ch. of Austin Friars through a para-mine. No other ch. in the City was so completely wiped out. All that remained were the outlines of three arches and a few flat gravestones. It had been a beautiful specimen of Decorated Gothic architecture.

The most memorable night, however, of the whole War was Sunday, 29th Dec. 1940, when attempts were made to set the City ablaze. At one time about sixty fires were counted, and the deaths numbered about two hundred. Whilst St. P.'s Cath. marvellously escaped, several chs., including St. Lawrence Jewry and Christ Ch., Newgate, were reduced to ruins. The Guildhall lost its roof; the Council Chamber had only bare walls remaining; the beautiful Aldermen's Room (early 17th century) was entirely obliterated. Almost the whole of Paternoster Row was burned out, and here and in the vicinity there were lost about four million books. The raid ceased about midnight.

In Jan. 1941 raids continued, though occasionally there was immunity for a night. In Jan. a land-mine fell on the Temple (previously damaged in several raids from Sept. to Dec. 1940), and Serjeants' Inn—later almost entirely destroyed, was hit. In March fifty incendiary bombs fell in the Temple, two on the Middle Temple Hall, and two on the ch. On 16th Apr. the biggest raid was launched on L. It was claimed that 100,000 bombs were dropped. It was then that the ch. of St. Andrew, Holborn, and the neighbouring City Temple were destroyed. Also—most lamentable—it was the night of the destruction of old Chelsea Ch. The next most memorable date was Saturday, 10th May. The Temple Ch. and St. Clement Danes were then reduced to ruins; Mercers' Hall, Cheapside, was one of five cos.' halls to be destroyed; the H. of C. was bombed to a shell; the Deanery of W.A. was burned out; the B.Mus. was hit; and Lambeth Palace had its hottest night. The chs. of All Hallows Barking, and St. Olave, Hart St., were practically destroyed; the Mansion House sustained damage.

Afterwards, at long intervals, there were raids in L., but seldom over the City. Early in 1944 bombs fell again in Fleet St., one damaging the ch. of St. Dunstan-in-the-W. Notwithstanding, it was found possible to hold a marriage service there the morning after.

On Tuesday, 13th June 1944 came the first flying bomb, and the incessant attacks—by day and night—were most harassing to Londoners. For the most part the suburbs were affected. In the last fortnight of June 400,000 houses were damaged in L. and its environs, and 462,000 people were found spending nights in shelters against 470,000 in Nov. 1940. Notable damage in central L. was to the Butchers' Hall, Bartholomew Close, Smithfield, in July 1944 and the almost entire destruction of charming Staple Inn in Sept. 1944. On Sunday, 18th June 1944 the Guards' Chapel, Birdcage Walk, St. James's Park, was hit.

The last weapons, the V2 rockets, commenced on 8th Sept. 1944. The first fell at Chiswick, and the report was heard at Westminster. On 26th Nov. 1944 one hit a Woolworth's stores at New Cross, causing 174 deaths. On 8th Mar. 1945, one fell at the corner of Farringdon Rd. and Charterhouse St. on the border lines of the City, the Bor. of Holborn, and the Bor. of Finsbury. This occurred at noon, and over a hundred people were killed.

The last notable bdg. to be destroyed was in the same month: this was Whitefield's Tabernacle in Tottenham Court Rd. The last explosive to fall anywhere in L. was the rocket that descended on Hughes Mansions, Stepney, on 27th Mar. 1945, at 7.20 a.m.; it hit two blocks of flats, and killed 134 people. In the L. area about 100,000 houses were destroyed or damaged beyond repair, and 1,650,000 houses sustained some injury.

The City's blitz record was as follows. Out of the total of 460 acres of built up land, bdgs. covering about 164 acres were destroyed.

The following is an epitome of the damage to bdgs. of historical interest.

City churches ('W' indicates that it was designed by Sir Christopher Wren).

All Hallows, Barking; All Hallows, London Wall; St. Anne and St. Agnes (W); St. Alban's, Wood St. (W); St. Andrew-by-the-Wardrobe (W); St. Andrew, Holborn (W); St. Augustine, Watling St. (W); St. Bride, Fleet St. (W); Christ Ch., Newgate (W); St. Dunstan-in-the-East; St. Giles, Cripplegate; St. Lawrence Jewry (W); St. Mary Aldermanbury (W); St. Mary-le-Bow (W); St. Magnus the Martyr (W); St. Michael Paternoster Royal (W); St. Mildred, Bread St. (W); St. Nicholas Cole Abbey (W); St. Olave, Hart St.; St. Stephen, Coleman St. (W); St. Stephen, Walbrook (W); St. Mary Abchurch (W); St. Swithin, London Stone (W); St. Vedast, Foster Lane (W).

Some of these have been restored and some demolished (See 'City Churches').

A number of chs. outside the City of antiquarian interest were destroyed or badly damaged. Amongst the former were St. Clement Danes, Strand, and Chelsea old ch. Chs. badly damaged were the Temple; St. James's, Piccadilly (W); St. Mary's, Islington; St. John's Clerkenwell; St. Nicholas, Deptford; St. George's-in-the-E.

The City's only Nonconformist ch., the City Temple, was reduced to a ruin, but has been rebuilt. The R.C. ch. of St. Etheldreda, Ely Place, sustained slight damage; The Great Synagogue, Duke's Place, Aldgate, was entirely destroyed, and all its treasures lost.

St. Paul's Cathedral. Damage to the high altar and the N. Transept.

Westminster Abbey. Some damage to Henry VII's Chapel which has been repaired. Damage to stained-glass. The Deanery almost entirely destroyed.

Southwark Cathedral. Most of the stained-glass windows commemorating literary worthies, including Shakespeare, were destroyed.

Temple. Middle Temple Hall was damaged. Middle Temple Library was also badly damaged. The Inner Temple Hall and Library were almost entirely destroyed.

Tower of London. There were fifteen direct hits, but the oldest parts of the bdg.—those shewn to the public—were little affected.

Guildhall. The roof was burned off, and some damage caused to monuments. Most of stained-glass was destroyed.

Mansion House. The Egyptian Hall sustained some damage. This has been restored.

Gray's Inn. Hall, Chapel and Library, were reduced to ruins.

Staple Inn, Holborn. The Hall and some of the chambers were destroyed. The Tudor houses—much restored at different times—survived.

Westminster School. Sch. Hall and Dormitory were badly damaged.

British Museum. Ten upper galleries were destroyed. About 150,000 books were lost. The Newspaper Repository at Colindale received a direct hit in Oct. 1940, and thirty thousand volumes of bound newspapers were destroyed.

Natural History Museum, Kensington. It received damage from incendiary and flying bombs.

Buckingham Palace. Kensington Palace. They sustained damage, but not of a serious character.

The following are particulars of damage to the companies' halls.

(*a*) Totally destroyed. Bakers; Barbers; Brewers; Carpenters; Clothworkers; Coach and Coach Harness Makers; Coopers; Cordwainers; Girdlers; Haberdashers; Mercers; Merchant Taylors; Painter-Stainers; Parish Clerks; Saddlers; Salters.

(*b*) Badly damaged. Butchers; Goldsmiths; Innholders; Leathersellers; Skinners; Wax Chandlers.

(*c*) Slightly damaged. Armourers and Braziers; Cutlers; Drapers; Dyers; Fishmongers; Grocers; Stationers; Tallow Chandlers.

The statues all survived. Slight damage was caused to those of Bacon (Gray's Inn); Milton (Ch. of St. Giles, Cripplegate; and Richard I (Old Palace Yard).

Other bdgs. which have been destroyed are: Chapel of the Ascension, Bayswater Rd., Moravian Chapel, Fetter Lane, and Staple Inn Hall.

The siren sounded 715 times; 415 in 1940. H.E. bombs of varying sizes numbering 417 were dropped in the City, together with 13 parachute mines, 2,498 oil bombs, and many thousands of incendiaries. 'Incidents' reported to the Report and Control centre numbered 1,300; 183 were on 29th Dec. between 6.20 and 11.40 p.m. One of the worst was on the night 10–11th Jan. 1941 when 111 persons were killed and 433 injured at the Bank Station, in Liverpool St., and Cheapside.

The warnings given over an area approximating to the County of L. were as follows: 1939, 3; 1940, 417; 1941, 154; 1942, 25; 1943, 5; 1944, 508; 1945, 22; total 1,224.

The largest shelter was in Southwark. It was the old City and S. London railway tunnel dating from 1890. It was 70 ft. deep, and held at least 10,000 people. Another large one, holding about 4,000, was at Clapham South tube station.

(See *The Lost Treasures of London*, by William Kent, 1947; *The Bombed Buildings of Britain*, edited by J. M. Richards, with notes by John Summerson. Second and Enlarged Edition, 1947; *Bombed London: A Collection of Thirty-eight Drawings*, by Hanslip Fletcher, 1947; *The British People at War*, 1943; *Hitler Passed this Way*, 1946.)

Bloomsbury derives its name from the manor of 'Blemundsbury,' owned in the 13th century by the De Blemontes, Blemmunds, or Blemmots. Their manor house stood somewhere between the sites of the modern Bloomsbury and Russell Squares.

St. Giles's in the Fields, par. generally, grew out of a hosp. for lepers on the triangular site now roughly bounded by High St., Charing Cross Rd., and Shaftesbury Av. The hosp., dedicated to St. Giles, was founded by Matilda, Q. of Henry I, in 1101. It does not appear to have been restricted to its original purpose; for, during the time of Edward II, non-leprous persons were introduced as residents, and it became, wrote Geo. Clinch,

'a sort of asylum for decayed domestics of the Court. Not only was this an injustice towards those whom the foundress of the hospital intended to benefit, but great danger to those who enjoyed sound health arose from mixing with the poor diseased inmates.'

Edward II issued a charter which forbade the quartering of old Court servants upon the hosp. without licence being first obtained from the master and brethren. The hosp. grounds covered at least eight acres; there was an oratory or small chapel. There are also references to a great gate and chapter-house. The wealth of the hosp. grew sufficiently to excite the avarice of Henry VIII, and in 1539 it was dissolved. The site was granted, 1545, to John Dudley, Viscount Lisle, afterwards D. of Northumberland, beheaded 1553. He turned the hosp. into a residence for himself; it became a manor, and was transferred about 1546 to Wymond Carew—Ld. Lisle seems to have remained as tenant. It reverted to the Crown, and was bestowed upon the D.'s heir, Ambrose Dudley. In 1565 it was in possession of Jas. Blount, sixth Ld. Mountjoy, in right of his wife, a daughter of Sir Thos. Leigh, of Yorkshire. It was next held by Sir Walter Cope, who had apparently been mortgagee: his daughter took it to Sir Henry Riche. It was sold, about 1617, to Philip Gifford and Thos. Risley, as trustees for Henry, E. of Southampton, for £600. It went, with the other Southampton estates, to the Russells, Ds. of Bedford, 1668. The manor-house, Dudley House, W. of the ch., stood on the plot now enclosed by Denmark St., Little Denmark St., and Charing Cross Rd. Sometime gallows stood at the NW. end of High St. Here in 1414 a Lollard, Sir John Oldcastle (the original name of Falstaff—but the real Oldcastle 'died a martyr,' says Shakespeare), was hanged in chains over a slow fire, he having planned a *coup d'état* in St. Giles Fields. At the hosp. gate, criminals were presented with a bowl of ale as their last refreshment on the journey to Tyburn. The Duchess Dudley, mentioned further on, allowed an annual stipend to the sexton of St. Giles Ch. to toll the great bell when the condemned prisoners were passing. Little is known about the early churches dedicated to St. Giles. Probably after the erection of the hosp. its chapel was the village ch. (there was a village from the 13th century), with a wall screening off the lepers. The first ch. of which any illustration is preserved has a curious round tower, capped by a dome. According to Noorthouck, it became parochial in 1547. In 1617 the tower was taken down and replaced by a larger and more ornamental steeple; but, the fabric of the bdg. being regarded as beyond repair, an order was made for considerable reconstruction. Then some of the pillars and walls 'were found so rotten and decayed as to be in great danger of falling down.' Rebuilding was undertaken 1623, principally at the charge of Dame Alice Dudley, the deserted wife of the self-styled D. of Northumberland, Sir Robt. Dudley: she became Duchess Dudley in her own right 1644; and she d. at Dudley House 1669. The new ch. was completed in 1630: it was a Gothic brick bdg.; it had a lofty nave, a poor chancel, and clerestory windows; it had some handsome wood carving and stained glass, and on some of the latter were the arms of the Fishmongers' Co. By 1715, the brick ch., less than a century old, was thoroughly decayed on account of damp. Yet, for want of funds, nothing was done until after St. George's Ch. had been erected in 1729. Flitcroft was the architect of the present Portland-stone ch., completed 1734. The body of this bdg. is plain; but there is a beautiful octagonal steeple, 160 ft. high, rising from an octagonal tower above the square bell-and-clock tower. Unusually, for a ch. in modern L., it dominates the neighbourhood. In 1634 Geo. Chapman, the Elizabethan dramatist, was bd. in the chyd. The monument, designed by Inigo Jones in the form of a Roman altar, is now against the interior W. wall of the ch. In 1648 Ld. Herbert, one of the first inhabitants of Great Queen St., d. there and was bd. in the ch.—according to one account in the chancel. A flat marble stone was placed over his grave, and a Latin inscription engraved upon it. He was the author of a·*History of the Life and Reign of Henry VIII, De Veritate*, and an autobiography. At the entrance to the chyd. on the W. side is a carving in oak of the Resurrection, similar to those at the chs. of St. Andrew's, Holborn, St. Stephen, Coleman St., and at St. Mary-at-Hill. This one was executed in 1687, and is supposed, like the others, to be based upon Michelangelo's 'Last Judgment.' The sum of £27 was paid to the carver, a

Mr. Lowe. Originally at the N. entrance it was removed about 1864. The most noticeable tomb in the chyd. is Richd. Pendrell's. To Boscobel, the seat of his family, Charles II went immediately after the battle of Worcester. The Pendrells (or Penderels) concealed him in their house, dressed him as a woodcutter, and used every means in their power to secure his escape. On the Restoration, Charles did not forget the friends of adversity. In 1662 £200 was awarded to Richd. Pendrell, 'whose services in a time of the greatest trial of his fidelity are known,' and other sums to his brothers. It is probable that the family settled in the par., as Wm. Pendrell was overseer of the poor 1702–3. The slab bearing the following original inscription is in the vestibule of the ch.:

'Here lies Richard Pendrell
Preserver and Conductor to his
Majesty King Charles the Second
after his Escape from Worcester Fight
in the Year 1651
who died Feb. the 8th 1671

The inscription on the modern tomb in the chyd. has a few variations and there the date of death is incorrectly given. In 1681, Oliver Plunket, Roman Catholic Abp. of Armagh, was tried for high treason committed in Ireland, found guilty, and executed. He had requested to be bd. with the fathers of the Soc. of Jesus who had been executed at the same place, and he was accordingly laid under the N. wall of St. Giles Ch. The most imposing tomb is Duchess Dudley's. There is a recumbent effigy. Sir Roger L'Estrange was bd. in the ch. in 1704 (age 88). He was captured by the Parliamentary army, and, although sentenced to death, survived to become Licenser of the Press at the Restoration. There is a neat white marble monument in the centre aisle of the ch. recording simply his name and dates of birth and death. There is a tablet to Luke Hansard (d. 1828). He was printer of the H. of C. Journals 1774–1803. In the N. porch is a tablet in memory of John Flaxman (bd. 1826). It was erected by the Royal Academy in 1930. In 1786 Edwd. Dennis, hangman (see 'Tyburn'), was bd. in the chyd.

A tablet once in the chyd. recorded the death of a parishioner, Eleanor Stewart (d. 1725), aged 123 yrs. 5 months. A flat stone, once richly carved, covers an empty grave, wherein was once the body of Jas. Radcliffe, E. of Derwentwater, executed after Culloden at the T.L. 1746. His body was disinterred and re-bd. at Thorndon (Essex). The famous St. Giles Rookery (possibly Tom-all-Alone's in Dickens's *Bleak House*) was bounded: N. by Great Russell St., W. by Tottenham Court Rd., SW. and S. by High St. and Broad St., E. by Dyott St.—for, though the Rookery extended farther E., St. Giles par. did not. A clearing-up began when New Oxford St. was cut through the Rookery in 1847. Dyott St. was named after a family prominent in the par. in Stuart times, who had a house in it—its earlier name was Maidenhead Close; for a while in the 19th century it was George St. Somewhere hereabout is the scene of Hogarth's 'Gin Lane' picture, for it gives a SW. view of St. George's Ch. steeple.

The most squalid part was comprised in Church Lane and Church St.—the former, and the lower end of the latter, are the Bucknall St. of to-day. There was a Buckbridge or Buckeridge St., crossing Church St.: it disappeared when New Oxford St. arrived. Church Lane was the last part of the Rookery to go.

S. of the old hosp. site runs Monmouth St. The previous thoroughfare of that name, which was from the eighteen-forties Dudley St., was swallowed up by Shaftesbury Av. in 1885. It was a Jewish mart of old clothes. There used to be a Monmouth Court between Monmouth St. and Little Earl St. (Seven Dials), where a famous press was founded by Jas. Catnach in 1813; it was noted for its chap-books and broadsides. From Broad St., southward, runs Drury Lane, partly in this par., as were the lands on each side of it anciently called 'Aldewych.' Great Queen St., which is St. Giles's eastward extension of Long Acre, contains the great new Freemasons' Hall (completed 1933) at Wild St. corner, and (on the N. side) the Kingsway Theatre— which began as the Great Queen Street Theatre in 1900. For Lincoln's Inn Fields see separate article.

The par. of St. George's, Bloomsbury, was cut out of the par. of St. Giles's in 1724; and a ch., erected in Hart St., was consecrated in 1730. The architect was Nicholas Hawksmoor, and his steeple was not worthy of a pupil of Wren's: it is a kind of pyramid, above whose apex, on a short column, is a statue of George I in

Roman costume, given by Wm. Hucks, an opulent brewer of St. Giles's par. Walpole stigmatized it as a 'masterpiece of absurdity.' At the bottom of the steeple were originally lions and unicorns, but they have been removed. It provoked an epigram:

'When Henry the Eighth left the Pope in the lurch
The Protestants made him the head of the Church;
But George's good subjects, the Bloomsbury people,
Instead of the Church, made him head of the steeple.'

The portico was copied from St. Martin in the Fields. The interior was fine but somewhat spoiled when in 1800 the sanctuary was moved from the E. end to the N. transept, to admit the handsome wooden reredos from the chapel of the recently demolished Southampton House. Bloomsbury Sq. was originally made about 1665, and was first known as Southampton Sq.—from the builder. (See 'Squares'.)

Great Russell St. and Russell Sq. derive their names from Ld. Wm. Russell, who m. the daughter and heiress of the last Ld. Southampton (see 'Lincoln's Inn Fields'). The sq. was laid out about 1804, and of the squares of L. only Lincoln's Inn Fields is larger. Torrington Sq. was laid out in 1800 on ground previously known as Long Fields. Here, by or on the site of the new bdgs. of L. University, was the 'Field of the Forty Footsteps.' The story was that about 1685 two brothers fought for the hand of a lady, who watched a duel which proved fatal to both men, and that ever afterwards the footsteps of the men were discernible, as the grass would not grow to cover them.

By reason of the B. Mus. (see 'Libraries') Bloomsbury is the district of the New Grub St. writers of whose woes Geo. Gissing was the plaintive portrayer. The coming of the L. University to its permanent home here has been preceded by the establishment of important schs. and colls. The London Sch. of Hygiene and Tropical Medicine and the Royal Academy of Dramatic Art are on the E. side of Gower St.

Books in London. L. may have been 'the flower of cities all,' but in the literary world it bloomed late. Students of early English literature must have noticed how long a period elapses before the incursion of the men of letters in L.

Nothelm was a pious priest of L. before he was Abp of C., and aided Bede in writing L. history. St. Dunstan, a Londoner at times, was a scribe and something of a bibliomaniac. For several centuries later, libraries are heard of only in ecclesiastical custody. In 1295 it is known from a visitation of St. P.'s Cath. by Ralph de Baudoke or Baldock, the Dean, afterwards Bp. of L., that there were found twelve copies of the gospels, all adorned with silver, some with gilding, pearls, and gems. The same bp. in 1313 bequeathed various volumes, including one of St. Thomas Aquinas and the *Chronicles* of Henry of Huntingdon. W.A. also had its library but there now remain only two mediæval books—the splendid *Litlington Missal* and the *Liber Regalis* containing the order of service for coronations, 'both 14th-century productions.

A 14th-century bibliophile who came to L. from time to time was Richd. de Bury. As Bp. of Durham he must have occupied Durham House (see 'Strand'), and probably wrote there some of his delightful *Philobiblon* (Love of Books). It was evidently penned by instalments, and perhaps he put that precious manuscript in his wallet and added a little, as the spirit moved, when ecclesiastical business ordered him S.

The library of the Dominicans in L. was at one time stored with valuable books. Leland mentions some he found there including those of Wycliffe. The library Richd. Whittington gave to the Greyfriars must also have been a fine one. An old MS. in the Cottonian library says:

'In the year of our Lord, 1421, the worshipful Richard Whyttyngton, knight and mayor of London, began the new library and laid the first foundation stone on the 21st day of October: that is on the feast of St Hilarion the abbot. And the following year before the feast of the nativity of Christ, the house was raised and covered; and in three years after it was floored, whitewashed, glazed, adorned with shelves, statues, and carvings and furnished with books, and the expenses about what is aforesaid amounted to £556 16s. 9d., of which sum, the aforesaid Richard Whyttyngton paid £400, and the

residue was paid by the reverend father B. Thomas Winchelsey and his friends, to whose soul God be propitious.—Amen.'

Through similar generosity, the Guildhall started its first library. (See 'Libraries.')

In 1506, the Inner Temple had a library; though it was evidently meagre, for there was no regular librarian, the care of the books being a subsidiary duty of the chief butler. Some yrs. later the Middle Temple were without one, 'so that,' said an anonymous writer, 'they cannot attaine to the knowledge of divers learnings, but to their great chardges by the buying of such bookes as they lust to study. They had a simple library in which were not many bookes besides the law, and that library by meanes that it stood allways open, and that the learners had not each a key unto it, was [at] last robbed of all the bookes in it.'

In 1476 Wm. Caxton set up his press in the 'Almonesrye' (the place where alms were distributed) in the precincts of W.A. His successor Wynkyn de Worde moved eastwards into the City—to Fleet St. The multiplication of copies must have been a boon to the hungry bookworm, their fewness having provoked a price that was prohibitive.

Fleet St. was the location of most of the early printer-publishers. Richd. Pynson, about 1502, moved from without Temple Bar to the 'George' in Fleet St. At the former works he had produced, in 1493 *Dives and Pauper* by Henry Parker, a Carmelite monk of Doncaster, who d. in 1470. This much-quoted work (see particularly *Parish Life in Medieval England* by Abbot Gasquet) begins with a treatise on holy poverty, points out the duties of the rich toward the poor, and expounds the ten commandments. Pynson became royal printer, receiving a salary of 40s. per annum, afterwards increased to £4. He printed numbers of proclamations, yr. books, and statutes; but in addition to this official work he produced also the works of Chaucer, Skelton, and Lydgate, Froissart's *Chronicles*, and the *Chronicles* of Alderman Fabyan in 1516. Another Fleet St. printer, Wm. Griffith, had a bookshop separate from his printing works, and in St. Dunstan's Chyd. sold copies of *Gorboduc*, by Thos. Norton and Ld. Buckhurst, the first

English tragedy, in 1565. In this era publishing was a much more risky business than now. Stow relates that Wm. Carter, a printer who had been imprisoned on divers occasions for printing 'naughty papysticall books,' was in 1584 drawn from Newgate to Tyburn, and there hanged, disembowelled, and quartered for having printed a seditious book entitled *A Treatise of Schisme*. In 1594 several stationers were fined for selling 'psalmes disorderly printed.' In 1559 John King was nned 2s. 6d. for printing *The Nutbrowne Mayde* without licence. In 1586 it was ordered that no further press be erected until such time as by death or otherwise they were reduced to the number which the Abp. of C. and the Bp. of L. should think requisite for the service of the realm. H. G. Aldis wrote:

'In London the localities most favoured by the booksellers of the Elizabethan period were St. Paul's churchyard, Fleet Street, and, towards the end of the century, Paternoster Row; but St. Paul's was quite clearly the focus of the trade. The business premises around the cathedral church were of two classes, the houses which bordered the churchyards, and the less substantial booths (or lock-up shops) and stalls which clustered round the walls, and at the doors of the building itself. Those stationers who dwelt at any distance from St. Paul's evidently felt the need of getting into closer touch with this business centre for some of them are found occupying stalls at the door.'

When John Day, the printer of Aldersgate (*q.v.*) found that his printing house was not advantageously situated for the sale of books:

'He got framed a neat handsome shop. It was but little and low, and flat-roofed, and leaded like a terrace, railed and posted, fit for men to stand upon in any triumph or show.'

It cost forty or fifty pounds.

It was in St. P.'s Chyd. that in 1597 the first issues of *Richard II* and *Richard III* appeared, and in 1600, from the same place, were published the only known quartos of *Much Ado about Nothing* and *Henry IV*. The first quarto of *Hamlet* was printed by Jas. Roberts in 1603, and the title-page of the second quarto (1604) states that it is to be sold 'at his shoppe under Saint Dunstons Church in Fleet Street.' Wm. Aspley of St. P.'s Chyd., together with John Wright, sold Shakespeare's Sonnets in 1609: in June of that yr. Edwd. Alleyn paid fivepence for a copy. The quarto plays were mostly produced for sixpence. The First Folio was published in 1623 at Barbican, and the price was £1. It was probably printed in the printing office of Wm. and Isaac Jaggard, near St. Dunstan's Ch.

In the 17th century a number of booksellers set up business on London Bridge. One, Wm. Pickering, had been there so early as 1557, selling mainly ballads. Henry Gosson's shop was 'on London Bridge, near to the Gate,' between about 1610 and 1635. A little later there was Chas. Tyus or Tyns, at the sign of the Three Bibles. In the 18th century Cocker's *Arithmetic* was sold on the bridge, and also printed there, as also a *Discourse of the Four Last Things, viz. Death, Judgment, Hell, Heaven; A Collection of Six New Delightful Novels; The Unlucky Fair One*, etc.; and W. Stow's *Remarks on London*. Gordon Home says:

'The large numbers of book printed and published on the bridge did not aspire to great literature; they were more on the level of the chapbook, or anything suited to the public of small means, and the majority were therefore little duodecimo volumes of modest price. The booksellers and printers catered for people up from the country, for sailors, servant maids, and any other who wanted a ready reckoner, and a cheap handy booklet of everyday knowledge.'

Another resort of booksellers up to about 1725 was Little Britain. There is an imprint of John Awdeley there in 1575. There the E. of Dorset found *Paradise Lost*, to the bookseller an unknown work which he was anxious to dispose of, as there was so little sale for it.

In 1711, in Little Britain, Samuel Buckley printed *The Spectator*. In 1712, Samuel Johnson, an infant of three, stayed there with John Nicholson, a bookseller. His father, Michael Johnson, was a bookseller, and perhaps had done business with Nicholson.

Paternoster Row (*q.v.*) succeeded Little Britain. *Robinson Crusoe* was published there in 1719, and a thoroughfare which before was famous for its mercers became the haunt of the booklover. Apart from

Longman's, however, it seems to have been given up to publishers of little note in the 18th century; and when John Murray started business in 1768 it was at 32 Fleet St.

Booksellers at this epoch had a rough-and-tumble life. Osborne, whose shop was at Gray's Inn Gate, was knocked down by a folio volume wielded by the strong arm of Samuel Johnson; and Curll, though he traded in Covent Garden under the sign of the Bible, stood in the pillory at Charing Cross in 1725, for 'printing and publishing several obscene and immodest books, greatly tending to the corruption and depravation of manners.' Another famous bookseller of the period was Thos. Guy, founder of Guy's Hosp. (see 'Hospitals'): his business was in Lombard St. He was able to acquire the privilege of printing the Bible, which he combined with less edifying business. The booksellers tended to scatter more; and Dodsley opened his shop in Pall Mall, then less fashionable than now; while Dilly, Dr. Johnson's friend, carried on business in the Poultry. John Newbery catered for children, publishing ('price 2d. gilt') *The History of Little Goody Two Shoes*, dedicated 'To all young gentlemen and ladies who are good, or intend to be good.' His shop was in St. P.'s Chyd. In the *Vicar of Wakefield* (published by Francis Newbery in two volumes at 6s. in 1766) there is a pleasing tribute to Newbery's goodness of heart when Dr. Primrose is sick and penniless at an inn and is succoured:

'This person was no other than the philanthropic bookseller in St. Paul's Churchyard, who had written so many little books for children: he called himself their friend, but he was the friend of all mankind. He was no sooner alighted but he was in haste to be gone, for he was ever on business of the utmost importance, and was at that time actually compiling materials for the history of one Mr. Thomas Trip.'

A publisher worthy of all praise was Chas. Knight, who started business in Pall Mall East in 1822. In 1832 he brought out the *Penny Magazine*; which, before the close of the yr., reached a sale of 200,000 in weekly and monthly parts. A *Pictorial Bible* was followed by *Illustrated London* (1843), the forerunner of Thornbury and Walford's *Old and New*

London. John Cassell made his first public appearance in L. in 1836, with a temperance speech in the New Jerusalem schoolrooms in Westminster Bridge Rd. He started with a tea and coffee business in Fenchurch St., to which was added a little publishing. He soon moved to La Belle Sauvage Yard, where he was associated with Messrs. Petter and Galpin. In 1850, the *Working Man's Friend* was the precursor of many serial publications, of which perhaps the best known was the *History of England*. John Cassell d. at his house in Regent's Park in 1865.

Secondhand-book shops make the most appeal to the hungry bookman, whose mind would fain banquet, even if the body pines. They were very elusive until modern times.

Stalls lined the walls of Bethlehem Hosp. in Moorfields. The shop where Chas. Lamb bought his prized Beaumont and Fletcher was in Covent Garden, where there are no book shops now. Geo. Gissing bought his Gibbon's *Decline and Fall of the Roman Empire* at a shop near Gt. Portland St. Station. This also has vanished: as has Vieweg's, a curiosity and secondhand-book shop E. of Westminster B. (County Hall covers part of the site) where Luke Ackroyd in *Thyrza* bought a volume. Gone, too, are the old familiar places for the book-browser in Booksellers' Row, otherwise Holywell St. Charing Cross Rd. is alone in its glory.

Bridewell. Bridewell Place, New Bridge St. (so called after the first Blackfriars Bridge), recalls a palace and a prison which were there from the 16th century. Stow conjectured a castle here in the reign of William I (1066–87), and a palace in the time of K. John; but in the latter part of the 10th century the site was a marsh; in 1375 a royal licence described it as a garden; and in 1422 it was simply 'a vacant and unenclosed waste.' In 1509 Henry VIII granted to Wolsey an orchard, twelve gardens between the vicarage of St. Bride's and the Thames, which Sir Thos. Docwra, Prior of the Knights Hospitallers of St. John of Jerusalem had leased to the notorious Empson, one of Henry VII's extortioners whom his son had executed. Wolsey probably designed to build a palace for himself; but he took a lease of Hampton Court manor from the Hospitallers in 1515, and Henry VIII decided to build a palace himself on the Bridewell estate.

It was commenced in 1515, and not completed until about 1523. The estimated cost was £25,000; the architect was Thos. Larke (d. 1530, bd. in Blackfriars Priory). There were three principal courts. The southernmost fronted the Thames. On the E. stood a small outer court. This led into an area or sq., which was bounded on the N. by Bride Lane, and on the W. by Dorset St. houses. At the beginning of the 20th century, when Graham House (at the junction of Water Gate and Tudor St.) was in course of erection, the foundations of an octagonal tower were discovered. This indicated the southern boundary of the palace, which—with its Tudor brickwork, small stone-framed windows, and hexagonal and octagonal towers—must have afforded a picturesque spectacle from the river.

In April 1523 Henry VIII was in residence there, and in June of that year Charles V of Spain was entertained by him. Charles and his cortège were lodged in the Blackfriars Priory; and to facilitate their passage to and from the royal apartments in Bridewell Palace, the Fleet River was bridged by a gallery which pierced the wall on its E. bank. In 1528 Henry VIII, in the Great Hall of the palace, received in audience Campeggio, the Papal legate, regarding the question of the divorce of Catherine of Aragon. In 1529, in the Parliament Chamber of the Blackfriars Priory, the protracted divorce proceedings began. It was probably in the palace that Catherine saw her husband for the last time, Henry inviting her to dine with him on 30th Nov. of the same yr.

From 1531 to 1539 Bridewell Palace was occupied by resident· ambassadors. In 1532 Hans Holbein the younger came to L., and as one of 'The Two Ambassadors' (in the famous picture in the N.G.) was Jean de Dinteville (1504–55), who was resident there, it is certain Holbein must have been a visitor from time to time, and possibly a resident. From 1545 to 1550 François van der Delft, the Spanish and Imperial ambassador, was a resident, and in 1553 there came Antoine de Noailles from France. In the following year his wife bore him a son in Bridewell Palace.

The palace can hardly have been ade-quately occupied by representatives of foreign courts, and it was not surprising, therefore, that better uses were suggested. The dissolution of the monasteries, and the surrender therewith of some of the hosps., had intensified the problems of poverty. Beggars, cripples, and other unemployed people swarmed in the streets. Ridley, Bp. of L., in a sermon preached before Edward VI at Whitehall Palace in Feb. or March 1552, drew attention to their condition. 'The young king was greatly moved, giving him hearty thanks for his sermon,' said Grafton, and at Ridley's request he gave him a letter addressed to the Ld.M., 'and commanded the bishop not only to deliver the same letter himself, but also to signify unto the mayor that it was the king's express commandment that the mayor should therein travail.' The sequel was that on 12th June 1553 an agreement was entered into between the C.C. and the K., bestowing upon the former Bridewell Palace, and on 28th June 1553 letters patent were granted, bestowing the lands and rents of the Savoy Hosp. to the value of £450 a yr., together with household stuff for its maintenance. Within a month the young K. was dead. In the hall of the present Bridewell Foundation there is still the painting of Edward VI presenting the charter.

Bridewell thereupon started a new era, and was formally inaugurated as a 'Hospital'—of moral not physical deformities—on 16th Dec. 1556. On that date a woman was whipped there, before being taken to the pillory in Cheapside, for abandoning a child in the streets of Southwark. Its business was to punish the wrongdoers, to protect the neglected child, and to put the vagrant and beggar to profitable employment. It became 'A House of Correction and House of Occupation.' In 1557 it was placed under the same management as Bethlehem Hosp. and this arrangement still prevails. In Q. Elizabeth's reign it became also a house of correction for what were deemed heresies, and in 1568 a number of Non-conformists, arrested at the house of a goldsmith in the par. of St. Martin-in-the-Fields, were taken there. One Richd. Fitz, regarded as the protomartyr of Congregationalism, died there. R.C.s were also confined there, and Margaret Ward, in 1588, was hanged and quartered at Tyburn for assisting the escape of Wm. Watson, a secular priest who had been imprisoned in some dark hole called 'Little Ease.' (There was a stained-glass window to her memory in Tyburn Convent.) In the 17th century many who were victims of religious vagaries were found within the walls of Bridewell Hosp. Richd. Lane and his wife were brought there in 1631, because their gospel of perfection in Christ had absolved them from solemnizing their marriage in their par. ch. Richd. Farnham came in 1637, believing that he was one of the 'anointed witnesses' of the book of Revelation, that he would be slain in the streets of Jerusalem, and rise again on the third day as priest and k. His faith, if it could not move mountains, was to have removed the plague, which he said would not come nigh him, but he caught it and d. 1641. In 1653 came Lodowick Muggleton, the prophet of Walnut Tree Yard. Quakers were included among its prisoners, including the notorious Jas. Nayler (c. 1617–60) who rode into Bristol to the shouts from female devotees of 'Hosanna! Hosanna! Holy, holy, holy, is the Lord God of Israel.' Thos. Ellwood, Milton's friend, was a prisoner in 1662, and his autobiography includes a detailed account of Bridewell. In the G.F. the S. quadrangle was entirely destroyed: the two N. ones suffered much less, the chapel court sustaining little damage. It was not until 1676 that the necessary rebuilding was completed. This included a new stone bridge built in 1672, to replace the wooden one over the Fleet erected for Charles V.

Maitland (1739) says that in the chapel of the Pre-Fire Bridewell, close by the pulpit, hung the picture of Edward VI with the lines under it:

'This Edward of fair memory the Sixt,
    In whom, with Greatness, Goodness
        was commixt,
    Gave this Bridewel, a palace in old
        Times,
    For a chastising House of vagrant
        Crimes.'

This was what Bridewell was most famous for. In 1633 a whipping-post and ducking-stool were installed, and it was a great L. sight to come and see the floggings twice weekly. After the G.F. these were administered in a special whipping-room, draped in black. In 1677 a balustraded gallery was erected for the public. The practice continued for another ninety yrs. Hogarth's picture of women at the hemp blocks (Plate IV of *The Harlot's Progress*) shows the Westminster Bridewell. The House of Correction was copied elsewhere, and there was a number also in the provinces. The Rev. E. G. O'Donoghue did not think that a time-honoured story, mentioned by Scott in one of his copious notes, could be associated with the original Bridewell. This was of Madam Cresswell, a notorious procuress, in the second half of the 17th century. She bequeathed £10 for a funeral sermon, on condition that the preacher was to say nothing but what was well of her. The parson was supposed to have won the legacy by concluding a conventional funeral sermon with the words:

'All that I shall say of her is that she
    was born-well, she married-well, and
    she died-well, for she was born in Shad-
    well, married Cress-well, lived in
    Clerken-well, and died in Bride-well.'
Clerkenwell had its own Bridewell, and probably she died there.

The 'No Popery' rioters threatened Bridewell, but, militiamen being quartered there for some sixty-four days, it escaped. Jonas Hanway visited it, and advocated solitary confinement as less demoralizing. John Howard, who came in 1787 and 1788, thought there should be more separation between the prisoners, although he commended the liberal allowance of food and the suitable employment given. Bridewell also provided medical attendance long before 1775, when it became general in prisons. In addition to the criminal population, there was the work of training boys (orphan and criminal) for various occupations under 'arts masters,' who were resident in the hosp. This system lasted until 1827, and in 1830 for the same purpose the 'House of Occupations' was opened in the grounds of Bethlehem Hosp. at Lambeth. In 1867 this institution (then called K. Edward's Sch.) was removed to Witley. As the result of unfavourable reports upon the prison, in some cases for evils which could hardly be remedied for lack of space and accommodation, it was closed in 1855. The bdgs. were demolished in 1863. Bridewell Place marks the centre of the site of the palace and prison. There still remain the Court Room and other offices. The former dates from 1865–70, and approximately occupies the site of the similar pre-Fire room. The Banqueting Hall of Henry VIII ran E.–W. parallel to Tudor St. The beautiful hammered iron gateway in the passage was presented by Sir Wm. Withers in the beginning of the 18th century. Up to 1803, when it was demolished, it was the entrance to the chapel. The New Bridge St. front with the carved head of Edward VI, was built about 1805. There still remain underground cells in which at one time refractory City apprentices were confined by order of the City Chamberlain. They have not been occupied for about forty yrs. The rector of St. Bride's Ch. holds the sinecure office of chaplain to these offenders!

Bridewell had three chyds. The first was S. of the chapel. The second was S. of Tudor St., the third was on a site between the modern Bridewell Place and Dorset St., and still remains, though without tombstones. The freehold of the chyd. was purchased from the De La Warr family (the modern representatives of the E.s of Dorset) in 1903 by Ward Lock & Co. Ltd., the publishers, and they were obliged to leave the ground vacant. A Bill to utilize the land for printing works passed the House of Lords in 1903, but was rejected by a large majority in the H. of C.

(See *Bridewell Hospital, Palace, Prison, Schools,* by Rev. E. G. O'Donoghue; Vol. 1, 1923, Vol. 2, 1929; and *Bridewell Royal Hospital,* by A. J. Copeland, 1888.)

Bridges. Exclusive of railway bridges, there are fifteen bridges over the Thames in the County of L.—E. to W. they are Tower B., London B., Southwark B., Blackfriars B., Waterloo B., Hungerford B., Westminster B., Lambeth B., Vauxhall B., Chelsea B., Albert B., Battersea B., Wandsworth B., Putney B., Hammersmith B.

LONDON BRIDGE alone has a lengthy history. It is possible there was a bridge not far E. of the present one—in A.D. 43. Dion Cassius (155–*c.* 230), referring to the pursuit of the Britons by the forces of Aulus Plautius, says the German troops swam across the Thames 'and some others got over a bridge a little way up stream.' If they swam across at Westminster, where the river would have been most fordable, this would seem to imply a bridge at a point where the Roman city afterwards sprang up. In 1887 H. Syer Cuming referred to the 'remains of stout oaken piles with iron shoes, and huge conglomerates composed of ferruginous matter, and numerous Roman coins, chiefly first and second brass of the higher empire' as being found a little to the E. of the present bridge. History is not reached regarding the bridge, however, until a date which can only be approximately fixed, 963–84. A woman and her son having been found guilty of that curious form of witchcraft which consisted in making a small figure of an enemy and piercing it with pins, the Codex Diplomaticus says the woman was drowned at London Bridge, and her son escaped and was outlawed. Amongst the laws of Æthelred (978–1016) are directions as to the tolls to be taken from fish-laden boats coming to the bridge.

In 1014 London Bridge figured in a fight between Æthelred, K. of the English, and the Danes. The former was supported by K. Olaf of Norway. According to the saga, they sailed into the Thames with their fleet, but the Danes had a castle in the City, and in 'Suthvirke' (Southwark) they had erected a great bulwark of stone, timber, and turf, and this was fortified by a strong army. Between the castle and Southwark there was a bridge, so broad that two wagons could pass each other upon it. On the bridge were raised barricades—towers and wooden parapets —and under it were piles driven into the river. On Olaf's suggestion ships lay alongside the bridge, great platforms of wood being made to cover them. These were sufficiently strong to withstand the missiles thrown by the troops that manned the bridge, and so cables were laid round the piles which supported it, and the ships, to which the other ends were attached, being rowed away, the bridge collapsed, and precipitated many of the men into the river. At the end of the saga which vividly portrays this remarkable exploit, there is inserted a vigorous poem by Ottar Svarte which opens:

> 'London Bridge is broken down, ,
> Gold is won, and bright renown,
> Shields resounding,
> War-horns sounding,

Hildur shouting in the din!
  Arrows singing,
    Mailcoats ringing—
  Odin makes our Olaf win.'

The next event was in 1023. Canute,
making such reparation as was possible
for the murder, in 1012, of Alphege,
Abp. of C., by the Danes, arranged for
his body to be transferred from St. P.'s
Cath. to Canterbury Cath. The bridge
was lined with troops, and Canute and
the Abp. of C. sat down on the Southwark
side until the cortège was well on its way.
In 1050, during the war between E.
Godwin and Edward the Confessor, the
former's fleet had to wait at Southwark
until the tide permitted it to pass through
the bridge. In 1136 one of a succession of
fires burned down the bridge. It was no
doubt speedily rebuilt. Apparently only
a temporary structure was raised; for
about 1163 there was another rebuilding,
this time in elm. This work was carried
out under the direction of Peter the
bridge-master, who was also chaplain of
St. Mary Colechurch. Probably the
expense of the work was borne by endowments, for in 1122 Thos. de Ardern and
Thos. his son gave to the monks of Bermondsey Abbey the sum of 5s. p.a. rent
(worth about £10 now) out of the land
belonging to the bridge.

In 1176 Peter of Colechurch decided
to erect something more substantial,
perhaps inspired by what he knew of the
Frères Pontifes, who built some famous
bridges on the Continent, notably one
at Avignon. The members of this fraternity (it was dissolved in 1459) wore a
white robe which had a representation
of a bridge and a cross on the breast.
The position chosen for the new bridge
was, according to Stow—

'near unto the bridge of timber, but
somewhat more towardes the west, for
I read that Buttolfe's Wharfe was in
the Conqueror's time, at the head of
London Bridge.'

Botolph's Wharf is a little to the E. of the
site of the N. end of the bridge which
Peter of Colechurch began to erect. The
latter d. in 1205, before it was completed.
He was bd. in the undercroft of the chapel
on the bridge dedicated to St. Thos.
à Becket, who was murdered six yrs.
before its erection was commenced, and
canonized three yrs. later. There is no

record of an inscription; perhaps its
absence was an implication that the
appropriate one would be similar to that
of Wren's in St. P.'s Cath. Four yrs.
before Peter's death a question of sup-
planting him had arisen, possibly because
he had been overtaken by an illness which
presaged his passing. In 1201 K. John
addressed a letter to the Ld.M. and
citizens advising them to make use of
'our faithful, learned, and worthy Clerk,
Isenbert, Master of the Schools of Xainctes.'
He had already constructed bridges at
Saintes and La Rochelle. There is,
however, no evidence that Isenbert
completed Peter's work, and Stow says
it was carried to its culmination 'by the
worthy Merchants of London, Serle
Mercer, William Almaine, and Benedict
Botewrite.'

The length of the new bridge, which
had nineteen pointed arches, was 905 ft.
The width was 20 ft., and the road-surface,
in the highest part in the centre, was
more than 31 ft. above low-water level
at common neap tides. In the letter of
K. John referred to, allusion is made to
houses to be erected on the bridge, so
presumably these were there from the
beginning of its history. In 1358 there
were 138 shops on the bridge, bringing
in rents amounting to £160 4s. There was,
in addition, the chapel mentioned. It
was on the ninth pier from the N. Referring to the Canterbury pilgrims, who
must of course have passed over London
Bridge, Gordon Home says:

'One can picture the little parties
soon after setting out for their journey
of sixty miles to Canterbury, stopping
on the bridge to implore the protection
of the saint during the perilous journey
they were just beginning.'

There was an entrance to the chapel from
the starling when exposed by the tide,
and Gordon Home adds:

'The picture that the chapel presented to the mariners from the water
must have been singularly attractive,
especially at dusk or dawn, when the
varied colours of the two storeys of
lighted windows were reflected in the
swirling waters, and when the Gregorian
chanting of the priests came pleasantly
to their ears, broken by the sounds of
creaking cordage, of lapping waves,
and of the cries of gulls.'

In a fire which occurred in 1212 or 1213,

and brought a big roll of casualties, part of the chapel was burnt, and restoration was required.

In 1240 a whale, 'a monster of prodigious size,' swam through one of the arches. It was pursued by sailors armed with ropes, slings, and bows, and, after a long fight, killed at Mortlake. In 1263 a contest of a more ignominious character was associated with the bridge. Q. Eleanor, consort of Henry III, when the City threw in its lot with the insurgent barons, desired to leave the T.L. and find protection at Windsor. As the royal barge passed under London Bridge she was assailed by stones, rotten eggs, and other garbage and wordy insults. In 1269, as if by way of sentimental compensation, Henry III gave 'to our most dear consort' custody of London Bridge. In 1281 a very severe winter brought great blocks of ice, which bore down upon the bridge with such force that five of the arches gave way. It is possible that this was the incident which gave rise to the song, *London Bridge is broken down, my fair lady*, though it has not been traced farther back than the time of Charles II. In 1301 a schoolboy was drowned from the bridge. (See 'Children's Memorials.')

In 1390 a joust took place upon the bridge between Ld. Welles, the English ambassador in Scotland, and Sir David de Lindesay, in the presence of Richard II. Ld. Welles was unhorsed and 'sore hurt'; but he recovered, and his adversary endeared himself to Londoners by his solicitude for his welfare. This incident is the subject of a large painting by Richd. Beavis in the Guildhall, and a tapestry at the Mansion House. Of the many processions across London Bridge perhaps the most solemn and imposing was when the embalmed body of Henry V was drawn by six richly caparisoned horses to its resting place in W.A. in 1422.

The grim spectacle of heads on the bridge began apparently with Wm. Wallace's in 1305. The body was quartered and hung on gibbets at Newcastle-on-Tyne, Berwick, Stirling and Perth. In 1403 the head of the old E. of Northumberland was on the bridge, together with part of the quartered body of his son, and the head of Ld. Bardolph, a name used in Shakespeare's *Henry IV*. Jack Cade's forces fought fiercely on the bridge in 1450. The same yr. he died fighting, and his head was exposed there. The heads of John Fisher, Bp. of Rochester, and Sir Thos. More were there in 1535, and Thos. Cromwell's in 1540. The D. of Stettin, travelling through England in 1602, saw 'the heads of thirty gentlemen of high standing, who had been beheaded on account of treason and secret practices against the Queen.' In 1661 the heads of the regicides and of the 'Fifth Monarchy Men' were exposed, and in 1678 the last on record—Wm. Staley, a R.C. goldsmith and banker, a victim of Titus Oates' machinations. The body had been bd., but the K. heard of the attention drawn to the obsequies by the singing of masses, and had it disinterred. Gordon Home relates a curious use made of the heads about 1562. A number of Germans employed in the Mint fell sick of noxious fumes from the molten metal. They were told that a cure was to drink from the skull of a dead man. The aldermen thereupon obtained a warrant from the Council 'to take off the heads upon London Bridge and make cuppes thereof, whereof they dranke and founde some relief, though the mooste of them dyed.' (Richd. Baxter recorded in his *Autobiography* that he was cured of a fit of bleeding 'by the mercy of God, and the help of Dr. Bates, and the moss of a dead man's skull.')

If the bridge was blatant in its display of tragedy it was not without a little romance. In 1536 a nursemaid was playing at a window with Anne the infant daughter of Wm. Hewet, a clothworker, whose premises were on London Bridge. The child lost her balance and fell into the cataract below. An apprentice named Osborne saw her fall and, without a moment's hesitation, plunged in after her. He succeeded in restoring the child to its parents. Money was bound to go with her hand when she grew to womanhood, and it is said she had many suitors. To these old Hewet turned a deaf ear. 'Osborne saved her,' he said, 'and Osborne shall have her.' They were m. in 1562, when she was eighteen, and in 1583 Osborne became Ld.M. The starlings (the name given to the wooden platforms which protected the piers) caused a perilous rush of water between them, and there was a proverb that 'London Bridge was made for wise men to go over and fools to go under.' Prudent people, navigating the river, disembarked, dragged their boats round the bridge, and entered them again on the other side. In 1428 the D. of Norfolk's barge collided with a starling. The D. and two or three of his companions sprang on to a starling, but others were submerged. Wolsey would not risk the rapids, but Henry VIII sometimes did. Pepys, Dr. Johnson, and Chas. Dickens allude to the risks of shooting the bridge. Mrs. Anne Kirke, a lady of the bedchamber to Henrietta Maria, was drowned through the overturning of the Q.'s barge at London Bridge. In 1689 John Temple, son of Sir Wm. Temple, the diplomatist, took advantage of this danger to commit suicide, flinging himself into the cataract after he had instructed the boatman to shoot the bridge. Narcissus Luttrell's *Diary* records that on 25th Nov. 1693 fifteen people were drowned.

Two important additions were made to London Bridge in the reign of Q. Elizabeth. In 1579 Nonsuch House was completed. The foundations were of stone, but the superstructure was entirely of timber. It was lavishly ornamented with sculptured wood and gilded pilasters. In 1582 Peter Morice, a Dutchman, was allowed to instal water-mills on London Bridge. 'The noise of London Bridge is nothing to her,' says a character in Beaumont and Fletcher's play, *The Woman's Prize*. That noise must have been considerably increased when to the clacking of the mills was added the swirl of the water.

It is not surprising that London Bridge aroused the admiration of Englishmen. John Lyly, John Norden, and Jas. Howell penned their eulogies. Foreigners also gave it their tribute of praise. Jacob Rathgeb, private secretary of Fredk. D. of Württemberg in 1592, described it as 'beautiful, with quite splendid, handsome and well-built houses,' and a remarkable testimony to its fame was a sculptured representation on a stone panel, dated 1617, in front of a house at Dordrecht in Holland. In 1633 a fire burnt down a third of its houses. Most of these were occupied by haberdashers, though in other parts there were printing and bookselling businesses. It was not until 1651 that the new houses were completed, and these were destined to be burnt in the G.F., which affected about a third part of London Bridge. In 1703 there were some

further repairs to the bridge, resulting in some widening. Pennant described it at a later period:

'I well remember the street on London Bridge, narrow, darksome, and dangerous to passengers from the multitude of carriages: frequent arches of strong timber crossed the street, from the tops of the houses to keep them together, and from falling into the river. Nothing but use could preserve the rest of the inmates, who soon grew deaf to the noise of the falling waters, the clamour of watermen, or the frequent shrieks of drowning wretches.'

Yet when the houses were removed, between 1756 and 1762, by Act of Parliament passed in 1755, a Mr. Baldwin, a haberdasher (aged 71), found himself unable to sleep at Chislehurst. He missed the familiar sound of the waters. During the alterations consequent upon the removal of the houses a temporary bridge was erected very close to the W. side, and on this a serious fire broke out in 1758, causing considerable damage to the old bridge. Strangely enough, the doomed houses were left unharmed. Two yrs. later, in 1760, the Southwark gateway, rebuilt in 1728, was demolished. After the houses were removed alcoves were placed at intervals along the bridge. It was in one of these that Dickens describes David Copperfield as lingering whilst awaiting the opening of the King's Bench Prison—and an interview with Micawber.

London Bridge had been patched and patched again, and in 1789 the *Quarterly Review* quoted Ben Jonson's lines about Pennyboy senior who minded

'A curtesie no more than London-
        bridge
What arch was mended last,'

and said further:

'This pernicious structure has wasted more money in perpetual repairs than would have sufficed to build a dozen safe and commodious bridges, and cost the lives, perhaps, of as many thousand people. Had an alderman or turtle been lost there, the nuisance would have been long removed.'

The stability of the old arches was affected by the freezing of the river. In 1800 Geo. Dance the Younger painted a design for two new parallel bridges (it is in the C.C. art gallery). In 1821 a committee of the H. of C. reported in favour of the bdg. of an entirely new bridge. In 1823 an Act was passed, and the first pile driven on 15th Mar. 1824, about 100 ft. W. of the old bridge. On 15th June 1825, the tenth anniversary of the battle of Waterloo, the first stone was laid by the Ld.M., Rt. Hon. John Garratt; the D. of York, brother of George IV (now exalted on the well-known column) being also present. A long inscription was deposited in a cavity, together with newly minted coins of George IV. On 1st Aug. 1831 the completed work was opened to the public by William IV and Q. Adelaide. The old bridge was demolished in 1831–2. Both the demolition of the old bridge and the opening of the new one are subjects of paintings in the C.C. Art Gallery. Nonsuch House, shorn of most of its architectural glory, had gone with the other bdgs. seventy yrs. before. The undercroft of the chapel of St. Thomas was still left, and there were found human remains, probably those of the architect Peter of Colechurch.

Other relics of old London Bridge can be definitely located. In 1921, when the foundations of Adelaide House were under excavation, an arch came to light in which three ribs of Portland stone, 4ft. in width, had been inserted in 1703. Two of the rib stones were preserved on the roof of Adelaide House, and others are in the chyd. of St. Magnus the Martyr. A sculptured stone shield, bearing three leopards, with angels on either side, from old London Bridge now forms the keystone of the tower arch of Merstham Ch. (The Rev. Wm. Joliffe, one of the contractors for the existing bridge, lived at Merstham House.) The royal arms, taken from the Southwark gate on its demolition in 1760, are to be seen in the modern front of the King's Arms Tavern in Newcomen St., Bor. High St. A portion of the 18th-century parapet is at Herne Bay, another at Ingress Abbey, Greenhithe. A house known as 'Stone House' at Wandsworth was built of the bridge materials. When it was pulled down, about 1909, the stone was reused in bdg. on the same site, No. 49 Heathfield Rd. In the grounds of Guy's Hosp. there is one of the alcoves mentioned; two are in Victoria Park. There are iron railings from the bridge in St. Botolph's Chyd., Bishopsgate. (See 'Companies of the City,' *Fishmongers'*.)

Instead of alcoves there were at intervals

recesses on the new bridge. Dickens alluded to these in *Oliver Twist*. Noah Claypole, wishing to track the footsteps of Nancy to her secret interview with Mr. Brownlow and Rose Maylie on the Southwark side, crouches down in one of them to allow her to pass. They disappeared with the widening of the bridge in 1905.

In 1967 began the construction of yet another London Bridge. The cost, 4 million pounds, is being met out of the private purse of the C.C.: thus the charge falls on neither taxpayer nor ratepayer, an outstanding example of the unique contribution of the C.C. to L. and indeed the country. The old bridge has been sold and is being re-erected, stone by stone, in Arizona.

(See *Chronicles of London Bridge*, 1839, and *Old London Bridge*, by Gordon Home, 1931.)

WESTMINSTER BRIDGE. There is nothing more surprising to the student of L. history than the discovery that London Bridge was alone in its glory until the middle of the 18th century. (It should be explained that the word 'bridge' was often used for 'pier' or 'landing place.' Addison refers to Strand Bridge; Foxe, in the *Book of Martyrs* to Westminster Bridge; and there are early references to Temple Bridge and Lambeth Bridge—all had the latter meaning.) This was due to vested interests. The Watermen's Co. found the ever-rolling stream of the Thames a source of great revenue. The devil's dislike of holy water was hardly more than the waterman's dislike of bridging the profane supply. Proposals for another bridge were made in the reigns of Elizabeth and James I, but they were opposed. Again, in the reigns of Charles I and Charles II, there were renewed proposals. In 1871 a Bill for a bridge at Putney was defeated by 54–67. In 1722, when one at Westminster was suggested, not only did the Co. of Watermen oppose it, but also the west-country bargemen, the Bor. of Southwark, the C.C., and the inhabitants of London Bridge. In 1734, however, the scheme was revived, and a small body of gentlemen, including the Abp. of C., joined in finding the money for preliminary plans and surveys. An Act for the bdg. of the new bridge was passed in 1736; and— financed by lotteries and grants—it was erected between 1739 and 1750. The architect was M. Chas. Labelye, a Swiss, and he spanned the river, here 1,223 ft. wide—300 ft. wider than at London Bridge, with a bridge of fifteen arches. This bridge, pleasing in appearance, had alcoves similar to those of old London Bridge. It was the bridge upon which Wordsworth composed his famous sonnet, commencing:

'Earth has not anything to show more fair.'

The arches, however, showed signs of giving way, and between 1854 and 1862 a new bridge was erected, at a cost of £250,000.

BLACKFRIARS BRIDGE was commenced in 1760, and opened in 1769. It was intended as a memorial to Wm. Pitt, E. of Chatham; and the foundation tablet (now in the G. Mus.) says:

'That there may remain to posterity a monument of this City's affection to the man, who by the strength of his genius, the steadiness of his mind, and a kind of happy contagion of his probity and spirit, under the divine favour and fortunate auspices of George the Second, recovered, augmented, and secured the British Empire in Asia, Africa, and America, and restored the antient reputation and influence of his country among the nations of Europe, the Citizens of London have unanimously voted this Bridge to be inscribed with the name of William Pitt.'

Adjacent streets were named Pitt and Chatham. It is remarkable, therefore, that it was called Blackfriars Bridge so soon. Robt. Mylne was the architect, and his proposal for elliptical arches instead of semicircular, was the subject of a controversy in which Dr. Johnson engaged. Boswell admitted it was quite out of Johnson's way, but ingeniously pointed out that it was no more so than the matters upon which barristers and legislators have to pose as authorities. There is a painting of the bridge in 1772 in the C.C. art gallery. On the first opening of the bridge there was a halfpenny toll, and it was increased to a penny on Sundays. The toll led to riots, and in 1780 the toll-house was burned down. The Govt. therefore, bought up the bridge and made it free. In 1833 it was thoroughly repaired at the cost of £100,000. In 1860 it was taken down, and a temporary bridge erected. In 1865 the foundation of the new bridge was laid, and in 1869 it was opened by Q. Victoria on the same day as Holborn Viaduct. It was widened between 1907 and 1909 from 80 ft. to 110 ft. to provide additional space for the L.C.C. tramways. It is now probably the widest bridge crossing a river in Gt. Britain.

SOUTHWARK BRIDGE was in course of construction at the same time as the first Vauxhall Bridge. It was commenced in 1815, and completed in 1819. The opening was at midnight—by lamplight. It was constructed of three cast-iron arches, the central one being of 240 ft. span. It was first known as the 'Iron Bridge,' and is so called in Dickens's *Little Dorrit*. It cost about £800,000, and was bought by the C.C. in 1866 for £218,868, having been made free of tolls in 1864. It was replaced by the present bridge, opened in 1921.

WATERLOO BRIDGE, first called Strand Bridge, was erected between 1811 and 1817. The architect was John Rennie. The cost was £565,000, but with the approaches and the bdgs. the total amounted to over £1,000,000. In 1877 the M.B.W. bought it, and opened it free of toll. Waterloo Bridge, with its gracefully curved arches, was considered by Canova to be the finest in Europe, and it was generally regretted when, in 1924, it was reported that one of the main arches had become weakened, so that it was necessary to close it for vehicular traffic for some months. Then followed ten yrs. of controversy as to whether there was to be restoration or entire reconstruction and, in 1935, the L.C.C. having failed to obtain any subsidy from the Govt., the latter was resolved upon, and the work of demolition completed in 1936.

Work on the new bridge was commenced in 1937. On 4th May 1939 the foundation stone was laid. A copper cylinder, containing a set of daily papers issued at the time of the L.C.C. Jubilee (Mar. 1939), and a set of current coins and stamps, were placed in the foundations. In 1942 the new bridge was made available for pedestrians and two lines of traffic; in 1944 it was entirely completed, affording space for six lines of traffic.

A lamp standard from the old Waterloo Bridge is now in Salisbury, Rhodesia.

TOWER BRIDGE. This was erected

1886–94, and cost over £1,000,000, exclusive of the approaches. The raised footway is 142 ft. above high water. This has been closed since 31st Dec. 1909. The design of the bridge was that of Sir John Wolfe Barry, so far as the engineering portion was concerned; that of Sir Horace Jones in respect of the Gothic architecture.

By Act of Parliament a tug has always to be in readiness for possible emergencies. The considerable cost of this service is met by the Bridge House Estates Committee of the C.C. out of private funds.

PUTNEY BRIDGE. It was erected in 1729 at an expense of £23,975, those interested in the ferry being compensated. The bridge was 789 ft. long and 24 ft. wide, with openings for vessels to pass through, the largest of which, in the centre, was named Walpole's Lock, in honour of Sir Robt. Walpole, who helped to procure the Act of Parliament. The plan was drawn by Cheselden, afterwards surgeon of Chelsea Hosp., where his tomb can still be seen. A toll of a halfpenny was charged foot passengers, and on Sundays this was doubled, for the purpose of a fund which was divided annually between the widows and children of poor watermen belonging to Putney and Fulham, as a recompense to the fraternity, who were not allowed to ply on Sundays after the bdg. of the bridge. The bridge was purchased by the C.C., and then transferred to the M.B.W., who pulled down the wooden structure, with a toll-house at each end, and erected in the yrs. 1884–6 a stone bridge. To meet the needs of the increasing traffic in this part of L., the bridge was widened in 1933.

BATTERSEA BRIDGE. The first one was erected 1771–3, where there had been a ferry in the reign of James I, which was granted to the E. of Lincoln by letters patent for £40. Ld. Spencer and seventeen associates financed the bridge, and the tolls were paid until 1879. In 1799 it was lighted by oil lamps, and in 1824 by gas, the pipes being brought over from Chelsea. In its later days, the bridge, whilst picturesque enough for Whistler to make it the subject of a picture, was too unsafe for comfort, and in 1890 it was superseded by the present bridge, designed by Sir Joseph Bazalgette, and opened by E. of Rosebery.

VAUXHALL BRIDGE was built 1811–16.

The first stone on the Middlesex side was laid (in 1811) by Ld. Dundas, as proxy for the P. Regent, and it was first called Regent Bridge. The first stone on the Surrey side was laid in 1813, by P. Chas. of Brunswick, who fell two yrs. later at Waterloo. Its proximity to Vauxhall Gardens soon led to a change in the name of the bridge. The new Vauxhall Bridge was opened in 1906, and had the distinction of being the first bridge crossed by tramcars. The cost, including the destruction of the old bridge and the erection of a temporary one, was about £600,000.

HAMMERSMITH BRIDGE. Erected in 1827, it was the first to be constructed on the suspension principle. It was designed by Tierney Clarke at a cost of about £80,000. The roadway was only 20 ft. wide. The present bridge, opened in 1887 by P. Albert Victor, D. of Clarence, is not much wider.

HUNGERFORD BRIDGE was completed in 1845, and was designed by the younger Brunel. It was named after the market. The centre span of this suspension bridge, the most notable part, was 676 ft. in length. It was removed in 1861, and now spans the River Avon near Bristol. In its place was erected the ugly Charing Cross Railway Bridge, with a footbridge alongside. These have been the target for aesthetic criticism ever since; but they still remain, despite many schemes for improvement. (See *Charing Cross Bridge*, by Arthur Keen, F.R.I.B.A.)

CHELSEA BRIDGE was opened in 1858, and crossed for the first time by the P. of Wales, afterwards Edward VII, and the P. Consort. It cost £85,319, and the imposition of tolls was strongly resented. It was freed from tolls in 1879. The toll-houses remained until the bridge was closed in 1935 for rebuilding. The present bridge was opened in 1937.

LAMBETH BRIDGE was opened in 1862, having been erected by a private co. at the very small cost of £40,000. As ugly as it was cheap, it was designed by Peter Barlow. On its erection the see of Canterbury was awarded £2,200 as compensation for the loss of the ferry, though by reason of the proximity of Vauxhall and Westminster bridges this must have been nominal at so late a date. Horseferry Rd. on the W. side recalls this. More worn by episcopal feet than any other, it might be called Bishops' Bridge. Bp. Gore's bio-grapher recalled his

'rather shabby-looking figure stand-ing on the summit of Lambeth Bridge against a sombre sunset, shaking his fist at Lambeth Palace, to the open-mouthed amazement of passing Lon-doners, and crying: "As for the bishops, they are hopeless; I have done with them." '

The old suspension bridge was pulled down in 1929, and a new bridge opened in 1932. It is a handsome structure, though there has been some criticism of the 'golden pomegranates,' which are similar to those over the pavilions of the Saracens in *The Talisman*.

ALBERT BRIDGE was built in 1873 and cost £200,000. Along with Lambeth, Vauxhall, Chelsea, and Battersea bridges it was freed from toll in 1879. Its length is 711 feet in three spans with towers which are 101 feet above high water.

WANDSWORTH BRIDGE was built in 1873 from the designs of J. H. Tolme. It is constructed of iron, and known as a lattice girder bridge. It was reconstructed 1936–40.

Buckingham Palace. Its site in the reign of James I was a mulberry garden, promoted by the K. for the benefit of the silk industry. In Charles II's reign, on the southern portion, was Arlington House, the occupant being the E. of Arlington, one of the Cabal ministry. On its demolition in 1703 the site was purchased by John Sheffield, D. of Buckingham, who built there a mansion of red brick. In 1762 George III removed from St. James's Palace where the P. of Wales, afterwards George IV, had been b., having bought Buckingham House for £21,000. All the rest of George III's children were b. there. In 1767 Dr. Johnson, in the Library, was interviewed by George III. In 1775, by Act of Parlia-ment, it was settled on Q. Charlotte in exchange for Somerset House. It was thenceforth called the Q.'s House. It was reconstructed between 1825 and 1836, in the Palladian style, from the designs of John Nash, and then known as Buckingham Palace. As William IV did not like the bdg., it was not occupied again until the succession of Q. Victoria. Most of the children of Q. Victoria were b. there, and in 1843 in the chapel of the

palace, the Princess Augusta of Cambridge was m. to Fredk. Wm. Grand D. of Mecklenburg-Strelitz.

An E. front was built in 1846, at a cost of £150,000, and a S. wing and ball-room, measuring 111 ft. were added in 1856. The other most important parts are the Marble Hall and Sculpture Gallery, the Grand Staircase, the Vesti-bule, the Drawing Room, the Throne Room, the Picture Gallery, and the Library. From the Library George IV transferred 120,000 volumes to the B. Mus.

The E. front was refaced by Sir Aston Webb in 1912, at a cost of £60,000. A model of the palace as it was previously is in the L. Mus. The pleasure grounds cover an area of forty acres, five of which are occupied by a lake. The royal stables are on the S. side. The Queen's Gallery containing a changing selection from the Royal collection is now open to the public (except on Mondays).

Until 1851 the Marble Arch was outside the principal entrance to Bucking-ham Palace.

During the Second World War there were fourteen 'incidents' at Buckingham Palace. One H.E. bomb went through the K.'s apartments; another fell on the Royal Mews.

Bunhill Fields Burial Ground. It is on part of an old prebendal estate con-nected with St. P.'s Cath. There is still in the latter the stall of 'Prebendarius de Haliwell et de Finesbiri,' and the pre-bendal estate thus commemorated was part of a great morass adjacent to Moor-fields. There is now no person attached to the prebend, and probably there was never much profit accruing from it. In 1315 the land was granted to the Mayor and Commonalty at the yearly rent of 20s., equal to nearly £20 to-day. For this sum there was transferred to the C.C. and their successors all right and claim to the property. This reads like a grant in perpetuity, but notwithstanding, in 1553, the C.C. obtained the lease for ninety yrs. at a rental of £29 13s. 4d. In 1561 a storm broke over L., houses were wrecked, and St. P.'s Cath. was struck. To repair the roof the C.C. provided about twenty tons of lead. In return for this favour leases of seventy yrs. each were granted, to date from the expiration of the existing lease.

During the Commonwealth — about 1650—when the lands of the Dean and Chapter were offered for sale, the C.C. bought them, and thus made themselves absolutely and unconditionally lds. of the manor. With the Restoration the new order changed, giving place to the old, the transaction was deemed to be cancelled, and in 1664 the C.C. was again paying rent. From 1665 it was in use as a graveyard and was known as 'Tindal's or the Dissenters' Burial Ground,' a man of the name mentioned having obtained a lease. This replaced the older name of Bonhil or Bunhill, probably dating from 1549 when bones from the charnel chapel of old St. P.'s Cath. were deposited here. After Tindal Bunhill Fields were in possession of Jas. Brown and Elizabeth Featherstonehaugh. In Tindal's time part of the land had been built upon, but in 1700 it was possible to extend the Burial Ground. About 1741 the C.C. took sole charge once more. With the growth of dissent the revenue from burials was considerable.

One stone was found inscribed 'Debora Warr Nov. 10 1623,' but this may have been the date of burial of a person who had been re-interred, as no others were found with a date approximating to this. The next in order of date was 'Joannes Seaman, natus 6 Feb. 1665, ob. Juli 23 1665.'

Southey called it the 'Campo Santo' of Dissenters. The principal burials are as follows:

DR. THOS. GOODWIN (d. 1680). He was President of Magdalen Coll., Oxford, under Cromwell, and was present at his death. He is regarded as the founder of the congregation known as the City Temple (q.v.).

DR. JOHN OWEN (d. 1683). He is said to have secured the release of Bunyan from Bedford Gaol. Charles II ridiculed him for going to hear a tinker preach. 'May it please your Majesty,' he replied, 'could I possess that tinker's ability for preaching I would gladly relinquish all my learning.'

JOHN BUNYAN (d. 1688) was bd. in a vault owned by one John Strudwick, in whose house on Snow Hill he d. He was the first of seven interments in the vault. In 1717 when Curll published the inscriptions in Bunhill Fields, there was no record of his name being on the grave.

There, in 1737, was bd. REV. ROBT. BRAGGE, Strudwick's son-in-law, and probably at that time Bunyan's name for the first time was inscribed. A monument with recumbent effigy was erected in 1851, and it was restored by public subscription under the presidency of the E. of Shaftesbury in 1862. For some yrs. the nose was absent. It was said to have been shot off by a bullet from the neighbouring Artillery ground. In 1922 it was replaced and there was a ceremonial performed by the widow of Dr. John Brown, Bunyan's greatest biographer. Two panels represent Christian with his burden and the burden rolling from his back.

CHARLES FLEETWOOD (d. 1692). He fought at Dunbar and Worcester, and m. Cromwell's eldest daughter Bridget. He was a member of Owen's congregation.

DR. DANIEL WILLIAMS (d. 1716). (See 'Libraries.')

DANIEL DEFOE (d. 1731). The entry of burial was 'Mr. Dubow,' Cripplegate.' There was only a shabby stone there until 1870, when an Egyptian pillar of Sicilian marble was erected by the subscriptions of 1,700 boys and girls of England, collected by the *Christian World*. In erecting the monument the grave was opened and the decayed coffin found. It was inscribed 'Foe' on the name-plate, and the skeleton was 5 ft. 4 in. in height, and had a massive under-jaw. Spectators wished to carry off the bones, and the police had to be called in. The coffin was then bd. in a concrete foundation.

Two tombs bear the name of Cromwell. One was erected by a grandson of Oliver in memory of his family. The other commemorates great-grandchildren of the Ld. Protector.

MRS. SUSANNAH WESLEY (d. 1742). She was mother of John and Chas. Wesley, and seventeen other children. John Wesley preached a funeral sermon at her grave. 'It was,' he wrote, 'one of the most solemn assemblies I ever saw or expect to see on this side eternity.' The stone—at least the third—was erected in 1936.

ISAAC WATTS. He d. (1748) at Abney Park. One of his hymns—'Our God, our help in ages past,' is probably the most familiar in the English language.

ROBERT TILLING, executed at Tyburn for murdering his master (1760). Rev.

Geo. Whitefield preached over his grave.

REV. JOSEPH HART (d. 1768). A red granite obelisk was placed on the spot in 1875. The inscription says it was 'erected by lovers of Hart's hymns'—published in 1759.

HESTER SAVORY (d. 1803). Chas. Lamb had a tender feeling for her, though it is said he saw her only once.

LADY ANN AGNES ERSKINE (d. 1804). A convert of Whitefield's, she was an intimate friend of Lady Huntingdon, and an executor of her will.

WILLIAM SHRUBSOLE (d. 1806). An organist, who composed the familiar tune, *Miles Lane*, the first bar of which is on the gravestone. It was so called because it first appeared in a collection of psalm tunes issued by the pastor of Miles Lane Chapel, near London Bridge.

REV. THEOPHILUS LINDSEY (d. 1808). He was the founder of Essex St. Unitarian Chapel.

HENRY FAUNTLEROY (d. 1824). He was a banker who was executed at Tyburn for forgery. In the L.Mus. there is a painting showing his being manacled at Newgate Gaol on the morning of execution.

WILLIAM BLAKE (d. 1827), and his wife (d. 1831).

THOMAS HARDY (d. 1832). His merits are fully set out in a lengthy inscription on an obelisk close to the railings of City Rd.:

'. . . One of the three who in 1792, commenced the formation of the celebrated London Corresponding Society, for the promotion of a radical reform in the Commons House of Parliament; he was appointed secretary to that Society in the same year and filled the office with diligence and ability till his arrest in May 1794, on a charge of High Treason, when he was committed to the Tower . . . [tried] at the Old Bailey, and triumphantly acquitted . . .'

Of the trial Dr. G. M. Trevelyan has written:

'Thanks to Erskine's persuasive eloquence, the sense of fair play that has often distinguished our countrymen caused the twelve Tory jurymen to acquit Hardy and his fellow prisoners, and to remind Pitt that the methods of Robespierre were not wanted over here. London, though strongly Anti-Jacobin, broke out into loud rejoicings at the acquittal.'

JOSEPH CHAMBERLAIN (d. 1837). Grand-father of the Rt. Hon. Jos. Chamberlain, M.P. The tall tombstone remains.

At one time Bunhill Fields was troubled by body-snatchers. This probably explained the spiked gate which, until the Second World War, was at the NE. corner. Bunhill Fields, too, had its 'Old Mortality.' This was the Rev. John Rippon, who was seen lying on his side, between two graves, and jotting down the epitaphs word for word by means of pen, book, and inkhorn. He said he had 'taken most of the old inscriptions,' and that he would 'if God be pleased to spare his days, do all, notwithstanding it is a grievous labour and the writing is hard to make out by reason of the oldness of the cutting in stone and defacing of other stones.' He d. in 1836 at the age of 86, and was bd. in Bunhill Fields. The results of his labours are now in the Coll. of Arms, and a copy of every inscription legible when the C.C. acquired Bunhill Fields is in the Guildhall Library.

The last burial was 5th Jan. 1854—Elizabeth Howell Oliver—15½ yrs. old. In 1852 an Order in Council had prohibited further interments, so presumably an old grave was allowed to be opened.

In 1867 the whole of the lapsed prebendal estate fell into the hands of the Ecclesiastical Commissioners for Ch. purposes, proposals for the renewal of the lease having been declined. Upon this becoming known, an application was made to the latter to give a pledge that the burial ground should be held sacred for ever. Their reply was that they were entitled to receive the ground free from encumbrance, that it was worth £100,000, but that they were willing, under the circumstances, to receive £10,000 by way of compensation. This demand, and the knowledge that offers were being made for portions of the ground for bdg. purposes, led to the C.C. being memorialized to seek parliamentary powers to prevent the secular use of the property. An Act was passed in 1867, and the C.C. having accepted the care and preservation of the ground on behalf of the public, it was opened in 1869. The intervening period had been used in raising tombs that had sunk, and restoring them, setting stones straight, deciphering illegible inscriptions, laying out paths, and planting trees. The Act safeguards the ground from bdg., and leaves it for all time to posterity as an open space.

There is a list of the principal burials on the wall pillars. It contains two errors. 'Samuel Wesley' should read 'Susannah Wesley,' and John Horne Tooke was bd. in Ealing chyd.

Bombs fell on the burial ground during the Second World War. No well-known monuments were damaged, but in some cases vaults were blown open. Restoration has been carried out by the C.C.

(See *Bunhill Fields*, by A. W. Light, second edition, 2 vols., 1915/1933. The official handbook has long been out of print. See also article 'Epitaphs' in this *Encyclopædia*.)

There was a separate Quaker burial ground in Bunhill Fields. It remains as a recreation ground in Roscoe St., and is said to have been the site of a plague burial-pit, where about 1,100 'Friends' were bd. It was the earliest freehold property possessed by the Soc. of Friends, and Edwd. Burrough was bd. here (1663).

A prisoner at the time of his death, he had engaged in a wordy warfare with Bunyan. In 1690 a large concourse followed the body of Geo. Fox. The plain wooden coffin had no bier or cover. In 1724 there was bd. here Daniel Quare, inventor of the repeating movement in watches, and in 1815 Dr. Lettsom (see 'Fleet St.'). In 1666 a minute read that 'ye washer-women and leather dryers be debarred at present,' and in 1716 sheep and cattle were pastured there. In that yr. it was ordered that all gates but one should be locked at dusk for fear of body snatchers. In 1855 it was ordered that the ground should be closed for burials. The M.B.W. purchased part of the property for widening the streets and some bodies were reinterred in the larger Bunhill Fields Burial Ground. In 1881 it was laid out as a garden, and the present small stone erected on a spot which was traditionally the place of Fox's interment,

Camberwell, now part of the L. Bor. of Southwark, was a met. bor. and ancient par. S. of the Thames, formerly in Surrey.

In Domesday Book the name was spelt 'Cābrewell,' later becoming 'Camerwell' and 'Camwell,' and finally Camberwell in the 18th century. The meaning of the name is uncertain.

The par. ch. dedicated to St. Giles, has occupied the same site since A.D. 670. It is mentioned in Domesday Book. With constant alterations and repairs from the 12th century onwards and—according to Lysons—much reconstruction in the time of Henry VIII, this ancient bdg. remained until the 19th century. The body of it was large and shapeless, with a square tower surmounted by a turret. It had a Lady Chapel, many ancient brasses and other monuments, and painted windows. From the 17th century onwards it underwent almost continuous modification. Galleries were added, and a new S. aisle was built in 1786. It was described in 1809 as being 'modernized' by coats of plaster and rough-cast. Further enlargement was carried out in 1825. Nevertheless, the interior had a very antique appearance; massive clustered columns, pointed arches, and a sedilia in the S. wall of the chancel. On the night following 7th Feb. 1841 it was totally destroyed by fire.

The present ch., designed by Sir Gilbert Scott and W. B. Moffatt, was opened in 1844. It was at that time one of the finest and largest par. chs. in the kingdom. In style, a transition between Early English and Decorated, it is cruciform, with a central tower and spire about 210 ft. high. There are brasses salved from the ruins of the former ch., and the glass in the E. window—damaged in the Second World War but reconstructed exactly in 1950—was partly designed by John Ruskin.

Amongst those bd. in the chyd. was the shrewish spouse of John Wesley (1781). Her grave is now under the widened roadway, and the headstone has gone. There is a large monument to the family of Champion de Crespigny, who gave their name to Champion Hill.

Other Camberwell chs. worthy of mention are St. George's, Wells St., built 1824 in the then popular Grecian style by Francis Bedford and altered internally in 1908; and the oddly named Camden Chapel, in the Peckham Rd., built 1797 by discontented members of the congregation of St. Giles and licensed as an Episcopal Chapel in 1829, after its use by the Countess of Huntingdon's Connexion. The pulpit was then occupied by Henry Melvill, afterwards Canon of St. P.'s Cath. He was a preacher of great eloquence and for a time the most popular in L. To this plain looking ch. there was added in 1854 a chancel in Byzantine style, designed by John Ruskin and Sir Gilbert Scott. It has been badly damaged by bombs. Also damaged was St. Antholin's, Nunhead. It had a fine 17th-century reredos from Wren's City ch. of St. Antholin, Watling St.

Denmark Hill recalls George, P. of Denmark, Consort of Q. Anne, who had a house nearby: Camberwell Grove is a pleasant 18th-century road which once led to a fine villa, standing in extensive grounds, occupied by Dr. J. Coakley Lettsom (1744–1815), a Quaker physician of more than local repute. In Southampton Way Robt. Browning was born: the site of the house is marked by a tablet.

Dulwich Village is in many ways the most attractive part of the bor. It has still an old-world and rather countrified air, and contains a beautiful park, a fine Art Gallery—almost demolished in a raid, but now rebuilt—and the Almshouses originally built at the same time as the College (1616), by Edwd. Alleyn, the Elizabethan actor, who lies in the College Chapel which he erected, and which was until 1894 the only ch. in the village.

In Dulwich College Rd. are the new bdgs. of 'The College of God's Gift,' erected by Sir C. Barry in 1870, and the only surviving toll-gate in L. A car 6d., a lorry 2s. 6d.

(See *Dulwich Village*, by D. H. Allport, revised edition, 1950, and *Dulwich Discovered* by W. Darby, 1966.)

Canals. L., for a city of its size, has not many canals, the chief being the Regent's Canal, and the Grand Junction Canal, which, though not so busy as formerly, still carry a fair amount of the less-hurried traffic in heavy goods.

There are three 'mouths' to the L. canal system: the mouth of the River Lea, by which barges can proceed northward; at Limehouse, where admission is given to the Regent's Canal, which goes northward for a while till it takes a westward turn to link up with the Grand Union system; and at Brentford, where the mouth of the partly canalized river, the Brent, is the main 'port' for inland navigation.

THE REGENT'S CANAL was begun in 1812 and opened in 1820. It commences at Paddington, at its junction with the Grand Junction, and passes beneath Edgware Rd., Maida Hill, and St. John's Wood by a tunnel about 370 yds long. Afterwards the canal goes on through Camden Town and Islington, where it runs through another tunnel by City Rd., Kingsland, Hackney, and Stepney, and so on to Limehouse, where it joins the Thames. It has in its course through L. forty bridges and twelve locks. The proper name of the Regent's Canal is 'The North Metropolitan Canal,' but it is never so called.

THE PADDINGTON OR GRAND JUNCTION CANAL runs westward through L., nearly parallel with Harrow Rd. It was opened for traffic in 1801, when the first barge arrived with passengers at Paddington Basin, from Uxbridge in Middlesex. It was made an occasion for great public rejoicings, bells were rung, flags hung out, and even cannon fired.

Harold P. Clunn (*The Face of London*, 1932), said:

'A century ago a passenger boat used to leave the Paddington Dock every day during the summer months, at eight o'clock in the morning, for Greenford Green and Uxbridge, returning in the evening. Breakfast was provided on board. The fares were most reasonable, being one shilling for six miles, eighteenpence for ten miles, and half a crown for the complete voyage to Uxbridge.'

This canal, now merged into the Grand Union system, though its festive appearance has long since departed, still carries large quantities of merchandise to and from the Midlands and the N. of England. At Brentford there are extensive docks and large goods sidings of the British Railways adjoining the waterside. Here are found many of the gaudily painted 'monkey barges.'

The chief L. canal S. of the Thames is the Grand Surrey Canal, which runs from the Surrey Commercial Docks through Deptford, across Old Kent Rd. to Camberwell, with a branch to Peckham.

The advent of the railways in the fourth decade of the 19th century led to the curtailment of many plans for fresh L. canals, including one to link up the whole of the SW. area by a system of waterways. Plans were drawn up so far as Clapham and district, but the scheme never materialized.

Cannon Street is first mentioned in records 1180–7, and is then 'Candelwrichstrete.' In the time of K. John (1199–1216) it is 'Candelwritestrate,' in Henry VII's reign (1485–1509) 'Canwikstrete,' and in Q. Elizabeth's (1558–1603) 'Canninge Street.' In Leake's map (1666) it appears as 'Cannon Street.'

In a will of 1372 direction is given for the purchase of cloth of 'Candelwykstrete' for the making of coats and hoods, and Dr. R. R. Sharpe says it was famous for its cloth so late as the time of Henry VI (1422–61). Budge Row recalls the old name for lambskin. The 'Burellers of Candelwykestrete' are mentioned in 1345. They were the makers of a coarse kind of cloth, brown in colour. Some forms of the name as given above justify Stow's assertion that it was derived from 'chandlers or makers of candles,' or of 'weeke' which is the cotton or yarn thereof.' In 1311 mention is made of 'John le Cierger de Kandelwikstrate,' and in 1326 of 'Matthew le Chaundler de Candelwykestrete.' (A block of modern offices at the E. end of Cannon St. is called 'Candlewick House.') There is no doubt with so many chs. and no other artificial light, the candle trade—divided between the tallow chandlers and the wax chandlers, both livery cos. now— was once most important. In 1558 the Paschal candle for W.A. (made under the superintendence of the Master and Wardens of the Wax Chandlers' Co.) contained 300 lb. of wax, and no tallow was allowed to be sent out of the city until the demands of the citizens had been met.

Edwd. de Vere, the E. of Oxford, regarded by some as the real Shakespeare, had a house close to St. Swithun's Ch. (Oxford Court commemorates it) and Stow says that in 1566 Robt. Dudley, E. of Leicester, was staying with him. Q. Elizabeth entered a wherry, probably at St. Mary Overies stairs, with only two of her ladies, and was rowed across to the 'Three Cranes' stairs opposite. Then 'she came out of her coache in ye highway and she imbrased ye earl and kissed him thrice and then they rode together to Greenwich.' This romantic episode, involving a little scandal about Q. Elizabeth, probably took place in Cannon St.

Originally Cannon St. did not extend beyond Walbrook, but in 1853-4 it was decided to continue it further W., and to make it a thoroughfare to St. P.'s Cath. For this purpose a number of small sts. were removed, e.g. Great St. Thomas Apostle, Basing Lane, Little Friday St., Great Distaff Lane, and at the same time the thoroughfare was widened. This scheme, opposed by many City men, was a vast improvement. Until 1866 the extension was known as Cannon St. W.

L. Stone, St. Swithun's Ch., and Cordwainers' Hall are dealt with elsewhere.

A number of modern office buildings, particularly those included in the rebuilt Cannon Street Station, have altered the appearance of the street.

Carlton House was first erected for Ld. Carlton in 1709, and was bequeathed to his nephew, the E. of Burlington, from whom it was purchased by Fredk. P. of Wales, father of George III, in 1732. The red-brick house was then new fronted with stone. In the gardens, which extended W. so far as Marlborough House, were statues by Rysbrack, of Alfred the Great and the Black P. It was modernized at a vast expense in 1788 and 1815. In 1816 here Princess Charlotte (daughter of George IV) was m. to P. Leopold of Saxe-Coburg. She d. a few yrs. later and Thackeray wrote:

'When I first saw England she was in mourning for the young Princess Charlotte, the hope of the Empire. With my childish attendant I remember peeping through the colonnade at Carlton House, and seeing the guards pacing the abode of the Prince Regent. I can yet see the guards pacing before the gates of the palace. What palace? The palace exists no more than the palace of Nebuchadnezzar. It is but a name now.'

It was pulled down in 1828. Some of the Corinthian columns which formed the colonnade of the house were used in the portico of the N.G., others in the chapel at Buckingham Palace. Carlton House Terrace (Waterloo Place) was built on the garden of the house in 1831.

Carlyle House. At No. 24 Cheyne Row, Chelsea, Thomas Carlyle lived from 1834 to his death in 1881. In the history of literary men in L. there is no equal to this 'stability of topographical centre,' as Lord Morley phrased it. After Carlyle's death the house was neglected, and Oliver Wendell Holmes, visiting it on his last visit to England in 1886, said: 'It was untenanted, neglected; its windows were unwashed, a pane of glass was broken; its threshold appeared untrodden, its whole aspect forlorn and desolate.'

In 1894 the lease was about to expire, and efforts were made to preserve the house as a national memorial, and the house was purchased for £1,750. It was opened on 26th July 1895 and on the following 4th Dec. (Carlyle's birthday) handed over to a trust. It is open daily to the public (except Tuesdays). There is a statue of Carlyle in the gardens facing the river. It is the most fascinating of literary shrines.

Central Criminal Court (Old Bailey). It was constituted by the Central Criminal Court Act, 1834. The present bdg. (on the site of Newgate Prison) was erected 1902-7. The architect was Edwd. W. Mountford, F.R.I.B.A., and the cost some £300,000. The exterior is faced with Portland stone, and the chief feature is a bold and lofty tower terminating in a dome, a lantern, and a bronze gilt figure of Justice with outstretched arms holding a sword and scales. The head of the figure (which is 16 ft. high) is 212 ft. above the level of the st. It was the work of F. W. Pomeroy, A.R.A., who also wrought the sculptured figures of Truth, Justice, and the Recording Angel over the main entrance, where appears the motto: 'Defend the children of the poor and punish the wrong doer.' This derives from the Prayer Book version of Psalm lxxii. It was selected by the Dean of Westminster, and approved by the Abp. of Canterbury. There is a splendid central hall, approached by a marble staircase, lined with slabs of marble, and surmounted by a dome ornamented with sculpture and with paintings. The latter are also by F. W. Pomeroy. There were four courts: one of 2,500 superficial ft. in area; one of 2,000 ft.; and two of 1,200 ft. From 1st May to 30th Sept. the judges, sheriffs, and the under-sheriffs all carry bouquets composed of old English garden flowers. On the floor of the Bench, and also on the ledges of the dock in each court, are strewn sweet herbs. This is an old custom originally designed to counteract the noisome smells emanating from Newgate Prison, which formerly adjoined the courts (see also 'City Corporation'). A tablet in the Central Criminal Court bears the following inscription:

'Near this site William Penn and William Mead were tried in 1670 for preaching to an unlawful assembly in Gracechurch Street. This tablet commemorates the courage and endurance of the jury, Thomas Vere, Edward Bushell, and ten others who refused to give a verdict against them although locked up without food for two nights and were fined for their final verdict of not guilty.'

There is also a statue of Mrs. Fry (1780–1845), modelled by Mr. A. Drury, R.A., after the famous portrait by Gibson. It bears the well-known lines from Browning, adapted to her sex:

'One who never turned her back
But marched breast forward,' etc.

The bdg. was twice hit by bombs, in 1940 and 1941. In the second attack the court of the Recorder of the City of London was demolished, as also the public waiting rooms. Mural paintings by Sir William Richardson were destroyed. Considerable extensions, necessitated by a steady increase in cases handled, were begun by the C.C. in 1967.

(See *The Old Bailey and its trials*, 1950, by B. O'Donnell.)

Charing Cross. The derivation does not imply a dear queen. Canon Westlake found evidence of a smithy kept by one Richd. at Charing at the end of the 12th century. A MS. entitled *Liber de Antiquis Legibus* in Guildhall Record Office mentions the village of Charing in 1260, thirty yrs. before the death of Q. Eleanor. It is probably derived from the Anglo-

Saxon *char*, whereby wood turned to coal becomes charcoal. Some have suggested that a charwoman is one who takes the turn of another. At Charing Cross the Thames turns E. There is a Charing in Kent which is situated at a deviation in the course of the Pilgrims' Way. At the time of the death of Q. Eleanor (1290) there was probably a small village half way between the City and Westminster. The funeral cortège would not be likely to stop where there were no inhabitants. It seems strange that a halt was made so near to W.A. where the body was laid. It may have been a short one, but possibly the cortège remained a whole night because the elaborate arrangements for interment were not complete. There is some reason to believe that there had been a cross of some kind before the Eleanor Cross, which was not completed until 1294. Whilst the cross at Waltham cost only £95, this one cost £650. The stone was brought from Caen, and the marble for the steps from Corfe, in Dorsetshire. The architects were many—Hubert de Corfe, Richd. and Roger de Crundale, etc. The sculpture was the work of Wm. de Ireland and Alexander de Abingdon. There are three drawings remaining—one in the Crace collection in the B.Mus., another in the Bodleian Library, and a third in the possession of the Soc. of Antiquaries. There appear to have been four steps, then an arcading, and above it eight figures of the Q., a further stage in a castellated style, and a topmost one somewhat Gothic in design. This was the last of twelve crosses erected between Harby (Notts) where Q. Eleanor d., and W.A., the others were at Lincoln, Stamford, Grantham, Geddington, Northampton, Stony Stratford, Woburn, Dunstable, St. Albans, Waltham and Cheapside. The cross was doomed by edict of Parliament in 1643, but not actually destroyed until 1647. Some amusing lines about its destruction appear in Bp. Percy's *Reliques*:

'Undone, undone the lawyers are;
  They wander about the towne;
Nor can find the way to Westminster
  Now Charing Cross is downe;
At the end of the Strand they made a stand,
  Swearing they are at a loss
And chaffing say, that's not the way
  They must go by Charing Cross.'

Some of the stone from the cross is said to have been used to pave the front of Whitehall Palace. The present cross, in the station yard, was erected at the expense of the London, Chatham, and Dover Railway Co. in 1863 at a cost of £1,800. The architect was E. M. Barry, son of Sir Chas. Barry, and the sculptor Thos. Earp. It does not follow very closely the drawings of the original cross. Four statues represent Q. Eleanor as Q., in two of the other four she is in the act of giving alms from a purse, and distributing bread, and in two more she is represented as the foundress of chs. and religious houses. The shields in the lower stage are accurately copied from those existing on the surviving crosses of Geddington, Northampton and Waltham. They display the three lions passant gardant, first assumed as the royal arms of England by Henry III in 1154; the arms of Ponthieu, which Q. Eleanor bore in right of her mother—three bends within a bordure; the arms of Castile and Leon, arranged quarterly.

Up to 1931 the N. end of what is now called Whitehall was in st. nomenclature 'Charing Cross.' Some of the other features of the district may therefore be mentioned, omitting those which more strictly appertain to the Strand. There was, about where Northumberland Avenue joins the Strand, a hosp., and chapel of St. Mary, belonging to the Priory of Rouncevall (Roncesvall) or De Rosida Valle, in the diocese of Pampelon in Navarre. It was founded by Wm. Marshall, E. of Pembroke. H. B. Wheatley plausibly suggested that this may explain the stoppage at this point of the funeral procession of Q. Eleanor. The house, as Stow records, was suppressed as an alien priory in the reign of Henry V, but restored under Edward IV. In the Yr. Books of Henry VII, the master, wardens, brethren and sisters of Rouncevall are mentioned, and these continued until it was suppressed under Edward VI. Near to this hosp., Stow says 'was an Hermitage, with a chapel of St. Katherine, over against Charing Cross.' In the Calendars of the Patent Rolls it is referred to as 'between St. Mary Rouncivall and the King of Scottis ground,' i.e. Old Scotland Yard, as it came to be called. N. of Charing Cross was the K.'s Mews, 'so called,' says Stow,

'of the king's falcons there kept by the king's falconer, which of old time was an office of great account.' So early as 1377 there was a bdg. here used for the K.'s hawks. ('Mew' was the name of a cage for hawks, especially when 'mewing' or moulting.) When, in 1537, Henry VIII's stables were burned down in Bloomsbury, and his horses removed here, the old name was retained, and so has become a generic term for a place for horses. During the Commonwealth Col. Joyce was imprisoned here by order of Cromwell. These Royal stables remained until 1829. The N. part was called 'Green Mews,' and that was the derivation of st. behind the N.G. which, until it was renamed in honour of Sir Henry Irving, was Green St.

Charterhouse is a name derived from Chartreuse, in France, where about 1084 six men, conducted there by the Bp. of Grenoble, started to erect an oratory surrounded by a number of small cells. Unlike the practice of the communal monastic orders, each monk worked, ate, and slept in his small apartment. The first English house was at Witham, on the borders of Selwood Forest, built by Henry II some time after the murder of Becket (1170), in fulfilment of a vow made at his tomb. The site chosen for the L. house was close to the priory of St. Bartholomew, Smithfield. It was a place where, in 1349, Sir Walter de Manny, a gentle, perfect knight, such as would have been beloved by Chaucer, and whose chivalry and courage were extolled by Froissart, had purchased thirteen acres for burial of the victims of the 'Black Death.' He also erected a chapel. The number of monks were to be twenty-four, and a prior; and a charter of incorporation, signed in March 1371, was confirmed by Richard II.

In 1372, when the prior's cell alone was ready, de Manny was bd. 'at the foot of the step of the great altar.' John Luscote, the first prior, held office for twenty-seven yrs., dying in 1398. At the time of his death five of the cells were still unfinished. Of those completed, five were the gift of the famous Sir Wm. Walworth, and four of Adam Fraunceys, Ld.M. The remaining cells, the refectory, the little cloister, with its guest-houses, the chapter-house, and the boundary wall were erected early in the 15th century. About 1430 a conduit was placed in the centre of the great cloister. The cells were arranged around a quadrangle.

There was a close connection between the priory of Charterhouse and the adjacent one of St. John of Jerusalem. When in 1381 the Wat Tyler rebels attacked the latter, they spared Charterhouse, perhaps because they esteemed the Knights of St. John as more men of the world and political in purpose. A fragment of eastern sculpture was once found embedded in a wall of the Charterhouse, and it is possible that this was part of the priory ruins used for repair there. In 1430 a document was drawn up, giving 'ghostly assistance to the Knights of St. John, in the masses, fasts, vigils, abstinences, and other spiritual exercises.' Moreover, Pardon chyd., adjoining which was the Charterhouse, was the place where the Knights of St. John bd. the bodies of those who, having given alms to their order, claimed the privilege of sanctuary.

Alone amongst the religious orders the Carthusians, in their strict 'rugorosite', remained vegetarians. It was probably this strictness that attracted Sir Thos. More. For about four yrs. 'he gave himself to devotion and prayer in the Charterhouse.' He lived there, Wm. Roper continued, 'religiously, but without vow.' There he learned to wear the hair shirt that he kept until death, and there he commenced to practise self-flagellation. Strictness of discipline, however, did not disarm the attack of Henry VIII. The priory had added field to field, and bgd. to bdg. In the early 16th century the ante-chapel, the guest-hall, the little cloister, and enlarged quarters for the lay brothers (Wash-house Court) had been erected. The priory was valued at £642 0s. 4½d. yearly. The K. found the prior (Houghton) less amenable to his wishes than the prior of St. John's, Clerkenwell. In 1534 Houghton, a man of sterling character, and his fellow-Carthusians, were called upon to swear assent to the Act of Succession. They had been averse to the divorce of Catherine of Aragon. After demur and delay they conferred with the father-confessor of Sion Monastery (Isleworth), and decided that it was a case in which consent might be given without hurt of conscience. In

1535, however, they were called upon to swear that Henry VIII was head of the Ch. This they refused to do. Houghton was soon sent to the T.L., with the Carthusian priors of Axholme and Beauvale. They were arraigned at Westminster Hall, and condemned to death. Sir Thos. More saw them leave the T.L. for their death.

'"Dost thou not see, Meg," he said to his daughter, Margaret Roper, "that these blessed fathers be now as cheerfully going to their deaths as bridegrooms to their marriage?"'

They were dragged on hurdles to Tyburn, where they were hanged and disembowelled, while still living. One of the limbs of Houghton was hung above the priory gate. A few weeks later three other monks suffered in the same way, and two more were sent to the Charterhouse of Hull, to be hanged in chains at York two yrs. later. Eleven monks were left in Newgate, and there Margaret Clements, the adopted daughter of Sir Thos. More, visited them and helped to alleviate their sufferings. Ten of them, chained upright in a Newgate dungeon, d. from filth and disease, and one only lived to be executed.

For several yrs. the priory, much dismantled, was left desolate. The K. took timber, stones, twenty-five loads of glass, and bay trees and orchard trees for his garden at Chelsea, also one hundred great carp from the pond which lay at the NW. corner of the present Pensioners' Court. The wainscoting was stripped from the cells. In 1545 Charterhouse was granted to Sir Edwd. North. Henry VIII had made him, as a lawyer with easy conscience, Chancellor of the Court of Augmentations —created for the handling of the revenues of the suppressed monasteries. In 1553 he conveyed it to John Dudley, D. of Northumberland, who possibly designed that Charterhouse should be a residence for his son, Ld. Guildford Dudley, and Lady Jane Grey. He himself never occupied it, for he was executed the same yr. North had signed at Greenwich a document in favour of Lady Jane Grey, notwithstanding which, for inexplicable reasons, he was pardoned, made a privy councillor, and granted Charterhouse again. His younger son was Sir Thos. North, the famous translator of Plutarch. When Elizabeth succeeded she honoured North by stopping with him at Charterhouse on her way from Hatfield to L. for her coronation. In 1561 Elizabeth spent three days at Charterhouse. North was negotiating for its sale when he d. on the last day of 1564. His son completed the transaction, and it passed into the possession of the D. of Norfolk, when it became known as Howard House.

The D. added the screen to the Great Hall, built the 'Tarrass Walk,' added the Great Chamber (Tapestry Room), and remodelled the Brothers' Library. He added the mantelpiece in the Master's Lodge. All of these have been destroyed by bombs. In 1568 Elizabeth was his guest, all these improvements being completed. In 1570 the D. was found intriguing with Mary Q. of Scots, whom he desired to marry. He was sent to the T.L., but, on an outbreak of plague there, was allowed to return to Charterhouse. He resumed his plotting, and in the Long Gallery received secret visits at night from John Lesley, Bp. of Ross, Mary's ambassador in L. Once the bp. brought a ring from her. In 1571, in the chapel of Charterhouse, dilapidated and disused since the days of the monks, the D. met De la Motte, the French ambassador, who lived in Charterhouse Sq. A bag with 600 crowns was handed to him; it was to help Mary's cause. On its way to her it was intercepted and sent to Cecil. Moreover Ridolfi, the agent of Philip of Spain and Alva, came to the gallery in Charterhouse by

'the Back Syde by the Long Workhouse at the furder end of the Lavendry Coort [Washhouse Court] and so up a new Payer of Stayers [the great staircast that still remains] that goeth up to the old wardrobe and so through the Chamber where my Lady Estrange used to dine and sup.'

The plot was that Alva was to land with troops at Harwich, and Norfolk and other nobles were to join him with 10,000 soldiers. Elizabeth was to be seized and Mary Q. of Scots proclaimed. Norfolk was suddenly arrested—tradition says on the great staircase—a 'fotecloth nag' was waiting at the gate and, unnoticed save 'by a number of idle raskall people,' he was taken to the T.L. Norfolk's fate was sure. The alphabet of a cipher was found hidden under tiles at Charterhouse. After one respite he was executed on Tower Hill in 1572.

Charterhouse, or Howard House, then passed to Philip, eldest son of the D. He does not seem to have lived there, for in 1574 and 1580 it was let to the Portuguese ambassador. In 1584 he joined the Ch. of Rome, and in 1585, having tried to escape to the Continent, was thrown into the T.L. (*q.v.*). An inscription of his remains in the Beauchamp Tower. He d. 1595, aged 38.

Charterhouse then passed under an entail to Thos. Howard, the son of the D. of Norfolk by his second wife, Lady Audley. He was a great admiral, and commanded the *Golden Lion* against the Spanish Armada. Elizabeth called him 'her good Thomas,' and a few weeks before her death she was once more at Charterhouse. James I, too, was there a few days before his coronation, the guest of the son of the man who aspired to marry his mother. Here he may have had the first interview with Raleigh which began a mutual dislike, for there was a great gathering of nobles. Here the K. created over a hundred knights—to his great profit—and created Howard E. of Suffolk. The new E. was in want of money for his new mansion at Audley End, so in June 1611 he conveyed Charterhouse to Thos. Sutton for £13,000.

The purchaser came of a good Lincolnshire family. He had probably been at Eton, possibly at Cambridge, and certainly at Lincoln's Inn. He had travelled much in Italy, Spain, and the Netherlands. He had been Master and Surveyor of the Q.'s Ordnance from Berwick to Edinburgh, and a keen business eye had suggested the possibility of exploiting the coalfields of Durham. He obtained leases for this purpose, and, marrying a wealthy widow, reaped a large fortune. He subscribed £100 to repel the Spanish Armada, and there was a bark *Sutton* fitted out. In 1611 letters patent were issued in which he was empowered to found a hosp. for eighty old men and forty boys under the name of the 'Hospital of King James in Charterhouse.' In the last days of the same yr. he d. at his house in Hackney, then a fashionable suburb. His executors gave instructions that his body should remain there till the roads into L. were in a fit and firm condition for a funeral procession. The body was embalmed at a cost of £40 4s. 8d., and the bowels buried at Hackney. The rest of the body was first bd. in a vault in Christ Ch., Newgate, until the new wing of Charterhouse chapel, added to the N. of the earlier monastic ch. was completed. A magnificent tomb was made there, the work of Nicholas Stone and Bernard Jansen (probably brother of Geraert Jansen, who is supposed to have made Shakespeare's bust at Stratford). There is much elaborate ornamentation, and a bas-relief represents the brothers assembled in their chapel. The iron grille is of much earlier date, and may possibly have belonged to one of the many tombs which had existed in the chapel or cloister. The founder's body still lies in the vault below, and there is a full-length effigy on the tomb which is described by Thackeray in *The Newcomes* with:

'Its grotesque carvings, monsters, heraldries, darkles and shines with the most wonderful shadows and lights. There he lies, Fundator Noster, in his ruff and gown, awaiting the great Examination Day.'

The first meeting of governors was held at Charterhouse on 30th July 1613, and it was decided that the brothers should be men

'such as could bring good testimony of their good behaviour and soundness in religion, and such as had been servants to the King's Majesty, either decrepid or old, captains either at sea or land, soldiers maimed or impotent, decayed merchants, men fallen into decay through shipwreck, casualty of fire, or such evil accident: those that had been captives under the Turks.'

Before the end of the yr. the eighty pensioners were elected. One of these was Capt. Geo. Fennar, buccaneer and patriot. He fought five Portuguese ships for two days, and commanded the largest private galleon against the Armada. He was the first of the brothers to die and was bd. in the chapel (*c.* 1617). These old sea-dogs were not easy to manage. One declining to apologize to the master, on his knees, was 'expulsed.' Another was expelled for a share in some coining venture outside. Some men were allowed to leave, to serve under Gustavus Adolphus. One was killed at Reval, another at Plymouth. In 1629 the governors were compelled to define the social status of the brothers as confined to 'gentlemen by birth.'

Among later brothers who have found Charterhouse a blessed haven of refuge in old age have been Elkanah Settle the City poet (d. 1724); Stephen Gray, F.R.S. (d. 1736), the pioneer of electric science; and Alex. Macbean, Dr. Johnson's amanuensis on the *Dictionary.* The last exchanged telepathic experiences with Johnson, and compiled a *Dictionary of Ancient Geography* for which the latter wrote a preface. He entered in 1781, on the nomination of Ld. Thurlow. In a letter to the Rev. Dr. Vyse, rector of Lambeth, about the matter, Johnson referred to the 'Chartreux.' Macbean d. there in 1784. Later brethren have been Maddison Morton, the author of *Box and Cox* (d. 1891), and Walter Greaves (d. 1930). The latter was a friend of Whistler and also an artist. His 'Hammersmith Bridge' is in the Tate Gallery.

The brothers must be of the 'distressed gentleman' class, officers in the army or navy, clergymen, doctors, lawyers, artists, or literary men, or men who have been engaged in mercantile or agricultural pursuits, and able to produce testimony to their good character.

To most of those to whom great books are part of the bread of life, Charterhouse stands for Thackeray, who introduced both brothers and scholars into his novels. Preacher's Court has been destroyed but there has survived the tablet on the staircase bearing the following inscription: 'In this room lived Captain Thomas Light, whom Thackeray visited when writing the last chapters of *The Newcomes.*'

There is some of the old priory still left, e.g. Washhouse Court, and the doors of one or two cells. The Chapel and the Guesten or Great Hall are now the principal parts of Charterhouse. In the first, in addition to the founder's tomb, there is a fragment of the tomb of Sir Walter de Manny, found some yrs. ago built into a wall. There are also monuments of Francis Beaumont (master 1617–24); Matthew Raine (master, d. 1811), by Flaxman; Chief Justice Ellenborough (d. 1818), by Chantrey. The last was a scholar here. The Great Hall has a fine ceiling of Elizabethan date, and a beautiful fireplace, which bears Sutton's arms. Here James I created the knights in 1603.

The Guesten Hall is 16th-century work, except the fireplace, some parts of which date from 1613. There was a hammer-beam roof, which was burnt off in the

Blitz; the music gallery with a magnificent screen, and beautiful panelling round the walls remain.

The sch. was at first for forty scholars; the number was afterwards raised to sixty. Amongst the scholars have been Richd. Crashaw, the poet; Isaac Barrow, the divine; Addison and Steele, as Thackeray reminded readers of *Esmond*. John Wesley entered in 1714, and was under Dr. Walker who, according to a memorial tablet in the chapel, had an exceedingly accurate knowledge of Hebrew, Greek, and Latin. Wesley suffered much privation here. The seniors robbed the juniors of rations, and he said that from ten to fourteen yrs. of age he had little but bread to eat. Wesley, however, thought that, far from hurting him, this restricted diet laid the foundation of good health. His father gave him strict injunctions to run round the playground—somewhat extensive—three times every morning, and Wesley obeyed. Other Charterhouse boys were Judge Blackstone, the historians Grote and Bp. Thirlwall, Sir Henry Havelock, Thackeray, John Leech, and Thos. Lovell Beddoes (poet). In the chapel cloister tablets commemorated Wesley, Roger Williams, Leech, and Thackeray. Only the tablet to the first-named remains. Leech was a great *Punch* cartoonist, and illustrated Dickens's *Christmas Carol*. Thackeray was at the sch. from 1822 to 1828. He referred to his old sch. by varying names. In *The Newcomes* perversely it was 'Greyfriars,' as though he desired to throw his readers off the scent. Roger Williams founded the settlement at Rhode Island in 1636.

During excavations consequent on the Blitz there was found a lead coffin which contained a well-preserved skeleton. It is believed to be that of Sir Walter de Manny, as in the coffin was a Papal Bull in the form of a leaden disc. Pope Clement VI issued a Bull to Sir Walter, who d. in 1373.

(See *Charterhouse*, by D. Knowles and W. F. Grimes, 1954; and *The London Charterhouse restored*, by A. Oswald, 1959.)

Cheapside. The earliest mention is 'Westceape' in 1067, distinguishing from 'Estchep' (Eastcheap). It was 'Westchep' *c.* 1214–22, and first called 'Chepsyde' 1510. It was so called from the market held there—Anglo-Saxon *ceap* barter or purchase.

Cheapside is said by Strype to be 28 ft. higher than when St. P.'s Cath. was first built. In 1845 when excavations for a sewer were made, 18 to 22 ft. down, there were found deep layers of ashes and burnt wood over the original gravel, and over that great quantities of debris of the Roman period, such as pottery and coins. Sir Geo. Laurence Gomme considered that this was definite evidence of a Celtic settlement here.

In medieval times Cheapside was probably broader than now, though it is unusual for a City st. to change in this direction with the passage of time. It was then the principal City market, and down each side of it were selds or warehouses for goods, many but one storey high; by Stow's time they had extended to four or five storeys. The st. was lined with small shops, with shutters instead of glazed windows, and called penthouses. There were also stalls, and from these the City authorities drew a rent. They were restricted to 22 ft. in height, and the C.C. reserved a right to remove them. In 1278, when Edward I was expected to arrive in L. from the Holy Land, where he was at the time of the death of his father, Henry III, an order was made for the removal of these stalls for the purpose of the great pageant. It then appeared from the petitions against it that at that early date some of the tradesmen were residing at 'Hakeney' (Hackney) and 'Stebney' (Stepney). It was this liability to get an unexpected notice to quit, that made it less profitable to own a stall in Westchepe than in some other parts of the City.

Starting from the W. end of Cheapside, near Foster Lane, was the place where the bread from Stratford was sold to the poor. The spot was familiarly known as 'The Cartes in Chepe.' This rivalry with the City bakers was resented at times, and by way of tariff a weekly charge was made of 2d. for the passage of the carts through Aldgate. This fact explains the Boy of Panyer Alley. It was more difficult to supervise a cartload of bread than the loaves sold in the stalls in Westchepe, and so, in 1392, says Chas. Pendrill:

'A rule was made that when any loaf from Stratford was found deficient in weight the whole cartload should be confiscated. Raids were frequently made upon these men by the officials, and on one such occasion in 1387, when the Mayor himself came to make inspection, one of them hastily inserted a piece of iron into a loaf to increase its weight, but was detected and seized.'

From the beginning of the 14th century the NW. end of Cheapside was the home of the Saddlers' Co. (see 'Companies; A'). Foster Lane derives from 'fusters,' or makers of wooden saddle-bows.

'There is an account,' says Chas. Pendrill, 'in 1300 of a saddler who had his workshop in the solar or first floor room of a house situated between Honey Lane and Milk Street, and keeping a plank of wood projecting from the window on which to hang his saddles to dry, it fell down and killed a man who was passing in the street below.'

Westchepe was famous for its goldsmiths' shops. In Tudor times they were particularly commented upon. In the beginning of the 16th century a Venetian traveller, mentioning Cheapside particularly, said that he did not think that in all the shops put together there would be found so many of the magnificences that were to be seen in L., and Thos. Deloney in *Thomas of Reading* (1600) said: 'Now when they were brought into Cheapside, there with great wonder they beheld the shops of the Goldsmiths.' In 1382, in one night, two burglaries were perpetrated on two shops, one at the corner of Friday St., and the other next door. The captures included silver girdles braided with silk, a silver-gilt chain, a silver chalice, two wooden mazers with bands of silver gilt, six silver spoons, two gold rings set with diamonds, a gold and ruby ring, three strings of pearls, and six gold necklaces. Strangely enough, it was at the same place that there was found in 1912, in the course of excavations, a fine collection of Jacobean jewellery, which was divided between the Guildhall Mus. and the L.Mus.

Gutter Lane is first mentioned as 'Godrunelane' in the reign of K. John (1199–1216). In 1240, when a murder was committed there, it was 'Goderonelane.' It has sometimes been derived from Guthrum, Danish K. of E. Anglia, with whom Alfred the Great made the Peace of Chippenham (inaccurately called the 'Peace of Wedmore') in 878. 'Godrun'

or 'Goderane,' however, appears in Domesday Book as the tenant of land here.

At the corner of Wood St. was the ch. of St. Peter, Westchepe (see 'City Churches; A') not rebuilt after the G.F. In front of the chyd. are now three shops, consisting of two storeys and two rooms, erected in 1687. They stand on the site of earlier shops, similarly small, which were built against the chyd. wall by permission of the C.C. Stow referred to 'the long shoppe or shed incroching on the high street before this Church wall,' and says it was licensed to be made in the yr. 1401. A clause in the lease forbids the shops being enlarged.

At the corner of Friday St. (believed to be the resort of fishmongers), up to about 1930, was a house which had an inscription claiming that it was the oldest in Cheapside, and it was said to have survived the G.F. W. G. Bell could not support the claim. 'Cheapside is all in a light fire in a few hours' time,' wrote the Rev. T. Vincent (*God's Terrible Voice*), and another contemporary said: 'You may stand where Cheapside was and see the Thames.' It was probably built soon after the G.F. Traditionally it was the shop from which John Gilpin set out.

'The stones did rattle underneath
  As if Cheapside were mad.'

The stone sign of a chained swan (the heraldic device of Henry IV) is now at the Guildhall. During repairs in 1920, below the second basement (it was the only house in Cheapside with two), a green bottle was found which was probably Roman work.

Between Friday St. and Bread St. was the famous 'Mermaid' (see 'Taverns'), and at the corner of Bread St. was the Mitre Tavern, which was in existence before 1475, and was not rebuilt after the G.F. On the right of Chepe, from Bow Lane to the corner of Bucklersbury, was the Mercery, a long row of shops kept by the Mercers. This was where Lydgate's Lickpenny found them:

'Then to the Cheap I 'gan me drawn
  Where much people I saw for to stand;
  One offered me velvet, silk and lawn;
  Another he taketh me by the hand,
  "Here is Paris thread, the finest in the
    land." '

In a house at the corner of Ironmonger

Lane Thos. à Becket was b. (*c.* 1118). There is a C.C. plaque. Up to the time of the dissolution under Henry VIII there was here the chapel of St. Thos. of Acon (from the title of an order instituted in the Holy Land, about the time of Becket's death, as a branch of the Templars, who had a house at Acre). The City gates had to be opened when the bell of this chapel rang for matins, so it must have been a loud-sounding one. Within the Hosp. precincts a small sch. was started (*c.* 1191). It remained until 1538. One of its scholars was John Colet, the famous Dean of St. P.'s Cath. At the E. corner of Ironmonger Lane was the shop of John Boydell. He was Ld.M. in 1790, and the printer and publisher of engravings. His most famous works were his illustrations of Shakespeare, engraved after the works of the most eminent contemporary artists. The originals were exhibited in his own gallery and by 1802 numbered 102. Financial difficulty compelled him to dispose of his property by lottery, in 1804, in which yr. he d. Boydell used to rise at 5 a.m., place his wig on top of a pump in Ironmonger Lane, and then sluice his head with water. Keats once lodged in No. 76 over Bird-in-Hand Court. In Keats's time the court led to the Queen's Head Tavern.

Cheapside might be described as the most public-spirited st. in old L. In the centre were a number of stationary objects of interest. Opposite Wood St. was the Eleanor Cross. It was erected in 1291, of Purbeck marble, as was the one at Charing. Around its base were carved in relief figures representing the Virgin Mary, Christ, Edward the Confessor, etc. Later there were added to it saints, martyrs, and popes. It is seen in considerable detail in a contemporary painting of the coronation procession of Edward VI (1553). In the first niche appears the effigy of a pope, below the base of the second stage are four apostles, each with a nimbus round his head, and above them the Virgin with the Infant Jesus. In this case, in contrast to the cross at Charing, Q. Eleanor seems to have taken a subordinate position. Possibly she was on the other side of the lowest tier. It was rebuilt in 1441, and it was probably then that the Q.'s figures disappeared. At the same time it was used as the terminus of an aqueduct, bringing water in leaden pipes from Highgate and Hampstead. Here also, at the same time, was placed the public granary. In 1484, the citizens of L. raised a subscription to repair and beautify it, and in 1522 it was new gilt with gold on the arrival of the Emperor Charles V. At the coronation of Edward VI it received a new polish, and for the coronation of Q. Mary all the possible popish decorations were lavished upon it. At the public entry of K. Philip of Spain (1554) it was again 're-touched and magnificently ornamented,' but under Elizabeth it fell into disfavour. In 1581 it was attacked. Edward the Confessor was mutilated, and the Virgin was 'robbed of her son and her arms broken by which she staid him on her knees, her whole body also haled by ropes and left ready to fall.' The Q. offered a reward for the discovery of the impious assailants, but with no result. In 1595 the effigy of the Virgin was repaired, and afterwards 'a new sonne misshapen (as borne out of time), all naked, was laid in her arms; the other images continuing broken as before.' In 1596 the Virgin was superseded by the goddess Diana—'a woman (for the most part naked), and water, conveyed from the Thames, filtering from her naked breasts, but oftentimes dried up.' This is the meaning of Rosalind's allusion in *As You Like It*: 'I will weep for nothing, like Diana in the fountain.' In 1599 Elizabeth ordered a plain cross to be placed on the summit, thinking that as the common symbol of the Christian faith it could cause no offence. The Virgin was also restored. This led to another attack, 'her crown being plucked off, and almost her head, taking away her naked child, and stabbing her in the breast.' In this condition it was left until 1600, when it was rebuilt. The universities were consulted as to whether a crucifix should be restored. They all sanctioned it except Dr. (afterwards Abp.) Abbot, but there was to be no dove. It was then surmounted by an iron railing, and what were considered superstitious images were replaced by effigies of apostles, Ks. and prelates. It is so seen in the well-known engraving of the pageant going along Cheapside on the occasion of the visit to L. of Marie de Medici, mother of Charles I's consort, Henrietta Maria, in 1638. In 1641 the cross was again defaced and there were agitations for its removal. In 1643 Parliament ordered its destruction, and a troop of horse and two cos. of foot carried out the work. The official account said: 'At the fall of the top cross drums beat, trumpets blew, and multitudes of caps were thrown into the air, and a great shout of people with joy.' In the same month the *Book of Sports* was burnt where the cross used to stand. Abp. Laud (in the T.L.) noted in his diary: 'The cross in Cheapside was taken down to cleanse that great street of superstition.' Evelyn himself saw 'the furious and zelous people demolish that stately crosse in Cheapside.'

A little E. of the cross was the little conduit of Chepe. It took the name of an old cross which was taken down in 1390. The Gt. Conduit of the City stood about opposite Old Jewry. These conduits were leaden cisterns cased in stone. The Gt. Conduit was built in 1237, merchants of Amiens, Corby, and Nesle in France subscribing £100 towards the expense. As the water came from Tyburn, via Leicester Fields, Strand, and Fleet St., through a pipe 4,752 yds. long, this must have required a large amount of capital. Money was frequently left in wills for the upkeep of the Gt. Conduit, which was under the care of a keeper, who held keys, so that water was only obtainable in his presence. In 1337 the L. brewers were found to be drawing so much water that everyone else had to go short. Their supply was curtailed, and eventually they rented certain pipes for their exclusive use. On any particularly joyous occasion conduits ran wine. This happened in 1274, when Edward I brought Q. Eleanor to L. In 1299, when his second wife came, he improved upon the first arrangement, and erected two large towers for the same purpose. Jack Cade (1450) in the Shakespearian *Henry VI*, sitting on L. Stone, orders that the conduit 'run nothing but claret wine this first year of our reign.' The Gt. Conduit remained until the G.F., and was not rebuilt.

Near to Honey Lane was the Standard. This seems also to have been a conduit, although it is not clear whether this was its original purpose. It is first mentioned in the C.C. Letter Books in 1337. It was the place of execution. Two fishmongers were executed here in 1340 for striking the Ld.M. during a riot. Wat Tyler, in 1381, executed several citizens at this spot; Jack Cade in 1450 executed here Ld. Saye and Sele. In 1461, at the Standard, a man had his hand struck off here for assaulting another in the presence of the judges at Westminster. In the 16th century a man who had ill-treated a child was thoroughly whipped at this spot by the 'beadles of the beggars.' At this spot occurred the diverse and piquant punishments for frauds in trade. In 1269, because the foreign merchants refused to weigh their merchandise at the official 'beam,' their scales were seized and burnt at. the Standard, and such parts as were non-inflammable smashed with hammers. In 1293 three men had their right hands amputated for rescuing prisoners. In 1311 forty grey and white hats were burnt. Here also the heads of rebels were often exposed to public view, before being taken to the T.L. or London Bridge. Here stood the pillory, and in 1703 Defoe was exposed in this way for publishing his *Shortest Way with the Dissenters*. The Standard was not rebuilt after the G.F.

Cheapside was also the most spectacular of all the City sts. There were joustings here. The most memorable was for Edward III in 1329. Sand was sprinkled, as now, before a procession, and bunting bedecked the houses and, by way of grand stand, an archway was erected across Chepe. Unfortunately when the K. and Q. ascended with their suite, the archway collapsed, and the royal dignity with it. Injuries were sustained only by a few knights beneath, but the K. was furious; Q. Philippa had to intercede to save the wretched carpenters, as she did later for the citizens of Calais. To avoid future accidents of this kind the K. had built beside the ch. of St. Mary-le-Bow (see 'City Churches; C'), a great house of stone, called the 'Crownsilde,' meaning the Royal House. It was used until the time of Henry VIII for viewing jousting, and the annual march of the watch on Midsummer Eve. When Wren rebuilt the ch. after the G.F. he placed a stone balcony in front, as a memorial of something no longer required, except for Ld.M.'s Shows. A house opposite the ch. is said to have offered accommodation for this purpose to Charles II, and several successive sovereigns, including the first three Georges.

Stranger exhibitions than Ld.M.s' Shows were to be seen in the medieval Chepe.

Bakers would be drawn along it on hurdles with short-weight loaves tied round their necks, butchers pilloried with stinking meat burned under their noses. In 1387 and 1388 there were three cases of penance being performed here. With head, legs, and feet bare, the culprit had to walk through Chepe carrying a lighted candle. The weight of the candle was specified. In one case it had to be deposited on the high altar of the ch. of St. Dunstan-in-the-W., in the other two in the same place in the Guildhall Chapel. The offenders had assaulted or insulted alder-men.

Hall, the tight-rope dancer of Bartholomew Fair, used to perform in Cheapside. In some lines on Bow Ch. and steeple, in Dr. Wild's *Rome rhymed to Death* (1683), it was said:

'When Jacob Hall on his high rope shows tricks,
The Dragon flutters: the Lord Mayor's horse kicks;
The Cheapside crowds and pageants scarcely know
Which most t'admire, Hall, hobby-horse, or Bow.'

The fact that Cheapside was so used as a place of pleasure and a place of penance, is an indication at once of the width of the thoroughfare and its importance in the public mind. Cade, announcing his programme in *2 Henry VI*, says: 'All the realm shall be in common and in Cheapside shall my palfrey go to grass.' In this way would the proud of L.'s citizens lie at the feet of the conqueror. Chas. Pendrill wrote:

'So famous did the streets identified with particular crafts become, that it is said that at the annual fair held at Stourbridge, each row of booths allocated to one trade was named after the corresponding street in London occupied by the same craft.'

Bread St., Milk St., Ironmonger Lane, and Honey Lane, are respectively the places where the trades indicated were in medieval times carried on. Friday St. was the resort of the fishmongers.

Cheapside suffered badly in the blitz.
(See *London Life in the Fourteenth Century*, 1925, and *Wanderings in Mediæval London*, 1928, by Chas. Pendrill; *Old Cheapside and Poultry*, by Kenneth Rogers, 1931.)

Chelsea, now part of the L. Bor. of Kensington and Chelsea (still called a Royal Borough) was a met. bor., comprising some 660 acres of land. This comparatively small triangular area is so rich in literary, historical, and royal associations, and exhibited, in bygone days, so many stately riverside homes, as to make its proud title of 'The Village of Palaces' no exaggerated appellation.

Concerning the derivation of the place-name, Reginald Blunt, in his admirable *Historical Handbook to the Parish of Chelsea*, has listed no fewer than five possible sources, viz. 'Chelcheya' (causeway), 'Cheselsey' (shelves of sand), 'Ceoles-ige' (the place of ships), 'Cealchyde' (cold harbour), and 'Cealchythe' (chalk wharf). He selects the last-named as the most probable source, since a wharf seems to have stood here from earliest times, and the most ancient parts of the old ch. were constructed of chalk.

At the S. end of Church St. stands the fine old par. ch., dedicated to All Saints; the greater part of it was demolished by a bomb in 1941 and rebuilt. The SE. or More Chapel remains, with the curiously carved capitals of Italian workmanship, probably designed by Hans Holbein, who was frequently the guest of Sir Thomas More at his nearby house. This was restored and in June 1950 opened for the first service in the ch. since 1941. The magnificent monument to Ld. Dacre of the South and his wife Anne, who d. 1595 and by her will founded Emanuel Sch. (now in Wandsworth), has survived almost intact, and with the monument to Sir Robert Stanley (1632) alone remains in its old position. By great good fortune almost every other monument was salvaged intact, or repairable, from the ruins, and they may one day be re-erected. Among the more important were those to Sir Thomas More (1535); Jane, Duchess of Northumberland (1555); Thos. Hungerford, 'gentilman pencioner' to Henry VIII (1581); Sir Arthur Gorges (1625); Sarah Lawrence (1631); Lady Jane Cheyne (1669), and tablets to Henry James (1916), and Wm. De Morgan (1917).

The best-known monument remaining in the little chyd. is that to Sir Hans Sloane, 'President of the Royal Society and of the College of Physicians who, in the year of our Lord 1753 the 92nd year of his age, without the least pain of body, and with a conscious serenity of mind, ended a virtuous and beneficent life.' His collections partly formed the nucleus of the B.Mus.

The new par. ch. of St. Luke, with its lofty tower, clerestory windows and flanking buttresses is a very fine bdg. of its kind and enjoys the distinction of possessing the first stone groined roof constructed in England since the Reformation. It was built in 1820–4, the architect being Jas. Savage. Chas. Dickens was married there in 1836. Of the other Chelsea chs. Holy Trinity, Sloane St., rebuilt by J. W. Sedding in 1890, contains much fine craftsmanship in glass and marble, bronze and mosaic; the R.C. Ch. of St. Mary, Cadogan Place, is the work of J. F. Bentley, architect of Westminster Cath.; Christ Ch. contains an organ and a well-carved pulpit which came from 17th century chs. in the City.

Of Chelsea's green spots the most pleasant are the Moravian Burial Ground, the Apothecaries' Garden, and the grounds of the Royal Hosp. The first-named—a haunting peaceful 'God's acre' lying in the angle between Milman's St. and King's Rd.—reminds the visitor that the benevolent Count Nicholas von Zinzendorf, leader of the 'Unitas Fratrum,' invited members of that body to settle on his Chelsea estate after their expulsion from Bohemia and Moravia in the first half of the 18th century. This hallowed ground is divided into four plots (married men, single men, married women, single women being separated): the gravestones are flat and record only the name and age of those who rest beneath. Among these worthies are Jas. Fraser, who made fifty-six heroic missionary voyages to and from Labrador; Jas. Hutton, the friend of Wesley and the originator of the Moravian movement in England; Jas. Gillray (father of the great caricaturist), who was sexton here for forty yrs.; and Nunak, an unbaptized Esquimaux Indian, who lies under an ancient mulberry tree. The burial-ground is further remarkable for its W. wall— the only surviving remains of Sir Thos. More's house. The Botanic (or Apothecaries') Gardens are situated between Royal Hospital Rd. and the Embankment. They were established by the Apothecaries' Co. (*q.v.*) in 1673 and were frequently visited by the famous Linnæus and by Mrs. Elizabeth Blackwell, who illustrated her *Herbal* from specimens which thrived here. Cotton seeds were first sent to America from this garden in 1732. In the centre of the grounds stands Rysbrach's fine statue of Sir Hans Sloane. The master's and warden's chairs of the Soc. of Apothecaries were made of wood from cedars grown in this garden. The Royal Hosp., home of some 600 Chelsea Pensioners, was founded by Charles II, it is erroneously said in compliance with a promise made to Nell Gwynne, and completed by William and Mary. Sir Christopher Wren designed the bdg., the fine façade of which fronts the river. The Great Hall and the Chapel, both wainscoted, are spacious and dignified, while in the cemetery lie Wm. Hiseland (see 'Epitaphs'); Dr. Burney (d. 1814), author of the *History of Music*, and father of Fanny Burney, who was for many yrs. organist here; and Dr. Wm. Cheselden (d. 1752), surgeon of Chelsea Hosp., who prepared the plan of old Putney B. (1729). Other 'pleasaunces' include the Embankment Garden, at the bottom of Cheyne Row, where stands Boehm's impressive statue of Thos. Carlyle, and the cool greensward in front of Crosby Hall (*q.v.*).

Famous men and women connected with Chelsea include Sir John Danvers; Geo. Eliot; Elizabeth Fry; Thos. Faulkner; Sir John Goss; Sir Isaac Newton; Jonathan Swift; P. B. Shelley; Tobias Smollett; Sir Richd. Steele; J. M. W. Turner; J. M. Whistler; Chas. Keene; Michael Fairless (author of *The Roadmender*); Dr. C. Burney; D. G. Rossetti; Thos. Carlyle; Holman Hunt; Mrs. Gaskell; Sir Thos More; Wm. De Morgan; and Robt. Falcon Scott. Many of these are commemorated by tablets on the houses where they lived. Carlyle House is dealt with separately.

Chelsea has been fortunate in its historian. Reginald Blunt, son of Rev. Gerald Blunt, its Rector, produced the following fascinating and informing volumes: *Carlyle's Chelsea Home* (1895); *A Handbook to Chelsea* (1900); *Paradise Row* (1906); *In Cheyne Walk and Thereabouts* (1914); *The Wonderful Village* (1918); *By Chelsea Reach* (1921); *The Lure of Old Chelsea* (1922); *Red Anchor Pieces* (1928).

(See also *Chelsea—from the Five Fields to the Worlds End*, by R. Edmonds, 1956.)

Children's Memorials in London. No record of child life in L. has come down to posterity. Old prints show them learning the humanities, with much flogging, as Lamb said, and generally it appears that they were expected to be adults in miniature from the beginning; of no interest except for their future.

Parenthood, however, had its pangs then as now. In the L.Mus. there is a small memorial stone with a Greek inscription which is translated: 'Dexios, son of Ditimos, excellent, farewell.' It was found during excavations in Drury Lane, and the brevity of the praise may be compared with Jane Lister's in W.A., referred to later. In the same mus. there is a small marble tablet inscribed: 'To Marcus Aurelius Eucarpus, my most devoted son, aged 15 yrs. 6 mos. Set up by his mother Aurelia Eucarpia.'

In the Guildhall Mus. is a stone with an inscription translated: 'To the god of the shades in memory of Onesimus well deserving son of Domitius Elianus who died in his 13th year.' It was found under Botolph Lane in 1852.

Leaving the Romans, there is a great gap. We have a few records; no memorials. Turning to the Middle Ages, Chas. Pendrill (in his admirable *London Life in the 14th Century*) says:

'That the proclivities of boyhood have not changed throughout the centuries, will be realized on reading of a boy climbing up to a gutter to retrieve his lost ball; of others playing on a heap of timber when one fell and broke his leg; and of another, a schoolboy, returning over London Bridge after dinner, who must needs climb out and hang his hands from a plank on the side of the bridge, and fell in and was drowned.'

This occurred in 1381, about the period of Chaucer's 'Prioress's Tale' of

'. . . a wydwes sone,
A litel clergeoun, seven yeer of age,
That day by day to scolé was his wone;'

and whose throat was 'kut unto my nekke boon' by the Jews, another example of the way in which records of that distant past children live only in death.

In W.A. there are monuments or graves of about fifty children. The first known is Katherine, a daughter of Henry III, who d. at five yrs. of age, in 1257. 'She was dumb and fit for nothing,' wrote Matthew Paris, 'though possessing great beauty.' Her mother fell ill, and nearly d. of grief at the loss of the child, who was bd. in an altar-tomb just outside the gates of St. Edmund's Chapel. It was once inlaid with marbles and mosaics, and had two images, probably one the princess herself. On the wall above are traces of gilding and colouring, which are supposed to be remains of a painting, of the Princess Katherine and two brothers who d. in infancy. Henry III suffered another loss in 1271. His youthful nephew, P. Henry, son of Richard 'King of the Romans,' was returning from a crusade and was stabbed whilst at mass by the sons of Simon de Montfort, a fearful revenge for the latter's death at Evesham, and their own banishment five yrs. before. The young P.'s body was bd. in the monastery of Hayles, which his father had founded, while his heart was brought to Westminster, and placed in a golden chalice near the shrine of Edward the Confessor. Matthew of Westminster adds:

'One of his murderers, Simon, died this year in a certain castle near the city of Sienna; who during the latter part of his life being, like Cain, accursed of the Lord, was a vagabond and a fugitive on the face of the earth.'

Edward I lost four children, and they are in the same tomb as his own brothers and sisters. One of these was P. Alfonzo. He came to L. from Wales in 1284, leaving his father there, and bringing with him Llewellyn's golden crown (traditionally that of K. Arthur), jewels and ornaments, 'applied to adorn the tomb of the blessed King Edward.' He d. the same yr. at the age of about twelve. Edward III lost four children in 1340, Wm. of Windsor, and Blanche de la Tour, both surnamed from their birth-places, the latter being born in the T.L. There are alabaster effigies of the two children, 20 in. in length, in the chapel of St. Edmund. The stonemason, who was also engaged on the tomb of their mother, Philippa, was John Orchard, and he received 20s. for his work. A brass inscription has disappeared, also small figures with which the panels appear to have been adorned. Two of the children of Wm. de Valence, cousins of Edward I, were bd. beneath the step between St. Edmund's Chapel and the tomb of

Henry V, one being a daughter, Margaret (d. 1276). In 1305, there were bd. in the chapel of John the Baptist, Hugh and Mary de Bohun, children of Humphrey de Bohun, E. of Hereford, and Elizabeth, daughter of Edward I. The material is grey Purbeck marble, once coloured, and round the sides runs a trefoiled arcade. It is unique in W.A., but resembles Abp. Theobald's tomb in Canterbury Cath. In 1472, in Edward the Confessor's Chapel, Margaret of York, infant daughter of Edward IV, was laid. She was nine months old. The little tomb is of grey marble; the brass effigy and inscriptions have been removed.

Next in order of death—but not of interest—are Edward V and his brother Richd., D. of York. What were believed to be their bones were found in 1674 in a wooden chest, 10 ft. below the ground, in the T.L. Charles II ordered the bones to be carefully collected and placed in a marble urn, designed by Wren, now to be seen in the N. aisle of Henry VII's Chapel. The following is a translation of a Latin inscription over them:

'Here lie the Reliques of Edward the Fifth, King of England, and Richard Duke of York. These brothers being confined in the Tower, and there stifled with Pillows, were privately and meanly buried by order of their perfidious Uncle Richard the usurper; whose bones, long enquired after and wished for, after two hundred and one years in the rubbish of the stairs (i.e. those lately leading to the Chapel of the White Tower) were on the 17th day of July 1674, by undoubted proofs discovered, being buried deep in that place. Charles the Second, a most compassionate Prince, pitying their severe fate, ordered these unhappy Princes to be laid amongst the monuments of their predecessors, Anno Dom. 1678, in the 30th year of his reign.'

The arithmetic was not quite correct. When the remains were discovered, the two Ps. had been dead 191 yrs. On 6th July 1933 the urn was opened in the presence of a number of gentlemen, including the Dean of Westminster and Prof. Wm. Wright (Dean of the L. Hosp. Medical Coll. and President of the Anatomical Soc. of Great Britain and Ireland). They were reburied on 11th July 1933,

together with a statement of the proceedings written on parchment, a part of the burial service being read. Prof. Wright had made an examination, and reported that they appeared to be the remains of children of the ages of Edward and his brother, i.e. twelve and ten yrs. Next comes Elizabeth, second daughter of Henry VII, who d. at Eltham Palace in 1495. She was only three yrs. old, but was given a State funeral. Her body was brought in a black chair drawn by six horses, received at the gate of the abbey by the prior, and borne ceremoniously into the ch. The tomb is a small one of Lydian marble. The gilt effigy and inscriptions have gone.

In 1605 there was bd. in the Chapel of St. Nicholas, Anne Sophia, infant daughter of the Count of Bellamonte, French ambassador at the Court of James I. The heart was placed in a vase on a pyramid of black-and-white marble.

In the N. aisle of Henry VII's Chapel (called 'Innocents' Corner') there are bd. two children of James I. Sophia d. in 1606, when three days old. She lies in a stone cradle which has a gorgeous coverlet, trimmed with lace. The arms of England, Scotland, and Ireland are on the back. The baby, much too large for its age, has also an expression beyond its days, and wears a close lace cap.

Next to this monument is Princess Mary's. She d. in 1607 at the age of two. Her body was brought in a barge covered with black velvet from Greenwich, where she d., and interred with 'all the great Lords of the Council and the heralds' present. The tombs cost respectively £140 and £215.

The first child of Charles I—a son—was b., baptized, and bd. in W.A. (by Laud) on the same day. A daughter, the Lady Anna, who d. before she was four yrs. of age, was bd. in 1641 in the tomb of her great-grandmother, Mary Q. of Scots.

Leaving W.A., there is a tombstone to children, passed daily by hundreds of people who probably never stop to read. It is in Bream's Bdgs., Chancery Lane, in a fragment still left of the chyd. of St. Dunstan-in-the-W. It reads:

'Here sleeps our Babes in silence, Heav'ns thaire rest
For God takes soonest those he loveth best.

'Samewell Marshall the 2 sonne of

Edwd. Marshall & Anne his wife.
Dyed May 27 1631 aged two yeares.
Anne Marshall, their first dau. dyed
21th of June 1635 aged one yeare
9 moneths. Nicholas Marshall their
third son dyed Decem. 5th 1635 aged
five yeares 6 moneths.'

Little thought those bereaved parents
(whose grave no man knows) that their
sorrow would be patent 300 yrs. after in
a city where now few children are b. and
fewer die.

To relieve this dance of death, the
incidents where life was the manifest
interest in the record of children may be
mentioned. One relates to the Plague,
and the other to the G.F. Pepys, in his
Diary—3rd Sept. 1665—says:

'Among other stories, one was very
passionate, methought, of a complaint
brought against a man in the town for
taking a child from London from an
infected house . . . the child of a very
able citizen in Gracious [Gracechurch]
Street, a saddler, who had buried all the
rest of his children of the plague, and
himself and wife now being shut up and
in despair of escaping, did desire only
to save the life of this little child; and
so prevailed to have it received stark
naked into the arms of a friend, who
brought it (having put it into new fresh
clothes) to Greenwich: where upon
hearing the story, we did agree it should
be permitted to be received and kept
in the town.'

Pepys was evidently much impressed
by the story, for he also mentioned it in a
letter to Lady Elizabeth Carteret. It was
made the subject of a painting, now in the
C.C. Art Gallery. With regard to the
G.F., writing of the ch. of St. Mary-le-
Bow, W. G. Bell says:

'The baptismal register has this entry:
' "Kasia, ye daughter of Morgan
Dandy was borne 2 Sept. 1666 (being
ye day ye dreadful Fire began in
London) and baptzd. in ye Country." '
'Two days after the flames were in
Cheapside, and the infant Kasia and
her suffering mother, carried in a bed
through the street surging with people,
left their home to its fate.'

Returning to W.A., in 1677 the son of
Sir Edwd. Carteret, Gentleman Usher of
the Black Rod to Charles II, was bd.
there. In the N. aisle of the nave is a
tablet which says his age was 'seven

yeares and nine monthes' and he 'was a
most beloved son.' In 1689 a tablet was
placed in the E. walk of the cloisters to
'Jane Lister, dear childe' (d. 1688).
She had been baptized in the Abbey in
1683. Her father was Dr. Martin Lister,
Court Physician to Q. Anne, and a contributor to the Proceedings of the Royal
Soc. He also wrote a natural history of
shells.

Within the same vault as Charles I's
children, are ten of the offspring of
James II, by his first wife, Anne Hyde,
and by his second wife, Mary of Modena.
There also are children of Q. Anne and
P. George of Denmark. Estimates of the
number vary from twelve to eighteen.
The longest lived was the D. of Gloucester.
He was delicate from the start, and spent
much of his early childhood at Kensington, much favoured for its air. He had
ague in his third yr., which was cured by
'Jesuit's Powder' or Peruvian bark. He
had a passion for soldiering, having
brought from Kensington village 'a little
company of twenty-two boys, wearing
paper caps and armed with wooden
swords, who enlisted themselves as his
guard.' At the age of seven he understood
the terms of fortification and navigation,
and he had a particular aversion to
dancing 'and all womanish exercises.'
When only six, meeting his uncle, William
III, who had just returned from a campaign, with a little musket on his shoulder,
he presented arms, saying: 'I am learning
my drill, that I may help you beat the
French.' The K. was so pleased that he
made him a Knight of the Garter a few
days after. Bp. Burnet, who was made
his preceptor, reported 'amazing progress'
in his studies. On the day after his eleventh
birthday he fell ill of a malignant fever,
which carried him off after a very brief
illness in 1700, and he was gathered to
his brothers and sisters in W.A. His death
led to the Hanoverian dynasty in England.
His portrait by Kneller is in Kensington
Palace.

There are instances of the casualties of
child life in the 18th century. In 1703 a
piece of coping fell off Bridewell Hosp.
many of the bdgs. being out of repair, and
killed a baby.

Cinema. The genesis of the cinematograph
may be said to have been at the L.

Exhibition of 1862, when Peter Hubert Desvignes, a Frenchman, demonstrated a 'Mimescope.' This apparatus was a horizontal rotating cylinder with narrow viewing slots cut opposite action pictures fixed internally, the 'live' reproduction, as in the case of all cinematograph viewing, being dependent upon the persistence of image on the human eye-screen; this method was used by Edward Muybridge, of Kingston-on-Thames, in San Francisco, who employed such a cylinder with twenty-four differing photographs taken of galloping horses. Earlier, in 1833, 'The Zoetrope,' or 'Wheel of Life,' invented by W. G. Horner, had, by the medium of a rotating cylinder, given image movement. In 1868 John A. Roebuck, an Englishman, obtained apparent movement in projected pictures, but it was not until 1888 that William Friese-Greene, a Bath photographer (b. Bristol, 1855, but living in London), succeeded, by methods indicated by J. A. R. Rudge, in manufacturing a celluloid film, having experimented with ribbons of paper soaked in castor oil to obtain transparency. His specification for cinematograph and film, which was an improvement upon his own earlier success in 1885, was lodged at the British Patent Office on 21st June 1889, and the resultant Patent No. 10,131 was subsequently held in the American courts to be the first cinematograph patent.

In 1890 Friese-Greene showed publicly the first moving picture, from a length of celluloid film, at 20 Brooke Street, Holborn, although it has been claimed that he had previously demonstrated projection before the members of the Bath Photographic Society on 25th Feb. 1890. The film shown at Holborn ran for twenty seconds and depicted a street scene taken at Hyde Park Corner in Jan. 1889; he also showed upon the window of his photographer's shop at 92 Piccadilly, an animated demon. In 1891 his affairs were involved and as a consequence his entire apparatus was dispersed by auction, but in 1892 he perfected the 'movie' camera which he and Mortimer Evans had worked on in 1889. In 1903 Friese-Greene was employed in research into colour photography. This inventor, who had spent more than £10,000 of his own money in developing his ideas, died almost penniless on 5th May 1921, his straitened circumstances having previously prompted a collection from those engaged in the cinema industry; this collection totalled £136. A memorial erected in Highgate Cemetery carries the following:

WILLIAM

FRIESE-GREENE

INVENTOR OF KINEMATOGRAPHY

HIS GENIUS BESTOWED UPON HUMANITY THE BOON OF COMMERCIAL KINEMATOGRAPHY, OF WHICH HE WAS THE FIRST INVENTOR AND PATENTEE.

In 1893, Edison's 'peep-hole' machine—the 'Kinetoscope'—was exhibited at Chicago. Work in various directions was continued by, amongst others, Louis and Auguste Lumière, of Lyons, France, and eventually C. Francis Jenkins, collaborating with Thomas Armat, produced the forerunner of the modern projector. This was called the 'Autoscope,' and the first commercial pictures were shown in New York City in 1896. Currently with this development, Robert W. Paul—a Hatton Garden diamond merchant—invented a stop-start mechanism to obviate blurring in reproduction, and on 28th Feb. 1896 (after initial success in Feb. 1895 at his studios at New Southgate) gave what he termed a 'Theatrograph' performance of film (a ship in motion) at the City and Guilds of London Technical College at Finsbury. In April 1896 he exhibited his first (hand) coloured picture; this manual tinting was too expensive for commercial exploitation and a modification was to print on to coloured film, red being used for fire scenes, blue for night scenes, etc. In 1896 R. W. Paul reproduced a picture of the Derby at the Alhambra, London, on the evening of the race. Following this success, he provided 'living pictures,' as they were then called, at that music hall for four years and also during that period showed his films at as many as eight L. music-halls, often covering twenty miles in an evening.

In Jan. 1896 Birt Acres projected motion pictures before members of two leading photographic societies. In 1896 also, 'Hale's Tours' began their showing at 165 Oxford St. W., the small audiences being seated in a railway carriage and deriving their entertainment from projected landscapes giving the illusion of travel. During this year the first cinema proper was opened in Fife Rd., Kingston-on-Thames, and in the following yr. many L. shops were rented and converted to cinemas, the first being in Old Kent Rd., SE. and Upper St., Islington, N.

In 1897 a studio for the taking of pictures was built at the back of the old Tivoli in the Strand and its erection was followed by that of the Cyril Hepworth Studio at Hurst Grove, Walton-on-Thames (1898/9) and the R. W. Paul Studio in Sydney Road, New Southgate (1899).

In the first yr. of the present century T. J. West presented *Our Navy* at the Polytechnic, Regent St., W., and the Lumières repeated at Marlborough Hall, Regent St., W., their show given at the Polytechnic, Regent St., W., on 20th Feb. 1896, when Mr. Trewey had demonstrated to the first paying audience.

A story film was presented at the Alhambra in 1902 being titled *A Trip to the Moon*; this was precursor to *The Great Train Robbery* presented at the Polytechnic, Regent St., W. in 1903 and *The Drunkard's Reformation*, marketed by Pathé Frères in the same year. Indicative of the growing strength of the story film are the following particulars of film length: 1898, 40 to 50 ft.; 1899, 60 to 75 ft.; 1902, 280 ft.; 1903/4, 440–500 ft.; 1906, 650 ft. The running time of the 650-ft. film was approximately 11 mins.; that of the 40-ft. film was 40 seconds.

It was not until 23rd May 1906 that the first news cinema—the 'Daily Bioscope' at 27/26 Bishopsgate Street Without, E.C.— opened, the programme being *The San Francisco Disaster*, *Lost*, *A Leg of Mutton*, *The Olympic Games at Athens*, and *A Naval Engagement*. It was the only cinema ever in the City. This was not due to any ban, but to the lack of residential population. In the previous year the emergence of the cinema as a serious challenge to the theatre had been signalised by the erection of cinemas in the W. End of L., the most notable being the West End Cinema and the New Gallery. Films of greater length were then made, and *Les Misérables* (1911) and *Quo Vadis* (1912) marked that phase of cinematograph progress.

In Aug. 1913 Eugene Lauste, in a house at Brixton, was successful in producing audibility on a film track, and his method, for all practical purposes, may be accepted as the system used to-day; yet amplification was not possible, although the thermionic valve (Sir Ambrose Fleming, 1903) and the amplifying valve (le Forest, 1907) had been invented— Londoners were not to hear their first 'talkie' until fourteen years later.

In 1926 a British experimental acoustic film was made at the Bell Telephone Experimental Laboratories; this was titled *Don Juan* and had musical accompaniment, and in the same year Fox Movietone succeeded in recording sound on and from film. The Derby of 1929, exhibited by The British Movietone News, was the first sound news item shown in this country. On 27th Sept. 1928 *The Jazz Singer*—the first part-talkie—was presented at the Piccadilly Theatre.

At its opening in Sept. 1931 the Granada at Tooting, seating 4,000 and one of the most beautiful cinemas within the L. area, was remarkable for its architecture, which was modelled on the Spanish-Moorish style of Granada City; stained-glass windows, pillars of marble in the foyer, and wall paintings of old illuminated manuscripts were some of its outstanding æsthetic attractions. The Trocadero, Elephant and Castle, which opened in 1937, seated 5,000 and was then the largest cinema in the world. Other cinemas in like style and size were Gaumont, Lewisham (3,300), Gaumont Palace, Hammersmith (3,600), Davis Theatre, Croydon (4,000), Orpheum, Hampstead Garden City (2,500), Gaumont, Streatham (2,500), Astoria, Finsbury Park (4,000) and the Rivoli, Whitechapel. Many of these, and other L. cinemas, have since closed or become Bingo halls or bowling alleys. Organ music was a feature of almost all London's leading cinemas, and broadcasts from such theatres were frequent. The last cinema to be completed in London up to the outbreak of the 1939 War was the Regal Cinema, Camberwell Road, S.E.5; it was opened without ceremony on 17th June 1940, the takings of the day amounting to £5. The oldest L. cinema still presenting programmes is the Biograph Cinema, 47/8 Wilton Rd., Pimlico, SW.1, which commenced its second half-century in 1949.

Very many L. cinemas were destroyed or irreparably damaged during the 1939–45 War.

Much early apparatus may be seen at the Science Mus., S. Kensington; this was collected by Mr. Will Day.

City and Guilds of London Institute. In 1876 a Provisional Committee was appointed by the City Livery Cos. to consider the possibility of the formation of a joint central body to promote and forward technical and scientific education. Its incorporation by royal charter originated in a meeting held at the Mansion House on 3rd July 1878, presided over by the Ld.M., and attended by representatives of the C.C. and the Livery Cos. The first Chairman was the E. of Selbourne, of the Mercers' Co.

Certification of teachers in technological subjects was amongst the early activities of the Institute. Examinations were held in the yr. 1879 in 28 centres in seven subjects for 202 candidates. In 1966 examinations were held in over 1,300 centres in more than 200 subjects for over 300,000 candidates. In addition to these enormous teaching and examining functions there is the City and Guilds College (Exhibition Rd., SW.7) which forms the Engineering Section of the Imperial Coll. of Science and Technology.

In the course of ninety years the Cos. have given more than one and a half million pounds to the City and Guilds of London Institute.

City Churches. According to Wm. Fitzstephen, in his account of London prefixed to a life of his master, Thomas à Becket, written about 1183, there were then 126 churches in L. How many of these were outside the walls it is impossible to say. The number cannot have exceeded a dozen. At the outbreak of the Second World War there were in the City 49, including the Dutch ch. of Austin Friars.

A few points of general interest in City chs. may be mentioned before attention is given to particular ones. There is rich material for history in their registers (made compulsory through the efforts of Thos. Cromwell, E. of Essex, in 1538), but few have the leisure to delve. Almost all of them are deposited in Guildhall Library and are readily available for study. Here may also be found the bulk of the civic parish registers, substantially augmented by information to be found in the archives of the Diocese and Archdeaconary of London.

Foundlings were named after the par. in which they were exposed. A James Garlickhithe was entered in the registers of that ch. in 1624, and twenty-three infants named Martin Outwich found by C. W. F. Goss in its registers between 1685 and 1738. A prominent athletic outfitter of Cheapside at the beginning of the 20th century had the name Benetfink. He may have worked his way up to success in making bats, as Bernard Shaw's Andrew Undershaft—also named after a City ch.—had done in making munitions. These cursory records show, too, how necessary was the Registration Act of 1836. For some par. clerks anything would do. Thus in the burial register of St. Martin's Outwich are these entries:

'1634. Alley's maid servant.'
'1652. A Barber's child.'
'1658. Mrs. Grundy's nurse.'

In 1646 there is one entry in the register of St. Andrew's, Holborn: 'A couple were married but it is not known who they were.'

Burials in City chyds. ceased under the provisions of an 'Act concerning the Burial of the Dead in the Metropolis' (1852), but an Order in Council had to be made in the case of each separate chyd., and having regard to the state of affairs sometimes revealed, this was highly desirable. In 1842, before a committee of the H.C., it was said that from a burial ground in St. Clement's Lane, Strand, sixty loads of 'loam of human remains' were shot into the making up of Waterloo Bridge Rd. (for further details see *The Face of London*, by Harold Clunn). The chyds. are much better cared for than when Dickens and Gissing wrote of them. They are protected from being built upon by the Disused Burial Grounds Act (1884), and even an underground chamber for an electric transformer, proposed to be placed in the chyd. of St. Nicholas Acon, was prohibited by the Privy Council in 1928.

There are three City chs. which are of unusual orientation, i.e. N. and S. St. Botolph's, Aldgate; St. Edmund King and Martyr, Lombard St.; St. Dunstan's in the West, Fleet St.

'Peculiars' were churches which were exempt from the jurisdiction of the Bp. of L. and the archdeacon, and subject only to the Abp. of C. who appointed to the living. There were once thirteen. At the outbreak of the Second World War, these were St. Dunstan-in-the-East; St. Mary Aldermary; St. Mary at Hill; St. Mary-le-Bow; St. Michael, Paternoster Royal; St. Vedast, Foster Lane. Only two of these were little damaged in the Blitz. 'Peculiars' demolished were: All Hallows, Bread Street; St. Dionis, Back-church; St. John the Evangelist, Friday St.; St. Leonard, Eastcheap; St. Mary Bothaw; St. Michael, Crooked Lane; St. Pancras, Soper Lane. Since 1841, when their special status was abolished by an Order in Council, they have been 'peculiars' only in name.

Of the 126 churches mentioned by Fitzstephen, the late Miss E. Jeffries Davis, M.A., F.S.A. (see *Norman London,* Historical Association Leaflets Nos. 93 and 94) traced 108. It may well be that Fitzstephen's calculation was inaccurate.

The Guild Churches Act of 1952 set aside 16 City Churches to minister to the spiritual needs of the daily workers in the City and to serve as centres for some special branch of the church's work.

Thirty-five chs. were not rebuilt after the G.F., twenty-five (nineteen of these were Wren's) have been demolished since and one (Holy Trinity, Minories) used for other purposes.

A. Churches Destroyed before or in the G.F. and not Rebuilt.

All Hallows the Less, Upper Thames St. It is known to have existed in 1240. It stood near the large mansion called Cold Harbour, belonging to Sir John Poultney. Up to 1941, when the bombs came, a few tombstones were left. One had an inscription partly in Welsh. It was that of Owen Jones, who d. in 1814. A furrier living in Thames St., he had always been interested in Welsh literature. He left a collection of Welsh MSS., which were bought and presented to the B. Mus. His son, also Owen, was better known. He was an architect, and designed and superintended the bdg. and decoration of the Great Exhibition in Hyde Park in 1851 and arranged the courts at the Crystal Palace. There is a C.C. plaque.

Holy Trinity the Less, Little Trinity Lane, Upper Thames St. First mentioned in 1266, it was called 'the Less' in distinction from the great priory at Aldgate. It was rebuilt 1607–8. After the G.F. the par. was united with St. Michael, Queen-hithe (*q.v.*). There is a C.C. tablet on the wall of Beaver House. (See St. James Garlickhithe—'City Churches—C.')

St. Andrew Hubbard. The first reference is as 'St. Andrew by Estchepe' (*c.* 1202). It stood on the S. side of Eastcheap, at the corner of Love Lane. 'Hubbard' and 'Hubert,' as sometimes it appears, was probably the name of a benefactor. In 1831 the foundations were discovered. It appeared to have been raised on a Roman edifice, for the walls had the aspect of Roman work and fragments of Samian pottery were found. After the G.F. the par. was united with St. Mary at Hill. There is a C.C. plaque on 16 Eastcheap.

St. Anne, Blackfriars. The first mention is in 1544 to the 'Parish of St. Anne within the site of the Friars Preachers.' It was the par. ch. for the inhabitants of the precincts of the Blackfriars, as distinct from the ch. of the Blackfriars Priory. It was pulled down by Sir Thos. Cawarden, as part of the priory precincts given to him, but Stow says in the reign of Q. Mary he was forced to find a ch. for the inhabitants, and allowed them a lodging chamber above a stair. In 1597 this fell down, and he thereupon built a ch. The Blackfriars Theatre was very close to the ch., and in 1596 complaint was made of the noise of drums and trumpets disturbing the services. In 1633 complaint was made to Laud, then Bp. of L., that christenings and burials had their solemnity impaired by those unhallowed sounds. Helen Burbage, daughter of Richd., was bd. in St. Anne's chyd. Sir Samuel Luke, from whom Butler is generally supposed to have drawn Hudibras, was a parishioner. His marriage in 1624, and the baptisms of several children, appear in the register. In 1633 Nathaniel Field was bd. here. He is in the list of twenty-six actors prefixed to the First Folio of Shakespeare, and his portrait, as he appeared in Ben Jonson's *Poetaster,* is in the Dulwich Art Gallery. Van Dyck was an inhabitant of St. Anne's par., but was bd. in old St. P.'s Cath. The par. after the G.F. was united with St. Andrew by the Wardrobe.

In 1691 Wm. Faithorne, the engraver, was bd. in the chyd. His engraving of Milton (in the N.P.G.) aroused the enthusiasm of one of the poet's daughters in 1725, fifty yrs. after his death. 'O Lord!' she said, 'that is the picture of my father. Just so my father wore his hair.' One part of the chyd. is in Ireland Yard, and another in Church Entry.

St. Benet Sherehog. There is much of an enigmatical character about the second half of the appellation of this ch. In a deed the date of which can only approximately be given (1111–31) is a reference to 'Alfwinus sacerdos Scerehog.' At the end of the 12th century it was called 'St. Benedict the Less,' perhaps to distinguish it from the ch. of St. Benet Fink. It was also dedicated to St. Osyth, and in 1363 both dedications are mentioned. Rev. W. J. Loftie found that a family named Serehog resided in the neighbourhood, Willelmus Serehog being mentioned as a witness to a deed of the 12th century, relating to the ch. of St. John, Walbrook. The name was probably added because a member of this family was a benefactor. The name of St. Osyth survives in Sise Lane. There was a chapel of St. Osyth—as also of St. Mary—in the ch. Stow says it was rebuilt in the reign of Edward II (1307–27). In 1547 Edwd. Hall, the chronicler (from the end of the reign of Richard II—1399—until his own death) was bd. here, and in 1573 Dame Joan White (she d. at Hinchinbrook in Huntingdonshire). Her second husband was Sir Thos. White (Ld.M. 1553), and founder of St. John's Coll., Oxford. Sir Henry Cromwell m. her daughter, and they were the grandparents of Oliver Cromwell. In 1664 Mrs. Katherine Philips, of Cardigan, the 'matchless Orinda' of Cowley's elegy, was laid to rest in the ch. A portion of the chyd. remains on the N. side of Pancras Lane, and exactly opposite the N. end of Sise Lane. There is a C.C. plaque.

St. Botolph, Billingsgate. This ch. is first mentioned in 1181. It was on the S. side of Lower Thames St. In 1392 a cemetery was made for the burial of parishioners, but its situation is unknown. After the G.F. the par. was united with St. George, Botolph Lane.

St. Gregory by St. Paul's. It was in existence in 1070, and is mentioned in an account of the translation of the body of St. Edmund when it was brought into the ch. of St. Gregory. In 1612 there was bd. in this ch. Alison, wife of Geo. Heriot, James I's goldsmith, the 'Jingling Geordie' of *The Fortunes of Nigel.* She was commemorated by 'a very goodly monument in the south ile of the quire uppermost,' with a long Latin inscription. When Inigo Jones was making his portico for the cath. about 1637 he began to pull the ch. down. The parishioners however

successfully petitioned; Jones was summoned to the bar of the House of Lords, prohibited from any further work of destruction, and the stones brought to the cath. for its reparation were given to them to repair their ch. In 1658 Dr. John Hewet, minister of St. Gregory's, was executed on a charge of conspiring against the Commonwealth, together with Sir Harry Slingsby. The latter had been a member of the Long Parliament, and one of Charles I's adherents. Clarendon mentions Hewet's ch. as one to which the K.'s party frequently resorted, and Sir Harry as 'a gentleman of good understanding, but of a very melancholic nature, and of very few words.' After the G.F. the par. was united with St. Mary Magdalene, Old Fish St. (*q.v.*), and on the demolition of its ch. in 1886, with St. Martin, Ludgate.

St. John the Baptist, Walbrook. The earliest mention is in 1182. Referring to the Roman midsummer water-festival, Sir Jas. Frazer writes:

'Water has always, down to modern times, played a conspicuous part in the rites of Midsummer Day, which explains why the Church, in throwing its cloak over the old heathen festival, chose to dedicate it to St. John the Baptist.' This ch. was on the bank of the Walbrook. It was enlarged in 1412.

According to Stow there were no monuments of importance. After the G.F. the par. was united with St. Antholin (*q.v.*). When the latter ch. was demolished in 1874 both pars. were united to St. Mary Aldermary. The site of St. J. the B.'s Ch. was enclosed for a chyd., but the greater part disappeared in 1884 for an extension of the District Railway. There is a memorial, surmounted by a small cross, on the N. side of Cloak Lane. The inscription is as follows:

'Sacred
To the memory of the dead
Interred in the ancient church and churchyard
of St. John the Baptist
upon Walbrook
during four centuries.
The formation of the District Railway
having necessitated the destruction of
the greater part of the
churchyard,
All the human remains contained therein

were carefully collected and reinterred in a vault

Beneath this monument
A.D. 1884.'

There had been a tablet placed on the site of the ch. in 1671. It was recut in 1830, and is still there. There is a C.C. tablet at the top of Dowgate Hill. A cross-head of Saxon date, found in 1856 in the chyd., is in the B.Mus.

St. John the Evangelist. The earliest mention is 'St. John the Evangelist and St. Wereburga,' 1349. St. Werburga was a Mercian princess, granddaughter of Penda, K. of Mercia. In the early part of the 8th century she was Abbess of Ely, and a number of English chs. were dedicated to her. It was a 'peculiar.' The par. was unique during the great Plague of 1665, inasmuch as it did not return a single victim. After the G.F. the par. was united with All Hallows, Bread St., and on the destruction of that ch. in 1876–7, both pars. were united to St. Mary-le-Bow.

St. John Zachary. It is first mentioned in 1181; it was 'St. John the Baptist.' In the 12th century it was granted by the canons of St. Paul's to Zacharie 'that he may visit the ch. regularly,' and hence the dedication. In 1390 the ch. was rebuilt by Nicholas Twiford, with a tomb for him and his wife. In 1577, Ralph Robinson, who in 1552 published the first English translation of More's *Utopia*, was bd. here. After the G.F. the par. was united with St. Anne and St. Agnes. A part of the chyd. remains, bearing a C.C. tablet at the corner of Gresham St. and Noble St. During the Second World War it was laid out as an attractive garden by A.F.S. workers.

St. Lawrence Pountney. The earliest record is 'St. Laurence next to the Thames,' and it was in existence in the 11th century. The chapel of Corpus Christi and College of St. Lawrence Pountney adjoining the ch. were erected by John de Poulteney (c. 1334), and this explains part of the later dedication. After the G.F. the par. was united with St. Mary Abchurch. The ch. was on the W. side of Laurence Pountney Lane. There is a C.C. tablet, and part of the burial ground (it was on the S. side) remains.

St. Leonard, Eastcheap. The earliest mention is c. 1214. It was dedicated to the hermit of France. Stow called it also

'Saint Leonard Milke Churche, so termed of one William Melker, an especiall builder thereof.' C. L. Kingsford suggested that this was William Melker of Eastcheap, whose will was proved in 1273. The vestry of this ch. was rebuilt in 1584, and a stone 25½ in. by 20 in., with the following inscription, put upon the new one:

'Time out of mind this vestry stood
Till crooked with age my strength
I lost and in November with full
Consent, was built anew at y parish
Cost, when queene Elizabeth ra-
ined had to England's peace.
26 yeares. John Herd Parson
Rich. Powntes & Harry Baker
Churchwardens. were Anno
Dom. 1584.'

In 1801, according to a correspondent of the *Gentleman's Magazine*, the stone was in a cellar in the house, No. 4 Eastcheap. It is now preserved at the Guildhall. After the G.F. the par. was united to St. Benet, Gracechurch St. When the latter's ch. was pulled down in 1867, the two pars. were united to All Hallows Lombard St. There is a C.C. tablet on 2 Eastcheap.

St. Leonard, Foster Lane. The first reference is 'St. Leonard near St. Martin' in 1278. Stow described it as a small parish ch. 'for them of St. Martin's le graund. A number of tenements being lately builded in place of the great Collegiate Church of St. Martin, that parish is mightily increased.' The ch. was repaired and enlarged in 1631. After the G.F. the par. was united with Christ Church, Newgate, and the ground adjoining St. Botolph's, Aldersgate (q.v.) includes the chyd. of St. Leonard's. The G.P.O. was constructed on its site (1825–9).

St. Margaret Moses. It was in existence by c. 1202, when it was at Fridai-strete. In 1299 it was 'St Margaret Moysy in Frydaystrate.' St. Margaret of Antioch was the saint. Stow said Moyses a priest 'was founder of new builder thereof.' Harben says he was one of the witnesses to a 12th-century deed concerning St. P.'s Cath., and he may have been founder or builder of the ch. John Rogers, the martyr, was instituted as rector in May 1550, but resigned the following yr. Sir Richd. Dobbs (Ld.M., 1551) was bd. here. He was one of a deputation that waited upon Edward VI with a request that he would place Bridewell Palace at the disposal of the City for the benefit of the poor. Ridley shortly before his martyrdom at Oxford in 1555, wrote him a remarkable testimonial:

'Thou in thy year didst win my heart for ever more for that most blessed work of God, of the erection and setting up of Christ's holy hospitals . . . which by thee and through thee were begun. . . . Thousands of poor members of Christ, which else for extreme hunger and misery should have perished, shall be relieved, and shall have cause to bless the aldermen of that time, the common council, and the whole of the city, but especially thee, O Dobbs, and those chosen men, by whom this honourable work of God was begun and wrought.'

After the G.F. the par. was united with St. Mildred, Bread St. A correspondent of the *Gentleman's Magazine* in 1830 complained that its chyd. (in Friday St.) had been paved over: 'the passenger walks little thinking that under his feet lies many a recently-interred corpse.'

St. Margaret, New Fish Street. The earliest mention is 'Sc̄i margaret ūs Pont̄ (1199–1211). Its usual name down to the 16th century was 'St. Margaret, Bridge Street.' It stood where is now the Monument. One of the City's ordinances was that lampreys brought from Nantes should be at once exposed for sale by the wall of St. Margaret's Ch. Stow says there were no monuments; no doubt he meant no notable ones. After the G.F. the par. was united with St. Magnus the Martyr. There is a C.C. tablet in Lower Thames St., E. of the Monument.

St. Martin le Grand Collegiate Ch. is said to have been founded in the 8th century. The first definite event in its history was in 1056, when it was founded or refounded by Ingelricus and his brother. This coll. of secular canons had its charter confirmed by William the Conqueror in 1067. There was a royal free chapel, and numerous privileges were conferred upon it by this charter. It had special rights of sanctuary, and the area remained a privileged one after the dissolution of the monasteries. A proclamation of the Ld.M., 1334, said:

'No person shall be so daring on pain of imprisonment, as to go wandering about the City after the hour of curfew rung out at St. Martin-le-Grand, unless it be some man of the City of good repute, or his servant, and that with reasonable cause, and with light.'

The curfew was also rung at St. Mary-le-Bow, St. Giles, Cripplegate, and All Hallows, Barking. Stow relates that in 1442 a soldier on his way from the Newgate Compter to the Guildhall was rescued by five of his comrades, who rushed out of Panyer Alley, and carried him into St. Martin's Ch. The sheriffs brought him out and returned him to jail, but were compelled to release him so that he could again take refuge in sanctuary. The City fathers were reminded, rather unkindly, that when they suffered from what Micawber called pecuniary embarrassment they had been glad to avail themselves of this protection! The Goldsmiths' Co. complained that their craft was illicitly carried on by sanctuary men there, but no redress followed. In 1450 Henry VI sent his officers to St. Martin's to claim for treason Wm. Cayme, one of Jack Cade's rebels, but Dean Cawdray convinced the K. that these things were not done. In this sanctuary Miles Forest, one of the murderers of the Princes in the T.L., 'rotted away piecemeal,' as Sir Thos. More says. In the reign of Henry VII the dean and chapter successfully vindicated the right of sanctuary when it was violated by the sheriffs, and the latter were 'grievously fined.' In 1503 the deanery and its possessions were granted to W.A., the abbots thenceforth assuming the office of dean. In 1533 the collegiate ch. was sold by John, the abbot, to John Russell. In 1548 it was surrendered to Edward VI, and the ch. pulled down, the bdgs. called 'New Rents' being erected on the site. Stow says that a wine tavern and other houses were built in the precinct, which for a considerable period possessed its own prison, bailiff, and court. It continued to be a refuge for debtors until about 1697. In 1815 all its privileges as a 'liberty' were abolished by Act of Parliament passed to provide a site for the new G.P.O. (*q.v.*), erected 1825–9. The precinct was then made part of the ward of Aldersgate. In 1818 an Early English crypt and foundations of an earlier date were found on the site.

St. Martin Orgar. The earliest reference is in the 12th century. The ch. was granted by Ordgar, the deacon, to the canons of St. Paul's to hold to him at a rent. It was 'St. Martin in Candelwrithtestrat' (1200–24); 'St. Martin Algar' (1259); 'St. Martin Orgor' (c. 1275). The saint was St. Martin of Tours (d. 397). Here Sir Wm. Huet (Ld.M. 1559) was bd. Part of the nave and the tower escaped the G.F., after which the par. was united with St. Clement, Eastcheap, and the French Protestants met in the ch. until 1820, when the bdg. was pulled down with the exception of the tower. This was demolished in 1851, but to mark the site a fresh tower was erected which had a projecting clock. This remains on the E. side of Martin Lane, Cannon St., where there is a C.C. plaque.

St. Martin Pomary. The first reference is to 'St. Martin Pomer' (1250). It stood on the E. side of Ironmonger Lane, Cheapside. Stow says that the name derived from the fact that apples once grew where houses had sprung up. Harben, however, points out that the Latin word 'pomarium' = orchard, 'pomerium' = an open space, and it has been suggested that the name was derived from the sacred belt of land outside a Roman city marking the limits of the first Roman Londinium. Stow said that there were no monuments 'to be accounted for.' After the G.F. the par. was united with St. Olave, Jewry. When the ch. of the latter was demolished in 1888 both pars. were united to St. Margaret Lothbury.

St. Martin Vintry. The ch. of St. Martin 'que est super Thamisiam' was granted to the monastery of St. Peter, Gloucester, 1100–7. Other names and forms are 'Sancti Martini ubi vina venditur' (1200), St. Martin de barmanne cherche otherwise 'Sancti martini in vinetrie' (c. 1210–11). Harben says:

'The name Baremannechurch is derived from O.E. "bærman"=carrier, porter—persons in the neighbourhood being largely employed in the wine trade. This seems to have been the first distinguishing appellation of the church, and it may have been erected in the first instance especially for the use of those employed in the great wine trade of the neighbourhood.'

Vintry merely indicates locality. In 1330–1 there is a reference to 'St. Martin de Garlekhuthe'; this is probably the same ch. Stow says that in this ch. was

bd. Sir John Gisors and two of his sons. Sir John (d. 1351) was Ld.M. in 1311, 1312 and 1314. He left to his granddaughter his tenement called 'Gysors halle' in Bread St. (See 'Gerards Hall.')

After the G.F. the par. was united to St. Michael, Paternoster Royal. The chyd. remains at the corner of Queen St. and Upper Thames St.

St. Mary Axe. The ch. was in existence by 1197. It was 'St. Mary del Axe' in 1231. The incident which the dedication of the ch. commemorates was recorded by Matthew of Westminster under date 393. It relates to a legend that eleven thousand virgins were slain by the 'lawless army of Wannius, K. of the Huns, and of Melga, Duke of the Picts' somewhere in the neighbourhood of Cologne. In most versions the virgins were slain by three axes, a suggestion that assists confirmation of the theory that through an error noughts were added to the number of the victims. The ch. claimed to possess one of the axes.

In 1514 a petition was presented to Henry VIII, asking for a brief or licence to collect money for repair, the parson having left the ch. in a dilapidated condition. Stow says that in 1561 the par. was united with St. Andrew Undershaft, and Wheatley adds, without quoting an authority, that the ch. was given to the Spanish Protestant refugees for worship. The date of demolition is unknown.

St. Mary Bothaw. The first mention is in 1117, in a gift of land near the ch. by the prior and convent of Christ C., Canterbury. It is 'Bothage' in 1150; 'Bothaw' in 1270. Stow derives the name 'Bothaw' from 'boat' and 'haw,' and says it was so called as 'adjoining to a haw or yard, wherein of old time boats were made, and landed from Downegate to be mended.' Stow mentions only two unimportant tombs. There was a small cloister adjoining the ch. After the G.F. the par. was united with St. Swithun's, and in 1669 an order was made for the removal of the walls and steeple of the ch., and for the materials to be used for the rebuilding of St. Swithun's Ch. The site of St. Mary Bothaw is now covered by Cannon St. Station.

St. Mary Colechurch. The first mention is in 1163, when Peter, chaplain of St. Mary Colechurch was also Bridge Master and carried out a rebuilding of L.B.

(see 'Bridges'). Stow said it was so called 'of one Cole that builded it: this church is builded upon a vault above ground, so that men are forced to go to ascend up thereunto by certain steppes.' The patronage (c. 1256–7) was given to the Hosp. of St. Thomas of Acon, perhaps because Thos. à Becket had been baptized there (1118). After the dissolution the patrons were the Mercers' Co. An earlier baptism said to have taken place in the ch. was Edmund, K. of E. Anglia (841). In Henry IV's reign there was a fraternity or guild of St. Katherine Colchirche. The ch. was repaired in 1623. After the G.F. the par. was united with St. Mildred, Poultry, and on the destruction of that ch. in 1872 both pars. were united with St. Olave, Jewry. When the latter ch. also disappeared in 1888 all three pars. were united with St. Margaret, Lothbury. There is a C.C. tablet at the S. end of Old Jewry.

St. Mary Magdalene, Milk Street. The earliest mention is in 1162—'St. Mary Magdalene in foro Londoniarum.' In 1203–15 it is 'St. Mary Magdalene, Milk Street.' After the G.F. the par. was united with St. Lawrence Jewry. The site was covered by Honey Lane market but has since been built on.

St. Mary Mounthaw. The earliest reference is to 'St. Mary de Muntenhaut' (1275). In 1298 it was 'St. Mary de Monte alto.' It was first built as a chapel for the Mounthaunts. Amongst the monuments Stow mentions:

> 'John Glocester, Alderman 1345, who gave Salt wharf for two chantries there; John Skip Bishop of Hereford 1539 . . . died at London in time of Parliament, and was buried in this church.'

After the G.F. the par. was united with St. Mary Somerset, and on the destruction of its ch. in 1871 both pars. were united with St. Nicholas Cole Abbey. The construction of Q. Victoria St. in 1871 took away so much of the par. that it then contained only six houses—at the corner of Q. Victoria St. and Friday St. Part of a tomb from St. Mary Mounthaw Ch.— possibly John Glocester's—was until 1940 on a wall on Lambeth Hill.

St. Mary Staining. The first mention is 'Ecclesia de Staningehage' (1189). Prof. Maitland suggested that the name was due to the fact that the neighbourhood once contained the haws of the men of Staines—the 'Staeningehaga'—within L. appertaining to the manor of Staines, included in the grant of that manor by Edward the Confessor to St. Peter's, Westminster (see also 'All Hallows Staining'). Stow says it had no notable monuments. After the G.F. the par. was united with St. Michael, Wood St., and on the destruction of that ch. in 1894 both were united with St. Alban's, Wood St.

St. Mary Woolchurch Haw. The earliest mention is in the 11th century. In 1260 it was 'St. Mary of Woollechurchehawe.' In Edward I's reign (c. 1282) the K. issued letters patent to 'the Mayor and Citizens empowering them to build on a vacant plot of land near the wall of the churche of Wollecherche.' On this vacant plot Henry le Wales erected the Stocks Market (see 'Markets'), the rents of which were to be applied to the maintenance and repair of L.B. In 1442 the ch. had become so 'old and feble' that it had to be rebuilt, and it was ordered that arrangements should be made to avoid any chance of the light of the City's house of 'le Stokkys' being obstructed. The vestry was to be pulled down and a new N. wall erected at a distance of 15 ft. from the 'Stokkes' so as not to obstruct the light of the market, while, in return, a footway was granted from the E. end of the 'Stokkes' under the parsonage to the 'Pultrie,' and a sum of money towards the rebuilding out of the revenues of L.B. 'Church haw'=chyd., and Stow says this is confirmed by the Liber Albus, that in the chyd. was the beam for the weighing of wool. Pendrill refers to a brewer bd. in the ch. in 1578 as illustrating

> 'the antiquity of the righteous minds of inn-keepers, that profound truth discovered by G. K. Chesterton, by leaving a barrel of beer to each of his customers.'

After the G.F. the par. was united with St. Mary Woolnoth. There is a C.C. tablet on the W. side of the Mansion House.

St. Michael le Querne. The first mention is of 'St. Michael que fundata est ante portam Sancti Pauli' in the 12th century. Other forms are 'St. Michael where corn is sold' (1258–9), and 'Sancti Mich' ad bladum' (c .1275). The ch. stood between St. P.'s Chyd. and Cheapside, and there was a right-of-way through it. In 1378 the rector stopped the passage by building a wall across the entrance, but he was soon compelled by the Mayor to remove the obstruction. John Leland, who was b. in L. about 1506, was bd. in the ch. in 1552. He was chaplain and librarian to Henry VIII, and was commissioned by him to search all the caths., abbeys, colls., etc., for their records. For six yrs. he perambulated the country, but he applied himself so intensely to the collation of his matter that he lost his reason. His monument disappeared with the ch., but his great work, *The Itinerary*, remains. Sir Thos. Browne was baptized here in 1605. After the G.F. the par. was united with St. Vedast, Foster Lane.

St. Nicholas Acons. The earliest mention is 'St. Nicholas' (1084). It is 'St. Nicholas Hacun' (1246). The dedications were to St. Nicholas, Abp. of Myra in Asia Minor in the 4th century. His remains were transferred to Europe in 1087. Probably the name Hacun (corrupted later to Acon) was added in the 12th century to commemorate a benefactor. Stow says that 'John Bridges Draper, Maior 1520, newly repayred this church and imbatiled it, and was there buried.' After the G.F. the par. was united with St. Edmund, Lombard St. The chyd., with a few tombstones, remains in Nicholas Lane. On the N. of it is a C.C. plaque inscribed: 'Site of the parsonage of St. Nicholas Acons, where scientific life assurance began in 1762.' The rectory had been leased to Edward-Rowe Mores, M.A., F.S.A., who took out the first policy with the Society for Equitable Assurances on lives and survivorships.

St. Nicholas Olave. It was on the W. side of Bread St. The first reference is to 'Sci Nicholai Bernard' (1242–59). In 1285 it is 'St. Nichi Olaui'; in 1303 'St. Nicholas Bernard Olof.' The St. Olave was Olaf the sea-king of Norway (d. 1030), and the ch. may have been built originally in the 11th century under Danish influence. 'Bernard' only occurs once or twice; it was probably the name of a benefactor. In 1537 almshouses were built in the chyd. by the Ironmongers' Co. Stow does not mention any remarkable burials. After the G.F. the par. was united with St. Nicholas Cole Abbey.

St. Nicholas Shambles. The first mention is 'St. Nicholas de Westmacekaria' (1196). In 1260 it is 'St. Nicholas Shambles,' the latter term referring to the butchers' quarter. The ch. was granted to the Ld.M. and citizens at the Dissolution, the par. being incorporated into that of Christ Ch., Newgate. It was demolished in 1547, fifty yrs. before the publication of Stow's *Survey*, and so no particulars of the building are available. Before 1941— it disappeared in the Blitz—there was a C.C. tablet on 77 and 78 Newgate St.

St. Olave, Silver Street. The first mention is 'St. Olave de Mukewellestrate' (1181). Other forms are 'St. Olave in Syrnerstrete,' and 'Sancti Olavi de Criplesgate' in the 13th century. Stow says of the ch.: 'a small thing and without any noteworthy monuments.' A daughter of one Mountjoy, a 'tire-maker' (theatrical costumier) m. Stephen Bellott, her father's apprentice, in this ch. Wm. Shakspere was a lodger in the house in 1604, and in 1612 his deposition was taken in an action arising out of the marriage. This was found in the Public Record Office by C. W. Wallace, an American professor, in 1910, and was hailed as an addition to the meagre information about our great national bard. It did not afford, however, any evidence of fame as a writer. Shakespeare was described as a 'gentleman of Stratford on Avon.' In 1923 a C.C. tablet was placed on the Coopers' Arms, the site of Mountjoy's house. Tavern and tablet were destroyed by German bombs. The par. after the G.F. was united with St. Alban, Wood St. The chyd. remains on the S. side of Silver St.

St. Pancras, Soper Lane. The first mention is in 1207. It is 'St. Pancras by Sopereslane' (1261). It was dedicated to a boy martyr (see 'St. Pancras'). In the tower of the ch. was a bell called 'Le Clok,' to the maintenance of which many citizens bequeathed money. In 1374 Wm., Abp. of C., granted forty days' indulgence to all true penitents who would contribute to it. In 1376 taverns were ordered to close as the tenth hour was sounded on the bell. In Stow the ch. is said to be in Needelars Lane (this was the name then of the western portion of the st.). Amongst the burials he mentions are John Barens (Ld.M. 1370), John Hadley (Ld.M. 1379), John Stockton (Ld.M. 1470), Richd Gardener (Ld.M. 1478). Of monuments which

'there doe remaine' is one 'to Robert Packenton, Mercer, slayne with a

Gunne shot at him in a morning as hee was going to morrow mass from his house in Chepe to S. Thomas of Acars [Acons].)

This was in 1536. The murderer

'was never discovered, but by his own confession made when he came to the gallowes at Banbury, to be hanged for felony.'

After the G.F. the par. was united with St. Mary le Bow.

St. Peter, Paul's Wharf. The first mention is 'St. Peter the Little' (*c.* 1170). It is 'St. Peter de la Wodewarve' (*c.* 1267). 'In this church no Monumentes doe remaine,' says Stow. On 25th March 1649, nearly two months after the execution of Charles I, Evelyn recorded in his diary that there he 'heard the Common Prayer (a rare thing in these days).'

After the G.F. the par. was united with St. Benet's, Paul's Wharf, and when that ch. ceased to be parochial in 1879 it was combined with St. Nicholas Cole Abbey. The 'parcel of land' devised to the par. for a graveyard remains, in Upper Thames St. There is a tablet with the following inscription on the W. wall:

'Before Y Late Dreadful Fire
This was Y' Parish Church
Of St. Peters Pauls Wharf
Demolished September 1666
And Now Erected
For a Church Yarde
Anno Domini 1675

St. Peter, Westcheap. The first mention is in 1196. In 1393 it is 'St. Peter at the Cross of Chepe,' the Eleanor Cross being opposite Wood St., near the corner of which the ch. stood. Stow says that John Sha (Ld.M. 1501, d. 1503):

'appointed by his Testament, the said church and steeple to be newly builded of his goods, with a flat roofe. Notwithstanding Tho. Wood, Goldsmith, one of the Shiriffes, 1491, is accounted principall benefactor: because the roofe of the middle Ile is supported by Images of Woodmen.'

Wood lived in the st. of the same name. Amongst the burials were Nicholas Farendon (Ld.M. four times, d. 1361), Sir John Monday (Ld.M., d. 1537), Sir Alexander Auenon (Ld.M., d. 1570). For an affray here in 1325 see 'Cheapside.' The City waits, a band of C.C.

musicians, were often posted on the leads of St. Peter's Ch. on the occasion of pageants. In 1559 Q. Elizabeth stopped here on her way through the City to be presented with a Bible in English at the ch. door. After the G.F. the par. was united to St. Matthew, Friday St., and when that ch. was demolished in 1881 both pars. were united with St. Vedast, Foster Lane. The chyd. remains (see 'Cheapside'). On the rails is a panel of St. Peter with a key. The plane tree therein is one of the oldest in the City. In *The Town* Leigh Hunt (writing in 1834–5) said:

'In Cheapside is an actual, visible, and even ostentatiously visible tree, to all who have eyes to look about them. It stands at the corner of Wood Street, and occupies the space of a house.'

It would appear that it was full grown in Hunt's time. Wordsworth's Susan saw the bird in a cage, not in the tree.

St. Thomas the Apostle. The earliest mention is in 1170. It was rebuilt by John Barn, Ld.M. in 1371, 'as appeareth by his arms there in stone and glass,' wrote Stow. Stow also mentions several chantries and the burial of Sir Wm. Littlesbery, alias 'Horne (for King Ed. the 4. so named him) because he was a most excellent blower in a horne.' He was Ld.M. 1487, 'and was buried in this Church, having appointed by his testament the Bels to bee chaunged for foure new Bels of good tune and sound, but that was not performed.' After the G.F. the par. was united with St. Mary Aldermary. There is a C.C. tablet on the W. side of Queen St. and the corner of Gt. St. Thomas the Apostle. On the opposite side—in a recess—is a tablet recording the interment in a vault below in 1851 of human remains from the ch.

B. CHURCHES DESTROYED OR DISUSED AFTER THE G.F.

All Hallows, Bread St. The ch. was in existence before 1227. Later, on the S. side of the chancel, was a small chapel called the Salters', having been founded by Thos. Beaumont of the Salters' Co. (d. 1457). In 1531 two priests of the ch. had a quarrel, and one wounded the other. In consequence, service was suspended for a month, and the priests, being enjoined to do penance, went at the head of a procession barefooted, bare-headed and bare-legged, with beads and books in their hands, from St. P.'s Cath. through Cheapside and Cornhill. In 1555 the rector, the Rev. Lawrence Saunders, after fifteen months' imprisonment, was burnt at Coventry. In 1559 the spire was struck by lightning and, to save the expense of rebuilding, taken down. John Milton was baptized here in 1608. The ch. was repaired in 1625.

The ch. was burnt in the G.F. and rebuilt 1680–4 by Wren, the par. being then united with St. John the Evangelist, Friday St. It was demolished 1876–7 by the Ecclesiastical Commissioners, and the par. was united with St. Mary-le-Bow.

All Hallows the Great. It is not known when the first ch. was erected. It was in existence in 1235, an early name for it being 'Allhallows at the Hay,' from an adjacent hay wharf (see 'All Hallows the Less'). It had a metrical memorial to Q. Elizabeth:

'Spain's Rod. Rome's ruine.
Netherlands' Relief
Heaven's Jem, Earth's Joy,
World's Wonder, Nature's Chief.
Britain's Blessing, England's Splendour
Religion's Nurse and Faith's Defender.

'Queen Elizabeth dyed 24th March 1602.'

Pepys (22nd Apr. 1660) mentions that about a month before Charles II landed in England, the K.'s arms were set up here, 'which being privately done was a great eyesore to people when they came to church and saw it.'

It was burnt in the G.F., and rebuilt by Wren in 1683. The tower of the ch. was taken down in 1876, and the body demolished in 1893, the site having been sold by auction the previous yr. A belfry which replaced the tower has now gone. The two large bells, dated 1670 and 1736, have gone to chs. in N. London. The proceeds of the sale of the site went to the erection of a new ch. of All Hallows, Gospel Oak, as also a small carved table. A beautiful carved oak screen, a gift of the Hanse merchants, in the early 18th century was transferred to St. Margaret, Lothbury, and the pulpit to the ch. of St. Paul, Hammersmith.

All Hallows, Lombard Street. This ch. is one of the few with a definite event in its history prior to the Norman Conquest. In 1053 Brihtmaer gave the rectory to the ch. of Canterbury. The first known

rector was Robt. de Kilewardby, who resigned in 1283. The ch. was rebuilt 1494–1516. Alexander Barclay became rector in 1552. He was a poet, who wrote *The Shyp of Folys [Fools] of the World.*

The ch. was burnt in the G.F. At first there was some hope of patching it up again, for the walls were coped with straw and lime to arrest further decay, and in 1679 a bell was hung in the steeple. It was found, however, that the damage was too great for satisfactory reparation, and it was rebuilt by Wren in 1694. Here in 1735 John Wesley preached his first extempore sermon. He had arrived without his manuscript, and was much perturbed. Seeking any ear into which to pour out his trouble, he told the caretaker. 'What,' said he, 'can't you trust God for a sermon?' Never again did Wesley take a manuscript into a pulpit. Pulpit, sounding-board, and altarpiece were fine specimens of wood-carving. The last displayed the figure of a pelican, and was surrounded by seven golden candlesticks, signifying the seven chs. of Asia which St. John saw in the Revelation. Above the N. door-case was a wooden figure of Death, about 4 ft. high, and the S. door-case supported a similar figure of Time. Above each of the door-cases was an ingeniously carved representation of a curtain. The C.C. pew had two swordrests, and the churchwardens' pews were carved with the lion and the unicorn. Both font and cover were finely carved. On the wall in the vestibule was a frame containing shelves for doles of bread. The gateway, removed in 1865 from its original position at the st. entrance, was characterized by a massed formation of skulls. All Hallows was so hemmed in by surrounding bdgs. that it was called 'The . Church Invisible.' In 1937 the Ecclesiastical Commissioners proposed that the ch. should be demolished and the benefice united with that of St. Edmund the King, Lombard St. The scheme was opposed by the C.C. and the Royal Academy of Arts, but was finally confirmed by the Judicial Committee of the Privy Council. It was demolished in 1938. The furniture and monuments were taken to the Ch. of All Hallows, Twickenham. It served four pars., i.e. St. Leonard Eastcheap, St. Dionis Backchurch, St. Benet Gracechurch and All Hallows. The one monument worthy of mention was removed from St. Dionis. It is Dr. Edward Tyson's, d. 1708. He was a physician of some note, as his long Latin inscription relates, and an F.R.S. Garth ridiculed him in *The Dispensary* under the name of 'Carus.'

All Hallows Staining. The earliest mention is 'Stanigrecherch' in 1177. Stow thought its name was derived from its having been one of the first chs. built of stone instead of timber. Other suggestions are that it belonged to a certain holding in the City mentioned in Domesday Book, and in a charter of Edward the Confessor, as belonging to the manor of Staines. Rev. A. Povah, the historian of the united parishes of St. Olave's and All Hallows, suggests that it may have been built after the fire of 1087 or 1136. It is said that here, on her release from the T.L. in 1554, Princess Elizabeth returned thanks. As, however, she was at once conveyed by barge to Richmond, the story deserves no credence. Stow enumerates some 'fayre monuments,' but adds that:

'The Churchwardens were forced to make a large account, 12 shillings that yeare for Bromes, besides the carriage away of stone and brasse of their owne charge.'

It was not burnt in the G.F., but collapsed in 1671, and a new ch. was built 1674-5. Dr. Dodd (see 'Tyburn') was once rector there. In 1870 the ch. was taken down, except the tower. The latter, in the Perpendicular style, is probably over 400 yrs. old. It was purchased, together with the site of the ch., by the Clothworkers' Co. from the Ecclesiastical Commissioners on the understanding that they would keep the tower in repair, and would not build on the site, except on defined portions fronting Mark Lane. A crypt of Norman architecture from Lamb's Chapel, Monkwell St., bequeathed to the co., was taken to the chyd. in 1873. After the almost total destruction of the Ch. of St. Olave, Hart St. in 1941, the crypt was fitted up as a chapel for the parishioners. Subsequently a pre-fabricated ch. was constructed which incorporated the old tower; the tower still stands.

A bell from All Hallows Staining is in the Grocers' Hall. It bears date 1458, and is of Flemish make. In 1587 it rang 'for joye of ye execution of ye Queene

of Scotts.' The churchwardens' minute-books cover four centuries. There is therein an account for bell-ringing in honour of James II, and two days later bell-ringing again for William III. The sword-rest, when the ch. was demolished, was purloined by the par. clerk. He took it to his own smithy, and after twenty yrs. it was discovered. It is now in the ch. of St. Andrew Undershaft. It has three shields— the Royal arms, the City arms, and the arms of Sir Wm. Stewart, Ld.M.

Holy Trinity, Gough Square. It was at the SE. corner of New St. It was erected in 1837 as a chapel-of-ease to St. Bride's Ch. The body was in the form of a hexagon, 47 ft. 6 in. in diameter, and the tower was designed in what Godwin and Britton called 'the Anglo-Norman style.' It was demolished in 1908.

Holy Trinity, Minories. The first allusion to the Minories as a par. is in 1657, when Julian Morgan of L., 'Gentallman,' bequeathed 'my body to be buried w^tin the churche of the Minores w^tout Allgate of London, where as I am a paryshoner.' It is evident that the ch. of the dissolved abbey (see 'Minories') became the par. ch., and was henceforth designated the ch. of St. Trinity or Holy Trinity in the Minories. The body of Sir Philip Sidney lay in state here for three months prior to burial in St. P.'s Cath. Between 1705 and 1708 it was rebuilt.

The new ch., a small structure, had some carvings dated 1620 from the old ch. There were a number of imposing monuments. The oldest was to the memory of Sir John Pelham and his son Oliver. There were figures of a knight in armour and a lady kneeling opposite, and a child kneeling behind the knight. The inscription was curious:

Death first did strike Sr John	Heare Tomb'd in claye
And then Enforst His Of Pelham's Line this	Sonne to Followe Faste
Knyghte	Was Chiefe and Staye,
By this Behold all Fleshe	Must Dye at Laste.
But Bletstowe's Lord thy Sister Most may Moane Both Mate and Sonn Hathe Lefte Her Heare alone.	

Sir John Pelham, died the 13 of October 1580
Oliver Pelham, his sonne, dyed 19 of Januarie 1584

This monument was removed, when the ch. was dismantled, to Stanmer, near Lewes. The next (in chronological order) was Col. Wm. Legge. He d. 1670, and the inscription said:

'He was Groom of ye Bedchamber

and Lieutenant General of ye Ordinance to King Charles ye first and in ye late Civil warr was Governour of Chester & Oxford & upon ye happy Restoration of ye Royal family in ye year 1660 was in consideration of his untainted fidelity to ye King and his many & great Sufferings during ye Civil war restored to his place of Lieutenant General of ye Ordnance and Groom of his Majesties Bedchamber by King Charles ye 2nd.'

Legge, as the inscription further said, m. Elizabeth Washington, eldest daughter to Sir Wm. Washington, and on the monument the Washington arms—stars and stripes—were impaled upon Col. Legge's escutcheon. Elizabeth Washington was the niece of Lawrence Washington, the great-great-grandfather of Geo. Washington. Another monument was to Ld. Dartmouth, another Master of the Ordnance, who d. 1688 (the Dartmouth family were bd. in the vaults until they were closed in 1847). A gravestone on the floor consisting of a slab of marble, recorded the death in 1596 of Constantia Lucy, daughter of Thomas Lucy Junr. This was a granddaughter of Sir Thos. Lucy, once supposed to be the original of Mr. Justice Shallow and Shakespeare's *bête noire*. The ch. was 'a royal peculiar,' and this right it maintained until 1730. When the parishioners voluntarily submitted themselves to the Bp. of L. in 1775 the privileges became extinct through acceptance of a grant from Q. Anne's Bounty.

In the yr. 1852, when the vaults were being cleared, a mummified head was discovered. In 1898 the Rev. Samuel Kinns, then Vicar, in a book dealing with eminent men and women connected with the ch., advanced a theory that it was the head of Henry Grey, D. of Suffolk, the father of Lady Jane Grey to whom, in 1552, Edward VI had granted the remains of the dissolved abbey (see 'Minories'). He was executed in 1554. In 1907, however, another vicar, Rev. E. M. Tomlinson, published *A History of the Minories*, and denied the whole story. He pointed out that in 1786 an infamous beadle had sawn up a number of coffins to utilize the wood, and in the process he did

'Cut and slash among the dead.'

In this way the amputation of the head might have occurred. An American offered £500 for it, but the Bp. of L. felt that no faculty could be granted for the sale.

This was the ch. attended by Sir Isaac Newton, when Master of the Mint. It was closed in 1899 and the par. united with St. Botolph, Aldgate. In 1941 what had been the ch. of Holy Trinity, Minories, was destroyed by German bombs, except for the N. wall and the vaults. The Lucy gravestone survived, and is now at the ch. of All Hallows, Barking.

St. Alphage, London Wall. The earliest mention is 'St. Elfego' (*c.* 1108–25). The saint to whom the ch. was dedicated was an Abp. of C. who was martyred by the Danes at Greenwich (*q.v.*). It is believed the first ch. was erected in 1013. It became dilapidated in the 16th century, and it was resolved to pull it down. Opposite was Elsing Spital, a hosp. founded by Wm. de Elsing in 1332 'for 100 blind people in honour of the Blessed Virgin Mary.' This priory was surrendered to Henry VIII. In its ch., according to Stow, John Northampton (Ld.M., 1381) was bd. He adds:

'The principáll Isle of this church towards the north was pulled down and a frame of foure houses set up in place: the other parte from the steeple upward, was converted into a parrish Church of St Alphage, and the parrish Church which stoode neare unto the Wall of the Cittie by Cripplesgate was pulled downe, the plot thereof made a Carpenters yearde, with saw pittes. The hospital itself, the Prior and Canon's house with other lodgings, were made a dwelling house, the church yeard is a garden plot, and a fayre gallery on the cloyster: the lodgings for the poore are translated into stabling for horses.'

Stow adds that the dwelling-house mentioned was destroyed by fire in 1541. In 1623 Sion College was erected on the site (see 'Libraries').

The remnant of the priory ch. which had thus become parochial, was extensively repaired between the yrs. 1624 and 1628, and in 1649 it was found necessary to rebuild the upper portion of the steeple. The ch. escaped the G.F., and was again repaired in 1701. In 1774, having become hopelessly dilapidated, it was taken down. The new ch. was erected by Sir Wm. Staines, and opened in 1777. In 1913 the N. porch of 1775 was taken down, and a new porch erected in the 14th-century style of architecture. The ch. was closed in 1920, and the par. united with St. Mary, Aldermanbury. In 1923 it was demolished with the exception of part of the tower (with pointed arches of early 14th-century work) and the porch, which remained as a chapel dedicated to St. John the Baptist. The porch was burnt out in the Second World War.

A monument to Sir Rowland Hayward remains. He was twice Ld.M. in Q. Elizabeth's reign, and had two wives and sixteen children, all represented in marble. He d. 1593. The registers and church-wardens' accounts, now in Guildhall Library, have some remarkable entries. There is 'A Register of those I have certi-fied who have been touched by His Majesty for the Evil'—forty-one names follow, dating from 1672 to 1686. There are the following items in the 'Inventory of Church Goodes':

'A cotte [coat] forr our Laydy.
Senser and Holy Water Stoke
Shepe [Ship] off Sylver and a Spone for Incense.'

There are entries relating to the purchase of books:

'The Book of the Papheas of Erasmus' (the *Book of the Paraphrase of Erasmus*), purchased in 1547.

'payde for a booke of Bishoppe Jewelles Works and for a chayne and a staple and a plate to make yt faste to yᵉ desks' (1610).

The par. also had its stocks, cage, and whipping post, all mentioned in the registers.

St. Antholin, Watling Street. The earliest mention is 'St. Antonin' (c. 1119). It was dedicated to St. Anthony the Hermit (d. 357), and 'Antholin' is a corruption. In 1345 a chapel of St. Anne and St. John the Baptist was annexed to it by John de Grantham. Stow says it was 're-edified' by Thos. Knowles (Ld.M. 1399 and 1410) in 1400, and his son of the same name, both of whom were bd. there. Henry Colet, mercer (Ld.M. 1486 and 1495), was a great benefactor. He was father of the famous Dean Colet, the founder of St. P.'s Sch., who was b. in the par. in 1466. The ch. appears to have been again rebuilt in 1513. Stow

mentions some interesting burials, and gives the epitaph on Thos. Knowles senior:

'Here lieth graven under this stone,
Thomas Knowles, both flesh and bone,
Grocer and Alderman yeares fortie,
Shiriffe, and twice Maior truly.
And for he should not lie alone,
Here lieth with him his good wife Joan.
They were togither sixtie yeare,
And nineteene children they had in feere.'

There was also bd. Hugh Acton, 'Marchant tayler,' in 1520. He gave '36. pound to the repayring of the steeple.' Simon Street, grocer, 'his arms be three Colts,' had a quaint epitaph:

'Such as I am, such shall you be,
Grocer of London sometime was I,
The kings wayer more then yeares twentie,
Simon Strete called in my place,
And good fellowship faine would trace,
Therefore in heaven, everlasting life
Jesu send me, and Agnes my wife:
Kerlie Merlie my wordes were tho,
And Deo gratias I coupled thereto,
I passed to God in the yeare of grace.
A thousand foure hundred it was,' etc.

Colet, Stow says, had:
'His wife, ten sonnes and ten daughters in the glasse window on the North side of the Church: but the said Henrie Colet was buryed at Stebunhith' [Stepney].

The celebrated St. Antholin lectures were first instituted in 1559 and were a great feature of City life in the 16th and 17th centuries. The bells began to ring at five in the morning 'after Geneva fashion,' as Machyn (the funeral furnisher and diarist) terms it. Among the State papers are orders relating to certain moneys given towards the maintenance of six morning lectures in the ch., endorsed by Laud, then Bp. of L. Sir Wm. Craven (Ld.M. 1610), the father of the E. of Craven, was a liberal contributor towards the endowment; the par. seems to have contributed £70. The Elizabethan drama-tists refer to these lectures. Heywood says: 'Instead of tennis court, my morning exercise shall be at St. Antlin's.' Davenant refers 'to two disciples of St. Tantlin that rise to long exercise before day.' Scott mentions them in *Kenilworth*. Clarendon relates that the chaplains to the Commissioners from the Ch. of Scotland to K. Charles I preached there in 1640, and that:

'Curiosity, faction, and humour brought so great a conflux and resort from the first appearance of day in the morning on every Sunday to the shutting in of the light, the church was never empty.'

The advowson belonged to the Dean and Chapter of St. P.'s Cath.

The ch. was burnt in the G.F. and rebuilt by Wren 1682–3. It had a beautiful octagonal spire, and an oval-shaped dome. John Wesley preached there several times, and in his diary mentioned the large attendance. In 1874 it was pulled down to make way for the new Q. Victoria St. The proceeds of the sale of the ch. were £44,900. A part of the money was devoted to the restoration of St. Mary Aldermary, and the remainder was utilized towards the erection at Nunhead of another ch. dedicated to St. Antholin. The spire is in an estate near to Forest Hill; the reredos was removed to the new ch., and the monumental tablets to St. Mary Aldermary. At the corner of Size Lane and Budge Row there was erected the most handsome memorial that existed to a departed City ch.: two stone columns with Corinthian capitals supported the architrave, and enclosed a monument with a medallion representation of the ch. On the bases of the columns were inscribed the names of the churchwardens of this and the neighbouring ch. of St. John the Baptist on Walbrook. An inscription recorded the fate of the ch., and stated that in a vault beneath were deposited the greater part of the human remains removed, and that the remainder were taken to the City of L. cemetery at Ilford. This memorial has now disappeared.

St. Bartholomew by the Exchange. The first reference is 1226. It was 'St. Bartholomew the Less' throughout the 14th and 15th centuries. Machyn referred to it as 'lytyll saynt Bathellmuw besyd sunt Antony's'; this was a reference to St. Anthony's Sch., a medieval foundation the site of which is marked by a C.C. tablet in Threadneedle St. The ch. was rebuilt about 1438 by Thos. Pike, alderman, and Nicholas Yoo, a sheriff. Sir John Lepington founded a chantry (c. 1482). Generally speaking, long

sermons were an outcome of Puritanism but a reference by Stow to this ch. suggests that they were known before its time.

'James Wilford Taylor, one of the sheriffes, 1499, appoynted by his Testament a Doctor of Divinitie everie good Fryday for ever, to preach there a Sermon of Christes passion from 6 of the clocke, till 8, before noone in the saide church.'

Miles Coverdale, one of the translators of the Bible, and Bp. of Exeter, was bd. in the ch. in 1568. In 1647 it was known as 'St. Bartholomew near the Exchange.'

The ch. was burnt in the G.F. and rebuilt by Wren in 1679. It was taken down 1840–1, and the materials sold by auction. The remains of Miles Coverdale were removed to the ch. of St. Magnus the Martyr (*q.v.*). Some of the carved masonry, the old pulpit, organ, etc., were preserved in a ch. erected in 1850 in Moor Lane, in the style of St. Bartholomew's and called by the same name. It was revealed during demolition that the walls of the structure were older than Wren's period, and a niche was found which was probably used for holding the vessels used for the water and wine in the Eucharist. There is a C.C. tablet at the corner of Bartholomew Lane and Threadneedle St.

St. Benet Fink. The earliest mention is 'St. Benet Finck' (1216). Stow says it was newly built by Robt. Finke the elder, who resided in Finke's (now Finch) Lane. Stow does not record any notable monuments. A son of John Speed (see 'St. Giles, Cripplegate'), was baptized there in 1608. The ch. was burnt in the G.F.. and rebuilt by Wren in 1673–6. Mr. Geo. Holman, said to have been a Roman Catholic, gave £1,000 towards the cost of adorning the ch., for which the par. presented to him and his heirs for ever two pews and a vault. The E. window contained his arms with the date 1695. There was a spring of water with a pump against the wall of the ch. Richd. Baxter was m. at this ch. in 1662, and the register records the burial in 1679 of Magdalen, the first wife of Alexander Pope the elder. John Henry Newman was baptized in the ch. in 1801, his father, a bank clerk, residing in Old Broad St. The ch. was demolished 1842–4 on the erection of the new Royal

Exchange, and the par. united with that of St. Peter le Poer.

St. Benet Gracechurch. There is a reference in 1053 to a ch. which was probably this one. In Henry III's reign (*c.* 1250) it is definitely mentioned—'St. Benedict of Garscherche.' Stow mentions three unimportant monuments, Weever records one with the following inscription:

'Prey for the saulys of Henry Denne and Joan his wyf, theyr fadyrs, theyr modyrs, bredyrs, and good frendys, and of all Christian saulys Jesus haue mercy, Amen, who departyd this lif. . . . MCCCCLXXXI.'

It was burnt in the G.F., and rebuilt by Wren in 1685, the par. of St. Leonard, Eastcheap, being united with it. It had a steeple 149 ft. high, and the ch. contained much good carving. It was demolished in 1867, and the par. united with All Hallows, Lombard St. The pulpit was taken to St. Olave's, Hart St. There is a C.C. tablet in Gracechurch Street.

St. Christopher le Stocks. The earliest reference is *c.* 1282; in 1348–9 it was 'St. Christopher upon Cornhull.' In 1361 it was 'St. Christopher near le Stokkes,' and it was probably dedicated to St. Christopher as being on the bank of the Walbrook. This saint was the patron of ferrymen, on account of his having carried the infant Christ over a stream; 'le Stokkes' referred to the City stocks, which at one time stood close to it. Stow mentions that there was bd. John Godnay (Ld.M. 1427), who

'in the yeare 1444 wedded the widdow of Robert Large, late Maior, which widdow had taken the Mantell and ring, and the vow to live chast to God during the tearme of her life, for the breach whereof, the marriage done they were troubled by the Church, and put to penance, both he and she.'

Wm. Hampton (Ld.M. 1472), he says, 'was a great benefactor and glassed some of the church windowes.' Another burial was Sir Wm. Martin (Ld.M. 1492).

The ch. was burnt in the G.F., and rebuilt by Wren in 1671, being the first he completed. It was demolished in 1781 to provide space for an extension of the Bank of England (*q.v.*). The chyd. remained—a delectable rural diversion in the City, particularly in the spring, when it was thick with such dancing daffodils

as those of which Wordsworth sung—but in 1934 this also vanished in the rebuilding of a considerable portion of the Bank. Then there was discovered the leaden coffin of Wm. Daniel Jenkins, who d. in 1798, aged 31. He was a clerk in the Bank, and was 6 ft. 7½ in. in height, and his relatives were permitted by the governors and directors to bury the body in the Bank garden, so that it should be safe from body snatchers. It was said that the surgeons offered 200 guineas for the corpse. The top of the coffin was 8½ ft. below the surface. It was removed to Nunhead Cemetery, where the other human remains had been conveyed in 1867.

St. Dionis Backchurch. The earliest mention is 'St. Dionis in Lime Street' (*c.* 1198–1214). In 1241–52 it was 'St. Dionis of Bakecherche'; in 1281 'St. Dionisius Batcherch.' Sometimes it was 'St. Dionysius.' The latter was correct, the dedication being to St. Denys or Dionysius, the patron saint of France, who since the 9th century has been identified with Dionysius the Areopagite. It is the only City ch. so dedicated. 'Backchurch' indicated that it stood back out of the main line of Fenchurch St. It was rebuilt in the reign of Henry VI.

John Stow said:

'John Bugge, esquire, was a great benefactor to that worke as appeareth by his armes three water Budgets, and his crest a Morians head graven in the stone work of the Quire, the upper end on the north side, where he was buried.

'John Darby Alderman added thereunto a fayre Isle or Chapple on the South side, and was there buried about the year 1466. He gave (beside sundry ornaments) his dwelling house and others unto the said church. The Ladie Wich, widow to Hugh Wich, sometimes Maior of London, was there buried and gave lands for Sermons, etc.'

Other burials were Sir Thos. Curtis (Ld.M. 1557) and Sir Edwd. Osborn (Ld.M. 1583). (For the latter see 'London Bridge'.)

The ch. was burnt in the G.F. and rebuilt by Wren in 1674. The tower was erected about ten yrs. later. There was a monument to Sir Thos. Rawlinson and his family, some of whom were eminent as bibliopolists and antiquaries. There was a tablet to Sir Arthur Ingram, an eminent Spanish merchant, who formerly resided in Fenchurch St. (d. 1681). The site of his house is marked by Ingram Court. Another tablet commemorated Sir Robt. Geffrey, Knight and Ld.M., who d. 1703 at the age of 91. In 1858 the crypt of the 15th-century ch. was discovered. At 23 Lime St. there is St. Dionis Hall, now offices and shops. The ch. was demolished in 1878 and the par. united with All Hallows, Lombard St. The bells went to that ch. and are, now that it is also demolished, on the ch. of All Hallows, Twickenham.

St. George, Botolph Lane. The first mention is in 1180 as 'St. George's in Estchepe.' In 1516 it is 'St. George in Podynge Lane.' It was the only ch. in the City with this dedication. It was repaired in 1627. Stow said 'the monuments are well preserved from spoyle.' These included one to Adam Bamme (Ld.M. 1396); Wm. Forman (Ld.M. 1538); and Jas. Mumford, surgeon to Henry VIII (d. 1544). It was burnt in the G.F. and rebuilt by Wren in 1674. The par. of St. Botolph's, Bishopsgate, was then united to it. Dr. Wm. Sherlock was rector for over twenty yrs. To the vexation of the nonjurors he renounced his Jacobite principles in 1691, on Tillotson's promotion to the primacy, and accepted the deanery of St. P.'s Cath. He d. 1707. Over the C.C. pew there was the following inscription:

'Sacred to the memory of that real patriot, the Right Hon. William Beckford; twice Lord Mayor of London; whose incessant spirited efforts to serve his Country hastened his dissolution on the 21st June, 1770, in the time of his Mayoralty, and the 62nd year of his age.'

His arms were on the sword-rest, together with those of the City of L. and the royal arms. The ch. being in a dangerous condition, was closed in 1899, and demolished in 1904. There is a C.C. tablet in St. George's Lane.

St. James, Duke Place, Aldgate. On the dissolution of the priory of the Holy Trinity (*q.v.*) the bdgs. were given by Henry VIII to Sir Thos. Audley. He pulled down the priory ch. and built houses on the site. After his death in 1544 the estate devolved on his son-in-law, Thos. D. of Norfolk, and was in consequence called 'Duke's Place.' The inhabitants had not then any special place of worship and resorted to St. Katharine Cree Ch. for baptisms and marriages and sometimes for worship. In the reign of James I (*c.* 1621) they applied for permission to build a ch. for themselves. This was granted partly through the exertions of Sir Edward Barkham (Ld.M.). He was characterised in some verses suspended in the chancel:

Barkham the worthy, whose immortal name,
Marble's too weak to hold, for this work's fame.
He's never ceased in industry and care
From ruins to redeem this house of prayer.

It was erected in 1623 and first called Trinity Ch. According to Strype (1720), in the Consecration Service, the bp. said that it was dedicated 'to the worship of the Holy and Undivided Trinity, and he named it the Church or Chapel of St. James within Algate.'

Strype refers to a tablet upon which were the lines:

'This Sacred Structure which this Senate Fames,
Our King hath stil'd The Temple of St. James.'

It was adjudged in Charles I's time that St. James's was a par. ch., and not a precinct of St. Katharine Cree Ch., and the privilege of marrying without licence was taken away by Act of Parliament. It escaped the G.F., and was rebuilt in 1727. The E. window displayed the arms of Barkham. It was pulled down in 1874, and the par. united with St. Kathérine Cree. Some of the monuments were taken to that ch. There is a C.C. tablet in Mitre Sq.

St. Katherine Coleman. The first mention was in 1301 as 'Sanctae Katerinae de Colman cherche.' Stow says it was dedicated to St. Katherine and All Saints, and it was probably identical with All Hallows Colemanch., to which there is documentary reference in the 12th century. It is referred to (*temp.* Henry II, 1154–89) as 'Colemaneschirche,' and this may have been the name of a builder or restorer. Stow says nothing of it beyond a reference to the derivation of the name from which it may be concluded there were no interesting monuments. About 1489 Wm. White, Ld.M., rebuilt or added the S. aisle. Amongst the epitaphs given by Strype—it is undated—was one worth preserving. It was on a monument to Mrs. Barners:

'In ancient times, the friends surviving gave
Some rich memorial to the dead friend's grave,
Gold, pearls, or gems, which custom did intend;
Our riches ought to wait upon our friend In life and death. O blessed ages, when Men parted fortunes, and not fortunes men!

'But now perverted are our present ends, That for wealth sell the fame of living friends;
The dead we live by, now can scant afford The rites and sacrifice of one good word: Of which, lest I be one, though I can bring (For worthy obsequie) no precious thing; My gratitude presents unto her hearse, My tears for balme, for offering my sad verse.'

The ch. escaped the G.F., was repaired in 1703, and in 1734 pulled down. The ch. which followed had no features of antiquarian or of architectural interest. Godwin and Britton remarked: 'It may be confidently stated that no parish in the metropolis would now allow such a piece of ugliness to be erected.' The last service was held in 1921, and it was no loss when it was demolished in 1925, and the par. united with St. Olave's, Hart St.

St. Martin Outwich. The earliest mention is *c.* 1217. About 1230 there was a grant of land in the par. by Matilda, late wife of Martin de Ottewich. It is referred to as 'St. Martin Oteswich' (*c.* 1253). Stow mentions a number of monuments, though none of any great importance. It escaped the G.F., and was repaired in 1681. It suffered considerably from a fire in Cornhill Ward in 1765, and in 1796 was taken down and rebuilt, the new ch. being consecrated in 1798. The Merchant Taylors' Co., patrons of the living, subscribed £500 and the South Sea Co. £200. In 1874 the ch. was demolished, and the par. united with St. Helen's, Bishopsgate. Eighteen monuments were taken to the ch. of the latter. These include 'the fair

monument' mentioned by Stow under which John Oteswich and his wife were bd., part of the monument of Hugh Pemberton, alderman (d. 1500), also mentioned by Stow, and brasses in memory of two rectors, John Brieux (d. 1459), and Nicholas Wotton (d. 1483). There is a C.C. tablet at the corner of Bishopsgate St. and Threadneedle St. The garden of the Fraternity of the Papey (an almshouse for poor and aged priests), was demolished about 1550. On the gateway, which remained until the Second World War, there were two serpents with tails in mouths—an emblem of eternity. (The history of the ch. and par. was written by C. W. F. Goss as a pamphlet in 1929.)

St. Mary Magdalen, Old Fish Street. The first mention is in 1162. In 1196 it was 'St. Marie Magdā in Piscaria apud Sanctum Paulum.' Little is known of the pre-Fire ch. It contained, like many others, a monument to Q. Elizabeth and the epitaph was as follows:

'Here lies her type, who was of late The prop of Belgia, stay of France, Spain's foile, Faith's shield, and Queen of State,
Of arms of learning, fate and chance; In brief a woman ne'er was seen, So great a prince, so good a queen. Sith virtue her immortal made, Death (envying all that cannot die). Her earthly parts did so invade, As in it wrackt self-majesty. But so her spirits inspired her parts, That she still lives in loyal hearts.'

The ch. was burnt in the G.F., and rebuilt by Wren in 1685. The par. of St. Gregory by St. Paul's was then united with it, that ch. not being rebuilt. The benefice of St. Mary Magdalen was a rectory in the gift of the Dean and Chapter of St. P.'s Cath., and the ch. of St. Gregory belonged to them and was served by a curate whom they appointed. The Rev. R. H. Barham, author of the *Ingoldsby Legends*, was rector from 1824 to 1842, when he removed to the neighbouring ch. of St. Augustine, Watling St. (see 'City Churches; D'). As several of his children had been bd. at St. Mary Magdalen's his remains were laid in the rector's vault there in 1845.

The ch. was seriously damaged by fire in 1886 and was thereupon pulled down to save the expense of repairs. The par. was then united with St. Martin, Ludgate. It stood on the N. side of Knightrider St. at the corner of Old Change. 'Old Fish Street' was the old name for part of Knightrider St., the fish market having been there in 1413, and probably much earlier. Billingsgate afterwards obtained the monopoly.

St. Mary Somerset, Upper Thames St. The earliest reference is in the time of Richard I (1189–99), 'St. Mary of Sumersetecherch.' There was a new chapel erected in the 15th century. Stow said little of it:

'It is a proper church, but the monuments are all defaced. I thinke the same to bee of olde time called Summers Hith of some man's name, that was owner of the grounds near adjoyning, as Edreds Hithe was so called of Edred owner thereof.'

The ch. was burnt in the G.F. and rebuilt by Wren in 1695, the par. of St. Mary Mounthaw being united with it. In St. Mary Somerset Ch., in 1701, Gilbert Ironside, Bp. of Hereford, was bd. He was Warden of Wadham Coll., Oxford, for twenty-five yrs., and was Vice-Chancellor of the University when the President and Fellows of Magdalene Coll. were ejected by James II. He opposed the latter to his face, and insisted on the rights of the fellows. Macaulay says that two months afterwards Col. Kirke and the K.'s commissioners invited Ironside to dine with them on the evening of the expulsion, but he declined saying: 'My tastes differ from that of Colonel Kirke, I cannot eat my meals with appetite under a gallows.'

The ch. was pulled down in 1872, and the body of the Bp. taken to Hereford Cath. (there is Ironside Court at the back of the tower). With the proceeds of the sale of the ch. a St. Mary Somerset Ch. was built at Hoxton. (It was destroyed in the Blitz.) The handsome tower, 120 ft. in height, was left.

St. Matthew, Friday Street. The first mention is *c.* 1261—'St. Matthew in Fridaistret.' In 1381–2 it was 'St. Matthew in Chepe.' Stow mentions a few monuments of aldermen, etc. and says that 'Thos. Warlington founded a chantry and Sir Nicholas Twiford Mayor gave to that church an house with the appurtenances, called the Griffon on the hope

in the same strete.' Sir Hugh Myddleton was bd. here (1631). It was burnt in the G.F. and rebuilt by Wren in 1685. The par. of St. Peter, Westchepe, was united to it. There was a monument to Sir E. Clark (Ld.M. 1696, d. 1703), and to Michael Lort, D.D., F.R.S., for twelve yrs. professor of the Greek language in the University of Cambridge (d. 1790). The ch., which was on the E. side of Friday St., was pulled down in 1884, and the par. united with St. Vedast, Foster Lane.

St. Michael Bassishaw. The earliest reference is to 'St. Michael de Bassieshage' (1187). It appears to have been founded about 1140, and the patronage then belonged to the prior and canons of St. Bartholomew's, Smithfield. In 1246 Henry III gave the advowson to Adam Basing, son of Salomon Basing (Ld.M. 1216). Stow was probably correct in deriving the second part of the name from the haw or estate of the Basing family. It was rebuilt in the 15th century by the help of John and Agnes Barton 'as appeareth,' said Stow, 'by his marke placed throughout the whole roofe of the Quier and the middle Ile of the Church.' He d. 1460, and Stow gives his epitaph:

'John Barton lyeth under here,
Sometimes of London Citizen and Mercer,
And Jenet his wife with their progenie,
Beene turned to earth as ye may see,
Friends free what so ye bee,
Pray for us we you pray,
As you see us in this degree,
So shall you be another day.'

Their remains were identified during excavations in 1896. Other burials noted by Stow were Sir Jas. Yarford (Ld.M. 1519, d. 1527): 'Buried under a fayre Tombe with his Ladie in a speciall Chappell by him builded on the North side of the Quire'; Sir John Gresham (Ld.M. 1547, d. 1554); Wolston Dixie (Ld.M. 1585); and Sir Leonard Halliday (Ld.M. 1605). The ch. was repaired in 1630, burnt in the G.F., and rebuilt by Wren 1676–9. The only monument of any note was a tablet with a Latin inscription to Dr. Thos Wharton, a physician of St. Thomas's Hosp. It stated that during the time of the Plague his resolution never wavered, and that he kept at his post ministering to his own patients and to the sick poor. He d. 1673, aged 59. The ch., which had a steeple 140 ft. high, got out of repair. It was closed in 1893 and demolished in 1897, the par. being united with St. Lawrence Jewry. The royal arms from the ch. are in the Guildhall Mus.

St. Michael, Crooked Lane. The earliest mention is 'St. Michael Candelwestrete' (*c.* 1271). In 1283 it was 'St. Michael towards London Bridge.' There was a chapel to St. Mary in the ch. in 1368, and 'Trinitie Chapell' in the chyd. Stow says that Sir Wm. Walworth built the choir and side chapels and founded in the ch. a coll. for a master and nine priests. He also says that Walworth was bd. there in 1385:

'But his monument being amongst other by bad people defaced in the raigne of Edward the sixt and again since renuwed by the Fishmongers for lacke of knowledge of what before had been written in his Epitaph, they followed a fabulous booke and wrote Jacke Straw, instead of Wat Tilar, a great error.'

It appears that there was also an error in their date. Dr. Hughson gives the original inscription as follows:

'Here under lyeth a Man of Fame,
William Walworth called by name,
Fishmonger he was in lefe-time here,
And twice Ld. Mayor, as in Books appear;
Who, with Courage stout and manly might
Slew Wat Tyler in K. Richard's sight:
For which Act done and true Intent,
The King made him Knight incontinent,
And gave him Arms, as here you see,
To declare his Fact and Chivalry.
He left his Life, the Year of our Lord,
Thirteen hundred fourscore three and odd.'

The ch. was very close to the Fishmongers' Hall, and Strype says 'the South ile or chapel was called the Fishmongers Chapel.' Stow calls the original ch. 'a small and homely thing,' but says that John Lofkin (he was Ld.M. 1348, 1358, and 1366) rebuilt it. He was 'there buried in the Quier under a faire tombe with the Images of him and his wife in Alabaster.'

The ch. was burnt in the G.F., and rebuilt by Wren in 1688; the steeple ten yrs. later. The ch. was removed in 1831, under an Act of Parliament of 1830 for the· formation of the approaches to the new London Bridge. On the occasion of the closing service (20th Mar. 1831) a fall of mortar from the cornice of the ceiling 'compelled the service to be abruptly concluded to the great injury of the collection for the charity' (*The Times*). During the demolition of the ch. two pointed arches were brought to light, and they appeared to be the remains of an old 12th-century crypt. The greater portion of the site is now occupied by the roadway of King William St. The name of the adjacent Miles Lane is a corruption of Michael's.

In Edward III's reign (*c.* 1346) a piece of land was granted, abutting on Eastcheap, for the enlargement of the cemetery of the ch. and for the reconstruction of two houses. These houses were afterwards known as Nos. 3 and 4 Eastcheap, the back of one forming part of the Boar's Head (see 'Taverns'). At the meetings of St. Michael's Vestry at the Boar's Head (it belonged to the ch. in medieval times) there used to be produced an Elizabethan drinking cup, 11¾ in. high, and weighing 15 oz. It is now in possession of the ch. of St. Magnus the Martyr. It is remarkable that in *2 Henry IV*, Act II, Sc. 1, Dame Quickly says:

'Thou didst swear to me upon a parcel-gilt goblet, sitting in my dolphin chamber, to marry me and make me my lady thy wife.'

Washington Irving in 1818 was shown the cup, and he associated it with this passage. There was also used at the vestry meetings of St. Michael's Ch. an iron tobacco box, given by Sir Richard Gore, and repaired by Mr. John Perchard in 1727. Its cover is painted with a scene of the exterior of the Boar's Head, showing Falstaff and Prince Hal, and this is said to have been the work of Hogarth. It also is in St. Magnus' Ch.

In its chyd. there is a tombstone to a drawer of the Boar's Head—Robt. Preston (see 'Epitaphs').

St. Michael, Queenhithe. The earliest mention is 'St. Michael de Aedredeshuda' —early 12th century. It was 'St. Michael, Queenhithe' in 1273–4. It was so called from the wharf or landing place nearby. (See 'Queenhithe.') Here was b. Richd. Merlawe who was Ld.M. when the Corpus Christi play was performed at Skinners' Well (see 'Clerkenwell'). Stow says all the monuments were defaced. It was burnt in the G.F. and rebuilt by Wren in 1677. It had an altar-piece painted on canvas, and including representations of Moses and Aaron, for retouching which Sr. Jas. Thornhill received the thanks of the par. in 1721. They were, however, destroyed through negligence when a new altar piece was set up. Over the doorway at the E. were some fine carvings of fruit and flowers. The tower was 135 ft. high, and had a gilded vane in the form of a ship in full sail, with a ball said to be capable of holding a bushel of wheat. The ch. was destroyed in 1876. Some part of the proceeds of the sale of the site was devoted to St. Michael's Ch., Camden Town. The organ is in Christ Ch., Chelsea. There is a C.C. tablet on 200 Upper Thames St.

St. Michael, Wood St. The first reference found is to 'St. Michael of Wood Street,' in 1170. In 1282 it was 'St. Michael in Wodestret near Hoggens lane.' Stow mentions a monument to

'John Lamberde, Draper, Alderman one of the Shiriffes of London, who deceased 1554, and was father to William Lambarde Esquire, well knowne by sundry learned bookes that he hath published.'

This Wm. Lambarde was the Keeper of the Records (then in the T.L.) to whom Q. Elizabeth said—referring to the Shakespeare play: 'I am Richard II, know ye not that?' He d. a few days after the interview in 1601. Stow proceeds to say;

'There is also (but without any outward monument) the head of James, the fourth king of Scots of that name, slayne at Flodden field, and buried here by this occasion. After the battell the body of the saide king being founde, was closed in lead and conveyed from thence to London, and so to the Monastery of Sheyne in Surrey, where it remayned for a time . . . but since the dissolution of that house, in the raigne of Edward the sixt, Henry Gray Duke of Suffolk being lodged and keeping house there, I have been shewed the same body so lapped in lead, close to the head and body, thrown into a wast roome amongst the olde timber, leade, and other rubble. Since the which time Workemen there, for their foolish pleasure, hewed off his head: and Launcelot Young Maister Glasier

to her Majestie, feeling a sweet savour to come from thence, and seeing the same dryed from all moisture, and yet the forme remayning, with the hayre of the heade and beard redde, brought it to London to his house in Woodstreet, where for a time he kept it for the sweetnesse, but in the ende caused the Sexton of that Church to bury it amongst other bones, taken out of their Charnell, &c.'

Some Scotch writers maintain that James was not killed, another individual having fought in habiliments similar to those of the K. It has been asserted that he escaped to Jerusalem, and d. there some time after. Weever, however, confirmed Stow as to the burial at Sheen. There was also a monument to Q. Elizabeth, with the usual eulogistic inscription. The ch. was burnt in the G.F., and rebuilt by Wren in 1675. The ch. of St. Mary Staining not being rebuilt, the two pars. were united. The ch., which had a spire 130 ft. high, was repaired in 1888, when the high pews were removed. The monumental tablets had no interest. The ch. was taken down in 1894.

St. Mildred, Poultry. First mentioned in 1175 as 'St. Mildrithe'; sometimes it is 'St. Mitheldrede upon Walebroc.' There was a chapel of St. Mary de Coneyhope annexed to the ch. In Henry VII's reign the latter was known as the chapel of Corpus Christi. The fraternity was suppressed by Henry VIII.

The ch. was rebuilt in 1457, the new choir standing on the course of the Walbrook. Cutberd Beechar, a draper bd. in the ch. in 1540, left a sum of money to purchase weekly thirteen 1d. loaves for a shilling, to be distributed every Sunday among thirteen poor persons of the par. Thos. Tusser was bd. in the ch. in 1580 with the following epitaph:

'Here Thomas Tusser clad in earth doth
  lie,
That some times made the poynts of
  husbandrie,
By him then learn thou maist, here learne
  we must
When all is done we sleepe and turne to
  dust,
And yet through Christ to heaven we
  hope to go:
Who reades his bookes shall find his
  faith was so.'

Tusser's book, *A Hundredth Good Pointes of Husbandrie*, was published in 1557. By 1573 he had expanded it into *Five Hundredth Pointes of Good Husbandrie*. The ch. was burnt in the G.F., and rebuilt by Wren in 1676. It had a bust by Nollekens of Mrs. Ann Simpson (1785). This is now in St. Margaret, Lothbury. The ch. was demolished in 1872. The pulpit and some of the carvings were erected in St. Paul's, Goswell Rd., but they were destroyed in raids in 1941. A new ch. was there endowed out of the sum obtained by the sale of St. Mildred's, the total amount of which was £50,200. The stones of the ch., purchased by Mr. Flytche, were taken to Lincolnshire and placed in a field called St. Katherine's Garth, near Thorpe Hall, Louth, where had stood an old priory of St. Katherine's. His intention was to rebuild on the site a domestic chapel for his house. The chyd. remained until about 1927, and was then sold to a bank. There is a C.C. tablet on 24–25 Poultry.

(See *A Site in Poultry*, by F. J. Froom, 1950.)

St. Olave, Jewry. The earliest reference is 'St. Olave in the Jewry' (1181). Stow says in 1320 it was called St. Olave Upwell. The chapel of St. Stephen was annexed to St. Olave in 1399, and a new aisle added to the ch., says Stow, by 'T. Morsted Esquire, Chirurgion to Henry the fourth, fift, and sixt,' one of the sheriffs, 1436. He was bd. in the ch. in 1450. Amongst other burials Stow mentions Robt. Large (Ld.M. 1440). He gave £200 to the ch. Also:

'Giles Dew, servant to Henry VII, and to Henry VIII, Cleark of their Libraries, and schoolemaister for the French tongue to Prince Arthur, and to the Lady Mary.'

He d. in 1535.

The ch. was burnt in the G.F., and rebuilt by Wren 1673–6. In 1804 John Boydell (see 'Cheapside') was bd. here. The inscription was extraordinarily long.

'Near to this place are deposited the mortal remains of John Boydell Esq born January 19th 1719, at Dorrington Hall, near the village of Woore in Shropshire: for many years a much respected member of the Company of Stationers, and the Lord Mayor of London in 1790. As an Engraver, he attained considerable eminence in his art, as a printseller, he caused its productions to become a source of commercial benefit to his country, and of such profit to himself, as to enable him to afford unexampled encouragement to the English school of Historical painting, and to form that splendid collection of British Art, the Shakespeare Gallery. As a magistrate, the conscientious discharge of his duties earned him the applause of his fellow citizens, as a man the singular simplicity of his mind, and the pure innocence of his heart, gained him the love and esteem of all that knew him; and as a Christian, he attended within these walls with exemplary constancy and fervent devotion. He departed from this life on the 12th day of December, 1804, aged Eighty-six years.'

Another memorial was to Mary Nichol of Pall Mall, bookseller to George III. She d. in 1820. This monument was removed to St. Margaret, Lothbury, when St. Olave's Ch. was pulled down in 1888, and the two pars. were united.

St. Peter le Poer. It is first mentioned in 1181. It is 'Sancti Petri de Bradestrate,' *c.* 1303; 'St. Peter Paupertatis' 1544. Stow says it was 'next unto Pawlet House,' and so called for a difference from other of that name, sometime peradventure a poore Parish.' Another suggestion is that it was not dedicated to St. Peter the Apostle, but to St. Peter the Hermit, who could appropriately be called poor to distinguish him from the former. The ch. was enlarged and very extensively repaired between 1615 and 1630, and Sir Wm. Garaway, a wealthy merchant, built a new N. aisle at his own expense. He d. 1625 at the age of 88, and had 'a fair and comely monument.' His wife and seventeen children were also bd. there.

Dr. Richd. Holdsworth, rector at the commencement of the Civil War, was sequestered and for a time imprisoned by the Long Parliament. He attended on Charles I during his confinement at Hampton Court and Carisbrooke, and d. a few months after his execution. He was bd. in the ch., and a monument set up to his memory. After the demolition of the old ch. it lay nearly a century hidden in the vaults. It was accidentally discovered and re-erected. Dr. Benjamin Hoadly, the famous Whig and controversialist became rector in 1704. In 1715 he was raised to the see of Bangor, but continued to hold the rectory till 1720. He d. in 1761 when Bp. of Winchester. The ch. escaped the G.F., but became much decayed, and it was an obstruction to the thoroughfare (Old Broad St.) in which it was situated. It was therefore removed by Act of Parliament in 1788, and rebuilt farther back, on the site of its cemetery. On the demolition of the Ch. of St. Benet Fink (1842) the two pars. were united with St. Michael's, Cornhill. St Peter le Poer Ch. was demolished in 1896.

C. EXISTING CHURCHES.

Under this heading are included only those churches which, at the time of writing, are open to the public.

All Hallows Barking (Mark Lane). Except to the student, the second half of the name is perplexing, and the ch. is now known as 'All Hallows by the Tower.' In the latter part of the 7th century, Erkenwald, Bp. of L., founded at 'Berkynge' in Essex, seven miles down the river, a Christian colony presided over by his sister, Ethelburga. When, in 675, he became Bp. of L., he granted to this religious house certain rights over the piece of land which to this day forms the par. of All Hallows, and a church was built. In return the Abbey of Berkynge undertook to provide a priest. The first ch., probably of wood, disappeared in a fire in 1087. This destroyed most of L. Nothing of it remained but some charred woodwork found beneath the paving in 1923, and now in the crypt. Another ch. was built while the T.L. was being erected. At the time of the blitz the piers of the nave and a fragment of medieval flooring remained. The date of completion of this Norman ch. cannot be ascertained. It probably suffered in the fierce fighting near the Tower incidental to the Civil War of Stephen's reign (1135–54). Richard I—Cœur-de-Lion—founded a Lady Chapel on the N. side of the ch. There was a tradition, as Stow records, that his heart was bd. under the high altar, but as he had given special instructions for its interment at Rouen, this is improbable. From the time of Richard I the chapel of 'St. Mary de Berking' became the care of the Ks. of England. Later prayer was specially ordained for the soul of Richard in the belief that his

heart was bd. in the ch. Edward I placed in it a picture of 'Our Lady'. Pope Adrian V (1276) granted an indulgence to all true pilgrims who worshipped before the shrine. Edward IV interested himself in the establishment of a brotherhood in connection with the chapel, by John Tiptoft, E. of Worcester and Constable of the Tower. A man of high scholarly attainments, he was one of Caxton's patrons. A zealous Yorkist, he was beheaded in 1470 when Henry VI, for a brief period, was restored to the throne by the E. of Warwick. Richard III rebuilt the chapel, and added a dean and six canons to the original foundation. As the ch. nearest to the T.L., it was the resting place of some of the executioner's victims. Bp. Fisher in 1535 was bd. there for a short time before his body was removed to the chapel in the Tower. From 1547 to 1614, when they were taken to Framlingham in Suffolk, the remains of Thos. Howard, E. of Surrey, the poet, lay there. From 1645 to 1663 the body of Abp. Laud was in the ch. At the latter date it was removed to St. John's Coll., Oxford, of which he had once been President. In the par. registers there are also recorded the burial of Sr. John Hotham, executed by order of Parliament in 1644 on account of conspiracy to surrender the important town of Hull, of which he was governor, to Charles I. In the same yr. Wm. Penn, the Quaker, was baptized in the ch.

The ch. survived the G.F., partly through the exertions of Admiral Penn, father of the Quaker, as Pepys recorded:

'Sept. 5th, 1666. About two in the morning my wife calls me up and tells me of new cryes of fire, it being come to Barking Church which is at the bottom of our lane. . . . But going to the fire I find by the blowing up of our houses, and the great help given by the workmen out of the king's yard sent up by Sir W. Pen, there is a good stop given to it as well at Mark Lane end as ours, it having only burned the dyall of Barking Church and part of the porch and was there quenched. I up to the top of Barking steeple and there saw the saddest sight of desolation that I ever saw.'

A window in the N. aisle (it is now in the porch chapel) was emblazoned with the arms of Sir Samuel Starling, and below them there was an inscription stating that they had been 'glassed' in 1666, the yr. of 'the conflagration of London.' Starling, who lived in Seething Lane, was Ld.M. in 1669, and was bd. here in 1674. According to Pepys, he was a man of no very liberal disposition. At the time of the G.F. the house adjoining his was in flames, and his only saved from destruction by the exertions of the poor. For this service he 'did give 2/6 among thirty of them'! In 1797, John Quincy Adams (President of U.S.A., 1824–8) was m. in the ch. A monument, damaged but restored, is to Alderman John Croke (d. 1477), who founded a chantry. There was a monument by Scheemakers, erected by Sir Peter Colleton, in memory of two daughters, a son-in-law, and four grandchildren. There was a large marble slab in memory of the widow of Admiral Sir John Kempthorne. He is several times mentioned by Pepys. There was a white marble tablet, tastefully ornamented, in memory of John Kettlewell, rector of Coleshill in Warwickshire, a non-juror. He d. 1695 at the age of 42; the epitaph was a glowing eulogy.

In brasses it came easily first amongst City chs. There are seventeen in all and, carefully covered, they have survived the Blitz. The most ancient is in memory of Wm. Tonge (1389); the finest is a Flemish brass representing Andrew Evyngar, a salter, with wife and children.

In the Lady Chapel is the shrine of Toc H. In a magnificent casket there was enclosed the first 'Lamp of Maintenance,' given by the P. of Wales as patron in 1922, in memory of those friends of whom the war bereft him. He unveiled it in 1923. A beautiful bronze effigy of a fallen soldier lies near it. The figure is that of Alfred Forster, son of Ld. Forster of Lepe, to whom Australia owes the beginning of Toc H in the Commonwealth.

Of recent yrs. there have been many interesting finds in this ch. In 1924 a chest of documents was found in the tower. The contents were edited by Miss Redstone, and they form the substance of the first part of Vol. XII of the L.C.C. *Survey of London.* In 1926 there was discovered beneath the S. aisle a mortuary crypt (14th century). This is now dedicated as a chapel to St. Francis of Assisi.

The ch. was reduced to a shell in 1941 and not re-dedicated until 1957.

The pulpit (1613), reredos (1685), altar table (1636) and chancel screen, the gift of the Hanseatic League (1705), have all been destroyed. The present pulpit came from St. Swithun, also bombed.

All the Toc H treasures survived; also the tomb of John Croke. The Colleton monument was badly damaged. The font (c. 1685) was destroyed, but the finely carved cover preserved by removal. A new bowl has been provided, made out of limestone from Gibraltar, and presented by tunnellers in memory of comrades who lost their lives in making the rock impregnable. The sword-rests remain; also figures of St. James and St. Roch. A tablet, erected by the Pennsylvania Society in 1911 in memory of Penn's baptism, was badly damaged. One of the last additions, a stained glass window, presented by the Port of London Authority, showing the City and old London Bridge, has been destroyed. Through the Blitz there were revealed a part of a Saxon cross, believed to be of 11th century date, and an archway ascribed to the 7th century. The tower up which Pepys climbed (it was erected in 1659) remains. So does the porch, with figures of St. Ethelburga, Virgin and Child, and Lancelot Andrewes (baptized in the ch. 1555). There are also displayed the arms of Barking Abbey and the Diocese of L.

The N. aisle of the ch., after re-roofing, was formally opened in 1949. Gifts of steel had come from U.S.A. and Canada. Other gifts were received from all parts of the Commonwealth.

There is a new carillon of bells, the gift of John McConnel of Montreal.

On 24th July 1950, on the outside of the N. porch, there was unveiled a new memorial tablet to Wm. Penn.

The inscription is:
'William Penn,
Quaker.
Born on Tower Hill.
Baptised in All Hallows Church.
25 Oct. 1644.
Founder of Pennsylvania.
In an adjoining garden is a tablet with a Latin inscription translated as follows:
'The ancient church of All Hallows. A.D. 675, Ethelburga founded me. 1666, Pepys from fire did ward me. 1940,

German bombs wounded me. 1948, loving friends restored me.'

All Hallows, London Wall. The associations of this ch. are inseparable from the old wall of the City. It stood just within it and in the chyd. a fragment is still left. The first authentic reference is to Matilda, Q. of Henry I, bestowing upon it the priory of Holy Trinity in Aldgate, *c.* 1108. Marriage entries include that of the union, in 1588, of Sir Francis Knollys, the Elizabethan statesman, to his second wife, Lettice Barratt. The ch. escaped the G.F., but in 1765, having fallen into disrepair so that after an Act of Parliament was obtained for the purpose, it was rebuilt by the architect, Geo. Dance, at a cost of £3,000 (1765–7). The body of the ch. is of brick, but the tower is of stone and presents the Corinthian design of architecture. In 1891 the interior was renewed and much improved by the vicar, the Rev. S. J. Stone—known as the author of two hymns, *The Church's One Foundation* and *Weary of Earth.* Excavations in 1905 revealed that the vestry had been built upon one of the bastions of the Roman wall. Above the altar stands a picture of St. Paul being restored to sight by Ananias at Damascus. It was presented by the architect, and is a copy made by his brother, Sir Nathaniel Dance Holland, of a painting in the ch. of the Conception at Rome by the Florentine artist, Pietro di Beretini di Cortona (1596–1669). Flanking the altar are figures of Moses and Aaron. (See 'London Guides.') Towards the W. end, on the N. and S. walls respectively, are marble monuments preserved from the old ch. of Edwd. Hammond, a benefactor of the par. who d. 1642, and Mrs. Joan Bence who d. 1684. S. of the chancel is a large monument to Joseph Patience, an architect, d. 1797; while on the N. side is a tablet to the memory of a former rector. Rev. Wm. Beloe, translator of Herodotus, d. 1817. It is a peculiarity of this ch. that the pulpit can be entered only from the vestry.

In 1950 a new garden was dedicated beside the ch., in the presence of the master and wardens of the Carpenters' Co., which has been connected with the par. since the 14th century. The ch. was badly damaged by bombs in 1941 and derelict for twenty years. It is now a Guild Church, serving at first as H.Q. of the Council for the Care of Churches (now at Fulham), and now as a Christian Arts Centre.

St. Andrew, Holborn. In a charter of K. Edgar in 951 there is a reference to a ch. of St. Andrew in connection with the boundaries of the original par. of Westminster, and this may have been on the same site. The first mention is 'St. Andrew Holbournestrate' in the 12th century. In 1291 it was 'S. Andrew de Holeburn.' The ch. was rebuilt during the 15th century, but by the time of Charles I it was in a dilapidated state. The work was long delayed, probably owing to the Civil War. It escaped the G.F., and was rebuilt by Wren in 1686. He left the tower which was in a better condition than the body of the ch., and in 1704 refaced it with Portland stone. T. F. Bumpus said 'it is one of the finest churches of the galleried basilican type in the country.' There was a fine altarpiece, and the E. window had stainedglass dating from 1718, whilst another window bore date 1687. A modern window was unique in L. inasmuch as it had a representation of a black man, the subject being 'the adoration of the magi.' There was a particularly fine lectern and a well-carved pulpit from which had preached Dr. Sacheverell, John Wesley, Chas. Kingsley, F. D. Maurice, and Canon Farrar.

After the Dissolution the advowson came into the hands of the Crown, and, in 1546, was bestowed by Henry VIII on Thos. Wriothesley, E. of Southampton and Ld. Chancellor. His remains were first interred here, but subsequently removed to Tichfield. It was forfeited to the Crown in 1601 through the Earl being involved in the Essex rebellion. His life was, however, spared, and James I restored him to all his honours and possessions, including the patronage of St. Andrew's. The male line of the Wriothesleys terminated in 1667 in the person of Thos., E. of Southampton, the father-in-law of Ld. Wm. Russell. The advowson passed to one of his daughters, and subsequently into the family of the D. of Buccleuch, in whose possession it remained at the time the ch. was almost entirely destroyed in 1941. At the outt break of the Civil War the rector wa-John Hacket. He was most intrepids He continued the use of the forbidden

Prayer Book. A sergeant and armed troopers were sent to the ch. to compel submission, but with a firm voice he read on. When a soldier put a pistol to his head and threatened instant death, he replied calmly: 'Soldiers, I am doing my duty, do you yours.' With a voice equally composed he resumed the prayers. The soldiers were awestruck by his courage and left in astonishment. Later he was elevated to the see of Lichfield, and became the biographer of Williams, Abp. of York. After the Restoration the living was held for some time by Edwd. Stillingfleet, who became Bp. of Worcester, and was one of the most eminent divines of his time. In 1713 the notorious Dr. Henry Sacheverell received the rectory as a reward for the trial he had undergone. This was mainly through the influence of Swift, who interested Bolingbroke on his behalf. Sacheverell continued rector until his death in 1724, and was bd. in the chancel. The site of the grave was marked by a stone with a simple inscription.

In 1697, in St. Andrew's Ch., Richd. Savage was baptized. His life was poignantly and realistically written by his friend Samuel Johnson, his one time companion in adversity. Here also was baptized Henry Addington, Speaker of the H. of C., and from 1801 to 1804 a Prime Minister on whom Canning conferred some unenviable fame:

'Pitt is to Addington
As London is to Paddington.'

There were several interesting marriages in the ch. In 1598 Sir Edwd. Coke (Chief Justice to James I and Charles I) m. the widow of Sir Christopher Hatton. She was the 'Lady of Bleeding Heart Yard' (see 'Ely Place') of the *Ingoldsby Legends*. Bacon had had designs upon her. In 1638 Hutchinson, Cromwell's colonel, m. the Lucy who was to write rather dull memoirs of her husband. In 1808 here Wm. Hazlitt m. Sarah Stoddart. Chas. Lamb was best man, and his sister Mary a bridesmaid. Lamb said he was—

'like to have been turned out several times during the ceremony. Anything awful makes me laugh. I misbehaved once at a funeral. Yet I can read about these ceremonies with pious and proper

feelings. The realities of life only seem the mockeries.'

Of burials several are of interest. It is said that John Webster, author of some of the most macabre Elizabethan tragedies (*The White Devil, Duchess of Malfi,* etc.), was bd. here. Nathaniel Tompkins certainly was. He was brother-in-law of Edmund Waller, and in 1643 was hanged for his complicity in Waller's plot against Parliament. In 1690 Haak, a Dutchman who translated much of *Paradise Lost* into his native tongue, was bd. here. In 1720 the interment is recorded of John Hughes, author of *The Siege of Damascus,* one of the best of the minor poets of the period of Q. Anne. Another entry (1770) records the burial of Thos. Chatterton, to whom Wordsworth referred as:

'The marvellous boy
The sleepless soul, that perished in his pride.'

He took his own life in his eighteenth yr., and was interred in the pauper ground in Shoe Lane. Its site is now covered by Farringdon Avenue. The 'Resurrection Stone' on the outside of the N. wall of St. Andrew's Ch. was originally over the entrance to that burial ground. In the chyd. Chas. Lamb's mother was bd. in 1796 his aunt Hetty (really Sarah) in 1797; and his father in 1798. Perhaps the most interesting entry in the registers is this:

'Baptized July 31, 1817 Benjamin said to be about twelve years old, son of Isaac and Maria Disraeli, King's Road. Gentleman. A clergy-man named Thimbleby performed the ceremony,' King's Rd. was the eastern part of what is now Theobalds Rd. There was in this ch. a memorial tablet to Dr. Marsden (see 'Hospitals').

The ch. was almost entirely destroyed in 1941 but has been reconstructed, and was re-opened in 1961.

The chyd. was once much more extensive, and in 1754 a new burial ground was opened in Gray's Inn Rd., now known as St. Andrew's Gardens. The ch. is much below the level of the roadway by reason of the construction of Holborn Viaduct (*q.v.*). Before then it was on Holborn, sometimes called 'Heavy Hill.'

St. Andrew Undershaft, Leadenhall St.

(entrance from St. Mary Axe.) The earliest reference to the ch. is in the 12th century, when it appears as 'St. Andre v ad Sanctam Trinitatem.' In 1268 it was 'St. Andrew juxta Alegate'—our Aldgate. In 1482 it was 'St. Andrew atte Shafte upon Cornhull.' A considerable portion of the ch. was rebuilt by Stephen Jennings, Ld.M. in 1508. He d. in 1523, but Wm. Fitzwilliams, who had been sheriff in 1506, continued the work and it was finally completed in 1532. The origin of the name 'Undershaft' has generally been accepted (Harben dissenting) as a long shaft or maypole higher than the ch. steeple, which was set up in the middle of Leadenhall St. in the 15th century before the S. door of the ch. every May Day until 1517. 'Evil May Day,' as it came to be called, because of the rising of the L. apprentices, led to the shaft being left recumbent beneath the eaves of a row of thatched cottages in Shaft Alley, when the curate of St. Katharine Cree Ch., Sir Stephen, preached against it at St. Paul's Cross as an idol. The result was that the parishioners took the pole off the hooks, sawed it up, and burnt it piecemeal. Nothing is known of the ch. preceding the present one, except that it was built in the early part of the 14th century. In 1561 the par. was united with the ch. of St. Mary the Virgin, St. Ursula, and the Eleven Thousand Virgins, commonly known as St. Mary Axe (*q.v.*).

This was John Stow's ch., and he referred to it as 'the fair and beautiful parish church of Saint Andrew the Apostle.' A beautiful late Perpendicular Gothic bdg., lofty and light, it deserved his praise. The roof of the nave is nearly flat, but slightly covered at the sides, and has transverse beams resting on corbels, on two of which the date is 1532. There are N. and S. aisles, and the aisles are divided from the nave by five clustered columns on each side, with pointed arches. There is a clerestory with six windows on each side, divided by mullions. Between these windows was formerly a series of paintings, representing the twelve apostles, and in the spandrels, formed by the arches, were painted various incidents illustrating sacred history. All these were executed in 1726 at the cost of Henry Tombes, an inhabitant of the par. Nicholas Leveson presented the NE. window of the N. aisle in 1532. He d. in 1539,

and was bd. in a tomb placed before the upper pillar of the N. side of the ch., between the high altar and the altar of the N. aisle. This N. aisle also had a screen; in the 18th century Mr. Geo. Mason gave £20 towards it. Some glass in the W. window was formerly in the E. window. No doubt the change was made because it was felt preferable to have more sacred subjects over the altar. It was the gift of Sir Christopher Clitherow, Ld.M. 1637. He was bd. in the ch. in 1642. In the upper part are portraits of Edward VI, Elizabeth, James I, Charles I, William III. Under Edward VI is an open book inscribed 'Verbum Dei,' and the royal arms. The fifth figure has been wrongly named Charles II. The E. window was presented by the Rev. Prebendary Blomfield, the rector, at the renovation of the ch. in 1875-6. The subjects are the Crucifixion and Ascension. The Royal Commission on Historical Monuments (1930), referring to heraldic glass, said: 'It is considered that perhaps the largest amount of pre-Reformation material (*c.* 1530) is in St. Andrew Undershaft.' The windows contain glass of the 16th century, 17th century, 19th century, and 20th century, including the arms of several of the City livery cos. The font (at the W. end) was the work of Nicholas Stone, master-mason to James I and Charles I. Stone's account book says it was 'to be of whit marbell 20 inches deameter and to stand on a piller of blak marbel fairly wrort and poleshed.' His note-book shows he received £15 for the work that can now be seen. There are two sword-rests. The one at the W. end formerly belonged to All Hallows Staining (*q.v.*).

There is a remarkable number of monuments in St. Andrew Undershaft Ch. The most imposing and the most important is to John Stow. It was provided by his widow and is of Derbyshire marble and alabaster. The following is a translation of the inscription:

'Acts worthy to be recorded or writings worthy to be read

'Sacred to the memory of John Stowe, a citizen of London who here awaits resurrection in Christ. He exercised the most careful accuracy in searching ancient monuments, English annals, and records of the City of London. He wrote excellently and deserved well both of his own and subsequent ages. The contest of a good and honest life being completed, he died in the year of our Lord on the day 5th April 1605. His sorrowing wife Elizabeth erects this as a perpetual witness of her love.'

Stow is represented by a well-carved figure, showing him old, bald-headed, and writing in a book, with other books about him. Annually, on a date near to the anniversary of Stow's death, under the auspices of the London and Middlesex Archæological Soc., a memorial service is held. It is attended by the Ld.M. and Sheriffs. After the service, which includes an address, a new quill pen is placed in the hand of the effigy by the Ld.M., and he awards a prize—a copy of Stow's great work—for the best essay on L. The discarded quill pen is placed in a case and presented to the headmaster or headmistress. According to Maitland, Stow's body does not lie there, the corpse having been removed in 1732 to make way for another. The monument was carefully restored by the Merchant Taylors Co. in 1905. A quaint and a beautiful monument is Sir Thos. Offley's. He was Ld.M. in 1556, and is shown with his wife and three sons. His wife, to whom he was m. fifty-two yrs., d. 1578, and he followed in 1582. Over the tomb are the lines:

'By me a lykelihood beholde
How mortal man shall torn to mold,
When all his pompe and glori vayne
Shal chaynge to dust and earth agayne;
Such is his great incertaintye,
A flower and type of vanitye.'

There is a monument to Alice Byng. She is represented with a large ruff round her neck in prayer at a desk. She d. in 1616, having had three husbands, 'all batchellers and stacioners.' There is a ponderous monument to Sir Hugh Hammersley (d. 1636). He was Ld.M. 1627, and was President of Christ's Hosp., and also President of the Artillery Gardens. He is shown in armour with his wife kneeling behind, and two mourning soldiers. There is a tablet to Sir Christopher Clitherow (d. 1642). He was Ld.M. 1635, and afterwards Governor of the E. India Co., and President of Christ's Hosp. There is a large mural monument to the Datchelor family, with a cherub weeping at either side. Mary (d. 1725) was a liberal benefactor to the par., and

in 1863 the trustees of her estate gave a portion for the foundation of a middle class sch. for girls, for which purpose they purchased for £4,500 a piece of land in Camberwell. There is a tomb to Mary Datchelor and her two sisters outside the ch. The memorial stone reads:

'Beneath is the original stone of Mary Datchelor, whose munificent gift to this parish founded the Mary Datchelor girls' school at Camberwell. "Let her own works praise her."—Prov. xxxi, 31.'

A monument concealed by the organ is Wm. Vansittart's. He was brother of Peter Vansittart, a director of the E. India Co., who named one of their ships after him. The latter's monument, adorned with cherubs and skulls, is on the S. wall. There is a plain monument to Elizabeth Manning, who d. 1780. She was the grandmother of the cardinal. There is a number of brasses. The two most notable are Nicholas Levison's and Simon Burton's. Levison was a sheriff and a distinguished member of the Mercers' Co. He and his wife are shown with his eight sons and ten daughters. Burton's brass Stow described as 'a faire gilded plate in the wall.' It shows his two wives and one son and three daughters. He was a Common Councillor and a Governor of St. Thomas's Hosp. He d. 1593 at the age of 85. On the S. wall is a brass tablet in memory of Hans Holbein, who is believed to have resided in the par. Amongst burials of note with no monument were Sir Robt. Dennie and Thos. Dennie, his son, in 1421, and Philip Malpas, sheriff 1439. This man's will showed remarkable generosity. He gave £125 to poor prisoners; to other poor, every yr. for five yrs., 400 shirts and shifts, 150 gowns and 40 pairs of sheets; to poor maids' marriages 100 marks; to the repair of the highways, 100 marks; to 500 poor people in L., 6s. 8d. each.

In 1930 the ch. was restored. The 125 carved and gilt oak bosses were then brought to light. They show the Paschal Lamb surrounded by arms of St. George, St. Andrew, the Diocese of London and the City. The paintings in the spandrels of the clerestory were restored at the same time and again in 1956. Some hammered iron communion rails, which were discarded in 1876 when also the fine Norway oak panelling was removed, were rescued from the heating chamber and reinstated. They probably date from 1704, and may have been the work of Jean Tijou, who did the gates of St. P.'s Cath. From among the old gravestones in the chyd. were rescued portions of a richly traceried wall tomb in Liege marble of the early part of the 16th century, with indents of some of the brasses on the upright slab at the back. There is a sanctuary knocker on the door.

St. Andrew by the Wardrobe (Q. Victoria St.). For the second part of its name see 'Wardrobe.' By reason of its proximity to the first Baynard's Castle (*q.v.*) the first reference to this ch. is Sci, andree de Castello' *c.* 1244. It is 'St. Andrew near Castle Baynard' in 1344. 'St. Andrew in le Wardroppe' in 1585-7. In 1213 the castle fell into the hands of the Fitzwalters, and with it also a certain area of land and houses around it. It is probable that the ch. was founded at this period; at any rate about 1303 it was a rectory, of which Robt. Fitzwalter was the patron. Later it was vested in the Crown, and afterwards in the Mercers' Co. The first ch. was burnt in the G.F.

Wren rebuilt the ch., completing it in 1692. It had two side aisles, divided from the nave by square pillars encased in wood to the height of the galleries. The walls were wainscoted to the height of 7½ ft.

A celebrated rector was Rev. Wm. Romaine, and there was a monument to him oddly showing a figure of faith pointing to a telescope; it was the work of Bacon. The inscription said he was 'for 30 years Rector of these united parishes.' The second par. was St. Anne, Blackfriars, the ch. was not rebuilt after the G.F. Romaine's evangelical zeal was copiously eulogized in the epitaph, but it was not to the taste of the church-wardens of St. Dunstan's-in-the-West, where he held a lectureship. At one time they would not open the ch. till the exact moment for beginning the service arrived, and then they refused to light it. Romaine then preached by the light of a candle, which he held in his hand. On another occasion the rector of St. Dunstan's sat in the pulpit so that Romaine had no room. However, the Bp. of L. happened one day to see the crowd outside the closed door, made inquiries as to the reason, and appointed him to the rectory of St. Andrew's. The galleries were erected in 1774, probably to accommo-

date the large congregations he attracted. The Rev. W. Goode, M.A., succeeded Romaine. In 1799 he established a soup house in Blackfriars, which was the origin of the Association for the Relief of the Poor of the City of London, and in 1809 he formed a Sunday sch. in the par., probably the first opened in the City. He d. in 1816. His monument showed an angel seated on a sarcophagus and grasping a testament, and was by Bacon the younger. The Rev. Isaac Saunders's, like Romaine's, had a bust. He succeeded Rev. W. Goode, and d. in 1836.

The Parish Clerks' Co. and the Apothecaries' Co. attended annual services here. In the N. wall was a stained-glass window representing St. Luke, the latter co.'s patron saint. It was presented by them in 1905. On the S. wall was a tablet in memory of Henry Hennel, who was killed by an explosion at the hall of the Apothecaries' Co. (see 'Companies A') in 1842.

The construction of Q. Victoria St. in 1871 placed the ch. in the prominent position it now occupies. Prior to that the entrance was on the N. side—from St. Andrew's Hill.

The ch. was almost entirely destroyed but has been rebuilt and re-opened.

St. Anne and St. Agnes (Gresham St.). The joint dedication is comparatively recent. (St. Anne is the mother of the Virgin; St. Agnes, a virgin martyr, who suffered about A.D. 304.) St. Anne's Ch. is said to have been attached to St. Martin's le Grand in the 11th century. It is mentioned in 1275 as 'St. Anne de Aldredesgate,' and in 1306 as 'St. Anne near Aldrichesgate' sometimes as 'St. Anne in the Willowes.' The adjacent ch. of St. John Zachary (the burial-ground of which remains on the N. side of Gresham St.) was not rebuilt after the G.F., and the two pars. were then united. Whilst the new ch. was in process of erection the parishioners carried on services in a shed among the ruins.

It was rebuilt by Wren in 1681, and was only 53 ft. square. The E. window had some good stained glass and there was a highly gilded altar piece. The ch. was badly damaged but has been restored and re-opened.

St. Bartholomew the Great (Smithfield). At the W. end of this ch. there is now a series of frescoes depicting the story of its foundation. Documentary evidence for the occurrences illustrated is in an account, interwoven with the life and miracles of, Rahere, the founder, written in Latin by one of the canons soon after that monk's death (1144). An illuminated copy, made at the end of the 14th century, is preserved amongst the Cottonian MSS. at the B.Mus.

Rahere was one of Henry I's courtiers. A man of humble origin, he won favour by the suavity of his manners, his witty conversation, musical ability, and flattering tongue. The manuscript says that

'when he attained the flower of youth, he began to haunt the households of noblemen and the palaces of princes where under every elbow of them he spread their cushions, with apings and flatterings delectably anointing their eyes, to draw him to their friendships.'

In 1120 a change was wrought in the K.'s character by the loss of his only legitimate son in the *White Ship*, on its voyage from Normandy to England, after which, it was said, he 'never smiled again.' An air of austerity thus replaced the atmosphere of frivolity; and thus, moved in spirit, and by a desire for adventure, Rahere started on a pilgrimage to Rome to do penance for his sins on the ground hallowed by the martyrdom of St. Paul, some three miles from the city. In a particularly unhealthy spot known as 'The Three Fountains,' he was attacked by malarial fever. In his distress he made a vow that if he were spared he would establish a hosp. for the poor as a thank-offering on his return to England. His prayer was granted, but recovery was retarded. During convalescence he had a vision wherein he saw a winged monster seizing him in its claws and about to drop him into a bottomless pit. A majestic form came to his rescue and revealed himself as St. Bartholomew. The saint declared that 'the will and command-ment of the Holy Trinity' was that a ch. should be founded in 'Smoothfield'—our Smithfield. Rahere promised compliance, and, as soon as he got back to L., first obtained the K.'s consent, and then:

'nothing omitting of care and dili-gence, two works of piety began, one for the vow that he had made, the other as to him by precept enjoined.'

Smoothfield was partly covered by water, the one dry spot—known as 'The Elms'—being reserved for public exe-cutions. The eastern portion of this waste land was granted by Henry I through the agency of Richd. de Belmeis, Bp. of L., and here in 1123 Rahere began building. He is said to have been assisted by Alfune (see 'St. Giles, Cripplegate').

On the south side rose the priory bdgs., and Rahere, having devoted himself to the monastic life, became the first prior. There were with him the sub-prior and twelve subordinates, all living under the Rule of the Canons Regular of St. Augus-tine. In 1133 a charter of privileges was granted by Henry I to the prior and canons. It ordained, *inter alia*, that

'they be free of all earthly servitude and all earthly power and subjection . . . and that as any church of all England is free, so this church be free, and all lands to it appertaining which it now has, or which Rahere the Prior, or the Canons, may be able reasonably to acquire, whether by purchase or by gift.'

It is probable that on Rahere's death in 1143 the choir had been completed, so that, save for the reinstated clerestory, the visitor to St. Bartholomew's sees it as he saw it. His tomb, as founder, is in the usual place—on the N. side of the sanctuary. A recumbent effigy represents him clad in the black habit of the Augustinian canons, the tonsured head rests upon a tasselled cushion, and the hands are in the attitude of prayer. At the feet is an angel with crowned head, and in its hands is the escutcheon of the priory. On each side of the figure is a monk of Rahere's own Order reading from a book. From the Latin discernible thereon ('Consolabitur' &c.) it is evident that the passage is Isaiah li 3:

'For the Lord shall comfort Zion: he will comfort all her waste places; and he will make her wilderness like Eden, and her desert like the garden of the Lord.'

This was chosen, no doubt, in allusion to the transformation effected in Smith-field by Rahere's enterprise. This group occupies an elaborately carved taber-nacle with a vaulted ceiling. Behind this runs the ambulatory, and pilgrims on that side would make their offerings through the small unglazed windows.

The design is continued in a fourth panel. Originally there were two other panels beyond this, similarly arcaded, and carried over the face of the adjacent Norman arch, which had a doorway beneath it leading into the ambulatory. The canopy and the quatrefoil panels date from 1405, the arms are considerably later. From left to right they are: (i) the City of L.; (ii) the Priory; (iii) England and France; (iv) Sir Stephen Slaney, Ld.M. in 1595. Rahere was succeeded by Thos. of St. Osyth, who increased the number of the canons to thirty-five. He erected the transepts and the easternmost bays of the nave in the Early English style. The latter style is still represented by the surviving western gateway, and the mutilated columns which remain at the western end of the ch. 'Infinity made imaginable' was the suggestive phrase of Coleridge about Gothic architecture. In St. Bartholomew's Ch. we get strength and solidity made impressionable. Matthew Paris relates an incident eloquent of the age of violence which the massive structure typifies. In 1250 Boniface, Abp. of C. (uncle of Henry III's Q., Eleanor), decided to include the ch. and priory in a general visitation. This was resented by the canons as being outside his jurisdiction, and the sub-prior manifested his disapproval. Boniface then rushed upon him, slapped his face, tore his cope to fragments, and trampled it underfoot, and, finally, being himself in full armour, finished by pressing him against a pillar so violently as almost to kill him. There ensued a skirmish between the canons and the archbishop's train, and as the inhabitants of Smithfield rallied to the former, Boniface was forced to fly whilst he was execrated as cruel, unlearned, a ruffian, a stranger, and as possessing a wife. The latter imputation, at a time when sacerdotal celibacy was imposed (though not infrequently evaded), was, of course, the 'unkindest cut of all.'

Perpendicular Gothic was introduced early in the 15th century, when Roger de Walden, Bp. of L. (1405–6), built a chantry chapel to the NE. of the choir, and inserted a new clerestory in the style then prevailing. He also substituted a square E. end for the semicircular apse. His work was interrupted by death, and he was bd. in his chapel instead of with his episcopal predecessors in St. P.'s Cath., as had been the custom. The Lady Chapel, with crypt, dates from about 1410. Further work was carried

on at this time, for Pope Alexander V, in a grant of indulgences to those who visited and gave alms to the ch. on certain holy days, mentioned the reconstruction of the chapter house and cloisters among the reasons which had induced the privilege. At this time there was a central tower which apparently dated from the 12th century. Prior Bolton (1505–32) inserted an oriel window on the S. side of the choir triforium, as well as a doorway in the S. ambulatory. Both of these bear his sculptured rebus, a bolt or arrow driven through a tun or barrel. In 1539 his successor, Robt. Fuller, the last of the Augustinian priors, surrendered the entire property to Henry VIII in accordance with the Act of Dissolution. Its value had been ascertained some four yrs. before, and the exact figures given by Dugdale are £693 9s. 10½d. The hosp. survived, but the whole of the monastic bdgs. were doomed. The nave was at once demolished, and only the choir preserved for the use of the par. With this reservation, the site of the priory and the bdgs. upon it, including the Lady Chapel, were sold in 1546 to Sir Richd. Rich (Attorney-General) for £1,064 11s. 3d., and the property remained in the hands of his descendants for over 300 yrs. There was, however, a brief interruption during Q. Mary's reign. In 1556 she lodged the Black Friars in the convent, and the reconstruction of the nave, which they began, would have proceeded to completion if the accession of Elizabeth had not involved a reversion to the old policy, and the restitution of the priory estate to Rich. During the reign of that Q. the ch. fell into a very dilapidated state, and there was a possibility of its being totally destroyed. In 1563, Grindal, Bp. of L., wrote to Sir Wm. Cecil, proposing to take the lead from the roof, and transfer it to that of the 'Mother Churche of Powles.' Ld. Rich—as he had then become—at first favoured the proposal, but apparently scruples arose in some quarter about the threatened vandalism, for Grindal wrote again thus:

> 'For S. Bartholomew's—I meane not to pull it downe, but to change it for a churche more conveniente . . . unlesse some strange opinion shulde arise that prayer were more acceptable under leade than under sclate.'

The Quaker-like simplicity of Grindal's

concluding remark sounds disingenuous. It was a plausible puritan excuse for a parsimonious person.

Documentary history of St. Bartholomew's offers nothing worthy of record for a long time after. In 1628 the ugly brick tower was erected. In 1697 Wm. Hogarth was baptized in the early 15th-century font, which stands in the S. transept. In 1747 John Wesley preached here.

'It was with much difficulty that I got in, not only to the church itself but all the entrances to it, being so thronged with people ready to tread upon one another.'

In 1789 the ch. was 'restored' by Geo. Dance, who was architect to the hosp. In 1809 two letters in the *Gentleman's Magazine* revealed the deplorable state of the bdg. The Lady Chapel still existed, but was filled up with modern tenements; the N. transept was more or less destroyed; and the S. transept—a roofless ruin—was walled off from the ch., and used as a burial-ground. The E. side of the cloister was all that remained of the quadrangle, and here was a comfortable 'eight stall stable.' The side of the N. cloister was occupied with 'a forge, a public house and certain private offices,' the S. and W. being covered with 'store-rooms and coach-houses.' Of the chapter house the remaining walls were 'no higher than a dado,' and under them the timber was stored after treatment in the sawpit of the enclosure. The dormitory to the S. of the chapter house had been demolished. A bdg. against the S. wall of the choir (probably the sacristy, though called a 'chapel'), which was a magnificent structure about the time of Edward III, was being used as a store-room for hops. The level of the ch. floor was raised by a thick deposit of earth, the walls were enveloped in whitewash concealing the ancient mural paintings and some delicate sculptured ornament. High pews had been erected. The openings of the triforium were bricked up, and above the altar-piece, contemptuously described as 'a painted theatrical scene of architecture,' was a brick wall pierced with two ugly round-headed windows filled with square panes of glass, and destitute of mullions and tracery. The space between the termination thus formed and the original apse went by the name of 'Purgatory,' as a receptacle for human bones,

some thousands of which were found to have accumulated when it was cleared out in 1836.

It is impossible to determine when the secular uses of the ch. commenced. In the 18th century there was a Nonconformist sch. in the triforium. This was connected with a chapel immediately outside, there being convenient access from its own galleries. There was also from 1833 a fringe factory which covered the remains of the crypt and Lady Chapel, and extended westward along the triforium, so as to include Prior Bolton's window. In 1830 the chapter house (which was S. of the S. transept with a slype between) was destroyed by fire. The dormitory extended still further S. from this. Its undercroft remained until about 1870. The real restoration was begun in 1863 by the rector, Rev. John Abbiss, who raised something like £5,000, and spent it in reducing the floor to its original level, removing the pews, repairing the walls and piers, and rebuilding the central part of the apse.

Three yrs. later there commenced the collection of a further sum of over £28,000, the chief individual contributor being the patron of the living, the Rev. F. P. Phillips, who at his own cost purchased the fringe factory for £6,500, and completed the restoration of the apse. At the same time the ch. was provided with a new roof, and the blacksmith's forge, which then occupied the site of the N. transept, was bought out. As a consequence a fine arcaded stone screen came to light. It was found bd. some 4 ft. in the earth, but the smithy's presence would have concealed it largely from view. It was of 15th-century date, and probably there was once another to match on the opposite side of the choir. In 1886 the restored portions were formally opened, the work having taken over two yrs. Between 1887 and 1893, under the Rev. Sir J. Borradaile Savory, who was then rector, the transepts were restored, both sides of the choir triforium opened out, while the W. front was refaced, the brick tower repaired, and the N. and W. porches erected. The N. porch, in Cloth Fair (1893), has over the doorway a figure of St. Bartholomew. He is raising his right hand in benediction, and in his left is a knife, the emblem of his 'passion.' A scroll entwined about the effigy bears the appropriate words from Rahere's vision: 'Almighty God this spiritual house shall inhabit and hallow.' In a niche above the arch of the W. front is a figure of Rahere, and in his right hand is a model of the ch. The design is taken from one of the ancient seals, and shows the central tower with a round turret at each end, and a small bdg. (probably the original Lady Chapel) projecting from the E. Rahere's features are copied from the effigy on his tomb.

In the early part of the 18th century the Lady Chapel was in use by a printer, in whose employment, in 1724, was Benjamin Franklin. In 1885 it was reclaimed by the clergy from the fringe manufacturers and restoration was completed in 1896. It is separated from the ambulatory by an elegant screen of ironwork, surmounted by a crucifix of metal which, though originally white has assumed the hue of the screen so as to be with difficulty distinguished in the dim light. As to the chapel, though every care was taken to preserve the older work in conformity with the general design, much is necessarily new. Its windows on the S. are entirely new, but the sills and jambs on the N. show a retention of 15th-century work. The sedilia were used by the fringe merchant for his safe! The crypt beneath is said once to have been used as a charnel-house for the dead exhumed periodically from the adjacent canons' cemetery. Passing into civil hands at the Dissolution, part of it was used as a coal-cellar and wine vaults by Rich, while subsequently the space was found convenient for the fringe factory. It is now equipped as a mortuary chapel. The archaic character is still represented in its walls, piers, and windows, the vaulting alone being new.

The cloisters were also profaned, and in 1742 there is a record of their use for stabling. The stables were later rebuilt and long left undisturbed. In 1900 negotiations were opened for the purchase of the freehold. In 1904 possession was obtained of three of the bays. In 1917, when some old houses were demolished in Cloth Fair, parts of the ancient fabric came to light. They consisted of the major arch of the groined arcade, the 12th-century arch of the triforium, the arch of the 13th-century aisle and the 13th-century clerestory window. In 1923, a Norman capital, a relic of the N. transept,

was unearthed on the N. side of Cloth Fair. In the same yr. possession of five more bays of the cloister was obtained, and restoration was carried out. Much of the vaulting had been destroyed in the fire of 1830. The restored bays were ceremonially opened by the Princess Mary in 1928 (the ninth bay had been destroyed). The cloisters are now used as a mus. Here is a fragment of Rahere's coffin, and also his sandal. Subsequent to the opening of the coffin in 1865 a pew opener confessed, when in a state of spiritual distress occasioned by illness, to having stolen the sandal. The doors leading to the cloister—fixed in a round-headed Norman arch—were found stowed among lumber. At the Dissolution they were removed, and were the western doors of the ch. for 350 yrs., after which they were returned to their original position.

The half-timber front facing Smithfield, dates from 1595. In the 18th century it was covered with facing tiles, made to resemble brick. A bomb from an air-raid in 1916 removed the tiles, exposing the timber beneath. The front was then restored to its original condition, with the addition of windows, including a dormer. In a niche was placed a statue of St. Bartholomew, in memory of a son of Sir Aston Webb, who was killed in the War. In 1930 the gate-house was officially condemned, and it was restored in 1932. There is a tablet recording that this was undertaken in memory of

'the two Brothers, Sir Aston Webb, R.A., and Ed. Alfred Webb, F.S.A., also of Frederick L. Dove, D.L., F.S.A., who worked together on the restoration of the fabric of the church for over 40 years.'

At the same time the beautifully wrought-iron gateway was constructed for the entrance to the chyd. It was designed by the firm of Sir Aston Webb & Son, and cost £500. It bears the arms of Rahere, as well as of the priory, and the emblem of St. Bartholomew. The archway through which there is access to Smithfield, is probably of 13th-century date. It may mark the western extremity of the nave of the medieval ch., of which the bases of pillars remain on the N. side of the chyd.

The ch. escaped the Blitz, except for slight damage by a flying bomb. A site has been prepared behind the altar for a shrine of Knights Bachelor.

St. Bartholomew the Less (St. Bartholomew's Hosp.). First mentioned *c.* 1150, this was originally the ch. of the hosp., which is a par. in itself. Stow mentions many monuments and brasses of the 15th and succeeding centuries. Some still exist. Amongst those that have vanished were two brass effigies 'in the habit of pilgrims,' with an inscription commencing:

'Behold how ended is
the poor old pilgrimage
of John Shirley Esquire
with Margaret his wife,'

and ending with the date 1456. Shirley was a traveller in various countries. He collected the works of Chaucer, Lydgate, and other learned writers,

'which works he wrote in sundry volumes to remain for posterity. I have seen them,' says Stow, 'and partly do possess them.'

Inigo Jones was baptized here 1573.

The ch. became dilapidated towards the end of the 18th century, and it was entirely remodelled on an octagonal plan by Geo. Dance the younger in 1789. Dance's work, being of timber, soon decayed, and in 1823 the ch. was practically rebuilt by Thos. Hardwick, who adhered to Dance's plan, but substituted stone and iron for timber. The ch. is now an octagon with almost square surrounding walls, and above the latter is a clerestory pierced with windows. Only the vestibule beneath the tower shows traces of the old work. The E. window had stained glass, presenting, in the upper part, figures of St. Bartholomew, Lazarus, and the four evangelists, and above and below the arms of Henry VIII, the hosp., and of some treasurers. It disappeared during the Second World War. On the pavement at the W. end are monumental brass figures of a man and woman, with this inscription beneath:

'Hic jacent Will'mo Markeby de Londoniis gentlemo'qui obiit xi die Julii A D'ni MCCCXXXIX et Alicia uxor ei . . .'

The remainder of the inscription, namely, 'Quorum animabus propitietur Deus, Amen' (May God be propitiated for their souls), has been deleted, by a Protestant, possibly by one who was also a puritan. There is a tablet in memory of the wife of Thos. Bodley, the founder of the Bodleian Lib. at Oxford. Below is a curious old stone, the inscription on which commences: 'Ecce sub hoc tumulo Gulielmus conditur.' Another large monument presents a kneeling figure beneath an entablature supported on two columns, and inscribed to Robt. Balthrope:

'Who Sergeant of the Surgeons sworn
Near thirty years had been.
He dyed at sixty nine of years,
December's ninth the day;
The year of grace eight hundred twice
Deducting nine away.'

There is a gothic tablet to Henry Earle, F.R.S., surgeon to St. Bartholomew's Hosp., which was erected in 1838 by his five junior pupils. In the lobby are two pieces of sculpture that belonged to the old ch.: a niche containing the figure of an angel bearing a shield, and beneath it the arms of Edward the Confessor, impaled with those of England; and a small figure, apparently of early workmanship. There is also here a canopied altar tomb; new stained glass windows have replaced those damaged in the Blitz. In one there is a figure of Rahere. In 1838 the sexton, in a fit of despondency, hanged himself in the lobby.

St. Benet, Paul's Wharf (now St. Benet Guild Welsh Church) (Q. Victoria St.). The earliest reference is 'Sancti Benedicti super Tamisiam' in 1111. At the end of the 12th century it is 'St. Benedict by the Thames.' The old ch. contained monuments to Sir Wm. Cheyney, Chief Justice of the K.'s Bench (d. 1442); Dr. Richd. Caldwell, President Royal Coll. of Physicians (d. 1585); and Sir Gilbert Dethike, who was Garter K. of Arms when Q. Mary granted Derby House, the former residence of the Stanleys, to be the Coll. of Arms (*q.v.*). The most illustrious of those bd. here was Inigo Jones. In accordance with his instructions the body was interred beneath the chancel close to the grave of his parents. A monument of white marble, for which he had assigned £100, was erected by his executor. It stood against the N. wall, showed in bas-relief the porticoes of St. P.'s Cath. and St. Paul's Covent Garden, and bore a Latin inscription recording that he was the K.'s architect, that he built the Banqueting House at Whitehall, and restored St. P.'s Cath. In the present ch. on the E. wall is a small tablet (near his grave) placed there in 1878 by a descendant, recording the original inscription. This would have pleased Peter Cunningham, who, in his *Life of Inigo Jones* said he 'could wish that Wren, in rebuilding the church, had rebuilt the monument.' In 1587 a Mr. David Smith was bd. in the old ch. The inscription to his memory said that he was 'an Imbroyderer to Queen Elizabeth,' and that in 1584 he built six tenements near the ch. for six poor widows under the care of Christ's Hosp. A tablet commemorating the bequest was until the Blitz on Lambeth Hill, built into the wall of premises belonging to the Salvation Army. Strype mentions a tablet in the ch. which represented a pre-Fire monument, upon which was mentioned a wife with the singular, and possibly justifiable, name of 'Obedience'!

The ch. is probably the one referred to in *Twelfth Night*, doubtless performed at the adjacent Blackfriars Theatre. 'The bells of St. Benet's, sir, may put you in mind,' says the Clown.

This ch. was burnt in the G.F., and rebuilt by Wren in 1683. It is built of red brick, relieved by stone quoins, and by stone festoons over the windows. Internally it has one aisle on the N. side, which is separated from the nave by two Corinthian columns. The walls are wainscoted to the height of 8 ft. The altar-piece is of oak, and is surmounted by a circular pediment of inlaid woods. Over the doorway at the NW. are the royal arms. The sounding-board of the pulpit is a ceiling in the base of the tower. There are a well-carved pulpit and font.

In this ch. Elias Ashmole, the antiquary, was m. to his first wife in 1638. In 1724 Mrs. Manley, the author of *The New Atlantis*, was bd. at St. Benet's. Here in 1747 Henry Fielding m. his second wife. It was, said Austin Dobson, 'like Mary-le-bone old church, much in request for unions of a private character.' The second Mrs. Fielding was the maid of the first, and she was described as 'of St. Clement's Danes, Middlesex, Spinster.' Wm. Oldys, 'Norroy,' the learned author of the *British Librarian* and the *Life of Raleigh*, was bd. here in 1761. The proximity of the ch. to the Coll. of Arms and Doctors' Commons explains the number

of burials of heralds and similar dignitaries. There is (N. of the reredos) a tablet, with a long inscription, commemorating John Chas. Brook,

'Somerset Herald, Secretary to the Earl Marshal of England and Fellow of the Society of Antiquaries.'

Later on the reader is told that:

'He lived in a strict intimacy with Persons of the highest Rank and of the first literary character without the smallest tincture of vanity.'

The moral comes appropriately at the end:

'Let us, instead of envying the possession, reflect on the awful uncertainty of these sublunary blessings for Alas he was in a moment bereaved of them in the dreadful calamity which happened at the Theatre in the Haymarket on the Third of February 1794 in the forty sixth year of his age.' (See 'Theatres.')

An imposing monument is Dr. Robt. Wyseman's (*temp.* Charles II). There is a monument in the gallery to the wife of the Rt. Hon. Sir Christopher Robinson, a member of the Privy Council, and an Admiralty judge, who d. 1830.

In 1879 the par. was united with St. Nicholas, Cole Abbey, and the ch. given over to the use of the Welsh Episcopalians, who formerly had the chapel of St. Etheldreda (*q.v.*). There are now two services each Sunday in the Welsh tongue.

St. Botolph, Aldersgate (Aldersgate St.), is first mentioned as 'St. Botulph without Aldredesgate,' and was in existence by 1260. Anciently it belonged to the dean and canons of St. Martin's le Grand, but in 1398 Richard II gave licence to the dean to unite and appropriate it to the Royal Chapel of St. Martin, reserving certain annual pensions for the Bp. of L. and others, and St. Botolph's was afterwards served by a curate. The patronage passed to the abbot and convent of Westminster in the reign of Henry VII, and their successors, the dean and chapter, now appoint the vicar.

Stow mentions that in 1377 was founded at the ch. a Brotherhood of St. Fabian and St. Sebastian, and another Brotherhood in honour of the Trinity in 1446. He also mentions a number of burials, including W. Marrow, a grocer, Ld.M. in 1455, and 'Katheren his wife,' also:

'Lady Anne Packinton, widow, late

wife to Jo. Packinton, knight, Chiro-grapher of the court of the common pleas: she founded Almes houses near unto the white Fryers church in Fleet-street.'

Her monument still remains. There is a brass in memory of John Brand (d. 1611). There is also a monument, with bust, to Elizabeth, daughter of Sir Wm. Hewitt, of St. Martin's in the Fields, and wife of Sir Thos. Richardson, of Honingham, in Norfolk, who d. 1639. The tablet in memory of Johannes Costin has a row of three skulls. There are tablets to two 17th-century practitioners, Sir John Mickle-thwait and Dr. Francis Bernard. The former was president of the Royal Coll. of Physicians, and d. 1683. The latter was ridiculed by Garth in *The Dispensary*, under the name of 'Horoscope.' An ornamental tablet commemorates Richd. Chiswell, a principal bookseller of his time, who was b. in the par., and became a benefactor to it. He d. in 1711. A white marble cameo bust of Elizabeth Smith, who d. in 1750 at the age of 15, was the work of Roubiliac. There is a tablet to the memory of Daniel Wray, who d. 1783, aged 82. He was for thirty-seven yrs. Deputy-Teller of the Exchequer, one of the original trustees of the B.Mus., part author of the *Athenian Letters*, and a particular friend of the poets Dyer and Akenside. His widow, who long survived him, is commemorated by a smaller tablet.

Zachariah Foxall's monument has also an interesting inscription, and another will appeal to Americans. It com-memorates 'Miss Cathe Mary Meade'—daughter of Geo. Meade, of Philadelphia who d. in 1791 at the age of 21. There are the following lines:

'Transferred from Pennsylvania's friendly coast
A father's blessing and a mother's boast,
On Albion's sea-girt shore, an early fate
Postponed each transport to a future state.
Death raised a barrier to each tender scene,
More fateful than the waves that roll between.'

The ch. was repaired in 1627, at which time a large portion of the steeple was rebuilt. It was but slightly damaged in the G.F., but, having become dilapidated, in 1790 it was pulled down and a new edifice erected at the cost of about £10,000. Externally it is perhaps the most unprepossessing of the City chs. Internally it is more attractive. It is divided into a nave and side-aisles by Corinthians columns. There are galleries on the N., S., and W. There is a large E. window. It shows angels ministering to Christ in the wilderness. The side-windows display figures of St. Peter and St. John. In 1950 St. Botolph's became a Guild Church; there is an after-care for prisoners centre at the church.

On the gateway of the chyd. is a tablet commemorating the conversion of John and Chas. Wesley in Aldersgate St. in 1738. This was when the former felt his heart 'strangely warmed.' A stained-glass window in City Rd. Chapel com-memorates the same incident. The garden inside is known as 'Postman's Park' by reason of its proximity to the G.P.O. It is made up of the chyds. of St. Botolph's, Christ Ch., Newgate, and St. Leonard's, Foster Lane, and an additional piece of land bought by subscription and opened by the Ld.M. and the Bp. of L. in 1900. It contains a statue of Sir Robert Peel and a loggia with seats and over these are more than fifty tablets commemorating heroes who lost their lives in endeavouring to save others. This fine conception was that of G. F. Watts, and it was to commemorate the Jubilee of Q. Victoria in 1887, although not until 1898 was the scheme inaugurated. Mr. Watts had files of newspapers searched to collect his examples, and about twenty-four were put up to begin with. In 1905 a statuette by the artist was unveiled by Sir Wm. Richmond. Mrs. Watts added a number after the death of her husband (1904), and in 1928 the last additions were made. These tablets, unveiled by Mr. Lees Smith, then Postmaster-General, were in memory of three metropolitan policemen and four employees of the East Ham Sewage Works who lost their lives trying to save comrades from asphyxiating gas. One of those commemorated is Alice Ayres. She d. (1885) from injuries received in rescuing her nephews and nieces from a fire in Union St., Borough.

St. Botolph, to whom this ch. is dedi-cated, was a Saxon renowned for piety. He built a large monastery near Boston in 654, and d. in 680. Boston is a cor-ruption of Botolph's town. He was the patron saint of travellers, and so chs.

dedicated to him are near city gates. There are also St. Botolph's, Aldgate, and St. Botolph's, Bishopsgate; St. Botolph's, Billingsgate, was not rebuilt after the G.F.

St. Botolph, Aldgate. The first reference is in 1125. It was included in a grant made in that yr. by the Knightenguild of their land to the prior and convent of Holy Trinity. The former consisted of burgesses who were descendants of thirteen knights who had land in the E. part of the City conferred upon them by K. Edgar, and were formed into a guild whose privileges were confirmed by Edward the Confessor, and subsequently by Wm. Rufus. The cure continued to be served by one of the canons till the priory was surrendered to Henry VIII in 1531. It was rebuilt by the prior just before this event. Not long after, in 1537, Ld. Darcy was bd. in the ch. He was beheaded on Tower Hill for his complicity in Catholic plots against Henry VIII. A yr. later the same fate overtook Sir Nicholas Carew for the same reason, and he was also bd. at St. Botolph's. Their monument, which stood in the chancel of the old ch., is in the W. gallery of the present one. Another interesting interment was made in this ch. This was Robt. Dowe, the charitable Merchant Taylor. His large monument with a sculptured and painted bust is now in the gallery; he wears a Geneva cap, and his hands rest upon a skull. He left £320 to Christ's Hosp., £20 p.a. to this par., and £50 to St. Sepulchre's Ch. (*q.v.*) for an interesting reason. On the S. wall there are two tablets from the old ch. One is inscribed to Robt. Tailor of Warton in Lancaster, 'a Drap (Draper) of London,' who d. 1577. The other is in memory of Sir Edwd. Darcy (d. 1612), third son of Arthur Darcy, Knight of the Privy Chamber to Q. Elizabeth. He was a grandson of Ld. Darcy.

The previous ch. escaped the G.F., but, having become very dilapidated, was pulled down. The present one was erected from the designs of the elder Dance, the architect of the Mansion House, and completed in 1744. It is built of brick, with stone dressings, and has a small spire surmounting the tower. The interior includes two side-aisles, separated from the central portion by Tuscan columns, and these support a flat ceiling. The altar, very unusually, is

placed at the N. The window over the altar, representing Rubens's 'Descent from the Cross,' is said to reproduce a similar window which used to be in St. Botolph's, Lincoln. The window to the W. of this is in memory of Sir John Cass; that to the E. of Sir John Gascoyne. The large windows are the work of Bentley, the architect of Westminster Cath. He also lowered the side galleries, put in light balustrades, and added plaster work to the ceiling and the undersides of the galleries, where the children of Sir John Cass's Sch. once sat. The chancel screen, as the tablet on the N. wall records, was the gift, in 1890, of Mrs. Rutson of Northallerton, in memory of her husband. There is a sword-rest for the Ld.M., and under it is a tablet (due to Sir Marcus Samuel, Ld.M. 1903) to Wm. Symington, an engineer, who constructed the *Charlotte Dundas*, the first steamboat that could be put to practical use. This was in 1802, and finding no support for his invention he d. in poverty (1831).

The ch. was badly shaken in the First World War, and one of the ball ornaments that was knocked by an air raid on to the roof is in the E. aisle. In the vestry is an excellent carving of a mother and babe, flanked by two older children. It was once on the shelves of the ch. of Holy Trinity, Minories (*q.v.*), where the dole of bread was placed. In a glass case, is the head found in the same ch., the two pars. having been united in 1909. The royal arms are outside the door. There is a small chyd., entered from Houndsditch. A tombstone against the wall of the ch. is in memory of Thos. Ebrall, a corn meter, who was 'shot by a lifeguardsman in April 1810 in the shop of Mr. Goodeve of Fenchurch Street.' There is a fountain (1903) of French manufacture, made in a thoroughfare named after Voltaire.

St. Botolph, Bishopsgate. The first reference is to 'Sc̄i Botulfi ex̄a Bissopeḡ,' 1212–13, but probably there was a ch. here long before the Norman Conquest, and Strype thought that the first might have been erected by Bp. Erkenwald. It was described by Stow as

'in a fair churchyard, adjoining to the town ditch, upon the very bank thereof, but of old time inclosed with a comely wall of brick, lately repaired by Sir William Allen, mayor in the year 1571, because he was born in that parish, where he also was buried.

Edwd. Alleyn (see 'Camberwell' and 'Southwark Cathedral') was baptized in 1566. Archibald Campbell, the seventh E. of Argyll, and father of the celebrated first marquis, was m. here in 1609 to his second wife, Anne, daughter of Sir Wm. Cornwallis. There were bd. here an infant son of Ben Jonson (1600); and (1623) Stephen Gosson, who had been rector for twenty-three yrs. (see 'Inns'). In 1650 Sir Paul Pindar was bd. His epitaph says that he was:

'His Majesties Ambassador to the Turkish Emperor Anno Dom. 1611, and Nine Years Resident. Faithful in Negotiation, Foreign and Domestick, Eminent for Piety, Charity, Loyalty, and Prudence.'

He lived to be 84. The façade of his house in Bishopsgate is in the V. & A. Mus.

In 1615, the burial-ground having become too small for their requirements, the City gave to the parishioners an additional plot on the W. Anthony Munday related a story of a curious interment a few yrs. after the enlargement of the ground:

'August 10th, 1626. In Petty France out of Christian buriall was buried Hodges Shaughsware a Persian Merchant, who with his sonne came over with the Persian Ambassador, and was buried by his owne Son, who read certain prayers, and used other ceremonies, according to the custome of their owne Country, morning and evening, for a whole month after the buriall; for whom is set up at the charge of his sonne a Tombe of stone with certain Persian characters thereon; the exposition thus: "This grave is made for Hodges Shaughsware, the chiefest Servant to the King of Persia, who came from the King of Persia and dyed in his service. If any Persian commeth out of that Country, let him read this and a prayer for him, the Lord receive his soule, for here lyeth Maghmote Shaughsware, who was borne in the Towne of Novoy in Persia." '

Stow described 'Petty France' at Bishopsgate (there was another in Westminster, and the name remains there) as 'a quadrant,' so called 'of Frenchmen dwelling there.'

The old ch. became ruinous early in the 18th century, and was demolished. The first stone of the new edifice was laid by Edmund Gibson, the learned Bp. of L. The new ch. was completed in 1729 at the cost of over £10,400. The architect was Jas. Gold. It is a spacious bdg., including two aisles separated from the nave by composite columns. There are galleries at the N., S., and W. There is a richly stained E. window. The W. window was destroyed in the Second World War, and replaced in 1948 by a window with a central figure of the risen Christ. The font and pulpit are of 18th-century date. Sir Paul Pindar's monument is above the staircase leading to the N. gallery. There is also in the chancel a brass plate in memory of Sir Wm. Blizard, President of the Royal Coll. of Surgeons, who resided many yrs. in the par., and d. 1835, aged 92. John Keats was baptized at St. Botolph's on 18th Dec. 1795, when he was seven weeks old.

Over a bdg. in the chyd. which used to be an infants sch. are figures of a boy and a girl in quaint costume. One is dated 1821; they are of Coade stone. (See 'South Bank.') In 1952 this became the Hall of the Fan-Makers' Co. (q.v.). Close by is the large tomb of Sir Wm. Rawlins, sheriff in 1801. He was an upholsterer, and Thos. Dibdin (song writer, and the son of another song writer, who is chiefly famous for *Tom Bowling*) was at one time his apprentice. Sir Wm. bequeathed £1,000 to the par. sch. The additional piece of ground opposite the chyd. was given to the par. by the Common Council in 1760. The houses on old London Bridge were then being demolished and the railings from a part of the bridge called 'London Square' were purchased by some of the parishioners and re-erected to fence this new enclosure.

There is a memorial cross in honour of John Cornwell of H.M.S. *Chester*, whose heroic conduct at the Battle of Jutland in 1916 brought a posthumous V.C.

The living used to be the richest in the City, possibly in the country. Rev. H. W. Clarke, in *The City Churches* (1898), said that the rector's net income was then £2,121. In the ch. is a list of benefactors commencing with 1481, and a list of rectors from 1323. Rev. Wm. Rogers, who became rector in 1863, was a great social reformer, and from his insistence on the practice rather than theory of religion, came to be known as 'Hang Theology Rogers.' His reminiscences were published in 1888, and there is a memorial tablet, with medallion, on the N. wall.

The ch. was restored and the organ rebuilt in 1912. There was another restoration in 1947/8.

St. Bride (Fleet St.) is dedicated to a 6th-century Irish saint, St. Bridget, who, according to Giraldus, was the cause of an inextinguishable fire being lit at her tomb in Kildare, it having been continuously fed by her vestal virgins. It is the only L. ch. so dedicated, and is mentioned in 1222. In 1234 *Liber Albus* (1419) records that Henry de Battle, a 'clerk,' slew Thomas de Hall on the K.'s highway and fled to the ch. At the close of the forty days allowed to a felon for sanctuary he confessed his guilt to a coroner, and was ordered to render his goods to the sheriff. He was thereupon passed from constable to constable until he reached a seaport, and was able to embark on a foreign-bound ship. Here, also, was held in 1356 an inquiry into the state of the Fleet River (see 'Lost Rivers'). The ch. had many chantries, and, says W. G. Bell:

'The Carmelites shared in the dead men's benefits, until the friars, too, came under the popular odium that had already overtaken the monks.'

In the ch. was bd. Wynkyn de Worde, who succeeded to Caxton's printing business and had premises opposite.

One vicar was John Taylor, who had the curious alias of 'Cardmaker.' A native of Devonshire, he became vicar in 1543. When in 1547 Edward VI came to the throne, he became lecturer at St. P.'s Cath. There he attacked Gardiner, Bp. 'of Winchester, and denied the ancient faith. He was made in Edward VI's reign prebendary and chancellor of Wells, and resigned the living of St. Bride's in 1551. Early in Mary's reign he was deprived of his new offices. He attempted to escape overseas, and came to L. disguised as a merchant. He was, however, committed to the Fleet Prison. He was

brought before a commission that sat in the Lady Chapel of St. Mary Overies Ch. (See 'Southwark Cathedral.') He was confined in the Bread St. Compter, where was also Laurence Saunders, rector of All Hallows Ch., Bread St. 'Cardmaker' seems to have been wavering up to that time, but the fellowship of these two kindred spirits, like that of Bunyan's Christian with Faithful, seems to have fortified the former vicar of St. Bride's. Saunders was burnt at the stake at Coventry, while 'Cardmaker,' after an imprisonment in Newgate, was brought to Smithfield on 30th May 1555, and 'went with bold courage to the stake and kissed it sweetly.'

In the pre-Fire ch. Sir John Denham m. his first wife in 1634. He was the author of *Cooper's Hill*, a poem admired by Pope and Johnson.

Sir Richd. Baker, author of the *Chronicles of the Kings of England*, which afforded so much pleasure and instruction to Sir Roger de Coverley was bd. here in 1645. It is possible also that here was interred Richd. Lovelace, the author of *To Althea from Prison*, in which occur the familiar lines:

'I could not love thee, dear, so much,
    Loved I not honour more.'

.   .   .   .

'Stone walls do not a prison make,
    Nor iron bars a cage.'

He was confined in the Gatehouse, Westminster (see 'Prisons'), and d. 1658 in Gunpowder Alley, Shoe Lane.

Samuel Pepys was baptised here (1633); the register remains. He visited it (18th March 1664),

'and, with the grave-maker, chose a place for my brother to lie in, just under my mother's pew. But to see how a man's tombs are at the mercy of such a fellow, that for 6d. he would (as his own words were): "I will jostle them together but I will make room for him," speaking of the fullness of the middle aisle, where he was to lie, and that he would for my father's sake do my brother that is dead, all the civility he can; which was to disturb others' corps that are not quite rotten, to make room for him.'

The earliest marriage mentioned in the

1 London Wall

2 Battersea Pleasure Gardens

3 Bank of England and Royal Exchange

4 Buckingham Palace

5 St Bride's, Fleet Street

6 Charterhouse, outer gate

7 Apothecaries' Hall: Courtyard

8 Goldsmiths' Hall

9 Vintners' Hall

par. registers was in Sept. 1587, and the earliest baptism Feb. 1588. Interesting entries in the marriage register are the names of Francis Drake and Mrs. Susannah Potts for 26th Dec. 1653, before Alderman Fawkes at the house of Nathan Wright, Esq. This is the first entry of a marriage before a Justice of the Peace.

At the time of the Plague Richd. Pearson was curate, and he signed the register all through its duration. A comparison of the number of deaths in the same months of 1664 and 1665 will give a notion of the ravages of the pestilence:

Aug. 1664 . 37   Aug. 1665 . 611
Sept. 1664 . 28   Sept. 1665 . 628

On 24th Aug. 1665 forty-two deaths were registered and 11,999 persons d. within the yr. As Rev. E. C. Hawkins wrote:

'The diminished population may account for the following entry under date 9th May 1668:

" 'John Childe, sworn parish clerk in which week not one died." '

Meanwhile—in 1666—the ch. had been destroyed in the G.F. Wren was the architect of the new structure which was completed in 1680 at a cost of £12,000. It was one of Wren's finest works, ranking perhaps next to St. P.'s Cath. and St. Stephen's, Walbrook. The pilasters finely set off the huge pillars. The roof of the nave was arched, and crossed by handsomely wrought bands connected at each extremity with the shields which embellish the tops of the columns.

The steeple dates from 1701, and was one of Wren's greatest achievements. It was originally 234 ft. In 1764 it was seriously damaged by lightning. When restored, the height of the spire was reduced by 8 ft., and is now 226 ft. Only the spire of St. P.'s Cath. and the tower of Westminster Roman Catholic Cath. are loftier amongst ecclesiastical bdgs. W. E. Henley called St. Bride's spire 'a madrigal in stone.'

The most important name associated with the ch. is Samuel Richardson. He was bd. here in 1761, with his first wife and two infant sons. There was a large gravestone in the centre aisle, and on the N. wall a tablet erected in 1889 by the Stationers' Co., of which Richardson was master, in commemoration of the bicentenary of his birth.

In 1756, Benjamin Annable, who broke bell-ringing records in his day, was bd. here.

This was peculiarly the pressmen's ch. There were memorial tablets to Sir Geo. Newnes (d. 1910), Sir Arthur Pearson (d. 1921), and Sir Edmund Robbins, manager of the Press Association for thirty-seven yrs. (d. 1922).

There was a tablet to Isaac Romilly, a L. merchant and uncle to Sir Samuel Romilly, who d. in 1759; and one commemorating Alderman Waithman. The inscription says he was—

'a friend of liberty in evil times and of Parliamentary Reform in its adverse days; it was at length his happiness to see that great cause triumphant of which he had been the intrepid advocate from youth to age.'

He was five times M.P. for the City, and Ld.M. 1823-4, as well as a member of the first reformed Parliament. His drapery shop was at Nos. 103-4 Fleet St., and he was one of the last City tradesmen to live over his business. The most recent memorial—a brass tablet to Thos. Weelkes, the madrigalist (see 'Music in London') also remains. There are wrought iron gates, erected by the Newspaper Soc. in memory of Valentine Knapp, its President from 1919-22. Inside the gate is the vault of the Holden family. It bears date 1657. They were hatters and haberdashers in Fleet St. and Pepys bought from them a hat for 35s., and a 'beaver' costing £4 5s. in 1661.

The church was gutted by bombs in 1940 and completely restored in 1957, the association with the press being strengthened by many new and restored memorials. Within the building were discovered a large number of human bones, and what is in effect a perfect medieval charnel-house. These relics are not of course on public view, but they are made available for scientific study, and have already proved of immense importance in such different fields as dental, forensic and social research. Many other discoveries were made including that of a Norman curfew tower: the undercroft has been laid out so that the exhibits form a history, not only of St. Brides, but of the Fleet St. district.

In 1959 an annual service was reinstituted to receive the Bridewell Governors and children into the city. It is held on the second Tuesday of March and includes the 'Bridewell Sermon'.

St. Clement, Eastcheap (Clement Lane, King William St.). The earliest mention is 'St. Clement Candlewickstrate' (11th century), the E. end of what is now Cannon St. having later become part of Eastcheap. There is, however, a reference to a ch. of St. Clement in a confirmation of grants to W.A. in 1067, and this probably referred to the first ch. here. The ch. was dedicated to the saint who was one of St. Paul's 'fellow labourers whose names are in the book of life' (Phil. iv.3), and who suffered martyrdom about A.D. 100 by being thrown into the sea with an anchor about his neck. Hence he became the patron saint of seamen. It came into the possession of the Crown, but by Q. Mary was invested in the Bps. of L. According to Stow, in his time it was a small ch., with no noteworthy monuments save those of Alderman Francis Barnham, sheriff in 1570 (d. 1575), and his son, Benedict Barnham, also an alderman and sheriff in 1591 (d. 1598). Francis Bacon m. a daughter of the latter.

Three theologians were commemorated in the ch. by a brass tablet (1878) and a W. window. The first is that quaint writer beloved of Elia, Thos. Fuller. On his return to L. after the surrender of Exeter to the Parliament in 1646, he held for a short time the position of lecturer. Pearson, afterwards Bp. of Chester, was appointed lecturer in 1650, and preached here a series of discourses on the Creed, which were afterwards incorporated in his renowned *Exposition*, published in 1659 and dedicated to the parishioners of St. Clement's. The third was Brian Walton, the learned compiler of the Polyglot Bible. He was rector of St. Martin Orgar (*q.v.*), the par. of which was united with St. Clement's after the G.F. Walton was deprived of the living by Parliament at the outbreak of the Civil War, and reinstated and made Bp. of Chester at the Restoration in 1660. A rector of St. Clement's who suffered similarly was Dr. Benjamin Stone of Corpus Christi Coll., Cambridge, who was presented to the living by Bp. Juxon in 1637. During Cromwell's domination he was deemed to have papist leanings, and was confined for a time in Crosby Hall (*q.v.*). From thence he was removed to Plymouth, where, after paying a fine of £60, he obtained his liberty. On the

Restoration he recovered his benefice, but d. 1665.

St. Clement's Ch., having been burnt in the G.F., was rebuilt by Wren in 1686. It has one aisle on the S. side, separated from the rest of the ch. by two columns on high bases. There is a clerestory with small windows. The ceiling is most ornamental. The walls are wainscoted to the height of 8½ ft., and the pulpit is handsomely carved. There is a most ornate reredos, and the altar is unusually elevated. In addition to a brass tablet, commemorating the three theologians mentioned, there are tablets also to Edwd. Purcell (d. 1740), son of the famous musical composer, Henry Purcell, and Jonathan Battishill, whose chants and anthems are still in use. Both were organists at St. Clement's. The ch. was rearranged and modernized in 1872. There is a nicely carved font; the cover has cherubs' heads. All the stained glass (including the Fuller window) was destroyed in the Blitz.

The vicar claims that his is the ch. referred to in the nursery rhyme, 'Oranges and Lemons,' but if there is any historical significance in the allusion, there is no ground for saying that it implies St. Clement's, Eastcheap.

St. Dunstan-in-the-West (Fleet St.). The earliest mention is 1185; later it was referred to as 'St. Dunstan over against the New Temple.' The advowson was in possession of W.A. until 1237, when the incumbents ceased to be vicars and became Custodians of the Liberty of the Rolls.

Wm. Tyndale, the translator of the New Testament (see 'Statues') was an occasional preacher at St. Dunstan's in 1523. He attracted attention by his reforming zeal. Dr. Thos. White, founder of Sion Coll. (see 'Libraries'), was presented to the vicarage in 1575. He became later prebendary of St. P.'s Cath. and canon of Windsor. He d. in 1623, and was bd. at St. Dunstan's, where he had endowed a lecture. His successor was Donne, the famous Dean of St. P.'s Cath. He held the living until his death in 1631. Izaak Walton was a parishioner when he resided in a house in Fleet St., two doors from the corner of Chancery Lane (see 'Fleet Street'). His first wife, Rachel, was bd. in St. Dunstan's in 1640. Walton became

Donne's biographer, and it was no doubt while he was a parishioner that he made his acquaintance. *The Compleat Angler* was published in St. Dunstan's chyd. in 1653.

Ralph Bane, Bp. of Lichfield and Coventry, and Owen Oglethorpe, Bp. of Carlisle, the prelate who officiated at the coronation of Q. Elizabeth, both d. 1559 —and were bd. at St. Dunstan's. Here were baptized the great E. of Strafford (who perished on Tower Hill) in 1593, and Bulstrode Whitelocke, ambassador and author of the *Memorials of English Affairs*, in 1682.

St. Dunstan's escaped the G.F. but narrowly. In 1671 a new clock was supplied by Thos. Harrys of Water Lane; a payment of £35 and the old clock was made. To the new clock two figures of giants were affixed; they struck the hours and quarters, and turned their heads. Accordingly this became the best-known clock in L. The figures are referred to by Tom Brown. Ned Ward in *The London Spy* (1698–9), at a music shop in St. Paul's Chyd., watching 'a little Red Fac'd Blade, beating Time upon his counter,' refers to the 'Conceited Motions of their Heads and Hands which mov'd too and fro with as much deliberate Stiffness, as the two Wooden Horologists at St. Dunstan's, when they strike the quarters.'

Goldsmith, in *The Vicar of Wakefield* (1766), makes Mr. Thornhill say, referring to an insinuation that he had been making some proposals to Miss Wilmot:

'Strike me ugly, if I should not find as much pleasure in choosing my mistress by the information of a lamp under the clock of St. Dunstan's.'

Cowper wrote in *Table Talk* (1782):

'When labour and when dulness, club in hand,
Like the two figures at St. Dunstan's stand,
Beating alternately in measured time
The clockwork tintinnabulum of rhyme,
Exact and regular the sounds will be,
But such mere quarter-strokes are not for me.'

Byron said, in a letter (1811): 'I would have raised all Fleet St., and borrowed the giant's staff from St. Dunstan's Church to immolate the betrayer of trust.'

In 1701 the ch. was extensively re-paired; the old arched roof was removed; and a square roof at a higher elevation substituted. In 1730 it was again threatened by a fire that came nigh, but not quite up to it. The ch. was demolished towards the end of 1829, and a new edifice erected 1831–3. The architect was John Shaw who designed the new hall of Christ's Hosp. He d. in 1832 and the work was completed by his son. The present ch. is farther back than its predecessor, which unduly narrowed Fleet St. The body is of brick, but the tower is of yellow freestone. It terminates in a pierced octagonal lantern, an uncommon form which is said to have been suggested to the architect by the steeples of St. Botolph's Boston and St. Helen's York. The tower contains eight bells which belonged to the previous ch., and theirs were 'The Chimes' of Dickens's Christmas story. The interior is octagonal in shape and contains seven recesses which are separated from each other by clustered columns and pointed arches supporting a clerestory. The altar, of elaborately carved oak, is in the northern recess. It is crowned by three carved canopies of Flemish workmanship. The stone font has angel figures.

On the walls are some monuments belonging to the old ch. The earliest is a brass showing two kneeling figures, male and female, with labels protruding from their mouths. Beneath is the following inscription:

'Here lyeth buryed ye body of Henry Dacres, Cetezen and Marchant Taylor and sumtyme Alderman of London, and Elizabeth his Wyffe, the whyche Henry decessed the . . . day of . . . the yere of or Lord God MDC . . . and the sayd Elizabeth decessed the xxiii day of Apryll the yere of or Lord God MDc and xxx.'

The omission of dates in the case of the man is mysterious. Probably Henry Dacres was alive when the brass was erected and for some reason was bd. elsewhere.

A monument with male and female figures commemorates Gerard Legh, a member of the Inner Temple who d. in 1563, and his wife. There is a long Latin inscription. Another Elizabethan monument is a square tablet with a long Latin inscription to Sir Matthew Carey, Doctor of Law. A monument which exhibits a female figure kneeling at the desk, and three children below, is that of Elizabeth North (d. 1612). The kneeling male figure is probably intended to represent her husband, Roger North. Cuthbert Featherstone, the K.'s door-keeper (d. 1615), has a tablet with bust in frame, and there is an oval tablet to Alexander Layton 'ye Fam'd swordman,' who d. 1679.

> 'His Thrusts like Lightning flew, more Skilful Death
> Parried 'em all, and beat him out of Breath.'

There is a monument with a curious Latin inscription commencing 'Quis es? Unde venis? Quo vadis?' (Who art thou? Whence comest? Whither goest?), com-memorative of Matthew, tenth son of George, Ld. Carew, a knight and doctor of the law. It states:

> 'I have lived under four kings, and two queens, and have attended the Court of Chancery 33 years, under five chancellors and keepers of the great seal.'

and ends thus:

> 'Oh! how many and how strange things have I seen. I have lived long enough for myself, if sufficiently for God. Thoroughly tired of the levity, vanity and inconsistency of this life, I seek an eternal one, that I may enjoy God, and rest in peace. Amen.'

There are also monuments to two Sir Richd. Hoares (d. 1718 and 1754), the Fleet St. bankers and both Ld.Ms., the elder in 1712, and the younger in 1745, the yr. of the Highlanders' march southwards. Of the latter the epitaph says:

> 'In which alarming crisis he dis-charged the great trust reposed in him with honour and integrity, to the approbation of his sovereign and the universal satisfaction of his fellow citizens.'

Their descendants were liberal benefactors to the new ch., to which they presented the window over the altar and the carved canopies of the altar-piece. A brass tablet to John C. Dwarler who d. 1890 at the age of 74, describes him as 'an ancient of the parish.' (For Hobson Judkin see 'Epitaphs.')

In 1895 a stained glass window close to the chancel was unveiled in memory of Izaak Walton. The centre is occupied by a figure of Walton and at the sides are half-length figures of his brother-in-law, Bp. Ken, and the subjects of those biographies which brought so graceful a tribute from Wordsworth:

> 'The feather, whence the pen
> Was shaped that traced the lives of these good men,
> Dropped from an Angel's wing.'

—Sir Henry Wotton, Geo. Herbert, John Donne, Richd. Hooker, and Dr. Robt. Sanderson. At the same time a tablet was affixed to the external wall of the ch., recording Walton's association with the par. On each side of the porch there are the sculptured heads of Tyndale (W.) and Donne (E.). There is also a bust of Ld. Northcliffe, unveiled by Ld. Riddell in 1930.

The ch. has had close association with the Cordwainers' Co. since the 15th century, and the benefaction of one of its members, John Fisher, provided gifts of money to poor householders and school children. These were distributed after a service, and before the Second World War infants ran round the ch. and received a penny for each time it was done.

A flying bomb caused some damage to the ch. in the summer of 1944, but notwithstanding, a wedding was cele-brated next day. It is now a Guild Church being concerned with good relations be-tween churches and with Christian Unity.

St. Edmund, King and Martyr (Lombard St.). Now known as St. Edmund the King. The earliest reference is to its being given by Q. Maud, wife of Henry I, to the prior and convent of Holy Trinity c. 1108. It was called 'St. Edmund towards Garcherche' c. 1292; in 1348 it was 'S. Edmund de Lombardestrete.' The dedication is to the K. of E. Anglia who, having been taken prisoner by the Danes in 1870, was shot by arrows. Over his remains was built the great abbey of Bury St. Edmunds. In the old ch. was a monument to John Shute, a painter-stainer. He studied architecture in Italy and, on his return, published *The First and Chief Groundes of Architecture*, one of the earliest works on that subject. He d. 1563.

The ch. was burnt in the G.F., and the ch. of St. Nicholas Acon (*q.v.*) not being rebuilt, the two pars. were united. St. Edmund's Ch. was completed by Wren in 1690, and the lantern of the tower (designed like a lighthouse—see 'St.

Nicholas, Cole Abbey') is ornamented at the angles by flaming urns in allusion to the G.F. It stands N. and S., the altar is in a recess. The position of the site left Wren no alternative. There are no aisles, and the walls and the bases of the pilasters attached to them are panelled with oak to the height of 8 ft. The door-cases at the NE. and NW. and the pulpit which stands on the W. side are also of dark oak, and are handsomely carved. Much stained glass was destroyed in the Blitz. In a recess at the SW., enclosed by rails, is a handsome font, with a beautifully carved oak cover. T. F. Bumpus says truly that:

'Within, . St. Edmund's, from its limited dimensions and the richness and beauty of its furniture and decoration, resembles the private chapel of a nobleman's house.'

There is a marble monument by the elder Bacon—a figure of Hope resting on an urn—in memory of Dr. Jeremiah Milles, Dean of Exeter, rector of the united pars., and president of the Soc. of Antiquaries, who d. 1784, and of Edith, his wife, who d. 1761, aged 35. Dr. Milles, who was rector of St. Edmund's Ch. for nearly forty yrs., was a strong advocate of the genuineness of Chatterton's Rowley poems. In 1782 he published a magnificent quarto edition, together with a *Preliminary Dissertation and Commentary*, in an endeavour to establish their authenticity. There is a brass tablet to Chas. Melville Hays, president of the Grand Trunk Railway, who went down with the *Titanic*. A memorial service was held here, and at the same time at Montreal. Here in 1716 Addison was m.—a real misalliance—to the Dowager Countess of Warwick and Holland.

On the W. wall is an ancient fresco found on the site of St. Nicholas Acon during the building operations of the banking co. who presented it to the ch. There is a brass tablet in memory of Canon Benham, rector (1882–1910).

St. Ethelburga the Virgin (Bishopsgate). The first reference is in 1250 to land in 'the parish of St. Adelburga, the Virgin.' In 1273 it is 'St. Edburga the Virgin within Bissopesgate'; in 1349 'S. Elburga.' The name has a number of variations. Two small relics of an earlier, perhaps the first, ch. have been discovered during repairs, one of which (a quinquefoil of a canopy) is now embedded in the N. wall, and the other, an Early English shaft, in the S. wall of the choir. The patron saint of the ch. was the first Abbess of Barking, and sister of Erkenwald, fourth Bp. of L.

The present ch. was built in the first half of the 15th century. This is borne out by the style of the architecture and references in wills. In 1429 Richd. Tepelane left 20s. to the churchwardens for the repairing and rebuilding of the nave, and in 1446 Richd. Person left 10s. to be expended by Joan, his wife, on the building of the body of the ch. It has suffered much disfigurement. The tracery in the windows has gone, save one piece now in the W. window. The windows on the N. and S. were blocked up about the beginning of the 19th century. The E. window was set in a classical framework until 1871, when the present one took its place. In 1629 a gallery was constructed. It was given, as the inscription at the E. end said, 'by Mr. Owen Saint Peere (being churchwarden) only for the daughters and maidservants of the parish to sit in.' It was removed in 1862. The S. aisle is lighted by four lancet windows, and separated from the main body of the ch. by four pointed arches, above which is a clerestory containing small windows. The walls of the chancel are panelled to a height of 5 ft. Between 1912 and 1914 a sum of £2,807 12s. 2d. was raised by the rector and the congregation for purposes of improvement. By means of this were added the oak screen and the oak gallery. The chancel was then refitted in oak and paved in stone; a parclose was erected between the chancel and the Lady Chapel. The porch was refloored, and a motto taken from an ancient temple of Asklepios (Aesculapius), let into the pavement. It runs: 'Bonus Intra Melior Exi' (Come in good, go out better). It is the smallest ch. in the city, measuring 60 ft. by 30 ft., while the height to the centre of the ceiling is under 31 ft. The font is old but of unknown date. It bears a Greek inscription, a translation of which is: 'Cleanse my transgression, not my outward appearance only.'

The earliest known of the rectors was Robt. de Meretsham, 1304. During the theological storms of the 16th century one or two of them found anything but smooth sailing. There was, for example, John

Larke. He was a pluralist, and while rector he was admitted to the rectory of Woodford in Essex at the presentation of Sir Thos. More. Having resigned Woodford in 1527, in 1530, again through More's influence, he became rector of the 'Church of Chelsey in Middlesex.' St. Ethelburga's he resigned before 1542, but 'Chelsey' he retained until he suffered attainder for denying the supremacy of Henry VIII, for which he was executed at Tyburn in 1544. (In the ch. there is a tablet and a remarkable modern painting of Larke.) His successor, John Deye, took the Protestant side, and came equally under the displeasure of Q. Mary's Govt. He was put in the pillory, and finally deprived, but escaped with his life.

From 1601 to 1632 Wm. Bedwell was rector. He was a pluralist, being also vicar of Tottenham from 1607 until his death in 1632. He was a considerable Arabic scholar, and some of his books and manuscripts went to swell Laud's collection, and others to Trinity Coll., Cambridge.

During the time he was rector occurred the incident related in the following extract from the log of John Pleyce, a member of the Moscovy Company:

'Divers Voyages and Northerne Discoveries of that worthy irrecoverable discoverer

'MASTER HENRY HUDSON

'his discoverie toward the North Pole set forth at the charge of certain Worshipfull Merchants of London in May 1607.

'Anno 1607, Aprill the nineteenth, at Saint Ethelburge in Bishops Gate street did communicate with the rest of the parishioners these persons, seamen, purposing to goe to sea foure days after for to discover a passage by the North Pole to Japan and China—First Henry Hudson master.'

Then follow the names of eleven others, the last being 'John Hudson, a boy.' In 1928, 1929, and 1930 three windows were placed in the ch. in honour of Hudson. The first (Hudson taking Communion at St. Ethelburga's) was the gift of the Governor and Co. of Hudson's Bay, whose office was S. of the ch., with a beaver as weather vane; the second (Hudson sailing up the Hudson river), of citizens of the U.S.A.; the third (Hudson cast adrift by mutineers), of citizens of

the British Empire. The artist was Leonard Walker, R.I. John Clarke, who became rector in 1633, was imprisoned as a malignant, and had his living sequestrated, 'a godly, learned and orthodox Divine,' being put in his place, according to the journal of the H. of C. in 1643. From 1645–59 in the Churchwardens' accounts, it is 'Parish of Ethelborough.' As Tom Brown said, 'the Saints were thrown out of doors and the parishes unsainted.' In 1693 Bp. Burnet preached at St. Ethelburga's, and the churchwardens honoured the occasion by the expenditure of 5s. 6d. in wine. Luke Milbourne, a hostile critic of Dryden, was rector 1704–20. Pope mentioned him in his *Essay on Criticism*, and in a passage in *The Dunciad*. He wrote a treatise on *Mysteries in Religion Vindicated, A Poetical Translation of the Psalms*, and *Tom of Bedlam's Answer to Hoadly*, besides publishing twenty-nine single sermons. John Wesley preached here in 1785. From 1900 to 1941 the rector was Rev. W. F. Geikie Cobb. The memorial window in the ch. (unveiled by the Ld.M. in 1947) says that he was a 'man greatly beloved.' In his time a feature of the church was a small printing plant at the rear where there were produced books on the ch. and other publications.

The date of the vane on the small turret of the ch. is 1671. In 1932 two shops which screened the W. end were demolished. They dated from 1570 and 1614, and since 1891 had been in possession of the City Parochial Charities. In the disused burial ground E. of the ch. there is a cloister and a fountain—the gift of the Billiter Literary Soc.—and it provides a pleasant lunch-time resort for City workers. The whole roof and much of the interior ceiling were badly damaged by a flying bomb: renewal and redecoration were completed in 1953. It is now a Guild Church with responsibility for the Church's Ministry of Healing.

St. Giles, Cripplegate (Fore St.). The first reference is a grant by Ælmund to the canons of St. P.'s Cath. of his Ch. of St. Giles, built outside the walls, in the time of Henry I (1100–35). Stow says it was built by Alfune about 1090, and the Cottonian MS which relates the history of the ch. of St. Bartholomew the Great (*q.v.*) says that:

'Rahere joined to him a certain olde

City Churches C

123

City Churches C

man, Alfun by name, to whom was sad of age with experience of long time. This same old man not long beforne had beldid ye Churche of Seynt Gyles at ye gate of the Cyte, that ynne Inglish tonge is called Cripilgate; and that good work happily he hadde endyd.'

Alfune, sometimes called Alfun and Alwin, was first almoner to the priory of St. Bartholomew. The dedication is to a saint who was b. in Athens of royal parentage, and went to France about A.D. 666. He was expert in physic as well as theology, and at first selected a retreat near Arles, afterwards, for more perfect solitude, retiring to a forest. According to a legend, one day Flavius Wamba, K. of the Goths, was hunting in the neighbourhood, and his dogs pursued a hind which took refuge in the saint's cave, and through his prayers the dogs were unable to pursue further. The protected animal furnished its patron with sustenance, and so it came about that St. Giles is the patron saint of maternity, as well as of the deformed and needy. The saint is depicted with a hind over the porch of the present ch., but, as one writer remarks:

'It is well to remember that a hind was a type of solitude and purity of life and is found accompanying several saints and that the legend may well have grown out of the symbol.'

In c. 1202 the name was 'S. Giles of Cruplegate.'

There has been much controversy over the meaning of Cripplegate. Harben says:

'It seems most probable that the name was Crepelsgate from the Anglo-Saxon "crepel" = "burrow" or "crypele" = "a den," a "burrow" of which the genitive form is "crypeles," and that the name denoted a "narrow underground passage or covered way" to which access was obtained through this gate.'

Harben mentions a postern on the wall of Shrewsbury, formerly named 'Crepulgate,' which was connected with the Severn by a narrow passage.

Nothing remains of the first ch. except possibly parts of the basement of the present tower. In the recess under that tower is a slab of Purbeck marble. It is said to have been the doorstep of this Norman ch. It was found during renova-

tions of the N. aisle. There was in connection with it, in the 13th century, a Fraternity of St. Mary and St. Giles. The first ch. was rebuilt about 1357. In 1545 a considerable part of this second ch. was destroyed by fire. The *London Chronicle* of 1545 records:

'The xij day of September, Satterday, in the Mornyng, above five of the klocke, was Saynt Jyles's Churche burned, belles and alle, wtout Crepellgate.'

It was rebuilt in the Perpendicular Gothic style, including a nave, chancel, and two side-aisles, which are separated from the central portion by clustered columns and pointed arches. In 1624–6 two side galleries were built, 'very fair and spacious,' says Strype. The steeple was raised 15 ft. between the yrs. 1682 and 1684. A new clock was then inserted, but in 1721 this was replaced by the recent one. In 1704 there was another internal restoration. The ch. was repewed, and the oak altar-piece erected. It consisted of three panels. The central one contained a painting of Christ seated on a throne, while on the smaller side panels were depicted St. Paul and St. Giles. In 1791 two additional windows were inserted on each side of the clerestory, and this innovation occasioned an extension of the roof of the middle aisle, and the consequent curtailment of the chancel. In the same yr. the E. window over the altar-piece was reglazed with a glory and cherubs' heads, surrounding the Sacred Name in Hebrew characters. The cherubs were obviously from Sir Joshua Reynolds, and his model is said to have been a daughter of the ranger of Green Park. This was one of the most charming ch. windows in L. In 1858 another restoration was carried out. An open roof and new chancel arch were constructed. The organ was moved from the W. end and taken to the N. of the chancel. A new font was placed at the W. end, and several new stained-glass windows inserted. One, at the W. end of the S. aisle, had as subjects: 'The Shepherds watching their flocks,' 'The Nativity,' and 'The Wise Men from the East,' with representations of St. Giles and St. Luke on the head-lights. This window was inserted at the expense of the neighbouring par. of St. Luke's, Old St., 'in grateful remembrance of Edward Alleyne, the founder of Dulwich

College (see 'Camberwell'). St. Luke's was originally part of St. Giles's par., but in 1732 was separated from it. Alleyn, who acquired some of his wealth here from the Fortune in Golden Lane, Barbican (see 'Theatres'), was a benefactor to his poorer neighbours.

The ch. narrowly escaped destruction in the G.F. In 1897 there was a still more narrow escape. The roof of the ch. was damaged, and the flames almost completely destroyed the roof of the vicarage. After this fire the Quest House, which stood at the NW. corner, was removed. Here was formerly the meeting-place of the Inquest, a body of men elected to regulate the internal affairs in the ward. They were abolished in 1857, and subsequently it was used for vestry meetings. The upper portion, since 1729 had been used as a lodging for the sexton. The removal of the Quest House added to the external beauty of the ch. It also exposed a turret which contained a stairway leading to a room above the porch. In 1901 the par. of St. Bartholomew, Moor Lane, was reunited to that of St. Giles, and the former ch. being demolished, the altar reredos and other fittings were removed to the N. aisle of St. Giles, into the Chapel of the Incarnation. Canon Newbolt preached a dedication sermon.

There have been notable burials here. John Foxe, author of the *Acts and Monuments* (the abbreviated title of what is known as 'the Book of Martyrs'). He, in his later years, resided in Grub St., and may have assisted at St. Giles' Ch. He declined all preferment, with the exception of a prebend in Salisbury Cath., bestowed upon him by Sir Wm. Cecil, owing to his conscientious objection to signing the thirty-nine articles. Foxe d. in 1587. Sir Martin Frobisher who sustained fatal wounds in action off Brest, was bd. here in 1594. In 1888, to commemorate the tercentenary of the defeat of the Spanish Armada, a memorial was erected. In 1629 John Speed was bd. here. He was the author of *The History of Great Britaine under the Conquest of ye Romans, Danes, and Normans.* Like John Stow he was a tailor by profession and Sir Henry Spelman said to Sir Wm. Dugdale: 'We are beholding to Mr. Speed and Stow for stitching up for us our English history.' Speed's half-length

effigy is placed in a sort of cupboard with open doors on each side. The right hand grasps a book, and the left a skull. The Latin inscription says he was 'a faithful servant of Queen Elizabeth, James I and King Charles I,' and died at the age of 77, and that although his wife brought him twenty-two sons and daughters, she lived to be at least a septuagenarian, and was m. fifty-seven yrs., dying in 1628.

Lancelot Andrewes was vicar from 1589–1604.

There are two most distinguished associations of St. Giles Ch.—Oliver Cromwell and John Milton.

Cromwell was m. here in 1620. The entry in the register reads: 'Oliver Crumwell and Elizabeth Bourchr.'

A stone in the floor of the chancel marks the spot where John Milton was bd. in 1674. Close by, his father had been bd. in 1647. The former was 66 and the latter 84 yrs. of age. There was a story that the grave was opened in 1793, when the body was exhibited for prices declining from 6*d.* to a pot of beer—and that then rib-bones and handfuls of hair were stolen. This occasioned Cowper's lines:

'Ill fare the hands that heaved the stones
  Where Milton's ashes lay!
That trembled not to grasp his bones
  And steal his dust away!'

There was, however, no real reason to think that the body was Milton's, and probably the hope of gain induced the ghoulish showmen to misrepresent them. In 1793, at the cost of Samuel Whitbread, a friend of Sheridan's, the celebrated sculptor, Bacon, made a bust of Milton, which was placed against a pillar near the grave. In 1862 a cenotaph of Caen stone, designed by Edmund Woodthorpe, was placed in the present position with the bust upon it. On the cenotaph are a snake and an apple.

In 1675 Richd. Smyth was bd. here. He was 85 yrs. of age, a well-known antiquary and book-collector, and author of the famous *Obituary*, published by the Camden Society. This consists of recollections of people known to him between 1627 and 1674. The monument represented him and his wife at a desk. Daniel Defoe was b. and d. in the par. of St. G.'s, but there is no memorial in the ch. A child of Jas. Shirley, the dramatist, was baptized here in 1625, and Holman Hunt, the artist, in 1827.

The rectory was in Well St., which takes its name from Crowder's Well, of which Strype (1720) wrote:

'The water of this well is esteemed very good for the eyes to wash them with and it is said to be also very good to drink for several distempers. And some say it is very good for men in drink to take of this water, for it will allay the fumes and bring them to be sober.'

It was not used after 1853. At the time of the Plague the pump was in the chyd., and this may have accounted for the fact that this par. suffered more than any other. In 1665 there were 8,069 deaths (4,838 attributed to the plague), and in 1666 only 776 deaths from all causes. From 29th Aug. to 5th Sept. 1665, there were 690 deaths, and one month's entries in the burial register required 99½ pages. The par. purchased four coffins for plague victims, solely to carry corpses to the pits, the cost being £1 6s., and, as a result of burial in the chyd., it was raised 2 ft. in level.

Thos. Hardy rarely introduces London scenes into his novels, but the chyd. of St. Giles appears in *The Hand of Ethelberta*, Ladywell says:

' "I had no idea there was such a lovely green spot in the city."

'The place was truly charming. The untainted leaves of the lime and plane trees and the newly sprung grass had in the sun a brilliancy of beauty that was brought into extraordinary prominence by the sable soil showing here and there, and the charcoaled stems and trunks out of which the leaves budded: they seemed an importation not a produce, and their delicacy such as would perish in a day.'

Hardy refers also to the iron grey bastion partly covered with ivy and Virginia creeper.'

' "What is this round tower?" Ladywell said, walking towards it. "Oh, didn't you know that was here? That's a piece of the old City wall," said Neigh, looking furtively around at the same time. Behind the bastion the churchyard ran into a long narrow strip, grassed like the other part, but completely hidden from it by the cylinder of ragged masonry.'

The ch. was the first in the City to suffer in the Blitz, being badly damaged on 24th Aug. 1940 and again later. The rectory has been demolished and the churchyard has disappeared in the rebuilding of the Barbican area, of which the ch. is now a feature. The E. window was destroyed but a new one has been built; there is a heraldic window created at the W. end. Many of the busts, including Milton's, remain but the external statue of Milton is now inside the ch. The memorial tablet to Foxe and the Frobisher memorial were both badly damaged, as was the monument to Speed.

The rebuilding of the ch. has taken many years but the result, in its modern setting, is well worth a visit. With the completion of the Barbican project the ch. will be the centre of both a working, residential and artistic area and should have a real part to play in the life of the community.

St. Helen, Bishopsgate (St. Helen's Pl.). There is a popular tradition that so long ago as the 4th century there was a Christian ch. on this site. It was supposed to have supplanted a pagan temple, and to have been erected by the Emperor Constantine on his conversion to Christianity, and dedicated by him to his mother Helena, the reputed discoverer of the true cross. She was a British lady, daughter of Coel II, P. of the Trinobantes, who later became none other than 'Old King Cole,' a name which Harold Bayley (*The Lost Language of London*) derives from 'Celi'—Celtic for the Concealed One. All that is known for certain is that a ch. was in existence in 1010, for in that yr. it is recorded in an extant document that Alwyne, Bp. of Helmeham, removed the remains of K. Edmund the Martyr from St. Edmundsbury to L., and deposited them there for sanctuary for three yrs. until the ravages of the Danes ceased in E. Anglia. In 1162 it is mentioned in a grant of land made by Peter Merewin and Goldeburg his wife to the ch. of St. Mary of Southwark (now Southwark Cath.), the land being 'ante ecclam sancte Elene.' In 1181 it is mentioned in a list of manors and chs. belonging to the dean and chapter of St. Paul's, wherein it is stated that the ch. of St. Helen is the property of the canons.

The priory of St. Helen was founded about 1212. The Dean of St. Paul's,

Alardus de Burnham (d. 1216), gave permission to Wm., the son of Wm. the Goldsmith, patron of the ch. of St. Helen, to found a convent for nuns of the Benedictine Order, reserving the ch. for all ecclesiastical purposes. They wore a black habit and cloak, a black cowl and veil. The nuns were sometimes 'human —all too human' for the ecclesiastical authorities. In the rules drawn up some time between 1385 and 1389 'it is to be enjoined on them that henceforth they abstain from kissing secular persons, a custom to which they have hitherto been too prone.' The prioress was ordered to give up some of her little dogs, and to be content with one or two. The nuns were to wear veils according to the rules of their order, and not such as were unduly ostentatious unless necessity so demanded. In 1432 it was reported that the service was hurried through at Easter and Christmas through a desire for dancing. Rules dated from the chapter house of St. P.'s Cath. in 1439, prescribe that there shall be service night and day, and that no secular women were to be allowed in the dorter without the consent of the chapter in the priory. Dancing and revelling were to be utterly forborne, except at Christmas. In 1308 Wm. de Basing, one of the sheriffs of L., became a great benefactor to the priory, augmenting it both in building and revenue, so that he came to be regarded as a second founder. Appropriate to the traditional story of the foundation of St. Helen's Ch., it was supposed to cherish a piece of the true cross, this having been presented by Edward I in 1285. The northern half of the present ch. was the ch. of the nunnery, and in the N. wall can still be seen the arched entrance from the latter into the choir,' a smaller door with a few steps, which probably led to the dorter (dormitory), and also a hagioscope or squint, consisting of six vertical oblique openings, so constructed as to afford a view of the high altar from the cloisters during the celebration of the mass. In the same wall are what were once thou to have been two aumbries for sacr. vessels. On examination from the outside they proved to be communication grilles between the nuns' ch. and a sacristy external to it. The recess above the hagioscope appears to have been used for an Easter sepulchre; in the

will of John Alfrey there is a direction for the remaking of a monument as he desired to be bd. in the 'quere under a tomb in the wall standing before the image of St. Helen whereupon the sepulchre of our Lord hath been yearly used to be sett.' The priory was surrendered in 1538, the estimated revenue being £10,000 p.a., and it passed into the possession of Sir Richd. Williams, the son of a sister of Thos. Cromwell, E. of Essex, who assumed the name of Cromwell in honour of an uncle who was great-grandfather of Oliver Cromwell. This gentleman sold the priory to the Leather-sellers' Co. (see 'Companies'). The co. used the nuns' refectory as their hall, and adapted some parts of the priory to their business requirements, and for the accommodation of their pensioners. There is a picture of the ruins in Wilkinson's *Londina Illustrata* (1819). In 1799 the whole of the old bdgs. was swept away, and it was said at the time that 'a more ruthless and unpardonable act of ignorant vandalism was perhaps never perpetrated.'

Probably about 1212, when the priory was founded, the original ch. was rebuilt, and the foundations of an apse, discovered in excavations in St. Helen's Pl. in 1922, may have appertained to this. A second nave and choir were added on the N. side of the par. ch. (as in the case of a ch. at Higham Ferrers), and so to-day there is a ch. of two naves of equal length, but slightly different in breadth, the nuns' nave being 26 ft. 6 in., and the par. nave 24 ft. The ch. also contains a S. transept, out of which open the two chapels of the Holy Ghost and the Virgin. The Norman and Early English structure was considerably altered in the reign of Edward II, when Wm. de Basing, sheriff of L., became a most liberal benefactor to the ch. and convent. F. T. Bumpus says:

'Of the work of this period, the outer piers and arch of the fifth bay, counting from the west, in the arcade dividing the two naves, and the jambs and arches of the great eastern window of the "nuns' choir" may be cited as specimens.'

Adam Francis, Ld.M., built the chapels mentioned, dedicated in accordance with his will. In the latter part of the 15th century, under the will of Sir John Crosby (d. 1475), the arcade between the two naves, with the exception of one arch, was entirely rebuilt, and the ch. reroofed. The lancet windows were either removed or blocked up, one, however, still remaining in the W. wall. To this period is assigned the framework of the window above the high altar, the two arches dividing the parochial chancel from the transept and its chapels, and the doorway leading from the nuns' choir to the priory. The two arches dividing the transept from the chapels were probably rebuilt about Henry VII's time. In 1631 Inigo Jones introduced the large three-light windows in the N. wall, and two yrs. later the fine S. doorway, bearing the date 1633 prominently displayed, in St. Helen's Pl.; in 1696 it was decided to consult Sir Christopher Wren, though it is not certain that this was done. About this time the bell-turret was erected; prior thereto the bells had hung over the gateway entrance. In 1744 a W. gallery was built by public subscription, and a screen which crossed the nave from the second pillar from the W. end, making an anti-nave, was removed. In 1865 the gallery was taken down, and in 1874–6 £1,560 was spent on restoring the chapels and chantry, and the floors lowered and the roofs renewed. In 1891, with a sum of £4,092 allotted by the Charity Commissioners, under the City of L. Parochial Charities Act, 1883, further repair and restoration took place, John L. Pearson preparing plans at the instance of the Merchant Taylors' Co. The stone work was re-dressed, the floors of the nave and N. aisle were lowered to their original level, and the whole ch. was repaved. The font and pulpit were refixed in new positions, and the eastern chapels and chantry rearranged. During this work, lasting nearly two yrs., the ch. was closed. The removal of the paving led to the disinterment of a number of bodies which were removed to the City of L. cemetery at Ilford. In 1909 further repairs to the walls were necessary, and to the stonework of some of the corbels on the roof.

In 1873 the benefices of St. Helen's, Bishopsgate, and St. Martin's Outwich (*q.v.*) were united. The latter ch. was demolished, the site was sold, and the principal monuments removed to St. Helen's Ch.

St. Helen's has been called the 'Westminster Abbey of the City' by reason of its tombs. It is unrivalled in this regard. The earliest is the tomb of Sir John Crosby (see 'Crosby Hall'), and his first wife, Agnes (d. 1466). There are recumbent effigies of both of them. This monument has been repaired by the Grocers' Co. (see 'Companies'). At the W. end of the nuns' choir is the tomb of Alderman Hugh Pemberton, Merchant Taylor, who was sheriff in 1490, and d. 1500, and Catherine his wife. At one time it had recumbent effigies. It was removed here from St. Martin Outwich Ch. About the same date (possibly earlier) is the tomb of John Oteswich and his wife. This is in the chapel of the Holy Ghost, and came from St. Martin Outwich. The latter is probably a corruption of the name of the same family, one of whose members founded or endowed the ch. of St. Martin. Immediately N. of the chancel is a monument to Sir Andrew Judd (d. 1558), represented kneeling in his armour with other figures, both male and female, at a desk. The inscription runs as follows:

'To Russia and Muscoua,
   To Spayne, Gynny without fable,
Traveld he by land and sea,
   Both mayre of London and Staple.

'The Commenwealthe he norished
   So worthelie in all his daies
That ech state full well him loved
   To his perpetuall prayes.

'Three wyves he had: one was Mary,
   Fower sunes one mayde he had by her,
Annys had none by him truly,
   By Dame Mary had one dowghtier.

'Thus in the month of September
   A thowsande five hundred fyftey
And eyght died this worthie Stapler
   Worshipynge his posterytye.'

Judde was sheriff in 1544 and Ld.M. in 1550. He founded a free grammar sch. at Tonbridge, his native town, and his L. property is commemorated by Judd St., St. Pancras.

On the N. side of the chancel is the most magnificent monument—Sir Wm. Pickering's (d. 1576). He distinguished himself as soldier and scholar, under Henry VIII, Edward VI, Mary, and Elizabeth, and the memorial is as handsome a one as can be found in a City ch. There is a rich marble canopy supported by Corinthian columns, and underneath a life-size recumbent effigy of Sir Wm.

In the nuns' choir is Sir Thos. Gresham's tomb. It is a large altar-tomb of Siena marble, with a surmounting slab of black marble, bearing the arms of Gresham. It was never completed, and the inscription on the top slab is simply copied from the par. register: 'Sir Thomas Gresham, Knight, bury'd Decembr. the 15th, 1579.' His helmet hangs close to his tomb. It is said to have been carried before his corpse at his funeral. The adjacent window, marking the eastern termination of the nuns' choir, was, during the restoration of 1865–8, filled with stained glass, representing St. Helen and the four evangelists, by the Gresham Committee in memory of Sir Thos. The latter is said to have promised to build for the par. a new steeple 'in recompense of ground in their church filled up with his monument.' He appears to have omitted to have provided for this in his will, and Stow's regret is general when he says St. Helen's 'is a fair parish church, but wanteth such a steeple as Sir Thomas Gresham promised to have built.' Almost in the centre, with a grate around it, is the tomb of Wm. Kirwin (d. 1594). He was a freemason, and the Latin inscription says:

'The fates have afforded this narrow house to me who have adorned London with noble buildings. By me royal palaces were built for others. By me the tomb is erected for my bones.'

A monument in the NE. corner is to Alderman John Robinson, Merchant Taylor and Merchant of the Staple of England, who d. 1599. The inscription states that 'the glass of his life held three score and ten yeares, and then ranne out.' There is also shown on the monument Christian his wife who 'changed her mortall habitation for a heavenly in 1592.' 'They spent together,' we read, '36 yeares in holy Wedlock and were happy besides other worldly things in nyne sonnes and seaven daughters.' These are shown, properly divided as to sex.

There is a Latin inscription to Albertis Gentilis, author of *De Jure Belli Commentationes Tres* (1589). He was Regius Professor of Civil Law at Oxford, and a friend of Sir Philip Sidney. He d. 1608, and is said to have been bd. in the same grave as his father, a physician (d. 1602). Alderman Staper (d. 1608) has a monument on the S. wall of the nave, removed from St. Martin Outwich Ch. His epitaph says he—

'was the chiefest actor in the discovery of the trades of Turkey and East India, a man humble in prosperity, painful and ever ready in public affairs, a discreetly liberal housekeeper, bountiful to the poor, and an upright dealer in the world, and a devout aspirer after the world to come.'

The most imposing monument is Sir John Spencer's. In the reign of Elizabeth, the part of Islington now known as Canonbury, and Islington Green, together with a large slice of Clerkenwell, was acquired by Sir John Spencer ('Rich Spencer')—once Ld.M.; who also owned Crosby Hall (*q.v.*). The monument is of the purest alabaster. There are recumbent effigies of Sir John, his lady and daughter, beneath a magnificent arched canopy. It was originally in the S. transept, and was removed here during the alterations 1865–8.

In the nuns' choir is a remarkable monument in memory of Sir Julius Cæsar. Born in 1557, he was a son of Q. Mary's Italian physician. He devoted himself to the law, his first appointment being as Admiralty Judge under Elizabeth. He m. three times. His last wife was a niece of Bacon, and he was present at the E. of Arundel's house when the great Ld. Chancellor d. 1626. The curious Latin inscription sets out that Cæsar:

'Chancellor of the Exchequer and Master of the Rolls . . . by this my act and deed confirm with my full consent that, by the Divine aid, I will willingly pay the debt of Nature as soon as it may please God. In witness whereof I have fixed my hand and seal February 27th, 1634.'

Here follows the signature 'Jul. Cæsar,' and below is another clause:

'He paid this debt being at the time of his death of the Privy Council of King Charles, also Master of the Rolls; truly pious, particularly learned, a refuge to the poor, abounding in love most dear to his country, his children, and his friends.'

while still lower is written in large letters: 'Irrotulator Caelo' (it is enrolled in Heaven). The 'debt' was paid in 1636. This is surely the most legal monument in existence. Cæsar's portrait is in the N.P.G.

There is an elaborate monument of black marble and alabaster to Capt. Bond (d. 1643), of the City Trained Bands at Tilbury in 1588, and subsequently M.P. for the City. He is represented seated at a table in his tent, while outside there is an attendant holding his horse, and two sentinels.

On the S. wall, close to the W. door, is a tablet to the memory of Dame Abigail Lawrence, wife of Sir John Lawrence, Ld.M. in 1665, the yr. of the Plague. He was conspicuous by his courage, benevolence, and energy, a marked contrast to the pitiable successor who was in office during the G.F. In the nuns' choir is a memorial of Francis Bancroft, an officer of the Ld.M.'s Court, who amassed a considerable fortune and, on his death in 1727, bequeathed over £28,000 to the Drapers' Co., in trust for the erection and endowment of almshouses for twenty-four poor old men of that co., and a sch. for one hundred boys. The almshouses, once in the Mile End Rd., have been pulled down; the sch. is at Woodford (Essex). He caused his tomb to be erected in his lifetime, and settled part of his estate, to quote an inscription he himself drew up, 'for beautifying and keeping the same in Repair for ever.' The tomb was of a square shape, and covered with a lid supplied with hinges so as to admit of its being opened for the purpose of viewing the corpse, which was embalmed in accordance with Bancroft's instruction. A solemn inspection of the body by officials of the Drapers' Co. took place periodically for over 100 yrs., but it became so unsavoury a task that it was abandoned. The position of the tomb is now marked by a brass fender.

On the floors of the chapels there are seven memorial brasses, commemorating the following: A merchant and his wife, name unknown, c. 1400; Thos. Williams and Margaret, his wife, 1495; a lady abbess, name unknown, temp. Henry VII; Robt. Rochester, sergeant of the pantry to Henry VII, 1510; John Brieux, rector of St. Martin Outwich, 1459; Nicholas Wotton, rector of St. Martin Outwich, 1483. In the Lady Chapel is a tablet bearing the names of those whose monuments were removed (in 1874) from St. Martin Outwich Ch. On the S. wall of the S. transept—behind the organ—is a marble scalloped shell and a scroll. It is of Arab or Moorish design, and almost exactly parallel with similar work at the Alhambra in Granada. The Purbeck marble round six foiled panels close by was part of the monument to one Clitheroe, bd. in St. Martin Outwich, and which was used to restore the Pemberton monument. The small statue of a woman reading a book, which is in the Lady Chapel, was formerly covered with black paint. On removal of this it was found to be composed of alabaster. Its origin is unknown. It is believed to have been Italian workmanship, anterior to the 16th century. There is a piscina on the E. wall of the Lady Chapel of early 14th-century date. There is an old oak register chest, 1692. The handsome font has its upper portion of the Charles II period. His arms are over the S. door. In the chapel is an old Jacobean table, formerly the communion table from St. Martin Outwich Ch. The Merchant Taylors (patrons) attend service twice a yr., the Leathersellers on election of master, and the Turners on St. Katherine's Day.

At the W. end is a stained glass window commemorating ten worthies of St. Helen's: Sir John Crosby, Sir Andrew Judd, Martin Bond, Sir W. Pickering, Sir Thos. Gresham, Sir John Spencer, Sir Julius Caesar, Albericus Gentilis, Robt. Hooke, Sir Francis Bancroft. Hooke was the City Surveyor, probably responsible for the Monument (usually ascribed to Wren), Bethlehem Hosp., Merchant Taylors' Hall, etc. He d. in 1703. There is old stained glass in one of the windows of the nuns' choir, and some more—coats of arms—in a window in the chapel of the Holy Ghost. In the nuns' choir is a memorial window to Shakspeare. It is known that Wm. Shakspeare was assessed for 5s. for a parly. subsidy, and was described in 1597 as of 'St Ellen's Parishe.' It is supposed, therefore, that he resided in this par., which was not far from the Shoreditch theatres. In 1884 Mr. H. H. Prentice, a Canadian gentleman, presented the window, which was unveiled by the Ld.M.

At the W. end in glass cases is a small mus., and a chest which held the sacrament plate, and is dated 1809. There is also a stone coffin.

St. James Garlickhithe (Garlick Hill). It is first mentioned in 1170. It was first called 'St. James apud Viniteriam' (St. James near the Vintry), 1177. Other forms are 'St. James by the Thames' (c. 1204), and 'St. James apud Tamisyam' (near the Thames) (1222). According to Stow the second part of the name was due to the fact that 'of old time, on the bank of the river of Thames, near to this Church, garlick was usually sold.' The ch. was rebuilt in 1326, probably by Richd. Rothing, sheriff, who left money for the support of the fabric, and was bd. there. Many other persons of note were interred in this ch. Amongst them was Richd. Lyons, a wine merchant and lapidary, who, in 1381, was beheaded in Cheapside by the Wat Tyler rebels. Six Ld.Ms. were bd. in the old ch.: John of Oxenford, vintner, Ld.M. 1341; Sir John Wrothe, fishmonger, Ld.M. 1361, d. 1407; Wm. More, vintner, Ld.M. 1395; Wm. Venour, grocer, Ld.M. 1389; Robt. Chichley, Ld.M. 1411 and 1421; Jas. Spencer, Ld.M. 1527. In 1555 £4 13s. 4d. was paid for the making of a rood, but on the death of Mary and the accession of Elizabeth roods became illegal, and about 1558 one was purchased from a neighbouring ch., and converted into pews. In the accounts for 1560 is a receipt of '8½d. for old parchment out of the old mass book.' In 1561 there was a charge of 30s. for making pews, and on a monument of 1588 in the old ch. there was an epitaph on the man concerned in making them:

'Here Edmund Chapman clos'd in Clay, undoubtedly doth rest
Who to his Neighbours (while he lived) the fruits of love exprest.
Fine pews within this Church he made and with his Arms support,
The table and the Seats in Quire, he set in comely sort.'

The earliest known of the rectors was Peter del Gannek in 1259. Robt. Freeman, who was rector in 1642, was forcibly ejected by order of Parliament in 1647 for continuing to use the Book of Common Prayer. On the Restoration he regained the living, and remained rector until his death.

The ch. was burnt in the G.F., rebuilt by Wren, reopened for worship in 1682, and completed in 1683. It contains two side aisles, separated from the nave by Ionic columns, elevated on lofty bases encased in wood. The gallery supports are finely constructed of Sussex iron. The walls are panelled with oak to the height of 9 ft., there are handsome door-cases at the NE. and SE., and the pulpit and large sounding-board, which are placed against a pillar of the N. side, are well carved. The staircase to the gallery is an excellent piece of woodwork, and the balustrade is undivided and seems to have been made from a single tree. There are high-backed churchwardens' seats, and the C.C. pews have elegant swordrests and figures of the lion and unicorn. The altar-piece is of oak, with Corinthian columns and entablature. The royal arms on the S. wall were originally above the altar. The picture of the Ascension above the altar-piece was the work of A. Geddes, A.R.A., and was presented to the ch. in 1815 by Dr. Thos. Burnet, then curate, and afterwards rector of the par. The font has a handsome cover. It has a steeple 125 ft. high, and similar in design to that of St. Michael's Paternoster Royal (q.v.). At the junction of the first and second stories of the tower there was a bracket supporting a clock, and above it, facing northward, a quaint gilded figure of St. James. These were destroyed in the Blitz. A figure of the saint is also on the beadle's staff, and on some ironwork in the ch.

The ch. is said to have been dedicated to St. James the Great, who was beheaded under Herod Agrippa at Jerusalem. The grottoes of oyster shells, still sometimes seen in the sts., had their origin in the story of St. James, whose day is 5th Aug. The shell is on the par. mark, the churchwarden's staff, and the chancel chair.

The ch. has more the aspect of a mus. than most City chs. It has even a mummy. In 1839 the vaults were being finally closed up, and, on digging in the chancel, there was found a body in almost complete preservation, except that the hair had perished. For many yrs. it was kept in the ch., and a man who was choir-boy in the 1880's asserts that the boys used to take the skeleton for a run round. It is now in a cupboard.

One of the registers of St. James Garlickhithe Ch. dates back to 1535, three yrs. before they were compulsory. An account book (belonging originally to the ch. of Holy Trinity the Less) from June 1593 to June 1594 has some curious drawings, including one of the Judgment of Solomon. The registers show an average of about 38 deaths a yr., until the Plague, when they rose to about 150.

On 13th June 1917 the windows of the ch. were seriously damaged by a bomb from a German aeroplane, which also nearly destroyed a neighbouring warehouse. From 1920 to 1930 an annual service of thanksgiving for this escape was held.

The Vintners' Co. sometimes have their annual service here, and sometimes at the ch. of St. Michael, Paternoster Royal. They have been several yrs. in succession now. They have been coming for about 400 yrs. The Joiners' Co.'s annual service here goes back 450 yrs., but they went elsewhere for a time. The Parish Clerks' Co. and Painter-Stainers' Co. also came for an annual service, the latter on the day of their patron saint, St. Luke— (18th Oct.), and the Glass Sellers' Co. twice a yr.

The ch. sustained some damage in the Blitz, and in 1954 was closed as a dangerous structure. It was rehallowed after restoration in 1963.

St. Katherine Cree (Leadenhall St.). The first reference is 'St. Katherine de Christchurch at Alegate' (1280). It was erected within the chyd. of the priory of Holy Trinity (*q.v.*), and previously the parishioners had worshipped at an altar therein. In 1303 it was referred to as 'Sanctae Katerinae Trinitatis.' 'Cree' is a corruption of 'Christ.'

The body of the ch. was rebuilt between the yrs. 1628 and 1630, the first brick of the new structure being laid by Capt. Martin Bond (see 'St. Helen's, Bishopsgate'), who was alderman and deputy of Aldgate Ward. The date 1630 is on the keystone of an arch in the NW. corner. The steeple (according to Stow, was erected until the beginning of the 15th century) was left untouched. The new ch. was consecrated by Laud, then Bp. of L., in 1631. Rushworth's *Historical Collections* give a full account of the ceremonial, superstitious in the extreme to Puritan minds. As Laud approached, persons stationed at the door shouted: 'Open, open, ye everlasting doors, that the King of Glory may enter in.' Laud fell on his knees, threw dust from the ground into the air, bowed to the chancel, pronounced curses on those who should profane this holy place, and blessings on those who should contribute towards its support. In a glass case in the chancel are a Bible and Prayer Book. The latter

is dated 1662, but it has the 1630 binding, probably from the book used by Laud.

The design of the ch. has been attributed to Inigo Jones. It is a combination of Gothic and Classical architecture, and internally one of the most bright and attractive of City chs. The brightness is due to the large E. window, constructed in the shape of a wheel, St. Katharine's traditional emblem, which has also given the name to a firework. According to tradition the saint was martyred under the Emperor Maximinus. She was to have been broken on a wheel, but the wheel, breaking at her touch, she was beheaded by sword (see 'Westminster'). The stained glass in the window was the gift of Samuel Stainer, Ld.M. 1713. The glass of the lower part of the window is of recent date. In a window on the N. side St. James, St. Katherine and Abp. Laud are shown. The two aisles are divided from the nave by Corinthian columns and round arches, which support the clerestory. There is one pier of the old ch. remaining—at the W. end of the S. aisle. The ceilings, both of the nave and aisles, are groined, and on the roof are displayed the arms of the City and some of the City cos. In the N. aisle, commencing from the E. window, they are: N. aisle: Mercers', Drapers', Skinners', Salters', Dyers', Pewterers'; nave: City; Fishmongers', Merchant Taylors', Ironmongers', Clothworkers', Leathersellers'; S. aisle: Grocers', Goldsmiths', Haberdashers', Vintners', Brewers'. The Cordwainers' arms are in the window by the side of the vestry. The window above the vestry door is in honour of St. Cecilia (1866). The lowness of the floor (it is probably about 15 ft. higher than once it was) was commented on by Stow:

'This church seemeth to be very old; since the building whereof the high street hath been so often raised by pavements that now men are fain to descend into the said church by divers steps, seven in number.'

The steeple was heightened early in the 18th century by erecting a Tuscan colonnade, supporting a cupola upon the old tower. On the S. wall between two of the windows is a curious old sundial. It bears the motto, 'Non sine lumine,' and was put up in 1706.

Beneath a canopy is a full-length recumbent figure of Sir Nicholas Throkmorton. He was one of the chamber-lains of England, and the ambassador to France from Q. Elizabeth. In the reign of her sister Mary he narrowly escaped death, having been tried for high treason owing to his connection with Lady Jane Grey. Throgmorton St. bears his name to-day. There is also a small tablet inscribed to Bartholomew Ellnor (d. 1636). It is supported by two figures of monks, and was executed at the commencement of the 17th century. There is a tablet to Richard Spenser, who,

'after he had seen prodigious changes in the state, the dreadful tryumps of death by pestilence, the astonishing conflagration of the city by fire, piously lamented the misery, and then in peace and charity, in the faith of Christ, in communion of the church, he finished his course, and left behind him a good name, a deare wife, a vertuous example, and three daughters.'

He d. 1667. A bas-relief at the W. end to Samuel Thorpe (d. 1791) was the work of the elder Bacon. Before the communion rails is a brass plate which marks the site of the burial place of Sir John Gayer. The inscription says it was placed there in honour of his memory by Mr. Edmund Richd. Gayer, of Lincoln's Inn, barrister-at-law, and others of his descendants, in 1888. Sir John was Ld.M. in 1646. As an adherent of Charles I, he was imprisoned by Parliament, and d. in T.L. He had traded in Turkey and the Levant, and once, when travelling in the former country, encountered a lion which did not attack him. The marvel of the deliverance has faded a little in the light of the common day of rationalistic criticism. Allen Walker coldly dismisses the suggestion of supernatural intervention.

'There is no doubt at all that the piety of Sir John Gayer saved his life. Sir John was doing the very best thing in dropping upon his knees and remaining motionless, though it is quite possible that he did not know that beasts of prey have been proved to be unaware of the existence of a motionless human being. This is because their sight seems to take cognizance of moving, rather than of stationary creatures, and hunters of great game have told of similar escapes.' One might also ask what kind of lions inhabited Turkey?

However, Sir John, who also gave the font to the ch., bequeathed at his death the sum of £200 to the par., partly for charitable objects, and partly for the preaching of an annual sermon, called the 'Lion Sermon.' The preachers was to have £1, the clerk 2s. 6d., and the sexton 1s. The Parochial Charities took over the money under the Act of 1891, but the sermon is still preached—on 16th October.

The pews have been converted into panelling for the walls. The sounding-board is made of seven different kinds of wood. At one time it was used as a vestry table. There is a fine door-case leading to the vestry, dated 1693. The silver gilt plate was presented by Charles I.

It is said that this was the first ch. where a flower service was held. This, however, held in the neighbouring St. James's Ch., 1852. The service continued until the First World War, when cigarettes for soldiers were brought instead. The flower services which then faded out were not revived. The vicar who instituted the flower service, Rev. Wm. Whittemore, also introduced the watchnight service into the Anglican Ch., as recorded on a tablet at the W. end. During restoration in 1920 there was found scratched upon one of the windows: 'Thomas Jordan cleaned this window and damn the job I say 1815.'

In 1873 the ch. of St. James's, Duke Pl., was pulled down, and the par. united with St. Katherine Cree. It was built upon part of the ancient priory site. The garden at the back of St. Katherine Cree Ch. belonged to the priory. The plane tree there is said to be the tallest and oldest in the City. There are a commemorative fountain and seat and the entrance gate of the old chyd.; in the tympanum of the arch is a nude stone skeleton.

St. Lawrence Jewry (Gresham St.). It was in existence by 1136. The saint to whom it was dedicated was martyred in Rome about the yr. A.D. 258. He was roasted on a gridiron, and by reason of the mode of his death, the domestic utensil became his emblem. Jewry was the Jews' quarter, and close by is the thoroughfare still known as Old Jewry.

There were chapels of St. Mary and St. John in the medieval ch. Amongst interesting burials were Geffrey Fieldynge (Ld.M. 1452); Richd. Rich, ancestor of the Earl of Warwick (d. 1469); 'Godfrey

Bollen Mercer' (Ld.M. 1457) and Thomas Bollen, his sonne Esquier of Norfolk' (d. 1471). This spelling (Stow's) is a variation of 'Bullen' or 'Boleyn.' The Ld.M. was the great-grandfather of Q. Anne Boleyn. Others bd. were Wm. Purchase (Ld.M. 1498); Sir Richd. Gresham (Ld.M. 1537); Sir Michael Dormer (Ld.M. 1541); Sir Wm. Rowe (Ld.M. 1593). Sir Richd. Gresham was the father of Thos. Gresham, and was bd. in the same grave as his first wife. Dame Alice Avenon vas also bd. here. She was a daughter of Thos. Hutchen, citizen and mercer, and was three times m.: firstly to Hugh Methwold, mercer; secondly, to John Blundell, likewise a mercer; and thirdly to Alexander Avenon, Ld.M. 1569. She was a benefactor to the poor of the par., and during her second widowhood, endowed a charity appointing the Mercers' Co. trustees.

The ch. was burnt in the G.F., as also was the neighbouring ch. of St. Mary Magdalene, Milk St. The latter was not rebuilt, and the two pars. were united. The first stone of the new ch. was laid in 1671; it was opened for service in 1677, and finally completed in 1680. One of the most handsome of Wren's chs., it had Corinthian columns, a richly worked entablature, and a fine ceiling of sunken panels and scrolls.

The ch. was reduced to a shell on 29th Dec. 1940 when German bombers attempted to set L. on fire. The same night the neighbouring Guildhall was badly damaged.

The only monument of importance was Abp. Tillotson. He was m. in the pre-Fire ch. and was lecturer in its successor when, in 1691, he became Abp. of C. There was destroyed a stained glass window in memory of Sir Thos. More, who in the medieval ch. in 1501 delivered discourses on Augustine's *City of God*. Destruction also came to the most beautiful vestry of any City ch. Its beautifully moulded ceiling was painted by Sir Jas. Thornhill, the subject was the reception of St. Lawrence, into Heaven after his martyrdom. The gridiron had been transformed into a harp. Over the fireplace was an old picture which depicted the manner of the saint's death. It was the work of Guiseppe Ribera, called 'Spagnaletto'—the little Spaniard (1598–1648). It was rescued at the time

of the G.F. by a youth. It was saved a second time in 1940.

In the ruins there is a tablet commemorating the visit to Vancouver of Sir Percy Vincent, Ld.M., during his term of office in 1936. The ensign referred to in the inscription has been destroyed.

The tower of the ch. remains and the weather vane (gridiron) which came down is now preserved in a small chapel constructed in 1943. Here also is a font brought from what was once the ch. of Holy Trinity, Minories. It dates from *c.* 1620.

The ch. of St. Lawrence Jewry is annually attended by the Ld.M. on 29th Sept., the day of election of his successor, who accompanied him to the service. There was a very large pew for their accommodation; the sword-rest has survived, but an arm-chair and table have gone.

There is a painting of the ruins by Denis Flanders, in the C.C. Art Gallery.

St. Magnus the Martyr (Lower Thames St.). The earliest reference is in confirmation of a grant by William I to W.A., dated 1067: 'lapidee eccle sci magni prope pontem' (stone ch. of St. Magnus near the bridge). A stone ch. at so early a date is unusual. Newcourt stated that the saint to whom the ch. was dedicated was a Christian who suffered in Caesarea in Cappadocia, in the time of Aurelian the emperor, A.D. 258. According to Prof. Worsaae (he came to England in 1846 to investigate Danish memorials) the dedication was to a Norwegian jarl, killed in the 12th century on one of the Orkney islands, and bd. in Kirkwall Cath., which is dedicated to him. This has been accepted of late yrs., and in the present ch., on the S. wall, is a figure of this St. Magnus, placed there in 1924. He is holding a model of the ch. Referring to Kirkwall Fair, Scott says:

'The fair is of great antiquity, and derives its name from Olaus, Olave, Ollaw, the celebrated Monarch of Norway, who, rather by the edge of the sword than any milder argument, introduced Christianity into these isles, and was respected as the patron of Kirkwall some time before he shared that honour with Saint Magnus the Martyr.'

The chs. dedicated to these two saints were opposite one another, with the Thames between. This is not surprising, as Southwark (under the name of 'Sydvirke' in the Scandinavian sagas) was fortified by the Danes.

The old ch. stood at the head of London Bridge. A few persons of note were bd. there. One was Henry Yeuele or de Yeveley, master-mason to Edward III, Richard II, and Henry IV. He was employed by Richard II on work at Westminster Hall, which still remains, and was bd. in 1400 under a monument still in existence in Stow's time. Others were Sir John le Blund, Ld.M. 1307; John Michell, Ld.M. 1436; Richd. Morgan Knight, Chief Justice of the Common Pleas (d. 1556); Mauritius Griffeth, Bp. of Rochester (d. 1558); Sir Wm. Garrarde, Ld.M. 1555—'a grave, sober, wise and discreet Cittizen, equall with the best and inferior to none of our time,' wrote Stow. He d. 1571. The most famous amongst the rectors was Miles Coverdale, translator of the Scriptures who was instituted in 1564. He resigned in 1566. He was bd. in the ch. of St. Bartholomew by the Exchange (q.v.), and when that ch. was demolished in 1840 his remains were transferred to St. Magnus by reason of the association mentioned. There is in the present ch., S. of the sanctuary, a panel of white marble, beneath a bp.'s mitre, with the following inscription:

'To the Memory of Miles Coverdale
Who, convinced that the pure word of God ought to be the
Sole rule of our Faith and guide of our Practice,
Laboured earnestly for its diffusion; and with the
View of affording the means and reading and
Hearing in their own tongue, the wonderful
Works of God, not only to his own Countrymen, but to the nations that sit in Darkness, and to every creature
Wheresoever the English language might be spoken, spent
Many years of his life
In preparing a translation
of the Scriptures
On the IV of October MDXXXV
The first complete English printed Version of
The Bible
Was published under his direction
The Parishioners of St. Magnus the

Martyr
Desirous of acknowledging the mercy of God,
And calling to mind that
Miles Coverdale
Was once Rector of their Parish
Erected this monument to his memory
A.D. MDCCCXXXVII
How beautiful are the feet of them that preach the Gospel of peace, and bring glad tidings of good things.
Isaiah lii. 7.'

From a curious compilation called *Arnold's Chronicle*, published about the end of the 15th century, it may be inferred that the ch. was somewhat neglected.

'First, that the churche and the chauncel is not repaired in glasinge in dyvers placis. Item we fynde not that cliere inventory is made of the goodis and landis of the chirche. Item that dyvers of the priestis and clarkes, in tyme of dyvyne service, be at taverns and alehowsis, at fyshing and other trifls, whereby dyvyne servyce is let [hindered].'

St. Magnus Corner was one of the places for piquant publicity. Machyn chronicles in his diary that this corner, with Cheapside and Leadenhall, were the three places from which the herald and trumpeter in the presence of the Ld.M. and sheriffs, with Ld. Admiral Howard, proclaimed Sir Thos. Wyatt a traitor and a rebel for his rising against Q. Mary (1554). The rebels were hanged at the gates of L., and in all the principal places of the City; among them three at St. Magnus and three at Billingsgate. In the Second Part of *Henry VI* Jack Cade is made to say: 'Up Fish Street. Down St. Magnus' Corner. Kill and knock down.' Machyn also records the funeral of Maurice Griffyth, Bp. of Rochester, and rector of St. Magnus in 1558. He was 'taken from the plasse in Sowthwarke into sant Mangus in London; for he was parsun ther; and he had herse of wax, and a v dozen pensels, and the qwyre hanged with blake and armes.' Recently there was discovered in the register (1594) the entry: 'Benjamine Johnson and Anne Lewis married.' As a child of Jonson's was baptized in the ch. of St. Botolph, Bishopsgate, in 1600, this was probably 'Rare Ben.'

St. Magnus's Ch. was burnt in the G.F. It was rebuilt by Wren in 1676, but the steeple was not added until 1705. The latter is one of Wren's best efforts, with its Ionic pilasters, stone octagonal lantern, lead-covered cupola, lead-covered lantern and spire, culminating in a finial and vane. It is 185 ft. high, only 17 ft. less than the Monument. The interior is divided into a nave and side aisles by slender Ionic columns. The ceiling is arched and ornamented with fretwork. The altar-piece is very handsome. It has four Corinthian columns, with entablature and pediment, and much carving has been bestowed upon it. The well-known medieval symbol of sacrifice, the pelican, figures here. An early addition to the ch. was the clock which is suspended from the tower. This was the gift, in 1709, of Sir Chas. Duncombe, alderman of the ward of Bridge Within, in which St. Magnus's Ch. is situated. He was Ld.M. in that yr. It is said that he was instigated to do this by a recollection of being late for an appointment when a youth through ignorance of the time. Originally the clock, which hung over the roadway of London Bridge, had gilded figures of St. Magnus and St. Margaret, Hercules and Atlas, and two cupids. All these have vanished. In one of his *Letters from the Dead to the Living* (1702) Tom Brown refers to the clock. Alderman Backwell, dead, writes to Duncombe, still of the living, and refers to 'your gilt oracle of time, that public monument of your generosity.' He refers also to 'your promise of a mansion house for the city-magistrate, and the twelve apostles to be elevated at the east end of St. Paul's.' These were not forthcoming. The organ of St. Magnus's was also given by Duncombe in 1712.

In the lobby of the ch. the Table of Benefactions gives an account of its narrow escape during the 'late terrible Fire on London Bridge,' and provides for a sermon every 12th Feb. to commemorate the preservation. This was the fire of 1633 (see 'London Bridge'). A tablet in the vestibule

'was here placed as a Memorial of a dreadful fire which suddenly broke out with great violence about ten o'clock in the morning on the 18th April 1760 at an OYL shop adjoining to the South East end of this Church, which instantly consumed the VESTRY ROOM, burnt most part of the roof of the Church, greatly

injured the ORGAN, and did very considerable damage to the whole Fabric.'

Close by another tablet informs the reader that in 1768 the vestry room at the NW. end and the SW. and NW. corners were taken down by the City of L. for the purpose of making a passage under the steeple, pursuant to an Act of 1756. Thus the length of the ch. was reduced for the footway, which stands isolated from the present London Bridge, opened in 1831 and erected 100 ft. W. of the previous one. There is a C.C. plaque in the chyd. There is also a piece of decayed timber, described as 'wood from the Roman wharf,' and a statue of 'The Good Shepherd,' which from 1881 to 1936 stood at the Convent and Hosp. for Incurable Children in Shoreditch.

The oak pulpit is beautifully carved, and two copies have been made, one for the ch. of St. Lawrence Jewry. There was a restoration in 1924, and before that the pulpit had been a three-decker in light varnished oak. The pulpit canopy, then replaced, was lying in the vestibule with carvings broken. The wrought-iron rails were on the top step, leaving a sanctuary only a few feet wide. N. and S. reredoses with altars were added, the southern one, where stands Wren's old communion table, being an old porch that had once stood at the central door on the N. side. Some yrs. ago a rich American would gladly have bought it for a house in New York. He had to content himself with a copy, very carefully made, costing £500. The N. one was erected in memory of the father and mother of the Rev. H. J. Fynes-Clinton. It was made of old carvings and wood from the ch., and brackets found in a cottage in the par. which was being pulled down. There is a new Ld.M.'s seat, a combined bp.'s throne and stall, and the seating is of Spanish prie-dieu motif, inviting to pray. The baptistery was formed at the same time, the font being removed from the E. end. A beautiful sacristy was made at the W. end. There was a number of box-pews dating from 1832, when the ch. was re-seated to accommodate the congregation from St. Michael's, Crooked Lane. They were removed save two; one at each end as historic momentoes and useful cupboards. The organ case is beautifully carved with musical instruments, etc. There are monograms of Q. Anne on the gallery front. The Ld.M.'s sword-rest bears Q. Anne's arms and monogram, and six shields; three of the latter commemorate Ld.M.'s of 1764, 1792, and 1824, two others bear the arms of the Salters' and Goldsmiths' Cos. The font was given by three parishioners in 1683. It is of marble, with a fine oak cover. There are two old chests bearing the dates respectively 1614 and 1670, and a sword-rest on a pillar near the sanctuary.

In the Lady Chapel is a copy 'with renaissance modification' of the famous figure in the Holy House at Walsingham, the shrine renowned from before the Conquest throughout Europe as 'England's Nazareth'. The fine wrought-iron candlestick, bearing the seven Fraternity lights, is believed to be 17th-century work, and was found by the rector in Paris. Among the pictures is a copy of Murillo's 'St. John the Baptist,' by Alfred Stevens. There is a fine Russian Icon from Moscow on the N. wall, and on the S. side a large cross of mother-of-pearl made in Bethlehem. The plate includes a pre-reformation paten of *c.* 1500, and four rare Puritan patens. There are also (brought from St. Michael's Ch.) a large silver 'basson for the ewse of the Porre,' dated 1524, and the old registers.

There are three interesting relics of St. Michael's, Crooked Lane: the Falstaff cup, a tobacco box, and a tombstone (see 'Epitaphs'). Before the restoration of 1924 there were two primitive fire-engines, which came from that ch. They are now on loan to Lloyd's. Two of these relics of St. Michael's (demolished 1831) are dealt with under the heading of that ch.

St. Magnus the Martyr's Ch. now represents three pars.: St. Michael's, Crooked Lane, and St. Margaret's, New Fish St. (not rebuilt after the G.F.), as well as St. Magnus the Martyr. Their par. marks are in the chyd., near the entrance to the ch. The Coopers', Plumbers', and Fishmongers' Cos. hold their annual services here. Up to the First World War the Fish Harvest Festival (afterwards held at St. Dunstan in the E.) (*q.v.*) was celebrated at St. Magnus the Martyr.

The ch. sustained some damage in the Blitz, but it has been restored. There is a painting of the ch. in the C.C. Art Gallery.

St. Margaret, Lothbury. The earliest mention is 'St. Margaret de Lodebure' (*c.* 1197). It was rebuilt in 1440. It stands over the course of the old Walbrook, and at the time of the rebuilding this was arched over at the expense of Robt. Large, who was Ld.M. in the preceding yr., and gave £200 to the ch. Here was bd. in 1383 Robt. Coleman,

'who,' said Stow, 'may be supposed the first builder or owner of Coleman street.'

Another burial was of Hugh Clopton, mercer, Ld.M. 1492 (d. 1496). He rebuilt the nave of the Guild Chapel at Stratford-on-Avon. There was also bd. at St. Margaret's Ch. Sir Brian Tewke, knight, Treasurer of the Chamber to Henry VIII. His wife was Dame Grisilde, suggesting a quality of submission and patience that would have been a requisite of any spouse of his master's.

There was also bd. here Sir Hugh Witch, Ld.M. (d. 1466), and Sir John Leigh (d. 1564), who built a chapel in Lambeth parish ch. (see 'Lambeth'). His epitaph was designed with something of the moral of the medieval morality play of *Everyman*:

'No wealth, no prayse, no bright renowne, no skill,
No force, no fame, no princes love, no toyle,
Though forraigne land by travell search ye will,
No faithfull service of the country soyle,
Can life prolong one minute of an houre,
But death at length will execute his power.
For Sir John Leigh to sundry countries knowne,
A worthy Knight well of his prince esteemed,
By seeing much to great experience growne,
Though safe on seas, though sure on land he seemed
Yet here he lyes too soone by death opprest,
His fame yet lives, his soul in heaven doth rest.'

The ch. was burnt in the G.F., rebuilt of stone by Wren, and completed in 1690. It consists of a nave, a chancel, and one aisle, on the S. side, separated from the main body of the ch. by two Corinthian columns. The walls are panelled to a height of about 8 ft. The S. aisle is railed off from the rest of the ch., and contains a side altar at the E., and at the W. end, on a marble pavement, is a remarkably handsome font, attributed to Grinling Gibbons. The bowl is sculptured with representations of Adam and Eve in Paradise, the Return of the Dove to Noah in the Ark; the Baptism of Christ in Jordan by John, and the Baptism of the Eunuch by Philip.

In 1781 the ch. of St. Christopher le Stocks (*q.v.*) was demolished and the two flat wooden painted figures of Moses and Aaron were brought from there. The screen was brought from the ch. of All Hallows the Great (*q.v.*). It was made at Hamburg, and presented to that ch. by the German Hanse merchants about the time of Q. Anne. The sounding-board also came from the same ch. The pulpit was also brought, but was afterwards transferred to Hammersmith. The candelabra within the sanctuary are other relics of All Hallows.

This small ch.—its dimensions are 66 ft. by 54 ft.—represents seven pars. St. Mary Colechurch and St. Martin Pomery were not rebuilt after the G.F.: The other four have been demolished—St. Christopher le Stocks (1781), St. Bartholomew by the Exchange (1841), St. Mildred in the Poultry (1872), and St. Olave, Jewry (1888). In the reredos there are six stone medallions of the saints of the associated pars. The gilded cross on the S. side of the sanctuary was made from a piece of the oak saved from old St. P.'s Cath. There are two interesting memorials. One is a metal bust inscribed to Petrus le Maire, 1631. This also came from the ch. of St. Christopher le Stocks. Sir Peter Le Maire, M.P., left an annuity of £5 to the poor of that par. The bust may have been the work of Hubert le Sueur. The other is a tablet in memory of John Boydell (Ld.M. 1790). Once surmounted by a bust, the latter has been detached from the monument.

St. Margaret Pattens (Eastcheap). St. Margaret of Antioch, a Christian martyr at the end of the 3rd and the beginning of the 4th century, is commemorated in the first part of the dedication. 'Pattens' has given occasion to much speculation. Stow said of the lane with a similar name, 'because of old time pattens were there usually made and sold.'

It has also been associated with Shakespeare's 'patines of bright gold' from some ornamentation of the roof. There is little reason to doubt that it was a proper name. The ch. was in existence in 1216. At the beginning of the 13th century it was 'Patynz'; in 1275 'St. Margaret de Patins.' C. L. Kingsford found the name 'Patin' in a 12th-century deed.

Notwithstanding all this diversity of opinion as to the origin of the name, pattens flaunt themselves as the real derivation. In the vestibule is a reproduction of an old notice: 'Will the women leave their pattens before entering the church and the men wipe their shoes on the mat?' In a glass case in the SE. corner there are two pairs of pattens. One pair is over 100 yrs. old, the other was made in 1928 in a Salford factory, and presented by a past master of the Patten-makers' Co., whose annual service has been held here in the octave of Epiphany since 1911. Rood Lane was originally, according to Stow, 'St. Margaret Pattens Lane,' but the name was changed, he says, because the old ch. was pulled down. A rood or cross was placed in the chyd. to obtain oblations from the devout towards the rebuilding. The cross was, however, destroyed in 1538, when iconoclastic zeal began to make its way.

The dates on the porch are 1067 and 1687. Of the first ch. nothing is known. It was rebuilt in 1530, and repaired between 1614 and 1632. It appears to have been remarkably destitute of interesting monuments, and of noteworthy history. The ch. was burned in the G.F., and rebuilt in 1687 by Wren. The par. of St. Gabriel, Fenchurch St. (*q.v.*) was then united with St. Margaret Pattens. The only external feature demanding mention at St. Margaret Pattens is the lofty spire—wood covered with lead—terminating now in a ball and vane. At one time it had a cross which was a replica of the one on St. P.'s Cath., but this was found too heavy to be safe, and it is now on the S. side of the ch. The spire attains a height of 200 ft.; St. Mary le Bow and St. Bride's are higher. Largely Gothic in conception, it is more like a medieval ch. spire than any other of Wren's. The S. wall of the present ch. is built partly of rubble and masonry from the old one. It consists of a nave, chancel, and N. aisle. A large E. window affords excellent light. The altar-piece has carvings of the Grinling Gibbons sch. A previous rector gilded the woodwork over and removed the altar gates. The altar was formerly painted red and varnished. The hour-glass dates from about 1750, and was presented by a former rector. At the back of the ch. are two canopied pews, unique in the City. This was the ch. regularly visited by Sir Christopher Wren, and his monogram is in inlaid wood in the N. pew. One of the pews has a carved lion, and the other a unicorn. The font, on the S. side, is of the Grinling Gibbons sch., it is a hundred yrs. older than the cover. The royal arms over the doorway are those of James II, the only example of his in the City. On the N. wall is a modern tablet to Charles I. The date is 1649, and it bears the text: 'Touch not mine anointed.' Hanging from the N. gallery (galleries were made spacious to accommodate both the pars. mentioned) is a painting of angels ministering to Christ in the garden of Gethsemane. It is said to have been the work of Carlo Maratti (1625–1713), a leading painter in Rome. This was the altar-piece twenty-five yrs. ago. There are fine sword-rests of Sussex iron. There is a chapel in the N. aisle with some finely carved woodwork, an altar surmounted by figures of the Virgin and Child. This is in memory, as a Latin inscription on the W. wall explains, of Thos. Wagstaffe, one of the ablest of the non-jurors, who was appointed to the rectory in 1684, and deprived in 1690 owing to his refusal to take the oath of allegiance to William III. There is also on the altar a beautiful glazed Della Robbia plaque, purchased in Florence, and presented to the ch. by the congregation. Here are also images of the three patron saints of the chapels of the Tudor ch.—the Virgin Mary, St. Mary Magdalene, and St. John the Divine. Here is also the shrine of a naval officer who, with a number of others, perished when a new submarine K4 was rammed by accident on 31st Jan. 1918. It is made of teak from the ship *Britannia*, on which he was trained. At the W. end of this chapel is a list of rectors. Beyond the pulpit to the S. of the altar are some pieces of old tapestry, one from Bruges. There is a Q. Anne chest, and against the E. wall a 'punishment bench,' with a devil's head in the carving at the back.

The most distinguished of past rectors was Dr. Thos. Birch (1705–66), secretary of the Royal Soc., of which he wrote a history. He was one of the principal contributors to the *General Dictionary, Historical and Critical* (1734–41). He was killed by a fall from a horse, and bd. in the chancel. Birch was succeeded by Rev. Peter Whalley. He was eight yrs. headmaster of Christ's Hosp., and amongst other works published *An Enquiry into the Learning of Shakespeare with Remarks on several Passages of his Plays*. He d. in 1791. The Rev. H. J. Newbury, M.A., was a remarkable preacher, who drew an audience of about 1,700 people. It was during his term of office that the ch. was 'beautified' in 1855.

On the N. side against the pillar is a monument erected in memory of his parents by Sir Peter Vandeput in 1686. He was a merchant of Flemish extraction, and was sheriff in 1684. He gave £100 to the poor of the par. On the S. wall is a large and elaborate monument to Sir Peter Delmé, Ld.M. in 1723, who d. 1728. It is the work of the famous sculptor, Rysbrack, a native of Antwerp. On the same side is a large tablet to John Birch, d. 1815, 'an eminent surveyor of this metropolis.' The inscription attains almost record length. He was a surgeon.

The ch. possesses a communion cup of 1543. It is of silver gilt, and it is claimed to be the oldest in the city. The baptismal register goes back to 1559. St. Margaret Pattens is now a Guild Church with present responsibility as H.Q. of the Mission to London Council.

St. Martin, Ludgate (*Ludgate Hill*). The first mention is 1174. The dedication is to St. Martin, Bp. of Tours (d. 397). Robt. of Gloucester (1260–1300) ascribed its erection to Cadwallo, a British p. of the 7th century, but the first recorded fact is that in 1322 Robt. de Sancto Albano was rector. The ch. contained several chapels and was well furnished with paintings, plate, and vestments. There was a monument to Wm. Sevenoke, Ld.M. 1418. His story, according to Lambarde in his *Perambulation of Kent*, had a flavour of Whittington's about it. He was said to have been found in the streets of Sevenoaks, his parents being unknown, and through the assistance of charitable persons made an apprentice to a City grocer, the first step on the road to the mayoralty. Stow, however, found him a father, though he does not explain why his name was Rumsched, and apparently knew nothing of his being a foundling. Certainly Sevenoke took his name from his native place, and there founded a free sch. and almshouses.

The right of presentation to St. Martin's belonged formerly to the abbot and convent of Westminster, and was exercised by them until Henry VIII suppressed the monastery, erected Westminster into a bishopric, and conferred the patronage of this living upon the new diocesan. Samuel Purchas became rector in 1614. He was known as the 'English Ptolemy.' Purchas fell into comparative poverty. He had been promised a deanery by Charles I at the time of his death (1626).

The ch. was burnt in the G.F. and rebuilt by Wren in 1684. It has a cruciform appearance from the introduction of four composite columns, a Greek cross being suggested by the long arms rather than a Latin cross. There is some good woodwork: the altar-piece and pulpit are well carved. The walls are panelled, and there are handsome inner door-cases at the SE. and SW. The font, of white marble, was presented by Thos. Morley, a native of the par., in 1673. It bears the same inscription as the one in St. Ethelburga's Ch. (q.v.). It reads in Greek the same backwards as forwards, and this probably explains its attraction. It is also on the font in Dulwich Coll. Chapel. The organ is by Renatus Harris (17th century). There are two Jacobean chests, and an older iron register chest, and a wooden cover of another chest. In a vestry is a leaden cistern dated 1779, and on the S. side of the ch. are the royal arms of the Stuarts. There is a wrought-iron sword-rest, with the City arms. There is a painting of St. Martin dividing his cloak with the beggar, by a Flemish artist, and other paintings of the Ascension (by Benjamin West), and of St. Mary Magdalene and St. Gregory. West's picture came from St. Mary Magdalene's Ch. Stained glass windows represent St. Peter, St. Paul, and the only Bp. of Westminster, Thirlby.

In 1886 the ch. of St. Mary Magdalene, Old Fish St. (q.v.) was burned and not rebuilt. A brass plate, saved from that ch. is in St. Martin's on the N. wall. It presents the figure of an old man in a gown, and the yr. 1586 over him. The verses are:

'In God the Lord put all your Truste,
    Repent your formar wicked waies:
Elizabeth our Queen most juste,
    Bless her, O Lord, in all her Daies.
So Lord encrease good Counselers
    And Preachers of his holie Worde;
Mislike of all Papistes' desicrs,
    O Lord, cut them off with thy Sworde.

'How small soever the Gifte shal bee,
Thanke God for him who gave it thee.
XII Penie Leaves to xii poor foulkes
Geve every Sabbath Day for aye.'

The figure is supposed to be that of Thos. Berry, a fishmonger, who 'gave a messuage in Southwark, called the Red Cross, with its appurtenances' to the poor of the par., subject to a small annual payment to the towns of Walton and Bootle in Lancashire. The Rev. R. H. Barham, author of the Ingoldsby Legends, was bd. in St. Mary Magdalene's Ch. in 1845. As its par. is now united with St. Martin's there are memorials to his children in the vestibule.

The height to the top of the tapering and graceful spire is 158 ft. The octagonal cupola is lead-covered. St. Martin-within-Ludgate Church is now a Guild Church associated with marriage guidance work.

St. Mary Abchurch (Abchurch Lane, Cannon St.). The earliest mention is c. 1198—'St. Mary of Abechurch.' About 1350 it was 'St. Mary Apechirch.' Stow construed the latter as meaning 'Upchurch,' or on rising ground, but H. A. Harben pointed out that this is not the earliest form, and that the use of the preposition 'of' negatived the idea. He concluded that it was from a proper name 'Aba,' 'Abba,' or 'Abbe.' There were in the ch. chapels of St. Mary and St. Trinity.

It was burnt in the G.F., and rebuilt by Wren 1686, the par. being then united with St. Lawrence Pountney (q.v.), the ch. of which was not rebuilt. St. Mary Abchurch is almost square, measuring 63 ft. in length and 60 ft. in breadth. It is surmounted by a cupola embellished with paintings once attributed to Sir Jas. Thornhill but now known to be the work of William Snow, citizen and painter-stainer. The ceiling is indeed a thing of beauty when the lights are switched on. In the possession of the ch. is a 'Vinegar' Bible, with drawings by Thornhill of similar design. There is also some remarkably good carving, by Grinling Gibbons, on the reredos, the pulpit, and the sounding-board. There is also much carving on the pews. It is the only City ch. where there is documentary evidence that the work was his. There are still preserved two letters of Gibbons, asking the churchwardens of St. Lawrence Pountney for their share of the cost. In the beadle's pew is the par. mace, presented by Dr. Bellamy, the rector, in 1822. At the same time a similar mace was given to Sion Coll. There are two gilded pelicans, one over the altar, and the other over a door. The pelican is a heraldic device attached to Corpus Christi. The ch. of St. Lawrence Pountney had had a coll. of Corpus Christi attached to it in pre-Reformation days, and Q. Elizabeth gave the patronage to the coll. of the same name at Cambridge. At the apex of the reredos (the largest of any City ch.) is the monogram of James II, supported by cherubs. The urns emitting flames here above the well-carved doors are reminders of the G.F. Stained glass windows were destroyed in the Blitz. The two westernmost of the central block of pews display at the ends opening into middle aisle, figures of the lion and unicorn bearing shields adorned with the City arms, and the high C.C. pews at the extreme W. have two elegant sword-rests. There is a marble font with a beautiful oak cover (1605), having four statuettes in niches. There is a 17th-century alms box. The pulpit dates from 1685. The register of marriages, births and deaths shows traces of the G.F.

Against the S. wall of the chancel is an ornate monument to Edwd. Sherwood, of the par. of St. Lawrence Pountney, who d. 1690. Against the E. wall is a monument to Sir Patience Ward (d. 1696), a zealous Whig, Ld.M. 1680 and M.P. for the City 1688–9.

The advowson belonged originally to the priory of St. Mary Overy, Southwark, but about the middle of the 15th century it came into the hands of the master and chaplains of the coll. of Corpus Christi already mentioned. This was surrendered to Edward VI and Q. Elizabeth, in the

tenth yr. of her reign, was induced by Abp. Parker, who had been educated at Corpus Christi Coll., Cambridge, to bestow the advowson upon the master and fellows there, and in their gift the living remains. The earliest rector known by name was Nicholas Woleye (1363). Jas. Nasmith (1740–1809) was one of the rectors. He was a learned divine, and an antiquary. The paved sq. by which the ch. is approached covers the site of the old chyd.

The ch. was seriously damaged by blast and water. Snow's painting has been repaired by Prof. Tristram. As a result of the Blitz vaults were discovered; part is probably of 14th-century date. St. Mary Abchurch is now the Guild Church of the Solicitors' Co.

St. Mary Aldermary (Queen Victoria St.). Stow ascribed the second part of the name to the fact of the ch. being older than any other in the City dedicated to the Virgin. As there is a reference to it *c.* 1080, this is probably correct. The name was then 'Aldermarie,' and in 1272–3 it was 'St. Mary de Eldemariechurche.' An early benefactor was Richd. Chaucer, who was bd. in the ch. in 1348. Stow thought this was the poet's father; it was in fact his grandmother's second husband. Stow says that Thos. Romeyn, Ld.M. 1310, had a chantry there, and that Wm. Taylor, Ld.M., was bd. there in 1483. A more distinguished burial was Chas. Blunt, Ld. Mountjoy (1545). 'He made or glased the East window,' says Stow.

Wm. Blunt, Ld. Mountjoy, was also bd. there in 1594, and two more Ld.Ms: Sir Wm. Laxton (1556) and Thos. Lodge (1563). In 1510 Sir Henry Keble, Ld.M., began to rebuild the ch. His epitaph, formerly in the old bdg., called him:

'A famous worthy wight,
Which did this Aldermary Church
Erect and set upright.'

Before the work was completed he d., but he bequeathed £1,000 to finish it. In 1835 when some houses were being pulled down in Watling St., up to the E. end of the ch., a bdg., which was probably the crypt erected by Keble, was revealed. Its course was from N. to S., and it was about 50 ft. in length. The width was 10 ft., and it had five arches on each side. There, in 1663, Milton m. his third wife.

The ch. was burnt in the G.F., with the exception of the tower. This was damaged in the great storm of 1703, and the upper part entirely rebuilt in 1711. The ch. was rebuilt by Wren in 1681, a sum equal to £5,000 being provided for that purpose by the widow of Henry Rogers, in pursuance of a will that directed that this amount should be expended in the erection or repair of some ch. An inscription in Latin over the W. door records this benefaction. Rogers's widow stipulated that the new ch. should be an exact imitation of Keble's ch., and so there is presented here an unusual specimen of Wren's genius, a Tudor Gothic bdg. It consists of a nave, chancel, and two side aisles, which are separated from the central portion by clustered columns and very slightly pointed arches. The ceiling, both of nave and aisles, is beautifully ornamented with fan-groining, and there are deeply-indented circular panels with a flower in the centre. The spandrels of the arches are adorned with foliage, and shields containing the arms of the archiepiscopal see of Canterbury, and those of Henry Rogers. This is the only City ch. with a ceiling comparable to that of Henry VII's Chapel in W.A. The ch. was much restored in 1876-7. There was then erected a new screen of carved oak at the W. to divide the ch. from the lobby, seats, and stalls, but Grinling Gibbons' pulpit has been preserved. The pavement was renewed, and new stained glass placed in the side windows. A new reredos was substituted for the old altarpiece presented by Dame Jane Smith, widow of Alderman Sir John Smith, who was sheriff in 1669, and was interred in the ch. in 1673. The old pulpit has been preserved, and also the old font—in the NW. corner. A Latin inscription states that it was given by Dutton Seaman, a parishioner, in 1627.

The ch. is as destitute of interesting monuments as it is rich in architectural beauty. In the chancel there is one beautifully sculptured by Bacon with no inscription. On the S. wall is a tablet to Percivall Pott, F.R.S., surgeon of St. Bartholomew's Hosp. for forty-two yrs., who d. 1788, aged 75. The epitaph says: 'He was singularly eminent in his profession, to which he added many new resources, and which he illustrated with matchless writings. He honoured

the collective wisdom of past ages: the labours of the ancients were familiar to him: he scorned to teach a science of which he had not traced the growth: he rose therefore from the form to the chair. Learn reader, that the painful scholar can alone become the able teacher.'

He gave his name to a Pott's fracture—a variety of broken ankle which he sustained when thrown from his horse in Kent St., Southwark, in 1756.

His grave is on the path leading to the ch. from Bow Lane. Another death recorded on a tablet (S. wall) is that of Jas. Braidwood. He was chief officer of the Metropolitan Fire Brigade, and d. on duty at the great Tooley St. fire in 1861. He was bd. at Abney Park cemetery.

In Henry VIII's reign the rector was Henry Gold. He became implicated in the visions of the 'Holy Maid of Kent,' with the result that he went before the Star Chamber and was duly sentenced. He was condemned first 'to stand in Paul's all the sermon time,' and thence he was taken to the Tower and finally to Tyburn for execution. At this ch. the St. Antholin lectures are given (see p. 91). The Cordwainer and Bread St. wards hold services here, as also the Skinners' Co., and the Guild of St. Peter. St. Mary Aldermary is now a Guild Church with the special assignment to promote retreats and the devotional life.

St. Mary at Hill (off Eastcheap). The earliest reference is 'St. Mary de Hull,' *c.* 1190. In 1336 Rose de Wrytell founded a chantry there, and there were four other chapels: St. Stephen's, St. Katherine's, St. Ann's, and St. Christopher's. There was, as at St. P.'s Cath., a pardon chyd., probably the 'litil chyrch-yerd' by the 'abbotes kechen,' closed 1495 or 1496. The abbot of Waltham was referred to. The N. aisle was reconstructed about 1487, and later the S. aisle which was on the site of the abbot's kitchen. According to Fabyan (1516) a coffin of decayed timber was found in 1497, whilst the work was in progress. It contained the body of a woman and the skin was whole and the joints pliable. After remaining above ground for some time an unpleasant odour was emitted, and it was reburied. An inscription showed that it was the body of Alice, wife of Richd. Hackney, sheriff in 1321. Other burials, mentioned by Stow, were:

Nicholas Exton, Ld.M. 1387; Wm. Cauntbrigge, Ld.M. 1420; Wm. Remington, Ld.M. 1500; Sir Thos. Blanke, Ld.M. 1582; Wm. Holstocke, 'Controller of the Queene's shippes'; Sir Cuthbert Buckell, Ld.M. 1594.

It was burnt in the G.F., and rebuilt by Wren, 1672–7, not, however, in its entirety, for the old tower and several of the walls were left standing. After the restoration the par. of St. Andrew Hubbard (q.v.) was united to St. Mary at Hill. The ch. has two side aisles, formed by four Doric columns. There is a cupola, and the central ceiling is arched to the E. and W. of it. The ceiling of each aisle is also elevated into an arch in the space between the columns, a cruciform appearance being thus given to the roof. There are large stained glass windows on the N. and S. walls. There is an abundance of carving, but all of a much later date than the bdg. It was executed by Mr. W. Gibbs Rogers in 1848–9 when the ch. was remodelled. The W. gallery and the pulpit, which has a large sounding-board, display excellent carving. The rector's pew and reading-desk have open tracery, and display the lion and unicorn, each bearing a shield carved 'V.R. 1849.' The C.C. pews have handsome sword-rests. They number six, a record for a City ch. There is an exquisite piece of ironwork from a font cover in a corner of the NW. end. It came from St. George's, Botolph Lane (q.v.). A relic of the G.F. is a piece of stone carving in the vestibule. It represents the resurrection and second coming of Christ. It probably once stood over a gateway. The organ is of particular interest. It was built by the famous Father Smith in the time of Charles II. He also made the organs for St. P.'s Cath. and W.A. The 'black' keys are of ivory and the 'white' ones of ebony.

There is a beautiful sculptured tablet to John Harvey (d. 1700). On the E. wall is a plain slab to the memory of Rev. John Brand, '22 years the faithful rector of this, and the united parish of St. Andrew Hubbard.' He d. 1806. This was the author of *Observations on Popular Antiquities* (1777). He was elected secretary to the Soc. of Antiquaries in 1784, the yr. in which he became rector of St. Mary at Hill. Edwd. Young, the poet (author of *Night Thoughts*), was m. in this ch. in 1731, his wife being Lady Elizabeth Lee,

daughter of the E. of Lichfield.

The existing brick tower replaced the one which survived the G.F. in 1780. Late in the 19th century there was a probability of the ch. being demolished for the purposes of a railway extension, but it was saved by the efforts of the City Church and Churchyard Protection Soc. It was closed for two yrs. whilst it was repaired and fitted with electric light, and re-opened in 1894, the Ld.M. and sheriffs attending in state. During the closure 3,000 bodies were removed and re-interred at Norwood Cemetery. The ch. became famous for the ministry of the Rev. Wilson Carlile, leader of the Ch. Army. There is a small chyd. with two fine ash trees. It is the church for Billingsgate Market.

The Fellowship Porters (q.v.) used to attend an annual service in this ch.

St. Mary-le-Bow, Cheapside. The earliest mention is 'Ecclesiae Sanctae Mariae quae dicitur ad Arcus' (The Ch. of St. Mary which is called 'at the Arch' or Bow) 1091. In 1193 it was 'St. Mary de Archis.' Stow says the ch. was built in William the Conqueror's reign. The derivation of 'Archis' or 'de arcubus,' which Stow called it in his first edition, has been much in dispute. There are chs. of St. Mary Arches in Exeter and St. Peter at Arches in Lincoln, but no derivation that assists here is reliable, the ch. at Lincoln being so called from its proximity to Stone Bow, a gateway with three arches across the High St. Stow, in his first edition (1598), said it derived from the stone arches or bows on the tops of the steeple, shown in the engravings of Visscher and others, and in a model of the ch. on the par. mace. In his second edition (1603), he favoured the notion that it was because it was built upon arches of stone—those still to be seen in the remarkable Norman crypt.

In its lower course the crypt is partly of Roman brickwork. (Wren found a causeway 18 ft. below ground when erecting the tower—it may have been part of the old Watling St.) The ashlar work is distinctly Norman, but the wallings were built by local Saxon masons. There are pillars with the Norman cushion capitals, and one of these has the carving of a spear head, a unique design. There are three apses and it is thought that here was a Roman basilica or hall of justice. The jambs of several windows are still plainly to be seen, showing that what is now correctly called a crypt was, at the time of its erection, level with the st. Only part of the crypt is now open; the other part is filled with bodies brought from the chyd., and in the crypt burials continued until 1860. There is also a deep splayed Saxon window, and a 12th-century staircase that once led to the ch. above.

The ch., says Stow, 'for divers accidents happening there, hath been made more famous than any other parish church of the whole city or suburbs.' He proceeds to say that in 1090, 'by tempest of wind, the roof was overturned wherewith some persons were slain.' Stow adds:

'Four of the rafters of 26 foote in length, with such violence were pitched in the ground of the high street, that scantly foure foote of them remayned above ground, which were faine to be cut even with the ground, because they could not been plucked out (for the Citie of London was not then paved and a marish ground).'

Stow was borrowing from Wm. of Malmesbury and Florence of Worcester. Matthew of Westminster also refers to 'a violent and mischievous wind' which struck L., shaking the towers and bdgs. and — a strange climax — 'fruit-bearing trees.' In 1271 a great part of the steeple fell down and killed a number of people. In 1284, one citizen having wounded another, fled for refuge into the ch., but some friends of the injured party got in during the night and killed him. In consequence sixteen men were hanged, and, says Stow, 'a certain woman, named Alice, that was chief causer of the mischief was burnt.' The ch. was interdicted, the doors and windows being stopped up with thorns. In Edward III's reign, in consequence of an accident that occurred to a grandstand erected for a joust (see 'Cheapside'), there was erected in front of Bow Ch. a house known variously as the 'Crownselde,' the 'New Seldam,' 'Tamarsilde,' and the 'King's Head.' It was a stone bdg., standing so close to the ch. as to cause windows and doors to be stopped up. It was used for the purpose mentioned until 1410, when Henry IV granted it to several mercers, at which time it was worth £7 13s. 4d. a

yr. The balcony which Wren placed on the present ch. to commemorate this can still be seen.

The steeple, says Stow, 'was by little and little re-edified.' Amongst the contributors was Robt. Harding, goldsmith, who was sheriff in 1478, and gave £40. The work was not completed until 1512. A few yrs. later—

'the arches or bowes thereupon with the lanthorns, five in number, to wit one at each corner and one on the top in the middle upon the arches, were also finished of stone brought from Caen in Normandy.'

In the latter half of the 14th century, and perhaps long after, the curfew was rung upon the bells of Bow Ch., together with the bells of All Hallows Barking, St. Bride, Fleet St., St. Martin le Grand, and St. Giles, Cripplegate. In 1469 the Common Council ordered that the great bell of Bow should be nightly rung at nine o'clock. This may have been to indicate the hour at which apprentices were expected to be within doors. Bow Ch. being in the heart of the city, the Bow bell was particularly important to them. Stow relates that:

'This bell being usually rung somewhat late, as seemed to the young men Prentises and other in Cheape, they made and set up a ryme against the Clarke, as followeth:

' "Clarke of the Bow bell with the yellow lockes,
For thy late ringing thy head shall have knockes."
'Whereupon the Clarke replying wrote:
' "Children of Cheape, hold you all still,
For you shall have the Bow bell rung at your will." '

The Court of Arches which sat at Bow Ch. took its name from it. The earliest reference to the court is in 1172, when Pope Alexander III wrote to the Abp. of C.'s judge under the title of Dean of the Arches. He presided over the Abp.'s Court of Peculiars, and of these chs. in the City St. Mary-le-Bow was the chief. It does not appear, however, that the court was always held in this ch., for in 1323 the Abp. of C. cited certain persons to appear before him in the ch. of St. Mary Aldermary. Pepys has an interesting entry in his diary regarding this:

'To Bow Church, to the Court of Arches, where a judge sits and his proctors about him in their habits, and their pleadings all in Latin.'

It is impossible to say whether the court sat in the ch. or the crypt. Dickens made lengthy reference to the court, then one of those included in Doctors' Commons, in *Sketches by Boz* (1836), and the case of Bumple *v.* Sludbury heard therein was based upon a case actually reported by him in the Consistory Court, closely allied to it. Dickens's shorthand note is still preserved in the archives of the ch. of St. Bartholomew the Great, the offence having occurred in that par. The Court of Arches ceased to meet at the ch. after the G.F. It now meets at Ch. House, Westminster. Up to the Second World War Bps. of the southern province still had their elections confirmed at Bow Ch.

The first rector known is Wm. de Cilecester, presented in 1287, and the earliest monument in the ch. of which there is record was to John de Holegh. He 'was buried under a slab of marble,' says Chas. Pendrill,

'surmounted by two images with prayers for his soul written round them. He founded several chantries in the church and took extraordinary precautions to ensure that his benefactions should not sink into oblivion with the passage of time. He provided that all articles in his will affecting the church should be written on parchment and placed on a tablet at the foot of the image of the Blessed Virgin, at the same time leaving 60s. for painting the image and providing it with a crown.'

De Holegh was a pious hosier of Cordwainer St., and bequeathed £20 to anyone who would make a pilgrimage in his name to the Holy Sepulchre in Jerusalem and the tomb of St. Katherine on Mount Sinai; also £7 to anyone willing to undertake the journey to St. James of Compostella in Spain. In addition he left money to all who were willing to go with naked feet to offer a penny at the shrine of the Blessed Mary at Walsingham.

The old ch., like the present one, had singularly few burials or monuments of importance considering its situation in the City. Stow mentions two Ld.Ms.— Sir John Coventrie, Ld.M. 1425, and Nicholas Alwine, Ld.M. 1499. The latter

appears in Lord Lytton's *The Last of the Barons*. Stow refers also to a proper 'Chappell on the south side,' where 'standeth a Tombe elevate and arched,' of 'Ade de Buke Hatter' who 'glased the Chappell, and most parts of the Church, and was there buried.' He refers also to chantries of Hawley and Sowtham.

The ch. of St. Mary-le-Bow was burnt in the G.F., and rebuilt by Wren. The work was not finally completed until 1680, and the cost—£15,400—was a larger amount by over £3,000 than was expended on any other of Wren's par. chs. Lady Williamson contributed £2,000, and her benefaction was commemorated by a tablet over the door of the vestry. The form of the ch. was taken from the Temple of Peace at Rome. It was almost square, measuring 65 by 63 ft. The interior was a handsome one. The two side aisles were separated from the main body by two Corinthian columns. There was an altar piece, richly gilded, set up in 1706. On it was a modern copy of Murillo's 'Holy Family' (in the N.G.). There was a carved oak pulpit with a monogram of two Cs., supposed to represent Charles II and his Q. Catherine. The font was modern; its predecessor, the gift of Francis Dashwood, for some reason had been removed to St. Alban's Ch., Westcliffe-on-Sea, in 1898.

The ch. was reduced to a shell by bombs. For twenty years it remained a shell but in 1961 the Bow Bells, re-cast and re-hung, heralded the start of reconstruction. The rebuilt church was opened in 1964.

In 1876 the par. of All Hallows, Bread St. (*q.v.*) was united with that of St. Mary-le-Bow, the ch. having been demolished. As this par. had been united with St. John the Evangelist (*q.v.*), St. Mary-le-Bow thus added two pars. at once. A tablet to John Milton, formerly outside All Hallows Ch., was brought to Mary-le-Bow Ch., and placed on the outside of the W. wall, when the former was demolished. Some time after a stained glass window was placed in the W. wall, close to the tablet, as a further memorial to Milton. It showed the expulsion from Paradise. This has been destroyed.

There also remains, though damaged, the only monument of any note. It was in memory of Bp. Newton, a native of Lichfield who became rector of the ch. in 1744. In 1757 he was created Dean of

Salisbury; in 1761 Bp. of Bristol, and in 1768 Dean of St. P.'s Cath. He was a man of letters and edited *Paradise Lost*, with annotations, in 1749. He subsequently published several more editions of the poet. Newton was also author of three volumes of *Dissertations on the Prophecies*. The first appeared in 1754; the last in 1758.

In modern days this ch. was most famous for its spire, which has survived. It is 221 ft. 9 in. high, and surpassed amongst City chs. only by St. Bride's, which is 226 ft. It was built of Portland stone and involved an expenditure of £7,388, almost one half of the total cost of the edifice. The tower has three storeys, of which the highest, or belfry, stage is ornamented with Ionic pilasters. Above the belfry is a cornice and balustrade, and at the angles rise tall finals, each supporting a vase. Still higher are twelve Corinthian columns, a dome, a lantern, and last the spire, culminating in a weather vane in the form of a dragon, the City emblem. The dragon was hoisted in 1679. It is 8 ft. 10 in. in length, and on each wing is a cross of gilt copper. An extract from Wren's account book mentions it:

> 'To Edward Pierce, mason, for carving of a wooden dragon for a modell for ye Vane of copper upon ye top of ye Steeple, and for cutting a relive in board to be profered up to discern the right bigness, the summe of £4.'

There was a popular Mother Shipton prophecy that if the grasshopper from the Royal Exchange and the dragon of Bow Ch. should meet, something would happen, and Swift said that 'when the Dragon on Bow Church kisses the Cock behind the Exchange great changes will take place in England.' 'The Cock behind the Exchange' was probably the weathercock of the ch. of St. Bartholomew by the Exchange, demolished in 1841. Haydon in his *Table Talk* says:

> 'Just before the Reform Bill of 1832, the Dragon and the Cock were both taken down at the same time to be cleaned and repaired by the same man and were placed close to each other. In fact the Dragon kissed the Cock, and the Reform Bill was passed.'

It was passed, too, without any bloodshed. In 1820 a young Irishman, Michael Burke, descended on the dragon's back, pushing with his feet from the cornices and scaffolding, in the presence of thousands of spectators. The walls of the tower are 7 ft. thick.

The tower and steeple of St. Leonard's Ch., Shoreditch, are an imitation by Geo. Dance the elder of those at Bow Ch., and something similar can be seen at Shadwell Ch. The bells were originally six in number, and on these were played the celebrated 'Whittington tune.' They perished in the G.F. A new set of eight were cast by 1680 by Hodsons of St. Mary Cray, Kent. In 1738 the tenor, which had cracked, was recast by Phelps & Lester of Whitechapel. In 1758 all the other bells were condemned, and replaced by the same firm. In 1881 Messrs. Mears & Stainbank, the successors of Phelps & Lester, added two bells at the top of the scale, making twelve in all. The bells, destroyed in the war but now replaced, are supposed to be of importance to the 'Cockney' (*q.v.*).

The ch. is in Cordwainer Ward, and at the Mansion House is the Cordwainer Cup, added during the mayoralty of G. S. Nottage. It has embossed representations of the two existing chs. in the ward, St. Mary-le-Bow and St. Mary Aldermary. There was until the Second World War annually preached in this ch. a sermon in commemoration of the Gunpowder Plot. It was not latterly preached on 5th Nov.; sometimes the Sunday nearest was chosen. This originated under the will of Mr. Theophilus Royley, citizen and draper of L., dated 12th Feb. 1655, whereby he directed that the sum of 20s. yearly should be 'paid to the Minister of the parish of St. Mary-le-Bow for the time being to preach a sermon yearly in the evening of the fifth day of November,' and the sum of 10s. yearly to 'the Clerk or Sexton for his pains and for candles to be spent every time.' The amounts were increased in 1841 to £2 and £1 respectively.

St. Mary Woolnoth (corner of Lombard St. and King William St.). The 'Parish of Wlnodmariecherche' is mentioned *c.* 1198, and 'St. Mary Wolnoth' 1273. C. L. Kingsford suggested that Wulfnoth de Walebroc, mentioned 1114–33, may have been the founder and H. A. Harben pointed out that 'Wulfnoth' was a name in general use and frequently appears in the form 'Wl' for 'Wulf.' The ch. was rebuilt in 1438 and, according to Stow, again in 1486—by Sir Hugh Brice, Ld.M., and a governor of the Mint, who also built a charnel chapel, as also the steeple. He was bd. in the ch. Simon Eyre (Ld.M. 1445), Stow further says, gave a tavern called the 'Cardinal's Hat,' in Lombard St., and other property towards a brotherhood of our Lady in the ch. He was bd. in this ch. in 1459. Three more Ld.Ms. were bd. here—Sir John Percivall, a Merchant Taylor, about 1504, and Sir Martin Bowes, 1566. His three wives were bd. there also. Sir Thos. Ramsey, Ld.M. 1577 (d. 1590), was the third. His second wife, who survived him, was Dame Mary Ramsey, the benefactress of Christ's Hosp.

The ch. was damaged in the G.F., but not destroyed, the steeple and part of the walls remaining. Wren repaired it in 1677, entirely rebuilding the N. side (facing Lombard St.), but constructing the remainder upon the old walls. Sir Robt. Vyner, Ld.M. 1674, contributed munificently towards the expense of restoration. He was a goldsmith, and had a mansion in Lombard St., and in compliment to him vines were spread about the ch. on the side fronting the house, 'insomuch,' says Strype, 'that the church was used to be called Sir Robert Vyner's Church.' Wren's patchwork proved insecure, and during the reign of Q. Anne it fell into an extremely dangerous state, with the result that it was pulled down in 1716, and the present ch. commenced. It was first opened for worship in 1727. The architect was Nicholas Hawksmoor, Wren's pupil, and it represents one of his finest works. The ch. is almost square. It contains twelve handsome Corinthian columns placed at the angles in groups of three. There is a clerestory, pierced on each of its four sides by a large semicircular window filled with stained glass. The altarpiece is of oak with twisted columns. The oak pulpit is a splendid piece of work. In 1876 the high pews were removed, and also the galleries at the N., S., and W. From the organ gallery at the W. project the banners of the Goldsmiths' Co. The handsome supports of the galleries remain against the walls. The organ, one of Father Smith's, is enclosed in an imposing case.

In 1779 Cowper's friend, Rev. John Newton, became rector of the ch. 'I am about to form a connection for life with one Mary Woolnoth, a reputed London saint in Lombard Street,' he remarked. It *was* for life, as he was still rector, after twenty-eight yrs., at the time of his death in 1807, at the age of 82. Newton contributed to the *Olney Hymns*, and his two best-known compositions are *Glorious things of Thee are spoken* and *How sweet the name of Jesus sounds*. On the N. wall there is a white tablet in his memory. It bears the epitaph he wrote for himself:

'John Newton, Clerk, once an infidel and libertine, a servant of slaves in Africa, was, by the rich mercy of Our Lord and Saviour, Jesus Christ, preserved, restored, pardoned, and appointed to preach the faith he had long laboured to destroy.'

The bodies of Newton and his wife were removed to Olney in 1893. In a case beneath the tablet are a biography of Newton, an autobiography (in letters), a portrait, a plate, and a Bible which belonged to him, one of his letters, and a copy of the *Olney Hymns*.

Here was bd. in 1695, without any memorial, Sir Wm. Phips, a treasure-seeker. (See *London for Americans*.)

Edwd. Lloyd was bd. here in 1712. There is a tablet to his memory, placed here by the Corporation of Lloyd's (*q.v.*) in 1931. The registers date from 1538. Geo. Stone, Protestant Primate of Ireland, was baptized here in 1708.

When the tube station was to be constructed underneath the ch. in 1897 there was a proposal to pull it down: again in 1926 it was one of those scheduled for destruction. It survives, and is externally an impressive ch. The tower is at the W., and the Composite columns in its upper storey and the two turrets surmounted by balustrades present an original appearance. There is a projecting clock attached by a bracket to the N. wall. Some carved cherubs belonging to an old doorway remain in the entrance to the station.

During the building of the station the ch. was closed for some yrs., and in 1900 all the bodies were removed from the vaults to the City cemetery at Ilford, where a rough granite block marks their final resting place. A copy of the inscription there is on the S. wall.

St. Michael, Cornhill. The earliest mention is that Alnothus the priest gave it to the abbot and convent of Evesham in 1055. The latter granted it to Sparling the priest about 1133. It is mentioned in an inquisition of L. chs. in 1181. It had a cloister on the S. side, and a pulpit cross in the chyd. In 1421 a new tower or steeple was commenced, and towards the expense Wm. Rus or Rous, sheriff of L., a great benefactor, contributed largely. Robt. Fabyan, author of *The Concordaunce of Historyes*, was bd. in the ch. (1513), and also the great-grandfather, grandfather, and father of John Stow. The grandfather, who d. 1527, directed his body 'to be buried in the little green churchyard of St. Michael's, Cornhill, nigh the wall as may be by my father and mother.' John Stow related 'a weird story of the tower.'

'Upon St. James' night certaine men in the loft next under the bells, ringing of a peale, a tempest of lightning and Thunder did arise, and an ugly shapen sight appeared to them comming in at the south window and lighted on the North. For fear whereof, they all fell downe, and lay as dead for the time, letting the Belles ring and cease of their owne accord. When the ringers came to themselves, they founde certain stones of the North Window to be raised and scrat, as if they had been so much butter printed with a Lyon's clawe: the same stones were fastened there againe and so remayne till this day. I have seen them oft, and have put a feather, or small sticke, into the holes where the Clawes had entered three or four inches deepe.'

The ch. was burnt in the G.F., with the exception of the tower, which contained a celebrated set of ten bells. The new ch. was built by Wren in 1672. The tower was left, but in 1721 this was rebuilt, one of Wren's last works. It is an imitation of the tower of Magdalen Coll., Oxford, and so there is a Gothic steeple attached to a semi-classical ch. Its total altitude is 130 ft., and it is one of the most pleasing in design of the City chs. The interior has two aisles, divided from the nave by Doric columns. The E. window is circular, and the W. oblong. These windows are filled with stained glass. The appearance of the ch. was greatly altered between 1858 and 1860 by Sir Gilbert Scott, who was also responsible for the porch facing Cornhill with a representation of St. Michael trampling down devils on the entablature. After the remodelling the P. Consort inspected the ch., and praised the work, as also did Tait, then Bp. of L., and afterwards Abp. of C. In the recess under the W. window is a fine representation of the pelican standing upon a nest and feeding her young. The group was formerly over the altar-piece, and was removed during the alterations. The poor-box is unusual in design. It is on an antique pedestal on clawed feet, and is inscribed: 'The poor cannot recompense thee, but thou shalt be recompensed at the resurrection of the just.' The vase for the money is supported on two dolphins. The font bears the date 1672. Here Thos. Gray (he was b. a few yards S. of the ch., and there is a tablet on No. 35 Cornhill) was baptized in 1716. To the sides of the tower arch are affixed brass tablets, recording the particulars of various repairs to the ch. and benefactors after the G.F.

In the vestibule are monuments to three members of the Cowper family. John was sheriff in 1551, and the founder of the fortunes of the family. His son, John (d. 1609), had 'a fair tomb in the Cloyster south' and 'a hatchment.' He was the father of Sir Wm. Cowper of Ratling Court, the first baronet, a zealous cavalier, who d. four yrs. after the Restoration. His successor in the baronetcy was Wm., whose son, also Wm., the third baronet, held the office of Ld. Chancellor in Q. Anne's reign, and became the first E. Cowper. He was the great-uncle of the poet, whose father, the Rev. John Cowper, rector of Gt. Berkhampstead, was the son of Spencer Cowper, younger brother of the Ld. Chancellor. Cowper's Court, Cornhill, marks the site of their residence. There is a monument to John Vernon, a Merchant Taylor, which was erected in place of one consumed in the G.F. It mentions several legacies to the poor. There is a half-length figure of Vernon. The Merchant Taylors' Co. carefully preserve it. This Co. and the Drapers' Co. attend an annual service here.

In a glass case are a walking stick that belonged to Gray, a piece of the Roman wall found under the ch., a pewter plate formerly used in the dinners of the Cornhill Ward, and a chained copy of

'The Book of Martyrs by Mr. Fox.' The book was stolen in 1607, but the thief was caught in the following yr.

The 'little green churchyard' was much built upon in the reign of Edward VI, and the successors of those bdgs. now hem it in. When in 1657 coffee was introduced into England, a tent was pitched for its sale in this chyd.

St. Michael Paternoster Royal (College Hill, Upper Thames St.). The earliest mention is 'St. Michael of Paternoster-chierch' (*c.* 1219). In 1361 it was 'S. Michael in the Riole.' 'Royal' is from 'Riole,' first a tenement and afterwards a st., so called from the town of la Reole, near Bordeaux, from which merchants imported their wine so early as 1282. The tenement was first mentioned in 1276 and in 1331 Q. Philippa was granted certain houses in 'La Reole' for her wardrobe, showing that the name had become attached to a thoroughfare. About 1370, Edward III (his Q. having d. the previous yr.), gave the Wardrobe to his newly founded Coll. of St. Stephen, Westminster. Froissart mentions an interview between Richard II and his mother, Joan of Kent, as taking place here in 1381, after the Wat Tyler rebels had been dispersed. Prior to 1483 it was for a time in possession of Henry D. of Somerset and Strype says that Richard III gave it to the D. of Norfolk. In 1529 it was granted to R. Radclyff, and in Stow's time Tower Royal was let out in tenements. The ch. seems to have occupied the N. end of 'La Reole.' It was mentioned in a list of churches compiled for taxation by Pope Nicholas IV in 1291. In 1409 part of a vacant plot of land in the st. called 'le Ryole,' in the par. of St. Michael Paternosterchirche, was granted to John White, parson, to build anew a par. ch. to St. Michael the Archangel, with a cemetery. This was due to the generosity of Rich. Whittington. He was bd. in the ch. in 1423. No account of Whittington's tomb or monument remains, but it was probably an imposing one. Stow says that the rector, Thos. Mountain, caused it to be broken up, and the body to be stripped of the leaden sheet and again bd. In Q. Mary's reign there was more disturbance; it was wrapped once more in lead, 'and so he resteth,' said Stow. Machyn mentions the event, and says he 'was new coffined

again,' and 'my lady ys wyffe at Wyttington College had durge over night and the morrow masse: the which was the founder of the same college and builded Nugate and other places and was mere of London.'

An inscription was placed over him, probably not a copy of the original. A free translation is as follows:

'As a fragrant odour was the fame of this Richard Whittington (Albificans villam, i.e. making white the town) who had justly obtained it. The flower of merchants, the founder of a College of Priests and also of an almshouse for the poor. So let these be a sure witness. He built this most beautiful Church to St. Michael; a Court of Hope close at hand, a place appointed for divine assemblies. He was a father to the poor and four times Mayor of this City. He lived until the fourth of March. Lo! the people tell thee he ceased to be on that very day. May he have rest in Christ. Amen.'

Whittington founded a Coll. of Priests (from which College Hill derives its name), the mayor and commonalty granting a piece of land for the purpose adjoining the ch. It was dedicated to the Holy Spirit and St. Mary. It was not completed at Whittington's death, but his executors faithfully carried out his wishes. In 1424 by licence of the Abp. of C. the masters of the coll. were to be rectors of the ch. The first master was Reginald Pecock, who became Bp. of St. Asaph in 1444, and of Chichester in 1449. In 1457 he was charged with Lollardism, tried at Lambeth Palace, and convicted of heresy. He recanted at St. Paul's Cross, and escaped with imprisonment for life. Sir Walter Besant says he was confined in Thorney Abbey, Isle of Ely, and

'kept in a single closed chamber in Thorney Abbey out of which he was not allowed to go: no one was to speak to him, except the man who waited upon him; he was to have neither paper, pen, nor ink nor any books, except a mass-book, a psaltery, a legendary, and a Bible.'

The ch. was burnt in the G.F., and rebuilt in 1694 by Edwd. Strong, Wren's master-mason, under the superintendence of Sir Christopher. The steeple was not added until 1713. The tower, with cornice and vases at the angles and with a steeple showing a colonnade of Ionic columns, is very pleasing. The height is 128 ft. 3 in. The interior is oblong in shape, 67 ft. long and 47 ft. wide. There is a fine oak altar-piece and some excellent oak carving, notably the pulpit and canopy, the choir screen, the lectern, stalls, and the panels in the W. screen. Portions of the woodwork, together with the two figures on the E. wall, came from the ch. of All Hallows the Great (q.v.). There are painted iron racks on each side of the choir stalls. One (N. side) was for the Ld.M.'s sword of state, the other (S. side) for the hats of his attendants. The beautiful brass candelabrum is dated 'Birmingham 1644.' Stained glass windows, inserted in 1866, when the ch. was restored, in memory of Whittington, who is believed to have been bd. on the S. side of the chancel of the old ch., have been destroyed. John Cleveland, the cavalier poet, was bd. here, but there is no memorial. His funeral sermon was preached by Dr. John Pearson, afterwards Bp. of Chester. Peter Blundell, founder of the famous Devonshire sch. at Tiverton, familiar to readers of *Lorna Doone*, was bd. here in 1601. The only monument of interest is to Sir Samuel Pennant; he d. whilst Ld.M., 1750. His death was caused through jail fever, which proved fatal to over sixty people having business at the courts, including two judges. It was from that time that sweet-smelling herbs were placed in the prisoners' dock to counteract the contagion.

The par. of St. Martin in the Vintry was united with St. Michael Paternoster Royal's after the G.F., that ch. not being rebuilt. All Hallows the Less was not rebuilt after the G.F., but its par. united with All Hallows the Great. The latter was demolished in 1894, and its par. united with St. Michael Paternoster Royal's, which therefore embraces four pars.

The Gold and Silver Wyre Drawers' Co. attend an annual service. The Vintners' Co. come annually, either to this ch. or St. James's Garlickhithe about 9th July.

The rector, Canon Douglas, in 1949, inaugurated a search for Whittington's tomb. It was unsuccessful. There was, however, found a mummified cat. Perhaps it was buried by one of Wren's workmen who had heard of the legend, which did not get going until Whittington had been dead 180 yrs.

The ch. was damaged by a flying bomb, but has been restored. It was rehallowed in December 1968, and the Whittington Hall at the W. end was added. The Church has beautiful stained-glass windows, one depicting Dick Whittington and his cat. A Mission to Seamen is associated with the church.

St. Nicholas, Cole Abbey (Knightrider St.). The first mention is 'Sancti Nichi Coldabbei' (1241–59). A variation occurs in the 16th-century, when it was 'St. Nicholas Wyllyms' (1553) and 'St. Nicholas Welleys' (temp. Q. Elizabeth). It appears that the name of some benefactor was temporarily added to the dedication. St. Nicholas, who lived in Asia Minor in the first half of the 4th century, is the patron saint of sea-farers, travellers, merchants, children, and those overtaken by sudden danger. He is supposed to have stood up in his bath on the day of birth, and given thanks to God for his advent; also to have restored to life three babies who were drowned in a pickletub. This perhaps accounts for his becoming Santa Claus through a corruption of his name. He was also believed to have appeared, with St. Thomas à Becket and St. Edmund Rich, to succour the fleet of Richd. I when, on the way to the Third Crusade, it encountered a terrible storm. This confirmed his interest in 'those in peril on the sea.' 'Cole Abbey' has provided matter for much speculation. Rev. W. J. Loftie plausibly surmised that the name was originally 'St. Nicholas Colby'; from a founder or restorer.

Stow says that about 1397—

'Thomas Barnarde-Castle, Clearke, John Sonderdash, Clerke, and John Nouncy, gave to the parsons and churchwardens of the said Church and theyr successors one messuage and one shoppe with the appurtenances for the reparation of the body of the church, the Belfry or steeple, and ornaments.'

The castle from which the first named donor derived his name was very close to the ch. (See 'Baynard's Castle.') Stow mentions a number of burials, including Walter Turke, Fishmonger, Ld.M. 1349 (d. 1352). On the N. wall was a list of prominent fishmongers bd. in the pre-Fire ch., and the existing one. Friday St. (see 'Cheapside') was a few yards from the N. door. Stow also says that—

'on the north side of this church in the wall thereof, was of late builded a

convenient cistern of stone and lead for receit of Thames water conveyed in pipes of lead to that place for the ease and commoditie of the Fishmongers and other inhabitantes in and about Old Fish Streete.'
and that Barnard Randolphe, Common Sergeant of the City, contributed £900 towards the cost. In 1628 new battlements were added to the tower. In 1629 Jas. Wood, Ld.M., and a member of the Bowyers' Co. was bd. there. The Co. in alternate yrs. used to attend a service here.

The Ch. was rebuilt by Wren in 1677. The walls were panelled to the height of 7 ft., and there were Corinthian pilasters. The stained glass over the reredos was the work of Burne-Jones. The ch. was reduced to a ruin by bombing. The steeple, shaped like a lighthouse in deference to the patron saint, has been destroyed, but the tower remains. Many treasures were lost, but the following survived: a chained commentary on the Prayer Book (1686); a fine old candelabrum; a sword-rest; an early 16th-century painting of the infant Jesus; a 16th-century lectern brought from Rome; a Flemish painting of the Madonna and Child (c. 1530).

The ch. represented five pars.: in addition to St. Nicholas, St. Mary Mounthaw; St. Mary Somerset; St. Benet, Paul's Wharf; St. Peter's, Paul's Wharf. On the panels of the destroyed pulpit the respective saints had been painted.

St. Olave, Hart St. The dedication is to the Norwegian K. Olaf, who d. in 1030. He assisted Ethelred the 'Unready,' to expel the Danes, and it is probable therefore that there was a ch. here before the Norman Conquest. It is said to have been referred to in a charter of Henry I (1109), but the first extant reference is to 'St. Olave towards the Tower' (1222). The name at later dates varies considerably. In 1368 it is 'St. Olave next the Friars of Holy Cross.' The latter were the Crutched Friars (*q.v.*), and so late as 1703 the *London Post Boy* announced that 'Samuel Pepys Esq. was buried in Crutched Friars Church.' In 1303 Theobald le Hurer 'leaves a tenement to Gunnelda his wife charged with maintaining a wax taper before the altar of St. Mary in the Church of S. Olave.'

The Ch. with which Pepys was familiar was probably built in the middle of the 15th century. Stow says that the principal builders and benefactors were Richd. and Robt. Cely, fellmongers (skinners), whose monuments were at one time in the ch. It was one of the smallest in the City, the length and breadth were 54 ft. It escaped the G.F., which came so near as All Hallows, Barking (*q.v.*). It was of Perpendicular Gothic architecture, and had a N. and S. aisle separated from the centre by clustered columns of Purbeck marble, and pointed arches. There was a clerestory with small windows, and a large E. window. In the mediaeval period there were at least three chapels: the Lady Chapel; the Chapel of St. Mary and St. George; and a Chapel of St. Stephen. There was a large image of St. Olaf in the N. aisle and probably some chantry chapels. In the 17th century the ch. was provided with a three-decker pulpit, and high pews. Pews were specially installed in 1660 in a gallery on the S. side for the use of the officials of the Navy Office in Seething Lane, there being added an external staircase for access to it. The principal occupants were Sir Wm. Batten, Admiral Sir Wm. Penn, father of the Quaker, and Samuel Pepys. The galleries and staircase were demolished in 1853. Samuel Pepys was bd. in the ch. in 1703, as, in 1669, his wife Elizabeth had been.

The ch. was almost destroyed by bombing but has been carefully restored. The finely carved pulpit (it came from the Ch. of St. Benet, Gracechurch St.) was preserved in the crypt of St. P.'s Cath. and re-erected after the war. The marble monument which Samuel Pepys erected to his wife was removed also and also restored. It was by John Bushnell, a well-known sculptor of the period. Pepys drew up the long Latin inscription, which says she bore no children because she could bear none worthy of herself. It was placed where her husband could gaze upon it from the Navy gallery. There was also a monument to Sir John Mennes (1670). As a member of the Navy Board, he figures much in Pepys's *Diary.*

The ch. is now most famous for its association with Pepys. In 1884, largely through the efforts of H. B. Wheatley, on the S. wall, where the Navy gallery had been, a memorial was unveiled by Jas. Russell Lowell, poet and essayist.

The memorial includes a medallion

from Hales's portrait in N.P.G. The entry in the burial register reads: '1703. June 4. Samuel Peyps Esq. buried in a Vault under ye communion table.' This monument was still in the ch. at the time of the bombing, but sustained little damage.

The registers date from 1563. From 1563 to 1893 there are entries of 9,818 baptisms, 3,179 marriages, and 11,533 burials. They have been transcribed from 1563 to 1700, and published by the Harleian Soc. An entry in 1563 gives the name of the child as 'Anne Bare,' and of the father 'Mr. Barre,' an example of the way in which spelling, as with Sam Weller followed the taste and fancy of the speller. In 1591 Robt. Devereux, son of Q. Elizabeth's favourite, was baptized in his father's house in Seething Lane, and the entry is in the register. Lancelot Andrewes officiated. This was the commander of the parly. forces at the battle of Edgehill. In 1667 a son of Dr. Daniel Mills, rector, was baptized. One of the godfathers was Sir John Minns (Mennes), and a godmother 'Madame Pepys.' (Dr. Mills, whose sermons sometimes sent Pepys to sleep, was bd. in the ch. in 1689.) In 1586 'Mother Goose' was bd. here. In 1647 there was bd. 'John Houlmes a porter who died suddenlie under his burden. God grant wee y^t survive may take warning.'

The communion plate is valuable. Two chalices and a paten of silver gilt date back to the beginning of the 17th century. The clock in the tower belonged to St. Olave Jewry, and was placed there in 1891. The clock in the ch. came from St. Katherine Coleman. The chyd. was probably much larger at one time. Pepys several times referred to it, particularly in connection with Plague burials. He said: 'It frightened me to see so many graves lie so high upon the churchyard where people had been buried of the plague.' Dickens referred to it in his delightful essay in *The Uncommercial Traveller*, entitled 'The City of the Absent':

> 'One of my best beloved churchyards I call the churchyard of Saint Ghastly Grim. It is a small, small, churchyard, with a ferocious strong spiked iron gate like a jail.'

This gateway remains intact. On the wall of the tower is a tablet with an inscription recording the miraculous pre-servation of the daughter of the Rev. John Letts, who fell from the top floor of the rectory on to the paving stones in the basement. There was a sanctuary knocker on the door in Hart St.

The Clothworkers' Co., whose adjacent Hall was destroyed at the time the ch. was reduced to a ruin, attend an annual service here, the rector being the chaplain. There is also a service in memory of Pepys on or near 26th May.

St. Peter, Cornhill. The earliest reference is 'St. Peter binnon Lunden' (*c.* 1040). It was afterwards called 'St. Peter de Cornhill' and 'super Cornhill,' and (1449) 'St. Peter Ledynhall in Corneyle.' It is claimed that it is the oldest in L., and a tablet in the vestry (said to be a copy of one in old St. P.'s Cath. before the G.F.) ascribes its foundation to K. Lucius in the yr. A.D. 179. It is also stated that he made it 'the metropolitane and chief church of this kingdome.' Stow mentions a similar tablet as having hung in the vestry of the ch. in his time. Thackeray took a fancy to Lucius, when editor of the *Cornhill Magazine* (the office of which was opposite the ch.), and babbled of him in the first of his *Roundabout Papers* (1860). Harben says that the Lucius legend appears first in *Liber Pontificalis* not later than A.D. 700, and thence found its way into the stream of medieval history by way of Nennius and Bede's *Ecclesiastical History*. With holy boldness the ch. celebrated its seventeen-hundredth anniversary in 1879. Tait, Abp. of C., was the preacher; he did not conceal his doubts. The Rev. G. B. Doughty, for many yrs. its rector, proudly claimed that he was the 'real Simon Pure.' In the Middle Ages right of precedence for this ch. was successfully maintained. On Whit-Monday a procession consisting of all the City rectors started from St. Peter's to march to St. P.'s Cath. There were also in the procession the mayor, recorder, aldermen, etc. A dispute continued for yrs. between the parishioners of St. Peter Cornhill, St. Magnus the Martyr, and St. Nicholas, Cole Abbey, as to which of their respective rectors should take precedence. After many yrs. the mayor and aldermen decided in favour of St. Peter Cornhill, on the ground that it was reputed to be the oldest in L. In 1230 one Geffrey Russel, who was implicated in a murder that took place in St. P.'s chyd., fled for sanctuary to the ch., 'and would not come out,' says Stow, 'to the peace of our Lord the King.' In 1243 a disturbance was caused in the par., by the murder of a priest attached to the ch. The culprit, who fled, is said to have been Walkelin, vicar of St. P.'s Cath. In 1411 Richd. Whittington conveyed the patronage of the living to the mayor and corporation, in whose gift it has remained. John Carpenter, Town Clerk, and Whittington's executor, was bd. here (c. 1441). There was a chapel of St. Mary in the chancel, and from about 1447 there was attached to the ch. one of the four parochial schs. directed by Parliament to be maintained in L., and there was a fine lib. attached to it. There was a gild of St. Peter (founded c. 1417), and tenements set apart for its maintenance. It was chiefly composed of members of the Fishmongers' Co. Sir Wm. Bowyer (Ld.M. 1543), and Sir Henry Huberthorn (Ld.M. 1546), were bd. there.

It was burnt in the G.F., and rebuilt by Wren in 1680–1. At that time Dr. Wm. Beveridge was rector. In 1704 he became Bp. of St. Asaph. He d. 1708, and was bd. in St. P.'s Cath. He wrote a learned treatise on the use of the eastern languages, and a most laborious work on the Apostolical Canons.

The ch. has two aisles, divided from the nave by Corinthian columns, which stand on high panelled bases. The chancel, on the N. and S. of which are side chapels, is separated from the nave by a carved wooden screen. All Hallows the Great and St. Peter Cornhill were the only Wren chs. so adorned. The screen is finely carved, and surmounting its centre are the lion and unicorn. Dr. Beveridge was instrumental in getting the screen erected, and mentioned it in his sermon at the opening of the ch., 27th Nov. 1681. The pulpit is well carved, and the walls are panelled to the same height as the pillars. The font was presented by Samuel Purchas in 1681. The excellently carved cover belonged to the old ch., and escaped the G.F. The reredos has an unusual design. There is the ancient Christian emblem of the Lamb that was slain, and blazing forth from it is the sun or morning star burning in its rays the sacred name Jehovah. There are, at the W. end, some nicely carved shelves, once used for the bread dole. The only interesting monument is referred to under 'Children's Memorials.'

In the vestry there is preserved the original keyboard of the organ (one of Father Smith's) upon which Mendelssohn played in 1840, with his autograph beside it. It was in the same yr. that George Borrow was m. in this ch. There is a long wooden table, once placed in the nave and used for communion by Puritans. There is a copy of Jerome's Vulgate (a translation of the Old and New Testament into Latin in the fourth century) made in 1290 by a scribe of St. Peter's Ch. There are 150 miniature paintings in its 586 leaves.

The Poulterers' Co. attend an annual sermon here. The steeple, 140 ft. high, is crowned with a representation of St. Peter's key, and there is another on the gate in St. Peter's Alley. There is no doubt that the chyd. is the one referred to by Dickens in *Our Mutual Friend*. Describing Bradley Headstone's unwelcome attentions to Lizzie Hexham, he said:

'They emerged upon the Leadenhall region, and Charlie directed them to a large paved court by the church, and quiet too. It had a raised bank of earth about breast high in the middle enclosed by iron rails. Here, conveniently and healthfully elevated above the level of the living, were the dead and the tombstones, some of the latter droopingly inclined from the perpendicular, as if they were ashamed of the lies they told.'

The stones are now more upright in disposition. A little later Lizzie is aroused from reveries by the striking of the clock. There is an illustration of the incident by Marcus Stone.

St. Sepulchre, Newgate (between Snow Hill and Giltspur St.) was originally dedicated to Edmund, the E. Anglian king and martyr (A.D. 870). For some centuries it was called 'St. Edmund without Newgate' or 'St. Edmund Sepulchre.' In 1137 it was bestowed by Roger, Bp. of Salisbury, upon the prior and canons of St. Bartholomew's. The second part of the name is curious. There was a 5th century saint named Pulcheria, and it has sometimes been called 'St. Pulchre's.' Stow once called it by this name. Swift used it in his *Description of a City Shower*. Augustus Hare (*Walks in London*, 1877) says, 'formerly St. Pulchre's.' It seems probable that about the beginning of the 12th century, when, according to Strype, the first crusade led to the foundation of the Order of Knights of the Holy Sepulchre, the name became 'St. Edmund and the Holy Sepulchre' and that the saint suffered from a later abbreviation. The par. was once much larger, and in 1308 the ch. was 'St. Sepulchre within Neugate.' In 1547 this portion of the par. within the gate, with the pars. of St. Audoen (*q.v.*) and St. Nicholas Shambles (*q.v.*) constituted the new par. of Christ Church, Newgate.

The ch. was the home of several fraternities; St. Katherine, St. Michael, St. Anne and Our Lady, and had a number of chantry chapels. About the middle of the 15th century it was rebuilt by Sir John Popham, Chancellor of Normandy and Treasurer of the K.'s Household. Sir John's statue once stood in a niche over the S. porch—this and the tower are all that remain of his ch., but 'silly churchwardens,' as Augustus Hare called them, removed it in favour of the oriel window. Popham, according to Stow, built a handsome chapel on the S. side. A rector of the ch., John Rogers, was a Protestant martyr at Smithfield (*q.v.*) in 1554, and is one of the three commemorated on the memorial tablet there. He helped Tyndale to translate the scriptures, and brought the work to England where it went under the name of Matthew's Bible. He was arraigned at John Rogers, alias Matthew, 'and had the courage, after Q. Mary had entered L., to call her religion at St. Paul's Cross 'pestilent popery, idolatry, and superstition.' He was degraded in the chapel of Newgate Gaol, his canonical dress being torn piecemeal from his person. When offered a pardon if he would renounce his heresy, he said: 'That which I preached have I sealed with my blood,' and he washed his hands in the flames.

In 1568 Roger Ascham, author of *The Scholemaster*, and tutor of Lady Jane Grey and Q. Elizabeth, was bd. in the ch., but he never seems to have had any memorial. Stow does not mention him. This is remarkable as Dean Nowell said that he had never seen or heard of any who lived more virtuously or d. more Christianly, and Q. Elizabeth said she would rather have lost £10,000 than her

Ascham! In 1631 Capt. John Smith was bd. there. In 1608 he became President of Virginia. His life had been saved by Princess Pocahontas, daughter of an Indian chief. She is supposed to have been in love with Smith, but as he left for England she found a husband in John Rolfe. She visited L. with him and d. on board ship when she was about to return (1617). She was bd. at Gravesend. A copy of the painting of her made during her stay in L. is on the wall of St. Sepulchre's Ch., near the brass tablet in memory of Capt. John Smith. The latter has a very eulogistic epitaph commencing:

'Here lyes one conquered that hath conquered kings
Subdu'd large Territories and done Things,
Which to the World impossible would seem,
But that the Truth is held in more esteem.'

He was supposed to have killed three Turks in single combat in 1602, and thereby to have had three Turks' heads on his shield of arms by command of Sigismund, K. of Hungary. The L. apprentices had a ballad recording his exploit of killing one Turk by a box on the ear. A statue to him was erected in Bow Churchyard in 1960 by the Jamestown Foundation of the Commonwealth of Virginia.

(See *Pocahontas*, by David Garnet, 1935, and *London for Americans*.)

A contemporary of Capt. John Smith's was Robt. Dowe. He was bd. in St. Botolph's, Aldgate (*q.v.*). In 1605 he gave the sum of £50 'for ringing the greatest bell' in St. Sepulchre's Ch. 'on the day the condemned prisoners are executed,' and 'for other services for ever, concerning such condemned prisoners.' There is believed to have been a tunnel beneath the road leading from St. Sepulchre's Ch. to Newgate, connecting with a crypt of the ch. An old man who was connected with the ch. as a boy, and rang the knell of prisoners executed at the Old Bailey, could recall it, and stated that it was filled up in 1879. Here, it is thought, condemned prisoners were brought to receive the last Sacrament, and this was the way that, in accordance with Dowe's further bequest, the sexton went on the eve of execution to the outside of the condemned cell to give 'twelve solemn towles with double strokes with a hand bell and deliver with a loud and audible voice' this exhortation:

'All you that in the condemned hold do lie,
Prepare you, for tomorrow you shall die;
Watch all, and pray, the hour is drawing near
That you before the Almighty must appear;
Examine well yourselves, in time repent,
That you may not to eternal flames be sent.
And when St. Sepulchre's bell to-morrow tolls,
The Lord above have mercy on your souls.
     Past twelve o'clock.'

Wesley, in his journal (13th Oct. 1784), referring to repentant prisoners he visited in Newgate Gaol, said:
'When the bellman came at twelve o'clock, to tell them (as usual), "Remember you are to die to-day," they cried out, "Welcome news, welcome news." '
The bell of the ch. commenced to toll when the procession left Newgate Gaol and outside the ch. a nosegay was presented to the criminal. John Rann ('Sixteen-string Jack'), executed in 1774, was one of the last to receive this favour. Dowe's gift of £50 is now vested in the Charity Commissioners. The handbell is probably the one alluded to by Lady Macbeth.

'It was the owl that shrieked, the fatal bellman
Which gives the stern'st good night.'

Macbeth was probably written about 1599, and this topical allusion added when Dowe's gift was made known. There is an allusion in Webster's *Duchess of Malfi* (1616):

'I am the common bellman
That usually is sent to condemned prisoners,
The night before they die.'

The bell was found in an old chest in 1896, and is now in a glass case on the S. wall of the ch.
St. Sepulchre's Ch. was, in the main,

destroyed by the G.F. It was rebuilt about 1670, some say under the direction of Sir Christopher Wren, but others maintain that the parishioners were in too great a hurry, and so carried out the necessary work themselves. It was extensively repaired in 1738, and again in 1790 and 1837, when a new roof was provided. In 1875 the tower and porch were refaced, and then Popham's statue disappeared. Between 1878 and 1880 the body of the ch. was completely transformed. New windows were inserted, and fresh buttresses and battlements substituted. Some interesting discoveries were then made. The remains of window jambs and arches of the 15th-century edifice were revealed, and a two-light window near the angle of the SE. wall, which had been filled up with brickwork when alterations were carried out in 1790. In the S. aisle there was discovered the remains of an old sepulchre or tomb of large size, with a moulded arch. This was not the tomb of Sir John Popham, as, according to Stow, he was bd. at Charterhouse. There was also found nearer the E. end the remains of a piscina. In 1879 the pews and galleries were removed.

St. Sepulchre's is an imposing ch. It has the largest area of any ch. in the City, being 150 ft. long by 162 ft. wide. There are a nave, chancel, and two side aisles and on the N. is the chapel of St. Stephen Harding. He was the founder of the Cistercian Order, and its head from 1109–31. There is a fine memorial window to Harding. The organ, one of Renatus Harris's finest productions, was formerly here. It is now in the N. aisle, and has a very handsome case. The font has a well carved cover bearing date 1670. There was no serious damage in the Second World War. The E. window was destroyed. This was replaced by another in 1949. It shows St. P.'s Cath., and some of the City chs.

In 1946 a fine stained-glass window was placed in the N. wall in memory of Sir Henry Wood. It shows him, as a young man, playing the organ in the ch., and, in later yrs., conducting a concert at the Queen's Hall. The inscription is as follows:
'This Window is dedicated to the memory of Sir Henry Wood, founder and for fifty years Conductor of the Promenade Concerts, 1895–1944. He

opened the door to a new world of sense and feeling to millions of his fellows. He gave his life for music, and brought music to the people. His ashes rest beneath.'
On a tablet under the window is inscribed:
'Here lie the remains of Sir Henry Wood, C.H., 1869–1944.'
The ch. has always been closely associated with crime. In a case in the vestibule is a piece of a charred beam from Newgate Gaol, believed to be a relic of the fire caused by the 'No Popery' rioters of 1780. There is also a plate bought at the sale of Newgate relics in 1903. Dickens several times alluded to the ch. In *Barnaby Rudge* the people waited for the victims of the riots mentioned to come out for execution 'with impatience which increased with every chime of St. Sepulchre's clock.' There are references to its ominous bell being heard by Fagin's young gentlemen in *Oliver Twist*.
The height of the tower to the top of the pinnacles is 150 ft. Howell, in one of his *Familiar Letters* (1632), refers to the 'fanes of St. Sepulchre's steeple which never look all four upon one point of the heavens.' In 1600 one Wm. Doddington threw himself from the steeple. This incident caused a great sensation at the time, Bacon referring to it in a conversation with Q. Elizabeth. When alluding to the affairs of the E. of Essex, he said: 'If I so brake my neck, I shall do it in a manner as Mr. Doddington did it, which walked on the battlements of the church many days and took a view and survey where he should fall.'
The greater part of the par. is situated within the City boundaries (in the ward of Farringdon Without), but as a small portion lies beyond the civic jurisdiction, two sets of churchwardens are annually appointed.
The chyd. was originally much more extensive than it is now, i.e. on the S. side. In 1760 the wall was pulled down, and the chyd. curtailed, and it was still further reduced in 1871 when many bodies were exhumed, and re-interred in the City Cemetery at Ilford.
There is a painting of the exterior of the ch. in the C.C. art gallery.
In 1949 the chyd. was dedicated and opened in honour of all ranks, past and present, of the Royal Fusiliers (City of L. Regiment). There is a chapel dedicated to their memory.

St. Stephen, Walbrook. The earliest reference is 'St. Stephen super Walbrock' (*c.* 1096). The first ch. was built on the W. side of the stream. In the latter part of the 15th century the patronage was given to the Grocers' Co., who still present to the rectory alternately with Magdalene College, Cambridge. The ch. was rebuilt (1429–39) on the E. side of the Walbrook. This was done largely at the expense of Robt. Chicheley (Ld.M. 1411 and 1421.) It had a Lady Chapel, and had chapels of St. Nicholas and Katherine. There was a cross in the chyd. Amongst monuments mentioned by Stow are Sir Richd. Lee, Rowland Hill (Ld. M. 1549), Sir John Yorke, knight (d. 1549) and 'Doctor Owyn Phisition to king Henrie the eight.'
The ch. was burnt in the G.F., and rebuilt by Wren 1672–9. 'The magnificent experiment of a prentice hand' is Miss Lena Milman's judgment upon it. Others have gone farther and called it his masterpiece, saving the one exception of St. P.'s Cath. Canova (1757–1822), the Italian sculptor, is said to have expressed a wish to revisit England, if only to see St. Paul's, Somerset House, and St. Stephen's Ch. The E. of Burlington (1695–1753), when in Italy, saw a ch. he much admired. He was told it was a copy of St. Stephen's. Amazed that he should have missed such an architectural gem in his own city, when he returned to L. he rushed round to St. Stephen's and viewed it by candlelight. John Wesley heard this story, and though usually giving but grudging praise to temples made with hands, as doomed to perish in the final conflagration of all things, was constrained to say that he was not surprised at the Earl's enthusiasm. Never was so 'sweet a kernel in so rough a shell,' said Cunningham, in 1850, referring to its exterior and the bdgs. that hem it in. It is oblong in shape, and only 82 ft. 6 in., though it appears much larger. There are four rows of Corinthian columns elevated on bases. It is divided into five aisles, the centre one being the broadest. An open space was made by omitting two columns from each of the two central rows, and the ch. is crowned by a circular dome, supported on eight arches. The height to the summit of the

dome is 63 ft., and the diameter of the dome at the base 45 ft. To Wren this probably represented an experiment for St. P.'s Cath., and on the W. wall are pictures of the two bdgs. That of the ch. shows the pews, which, like the wainscoting, were presented by the Grocers' Co. when it was rebuilt. The pews were removed in 1888, and at that time the mosaic pavement was laid down. The arms of the Grocers' Co. are on the organ gallery. A picture of the Burial of St. Stephen by the American, Benjamin West, was presented to the ch. by the rector, Dr. Wilson, in 1779, and was at first placed over the altar, where it blocked the E. window. During repairs in 1847-8 it was removed to the N. wall. There is a monument on the N. wall to Dr. Geo. Croly, rector, who d. in 1860. Charlotte Brontë visited this ch. in company with her sister Anne in 1848. They were disappointed not to hear Dr. Croly preach.

The oldest monument in the ch. is one of white marble on a pillar at the SE. It is in memory of John Lilbourn, citizen and grocer of L., who d. 1678. On the N. wall is a tablet to Nathaniel Hodges, a physician who wrote a treatise on the Plague called *Loimologia*. He was then made a fellow of the Coll. of Physicians. He d. in Ludgate debtors' prison having fallen into poverty. Dr. Johnson once was moved almost to tears by the fate of a physician so devoted to duty at so difficult a time—he was probably the original of Defoe's Dr. Heath—and said he would not so have perished in his day. The following is a translation of the Latin inscription:

'Take heed of all thy days, O mortal man, for time steals on
With furtive step. Death's shadow flits across the sunniest hour,
Seeking to prey 'mong all who mortal are.
He is behind thee; and even though breath be in thee
Death has marked thee as his own.
Thou knowest not the hour when Fate shall call thee.
E'en while this marble thou regardest, time is irrevocably passing.
'Here lies in his grave Nathaniel Hodges, Doctor of Medicine
Who while a child of Earth lived in hope of Heaven.
He was formerly of Oxford, and was a

survivor of the Plague
Born, September 13 A.D. 1629
Died 10th June 1688.'

On a pillar at the NE. is a memorial to Robt. Marriott, a rector. The Latin epitaph says he was a divine man, and emigrated to the celestial country in 1699. There is a white marble monument, with bust to Percival Gilbourne, an apothecary (d. 1694). In the vaults was interred Sir John Vanbrugh (d. 1726). He was a dramatist (author of *The Relapse, The Provoked Wife*, etc.), and architect—of Blenheim Palace and other 'splendid creations,' as Benjamin Disraeli called them. Dr. Evans suggested as his epitaph:

'Lie heavy on him, earth, for he
Laid many a heavy load on thee.'

One rector, Dr. Wilson, made himself notorious by placing (*c.* 1769) within the altar rails of the ch. a white marble bust of Mrs. Catharine Macaulay. She was the author of a *History of England 1688-1715*, and other works, and was described by Dr. Johnson as a 'female patriot.' She visited America in 1785, and was received by Geo. Washington. When she m. a second time the rector removed the bust, some say at the request of the bishop, others because she did not find the husband in Bath, where he was living in retirement. It was returned to its sculptor, Moore, 'with full permission to do whatever he pleased with it.' What that was history does not record.

The ch. represents also the par. of St. Benet Sherehog (*q.v.*).

The Ch. was badly damaged by fire and blast. Stained-glass windows were destroyed, and there was serious damage to the dome. The church has been restored to the original Wren design.

There is a painting of the ch. in the C.C. Art Gallery. The present Rector has built up a 'Samaritan' organization attached to the church.

St. Vedast (Foster Lane, Cheapside). The earliest mention is as 'Sancti Vedasti' in the 13th century. It was 'St. Faster,' 1315-16, and in 1352 'SS. Vedast and Amandus.' St. Vedast was a Bp. of Arras (d. A.D. 540), who worked great marvels, according to tradition. John Throwstone gave £100 to the rebuilding of the ch. in 1519. Robt. Herrick, son of a Cheapside goldsmith, was baptized here in 1591. It was repaired and 'beautified' in

1614, and 20 ft. of ground added out of a 'fair court' belong to Saddlers' Hall.

It was burnt in the G.F., and the ch. of St. Michael le Querne (*q.v.*), not being rebuilt, the pars. were united. It was rebuilt 1697–8, mostly upon the old walls. The old steeple also had survived, but owing to injuries through the flames it was found necessary to take it down. There is a peculiar grace about the one Wren then erected with a concave stage, a convex stage, and surmounting these an obelisk-shaped spire, ball, finial and vane. The ch. had a handsome altar-piece, sometimes attributed to Grinling Gibbons. It included four Corinthian columns, and displayed cherubim, a pelican, urns, palm branches, and other embellishments.

The ch. was badly damaged by bombs and has since been rebuilt.

In addition to St. Michael le Querne, St. Vedast's Ch. represents the pars. of St. Peter, Westcheap (*q.v.*). Thos. Rotherham was rector 1465–7, when he resigned on being promoted to the see of Rochester. He was translated to Lincoln in 1471, and in 1474 Edward IV made him Ld. Chancellor. In 1480 he became Abp. of York, an office he held until death (1500). In 1880 the rector, Pelham Dale, went to Holloway Gaol after proceedings for ritualistic practices. Dr. Sparrow Simpson (author of three learned volumes on St. P.'s Cath.), who had previously been at St. Matthew's Ch., succeeded him. Dr. Simpson visited Arras in 1894, having become particularly interested in the saint to whom the ch. was dedicated. The result was a lengthy and minute biography. At Tathwell (Lincs.) is the only other ch. dedicated to St. Vedast.

In 1836, in a vault under a small burial ground, on the N. of the ch., a curious stone coffin was discovered. It consisted of a block of freestone, about 7 ft. long and 15 in. thick, hollowed out to receive the body, with deeper channel for the head and shoulders. It contained a skeleton. Other relics were found at the same time 10 to 12 ft. below the level of the road. In a small garden attached to the ch., in the autumn of 1934, there were picked 1½ pounds of blackberries.

There is a painting of the exterior in the C.C. Art Gallery.

(See *Ancient London Churches*, by T. F. Bumpus (1923); *A Dictionary of London*, by H. A. Harben (1918); *Parish Churches of London*, by B. F. L. Clarke (1966); *Old London Churches*, by E. A. H. and W. H. Young (1956).

D. CHURCHES REDUCED TO RUINS.

Christ Church, Newgate. The history of this ch. commences with the Franciscans, called Grey Friars, from their costume which was a loose garment of a grey colour reaching down to the ankles, with a cowl of the same hue, and a cloak for outdoor wear. They came to L. in 1224, living for a few days in the Dominicans' House in Holborn (see 'Blackfriars'). They then hired a house in Cornhill. They increased rapidly, and John Ewin, a mercer, gave for their use a piece of ground within Newgate, and in the par. of St. Nicholas Shambles (*q.v.*). Of the first ch. erected here hardly anything is known. In 1306 the Grey Friars commenced a magnificent new edifice. It was probably the largest ch. in England. A. W. Clapham, F.S.A., and Walter H. Godfrey (*Some Famous Buildings and their Story*) wrote:

'This building, with its 300 feet of length, its slender piers, its long range of clerestory, aisle, and end windows is a type which is without parallel of its own date and outside its own order as the expression of a new and original idea in church building, departing equally from the insignificant dimensions of the contemporary parish church and the massive and cavernous construction of the monastic nave.'

The chapels were dedicated to St. Francis, the Apostles, All Hallows, and St. Mary. There were the usual cloister and chapter house. The principal benefactors of the bdg. were Q. Margaret, the second wife of Edward I; Isabella (Edward II's Q.); Q. Philippa (consort of Edward III); John of Brittany, E. of Richmond; and Gilbert de Clare, E. of Gloucester.

'No order of monks,' said Pennant, 'seems to have had the powers of persuasion equal to these poor friars. They raised vast sums for their buildings among the rich: and there were few of their admirers, when they came to die, who did not console themselves with the thoughts of lying within their expiating walls; and if they were particularly wicked, thought themselves secure against the assault of the devil, provided their corpse was wrapped in the habit and cowl of a friar.'

Pennant added:

'Multitudes therefore of all ranks, were crowded in this holy ground. It boasts of receiving four queens: Margaret, and Isabella, Joan, daughter to Edward II and wife of Edward Bruce, King of Scotland; and to make the fourth, Isabella, wife of William Warren, titular queen of Man is named. Of these Isabella, whom Gray so strongly stigmatizes,

"She-wolf of France, with unrelenting fangs,
That tear'st the bowels of thy mangled mate,"

Here was also buried Isabella, daughter of Edward III, and wife of de Courcy. E. of Bedford; John Hastings, E. of Pembroke (slain in Woodstock Park at a Christmas festivity), 1389; John, Duc de Bourbon, taken prisoner in 1415 at Agincourt, 1443; Walter Blount, Ld. Mountjoy, Ld. Treasurer in the time of Edward IV, 1474; Sir John Dinham, K.G., who held the same office under Henry VII, 1500. The heart of Q. Eleanor, consort of Henry III, was bd. here (1291). In all 663 persons of nobility are said to have been interred in the ch. or cloisters of the Grey Friars. Amongst others should be mentioned Roger Mortimer, E. of March, who was hanged in 1327 on Edward III's succession, and Elizabeth Barton, 'Holy Maid of Kent,' who was executed at Tyburn in 1534. She was unwise enough to prophesy that if Henry VIII m. another woman he should not be K. a month later. Her indiscreet revelations of the will of Heaven regarding Henry's matrimonial projects not only brought her to her end, but unfortunately embroiled a person of far greater value, Sir Thos. More. No doubt the friars regarded her as a martyr. A lesser known interment is recorded by Pennant:

'A murderess, a lady Alice Hungerford. . . . She had killed her husband; for which she was led from the Tower to Holborn, there put into a cart with one of her servants, and thence carried to Tyburn and executed.'

Stow gives an account of the monuments of noble personages who were bd. in the Grey Friars' ch. The priory having surrendered in 1538, in 1546 many of

them were bought for about £50 by Sir Martin Bowes, Ld.M., some being of alabaster and some of marble. In 1547 a grant was made to the Ld.M. and citizens of the ch., the lib.', the dorter (dormitory), the chapter house, the great cloister, the little cloister, and houses on the N. of the little cloister; the Grey Friars' ch. thereupon became a par. ch., the pars. of St. Ewin or Audoen (q.v.) and St. Nicholas Shambles (q.v.) being combined with it. Probably the family of the early benefactor of Christ Church already mentioned had taken their name from the saint. Apparently both the chs. wer almost immediately pulled down.

There were three burials of note in the pre-Fire Christ Church. Lawrence Shyrfe (Sheriff), founder of Rugby Sch. (1567). In 1596 Dame Mary Ramsey, the widow of Sir Thos. Ramsey, Ld.M. 1577. She was very charitable and a benefactress to Christ's Hosp. and other deserving institutions. There was a tablet recording her good deeds. In 1633 there was interred Venetia, the wife of the learned and eccentric Sir Kenelm Digby, son of Sir Everard Digby, who was a 'Gunpowder Plot' conspirator. Sir Kenelm was the author of a criticism of Sir Thos. Browne's *Religio Medici*, which helped to expedite its sale. He was also bd. in the ch. in 1665.

The ch. was burnt in the G.F. and presumably then also disappeared a library which had been provided for the Greyfriars, together with desks and settles for students in 1429 under Whittington's will. The ch. of St. Leonard, Foster Lane was not rebuilt, and the pars. were united. The ch. was rebuilt by Wren in 1687; the steeple was not completed until 1704. It represented in its state only the choir of the Greyfriars ch. Greyfriars Passage (the only commemoration in L. nomenclature of the Franciscans) marks the division between choir and nave, the site of which is now the part of the burial ground which is W. of the ch. The walls and columns occupy the actual sites of their predecessors, and the bases of some of the original buttresses against the S. wall were found below the ground level some yrs. ago. Richd. Baxter, author of *The Saints Everlasting Rest*, and of an interesting autobiography (in Everyman's Library) was bd. here (1691). His wife, who predeceased him by ten yrs., had been buried here in 'the ruines in her own mother's grave.' No doubt 'the ruines' were those left after the G.F.

In 1940 the ch. was reduced to a shell by German bombs. The beautifully carved fronts of the choir stalls—made from a ship of the Spanish Armada, and the Sicilian marble font were all destroyed. There also disappeared tablets in memory of Shyrfe, and Baxter, unveiled respectively in 1932 and 1924. Part of the gravestone of Richd. Roystone, 'Bookseller to three Kings,' who d. in 1686 at the age of eighty-six, and Thos. Hollies, a 'chirurgeon' who d. in 1690, remain. There were in the extensive galleries, tall desks in which sat the 'Grecians' of whom Coleridge was one. After the sch.'s removal to Horsham in 1902, on St. Matthew's Day (21st Sept.), a large number of boys come up to hear a sermon by an 'old Blue.' Since the Blitz the service has been held at St. Sepulchre's Ch. Girls from the sch. at Hertford are now included, and all the scholars, after service, attend the Mansion House to be there regaled with tea and presented with gifts of coin.

Early in 1935, at the instigation of the Elian Club and in commemoration of the centenary of his death, a bust of Lamb was erected outside the W. wall of the ch. This survived the Blitz, and was removed to Horsham.

Before the ch. was so badly damaged the Spital Sermon (see 'Customs') was preached here.

There is a painting of the exterior in the C.C. Art Gallery. The tower of the church still stands.

St. Alban, Wood Street. Amongst City chs., only St. Peter's, Cornhill, claims a longer history. It is the only one in the City dedicated to the proto-martyr of Britain, and it is believed that on its site was a palace of Offa, K. of Mercia, which had a chapel. Offa founded the abbey of St. Albans in 793, and subsequently there were several chs. in L. which belonged to that monastery. Strype thought there was proof of its antiquity in the Roman bricks inlaid in the walls, the turning of the arches, and the heads of the pillars, and some old work seems to have survived much rebuilding. The par. clerks' account of the ch. dates it from about 930. It was certainly in 1077 in the patronage of the abbey of St. Albans, for

in that yr. the abbot exchanged the right of presentation for the patronage of another belonging to the abbot of Westminster. It is now a rectory, and the presentation is alternately with the dean and chapter of St. P.'s Cath and the provost and fellows of Eton Coll. Its more modern name first appears in the time of K. John—'St. Alban Wudestrate.'

In the old ch. was a monument to Sir John Cheke, an eminent Greek scholar and tutor of Edward VI, who was bd. in 1557. Stow gives a long list of monuments, including Sir Richd. Illingworth, Baron of the Exchequer; and Thos. Catworth, grocer and Ld.M. (d. 1443). A curious epitaph in the pre-Fire ch. is said to have been the following:

'Hic jacet Thom Short-hose
Sine tombe, sine sheets, sine riches;
Qui vixit sine gowne,
Sine cloak, sine shirt, sine breeches.'

The earliest known monument of which there is record was to Wm. Linchlade (d. 1392). The first rector mentioned is J. Ewell, 1346. In 1633, the ch. having become much dilapidated, Inigo Jones, Sir Henry Spiller, and others were deputed to examine its condition, and report upon means for its preservation. It was found to be beyond restoration, was pulled down in 1633, and rebuilt the following yr. This ch. was burnt in the G.F.

The new ch. was completed by Wren in 1685, and, as St. Olave, Silver St., was not rebuilt, the pars. were combined. Unusually, for Wren, it was built in a style that has been described as Tudor Gothic. It has an elegant tower, the pinnacles of which had to be replaced about 1890. The interior had been much altered and modernized since Wren built it. In fact, said A. E. Daniell, 'no pains seem to have been spared to render a once interesting and dignified interior as commonplace as possible.' The handsome marble font was presented by Benjamin Harvey in 1684. His monument was on the N. wall. He was 'Major to the Yellow Regiment of Trained Bands.' Another monument, also of marble, was to Richd. Wynne, a merchant and a benefactor to the poor (d. 1688). Amongst the rectors have been Dr. Watts (d. 1649), who assisted Sir Henry

Spelman in his *Glossary*, and edited Matthew Paris's *Historia Major*, and Edwd. Jas. Beckwith, minor canon and succentor of St. P.'s Cath. He was presented to the living by the dean and chapter in 1799. He was a good musician, and some of his chants are still sung.

The church has been completely removed but the tower remains, an attractive feature, in the middle of Wood Street.

St. Augustine (Watling St.). The earliest mention is 1148. The dedication was probably to Augustine, the first Abp. of C., and H. A. Harben remarked that:

'It is noteworthy that the church so dedicated stood near to the church dedicated to St. Gregory the Great to whose inspiration and determination the Anglican Church is indebted for the mission of St. Augustine.'

In 1309 it was referred to as 'St. Augustine's near St. Paul's Gate,' and this gate, which stood at the SE. corner of Watling St., and was not rebuilt after the G.F., was sometimes called 'St. Augustine's Gate.' Stow called St. Augustine's 'a fair church,' and adds that it had been lately 'well repaired.' It was destroyed in the G.F.

After the G.F. the par. of St. Faith's (see 'St. Paul's Cathedral') was united with St. Augustine's. St Augustine's, like St. Faith's, possessed no proper burial-ground of its own, so both pars. used the crypt of St. P.'s Cath. for a time. The ch. was first opened after the G.F. for worship in 1683, but the steeple was not finished till 1695. It was divided into a nave and side aisles by six Ionic columns.

Dr. John Douglas, who defended the reputation of Milton against the attacks of Lauder, and defended the New Testament miracles against the onslaughts of Hume, was rector of St. Augustine's from 1764 to 1787. He resigned on being given the bishopric of Carlisle. In his younger days he was an army chaplain, and was present at the battle of Fontenoy. The Rev. R. H. Barham, author of the *Ingoldsby Legends*, was rector from 1842 until his death in 1845. He was very popular with his parishioners, and their faith in him was such that they felt they could not do better than get his son as successor. The latter, however, would not consent to their petitioning the dean and chapter of St. P.'s Cath. to that effect. The boys of St. Paul's Sch. used to attend

here when the sch. was in St. Paul's Chyd. Mrs. M. V. Hughes tells of one worshipper who came in every day for forty yrs. for private prayer.

A cat connected with the ch. inspired a leading article in *The Times* in 1948. Its name was Faith, and in the tower is a record of its bravery. On 9th Sept. 1940, it is recorded, Faith shielded her kitten in a corner of the rectory, where she remained through bombing and fire: 'Roofs and masonry exploded and the whole house blazed. Four floors fell through in front of Faith; fire and water and ruin were all round her. Yet she stayed calm and stedfast and waited for help. We rescued her in the early morning while the place was still burning and by the mercy of God she and her kitten were not only saved but unhurt. God be thanked for his goodness and mercy to our dear little pet.' Also in the tower there was hung a certificate awarded by the People's Dispensary for Sick Animals of the Poor—'for steadfast courage in the Battle of Britain,' and there was also a certificate of honour presented to Faith by the Greenwich Village Human League Inc. of New York. The cat had strayed into the ch. about 1936. It died in 1948.

Only the tower of the church now remains as part of the new Choir School buildings.

St. Dunstan-in-the-East (Lower Thames St.). The earliest mention is 1272. It was sometimes called 'St. Dunstan by the Tower' and 'St. Dunstan near Fanchurch.' It was dedicated to that scheming and ambitious 10th-century prelate whose canonisation caused Chas. Dickens—in his *Child's History of England*—to wax sarcastic:

'When he died, the monks settled that he was a saint, and called him St. Dunstan ever afterwards. They might just as well have settled that he was a coach horse, and could just as easily have called him one.'

Stow recalls the burial of John Kennington, parson, in 1374, the earliest he seems to have found; in addition to aldermen and a sergeant-at-arms, he mentions the burial 'under a fayre monument' of Sir Bartholomew James, draper, who was Ld.M. in 1479, William Hariot, draper, Ld.M. in 1481; Sir Christopher Draper, Ld.M. in 1566; Sir Richd.

Champion, draper, Ld.M. in 1565. Stow described St. Dunstan's as 'a fair and large church of an ancient building, and within a large churchyard.' There was a monument to Sir John Hawkins, who d. at sea—off Porto Rico—in 1595. Here was bd. Alderman Jas. Bacon, fishmonger, a sheriff in 1569, who d. in 1573. He was the youngest brother of Sir Nicholas Bacon, the Lord Keeper. (See 'York House.') Here also was bd. Admiral Sir John Lawson, who was mortally wounded in the sea-fight with the Dutch off Lowestoft in 1665. The ch. extensively repaired and almost rebuilt in 1633, was practically destroyed in the G.F. The outer walls remained for the most part, but the tall lead-covered spire and the whole of the interior were consumed. Wren was consulted in 1671 and, in the work of rebuilding, the parishioners were materially assisted by the generosity of Dame Dyonis Williamson, of Hale's Hall, Norfolk, whose grandfather, Richd. Hale, had been bd. in the old ch. She gave £4,000 towards the cost, in addition to contributing £2,620—the largest individual subscription—for the rebuilding of St. P.'s Cath, and £2,000 for rebuilding the ch. of St. Mary-le-Bow. The steeple was not completed until 1699. Wren's ch. was divided into nave and aisles by means of Doric columns. By 1810 there was considerable decay manifest, and the walls were found to have been forced so much as 7 in. out of the perpendicular by the pressure of the roof on the nave. The ch. was thereupon pulled down with the exception of the steeple, and a new edifice erected between 1817 and 1821. The architect was David Laing who, a few yrs. before, had built the Customs House, and he was assisted by Sir Wm. Tite, who later rebuilt the Royal Exchange. The style of the ch. was perpendicular Gothic. It had two side aisles, divided from the centre portion by slender clustered columns and pointed arches; there was a clerestory.

The par. registers are complete from 1558. Fredk. Thesiger, who became Ld. Chelmsford, and was twice Ld. Chancellor, was baptized here in 1694. Dr. John Jortin, author of *Remarks on Ecclesiastical History* and the *Life of Erasmus*, was rector from 1751 till his death in 1770. He was bd. at Kensington, of which he was also vicar, but there were tablets at St. Dunstan's to some of his family. Another rector was Rev. Thos. Bowles Murray (d. 1860). He published the *Chronicles of St. Dunstan's Church* in 1859.

The ch. has been reduced to a shell by bombs. There has been destroyed the window in memory of the Rev. T. B. Murray, and one of the flags of the City trained bands of which John Gilpin was a member. Also a monument to Sir John Moore. The epitaph said he was—

'one of the Representatives of this City in Parliament and President of Christ's Hospital, Who, for his great and exemplary loyalty to the Crown, was impowered by King Charles the Second to bear on a canton one of the Lions of England, as an augmentation to His Arms.'

The steeple happily survived, but in 1950 it was dismantled and stored in the ruins. It is Wren's most charming work in this regard, four arched ribs supporting a graceful spire. The steeples of St. Nicholas, Newcastle-upon-Tyne, St. Giles's, Edinburgh, and King's Coll., Old Aberdeen, are of similar construction. There is a tradition that the idea was suggested to him by his only daughter Jane, who d. three yrs. after its completion, at the early age of 26. A further tradition that the young lady lay down beneath it, when the props were removed, by way of a spectacular assurance to the sceptics that the spire would not fall, is much more incredible. The rector, the Rev. Arthur West, says:

'You must go down St. Dunstan's Hill to within a dozen paces of the Customs House. Then the narrow shaft can be seen from the bottom to the top, framed in the counting-houses which flank it. It expands lily-like, lighter and whiter as it rises with unique symmetry and grace as seen through the frosted tracery or abundant foliage of a plane tree, which was 41 feet high in 1720 and which is mentioned by Sir Walter Raleigh. . . . Giotto's Baptismal Tower in Florence does not expand more flower-like, and our Portland stone has somehow learnt to wash itself white in October gales from smoke and City murk.'

St. Mary Aldermanbury. It was in existence in 1148. 'Aldermanbury' apparently derives from the alderman's hall. Newcourt records that in the reign of

Henry III, *c.* 1232, the living was presented to one Wm. de Alerrmanbir. His name, however, probably followed that of the locality where his family had resided. Originally the ch. appears to have belonged to the dean and chapter of St. P.'s Cath., but in 1331 it was appropriated by them with the consent of the Bp. of L., to the Elsing 'Spittle' or Hosp. (see p. 90), providing, however, that the patronage of both should be vested in them, and that a pension of one mark p.a. for St. Mary Aldermanbury Ch., and 6s. 8d. for the hosp. should be paid to them. Under this arrangement it remained until after the dissolution of religious houses by Henry VIII, when the advowson was granted to certain persons in trust for the parishioners, by whom, in consequence, the minister has since been elected. The living is a perpetual curacy. Nothing is known of the original bdg. The ch. appears to have been partially rebuilt in the beginning of the 15th century by Sir Wm. Eastfield. He also presented five bells for the tower. Stow calls it—

'a fayre Church with a churchyeard, and cloyster adjoyning, in the which cloyster is hanged and fastned a shanke bone of a man (as is said) very great and larger by three inches and a halfe than that which hangeth in S. Lawrence church in the Jury, for it is in length 28 inches and a halfe of assisse, but not so hard and steely, like as the other, for the same is light and somewhat porie and spongie. This bone is said to bee found amongst the bones of men removed from the charnel house of Powles, or rather from the cloyster of Powls church of both which reportes I doubt. . . . True it is, that this bone (from whencesoever it came) beeing of a man, as the forme sheweth, must needes be monstrous, and more then after the proportion of five shanke bones of any man now living amongst us.'

Stow mentions, amongst burials, Sir Wm. Estfeld, Knight of the Bath, Ld.M. 1438,

'a great benefactor to that church, under a fayre monument: hee also builded their steeple, changed their old Bels into 5 tunable bels, and gave one hundred poundes to other workes of that church. Moreover hee caused the Conduit in Aldermanbury which he had begun, to be performed at his charges, and water to be convayed by pypes of leade from Tyborne to Fleetstreete.'

John Middleton (Ld.M. 1472) and Sir Wm. Browne (Ld.M. 1507) were also bd. here. John Heminge and Henry Condell, friends of and fellow-actors with Shakespeare, were associated with the ch. Heminge lived in the par. upwards of forty-two yrs. He was m. in the ch., and had fourteen children, thirteen of whom were baptized, four bd., and one m. here. He was bd. in the ch. also in 1630, as his wife was at a date unknown. Condell lived in the par. more than thirty yrs. He had nine children, eight of whom were baptized here, and six bd. He was bd. here in 1627, and his wife also. These particulars are given on the Shakespeare monument in the chyd., which dates from 1895. It is based upon the Chandos portrait in the N.P.G. The pedestal also commemorates Heminge and Condell; they signed the dedications to the First Folio (1623), and a representation of the title page is carved in stone. They were parishioners, and both were bd. in the pre-Fire ch. Their burial records are in the registers in Guildhall Library. In the pre-Fire ch., in 1656, Milton m. his second wife. Edmund Calamy, the celebrated Presbyterian divine, was appointed to the ministry of St. Mary Aldermanbury in 1639, and remained all through the Civil War and the Commonwealth. *The Soldier's Pocket Bible*, issued to Cromwell's army, has on the title page, 'Compiled by Edward Calamy, and issued for the use of the Commonwealth Army in 1643.' There is a copy in the B.Mus. He, however, warmly favoured the Restoration of Charles II, and when it occurred was offered the bishopric of Coventry and Lichfield. This he declined and, on the passing of the Act of Uniformity, he threw in his lot with the Nonconformists. He continued to reside in the par., and to attend the ch. He d. 1666, a few weeks after the G.F., and was bd. beneath the ruins of the ch. where his wife had been laid many yrs. before. One of his sons, Dr. Benjamin Calamy, was at St. Mary Aldermanbury from 1677 to 1683, when he obtained the benefice of St. Lawrence Jewry. He was a zealous High Churchman. A grandson, Dr. Edmund Calamy, himself a leading Nonconformist minister, was bd. at St.

Mary Aldermanbury in 1732. He was a voluminous writer, and compiled biographies of ministers ejected by the Act of Uniformity, and a *Historical Account* of his own life containing much interesting matter.

The ch. was burnt in the G.F., and was rebuilt by Wren in 1677. It was built of stone. It included two side aisles, each divided from the main body by Composite columns.

The remains of Judge Jeffreys, first interred in the T.L. (*q.v.*), were removed here in 1693. While Common Sergeant and Recorder of the City, Jeffreys had been a prominent inhabitant of the par. His son, the second and last Baron Jeffreys, and several other of his children were also bd. here. A small tablet that has gone bore the significant text: 'The Lord seeth not as man seeth.' Jeffreys' remains were seen so recently as 1910. On the E. wall was a white marble monument to Lieut. John Smith, who was drowned off Staten Island in 1782 at the age of 24. It represented a female figure, seated on a gun, while above her rose a broken column.

Externally St. Mary Aldermanbury Ch. had a somewhat handsome appearance, with its cornice and pediment, and large carved scrolls at the sides of the central window. The dedication is indicated by a carving of the Virgin and Child over the doorway. The church was dismantled stone by stone and lovingly re-erected at Westminster College, Fulton, Missouri, as a memorial to Sir Winston Churchill when there made a celebrated speech and first used the phrase 'The Iron Curtain'.

St. Mildred, Bread St. The earliest reference is 'St. Mildrid in Bredstrate' (1223–52). St. Mildred was daughter of a Saxon p. and abbess of Minster (Isle of Thanet), which was founded by her mother at the beginning of the 7th century. Stow said that 'Lord Trenchaunt of St. Alban's, Knight (bd. there about 1300) was supposed to be either the new builder of this ch. or best benefactor to the works thereof.' Another benefactor was Sir John Shadworth (Ld.M. 1401), who gave the parsonage house, a revestry, and chyd. to the par. in 1428. He was bd. in the chancel, where a monument was erected. Stow mentions also a monument to 'Stephen Bugge Gent., his Armes to be three water bugges.' He

says also Henry Bugge founded a chantry in 1419. Stow also records that in 1485 the parsonage was 'burned to the ground, together with the parson and his man.' There was also a monument to Christopher Turner, 'Chirurgion' to Henry VIII (d. 1530). The most distinguished rector was Hugh Oldham (1485–8). He was chaplain to Lady Margaret Beaufort, Henry VII's mother, and through her obtained, in 1504, the bishopric of Exeter, which he retained until his death (1519). He was a benefactor to Corpus Christi Coll., Oxford, and founded a free sch. at Manchester, where he was b. The rectory was first in the gift of the priory of St. Mary Overy, Southwark, but since the reign of Henry VIII has been in private hands. In the 17th century the advowson was in possession of the Crispe family. Alderman Ellis Crispe, sheriff in 1625, was a victim of the outbreak of plague in that yr., and d. almost as soon as he attained that office. He was bd. in the family vaults of the Crispes on the S. of the chancel. One of his sons was Sir Nicholas Crispe, a capt. of the trained bands, and a devoted adherent of Charles I. He was praised by Dr. Johnson as—

'a man of loyalty that deserved perpetual remembrance: when he was a merchant in the city he gave and procured the king in his exigencies a hundred thousand pounds: and when he was driven from the Exchange, raised a regiment and commanded it.'

At the Restoration Crispe returned from exile and was created a baronet. He then took possession of a house at Hammersmith which he had built before the Civil War commenced. On his death in 1666 his body was bd. at St. Mildred's, and his heart in the par. ch. of Hammersmith (*q.v.*). Crispe was a great benefactor of St. Mildred's Ch. and in 1628, when it was repaired, erected at his sole cost an E. window representing the Spanish Armada, Q. Elizabeth, Gunpowder Plot, the Plague of 1625, and figures of the donor himself with his wife and children.

The ch. was burnt in the G.F., and rebuilt by Wren in 1683. Its par. was then united with St. Margaret Moses (*q.v.*). It was the one City ch. that remained practically as Wren left it. The pews remained, and there was some handsome wood-work. The walls were panelled;

there was some fine carving, and the C.C. pew was adorned with the lion and the unicorn, and had a handsome sword-rest. There was a tablet to Sir Thos. Crispe, son of Sir Nicholas: the epitaph made mention of his father's fidelity to Charles I and Charles II.

Nothing now remains of the ch. except the lower part of the tower. The par. registers remain in Guildhall Library and in one is a record of the marriage of Shelley and Mary Wollstonecraft Godwin on 30th Dec. 1816. This once took Thos. Hardy to the ch.

In 1932, through the generosity of Viscount Wakefield, there was placed outside the ch. a huge memorial to Admiral Philip, first Governor of Australia (1788–92). He was b. in Bread St. Ward in 1738 and d. in 1814. A map of Australia was at the top, above a bust of the Admiral, and at the sides panels showing the discovery of the site of Sydney (1788) and supplies being left there.

St. Stephen, Coleman St. It is claimed that the first ch. was built in 1181, but the first definite mention is *c.* 1214, 'Parish of St. Stephen Colemanstrate.' In Henry III's reign (*c.* 1268) it was 'St. Stephen in the Jewry.' It was described as a chapel annexed to St. Olave's, Old Jewry, in 1317, and also in the will of John Sekelyng (*c.* 1431). By Inquisition of 15 and 29 Henry VI, however, it was found to be a par. ch., and not a chapel. In 1456 a vicarage was ordained and endowed by Thos. Kemp, Bp. of L., who arranged matters with the prior and convent of Butley in Suffolk, who had held the advowson from the canons of St. P.'s Cath. The patronage remained with the prior and convent till the dissolution, but since the reign of Q. Elizabeth has been in the gift of the parishioners. Amongst the burials Stow mentions Wm. Crayhag, who founded a chantry in the reign of Edward II; and Thos. Bradberie (Ld.M. 1509).

One of the monuments was:

'To the memory of that ancient servant to the city, with his pen in divers employments, especially the Survey of London, master Anthony Munday, citizen and draper of London.'

From 1580 to 1621 Munday arranged the City pageants and shows. Some lines on the monument referred to him as:

'He that hath many an antient tomb-stone read,
(I' th' labour seeming more among the dead
To live, than with the living) that survaid
Abstruse antiquities, and ore them laid
Such vive and beauteous colours with his pen,
That, (spite of Time) those old are new agen.'

The revised edition of Stow was referred to in the epitaph. This was prepared upon the instructions of the C.C., and printed in 1618. Munday d. 1633, in his eightieth yr. John Hayward, under-sexton of the ch., made himself particularly active in the Plague and is mentioned by Defoe.

The ch. was burnt in the G.F., and rebuilt by Wren in 1676. It was a plain bdg. without aisles, measuring 75 ft. in length and 35 ft. in breadth. The oak pulpit was well carved, and the altar-piece of oak had Corinthian pilasters. The E. window inserted in 1843 was destroyed by a German bomb on 7th July 1917. It was replaced in 1919. There was a large marble monument to Henry Vernon, an Oriental merchant, who d. at Aleppo in 1694, in his thirty-first yr.

The ch. was entirely destroyed in 1941 and has been built over.

St. Swithun, London Stone (Cannon St.). The first mention is 'St. Swithun de Candelwryhttestrate, 1272.' In 1557 it was 'St. Swithun at London Stone.' It was rebuilt largely at the expense of John Hend (Ld.M. 1405), *c.* 1420. In the old ch. were bd. Sir Wm. Crowmere (Ld.M. 1413 and 1423), Sir Ralph Josselyn (Ld.M. 1464 and 1476), Wm. White (Ld.M. 1489), Sir John Allott (Ld.M. 1589), Sir Stephen Slaney (Ld.M. 1595), and Sir Geo. Bolles (Ld.M. 1617).

The ch. was burnt in the G.F., and rebuilt by Wren in 1678. It had a fine octagonal domed roof, and was of pleasing proportions. The lower portions of the walls were panelled. The ch. was destroyed by bombing and the site built on. The only monument of note was to Michael Godfrey, who was killed by a cannon ball at the siege of Namur in 1695, and his body brought home for interment. Godfrey was a prominent figure in the establishment of the Bank of England, and on its incorporation was made its first deputy-governor. He was not a soldier, but was at Namur on business. Just before he was killed William III had been remonstrating with him upon his rashness in exposing himself.

The list of rectors contained forty-six names from the priest Alexander (1236). Two rectors were deprived, presumably for Romanizing tendencies: Geo. Barton in 1561, and Wm. Jackson in 1605. The Rev. Richd. Owen was for seventeen yrs. ousted from the cure by a Puritan preacher, but was restored just before the death of Cromwell.

London Stone (*q.v.*) is embedded in the wall of a bank building in Cannon Street.

City Corporation. Glimmerings of a govt. of L., apart from the nation of which it formed a part, are discernible in the days of Alfred the Great. In 886 he appointed Ethelred, his son-in-law, its alderman. It is plausibly assumed that at this time Anglo-Saxon practices must have been paramount in the City, and when this alderman was agitated by any vital question of public policy he consulted the citizens at their moot or meeting-place. This was probably at the E. end of St. P.'s Cath., and this fact, at a time when the population was too large for any general assembly to have gathered in one place, may have suggested the site of Paul's Cross. At any rate, it was only in the ordinary course of things that the bell of the cathedral should summon the citizens, as this transcended all other bdgs. in importance and significance. Probably the alderman was elected here.

The next historic landmark is William the Conqueror's charter *c.* 1066 (see 'Guildhall'), in which a portreeve is referred to. As he is mentioned immediately after the bp., he may be assumed to have been the premier civic authority. He was evidently in the City what the shire-reeves or sheriffs were in the shire, and held a position somewhat analogous to that of a mayor. This charter was a confirmation of old, rather than a grant of new, privileges. Next comes Henry I's charter, granting the City the right to elect its own justiciars, the foundation of the City's present privilege of holding the trials of the King's Pleas in the chief

court of criminal justice in the realm, the Central Criminal Court, commonly called 'the Old Bailey,' which is maintained by the C.C. There aldermen have the right to sit alongside the judges, and in addition there are courts peculiar to L.—the Ld.M.'s Court and the City of L. Court. The former—at the Mansion House—is analogous to a police court, and there is a similar court at the Guildhall; the latter, in a bdg. adjacent to the Guildhall, does the same work as an ordinary county court.

MAYOR. The first Mayor specifically named (and there is no reason to suppose he had any predecessor), was Henry FitzEylwin, who assumed office about 1191, and d. in 1212. Not much is known of him. He was described as of 'Londenestone'; and it may be assumed that his house was near what is still known as 'London Stone' (*q.v.*). He was not called '*Lord*' Mayor. The first allusion to the latter is in 1283, when there is a record of proceedings taken 'coram domino Maiori' (before the Lord Mayor). A report of Common Council in 1414 is addressed to 'The worshipful Lord Mayor.' In 1440 'dominus Maior' (The Lord the Mayor) is recorded to have received letters from Henry VI regarding the interference of the sheriffs with the rights of sanctuary of the ch. of St. Martin le Grand. The 'Lord' Mayor is referred to thereafter intermittently until 1545, and after that it was the regular title. In 1215, three yrs. after the first Mayor had terminated a period of office lasting at least twenty-one yrs., K. John—in a charter a few weeks earlier in date than Magna Carta—granted the citizens the right to elect annually their Mayor.

There have been about 570 Mayors. Five are known to have been of foreign extraction. The last of these was Polydore de Keyser (1887). The salary is now £18,750 per annum. The expense of maintaining the office is much greater.

ALDERMEN. The 'Court of Aldermen' first appears out of the 'dark backward and abysm of time' in the yr. 1200. Then there were chosen, says an ancient chronicle,

'five and twenty of the more discreet men of the City, and sworn to take counsel on behalf of the City, together with the Mayor.'

In 1319, Edward II decreed that all

the aldermen should be retired annually, and not be subject to re-election. From 1377 to 1393, however, each ward annually elected its own aldermen, after which the aldermen retained their office for life, unless removed therefrom for some reasonable and justifiable cause, and this rule prevails still. The oath taken by aldermen in medieval times prescribed, inter alia, that they should sell 'no manner victual by retayle, as bread, ale, wyne, flesh ne fyshe, by your apprentices, allowes, servaunts, ne by any other way. No proffit shall ye none take of any such manner victuall so sould during your office.'

The inhabitants on the electoral roll of every ward have the right to elect a freeman to be their alderman, but before he can sit he must be approved by the Court of Aldermen. If the electors of any ward return a person who has not been so approved, the court may, after rejection three times in succession, themselves nominate, elect, and admit a fit and proper person to fill the office. Every alderman of the City of L., by virtue of his office, is a justice of the peace, with exclusive powers as such. Every alderman may, within his ward, execute such duties as are prescribed for one or two justices of the peace of any county. He can also, when sitting at either of the City justice rooms (Guildhall and Mansion House), do alone any act, which by any statute, past or future, is directed to be done by more than one justice, and the court is deemed to be a court of summary jurisdiction, consisting of two or more justices. All the aldermen are justices of oyer and terminer, and are, as such, named in the commission for holding the Old Bailey sessions. They also discharge important duties under the City Police Act, 1839, and the various licensing acts. The aldermen also appoint a number of their body as visiting justices of H.M. Prisons of Brixton, Holloway, and Pentonville. They are severally governors of the five royal hospitals, viz. St. Bartholomew's, Christ's, Bridewell, Bethlehem and St. Thomas's. Each alderman has the government of his own ward, and has to appoint a deputy from its common councilmen. A person who refuses to serve as alderman on being elected is liable to a fine unless he is in the position to satisfy the Court of Aldermen that at the time, he was not rich enough to serve.

COMMON COUNCIL. The earliest known list of members is found in the City archives c. 1285: 'the names of the good men of all the wards sworn to consult with the aldermen on the affairs of the City of London.' It contains 40 names; another list of 133 names dates from 1347. In 1341 Edward III granted the City a charter empowering the citizens, in their corporate capacity, to amend customs found oppressive or defective. The craft guilds, seizing the exercising of this freedom, claimed a more direct participation in the government of the City than hitherto they had attained, and in 1376 succeeded in wresting the election of the Common Council and of the Ld.M. and sheriffs from the wards, and vesting it in the guilds. In 1384 the election had reverted to the inhabitants of the wards, being freemen, each ward electing representatives as before in proportion to its size. The system has continued to the present day—except as to the necessity of the electors being freemen. By virtue of the charter of 1341, the Court of Common Council has from time to time fixed the number of annually elected representatives (now 206; it was 240 up to 1840), has settled the qualifications required for electors and elected, and has made any changes it thought fit in the machinery of the City's municipal government. The Court has the exclusive power of conferring the honorary freedom of the City and of voting corporate addresses to distinguished personages. All documents requiring the common seal of the C.C., and also leases granted by the royal hosps. (of which the Chamberlain holds the corporate seal), must be sealed in open court at a meeting of the Common Council. Every candidate must be a freeman of the City, a householder or freeman and occupier of premises worth £10 p.a., and a registered voter. The electors' qualifications are similar except they need not be freemen. The Court of Common Council thus consists of the Ld.M., 25 other aldermen, and 206 commoners, making a total of 232. There are no political parties.

WARDS. These number twenty-six. They are Aldersgate; Aldgate; Billingsgate; Bishopsgate Within; Bishopsgate Without; Bread St.; Bridge Within; Bridge Without;

City Corporation

Broad St.; Candlewick; Castle Baynard; Cheap; Coleman St.; Cordwainer; Cornhill; Cripplegate Within; Cripplegate Without; Dowgate; Farringdon Within; Farringdon Without; Langbourne; Lime St. ; Portsoken ; Queenhithe ; Tower ; Vintry; Walbrook. The significance of most of these names is explained in the course of this Encyclopædia. Candlewick retains the old name of Cannon St., Cordwainer recalls the shoemakers who—until it was bombed—had their hall in Cannon St.; Langbourn was not the name of a stream but a corruption of the Langobards or Lombards who settled there (the Bank of England is within it). For Portsoken, see 'Holy Trinity Priory.' Bridge Without (a ward formed in 1554) is the Bor. of Southwark. In 1327 Edward III brought it under the jurisdiction of the City of L., chiefly because the link of London Bridge so closely united them. The alderman is not directly elected, and the senior alderman who has passed the chair becomes alderman for this ward, but it is not compulsory.

SHERIFFS. The sheriffs have a longer history than the Common Council, the aldermen, or the mayor. They are referred to in the early charters. Until the beginning of the 14th century they were elected by the mayor, aldermen, and the commonalty. In 1347 one of the sheriffs was elected by the mayor, and the other by the commonalty, and this practice was maintained down to 1638. From 1642 to 1651 the mayor's claim to elect a sheriff was always contested. He was allowed to nominate, but not to elect, although often his nominee was accepted by the citizens. For the yr. 1652, and for some yrs. afterwards, the mayor neither nominated nor elected a sheriff, but in 1662, when he wished to resume the ancient right, there was again disputing, although eventually his nominee was accepted. Until 1673 his right was unchallenged. In 1674, when objection was again raised, a committee was appointed to inquire into the whole matter. In its report is found a reference, for the first time, to the custom of the Ld.M. electing, or at least nominating, a sheriff for the yr. ensuing by drinking to him on some public occasion. The custom is said to have arisen in the reign of Elizabeth. In 1878, by act of Common Council, it was declared that the right of

election should vest in the Liverymen of the several cos. of the City in common hall assembled, the 24th day of June in each yr. A fine of £200 was made payable by any person duly nominated, who should decline to take upon himself the office. The election takes place on the 'hustings' erected at the E. end of the Guildhall, the Ld.M. going in full state from the Mansion House to the Guildhall for the purpose. The duties of the sheriffs are many, and almost unintermittent. They wait upon the sovereign, attended by the City Remembrancer, regarding any proposed address to the Crown; they have the duty of presenting at the Bar of the H. of C. petitions to Parliament on behalf of the C.C., attended by the City Remembrancer. They are expected to be in attendance on the Ld.M. in many of his official functions; they preside in common hall during the absence of the Ld.M., and they are required to attend every session of the Central Criminal Court.

Recorder. He is first heard of in 1298. He is the senior law officer, by charter of 1304 the mouthpiece of the C.C. in declaring and protecting the ancient privileges of the City. He attends as one of the judges at the Central Criminal Court, and sits as judge in the mayor's court. He attends the Ld.M. upon presentation of addresses from the Courts of Aldermen and Common Council to the sovereign. He has to present the Ld.M. to His Majesty's judges on his being sworn into office.

Chamberlain. He is mentioned in 1276. He is elected by the Livery, and is the treasurer. He is also Keeper of the Roll of Freemen.

Town Clerk. Called in ancient times the 'Common Clerk,' his office is mentioned in 1284. He attends to advise the Court of Aldermen and Common Council, and minutes their proceedings. He issues the precepts and writs for civic elections, and is keeper of the charters and archives.

Common Serjeant. An office named in the constitutions of 1319. He sits in the Central Criminal Court, and is junior to the recorder. More often he presides in the Ld.M.'s court, and he is one of the law officers of the C.C. In 1888 the appointment was taken out of the hands of the C.C., and conferred upon the Crown.

A well-known Common Serjeant of recent yrs. was H. F. Dickens, K.C., son of the novelist.

Comptroller and City Solicitor. He is a law officer and conveyancing solicitor. His duties are the custody of the title deeds of the City's properties. He executes all leases and agreements, and controls the rentals of the City and Bridge House Estates. He drafts the City's by-laws and prosecutes offenders.

Remembrancer. He is a law officer, and attends daily at the H. of C. during its sittings to watch the City's interests. He is responsible for the formal invitation of the officers of state and others to the Guildhall banquet, and the reception in the library He is also responsible for the order of the procession on Ld.M.'s Day.

Lord Mayor's Election. The first step—not the first in the Ld.M.'s career, as he must previously have been elected an alderman and a sheriff—is a precept from the Ld.M. for the time being, addressed to the masters and wardens of the various cos. to summon their liverymen to the Guildhall, and from thence to go to St. Lawrence Jewry for service and sermon, and afterwards to return to the Guildhall for the election of a Ld.M. for the yr. ensuing. The aldermen, sheriffs, and high officers receive a summons to the same effect from the swordbearer's office. The religious service dates from Whittington's second election when there was a solemn mass in the Guildhall Chapel before election. It was then ordained that the religious ordinance should be an annual observance, and subsequently this was held in the Guildhall Chapel.

The Ld.M., sheriffs, and aldermen (all in full ceremonial dress) go from the Mansion House to Guildhall. A nosegay is presented to each by the hall keeper. Conducted by the City marshals, the procession then proceeds to the ch., the Ld.M. bringing up the rear. The sermon is preached by the Ld.M.'s chaplain. The procession then proceeds to the Guildhall—a part of which is reserved for the Aldermen (the beautifully painted and panelled room set apart for them was destroyed in the Blitz) and from there they proceed to the hustings. These are erected at the E. end, and strewn with sweet-smelling herbs—a relic of the time when L. was insanitary and odoriferous. There the Liverymen are gathered, and the 'Common Hall' is opened by the common crier repeating the following proclamation:

'Oyez, Oyez, Oyez. You good men of the Livery of the several Companies of this City, summoned to appear here this day, for the election of a fit and able person to be Lord Mayor of this City for the year ensuing, draw near and give your attendance.'

Then the Recorder (or in his absence the Common Serjeant) informs the Livery that in order that their choice may be unfettered the Ld.M. and the aldermen who have passed the chair will retire. When they have retired, the sheriffs, with the Common Serjeant between them, advance to the front of the hustings; the Common Serjeant reads to the Livery a list of the names of those aldermen below the chair who have served as sheriffs, and intimates that out of the aldermen named they are to return two to the Ld.M. and aldermen, for them to choose which of the two shall be Ld.M. for the yr. ensuing. Hands are then raised in turn for each of the aldermen on the list. The Common Serjeant then declares to the Livery that the sheriffs are of opinion that their election has fallen upon two who are named, together with their respective companies. The two sheriffs and the Common Serjeant then report the result to the aldermen who have remained apart (ex-Lord Mayors) and the election from the two is made by them. Then the result is declared by the Recorder, and the sword-bearer hands the Ld.M. elect to his place on the left hand of the Ld.M. The former then addresses the Court of Aldermen, thanking the court for the honour conferred, and requesting their aid in the execution of his office. The aldermen present, in order of seniority, come up and congratulate the Ld.M., as also do the officers. All of them then proceed to the great hall and the Recorder declares the election to the Livery. The Ld.M. elect is called upon by the Town Clerk to declare his assent to assuming the office, after which the sword-bearer places the chain upon the Ld.M. elect, who makes a speech. At this point the Ld.M. and sheriffs are thanked by the Livery for their services during the past yr., and very rarely has a vote of thanks been refused. The 'Common

Hall' is then dissolved, the common crier repeating from the Town Clerk the following formula:

'You good men of the Livery of the several Companies of this City, summoned to appear here this day for the election of a Lord Mayor of this City for the year ensuing, may depart hence at this time, and give your attendance here again upon a new summons.'

The Ld.M. takes the Ld.M. elect to the Mansion House in his state coach, the Ld.M. elect sitting on the left of the Ld.M. They are attended by the aldermen, the sheriffs and the officers.

On 8th Nov. the Ld.M. elect is sworn in at the Guildhall. Both he and the retiring Ld.M. leave the Mansion House in private carriages. The Town Clerk administers the following Declaration:

'I . . . do, solemnly, sincerely and truly declare that I will faithfully perform the duties of my office of Mayor of the City of London required by the 12 sect. of 31 and 32 Vic. cap 72.'

After the oath has been taken the late Ld.M. surrenders his seat to the new Ld.M., and takes his place on the left.

The Chamberlain then presents the City sceptre to the late Ld.M., who presents it to the new one. The sceptre measures $1\frac{1}{2}$ ft., and the shafts and knobs are of crystal, mounted in gold, and jewelled. The date is unknown. The head appears to be 15th-century work; the shaft may possibly date back to Saxon times. It was carried by the Ld.M. in discharging the office of chief butler at coronations, and is now borne at coronation processions. The large faceted boss halfway up the shaft is of glass and dates from 1845. The Chamberlain then presents the seal of office and the purse; after that the sword-bearer presents the sword in the same way. The latter has a scabbard studded with pearls; it is said to have been presented by Q. Elizabeth when she visited the first Royal Exchange in 1571. The common crier then presents the mace, which is seen protruding from the window of the Ld.M.'s coach whenever he goes in civic procession from the Guildhall. It dates from 1735, is of silver gilt, and is 5 ft. 3 in. in length. These emblems of office are then all received back by the officers who tendered them with more ceremonial. The Comp-

troller then presents the indenture for the City plate, which the Ld.M. signs. The late Ld.M. then delivers up the key of the City and seal to the new Ld.M. The obverse of the latter bears a figure of St. Paul, the patron saint of the City, with a sword in his right hand, and in his left a banner of England. The reverse once included a figure of St. Thomas à Becket, but he disappeared here, as everywhere, at the Reformation. It now bears the City arms, helmet, and crest.

LORD MAYOR'S SHOW. This, the last surviving pageant in the City of L., goes back to immemorial antiquity. From the first institution of the mayoralty the election had to be confirmed by the sovereign or his justices, and it is therefore probable that there was a procession to Westminster from the beginning of the 13th century. In 1422 it is known that the procession was partly by water. This continued until 1856. Such of the companies as had barges followed the Ld.M. on the water. Particulars of some interesting shows are given in *My Lord Mayor*, by William Kent and S. Van Abbé (1947).

The business of the C.C. is carried on by the following committees, composed of four aldermen and twenty-nine common councillors; City lands; Bridge House Estates; Coal and Corn and Rates; Finance; Improvements and Town Planning; Streets; Port and City of London Health; Central Markets; Billingsgate and Leadenhall Markets; Spitalfields Market; Police; Library (Library, Records, Art Gallery); Housing; Establishment; City of London Schools (Freemen's School, Guildhall School of Music and Drama); General Purposes; Civil Defence. There are also a number of Special Committees.

The Honourable Irish Society, which manages the Corporation's estates in Ulster, consists of the Governor and five other aldermen, the Recorder, and 19 members of the Common Council, of whom one is elected Deputy Governor.

The City of L. Mental Hosp. is at Stone (Kent). It was opened in 1866. It accommodates about 600 patients. It was transferred to the Ministry of Health in 1947.

The resident population of the City of L. has never been so few. In 1841 it was 124,717; in 1947, 6,014; in 1967, 4,600. The day population is estimated at 500,000.

(See *The Corporation of London*, 1950.)

City Press (The) was founded in 1857. With the development of the L. Press into a national Press the affairs of the City of L. tended to be left unrecorded unless such affairs had national implications. At the time there was an intense local life and the older citizens had keen memories of the old rights in parish and ward; of their wardmotes; and of their ancient fight to preserve their liberties.

Mr. W. H. Collingridge, the printer and publisher of Aldersgate St., then at the head of the old City Press, undertook to found a newspaper for the City of L. This he did and named it the *City Press*, after the then old publishing house, of which he had become the chief with his brother Leonard.

The *City Press* has had a long and honourable career. From the start it has devoted space to matters of antiquarian and historical interest. The first Editor was W. H. Collingridge, the founder. It publishes also the annual *City of London Directory and Who's Who* (with Livery Companies Guide).

City Temple has a history dating back to 1640. In that yr. Dr. Thos. Goodwin (see 'Bunhill Fields') founded a ch. in Anchor Lane, Lower Thames St., resigning in 1650 when appointed President of Magdalen Coll., Oxford. His successor was Dr. Thos. Harrison, and, according to a contemporary record, 'the Meeting House was crowded every Lord's Day.' At the beginning of his ministry the ch., for some inexplicable reason, left Anchor Lane and assembled at a meeting house in Paved Alley, at the Leadenhall St. end of Lime St. This apparently was only temporary, and in 1672, the Declaration of Indulgence having afforded full liberty to dissent, a ch. with three capacious galleries was built on an adjacent site. Dr. Harrison's ministry had terminated by 1657, perhaps earlier. He was succeeded by Rev. Thos. Mallery, who was also lecturer at St. Michael's Ch., Crooked Lane. Of him little is known. He had 'a considerable congregation' to the end.

When the ch. premises were demolished in 1755 a serious division manifested itself amongst the members. A minority established itself at a meeting house in Artillery St., whilst the majority moved to Miles

Lane, Cannon St. (see 'Bunhill Fields'), and appointed as their minister Rev. Wm. Porter. The chapel there had been erected in the early part of the reign of Charles II, and the congregation went at the invitation of its pastor, Rev. Timothy Jollie, holding only a Sunday morning service. In 1766 a new ch. was opened in Camomile St. In 1819 the ch. was moved to the Poultry, where Rev. John Clayton closed his ministry in 1845. In 1869 commenced the historic ministry of Dr. Joseph Parker, and in 1874, owing to his success, the City Temple was erected at Holborn Viaduct. It was designed by Messrs. Lockwood & Mawson in a light Italian style, and was built on a site acquired from the C.C. at a cost of £25,000. The memorial stone was laid by Dr. Binney, and the ch., which could accommodate at least 2,500, was opened in 1874. The Ld.M. attended in state, there was a luncheon, over which he presided, at the Cannon St. Hotel, and an address was delivered by Dean Stanley. The pulpit, of Caen marble, cost 300 guineas, and was the gift of the C.C., possibly in recognition of the fact that this ch. had always been within the City. Round the walls of the C.T. were painted the following names—they were chosen by Dr. Parker in collaboration with his deacons: Spurgeon, Binney, Whitefield, Baxter, Wesley (C.), Wesley (J.), Askew (Anne), Bunyan, Howe, Moffatt, Fry (Elizabeth), Luther, Cromwell, Parker. The last was presumably chosen by the deacons alone, although a gentleman whose telegraphic address was 'Preacher London' might not have been backward in the proposal. Dr. Parker's oratory and daring ('God damn the Sultan,' he once said) drew large crowds to the City Temple. He instituted at the beginning of his ministry a Thursday midday service. Dr. Parker d. 1902, and his successor was Rev. R. J. Campbell, whose so-called 'New Theology' produced a 'buzz of excitement never before known in the church.' This was assisted by the popular religious weekly, the *Christian Commonwealth*, which was in all but name the official organ of the City Temple. Rev. R. J. Campbell resigned in 1915. From 1916 to 1919 Dr. Fort Newton was minister. He was assisted by Miss Maud Royden, and the first appearance of a lady in the famous pulpit in the summer of 1917 packed the bdg. to the doors.

The City Temple was reduced to a ruin by German bombs in 1941. A bust of Dr. Parker was saved. Only the front and rear walls were left after the fire.

Subsequently the congregation assembled at the Ch. of St. Sepulchre, Newgate; the Friends' Meeting House, Euston Road; and the Marylebone Presbyterian Ch., George St. After an appeal for funds the Temple was completely rebuilt with a modern interior and re-opened in 1958.

(See *The City Temple 1640–1940*, 1940.)

Clement's Inn derives its name from the par. of St. Clement Danes. It was attached to the Inner Temple, from what date cannot be ascertained. In 1479, according to Dugdale, it was a house of law, and in 1486 it was leased by Sir John Cantlowe to Wm. and John Elyot, probably in trust for legal students. In 1528 it passed to Wm. Holles, afterwards Ld.M., and from him it came down to John E. of Clare, the son and heir of Sir John Holles, the first E., whose title is recalled by Clare Market. Stow referred to it as near 'the fair fountain called Clement's Well.' In 1560 Machyn recorded a great robbery 'with-in Clementts inn withowt Tempulle bare, by on master Cutt and iij mo and iij of them was taken on led into Newgatt and anodur in Wostrett (Wood Street) contur, and anodur in the contur in the Pultre.'

Mr. Justice Shallow of Shakespeare's creation lodged there.

' "I do remember him at Clement's Inn," says Falstaff; "when 'a was naked, he was, for all the world, like a forked radish, with a head fantastically carved upon it with a knife." '

Perhaps the chimes he heard at midnight were those of St. Clement Danes Ch. Another graceless creature found its rural surroundings convenient. Nicholas Jennings, one of the most notorious beggars of the Elizabethan underworld— 'about twelve of the clock went on the backside of Clement's Inn without Temple Bar. There is a lane that goeth into the fields. There he renewed his face again with fresh blood, which he carried about him in a bladder, and daubed on fresh dirt upon his jerkin, hat and hosen, and so came back again into the Temple, and

sometime to the waterside, and begged of all that passed by.' (*Caveat for Common Cursitors*, by Thos Harman, 1567.)

Wenceslaus Hollar lived in Clement's Inn, and was most precise in describing his whereabouts to Aubrey:

'Myself doe lodge withowt St. Clement's Inn back dore, as soon as you come up the steps and owt of that house and dore on your left hand two payre of stayres, into a little passage right before you. If you have occasion to ask for me, then you must say the Frenchman limner, for the people of the house know not my name perfectly for reason's sake.'

Hatton (*New View of London*, 1708) says:

'There was a Hall and many handsome chambers, built round three Courts, through which is a Passage from St. Clement's Church to Clare Market in the Day-time, when the gates are open.'

The old hall was rebuilt in 1715. The original entrance to the bdgs., before the advent of the Royal Courts of Justice, was beneath an archway in Pickett Place, cut through some new houses which were erected on the site of Butchers' Row, immediately to the N. of St. Clement Danes Ch. When, however, it was decided to erect the Courts, all this part of Clement's Inn was demolished, and the material sold in 1868. A row of new bdgs. then appeared, bearing the same name, W. of the new Courts, and the hall was refaced and somewhat altered. The hall was demolished in 1893. Sir George Buc (1615) said the device of the Inn was—

'an anchor with a stocke, with a capital C couchant upon it, and this is graven in stone over the gate of Clement's Inne.'

The carving of an anchor was on the front of Clement's Inn Hall when it was destroyed. This can still be seen lying flat in Clement's Inn. In (Dr.) Philip Norman's *London Vanished and Vanishing* (1905) there is a charming picture of the garden of Clement's Inn, showing the leaden blackamoor now in the gardens of the Inner Temple (see 'Temple').

Cleopatra's Needle (Victoria Embankment) has no connection with the Egyptian Q. It was originally one of two obelisks erected at Heliopolis by Thothmes III (c. 1450 B.C.) and dedicated to Tum of Heliopolis. The centre column of hieroglyphics are believed to have been the work of Thothmes, and the side columns that of Rameses II (c. 1300 B.C.). The two obelisks were first set up in front of the great temple of the sun. In 23 B.C. the Emperor Augustus Cæsar had them taken down and transported to Alexandria to adorn the palace of the Cæsars. Cleopatra had died there seven yrs. before, and so the obelisks became associated with her. Through encroachments of the sea their stability became affected, and about the middle of the 16th century one of them fell. In 1798 Nelson won the Battle of the Nile, and in 1801 Sir Ralph Abercrombie completely defeated the French army. Some of the conquering soldiers and sailors conceived the idea of bringing home a trophy, and subscribed towards a fund for the removal of the prostrate obelisk. After considerable exertions, they could move it only a few feet, and, the project not meeting with official approval, it was abandoned. Part of the pedestal, however, was uncovered and raised, and a brass plate was inserted on which was engraved a short account of the British victories.

George IV, on his accession to the throne in 1820, was offered it as a gift from Mehemet Ali, then ruler of Egypt. For some reason it was not accepted. In 1831 the latter renewed the offer to William IV, and promised also to shift the monolith free of charge. This proposal was also declined. In 1849 the Govt. announced in the H. of C. their desire to transport it to L., but as the Opposition demurred on the ground that 'the obelisk was too much defaced to be worth removal,' the proposal was again abandoned. In 1851, the year of the Great Exhibition, the question was again broached in the House, but the estimated outlay of £7,000 for transport was considered too large. In 1853 the Sydenham Palace Co., desiring to have the obelisk in their Egyptian court, offered to pay all expenses. As, however, it was national property, and it was urged it could only be lent, and not given, the matter again dropped. In 1867 the Khedive disposed of the ground upon which the Needle lay, and the purchaser, a Greek merchant,

insisted upon its removal. The appeal of the Khedive was futile, and it seemed probable that the purchaser of the ground would break it up for building material. General Alexander, who had pleaded for ten yrs. with learned socs. and with the Government, then went out to inspect it. He found it buried in the sand, but was able to uncover it. On his return to England he obtained the enthusiastic assistance of Prof. Erasmus Wilson, who signed a bond for £10,000 to be paid to Mr. John Dixon, C.E., when Cleopatra's Needle was set up in L. The M.B.W. offered a site on the Victoria Embankment. A cylindrical vessel had been specially designed to carry the obelisk, and in 1877 the tug *Olga*, with the whole in tow, steamed out of the harbour of Alexandria. There was a storm in the Bay of Biscay, and after much difficulty in saving the crew, the vessel bearing Cleopatra's Needle was abandoned. It did not, however, sink. It was found by the steamer *Frogmaurice* (Jas. Sexton, later the dockers' M.P., was one of the crew) and towed to Vigo, whence it was brought to England after a few weeks' delay, and erected in its present position in 1878. The sphinxes, through the error of the contractor, were so placed that their faces were towards the pillar. In 1879 the companion obelisk was removed to New York.

The obelisk is 68½ ft. high, and is on a pedestal of grey granite, 18 ft. 8 in. high, including the steps. The inscription covers three sides of the base, while on the fourth side is a memorial tablet to six sailors who perished in a bold attempt to succour the crew of the obelisk ship. In the centre of the pedestal are two large earthenware jars containing the following articles: standard foot and pound; bronze model of the obelisk, ½ in. scale to the foot; copies of *Engineering* printed on vellum, with plans and details of transporting and erecting the monument; jars of Doulton ware; a piece of the obelisk stone; complete set of British coinage, including an Empress of India rupee; parchment copy of Dr. Birch's translation of the obelisk's hieroglyphics; standard gauge to one-thousandth part of an inch; portrait of Q. Victoria; Bibles in various languages; Bradshaw's Railway Guide; Mappin's sculling razor; case of cigars; pipes; box of hairpins and ladies' ornaments; Alexandra feeding bottle and children's toys; a Tangye's hydraulic jack as used in raising the obelisk; wire ropes and specimens of submarine cables; map of L.; copies of daily and illustrated papers; photographs of a dozen pretty English women; a 2-ft. rule; a L. directory; *Whitaker's Almanack*; copy of *The Times* for the day the obelisk was set up.

The obelisk, which is maintained by the G.L.C. as successors to the M.B.W., was slightly damaged by an air-raid in Sept. 1917.

(See *Cleopatra's Needle*, by Rev. Jas. King, 1893.)

Clerkenwell is the most interesting part of the bor. of Finsbury, now in the L. bor. of Islington. The name is literally 'Clerks' Well,' 'en' being plural in Anglo-Saxon. It was not mentioned in the Domesday Book and is supposed to have been included at that time in Islington.

Its early history is connected with the Priory of St. John of Jerusalem. This was founded by Jordan Briset, *c.* 1140. In 1185 Heraclius, Patriarch of Jerusalem, consecrated the newly built ch. of St. John here. K. John stayed at the priory for a month in 1212, P. Edward and Q. Eleanor of Castile were guests in 1265. Hospitality was a religious duty, and an expensive one. It is not surprising to find that, in a sort of balance sheet drawn up by the Prior of Clerkenwell in 1358, it was said:

'There was much expenditure which cannot be given in detail, caused by the hospitality offered to strangers, members of the royal family, and other grandees of the realm who stay at Clerkenwell and remain there at the cost of the house.'

There was an adverse balance of £21 11s. 4d! In 1381 the Wat Tyler rebels burnt the ch. and part of the priory, and then the round nave (the area of which is shown by paving-stones arranged in a circular formation outside the present ch.) disappeared and was replaced by one of the usual rectangular form. In 1911 the foundations of the N. wall of this nave were found in St. John's Sq., showing that it was some 90 ft. in length. At the NW. corner was a great tower, described by Stow. It was built with the sum of £3 6s. 8d. bequeathed by Wm. Massett, citizen and grocer of the par. of St. Sepulchre.

In 1399 Henry IV spent a fortnight at the priory before his coronation, and in the third yr. of his reign the emperor Constantine came to England and lodged here. A few yrs. later Henry IV again came to stay. The knights possessed considerable property wherewith to meet the cost of entertaining royalty and a charter of Henry VII, confirming previous ones, mentions 'woodland, meadows, pastures, waters, and mills.'

The priory occupied a considerable area, extending from what is now Clerkenwell Green on the N. to the gatehouse (still existing) in St. John's Lane on the S., and from St. John's St. on the E. to Red Lion St. on the W., covering some 10 acres. The gatehouse mentioned, as appears from an almost illegible inscription on the N. side, was erected in 1504 by Sir Thos. Docwra, prior 1501–27. Docwra also rebuilt the tower of the ch. and inserted Perpendicular windows. He added also on the S. side of the choir 'my lord Dockery's chapel, which is in length 12 yards.' Docwra was visited here by Henry VIII who employed him on embassies and commissions. On Docwra's death, Henry tried to force a nominee of his own upon the knights; but they elected Sir Wm. Weston, who had fought in the siege of Rhodes when the knights defended it unsuccessfully against the Turks. When the dissolution came, Henry VIII, in the words of Stow:

'tooke into his own handes all the landes that belonged to that house and that Order, wheresoever in England and Ireland, for the augmentation of his crowne,'

which Stow says were valued at £262 19s. a year. Sir Wm. Weston did not defy the royal power like the heroic brothers of the Charterhouse: he accepted a pension of £1,000 a yr. He did not want it long. In the quaint words of Weever:

'It fortuned on the 7th day of May, 1540, being Ascension Day, and the same day as the dissolution of his house, he was dissolved by death, which strooke him to the heart at the first time when he heard of the dissolution of his Order.'

He was bd. in St. James's Ch. His figure —all that remains of the monument, the canopy and upper part of the tomb are lost—is in the crypt, having been removed from that ch. in 1933. A number of the knights fled to Malta, and some of those who remained suffered execution.

Princess Mary seems to have taken up her abode there during the reign of her brother Edward VI. Machyn wrote in his diary (1551):

'The XVth day the Lady Mary rode through London into St. John's, her place, with fifty knights and gentlemen in velvet coats and chains of gold afore her, and after her iiij score gentlemen and ladies, every one having a peyre of beads of black.'

In tiles at the entrance to the Metropolitan Tavern (at the corner of Farringdon Rd. and Clerkenwell Rd.) there is a pictorial representation of Princess Mary leaving the priory on a visit to her brother. The tower and much of the ch. was destroyed by the D. of Somerset in Edward VI's reign. There still remains, however, a beautiful crypt, of Norman architecture in parts, and elsewhere of Early English transitional style. When an excavation was made for the purpose of examining the walls, three medieval skeletons were found, one minus its skull. It is on record that Grand Prior Langstrother was taken prisoner and beheaded by Edward IV after the Battle of Tewkesbury in 1471, and that he was bd. in the ch. It is probable that this skull was the Prior's.

On Q. Mary's accession she invited the knights to return. They found the nave and tower of the ch. destroyed; the choir roofless and exposed to the weather. Stow says:

'That part of the Quire which remained, with some of the Chappels, was by Cardinal Poole in the raigne of Queene Mary closed up at the west end and otherwise repayred.'

The Order was revived, with all its ancient privileges, in 1557. Q. Elizabeth dissolved the Order, and seized the property of the knights, who fled to Malta. Under her the priory was used as the office of Edmund Tylney (see 'Wandsworth') from 1579 to 1610. Rehearsals took place in the Great Hall, 105 ft. long by 60 ft. wide. In 1612 James I gave the premises to Ld. Aubigny, and allowed Tylney's successor £15 p.a. for house rent in lieu thereof. Later the priory came into possession of Wm. Cecil Ld. Burghley, and from Fuller we learn that 'his countess was very forward to repair the ruined choir.' She was bd.

in St. James's Ch. The tablet to her memory is in the present bdg. The Countess d. in 1653, and was then above eighty yrs. of age.

The ch. was solemnly reopened in 1623, and when, by marriage and descent, the priory house passed to Ld. Aylesbury, the choir was known as Aylesbury Chapel. Fuller, writing in 1655, thought that it was—

'one of the best private chapels in England discreetly embracing the mean of decency between the extremes of slovenly profaneness and gaudy superstition.'

In the early part of the 18th century the ch. had become a Presbyterian meetinghouse. Burnet says it was sacked during the Sacheverall riots, and its contents were burned before the door. In 1716 it was advertised for sale as 'the remains of the once famous Abbey of Clerkenwell.' In 1721 it was bought by one Simon Michel who was responsible for a hideous W. front and ugly galleries. In 1723 Michel sold the ch. to the Commissioners of Q. Anne's Bounty for £2,500, when it was reconstructed as the par. ch. of St. John's, Clerkenwell. In 1747 John Wilkes was m. in this ch.

In the crypt, in 1762, was bd. Fanny Kent, whose murder was said to have been revealed by the 'Cock Lane ghost.' (q.v.) In 1893, when 325 coffins were removed, a Sunday paper reported that one was found stained with arsenic! The coffin was never identified. It probably had no plate. It remained the par. ch. until 1931 when the par. was united with that of St. James's Clerkenwell and the ch. assigned solely for the Order of St. John of Jerusalem. Much of the medieval wall had survived. The ch. was reduced to a ruin by German bombs in 1941 but rebuilt in 1958.

The gatehouse has not always been as now seen. In the earliest representation— that of Hollar, 1656—there is an inner wooden gate divided into two passages, one for vehicles and one for pedestrians. In 1733 the double entry remained, and there were battlements, according to a print in the *Gentleman's Magazine*, which had commenced publication two yrs. before. The title-page always bore a print of the gate where it was published, and there was a representation of it on the panels of the coach in which rode Edward Cave, its founder and first editor. In the room over the gateway young Samuel Johnson wrote. Here he had dinner behind a screen; he was too shabby to be seen. Here his fellow townsman, David Garrick, gave his first dramatic performance in L.—to Cave's workmen. After Cave's death (1754) the *Gentleman's Magazine* continued to be issued here from St. John's Gate until 1781. In 1771 the secondary arch of the gate was removed. In 1831 a revival of the Order of St. John under a fresh constitution was decreed. The Order, obtaining a freehold of the old gate completely redecorated it, and made it their headquarters. The St. John's Ambulance Association was an offshoot of this Order in 1877. The Grand Hall over the roadway was entirely renovated, re-panelled, and fitted with a decorative skylight of carved oak. Leading to it is a spiral staircase made of solid oak blocks, some dating from Docwra's time. There is a most interesting mus. in the gatehouse, part of which, in the 19th century, was the Jerusalem Tavern. In 1893 the shields above the gateway on the S. side were so badly decayed that they had to be replaced by the present ones. Here there is an inscription in memory of the D. of Clarence, sub-prior at the time of his death. On the N. side are the arms of the Order and those of Docwra. There is no other thoroughfare in L. spanned by an arch of any antiquity. In St. John's Lane was the 'Baptist's Head,' for about 200 yrs. an inn, now a modern tavern. It was once the house of Sir Thos. Forster, Judge of Common Pleas, who d. there in 1612. A handsome chimney-piece, a magnificent example of English Renaissance work, was taken from the taproom on the demolition of the inn in 1895 and placed in the chancery of the gatehouse.

A short distance to the W. of the priory a Benedictine nunnery was founded about 1140, also by Jordan de Briset—for the good of his soul, that of Muriel, his wife, and the souls of his parents and friends, living and dead. (Briset St., off St. John's Lane, commemorates the founder.) According to a document of Richard I's reign, the lands belonging to the nunnery were more extensive than those of the priory, amounting to 14 acres. It was suppressed in 1539, the last prioress being bd. in 1570 before the high altar of St. James's Ch. The nuns' hall was in use

as a workshop so late as 1773, and at the end of the 19th century, a few feet below the surface, part of the pavement of a walk, evidently of the date of the nunnery, was unearthed. A few fragments of pillars, etc., dug up at the same time, are preserved in the nearby Public Library in Skinner St. Clerkenwell Close was originally the nunnery close. It was built over in the time of the Stuarts, thirty-one houses being rated there in 1661. Here lived Sir Thos. Challoner, an ambassador under Q. Elizabeth and author of *The Right Ordering of the English Republic*, incomplete in five volumes. The par. register records his death, but he was bd. in St. P.'s Cath. His son was the first to discover alum in England. From a house in Clerkenwell Close John Weever issued his *Ancient Funeral Monuments* (1632).

Stow said that the ch. of the nunnery became the par. ch. This, however, was an error. The existence of the ch. in 1478 is proved by its mention in a papal bull; it was then quite new. Apparently the growing needs of the expanding village of Clerkenwell necessitated a par. ch. The ch. of the nunnery was probably only for its inmates.

In 1556 John Bell, Bp. of Worcester (1539–43) was bd. in the ch. He spent the last thirteen yrs. in retirement at Clerkenwell. On the N. wall there is a brass to his memory. This was apparently stolen and it was restored to the ch., at the cost of Stephen Tucker Esq., Somerset Herald, in 1884. In 1632 John Weever was bd. in the ch. His epitaph happily commemorated his work. It opened as follows:

'Weever, who laboured in a learned strain
To make men long since dead to live again,
And with Expense of Oyle and Ink did watch
From the worm's mouth the sleeping corse to snatch.'

Another Clerkenwell resident was Izaak Walton (*c.* 1643–53); two of his infant children were bd. in the ch.

In 1691 a famous archer Wm. Wood was bd. here. He lived to the age of 82. The epitaph on a tablet on the S. wall, is as follows:

'Sir WILLIAM WOOD lyes very near this

stone.

In's time in archery excelled by none.
Few were his equals of this noble art,
Has suffer'd now in the most tender part.
Long did he live the honour of the bow,
And his long life to that alone did owe.
But how can art secure or what can save
Extreame old age from an appointed
    grave?
Surviving archers much his loss lament
And in respect bestow'd this monument
Where whistling arrows did his worth
    proclaim,
And eterniz'd his memory and name.'

Three flights of arrows were discharged
over the grave of Wood, author of *The
Bowman's Story*.

The most important figure associated
with Clerkenwell was Thos. Burnet, Bp.
of Salisbury. He was author of *The History
of My Own Time*, published posthumously
(1724–34), and *The History of the Reformation*. According to J. P. Malcolm (*London
Redivivum* (1803–7)), Burnet was unpopular
with the mob, and his hearse was pelted
with stones and dirt. No reason is assigned
for this hostility. Burnet's gravestone, for
long in the vaults, is now under the
Communion table. There is a large
monument in the vestibule, with a long
Latin inscription. It says he ever opposed
tyranny and superstition, as his excellent
works show, and earnestly defended the
liberties of his country and true religion.

The ch., which had been partly rebuilt
in 1625, remained in private hands until
1646, when it was purchased by the
parishioners. It has been theirs ever since,
and accordingly the vicar is elected by the
par. In 1788 an Act of Parliament was
passed for its rebuilding, and in 1792 the
present ch. was completed. An extraordinary feature of the interior is a double
gallery. The upper one is now only at
the W. end of the ch. When Wm. Pink's
Clerkenwell was published in 1865 it was
also round the N. and S. walls. The font
dates from 1850. The most interesting
memorial tablet is to the victims of the
explosion at Clerkenwell House of Detention, caused by Fenians in 1867. This is
in the vestibule. (See 'Prisons.')

The spacious chyd. was purchased in
1673. It is now charmingly laid out as a
garden in happy contrast to its condition
when it was described by Gissing in the
opening chapter of *The Nether World*

(1889). (For the record of a murder on a
tombstone see 'Epitaphs.')

The Clerks' well is about 100 yards W.
of the ch. It is one of those referred to by
Wm. Fitzstephen, in the account of L.
prefixed to his biography of his master,
Thomas à Becket.

'There are also round London on
the northern side, in the suburbs,
excellent springs, the water of which is
sweet, clear and salubrious.

    ' "Mid glistening pebbles
      Gliding playfully."

amongst which Holywell, Clerkenwell
and St. Clement's Well are of most
note, and most frequently visited, as
well by the scholars as by the youth
of the city when they go out to take
the air in the summer evenings.'

John Stow, in his *Survey of London*
(1598), wrote:

'Clarkes' well or Clarkenwell, is
curbed about square with hard stone,
not far from the west end of Clerkenwell
church, but close without the wall that
incloseth it. The said church took the
name of well, and the well took the
name of the parish clerks in London,
who of old time were accustomed there
yearly to assemble, and to play some
large history of Holy Scripture. And
for example, of later time, to wit, in
the year 1390, the 14th of Richard II,
I read, the parish clerks of London,
on the 18th of July, played interludes
at Skinners' well, near unto Clarkes'
well, which play continued three days
together; the king, queen, and nobles
being present. Also in the year 1409,
the 10th of Henry IV, they played a
play at the Skinners' well, which lasted
eight days, and was of matter from the
creation of the world. There were to
see the same the most part of the
nobles and gentles in England etc.'
The exact site of Skinners' Well is not
known. There is reason to believe that it
was a few yards W. of the Clerks' well.

John Strype, in his augmented edition
of Stow's *Survey* (1720) wrote:

'I was there and tasted the water;
and found it extremely clear sweet and
well-tasted. The Parish is much displeased (as some of them told me)
that it is thus gone to decay: and
think to make some Complaint at a
Commission for Charitable Uses, hoping

by that means to recover it to common Use again, the Water being highly esteemed thereabouts; and many from these Parts send for it.'

In 1765 a carpenter, sent to repair the well, found it extremely hot. Then there was a large drain inserted in it for the purpose of a distillery. In 1800 a pump made the water available for the inhabitants of Clerkenwell. In 1857 the well was closed and, having become polluted, it was covered with rubbish. In 1878, on the demolition of the pump-house, a tablet with an inscription relating to the well was removed to the W. wall of St. James's Ch. The inscription is as follows:

'A.D. 1800.   William Bound ⎫ Church-
                     Joseph Bird ⎰ wardens.

'For the better accommodation of the neighbourhood this pump was removed to this spot where it now stands. The spring by which it was supplied is situate 4 feet eastward and round it as history informs us, the parish clerks of London in remote ages annually performed sacred plays. That custom caused it to be denominated Clerks' well and from which this parish derived its name. The water was greatly esteemed by the Prior and Brethren of the Order of St. John of Jerusalem and the Benedictine nuns of the neighbourhood.'

It is probable that the Prior and Brethren referred to found a water supply nearer. In his *London Signs and Inscriptions* (1897), Dr. Philip Norman mentions the well. Thereafter knowledge of its whereabouts seems to have been lost.

In 1924, during excavations on an adjoining site, it was rediscovered by Wm. Barrett. The well was under a wood and stone floor, covered with brick rubbish, earth, pieces of chalk and ragstone, and below this, at a depth of 2 ft. 9 in., was the circular well covered with thick elm boards, resting on a beam, all badly decayed, 13 ft. 6 in. below the street footway and half full of water. The brickwork was 14 in. thick, and might have been of 17th or 18th century construction.

The well can now be seen at 18 Farringdon Rd., on application to the Librarian of the Borough. The N. wall of the well-chamber is believed to have been part of the Benedictine nunnery. The tablet bearing the inscription quoted above is in the chamber, together with the nozzle of the pump.

Newcastle Row, behind St. James's Ch., is on the site of Newcastle House where resided Wm. Cavendish, 1st Duke of Newcastle, and his duchess, Margaret Lucas.

The Duke and Duchess were bd. in W.A., and on a monument, inside the N. door, their effigies lie side by side. On the breast of the Duchess is an ink well. Newcastle House was demolished in 1793, a date inscribed on a building in Newcastle Row.

A prominent feature of Clerkenwell Green (in the 1880's a place of public meeting—see Gissing's *Demos*, 1886) is the old Sessions House. It was erected 1779–80, and the medallions (enclosing allegorical figures of Justice and Mercy, and the arms of the county) were the work of Nollekens. The Sessions' House is judicially the descendant of Hicks' Hall, named after Sir Baptist Hicks, one of the justices of the county, who built it about 1612. This, however, was in St. John St. For the later Sessions House there were brought from Hicks's Hall (demolished *c.* 1777) a fine wooden varnished overmantel in Jacobean style ornately carved, with an inscription relating to the gift by Sir Baptist Hicks of the Sessions House, and a pair of heavy iron fetters—traditionally those worn by Jack Sheppard (now at Newington). The building was enlarged and considerably altered in 1860, there were further additions in 1876, and in 1889 it was taken over by the L.C.C. The sessions were, however, removed to Newington Causeway in 1921.

(See *Clerkenwell*, by Wm. J. Pinks, 2nd ed., 1881; *Clerkenwell*, by G. E. Mitton (1906); for Clerks' well, *Transactions of London and Middlesex Archæological Society*, New Series, v, 67; for St. Mary's Nunnery, *Ibid.*, VIII, Pt. II, 234.)

Clifford's Inn (Fleet St.) was leased in 1345 by the widow of the sixth Baron de Clifford to certain lawyers, Edward II having granted the baron a messuage and garden there *c.* 1317. It was an Inn of Chancery, entirely independent, and with a constitution of its own. It was governed by a principal, and twelve 'Rules' (as the Ancients here were called); the juniors sat at a separate table, which for no known reason was called the

'Kentish Mess.' In the reign of Q. Elizabeth it had over 100 members, many of whom had to reside outside the inn, in Fleet St. or Ludgate Hill. Edward Coke (1552–1634) and John Selden (1584–1654) were students of Clifford's Inn.

The G.F. caused very little damage to Clifford's Inn and in 1670, in its hall, the judges commenced to meet to settle all disputes arising out of boundaries, etc., caused by the wholesale destruction of property. Their portraits were afterwards painted and until recently could be seen in the C.C. Art Gallery. In 1767 a new hall was erected, incorporating some of the medieval work. From 1792 until his death in 1841 Chas. Lamb's quaint friend, Geo. Dyer, lived in Clifford's Inn.

In 1833 a serious dispute took place as to the election of principal. Mr. Jessop, a barrister, trying to exclude a solicitor named Allen who had been elected. It ended in a law-suit, in which Jessop was unsuccessful, although he had some support from the benchers of the Inner Temple.

Dr. Philip Norman wrote:

'Clifford's Inn was nominally dependent on that Society, but it was then declared in court by one of the judges that no instance had been adduced of the governing body of the Inner Temple having exercised authority over it by compulsion.'

After 1877 no new member was admitted, and shortly after the dinners were reduced to two in each term. There was a curious ceremony on these occasions. The President took up four little loaves baked together in the form of a cross; he knocked them twice on the table and then slid them down the middle of it. Finally they reached the porter, standing at the lower end, who removed them to the back of the screen, and they were distributed to poor people. It is possible that the knocks were in honour of the Holy Trinity.

In 1903 the then 'Rules' of Clifford's Inn, probably incited by the encouraging example of Serjeants' Inn (q.v.), decided to wind up their affairs and sell. A judgment of the High Court, however, forbade them to put the entire proceeds into their own pockets and a large portion of the purchase money had to be assigned for the purpose of legal education. At the auction William Willett, of 'daylight saving' fame, was the only bidder, and his price was £100,000. His contemplated schemes did not mature, and Clifford's Inn continued to be occupied by lawyers. It included also a restaurant and the offices of the London Topographical Soc. The Hall was leased by the Knights Bachelors, and used by the Dickens Fellowship from 1918–25.

In 1934 Clifford's Inn was doomed, and in 1935 the whole of it, with the exception of the modern gateway—dating from the 1840's, was demolished. This bears the arms of the Barons Clifford. Dr. Philip Norman thought that No. 12 dated back to 1624. At No. 3 was once some finely carved woodwork worthy of Grinling Gibbons. This had been taken to the Victoria and Albert Mus. many yrs. before.

Coal Exchange. Coal dug up by the people of Newcastle came to L. in the time of Henry III (1216–72), dyers and brewers taking to it for fuel. The landowners and gentry raised a loud complaint that the smoke caused thereby was unendurable. Edward I therefore issued a proclamation forbidding its use. Nevertheless, a charter of Edward II shows that Derbyshire coal was being used in L. In 1591 the Ld. High Admiral claimed the coal metage in the port of L. The Ld.M. and citizens disputed and overthrew his claim, and by the influence of Ld. Treasurer Burghley, obtained the Q.'s confirmation of the City's right to this. It was for long a dutiable article, and in 1655 Cromwell allowed the C.C. to import 400 chaldrons every yr. for the poor citizens duty free. Out of these duties on coal St. P.'s Cath. and other bdgs. were rebuilt after the G.F. The C.C. had been allowed a metage or weighing charge of 8d. a ton from the time of James I on all coal entering L., and in 1667 a duty of 1s. a ton was imposed. This was raised to 7s. in 1704.

The coal factors in the 13th century conducted their business in an open space near Billingsgate Market. It was known as 'Romeland'—derived from A.S. ram = open, cleared. There they met the captains from the colliery vessels, and concluded the bargains in a neighbouring tavern. The first exchange was erected on the site of one of these—the 'Dog.' The first mention of the exchange is in a L. guide of 1758. It was the property of the Coal

Factors' Soc., an exclusive body of traders with a restricted membership. There was, however, some criticism of their methods, and in 1803 powers were obtained from Parliament for the compulsory purchase of the exchange by the City from the soc., for the sum of £25,600, and the opening of its doors to all who desired to attend. The old bdg. became inadequate, and in 1847 the foundation of the exchange at the corner of Lower Thames St. and St. Mary-at-Hill was laid. It was opened in 1849. A remarkable feature of the bdg. was the floor, in the form of a mariner's compass, with the City shield and an anchor represented in the centre. Over 4,000 different pieces of wood were used, including black oak from an old tree removed from the bed of the Tyne in 1848. This fine floor was destroyed by water as a result of bombing which gutted the building, and from 1941 until 1950 it was in ruins. It was repaired and reopened in 1950 but events were against its continuance: because of changes in the trade (culminating in nationalization), there was no longer a need for a free market in coal, and moreover the site was needed for road widening. After several years of controversy while lovers of Victoriana proposed ever more expensive and impractical schemes to save it, and the C.C. showed exemplary patience, demolition began. If demolition was unfortunate in one sense, it showed profit in another, as the opportunity was taken by the C.C. to investigate traces of a Roman bath under the site.

Cock Lane (Smithfield). It is first heard of as 'Cockes Lane' (c. 1241–50). Having existed an age without a name, it had a few weeks of notorious—if not glorious—life in the yr. 1762. One Mr. Kent lost his wife in 1757, and then fell in love with her sister Fanny. In 1759 they were both in L., and took lodgings in the house of Parsons, the clerk of St. Sepulchre's Ch. in Cock Lane. Kent left Fanny there whilst he went into the country to attend a wedding, and she thereupon invited the daughter of the landlord, whose Christian name was Elizabeth, to share her bed. They were disturbed by strange scratchings and rappings. At first these were attributed to a neighbouring cobbler, but when it was observed that they continued on Sundays when he rested from his labours, this idea was abandoned. Fanny is then supposed to have believed that they were warnings of her impending death. Fanny and Kent again lived together in Bartlett Court, Clerkenwell, and there, on 2nd Feb. 1760, she d. of smallpox, according to the certificate of her physician and apothecary. She was bd. in the vaults of St. John's Ch. After cessation for a yr. and a half, the noises returned in the Cock Lane house, and seemed to come from the bed of Elizabeth Parsons. Mary Fraser, a nurse, suggested a code; one knock for 'Yes' and two for 'No.' In this way it was supposed to be divulged that Kent had poisoned Fanny with red arsenic in a glass of purl, and that the once dear departed wished to see him hanged.

The ghost story became the talk of the town. Horace Walpole, who was as alert for sensation as his contemporary Jas. Boswell, wrote to Horace Mann:

'I am ashamed to tell you that we are again dipped into an egregious scene of folly. The reigning fashion is a ghost—a ghost that would not pass muster in the paltriest convent in the Appenines. It only knocks and scratches: does not pretend to appear or to speak. The clergy give it their benediction: and all the world, whether believers or infidels, go to hear it. I, in which number you may guess, go to-morrow.'

Walpole duly went, having changed his clothes at Northumberland House, together with the D. of York, Lady Northumberland, Lady Mary Coke, and Ld. Hertford. He wrote:

'The house is wretchedly small and miserable. When we opened the chamber, in which were fifty people with no light, but one tallow candle at the end, we tumbled over the bed of the child to whom the ghost comes, and whom they are murdering by inches in such insufferable heat and stench. At the top of the room are ropes to dry clothes. I asked if we were to have rope-dancing between the acts. We heard nothing. They told us (as they would at a puppet-show) that it would not come that night till seven in the morning, that is when there are only 'prentices and old women. We stayed however till half an hour after one. The Methodists have promised them contributions. Provisions are sent in like forage, and all the taverns and ale-houses in the neighbourhood make fortunes.'

The spirit was supposed to intimate that it would rap on its own coffin so a small company, including Samuel Johnson, went into the vaults of St. John's Ch. Johnson's account (Goldsmith also wrote on the subject) was as follows:

'The spirit was then very seriously advertized that the person to whom the promise was made of striking the coffin was then about to visit the vault, and that the performance of the promise was then claimed. The company at one o'clock went into the church, and the gentleman to whom the promise was made went with another into the vault. The spirit was solemnly required to perform its promise, but nothing more than silence ensued. The person supposed to be accused by the spirit then went down with several others, but no effect was perceived. Upon their return they examined the girl, but could draw no confession from her. Between two and three she desired, and was permitted, to go home with her father. It is therefore the opinion of the whole assembly, that the child has some art of making or counterfeiting a particular noise, and that there is no agency of any higher cause.'

At length the girl was detected. When she was bound hand and foot the ghost was always silent. When threatened with Newgate if she did not arouse the ghost, she was found to have concealed a small board beneath her stays. Kent with the secret out, felt justified in vindicating his character. The father, the mother, and Nurse Fraser were indicted at Guildhall. Parsons was sentenced to be placed three times in the pillory at the end of Cock Lane, and to be confined for two yrs. in the King's Bench Prison. When in the pillory he was not molested; later a public subscription was raised for his benefit. Mrs. Parsons was sentenced to one yr.'s imprisonment, and Nurse Fraser to six months. Miss Parsons m. twice, and d. in ·1806.

(See *The Cock Lane Ghost*, by W. D. B. Grant, 1965.)

Cockney. The *Oxford English Dictionary* gives the first use of the word in its present connotation as in 1521, by a writer named Whitinton. In 1594 Sir Hugh Platt (*Jewell House of Art and Nature*),

says: 'The Country people will go near to rob all cockneys of their breakfast.' John Day (*Blind Beggar of Bednell Green, c.* 1600) said: 'I think you be sib to one of the London cockneys that ask whether Haycocks were better meat broyl'd or rosted.' Samuel Rowlands (*Letting of Humours Blood in the Head-Vaine*) in 1600: 'I scorne to let a Bow-bell cockney put me downe.' John Minsheu (*Ductor in Linguas,* 1617) gives a derivation of the word:

'A cockney or cockny—applied only to one born within the sound of Bow bell, that is within the City of London, a tearme coming first out of this tale. That a cittizen's sonne riding with his father in the country, asked when he heard a horse neigh what the horse did; his father answered "neigh." Riding further he heard a cock crow, and said: "Does the cock neigh too?"'

The word was originally applied to a small or misshapen egg, occasionally laid by fowls, these being sometimes called cock's eggs. Probably therefore it was a synonym for anything odd or out of place.

Cockpits. Henry VIII had a cockpit added to Whitehall Palace. It was the first bdg. specially erected for the purpose. It stood where is now the office of the Privy Council. A 'new Cocke-pitt, by the King's gate' (see 'Whitehall'), is mentioned by Pepys (6th Apr. 1668). This was evidently close to the old one. Pepys (21st Dec. 1663) refers to one in Shoe Lane.

In the reign of Q. Anne a new pit was made 'by the Bowling Green behind Gray's Inn Walks.' Von Uffenbach, a traveller from Frankfort, visited it in 1710 and gave a detailed account (see *Mine Host London*). At the beginning of the century another was constructed in Dartmouth St. by Q. Anne's Gate (there are still Cockpit Steps, leading to Birdcage Walk). It seems probable that this succeeded the one at Whitehall, and that it was the one so finely drawn and engraved by Rowlandson and Pugin, though it has been labelled 'The Cockpit, Whitehall.' There was also a view in Ackerman's *Microcosm of London,* 1808. Boswell spent five hours there in 1762. Wm. Windham went in 1796, after a dinner at Wm. Pitt's. It was demolished in 1816. Cock-fighting also went on at Hockley-in-the-Hole, Clerkenwell; Jewin St., Cripplegate; Duck Lane; Orchard St., Westminster; Crawford Passage, Clerkenwell—about 1775; Henry St., off Doughty St.; Tufton St., Westminster. The latter was there about 1821, and was probably the last of all. Cockfighting was made illegal in 1849, though it has been surreptitiously practised from time to time, and in Glasgow a man was fined in 1917 for this offence. Up to the outbreak of the Second World War part of the old pit remained in Henry St., N. of Theobald's Rd. It was probably the one behind Gray's Inn Walks. Cockspur St., no doubt, derived its name from its proximity to the Whitehall pit. 'Here,' says Jas. Bone, 'Indian rajahs still buy spurs for their cock-fighting.'

Coffee Houses. The coffee houses of 17th- and 18th-century L. were as integral part of the social life of the times, and not merely houses of refreshment. They were the meeting places for the wits and men of fashion, as well as for learned men, merchants, and politicians, supplying in fact, the place of the modern club for all intents and purposes.

The first coffee house was opened in L. in 1652 in St. Michael's Alley, Cornhill, by a Ragusan named Pasqua Rosea at the 'Sign of my own head.' He announced that 'it is a very good help to digestion, quickens the spirits, and is good against sore eyes,' etc. The new beverage took the public fancy. So numerous did the coffee houses become that their political influence began to be feared, and Charles II tried to suppress them in 1675 with, however, little result, as they continued to increase rather than diminish in number. The frequenters of these places naturally soon began to form themselves into coteries; each section made its headquarters at some particular place, and these humble beginnings often had far-reaching effects. Thus in the days when no telegraph or wireless existed, and there were few posts, houses were frequented by business men who desired to know from personal intercourse the latest news affecting their interests. The famous institution known as Lloyd's (*q.v.*) grew out of a coffee house.

The American Coffee House in Threadneedle St. was used in a similar way by those interested in the trade with the colonies. Merchants with interests in the East used to meet at the Jerusalem Coffee House in Cowper's Court, Cornhill, while the West Indian traders met at the Jamaica Coffee House in St. Michael's Alley, and those in the Russian trade frequented the Baltic (*q.v.*). In Change Alley (Lombard St.) were two famous commercial coffee houses, Garraway's and Jonathan's. In addition to merchants, many medical men made Garraway's their meeting place. A tablet was placed on its site in 1930. The Chapter Coffee House, in Paternoster Row, was the resort of booksellers. Will's Coffee House (formerly called the 'Rose') in Russell St. was the favourite haunt of Dryden, and near here stood the equally famous Button's, also celebrated as a resort of the wits and poets of Q. Anne's reign. Pope, Steele, and Addison were its most notable members. Another place where literary men foregathered was the Grecian. Also in Devereux Court was Tom's, much used by David Garrick and his circle, and by Akenside, the poet.

There is sometimes a little confusion over the name of Tom's coffee house, as there were three in all: the one above mentioned; another in Russell St., which was largely patronized by the theatrical profession and those interested in the theatre; while still a third Tom's was in Birchin Lane, in the City. Different records say that Garrick was a member of all three; this is possible, but rather unlikely. Nando's was another famous coffee house; it stood in Fleet St., while the equally well-known Piazza was in Covent Garden, and each had its own particular following. The Rainbow coffee house, near Temple Bar, though it became one of the most popular and fashionable of such places in town, was in the early days of its existence actually sued for the 'nuisance of selling coffee'!

Dick's coffee house, also by Temple Bar, was a resort of Isaac Bickerstaff, of the *Tatler*, who led the deputation from here of the 'Twaddlers' across Fleet St. When Cowper lived in the Temple he used to breakfast almost daily at Dick's (sometimes called Richard's, its earlier name), and it was naturally, from its position, a great resort for many generations of Templars.

Going further W. there was the British coffee house in Cockspur St., largely

G

frequented by Scotsmen; while the King's Head, which stood in King St., Westminster, was much used by Pepys; and the St. James's, in St. James's Sq., was a noted resort of the Whig party in the reign of Q. Anne. Another famous house was Don Saltero's at Chelsea (see 'Museums').

The coffee houses mentioned above, though by no means all, represent the chief ones, and as is only to be expected concerning such places where 'all the Town' met for business or gossip, the allusions to the various coffee houses of L. are innumerable. The following is a brief selection from this inexhaustible supply.

Sir Richd. Steele, in the first number of the *Tatler*, touches upon the differing characteristics of the various coffee houses when he writes:

'I date all gallantry from White's; all poetry from Will's; all foreign and domestic news from St. James's, and all learned articles from the Grecian.'

In Mrs. Centlivre's play, *A Bold Stroke for a Wife* (1717) there is a scene laid at Jonathan's coffee house, which gives a good idea from a contemporary source of how such places were conducted. While the business and pleasure goes on she makes the 'Coffee-boys' march up and down with the cry: 'Fresh coffee, gentlemen, fresh coffee! Bohea tea, gentlemen!'

In 1722 Daniel Defoe mentions Garraway's coffee house as frequented about noon by people of quality who had business in the City, while Dean Swift, in his ballad on the South Sea Bubble, calls Change Alley 'a narrow sound, though deep as hell,' and elsewhere describes the wreckers watching for the shipwrecked dead on 'Garraway cliffs.'

Coffee drinking, which became so popular quickly after its introduction, had its detractors in the early days, usually wine merchants and brewers, who used to employ lampooners to ridicule the 'new-fangled drink,' and declared that to drink this new liquor was to ape the Turk and to insult one's canary-drinking ancestors! They even issued a pamphlet on the subject, entitled *Cofee in its Colours* (1663), which declared that were it 'in the mode men would eat spiders!'

Although so famous as a coffee house, Garraway's was the first place in England where tea was sold to the general public.

A circumlocutory announcement, issued about 1660, ran:

'Tea in England hath been sold in the leaf for six pounds and sometimes for ten pounds the pound weight, and in respect of former scarceness and dearness it hath been only used as a regalia in high treatments and entertainments, and presents made thereof to princes and grandees, till the year 1657. The said Thomas Garraway did purchase a quantity thereof, and first publicly sold the tea in leaf and drink made according to the directions of the most knowing merchants and travellers into those eastern countries, and upon knowledge and experience of the said Garraway's continued care and industry in obtaining the best tea, and making drink thereof, very many noblemen, physicians, merchants and gentlemen of quality, have sent to him for the said leaf, and daily resort to his house in Exchange Alley aforesaid to drink the drink thereof. This is to give notice that the said Thomas Garraway hath tea to sell from 16 shillings to 50 shillings the pound.'

(See *London Coffee Houses*, by B. Lilly-white, 1963; and *The Penny Universities* by A. Ellis, 1956.)

Cogers. The oldest debating soc. in L. was founded in 1755 by Daniel Mason, a freeman of the Tallowchandlers' Co., at the White Bear Tavern, 15 Bride Lane. The name was derived from the Latin cogito—I think—and its motto is 'Cogito, ergo sum' (I think therefore I am), a phrase which provided the basis of the philosophy of Descartes, and led Carlyle to remark: 'Alas, poor cogitator!' A short 'o' in pronunciation is a gross offence to any member. In 1793 a minute book gave the following record:

'The society originally consisted of citizens of London who met to watch the course of political events and the conduct of their representatives in Parliament.'

There are no details of early meetings, but it is known that between 1756 and 1768 1,192 members were elected. The first President (he is called 'Grand Coger,' for short 'My Grand') is said to have been John Wilkes. Other early members were: (1793) Sir Richd. C. Glynn, M.P. (Ld.M. 1798); (1812) Sir Jas. Shaw, Bt., alderman; (1817) Sir Jas. Williams, chairman of the Middlesex Sessions. Other members, who cannot be associated with precise dates, were J. P. Curran, afterwards Master of the Rolls (Ireland); Daniel O'Connor; Judge Keogh; Ld. Brougham; Thos. first Ld. Denham, afterwards Lord Chief Justice; Robt. Waithman (Ld.M. 1823), five times M.P. for the City of L. (see 'City Churches; C'—St. Bride).

The meetings were held in a front room on the ground floor of the 'White Bear,' and the entrance had over it a lamp bearing the words 'Cogers Hall.' It is said that a stone tablet within the hall recorded the name of the soc., its founder, etc. Peter Cunningham (*Handbook of London*, 1849) wrote:

'Cogers Hall. The name of a public house in Bride Lane where a set of politicians, or thinkers, collect at night in large numbers and discuss the affairs of the State over porter etc.'

The soc. left there in 1856. The old hall, remodelled in 1887, was demolished in 1903. The next meeting-place was in Shoe Lane, on a site now covered by the *Evening Standard* office, near St. Bride St. It is claimed that here, and at the previous hall, Dickens was a frequent attender. As, however, he was a very busy man, and not one of his many biographers has mentioned it, it is probable that his visits were rare. It is inconceivable that Dickens should have missed all the opportunity for copy the Cogers would have afforded, and there is no reference to it in any of his many essays on L. life. In 1868 an article on the Cogers appeared in *All the Year Round*. It opens: 'My grand is not a piano.' It was the work of Mr. T. C. Parkinson (afterwards republished in *Places and People*). Therefore, the idea that Dickens found models for his characters amongst the Cogers, that there was 'Dick Swiveller to the life,' and that a frothy waiter named Piper was the original of Simon Tappertit, must be taken as pleasing conjectures, like some other things in the volume of its history. In 1871 another move was made—to the 'Barley Mow,' Salisbury Sq. On this tavern was a tablet indicating the meeting place of the Cogers, and mentioning amongst members Dr. Johnson, Oliver Goldsmith, John Wilkes, Macaulay, Dickens, Bradlaugh, Sir Edwd. Clarke, T. P. O'Connor. The names of Johnson,

Goldsmith, and Macaulay are quite unsupported by any known writer. After a brief period in 1887 at the Oriental Hotel, over Blackfriars Station, the soc. returned to the 'Barley Mow,' and remained until 1904. It then moved to the 'Rainbow,' in Fleet St., and in 1908 to Clifford's Inn. Later it was at Bride Lane (for a second time), Memorial Hall, Farringdon St., Red Lion Court, Fleet St., Cock Tavern, Fleet St., Dyers' Arms, Cannon St., Peacock, Maiden Lane (for a short time it was outside the City); White Lion, Lower Thames St.; White Horse, Fetter Lane; now at 'The Cogers,' on the site of the 'Barley Mow' in Salisbury Square.

During the First World War, when there was a temporary split, one section, meeting in Bride Lane, had sometimes to bolt into the machine-room of the *Daily Chronicle*. The soc. carried on through the Second World War, though sometimes the attendance was very small.

The soc. meets every Saturday at 7 p.m., missing only Saturdays before Bank Holidays and when one of the Christmas holidays falls on a Saturday. The opener is allowed forty minutes; the first speaker in the discussion fifteen minutes; and subsequent speakers ten minutes. The opener may correct an error of fact on the part of subsequent speakers, but has no right of final reply. The subject is always the events of the week. Membership was always confined to men but from October 1968 ladies have been admitted on equal terms and it remains to be seen how this will affect the life of the club. Visitors are welcome, and are allowed to speak with the consent of 'the Grand,' who is elected annually. The latter's chair, which was slightly damaged by bombs, is well carved, and is said to be as old as the soc. On the table at which 'the Grand' presides there is always a waxen apple—a symbol of discord.

(See *Ye History of Ye Ancient Society of Cogers*, by Peter Rayleigh, 1903, and article by 'Past Grand' Thomas in *Chambers's Journal*, Dec. 1949.)

College of Arms (sometimes inaccurately called the Coll. of Heralds) now fronts Q. Victoria St. It stands on the site of Derby House, built by the Thos. Stanley, later first E. of Derby, who m. the Lady Margaret, Countess of Richmond (mother of Henry VII). In 1555, by gift of Q. Mary, Derby House became the Coll. of Arms—

'to the end,' said Stow, 'that the kings of arms, heralds, and pursuivants of arms and their successors, might at their liking dwell together, and at meet times to congregate, speak, confer and agree among themselves, for the good government of their faculty, and their records might be more safely kept.'

Previously they had been housed in Poultney (Pountney) Lane, and, in the reign of Henry VII, at Rouncevall Priory, near Charing Cross (*q.v.*). Derby House was burnt in the G.F., and this pleasing red-brick structure was designed by Wren, and completed in 1683. The coll., whose business it is to deal with all matters of heraldry, consists of three kings of arms—Garter, Clarenceux, and Norroy; six heralds—Somerset, Richmond, Lancaster, Windsor, Chester, and York; and four pursuivants—Rouge Dragon, Blue Mantle, Portcullis, and Rouge Croix. All these officers are appointed by the D. of Norfolk, in the capacity of Earl Marshal. The existing quadrangle of the coll. is not proportionate to the bdg., as a considerable slice was removed on the formation of Q. Victoria St.

Companies of the City of London.

The origin of the Companies is a matter for historical speculation (See *The Gilds and Companies of London*, by George Unwin, 4th ed., 1963). William Kent's version is given here.

The earliest form of guild, from which the companies derive, is found in Saxon times. This was the Frithgild. It is said to have been composed of ten families that jointly provided a stock fund from which compensation could be made to anyone offended by a member of the covenanting family. In the meantime, that they might better identify each other as well as ascertain whether any man was about an unlawful business, they assembled at stated periods at a common table where they ate and drank together.

There was too a Knightengild which had a district or soke assigned to it. According to Stow, this was in existence in the reign of K. Edgar (944–75), and the latter granted them a charter, probably the first obtained by a fraternity of this sort. The soke was in the vicinity of Aldgate; this was given by Matilda, consort of Henry I, to the priory of Holy Trinity, which she founded in 1108. Hence there is to-day a Portsoken Ward thereabouts.

These two guilds seem to have been devoted to mutual defence rather than trade interests. The beginning of organization for the benefit of the latter seems to date back to the 11th century. The word 'gild,' as it was originally spelt, is of Saxon origin and meant a payment, made by these early fraternities towards a common stock. They were always connected with some ch. convenient to the quarter of the town occupied by a particular industry. They had a patron saint, and sometimes maintained a chapel in the ch. Under Henry II the Saddlers' were connected with the canons of St. Martin's le Grand. They were joined with them in masses, orisons, etc. About the same date (the honour of being the pioneer livery company is still disputed), there was in existence a Guild of Weavers. The latter seem to have had a charter in the reign of Henry II. In the same reign (1180) eighteen L. guilds were amerced as adulterine, i.e. set up without licence. The names of two of these guilds are still represented by livery companies—the Goldsmiths' and Butchers'. Others were Pepperers, Travellers, and four gilds de Ponte (concerned with London Bridge).

The guilds in due course became authorized by the K. They were granted charters, and in time of strict regulation of dress, members were allowed to wear certain distinguished robes. Hence the term 'livery company.' Now, however, the livery is never more than a fraction of the membership or 'freedom' of the Co., and some of the companies have no livery. There is only one instance—the Ironmongers' Co.—in which the livery is the governing body. In all other cases, however, it is the source from which the court of assistants is chosen. Vacancies in this court are usually filled by co-opting from the livery. This is usually in order of seniority, but capability and celebrity are taken into account. The court is usually ruled by a master and two, three and sometimes more wardens, taken from its own members; each step upward is usually a matter of seniority. The selection of freemen of a co. to fill up the quota of livery is in the hands of the court of assistants; which has also, in most companies, immemorially exercised the power of allowing outsiders to purchase the freedom of membership.

So far back as the 15th century it was possible to become free of a Co. by patrimony—that is, the lawful issue of a freeman could be admitted without becoming a craftsman; in this way a family often became strongly represented in, and influential as regards the government of a co. with whose industry it had long ceased to have any connection. This practice, and the custom of admission by purchase, together with changes of conditions in industry and commerce, gradually deprived nearly every co. of all concern with its nominal purpose. While active the cos. pursued a monopolistic and protectionist policy. This, when successful, rendered them wealthy and their gains were invested in land in or near the City. This increased in value from century to century. The Tudor and Stuart monarchs oppressed and despoiled the Cos. by requisitions for their wars. James I induced the Great Cos. to finance his plantation of Ulster; and from 1613 the Ulster enterprise—except a part (the city of Londonderry reserved to the Irish Soc. of the City of L.) was divided into twelve portions: each of the said Cos. taking one portion, some of them in partnership with some of the minor cos. The Merchant Taylors', Clothworkers', Mercers', and Ironmongers' have parted with their Ulster holdings.

The G.F. caused the cos. enormous losses; and in 1684 Charles II, in his dispute with the City, demanded by writ of *Quo Warranto* and obtained surrender of nearly all the charters. In exchange limited charters were granted; but in 1690 an Act of Parliament annulled the *Quo Warranto* proceedings.

The Companies are divided into two classes, the Great Cos. and the Minor Cos. The former, in order of precedence, are as follows: Mercers'; Grocers'; Drapers'; Fishmongers'; Goldsmiths; Skinners'; Merchant Taylors'; Haberdashers'; Salters'; Ironmongers'; Vintners'; Clothworkers'. The Skinners and Merchant Taylors take position as 6 and 7 in alternate years: hence (probably) 'Sixes and Sevens.' This division seems to have subsisted from the time of Richard II (1377–99); and from that time till 1743 the Ld.M. was neces-

sarily a member of one of the twelve great Cos. These were at first the wealthiest, but in the race for wealth some of them have been outstripped by certain Minor Cos., e.g. the Brewers'. One of the two companies with the longest history, the Weavers', is No. 42 on the list. The minor companies now in existence, including five created in the present century, number seventy-two. Every Co. has a number; it is placed in parentheses after its name at the beginning of each of the following accounts. Besides the subjects of those accounts, there are a number of cos. no longer in existence, viz. Comb-makers': Silk-throwers'; Silkmen; Pin-makers'; Soapmakers'; Hat-band Makers'; Longbow string Makers'; Woodmongers'; Starchmakers'; Fishermen's; Porters'; Surgeons'.

In early times the representatives of the wards were the electors for parliamentary purposes in the City; but from 1375 till 1835 the livery of the Cos. were sole possessors of both the municipal and the parliamentary franchise. The whole body of the Livery Companies called the Common Hall, elect the Sheriffs and the Ld.M.; the latter must previously have been through two other elections. (See 'City Corporation.')

As the Cos. became richer and thereby more unrepresentative, the exercise of their powers was resented and resisted, probably with reason, since the searchers would of necessity be influential trade rivals of the subjects of search. Therefore, for the most part, the Cos. retired from business. The Fishmongers', the Goldsmiths', and the Gunmakers' have maintained their chief functions uninterruptedly: about half a dozen other Cos. maintained some of the old functions or acquired new ones: but by the 18th century, the Cos. of the City of L. were as a rule friendly societies, with fancy names and imposing armorial bearings.

A Commission appointed in 1833, to inquire into the state of municipal corporations inquired as to the L. Cos. and Sir Francis Palgrave reported on them. There were various Government inquiries as to their charities in the 19th century. In 1880 a movement hostile to the Cos. induced the Government to appoint a royal commission to inquire. Many Cos. furnished full answers from which much of the information now obtainable about them is derived. Most

Cos. protested: a few refused to make any return. It is said that the companies that furnished full particulars derived considerable benefit from the publicity. The public had not till then realized to what extent they promoted education: many schs. of various grades were maintained, and a conference of the companies had founded in 1878 the City and Guilds of L. institute (q.v.).

The Weavers' is probably the oldest Co. The newest is the Scientific Instrument Makers. Many of the extant records of the Cos. (Apprentice Rolls, order books, charters) are deposited in Guildhall Library and are a rich quarry for historians.

(See *The History of the Twelve Great Companies*, by Wm. Herbert, 1836; *The Livery Companies of the City of London and their Good Works*, by P. H. Ditchfield, 1904; *The City of London Livery Companies*, by Bryan Pontifex, 1939; *The Guilds of the City of London*, by Sir Ernest Pooley, 1945.)

1. COMPANIES WITH HALLS AT OUTBREAK OF THE SECOND WORLD WAR (35).

Apothecaries' (58). It has from the first been termed a Soc., though it is one of the Livery Cos. Of old, drugs were sold by the Grocers. *Apotheke*, in Greek, means a storehouse: in the Middle Ages it came to mean a storehouse for drugs. The right to practise surgery and physic having been made a matter of examination in 1511, the admitted physicians 'sued, troubled, and vexed' certain persons that had not been examined but nevertheless cured poor people for nothing: so, to check the pride of these professionals, an Act was passed in 1543, giving the aforesaid charitable persons leave to 'minister medicines' in their own humble way. These were the germ of the Apothecaries of L. They came to be keepers of what were later called doctors' shops. When the Grocers received a charter from James I in 1606, the Apothecaries were united with them; but such was the outcry at the incompetence of the Grocers' Co. in this department that the Apothecaries were made into a separate Soc. within twelve years.

The Soc.'s charter was an exceedingly long document, drafted by Bacon, and granted by James I, 6th Dec. 1617. Fifty years before Charles II made a business of such things, the Soc. in 1634–5 had to defend itself against a writ of Quo Warranto. With other Co. charters it was surrendered 1684—it was not completely restored until Nov. 1688. It still governs.

Toward the end of its first century its members had begun to prescribe, defeating efforts of the physicians to monopolize that practice. The Soc. accumulated a stock for use by its members, and a laboratory was instituted 1671–2. Out of these was developed a wholesale drug business which obtained a monopoly of the supply of drugs to the fleet, the East India Co., and (in the 19th century) the Army. By the Apothecaries Act of 1815 (amended 1874), the Soc. obtained the power to examine all persons intending to practise as apothecaries throughout England and Wales. In 1822 it established a retail drug business. The Pharmacy Act of 1852 put the chief powers of regulating pharmaceutical chemistry into the hands of the Pharmaceutical Soc. of Great Britain, so the apothecaries turned their attention to the licensing of practitioners. They obtained recognition as practitioners under the Medical Act of 1858; and, until the law was altered in 1886, it was usual for a surgeon who intended to become a general practitioner to take his degree as licentiate at Apothecaries' Hall. Afterwards, the examiners there came to be appointed by the General Medical Council; and the Soc.'s licence (of which the title was, in 1907, changed to L.M.S.S.A., i.e. Licentiate in Medicine and Surgery of the Soc. of Apothecaries) is now a complete qualification for a general practitioner—it is sought also by those that wish to qualify as dispensers without serving apprenticeship in a shop. The Soc. has also instituted the special degree of Master in Midwifery. Its physic garden at Chelsea, originally leased to it by Chas. Cheyne in 1673 (and given at a quit-rent by Sir Hans Sloane in 1731), was transferred to the Charity Commissioners in 1893. The retail drug business was closed down in 1922.

The hall is on the E. side of Blackfriars (formerly Water) Lane. The first hall was Cobham House on the same site, purchased in 1632 from Lady Howard of Effingham. That house was burnt in the G.F. In succession to it, the present hall was built in 1670. Much of it was let, the Co. being in very poor circumstances. It is best described as a quaint old house—with its long library and banner-decorated great hall, its kitchen of the real old-fashioned kind, and its retired 'front court.' It was restored, and the staircase rebuilt on the well pattern 1929. There is a chest dating from 1668, the carved pine mantelpiece was by Wm. Kent (1726). The Hall survived the Second World War undamaged.

The greatest benefactor to the Co. at its inception was Gideon Delaune (master, 1637): he was the son of a Huguenot refugee, and Apothecary to James I's Q.; he d. 1659 at the age of 97—having been (his profession makes the fact relevant) a prolific father. He had seventeen children, many stillborn. He is said to have died worth about £90,000, much of the money being made by pills.

Members whose names are household words: Thos. Sydenham; Tobias George Smollett; Oliver Goldsmith; John Hunter; John Keats—one of the first to obtain the licence of the Soc. under the Act of 1815; Edwd. Jenner; Sir Humphry Davy; Geo. Crabbe.

There are many portraits—most of past masters; but also of James I, Charles I, and William III entering Exeter. There are a bust of Gideon Delaune presented in 1641, a contemporary painting of the Spanish Armada, and a pre-Fire oak table. There are a great many old and good chairs in the parlour and the court-room. There is a wooden mace, whose silver head bears the arms of the Co. There is a chest presented in 1668. The only old plate is two salvers, a monteith, a ladle, and a coffee pot.

There are charitable funds for the support of necessitous members and their dependants. A scholarship, value £90 p.a., was founded under the will of Wm. Edward Gillson, one of the Soc.'s licentiates: it is for research in pathology.

(See *History of the Society of Apothecaries*, by C. R. B. Barrett, 1905; *The London Apothecaries*, by Cecil Wall, 1932.)

No. of Livery, 378.

Armourers' and Brasiers' (22). The Armourers were in existence as a gild long before their incorporation, and had a chapel in St. P.'s Cath. In the reign of Edward II they were successful in the court of aldermen in a dispute over privilege with the Blacksmiths

The Armourers' earliest charter, granted by Henry VI, is dated 1453; it was re-newed by Elizabeth 1559. James I granted, for a consideration of £100, letters confirming the Co.'s title to its lands. In 1685 James II made an order for all edged tools, armour, and copper and brass work hammered, within the City, to be approved by the Co. There ensued difficulty with the Brasiers, whose organization was not a recognized Livery Co.; so the present charter, of Q. Anne's reign, dated 1709, amalgamated the Brasiers with the Armourers, and gave the Co. control of all weapons, and all work of brass and copper, in the City and for eleven miles round.

The present hall is in Coleman St., on the site of the one that was standing when the Co. was first incorporated. The Armourers acquired the freehold in 1428. By 1795 the 15th-century hall, despite recent repairs, was tumbling down, and had to be entirely rebuilt: it still had a central courtyard. The new structure lasted only till 1840: the present hall, designed by Joseph Henry Good, was erected 1840–1: its front is impressively plain and respectable. The interior was extensively altered and decorated in 1872. The Hall sustained slight damage in the Second World War.

Although under Henry VIII the Co. was obliged to sell its plate, its collection is one of the finest in the City: the Richmond Cup, made about the middle of the 15th century, was presented by John Richmond in 1557. There is a representative collection of armour—the most famous piece being the Lee suit: the armour of Sir Henry Lee, Q. Elizabeth's champion, who retired 1590; it was made by Jacobe Halder, an immigrant member who was master-workman in Greenwich armouries. The Co. acquired this suit in 1767.

The Co.'s abandonment of its right of search in 1785 may be taken as its formal abdication of craft-function. Yet, in recent times, it has become active in a kindred sphere. It attempted, a good while ago, to stimulate the brazier's art by the offer of prizes; but results were unsatisfactory. Progress in metallurgy it specially encouraged. A grant is given annually to the Sheffield industries and to the City and Guilds of L. Institute. In the 16th century there were almshouses in St. Olave, Jewry, founded by Dame Elizabeth Morrys. Later there were twenty-four almshouses in Britannia Pl., Bishopsgate.

No. of Livery, 93.

(See *The Worshipful Company of Armourers and Braziers*, by H. W. Wills, 1917; *Some Notes on the History of the Worshipful Company of Armourers and Braziers*, by S. H. Pitt, 1930.)

Bakers' (19). The fraternity of Bakers was strong enough in 1155 to compound with the Govt. for the toll on baking. From before the Conquest, the regulation of bread-baking was strict, and punishment for transgression severe—a third offence entailing lifelong disqualification. Stow says it was recorded that in 1302 the bakers were forbidden to sell in their shops or houses, but were obliged to bring it all to the market, which was in Bread St. In the 13th century it was customary for the bakers to assemble in court four times a year for reading of rules and punishment of offenders. In 1281 the Ld.M. had a special house erected for weighing of all grain before sending it to be milled, and when it came back ground. (By the end of the 15th century the bakers were allowed to do their own weighing.) Two members of the mistery were on the common council in 1376. Antipathy between bakers of brown bread and those of white has complicated the history of the Co. The bakers of each variety were required to keep to it strictly; but, as the White Bakers catered for the better-off customers, they were usually the more active in enforcing the rule, which was declared at a hall-mote of 1321 to be immemorial, and which was maintained till 1654. The White Bakers defined brown bread as bread made from a mixture of grains; whereas the original idea was that brown bread was wholemeal bread—not even bread made from a mixture of white flour and bran. As Brown Bakers dwindled in number, and White Bakers increased, brown bread deteriorated and White Bakers grew arrogant: they procured the charter of the Co. in 1486 (order of precedence settled 1515), and compelled the Brown Bakers to come in—though these remained inferior in status. By 1544 the City had allowed the Brown Bakers to secede; but their Co. was left almost powerless, and their endeavour in 1568 to obtain a charter was frustrated. Next year the White Bakers followed up their

victory; but many provisions of the new charter they got were suspended, and in 1580–1 the Brown Bakers were again separate by official permission. By 1586 they had lost all advantages of separateness, by reason of the White Bakers defiance of regulations. At last, in 1621, the Brown Bakers obtained separate incorporation. But their trade was out of date: they had become mere makers of inferior bread; and though in 1635 (after being tenants at Founders' Hall) they acquired lease of a hall outside Aldersgate, in 1645 they were finally reabsorbed. The powers of the Bakers' Co. as settled under James II were extinguished by 3 George IV, local Act c. cxvi.

The first charter was granted by Henry VII in 1486. Q. Elizabeth in 1569 granted the uniting charter that led to more dispute and disunity. The Brown Bakers' charter, which did them so little good, was granted 1622 by James I. The final uniting charter was granted by James II, *c.* 1686.

The first hall is believed to have been at Dowgate, 1490. In 1506 the Bakers moved into the first of their halls on the present site, on the E. side of Harp Lane. It stood back from the lane, round a little courtyard. The G.F. demolished it. Rebuilding was complete by 1675. This second hall on the site was burnt 1715. There followed a sojourn at the halls of the Butchers and the Brewers. The third hall was begun 1719, and finished 1722. Further wainscoting was done in 1772. A new roof was built in 1806; the court-room was redecorated in 1882; further changes were made in 1897, and an entire renovation was begun in 1932—in order to remove disharmonies introduced in the 19th century. The doorway of the court-room was from the E. of Chesterfield's mansion at Holme Lacey. This hall was entirely destroyed by German bombs in 1940. A new Hall on the Harp Lane site was opened in 1963.

Twelve almshouses were built at Hackney in 1828. They were demolished in 1931—the Co.'s charity being otherwise directed. Pensions for poor members have been provided by wills and donations: the benefactions including those of Henry Elsing (1577); Barbara Snow (1656); Edwd. Cooper (1659); Thos. Cooke (1706); Thos. Bradley (1728); Edwd. Grose (1733); Richd. White, £500 (1748);

Joseph Read, £500 (1816); Thos. Webber, £500 (1895).

No. of Livery, 260.

(See *A Short History of the Worshipful Company of Bakers of London*, 1933.)

Barbers' (17). The action of the Council of Tours in 1163, prohibiting the clergy from the practice of surgery, stimulated its exercise among Barbers. A Barbers' gild, ruled by a master, existed 1308; by 1376 it prohibited the unqualified and had come to have two masters. The election in 1308 was on the Tuesday before the feast of St. Lucy the Virgin, and the Co.'s meetings have been on Tuesdays ever since. From the earliest times its members that were Barbers only were distinguished from those that were Barber-Surgeons. One of the fraternity's duties was to maintain watch at the City gates to see that no lepers entered. Such dentistry as was then known was part of the Barber's business. There coexisted an independent fraternity of Surgeons, with which there were differences: in 1376 the Barbers obtained an ordinance giving them scrutiny and correction of all Surgeons. The Barbers is the only extant one among all the returns made in 1388 to the writs issued by Richard II to all gilds. In 1390, women were practising surgery. Thos. Arundel, Abp. of C., in 1413 objected to the Barbers' custom of opening shop on Sunday, but they have done so ever since. From their incorporation in 1462 Barbers were exempted from jury-service. In 1493 an agreement with the Surgeons' gild was arrived at. One of the orders minuted in 1566 contains the earliest known mention of the barber's pole—which developed from the stick grasped by a patient during blood-letting and the bandage that was twisted round the stick when not in use. In 1745 the Barbers were separated from the Surgeons by 18 George II, c. 15; yet it is now customary for eminent surgeons to be elected to the Livery.

Edward IV granted the first charter in 1462; it gave the Co. control of the Surgeons. An inspeximus was granted by Henry VII in 1499, another by Henry VIII in 1512. The incorporation of the Surgeons with the Barbers, commemorated in Holbein's picture, was effected, not by charter, but by statute, in 1540. Philip and Mary granted a charter in 1558; Elizabeth, in 1560; James I, in 1605; Charles I, in 1629; and, after the general surrender of charters to Charles II in 1684, James II in 1685 granted a long charter full of reservations and limitations —but in 1688 came the general redelivery, merely anticipating the action of the Bill of Rights.

There was once a hermitage of St. James, close by St. Giles Ch., Cripplegate, accommodating a hermit and two Cistercian friars; it was on the site of one of the Roman bastions on London Wall. In 1381 it had been superseded by the hall of the Barbers, their freehold from 1490. There was a physic-garden on the Monkwell St. front, to the E. About 1636 Inigo Jones was employed to build a court-room, and also (upon a piece of land to the NE., leased from the C.C.), a surgical theatre. The G.F. destroyed most of the hall-buildings, but spared the court-room and the theatre. Restoration was completed in 1678. A cupola was added, and extensive repairs were done, 1752–3. Soon afterwards, it would appear, the theatre (not needed since the departure of the Surgeons) was demolished. In 1863–4 the bulk of the hall was removed to make way for warehouses; but the court-room, whose W. wall follows the line of the old bastion, was preserved, and reserved to the Co. It was entirely destroyed in the Second World War and a new one is being built there.

There have been noble and non-practising members since early in the 16th century. Of the active members the famous ones are (as might be expected) famous chiefly as surgeons: Thos. Vicary (master 1541, 1546, 1548, and 1557), surgeon to Henry VIII and serjt.-surgeon, governor and director of St. Bartholomew's Hosp.; Wm. Clowes the elder (1540?–1604), surgeon in army and navy abroad, surgeon in St. Bartholomew's and Christ's Hosps.; Wm. Clowes the younger (1582–1648), surgeon to Charles I, and prosecutor of a gardener named Jas. Leverett for infringing the King's prerogative of touching for the evil; John Gerard (master 1607), author of the famous *Herbal*; Sir Chas. Scarburgh, physician to Charles II and James II; Sir Humphrey Edwin (master 1688), Ld.M. 1697 (he belonged also to the Skinners), was a wool-merchant by occupation; Wm. Cheselden, one of the wardens of the Surgeons' Co. at the separation in 1745, was inventor of the lateral operation for the stone; Sir Caesar Hawkins, surgeon to George I and George III, made baronet 1778, inventing the cutting gorget.

The greatest treasure is Hans Holbein's enormous picture of Henry VIII and the Barber-Surgeons: it was kept underground at Trafalgar Sq. during the First World War and again removed in the Second World War. Although the King is depicted as granting a charter, it is (as the persons introduced prove) really a commemoration of the statutory union of the Barbers and Surgeons. The kneeling figures, left to right in the lower row, are Thos. Alsop; Wm. Butts; John Chambre; Thos. Vicary; Sir John Ayleff; Nicholas Simpson; Edmund Harman; Jas. Nonforde; John Pen (the King's barber); Nicholas Alcocke; Richd. Ferris. Of the back row of seven, only two are known, Christopher Salmond and Wm. Tilney. The plate has survived. This includes a silver-gilt grace cup, given by Henry VIII. Having been stolen in 1615, it was found in a garret in Westminster; sold to raise money for the war, 1649; bought in by Alderman Edward Arris. There is also Charles II's Royal Oak cup, of hammered silver. There are a master's hammer of 1540, wine cups of the Charles I period, and two loving-cups of Commonwealth date. Q. Anne's punch-bowl made by Pierre Harache, weighs 160 oz. There are portraits of Charles II, Q. Anne, and Inigo Jones (by Van Dyck).

In the *Gentleman's Magazine* for 1740 under date Monday 24th Nov. of that yr., appeared the following:

'Five malefactors were executed at Tyburn, viz. Thomas Clack, William Meers, Margery Stanton, Eleanor Mumpman, for several Burglaries and Felonies; and William Duell for ravishing, robbing, and murdering Sarah Griffin at Acton. The Body of this last was brought to Surgeon's Hall to be anatomiz'd; but after it was stripp'd and laid on the Board and one of the servants was washing him in order to be cut, he perceived life in him, and found his Breath to come quicker and quicker; on which a Surgeon took some Ounces of Blood from him; in two Hours he was able to sit up in his Chair and in the evening was again

committed to Newgate.'

In his *Annals of the Barber Surgeons*, 1890, Sidney Young (afterwards master) wrote: 'A popular impression prevails, and frequently currency has been given to it, that Duell subsequently made a fortune abroad and out of gratitude to the Barber-Surgeons for saving his life presented them with the handsome leather folding screen now in the Court Room, the best answer to which is that the screen in question is referred to in the Company's Inventory some thirty years previously to Mr. Duell's visit to Tyburn.'

All the trust charities are for poor members.

No. of Livery, 160.

(See *The Annals of the Barber Surgeons of London*, by Sidney Young, 1890.)

Brewers' (14). The craft of brewing was in early times of low repute; its practitioners were chiefly brewsters (i.e. breweresses). By 1345 the Brewers, growing in importance and dignity, had to be forbidden to take any of the City water. Then some of them got on the Common Council, but they were soon disqualified because of unseemly conduct. Richd. Whittington, when mayor for his last term, 1419–20, 'harassed them with domiciliary visits in person' (Unwin). He even fined them £20, and in default imposed imprisonment. After that, they appeared to have bribed him, through his butler, with two pipes of wine.

The original charter was granted by Henry VI in 1437; confirmed in 1560, by Elizabeth—who modified it, and granted a further modifying charter in 1563. An inspeximus charter was granted by Charles I in 1641. The charter was surrendered by deed to Charles II in 1660, and a new one was then granted— it was confirmed and enlarged by James II.

There was a hall in 1420, in Addle St. —where its successor, built in 1673 after the G.F. had destroyed the original, was up a court in the centre of the block bounded by Addle St., Philip Lane, Aldermanbury Av., and Aldermanbury. It was repaired 1828, and the houses in front were rebuilt 1875. The bdgs. were in the form of a quadrangle; the hall was wainscoted and had oak carvings. There were old-fashioned kitchens with wide fire-places and spits, and a court-room with port-hole windows. The hall was destroyed in Dec. 1940 and has been re-built in Aldermanbury Square. The charters have survived.

Only persons connected with the trade are admitted to this Co. Harvey Christopher Combe, Brewer, was Ld.M. 1799–1800; he was a gambler.

Richd. Platt, alderman, in 1596 bequeathed property to educate young and to maintain old poor people at Aldenham (Herts.). At the same place he founded a grammar sch.—still mainly governed by Brewers. The Co. built and endowed lower schs. at Aldenham and Medburn; and it has six almshouses at Delrow, near Aldenham. 'Dame' Alice Owen in 1609 left an estate, including the 'Ermytage Field' in Clerkenwell par., and a farm at Orsett (Essex), for the relief of poor in the pars. of Islington and Clerkenwell and for the instruction of their children: the original almshouses and sch. were on the east side of St. John Street Rd. (northern part of St. John St.), between the Old Red Lion tavern and the Crown and Woolpack tavern, below the road-level; in 1840–1 these were superseded by a new sch.-house on the N. side of neighbouring Owen St., and new almshouses on the S. side thereof opposite the sch.; in 1878 the sch. was divided into a boys' and a girl's department—displacing the almshouses. Alderman Hickson, in 1686, left an estate for founding a sch. and almshouses: the first sch. was at Plough Yd., Seething Lane; in 1852 a new sch. was built in Trinity Sq., Tower Hill—it has since been closed. Samuel Whitbread, 1794, bequeathed estates at Great Barford and in Whitecross St., for the poor of the trade. John Baker, 1813, bequeathed an endowment of six almshouses in Mile End Rd., erected 1825. Other almshouses of the Brewers are now at South Mimms (Herts). Grants and scholarships are made to Aldenham and to the North London Collegiate Sch. for Girls. No. of Livery, 14.

Broderers' (48). Their existence is recorded in the *Oxford Dictionary* under 'Broderer' as early as 1430. They received a Charter from Q. Elizabeth I in 1561. In the late nineteenth century they held exhibitions of embroidery and today they encourage the study and practice of the craft by making grants to the Royal School of Needlework, the City of London School for Girls and the Embroiderers' Guild. An early Hall was in Carey St., the site is marked by a plaque. The later Hall stood in Gutter Lane but was destroyed by bombing in 1940 and has not been rebuilt. No. of livery, 59.

Butchers' (24). The Butchers—real killing: Butchers—were included in 1180 in the list of adulterine gilds fined for going without a licence. They were in Eastcheap, in the Stocks' Market (see 'Markets'), and in St. Nicholas Shambles, in the middle of the roadway at the E. end of Newgate St. Later they obtained additional space at Leadenhall. They sold their meat on London Bridge until forbidden in 1277: they were also, in early times, prohibited from selling their ware on the highway, yet the practice seems to have persisted. Also, their trade activity was confined by order to daylight hours. They acquired a place of their own, near Baynard's Castle known as Bochers-Brigge. Noblemen residing in the vicinity complained of the pollution of the river thus caused by offal being cast into it. 'No one can hardly venture to abide in his house.' This was stopped by an order of 1369. Though the Company's members are no longer butchers in the true sense, and though by 1863 their authority was completely abrogated, they are all connected with or interested in what in Scotland would be called the fleshers' business, the members and dependants of members whereof engross all their attention.

The first charter was granted by James I in 1605. Charles I granted a second in July 1638: this was surrendered to Charles II in 1682 and restored by James II in 1685. The present charter was granted by George II, 1749.

The first hall was in Monkwell St. In 1548 the Company obtained a lease of what had been the parsonage of St. Nicholas Shambles (between King Edward St. and Roman Bath St. of to-day); and there the second hall stood until destroyed, with most of the Co.'s records, in the G.F. The next hall was up a court on the S. side of Eastcheap, between Pudding Lane and Botolph Lane: it was finished before 1677. Extensive alterations were undertaken, 1828–9; but before these were complete the premises were gutted by fire. A new hall was built on the same site, 1829–30. In 1882 the site was acquired for the purposes of the underground railway. In 1883 the Co. purchased 87 and 88 Bartholomew Close, West Smithfield; on this site, enlarged by the later purchase of 10 Duke St. (i.e. Little Britain), the present hall was erected by 1885. It was enlarged, 1915. In Sept. 1915 it was severely damaged in a Zeppelin raid, all the stained glass windows (including one in memory of Defoe) being destroyed. The hall was reinstated in 1916—the Co. meanwhile meeting in the Guildhall. The Livery Hall was wainscoted in light oak, and lighted by nine stained glass windows—portraying Shakespeare, Cardinal Wolsey, James I, Charles I, George II, Daniel Defoe, Q. Victoria, a figure of 'Peace,' and George V. The hall sustained damage in the Second World War—by blast in 1941 and by flying bomb in 1944. It was rebuilt in 1960. The windows dedicated to Shakespeare, Wolsey and Peace have survived. The second window in memory of Defoe suffered destruction. The plate, which included a silver goblet of 1669, escaped, as also a chair made of wood from a cattle pen in Smithfield Market.

There is a tradition that Cardinal Wolsey was master long before the incorporation. Shakespeare is presumably commemorated because one of the many occupations ascribed to his father was that of a butcher. The most celebrated member was Daniel Defoe, admitted to the freedom by patrimony in 1687. The entry in the Co.'s books remains.

The Co. is peculiar in having a deputy master who is a permanent official.

The Co.'s energies are devoted to assisting necessitous members and dependants of members of the meat purveying trade. The principal bequests and gifts are devoted to assisting necessitous members; for this purpose are those of Jas. Leverett (1662); Ruth Bayley (1840); Emily and Anne Game (1890); Alfred Lyon (1892); and Benjamin Bloomfield Baker (1896).

No. of Livery, 387.

(See *A History of the Butchers' Company*, by A. Pearce, 1929.)

Carpenters' (26). The Carpenters, very important in ancient times on account of the prevalence of wood as a building material, had a book of ordinances lodged at Guildhall in 1333: they were, even then, chiefly a friendly Soc. After the G.F. the importance of the craft waned, owing to the demand for fire-resisting houses. During the first part of the 18th century the Co.'s activities were almost entirely confined to the binding and transferring of apprentices: it appears from their books that by 1739 they had surrendered all control of the craft. The Co., in association with the Armourers, Joiners, Glaziers, Painter-Stainers, Pewterers, Plasterers, and Tylers, established the Trades Training Schs. Technical lectures were given also at the hall.

A charter was granted by Edward IV in 1477: it was renewed by Philip and Mary in 1558, by Elizabeth in 1560. Another was granted by James I in 1606; confirmed by Charles I in 1640, and by Charles II in 1674—afterwards surrendered, re-granted by James II in 1685-6, confirmed by Act of 2 William and Mary.

The first hall was erected 1428-9. The hall escaped the G.F., and was used by the Ld.M. as his mansion-house temporarily. In 1876, pursuant to an arrangement with the Drapers' Co., the old hall was pulled down to make the thoroughfare known as Throgmorton Av.; and the last hall was built of Portland stone, and in a Renaissance style, of course, on part of the old site—it was on the S. side of London Wall; NE. corner of Throgmorton Av., which it faces. It was not completed until 1880. The oak furnishings of the old hall were used to decorate the new one; and three of the four old mural paintings of biblical subjects were successfully transferred. The Livery hall on the first floor was destroyed in the Second World War and rebuilt in 1957-9. In the L. Mus. there are two of these mural paintings from the old hall (*c.* 1540): one showing K. Josiah commanding money to be given to the carpenters for the repair of the Temple, and the other Jesus in the carpenter's shop and Jesus in the Temple.

A notable member was Sir John Cass (1666-1718)—who, however, transferred from the Carpenters to the Skinners—famous for his charitable bequests, and founder of a sch. in Aldgate. His estate is administered by a separate foundation, though he had nominated the Carpenters. Sir Wm. Staines (Ld.M. 1801) and Wm. Lawrence (Ld.M. 1863) were Carpenters.

There are portraits of: Wm. Portington, king's carpenter *temp.* Elizabeth and James I; and John Scott, carpenter to the office of ordnance, *temp.* Charles II. A carved octagonal oak table bears an inscription dated 1606. An ornamental carving with the arms of the Co., and two other carvings, are dated 1579. The master's chair is of solid mahogany. There are four silver-gilt cups of elaborate workmanship, with spire-like covers—the master's cup presented by John Reeve (twice master), 1611; three wardens' cups presented respectively by John Ansell (twice master), 1611; Thos. Edmones, 1612; and Anthony Jarman, 1628.

Richd. Wyatt (thrice master), a great benefactor of the Carpenters during his life, left property at Henley-on-Thames to maintain allowances he had been making to the poor; also £500 to build ten alms-houses at Godalming: these were built in 1622. In 1947 there was a reversionary bequest of silver under the will of Mrs. Aida Wyatt. This included two silver-gilt tankards inscribed 'Richard Wyatt, Citizen and Carpenter of London, 1619.' John Read (master), who d. 1650, left property in Southwark which was, in the 19th century, exchanged for property at Stratford (Essex); the income is used to supplement the Co.'s maintenance of an exhibition at Cambridge University: the Co. also maintains two exhibitions at either Oxford or Cambridge. It established schools at Godalming and Derry early in the 19th century. In 1841 almshouses were erected at Twickenham, and a system of pensions was instituted. The Co. contributed continually to funds raised in cases of emergency.

No. of Livery, 150.

Clothworkers' (12). The Clothworkers were originally two gilds—the Shearmen and the Fullers. The Shearmen were those that sheared away the superfluous nap of cloth: they were an offshoot of the gild of Tellarii, composed of Woollen-weavers, Burrellers (or width-measurers), and Testers. The Fullers were incorporated by charter of Edward IV (1480), they inhabited Whitechapel; and Ditchfield derives the last word of the name of St. Mary Matfelon from the teasel used in their trade, but the *Oxford Dictionary* defines 'matfellon' as the knapweed. The Shearmen did not receive a charter until Jan. 1508. In 1528, on their joint petition, the Fullers and Shearmen were united by a charter conferred on them as Clothworkers. There are inspeximus charters of 29 Elizabeth and 9 Charles I.

The site of the Clothworkers Hall, in Mincing Lane, was demised to Shearmen in 1455 by John Badby. The Fullers had a hall in Billiter St. until the union of the Cos. The original Clothworkers Hall, a small bdg. of red brick, made a grand flare in the G.F.—its cellars being, as Pepys remarks, full of oil. The succeeding hall, spoken of by Hatton (1708) as 'a noble rich building,' was demolished in the eighteen-fifties. The third hall, designed by Samuel Angell, was built 1856–60; it was opened by P. Consort. The front was of Portland stone with Corinthian pilasters. There were five stained glass windows, with the arms of the Co. and its past masters and benefactors. The hall was bounded on the E. by the chyd. of All Hallows Staining (see 'City Churches; B'), where the ancient ch. tower alone stands. The responsibility of preserving it rests with the Co. The hall was destroyed by enemy action in 1941 and rebuilt in 1958.

Notable members: Sir Wm. Hewett—who, when first elected alderman, refused to serve and was punished by imprisonment—as sheriff in 1553 he had charge of the executions of Lady Jane Grey, her husband, and the adherents of Wyatt —he was Ld.M. in 1560; Wm. Lambe (master 1569–70), benefactor; Sir John Spencer, Ld.M. 1595 (see 'City Churches; C'—St. Helen, Bishopsgate); Sir John Wattes, volunteer serving against Spanish Armada, 1588, Ld.M. 1607, one of the founders of the East India Co., and governor of it, member of the Virginia Co.; James I, admitted 1607; Sir Richd. Gurney, Ld.M. 1641–2, on the K.'s side in the matter of the five M.P.s committed to the Tower by Parliament; John Ireton. Ld.M. 1659, brother of Cromwell's general; Sir Joseph Williamson (master 1676), Sec. of State 1674, and victim of the 'popish plot' mania, president Royal Soc.; Samuel Pepys (master 1677). Alderman Cooper, a prominent member of the Co., who d. early in the 18th century, left money to provide 'fine cognac' at the dinners; and his wife, dying soon after, left money for 'other liqueurs'—therefore, at the banquets, the answer to the question 'Do you dine with Alderman or Lady Cooper?' indicated the liqueur preferred.

Notable members include Albert, P. Consort; Baroness Burdett-Coutts; the first

Ld. Dufferin; the eighth D. of Devonshire; Ld. Kelvin; and the tenth D. of Leeds. More recent members include: Field-Marshal Smuts; Sir Robert Menzies; and Field Marshal Viscount Slim.

The Co. has preserved some of its pre-Fire records. During the Civil War it had to sell nearly all its plate: it still has a rosewater - dish presented by John Burnell, master in 1593. It has a caudle-cup of 1654, a salt of 1661, a loving-cup presented by Pepys when, in 1677, he was master, and much modern plate.

Wm. Lambe in 1576 founded the grammar sch. of Sutton Valence, near Maidstone; but, as the endowment was only £30 p.a., the Co. supplemented it, giving more than £1,000 p.a. In 1910 the Governorship was taken over by the United Westminster Schools Foundation. Lambe also endowed 'Lambe's Chapel' in the City wall at Cripplegate, entered through a yard from the top of Monkwell St.: it was rebuilt about 1825, and finally pulled down in 1872; and, instead, the ch. of St. James, Prebend Sq., Islington, was erected—the Co. augments the vicar's stipend, and contributes to the mission work. Philip Christian in 1655 founded a sch. at Peel, I.O.M.; and the Co. has spent £10,000 on new sch. bdgs. there. These schs. were handed over to the local Rector and the Isle of Man Education Authority in 1936. On technical and secondary education in various parts of the country the Co. annually spends generously from its corporate income. The Company is very closely connected with the City and Guilds of London Institute for Technical Education, of which they were one of the founders in 1878. Their grants in aid of the Institute and its Engineering College at South Kensington exceed £320,000. It has been especially generous also to the University of Leeds, to which its benefactions amount to over half a million pounds. They are the Estates Governors of the Mary Datchelor Schs. at Camberwell. Margaret, Countess of Kent, in 1538 established almshouses in Whitefriars; and John Heath, in 1640, established a set at Islington. There are about 1,000 blind pensioners of the Co. receiving gratuities; it also subscribes largely to institutions for the blind. In 1889 Thos. Wm. Wing bequeathed £70,000 to the Co. in trust for the blind.

No. of Livery, 180.

Coach-makers' and Coach Harness Makers' (72). By reason of the badness of English roads, coach-making was unknown here in the Middle Ages. The Co., before obtaining its charter, was called the Chariot-makers' Co. When its powers were exercised in the 17th and 18th centuries, they extended twenty miles round L. It tried to limit coach-making and harness-making to British-born persons, and succeeded in making the craft very exclusive in the 18th century. The earliest coach-makers were found at Cow Lane, West Smithfield. Other quarters were: Hosier Lane, Aldersgate St.; Bishopsgate; 'Shandois' (Chandos?) St., Bedfordbury, Haymarket, and Long Acre—the last-named was associated with coach-making for 300 years. In 1864, the Co.'s authority having then decayed from disuse, it gave its hall for the purposes of the Coach Makers' Industrial Exhibition. From that time the Co. has continually offered prizes in connection with the trade, and there are always craftsmen among its members.

Charters were granted by Charles II in 1677, and by James II in 1687, when Livery was obtained.

The court was at one time held at the 'White Hart,' Old Bailey. The hall, in Noble St., was on the site of the house of Sir Thos. Shelley, attainted in Henry IV's reign for supporting Richard II. This house, or a new one on the same site, was afterwards occupied by Sir Nicholas Bacon, before he got York House in 1558. In 1642 the place was disposed of by the executors of one Geo. Smythes to the Scriveners' Co.: thenceforward it was Scriveners' Hall—it was burnt in the G.F. The Scriveners rebuilt it; and in 1703, being hard up, sold the place—except the Noble St. frontage—to the Coach Makers. In 1780 the hall was used by 'a sort of religious Robin Hood Soc.', closely connected with Ld. Geo. Gordon's 'Protestant Association.' Great alterations were made 1841–3, and the hall was rebuilt 1867–70. The hall was entirely destroyed by enemy action in 1940.

The Co. possesses the original model (one-sixth actual size) from which was made the royal state coach that has been in use since the wedding of George III and Q. Charlotte. Like the Ld.M.'s coach it has panels by Cipriani. As to plate, it has the Cheslyn flagon, mid-17th century, presented by its clerk, Richd.

Cheslyn; cup with cover, given by Samuel Aubrey in 1677; elaborately carved tankard, presented by Samuel Wright, currier, 1703. There is an alms box with carvings of the four evangelists, dating from 1680.

Amongst freemen of the Co. have been Quintin Hogg, founder of the Poly-technics, and Baroness Burdett-Coutts, in recognition of assistance to the craft of coachmaking.

The charities connected with the craft are in the hands of other organizations.

No. of Livery, 356.

(See *History of the Worshipful Company of Coach-makers and Coach Harness Makers of London*, compiled by direction of Lord Iliffe, C.B.E., Master, 1937.)

Coopers' (36). The Coopers were in existence as an unchartered Co. in the reign of Edward II. The abuses of selling casks below measurement, and old con-taminated ones for new, were checked by the C.C. on several petitions of the Coopers, and the custom of specially marking each individual's manufacture was introduced.

A long Latin charter was granted the Co. by Henry VII in 1501. Its second and governing charter was granted by Charles II in 1661: it had a re-grant in 1685; it also had powers conferred on it by statute.

Coopers' Hall, in Basinghall St., formed the NE. corner of the Guildhall block, being on the S. side of the space on whose W. side there stood until 1900 the ch. of St. Michael Bassishaw (see 'City Churches, B'). It was the third Coopers' Hall to stand on the site, which came to the Co. under the will of John Baker, dated 1490—the first hall, however, was not built until 1547: it was of timber, and burnt in the G.F. The second hall, costing over £5,000, was built 1669–78—the site having been enlarged. Lotteries used to be drawn in this hall: the last state lottery was drawn in it in 1826. It was pulled down in 1867, and part of the site was given up for extension of the Guildhall. The third hall, designed by Geo. Barnes Williams, was built 1868. The court-room on the first floor was used as common hall—but not for banquets, being too small. The hall was destroyed in the Second World War; a stone on the Guildhall office building marks the site.

Notable members: Sir Robt. Willi-mott, who (before his knighthood) broke (1742–3) the rule that a Ld.M. on election must join one of the twelve great Cos.; Sir David Salomons (master 1841), at first on election as alderman excluded because a Jew, alderman for Cordwainer ward 1847, Liberal M.P. for Greenwich 1851 and 1859–73, Ld.M. 1856. Jas. F. Firth, author of a history of the Co. from its beginning till 1848.

There is a 'Coopers' Song,' with a 'derry-down' chorus, dating from the 17th century.

The Co. on 1st Jan. every year makes a state attendance at St. Magnus's Ch. This ceremony was held at St. Michael's, Crooked Lane, until demolition of that ch. in 1830: it is connected with tenure of property bequeathed by Henry Cloker in 1574.

Much of the Co.'s ancient belongings escaped the G.F. There are portraits of Sir Anthony and Lady Alice Knyvett (see *infra*), James I, Sir Felix Booth, J. F. Firth, and Sir David Salomons. As to plate there are, *inter alia*, two silver tankards—one 17th, the other 18th, century; model of Westminster clock-tower in oxidized silver, presented by Sir D. L. Salomons, 1893; pewter cup with glass bottom and three handles, known as the Co.'s 'cheese cup,' presented by Robt. Major Holborn.

Lady (or Dame) Alice Knyvett in 1552 transferred to the Co. the remainder (in the legal sense) in her estate in Stepney, to endow sch. and almshouses founded at Ratcliff by her former husband, Nicholas Gibson, in 1536: these were managed by the Co. from 1554. John Charley (master 1543) gave property known as Old Wool Quay, in the par. of All Hallows, Barking, for the Ratcliff charity—this was sold to the Crown in 1558 for £400. Tobias Wood in 1611 left £600 to found six almshouses, built 1613, and forming part of the Ratcliff charity. Henry Strode in 1703 benefited the same charity, endowed the Egham charity, and left £500 more for the Ratcliff charity. Wm. Alexander in 1725 left a freehold estate of 308 acres at Woodham Mortimer (Essex), for charitable purposes. The Ratcliff institu-tion was burnt down in 1794, and rebuilt. In 1891 the schs., which are at Tredegar Sq., were organized under a new scheme by the Charity Commissioners—they are now under the G.L.C. as secondary schs., the Co. still sharing in their management, and in that of the Coborn Sch. for Girls, under same foundation. Strode's Egham Charity Sch. was in 1912 organized by the Charity Commissioners as a separate foundation. The Ratcliff almshouses were pulled down in 1898: they are superseded by a pension system.

No. of Livery, 210.

(See *The Coopers' Company and Craft*, by G. Elkington, 1933; *The Coopers' Company*, by Sir Wm. Foster, 1944.)

Cordwainers' (27). Cordwainer means Cordovan-er, a dealer in Cordovan leather. It came to be synonymous with Shoemaker. The first known ordinance was made 56 Henry III, 1272. The Cordwainers, anciently called Alutarii, sent members to the Common Council in 1351. In 1409 an ordinance made a distinction between Cordwainers and those that dealt in *old* leather, i.e. cobblers; the signatures to this include that of John Yonge (see *infra*). An Act of 1824 rendered the Co.'s control of the trade obsolete. It now concerns itself with training for the craft: it assisted in founding the Leather Trades Technical Sch., formerly at Bethnal Green. In 1913 the Co. took over responsibility for the sch. now known as the Cordwainers' Technical College, Mare St., Hackney. It also maintains an inspector who visits schs. and classes in which the art is taught.

A charter was granted by Henry VI in 1439. It was confirmed in 1557 by Philip and Mary, and in 1562 by Elizabeth. In 10 James I (*c.* 1613) another charter was granted. A new one was granted by James II (1685).

John Yonge, a member at the first incorporation, in 1440 presented to the Co. a plot of land in Great Distaff Lane, on which its successive halls have ever since stood. There have been six halls on the site. The first was probably erected in 1393. Another, perhaps the third, was built 1577 out of funds provided by Thos. Nicholson (master): this was burnt in the G.F. with many ancient documents; so much of the Co.'s other property in the City was burnt that it had to sell its Irish estates. The fourth hall was completed by 1670; it was replaced in 1788 by the fifth, covering only part of the original site; and again rebuilt 1910. This last hall was entirely destroyed in the Second World War. The foundation stone was removed on 11th July 1950. Beneath were coins, including a golden sovereign, and a copy of the *City Press* dated 27th Nov. 1909.

The Chamberlain family, long prominent in politics, were connected with this Co. since the fourth generation before the Rt. Hon. Joseph Chamberlain, whose father was master. The famous statesman was himself a member, as also was his son the Rt. Hon. Sir Austen Chamberlain, K.G., who was master 1936 and died in office. Portraits of both are preserved. Ld. Wakefield of Hythe was master (1915) of this as of several other companies.

Among the charities administered by the Co. is one founded by John Came, who d. in 1796. There was an urn and tablet to his memory. The sum was £40,000; it produces £1,000 p.a. for clergymen's widows and blind and deaf and dumb persons. Another charity is Milner's, for 'poor distressed fathers of families,' £120; Love and Woolnough's, for augmenting Came's Blind Pension. It contributed towards the building of the City and Guilds of London Institute, and subscribes to it.

The Co. received a handsome present of plate from the Rt. Hon. Joseph Chamberlain to supplement older treasures such as a porringer of 1666 and a tankard of 1679. Amongst the most recent acquisitions are silver models of the Nelson column of Trafalgar Sq. and of the fifth hall.

There survived the Blitz a window in memory of Came, the portraits, and plate.

No. of Livery, 121.

(See *A Descriptive and Historical Account of the Guild of Cordwainers of the City of London*, by C. H. Waterland Mander, 1931.)

Cutlers' (18). An inquisition in Edward I's reign (1285–6) mentions a house of the Cutlers, opposite the Conduit (see 'Cheapside'). The neighbourhood of Fleet Bridge was another home of the craft; London Bridge another. By the 14th century there were yet other local settlements. In 1328 seven prominent Cutlers were sworn before the Ld.M. and aldermen for govt. of the craft. Articles investing certain rulers with its control were passed, 1344. Rules made for it in 1370 are said (by the Co.'s historian, Chas. Welch) to have been those of 'a sister fraternity'—

which appears to have been chiefly concerned with religious duties. Further ordinances were sanctioned 1379–80. There were women Cutlers. There was an early division of Cutlers into Bladesmiths, Hafters, and Sheathers—the Cutlers proper assembled the parts. The Sheathers had an old independent organisation; complaints against them by the Cutlers were heard early in the 15th century: late in the same century the Cutlers seemed to have absorbed the Sheathers. The Furbers or Furbishers were allied to both the Armourers and the Cutlers. In 1376 the Cutlers sent two to the Common Council. There was a long controversy with the Goldsmiths in the 14th and 15th centuries, the Cutlers being in the habit of working in gold and silver upon knives, daggers, etc. The affair was settled by leaving the Goldsmiths the right to assay all gold and silver work made by the Cutlers. In the 15th century there was rivalry with the Bladesmiths, but there were many bladesmiths in the Cutlers' Co. The Bladesmiths ceased to be a separate craft in 1515: they were amalgamated with the Armourers, but shortly afterwards began to drift away into the Cutlers' Co. The Cutlers' Co. of Sheffield, formed 1624, soon overshadowed the L.Co. and the craft in Sheffield dominated all depts. except that of surgical instruments. The L.Co. in later times complained that Sheffield was trying to legislate for the cutlery trade of Britain.

The first charter was granted by Henry V in 1416: it was obtained chiefly for the purpose of enabling the Co. to hold property in Watling St. held in trust for it since 1408. This charter was confirmed by letters patent of Philip and Mary in 1557, and by inspeximus of Elizabeth in 1560. A new charter was granted by James I in 1606—this contained clauses that seemed intended to disfranchise all non-craft members; and the result of objections upheld by the Court of Aldermen was the substitution of a newer charter, 1607, omitting the obnoxious provisions. This had to be surrendered in 1684 to Charles II, who imposed his closet-keeper, Wm. Chiffinch, on the Co. as master. By Act of Parliament of 1 William and Mary the second charter of James I was restored, and it is the working charter of the Co.

The first hall was 'between the door of the church of St. Thomas of Acres and the church of Colchurch,' i.e. near where Mercers' Hall now stands. The Cutlers probably remained here until they settled in Cloak Lane—called, when they went there early in the 15th century, Horseshoe Bridge St., for it led E. to a bridge over the Walbrook, to the bank of which the new property of the Cutlers extended. The Cutlers became its owners in 1451. Their hall, an old house when they came to it, was on the S. side of the lane, a little to the E. of College Hill, in the par. of St. Michael, Paternoster Royal; it was spacious, and had gardens and a vinery. At the high table the benches were supplied with leather-covered cushions in 1485. The hall was often let to other Cos. Soon after the Restoration the hall was so much decayed that rebuilding was begun: it took four years; and, after standing a few months, the new hall was swept away in the G.F. The records and plate were preserved by the activity of the clerk. The next hall was opened in 1670. There appears to have been an open yard in place of the former gardens. Letting to other Cos. was continued; religious bodies and dancing-masters were also taken as tenants. Extensive repairs were made, and the tapestry sold, 1769. A music-gallery was erected 1778. There was a slight fire in 1803. The Co. at banquets were still sitting on forms in 1842. Repairs, amounting almost to rebuilding, took place in 1853–4. In 1878 the site was required by the District Railway; it was given up by the Co. in 1882. For six years its members were guests of the Salters' Co. On the W. side of Warwick Lane, a site that had been occupied 1674–1825 by the Royal Coll. of Physicians, was fixed upon for a new hall—the present one, opened 1887, built in 'modern Tudor' style from designs by T. Tayler Smith. In it is inserted the valuable and interesting stained glass taken from the old hall. Outside is some stone carving, representing various processes in the craft.

Among the members that attained civic honours were Sir Richd. Hopkins (d. 1736), sheriff and M.P. for the City 1724, a strong Whig, director and sub-governor of South Sea Co., transferred to Fishmongers 1730; Wm. Bridgen (c. 1709–79), who, though he served apprenticeship to a Cutler, became a wine-merchant—Ld.M. 1763-4, then withdrew entirely from City affairs and d. 'in inglorious retirement' at Enfield; Henry Winchester (*c.* 1776-1838), though a Cutler (twice master), a stationer by trade, Tory M.P. for Maidstone 1830, strong opponent of Reform, Ld.M. 1834-5, extremely unpopular with Common Council, left some beautiful plate to the Co., went bankrupt 1838, d. in a lunatic asylum; Sir Walter Vaughan Morgan (1831-1916), Ld.M. and baronetted 1906 (master 1911); he was first a bank clerk, afterwards member of firm of Morgan Bros., who founded two papers, the *Ironmonger* and the *Chemist and Druggist*.

Since 1772 the Co. has presented a medal to each member of the Livery and the court of assistants.

There are many modern paintings in the hall, and also portraits of the widow of John Craythorne, who left the Belle Savage Inn to the Co., 1569; Henry IV (traditional); William III, by a pupil of Kneller; Q. Anne, perhaps by Edwd. Lilly. There are two water-colour drawings of Belle Savage Inn and yard (*q.v.*) (a famous property of the Co.), presented by Richd. Tress, 1846. Of plate the Co. has six silver loving-cups—one of them (with cover) dated 1616, an old possession ; two-handled silver cup with arms of Co. and donor, 1689; salt, in form of an elephant and castle (the Co.'s crest), profusely jewelled, 1658; silver strainer, 1686; beadle's silver staff-head, 16th century. There are an ivory hammer dated 1603; two Chinese bronzes of the Ming period; and a snuff box made of oak from the London Bridge that was demolished in 1176; presented 1838. By reason of the crest, elephants of various descriptions abound in Cutlers' Hall. In one room there are thirty. The knockers are elephants' trunks.

Thos. Buck, in 1566, left £3 6s. 8d. per annum for the support of a scholar at St. John's Coll., Cambridge—this amount has been increased by the Co. John Craythorne (see *supra*) in 1568 left £6 13s. 4d. yearly for a scholarship at each of the two older universities, this has been proportionately increased. The Co. has also established scholarships and exhibitions out of its own funds, and has spent liberally on technical education from the middle of the 19th century.

There were almshouses attached to the old hall, which were not rebuilt after the G.F.; in 1838 seven were authorized, and they were built at Ball's Pond—these were added to; but applications for admission fell off, and they were let.

No. of Livery, 95.

(See *History of the Cutlers' Company of London*, by Chas. Welch, 1916.)

Drapers' (3). There is written mention of it in 1180. Edwd. Hatton (*New View, of London*, 1708), disagreeing with Stow, states that FitzEylwin, the first Ld.M., was a member. He certainly left the Co. all his lands in the par. of St. Mary Bothaw. Drapers were makers of woollen cloth. There are charters of 38 Edward III, 17 Henry VI, 6 Edward IV, 4 and 5 Philip and Mary, 2 Elizabeth, and 4 James I—confirmed 9 James I: this last granted a new constitution.

In 1397 Blackwell Hall was appointed the market. The first hall of the Co. (mentioned 1405) was in St. Swithin's Lane. The site of the present hall in Throgmorton St. was purchased from Henry VIII in 1541: it was occupied by the house of the attainted Thos. Cromwell. This house went in the G.F.: the records, kept in another bdg., were preserved. The hall, built 1667, designed by Edwd. Jerman, was rebuilt 1774, after partial destruction by fire. The present bdgs. date from 1870: they have a quadrangular garden with trees and a fountain. It sustained some damage in the Second World War, but not of a serious character.

Notable members: Sir John de Pultney, four times Ld.M. *temp.* Edward III, ancestor of the Es. of Bath; John de Northampton, M.P. for the City 1378, Ld.M. 1382, a demagogue, head of John of Gaunt's party, condemned to death for sedition, but released 1387; John Heende, Ld.M. 1392 and 1405, rebuilt St. Swithun's Ch.; Sir Thos. Cooke, Ld.M. 1463, intermediary between the citizens and Jack Cade; Sir Wm. Capel, Ld.M. 1503, ancestor of Es. of Essex; Sir John Brugges, Ld.M. 1520, ancestor of the Brydges (D. of Chandos) family; Sir Wm. Chester, Ld.M. 1560, M.P. for the City 1563, partner in the first sugar-refinery in England; Sir Henry Garraway (master), Ld.M. 1640—governor of the Greenland, Russia, and Turkey Cos., expelled from court of aldermen and imprisoned for royalism; Sir Thos. Adams (master), Ld.M. 1646, imprisoned for royalism, founded Arabic lecture at Cambridge; Sir Thos. Davies, Ld.M. 1677, bookseller, twice master of Stationers' Co.; Sir Robt. Clayton, Ld.M. 1680, M.P. for the City 1679–81, advocated Exclusion Bill, on committee to defend City charter 1682, benefactor of St. Thomas's and Christ's Hosps.

The Co.'s connection with the cloth trade was already weakened by admissions 'by redemption,' in Elizabeth's reign; since the 17th century it has had nothing to do with the industry. Its valuables include a silver-gilt cup presented by Mr. William Lambard in 1578; a monteith, hall-marked 1685; a voiding-knife (precursor of the crumb-brush), dated 1678; tapestries in the court-room.

Amongst the portraits is one purporting to be Fitz-Eylwin; there are also portraits of Mary, Q. of Scots, Charles I, William III, Q. Anne, George IV, William IV, Q. Victoria, Edward VII, George V, Princess Elizabeth, the D. of Marlborough, Ld. Nelson, the D. of Wellington.

The most prominent institution associated with the Co. is Bancroft's Sch., Woodford, founded under the will of Francis Bancroft, dated 1727. (See City Churches—C.; St. Helen, Bishopsgate.) It was originally at Mile End, and was transferred to its present position in 1886.

There is also Howell's Sch. at Denbigh, due to the charity of Thos. Howell whose will was dated 1540.

There are almshouses: Queen Elizabeth's Coll., Greenwich, founded by Letters Patent of 1574, and endowed by Wm. Lambard; Bruce Grove; St. Mary, Newington; St. George, Southwark; St. Leonard, Shoreditch Almshouses are now at Wood Green; there is also Lucas's Hosp., Wokingham.

The Co. has the presentation to the living of St. Michael's, Cornhill.

No. of Livery, 200.

(See *The History of the Worshipful Company of the Drapers of London*, by A. H. Johnson, 1914.)

Dyers' (13). The first positive reference to an existing gild of Dyers is in 1188. They disputed precedence with the Shearmen; and, when the Shearmen and Fullers became united as the Cloth-workers, the Dyers had a long contest—settled, 7 Henry VIII, in favour of the Clothworkers. Since then the Dyers have been first on the list of minor Cos.

The industry is native, and possibly a development of the body-staining practice of the early Britons. Wool, silk, and leather were dyed: in 1372, in an agreement by the Leathersellers, Pursers of the Bridge, and Dyers, the Dyers' wives are associated as parties. By the 15th century the art had attained great perfection in all varieties of colour, exhibited in the holiday dress of all classes. The last confirmation of by-laws was in 1705: the Co. is now a charitable concern, and one of the three authorities (the Crown and the Vintners' Co. are the others) for looking after the swans on the Thames: however, since the time of the First World War it has interested itself in the improvement of British dyeing.

A charter of incorporation was granted by Henry VI in the last year of his life (1471) during his brief restoration: Edward IV gave a re-grant in 1472. The charter was confirmed by Henry VIII and all succeeding monarchs (James I in 1606) until James II (1686). Q. Anne granted a new charter in 1704, giving authority over the craft in L. and ten miles round.

The first hall was in Anchor Lane in the Vintry (1483). The second was on land given to the Co. by Sir Robt. Tyrwhitt in 1545: its site is marked by Dyers Hall Wharf. This was burnt in the G.F. A third hall, apparently on the same site, was burnt in 1681. About 1657 the Co. had acquired land on Dowgate Hill, where there had stood a coll. (for priests) called Jesus Commons—till Henry VIII's reign. After the G.F. the Co. leased part of this land to the Skinners' Co.; and, on the expiry of the lease, two houses formerly used by the Skinners were turned into a hall for the Dyers. The Skinners apparently ceased to occupy in 1731—whether occupation by the Dyers was deferred till then is not clear: however, this makeshift hall fell down in 1768. The next hall, which they built on the same site in 1770, was a dangerous structure and unusable by 1831: it was taken down in 1838—it had faced S. on College St., formerly called Elbow Lane. The present hall, on Dowgate Hill, was erected in its place by 1840. By 1856 the rest of the Dyers' Dowgate Hill site was cleared; the new bdgs. then erected (as offices, etc.) were surmounted by a pediment displaying the Co.'s arms, and the covered way to the hall from the E.

was made to supersede the College St. entrance. The hall sustained some damage in the Second World War.

The Co. possesses an ancient muniment chest, of unknown workmanship, the mechanism of which is complex and the ornamentation elaborate. There are portraits of benefactors.

Sir Robt. Tyrwhitt, in 1545, founded a charity for the erection of almshouses; Henry West, 1551, a similar charity. Other benefactors were: Henry Trevillian, 1636; Wm. Lee, 1719; John Peck, 1739; and Geo. Maguire. The earliest alms-houses adjoined the first hall in Upper Thames St.: in 1777 they were removed to City Rd.; in 1850 to King Henry's Walk, adjoining Ball's Pond.

The Dyers still retain connection with the craft of dying and its practical applica-tion.

The Co. is responsible for the manage-ment of charitable trusts. It donated £1,000 towards the post-war requirements of Westminster Sch.

No. of Livery, 109.

Fishmongers' (4). The ware of the Fish-mongers of old L. consisted mainly of salt fish and stock-fish; and there were originally two companies dealing in those articles respectively, but the dealers in salt fish were the earlier. Henry III, in the interest of his Queen's customs, restricted the landing of fish to Queen-hithe (*q.v.*). Consequently a new fish-market was established N. of Queenhithe, in what came to be called Old Fish St.— the E. end of what is now Knightrider St. Edward I removed the restriction, and the Fishmongers removed to Bridge St. (Fish Street Hill), where they had their hall in 1321. They also used the Stocks Market (see 'Markets'); and the new company of Stock-fish Mongers occupied in 1399 Stock-fish Monger Row in Lower Thames St. (from Fish Street Hill to Old Swan Lane). The Fishmongers had a dispute over precedence with the Skinners which led to bloodshed in Cheapside, 1340. In 1377 the craft returned six members to the Common Council, and occupied fourth place among the Cos.— as they have done ever since. In 1380 and 1382 Parliament made enactments that disfranchised the Fishmongers; they pro-tested, and a compromise was arranged in 1383. Between them, according to Stow, the Cos. had six halls both in Stock-

fish Mongers' Row, in Old Fish St., and in Bridge St. It would appear that in later times (1632) the Fishmongers had a monopoly of the export trade in salt. They remain to this day in their old locality: Fish Street Hill has never lost its fishlike smell.

Charters, not now extant, were granted by Edward I and Edward II. A patent in French of 37 Edward III (1363) con-firms grants made by that king's 'pro-genitors immemorial.' Richard II altered the rules in the seventh year of his reign. Henry V, in the fifth year of his reign, issued a mandate alluding to the early charters and confirming them. Henry VI granted an inspeximus charter in his sixth year, and by a new charter in his eleventh year (1433) united the Stock-fish Mongers with the other Fishmongers'; but by charter of 21 Henry VII (1505) they were separated into two Cos. Letters patent of 28 Henry VIII (1536) finally united them. There followed charters of: 1 Edward VI (1547), 1 Mary (1553), 1 Elizabeth (1559), 11 Elizabeth (1569), 2 James I (1604— the working charter), '36' Charles II (1685)—annulled by 2 William and Mary.

The earlier halls, mentioned above, were superseded by a hall on the site of the present one, which was the site of one of the two halls built by the respective Cos. in Stock-fish Mongers' Row. Various tenements thereabout had been acquired by the Cos., and in 1504 they fixed on 'the Lord Fanhope's house' to accommo-date them both: its site had belonged to John Lovekyn in 1369. It is in the par. of St. Michael, Crooked Lane. In Richard II's time Sir Wm. Walworth occupied it; and in 1433 it came into the possession of John Cornwall, Baron Fanhope, from whom at one remove it came to the Fishmongers' in 1434. Stock-fish Mongers' Hall, which was in the par. of St. Magnus, was let, and apparently was still standing in 1615. The castellated bdg. here was swept away by the G.F. The next hall was designed by Edwd. Jerman, and completed 1671—a stately structure. It was pulled down and the present hall built 1831-3; on account of the building of new London Bridge; the northern approach to which, called Adelaide Pl., bounds the hall on the E. It is the most conspicuous of all the Companies' halls— the classical portico that faces the river on the high bridge-level being a wonderful contrast to hideous 'Adelaide House.' It sustained considerable interior damage in World War II. There is an old oak statue of Sir Wm. Walworth, by Edwd. Pierce, with an inscription erroneously identifying the dagger of Sir Wm. with the weapon in the City arms (see 'City Corporation').

The Fishmongers' first mayor was John Lovekyn, aforesaid—1349, 1359, 1366, and 1367—a stock-fish mongering pioneer, M.P. for the City 1347–8 and 1365. Sir Wm. Walworth, mayor 1375 and 1381, who slew Wat Tyler, was their sixth. Their twenty-second was Sir John Leman, 1617—the first bachelor mayor since 1491, he had an unusually magnificent pageant, composed by Anthony Munday, the City poet. There was a huge representation of a lemon—a punning device typical of the time. Their twenty-third was Sir Isaac Penington, 1643—a staunch Puritan, and one of the judges of Charles I; but he declined to sign the death-warrant, and was allowed to die in the Tower after the Restoration. Their twenty-fourth was Sir John Gayer, 1647, a royalist (see 'City Churches; C'—St. Katherine Cree).

The Co. possesses a chair made of stone and wood taken from the foundations of old London Bridge. The pictures include portraits of royalty and nobility and scenes from the neighbourhood in past times. There is an ancient pall, commonly but wrongly called Walworth's—it is Elizabethan. The Walworth dagger is also preserved. Plate includes: 2 large silver monteiths, 1696 and 1698; antique ladle, 1698; parcel-gilt silver salt, 1654; rosewater dish, 24 in. in diameter, 1676; silver loving-cup, 1676; circular silver tankard, 1667; 2 tankards with covers, 1681 and 1682; 2 silver salvers, 1697 and 1698; 5 silver cups of 17th century.

There is a scale model of the Co.'s last state barge (built in 1773, and broken up in 1850), presented by Major Edward Miller, Prime Warden in 1935–6.

This is one of the few Cos. still on the active list as to craft: its charter of James I is no dead letter. It appoints fishmeters, who are the officers that attend Billingsgate market and seize unsound fish. It assists in maintaining a biological laboratory at Plymouth for the study of marine life. There are four trust charities: Sir John Gresham's (1554), a sch. at

Holt (Norfolk); Wm. Goddard's (1618), Jesus Hosp. at Bray (Berks.)—a fine set of old almshouses; Mark Quested's (1642), almshouses at Harrietsham (Kent); Jas. Hulbert's (1719), for renewing the Co.'s then existing almshouse (St. Peter's Hosp.), formerly at Newington, were at Wandsworth until 1924. They were then sold under an order of the High Court and the former inmates granted pensions. The Co. manages the annual competition for Doggett's Coat and Badge (see 'Customs). It helped to found the City and Guilds of London Institute. No. of Livery, 275.

Girdlers' (23). In ancient days the girdle was an important, and with the well-to-do an elaborate article of dress; being that to which weapons, purses, and other portable conveniences were attached: moreover it was often elaborately worked and even jewelled. Besides the girdle, Girdlers made the garter and the bandolier—a belt worn over the shoulder for suspension of a wallet. The first hint of a fraternity of Girdlers is the amercement in 1180 of an adulterine guild of St. Lawrence whose master was Ralph de la Barre— he was probably master of the Girdlers: their patron was St. Lawrence, whose ch. in Jewry was the centre of their colony; and girdles were sometimes called bars, from the transverse bands with which they were ornamented. The history of the Co. is rendered meagre by the loss of its records in the G.F. In 1927 it celebrated the 600th anniversary of its grant of letters patent.

A charter was granted by Henry VI in 1448. Philip and Mary granted one in 1557. Elizabeth's charter (1567) effected the amalgamation of the Pinners and Wireworkers with the Girdlers. A charter by Charles I in 1640 separated the Pinners and made them again a distinct Co. His charter was surrendered to Charles II in 1684, and superseded by a charter granted by James II in 1685; this remains the working charter.

It is probable that the Co.'s first meeting-place was a shop in Westcheap called 'Girdlersselde,' alluded to as the property of John Potyn, Girdler, in 1332. In 1431 Andrew Hunt, Girdler, gave two tenements and a parcel of land in the par. of St. Michael, Bassishaw, to the wardens of 'the mistery.' Robt. Belgrave, in 1505, left the Co. the ground that became the hall garden. The site of the hall on the N. side of Basinghall Av. is still the same. The first hall was burnt in the G.F. The new hall was not ready until 1681: the court-room (formerly the 'ladies' parlour') was enlarged 1735; the whole bdg. was restored and altered 1878-9. There was further rebuilding in 1887. This hall was destroyed in 1940 and has been rebuilt on the same site.

A few of the Co.'s treasures were saved. These included a carpet, presented 1634 by Robt. Bell, master. It was made in Lahore, and is about 8 by 2½ yards. It has the Co.'s arms in the centre. It survived the G.F., and being for many years used as a table cover, it became covered with ink-stains. It was carefully cleaned. The minute books and glass were sent to the Clothworkers' Hall, where subsequently they were lost by bombing.

Cuthbert Beeston in 1580 bequeathed a messuage in Southwark, known as the Cage, and seven other tenements for a variety of charitable uses. The estate was sold on the widening of London Bridge approaches in 1824; and in 1825 the Charity Commissioners sanctioned a new scheme: seven almshouses were built at Albert Rd., Peckham Rye—where they still flourish. George Palyn in 1609 left £900 to build 'an almshouse': six houses were therefore built without Cripplegate; on their destruction in the G.F. houses were built in Pesthouse Row (Bath St. off City Rd.), and rebuilt 1745; about 1849 they were superseded by new houses erected at Choumert Rd., Peckham. There is also a pension-charity founded by Richd. Andrews (master) in 1637. Henry Flycke in 1559 left the George Inn, Hammersmith, for charitable purposes. The Co. has also other property in that district. There are sums payable to various pars. under the will of Thos. Nevitt, 1633. There is a small scholarship in the Guildhall Sch. of Music, and a Girdlers lectureship in economics at Cambridge.

No. of Livery, 80.

(See *An Historical Account of the Worshipful Company of Girdlers, London*, by W. Dunville Smythe, 1905.)

Goldsmiths' (5). An adulterine Co. of Goldsmiths was heavily amerced in 1180. Herbert says their habitations on the E. side of Foster Lane were called Gold-

smiths' Row: Sir Walter Prideaux states that this name was given to the S. side of Cheapside from Bread St. to the cross. Mention of the warden of the craft in a statute of 28 Edward I (1300) shows continuance of the gild, unincorporated, but possessing power and recognized privilege. At the beginning of Edward III's reign, the genuine goldsmiths were said to 'sit in their shops in the high street of Cheap'; and it was ordered by that king that the trade should not be practised elsewhere except at his exchange. There was special trouble with the Cutlers, who were alleged to defraud purchasers of gold and silver. The Goldsmiths' Co. had an assay office early in the 14th century; and the statute of 1300 enacted that no vessel of gold or silver should depart out of the hands of the workman until it had been assayed by the wardens of the craft and stamped with the leopard's head—the royal mark. All the wardens were reported dead in 1350, in consequence of the plague ('Black Death'). Even in those early times the Co. and its members seem to have acted as bankers and pawnbrokers—taking as pledges, besides plate, cloth of gold and pieces of napery. There were many different grades—freemen who were full members; and 'allowes' or permitted practitioners of various kinds, English and foreign. The Co.'s powers were exercised under its charters till 1739, when a change was deemed necessary, and an Act of Parliament, 12 George II, c 26., was obtained. Other statutes have followed: the principal one being 7 & 8 Victoria, c. 22 (1844), regulating the assay office in charge of the Co., which has extensive powers for the superintendence of the manufacture and sale of gold and silver articles: these must bear its stamp, called the hall-mark. The Assay Office for hall-marking gold and silver plate is conducted by the Co. under statutory authority, the charges for marking being applied in payment of the expenses of the office and the prosecution of offenders against the hall-marking laws. The annual deficit is met by the Co. The plate duties, formerly collected by the Co. through the Assay Office for the Government, were abolished in 1890. The Antique Plate Committee was formed in September, 1939, from members of the Co. to assist the Court in carrying out their statutory duties with regard to plate contravening the hall-marking laws. The committee is elected from members of an advisory panel of trade experts and holds monthly meetings. Memoranda have been issued to the trade on the hall-marking laws. The committee is in touch with the British Antique Dealers' Association, the Auctioneers' and Estate Agents' Institute, Board of Trade and the Customs authorities. The Assay Office building in Gutter Lane was burnt down in Dec. 1940 and the whole office is now established in the Hall.

The Trial of the Pyx. The trial of the coins in the Pyx of the Royal Mint is conducted at Goldsmiths' Hall by a jury of members of the Co., sworn in and charged by the King's Remembrancer. The Trial takes place in March and the Verdicts are delivered in May to the King's Remembrancer in the presence of the Chancellor of the Exchequer, who attends as Master of the Mint. The Goldsmiths of L. have, since 1248, made these trials, which formerly took place at the Exchequer but were, in 1844, moved to Goldsmiths' Hall, and have taken place annually since the Coinage Act, 1870. Books of record date from 1604.

Imperial gold coins made at the branch mints at Perth, Sydney, Melbourne, Ottawa, Bombay and Pretoria were tried at the Hall between 1906 and 1914, but no such coins have been made in recent years. Silver coins made at the Royal Mint for the Governments of New Zealand and Southern Rhodesia have been tried each year since 1934. The standard trial plates used for the Trial of the Pyx and by the Royal Mint and the Assay Offices throughout the United Kingdom are prepared by officers of the Mint for the Board of Trade and are submitted to the Company for verification. Trial plates were made and verified in 1873 and 1900; new gold trial plates were made in 1927 and 1929. Trial plates of copper and nickel were verified in 1948. The first trial of cupro-nickel coins took place in 1948.

The yr. 1327 is usually regarded as that of incorporation: it was then that Edward III issued letters patent empowering the Co. to remedy the trade abuses recited therein. He confirmed this power in his second year, and granted two charters, conferring new privileges, in his third and fourth years respectively. In 16 Richard II (1393) letters patent constituted 'a perpetual community.' There is an inspeximus of 3 Henry IV, one of 5 Henry V, and one of 1 Henry VI. In 2 Edward IV (1462–3) was granted a charter conferring further privileges and a common seal. Another was granted 20 Henry VII (1504–5). Confirmations were granted: 1 Henry VIII, 1 Edward VI, 1 Mary, 3 Elizabeth, 2 James I. These charters were ratified by every monarch till William and Mary. (In 2 James II some powers were withdrawn, but that K.'s successors restored them.)

The site of Goldsmiths' Hall in Foster Lane belonged, in the reign of Edward II, to Sir Nicholas de Segrave, Ld. of Stowe. It was 'in the way called St. Vedast in the parish of St. John Zachary,' and was bounded on the N. by Ing Lane —now part of Gresham St. In 1366 an ordinance mentioned a 'common place,' of meeting in the said par. In 1401 there was recorded an assembly of the Co. 'in their hall in Fasteres Lane.' Previously — 1380 — there had been expenses of building a new parlour and a cellar: the walls were of rubble and chalk, the roof of the parlour was leaded; the inside was wainscoted with 'planche bord' and painted in oil; and there were two chimneys. What is believed to have been the second hall was built by Sir Dru Barentyn early in the 15th century: it had a chapel, the 'Chamber,' an armoury, a granary, a gallery, an assay office, vaults, a court-yard or garden, and an entrance gate-house. It had a bay-window, with armorial bearings, on its E. side, next Huggin Lane. In the time of Henry VIII the reredos or screen of the Livery hall was surmounted by a silver-gilt statue of St. Dunstan (patron saint of the craft); it was broken and sold at the Reformation. From 1641 till the Restoration Goldsmiths' Hall was the exchequer of the Parliamentarians. It was burnt out in the G.F.; most of the valuables having been previously removed. In Sept. 1666 temporary premises were taken in Grub St. Partly by rebuilding and partly by repair, the hall was restored in 1669—Jerman being the 'surveyor.' This old hall was of red brick: it surrounded a small square paved court. The staircase was ornate, and the court-room still more so. This renovated medieval bdg. lasted till 1829. On its site was built the present hall, by Philip Hardwick, in the Italian style, opened 1835. In digging the foundations a little altar of Diana was turned up. It is kept in the courtroom (see 'St. Paul's Cathedral'). The hall is, as to interior, the most sumptuous of all the companies' halls; and, with its Corinthian columns, etc., it would be imposing outwardly if it were not entirely surrounded by narrow ways. In 1871 the hall and staircase were entirely lined with costly marbles of different sorts and colours. On the balustrade are four statuettes of the Seasons, by Samuel Nixon; and there are numerous statues and busts. The wainscoting of the old hall has been used in the court-room where, on special occasions, candles are still used in the chandeliers.

A number of incendiary bombs fell on the Hall during the war, but little serious damage ,was caused until the 17th Apr. 1941, when a high explosive bomb destroyed the tea-room, drawing-room, court dining-room and the offices below. Rebuilding began in the summer of 1947 and the plans included a library and exhibition room, and accommodation for the Design and Research Centre for the gold, silver and jewellery industries. The work was completed in 1950.

In the reign of Henry I, one Leofstane, a Goldsmith, was Provost of L.; and an earlier Leofstane, joint-portgrave of L. temp. Edward the Confessor, is supposed to have been a Goldsmith. Gregory de Rokesley, Ld.M. 1275–81 and 1285, chief assay-master of the mints and keeper of the king's exchange, was a famous Goldsmith who in 1285 asserted the rights of the City against the lord treasurer, John Kirkby, Bp. of Ely, by taking off his mayoral robes (in All Hallows Barking Ch.) before obeying the treasurer's summons to the Tower—with the result that Kirkby deprived the City for a while of its mayoralty. (Rokesley's long term of office is commemorated by a C.C. tablet in Lombard St.) Sir Nicholas Farindon, Ld.M. 1308, 1313, 1320, and 1323 (appointed to office by Edward II), son of Wm. Farindon, who purchased and bequeathed to Sir Nicholas the aldermanry of his ward, and gave it its name of Farringdon (afterwards it was split into two, Within and Without), was a warden of the Co. in 1338: he must

have been very old when he d., not before 1361. Sir Dru Barentyn, refounder of the hall about 1410, and a great benefactor of the Co., was several times warden, M.P. for the City 1391 and 1413, Ld.M. 1409. Another benefactor, Sir Martin Bowes, M.P. for the City 1547, 1553, 1554, 1555, and 1558, Ld.M. 1546, was a well-known jeweller and Goldsmith, and deputy-keeper of the exchange. Sir Francis Child the elder, successor to the Goldsmith business of Wm. Wheeler, Ld.M. 1699, M.P. for the City 1702, was the first Goldsmith to cease practise of the craft in order to devote all his energies to banking. Sir Chas. Duncombe, apprenticed to a Goldsmith, also became a banker, and was receiver of customs under Charles II and James II; he was expelled from Parliament 1698 on an accusation of falsely endorsing exchequer bills; Ld.M. 1709 (see 'City Churches; C'—St. Magnus the Martyr). Sir Francis Child the younger was Ld.M. 1732.

There is a great store of pictures, mostly portraits of famous members. The Co. has a large collection of silver plate, illustrating most of the changes of style and fashion which have marked the craft of the silversmith in this country during the past four centuries. It may be seen on inquiry in writing. With the object of keeping up the standard of design and craftsmanship and to facilitate the selection of silver for exhibitions, the Co. has formed a collection of examples of silver work by the best manufacturers and craftsmen of the present day. This collection has been seen in many parts of this country as well as abroad.

The Company's charities are as follows:
1. The Goldsmiths' Consolidated Charities. This is the largest fund and is primarily a L. Charity and is available for the following objects amongst others: Pensions and grants for the poor members of the Co., their widows and widowed and unmarried daughters; for poor persons resident or employed in the Administrative County of L. Apprenticeship premiums. Donations to convalescent homes, orphanages, etc. Provision of libraries, museums, recreation grounds, open spaces, etc. Provision of dwellings for the poor. Technical and other education. To assist L. boys who are in exceptionally difficult circumstances to complete

their training at places of higher education.

2. The Charity of John Perryn of Acton. The Co. has been responsible for many exhibitions and studentships for under-graduates and graduates at Oxford and Cambridge. These exhibitions have been discontinued, owing to the greatly in-creased facilities provided by the State. The funds are available for general charitable purposes. Exhibitions for sons and daughters of freemen, to help mem-bers of the Co. in the education of their families, were introduced in 1946. A scheme for sending selected post-graduate students from British universities to work at universities in the Dominions under special teachers was started in 1946. John Perryn's Almshouses at East Acton were built in 1912 at a cost of £12,000. There are twenty houses for freemen, the widows or the widowed or unmarried daughters of freemen of the Co., who receive pensions and medical and other comforts in addition to their houses. The Wardens visit the Almshouses every summer.

3. Sir Martin Bowes Charity. For pensions to poor women of Woolwich.

4. Mrs. Jane Clarke's Charity. For pensions to poor men of Putney.

5. The Queen Victoria Commemoration Charity. Founded in 1897 out of Corporate Property for giving help to poor gold-smiths and silversmiths in the L. area who are not members of the Co. and their widows. The necessary funds are now provided from the Consolidated Charities.

There have also been donations to Oxford and Cambridge Universities, to University College, L., and various other colleges. The City and Guilds of L. Institute (*q.v.*) has received from the Co. contributions exceeding £274,000. The sum of £89,000 was given to the Imperial Coll. of Science and Technology for the Goldsmiths' Extension of the City and Guilds' Coll. at S. Kensington, which was formally opened in 1926. Goldsmiths' Coll., New Cross, was maintained out of the Co.'s corporate funds from 1890 until 1904. It is now used as a Training Coll. for Teachers, a School of Art, and an Evening Institute. The Co. is repre-sented on the delegacy of the Coll.

Among many other benefactions, St. Dunstan's Ch. and Vicarage, E. Acton, were built and endowed in 1878 at a cost of £30,000, out of corporate property,

on land adjoining the estate of John Perryn. A further endowment was pro-vided in 1929.

No. of Livery, 233.

(See *Memorials of the Goldsmiths' Com-pany*, by Sir W. S. Prideaux, 1896).

Grocers' (2). They were at first the Pepperers. Dealers in gross, i.e. whole-sale, were called gross-ers; and the group of wholesalers that became the Grocers' Co. happened to be dealers in spices, pepper, and other foreign articles of semi-luxury; which seem to have been called 'grocery,' even when retailed, as early as the 15th century. The Pepperers are first mentioned as a fraternity amongst the amerced gilds of Henry II, but prob-ably existed as a gild long before. They were mostly of Italian descent. Andrew de Bokerell, Pepperer, Ld.M. from 1231 to 1237, was of the Bocherelli family, Sir John de Gisors, Ld.M. 1311, 1312, and 1314, a member of the Gisorio. The statutes and ordinances of the Pepperers made in the reign of Edward II were amongst the City Records, under the title *Ordinatio Pipero-rum de Sopers Lane.* Stow wrote: 'By the assent of Stephen de Abunden [Ld.M. 1315] the Pepperers in Soper's lane [Queen St.] were admitted to sell all such spices, and other wares, as Grocers now sell, retaining the old name of Pepperers of Soper's lane.'

The Grocers' Co. was founded by 22 pepperers in 1345, and was originally known as the Fraternity of St. Anthony, but they did not obtain a charter until 1428. By this the Co. was appointed the official garbellers, i.e. inspectors of mer-chandise, such as spices, drugs, etc. Further charters were granted: 4 & 5 Philip and Mary, 2 Elizabeth, 2 James I, 15 Charles I, '36' Charles II (1685), 1 James II, another by the same K. in 1688, 2 William and Mary, 9 Anne, and 12 George I. The Grocers were therefore 'only a separation from the parent society of Pepperers . . . which . . . long afterwards formed a distinct and independent body. . . . From 1350 to 1375 the society's meetings continued to be held regularly . . . and it kept increasing in wealth and numbers. . . . Sixteen aldermen were members in 1383' (Herbert). They were called grossers in an opprobrious sense in a petition to the Commons in 1361 accusing them of being 'engrossers of all sorts of wares.' They did not call themselves Grocers until 1373. Stow continued: 'At length, in the reign of Henry VI, the said Soper's lane was inhabited by Cordwainers and Curriers; after that the Grocers had seated themselves in a more open street, to wit, Buckler's-bury, where they still remain.' At this time the Grocers were also druggists and herbalists. Hence Falstaff's reference (*Merry Wives of Windsor*) to 'A smell like Bucklersbury in simple time.' They appear to have dealt in whale-oil, even cotton and wool, are mentioned as among their goods. For a time they were foremost among the Cos. in order of precedence. In 1607 the Apothecaries were incorporated with the Grocers, but this union was dissolved in 1615. As the Co.'s wealth increased, it was mulcted in war-contributions in times of stress. The G.F. practically destroyed all its house property except a few small tenements in Grub St. It does not appear to have exercised any authority over the craft afterwards. The Company was ejected from its hall on account of debt in 1679. After that it managed its estates (all in the City, except the Irish estates) so well that it became exceedingly prosperous.

The meeting-place at first, 1345–6, was the town mansion of the abbot of Bury, in what is now called Bevis Marks. In 1347 it was 'the abbot's place of St. Edmund.' In 1348 it was 'the house of one Fulgham, called the Ryngdehall,' near Garlickhithe; where, at the hotel of the abbot of St. Cross, the Co. continued till 1383. It then took up residence at a place in Bucklersbury called Cornet's Tower, formerly used by Edward III as his exchequer. In 1426 it purchased from Ld. Fitzwalter his town mansion and raised money for building their hall on its present site—in the centre of the block next the Bank of England on its W. side. The first stone was laid 8th May 1427, and the completion was celebrated by a dinner, 5th Feb. 1428. It was not wainscoted till after 1594. The floor of the great parlour was not boarded till 1631—before that, the ground was strewed with rushes. There were vines in the garden, which was so spacious and pleasant that it was sometimes borrowed for public recreative purposes. The G.F. destroyed the roof and woodwork; but there remained the old walls, and an old turret in the garden that was probably part of Ld. Fitzwalter's house. Rebuilding lan-

guished; the generosity of Sir John Cutler enabled its completion by 1668: however, it was ruinous in 1681, and repaired that year at the cost of Sir John Moore. In 1694 it was let to the Bank of England, which held its courts there till the building of the Bank in 1734. The garden remained unchanged till 1798, when it was encroached upon by the building of a new and larger hall. About half of the remainder disappeared in 1802, at the straightening-out of Prince's St., north-westwards. The hall was rebuilt that year from designs of Thos. Leverton—but so insecurely that in 1827 repairs amounting almost to rebuilding had to be done: Joseph Gwilt directed them. The present imposing hall was built in 1893. The entrance is in Prince's St. It was badly damaged by fire in 1965 and is being rebuilt.

The Co.'s first Ld.M., 1231–7, was Andrew Bokerel, Pepperer. Its second, 1245–6, was Sir John Gisors: his son built Gisors's or Gerard's Hall (Basing Lane, near Bread St.), which stood till 1853. Sir Nicholas Brembre, Grocer, after disputes over a riot, was appointed Ld.M. by king's writ, 1377; he represented the oligarchy of the great Cos. and the opponents of John of Gaunt, and was with the K. at Smithfield in the rising of 1381; in 1383 he was elected Ld.M., and he held office till 1385—by main force; he was one of the royal councillors found guilty of treason in 1388, and was hanged at Tyburn. Sir John Philpot, most famous of Grocers, held important office under Edward III at Calais, M.P. for the City 1371: during the crisis caused by French and Scottish invasions at the beginning of the reign of Richard II, Philpot fitted out a squadron that punished the Scots— he was Ld.M. 1378. Sir Wm. Sevenoke (joint master 1406), M.P. for the City 1417, Ld.M. 1418—a great benefactor. Sir John de Welles, Ld.M. 1431, 'builded the Standard in Chepeside' (Stow). Sir John Crosby, sheriff 1470, mayor of the staple at Calais (see 'Crosby Hall'). Sir Wm. Laxton, Ld.M. 1544, founded Oundle Sch. Laurence Sheriff, d. 1567, bequeathed the means, and directed the foundation, of Rugby Sch. Sir Thos. Lodge (master 1559), Ld.M. 1562, is usually regarded as the founder of England's slave-trade. Thos., first Baron Coventry, Lord Keeper, was admitted member 1627. Charles II was master in 1660: in that yr. also Gen. Geo. Monck (D. of Albemarle), and Geo., E. of Berkeley, were admitted. Sir Geoffrey Palmer, Bart., Attorney-General, was admitted 1661. Heneage Finch, first E. of Nottingham, Ld. Chancellor 1674, was admitted 1665. Sir John Moore, Ld.M. 1682, was autocratic, and had a tumultuous yr. of office. John Sheffield, D. of Buckingham, was master 1685. Sir John Cutler, a miser with fits of public generosity, satirized by Pope (*Moral Essays*, Ep. iii), was master-warden 1652–3. William III was master 1689. Chas. Sackville, E. of Dorset, author of the song *To all you ladies now at land,* was master 1691. Sir John Barnard, Ld.M. 1738, M.P. for the City 1722–61, authority on finance, was an ordinary member of the Co. All later notable members were national rather than City personages. Amongst these was Wm. Pitt the Younger. There is still at banquets a toast to his immortal memory. It was his membership that led to James Boswell's ridiculous behaviour at a dinner at the Guildhall in 1785. In Pitt's presence—'he sat with all the dignified silence of a marble statue'—Boswell sang a song of his own composition entitled 'A Grocer of London.'

There are two schools—at Oundle (Northants), the original Free Grammar School, founded under the bequest of Sir Wm. Laxton in 1556, and called by his name; and a bigger public sch., established in 1876, known as Oundle Sch., for which a charter was obtained in 1930. The Co. appoints representatives on the governing bodies of the sch. at Colwall (Herefordshire), founded by Humphrey Walwyn, and at Witney (Oxfordshire), founded by Henry Box. Mrs. Emma Bacchus in 1587 founded exhibitions for poor scholars. A bequest by Lady Slaney in 1704 placed the Co. in a position to purchase ch. benefices—it has taken advantage of this in such a way as to multiply churches in 'developed' localities. Lady Middleton, in 1645, bequeathed £20 p.a. for clergymen's widows; the Co. has given about £1,000 p.a. for the same object. There is a sch. at Hackney which was built and equipped at the cost of £30,000 of which some £23,000 was obtained by the redemption of old charities, and this was financed by the Co. from 1873 to 1903. It was then transferred voluntarily as a gift to the L.C.C.

The Medical Research Scholarships scheme was revised a few years ago, and now one is offered every yr. tenable for two yrs.; a further sum is also available for the scholars' expenses.

Since 1883 the Co. has given three scholarships for original research in sanitary science. Despite the Second World War, the Co. continues to give considerable sums to charitable institutions of all kinds, e.g. to the City and Guilds of London Institute. It also assists members of the Co., and their widows and children who are in poor circumstances.

No. of Livery, 222.

Haberdashers' (8). The Haberdashers' were a branch of the Mercers': their name is of uncertain etymology. They were originally called Hurrers, i.e. Capmakers; but a section having added to capmaking the vending of small articles of adornment (chiefly from Milan, whence they got the name Milliners), the Capmakers became a separate body for a while. The first ordinances of the other body were promulgated 1372, when they returned two members to the Common Council as a gild distinct from the Hurrers. As the fraternity of St. Katherine, they are first mentioned in the Bp. of London's Registry in 1381. In 1448 they received a charter of incorporation. Other charters were granted: by Henry VII in 1502, this apparently uniting them with the Hurrers (they are termed Merchant Haberdashers); by Henry VIII, 1510 (calling them simply Haberdashers) confirmed 1558 (Philip and Mary) and 1578 (Q. Elizabeth).

The site of the hall which was destroyed by bombs in 1940, was bequeathed to the Co. in 1478 by Wm. Baker. It was in Gresham St. The first hall on this site was destroyed with the records, in the G.F. The rebuilding 1667, was by Sir Christopher Wren: his court room (with the original ceiling and drawing room alone) remained until the Blitz, the rest having been burnt in 1840. The new hall is in Staining Lane.

Notable members: Sir Geo. Whitmore (master), Ld.M. 1631, master of the Virginia Co., imprisoned (1642–3) for refusing to pay taxes levied by Parliament; Thos. Aldersey, founder (1594) of the Co.'s sch. at Bunbury; Wm. Jones, founder of the sch. at Monmouth; Robt.

Aske, founder of a sch. and almshouses at Hoxton; and the following masters: Sir Geo. Wyatt Truscott, Ld.M. 1909, and Viscount Wakefield of Hythe (an alderman).

The plate, including a gilt salt cellar of 1595, has been saved, as also portraits including one by Gainsborough and two by Reynolds.

The Co.'s only business now is the administration of its charities. The elementary sch., formerly a grammar sch. at Banbury (Cheshire) was founded 1594, and rebuilt 1875. The grammar sch. at Monmouth was founded 1614, with a gift of £40,000 from Wm. Jones; a girls' sch. has been added. The grammar sch. at Newport (Shropshire) was founded 1656 by Wm. Adams for about eighty boys of that town. A free elementary sch. at Cripplegate, founded 1663 by Throgmorton Trotman, has been discontinued.

The sch. founded in Hoxton, 1692, by Robt. Aske, has been removed; the boys are at Cricklewood, the girls at New Cross. Singleton Manor at Great Chart, near Ashford, Kent, part of the estates administered for the Aske Charity, was sold. There used to be almshouses at Hoxton under the same foundation: but relief has been substituted. The Co. has spent £64,000 on the schools founded by Aske and has built day-schools at Hatcham for boys and girls. Altogether the Co. educates about three thousand children. It is trustee for fourteen exhibitions at the universities; and it maintains five scholarships and four exhibitions for those at the Monmouth sch. that go to the universities. There are almshouses for sixteen founded by Wm. Jones at Newland (Glos.): there are four almshouses at Newport (Salop). The Co. administers many funds for the benefit of poorer members, also some miscellaneous charities, e.g. Jeston's Gift to the poor of the Co. of Lambeth, and of Kinver (Staffs.); and Jones's preacherships.

No. of Livery, 310.

Innholders' (32). In 1327, Hostelers and Haymongers, apparently one body, were cited in a petition regarding the irregular sale of hay. In L. the practice of furnishing entertainment and sleeping accommodation for reward came earlier than elsewhere in the kingdom. In 1446 certain Hostelers of the City petitioned the Ld.M. for confirmation of ordinances.

In 1473, the warden and others of the mistery of Innholders represented that they had been theretofore improperly designated Hostelers, a word that signified their servants: since then the Hostler or Ostler has been the underling. In 1501 the Innholders possessed a Livery of sixteen by prescription. In 1515, among the forty-eight recognized misteries, Innholders were ranked between Plumbers and Founders. Application was made in 1509 for a charter, granted five years later. In 1757 the opinion of counsel, sought by the Co., was that the provisions in the charter purporting to control persons living in the City and within three miles of the City were not enforceable except in the City. Thenceforward the membership dwindled. However, under modern conditions, in which connection with the craft is not indispensable, the Co. has furnished some Ld.M.s and sheriffs.

Charter was granted by Henry VIII in 1515. A second charter was apparently granted by Charles II in 1663 or 1664—the official history of the Co. contains obscurities and incompatibilities; but James II in 1685 granted a charter, and there was restoration of the older charter or charters by the Act of Parliament of 1691.

Strype mentions a hall in Gutter Lane, a little to the S. of Goldsmiths' Hall; but the records of the Co. mention only one site—that on the S. side of Elbow Lane (i.e. College St., just E. of Little College St.) in Dowgate ward. The land came into possession of the Co. in 1613. The hall was burnt in the G.F. A new hall was completed by 1670: Wheatley states it was designed by Sir Christopher Wren and Jerman, but gives no authority. By 1882 it was dangerous; and it was restored, and partly rebuilt, under the management of J. Douglass Matthews. The plaster ceiling in the court-room, the wainscoting, the musicians' gallery, and other features, are taken from the older bdg. The hall suffered slightly during an air-raid in the First World War and more heavily from a rocket near by in the Second World War.

There are some interesting pictures, including three 'pyrographic' ones by Jeremiah Smith, dated 1801. A lead cistern dates from 1685. Of plate, the most notable article is the Anne Sweete salt (1635), built up like a steeple in three storeys. There are many other 17th-century salts; and of cups—the Grace Gwalter (1599), the Thos. Hinde (1654), the Nicholas Cooke (1654), the Edwd. Osborne (1658), and the Stockton (1682). There are two tankards: Thos. Charlett (1656), Wm. Pennington (1661). When the hall was damaged in 1941 these treasures were saved.

The most remarkable member appears to have been Wm. Jas. Chaplin (1787–1859)—a native of Rochester, son of a coach-proprietor: he succeeded the only less famous Wm. Waterhouse as proprietor of the 'Swan with Two Necks,' Lad Lane: he was also proprietor of the 'White Horse,' Fetter Lane; the 'Spread Eagle' and the 'Cross Keys,' Gracechurch St.; and the 'Spread Eagle West-End coaching-offices in Regent Circus.' In 1838 he owned sixty-eight coaches. He was M.P. for Salisbury 1847–57, and master of the Co. 1854–5.

There was a gift, 1639, by Mrs. Margaret Astill, for the preaching of a sermon—Ditchfield (1904) stated that no arrangement had been made about it for many yrs., and added: 'We trust it is not because the worshipful company dislikes sermons.' Benefactors of the poor of the Co., according to Ditchfield, were Thos. Bayley (1543), Thos. Hyne, Henry Scrambler (1845), and Richd. Bailey (1861). In 1946 the Prime Minister, Rt. Hon. C. R. Attlee, attended the hall to receive the freedom of the Co. His family has been connected with it through the firm of Druces and Attlee, solicitors, who have been clerks to the Co. for nearly 250 yrs.

No. of Livery, 104.

(See *History of the Worshipful Company of Innholders*, 1922.)

Ironmongers' (10). Regulations were made respecting the Ironmongers, although they were not mentioned as a gild, so early as in the reign of Edward I (1272–1307). The earliest account of the Ironmongers as a gild is in 1364. In 1377, the last yr. of Edward III's reign, four members were sent to the Common Council. The trade congregated in Ironmonger (or Isemonger) Lane, Cheapside, and their patron saints were St. Lawrence (whose ch. was close by until its almost entire destruction in 1940), and St. Eligius, Bishop of Noyon,

who died in 659. He is known in Latin as St. Eligius, and in English sometimes as St. Loo. According to legend, there was a horse that was possessed of the Devil, and would not stand still to be reshod. The owner took the horse to the saint, who cut off a leg, nailed the shoe on and then put the leg back on the stump. On his making the sign of the cross, the leg was miraculously reunited. The Co. were afterwards in the par. of St. Dunstan's-in-the-East. Their charter, apparently the only one, was granted by Edward IV in 1463.

There is no record of any hall until 1457; when, under the will of Alice Styward, they obtained the site on which their halls successively stood for about 460 yrs. It was on the N. side of Fenchurch St., at the corner of Fishmonger Alley, between that and Billiter St. In 1587 it was rebuilt. This second hall escaped the G.F. In 1694, it was let to one Thos. Hatfield for the holding of a lottery. The last hall on the site was erected 1750—not conspicuous externally, but richly decorated within: it had a drawing-room with Corinthian pillars; and it contained a statue of Beckford (see 'Guildhall') and the figurehead (an ostrich) of the Co.'s old barge. Early in the 20th century, rebuilding was proposed; but the 18th-century hall stood until the forenoon of Saturday, 7th July 1917, when it was utterly destroyed in the famous daylight bombing-raid by German aeroplanes.

While without a hall, the Co. was accommodated in Waxchandlers' Hall, Gresham St. A new site was chosen in Shaftesbury Pl., a cul-de-sac off the E. side of Aldersgate St. The ground hereabout was reclaimed from marsh, 1606–16, by an ironmonger—Nicholas Leat (thrice master), alderman, and enthusiast for gardening. The new hall was opened 17th June 1925. A tablet in the vestibule sets out its history. It is in Tudor style, Portland stone and thin hand-made red bricks, heavily timbered in the upper storeys. Inside, there is much carved English oak, giving the impression of a 16th-century house. The lofty banqueting-room has panelling to a height of about 10 ft., a buffet at one end and a minstrels' gallery (supported on oak pillars) at the other. There are many past masters' shields, a chandelier of Waterford glass that escaped the bombs, and Morris tapestry (in library). At the SE. corner of the bdg. there are cloisters and a fountain-court, overlooked by the lunch-room. The staircase is notable for its carving and its wide landing. There are arms and other devices on the windows. Outside are figures of the two patron saints. The hall sustained no noteworthy damage in the Second World War.

Notable members: Rowland Heylin (master), sheriff 1624, published the Bible in Welsh; Sir Jas. Cambell (thrice master), Ld.M. 1630 (pageant by Dekker), a governor of the East India Co.—a benefactor, as was also his lady; Izaak Walton, most notable of all Ironmongers; Sir Robt. Geffery (master), Ld.M. 1686, the president of Bethlehem and Bridewell Hosps., and benefactor (see *infra*); Wm. Beckford; Edwd. Pellew, Viscount Exmouth, an admiral—who, upon retirement from foreign service, was made free of the Co. 1816; Sir Edwin Durning-Lawrence, the Baconian.

The Co., unlike all other City Cos., has no court of assistants—it is governed by the whole Livery.

Most of its plate was sold long ago (especially in 1644) to pay contributions levied by Govt. The only noteworthy specimens that came down to recent times were a mazer, a pair of hour-glass saltcellars (16th century), and a mounted coco-nut called a hanap. There is an ancient chest of unknown date.

Of the charities, the most important is that of Thos. Betton; whose money is used mainly for education—since the redemption of Christian slaves, to which he devoted half his bequest, is no longer exigent. Sir Robt. Geffery (see *supra*) gave an annuity to the sch. at Bishop's Stortford, and a sum toward founding free schs. at Landrake and South Erny (Cornwall): his donation goes toward maintenance of almshouses in the Kingsland Rd., otherwise supported by the Co.: the Landrake sch. was rebuilt 1877, and accommodates 150 children. Minor charities include those of Thos. Lewen (1555), bequest formerly devoted to the upkeep of four almsmen in premises on Bread St. Hill, burnt in the G.F.; the rebuilding was in Old St., outside the City, where they were burnt in 1785 and once rebuilt —the charity now maintains a scholarship at either of the two old universities; two similar scholarships are maintained out of other bequests. Other charities are: Chapman's, Margaret Dane's, Hallwood's, Handson's, Westwood's, and Wild's.

No. of Livery, 40.

(See *Some Account of the Ironmongers' Company*, by John Nicholls, Second Edition, 1886.)

Leathersellers' (15). The Leathersellers were probably an offshoot of the White Tawyers, who made white leather by treating skins with alum and salt, and who had by-laws made for their craft in 1346. As a distinct fellowship, the Leathersellers, who were manufacturers to some extent, first made their appearance in 1372: in which yr. they elected two members of the Common Council, and petitioned for regulations to prevent frauds. Ordinances were made in 1398, 1438–9, and 1443—the yr. before incorporation. Within a few months of the latter event the Co. came into possession of the first parcel of its London Wall property: the rest of which came to it on the death of Robt. Ferbras, by his two wills, on his death in 1473. In 1502 the Glovers-Pursers were incorporated with the Leathersellers, who then transferred themselves from the patronage of St. Mary Magdalen's chapel at Guildhall to that of the Virgin at St. Thomas of Acon (site of Mercers' chapel). At the coronation of Henry VIII the Co. was reckoned eighteenth; by 1515 it had attained fifteenth place. In 1517 the Pouchmakers, who made almost everything in the way of bags and trunks, joined the Co. In 1591 there was a dispute over a monopoly for the searching and sealing of leather, granted by Q. Elizabeth to Edwd. Darcie, culminating in assault and battery by Darcie upon an alderman: the matter was not settled till 1595. In 1604 there was statutory confirmation of the right of search in Southwark Market and Bartholomew Fair—this continued till 1679. When the Co. was in low water about 1620 there was discussion of a project for another monopoly. Through its fortunate acquisition of land in the City and elsewhere, the Co. became very wealthy. It long used its wealth for encouragement of the craft by means of education —giving largely to the City and Guilds of London Institute, and supporting the National Leatherseller's College.

Charters, the originals of which are

still in existence, were granted by Henry VI in 1444 and by James I in 1604. (Q. Elizabeth granted, in 1559, an inspeximus that somewhat belied its name by reciting the first charter as of Henry VII.) Charles II had these charters surrendered, and issued one of his own in 1685. The former charter was restored in 1689.

The first hall was at London Wall, in the E. part of the Co.'s estate there, at a place for centuries afterwards called Leathersellers Bdgs.—now covered by the N. end of Copthall Av. It was all upstairs: the lower part probably let. In 1543 the Co. acquired the St. Helen's estate in Bishopsgate, and occupied the bdgs. of the dissolved priory of Benedictine nuns. Immediately S. of St. Ethelburga's Ch. there used to be a narrow entry, leading into a close called Little St. Helen's. On the S. side of this close, backing upon the ch. of Great St. Helen's, stood the priory that was Leathersellers' Hall for two centuries and a half—with its refectory, capacious vaults, and dormitories; and adjoining it on E. and NE. were the garden and dovecot, let to tenants. To its lasting shame, the court of the Co. in 1797 passed a resolution in accordance with which every fragment, even of the cellarage, was swept away in 1799, with the 'curious antient pump' made by Caius Gabriel Cibber. The excellent pictures in Wm. Henry Black's history of the Co. (1881) show what the hall was like, inside and out. The Co. migrated to an old house at the E. end of Little St. Helen's, where it was burnt out in 1819. It was accommodated at Brewers' Hall pending the erection of a new hall in St. Helen's Pl., which had by then superseded Little St. Helen's; it was apparently on the site of the one lately burnt; was designed by Wm. Fuller Pocock, and was opened Jan. 1822—a Leathersellers' Song by Geo. Tomkins being sung by him on the occasion. In 1878 a fourth hall was erected 'immediately opposite'—i.e. to the W.: the third being used as offices.

The old charters, and caps of state given in 1539, seem to be the Co.'s chief remaining treasures.

This hall was almost destroyed by bombs in 1941 and rebuilt in 1960. The charters and plate were saved.

Secular and theological exhibitions tenable at Oxford and Cambridge and theological exhibitions at L. University, have been established. There are almshouses at Barnet and in Lewisham High St.

No. of Livery, 147.

(See *History and Antiquities of the Worshipful Company of Leathersellers*, 1881.)

Mercers' (1). Though by etymology, mercer means simply a merchant, a mercer is one who deals in textile fabrics—especially in silks, velvets and other costly materials. For a long time mercer meant a dealer in small ware, 'the stock of a general country shopkeeper.' The silk trade, which in later yrs. was the chief element in mercers' business, was, so late as the time of Henry VI, carried on by 'the silkwomen and throwsters.' The Mercers were a gild by 1172. In Henry II's time their station was the neighbourhood of Mercers' Hall of to-day. Gilbert à Becket, father of St. Thomas so surnamed, was a Mercer, with a shop on the site of the hall—N. of Cheapside and E. of Ironmonger Lane. Somewhat later the Mercers removed to the S. side of Cheapside, between Bow Ch. and Friday St., giving that locality the name of the Mercery. Here they sold their mixed wares at little stalls. In 1351, violent assaults were made on certain Lombard competitors by Mercers of Old Jewry. The Sumptuary Act, 37 Edward III (1363), proves the Mercers to have then sold woollen cloth but not silk. By the reign (1422–61) of Henry VI the Mercers had become extensive dealers in silks and velvets, and had resigned their trade in small articles of dress to the Haberdashers. They built themselves fine houses in the Mercery, four and five storeys high, and encroaching on the roadway—Cheapside is narrower than in the Middle Ages. Kings came heavily upon them for war-contributions. Their Co. spent £4,000 in buying back property taken from it by Henry VIII. It was hard hit by the G.F.; and a grandiose scheme for raising money from clergymen on an engagement to pay pensions to their widows, landed it in bankruptcy, 1745–7. By an Act of 4 George III it was enabled to regain solvency by means of a lottery.

Although it holds first place among the Cos., the Mercers' Co. stands only fourth in order of incorporation. This was effected for it by letters patent of Richard II in 1393 (the document is lost). In the twentieth year of Richard II (1396) it received additional privileges. An inspeximus charter was granted 1424-5 by Henry VI at the request of Whittington's executors: in 1461 (1 Edward IV) an Act was passed confirming this among other charters granted by Lancastrian kings. Elizabeth granted a charter in the second year of her reign. Charles II, after receiving surrenders of the old charters in 1684, granted another: confirmed in 1685.

The ground round about where the hall stood, from Ironmonger Lane to Old Jewry, and from Cheapside to St. Olave's Alley (Church Court), was covered, at the beginning of the 13th century, by the coll. and hosp. of St. Thomas of Acon (see 'Cheapside'). In 1413-14 the Co. hired or borrowed from the master of St. Thomas's 'a small room which at once served as an office and a chapel.' It probably owed this accommodation to Gilbert à Becket's having been father of Agnes, wife of Thos. Fitzthebald, who with her founded the institution. A new hall was built, slowly, 1517-52. On the suppression of the coll. in 1538, the Co. purchased the whole site and the bdgs. (including the conventual ch., chapter-house, etc., and the ch. and advowson of St. Mary Colechurch). The hall was burnt in the G.F. The Co. took refuge in Gresham Coll. until the last hall was built, 1672. It was said to have been designed by Wren. An ornate front in Cheapside—later in construction, and subject of much artistic dispute—was superseded by a plainer one in 1879. The old front is now part of the façade of the Swanage town hall. The hall was supported by Doric columns. Adjoining was a chapel, neatly pewed and wainscoted, and ornamented with ionic pilasters and much fine carving. It was the only chapel owned by a City company. Both chapel and hall were destroyed by bombs in 1941 but have been rebuilt.

The Mercers' first Ld.M. was Robt. Searle, 1214 and 1217-22. Richd. Whittington has been the most famous member. Sir Geoffry Bullen, Ld.M. 1457, was great-grandfather of the Q. commonly called Anne Boleyn. Sir Henry Colet, twice Ld.M. (see 'Schools'), rebuilt the cross in Cheapside. Sir Hugh Clopton, Ld.M. 1492, was b. near Stratford-on-Avon, and owned the property in that town afterwards called New Pl. where

Wm. Shakespeare died. Sir Ralph Warren (master 1530 and 1542), Mayor 1536 and 1544, took over the conventual property in trust for the Co., was mayor of the staple at Westminster, occupied important judicial positions, and had a country-house at Bethnal Green. Sir Richd. Gresham (master 1533, 1539 and 1549), Ld.M. 1537, a friend of Wolsey, was father of another noted Mercer—Sir Thos. Gresham. Sir John Gresham, Ld.M. 1547, was a younger brother of Sir Richd.'s, and his famous nephew Sir Thos. was his apprentice. Sir Rowland Hill (four times master), Ld.M. 1549, was the first Protestant to be elected Ld.M. Sir Baptist Hicks, who became first Viscount Campden, was a Mercer and a moneylender—made baronet 1620, M.P. once for Tavistock, and four times for Tewkesbury, built Hicks's Hall (see 'Clerkenwell'). Royalty has of late been admitted to honorary membership. Richard II and Q. Elizabeth I received the freedom of the Co.

In 1542 a member was dismissed from the Livery for refusing to be shaved; and in 1545 certain freemen were not called on the Livery because they 'obstinately and frowardly persisted in wearing beards.' The Mercers' Song, which begins with an allusion to the Virgin on their crest, claims that among the trades they are 'first in time and place'—a manifest impossibility.

There is a great collection of plate, including a silver-gilt wagon and tun, weighing 64 oz., which moves along the table by clockwork—it was given by Wm. Burde during his wardenship in 1573; Wm. Hurt's loving-cup, 1673; two loving-cups given by the Bank of England in 1694 as an acknowledgment for the Bank's use of the hall; two flagons given for a similar reason, 1702, by the East India Co.; two monteiths with lion handles given by W. Sydenham, 1699; loving-cup and two salts belonging to Trinity Hosp., Greenwich—one of the Co.'s trusts. The plate and portraits have survived.

Many charities are administered by the Co. The oldest is Richd. Whittington's almshouses (see 'Highgate'). St. Paul's Sch. (q.v.) was founded 1509 by Dean Colet. Mercers' Grammar Sch., dating formally from 1542, is really a continuation of the sch. attached to the hosp. of St. Thomas of Acon: at first it was held in the chapel or in the ch. of St. Mary Colechurch; after the G.F. its house was built on the W. side of Old Jewry; in 1787 it moved to 13 Budge Row; in 1804 to 20 Red Lion Court, Watling St.; in 1808 to 20 College Hill (on the site vacated by Whittington's Coll.), which was rebuilt for it in 1832; and thence, in 1894, it removed to Barnard's Inn, Holborn (*q.v.*) which it left in 1959. Henry, E. of Northampton, in 1613, founded Trinity Hosp., Greenwich—a 'college' for the maintenance of 'decayed housekeepers' of Greenwich and of Shottesham (Norfolk). Richd. Fishbo(u)rne, 1625, left money for lectures in various places, and to maintain Huntingdon Grammar Sch. Lady Mico, 1670, founded almshouses at Stepney chyd. Besides, there are charities—for the poor of various grades—Banck's (1619), Bennett's (1616), Chertsey's (1555), Walthall's (for poor scholars), Morley's; for exhibitions—Barrett's (1584), Lady North's (1574), Robinson's (1618). The Co. has founded charities of its own. No. of Livery, 194.

Merchant Taylors' (6 and 7). The first notice taken of L. Taylors in a corporate capacity is connected with a fatal riot with the Goldsmiths in 1267. The first licence is stated by Stow to have been granted 28 Edward I—they were 'Taylors and Linen Armourers.' The first charter is dated 1 Edward III—confirmed 14 Richard II, 2 & 9 Henry IV (they were called 'Scissors' by then), 18 Henry VI, and 5 Edward IV. The present 'acting' charter, giving the name 'Merchant Taylors,' is dated 18 Henry VII—confirmed, by inspeximus, by Henry VIII, Philip and Mary, Elizabeth, and James I. These all remain.

The first hall was 'at the back side of the "Red Lion" in Basing Lane'—a thoroughfare extending from Bow Lane to Bread St., over ground now covered by Cannon St. In 1331 was acquired the present site in Threadneedle St.: it was purchased from Sir Oliver de Ingham for the Co. by Edmund Crepin. The Oteswich or Outwich family granted additional land and the advowson of St. Martin Outwich Ch. (see 'City Churches; B'). The Ingham hall was adorned with tapestry depicting the history of John the Baptist, the Co.'s patron saint—it had a garden and terrace at rear. Much of it was destroyed in the G.F.; restoration

(conducted by Jerman, who carefully followed the original design) was completed by 1671: new bdgs. were added, and there was much restoration, but it retains a crypt of 1375 and a kitchen dating from 1425, with an ancient spit. The hall proper was the largest Co. hall in L., 82 ft. by 43 ft. by 43 ft., 'an accurate representation of one of the 14th century' (Clode's *Early History* of the Co.). There was severe damage by enemy action; it has since been rebuilt.

Notable members: Sir Wm. Fitzwilliam (master), sheriff 1506, obtained new charter for Co., chamberlain to Wolsey and his friend after disgrace; Sir Thos. White, Ld.M. 1553, founder of St. John's Coll. (Oxford), and one of the founders of Merchant Taylor's Sch.; Richd. Hilles (master), principal founder of Merchant Taylors' Sch. (1561), early suffered persecution for Protestantism; Sir Thos. Offley (master), Ld.M. 1556, originated night-bellmen; Sir Wm. Harper (master), Ld.M. 1561, helped to found Merchant Taylors' Sch., founded sch. at Bedford; Sir Wm. Craven (warden), Ld.M. 1610, founded sch. at Burnsall (Yorks.), president Christ's Hosp.; Sir Abraham Reynardson (master), Ld.M. 1648—deposed and fined for royalism; Sir Patience Ward (master), Ld.M. 1680, supposed author of the anti-papal inscription (assailed by Pope), formerly on the Monument, fled the kingdom on conviction for perjury in Pilkington case (see 'Companies'—Skinners'), a City member of the Convention to meet William of Orange; Sir Wm. Pritchard, Ld.M. 1682, court favourite, M.P. for the City 1702.

Many fine portraits used to hang in the hall, but some were destroyed by enemy action. The plate includes a 16th-century silver basin, and a salver and an Irish tankard of the 17th century; the silver badge of the old barge-master is mounted on an oak snuff-box. The Company possesses two Italian hearsecloths of the early part of the 16th century.

Since the reign of James I the Co. has had no craft functions. Merchant Taylors' Sch. (see 'Schools') is no longer in L.

The Co. also founded a sch. at Great Crosby, near Liverpool, in 1618, rebuilt 1878: a girls' sch. has been added. It built a new elementary sch. at Ashwell (Herts.) in 1875. Many closed scholarships at the universities are open to Merchant

Taylors' schoolboys and the Co. contributes to the City & Guilds of London Institute. It has built chs. in the East End, and restored St. Helen's, Bishopsgate—its par. ch. since the demolition of St. Martin Outwich. It maintains a convalescent home at Bognor. Its almshouses, formerly on Tower Hill, are at Lee (Lewisham).

There was a dispute as to the order of precedence of this Co. and accordingly, with the Skinners' Co., it is in alternate years 6 and 7.

No. of Livery, 350.

Painter-Stainers' (28). It is believed that the art of the Stainer was that of producing, on plain woven fabrics, both coloured and figure subjects in imitation of tapestry; and probably actual painting on canvas were included as stained cloth. Painting meant primarily painting on wood: painting on cloth is supposed to have been an English invention. In 1466 an important set of ordinances was granted to the Painters. In 1469 the Painters contributed twenty men to the City watch; the Stainers, fourteen. A grant of arms was made in 1486. In 1500 occurred the union of the Painters and Stainers: in the words of their joint petition to the C.C., they were 'knyt joyned and unyd to giders.' The united gild was twenty-ninth in 1515; thirty-ninth in 1532. In 1575 it petitioned Q. Elizabeth, complaining of the practice of painting by persons that had never been apprentices; and the result was incorporation six years later. By this time portraiture and landscape were important branches of the craft, and a particular grievance against the unauthorized was concerned with alleged portraits of the queen. The Co. was sometimes called upon by the Crown to assess the value of work done. A statute, 1 James I, c. 4, allowing the Plaisterers to lay six colours with size only, was the beginning of a long dispute. Pepys, 23rd Apr. 1669, records his listening to a cause in the council-chamber at Whitehall, wherein Sir Philip Howard and one Watson claimed to be inventors of 'varnishing and lackerworke' as against the Painters' Co.—it is not clear from Pepys's account which way the decision went, but from the Co.'s books it seems that it lost. The right of search was abandoned about the beginning of the 18th century. Several times in the 17th century, and again in 1738, the Co. was

in dispute with the Heralds' Office as to the right to paint arms: the Co. was finally victorious. In 1766 it obtained an Act of Common Council compelling all that carried on the trade of painting and applied for the freedom of the City to take up the freedom of the Co. In 1769 it established a labour exchange for the house-painting trade at 2 Ironmonger Lane. About 1775 there was lively renewal of action against Plaisterers who were stretching the Act of James I. Rates of wages for journeymen were revised in 1799, and orders given for enforcing the new Act against workmen's combinations. Further revisions took place in 1836 and 1851. A period of litigation against persons practising the craft in the City without taking up the freedom began Aug. 1823. A decision was given against the Co. in this matter in 1829; and, though litigation did not immediately cease, it began to slacken. From 1875 there have been annual awards of medals to students in specified schs. In 1880 Geo. Mence Smith instituted a travelling studentship: other studentships have followed. In 1893 a conference of painters and decorators at the Co.'s hall resulted in the establishment of a technical class at the Carpenters' premises in Great Titchfield St. The Institute of British Decorators, incorporated 1899, was inaugurated at the Co.'s hall.

Charter was granted by Q. Elizabeth in 1581: it was surrendered to Charles II; and in 1685 James II granted a new charter conferring powers in L. and Westminster and six miles round. Although the statute 2 William and Mary, c. 8, nullified the surrender, it is on the charter of James II that most of the routine of the Co. is based.

Sir John Browne, serjeant-painter to Henry VIII, and alderman of Farringdon Without (1523) and Within (1524), d. 1532, and left to his brother Painter-Stainers his house on the W. side of Little Trinity Lane in Queenhithe ward. This became Painter-Stainers' Hall. It was ornate. John Evelyn in his *Diary* states that a commission for supporting the sick and wounded in the war had permission to meet there: under date 16th Nov. 1665 he notes some good pictures in it. After its destruction in the G.F. (just before which Charles II is reported to have rested in it after viewing the approaching conflagration) a new hall was ready by 1670—though additions and improvements continued to be made. In 1682 it was insured against fire. Extensive repairs were carried out 1776–7. A new wing was built 1880. The Little Trinity Lane front was reconstructed, and new bdgs. were erected on the adjoining site— 5, 6, and 8, in the lane, in 1914–16. The hall was destroyed by bombs in 1941 but was rebuilt in 1961.

No other Co. has had more distinguished members. A few of the names: Sampson Camden, father of the historian; Sir John Browne, before-mentioned; Richd. Lovelace, the soldier-poet; Thos. Rawlins (1620?–70), graver of the Mint; Sir Peter Lely; Sylvanus Morgan (master 1676), arms-painter and author; Antonio Verrio (1639?–1707), decorator of Windsor Castle and Hampton Court; Sir Godfrey Kneller; Sir Jas. Thornhill (master 1720); Peter Monamy (1670?–1749), marine-painter, and decorator of Vauxhall; Chas. Catton the elder (upper warden, 1782), who painted coaches and landscapes; Geo. Mence Smith (master 1893), before-mentioned, oilman, pioneer of the 'multiple-shop' method of retail.

There are the following among other portraits: Wm. Camden, presented by Sylvanus Morgan; Charles II, painted by Jan Baptist Gaspars. There are several 17th-century cups—the largest, with a cover, bought with a bequest of Wm. Camden, 1623; others—the Fryer, 1605; the Willingham, 1645; the Monke, 1650. The Beeston salt, with a steeple cover, is of 1614. There are twelve small salts or wine-cups of quatrefoil shape, 1662; six flat-handled spoons with trefoil ends, made 1686; large tankard and cover, with Chinese figures, made 1685; pair of tankards with domed tops, 1687; Thornhill loving-cup and cover, gift of Sir Jas. when master. The portraits and plate have survived.

John Stock, who had previously benefited the Co., d. 1781, leaving about £55,000 to this Co. and the Drapers', in trust for blind and distressed people; and the Painter-Stainers' Co., administers the whole. This is supplemented by bequests of Jane Shank, Mrs. Dorothy Smith and Mrs. Anne Yeates—all in the 1790s, and of Mrs. Mary Grainger (£1,000) in 1806, in which yr. John Fairchild left £1,000 for the Co.'s poor.

No. of Livery, 270.

Parish Clerks'. According to Stow, the Clerks' 'Fraternity of St. Nicholas' was registered in the books of the Guildhall in 1233. They were originally a kind of inferior clergy; upon whom, however, the rule of celibacy was not imposed. A Clerk's duties included leading the choir, accompanying the priest on visits to the sick, attending to certain subordinate parts of ch. routine (especially in pre-Reformation days), and sometimes the care and ringing of the bells. In L., from the reign of Henry VIII, the Parish Clerks prepared the Bills of Mortality until 1859, although in 1836 the central government established public registration of deaths. Ditchfield remarks that the only civil right retained by the Parish Clerks is that the prospectors of new railways are obliged to deposit their plans and maps with him, and that—so little is known of this right, or even of parish clerkship— a postman outraged the feelings of one holder of the office by delivering some such plans to the clerk of the par. council.

Charter was granted by Henry VI in 1442. This was surrendered and superseded by a new charter of the same K., in 1449. On petition, another charter was granted by Edward IV in 1475; so as to relieve the Co., which was poor, of some of its expensive obligations. A statute against fraternities passed in the reign of Edward VI raised a continuing doubt whether the Co. were still incorporated. James I accordingly granted a charter in 1611–12. This being soon found insufficient, another charter was granted by Charles I in 1636. Still unsatisfied, the Clerks obtained their last charter in 1640: it extended their jurisdiction over Westminster, Southwark, and fifteen out-parishes, besides nine out-parishes already included: that is to say, over the 'Bills of Mortality' area. It would appear that this last charter was not interfered with by the *Quo Warranto* of 1684—at any rate since 1688 it has been valid.

In 1274 the Clerks, then unincorporated, acquired, through their trustees, certain lands in the par. of St. Ethelburga (Bishopsgate). Further lands in that neighbourhood were acquired during two centuries following. The Wrestlers Inn was on the property; and Wrestlers Court (off Camomile St.) and Clark's Place (Bishopsgate) commemorate the old associations. The entry from Bishopsgate St. led first to the Co.'s almshouses, and beyond them to the hall. As a place devoted to superstitious uses, the whole of the Clerks' enclosure was seized in 1548 and sold to Sir Robt. Chester. Litigation went against the Clerks; and, when the accession of Q. Mary promised them better fortune, Chester pulled down the bdgs. and sold the materials and the land. In 1562 the Co. were occupying a hall at the NW. corner of Brode Lane (i.e. Queen St.), Vintry: this was burnt in the G.F. A new hall was built 1669–71; W. of Wood St. and S. of Silver St. In 1765 it was seriously damaged by fire. It was subsequently enlarged and repaired. Entrance was transferred from Wood St. to Silver St. in 1848. The hall—of which there is a painting in the C.C. Art Gallery, has been destroyed by bombs, and some treasures lost, including a snuff-box made from the wood of Nelson's ship the *Victory*.

It is not a livery co. No. of members 53. (See *Some Account of Parish Clerks*, by James Christie, 1893.)

Saddlers' (25). As a traveller's journeying about England, in medieval times, depended entirely on his own feet or his horse's, it is natural to find that the important business of saddling was early organized. The district called the Saddlery in L. was under the eastern boundary-wall of the ch. of St. Martin le Grand —that is, in and about Foster Lane. Discoveries made in the area as a result of bombing confirmed an early settlement of saddlers here. There is, in possession of the chapter of Westminster, a parchment agreement as to masses, etc., between the convent and the gild of Saddlers: undated, but probably made about 1154— not later than 1216: and, from its language, it seems very likely that the Saddlers' gild was then an ancient body, dating from Saxon times. It is not enumerated among the adulterine gilds in the list of 1180. A charter was granted by Edward I in 1272; not to the L. gild specially, but to the general body of Saddlers throughout the kingdom, giving them authority to appoint two of their number in every town to oversee the craft. This instrument was renewed by Edward III in 1364, by Henry VI in 1424, by Henry VII in 1495, and by Henry VIII in 1540; so its provisions were

long concurrent with those of the L. Saddlers' charter. There is a record of ordinances made 1309, not now extant. In 1327 there was a bloody affray in Cheapside, between the Saddlers on one side and the Joiners and Painters and Loriners on the other. The earliest ordinances known are dated 1365. The Saddlers addressed the Crown directly, as spokesmen for the citizens oppressed by Sir Nicholas Brembre. The charter of 1394–5 indicates that the gild had then many aged and indigent members.

The right of search came with the charter of 1558. In 1607 it was ordered that certain long-haired apprentices be 'polled close.' In 1608 the government of the Co. was turned into an oligarchy by new ordinances vesting all power in the wardens and assistants. The Co. opposed the introduction of coaches, 1620. Frederick, P. of Wales, was master 1737–51. A search (in Holborn) was carried out, and worthless saddles were destroyed, so late as 1822. In 1873–4 an exhibition was held in the hall. In 1882, twenty-two members were in the Saddlers' trade in the City.

The first charter to the Saddlers of L. as a separate body was granted by Richard II in 1394–5. It was confirmed in 1446 by Henry VI. An inspeximus was granted by Edward IV in 1463. Another charter was granted by Elizabeth in 1558: by it, it would appear, the national organization was merged. An inspeximus was granted by James I in 1607. The charter was surrendered in 1684, and a limited one substituted by Charles II. The surrender was cancelled in 1688.

The hall stood, as all Saddlers' halls have, in the old Saddlery district, abutting on the S. of St. Vedast's Ch., with entrances from Foster Lane and from Cheapside. In 1393 Wm. de Lincoln, Saddler, bequeathed ten marks toward a common hall on condition that it was built within three years. The next news of a hall is in 1545, when Anne Askew underwent her first examination in it. It was used for meetings of the commissioners collecting funds for the relief of inhabitants of the town of Marlborough, after the fire of 1653. It was itself destroyed in the G.F. By 1670 it was rebuilt; and, the Co. being impoverished, it was frequently let—but not to conventicles or dancing-masters. From 1721 it was often let for funeral ceremonies. It was 'at the upper end of an handsome alley,' apparently (see Strype's map) from Cheapside. It was injured in 1815, and totally destroyed in 1821, by fire. The furniture, wine, plate, and (to some extent) painted glass, were saved. The hall, which was destroyed in the Blitz and was replaced by the present Hall in Gutter Lane nearby, was erected in 1822. The plate and some of their other treasures have survived.

Among the members' were: Francis Dashwood (d. 1683), who was a rich Turkey merchant (master 1653), father of Sir Francis Dashwood (1st Bart.), and grandfather of Ld. le Despencer; Sir Peter Rich (master 1678 and 1680), a court favourite, with whom the popular party in the City had frequent collisions; and Sir Peter Laurie (see 'Bridewell'). The late E. of Halsbury, so long Ld. Chancellor, was master; so was Mr. Justice Travers Humphreys. In 1906 the D. of Connaught was made master for life.

The Co. used to attend St. Vedast's Ch. in state every July.

There were portraits of Frederick, P. of Wales; of Q. Anne; of Pitt (by Romney); and of Sir Peter Laurie. They were destroyed as were most of the Company's records both ancient and modern. The plate, which has survived, includes: coco-nut cup, bequeathed 1627 by Robt. Labourne; two-handled cup, presented 1681 by (Sir) Peter Rich; silver-gilt standing-cup, presented 1654 by Francis Dashwood; another, presented 1662 by Wm. Fisher; three 17th-century tankards; silver ewer and basin, same period; two monteiths, 1699 and 1720; various old salts and candlesticks and ladles. There are also, according to Hazlitt, 'an ancient treasure-chest of Flemish workmanship, with a most elaborate lock, a ballot-box or *cadet*, which was once used for elections, and a MS. copy of the Gospels, on which the officers of the Co. are still sworn.' But the most ancient treasure is a gorgeous funeral pall, dating from the beginning of the 16th century.

Pensions and gifts to poor amount to more than £2,000 a yr. Young (a Christian name, not an adjective) Geo. Honnor (master 1765) founded a trust for relief of decayed members; from a portion of the fund the Co.'s almshouses at Spring Grove, Isleworth, were built in 1859. The charities were not much affected by the Company's losses through enemy action.

No. of Livery, 85.

(See *History of the Guild of Saddlers*, by J. W. Sherwell, 1937.)

Salters' (9). The Salters were those that salted provisions—especially fish ; and the motto of the Co. is 'Salt savours everything.' There were brethren and sisters in the fraternity (established in the par. of All Hallows, Bread St.) when it was incorporated in the reign of Edward III. About 1364 liberties were granted to the salters of L. and elsewhere: a yr. later, protection was granted to those of L. There was confirmation, and grant of livery, in 1394. Confirming charters were granted: 3 and 24 Henry VI; 3 Edward IV; 1 Elizabeth; and one by James I. The last-mentioned, dated 1608, is the only one now remaining.

The first hall, in Bread St., was erected about the middle of the 15th century; and there were six 'mansions' (almshouses) adjoining. The site, on which the hall had already been built, was in 1451 bequeathed to the Co. by Thos. Beamond. This first hall was so much damaged by fire in 1553 and 1559 that rebuilding was necessary. The second hall, so built, was completely burnt in 1598. The Co. appears to have remained without a hall until 1641; when it took the 'town inn' or mansion of the priors of Tortington—otherwise 'the great house, called London Stone or Oxford House' (after the E. of Oxford)—adjoining the W. end of the ch. of St. Swithun, London Stone. This old house went in the G.F. The fourth hall, which succeeded, was 'a small structure of brick, the entrance opening within an arcade of three arches, springing from square pillars, fluted.' There was a large garden adjoining; and next to it was Salters' Hall Meeting-House, rented of the Co. by dissenters. The hall and the meeting-house and the clerk's house were demolished after about 150 yrs.' use, and the material sold, 1821. The last hall, the fifth, designed by Henry Carr, was built 1823–7 on the same site: its entrance was one of the most pleasing of the Co.'s hall-fronts in the City; the four Ionic columns of the porch made it particularly imposing. The interior of the hall was fine, and adorned with portraits—two of them reputed to be by Reynolds. There was also a portrait of Charles I purchased in 1634. These were saved when the hall was practically destroyed in 1941. The columns and part of the façade which remained were demolished in 1950. The fine wrought-iron gateway, erected in 1887, was removed. An odd survival was the stone figure of 'the maid'—representing her scrubbing.

The industry has lost its importance, and the Salters' Co. now has nothing to do with it. A prominent salter was Sir Robt. Nicholas Fowler, Bart., M.P. for the City 1880–91, d. 1891: he was Ld.M. 1884 and 1885—twice in succession, through the death of Ld. M. Nottage (see 'St. Paul's Cathedral'). At one time a service was held in St. Magnus's Ch. in memory of John Salter (d. 1605). Pursuant to his will it took the form of a procession to his tomb upon which each person knocked with a stick and said three times, with a loud voice: 'How do you do, Brother Salter? I hope you are well.' Sir Ambrose Nicholas, a salter who was Ld.M. in 1576, founded almshouses on the E. side of Monkwell St. These were destroyed in the G.F.; after which, since rebuilding, the charity has been supported out of the Co.'s funds; and in 1863 the inmates (18) were removed to new premises at Watford, costing £11,000 and more. Money is also given for persons in distress. The Co. was at one time possessor of the advowson of St. Swithun's. One 17th-century bequest is of £30 a yr. to support a lectureship in the ch. of St. Mary-at-Hill. £40, formerly added by the Co. to this bequest, is now given to a scholarship at St. Paul's Choir Sch. The Co. pays towards bdg. and restoring chs. in England, and has built chs. and chapels (a R.C. chapel at Magherafelt) on its estates in Ireland—spending over £9,000. Wm. Robson, in 1633, bequeathed £5,000: out of which many purposes are served, including two scholarships at St. John's Coll. (Camb.). Jas. Smith, in 1661, founded 'an almshouse' at Maidenhead; and his bequest for the maintenance is liberally supplemented by the Co.

No. of Livery, 150.

Skinners' (6–7). The Skinners traded in furred pelts. They had a hall in the reign of Henry III. Their first charter, however, is dated 1 Edward III (1327). Other charters: 16 Richard II, 16 Henry VII, 4 & 5 Philip and Mary, 2 Elizabeth (a mere inspeximus), and finally the 'acting' charter of 4 James I—an abortive charter of the previous year having contained democratic provisions that the Co. would not accept.

Notable members: Sir Thos. Legge, Ld.M. 1348–55; Sir Henry Barton, Ld.M. 1417–29, who ordained lanterns to be hung out on evenings between Allhallows and Candlemas; Sir John Champneys, Ld.M. 1534; Sir Andrew Judd, Ld.M. 1551, a great traveller, and founder of Tonbridge Sch.—endowed with lands in St. Pancras, where Judd St. is named after him (see 'City Churches; C'—St. Helen, Bishopsgate); Sir Wolstan Dixie, Ld.M. 1585 (his pageant written by Geo. Peele), president and benefactor of Christ's Hosp., benefactor of Emmanuel Coll. (Camb.) and Market Bosworth Sch.; Sir Richd. Saltonstall (master), Ld.M. 1597, governor of Merchant Adventurers' Co.; Sir Thos. Smythe, sheriff 1601, and suspected of implication in the E. of Essex's raid into the City; Sir Wm. Cokayne, governor of the Ulster colonists 1612, Ld.M. 1619; Sir Robt. Tichborne, regicide, Ld.M. 1656 d. a prisoner in the Tower; Sir. Thos Pilkington, imprisoned 1682–6 for *scandalum magnatum* against the D. of York, M.P. for the City 1689, Ld.M. 1689–91; Sir Humphrey Edwin, master of the Barber-Surgeons' Co., cashiered from military appointments for nonconformity, Ld.M. 1697.

The first hall, called Copped Hall, stood on or near the site of the present one, which has frontages on College St. and Dowgate Hill. There were two branch establishments—one in St. Mary Axe, the other in St. Mary Spital (Bishopsgate Without). Copped Hall was destroyed in the G.F., but the valuable contents had been removed in time. The present hall was built 1668–9. A new front was added 1791. Fittings and decorations were partially altered 1847–8. There is a fine old staircase.

The hall survived the Second World War (it is panelled with paintings by Sir Frank Brangwyn, R.A.), but the oak parlour and clerk's room were damaged. There is a bell in the entrance hall which is said to date from the 12th century.

The Co. formerly had the chantry of Corpus Christi annexed to the ch. of St. Mildred, Poultry. On Corpus Christi Day each year the members march from the hall to the ch. of St. Mary Aldermary to hear a sermon—formerly torchlights were carried; bouquets have replaced torches and the procession includes boys from Christ's Hosp. On the same day the master is elected—by trying the fit of the master's cap on several at the hall: it never fits anybody but the senior warden!

The Co.'s plate includes five silver-gilt loving-cups in the forms of cocks, of which the heads must be removed for the purpose of drinking. They were bequeathed by Wm. Cokayne, 1598. There are several other cups formed like birds, and a snuff-box in the form of a leopard—the dexter supporter on the Co.'s arms.

The Co. has no craft-functions. Its most important charity is the grammar sch., founded by Judde in his native Tonbridge in 1553, and by his will entrusted to the Co.: it has nearly 400 scholars. In 1888 this sch. was supplemented by a commercial sch., which has more than 100 boys. The Co. has founded scholarships and exhibitions, at the universities, at King's College Sch., at the Central Foundation Sch. (Cowper St.), and the City of London Sch., at Girton Coll. (Camb.), and at Alexandra Coll. (Dublin). It liberally supports the City and Guilds of London Institute and other Schs. In 1887 it opened a sch. for boys at Tunbridge Wells, in 1890 a girls' sch. at Stamford Hill. It helps to support poor clergymen. Its almshouses are, since 1894, at Palmer's Green.

No. of Livery, 265.

Stationers' and Newspaper Makers' (47). A stationer was, according to some, a bookseller that was not itinerant (as most booksellers were of old), but had a station or shop: it is most probable, however, that the name was popularly transferred to dealers in writings and writing-materials from the *stationarii*, appointed by the universities as keepers of their stations or depots of standard texts. In 1403 the C.C. allowed an ordinance 'of the Writers of Text-Letter, Limners, and others, who bind and sell books'; whereby two wardens were appointed—one for the Limners and one for the Text-Writers. The Limners are taken to have been those that drew initials and marginal decorations. At some unknown early date, the Stationers formed for themselves several common stocks, held by different groups of members: one of these stocks,

the English stock, survives; the members are the shareholders, and can dispose of their shares to their widows only. In 1501–2 the Co. was reckoned fifty-third. The reason for giving it a charter in 1557 was the desire of the Govt. to check heretical publications. Unlimited Livery was granted it in 1560. In 1563 it answered the C.C.'s inquiry as to its lands, plate, jewels, and money, that it had none. From the first year of the reign of James I the Co. had a monopoly of almanacs, primers, psalters, the A B C, the Little Catechism, and Nowell's Catechism: and well into the 19th century it continued to print Old Moore's and other astrological almanacs. The register of printed books—valuable to the Shakespeare student as possessing the entry of so many plays—that has been kept by the Co. since the beginning of the 16th century, was at first merely for the convenience of its members; but by an Act of 1662 (13 & 14 Charles II, c. 33) registration was made general and compulsory. After several renewals, this Act expired in 1692, and in 1695 the Commons refused to renew it; but, so far as concerns the securing of copyright, registration in Stationers Hall books was imposed by an Act of 1709, continued by the Copyright Act of 1842, and not abolished until 1911. The right to print the Bible was, after the appointment of Richd. Jugge as Queen's printer in 1560, a subject of controversy between him and the Co., of which he was a member. Compromises were effected with him and with the universities in this matter; and all that remained of the Co.'s monopolies—psalters, primers, almanacs, etc.—faded away in consequence of a legal decision in 1775.

Sir Walter Besant wrote:

'The Company has continued ever since its incorporation, and still is, a trade guild consisting exclusively of members of the trade of a stationer, printer, publisher, or bookmaker, and their children, and descendants born free.'

Most printers' apprentices in the City are bound at Stationers' Hall, they are each given a Bible and Prayer Book.

Charter was granted by Philip and Mary in 1557, giving the Co. jurisdiction as licenser throughout the realm. Elizabeth granted confirmation in 1559. Both these charters were burnt in the G.F. A writ of *Quo Warranto* was issued in respect of them in 1663, because of the Co.'s alleged neglect of duty. Similar proceedings suspended the charter from 1684 until the Act of 1690.

Before incorporation, there was apparently a hall in Clement's Court, Milk St. Between 1550 and 1570 the Co. removed to Peter Coll., at the SW. angle of St. Paul's Chyd.—these premises it leased in 1606, and they became the Feathers Tavern. The partners in the Co.'s English stock had in 1611 purchased Abergavenny House—which had belonged to John, E. of Richmond, in the reign of Edward II; afterwards to Wm. Herbert, E. of Pembroke; who sold it to Ld. Abergavenny: the site was just inside the City wall, to the N. of the ch. of St. Martin, Ludgate, and was bounded on the N. by the chapter-house estate, and on the E. by the garden of London House. This mansion, adapted as the Co.'s hall, was destroyed in the G.F.: the Co.'s losses were terrible, £200,000 worth— only the registers were saved. The new hall on the same site was not complete till 1674: it was wainscoted by Stephen Colledge (an ultra-Protestant joiner, who was executed at Oxford on a charge of treason in 1681). In 1677-8 it was used as par. ch. while St. Martin's was being repaired; and, toward the end of the same century, it became the scene of an annual musical festival on 22nd Nov. in honour of St. Cecilia—settings of Dryden's and Pope's odes were among the pieces performed: *Alexander's Feast* was performed in 1697. After 1703 these festivals were held but occasionally—until the Musicians' Co. revived the annual celebration in 1903. The hall, which is brick-built, was faced with Portland stone in 1809. It was slightly damaged by bombs. The beautiful north window of the hall picturing Caxton and Edward IV, was presented by Joshua Whitehead Butterworth in 1894. There are also windows depicting Wm. Tyndale, Cranmer, Shakespeare, St. Cecilia, and Caxton separately. The entrance-screen is a fine piece of carving of the time of William III. The court-room to the W. of the hall received its present guise in 1757. It sustained damage in the Second World War. An octagonal card-room, designed by Wm. Chadwell Mylne, was opened

out of it in 1825. On the opposite side of the hall is the stock-room, erected 1887, decorated with beautiful carvings; it is used for meetings of the stock-board. A new muniment room was opened in 1949. A courtyard that lies to the W. contains a plane tree marking the spot where seditious books used to be burned.

To attempt an enumeration of notable members would be to recite all the famous names in the history of English publishing. Samuel Richardson the novelist was master, 1754; Jacob Tonson the younger, 1759. The Rivington family have furnished eight masters and four consecutive clerks. Stationers who became Ld.M.s: Sir Thos. Davies, 1676-7; (Sir) Stephen Theodore Janssen, 1754-5; Thos. Wright, 1785-6; Wm. Gill, 1788-9; John Boydell, 1790-1; Sir Wm. Domville, 1813-14; Christopher Magnay, 1821-2; Wm. Venables, 1825-6; John Crowder, 1829-30; Sir John Key (twice), 1830-2; Sir Wm. Mafnay, 1843-4; Sir Francis Graham Moon, 1854-5; Sir Sydney Waterlow, 1872-3; Francis Wyatt Truscott, 1879-80; Sir Geo. Robt. Tyler, 1893-4—all these held the office of master. More recent of the Co.'s twenty-seven Ld.M.s are: Sir Frank Green, 1900; Sir Geo. Wyatt Truscott, 1908; Sir Thos. Vezey Strong, 1910; Ld. Marshall of Chipstead, 1918; Sir J. J. Baddeley, 1921; Ld. Ebbisham of Cobham, 1926; and Sir William Waterlow, 1929. Perhaps the most distinguished member of the Co. was Bernard Shaw.

There are the following pictures: 'Mary Q. of Scots escaping from Lochleven Castle,' by J. Graham, acquired 1791; portraits of—Henry Chicheley, Abp. of C. (the one in Shakespeare's *Henry V*); John Tillotson, Abp. of C., by Kneller; Matthew Prior; Sir Richd. Steele; Samuel Richardson; Tycho Wing, astrologer, d. 1750; Benjamin Hoadly, Bp. of Winchester; Robt. Nelson, religious writer, d. 1715; Wm. Bowyer the elder, printer, d. 1737; Wm. Bowyer the younger, printer, d. 1777; portraits of John Boydell (by Jas. Graham), and Sir Wm. Domville (by Wm. Owen, R.A.), beforementioned. 'K. Alfred dividing his last loaf with the pilgrim' (doubtful history), by Benjamin West; and portraits of four masters— Wm. Strahan (1774), Thos. Cadell (1798), John Nichols (1804), and Andrew Strahan (1816).

The oldest plate is of the 17th century:

two two-handled cups; four other silver cups; silver flagon, given by Abel Roper; silver salver; silver-gilt dish, given by Thos. Newcomb the elder; two silver candlesticks.

The Co.'s barge (represented in the N. window), one of the finest of the old Co. barges, was still in existence when Hazlitt wrote (1892)—in the club-house at Oxford. Its subsequent fate is unknown. It was rowed by twenty men. There is a model at the hall.

Alderman John Norton (thrice master), who d. 1612, left to the Co. in trust two sums, £150 and £1,000—the former for the poor of the par. of St. Faith, the latter (invested by the Co. in house-property in Wood St.) for loans to young men in business. The latter practice becoming obsolete in the City, the Co. obtained leave from the Court of Chancery to use the income for founding and maintaining a sch.; which was established in 1861 in Bolt Court. It has since been removed to Mayfield Rd., Hornsey. In 1949 Norton was commemorated by a plaque in the crypt of St. Paul's Cathedral. There are many other trusts, all for the benefit of those connected with the Press or their dependants: Blackwell's (1818), Bowyer's (1777), Cater's (1718), Clarke's (1838), Compton's (1862), Davis's (1850), Dilly's (1803), Figgins's (1884), Guy's (1717), Hamblin's (1818), Hansard's (1818), Johnson's (1795), Nichols's (1817 and 1855), A. Strahan's (1815), W. Strahan's (1784), Whittingham's (1840), Wilkins's (1773), Wright's (1798).

No. of Livery, 380.

(See *The Stationers' Company: a history, 1403-1959,* by Cyprian Blagden, 1960.)

Tallow Chandlers' (21). R. H. Monier-Williams, the Clerk to the Co., in a paper read to the London Society in 1932, gave an interesting account of the commencement of the craft.

'Our story opens with a little colony of tallow-chandlers in the reign of Edward I, plying their trade in what was then the great forum or market-place of London, called West Chepe. The reference to this colony occurs in 1283, in Letter Book A, the first of the memoranda books kept by the City Corporation, so that the Company can claim for their forbears the distinction of having received one of the earliest notices possible of a London craft.

'The entry is, of course, in Latin, and the name given to these early merchants in grease (for that is what they were) is "unctuarii." When cataloguing the entry in the *Liber Albus* a little over a century later, John Carpenter, Town Clerk, had no hesitation in rendering "unctuarius" by "candelarius" or "chandler," and although that rendering presents only one aspect of the trade it is broadly speaking correct. . . . The entry to which I have referred was, in fact, an order issued against them by the civic authorities giving them a month's notice to betake themselves elsewhere. One suspects their next door neighbours of having instigated this expulsion order for candlemakers, soap-boilers, and the like have never been popular, on account of the unsavoury odours associated with their trade and the danger of fire.'

The order seems to have been inoperative. There is reason to believe that a move was eventually made to the neighbourhood of Bishopsgate, but there is no reason to believe that it was upon compulsion. Wills testified to the increasing importance of the craft, and in 1339 there was a reference to 'masters' elected to office by the C.C. It is questionable if at this time there was any formal soc., but they were representative chandlers, and were authorized by the C.C. to function in various ways and to seize candles of deficient weight. An edict of 1362 regulated the sale of tallow and candles, and in 1363, in which yr. it was ordained that 'handiscraftsmen shall use but one mistery,' the chandlers are enumerated among 'misteries' offering money to the K. of France. From early times they were in close relation to the Salters. Four masters were attributed to the craft in a list of 1393. A grant of arms was obtained in 1456: incorporation came six yrs. later. Confirmation of the fact that the Co. owned property round the Ch. of St. Botolph, Bishopsgate, has been found in the fact that there used to be a Soper's Alley among the thoroughfares obliterated by the construction of Liverpool St. Station. Soap was possibly one of the craft's principal wares.

The Co. had powers of search in and around the City of L. for bad tallow and candles, as well as other commodities such as soap, vinegar, barrelled butter, oil, and hops. Searches were also carried out with a view to regulating supplies. For this purpose the Co. obtained several grants from the Crown, among which were the Letters Patent of Henry VIII (1512) giving the Co., in conjunction with the Ld.M., 'the search of oils' and therewith the control of soap-making in the City, and the Letters Patent of Elizabeth (1577) by which they were appointed 'viewers and triers of soap, vinegar, butter, hops and oil,' not only in the City but in Southwark, St. Katherine's, Whitechapel, Shoreditch, Westminster, Clerkenwell, and St. Giles. Fees were to be imposed for searches: twopence for a barrel of soap; eightpence for a barrel of butter; eightpence for a ton of Seville oil; eightpence for a sack of hops. W. C. Hazlitt, noting from the records of the Drapers Co. that earlier there had been mention of dealing with salt, packthread, lathes, galley-pots, pans and brooms, thought he recognized here 'the parentage of the modern chandler's shop and its almost inexhaustible resources.'

The Co.'s books of the 16th and 17th centuries contain many references to searches, such as the following:

'Paid at the Guildhall when we were before my Lord Mayor and Mr. Chamberlain with ill candles . . . 6s. 8d.

'Paid to two porters for carrying naughty candles to the Chamberlain, 6d.

'Spent at the Red Lion when we went to search for oils . . . 2s. 1d.

'Received of F.S. for a fine for unclean and naughty vinegar . . . 6s. 8d.' Although granted by royal charter the above powers could only, in practice, be exercised with the consent of the C.C. and, at times, they were strenuously opposed.

A most elaborate set of by-laws was framed in 1639: from these it appears that the Co.'s yeomanry had a separate and complete organization. From Charles II the Co. obtained a grant whereby in addition to previous powers of search, they were authorised to break and destroy inferior candles.

About this time the Co. awoke to the fact that forms of illumination other than candles were finding increasing favour. In 1692 they petitioned against the monopoly granted to certain persons for lighting all public places in the City with what were called convex lights or lamps. By this time, however, the Co.'s powers had waned. In 1708 they lost an action brought by a tallow chandler who claimed damages for stock which they had destroyed in exercise of their alleged rights, and thereafter they discontinued their searches.

There were inspeximus charters by Edward VI in 1547–8; by Philip and Mary in 1558, and by Elizabeth in 1560–1. Letters patent of James I in 1620 gave confirmation. In common with other companies, there was a temporary suspension by the *Quo Warranto* proceedings of 1684. The Grant of Arms of 1456 is one of the finest specimens of heraldic work in existence. In 1602 the Co. acquired Supporters to Arms. They are picturesquely described in the instrument as 'angells crowned with starrs in token of light, whereof your mistery is a beautifull imitacion.'

Probably the original hall was in the Bishopsgate colony. In 1476 the Co. bought the site of the present hall, on the W. side of Dowgate, from the Executors of Sir Richard Alley, citizen and alderman of L. The price was £66 13s. 4d. in cash, payable by three annual instalments, and an annuity of £10 payable quarterly for ten years to Dame Margaret Alley, his widow. The Co. possesses the title deeds of the site commencing in 1335. The Skinners' Hall was already on an adjoining site when the Tallow Chandlers obtained theirs.

Little is known of the old hall which was destroyed in the G.F. Every effort was made to carry on business despite the calamity. The Clerk and Beadle both lived on the premises, and instructions were given 'that a shed should (at the charge of the Company) be erected within the ruins of their late Common Hall, wherein their said Beadle might dwell and inhabit during the pleasure of the Court, and might therein sell drink and chandlery ware during so long time as to the Court should seem convenient.'

The exterior of the new hall was completed in 1672, and the interior some four yrs. later. The parlour was wainscoted at the expense of Sir Joseph Sheldon, who was master in 1667, and later Ld.M. Through his generosity the Co. was presented with a barge in 1668. For the purpose of housing it, together with the Weavers' Co., a piece of land was acquired in Cheyne Walk, Chelsea, from the Soc. of Apothecaries where there was a large garden that still exists. The barge was disposed of for £5 in 1694.

There is no evidence that Sir Christopher Wren himself was directly concerned in the design of the hall, but it is presumed that Captain John Caines, the Company's Surveyor, was inspired by Wren.

Alterations were subsequently made. In 1764 the music gallery was partitioned off 'to make the hall warmer and more commodious.' The original moulded plaster ceiling in the parlour was obliterated and there was substituted graining and varnish in imitation of oak. The oak panelling in the hall and in the parlour was varnished and the mouldings gilded. Sash windows were later removed, and the openings filled with heraldic painted glass. In consequence of the demolition of the four old houses fronting Dowgate Hill, and the erection in 1882 of an office bdg. occupying the E. wing of the court-yard, a bay was lost. With the beginning of the 20th century came improvements. An oak staircase was erected in place of the previous one made of elm. In 1905 the acquisition of a strip of land, giving access to Cloak Lane, provided the occasion to incorporate in a new entrance the carved canopy bearing the arms of the Co., originally erected over the gate on Dowgate Hill. This bears the Co.'s motto: *Ecce Agnus Dei qui tollis Peccata Mundi* (Behold, the Lamb of God which taketh away the sins of the world).

Damage was sustained during the Second World War on 10th May 1941. The wing furthest removed from the parlour and the hall was practically demolished, and with it the SE. corner of the banquet hall; the ceiling was also damaged. Later flying bombs removed most of the heraldic glass, including that of the parlour. It has since been repaired.

Amongst the Co.'s present possessions are portraits of William III and Q. Mary by Kneller. Another picture, reputed to be by Matthew Brown, depicts the marriage of Henry VII with Elizabeth of York, daughter of Edward IV. The donor of these pictures was Roger Monk of His Majesty's Bodyguard. He also included in the presentation in 1826 a portrait of himself. There is also a book of accounts from 1550 in the original

binding; an early 17th-century oak table; a tall case clock of walnut (*c.* 1700).

In 1948 a new memorial window was unveiled. It commemorates two Liverymen who lost their lives in the Second World War. The donor was their father, H. M. Humphrey, a Past Master.

No. of Livery, 125.

(See *Records of the Worshipful Company of Tallow Chandlers, London*, 1897.)

Vintners' (11). Dealers in wine were of two classes; the Merchant Wine-tonners of Gascony, and the Tabernarii or Taverners to whom they consigned the wine on sale. In 1282 Edward I granted to Henry de Kingston for the use of the Vintners (or Wine-tonners) of L., Botolph Wharf by Billingsgate. In 1300 the merchants complained of want of accom-modation; by K.'s writ the difficulty was removed, and large houses with vaults were built where before there were only cooks' houses—in the district round about Queenhithe, and where the N. end of Southwark Bridge now is: it was called the Vintry by the time of Edward II (1307–27). Stow says that till about 1300 it was the place where Bordeaux merchants unloaded and sold their wines. In 1365 Edward III granted a charter, not of incorporation, but giving the Vintners exclusively the wine-trade with Gascony. As part of its power over the craft after incorporation in 1437, the Co. was virtually the licenser of inns. Limitation by statute (1552) of the number of inns and taverns troubled it seriously in the reign of Edward VI: Justices were then given the task of granting and renewing licences. Under Elizabeth it had an opposite grievance, the multiplication of irregular taverns: it was also harassed by the granting, to court favourites, of monopolies—e.g. Robt. Devereux, the ill-fated E. of Essex, drew most of his income from a monopoly of sweet wines. In 18 Charles II an unsuccess-ful attempt was made, by a prosecution, to invalidate the free Vintners' power to trade without further licence. However, legislation, long busier with the liquor trade than with any other, has now placed in other hands the authority the Co. formerly wielded.

Notwithstanding, the Vintners still retain some of their privileges. Fifteen freemen of the Co. have the right to sell wine without applying for a licence.

The only condition imposed within the City and a three-mile radius thereof is for the premises to be approved by officials from the Customs and Excise. At one time this led to fraudulent misrepresentation, and there is a reference to this in Michael Sadleir's fine novel *Fanny by Gaslight* (1940):

'There were so-called Supper Houses —every second house in Bow Street and Brydges Street and Phoenix Alley was one—which were unlicensed yet sold drinks freely. They used to pay some Free Vintner to paint his name over the door, and then, if ordered to show a licence, said they were employed by such and such a Free Vintner and need not have one.'

The right of exercising the ancient right is a family one and is handed down from generation to generation.

In 6 Henry VI (1427), an inspeximus of Edward III's said non-incorporating charter was granted; and in 16 Henry VI (1437) the Vintners were at length incorporated. Confirmation was granted 1 Henry VII (1485). A temporary charter of 2 Philip and Mary (1554) relieved the Co. from observing the onerous conditions imposed under Edward VI. Philip and Mary granted another charter in 1558: confirmed in 1559 by Elizabeth, who granted very full powers by another charter in 1567. A third charter of Elizabeth, granted 1577, continued the relief granted by Mary's temporary charter. James I in 1604 confirmed only the first of Elizabeth's charters; but in 1612 he granted an entirely new charter, giving full power with regard to taverns in L., and three miles round. A charter of James II in 1685 confirmed and extended privileges, but interfered in the internal management of the Co.: this interference was removed by another charter of the same monarch in 1688. The charter of 1612 then became the working charter.

There was a thoroughfare called Stody's Lane, where now is that part of Queen St. which forms the N. approach to Southwark Bridge. Land abutting on this lane came to the Co. through one of the craft, Sir John Stody, who bequeathed it in 1357. Here was the first hall—perhaps merely an old house used as hall. In 1446 Guy Shuldham devised to the Co. adjacent lands, in the pars. of St. Martin-in-the-Vintry and St. James Garlickhithe,

subject to a rent of £5 6s. 8d. and to the condition that the Co. should maintain thirteen almshouses on the spot. The Co. then built there the almshouses and a new hall, between Thames St. and the river. Gen. Monk was feasted here in 1660. Five years later the G.F. came, and the hall went. Rebuilding, partly on the old foundations, of the hall as it now stands, at the corner of Anchor Alley, near Queen Street Pl., was completed in 1671. Hatton, in 1708, described it as 'well built of brick, and large and commodious,' and continued:

'The room called the Hall is paved with marble, and the walls richly wainscoted . . . enriched with fruit leaves, &c., finely carved, as is more especially the noble screen at the east end, where the aperture into the hall is adorned with columns, their entablature and pitched pediment; and on acrosters [acroters] are placed the figures of Bacchus between several Fames, and these between two panthers; and there are other carved figures, as St. Martin, their patron, and the cripple, and pilasters.'

A smoking-room on part of the site of the garden was a 19th-century addition.

The first Vintner Ld.M. was John Adrian, 1271. Henry Picard was Ld.M. 1356–7: he lived over against St. Martin's Ch., in a large house in which he entertained five kings in 1363. This is the most renowned event in the history of the Vintners' Co., and until the damage to the Guildhall was commemorated by a stained glass window there. A tablet in Vintners' Hall records it. The names of the monarchs are given as Edward III of England; David, K. of Scotland; John, K. of France; Waldemar, K. of Denmark; and Amadeus, K. of Cyprus. The tablet is said to be a copy of a similar one destroyed in the G.F. It is unfortunate that historical criticism cannot support the view that all these five sovereigns 'banqueted splendidly' at Picard's mansion. No K. of Cyprus has ever borne the name of Amadeus, and probably Peter II was meant. Waldemar did not come to England till a yr. after K. John of France was dead. It is for this reason that the toast of the Vintners' Co. is always drunk with five cheers. In 1935, when the E. of Athlone, K.G., was Master, there was a Commemoration Feast at Vintners' Hall. The five kings were to be represented by the P. of Wales (afterwards Edward VIII), the D. of York (later George VI), the D. of Gloucester, the D. of Kent, and P. Arthur of Connaught. There were only four, as finally the illness prevented the last from attending.

There have been notable Vintners. Sir John Stody, or Stodeye, Ld.M. 1357–8, was M.P. for the City 29 and 31 Edward III. Sir John Lewis, a member of the Co., entertained Henry IV's four sons at his house in the Vintry, to a supper, at which they received a commemorative ballad from Henry Scogan. Sir Thos. Bloodworth (master 1665) was Ld.M. 1665–6; his conduct during the G.F. is described by Pepys. Sir Samuel Dashwood (master 1684), upon his inauguration as Ld.M. in 1702, had a 'highly classical pageant'—and entertained Q. Anne at the hall. Sir Gilbert Heathcote, Bart. (master 1700), was Whig M.P. for the City, 1700–10—afterwards sat for other places, Ld.M. 1710–11, and was ridiculed by Pope (*Imit. of Horace*, bk. ii, ep. 2) for his parsimony: he was the last Ld.M. to ride to Westminster on horseback on Ld.M.'s Day. Brackley Kennett, Ld.M. 1779–80, is the one who comes on the scene for a moment in Dickens's *Barnaby Rudge*—he was subjected to actions at law arising out of the 'riots of 'eighty'; and his death, 12th May 1782, is stated by Milbourn (historian of the Co.) to have been by suicide. Benjamin Kenton (Master, 1776), a Whitechapel charity-boy, became a tavern-keeper, and a great benefactor.

Among the elected officers of this Co. is a 'Swan Warden.' His office directly relates to the little known fact that some of the swans which grace the upper reaches of the Thames are owned by the Vintners' Co. The King is 'Seigneur of the Swans' but he has allowed to the Vintners' and the Dyers' Cos. the privilege of keeping a 'game' of these royal birds upon the Thames 'from time beyond legal memory.'

The earliest existing record relating to this custom is in the accounts of the Master and Wardens, now in the British Museum, of about the year 1509.

In Dec. of each yr. the Vintners used to hold a Swan Feast. At this banquet the Swan Warden, with a retinue of 'Swan Markers and Uppers' and attended by musicians playing wood wind instru-

ments, presented roast cygnets to the Master 'For the delectation of your guests.' 'Let them be served, Mr. Swan,' was the Master's reply.

During July, when the cygnets are about two months old, the annual Swan Voyage takes place. The three Swan Markers, of the K., the Vintners, and the Dyers, assemble at Vintry Wharf at such an hour as may be appointed by the Ld. Chamberlain.

From Vintry Wharf they, together with their Uppers, proceed on their week's journey up the river. The Vintners' birds are marked by having two nicks in the upper mandible and the Dyers' by one nick. The K.'s birds have no mark, and all swans not marked are the property of the 'Seigneur of the Swans.' Swans with nicks are in the wrought-ironwork of the gate in Upper Thames St.

The Vintners have a song, composed by Elkanna Settle, the City poet, for the visit of Q. Anne in 1702. The last lines run:
'Come, come let us drink the Vintners' good health,
'Tis the cask, not the coffer, that holds the true wealth.'

The wine porters, with their white smocks, take part in an annual procession. (See 'Customs.')

A writer in the *City Press* said:
'The ceremony of the Loving Cup is common to all City Livery Companies, but its origin is not always understood. When the loving cup passes there must always be three standing so that the one who is holding the cup and is then defenceless is fully protected; the one behind him should be standing back to his back, that his sword arm be free, and the one in front holds aloft the cover of the Cup in his right hand.

'The custom arose from the murder nearly one thousand years ago of Edward the Martyr, who was stabbed in the back while drinking. All good Vintners consider this the foulest crime in history.'

The Co.'s collection of muniments is unusually good: most of the ancient charters are preserved. The master's chair is pre-Fire. In the court-room, amid carvings ascribed to Grinling Gibbons, are paintings: 'St. Martin and the Beggar,' and portraits of Charles II, James II, William III and his Q., and four of the masters. There is a fine piece of tapestry, dating from 1466, 6 ft. 7 in. by 3 ft. 7 in. —one half depicts St. Martin and the Beggar; the other, St. Dunstan and a Choir. There is an ancient hearse-cloth. The earliest specimens of plate are a coco-nut cup of 1518, mounted in silver gilt, and a Delft tankard of 1563. A silver-gilt cup has as pedestal a milkmaid holding it over her head—it moves on pivots, so that, on the maid being inverted, her skirt forms another cup: both cups are filled, and it requires skill to drink from one without spilling from the other. There is an ornate stoneware jug of 1562.

The hall, superficially damaged during the Second World War, was restored so far as possible to its original condition. It was formally re-opened on 21st June 1949. Amongst those attending were the Ld.M. and Sheriffs, the Bp. of L., Earl Wavell, and the D. of Wellington.

Shuldham's almshouses (named after Guy Shuldham who gave land to the Co. in 1446), burnt in the G.F., were rebuilt on the Mile End Rd. Benjamin Kenton in 1802 left money for rebuilding, which was then done. They have been ruined by bombs. They were for women only. There are various other gifts for the poor, but no educational endowments.

No. of Livery, 300.

(See *The Vintners Company*, edited by T. Milbourn, 1888.)

Watermen's and Lightermen's. This Co. has never had either Livery or charter. Its constitution has always been settled by statute. The boatmen who, in 1372, were commanded by the City authorities not to take more than twopence as a fare between L. and Westminster, and also those that were the subject of regulation by 6 Henry VIII, c. 7 (1515), were probably destitute of organization. By the Act 2 & 3 Philip and Mary (1555), c. 16, the Court of Aldermen were authorized to select, from the whole body of Watermen plying between Gravesend and Windsor, eight overseers or rulers of the rest. By 1 James I, c. 16 (1604), regulations as to apprenticeship were made. Naturally the oligarchic character of its government was a lasting source of discontent in the Co. Watermen were always specially liable to be pressed into the navy, and they were forbidden to go to a distance to avoid impressment. They often had disputes with the Lightermen

or cargo shifters, who poached on the Watermen's business. They waged a long battle against the introduction of coaches, opposed the building of new bridges, and fought against the possible transfer of playhouses from the south bank to the north of the river.

In 1641 in reply to an appeal for better representation of the Watermen on the ruling body, fifty-five of 'the most honest and sufficientest' were given authority to nominate twenty from whom the Court of Aldermen might choose the overseers: this twenty in time began to be called the assistants, though they were not legally so. A court of assistants would appear to have been appointed in 1682: they are possibly of the same as the thirty-two 'of good loyalty and best ability' mentioned in a mayoral order of 1683, from whom only the overseers were to be selected. From the reign of Elizabeth to that of Anne there were about 40,000 watermen engaged on or about the Thames. In 1700, by 11 & 12 William III, c. 21, the Watermen and Lightermen were formed into one Co.: the Watermen were to nominate yearly from forty to sixty assistants; the Lightermen nine—but as the assistants were from yr. to yr. to nominate the electing Watermen, there was no rash experiment in democracy. In 1729 the number of assistants was reduced to thirty. In 1808 the Co. made its last great protective effort by petitioning against the erection of Putney and Strand (i.e. Waterloo) bridges. In 1827, by 7 & 8 George IV, local and personal acts, c. lxxv, the Co. was reincorporated; the limit at Gravesend was removed E. to Yantlet Creek, and for the first time a master and wardens were appointed. In 1859 the assistants were empowered to fill up vacancies in their body. The licensing of boats and pilots, formerly the business of the Co., since 1939 has been done by the Port of London Authority at their headquarters in Trinity Square.

A hall is mentioned in the Act of James I. The first indication of its locality comes with an engraving of it by Hollar in 1647. It was S. of Upper Thames St. The site is on the quay called Waterside, E. of Cannon St. Station, to the S. of the chyd. of All Hallows-the-Great. It was burnt, with nearly all the Co.'s records, in the G.F. It is supposed to have been rebuilt 1670. It was again rebuilt on the same site 1719–22. In 1776 the present premises on the W. side of St. Mary-at-Hill were purchased. The process of building was interrupted by disputes with adjoining occupiers, concerning party walls, etc.; for some time the workmen were driven away by a display of firearms. Removal to the new hall took place in 1780. It has a neat pilastered façade, with a pediment, and an ornamental fanlight over the three-light window on the first floor. The hall mantelpiece is of marble, with a figure 'of the God Thames.' The hall was badly damaged in 1944 but has since been restored.

The most notable member was John Taylor, the 'water-poet' — 'a literary bargee,' the late Harold Child dubbed him—a friend of Ben Jonson. He once nearly drowned himself trying to row a brown paper boat from L. to Queenborough. He was voluminous in verse and the legend of 'Old Parr' (see 'Westminster Abbey') owes almost everything to him. His portrait hangs in the hall. There is also a portrait of the first winner of Doggett's Coat and Badge, 1715. (See 'Customs.')

There used to be a custom of appointing one of the Co.'s oldest widows to give a draught of ale to each new freeman when he was sworn, in return for which he gave her a shilling. There is record of a succession of these widows from 1706 till 1793: in 1827 it is noted that the widow no longer attends with the ale, but gets the shillings all the same. The drink was given in a silver bowl which has the inscription 'Batchelors Bowl' together with the Co.'s arms. It has the hall-mark 1659.

There is a tradition of almshouses at Blackwall established under the will of John Fell in 1742, and lost to the Co. by negligence—being appropriated and sold by descendants of their Watermen inmates. In 1837 a meeting was held at Blackwall to consider the matter, and in consequence new almshouses were built at Penge and occupied by 1843: the Co. also founded the adjoining ch. of St. John. There is an interesting account of the Penge property in Walford's *Greater London.*

The number of Members runs into thousands.

(See *History of the Origin and Progress of the Company of Watermen and Lightermen,* by Henry Humpherus, 1887.)

Waxchandlers' (20). To this day the Goldsmiths and the Armourers and Braziers sometimes light their halls with wax candles. Catholics, for religious uses, insist on a percentage at least of beeswax in candles. But, for all utilitarian purposes, the wax-candle industry is dead—buried first under spermaceti; next under paraffin, stearin, gas, and cheap oil; and lastly under electricity. The supply of candles to churches and other public establishments was the chief business of the medieval Waxchandlers: private illuminations, except in houses of the wealthy, being small and brief. A common custom was for churches to supply their own wax by keeping bees. The Waxchandlers made torches as well as candles—customers often supplying the material. In reply to one of the usual complaints as to incompetent practitioners, the C.C. in 1358 gave the Waxchandlers' gild liberty to fix its own governing body at from two to four wardens. Two was the number in 1371. The Livery, customary in origin and unlimited, rose to 101 in 1724; by 1892 it was down to 27. But the Co. owns property—it first acquired the land on which its hall has always stood; during the 16th century and later it acquired land in Coleman St., Upper Thames St., and Old Change. Appropriately, there are clergymen on the Livery.

Charter was granted by Richard III in 1484, giving a very limited licence in mortmain—five marks. Confirmations were granted by: Philip and Mary, 1557; Elizabeth, 1560; and James I, 1604. Charles II granted a charter with extended powers in 1663; James II's charter of 1685 was only temporarily in use.

In 1493 the Co. was in possession of a hall on the present site at the NE. corner of Gutter Lane—viz. 2A Gresham St.: that portion of Gresham St. which was formerly called Maiden Lane and other names. Harben says the hall was rebuilt 1657. It was burnt in the G.F. and presumably rebuilt soon afterwards. Of the 17th-century hall, there is a water-colour drawing by Geo. Shepherd, made 1811. In 1852 it was demolished and the present small hall erected; it was badly damaged in the Second World War but rebuilt in 1958.

Ditchfield gives the names of the founders of charities as: John Thompson, Wm. Parnell, Nicholas Frankwell, Wm. Caldwell, and Kendall.

No. of Livery, 20.

Three Companies have acquired halls since 1939:

Fanmakers' (76). The stimulus for the formation of a guild of fanmakers is said to have been due to the influx of large numbers of Protestant fanmakers from the Continent after the revocation of the Edict of Nantes in 1685. To prevent the dilution of their trade by aliens, the native craftsmen formed themselves into an organized body. A Charter was granted by Q. Anne in 1709, but increasing pressure by nonfreemen and from foreign imports broke down the Co.'s control of the trade and after a petition of 1806 against the 'extinction by foreigners of British fan craft' had failed, the Co.'s powers were finally abandoned. The Co. was revived in 1877 as a traditional trade guild, showing a benevolent interest in the development of the mechanical fan, making grants in the field of fan engineering. In 1950 it took over the small hall in the churchyard of St. Botolph, Bishopsgate, as its Company Hall.

Master Mariners (78). This was at first a Co. formed (1926) under the Companies' Acts, 1908-17. In 1928 George V gave it the privilege of being called the Honourable Co. It was incorporated by Charter of George V in 1930, in which yr. the P. of Wales, afterwards Edward VIII, was Master. In 1932 it was granted Livery up to 200 by the Court of Aldermen. Its objects are to provide senior officers of the merchant navy with a central body representative of and qualified to represent them, only British master-mariners being eligible for membership; to encourage a high standard of proficiency and professional conduct; to co-operate with the royal navy; to forward nautical study and seamanship; to endow professorships, scholarships, etc.; to establish places of instruction; to provide for education of master mariners' children; and where necessary for master mariners' dependants; to make pilots; and in many other ways specified in the charter, to act for its members collectively. Membership is limited to 500 ordinary members.

In 1948 the Master Mariners' Co. became the first Livery Co. to have a floating hall. By the contributions of its members, the sloop 'Wellington' (900 tons), at one time in service on the coast of New Zealand, was bought from the Admiralty, and fitted up as the headquarters of the Co. From Chatham Dockyard, where it was converted, it was brought to its moorings at Temple Stairs.

The Court Room is panelled in oak, and behind a dais at one end is Sir John Lavery's oil painting of the handing over of the Co.'s livery by the P. of Wales. There is a handsome double staircase, which formerly belonged to the 'Viper,' a passenger ship in the Isle of Man and Clyde region for many yrs. There is also a mus. and library. The steering wheel of the barque *Otago*, the first command of Joseph Conrad, was given to the Co. and is on display.

There is a Marchwood Scholarship to perpetuate the name of a former Master; it is tenable for two years at a residential school for officers of the Merchant Navy.

No. of Livery, 200.

Pewterers' (16). 1348. A charter was granted by Edward IV in 1473. The craft was very prosperous in Elizabethan times, but by the 18th century there had been a great decline accompanying the rise of designs in silver. Later the collection became a hobby and led to trade in sham antiques.

The new Hall in Oat Lane was opened in 1961 and incorporates panelling and chandeliers from the old Hall in Lime St. The Co. has a fine collection of pewter ware in its hall; it has for many years contributed to the development of technical training and education.

No. of Livery, 100.

2. COMPANIES WITHOUT HALLS (49).

Air Pilots and Air Navigators, Guild of (81). Founded in 1929 for men qualified in these professions; received grant of Livery in 1956. Present trophies and medals for aerial skills.

Basket Makers' (52). They are mentioned as a craft in the books of the Brewers' Co. in 1422. They received their only known constitution from the Court of Aldermen in 1569. Issues certificates of basketmaking to apprentices.

Blacksmiths' (40). First mentioned in 1325 but incorporated by letters patent of Q. Elizabeth in 1571 as the Art and Mistery of Blacksmiths-spurriers. Now interests itself in technical education and issues medals and diplomas in ironwork.

Bowyers' (38). Before 1370; in L. the provision of archers' equipment depended on three separate crafts: the bowyers, the fletchers or arrow-makers, and the stringers or longbow string-makers. The first two were originally a single trade but in 1371 the bowyers and fletchers are found enforcing an ordinance of mutual exclusion for the two crafts. The military pre-eminence of the English archer declined steadily with the coming of guns but constant pressure was applied by the Crown to keep archery as a national skill. James I granted a charter in 1621 but archery continued to decline as a force in war; with its rise as a sport the Co. transferred its support and now grants prizes and presents medals for skill in archery.

Carmen's (77). Carmen plied for hire for the transport of goods both within the City and to distant towns. In 1517 a Fraternity of St. Katherine entered into an agreement with the Ld.M. and Aldermen to govern the carmen's trade. The woodmongers, whose major occupation was the supply of fuel, were more numerous than the carmen and soon dominated the fraternity. In 1605 the Woodmongers, by Royal Charter, secured control over the carmen but in 1665 the carmen became answerable directly to the City authorities and the Keeper of Guildhall still conducts an annual sealing of carts plying for hire within the City. The Co. obtained Livery from the Court of Aldermen in 1848 and was granted a Charter in 1946. Awards prizes in the field of modern transport.

Clockmakers' (61). Originally within the Blacksmiths' Co. but granted a separate Charter in 1631 and Livery in 1766. Closely connected with the trade and with collectors; maintains a library and a magnificent exhibition of clocks and watches of all ages in Guildhall Library.

Cooks' (35). Mentioned in 1311 but some confusion exists as to the early function of the cooks, the pastelers and the pie-bakers, each of which seems to have existed as a separate mistery. By the end of the 15th century the terms cook and pasteler seem to have been used indiscriminately and it appears that pastelers and pie-bakers were absorbed into the general description of cooks, the Co. receiving its Charter in 1482. Still connected with the trade, the Co. grants prizes and finances classes in cookery.

Curriers' (29). To curry is to dress tanned leather by various scraping, beating and colouring processes. Originally part of the Cordwainers' guild but separation was foreshadowed by a civic ordinance of 1272. Full self-government was achieved with the approval of ordinances in 1415. Obtained a grant of Arms in 1583 and a charter in 1606. Its Hall, in London Wall, was sold in 1920; makes grants to Cordwainers' Technical College.

Distillers' (69). Obtained a Charter from Charles I in 1638 but this was opposed by the City on the grounds that it would weaken other Cos. of which distillers were then members, and not enrolled in the Chamber of L. until 1658. Under its Charter the Co. was entrusted with the control of all makers of vinegar, spirits, beergar and alegar within the City of L. and an area 21 miles therefrom. No longer exercises any control but still connected with the wine and spirits trades by scholarships.

Farmers' (80). Began as a Guild in 1938 and in 1946 became a voluntary body as the Farmers' Co., after useful work in wartime. Granted Livery in 1952, its aims are to foster agriculture and its allied occupations and it gives scholarships and prizes in this field as well as encouraging research into soil fertility and pest control.

Farriers' (55). Existed since the 13th century and in 1356 is recorded as a Fellowship under the name 'Marshalls of the Citty of London.' Was incorporated by Charles II in 1685 and as a Livery Co. by the Court of Aldermen in 1692. Has examined and registered shoeing smiths for over 70 years.

Feltmakers' (63). First mentioned in 1180 but in the Middle Ages the process of making felt was shared in L. between the fullers and the hatters or cappers. In 1501 the fraternity of hatters was subordinated to the Co. of Haberdashers but in 1604 James I granted a Charter to the Art or Mistery of Feltmakers of L. and this was confirmed by Charles II in 1667. Livery was granted in 1733 but the coming of the silk hat in the 19th century was a blow and the Co. lost its connection with the trade. Has more recently revived its interest by grants to the trade Research Association.

Fletchers' (39). Fletchers were arrow-makers and in 1371 agreed before the Ld.M. and Aldermen that they and the bowyers should respect each other's different crafts. Ordinances were proclaimed in 1403 and later a Charter granted by Edward IV. With the decline of archery as a military force transferred its interests to the support of it as a sport.

Founders' (33). Thirteenth-century existence as metal founders, and Ordinance of 1365 refers to the casting of small brass and copper objects, such as candlesticks, pots and stirrups. During the 16th century acquired the right of sizing and marking brass weights and this privilege was confirmed to them in their first Charter of 1614. These powers fell into disuse in the 19th century. Hall (1531) destroyed in G.F.; second hall, still standing, has been let as offices for many years.

Framework Knitters' (64). The development of the invention of the stocking frame to knit silk hose led to the grant of a Charter by Cromwell in 1657 and the powers were widened by another Charter in 1663. During the 18th century L. lost its position as centre of the stocking trade to the Midlands but the Co. still retains considerable connections with the trade.

Fruiterers' (45). Has existed since the 15th century and in 1463 an Ordinance of the mistery of Fruiterers' was approved by the Ld.M. and Aldermen. Received a Charter from James I in 1605. Each year the Co. presents the Ld.M. with baskets of English-grown fruit in amicable commutation of the ancient rights of the City authorities, as City fruit-meters, to a toll in kind of all produce of this sort brought into the City. Identifies itself with the industry by co-operation with horticultural organizations and centres of research in the trade.

Furniture Makers' (83). Inaugurated in 1952. Has very close associations with the craft and awards scholarships in the furniture industry.

Gardeners' (66). 1345. Incorporated by Letters Patent of James I in 1605. Presents annually a basket of flowers and vegetables to the Ld.M. Supports scholarships for the Royal Horticultural Soc. etc. Maintains a horticultural library at Guildhall and sponsors window-box displays in the City. Since the war has built a garden and wall fountain on the site of Old Change, near St. Paul's.

Glass-sellers' (77). Home production of glassware was stimulated by Venetian immigrants in the 16th century; to protect themselves against the growing production

of inferior glass in the 17th century, the glass-sellers of L. petitioned for a Charter in 1635 but it was not granted until 1664. The Co. played a prominent part in the development of English glass but with the decline of control of trade by the guilds, the Co. made its contribution by technical scholarships and grants to university work in this field.

Glaziers' (53). Early references to L. glaziers term them 'verrers,' a term replaced by glaziers after the 14th century. Ordinances were granted to the Verrers of the City of L. in 1364 and new ones to the Misterie of Glaziers in 1474. The Charter of 1637 makes it clear that glaziers were concerned with the glazing, leading and painting of windows. Closely concerned with the trade and with glass painting, maintaining classes and scholarships.

Glovers' (62). Recorded in 1327, Ordinances being obtained in 1349. In 1498 the Glovers were united with the Pursers and in 1502 with the Leathersellers. Received a Charter as a separate Co. in 1639. Its Hall, in the Cripplegate area, disappeared many years ago; the connection with the trade however remains very strong.

Gold and Silver Wyre-Drawers' (74). This craft, embroidering with precious metals, was under the control of the Goldsmiths from early times. The age of adornment under the Tudors and Stuarts caused the trade to prosper to such an extent that the supply of bullion became affected and attempts were made to control it. After attempts to secure a Charter from 1623, it was not until 1693 that one was finally obtained. Nowadays the wares are still in demand for military and ceremonial uniforms.

Gunmakers' (73). Prior to the formation of the Co. by its Charter of 1637, working gunsmiths of the City were members of either the Armourers' or the Blacksmiths' Cos. Because of the opposition of these Cos. it was not until 1656 that the Charter was enrolled. Livery was granted in 1778. The Co. still exercises its powers in viewing and testing smallarms and handguns, in association with the Proof House at Birmingham.

Horners' (54). The making of articles of horn is a craft of great antiquity. There is a reference to 'Statutes of the Horners' in City records in 1284 and an ordinance for the misterie in 1391. In 1475 the Horners and the mistery of Bottlemakers (makers of leather bottles) were united at their own request. The increasing use of glass caused a decline in the demand for horn but it revived again under the demand for snuff-boxes and for horn-books. A Charter was obtained in 1638 but the trade continued to decline and the Co. now has strong associations with the plastics industry.

Joiners' (41). 1309, Ordinances being received in 1400 and a Charter in 1571 to the faculty of Joiners and Ceilers. The original function of the joiner was the joining of timber by mortice and tenon but large-scale timber house-work was the prerogative of the carpenter, so that the joiner became more concerned with furniture work and carving, the secondary title 'ceilers' being derived from the Latin word for a carver. Until 1939 part of the Jacobean gateway of the last Hall remained in Joiners' Hall Buildings, Upper Thames St.

Loriners' (57). The Loriners' Ordinances of 1260 are among the oldest known rules of self-government granted by the Ld.M. to the City misteries. Among the requirements is one to provide the Ld.M. with a bridle and bit every Easter. Later ordinances of 1313 and 1393 permit the election of wardens to survey the craft of 'loremerie.' A Charter was granted by Q. Anne in 1711; control of the trade was lost early and the Co.'s main association with it now is through horse shows.

Makers of Playing Cards (75). The craft was in operation early in the 15th century; the manufacture was a monopoly of Sir Walter Raleigh in the reign of Q. Elizabeth. The Co. was granted a Charter in 1628 by Charles I who levied an excise of 36s. per gross on all packs. From 1882 each liveryman has yearly a pack with a portrait of the reigning Master on the ace of spades. It maintains a fine collection of cards in Guildhall Library.

Masons' (30). Although domestic buildings were made of timber, the important public buildings, for example bridges and churches, were made of stone. Masons therefore were important craftsmen and references to a mistery occur in 1376. Ordinances were approved in 1481 but the decline of guild powers was accelerated in the case of all building crafts by the G.F. The urgent need for rebuilding swept away the guild restrictions and even the grant of a Charter of 1677 did nothing to restore the position. All the membership of the

Co. is admitted into the Livery; has strong association with the training of apprentices in the trade.

Musicians' (50). Ordinances dated 1350 indicate that a fellowship of minstrels of L. existed in the 14th century. At the same time another body known as the King's Minstrels flourished and obtained a royal charter in 1469. Despite this, the City supported its own body which in its turn received a royal charter in 1604. Conflict ensued and the latter charter was revoked in 1634, but the City Co. continued to exercise control within the City. By the middle of the 18th century however, in common with other guilds, its functions had ceased and it has continued as a benevolent and educational body, founding, for example, scholarships at the Guildhall School of Music.

Needlemakers' (65). The trade in L. dates from the early 16th century; a Charter was granted by Cromwell in 1656 and another by Charles II in 1664. By the 18th century the centre of the trade had moved to Redditch but the Co. still maintains close associations with the modern trade.

Pattenmakers' (70). In the 14th century there were separate misteries of pattenmakers and galochemakers; a patten was probably ironshod, while a galoche was a clog with a wooden sole. Both misteries became closely associated with the Pouchmakers, possibly because of the use of leather for shoe ties. The Pouchmakers eventually merged with the Leathersellers but the Pattenmakers obtained their own Charter in 1670. With the decline of the trade the Co. has maintained its association with the manufacture and sale of rubber footwear.

Paviors' (56). A code of ordinances was granted in 1479 and in 1673 the Co. sought a royal charter from Charles II but the move was opposed by the Court of Aldermen. A later attempt also failed and the Co. has remained an unincorporated guild. Has many members who are prominent in road engineering and exercises a considerable influence in the trade and its education.

Plaisterers' (46). An important craft, it is mentioned in the City archives in the 14th century. Received a Charter of incorporation in 1500 and a later one in 1679. After the G.F. the Co. had a Hall; for many years has offered prizes for outstanding art-work in the trade.

Plumbers' (31). Ordinances were granted in 1365, 1488 and 1520, and in 1611 received a Charter of Incorporation. Although it no longer controls the trade it strongly supports technical training and is still the registration authority for qualified plumbers.

Poulters' (34). As early as 1299 is recorded as electing members to supervise the trade, and ordinances are known to have existed before 1370. A Charter is said to have been granted by Henry VII in 1504 but does not now exist, the earliest recorded Charter being of 1665. The L. Poulter was a seller of table-birds, rabbits, butter and eggs but the Co. now is only associated directly with the trade by the prizes it gives at shows.

Scientific Instrument Makers' (84). The most recent of the Cos., it began only in 1956. Was granted Livery in 1964 and is very closely associated with its industry.

Scriveners' (44). The Scriveners were a branch of the Text-writers (whose other branch developed into the Stationers): they acquired skills in drafting legal forms and became lawyers to the extent of drawing up wills and legal deeds. A Charter was granted by James I in 1617. The father of John Milton was Master in 1634. Their early declaration book (in Guildhall Library) is most valuable evidence of the state of official handwriting over the centuries.

Shipwrights' (59). The shipwrights of L. have existed, as an entry in their archives of 1483 puts it, 'of tyme out of minde.' During the 16th century there was conflict between the shipwrights of the City and those of 'Redrith' (i.e. Rotherhithe), the latter being granted a royal charter in 1605 and another in 1612. Despite these charters, the City body successfully maintained its independence and the struggle went on. With the loss of control over the now highly industrialized trade, the Co. maintains its interest in educational work, giving scholarships at colleges and universities in Greenwich, Glasgow and Durham.

Solicitors of the City of London (79). A strict craft guild in that its membership is confined to those who practise, or have practised, within one-mile radius of the Bank of England. Formed in 1909, it received a grant of Livery in 1944. Awards prizes at Law Society examinations.

Spectacle-makers' (60). 1563. Granted a Charter by Charles I in 1629; the Co. has always been concerned with optical instruments as well as spectacles. Is now the body holding examinations and issuing diplomas in optical subjects.

Tin-plate Workers' (67). Charter was granted by Charles II in 1670. The Co. was an offshoot of the Wire Workers or Wire Drawers, first heard of in 1469. The Co. awards prizes for inventions of commercial utility and also scholarships.

Tobacco Pipe Makers and Tobacco Blenders' (82). Incorporated 1619, confirmed in 1675; the Co. prospered until the decline of smoking in the 19th century and became extinct. Revived in 1954, granted livery in 1961. Still closely associated with the trade.

Turners' (51). 1310. A charter was granted by James I in 1604. In the 19th century the Turners' was the first Co. to pay attention to technical education. It has held many exhibitions and gives prizes for amateur work. Turning-lathes have been presented to schools.

Tylers and Bricklayers' (37). 1416. A charter was granted by Q. Elizabeth in 1568. Formerly possessed a hall in Leadenhall St. The Co. has promoted building exhibitions and maintains classes at Trades Training Schools.

Upholders' (49). The craft was originally fripperers: those that repaired old clothes. Fripperers are heard of in the 14th century. In 1502 there was a guild of upholders. In 1626 a charter was granted by Charles I.

Weavers' (42). This is probably the oldest of all the guilds; it is the first recorded as having a charter—granted by Henry I around 1155 and now in Guildhall Library. There are also existing ordinances attributed to the reign of Edward I. Its last hall—in Basinghall St.—was demolished in 1856. Gives scholarships in Textile Technology and maintains almshouses.

Wheelwrights' (68). A charter was granted by Charles II in 1670. Associated with trade classes in Trades Training Schools.

Woolmen's (43). The only surviving document is a book of ordinances (1587). Till 1779 every woolwinder required a licence from the Co. Connected with the wool industry, where it awards scholarships.

The following Cos., like the Parish Clerks' and the Watermen's, have no livery or number in precedence: Launderers';

Builders' Merchants.'

Compters were prisons immediately under the supervision and control of the sheriffs. The *Liber Albus* gives various orders of Henry VI's reign for proper conduct, and it appears that they were sometimes designated by the names of the respective sheriffs who presided over them. Probably they were sometimes in the sheriff's own house. In Stow's time there was one in Poultry, and one in Wood St. Of the former he says:

'This hath beene there kept and continued time out of minde, for I have not read of the originall thereof.'

It had a number of interesting prisoners. In 1598 Henslowe provided 40s. to secure the release of Thos. Dekker from the 'Counter in the Poultrey.' In 1628 Dr. Lambe, a man charged with 'certaine Evill Diabolicall and Execrable arts called witchcraft,' and who is said to have supplied the D. of Buckingham with love philtres, d. here. Ned Ward (1698-9) gave an odious picture of it. There was

'a mixture of scents from mundungus, tobacco, foul feet, dirty shirts, stinking breaths, and uncleanly carcases . . . far worse than a Southwark ditch, a tanner's yard, or a tallow chandler's melting-room. The ill-looking vermin, with long rusty beards, swaddled up in rags, and their heads—some covered with thrum caps, and others thrust into the tops of old stockings.'

Between 1740 and 1749 Boyse, the Grub St. poet, spent much of his time here. With no covering but a blanket, he had two holes made in it, that he might put his arms through and write. In 1765, Jonathan Strong, an African slave, having been freed by his master after most brutal treatment, was kidnapped by his connivance and sent to the Poultry Compter. Through the exertions of Granville Sharp he was discharged by the Ld.M. This compter was pulled down in 1817, and on its site the Poultry Chapel was built (see 'City Temple'). The Wood St. Compter was erected in 1555, having been previously in Bread St. Fennor, an actor, in 1617, wrote a pamphlet on the abuses of this Compter, where there were three sections—the master's side, for the wealthy; the knight's ward for those of moderate means; and the 'hole' for the riff-raff. Thurston Hopkins thinks that the Hole-in-the-Wall Tavern, which until the Second World War was in Mitre Court, was a survival of the last. Underground there are still some of the dungeons and old oaken iron-plated doors. Dr. J. C. Lettsom said in 1773 that it consisted of one room, 33 ft. long, 12 ft. high and 15 ft. broad, and this was the only accommodation for 40 prisoners. This compter was removed in 1791 to Giltspur St.—a bdg. opposite St. Sepulchre's Ch., which was designed by Geo. Dance, Junior. Hepworth Dixon wrote a vivid account of it. It was supposed to accommodate 203, yet the prisoners in 1850 numbered 246. It was closed in 1854, and demolished in 1855.

Corn Exchange (Mark Lane). To prevent cornering of wheat, in 1438 Stephen Broun (Ld.M.) established a public granary, and a few yrs. later Simon Eyre set up another in Leadenhall. The City Livery Cos. were required to supply certain quantities of corn to these granaries. At length they turned stubborn, and refusing to buy corn, provoked much friction with the C.C. This was terminated by the G.F., which burnt the Bridgehouse (immediately to the E. of St. Olave's Ch., Tooley St.), this having been the main store, and the granary of the cos. It was here because of its proximity to the corn mills on London Bridge. In the 18th century the met. corn market was held at Bear Quay in Thames St. The farmers of Essex brought their waggons to the neighbourhood of Tower Hill, and in the Ship Inn in Water Lane, and Jack's Coffee House in Lower Thames St., they transacted business. In 1747 thirty-five factors called a meeting at the Ship Inn, and formed a small co. to build a market in Mark Lane. It was a quadrangle, and on three sides were piazzas supported by pillars, and under them were sixty-four stalls, with bins for exhibiting samples on market days. At times these had to be examined by rushlight, and they were drenched by rain or snow which fell from the open roof. In 1783 Christopher Atkinson, M.P., stood in the pillory outside the Corn Exchange on conviction for perjury. He was a standholder. He was also expelled from the H.C., and sentenced to twelve months' imprisonment, and a fine of £2,000. In 1827 the market had become too small, and was partly rebuilt, and at the same time another group of traders, who had developed a market for corn and seed, had another exchange built for them at the back of 27 Mark Lane. The new bdg. adjoined the old on the N. side. The old Corn Exchange was rebuilt in 1881, so the older in name is the newer by date. The newer one had a Doric portico, which was demolished in 1931.

The two markets were amalgamated in 1929 under powers granted in the Corn Exchange Act of that yr. The exchange was partly destroyed by enemy action in 1941. It has been rebuilt, modernized and expanded.

County Hall. The central offices of the G.L.C. (*q.v.*), are situated at the junction of Belvedere Rd., Lambeth, and Westminster Bridge. The council, in 1889, took over the offices of the M.B.W. in Spring Gardens. They were inadequate, and for about a year the new council met at Guildhall. It was not until 1906 that the L.C.C. obtained the authority of Parliament to acquire the site of the present bdg., part of which is Pedlar's Acre (see 'Lambeth'). It was the cheapest of several suggested, e.g. Parliament St., Trafalgar Sq., and the Adelphi. The architectural features of the central part of the river wall were designed by Ralph Knott, F.R.I.B.A., the construction being carried out by the council's chief engineer, the late Sir Maurice Fitzmaurice, C.M.G., and his successor, Mr. G. W. Humphreys (now Sir Geo. Humphreys, K.B.E.). The architect chosen for the bdg. was Ralph Knott, and he was accordingly appointed in association with Mr. W. E. Riley, the official architect. The foundation stone was laid by George V in 1912, and work commenced in the spring of 1913. This excluded the N. section of the bdg., for which the site was not then available. The outbreak of war delayed progress, and in Feb. 1916 work was stopped by the Ministry of Munitions. During the summer of 1917 part of the completed portion of the bdg. was taken over by the Army Council, and used chiefly by the Ministry of Food and H.M. Office of Works. After the return of the bdg. to the council in 1919, work was resumed, and carried to completion. The opening ceremony was performed by George V on 17th July 1922. The N. section was opened by (Sir) Angus Scott, then Chairman of the Council, on 27th Jan. 1933. In 1939 the two central sections of the north and south blocks were completed on a site to the east of the main building. The extension to the north block was completed in 1958 and to the south block in 1963.

The approximate total cost of the bdg. amounted to £3,636,533, made up as follows: (i) site, £620,911; (ii) river embankment, £114,040; (iii) raft foundation, £117,117; (iv) superstructure, including both the original and N. sections, £2,784,465. The area of the site is about 750 ft. in length, with an average width of rather more than 300 ft. There are nine floors, the first being reserved generally for the use of members, heads and deputy-heads of departments. The entrance hall is lined with Roman marble, and has a marble mosaic floor, plaster ceiling, and end fireplaces, treated in Verde Prato marble, the gift of the Italian Govt. The ceremonial staircase is treated in Pentelic, black Belgian, and Ashburton marble, and has a groin-vaulted ceiling. The council chamber is octagonal in plan, and has accommodation for 200 members. The seating is of oak; the seats of the chairman, the vice-chairman, and the deputy chairman being made of bog-oak, believed to be several thousands of yrs. old. It was found some 35 ft. below the level of Villiers St. during excavations at the Charing Cross Station of the Charing Cross, Euston, and Hampstead Railway. The plinth and capping of the dado round the walls, and the framing of the doorways, are of black Belgian marble: the greenish-grey filling is of Cipollino marble from the island of Euboea. The columns and pilasters above are monoliths of Veine Dorée, an extremely beautiful marble quarried over 5,000 ft. above sea-level in the Italian Alps. There is a public gallery. The malachite vases at the entrance to the council chamber were bequeathed to the council in 1914. The conference hall in the N. section is on the elliptical plan, the extreme diameters being 66 ft. and 56 ft. respectively.

There is a remarkable collection of records at County Hall. When the L.C.C. took over Poor Law administration from the Boards of Guardians it had also to take

800 tons of documents, and the Clerk's Department alone has 8 miles of steel shelving. The earliest records are the rolls of Tooting Bec Manor, dating from 1394. These are the minutes of the Commissioners of Sewers for Kent and Surrey from 1569 to 1847.

The members' library includes the collection of L. books left by John Burns, and presented by the late Viscount Southwood.

County Hall sustained damage in the Second World War. The council chamber was little affected, but committee rooms were rendered useless and pillars along the crescent were badly damaged.

Cripplegate. For derivation of name see 'City Churches; C'—St. Giles, Cripplegate. The first reference is in the Laws of Ethelred (*c.* 978–1016). It is 'Crepelesgate' in a charter of William I, 1068. Harben says:

'There are one or two transcripts of this charter, in the Register, in Anglo-Saxon and in Latin; in one it is described as "posterulam que dicitur Crepelesgate," as though it were one of the smaller gates or posterns.'

Maitland (1739) was of opinion that in 1010 it was the only gate in the N. wall of the City, and that it was originally erected over a Roman military way, which led from L. to Hornsey. It has been remarked that the custom of making proclamations at the end of Wood St. may have arisen from its having been one of the old military ways, but the presence of one of the Eleanor crosses might suffice as an explanation. Some colour is given to the suggestion that the gate, in medieval times, opened on to an important thoroughfare, by what occurred in 1461, when Q. Margaret, Henry VI's consort, having defeated Warwick 'the King-maker' at St. Albans, marched on L. The Q. and her feeble husband promised that the rabble that followed them should not enter the City, so long as the citizens undertook to provide them with provisions. When the rations were about to be conveyed news came that the E. of March (afterwards Edward IV) had rallied the remainder of Warwick's army and was marching on L. A determined crowd rushed to Cripplegate, and prevented the wagons from passing through. As a result, faced with the alternative of attempting to storm the City or retiring

to the north, Q. Margaret and her forces chose the latter course and shortly after Edward and Warwick entered L.

Stow called Cripplegate a postern, and said:

'It was sometimes a prison, whereunto such citizens and others, as were arrested for debt or common trespassers, were committed as they be now to the compters.'

He adds that it was rebuilt by the brewers of L. in 1244. In 1336–7 pieces of wood from the Guildhall were used for its repair. Its custody was committed to Chepe, Crepelgate, and Bassieshaw wards. It was again rebuilt in 1491. It was repaired and 'beautified,' a foot postern being added in 1663. Threatened by the G.F., it was saved through the blowing up of a number of houses. In 1760 the materials were sold for £91, and the gate demolished that yr. A fragment of the gate for some time remained in the White Hart Inn on the N. side of Fore St. The C.C. plaque on Cripplegate Bdgs. disappeared during the War. There is a model of the gate in the L.Mus.

Crosby Hall was first on the E. side of Bishopsgate. The site is now covered by Crosby Sq. It was built in 1466 by Sir John Crosby. He was a soldier as well as a captain of industry, being warden of the Grocers' Co., and a distinguished member of the Woolmen's Co. He became an alderman; he was also a diplomatist, who was sent on foreign missions. He had a large business. C. W. F. Goss in his excellent monograph on Crosby Hall (1908) says:

'Sir John's business is said to have been so extensive that he must have employed a large staff, including apprentices, who lived, as was the practice, above the warehouse. According to time-honoured custom, no great dinner or entertainment was ever given by the rich merchant in that noble hall in Bishopsgate Street, without the apprentices and clerks being included among the guests.'

Sir John was evidently a forerunner of Fezziwig. He did not long enjoy what Stow called 'his large and sumptuous building,' for he d. 1475. He was bd. in the adjoining St. Helen's Ch.

The house had a frontage of about 240 ft., and in places went back from

Bishopsgate St. about 300 ft. It consisted of the great banqueting hall, the smaller dining parlour, the chapel, State apartments, noblemen's lodgings, butler's and bursar's lodgings, porters' quarters, the great kitchens, brewhouse, bakehouse, larders, stables, together with courtyards and various outhouses. There were probably extensive gardens, and a large bowling green. In 1483 Richd. of Gloucester was domiciled at Crosby Hall, probably he held it from Sir John's executors. This accounts for its appearing three times in the play of *Richard III* (Act I. Sc. ii, Act I. Sc. iii, Act III. Sc. i). Mr. Goss points out that as the two earlier events recorded took place in 1471 and 1478, the allusions must be regarded as anachronisms. Richard was tenant but a short while. On accepting the crown he made the Palace of Westminster or Baynard's Castle his residence. Subsequent occupiers were Sir Bartholomew Reed and Sir John Rest. The latter remained until 1517 or 1519. In the summer of 1523 it came into the hands of Sir Thos. More. It is not known whether he lived there; it cannot be associated either with his *Richard III* or *Utopia*. In Jan. 1524 More sold his remaining term of forty-one yrs'. interest in Crosby Hall for £207 to Antonio Bonvisi. There followed a succession of tenants, of whom the only noteworthy one was Wm. Roper, More's son-in-law and gifted biographer. He went to Crosby Hall in 1547, having as co-lessee Wm. Rastell, a nephew of More. The latter also wrote a life of the great Ld. Chancellor, but fragments only have survived. In 1566 Alderman Wm. Bond came into possession, paying £1,600. Bond d. 1576, and was bd. in St. Helen's Ch. In 1594 Alderman Sir John Spencer—known as 'Rich Spencer,' purchased it from Bond's sons. He d. 1609, and was also bd. in St. Helen's Ch. It then came into the hands of Wm. Compton (afterwards first E. of Northampton) who, to the vexation of Spencer, had contrived to marry his daughter (see 'City Churches; C'—St.Helen, Bishopsgate). Apparently his residence there was very brief, for in the yr. of Spencer's death, the Countess of Pembroke was a resident, her house in St. Martin's le Grand being used for a time for some other purpose. She was followed by Wm. Russell, and in 1618, during his tenancy, two Russian ambassadors were lodged at Crosby Hall. They came to raise a sum of £600,000 from the L. merchants. In 1621 the East India Co. came, and remained until 1638, the rent being £100 p.a. In the yr. they quitted Spencer Compton, second E. of Northampton, came to live at Crosby Hall. He had, like Pope's uncle, according to Johnson, 'the honour of being killed in the service of Charles I,' meeting his death at Hopton Heath in 1642. He had already thought it prudent to lease Crosby Hall, as the City was a parliamentary stronghold, and had written to his wife as follows:

'We hear of Mr. Pym's motion for searching our houses. I hope you have taken care he shall not find much at Crosby House, and for the future we shall take such order that the searching of our country houses will be in little danger. Take care that your coach horses be not appointed for the militia.'

Alderman Sir John Langham, a Presbyterian, was then a lessee, and after him his son, Sir Stephen Langham. In 1672 it became a Presbyterian meeting-house, and for this purpose a new floor was put into the banqueting hall, level with the minstrels' gallery In 1676 the ground floor was let for a grocer's warehouse. The Presbyterians remained until 1769, and for another nine yrs. their hall was used by another dissenting body. In 1778 Messrs. Holmes & Hall secured a lease. A third floor, just below the corbels of the roof, was then inserted. This firm remained in possession until 1831. In that yr. the premises became untenanted, and fell into a state of dilapidation. A placard appeared, advertising the premises to be let on a building lease, and it looked as if the destruction of the hall were imminent. Happily a meeting was called at the London Tavern, resolutions were passed, and it was saved. A Restoration Committee carried out the necessary repairs, and in 1836 the Ld.M. laid the first stone of the new works of the so-called Council Chamber and Throne Room. Miss Maria Hacket, of 8 Crosby Sq., a most public-spirited lady, had taken a lease of the premises, and undertaken to uphold the fabric in accordance with its provisions.

From 1841 it was occupied by the Crosby Hall Literary and Scientific Institute. In 1852 the P. Consort visited the hall for the purpose of inspecting some new evening classes for young men which were being conducted. After these classes removed elsewhere it was used for lectures and concerts. In 1862 it was leased to Messrs. H. R. Williams & Co., wine merchants, who converted it into a storehouse. Some protest was made against what was termed 'vandalism,' but the wine merchants used the hall well. They left in 1867. The premises were empty for a few months, and in 1868 leased, at about £1,000 a yr. rental, to Messrs. F. Gordon & Co., who converted the place into a restaurant, as which the hall was used until 1907. In that yr. the freehold was sold for £175,000 to the Chartered Bank of India, Australia, and China, and antiquaries, and all with any feeling for the past, received a shock when it was announced that it was intended to destroy the bdg. and to use the site for business premises. The huge sum of £120,000 was asked for their retention, although it represented less than half the site, and at this time the timbered façade in Bishopsgate (a reproduction of the timber houses of the 15th century) was demolished. The sum of £60,000 was subscribed and, as this did not suffice, an alternative scheme of removal was adopted. This was happily carried out by the Crosby Hall Preservation Committee, and since 1910 the hall has been in Chelsea.

Happily, when the neighbouring ch. was almost destroyed by bombs, only slight damage was caused to this building,

Crutched Friars. The Order is said to have been instituted by Gerard, Prior of St. Mary of Morella at Bologna, and confirmed in 1169 by Pope Alexander III, who brought them under St. Augustine's rule. They came to England in 1244, and had their first house at Colchester. About 1298 they came to L., and settled in the par. of St. Olave, Hart St. The name was derived from the cross, forming part of the staff carried by them, which was called a crutch. (In Middle English 'cross' was 'crouche' from Latin *crux*.) This was afterwards given up, and a cross of red cloth placed upon the breast of the gown. According to Stow, it was not until 1319 that they built their house. He mentions a number of burials in the ch., including John Rest, grocer

(Ld.M. 1516); Sir John Milbourne, draper (Ld.M. 1521). The latter's body, he says, was removed afterwards to the ch. of St. Edmund, Lombard St.

Milbourne was the founder of certain almshouses in the par. of St. Olave's, the bedesmen getting 2s. 4d. a month. For this they had to go daily to the Crutched Friars Ch., and pray for the souls of Sir John and Dame Johan, and Margaret, Sir John's first wife, and the souls of their fathers, mothers, children, and friends, and 'for all Christian souls.' Also under his will, thirteen penny loaves were to be given to thirteen poor people at the chs. of St. Edmund, Lombard St., and St. Michael, Cornhill. Sir Rice Griffith, beheaded on Tower Hill in 1531, was bd. here. Stow says in his time,

'in place of this church is now a carpenters yard, a Tennis court and such like: the Fryers hall was made a glasse house, a house wherein was made glasse of divers sortes to drink in, which house in the year 1575 on the 4 of September brast out into a terrible fire.'

The earliest reference to the thoroughfare is 'le Crouchedfrerestrete' (1405). In Stow's time it seems to have been called Hart St.

Customs.

BEATING THE BOUNDS. Before the Second World War this old practice was regularly carried out on Ascension Day in the pars. of St. Clement Danes, Strand, and St. Dunstan-in-the-East; also round the Duchy of Lancaster Estate, of which the ecclesiastical centre is the chapel of the Savoy, though here not always on Ascension Day. Once every five yrs. there was a perambulation of the par. of St. Giles, Cripplegate. Naturally the almost entire destruction of the ch. of St. Clement and St. Giles has led to the discontinuance of the practice there.

Since 1939 it has been carried out only in the par. of St. Dunstan-in-the-East and at the T.L. The former was the first—in 1946. The Rector led the party which came from the choir of St. Dunstan's Coll., Catford, one of six grammar schs. in the City, which was removed in 1888. Wearing white surplices, and carrying staves, to the end of which they tied posies of herbs and flowers—a custom that originated in the days of plague—the boys moved off from the Chapel of St. Dunstan in Idol Lane, singing a hymn. On the site of the Cloth-workers' Hall the boys were addressed by the Chairman of the Governors of the Sch. Services were held at various points, and at Custom House jetty the boys boarded a motor launch. In mid-river between London Bridge and Tower Bridge, a boy was lowered over the side of the boat, and while buglers sounded a call, he placed his hand in the water to mark the limit of the par. boundary. The ceremonies ended with a service at the ruined church of St. Dunstan.

At the T.L. the practice has always been to make the ceremony triennial. The procession there assembled on Tower Green. It was headed by the Chief Warder; his mace was surmounted by a silver miniature of the White Tower. Next came the chaplain, and a score of surpliced choir boys of the Chapel Royal of St. Peter ad Vincula, followed by other boys and girls whose homes are in the Tower. Two detachments of Yeomen Warders who marched behind were in full state uniform, and carried their damascened halberds, the Yeoman Gaoler bringing up the rear with the symbolic axe. With them was the Resident Governor, in full-dress uniform of scarlet and cocked hat. Women residents of the Tower, who like the children, bore long osier wands, completed the procession. A Special Correspondent of *The Times* wrote:

'At the first of the 31 boundary marks, which is on the water-front near Tower Pier, outside the Tower gates, Mr. Cook raised his mace high to halt the procession. Pointing to the stone, he ordered, as custom ordains, "Whack it boys, whack it!" They thrashed it joyfully as the chaplain uttered the fearful scriptural warning: "Cursed is he that removeth his neighbour's landmark." Most of the boundary stones are small iron plates at the foot of a wall prosaically inscribed with a broad arrow, "W.D.", and a number, and newly repainted for yesterday's occasion, but some are sunk in the roads about Tower Hill. It took about an hour to belabour them all. Then the procession returned through the workaday traffic of the streets to Tower Green and sang the National Anthem before dismissing.'

CHARLES I SERVICE. Of recent yrs. much interest has been aroused in the second Stuart king who from the point of view of personal character stands highest. It was partly due to the fifth E. of Ashburnham, whose ancestor was his Groom of the Bedchamber. He was an enthusiastic Jacobite, and through him the Order of the White Rose was resuscitated, and several new clubs formed in various parts of the country. A Stuart calendar was published, and a Stuart exhibition held at the New Gallery in 1888. Ch. services in honour of the 'royal martyr' were held, first at St. Margaret Pattens (see 'City Churches; C'), and, after the death of the vicar, the Rev. J. Leonard Fish, in 1907, at St. Cuthbert's in Philbeach Gardens. There is a ch. dedicated to K. Charles the Martyr at Potter's Bar (Mdx.). The Royal Martyr Church Union was established in 1906 with the object of restoring the service in honour of the king to the Book of Common Prayer. This had been omitted (together with services in memory of the Gunpowder Plot and the Restoration of Charles II) by royal warrant in 1859.

The custom of decorating the statue at Charing Cross commenced in 1892, but it was stopped by the police. In the following yr. application in the proper form was made to the authorities, and, although at first refused, was granted at the last moment. Since then the statue has been decorated annually, with the exception of 1901, when it was prohibited on account of the death of Q. Victoria. For many yrs. past there has also been a service, but in 1936 this was deferred from 30th Jan. to 27th Mar. (the date of Charles I's accession) on account of the death of George V. The choristers attire themselves at the ch. of St. Martin in the Fields, and walk in procession to the statue. The prayers, once in the Prayer Book, are read. There is no discourse. The Soc. of King Charles the Martyr, founded in 1894, is now most active in the arrangements. Its objects are:

'To promote the restoration of the name of Charles, King and Martyr, to its proper place in the Kalendar of the English Church and the observance of January 30th, the day of his Martyrdom by a suitable service in the Prayer Book.

'To maintain the principles of Faith and Loyalty for which the King died—the Faith of the Church and Loyalty to the Crown.'

With the removal of the statue for the duration of the Second World War the service was discontinued although wreaths were placed against the plinth which remained. The statue was returned in 1947, and the service was resumed on 30th Jan. 1948.

OUR LADY OF MOUNT CARMEL. Annually on a Sunday in July there is a long and picturesque procession from St. Peter's Italian Ch., Clerkenwell Rd. in her honour. It parades the district known as 'Little Italy.'

DOGGETT'S COAT AND BADGE. 'The Watermen's Derby' dates back to 1st Aug. 1716. The previous night a placard was set up on London Bridge which ran as follows:

'This being the day of His Majesty's happy accession to the throne there will be given by Mr. Doggett an orange colour livery with a badge representing Liberty to be rowed for by six watermen that are out of their time within the year past. They are to row from London Bridge to Chelsea. It will be continued annually on the same day for ever.'

Thos. Doggett (comedian and joint-manager of Drury Lane Theatre) conceived a remarkable enthusiasm for the new dynasty, and at this time had retired to Eltham. He d. there in 1721, and left directions in his will that out of his personal estate freehold lands should be purchased to the value of £10 p.a.,

'and conveyed unto Edward Burt of the Admiralty Office, Esqr. his Heirs and assignes subject to and charged and for ever chargeable with the laying out ffurnishing and procuring yearly on the ffirst day of August for ever the following particulars, that is to say, ffive pounds for a Badge of Silver weighing about twelve ounces and representing Liberty to be given to be rowed by Six young Watermen according to my Custom eighteen shillings for Cloath for a livery, whereon the said Badge is to be put, one pound one shilling for making up the said Livery and Buttons and appurtenances to it and Thirty Shillings to the Clerk of the Watermens Hall All which I would have to be continued for ever yearly in Commemoration of his Majesty King George's happy accession to the British Throne.'

The course was from the Old Swan Pier, London Bridge, to the Old White Swan Inn at Chelsea. On the demolition of the latter in 1873 (the site is now marked by Swan House, Cheyne Walk, designed by Norman Shaw, which has a sculptured swan on the façade) the race finished at Cadogan Pier. The race has to be rowed against the tide, at the time when it runs the strongest. The distance covered is 4½ miles. Edwd. Burt transferred his responsibility by an indenture of 1721 to the Fishmongers' Co., and the latter have had the superintendence of the race ever since. In addition to the coat and badge (the prancing horse of the House of Hanover), the winner receives £20. There are further prizes of £12, £10, £4, £3, and £2.

In 1920 there were six races to cover the yrs. lost by the war, 1915–20, and in 1947 eight races to cover the yrs. 1940–47. The date varies but is usually in July.

(See *Thomas Doggett, deceased*, by T. A. Cook and Guy Nickalls, 1908.)

LITERARY CELEBRATIONS. On the Saturday nearest to the birthday of Charles Lamb (10th Feb.) the Charles Lamb Society commemorates the author by placing a wreath on the bust in Giltspur Street. Usually on the same day the birthday of Dickens is commemorated, the exact date being 7th Feb. There is a luncheon arranged by the Dickens Fellowship, and the Tabard Players (led by Ross Barrington) perform scenes from an adaptation of a novel in the yard of the old George Inn, followed by further scenes in the Chas. Dickens Sch., Lant Street, where a laurel wreath is placed upon the bust by the Mayor of Southwark. On the Saturday nearest to 23rd Apr. a birthday performance of an Elizabethan play is given in the yard of the George Inn. On 9th June, the anniversary of Dickens's death, a wreath is placed on his grave in W.A. On the anniversary of the death of Dr. Johnson (13th Dec.) the Johnson Soc. of London place a wreath on the grave in W.A., when a short address is delivered by one of its members.

MAUNDY THURSDAY originated in a custom of the medieval abbots of Westminster of sitting in the E. cloister on the day before Good Friday, and washing the feet of thirteen poor men. Having 'clean washed' their feet the abbot wiped them with a towel and kissed them, bestowing money also with food and beer. The first reference to the practice was in 1300. The word 'Maundy' is derived through *mandé*, old French from the Latin *mandatum* (a command), in this case of Christ to His disciples to wash one another's feet as He had washed theirs (John xiii. 14). The practice was not restricted to W.A. It took place in all cath. chs., and in the greater par. chs., and some of the smaller ones. Once at Magdalen Coll., Oxford, the president washed the feet of seven choristers on Maundy Thursday. After the Reformation the practice continued, Cranmer participating in and defending the custom. The monarch sometimes took the place of ecclesiastics then. Q. Elizabeth deigned to wash the feet of the poor. Thos. Rugge (*Mercurius Politicus Redivivus*) records that Charles II in 1661 was—

'pleased to wash 31 poor men's feet in the great hall in Whitehall, and gave every man a purse of white leather, in it 31 pence, and a red purse, in it a piece of gold, and a shirt, a suit of cloathes, shoes and stockings, a wooden dish, and a basket wherein was four loaves, half a salmon, a whole ling, and herrings red and white. Every man drank claret wine in the Hall, and after service was done by the usual Vicar, that belonged to the King's Chapel, also the sound of the organs, they all departed and said—God save the King.'

This humility of Charles was no doubt a piece of Restoration enthusiasm, for in 1667 Pepys records that 'the King did not wash the poor people's feet himself, but the Bishop of London did it for him.' James II was the last monarch to do it in person. The Hanoverian monarchs declined the office, but in 1731 it was performed by the Abp. of C. as George II's deputy. In 1737 the washing was dropped, but the custom of giving alms, food, and clothing was retained. Money is now given in lieu of the last named. The ceremony took place at the Chapel Royal, Whitehall, until 1891, and on that bdg. being closed as a place of worship it was transferred to W.A. The almoner and his assistant are still girded with long towels, by way of a reminder of the original ceremony. The number of poor men and the number of poor women who are recipients of this bounty always equals the age of the monarch. The gift to men is of £4 15s. in cash and copper coins

to the amount of a penny for each yr. of the monarch's age. Women receive ten shillings less. The Maundy Money, specially struck by the Mint, can be sold at much more than face value. The money is brought in procession by two members of the Yeomen of the Guard, who carry a silver-gilt alms dish filled with little red and white leather purses.

FLORENCE NIGHTINGALE. Annually on her birthday, 12th May, the Women's Section of the British Red Cross Soc. place a wreath on her statue in Waterloo Place.

QUIT RENTS. The payment of the quit rent, made every Michaelmas at the Royal Courts of Justice, is probably the oldest L. custom. Its history commenced in 1235 with an entry in the Great Roll of the Exchequer (the Pipe Roll) of a payment of six horseshoes by one Walter le Brun, le Mareshal or farrier, for a plot for a smithy in the par. of St. Clement Danes. J. Bruce Williamson (*The Temple, London*) mentions that the Knights Templars were in possession of two forges, and he quotes a petition of 1446 which said:

'One of theym was edified and sett a little from the Churche of Seint Dunstene in Flete Street, upon the Est partie thereof and conteyning in length 18 footes of assize and in brede 14 footes; and the other Forge was edified and set upon the west side of the same Churche in the same streete whiche conteyned in length 15 footes of assize and in brede 11 footes.'

It would appear that one of these was the one existing in 1235. A. E. Stamp (*The Times*, 28th Sept. 1935) states that in 1261 Henry III gave to Walter, the smith of the time, some extra land 'for the enlargement of the smithy,' which may be assumed to imply an additional forge. He adds that

'the smithy is said to be in the Gore of St. Clement between the Church of the Danes and the Stone Cross, on the north side of the road to Westminster.'

No doubt the forges were required for shoeing horses and repairing armour and weapons at Fiketscroft or Fikettsfield, used by the Knights Hospitaliers and the Knights Templars for their martial exercises.

The last male Mareshal d. 1343, and one of his daughters, Joan, m. Thos. of Waltham Cross. They eventually sold the smithy to Wm. of Evesham. He d.

1351, holding 'of the King in chief, a messuage formerly having a forge before the door but long since demolished.' Still however there was due the annual rent of horse-shoes and nails. It is not known that the property came into the possession of the City, but in course of time it became the practice for the City authorities to collect numerous small rents due to the Crown and pay them into the Exchequer. By the end of the 14th century the occupant of the property was practically a freeholder, and his payment of shoes and nails an antiquarian gesture. The six shoes and 'sixty and one more' nails (ten to each shoe) are those paid over from time immemorial. After the warrants have been read in court the summons goes forth:

'Tenants and occupiers of a certain tenement called "The Forge" in the parish of St. Clement Danes in the County of Middlesex, come forth and do your services.'

The City Solicitor then steps forward, counts the shoes and nails, and presents them to the King's Remembrancer, to whose office they are then returned for another yr.

At the same time another quit rent is paid for a piece of land called The Moors in Shropshire, which came into the possession of the City in the time of Henry VIII. It was probably in the neighbourhood of Alveley. The City Solicitor tenders for this property an axe and a billhook, using the former on a bundle of faggots to prove its keenness. There is a record that once the payment was two knives, one good and the other bad, and this no doubt was a test required thereafter. However, both knives were not expected to be of equal keenness, for one was to cut through a hazel rod, and the other to be a flexible one.

The ceremony is open to the public, and is preceded by an introductory essay by the Queen's Remembrancer. It is probable that at one time it took place at the Stone Cross in the Strand (*q.v.*).

The payment of a single rose—as a quit rent—is made annually in respect of an illicit obstruction made in Seething Lane.

In 1370 Thomas de Brandon, mercer, sold to Sir Robert Knollys and Constance, his wife, a property on the W. side of Seething Lane, in the par. of All Hallows,

Berkyngechirche. In 1379, when Knollys retired, he and his wife bought another house on the E. side of the same lane. These they connected with a *haut-pas* 14 ft. above the level of the lane. This caused some obstruction, and the matter was reported to the Guildhall. Sir Robert, having been a close friend of the Black Prince, seems to have assumed that any infringement of the City's rights would be overlooked. The C.C. did not do so, although they took a lenient view of the offence. Instead of a monetary quit rent, it was ordained that every yr. upon the festival of St. John the Baptist (Midsummer Day), Sir Robert should present himself at the Guildhall, bearing a red rose fresh, as plucked out of his garden. Sir Robert obeyed, it is believed, until old age made the journey to the Guildhall impossible.

Annually (now at the Mansion House) a red rose is presented to the Ld.M. on a black velvet cushion. It is only fair to point out that the authenticity of the legend is much in doubt. A stained-glass window in the Ch. of All Hallows Barking, commemorates Sir Robert Knollys and his quit rent.

ROYAL COURTS OF JUSTICE. On the first day of Michaelmas sittings, after the Long Vacation, the whole body of judges (fully robed) breakfast with the Ld. Chancellor, attend service at W.A., and then proceed to the Law Courts.

Once a yr. new K.C.s (at present Q.C.s)—or 'silks,' as they are colloquially called from the material of their gowns, present themselves in each of the courts. They are attired in full-bottomed wigs, silk gowns, and knee-breeches. The judge looks down and calls a name; the new K.C. advances, and sits down in the middle of the leaders' benches. The judge says: 'Mr. Jones, do you move?' Mr. Jones gets up, bows to the judge, bows to any K.C. that is present on his right, then on his left, then turns round to the Junior Bar, and bows to them; they rise and bow back to him. He then goes out, and another K.C. takes his place. As there are sometimes fifteen new K.C.s at one time it is a lengthy business, and judges have been known to take them in batches. The full dress worn (plus a sword, which is left at home) costs well over £100.

ST. BARTHOLOMEW'S CHURCH. On Good Friday morning about 11.30 a number of widows pick up sixpences from a tombstone in the chyd. of St. Bartholomew the Great. The origin of the custom is unknown. It has been suggested that it is due to the diversion of a pre-Reformation fund designed to furnish masses for the dead. The first reference is in 1686, and therefore the money is not laid upon the tombstone of the benefactor. In cases of extreme decrepitude the money is taken to their homes. Now invariably more than 6d. is given, and in 1950 12s. 6d. was added to the sixpence formally picked up, with a hot cross bun. Owing to the diminution of the population, in 1950 only about nine qualified. The source of income is a gift of £22 10s. made in 1885 and the collection at the preceding service.

ST. ETHELDREDA'S (R.C.) CHURCH. On 3rd Feb. is celebrated St. Blaise's Day. St. Blaise (or Blasius) was a physician who entered the church, and became Bp. of Sebaste (Armenia), at the beginning of the 4th century. He became a martyr and whilst in prison, is said to have performed a wonderful cure of a boy who was nearly choking through having swallowed a fish bone. On his day (3rd Feb. in the Latin and 11th Feb. in the Oriental churches) two consecrated candles, held in the form of a cross, are applied to the throat of any sufferers from complaints affecting that part of the body. A number of patients annually present themselves in St. Etheldreda's Church (Ely Place, Holborn) for this purpose. (In pre-Reformation days there was a chapel dedicated to St. Blaise in W.A. where is now 'Poets' Corner.)

ST. JOHN'S CHURCH, CLERKENWELL. Annually, on 24th June, there is a procession of the Knights of the Order of St. John of Jerusalem from the gatehouse in St. John's Lane to the neighbouring ch. of St. John, now exclusively the ch. of the order. The ch. has been reduced to a ruin by bombs, but notwithstanding the service is still held there. In 1931, to commemorate the centenary of the reconstitution of the English branch of the Order, the service was held in W.A. (See 'Clerkenwell.')

SPITAL SERMONS derive their name from the priory of St. Mary Spittle (Hospital), founded by Walter Brune and his wife, Rosia, in 1197. It was in the par. of St. Botolph Without, Bishopsgate, and the site is now covered by Spital Sq., Spital Yard, etc. Stow mentions them as being preached in 1477. The priory was surrendered at the dissolution to Henry VIII, but long after a portion of the large chyd. of the hosp. remained, with a pulpit cross within a walled enclosure, similar to the one at St. Paul's Cath. Here, every Easter, the sermons were preached and, in a small two-storied bdg. opposite, the aldermen and sheriffs sat to listen. Foxe, in his Acts and Monuments, many times alludes to these. Q. Elizabeth went in 1559. In 1594 a gallery was built near the pulpit for the governor and children of Christ's Hosp. In 1617 many of the Lds. of K. James's Privy Council attended the Spital Sermons, and afterwards dined with the Ld.M. at Billingsgate. On Good Friday Christ's Passion was usually the subject of the sermon at Paul's Cross, and on the following Monday, Tuesday, and Wednesday a bp., a dean, and a doctor of divinity preached at the Spital concerning the Resurrection. On Low Sunday another learned divine at Paul's Cross rehearsed the substance of the previous four in a fifth sermon. The Ld.M. and C.C. always attended, robed in violet gowns, on Good Friday and Easter Wednesday; on the other days in scarlet. In 1642 the custom was discontinued. It was, however, revived at the Restoration, except that the two sermons formerly preached at St. Paul's Cross were then preached inside the Cath., the Cross having been destroyed, and the others at one of the City chs. Some of these sermons were very lengthy. Dr. Isaac Barrow (1630–77) preached once for three and a half hours. He was asked, on coming down from the pulpit, if he was not tired. 'Yes, indeed,' said he, 'I began to be weary with standing so long.' This was probably at St. Bride's Ch., where the sermons were regularly preached as soon as it was rebuilt. From 1797 they were preached at Christ Ch., Newgate. The object is not charitable, and there is now only one sermon, on the second Wednesday after Easter. It is now attended by the governors of the two royal hosps.— Bridewell and Christ's. Formerly there were three others—St. Bartholomew's, St. Thomas's and Bethlehem. 'Blue-coat' boys attended before the sch. was removed to Horsham. Dr. Parr, a rather eccentric divine, who argued with Dr. Johnson, preached the Spital Sermons on more than one occasion. Once it was at the invitation of the Ld.M. (Harvey Combe), and as they were coming out of the ch. together Parr said: 'Well, how did you like the sermon?' 'Why, Doctor,' replied his Lordship, 'there were four things in it that I did not like to hear.' 'State them,' said the preacher. 'Why, to speak frankly then, they were the quarters of the church clock, which struck four times before you had finished.' Parr's Spital Sermon in 1799 occupied nearly three hours in delivery.

On the destruction of Christ Ch., Newgate, the sermon was preached at St. Stephen's, Walbrook, and when the latter Ch. was gutted it was transferred to St. Mary Woolnoth, later to St. Lawrence Jewry and now to St. Sepulchre. The preacher is always a bishop, who is appointed by the Abp. of C., and is taken in order of seniority on the bench.

STATIONERS' HALL. On Ash Wednesday the Stationers' Co. hold an annual service in the ch. of St. Faith in the crypt of St. Paul's Cath., about 2.40 p.m., after which buns and ale are consumed in the Stationers' Hall. The custom originated under the will of Alderman John Norton dated 21st May 1612. (See Companies —Stationers.)

TOWER OF LONDON. Annually on 21st May, the anniversary of Henry VI's murder (1471), lilies from Eton Coll. and white roses from Kings Coll., Cambridge, both of which he founded, are placed in the chapel in the Wakefield Tower, where he is believed to have been engaged in devotions at the time of his death. For this purpose a sum of £10 was given to Sir Geo. Younghusband in 1923 by the Soc. of the Blessed Mary of Eton, and the Eton lilies, which are tied together with blue ribbon, are in accordance with a similar offering which yr. by yr. was placed on the tomb in St. George's Chapel, Windsor. The flowers are deposited in the oratory in the chapel at 6 p.m., on the date mentioned, and burned the following day.

VINTNERS' COMPANY. Annually, on a Thursday in July, members of the Vintners' Co. walk in procession from their hall in Upper Thames St. to the ch. of St. James Garlickhithe. They are preceded by two men in top hats and white smocks, carrying brooms, with which, merely as a gesture, they sweep the road, whilst others in the procession carry flowers. The custom dates back to 1205, when it was laid down by the court that

'the wine porters should sweep the roads with full besoms that the Master and his Wardens and Brethren of the Court of Assistants slip not on any foulness in our streets; and further, that each such Master, Warden, and Brother of the Court of Assistants be provided with a nosegay of sweet and fine herbs that their nostrils be not offended by any noxious flavours or other ill vapours.'

WESTMINSTER SCHOOL. On Shrove Tuesday the chef of the sch. tosses a small pancake from a small frying-pan over the bar across the great schoolroom. One boy from each form is chosen to scramble, and he who captures the largest piece is awarded a guinea by the dean. The date of the origin of the custom is unknown. Some writers on the sch. take it back to the early 17th century. The first known reference, however, is in some autobiographical notes of Jeremy Bentham's—a scholar from 1755 to 1762. He says:

'The higher school was divided from the lower by a bar, and it was one of our pastimes to get the cook to throw a pancake over it.'

The pancake is the genuine article, not a putty one, as one historian will have it. In 1947 the bar was fixed across the ruined schoolroom when, for the first time after the Second World War, the pancake 'greaze' took place at the old sch.

WIDOW'S SON (Devons Rd., Bromley-by-Bow). The story is that a widow had an only son who went to sea. He endeavoured to console her, on parting with the hope that he would be back by Easter, when they would have hot-cross buns together. He went down with his ship, but the widow refused to believe he was lost, and on Good Friday sat waiting all day with a table spread for two. On every anniversary of his death thereafter she religiously laid aside a bun for him. Upon her decease a kindly neighbour collected these tokens of affection and suspended them from a beam, and locally the cottage became known as the 'Bun House.' Eventually it fell into decay, was demolished and a tavern erected on the site. The addition of a hot-cross bun to the cluster hanging from the ceiling is required by the lease, and this is made every Good Friday morning. It is said that once there were as many as 120 to be seen, but they are much fewer now.

Special sermons are mentioned under 'City Churches.' For Gunpowder Plot, see 'St. Mary-le-Bow Ch.' For 'Lion Sermon,' see 'St. Katherine Cree Ch.' For Stow Service, see 'St. Andrew, Undershaft Ch.'

(See *Quaint Survivals of Old London Customs*, by H. E. Popham, 1928; *Ghosts of London*, by H. V. Morton, 1939; *English Custom and Usage*, by Christina Hole, 1942.)

Customs House (Lower Thames St.). The first Customs House was erected by John Churchman, sheriff, in 1382. It was E. of the site of the present bdg., in a 'Wool Wharf,' the king 'granting that the tronage of wools should be kept in the house and a counting place for customers,' etc. This bdg. was burnt in the reign of Elizabeth. The second Customs House was burnt in the G.F. The third, designed by Wren, was also burnt (1718), and the fourth again (1814). The present Customs House was erected 1815–17, the architect being David Laing. The foundations were found to be defective and in 1828 the long room had to be taken down, and the foundations relaid. The new work was carried out by Sir Robt. Smirke. The imposing river front of Portland stone is 488 ft. long, and the long room (where most of the documents required by the Custom laws are received by officials) is 190 ft. long and 66 ft. wide. There is a handsome board room for the commissioners, a library, a collection of curios appertaining to customs, and old-fashioned armed equipment.

10 Barges, Limehouse

11 *Jason* on the Regent's Canal

12 The Post Office Tower

13 *Cutty Sark*, Greenwich

14 Royal Naval College, Greenwich

15 Ken Wood

16 Guildhall

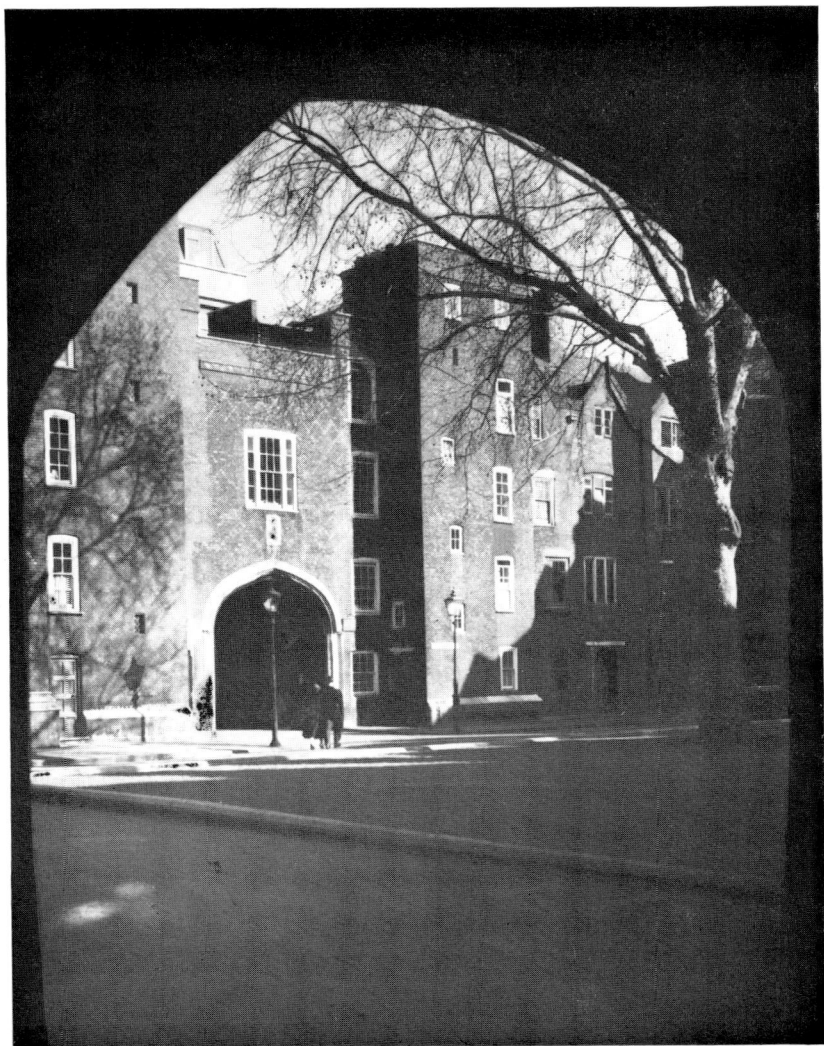

17 Old Gate, Lincoln's Inn

18 Boodles Club, St James's

D

Deptford, now part of the L. Bor. of Lewisham, was a met. bor. S. of the Thames. There was originally but one par. of the name, St. Nicholas, part of the area of which, including the ch., has now somewhat oddly been included in the bor. of Greenwich. The river Ravensbourne, called at its mouth Deptford Creek, forms the chief eastern boundary line, and on the site of the ancient deep ford, from which the place most probably takes its name, is now Deptford Bridge; the present structure dating from 1883.

The original name of the place, as recorded in the Anglo-Saxon Chronicle and in Domesday Book, was Mereton, the town in the marsh, and it did not receive its present designation until after the Norman Conquest. The manor of Deptford, or W. Greenwich, was then given to Gilbert de Magninot or Maminot, from whom it descended to the Saye family. The manor was later known as Sayes Court, and in 1653 was purchased by John Evelyn, diarist and author of *Sylva*. Here he entertained Charles II and other distinguished visitors, and tended his gardens of which he was very proud. The house was let in 1698 to Peter the Great of Russia, who left it and the gardens in a terrible condition, much to Evelyn's disgust. According to Lysons, the house was pulled down about 1728. The small Sayes Court Park is now a reminder of his estate.

Other lesser manors were Deptford-le-Strond, or Strand, the original home of Trinity House; Hatcham, partly in Camberwell, and Brockley, partly in Lewisham.

The ancient ch. of St. Nicholas stands on Deptford Green near the river, and dates from the 12th century. Rebuilt except for the tower in 1697, it was burnt during the Second World War, but most of its beautiful fittings and monuments were saved. Among the latter were memorials to Edwd. Fenton (1603) sea captain and companion of Sir Martin Frobisher; Peter Pett (1652) master shipwright; George Shelvocke (1742) privateer; and a modern tablet to Christopher Marlowe, slain in a tavern brawl at Deptford 1593 and bd. in the chyd. The ch. also contained a wonderful piece of woodcarving representing Ezekiel's vision of the valley of dry bones. It was the work of Grinling Gibbons who was 'discovered' by Evelyn who found him 'in a poor solitary thatched house in a field . . . near Sayes Court.' Over the gateway are carved stone skulls sometimes known as Adam and Eve.

St. Paul's Ch., built to designs of Thos. Archer in 1730, is an interesting bdg. of its period, and though re-arranged in 1883 contains some magnificent Dutch oak fittings. There is a bust of a former rector, Chas. Burney, brother of Fanny Burney, and a tablet to John Harrison (1753) founder and first surgeon of the London Hosp.

Immediately to the E. of this ch. is a little Baptist chapel, built in the early 18th century, and now the oldest in the L. area.

Of the more modern chs. St. James', Hatcham, consecrated 1854, has had a stormy history, and the misfortune to have been twice burnt out. During the incumbency of Rev. Arthur Tooth, 1863–77, his insistence on holding extreme 'high-church' services in defiance of his Bp. led to his being deprived of the living and imprisoned in Horsemonger Lane Gaol.

Deptford Dockyard was founded by Henry VIII in 1513, and was closed in 1844. Here Drake's famous ship the 'Golden Hind' lay in dry-dock until it literally fell to pieces through age. Part of the bor.'s small river front was occupied by the Royal Victualling Yard established in 1742 but now is used for other purposes. In the premises occupied by Convoys Ltd. may still be seen parts of one of the original Tudor bdgs. of the once famous Deptford Yard.

Dickens House. Chas. Dickens resided at 48 Doughty St. from Mar. 1837 to the end of 1839. He removed here from Furnival's Inn (*q.v.*). There was one child, Chas. Dickens the younger, then a few weeks old. Other members of the household were his brother Fredk. and his sister-in-law, Mary Hogarth, who was seventeen yrs. of age. On 7th May 1837, in the top back room of the house, she died in Dickens's arms. This blow suspended the publication of *Pickwick Papers* for two months. In Mar. 1838 his first daughter Mary was born here. She died in 1896 leaving a small book on her father, which was published in 1885. This was entirely a eulogium, and contrasted strangely with *Dickens and Daughter* (1939), the volume instigated by her sister Kate who was born here in October 1839 and wrote more candidly and truly. The latter became first Mrs. Collins, afterwards Mrs. Perugini; she died in her ninetieth yr. in 1929. In Doughty St. Dickens completed *Pickwick Papers*, and wrote *Oliver Twist* and *Nicholas Nickleby*. Here he planned *Barnaby Rudge*. He moved from here to a house in Devonshire Terrace, Marylebone High St., which still remains.

The acquisition of the Doughty St. house by the Dickens Fellowship was mainly due to B. W. Matz, a foundation member, first secretary, and past president (1920–1) of the Fellowship. It was formally opened on 9th June 1925 (the fifty-fifth anniversary of Dickens' death) by the E. of Birkenhead. The only literary notability present was Sir Edmund Gosse. The Dickens family, holding the view that it was contrary to the novelist's wishes forbidding a national memorial, was not represented. It was B. W. Matz's last public appearance. On 17th July 1925, he died at the age of sixty. His fine collection of Dickensiana had been lent to the house. It was purchased for a thousand pounds from his widow by Viscount Wakefield, and presented to the trustees. The Dickens House happily escaped the blitz.

Amongst personal relics of Dickens on show are a lock of his hair; a portrait by Samuel Drummond (painted at the time of his residence here); a collection of letters; a writing table used at Gad's Hill Place; his Reading Desk—taken to America; a wardrobe from Gad's Hill Place; a portrait of Mary Hogarth; desk at which Dickens sat, as a youth, in the office of Messrs. Ellis & Blackmore, Gray's Inn. The MSS. exhibited are: small parts of *Nicholas Nickleby* and *Oliver Twist*; one page of *Pickwick Papers*; *Our Commission* (*Household Words*); *The Schoolboy's Story* (*Reprinted Pieces*).

The House is the headquarters of the Dickens Fellowship, and from here *The Dickensian* appears quarterly.

Directories. The earliest known was published in 1595, having been printed by S. Bentley, Dorset St. It consists of 'the names of all suche gentlemen of accompte, as were residing within ye Citie of London, Liberties and suburbes thereof, 28 Novembris 1595 Anno 38 Elizabethae Reginae.' The list in manuscript is in the Burghley papers in the Lansdowne MSS. It is endorsed: 'Strangers beyng not citizẽs lodgỹg in London.' It was republished (fifty copies only) in 1830 by York Herald, Chas. G. Young. There are only 118 names, arranged under twenty-one wards. Next comes a series of Returns in 1638, now in the lib. of Lambeth Palace. These were prepared by the various incumbents for submission to the Privy Council, and cover 13,500 householders in 93 pars. in the City and the liberties. This return was published in 1931 by the Soc. of Genealogists, the volume being edited by Rev. T. C. Dale, B.A. The editor regrets that rarely do the clergy indicate with any precision where the citizens lived, but the incumbent of St. Margaret's, New Fish St., was quite detailed in his addresses, e.g. under Pudding Lane—'Mr. Shaw costermonger next below the star backdoor,' and 'Mr. Pinn by the stayers above Shaw's house.' In 1640 there was prepared a *List of principal inhabitants of the City of London*. This is a manuscript in the Public Record Office. The list was compiled by the aldermen in obedience to an order of the Privy Council, and 1,518 persons are enumerated as being reputed able to lend money to Charles I. This list was published in 1886, edited by W. J. Harvey.

In 1677 the first real directory appeared. It was entitled *A Collection of the Names of the Merchants living in and about the City of London*, and said to be 'very useful and necessary, Carefully Collected for the benefit of all dealers that shall have occasion with any of them, Directing them at the first sight of their name to the place of their abode.' It was 'printed for Sam Lee,' and was 'to be sold at Lumbard Street near Pope's Head Alley, and Dan Major at the Flying Horse in Fleet stret.' This gives a list of 1,953 merchants and traders, and the names of the streets in which they lived or conducted business. Of the numerous shop signs only half a dozen are mentioned apart from the goldsmiths,' i.e. 'to be spoken withal at the sign of the Purse in Loathbury'; 'at the Sun, Lumbard Street'; 'At the Angel near Bread Street'; 'at the Pewter Platter,

Cannon Street'; 'Bankside, near the Wind Mill'; 'Clement's Lane at a Milliner's.' Only in a few instances is the precise nature of the business given apart from goldsmiths. There were thirty-eight factors carrying on business at Blackwell Hall, there were eighteen packers, four upholsterers, two confectioners, one barber, one cheesemonger, one stationer, and one apothecary. Of the fifty-eight goldsmiths mentioned, only two survive to this day—Child's Bank, formerly Blanchard & Child of 'ye Marygold in Fleet Street,' and Hoare's Bank, formerly James Hore at the sign of the Golden Bottle. Both are still within a few yards of one another. There are copies of this first directory in the B.Mus., the Bodleian Library, and two copies at the Guildhall.

In 1732 James Brown (b. at Kelso 1709, d. at Stoke Newington 1788) made a list of the principal traders of L. He gave it to Henry Kent, printer, of Finch Lane, Cornhill, and in 1734 the latter published it. This appeared annually until 1771, so evidently was found lucrative. It was then passed on to Richd. Causton, who published until 1776. It was then continued by Richd. and Harry Causton, and then by Henry Kent Causton. Ninety-six issues had appeared when it ceased publication in 1828. These directories consisted simply of alphabetical lists of names, occupations, and addresses. In 1763 a 'Mr. Mortimer' published a directory with a section devoted to trades. The first directory divided into streets was P. Boyle's, published in 1792. In 1799 appeared the first Post Office Directory under the title *The New Annual Directory.* This was prepared by postal officials, and issued under the patronage of the Postmaster-General. It was therefore surprising that the innovations of Messrs. Boyle and Mortimer were ignored, this volume consisting simply of an alphabetical list of names, occupations, and addresses. In 1817 Andrew Johnstone, a commercial broker, produced the first directory that combined all the advantages of a modern one. He gave streets arranged alphabetically, and a topographical description of them, also their length, the number of houses in each, and the names and occupations of the residents. He gave also the names of individuals, their occupations, and addresses, with the names of persons engaged in them and page refer-

ences for all trades. There was also a mail-coach and wagon conveyance guide. This directory had about 27,000 names. In 1837 the copyright of the Post Office London Directory passed to Fredk. Kelly. It was not until 1840 that anything better was offered than in 1799. Then there was a trades section, and in 1841 the streets were given separately. Kelly's Directory since then has established supremacy.

(See *London Directories,* by C. W. F. Goss, 1932.)

Docks. L. has been a port as long as it has been a city, but its docks are of more recent origin. The growth of overseas trade during the 17th and 18th centuries led to congestion of shipping in the river, and the berthing and warehousing accommodation of the 'legal quays' and 'sufferance wharves' became inadequate. Various schemes for docks were put forward, and eventually the W. India merchants obtained parliamentary powers to build L.'s first commercial dock. This was the W. India Dock, which was opened in 1802, and by the end of the 19th century most of the other docks had been built.

To-day L. is the Commonwealth's greatest port. The shipping which arrived and departed from the Port of L. in the year 1966 amounted to over 91 million net register tons; and the quantity of imports, exports, and trans-shipments amounted to approximately 59 million tons.

The modern Port of L. comprises four large dock systems, viz. the India and Millwall; Surrey Commercial; Royal; and Tilbury Docks. The port also includes the tidal reaches of the Thames from Teddington to about 22 miles eastward into the Thames Estuary. The whole of the docks (with the exception of the Regent's Canal Dock) and the tidal river come under the jurisdiction of the Port of L. Authority (*q.v.*).

The former London and St. Katharine Docks were situated immediately to the E. of the T.L. The St. Katharine Docks were opened in 1828, and were built on the site of the old royal and collegiate chapel of St. Katharine by the Tower. The London Docks were opened in 1805 and were used by vessels engaged in the short sea trade and coastal services. In 1968 the London and St. Katharine Docks were closed because they are no longer economic. New methods of cargo-handling and growing ship sizes demand more modern facilities such as are being developed down-river at Tilbury. The dock area will be used for housing, but the old warehouses will remain as buildings of historic interest. L.'s is the world's greatest market for tea, and most of this is stored at the Commercial Rd. warehouse. Carpets, curios, silk, feathers, cigars, and drugs are stored at the Cutler St. warehouses.

The India and Millwall Docks are on the Isle of Dogs.

The West India Dock, built for the W. India trade, are still the most important storage centre for sugar, and have specially equipped sheds for the storage of hardwood.

The south *West India Dock* was built in 1805 as the City Canal to save sailing vessels the long détour round the Isle of Dogs. The canal was acquired by the W. India Dock Co. in 1829, and reconstructed as a dock. In recent yrs. these docks have been completely remodelled, and are now intercommunicating by means of deep-water passages, and are served by a modern entrance lock in Blackwall Reach. There are specially equipped berths in the W. India Docks for the discharge of bananas.

The *Millwall Dock*, connected to the south W. India Dock, was opened in 1868. In addition to a large general trade, these docks are the centre of the grain trade, the central granary having a capacity of 24,000 tons.

The East India Docks are situated at Blackwall, and were built in 1806 by a subsidiary co. of the famous E. India Co. They are used mainly by vessels trading coastwise.

The Surrey Commercial Docks, the only dock system on the S. bank of the river, are about two miles below London Bridge. They originated in 1696 with the Howland Great Wet Dock, a harbourage for sailing vessels, and have been added to from time to time, and now have nearly 9 miles of quay. The Greenland and South Docks accommodate vessels from N. America which bring lumber, wheat and general cargoes. The eight docks in the northern portion of the system are used exclusively by timber-carrying ships from N. European and Canadian ports. Specially constructed sheds, and open storage ground, provide accommodation for 500,000 tons of timber.

The Royal Docks. The Royal Docks consist of the Royal Victoria, Royal Albert, and K. George V Docks, and are intercommunicating by means of deep-water passages. Together, these three docks have a water area of 230 acres—the largest enclosed area of impounded dock water in the world.

The Royal Victoria Dock, the oldest of them, was opened in 1855, has, in recent years, been completely modernised. It possesses a fine range of warehouses in which are stored thousands of tons of tobacco. There are specially equipped berths for the discharge of chilled beef, and on the S. side four of the largest flour-mills in the country.

The Royal Albert Dock was opened in 1880 as a transit dock, and parallel to its 3 miles of quays are transit sheds covering an area of 30 acres. The dock is equipped with special berths for the discharge of frozen meat, and has cold stores, the largest of which has accommodation for 250,000 carcases of mutton.

The King George V Dock is L.'s most modern dock, and was opened by George V in 1921. This dock cost £4,500,000 to build, and can accommodate vessels up to 37-ft. draught.

The Tilbury Docks are 26 miles down the river from London Bridge, half-way between the City and the sea. They have a water area of 104 acres, 4 miles of quay, and 35 miles of railway sidings. These docks are used by some of the largest vessels which come into the Port of L. A £6 million extension, begun in 1963, has provided four new berths.

The River Cargo Jetty, adjacent to Tilbury Docks, is used by vessels discharging or loading part cargoes.

The Tilbury Passenger Landing Stage accommodates large liners at any state of the tide, and is connected by covered ways with a commodious and artistically designed customs baggage examination hall, and the adjacent Tilbury Riverside station.

The War. During the war years it became necessary for security reasons to divert much ocean shipping from L. to other ports, but coastwise shipping was maintained. 3,000 convoys sailed from L. during the war yrs. In preparation for the allied invasion of Europe, L. received immense cargoes of munitions of war from Canada and the U.S.A. Later, immediately prior to D-Day, a fleet of over 200 merchant ships left L. for the beachhead with tanks, military vehicles, ammunition and stores. Between D-Day and VE-Day no less than 2¾ million tons of military stores were shipped from L.

Aerial attacks on the Docks were severe and sustained, and by the end of the war the damage amounted to £13,500,000. Major works for the rehabilitation of the Docks, authorized, in hand, and contemplated, amount to £10,500,000.

Visits to the Docks. During the summer months the Authority organizes afternoon cruises down the river and through the Royal Docks.

Doctors' Commons is first mentioned in 1532. The civilians and canonists then lodged in a small, inconvenient house in Paternoster Row, afterwards the Queen's Head Tavern. It was a coll. or common house for the doctors of law, for the study and practice of the civil law. In 1570 a house called Montjoye Place ('in Knight Rither' Street) was leased for the coll. from the dean and chapter of St. Paul's, by Master Henry Harvey, Master of Trinity Hall, Cambridge, Prebendary of Ely, and Dean of the Arches—according to Sir Geo. Howes, 'a reverend, learned and good man.' It was burnt in the G.F. and rebuilt. There were five courts, viz. (1) Court of Arches; (2) Prerogative Court; (3) Court of Faculties and Dispensations; (4) Consistory Court of the Bp. of L.; (5) High Court of Admiralty. Doctors' Commons appears in several of Dickens's books, for he was a shorthand-writer for the proctors—'a sort of monkish attorney,' says Steerforth. It is described as:

'A quiet and shady court-yard, paved with stone, and frowned upon by old red-brick houses. . . . A lazy old nook near St. Paul's Churchyard. . . . a little out-of-the-way place, where they administer what is called ecclesiastical law, and play all kinds of tricks with obsolete old monsters of Acts of Parliament, which three-fourths of the world know nothing about. . . . The place where they grant marriage licences to love-sick couples, and divorces to unfaithful ones : register the wills of people who have any property to leave.'

Regarding the first purpose, Sam Weller mentioned two porters who were touts for licences, and a letter in *The Times* in 1833 complained of this. 'They puts things into old gen'lm'n's heads as they never dreamed of,' says Sam. The buildings were extensive, and included a large court room. They were demolished in 1867, but the 'low archway,' mentioned by Sam Weller (when Jingle, who had gone there for a marriage licence, was being pursued), remained until 1894. There is a C.C. tablet on Faraday House, Queen Victoria St. In 1857, ten yrs. before the demolition, the occupation of Doctors' Commons had gone, partly through the reforms introduced by the Probate Act of 1857. Now the Probate, Divorce, and Admiralty Division of the High Court of Justice deals with a considerable amount of business formerly done at Doctors' Commons. The proving of wills and testaments, however, is carried on at Somerset House, and the Court of Arches meets at Westminster.

Downing Street. It took its name from Sir Geo. Downing—son of a L. barrister, who was b. in Dublin 1623. He was taken by his parents to America in 1638, and became an undergraduate of the new Harvard Coll. About 1643 he returned to England, and became a chaplain in the Parliamentary forces. In 1655 he was one of a group who wished Cromwell to be king. After this he became ambassador at the Hague, and, notwithstanding his support of the Commonwealth, he managed at the Restoration to be made teller in the Exchequer, having Samuel Pepys as his clerk. The latter thought less of him than did his king. Charles II knighted Downing a week before he reached L. in 1660. Pepys wrote a few weeks later: 'He is so stingy a fellow I care not to see him; I quite cleared myself of his office, and did give him liberty to take anybody in.' In Mar. 1661 he was 'a perfidious rogue.' Downing was certainly a bit of a Vicar of Bray, and played his cards well.

In 1681 he bought 'a messuage' in Whitehall, and built four houses. In 1698 Downing St. was described as

'A pretty open space, especially at the upper end, where are four or five very large and well-built houses, fit for persons of honour and quality, each house having a pleasant prospect into St. James's Park, with a Terras-walk.'

No. 10 had been part of the forfeited property of the E. of Lichfield, who retired with James II, to whom he had been Master of the Horse. As Crown property George I gave it to Baron Bothmar, the Hanoverian minister, for life. On his death in 1731 George II offered it to Sir Robt. Walpole as a personal present. Walpole declined it as such, and it was agreed between that monarch and his minister that for the future it should go with the offices of First Lord of the Treasury and Chancellor of the Exchequer. Walpole went there from St. James's Sq. in 1735, and remained until 1742, when he left for a small house in Arlington St. Lady Walpole d. in Downing St. in 1738.

To the house in Downing St., Wm. Pitt, E. of Chatham was conveyed when he swooned in the House of Lords. His death followed in three weeks (1778). Here his son Wm. Pitt the younger lived. Later came Earl Grey, Lord John Russell, and W. E. Gladstone. The last went into residence in Downing St. first in 1853, but then as Chancellor of the Exchequer he occupied No. 11. Here his son Herbert (made Home Secretary in 1905), was b. in 1854. In 1868 Gladstone went to No. 10 as Prime Minister, after Disraeli had been there for a few months. Gladstone's residence was famous for Thursday breakfasts. Ld. Salisbury used it only for official purposes (like Ld. Melbourne and Sir Robt. Peel before him). Whilst Salisbury was premier, in 1887, Ld. Iddesleigh, formerly Sir Stafford Northcote, d. in an ante room of 10 Downing St. in his presence. Ld. Rosebery occupied it for a yr., but was known to dislike it. All subsequent Prime Ministers have occupied it. On the staircase leading to the reception rooms there is a portrait of every premier since Walpole.

Every precaution is taken against leakages. The windows of the Cabinet Room have double sashes, and there are double doors so that no conversation within can be heard without. As soon as a Cabinet meeting is concluded, every scrap of paper, including the blotting paper, is burned. Minutes are printed in a secret press in the basement by a special staff sworn to secrecy. Every scrap of paper has to be accounted for, and all waste is burned at once.

It was not until Lloyd George took possession in 1916 that No. 10 Downing St. had a bathroom.

The official residence of the Prime Minister of Gt. Britain has made Downing St. perhaps the best known thoroughfare in the world. Other people of note have lived there. G. H. Cunningham says that Aubrey de Vere, the twentieth and last E. of Oxford, d. there in 1703. He was a descendant of Edwd. de Vere, the seventeenth earl, one of the Shakespearean pretenders. Smollett lived in Downing St. in 1744, when seeking practice as a surgeon; Boswell lodged there in 1763; Gibbon stayed there as a guest of Ld. Sheffield.

Dulwich. *See* Camberwell.

E

Eastcheap is first mentioned *c.* 1214 as 'Estchepe.' The name Eastcheap was in use for the whole of the st. up to the 16th century, and then it appears to have included some of the E. end of what is now Cannon St. Stow, however, mentions Great Eastcheap and Little Eastcheap; the latter ran from St. Mary Hill to Fish St. Hill, and the former from Fish St. Hill to St. Martin's Lane. In Horwood's map (1799) Eastcheap ends at Crooked Lane. By 1827 'Great Eastcheap' had disappeared in nomenclature and it was simply 'Eastcheap.' The construction of London Bridge brought about considerable changes here between 1829 and 1831, some portion of Eastcheap being swept away for the approaches. The W. end ceased to exist, and the eastern portions were known respectively as 'Eastcheap' and 'Little Tower St.' In 1884 the whole street was widened and, as formerly, known only by the present name.

The earliest reference shows it to have been a place particularly for the resort of butchers, and a patent *c.* 1324 provides that a market for flesh and fish should be held as of old. Stow says:

'This Eastcheape is now a flesh Market of Butchers there dwelling, on both sides of the streete, it had sometime also Cookes mixed among the Butchers, and such other as solde victuals readie dressed of all sorts. For of old time when friends did meet, and were disposed to be merrie, they went not to dine and suppe in Taverns, but to the Cookes, where they called for meate what them liked, which they alwayes found ready dressed at a reasonable rate.'

At 'East Cheap,' in John Lydgate's *London Lickpenny*:

'One cries Ribs of beef and many a pie.'

Jas. Thomson is associated with the thoroughfare. In a letter to Aaron Hill, dated 24th May 1726, he said:

'I go on Saturday next to reside at Watts' academy, in Little Tower Street, in quality of a tutor to a young gentleman there.'

In 1727 he wrote his poem *Summer* there. He resided in what was the E. end of the thoroughfare now called 'Eastcheap.' G. H. Cunningham says that at No. 1 Little Tower St. was the 'Crooked Billet' in *Barnaby Rudge* where Joe Willet enlisted, and in which he was locked up for the night after his supper of tripe and onions. (The 'Boar's Head' is treated under 'Taverns.')

East India House was in Leadenhall St. from the date of the incorporation of the East India Co. in 1600. According to Strype the original edifice was Sir Wm. Craven's house, and it was let to the co. by him. It was rebuilt in 1726, and this was the house in which Chas. Lamb served as a clerk for thirty-three yrs. During his time, i.e. in 1799, an Ionic portico and an E. wing were added. On the shelves in Leadenhall St., Lamb said, were to be found his true works. 'There is corn in Egypt while there is cash in Leadenhall.' The building was sold in 1861 and demolished in 1862. There is a C.C. plaque on 15 Leadenhall St.

Eastminster. This name is sometimes said to have been borne by the abbey at E. Smithfield which Stow says was founded by Edward III in 1349. It was described in a Patent Roll 1348–50 as:

'The house of the Cistercian order to be called the royal free chapel of St. Mary Graces, which the king decided to found and endow in the new graveyard of the Holy Trinity by the Tower of London.'

According to Stow the K. who had been 'in a tempest on the sea and peril of drowning, made a vow to build a Monastery to the honour of God, and our Lady of Grace, if God would grant him grace to come safe to land.'

It was suppressed in 1539, and the site granted to Sir Arthur Darcy. He demolished the abbey, and erected on the site a store-house for victuals. The Mint (*q.v.*) now stands on the site.

There is no medieval authority for 'Eastminster' as applied to this abbey; neither is it so called by Stow. Erasmus, in a biographical sketch of Dean Colet, called St. P.'s Cath. by that name.

Ely Place. (Holborn) commemorates a L. palace of the Bps. of Ely. In 1286 the bp. was John de Kirkby; and, in accordance with custom, he had property in L. Dying in 1290, he bequeathed a messuage and nine adjoining tenements to his successors. The will refers to the property as in the par. of St. Andrew near Holborn. Kirkby's successor was Wm. de Luda. He held the see from 1290 to 1298, increased the demesne, and bequeathed fresh property to the see. It appears that it was during his episcopate that the chapel was built on ground left by Kirkby. The names of Kirkby and de Luda are remembered now in the chapel on the Sunday nearest to their anniversaries, viz. the last Sunday in Mar. or the last but one, and the former's name is preserved in Kirby St. The palace of the bp. is twice referred to in 1302; and, as on these occasions a knight and a baron 'did homage and fealty,' probably it was the chapel that was particularly referred to. In 1327 Philippa of Hainault spent her Christmas at Ely Place on her way to be m. to Edward III at York, and no doubt attended Mass in the chapel. The Black Prince was there in 1357; and in 1381, when the palace of the Savoy was gutted by the Wat Tyler rebels, John of Gaunt, 'time-honoured Lancaster,' came to the bp.'s palace where he appears to have remained until his death in 1399. Modern editions of Shakespeare (there are no scenes given in the First Folio, 1623) assign Act II, sc. i of *Richard II*, which includes John of Gaunt's fine speech about England, to 'Ely House.' The authority is Holinshed's *Chronicle*, so largely used in the Shakespeare plays—'The Duke of Lancaster departed out of this life at the Bishop of Elies place in Holbourne.'

In 1405 extensive repairs were done to the chapel, and Wm. the Glazier of Hitchin was paid 13s. 4d. for glazing the windows. In 1464 the serjeants held their banquet at Ely Place, and amongst the guests were the Ld.M. and aldermen. In the words of the Rev. J. A. Dewe:

'In accordance with the custom prevalent in places pertaining to their jurisdiction they expected the first places at the banquet; but, like the imprudent man mentioned in the gospel, they were requested to take a lower place, Guy de Ruthin, Ld. Treasurer, being honoured instead. The chief magistrate of the city, being deeply incensed, took his departure, and is reported to have consoled himself and his associates by a feed on their own account.'

The next historical event of interest was in 1483, and is recorded in the play of *Richard III*. The D. of Gloster, as the latter then was, says: 'My Lord of Ely, when I was last in Holborn, I saw good strawberries in your garden there, I do beseech you send for some of them.' The bp. replies: 'Marry and I will, my lord, with all my heart.' The garden at Ely Place was noted for its strawberries, and in the B.Mus. is a Latin play in which is a dialogue descanting upon their merits and styling them *decora fragra*. The gardens of the bp. sloped down to the River Fleet; and probably Plum Tree Court (from Farringdon St. to Shoe Lane), Saffron Hill, and Vine St. derive their names from them. It is remarkable that there is a threefold account of the trifling incident of Gloster's remark—in Holinshed's *Chronicle*, in Sir Thos. More's *History of Richard III*, and in the Shakespeare play quoted. It was probably deepened in the memory of all present by the hasty execution of Hastings which immediately followed. The bp. was sent to prison the following day. In 1531 a sumptuous banquet was held here, when eleven new serjeants were made. The hall, standing E. to W., is said to have been 74 ft. long; it was lighted by six Gothic windows. The entertainment lasted five days, and Henry VIII and Catherine of Aragon, with the foreign ambassadors, were present. Among the guests were the judges, the Ld.M., and aldermen. Stow gives full details of the dinner. In 1459 there was residing at Ely Place John Dudley, D. of Northumberland. He followed the D. of Somerset as Protector of Edward VI, and, on the accession of Q. Mary, followed him to the block.

In 1576 a change which left its mark on L. topography took place. The Bp. of Ely was obliged to surrender part of his property to Sir Christopher Hatton, Q. Elizabeth's 'dancing Chancellor.' He wound his way into her affections by insinuating flattery. 'To serve you is Heaven, and to lack you is more than Hell's torments,' he wrote. 'Pain overcomes me, I can write you no more. Love me for I love you.' The bp., Dr. Cox, was obliged to grant a lease of the gate-house and other portions of the palace in the first courtyard, together with the keeping of the garden and orchard for 21 yrs. The rent to be paid was a red rose for the gate-house, ten loads of hay and £10 p.a. for the garden. Sir Christopher wanted even more. He spent £2,000 in repairing the gate-house and making it into a more convenient dwelling, and he used this expenditure as a plea for obtaining the entire palace. Bp. Cox protested in a well-written Latin letter. The matter was referred to the Q., who decided that the property should remain in Hatton's hands until such time as the bp. should repay to him the money he had lavished upon it. The bp. d. in 1581; and, perhaps because other ecclesiastics were shy of what was a bed of roses in a literal but not in a metaphorical sense, the see remained vacant until 1599, when Dr. Martin Heton became bp. In 1591 Hatton had died at Ely Place, Q. Elizabeth visiting him there in his last illness. The new bp. resumed the fight where his predecessor had left it, but with no success. It is to him that the Q. is said to have written: 'I would have you to know, that I who made you what you are, can unmake you, and if you do not forthwith fulfil your engagements by ——, I will immediately unfrock you.' The engagement presumably was to continue to repay money to Hatton's estate. (The letter quoted, said to have come from the Register of Ely, appears to have been unknown before it was printed in the *Annual Register* for 1761, and is therefore of doubtful authenticity.) No attempt was made to pay off the mortgage until the time of Bp. Lancelot Andrewes, who accepted the see in 1609, and his translation to Winchester came before anything was done. Eventually, after long disputes with the owners of the Hatton property, it was agreed that £100 p.a. should be paid to the bps. in compensation for what they had lost. In the Harleian MSS., in the case between the Bp. of Ely and my Ld. of Hatton, it is stated that:

'Several cellars are possessed by others, even under those rooms of the house which the Bishop hath now left to dwell in, and they are intermixed with the cellars which he uses, having lights and passages into the cloisters and the most private parts of the house. Even half of the vault or burying place under the Chapel is made use of as a public cellar, or so was very lately, to sell

drink in, there having been frequently revellings heard during divine service.' 'My Lord of Hatton' referred to was Sir Christopher's nephew Newport; who, on entering into possession of the property, assumed his uncle's name. Hatton had died indebted to the Crown in the sum of £40,000, and this no doubt enhanced Q. Elizabeth's desire for her dues from the bp. Lady Hatton lived on on her husband's premises, and eventually m. Sir Edwd. Coke, the eminent lawyer. The wedding took place at Hatton House, as it was called; and, despite Abp. Whitgift's warning that the infringements of the Ch.'s regulations would be followed by excommunication and imprisonment, she insisted on being m. at night without banns or licence. Sir Edwd. took possession of her entire estate, and administered it according to his own wishes. Her reprisal was to refuse him admission to this house. The sordid story of this matrimonial strife is related in *The Lady of Bleeding Heart Yard*, by Laura Norsworthy (1935).

Between 1620 and 1624 the Spanish Embassy under Gondomar and his successor Colonna occupied Ely Place, and Mass was again said in the chapel. Catholics were admitted privately, and the services were much frequented. As, about this time, 16 priests were drawn, hanged, and quartered, and 400 cast into prison, such a privilege, however illicit, was a valuable one. It is recorded in Malone's *History of the Stage* that the last passion-play performed in England was acted before Gondomar during his residence in Ely Place. Later the D. of Richmond occupied the gate-house and d. there. Afterwards the duchess retired into the bp.'s part of the buildings, and there had Lenten services conducted 'as orderly' as they were at Whitehall Palace. The chapel was thus again in Protestant hands. From 1638 to 1667, Matthew Wren, uncle of Sir Christopher, was Bp. of Ely. In 1640 he was committed to the T.L. for endeavouring to restore Catholic practices in his diocese. He remained there until the Restoration in 1660. During this time much of Ely Place disappeared, the hall and chapel alone being left.

In 1643 Ely Place was made a prison by the Long Parliament, and the Serjeant-at-Arms was appointed keeper, with a charge that the chapel and the garden should receive no injury. It became also a hosp. for wounded soldiers, numbers of whom were bd. in the chyd. of St. Andrew's, Holborn. After Matthew Wren's return his eldest daughter Anna was m. in the chapel to John Ball of the Inner Temple. Evelyn mentioned the chapel several times. In 1661 he went there to hear Dr. Boldero preach. In 1668 he was present at the consecration of Dr. Williams as Bp. of Chester, and in 1675 at the consecration of Dr. Barlow as Bp. of Lincoln. In 1693 Evelyn's daughter Susanna was married there. Q. Anne, when princess, went to the chapel to hear Bp. Ken—author of the hymns *Awake my soul, and with the sun*, and *Glory to thee, my God, this night*.

In 1772, when Dr. Edmund Keene was Bp. of Ely, the whole of the property was transferred to the Crown. The sum paid to the see was £6,500, while a further sum of £3,600 was paid over to provide for another town residence for the Bps. of Ely. This was erected on the site of Clarendon House, Dover St., Piccadilly; and £200 annually was settled on the Bps. of Ely for ever. Mr. Cole, architect and surveyor, purchased the premises, and presumably demolished all that remained of the hall when he built his houses. The chapel, however, was left for the use of his tenants. When Mr. Cole died, the chapel was let to a Mrs. Faulkner for the sum of £125 p.a., and in 1814 to Rev. J. Wilcox. In 1815 it passed into the hands of the National Soc. for Promoting the Education of the Poor in the Principles of the Established Church, and then galleries were erected. In 1844 the chapel was leased to the Welsh Episcopalians, and it remained in their hands until the whole property was sold under an order of the Court of Chancery to finish a lawsuit between the descendants of the original purchaser. The chapel then passed again into Roman Catholic hands —for £5,400.

Much restoration was required. The chapel had

'a coved or segmental plaster ceiling; this was quickly removed amid inconceivable filth, living and dead. The lath and plaster had been hung from the old coupled rafters; these were all in their places; they were of chestnut: they were eight inches by six inches, laid flatways, so that the greater thickness should be seen from below: a few of them were decayed: they were replaced in oak, as chestnut was not obtainable.' Through long neglect, much more besides the roof needed attention. On St. Etheldreda's Day, 23rd June 1874, the first Mass for 250 yrs. was said, the crypt was opened for services by Cardinal Manning on the same day in 1876, and again, on the same day in 1879, the cardinal opened the chapel.

The windows were gradually filled with stained glass. That in the E. window was the gift of the D. of Norfolk, in memory of his sister Etheldreda. The two outer figures—St. Etheldreda and St. Bridget— commemorate the saints to whom this chapel and an old Catholic chapel in Baldwin's Gardens were respectively dedicated. There was also a Mission of the Holy Family in Saffron Hill; and figures of Joseph, Mary, and Christ signify this. Below the altar is a gilded and jewelled reliquary purporting to contain a portion of the incorrupt hand of St. Etheldreda, Q. of E. Anglia (d. 679). She was twice m., but twice maintained her virginity. She founded the abbey of Ely. Her shrine is on the N. side of the sanctuary, and her statue is clothed in garments showing her double dignity of q. and abbess. The eight side-windows have subjects ranging from the Creation to the birth of Christ. The screen is modern—the work of J. F. Bentley (1899). The W. window, in memory of Catholic martyrs, was completed shortly before the Second World War, and damaged when it came. There were depicted St. Thos. More, and St. John Fisher, Bp. of Rochester; also the Carthusian martyrs (see 'Charterhouse'), and their brethren of the York Charterhouse. The SW. door is a beautiful specimen of Early Gothic architecture. The royal arms (Charles II), rejected by the Catholics, are in the vestibule: formerly they were over the communion table where the altar had been. F. T. Bumpus says of this chapel:

'For its size it is one of the most beautiful specimens of Geometrical Decorated art in Christendom, and from the resemblance it bears to such works as the tombs of Edmund Earl of Lancaster and Aveline his wife at Westminster and of Archbishop Peckham at Canterbury and of Bishop de Luda in the presbytery of Ely, may have been designed by the same hand.'

The undercroft is extensive, and the

walls are in places 8 ft. thick. From this, and the improbability that one so large would be specially constructed for a private chapel, it has been plausibly suggested that a Romano-British ch. stood upon the site. Such chs. were frequently erected near a river, as this would have been near the Fleet. By way of support of this idea, bd. in the centre of the undercroft was found what Sir Gilbert Scott considered was a holy water stoup, older than the Saxon period. The undercroft for many yrs. was a wine vault, drinking proceeding during service hours. It is now used as a chapel, and there are statues of the Virgin Mary and Joseph and one of St. Bridget—brought from the chapel in Baldwin's Gardens when it was demolished. (See 'Customs.')

The thoroughfare known as Ely Place is unique in several respects. The gate is closed nightly at dusk, and up to 1939 from then until 6 a.m. one of the three watchmen, on duty in turn, paraded round the cul-de-sac calling out the hour. At one time he also announced the weather! The police do not patrol Ely Place, but, of course, come if summoned. Next to the chapel is St. Audrey's House. St. Audrey was a popular name for St. Etheldreda, who, according to Bede, died of a tumour in the throat caused through an early love of necklaces. At the fair at Ely, necklets were sold, and lace, as 'St. Awdrey's'—thence our word 'tawdry':

'You promised me a tawdry-lace and a pair of sweet gloves.'
Winter's Tale, IV. iv.
For the Mitre see 'Taverns.'

Epitaphs. There could be found enough interesting epitaphs recorded of L. citizens to make a small volume. A few of note that can be reliably accepted as once extant, but no longer to be seen, are as follows.

Stow records the epitaph on Robt. Trappis in the ch. of St. Leonard, Foster Lane, in 1526.

'When the bels be merily roong,
And the mass devoutly sung,
And the meat merrily eaten,
Then shall Robert Traps his wives
And children be forgotten.

A pathetic inscription before it dis-

appeared in the blitz was in the Temple Ch. It was in memory of Miss Mary Gaudy, who d. of smallpox in 1671, at the age of twenty-two.

'This fair young Virgin, for a nuptiall Bed
More fitt, is lodg'd (sad fate) among ye dead;
Stormed by rough windes, soe falls in all her Pride
The full blowne Rose design'd to adorne a Bride.'

There is a quaint epitaph, relating to the same disease, in the Little Cloisters of W.A.:

'In memory of Mr. Tho: Smith. of Elmly Lovet, in ye County of Worcester, & Bach: of Arts, late of Ch: Ch: Oxford, who through ye Spotted Vaile of the Small Pox, rendred a Pure and Unspotted Soul to God, Expecting but not fearing Death, wch ended his dayes,

'March the 10th Anno Dom 166$\frac{3}{4}$ Aetatis Suae 27.

'The virtues which in his short Life were shown,
have equall'd been by few, surpass'd by none.'

In Chichester Cath. the 'spotted vale' is also referred to in an inscription.

Two inscriptions that seemed rude to the deceased in their perhaps significant terseness were the following. One was in the Ch. of St. Michael, Crooked Lane (demolished on the construction of the new London Bridge):

'Here lyeth wrapt in Clay
The Body of William Wray
I have no more to say.'

The other was in the Ch. of St. Dunstan, Stepney:

'Here lies the body of Samuel Saul
Spitalfields weaver, and that is all.'

A refined, brief, but eulogist epitaph was in old Chelsea Ch.:

'Erected to the memory of Admiral Matthew Squire, d. 1800.

'His Virtues are too well known to be recorded here, being sincerely regretted by all his friends.'
Another—equally favourable and a little more expansive—was in the Ch. of St. Giles-in-the-Fields:

'Here lyes the best of Men, whose Life is at an end.
The best of Husbands, and the truest Friend:
Who rests, I hope, as I do hope to be
Happy with him to all eternity.'

A tribute to a wife until recently was in the Chyd. of St. James's, Piccadilly:

'She was, but words are wanting to say what.
Think of a good mother, wife and friend and she was that.
                    'Elizabeth Jones, 1828.'

In Islington parish ch. was another fine epitaph to a woman—Elizabeth Emma Thomas (d. 1808, age 27):

'She had no fault, save what travellers give the moon;
Her light was lovely, but she died too soon.'

The pendant to this, for a man, was once in the chyd. of St. Giles-in-the-Fields:

'In sense a Man, in innocence a child.'

Some inscriptions which were humorously devised are also recorded. At one time there seems to have been no attempt to censure an epitaph, however faulty in matter of taste. Augustus Hare recorded a punning one in the chyd. of St. Benet's, Paul's Wharf:

'Here lies one More, and no More than he.
One More and no more! how can that be?
One More and no More may well lie here alone;
But here lies one More, and that's more than one.'

Another example—gruesome as the former was not—was in the Ch. of St. Olave, Tooley St. (demolished 1926):

'Hallowed be the Sabaoth,
And farewell all worldly Pelfe;
The Weeke begins on Tuesday,
For Munday hath hang'd himself.'

There are occasionally amusing references to the profession of the deceased. 'Born a man, and died a grocer' was said to be the suggested epitaph of a man who despaired of rising higher in the world. In the epitaph of John Jarret (d. 1626), once in Southwark Cath., there is some comfort for such:

'Some called him Garret, but that was too high,
His name was Jarret that here doth lie:
Who in his life was tost on many a wave,
And now he lies anchored in his own grave.
The Church he did frequent while he had breath.
He desired to lie therein after his death.
To heaven he is gone, the way before,
Where of grocers there is many more.'

The following are inscriptions that remain.
In St. Bartholomew-the-Great Ch. there is a tablet, showing figures of husband and wife lying together, in a nude state on a couch. Underneath are the lines:

'Behowlde youreselves by us;
    Sutche once were we as you;
And you in tyme shal be
    Even duste as we are now.'

It was of this kind of inscription that Chas. Lamb wrote:
'Every dead man must take upon himself to be lecturing me with his odious truism that "Such as he now is I must shortly be." Not so shortly, friend, perhaps as thou imaginest. In the meantime I am alive. I move about. I am worthy twenty of thee. Know thy betters.'
Inside the ch. of St. Andrew Undershaft —it was once outside—is another of this kind, but more courteous to the living:

'Stay Courteous Reder spend a teare
Uppon the dust that slumbers here
And whilest thou Readst ye state of mee,
Thinke on the glasse that runns for thee.'

This was probably the Uncle Wight of Pepys, many times mentioned in the Diary. Charles Williams (St. John's, Hackney Ch.) so late as 1841 gave the old admonition:

'Remember me as you pass by
As you are now so once was I.
As I am now so you must be.
So be prepared to follow me.'

It is said that a waggish fellow once added to a similar inscription:

'To follow thee is my intent,
But you've left no word which way you went.'

It is certainly better for the dead to lecture the living than for the living to seem to lecture to the dead, as the latter cannot answer back. In the chyd. of St. George, Southwark, appear the following lines from Pope's *Elegy to the Memory of an Unfortunate Lady*:

'How Lov'd, how Valued Once, avails thee not!
To whom related or by whom begot!
A heap of Dust alone remains of thee;
'Tis all thou art and all the Proud shall be.'

Lamb would have desired to feel the bumps of the person who so adorned another's grave.

Stephen Pounds (bd. in the chyd. of St. John, Hackney, 1825) told the living how indifferent he was to their opinion of the dead:

'Farewell vain world
I have had enough of thee,
And now I fear not what thou sayest to me.'

A variation of this epitaph is in the chyd. of Wingham (Kent):

'Farewell, vain world, I've had enough of thee,
And now am careless what thou sayest of me.
What fault you've seen in me take care to shun
And look at home—enough there's to be done.'

Perhaps because psychic phenomena had not illumined the tomb, up to a century ago Death was usually represented as a King of Terrors. Even when, seemingly he might come in mercy, he must be represented as fearsome. Thus of John Godfrey Harman (d. 1792 at the age of 72), on a stone in the ch. of St. Katharine Cree the reader is told:

'Long dropping toward the grave
Our Friend remained, and many a wish and many a sigh
transpired for death ere he the grant obtained
 at Length his prayers are heard
 the grisly King approached his Bed.'

Geo. Jacob (bd. in the chyd. of St. John, Hackney 1825) was represented as having very uncomfortable lodgings.

'A faithful friend, a father dear

A loving husband buried here
In prime of life Death did him take
In this cold earth his bed to make.'

On the other hand, John Gardner, who was bd. in the chyd. of St. Leonard, Shoreditch, would fain suggest that he was more pleased with his present than his past lodgings:

'1807
'John Gardner's last and best bedroom.'

Another curious characteristic of some minds is unnecessary precision about details of death. On the stone in memory of Geo. Cruikshank in the crypt of St. P.'s Cath. the information is given that he d. at 263 Hampstead Rd. In old Chelsea Ch. is the tomb of 'Edmond First Lord Bray died 1539,' also his son, John de Bray 'who died wythyn Blackfryers at 3 of yᵉ clocke in yᵉ afternone Thursdaye 18 Novembre 1557.' (This monument survived the Blitz.) Those who visit the ch. of St. Mary Aldermary, pass over the gravestone of Mrs. Ann Catharina Schneider, 'died 15 of June 1798 at half past six o'clock in the evening, age 37 years 6 months and nine days.' On a tombstone —to Geo. Higgs, in Battersea chyd. (d. 1807) it states that his age was '21 yrs. 3 days and he died at 10 minutes past 11 o'clock.'

Reference has been made to epitaphs which have disappeared which seem cruel in their brevity. There is still extant one of these in the ruins of St. Giles, Cripplegate. It commemorates Thomas Stagg. He is said to have been

'Attorney at Law
Vestry Clerk of this Parish
From the 8th day of March 1731
to the 19th day of February 1772
on which Day he died
In the 76th year of his Age.
That is all.'

The last phrase may convey more unkindness than was intended. It is possible that the composer of the inscription, on being asked if he did not wish to add to it, so replied and the mason, too literally, carved his words.

Other tombstones seek to enlist the sympathy of the living, not so much for death as for a painful life. A striking example of this is in Bunhill Fields Burial Ground. There, in letters about 4 in.

long, is the following inscription:

'HERE LYES DAME MARY PAGE
RELICT OF SIR GREGORY PAGE BART,
SHE DEPARTED THIS LIFE
MARCH 11 1728
IN THE 56TH YEAR OF HER AGE.'

On the other side the reader was informed:

'IN 67 MONTHS SHE WAS TAP'D 66 TIMES
HAD TAKEN AWAY 240 GALLONS OF WATER
WITHOUT EVER REPINING AT HER CASE
OR EVER FEARING THE OPERATION.'

Sir Gregory and his wife were members of the dissenting congregation at Devonshire Sq., Bishopsgate.

In the chyd. of St. James's, Clerkenwell, a tall tombstone records a gruesome murder:

'Beneath this stone
are deposited the remains of
Ellen Lefevre
Aged 23 years
and her four children
Henry aged 5 years and 6 months
John aged 4 years and 6 months
Ellen aged 2 years and 6 months
Philip aged 8 months,

who were murdered at their residence in Southampton Street Pentonville during the night of Monday 8th September 1834 by Johann Nicholas Steinberg aged 45 years a native of Germany and father of the above children who afterwards murdered himself and was buried according to law.'

Then follow texts and pious verse, and the inscription concludes:

'This stone was erected by public inscription to commemorate the lamentable event.'

The burial 'according to law' was probably a reference to burial at cross-roads with a stake through the body. This does not appear to have been carried out. The body of Steinberg was, however, turned out of the shell containing it, and the skull broken with an iron mallet. Puppets to represent the murdered family were dressed up in their own clothes and exhibited in the house where the crime was committed.

It is pleasing to know that what may be the oldest epitaph now to be seen in L. is of a good husband, prepared at the instigation of a grateful wife. In the L.Mus. there is a tombstone with the inscription:

'In memory of Flavius Agricola, private of the Sixth Victorious Legion, aged 42 years and ten days; erected by Albia Faustina to her peerless husband.'

It was found in Goodman's Fields, Whitechapel, in 1787.

Wifely submission is magnified in Streatham par. ch., on a monument to Elizabeth Hamilton, wife of Major-General Hamilton, which may have been Roubiliac's. The lady d. in 1746, and the inscription concludes:

'She was married near 47 Years, & never did one thing to displease her husband, who has Caused this Monument to be Erected, in Testimony of His never-dying Affection for her.'

Strype mentioned a lady named 'Obedience' commemorated on a tablet in the ch. of St. Benet, Paul's Wharf.

Of blissful relations between husband and wife, there is no more tender allusion than is to be found on a stone in the ch. of St. Bartholomew the Great. It commemorates John and Margaret Whiting who d. respectively in 1681 and 1680. The epitaph is Sir Henry Wotton's with sexes transposed.

'Shee first deceased, Hee for a little Tryd
To live without her, lik'd it not and dyd.'

Very different seems to have been the relation between a pair who are bd. in the par. chyd. of Fulham. The stone, which remains, says:

Sacred
To the Memory of
Isabella Murr
of this Parish,
who departed this Life
the 29th November 1829
in the 52nd Year of her Age

'Ye who possess the brightest charms of life,
A tender friend, a kind indulgent Wife:
Oh, learn their worth! In her beneath this stone
These pleasing attributes together shone,
Was not true happiness with them combined?
Ask the spoil'd being she has left behind.'

A little distance below, in larger letters, the words are added:

'HE'S GONE TOO!'

The husband was a tippling schoolmaster and so there was nothing to report of him but departure.

In the graveyard of Chelsea Hospital is

the following inscription:

Here lies WILLIAM HISELAND
A Veteran if ever Soldier was,
Who merited well a Pension—
If Long Service be a Merit,
Having served upwards of the Days of Man
Antient but not Superannuated.
Engaged in a series of wars
Civil as well as Foreign,
Yet not maimed or worn out by either
His Complexion was fresh and florid
His Health hale and hearty
His Memory exact and ready
In Stature
He excelled the Military size
In Strength
He surpassed the prime of Youth
and
What rendered his Age
Still more Patriarchal,
When above an Hundred Yeard Old
He took unto him a Wife
Read Fellow Soldiers and Reflect
That there is a Spiritual Warfare
As well as a Warfare Temporal
Born VI: of August, 1620 } Aged 112.'
Died VII: of Febru^r 1732 }

It might appear that to this veteran the warfare temporal was the state of holy matrimony. His portrait, painted when he was a centenarian, hangs in the hall of the hosp., and he looks hale and hearty. There is no documentary evidence of his great age and it is very doubtful. Strangely, W. J. Thoms did not mention him in his book *Human Longevity* (1873).

The finest expression of deep affection between parents and son was in St. Dunstan's in the East. Of Thomas Turner (d. 1771) it is said:

'He knew no joy but friendship might divide,
Nor gave his parents grief, but when he died.'

This can be matched by an epitaph in Hampstead chyd.:

'Brief was his span of life sweet was his rest,
He left no trace behind save in a parent's breast.'

Pope wrote some lines which are favoured for sepulchral purposes. On the walls of St. Margaret's Ch., Westminster, is his famous epitaph to Mrs. Elizabeth Corbet, daughter of Sir Uvedale Corbett of Longnor:

'Here rests a Woman Good without pretence,
Blest with plain Reason and with sober Sense;
No conquests she but o're her Self desired,
No Arts essay'd, but not to be admir'd.
Passion and Pride were to her Soul unknown,
Convinc'd that Virtue only is our own.
So Unaffected, so Compos'd a Mind;
So firm, yet soft, so strong, yet so refin'd:
Heav'n, as its purest Gold, by Tortures try'd,
The Saint sustain'd it, but the Woman dy'd.'

Johnson praised these lines, though he reported:

'I once heard a Lady of great beauty and excellence object to the fourth line "that it contained an unnatural and incredible panegyrick." Of this,' he added, 'let the Ladies judge.'

The epitaph can also be found in Bunhill Fields Burial Ground on the tombstone of Mrs. Mary Bland (d. 1767)—slightly curtailed. It was rather basely corrupted in the following singular epitaph in Stoke Newington Chyd., now becoming illegible:

'This tomb was erected by William Picket, of the City of London, goldsmith, on the melancholy death of his daughter Elizabeth.
A testimony of respect
from greatly afflicted parents
In memory of Elizabeth Picket, spinster
who died December 11, 1781
Aged 23 years
this much lamented
young person expired in consequence
of her clothes taking fire
the preceding evening
Reader, if ever you should witness such an affecting scene; recollect that the only method to extinguish the flame is to stifle it by an immediate covering.

So unaffected, so composed a mind,
So firm, yet soft, so stout yet so refined;
Heav'n as pure gold, by flaming tortures try'd.
The angel bore them, but the mortal dyed.'

There is a number of what may be called occupational epitaphs. Perhaps the longest of all L. epitaphs is a brass in St. Margaret's Ch., Westminster, in memory of one Cole who d. in 1597. It runs to fifty two lines. We are told:

'In Parliament a Burgess, Cole was placed;
In Westminster the like for many yeares:
But now wth saints above his soule is graced,
And lives a Burgess wth heavns royall peares.
O blessed chaunge from earth, where death is kinge,
To be united there, where Angells singe.'

There is a long inscription (now hardly legible) in the W. Walk of the Cloisters of W.A.:

'With Diligence and Trust most exemplary
Did WILLIAM LAURENCE serve a Prebendary;
And for his Paines now past, before not lost,
Gain'd this Remembrance at his Master's cost.
O read these Lines againe: you seldome find
A Servant faithfull and a Master kind.
Short Hand he wrot: his Flowre in prime did fade,
And hasty Death Short Hand of him hath made.
Well couth he Nu'bers, and well mesur'd Land;
Thus doth he now that Ground where on you stand,
Wherein he lyes so Geometricall;
Art maketh some, but thus will Nature all.'

Laurence d. in 1621. This was the first reference to shorthand in any L. inscription. He probably had used Shelton's *Tachygraphy*, the system employed by Pepys in his Diary.

A happy tribute to a humbler worker is once said to have been in St. Pancras chyd.:

'Underneath this stone doth lie
The body of Mr. Humpherie
Jones, who was of late
By trade a plate
Worker in Barbicanne;
Well known to be a good man
By all his friends and neighbours too,
And paid everybody their due.
He died in the year 1737
August 4th, aged 80, his soul we hope's in heaven.'

In Southwark Cath.—at the time of his death the par. ch. of St. Saviour—there was bd. in 1672 Lionel Lockyer, a quack doctor. His monument showing a recum-

bent and somewhat drooping figure, has the following epitaph:

'Here Lockyer lies interr'd, enough; his name
Speakes one hath few competitors in fame:
A Name soe Great, soe Generall't may scorne
Inscriptions wch doe vulgar tombs adorne
A diminution 'tis to write in verse
His eulogies, wch most men's mouths rehearse.
His virtues & his PILLS are soe well known
That envy can't confine them under stone,
But they'l survive his dust and not expire
Till all things else at th'universall Fire.
This verse is lost: his PILL Embalmes him safe
To future times without an Epitaph.'

The pills were said to be partly compounded of extracts from the rays of the sun. They were even an antidote against London fogs, and promised to make old age comely.

An important feminine occupation, that of a midwife—Margaret Hawtrees—bd. in St. Paul's chyd., Deptford (1734), is commemorated in this way:

'She was an indulgent mother, and the best of wives;
She brought into this world more than three thousand lives.'

A temperate drawer is commemorated in an inscription in the chyd. of St. Magnus the Martyr. It was brought there from St. Michael's, Crooked Lane. It commemorated Robert Preston of the 'Boar's Head' Tavern:

'Bacchus, to give the Toping World surprize
Produc'd one Sober Son, and here he lies.
Tho' nurs'd among full Hogsheads, he defy'd
The charms of Wine, and ev'ry vice beside.
O Reader! if to Justice thou 'rt inclin'd,
Keep Honest Preston daily in thy mind.
He drew good Wine, took care to fill his Pots,
Had sundry virtues that outweigh'd his faults.
You that on Bacchus have the like dependence,
Pray copy Bob in Measure and Attendance.'

His temperance did not bring long life, but L. water was as dangerous as L. beer!

Lawyers have attracted most derision. In St. Pancras chyd. there is said once to have been the following inscription:

'Here lies —— believe it if you can
Who though a lawyer was an honest man.
To him the gates of heaven shall open wide
And quickly close 'gainst all the tribe beside.'

In St. Dunstan's in the West Ch. can still be seen the following inscription:
'To the Memory of Hobson Judkin Esq. late of Clifford's Inn. The Honest Solicitor. Who departed this Life June 30 1812. This Tablet was erected by his clients as a token of gratitude and respect for his honest, faithful and friendly conduct to them through Life. Go reader and imitate Hobson Judkin.'
In the ch. of St. Lawrence Jewry, before the Blitz, there was a tablet in memory of another lawyer, Thos. Loggan, who d. 1810, and is described as 'of un-blemished purity of conduct and open probity of character.'

A somewhat snobbish inscription is in W.A. (Chapel of St. John the Baptist). Mrs. Kendall (d. 1710) was equipped for the highest society.

'Those admirable qualitys
in which she was equalled
By few of her sex.
Surpass'd by none
Render'd her every way
Worthy of that close
Union and Friendship,
In which she liv'd with
The Lady Catherine Jones.'

This is such an one as Jane Austen's Rev. Mr. Collins might have desired for himself, regarding his relations with Lady Catherine de Bourgh.

Some tombstones set out in great detail the benefactions of the deceased. Two such could once be seen in the ch. of St. Giles, Cripplegate (see 'City Churches; D'). There the epitaphs (now destroyed) said:

'And let this good example move such men as God hath blest
To doe the like before they goe with Busby to their rest.'

Whilst of Langlie the reader is told:

'A sermon eke he hath ordayned That God may have his praisee
And others might be wonne thereby To follow Langlie's waies.'

This monument has survived the Blitz.

Thos. Leverton (d. 1814), according to a tablet in St. Giles-in-the-Fields Ch., left 3 per cent. Consuls 'the interest to be applied annually for the benefit of deserving females.' In another case details of investment are given. On a large table tomb, in the chyd. of St. Katharine Cree, is an inscription to Gale Middleton, who d. in 1732. The reader is told that she 'left £500 £3 per cent to Aldgate Ward School on condition that this tomb be kept in repair.'

The condition is vexatious when un-accompanied by a charitable bequest. Mary Anne Chase left £100 in 1796 to keep her tomb in Bermondsey chyd. in good repair for ever. The rector has sometimes been upbraided for spending money for this purpose by people who do not understand the sacredness of such a trust.

Confidence in awaking, so common as to be unimpressive, is expressed in the case of Sir Arthur Gorges (d. 1689) who is bd. in Chelsea Ch. where the tablet has been damaged.

'Let him rest free from envy as from paine
When all the Gorges rise heele rise againe.'

Less jarring is the couplet in the crypt of St. Martin's-in-the-Fields Ch. regarding Mary White, who d. 1687:

'A friendly neighbour and a virtuous wife
Doubtless she's blessed with everlasting life.'

In contrast to both of these is the inscription on the grave in Highgate Cemetery of Prof. W. K. Clifford, scientist and atheist, who d. in 1879, aged thirty-four:

'I was not and was conceived.
I loved, and did a little work.
I am not, and grieve not.'

On the tablet in St. Giles-in-the-Fields Ch. to Thos Burrows (d. 1815) doubt is expressed about monumental praise:

'If ever truth in epitaph be told.'

Perhaps the best conclusion of the whole matter is to be found in the couplet on the tablet to Mr. W. Pinder (d. 1806) in St. Botolph's Ch., Aldersgate:

'Praises on tombs are trifles vainly spent,
A man's good name is his best monument.'

F

Fellowship Porters. A brotherhood incorporated in 1155 (Henry II), and re-incorporated in 1603 (James I). Their business was to carry or house corn, salt, coals, fish, and fruit of all descriptions. By an Act of Council of 1646, they had the power to choose twelve rulers, the Ld.M. and aldermen reserving the right to appoint one of the number. The co. had no livery or arms, but a hall, first in St. Mary at Hill and afterwards in Beer Lane. The members wore badges or tallies. Annually, every Sunday before Midsummer Day, they attended a service in the ch. of St. Mary at Hill. They previously furnished the merchants and families above Billingsgate with nosegays, and proceeded from the hall to the ch. carrying nosegays. The co. was dissolved by Act of Common Council in 1894, and the hall sold in 1907. The 'Six Jolly Fellowship Porters' as a name for a riverside tavern in *Our Mutual Friend* was probably suggested to Dickens by this co., as no tavern of that sign is known.

Finsbury, now part of the L. Bor. of Islington, was a met. bor. It is mentioned by Fitzstephen and by Stow as '*Fens*bury,' suggesting a plausible etymology; but the official *Guide* to the bor. endorses a statement in John Mitchell Kemble's *Saxons in England*, that the name is derived from a family called 'Finnes,' 'Fynes,' or 'Fiennes.' The name has connoted various areas. Wheatley defines Finsbury as a lordship without the postern of Cripplegate. There is a Prebend of Finsbury in St. P.'s Cath., whose property included the site of Bunhill Fields.

The locality situated to the W. is called St. Luke's—a par. carved out of the City ward of Cripplegate Without (being the part outside the City liberties as well as outside the wall) and constituting what may be called Finsbury proper—for there is no par. of Finsbury. Here in the City Rd. is the new Artillery Ground, headquarters of the Honourable Artillery Company—recalling the days before fire-arms when bows and arrows were artillery and the butts were in Finsbury Moor, a marshy waste extending to Islington.

St. Luke's Ch. in Old St. was built by George Dance senior in 1732, and the tower is conspicuous by reason of its being surmounted by a tall fluted obelisk. It was called 'Lousy St. Luke's' by reason of the weather vane which was said to represent a louse but is a dragon. It has an attractive Georgian interior. In the chyd. lies Thos. Allen (1833) the historian of L., and there is a memorial to Wm. Caslon the typefounder. St. Luke's par. contains John Wesley's Chapel, on the E. side of City Rd., opened 1778; also his house adjoining (a show-place); and also directly opposite, the burial-ground of Bunhill Fields (*q.v.*). The chapel was badly injured by fire in 1879: it has a statue of Wesley, erected 1891, in front; and his grave in a yard at the back. The Roman Catholics have St. Joseph's, Lamb's Bdgs., Bunhill Row. It is a mistake to identify with Bunhill Fields the 'great pit in Finsbury' used for disposal of the bodies of those that d. in the Plague of 1665: the pit was at Mount-mill, at the other side of St. Luke's par., near the junction of Old St. and Goswell Rd.

The LIBERTY of GLASSHOUSE YARD is a small area, where there was once a glasshouse, between the Charterhouse and Aldersgate St., in the par. of St. Botolph Without Aldersgate.

John Keats was born at 24 Finsbury Pavement—now numbered in Moorgate, for it was inside the City liberties and not in Finsbury. Milton, in his later yrs., lived in 'Artillery Walk' (125 Bunhill Row is the site), and in his Old St. garden cultivated the choicest fruits of the kingdom. Samuel Daniel (d. 1619) and George Psalmanazar—the self-styled 'Formosan Christian' (d. 1763), lived in Old St.

Fleet Street. It takes its name from the River Fleet. (See 'Lost Rivers.') W. G. Bell considered that it had not come into existence before the 12th century had drawn to a close. He, however, admitted a conflict in this regard with many authorities. As there was a palace of Westminster, at latest in the time of Edward the Confessor, it is difficult to believe there was not some highway connecting the City therewith at a much earlier date. H. A. Harben, however, found no documentary evidence earlier than 1228 when, according to the *Liber Albus*—

'Gervaise le Cordewaner being Chamberlaine and the aforesaid persons being sheriffs, it happened that one Henry de Buke on the Monday next after the feast of St. Ethelburga, slew Ireis le Tyulour, in the street of Fletebridgge with a knife, and then fled to the Church of St. Mary in Suthwerke, and having there acknowledged the deed in the presence of the said Chamberlain and sheriffs abjured the realm.'

In 1384 a grant of pavage for three yrs. was made for the paving and repair of Fleet St. from Temple Bar to the Savoy. It appears from this that the Strand was then shorter, and Fleet St. longer, than at present. John Allin, in 1272, left 'his estate in a stone house in Fletestrete' to his two sons; in the City letter-books there is a reference to Richard de Fletbrigge, and in 1315 William de Flete was elected M.P. for the City. A reference to the 'Menters House' in Fleet St. in 1309 may indicate a mint there.

North Side going West

POPPIN'S COURT is one of the earliest courts off Fleet St., having been 'Popyngay Aley' when Henry VIII seized the messuage in the par. of St. Bride's bearing the sign of the Popinjay, which had belonged to the monks of Cirencester, Gloucestershire. In 1428 Roger Lardener, a baker, in a codicil to his will, left to his brother his leasehold interest in the hostel of the abbot and convent of Cirencester called the 'Popyngaye' in 'Fletestrete.'

RACQUET COURT, which is next, may date from the time of Charles I, when the game became popular, though it is first mentioned by Strype (1720). In 1721 Thos. Wicks killed Dennis Connel here in a duel. Here are some old houses of the early 18th century. The wrought-iron work suggests that it had once a gate. Passing the offices of the *Daily Express*, with the unsightly steel-glass façade, the next turning is:

SHOE LANE. In Henry III's reign (*c*. 1272) there is reference to a st. called 'Sholand,' in the par. of 'St. Andrew of Holebourne,' and about ten yrs. before there is mention of a well—'Showelle'—at the upper end of the lane. Here was one of the cockpits (*q.v.*). G. H. Cunningham says that John Florio, the translator of Montaigne, lived here in 1624, and that in the Windmill Tavern Felton read in 1628 the Parliamentary Remonstrance against the D. of Buckingham, and formed the determination to kill him. In Shoe Lane, on the site of what is now Farringdon Av., was the pauper burial ground, where the body of Thos. Chatterton was bd. after his suicide by swallowing arsenic in Brooke St., Holborn, in 1770.

PETERBOROUGH COURT is the next. Here the Abbot of Peterborough had his hostel with a large garden. In 1863 the ground was still in possession of the Ecclesiastical Commissioners, who then sold it to the *Daily Telegraph*. This explains Matthew Arnold's reference to the 'young lions of Peterborough Court.'

CHESHIRE COURT, according to H. A. Harben, has only borne the name since 1905, having previously been 'Three Falcon Court.' For 'Cheshire Cheese' see 'Taverns.'

WINE OFFICE COURT took its name from the office for the receipt of customs on wines which was there in Pepys's day. Goldsmith lived here.

HIND COURT was so named from a house sign. It is first mentioned in Ogilby and Morgan's map of 1677.

THREE KINGS COURT probably recalls the Kings and Key Tavern, which was hereabouts, perhaps so early as 1600. Larwood and Hotten plausibly suggested that this was originally 'Three Kings and Cross Keys,' the kings being the three wise men from the east. There is such a sign in the Guildhall Mus.

BOLT COURT is also first mentioned in the map of 1677. It derives its name from the 'Bolt-in-Tun' on the opposite side of Fleet St. (see p. 266). Dr. Johnson d. here. At No. 3, which remains, lived Dr. John Coakley Lettsom, who was with Johnson in 1776 at the famous dinner at Dilly's at which Wilkes was present. In 1787 Lettsom brought the Medical Soc. of L. (founded in 1773) to this house. It was his freehold and in 1790 he gave it to the council; he also contributed money and a library. His prescriptions were always signed with the old-fashioned initial 'I,' and from this fact an epigram was made:

'If any folk applies to I,
  I blisters, bleeds, and sweats 'em;
If after that they please to die,
  Well, then—I Lettsom.'

This hardly suggests the kind, humane man that this Quaker physician was. At No. 4 Jas. Ferguson, the astronomer, d. in 1776. From here in 1802 Wm. Cobbett commenced to publish the *Political Register*.

ST. DUNSTAN'S COURT. In the will of Dr. White (see 'City Churches; C'—St. Dunstan in the West), the property mentioned included the 'Hole-in-the-Wall' public-house, to which this court led. It disappeared in 1860. W. G. Bell says:

'The curious name describes its situation, behind the main line of buildings, and approached through a passage or hole in the wall of the front house. Carlin Sunday was regularly celebrated at the Hole-in-the-Wall, where one learns from an old newspaper of about 1830 that upwards of twelve bushels of grey peas were prepared for the men of the North. The origin of the famous feast was said to be this. Centuries ago a battle was fought at Newcastle. When the inhabitants were on the eve of starvation, a vessel entered the port (on the fifth Sunday in Lent) filled with grey peas. These were promptly fried in oil, and were the means of saving the lives of several thousand persons. A like legend is told of Leith and Marseilles.'

JOHNSON'S COURT preserves the name of an Elizabethan worthy, Thos. Johnson, citizen and merchant tailor, and a member of the C.C. from 1598 to 1626. It is mentioned in the registers of St. Dunstan's in 1622 and 1647—in the latter year as 'Mr. Johnson's Court.' Dr. Johnson lived here. *John Bull* was started here (at No. 11) in 1820 by Theodore Hook. It was prosecuted for libelling Q. Caroline, and notoriety thus achieved increased the circulation to 12,000 copies by the twelfth number, although the price was 7*d.* Johnson's Court was 'the dark court in Fleet Street' where 'in a dark letter-box in a dark office' Charles Dickens dropped his manuscript entitled 'A Dinner at Poplar Walk,' called in *Sketches by Boz* 'Mr. Minns and His Cousin.' It was his first publication when it appeared in the old *Monthly Magazine* in December 1833. John Watts, uncle of Chas. Watts, editor

of the *Literary Guide*, in 1864 made No. 17 the offices of the *National Reformer*; since then this court has been the headquarters of rationalism. The Rationalist Press Association was established at No. 17 in 1899, and the bdg. remained until 1924, when it was demolished to make room for Messrs. Benn's new bdg.

RED LION COURT is named after a tavern of that name mentioned in 1571, and is in Ogilby and Morgan's map (1677). Here is the old printing house of Taylor & Francis, successors of Valpy, originator and printer of the Delphin Classics reprints in 144 volumes. All of these were edited by Lamb's friend Geo. Dyer, who lived near (see 'Clifford's Inn'). Richd. Taylor came here in 1837. He was under-secretary of the Linnean Soc. for nearly fifty yrs., a fellow of the Royal Astronomical and of the Philological Socs., and of the Soc. of Antiquaries and the British Association. Dr. Wm. Francis entered the business in 1852. The firm have produced many important works in natural history, as well as beautiful editions of classics. The printing premises, which date from shortly after the G.F., include fine door-cases, panelling, and a remarkably beautiful ceiling, similar to one which was in St. Vedast's Ch., Foster Lane (see 'City Churches; C'). Valpy's sign, the Greek digamma, still stands fixed on the exterior wall, with the Latin motto: 'Alere Flammam' (to feed the flame).

CRANE COURT is first mentioned in 1662; it was burnt in the G.F. and rebuilt. No. 5 is a good specimen of the bdgs. erected immediately after the conflagration. In a house at the end of Crane Court lived Dr. Edwd. Browne, eldest son of Sir Thos. Browne. He was physician to Charles II. From 1710 to 1780, in the same house, the Royal Soc. met, so the figure of Sir Isaac Newton must have been very familiar in that court. The council of the Soc. recommended the situation as 'being in the middle of the town out of the noise,' and 'very convenient for the society.' On meeting nights, by Newton's order, a lamp was hung above the entrance to the court from Fleet St. In 1780 the soc. was moved to Somerset House and the Philosophical Soc. rented the old meeting-place. Under its auspices, in 1819-20, Coleridge gave there his course of lectures on Shakespeare. Later there came the Scottish Corporation. They reverently preserved the room in which Newton used to preside over the meetings of the Royal Soc. until, in 1877, the whole bdg. was destroyed by fire. The new large castellated premises stand both in Crane Court and Fleur-de-Lis Court. The Soc. of Arts (*q.v.*) met in Crane Court in 1754, and awarded their chief prize of £15 to Cosway, then a boy of 15, who afterwards became the fashionable painter of miniatures. The soc. afterwards moved into the hall specially built for them by the Adam brothers. In the first house on the right in Crane Court lived Dryden Leach the printer, who in 1763, was arrested on a general warrant upon suspicion of having printed there Wilkes's *North Briton*, No. 45. The ground of the arrest was a report that Wilkes had been seen going into the house. Leach eventually obtained £300 damages from three of the King's messengers who had executed the illegal warrant. In this court there is a new block of 'luxury flats.' Two par. marks of St. Bride's and St. Dunstan's indicate the par. boundary here.

FETTER LANE. Its earliest name is 'Faytures-lane' (1292); in 1312 it was 'faiterslane'; in 1357 the new lane called 'Faiturlane'; it is Fetter Lane for the first time in 1612. Stow said the name was derived from 'Fewters' or idle people. Halliwell's *Dictionary of Archaic and Provincial Words* gives the word as 'Faitour'—an idle lazy fellow, a deceiver, a flatterer, a vagrant.' It is, however, difficult to understand why such people should have been associated with any one spot, and it seems probable that there is a personal name at the back of the derivation. Harben said that one Viteri or Viter had property mentioned in a will in the 14th century, but strangely, dismissed his association with the name of Fetter Lane because the property was in the par. of St. Sepulchre, Newgate. He may have lived here, and had his property elsewhere.

HEN AND CHICKENS COURT, first mentioned by Ogilby and Morgan in 1677, takes its name from a house sign. At the E. corner of Chancery Lane stood the King's Head Tavern from 1291 to 1770.

CLIFFORD'S INN PASSAGE. See 'Clifford's Inn.'

CHANCERY LANE. At the W. corner here was, until 1799, an old house

elaborately constructed of oak and richly ornamented. A model is in the L.Mus. It is erroneously labelled 'Izaak Walton's House.' Walton's linen-draper's shop was two doors W. of Chancery Lane. He came to Fleet St. in 1624 and in 1632 moved to Chancery Lane. Outside Attenborough's is a statuette of Kaled; she was the page who attended Byron's Count Lara on the battle-field and mourned his death. The lines inscribed are:

'They were not common links that formed
    the chain
That bound to Lara, Kaled's heart and
    brain.'

It belonged to the founder of the business, who selected the lines quoted when the statuette was placed upon the new bdg. in 1883. Bell Yard runs over the site of a house and grounds known as the 'Bell,' belonging to the Knights Hospitallers. In Bell Yard was exhibited in 1702 a model of Amsterdam 30 ft. long by 20 ft. wide, which had taken twelve yrs. in constructing.

TEMPLE BAR is dealt with separately and CHILD's BANK under the head of 'Banks.'

South Side, going East

MIDDLE TEMPLE LANE and INNER TEMPLE LANE are under 'Temple.'

FALCON COURT is first mentioned in Ogilby and Morgan's map (1677). Walking in Fleet St., Boswell met Johnson:

'He stepped aside with me into Falcon Court, and made kind inquiries about my family; and as we were in a hurry going different ways, I promised to call on him next day; he said he was engaged to go out in the morning. "Early, sir?" said I. Johnson: "Why, sir, a London morning does not go with the sun." '

NO. 32 FLEET ST. Here were the premises of John Murray. Amongst their early publications here were Walpole's *Castle of Otranto*, Ld. Lyttleton's *Dialogues of the Dead*, and Isaac D'Israeli's *Curiosities of Literature*. The firm, however, advertised as 'Bookseller and Stationer,' and announced that it 'sells all new books and publications. Fits up Public or Private Libraries in the neatest manner with Books of the choicest editions, the best Print, and the richest Bindings.' There is a C.C. tablet on the site of the 'Mitre' (see 'Taverns'), associated with Johnson.

HARE COURT was named after Hare House in Ram Alley, an old house left to the par. of St. Dunstan's in 1584.

SERJEANTS' INN (*q.v.*) comes next.

PLEYDELL COURT (it takes its name from a ground landlord) was the one referred to by Dickens when (1846), after his brief editorship of the *Daily News*, he wrote to Forster:

'There has been small comfort for either of us in the *Daily News* nine months. Make a vow (as I have done) never to go down that court with the little news shop at the corner any more.'

BOUVERIE STREET. Hazlitt lived at No. 3 in 1829. There is a C.C. plaque on the site. He left here for Soho (*q.v.*).

BOLT-IN-TUN COURT seems to derive its name from Le Boltenton (*c.* 1442), and, if so, there can be no connection with the prior of St. Bartholomew's as he must have been born a generation, later. There was here a coach office (demolished in 1921), which was in Dickens's young days the L. terminus of the service of coaches running to Bath. The proprietor was Moses Pickwick of the 'White Hart' in the latter town. Here, doubtless, Dickens first met the name, the centenary of which, as a literary creation, was celebrated in March 1936.

BOAR'S HEAD COURT. It takes its name from 'Le Borys Heade,' an inn granted to the Carmelite Friars in 1443. It was burned in the G.F. and rebuilt. As a tavern it survived until the middle of the 19th century.

WHITEFRIARS STREET (see 'Whitefriars'). At the corner were the offices of the Anti-Corn Law League, associated with Cobden and Bright. There is a C.C. plaque. Here also was the shop of Graham and Tompion (1639–1713), both clockmakers who were bd. in W.A. There is a plaque bearing their names. On the E. side is Hanging Sword Alley, well known to Dickensians as the residence of Jerry Cruncher in *A Tale of Two Cities.*

HOOD COURT was Hanging Sword Court in Ogilby and Morgan's map (1677). A former name was Crown Court, first found in 1758.

SALISBURY COURT takes its name from the L. house of the bps. of Salisbury. On the E. side there is a C.C. plaque commemorating the birth here of Samuel Pepys. The date given is 1632, but this is Old Style. To moderns it is 1633,

Pepys having been b. on 23rd Feb.

Salisbury Court leads to SALISBURY SQUARE. Here were the printing office of Samuel Richardson, the 18th-century novelist. Close by is a plaque commemorating the Salisbury Court Theatre (*q.v.*).

St. Bride's Ch. (see 'City Churches; C') Milton lived in the chyd. (1639–40) A fire in 1824 burned a number of houses which screened the ch. from Fleet St This provided an opportunity for purchasing the site, and a broad open way was then made to the N. porch. *Punch* had offices for many yrs. in this passage until about 1852 they moved to White friars St. The Punch Tavern commemorates the association, and stands very close to the site. In Bride Lane there was the mouth of a pump which, it is said used to supply water from St. Bride's well Hone (*Every Day Book*) said it was exhausted on the occasion of the coronation of George IV. Mr. Walker at a hotel in Bridge St. engaged several men a day or two before to fill thousands of bottles.

For statues of Q. Elizabeth and Mary Q. of Scots, see 'Statues.' For 'Devil, and 'Cock,' see 'Taverns.'

Fleet St. began to be a 'street of ink' in 1825 when the *Morning Advertiser* office were transferred there from the Strand The two most imposing bdgs. are now the offices of the *Daily Telegraph* (founded 1855) and the *Daily Express* (founded 1930).

Fog cannot be dated. It is not heard o in Roman times in L., though in th Channel it appears to have embarrassed a Roman fleet bound for our shores E. K. Adler (*London*) says that in a Jewish commentary on Exodus, written in 1166 in explanation of the plague and darkness there is an obvious reference to a L. fog In 1306 the problem of air pollution and consequent fog-raising, figured so prominently in the schedule of publi nuisances that the unforgivable sin c burning smoke-producing coal was punish able with death and at least one mai was executed for the offence. It does not however, appear to have become a seriou nuisance before the 17th century. I 1661 John Evelyn told Charles II som straight truths about the clouds of smok which hung about the City. They wer 'so full of stink and darkness,' he said that the inhabitants breathed nothing bu 'impure and thick mist, accompanied with fuliginous and filthy vapour,' so that 'cathairs, phthisicks, coughs and consumptions reach more in this one city than in the whole earth besides.' The traveller 'smelt' the city many miles away, and one poor country cousin became so indisposed within an hour or two of coming to town, that he was regularly forced to take horse and ride for his life back to the open fields.' Once, he said—

'as I was walking in your Majesty's palace of Whitehall (where I have sometimes the honour to refresh myself with the sight of your illustrious presence, which is the joy of your people's hearts) a presumptuous smoke issuing from one or two tunnels near Northumberland House and not far from Scotland Yard, did so invade the court that all the rooms, galleries and places about it were filled and infested with it; and that to such a degree as men could hardly discern one another for the cloud and none could support without manifest inconveniency. . . . That this glorious and ancient city . . . should wrap her stately head in clouds of smoke and sulphur, so full of stink and darkness, I deplore with just indignation.'

These quotations are from *Fumifugium: or the aer and smoak of London dissipated. Together with some Remedies humbly proposed*, which, published in 1661, was sensibly republished by the Coal Smoke Abatement Soc. in 1933.

Anthony à Wood on 11th Nov. 1667, noted in his diary:

'Nov. 11, being munday, was such a great mist at London that never the like before was knowne. Horses ran against each other, carts against carts, coaches against coaches, etc. One could not see the length of a man before him. The mist, though not soe great, was 10 or 16 miles westward from London and likely on other sides.'

Perhaps Wood exaggerated. All Pepys said was that it was a 'foggy, dark, thick day.'

Evelyn entered in his diary under 5th Nov. 1699:

'There happened this week so thick a mist and fog that people lost their way in the streets, it being so intense that no light of candles or torches yielded any (or but very little) direction.

I was in it and in danger. Robberies were committed between the very lights which were fixed between London and Kensington on both sides, and whilst coaches and travellers were passing. It was begun about four in the afternoon, and was quite gone by eight, without any wind to disperse it. At the Thames they beat drums to direct the watermen to make the shore.'

Ld. Boyle wrote to a friend from Tunbridge Wells in 1728:

'The Diversions and Amusements of the Place sent us home again chearfull, and the foggy Air of London with the common Disappointments of Life urge our Return the following year.'

Benjamin Franklin wrote to his wife in 1758:

'The whole town is one great smoaky house, and every street a chimney, the air full of floating sea-coal soot, and you never get a sweet breath of what is pure, without riding some miles for it into the country.'

Another bad fog is recorded in 1772:

'In the morning of 23rd December there happened one of the greatest fogs in London that had ever been remembered, by which great damage was done. The darkness was so great that the carriages of the nobility and gentry were attended by lights the same as at midnight. Many incidents occurred during the continuance of this fog, which lasted through the night; and in the morning several people were found dead in the fields round the metropolis, who not being able to find their way, were supposed to have perished from the inclemency of the weather.'

Lambert's *London*, 1806.

Dickens's Mr. Guppy popularized what has become a classic phrase for a L. fog—Says Esther Summerson in *Bleak House*:

'As he handed me into a fly, after superintending the removal of my boxes, I asked him whether there was a great fire anywhere. For the streets were so full of dense brown smoke that scarcely anything was to be seen.

' "Oh dear no, miss," he said: "this is a London particular."

'I had never heard of such a thing.

' "A fog, miss," said the young gentleman.

' "Oh indeed," said I.'

Mazzini was one of the few to have some affection for it. When he returned to Italy he said he grew tired of the eternal blue of the Italian skies and would have liked some fog for a change.

In a leading article on 'The Fog' in Dec. 1948 *The Times* said:

'What is said to have been the longest fog of more or less recent times lasted from November, 1879, until March, 1880, and provoked angry demands for science and legislation to combine in putting a stop to a dangerous and unhealthy nuisance. Much activity in both these spheres of human self-help, leading to only modified results, has bred a spirit of more or less philosophic resignation.'

Such resignation has been less called for of late. During the last few years the beneficial effect of the Clean Air Act has been noticeable and it may well be that the 'London particular' is a thing of the past.

There is a description of a fog in E. F. Benson's novel *The Image in the Sand* (1905); and an essay 'In Praise of London Fog' by M. H. Dziewicki (*London as Seen and Described by Famous Writers*, edited by Esther Singleton, 1902). (See also *The Climate of London* by T. J. Chandler, 1965.)

Foundling Hospital. This was the noble conception of Capt. Coram, mariner and shipwright. On his journeys to and from Rotherhithe, he was distressed by the sight of half-clad infants, dead or dying as often as alive. They were left in the streets by heartless parents. He obtained a charter in 1739, and in 1741 opened a house for foundlings in Hatton Garden. There was accommodation for only twenty children. Any person who brought a child rang the bell, and waited to hear if the child was accepted, or rejected (because of disease). One of the regulations said that

'All persons who bring children are requested to affix on each child some particular writing, or other distinguishing mark or token, so that the children may be known hereafter if necessary,'

and it was stated that

'No questions whatever will be asked of any person who brings a child, nor shall any servant of the house presume to endeavour to discover who such person is, on pain of being discharged.'

Sometimes there were a hundred wome at the door, when twenty only could b received, and there was much scramblin and fighting, before the 'House Ful notice was displayed. In consequence a ballot was contrived with white ball for admission, and red for rejection This system prevailed from 1741 to 1756 during which period 1,384 children wer received.

The hosp. was in Hatton Garden onl for four yrs. In 1745 a new site wa obtained in Lamb's Conduit Fields. Her 55 acres of ground were obtained fo £3,500, and a spacious bdg. erected, t which a chapel was added in 1747. Capt Coram d. in 1751, and by his own desir was bd. in the chapel. The long inscrip tion said that

'his name will never want a monumer as long as this Hospital shall subsist,'

that he was

'a man eminent in the most eminen virtue, the love of mankind; littl attentive to his private fortune, an refusing many opportunities of increa ing it, his time and thoughts wer continually employed in endeavours t promote the public happiness, both i this kingdom and elsewhere.'

The managers of the Foundling Hosp were ambitious to open it upon the mo unrestricted plan. They ascertained tha George II was well disposed towards i and in 1756 resolutions were passed by tł H. of C. approving the charity, an guaranteeing liberal grants of money, s that 'it should be enabled to appoir proper places in all counties, ridings, divisions of this kingdom, for the receptio of all exposed and deserted your children.' A basket was thereupon hur outside the gate and an advertisemer publicly announced that all childre under the age of two months, tendere for admission, would be received. O the first day of general reception, 2n June 1756, 117 children were deposite The whole month produced 425, all suj posed not to be above the specified ag limit. The next yr. £30,000 was vote and the age was extended to six month Later it was extended to twelve month A regular carrying trade in childre went on. Wagons brought them fro the country; sometimes seven out eight would be dead when the bell wa rung at the gate to signalize new arrival

One parent who thus easily disposed of a child to the Foundling Hosp. was tried for infanticide, and would probably have been hanged, but for his ability to prove that the crime was committed by the carrier. In order to enable inquiries to be made if there was cause for suspicion, in 1757 it was ordained that all persons bringing children should leave some token with them. A collection of these is in the mus. of the Foundling Hosp. There is a card with the ace of hearts, and a verse written upon it; an ivory fish; a gold locket; a lottery ticket; a book-marker with the inscription: 'Cruel separation'; a piece of brass in the shape of a heart inscribed: 'You have my heart though we must part.' Previously identification had been possible only by the clothing, which was sometimes therefore minutely described. About 15,000 children were received between 1756 and 1760. Of these only about 4,400 lived to work as apprentices, or, in the case of the girls, to enter domestic service. The amount expended had been about £500,000. After the withdrawal of Govt. support in 1760, the governors decided to take all children offered with a £100 note, no questions being asked. This system lasted until 1801. Since then admission has been upon the personal application of mothers, and the committee have to be satisfied of the previous good character and present necessity of the mother, and that the father had deserted it and her; also that the reception of the child would 'in all probability be the means of replacing the mother in the course of virtue and the way of an honest livelihood.' No money has since been demanded.

The Foundling Hosp. has a good collection of pictures, including Sir Godfrey Kneller's portrait of Handel, who gave an organ to the chapel, and often presided at performances of the *Messiah* given for the benefit of the institution. There is also Hogarth's portrait of Capt. Coram, painted in 1740. According to the artist, this was the portrait which he painted with most pleasure, and in which he particularly wished to excel. It was at his suggestion that a collection of pictures was made. This drew visitors and benefited the charity. There is also a bust of Handel by Roubiliac, and Raphael's cartoon of the 'Murder of the Innocents,' bought for £26 by Prince Hoare.

Dickens took much interest in the Foundling Hosp., and whilst residing in Doughty St. took sittings in the chapel. His letter resigning them is preserved in the Hosp. Mus. Tattycoram in *Little Dorrit* was a foundling, really Harriet Coram, the surname after the founder. The governors favoured famous names for the children, and there were Wickliffes, Lauds, Chaucers, Shakespeares, Miltons, Cromwells, Hampdens, and one Izaak Walton. Popular novels also were utilized. There were children named Chas. Allworthy, Tom Jones, Sophia Western, and Clarissa Harlowe. The last child received under the parliamentary system was named Kitty Finis.

In June 1926 the Foundling Hosp. left Bloomsbury for temporary quarters at Redhill and in autumn 1935 it moved to Berkhamstead. It is now called the Thomas Coram Foundation for Children. The familiar statue of Capt. Coram (with flowing wig and broad-tailed open coat), holding in his hand the charter of the hosp.—it was erected in 1852—departed with the institution.

The estate was sold to a syndicate, but was subsequently saved as a playground for the children of a densely populated area by raising some £475,000 in 4½ yrs. The subscribers included the late Ld. Rothermere (£170,000), the Pilgrim Trust, and the City Companies.

In 1936 a handsome bdg. was erected in Brunswick Sq. for offices. Here also is the picture gallery, and museum. It is open to the public.

Fulham, now part of the L. Bor. of Hammersmith, was a met. bor. situated on the N. bank of the Thames in the county of Middlesex: it was bounded by Chelsea, Hammersmith, and Kensington; it possessed the longest river frontage of any met. bor.

There has been much speculation about the origin of the name, two commonly accepted explanations being 'foul-town' on account of its muddy ways, or 'fowlham' because of its being the haunt of wild-fowl. The manor of Fulanham is mentioned as early as 691.

The ch., dedicated to All Saints, is not mentioned in Domesday Book, but was in existence in 1242. The oldest part is now the tower, built in 1440, the remainder of the bdg. having been rebuilt in 1880–1 by Sir A. Blomfield. A number of interesting monuments from the older ch. remain, and the 17th-century organ and font were also retained. In the tower is a fine statue of Viscount Mordaunt (1675), and in the chancel an attractive memorial to Lady Margaret Legh (1603), seated with an infant in her arms. There is a fine Flemish brass to Margaret Svanders (1529), and a stone slab commemorating Thos. Carlos, son of that Col. Wm. Carlos who aided Charles II to escape by hiding in the oak tree at Boscobel. There are also tablets to Bridget Holland, daughter of Lancelot Brown, the 18th-century landscape gardener; her husband, Henry Holland, the architect of Carlton House and the Pavilion at Brighton, and Theodore Hook (d. 1841). In the chyd. lie fourteen Bps. of L. and two Ld.Ms.; and it contains an amusing epitaph, quoted under that heading.

St. John's, Walham Green, is an early Gothic revival ch. by Taylor, 1828. The chancel is a later addition. The Roman Catholic Ch. of St. Thomas in Rylston Rd. is from designs by Pugin (1848), and three chs. in the bor. contain relics of those demolished in the City—St. Clement, Fulham Rd. (a font); St. Peter, Reperton Rd. (a pulpit); and St. Dionis, Parson's Green (pulpit, font and altar).

Of its ancient houses very few remain, and only four need mention here. The oldest, Sandford Manor House, now stands within the confines of the Gas Works on the borders of Chelsea, and is said to have been the home of Nell Gwyn. It is well worth a visit for its own sake. Two 18th-century houses with literary associations remain: Fulham House, once the home of Jacob Tonson 'the Prince of Publishers' is now occupied by a unit of the Royal Signals (T.A.), and North End House, in private occupation, was the residence of the novelist Samuel Richardson, and later of the famous Pre-Raphaelite painter, Sir Edward Burne-Jones. Lastly there is the impressive mansion belonging to the Hurlingham Club, which overlooks the river and was re-modelled as it now stands about 1797.

In 1671 the K. granted to John Dwight, the famous potter, a licence to make stoneware, 'vulgarly called Cologne ware,' and earthenware at Fulham, and the

Fulham pottery remains to-day on its old site. Dwight d. in 1703, and was buried at Fulham. His wonderful busts and statuettes, which have justly been called 'the finest example of white salt-glaze portraiture,' may be seen in the museums. Most notable are the busts of P. Rupert and Mrs. Pepys at the B.Mus., and the charming statuette of the potter's little daughter Lydia at the V. and A. Mus.

Fulham Palace. The Manor House, better known as the Bishop's Palace, is without doubt the oldest bdg. in Fulham. Save for the brief interregnum of Col. Harvey in Cromwellian times, the manor shows an uninterrupted ecclesiastical tenancy of 1,200 yrs. Of the manor-house of pre-Tudor days, however, no vestige remains. Fulham Palace is approached by way of Bishop's Av., passing the porter's lodge (built by Bp. Howley, who occupied the Palace from 1813 to 1828) on the left and a still rural paddock on the right. The massive gateway that guards the Fitzjames quadrangle—the oldest portion of the palace—was built by Bp. Fitzjames (1506–22). The quadrangle is flanked by low and homely bdgs. of red and black brick, repeating everywhere the characteristic Tudor diamond pattern, and there is a stone fountain in the centre. The entrance to the palace proper lies on the E. side of the quadrangle under a squat but picturesque clock-tower. There is a doorway over which are the arms of Bp. Terrick, which leads to the Fitzjames Hall, a noble apartment measuring 50½ ft. by 27 ft. The room is panelled with carved oak wainscoting which originally belonged to the chapel at London House, Aldersgate St. The windows contain some old and exceedingly interesting armorial glass. Over the deeply recessed fire-place is a large tablet, encased in a massive carved frame, which records that

'This Hall, with the adjoining quadrangle, was erected by Bishop Fitzjames in the reign of Henry VIIth, on the site of buildings of the old Palace as ancient as the Conquest. It was used as the Hall by Bishop Bonner and Bishop Ridley, during the struggles of the Reformation; and retained its original proportions, till it was altered by Bishop Sherlock, in the reign of George IInd Bishop Howley, in the reign of George IVth, changed it into a private uncon secrated chapel. It is now restored to its original purpose, on the erection, by Bishop Tait, of a new chapel of more suitable dimensions. A.D. 1866.'

his hall was used by Bonner for the trial f heretics and is clearly shown in the lustrations of Foxe's *Acts and Monuments* 563). Bonner's bedroom—said to be aunted by the ghost of that prelate— es on the N. side of the quadrangle: his ed was taken down so recently as 1894. Another apartment is the Bp.'s Vestry, eautifully panelled with old oak from the audian quarters of the palace. There is so the Tait Chapel, the sanctuary floor f which is laid in marble brought from te hall. The Bp.'s drawing-room, on the . front of the palace, is a spacious apart- ent commanding a fine view of the rounds, and next to it is the dining-room, ontaining a magnificent collection of ortraits of later bps. The dining-room ads to the Porteus Lib., which stands n the site of the historic Old Chapel. his imposing apartment, with a vaulted iling, is named after Dr. Beilby Porteus, p. of L. (1787–1808), who was instru- ental in forming the collection of eological works housed herein. Round e walls hang portraits of earlier prelates llected by Bps. Porteus, Randolph, and owley.

Not the least interesting of the palace oms is the great kitchen, formerly the ning-room, in which the Bps. of L. dined om the time of Bp. Sherlock (1748–61) that of Bp. Howley. Its fine ceiling is orthy of special notice. The cellars have out staples and rings affixed to the walls testify to their former use as dungeons; e Armour, or Guard Room, possesses a ancient hearth, surmounted by some fine old carving; there is also the brew- house in which the famous 'Bishop's Ale' was brewed of old, and the Tithe or Hay Barn, built in the time of Col. Harvey (1654). The grounds, which were the joy in old days of such ardent horticul- turists as Bp. Grindal and Bp. Compton, are still delightful, but the ancient moat (fully a mile in circumference, and attributed to the Danes) was filled in in 1921 with builders' rubbish, the Bp. of L. not feeling justified in incurring the expense of cleaning it.

Furnival's Inn (Holborn) took its name from the Lds. Furnival, whose town house it was. Sir Wm. Furnival (*c.* 1383) had two messuages and thirteen shops here. It became an Inn of Chancery about 1408, and by 1422 was attached to Lincoln's Inn. Sir Thos. More was reader there from about 1498 to 1501. It was partly rebuilt in 1640, and wholly rebuilt about 1818. Dickens lived there 1835–6. Here he was residing at the time of his marriage, and the publication of the earlier part of *Pickwick Papers*. Wood's Hotel, which figures in *Edwin Drood*, was demolished in 1895 and the rest of Furnival's Inn in 1897. A watchman's box from there is in the Maidstone Mus. The site of Furnival's Inn is now covered by the huge offices of the Pru- dential Insurance Co., and there is a C.C. tablet on the E. side of the entrance gate. Furnival St. is on the S. side of Holborn. There is also a bust of Dickens, on the W. side of the gateway. It was the work of Percy FitzGerald, and was cautiously described by *The Dickensian* at the time of its erection (1907) as 'a recognisable like- ness.'

G

General Post Office. In the Middle Ages there was a regular, if rudimentary, system of postage between the various courts of Europe. By 1548 it is evident that there was a regular system of private postage, for a statute of that year fixed a penny a mile as the rate of hire, and later Camden, the Elizabethan antiquary, mentions Thos. Randolph as the chief postmaster of England. James I seems to have taken unusual interest in the matter, because he detected deficiencies in the postal system of England as compared with that in practice over the border and instigated some improvement. In 1635 there was a proclamation which said 'that there hath been no certain or constant intercourse between the kingdom of England and Scotland,' and commanded

'Thomas Witherings Esq., his Majesty's postmaster of England for foreign parts, to settle a running post or two to run night and day between Edinburgh and the City of London, to go thither and come back in six days';

and directions were given for the management of the correspondence between post-towns on the line of the road, and other named towns; and similarly in Ireland. The first metropolitan postal system was organized in 1680 by Wm. Docwra, who carried and insured letters and parcels up to £10 in value, and a pound in weight, for 1*d*. He originated post-marks and provided a more remarkable service than is available even to-day. Between four and five hundred post offices were opened in a single morning, and the letters received there were delivered at places of business in L. and at the Inns of Court virtually once an hour during the day, and at other places, according to distance, from four to eight times a day. Whilst he lost money Docwra was undisturbed; when profits were reported James, D. of York, who was entitled to post office revenues, went to law in defence of his monopoly. Docwra was mulcted in damages, and in less than five yrs. from its foundation, his penny post was annexed by the G.P.O. During James's reign he received no recognition of the service he had done the capital, but under William and Mary he was pensioned, and in 1697 was appointed Comptroller of the penny post at a salary of £200. Soon afterwards,

however, he was dismissed by the Lord of the Treasury, on complaint made by subordinates, and both salary and grant came to an end. His penny post for L. survived until 1801, when 2*d*. was made the minimum charge.

The first G.P.O. known was at Cloak Lane, Dowgate Hill. At the time of the G.F. it was the 'Black Swan,' Bishopsgate. Pepys mentions it, and twice in 1664 went to 'musique' meetings there. In Ogilby and Morgan's map (1677) it is shown on the E. side of Bishopsgate, and this was when it was established at Crosby Hall. Later, Harben says, it was in Star Court, Cornhill. In 1688 it was in Lombard St., and the site of the bdg. is now indicated by Post Office Court there. It is said formerly to have been Sir Robt. Vyner's house. Here it remained until the bdg. in St. Martin's le Grand was erected 1825– from designs by Sir Robt. Smirke. This was an imposing structure, with pillars of the Ionic order and a central portico surmounted by a pediment. The G.P.O. West was built opposite, 1869–74, from designs by Jas. Williams of H.M. Office of Works. In 1880 the business of the Savings Bank was transferred to a bdg. in Q. Victoria St. and in 1903 again removed to W. Kensington. In 1890–5, to the N. a G.P.O. West, another bdg. was reared. This was known as G.P.O. North. In 1901 pressure upon accommodation was relieved by transferring the country mail to Mount Pleasant, where the Parcel Post, established in 1883, was already installed. In 1903 3½ acres of the site of Christ's Hosp. was obtained, and in 19— new bdgs. were opened there. Outside there is a statue of Rowland Hill (1882) once outside the Royal Exchange. The premises are again being enlarged. Statistics of the present London post office Service are:

Telephone Exchanges 350

Residential Subscribers:

Exclusive	1,008,000
Shared	3,700

Originated calls in year:

Local	2,845 million
Trunk calls	167·1 million
Overseas	9.948 million
Inland telegrams	2·7 million

Post offices:	2,041
Letters posted:	3,243,257,000

Parcels posted:	85,742,000
Radio licences:	513,600
Television licences:	2,187,700

A striking development of the G.P.O. is the Post Office Tower near Tottenham Court Road. 580 feet high (excluding the 40-foot mast) it is the tallest building in Britain. The Tower was built primarily to deal with the ever-increasing number of trunk telephone calls and will eventually provide for 150,000 simultaneous telephone conversations and up to 40 television channels. Two high-speed lifts carry visitors to three viewing platforms and the restaurant at 1,000 feet per minute. The restaurant, the highest in England, revolves every 25 minutes. Including equipment, the Tower cost £9 million and was completed in 1965.

Gerard's Hall was originally the hall of John de Gisorcis in the par. of St. Mildred de Bredstrete, erected about 1296. In 1430 it was 'Gisoreshalle.' Stow called it 'Gisors Hall,' but said by corruption it was called 'Gerardes Hall,' and was then 'a common Ostrey [hostelry] for receipt of travellers.' In the high-roofed hall, Stow says:

'sometimes stoode a large Firr Pole, which reached to the roofe thereof, and was sayd to bee one of the staves that Gerrard the Gyant used in the warres to runne withall. . . . The Hostelar of that house sayde to me, the Pole lacked halfe a foote of fortie in length. . . . Reason of the Pole could the master of the Hostrey give me none, but bade me reade the great Chronicles, for there he heard of it.'

Stow adds: 'Which aunswere seemed to me insufficient,' and after a few reasons for this conclusion decides 'to leave these fables.' He suggests the pole may have been used for May Day celebrations. Gerard's Hall was burnt in the G.F. and on being rebuilt about 1672 seems to have been called 'Garrett's Hall,' being used again as an inn and later as a hotel. Here in 1844, says Walter Thornbury:

'Mr. James Smith, the originator of early closing (then living at W. Y. Ball & Co.'s, Wood Street), learning that the warehouses in Manchester were closed at one p.m. on Saturday, determined to ascertain if a similar system could not be introduced into the metropolis. He called a meeting at Gerard's Hall, and the only result was that for eight months in the year the London warehouses were closed at six o'clock, and for four months at eight o'clock.'

The fine Norman crypt remained until everything was demolished for the western extension of Cannon St. 1853–4. A figure of a smaller giant than would have been required to handle the pole mentioned by Stow was outside the hotel, and is now in the Guildhall Mus. There is a C.C. tablet in Queen Victoria St.

Gray's Inn is situated in what was known as the 'Manor of Portpoole.' The name is said to have been derived from two words meaning the 'market by the pool.' The market of Portpoole, held at Holborn Bars, was known in the 13th century as the Bp. of Ely's fair. The name is commemorated in Portpool Lane—off Leather Lane. Residing here at the beginning of the 13th century was a family of de Greys. Walter de Grey was chancellor (1206–14) under K. John, and his nephew became Justice in Eyre 1260, and the latter's son, Reginald, Chief Justice of Chester in the reign of Edward I, and first Ld. Grey of Wilton. When this last d. (1308) the property consisted of a messuage with gardens and one dove-house and a windmill. Probably—it was the custom in other cases—here resided the judges, clerks, and other officers of their court and law students. With the death of the first Ld. Grey de Wilton, the family ceased to live in the Manor of Portpoole. It is not known who succeeded to the property; Hugh H. L. Bellot pointed out that in 1370 it was described as 'Hospitium,' and was inclined to the belief that the Soc. of Gray's Inn came into possession on the death of the first Ld. Grey. Simon Segar (librarian of the Inn in the reign of Charles II) compiled a list of Readers, and this mentions Wm. Skipwith, 1355. It is possible, therefore, that Gray's Inn may antedate both socs. of the Temple. In 1513 the manor was sold to the convent of the Charterhouse at Sheen, subject to licence of the Crown, which was obtained three yrs. later, and the benchers held the Inn of the prior and convent at an annual rent of £6 13s. 4d., which continued to be so paid until the dissolution of the monasteries in 1539, when the rent became due to the Crown. The extant records of the Soc. of Gray's Inn open in 1569. At the head of the fellowship stood the masters of the bench and readers, as they are also frequently termed. Next came the utter barristers, and of these, those who had been called ten yrs. formed the Grand Co. of Ancients, and took precedence of the remainder of the utter barristers in hall. From their ranks was chosen the reader. The third class consisted of inner barristers and students. The dean of the chapel took rank next the reader in the Elizabethan period. He was usually master of the bench, and it was his duty to enforce attendance at ch., to receive and distribute alms received at Holy Communion, and the taxes levied for the stipend of the clergy. He was also responsible for the furniture of the chapel. Of the servants of the Inn, the four chief officers were, in 1570, the steward, the butler, the priest, and the master cook.

The hall dated from 1556–60. It was 75 ft. in length, 35 ft. in width, and 47 ft. in height; a fine specimen of Tudor architecture. It had a magnificent oak screen, and this and some of the dining-tables are said to have been presented by Q. Elizabeth. Above the screen was the minstrels' gallery, with a richly carved front, and at the W. end the hall was lighted by a large window over the minstrel's gallery, and on the E. by a similar window, both emblazoned with armorial glass. There was an oriel window similarly decorated. On the oak panelling were the armorial bearings of a long succession of Readers and Treasurers. There was a bench table and a cupboard, as in the Middle Temple hall. Here were held from time to time the serjeants' feasts and banquets to distinguished guests. Here were performed masques and plays, including the *Comedy of Errors* in 1594. On Grand Day in every term, the guests still drink to the 'glorious, pious, and immortal memory' of Q. Elizabeth. There is a portrait of the latter in the twenty-sixth year of her age. Amongst other portraits are Charles I, Charles II, James II, Sir Nicholas Bacon, and Francis Bacon, Baron Verulam. The chambers occupied by the last disappeared in fires in 1684 and 1717. The hall had a narrow escape during the German air-raids of 1914–18, the robing-room adjoining being fired by an incendiary bomb. It was reduced to a shell by German bombs in 1941. The panelling was saved.

There was a chapel at Gray's Inn between 1305 and 1315, and possibly some of the original bdg. remains. Great reconstruction, however, was carried out in 1615–34, and in 1689 surveyors were summoned to 'repaire, alter and modell' the chapel to the best of their ability. In 1893 the bdg. was transformed. The roof dated from this period. The Tudor windows were discovered concealed by plaster. The E. window (1895–9) contained five figures: Becket, Abps. Whitgift and Laud, Bp. Juxon, and Abp. Wake. Whitgift, Laud, and Juxon were members of Gray's Inn. Laud was represented on the scaffold at Tower Hill. Wake was preacher 1688, and was represented preaching in the chapel. In the N. window were the arms of Juxon, Abp. Sheldon, etc. The chapel suffered the same fate as the hall in 1941. Hall, chapel and library have now been restored. The library bdg. was also burnt out, and about thirty thousand books destroyed.

The present gatehouse in Gray's Inn Sq. is approximately on the site of the original gatehouse to the old manor-house of Portpoole. It dates from 1688. Here Jacob Tonson had his bookshop. He was the purchaser of the copyright of *Paradise Lost*. He was also Dryden's publisher, and the poet, growing exasperated in the course of some dispute, sent him a word-portrait of himself:

'With leering looks, bull-faced, and freckled fair,
With two left legs, and Judas-coloured hair,
And frowzy pores that tain the ambient air.'

'Tell the dog,' said the poet to the messenger, 'that he who wrote these can write more.' Tonson subsequently had also a shop in the Holborn gate. Osborne, who was supposed to have been felled to the ground by Johnson, also had a shop in the Holborn gate. The latter was erected in 1594, and in 1867 the original red bricks were shamefully covered with cement. In South Sq. is Bacon's statue, unveiled by Mr. Arthur Balfour (1912). At No. 1 Dickens was a clerk in 1827 (the chambers have been badly damaged); No. 2 Holborn Court, where Traddles had chambers, is now No. 2 South Sq. The gardens were probably laid out largely through the influence of Bacon, who set up a mound and a summer-house with a Latin inscription. They were removed in 1755. In Pepys's time the walks were fashionable. He went there on a 'Lord's Day' in 1661, 'seeing the fine ladies walk there.' In 1662 he took his wife there 'to observe fashions of the ladies, because of my wife's making some clothes.' Addison's Sir Roger de Coverley walked there; and there John Wesley and Count Zinzendorf held their final interview and 'parted without the least prospect of a reconciliation.' Lamb cursed Verulam Bdgs. for encroaching upon these gardens, and said:

'They are still the best gardens of any of the Inns of Court, my beloved Temple not forgotten—have the gravest character, their aspect being altogether reverend and law-breathing. Bacon has left the impress of his foot upon their gravel walks.'

Bacon is also supposed to have planted the catalpa tree, now more bowed to the ground than the man with the crooked sixpence, and on this false assumption (catalpa trees had not then been introduced into England) slips from it have been planted in America. The gates in Field Court were erected in 1723 and bear the initials of Wm. Gilby, treasurer at the time. They used to bear the arms of Gray's Inn with those of the Inner Temple. Gray's Inn had its curfew. It tolled forty times at 9 p.m., and the gates were then closed.

Famous members of Gray's Inn not already mentioned are Thos. Cromwell, afterwards E. of Essex, Sir Thos. Gresham, Wm. Cecil, afterwards Ld. Burghley, Wm. Camden, the antiquary, and, amongst moderns, E. of Birkenhead. The body of the latter lay in state in the chapel in 1930.

(See *Gray's Inn and Lincoln's Inn*, by H. H. L. Bellot and *A Prospect of Gray's Inn*, by F. Cowper, 1951.)

Greater London Council. Under the London Government Act 1963, the London County Council, the Middlesex County Council, 3 county bors., 28 met. bors., 39 non-county bors. and 15 urban district councils were abolished. In their place, since 1st April 1965, London has been governed by the Greater London Council and 32 London Borough Councils. The C.C. was not affected.

The G.L.C. consists of 100 councillors and 16 aldermen: elections are held every third year. The area of Greater London which the Council serves is 620 square miles and its population (in 1965) was 7,948,800. Among its many functions are: housing (it is the world's biggest landlord and has 230,000 families housed within 25 miles of Charing Cross), planning, roads, traffic management and control, fire and ambulance services, refuse disposal, parks, licensing, main drainage and sewage disposal. One of its committees is the Inner London Education Authority, the largest education authority in the country, with more than 800,000 pupils and students attending 1,450 schools and colleges. Its revenue expenditure in 1967/8 was £115·5 million.

The electorate of the G.L.C. is 5,323,719; the rateable value of the G.L.C. area is around £600 million (nearly one-third of the total for England and Wales). The Council's total estimated expenditure in 1967/8 was £300 million.

From 1969 (or thereabouts) the G.L.C. takes over the London Transport Board (q.v.).

Greenwich, now part of the L. Bor. of Greenwich, was a met. bor. bounded N. by the Thames, E. and SE. by Woolwich, SW. by Lewisham, and W. by the River Ravensbourne and Deptford. The ancient par. of Greenwich was originally E. Greenwich, Deptford being known as W. Greenwich. The ch. is dedicated to St. Alphege, an Abp. of Canterbury who was murdered here by the Danes in 1012. It was rebuilt in 1718, probably from designs by Nicholas Hawksmoor, with a steeple by a local architect, John James. Burnt out during a raid in the Second World War, it has now been restored. Among the more important monuments were those to T. Tallis (1585), General Wolfe (1759), and John Julius Angerstein (1823), whose collection of paintings formed the nucleus of the N.G.

The hosp. retains its name; but it ceased to be the residence of aged seamen of the fleet in 1873, and is now partly a show-place but mainly a naval sch. It is the direct successor of the Palace of Placentia, where Henry VIII, Q. Mary I, and Q. Elizabeth were born, and Edward VI died. Alterations and additions to the palace were made by Edward IV, Henry VII, and Henry VIII; and Anne of Denmark, on whom (together with E.

Combe) it was settled in 1613, laid the foundation of the 'House of Delight' (finished by Inigo Jones for Henrietta Maria 1635). In this beautiful bdg., usually known as 'The Queen's House,' the body of Admiral Blake lay in state before burial in W.A. (1657). It is now part of the National Maritime Mus. In 1652 Parliament tried to sell the palace. Charles II pulled it down in 1662, and had the NW. wing of the present hosp. built, 1664, as the beginning of a palace on the river front. The nominal architect was Sir John Denham; the real one was John Webb, Inigo Jones's nephew, who adopted designs by his uncle. Lysons says this wing was built on the site of the convent of the Friars Observant of the Franciscan Order, settled in Greenwich by Edward IV and confirmed in their possessions by Henry VII in 1486: Grey Friars replaced them when they were turned out by Henry VIII for objecting to his proceedings against his first Q., 1534; they were reinstated by Mary, and suppressed 1559. Nothing more was done to the palace Charles II began until the reign of William III; whose Q., Mary II, in the year of her death (1694), made arrangements for turning it into a hosp. for superannuated and disabled seamen of the navy. Funds were raised by lottery among other means; and the SW. wing, called K. William's bdg., was erected by Sir Christopher Wren 1698-1703; the W. front was finished by Sir John Vanbrugh 1726. The SE. wing, called Q. Mary's bdg., is similar, and was built 1692-1752: but in 1779 a fire destroyed the chapel (designed by Ripley) and much adjoining; the present chapel was built by James ('Athenian') Stuart. The altar-piece is 'The Ship-wreck of St. Paul,' by Benjamin West. There was a font which had been carved by a Chatham prisoner in 1883. This has recently been removed to replace Stuart's Font, which was re-discovered. There is a 'butterfly' window and a spiral staircase of Wren's design, 30 in. in diameter. Q. Anne's bdg. is the NW. wing, almost a reverse copy of K. Charles's NE. wing; it was built 1698–1728. The Painted Hall is in the K. William bdg.: the painting of the walls and ceiling is by Sir Jas. Thornhill. For three days the body of Ld. Nelson lay in state here (1806). In the great quadrangle is a statue of George II by Rysbrack.

Trinity Hosp., in 2½ acres of its own ground, faces the Thames: it was established 1613 by the E. of Northampton for the accommodation of aged bachelors and widowers of Greenwich.

S. of Greenwich Hosp. is the park; and on a hill therein is the Royal Observatory, from whose meridian all longitudes are calculated—it was built 1675 in place of D. Humphrey's tower of Greenwich Castle, for the express purpose of longitude calculations: the site was selected, not by Flamsteed the Astronomer Royal, but by Wren. In 1950 it was removed to Hurstmonceaux, Sussex, because of the impurity of the atmospheric conditions over modern L. The old building is open to the public and there is a planetarium in the grounds. An extensive view of the river is to be had from this hill upon which is a statue of Gen. Wolfe, unveiled by the Marquis de Montcalm in 1930. Greenwich Park is still a beautiful spot, and on its W. side are two historic houses, the Ranger's Lodge, once the home of the E. of Chesterfield, and Macartney House, an early home of Gen. Wolfe. On Maze Hill, E. of the park, stands Vanbrugh Castle, a castellated brick mansion erected by Sir John Vanbrugh, now a sch. The statue of K. William IV (see 'Lost Monuments') marks the site of St. Mary's Ch. (1825).

Charlton (chorl-ton or farmer-town) is a picturesque spot with an old red-brick ch. and a magnificent manor-house. St. Luke's Ch. was almost rebuilt in 1630–40, and contains a number of interesting monuments and some old stained glass. There is a memorial bust by Chantry to Spencer Perceval, the Prime Minister assassinated in the H. of C. in 1812. The Ch. suffered considerable blast damage during the Second World War, as did Charlton House, now used as a Public Library. The house was built by Sir Adam Newton, who is bd. in the Ch., and was completed about 1612. It is a splendid example of Renaissance Architecture, with a well preserved interior.

Morden Coll., a very delightful example of Wren's work, was built in 1695 as a retreat for aged and necessitous merchants; the founder being Sir John Morden, a rich Turkey merchant whose statue, with that of his wife, is over the main entrance.

Blackheath is mainly in Lewisham bor.,

though connected historically with Greenwich. The Danes camped there in 1011; Wat Tyler and his followers 1381; Jack Cade in 1450; Henry VI with his Lancastrians 1452; Ld. Audley and the Cornish rebels 1497. Famous meetings on the heath include Henry IV and the Emperor of Constantinople 1400; the Citizens of L. and Henry V after Agincourt 1415; the Citizens and Edward IV on his return from France 1474; the Admiral of France and the E. of Surrey, High Admiral of England, 1519; Cardinal Campeggio and the D. of Norfolk 1519; Anne of Cleves and Henry VIII 1540. Here also James I introduced golf to Englishmen, and highwaymen menaced the unwary traveller.

Gresham College. Under the terms of Sir Thos. Gresham's will (made in July 1575), his house in Bishopsgate St. was to go to his wife for her lifetime, and thereafter to become Gresham Coll., an institution where free lectures were to be provided for all who cared to attend. Seven subjects were to be dealt with, one on each day of the week, i.e. divinity, astronomy, music, geometry, law, medicine, and rhetoric. For each of these there was to be a professor, who was to be unmarried and to reside in the coll. The professors' salaries—£50 each—were to be derived from the rents of the shops in the Royal Exchange. The actual bdgs., and the govt. of the institution, were vested jointly in the C.C. and the Mercers' Co. Lectures were given at Gresham House until 1768, when the trustees complained that the rents from the shops in the Royal Exchange did not produce the necessary income. The lectures were then given at the Exchange, afterwards at the City of L. Sch., then in Milk St., until 1843, when the Coll. was removed to the corner of Gresham St. and Basinghall St. The present building was erected in 1912. From 1966 the lectures have been given under the auspices of the City University, one of whose departments now occupies the College.

Greyfriars. See 'Christ Church, Newgate—City Churches, D.'

Grub Street was first known (1217–43) as 'Grobstrat.' It was 'Grubbestrate' in 1281. The derivation is much in dispute.

The most likely is from *grube*, a ditch or drain. John Foxe, the martyrologist, lived here from 1571 to 1587, and another resident was John Speed (for both see 'City Churches; D'—St. Giles, Cripplegate).

There was 'a hermit of Grub St.'; his name was Henry Welby. It is said that for forty-four yrs. he was never seen by any human being except an old female servant, and by her only in cases of great necessity. His diet was bread, oatmeal, water gruel, milk, vegetables, and—as a great indulgence—the yolk of an egg.

The thoroughfare seems to have been associated with hack writers from the middle of the 17th century. In 1649 Allsop, a printer of Grub St., was bound over in the sum of £3,000 and two sureties of £200 each 'not to print any seditious or unlicensed books or pictures, or suffer his press to be used for any such purpose.' Swift, in 1710, wrote:

'Grub Street has but ten days to live, then an Act of Parliament takes place that ruins it by taxing every half-sheet a half-penny.'

From 1730–7 there was published the *Grub Street Journal.* Its object was to satirise the personages of the *Dunciad*, and the productions of Cibber, Curll, Dennis, etc. One of these contributors, writing in 1730 in honour of Humphry Parsons, a Ld.M. who was a brewer, said:

'Grubean authors malt's strong juice inspires
The coldest genius warms, and warmest fires
If Parsons' noblest tun inflame their brains
They soar in epic or Pindaric strains.'

Hoole, the translator of Tasso, is the only man of letters whose residence can be definitely located in a thoroughfare which was the resort of those who had abandoned hope of literary fame. Samuel Johnson in his *Dictionary* (1755) included this topographical tit-bit:

'Grubstreet. The name of a street in London, much inhabited by writers of small histories, dictionaries, and temporary poems; whence any mean production is called grubstreet.' Johnson did not himself know it as a resident, though in his earlier L. days he had qualified. In 1780 Fanny Burney, in a letter to Mrs. Thrale, said:

'I have had the pleasure to meet him again at Mrs. Reynolds's, when he offered to take me with him to Grub Street, to see the ruins of the house demolished there in the late riots, by a mob that, as he observed, could be no friend to the Muses! He inquired if I had ever yet visited Grub Street? but was obliged to restrain his anger when I answered "No," because he acknowledge that he had never paid his respects to it himself. "However," says he, "you and I, Burney, will go together; we have a very good right to go, so we'll visit the mansions of our progenitors, and take up our own freedom together." '

In 1829 the householders petitioned for a change in the name, and suggested 'Milton Street,' a name, they said—

'calculated to show that while the Inhabitants of the greatest commercial City in the world are attentive to their own interests, they are not unmindful of the claims of Literature and Science.'

The name was therefore changed as requested. Geo. Gissing wrote a novel entitled *New Grub Street* (1891). This, he suggested, was the area round the B.Mus.

Guildhall. Nothing is known of the first building on the site, although excavations during the current rebuilding have revealed evidence of a Guildhall earlier than the present 15th-century one. The existence of the arms of Edward the Confessor (five martlets round a cross) in the porch of the present hall alongside those of Henry VI in whose reign it was completed indicate that there was a hall of some kind in his reign (1042–66). Fabyan, in his Chronicles (1490), recorded the erection of the new building:

'1411. In this yere was ye Guyld Halle, of London, began to be new edyfied, and of an oylde and lytele cotage made into a fayre and goodly house as it now apperyth.'

Stow says that—

'towards the charges thereof the companies gave large benevolences: also offences of men were pardoned for sums of money towards this work, extraordinary fees were raised, fines, amercements and other things employed during seven years with a continuation

thereof three years more all to be employed to the building.'

In 1422 John Coventry and John Carpenter, executors of Whittington, contributed £20 towards the paving of the great hall and £15 more 'to the said pavement with hard stone of Purbeck.' They also glazed some windows thereof 'on every which window the arms of Richard Whittington are placed.' In 1439 the executors of another citizen's will brought in £20 'towards the sustentation of the work at the Guildhall.' Stow records that in 1505 Nicholas Alwyn left £73 6s. 8d. 'for a hanging tapestry to serve for principal days in the Guildhall.' Two lanterns were added in 1499.

The hall was damaged by the G.F. Thomas Vincent (*God's terrible Voice in the City*, 1667) wrote:

'That night the site of Guildhall was a fearful spectacle which stood, the whole body of it together in view for several hours together after the fire had taken it without flames (I suppose because the timber was such solid oake), in a bright shining coale as if it had been a pallace of gold or a great building of burnished brass.'

The roof was so much injured that it was necessary to take it down. In rebuilding, the walls were considerably heightened. Richd. Blome said:

'The roofs, floor, and what else was therein, were consumed—these rooms, courts, and offices are appropriated to the same place wherein they were kept formerly, but much more regular and loftier, and more substantially built.'

The old timber roof gave way to a flat one, attributed to Wren. He is said to have built it in haste for immediate use, and only as a temporary measure. It remained, however, for nearly 200 years, being replaced in 1864 by the recent handsome roof, from a design of the late Sir Horace Jones, the City architect, consistent in design with the style of architecture in fashion at the period when the hall was built. The floor is paved principally with Portland stone, arranged in panels of large dimensions. The panels are enriched with incised quatrefoils and ornamental figures. In the panels in the centre of the pavement, commencing from the E. end, are first the arms of Henry VI, in whose reign the Guildhall was built, and then alternately the arms of the City and the royal arms. In the side panels are the arms of the following Ld.M.s: N. side—Henry FitzEylwin (1191–1212), Richd. Whittington (1396, 1397, 1406, 1419), Sir Richd. Gresham (1537), Sir Edwd. Osborne (1583), Sir Henry Tulse (1684), Wm. Beckford, Esq. (1763), S. side—Sir Wm. Walworth (1374, 1380), Thos Knolles (1399, 1411), Sir Thos. White (1553), Sir Thos. Myddleton (1613), Sir Richd. Hoare (1713), Sir Thos. Gabriel (1867). These arms are all filled in with lead. The official standards of length are in brass plates across the floor. They were laid under the superintendence of the late Sir Geo. Airy, Astronomer Royal, and certified by the Board of Trade.

In 1789, Geo. Dance the younger reconstructed the front of the Guildhall. The 'images of stone' with which Stow said the front was beautified then disappeared, but since have been lost sight of. In 1846, according to C. G. Harper, they were sold for £100 to Henry Bankes, M.P. for Corfe Castle. They were seven in number, representing Christ, Law, Learning, Discipline, Justice, Fortitude, and Temperance. The pile of bdgs. on the W. dates from the same time. The E. wing was re-erected in 1909. From 1828 until 1873 (when the present library was opened) the rooms above the porch were used for that purpose. The Guildhall Chapel, which had stood since 1299, was demolished in 1822. Statues of Queen Elizabeth, Edward VI and Charles I—once on its façade—are now on the staircase leading to the library.

SIZE. The hall is 152 ft. long, 49½ ft. wide, and 89 ft. high. (Westminster Hall (q.v.) is larger.)

There were two large stained-glass windows at the E. and W. ends. The former was presented to the C.C. by the Operatives of Lancashire and the cotton districts on 15th July 1870, in acknowledgment of assistance given them during the Cotton Famine (1862–5). The inscription stated that it was

'The Grateful Memorial of the Operatives of Lancashire and the Cotton Manufacturing District to the Mansion House Relief Committee, who as almoners of a world's benevolence, distributed to them more than £500,000 during the Cotton Famine 1862–5.'

The other large window was in memory of the P. Consort. It was unveiled by P. Arthur, later D. of Connaught, in 1870. It included a figure of the P. Consort unveiling the Great Exhibition of 1851. Both of these windows have been destroyed, as also a number of smaller ones depicting interesting historical incidents, from the granting to the City of its first charter (c. 1067), to one commemorating the first Jewish Ld.M.—Sir David Salomans, who took office in 1855. Other windows destroyed represented Sir Wm. Walworth striking down Wat Tyler (S. side) and the old myth of Richard Whittington—with Henry V and his Q. at the Guildhall—throwing bonds into the fire. As usual, the cat was in evidence. The window was the last in date. It was presented by Viscount Wakefield in 1931. An earlier window commemorating Whittington—it was over the door leading to the Council Chamber—was also destroyed.

The destruction mentioned occurred on the memorable night of 29th Dec. 1940 when the neighbouring ch. of St. Lawrence, Jewry, was reduced to a shell. The roof of the Guildhall was destroyed and the figures of Gog and Magog burned to ashes. These figures, formerly on each side of the door leading to the council chamber, were in 1869 removed to the new gallery. They were the successors of previous ones of wicker and pasteboard referred to by Ned Ward

'I asked my friend the meaning and design of setting up these two Lubberly Preposterous Figures, for I suppose they had some peculiar end in 't? Truly, says my friend, I am wholly ignorant of what they intend by 'em, unless they were set up to show the City what huge Loobies their Forefathers were, or else to frighten stubborn apprentices into obedience for the threat of appearing before two such monstrous logger heads will sooner reform their manners or mould 'em into compliance with their masters will, than carrying of 'em before my Lord Mayor so some of them are as much frighted at the names of Gog and Magog as little children are at the terrible sounds of Raw-head and Bloody-bones.'

These figures were carried in the Ld.M.'s Show till 'Old Time with the help of the City rats and mice had eaten up all their entrails.' The later ones had never been out. The latter were carved by Richd.

Saunders in 1708 for £70. (He also carved, for the ch. of St. Giles, Cripplegate, a figure of Father Time now in the Guildhall Mus.) They measured 14 ft. 6 in. in height and were hollow. Gog held a long pole, from which was suspended a chain to which was attached a globe studded with spikes. This weapon in the Middle Ages was known as a 'morning star,' and Dion Cassius, the Roman historian (155–230), referring to the weapons of the ancient Britons, said that among them

'are a shield and a short spear, having a piece of brass at the lower end shaped like an apple, designed by its shaking to terrify their enemies.'

Magog was armed with a shield and spear, and was attired in conventional Roman costume. The heads of both were wreathed in laurel. Gogmagog was originally the name of one giant (there are Gogmagog Hills in Cambridgeshire to-day), and the other giant was Corineus. The latter's name seems to have been forgotten and the former's divided. They were supposed to represent the giants who fought against the Trojan invaders under Brute, who was fabled to have given his name to Britain. Gog and Magog are mentioned in the Book of Ezekiel and the Book of Revelation. One version of their story was given in the *Chronicles of England*, by William Caxton (see W. G. Bell's *More about Unknown London*). New figures carved by Mr. David Evans, F.R.B.S., replaced them in 1953.

MONUMENTS. Of the five statues in the Guildhall, the most notable is Ld.M. Beckford. It shows him with hand uplifted, making a speech to George III. This was the notable occasion when he attended the K. at St. James's Palace and felt the latter was not sufficiently courteous in respect of a petition which he had presented from the C.C.

On one side of the figure of Beckford is represented the City of L. in mourning, and on the other Trade and Navigation in a drooping condition.

Beckford had served the office of Ld.M. in 1762, and against his wish, being of a great age and in an infirm state of health, was again elected in 1769. He d. suddenly on 21st June, 1770. The erection of the monument (with the inscription) was voted by the Common Council on 5th July following, and it was unveiled on 11th May,

1772. It cost £1,300. Beckford, strangely, is the only Ld.M. to have a monument in the Guildhall, and only Whittington has one elsewhere. His son, also Wm., was the eccentric owner of Fonthill Abbey, and the author of *Vathek*.

The other monuments are: Wm. Pitt E. of Chatham, by Bacon (1782); Ld. Nelson (1810); Wm. Pitt the younger (1813); D. of Wellington—the last charge at Waterloo is represented in relievo—(1857). The monuments of Nelson and Wellington sustained some damage in the Second World War. A bronze statue of Sir Winston Churchill, the work of Oscar Nemon, was unveiled in June 1955.

TRIALS. On the N. wall (E. end) is a tablet recalling notable trials in the hall: Anne Askew (1547), the E. of Surrey (1547), Lady Jane Grey (1554), Dr. Lopez (1594), and Dr. Garnett (1606). The first was arraigned 'for speaking against the sacrament of the altar.' She was burned at Tyburn. Surrey was a beautiful sonnet writer. Lady Jane Grey is the best known of all. Dr. Lopez was a Spanish Jew and a physician to Q. Elizabeth, whom he was accused of attempting to poison. He was hanged at Tyburn, and anti-Semitic feeling aroused led to a revival of Marlowe's *Jew of Malta*, and possibly the Shakespearian *Merchant of Venice*. Garnett was superior of the Order of Jesuits in England, and was accused of complicity in the Gunpowder Plot.

The Aldermen's Court Room, most sumptuously decorated, and adorned with a ceiling and chimney-piece painted by Sir Jas. Thornhill, suffered entire destruction. The Thornhill paintings were, however, evacuated during the war. It was probably of early 17th-century date, though undergoing necessary restoration in 1670–80 consequent on the G.F. The Council Chamber is represented only by the remaining pillars. This was erected in 1884 on the site of a previous one which was built in 1614. In a still earlier chamber there occurred a famous historical incident, commemorated by a tablet bearing the following inscription:

'On this site stood the Council Chamber (built 1614, vacated 1777, burnt 1786) wherein Charles I came to demand the surrender of the five members of Parliament, on the 5th January, 1641–2.'

THE CRYPT is the same date as the Guildhall, and the most extensive in L. Its dimensions are 77 ft. by 46 ft. It is divided into equal bays, four from E. to W. and three from N. to S. by six clustered pillars. At the intersections and points of the ribs are carved bosses, including the arms of Edward the Confessor, the See of L. (two crossed swords), and the City. Only the eastern half of the crypt was open to the public, the western half being used for heating and storage purposes. In the NW. corner is an old doorway which once led to a bdg. on the W. side of the Guildhall. There are staircases remaining, in the thickness of the wall, where the mus. was entered from the crypt, and a circular staircase in the SW. corner. In 1851, the yr. of the Great Exhibition, the crypt was fitted up as a baronial hall. Suitable furniture was hired, and some of the City Companies' plate was placed on oak sideboards. There were mirrors in recesses, tapestries from Bayeux examples, and City policemen in suits of armour from the T.L. The crypt has now been restored to its original state and is open to the public.

The great treasure of the Guildhall is in the custody of the town clerk. This is the charter granted to L. by William the Conqueror *c.* 1066. It consists of sixty-six words in Anglo-Saxon, inscribed upon a slip of parchment 6 in. long and 1⅝ in. broad. It does not bear a cross traced by the Conqueror's own hand, as Freeman, the historian, stated. It was completed by the Great Seal. It is translated:

'William King greets William, Bishop, and Gosfregdh Portreeve, and all the burgesses within London, French and English friendly. And I give you to know that I will that ye two be of all the laws worthy which ye two were in Edward the King's day. And I will that each child be his father's inheritance taker after his father's day and I will not suffer that any man to you any wrong offer. God you keep.'

In 1927 fragments of the detached seal were found in the muniment room.

Another treasure is the charter of K. John, 9th May, 1215, providing for the annual election and presentation of the Mayor. The seal is attached.

THE ART GALLERY was first established in 1885, and formally opened, free to the public, in 1886. It was enlarged in 1890, but was burnt out in 1940. A temporary gallery has been built within the old walls. Amongst its treasures is a number of interesting portraits and paintings of scenes in the City's history. They include views of Guildhall in 1782, 1900 (welcome home of C.I.Vs.), and 1911 (coronation of George V). A painting now always on view shews the Freedom of the City being presented to the Rt. Hon. Winston Churchill, when Prime Minister, while others depict various ceremonies held in Guildhall.

The Gallery's present policy in acquiring pictures is to confine accessions to paintings of L. interest and such other works as may be of sufficient artistic merit to claim a place on its walls. The former include large ceremonial paintings by Solomon, Salisbury, Dring and Cuneo, and the latter a fine portrait group by Lely and the splendid 'Fording the river,' by Constable.

Exhibitions are of three classes: selections from the Corporation's permanent collection; loan exhibitions of master paintings from other collections; and annual shows by art societies. Recent ventures are the City of L. Art Exhibition, to which all who live or work in the City boundaries are eligible to submit work; and the Lord Mayor's Art Awards for works showing aspects of the City and its life.

The Future. In 1967 work began on the first phase of the Guildhall Reconstruction Scheme which has as its aim the creation of new offices, library, art gallery etc., and which will form an appropriate grouping around the historic centre of City government. The scheme is due to be completed in 1972.

H

Hackney, now part of the L. Bor. of Hackney, was a met. bor. and ancient parish in the NE. It bordered Tottenham, Walthamstow, Leyton and E. Ham. On the S. are Poplar, Bethnal Green and Shoreditch and on the W. Islington and Stoke Newington. The name probably originated as 'Hakon's Ey' (Ey = island).

The middle portion of the thoroughfare that begins at Mile End in Stepney, and runs N. through Bethnal Green and Hackney proper, and then NW. through Clapton to join the Ermin St. at Stamford Hill, is Mare St., on whose E. side, and in the narrow part (N. of Hackney Station, and by Hackney Brook—which flows underground SE. from Stoke Newington), stood the old par. ch. (St. Augustine's). Of its founding there seems to be no information; but repairs that amounted almost to rebuilding—apparently at the cost of Sir John Heron, master of the jewels, and of Christopher Urswick, the rector—were carried out in the reign of Henry VIII. Lysons's *The Environs of London* gives a full account of this ch.; which was demolished 1798—except that the old tower (probably 14th century) still stands behind what was the ch.-house and afterwards the vestry-hall and is now partly occupied by a bank. The monuments in the old ch. were mostly destroyed in the demolition; some are preserved in the new ch. The chyds. of old ch. and new ch. are continuous. Here was first bd. Edwd. de Vere, the 17th E. of Oxford, to some the real 'Shakespeare' (1604). There is reason to believe that his body was afterwards removed to W.A., where his son, the 18th E., was bd. In this ch. Wm. Hall, probably 'the onlie begetter' of the sonnets, was married.

The present par. ch. of 'St. John at Hackney' stands NE. of the old site; its chief entrance is at the N., from the eastward-bending continuation of Mare St. called Lower Clapton Rd. It was built very slowly, 1791–7. It is a square brick structure, with a convex stone portico at each side. Among the monuments brought from the old ch. are those of: Lady Latimer, 1582 (recumbent effigy); Christopher Urswick aforesaid (brass effigy under marble canopy); David Dolben, vicar of Hackney and afterwards Bp. of Bangor, 1633 (half-length effigy): these are in lobbies of the N. portico. An old hand-pillory is preserved in the chyd. On the railings round a tomb is a metal tablet which says: 'Hereby was seen for many years Blind Fred, a sunny soul.' Beneath this are three lines of raised dots which only the blind can read, for it is a message in braille. 'One thing I know; whereas I was blind, now I do see.' The ch. registers record the marriages of: Sir Robt. Rich, afterwards second E. of Warwick, 1604; Richd. Lovelace, afterwards Ld. Lovelace, 1608; Sir Christopher Hatton, cousin of Q. Elizabeth's 'dancing chancellor,' 1630; E. of Westmorland, 1638; also, baptism of Sophia, daughter of Daniel Defoe, 1701.

In Mare St., just N. of the railway on the E. side, stood the 'Black and White House' built 1578 by a citizen of L., later becoming a country house of Elector Palatine in the reign of James I; it afterwards came to the Vyner family. Popularly known as Bohemia Palace, its site is now marked by Bohemia Place, 1796. Brooke House, a Manor House of Hackney was granted by Edward VI to the E. of Pembroke, Edward de Vere, after residing therein for some yrs. died at the house. It was visited by Samuel Pepys and John Evelyn. It was damaged by bombs in the Second World War and demolished. Further S. is the old-fashioned St. Thomas's Sq., and running from it Loddiges Rd., which commemorates Conrad Loddiges, an 18th-century market gardener who first introduced rhubarb as an edible plant. To the W. of Mare St. in Hackney Grove are the almshouses founded by Wm. Spurstowe, Vicar of Hackney in 1666, rebuilt 1819, demolished 1967.

In 1835 two distinct pars. were carved out of the mother par.—South Hackney, whose large ch. is dedicated to St. John of Jerusalem (1845) in Lauriston Rd., and West Hackney, where the little Grecian ch. of St. James, erected in 1824, was destroyed during the Second World War. It was rebuilt and rededicated as St. Paul's in 1960. Stamford Hill to the N. was served by a proprietary chapel built *c.* 1774 on Clapton Common, enlarged as St. Thomas's Ch. 1827: it too was almost destroyed in a raid.

Homerton lies E. of Hackney, and its little Episcopal chapel founded in 1729 by Stephen Ram was demolished as a dangerous structure in 1934. In the High St. is an interesting Tudor house, now St. is Sutton House, an interesting Tudor house, which contains good linenfold panelling and is the property of the National Trust. It was the residence of Thomas Sutton (see 'Charterhouse').

In the SE. of the bor. lies Hackney Wick, a busy industrial district. It has a fine ch., St. Mary of Eton, by Bodley, 1893. Here are the Hackney Marshes—for the most part used as playing fields.

Hammersmith, now part of the L. Bor. of Hammersmith, was a met bor. situated on the Middlesex bank of the Thames.

Of the derivation of its name no satisfactory explanation has been offered. Bowack stated that its earliest name was 'Hermoderwode,' which, in ancient Exchequer deeds, became 'Hermoderworth.' The present form of the name (which dates from the end of the 15th century) is derived, say some writers, from *ham* (a town), and *hythe* (a haven). However ancient the place-name may be, there are very few visible remains of the 'hamlet' of Hammersmith which date earlier than the 17th century.

The pars. of Fulham and Hammersmith from time immemorial formed a manor, the lords of which (except during the Protectorate) were the Bps. of L. Down to 1834 the two places formed a single par., the component parts being styled 'Fulham-side' and 'Hammersmith-side' respectively. In that year, however, an Act of Parliament was passed making the Hamlet of Hammersmith into a separate par. and the perpetual curacy into a vicarage.

The par. ch. of St. Paul in Queen St., near the Broadway, dates back to 1631, its chief benefactor being Sir Nicholas Crispe, who gave £700 towards its erection. It was restored and enlarged in 1864, but the rapid growth of the par. made the bdg. inadequate. It was accordingly demolished in 1882–3 and the present imposing ch. was erected on its site, the first stone being laid by the D. of Albany. Within may be seen many memorials which formerly stood in the old ch., the most interesting being a monument of black and white marble to Sir Nicholas Crispe himself. It is surmounted by a fine bronze bust of 'that

Glorious Martyr Kinge Charles the first of blessed Memory,' beneath which, on a pedestal of black marble, is an urn containing the heart of Sir Nicholas. The inscription runs:

'Within this Urne is entombed the heart of Sʳ. Nicholas Crispe, Knighte and Baronet, a Loyall Sharer in the suffrings of his Late and present Majesty. Hee first Settled the trade of Gould from Guyny and there built the Castell of Cormantine. Died the 26 February, 1665, aged 67 yeares.'

In Miss Hartshorne's book, *Enshrined Hearts*, it is stated that this loyal knight left provision in his will that his heart might be annually refreshed with a draught of wine, which practice was faithfully observed for a full century, and was only discontinued when that member became too decayed for further treatment! (See also 'City Churches; D'—St. Mildred, Bread St.)

Other monuments worthy of special notice are those to the octogenarian E. of Mulgrave who served Q. Elizabeth faithfully and valiantly against the Spaniards and 'in the Irish warres'; to Sir Edwd. Nevill, Justice of the Court of Common Pleas (1705); to Thos. Worlidge, the painter (1766), whose rhymed epitaph is both quaint and pleasing; and to Arthur Murphy, barrister-at-law, dramatist, essayist, and friend and biographer of Dr. Johnson (1805). In the chyd. is the tomb of Sir Nicholas Crispe and that of Louis Weltje—K. George IV's favourite cook.

The most picturesque portion of the bor. is undoubtedly 'The Mall'—a riverside promenade stretching from Hammersmith to Chiswick. Foremost in point of interest among its notable residences is Kelmscott House, formerly the home of Geo. MacDonald and later of Wm. Morris, who renamed the house (formerly called The Retreat) after his Oxfordshire home. He d. there in 1896. Nearby is the quaint old riverside tavern 'The Dove,' frequented by the poet Jas. Thomson in the 18th century. Other famous residents of the Mall were J. M. W. Turner, Sir Wm. Richmond, Capt. Marryat, Sir Godfrey Kneller, and Q. Catherine of Braganza, who is said to have come to live here after the death of Charles II in a house later tenanted by Dr. Radcliffe, physician to Q. Anne.

In Hammersmith Rd. stand the modern

bdgs. of Colet's famous foundation, St. Paul's Sch., removed here in 1884, and also in the bor. are the various schs. endowed by the bequests of a 17th-century benefactor to the par., Edwd. Latymer.

There are two chs. built by notable architects of the last century, St. John's, Glenthorne Rd., by W. Butterfield, 1859; and Holy Innocents, Dalling Rd., by Jas. Brooks, 1890.

Hammersmith's most attractive pleasaunce—Ravenscourt Park—was anciently the manor granted by Edward III to Alice Perrers, the notorious favourite who, as that forsaken monarch lay dying at Sheen, 'made her re-appearance only to strip the rings from his cold fingers.'

Hampstead, now part of the L. Bor. of Camden, was a met bor., an area formerly in Middlesex, 4 miles NW. of the City. It stands upon one of the highest hills round L. The town occupies its southern slopes, the Heath its summit—it is 443 ft. above sea-level. The name is clearly derived from *ham* or *hame*, a home, and *steede*, a place, and has consequently the same meaning as 'homestead.'

There is a charter of K. Edgar (d. 975) which granted the land at 'Hamstede' to one Mangoda, though the genuineness of this document is not established. The Domesday Book records the manor as being in possession of W.A. One of the abbot's sixteen gallows (he had power to inflict capital punishment) was on Hampstead Heath. To Hampstead the abbot and some of the monks retired in 1349 to avoid the 'Black Death.' It remained in possession of W.A. until 1550, the yr. in which Thirlby, the first and only Bp. of Westminster, was translated to Norwich. Edward VI then gave it to Sir Thos. Wroth, whose family retained it until 1620, when it was acquired by Sir Baptist Hickes, afterwards Viscount Camden. In 1818 it became the possession of Sir Thos. Maryon-Wilson. In addition to the manor of Hampstead there is included in the bor. the ancient manor of Belsize or Belsea, owned by Sir Roger de Brabazon, who, in 1317, gave an estate to W.A. to found a chantry for himself, Edmund, E. of Lancaster, and Blanche, his wife. After many changes the house was occupied by Ld. Wotton, who had been created a baron by Charles II. It was visited by Pepys in 1668 and by Evelyn in 1677. Ld. Wotton's half-brother Philip, E. of Chesterfield, succeeded him, and the family held the Belsize estate until 1807. The house was afterwad turned into a popular place of amusement, and was demolished in 1852.

Up to the beginning of the 18th century, Hampstead was only a small village. Defoe waxed almost lyrical about its charm:

'On top of the hill indeed, there is a very pleasant plain, called the Heath, which on the very summit, is a plain of about a mile every way: and in good weather 'tis pleasant airing upon it, and some of the streets are extended so far, as that they begin to build, even on the highest part of the hill. But it must be confest, 'tis so near heaven, that I dare not say it can be a proper situation, for any but a race of mountaineers, whose lungs have been used to a rarify'd air, nearer the second region, than any ground for 30 miles round it.'

At that time its chalybeate springs came into popularity. A resident physician, Dr. Gibbons, praised the water, and crowds flocked to drink. Those who could not travel so far were offered it in flasks at the 'Eagle and Child' in Fleet St., at the 'Sugar Loaf,' Charing Cross, and Nando's Coffee House, Temple Bar, etc. Well Walk commemorates the site of the springs, and here was the Pump Room where a concert is recorded to have been held in 1701. It was pulled down in 1880. Until 1949 there remained Weatherall House, with its Long Room, famous for dances and assemblies. There once went Sir Joshua Reynolds, Johnson, and Fanny Burney. The last was a great object of interest—'second only after the balloon which goes up from the Pantheon,' said Mrs. Barbauld, a Hampstead resident —perhaps a little jealous of a rival author's fame. At Hampstead marriages on easy terms could be arranged. A newspaper advertisement in 1716 said:

'Sion Chapel at Hampstead, being a private and pleasure place, many of the best fashioned persons have lately been married there. Now, as a minister is obliged constantly to attend, this is to give notice that all persons bringing a licence and who shall have their wedding dinner in the gardens may be married in the said chapel without giving any fee or reward whatsoever:

and such as do not keep their wedding dinner at the said gardens, only five shillings will be demanded of them for all fees.'

Seymour praised the refinement of Hampstead in 1735:

'This village is much more frequented by good company than can well be expected considering its vicinity to London, but such care has been taken to discourage the meaner sort from making it a place of residence that it is now become, after Scarborough and Bath and Tunbridge, one of the Politest Public Places in England.'

In 1766 the E. of Chatham went to Hampstead to live in what was then called 'North End House,' and now, much altered, is known as 'Wildwood House.' In 1767 he was there again when afflicted, in the words of the E. of Stanhope, 'by a strange and mysterious malady . . . able at intervals to take the air upon the heath, but still at all times inaccessible to all his friends.' At the time of the 'No Popery' riots of 1780 Ld. Mansfield had a country house at Hampstead (now Ken Wood House). It was near the 'Spaniard's.' The strategy of the landlord of the latter, who plied the rioters freely with liquor until a detachment of soldiers arrived, averted an attack. Ld. Erskine, the famous advocate, purchased another house in the same neighbourhood. He spent a lot of money upon it, and, in the words of Park, Hampstead's historian, 'having surrounded it with evergreens of different descriptions has lately given it the name of "Evergreen Hill.' " The garden was on the opposite side of the road, and connected by a subterranean passage. In this house Erskine was visited by many of the famous politicians of his day, and here occurred his last meeting with Burke. Erskine lived here for about twenty-five yrs., during which period he lost his first wife. The house remains.

Hampstead has had so many distinguished residents that a catalogue only is permissible: Canon Ainger, Mary Anderson; H. H. Asquith; Joanna Baillie; Mrs. Barbauld; Canon Barnett; Barrett (the historian of Hampstead); Sir Walter Besant; Bp. Bickersteth; Gordon Craig; Sir Hall Caine; John Constable; Thos. Day; Chas. Wentworth Dilke; Austin Dobson; Geo. Du Maurier and his son Sir Gerald; Ld. Erskine; John Galsworthy; Kate

Greenaway; H. M. Hyndman; Leigh Hunt; Henry Holiday; Samuel Hoare; Samuel Johnson; John Keats; Ramsay MacDonald; F. D. Maurice; Ld. Mansfield; Dr. Joseph Parker; Thos. Park; Geo. Romney; Sir Gilbert Scott; Sir Richd. Steele; Dr. Thos. Sadler; Mrs. Siddons; Sir Herbert and Lady Tree; Sir Harry Vane; H. G. Wells.

Johnson lodged at Frognal with his wife about 1748, and there wrote much of *The Vanity of Human Wishes*. He once complained to Mrs. Desmoulins, who had known Mrs. Johnson before her marriage with him, that 'Mrs. Johnson there indulged herself in country air and nice living at an unsuitable expense while her husband was drudging in the smoke of London.' Romney's studio remains on Holly Bush Hill. It is marked by a tablet. The cottage of Leigh Hunt was in the Vale of Health. Constable's house in Well Walk remains; it is marked by a Soc. of Arts tablet. 'Our little room commands a view unsurpassed in Europe,' from Westminster Abbey to Gravesend,' he wrote to Dean Fisher. Joanna Baillie's large house is very close to Romney's, and is also marked. Here she was visited by Sir Walter Scott. Mary Anderson was m. at St. Mary's Roman Catholic Ch., Holly Place. Mrs. Barbauld (one of Lamb's two bald authoresses—the other was Elizabeth Inchbald), Lucy Aikin, Thos. Park, Austin Dobson, and H. G. Wells lived in charming Church Row. John Galsworthy (d. 1933) in a house near The Grove, next to 'Admiral's House,' a picture of which by Constable is in the N.G.

The par. of Hampstead was originally included in that of Hendon. The registers commence in 1560, and until 1561 it was considered as a free chapel served by priests from Hendon. Thereafter it became a perpetual curacy, subject to the jurisdiction of the bp. and the archdeacons. The churchwardens first appear in 1598, and then probably it commenced as a separate par. The first ch. was a low-pitched Gothic bdg. with a wooden belfry. It was dedicated to St. Mary, and the date of its origin is unknown. The present ch., dedicated to St. John, dates from 1745, as is blatantly displayed at the E. end. The conical copper spire was added in 1784. In 1878 it was desired to enlarge the ch. by projecting a chancel. It was found that to do this at the E. end would involve the demolition of the tower. A chancel was therefore built at the W. end, so the orientation is unusual. The only noteworthy memorials are a mural monument to Ld. Erskine's first wife (d. 1809). She is described as 'the most faithful and the most affectionate of women.' It was the work of the younger Bacon. There is also a bust of Keats (see 'Keats House'). In the N. chapel is a copy of a picture by Fra Lippo Lippi in the N.G. In the chyd. are the graves of Joanna Baillie (1851, aged 100), Constable (1837), Sir Jas. Mackintosh (1832), and Lucy Aikin (1864). The last wrote memoirs of the courts of James I and Charles I. She said she would not proceed farther—'Charles II is no theme for me. It would make me condemn my species.' Macaulay criticized her *Life of Addison*. In the extension of the chyd. there are the graves of one of Thackeray's daughters—Lady Ritchie, who edited her father's work (1919); Du Maurier (1896); Sir Walter Besant (1901); Stopford Brooke (whose primer of English literature sold about half a million copies) (1916); Sir John Hare (1921); an adopted son of Sir J. M. Barrie; Norman Shaw, architect (1912), and Sir Herbert Beerbohm Tree (1917).

Of the other Anglican churches, the most conspicuous is Christ Ch., designed by Sir Gilbert Scott in 1852, and enlarged in 1882. Its tall and graceful spire is a landmark for miles round. An older but much uglier ch. is St. John's, Downshire Hill. This dates from 1818; and there is a painting of it in the N.G. There represented as snow-covered, it is somewhat picturesque. The most important Nonconformist ch. is Lyndhurst Rd. Congregational, where from 1883 to 1930 Dr. R. F. Horton was minister. This record was probably only exceeded by that of the Rev. S. A. Tipple at Norwood.

For most people Hampstead is principally famous for its Heath. At one time it was famous for highwaymen:

'As often upon Hampstead Heath,
Have seen a felon long since put to death,
Hang, crackling in the sun, his parchment skin
Which to his ear had shrivell'd up his chin.'
      *The Triennial Mayor, or The
      New Repartee*, 1691.

In 1673 Jackson was executed there. In 1674 there was published *Jackson's Recantation . . . wherein is truly discovered the whole mystery of that wicked and fatal profession of Padding the Road*. In 1866 Sir Thos. Maryon Wilson, as ld. of the manor, claimed the right to build upon the Heath. A Hampstead Heath Protection Fund was raised by public subscription, and the issue carried to the courts. Sir Thos. Wilson died before the dispute was settled, and his successor, Sir John Wilson, made a compromise, by which the Heath was purchased by the M.B.W. for £55,045. The area sold was 226 acres in extent, and in 1889 another 260 acres were added, partly by public subscription and partly by grants from the L.C.C. and the vestries of Hampstead and St. Pancras, the total purchase price being £302,000. This was called Parliament Hill Fields. Divided from the Heath and more formally laid out is Golder's Hill Park. Ken Wood was added largely through the energy of the Mayor of Hampstead (F. G. Howard). It was formally handed over to the care of the L.C.C. in 1924. In 1927 Ld. Iveagh presented Ken Wood House, whose library was designed by Robt. Adam, one of the Adelphi brothers. There are some sixty beautiful pictures, many by old masters, and period furniture. They were in the N.P.G. for the duration of the Second World War. The house was re-opened in 1950.

The Spaniard's Tavern is not in the bor., but it is very close to the border, and so indissolubly associated with the Heath that it justifies reference here. Its history probably commenced with the early 17th century, when an hostelry was opened by a servant of the Spanish ambassador. His name was unpronounceable, and so it became known as 'The Spaniard's.' The present structure may not be so old. It has Dickens associations, as here Mrs. Bardell and her friends resorted. Dickens himself seems to have gone more to Jack Straw's Castle. The latter took its name from one of Wat Tyler's lieutenants, but it is not known that his followers went to Hampstead, though they visited Highbury.

(See *The Story of Hampstead*, by J. H. Preston, 1948 and *The Book of Hampstead*, by M. and I. Norrie, 1960.)

Highgate, as its name implies, is situated on high ground. Municipally it belongs mainly to Hornsey, with other portions in St. Pancras and Islington. With Hampstead, it is invariably shown vaguely in the background of maps and view-plans of old L. To reach Highgate from the City, the usual route is via '*High*-bury' and the '*Hollow*-way,' both significant names. No doubt this was the way Pepys came in Feb. 1664: 'We set out from an inne . . . and round about the bush through bad ways to Highgate.' Here Q. Elizabeth (1558) was met by the Ld.M. and City fathers on her entry into L. at her accession. John Norden, writing in 1593, said:

'Upon this hills is most pleasant dwelling, yet not so pleasant as healthful; for the expert inhabitants there report that divers that have beene long visited with sickness, not curable by physicke, have in short time repayred their health by that sweet salutarie aire.'

Owing to its healthy situation—over 400 ft. above sea-level—the village, as it is still called, has been the temporary or permanent home of many famous folk, and several of its old Georgian houses still exist, though a few have recently given way to barrack-like flats.

As regards the origin of the name, it is usually supposed to be derived from some gate erected on the hill. But there is no record of any such gate until late in the 14th century, and gate may have meant road, as in Stangate, Westminster. Its history proper dates from the Norman Conquest.

Until the 14th century there was no public road over the hill; the many pilgrims who went to the shrine of St. Alban did so via Crouch (i.e. Cross) End, and 'Muse-well' or 'Muswell' Hill. So Leofstan, twelfth abbot of St. Albans, cut down undergrowth, made rough places smooth, and built bridges. This road was in use until a quarrel occurred between the monks of Westminster and St. Albans, which led the former in 1386 to make a new road guarded by a gate. This road ran through the Bp. of L.'s park, with a toll-gate at the entrance across the road from a gatehouse. The gate was removed in 1769; the house itself stood till 1892. Local names like Bishopswood and Winnington Rd. to-day form a link with the see of L., while Ken Wood is all that remains of the old Middlesex forest.

The Islington portion of Highgate is mainly associated with legends of the famous Dick Whittington. Here on the slopes are Whittington Stone (modern), 'an imposition upon the credulous,' says Mr. Walter G. Bell, two taverns, a council sch., a Pauntley St., named from his native Gloucestershire village, and the Almshouses, originally in the City. In 1822 the Mercers' Co., having about £6,600 in hand from estates, began the present almshouses, on a lease of 999 yrs., at £120 p.a. ground rent. There are apartments for a tutor, who must be in Holy orders, and twenty-four suites for single women, over 55 yrs. of age. They were opened in 1828, and a small statue of Whittington is in the grounds.

The most prominent feature in this locality is the Highgate Archway, built of iron from the design of Sir Alexander Binnie, chief engineer to the L.C.C. Its predecessor was a massive structure in stone, flanked with brickwork, a marvel of engineering in its day, and often referred to as London's 'Bridge of Sighs.' This was opened in 1813, and lasted until 1900.

Three boroughs, each with its boundary mark, join in Highgate village, which has 18th-century houses. In Islington stands the monastery and ch., known as St. Joseph's Retreat, opened in 1876 by Cardinal Manning, on a site occupied by the old Black Dog Inn. On the same side, but in the bor. of St. Pancras, is the picturesque, undulating Waterlow Park, of about 29 acres, given to the people of L. in 1889 by Sir Sydney Waterlow, who was Ld.M. in 1872-3.

Lauderdale House (now the refreshment rooms) was built about 1661 by the renegade Covenanter, Lauderdale, member of the cabal ministry of Charles II. While he was away in Scotland, his royal master installed Nell Gwynne here, and what purports to have been her bath is still shown. Pepys came here on 28th July 1666, and thus records his visit:

'Thence with my Lord [Bruncker] to his coach-house, and there put in six horses into his coach, and he and I alone to Highgate. . . . Being come thither, we went to my Lord Lauderdale's house to speake with him . . . we find him and his lady, and some Scotch people at supper. Pretty odd company, though my Lord Bruncker tells me, my Lord Lauderdale is a man of mighty good reason and judgment. But at supper there played one of their servants upon the viallin some Scotch tunes only. . . . But, strange to hear my Lord Lauderdale say himself that he had rather hear a cat mew, than the best musique in the world; and the better the musique, the more sick it makes him; and that of all instruments, he hated the lute most, and, next to that the baggpipe.'

Later the mansion became a private residence, occupied by Ld. Chancellor Westbury, who 'dismissed hell with costs.'! From 1872 to 1893, it was a convalescent home in connection with St. Bartholomew's Hosp. It was then acquired and altered by the L.C.C. Adjoining it, on land belonging to Lauderdale, stood what was known as Andrew Marvell's cottage. This great political debater is said to have occupied it prior to 1653, but the L.C.C. survey volume on Highgate (1936) does not confirm this. The cottage was built mainly of timber and plaster with trees in front, and when demolished in 1868, a stone step was built into the wall, on which is a tablet.

Across the road is Hornsey, where is the fine brick mansion known as Cromwell House, and next it is Ireton House, though neither has any connection with Oliver nor with his son-in-law. There is a date 1614 on a party wall at the back. Cromwell House was built in 1600, and contains some handsome ceilings, but its chief glory is the staircase, with carved figures 1 ft. $7\frac{1}{2}$ in. high, representing various grades of the army of Cromwell, of which there are replicas in the T.L.

Here at the top of the hill is the nucleus of both historical and literary Highgate, and the junction of the two bors. of St. Pancras and Hornsey, as shown by the boundary marks in the wall of the modernized Ye Olde Gate House Tavern. This is the principal and most far-famed of all the Highgate inns, built in 1380 beside the toll-gate on the fringe of the landed estate of the Bps. of L., whose own servant collected the tolls. Its second floor was the ancient court room, in which the respective magistrates tried prisoners at each end simultaneously, and, at one time, the house was said to contain about eighty doors. Within its walls Chas. Whitehead wrote his novel on the life of the ill-starred Richd. Savage

(1842), and Henning drew the very first cartoon that appeared in *Punch*. Among regular visitors were Byron, Cruikshank, E. L. Blanchard, Dickens, and Balfe. It is mentioned several times by Lamb, when on visits to Coleridge. In recent years, the ancient custom of 'swearing on the horns' has been revived by the Highgate Thirty Club, which meets here. In 1826 there were nineteen taverns in Highgate where this ceremony took place, the origin of which is obscure, but doubtless as old as the Reformation, and of some religious significance. Later, Highgate being the nearest spot to L. where cattle rested on their journey from the north to Smithfield, many graziers put up at the taverns for the night, whose landlords, to attract customers, introduced the humorous ritual. Harrow Sch. boys came and were sworn in numbers, including Byron, who in *Childe Harold*, canto i, wrote:

'Many to the steep of Highgate hie.
Ask ye, Boeotian shades! the reason why?
'Tis to the worship of the solemn Horn,
Grasped in the holy hand of Mystery,
In whose dread name both men and
    maids are sworn,
And consecrate the oath with draught,
    and dance till morn.'

The horns used at the various taverns were those of bullocks, stags, and rams.

Opposite the Gate House stands Highgate Sch. and Chapel on the most historic site of all. There had been a chapel on this spot from at least the 14th century, for, in the year 1386, Bp. Braybrooke gave 'to William Lichfield, a poor hermit, oppressed by age and infirmity, the office of keeping our chapel of Highgate,' etc. Then came the sch., founded by Sir Roger Cholmeley, of which it is recorded

'that the fyrst stone of the Chapell and free Scoole at Higate was leyd the 3rd day of Julye 1576, and the same Chapell and Scoole was finished in Septr 1578.'
And later, in 1596:

'Where now the Schole standeth was a hermjtage, and the hermjte caused to be made the causeway betweene Highgate and Islington.'
The chapel was granted to the grammar-sch. (the present one was opened in 1866), and remained as the par. ch. until 1833. Under the present edifice lies bd. Samuel

Taylor Coleridge, his wife, daughter Sara, son-in-law, and grandson. The tomb was visited by two emperors (of France and Brazil) on the same afternoon. During the last eighteen yrs. of his life, i.e. from 1816, Coleridge lived at No. 3 The Grove (a house dating from *c.* 1688), with his friend Dr. Gillman, who strove to cure the poet of his drug-taking habit. A Harvard graduate, Washington Allston, described Coleridge's room at the back—specially constructed by Dr. Gillman to view the fine scenery of Ken Wood, as 'a small chamber looking out upon Caen Wood, a noble park, full of forest trees.' The room was, in the poet's own words, 'under the roof of my dear, and, under God, my most precious friends, James and Ann Gillman.' The room in which he d. 25th July 1834 still exists, though the rest of that storey was modernized by its recent occupier, J. B. Priestley. Thos. Carlyle, in his *Life of John Sterling* (1851), recalled visits to Coleridge, where 'on the brow of Highgate Hill' he was 'looking down on London and its smoke-tumult, like a sage escaped from the inanity of life's battle.' From 1826–8 Leigh Hunt was living here, and once said of Coleridge:

'I did not know (much as I admired him) how great a poet lived in that grove at Highgate, or I would have cultivated its walks more. . . . He was the finest dreamer, the most eloquent talker, and the most original thinker of his day.'

In the adjacent par. ch. of St. Michael, successor to the sch. chapel, is a tablet with a long inscription written by Dr. Gillman, ending with:

'Reader, for the world mourn!
A light has passed away from the earth:
But for this pious and exalted Christian,
Rejoice! and again, I say, "Rejoice!"''

Arundel House covered part of the site of the modern St. Michael's Ch. (1832). There Bacon d. 1626. Aubrey related the cause of his death:

'Mr. Hobbs told me that the cause of his Lordship's death was trying an experiment, viz., as he was taking the Aire in a coach with Dr. Witherborne (a Scotchman, Physitian to the King), towards Highgate, snow lay on the ground, and it came into my Lord's thoughts, why flesh might not be preserved in snow, as in salt. They were resolved they would try the experiment presently. They alighted out of the coach and went into a poore women's house at the bottom of Highgate Hill, and bought a Hen, and made the woman exenterate it, and then stuffed the body with Snow, and my Lord did helpe to doe it himselfe. The snow so chilled him that he immediately felt so extremely ill that he could not returne to his lodgings (I suppose then at Graye's Inne), but went to the Earl of Arundel's house at Highgate, where they put him into a good bed warmed with a Panne, but it was a damp bed that had not been layn-in about a yeare before, which gave him such a colde that in 2 or 3 dayes, as I remember Mr. Hobbes told me, he dyed of suffocation.'

Bacon wrote a letter to the earl apologizing for occupying his house and mentioning the experiment. Arundel House was subsequently occupied as a sch.; it was demolished in 1825.

On the slope of West Hill, adapted for a private residence, stands the house formerly known as the Fox under the Hill Tavern, later the 'Fox and Crown,' which possessed a royal coat of arms, now in the Highgate Literary and Scientific Institution, bearing the following inscription:

'6th July 1837. This coat of arms is a grant from Queen Victoria for services rendered to Her Majesty while in danger travelling down this hill.'

The Q. was being driven with her mother, the Duchess of Kent, in a carriage without a drag chain. The horses became 'restive and plunged violently, and an accident was only avoided by the prompt assistance of Mr. Turner, landlord of the 'Fox.' Her Majesty alighted for a short time and rested in the house.

Near the bottom of the hill was 'The Hermitage,' an old cottage, residence of Wm. and Mary Howitt, demolished in 1860. The Howitts had, in 1837, moved higher up to West Hill Lodge, pulled down in 1926. Here Mary wrote *The Northern Heights of London*, in which she described the Q. Victoria incident, and adds:

'Highgate . . . became our settled place of residence, and in 1857 we quitted the "Hermitage" for West Hill Lodge, pleasantly situated higher up on the same ascent, and possessing from its flat, accessible roof a magnificent survey of London.'

In a house close to the par. ch. of St. Michael lived the Tory preacher, Dr. Sacheverell, who d. here 1724.

The Flask Inn, near by, faces the old-time Highgate Green or The Grove, where a fair was held in July, and was formerly the headquarters of the revellers. In a comedy, *Jack Drum's Entertainment*, dated 1601, occurs:

'Strike up the tabor, for the wenches' favour,
Tickle it, tickle it lustily!
Let us be seen on Highgate Green,
To dance for the honour of Holloway.'

From the inn, flasks could be obtained to be filled with water from Hampstead wells, near which was another tavern of the same name.

Moreton House, in South Grove, was the home of Dr. Gillman and Coleridge for a short time prior to occupying No. 3 The Grove. Here Chas. Lamb, one day, was waiting in the Highgate stage-coach, when a woman came to the door, and inquired in stern voice: 'Are you quite full inside?' 'Yes, ma'am,' said Chas., 'quite; that plateful of Mrs. Gillman's pudding has quite filled us.' No. 10, known as Church House, was the home of Sir John Hawkins, the literary executor of Dr. Johnson, and author of a *History of Music* (see 'Westminster Abbey'). This house, too, is one of four in Highgate which claims to be the home of the Steerforth family of *David Copperfield*, and fits the description best of all. There are many references to Highgate in Dickens's works, from *Pickwick* onwards. This may be due to the fact that in Jan. 1831 his parents and other members of the family, including himself, took lodgings for a change of air at 'Mrs. Goodman's, next door to the Red Lion,' which happily survives. A. E. Housman lived at Byron Cottage, 17 North Rd., Highgate, from 1886 to 1905, and there wrote *A Shropshire Lad*.

The Highgate Literary and Scientific Institution, previously mentioned, is in South Grove. It was established in 1839. Here is an interesting collection of prints and pictures, a portrait of Coleridge, a mahogany table from Andrew Marvell's cottage, and a pair of horns once used for the swearing.

Amongst about 45,000 graves in Highgate cemetery lie Dickens's parents, his wife, his child Dora, and other members of his family; also Geo. Eliot, Herbert Spencer, Karl Marx, F. D. Maurice, and many other celebrities (see 'Epitaphs').

Old 'Mother Shipton' prophesied that:

'Before the good folk of this kingdom be undone,
Shall Highgate Hill stand in the midst of London.'

In real life she was Ursula Southill, an English prophetess (1488–1560) of great reputation, consulted by Henry VIII and Elizabeth. Happily her prophecy remains unfulfilled!

(See *Old Highgate*, by F. W. Kitchener, 1949, and *The Literary Associations of Hornsey*, by Dr. F. W. M. Draper, 1949.)

Holborn, now part of the L. Bor. of Camden, was the smallest of the met. bors. (405 acres) and the probable meaning of its name is 'the brook or bourne in the hollow.' It comprises four pars.—St. Giles' in the Fields; St. George's, Bloomsbury; St. George the Martyr, Queen Sq.; St. Peter's, Saffron Hill; and the part of St. Andrew's, Holborn, which is outside the City.

In Woburn Sq. is a little early Gothic revival ch. by Vulliamy (1833) containing a reredos designed by Burne-Jones in memory of Christina Rossetti, who lived nearby and in Gordon Sq. is the great Catholic Apostolic Ch. by Brandon (1854).

St. George the Martyr is a par. carved out of St. Andrew's Holborn in 1723, the ch. in Queen's Sq. having been built in 1706 as a Chapel of Ease. It was so completely transformed in 1867 that it is of little interest. The sum of £11,000 was required for repairs, and it will probably be demolished. Wm. Stukeley, the eccentric antiquary, was rector here from 1747 until his death in Queen's Sq., 1765. Another resident there was Jonathan Richardson, the painter. There is a beautiful lead statue in the Sq. garden, it used to be said to represent Q. Anne, but now it is generally accepted for Q. Charlotte, consort of George III. For Red Lion Sq. see 'Squares'.

In the par. of St. Andrew's Holborn was Furnival's Inn (q.v.). Bedford Row is a street of fine old 18th-century houses mostly occupied by the legal profession. The name, like that of nearby Harpur St., is due to a local benefactor, Sir Wm. Harpur of Bedford (d. 1573) who was Ld.M. in 1561. Theobalds Rd. was part of the route to the favourite country resort of James I, Theobalds in Herts. Old Temple Bar now forms the entrance to that estate, but the mansion has been rebuilt. In Brook St. stands one of Butterfield's finest chs., St. Alban's, now but a burnt-out shell containing a temporary ch. There from 1887–1913 Father Stanton was curate.

Saffron Hill—once a 'liberty' or area free from the jurisdiction of county sheriffs and magistrates, and the haunt of undesirable characters. It is the background of much of *Oliver Twist*. It was bounded on the E. by the Fleet Ditch, a most unsavoury stream. St. Peter's Ch. was an early work by Sir Chas. Barry (1832), and is now a ruin.

To the W. is Ely Place (*q.v.*) and Hatton Garden, taking its name from Sir Christopher Hatton who acquired the property from the Bps. of Ely. Its famous residents include Dr. Geo. Bates, physician to Charles I, Cromwell, and Charles II; John Stanley, the blind organist of St. Andrew's and Master of the King's Musick (d. 1786); Capt. Thos. Coram, who here began his Foundling Hosp. (*q.v.*), Joseph Mazzini, Samuel Plimsoll, and Sir Hiram Maxim. Here there is, in a somewhat dilapidated condition, a charity sch., designed by Wren in 1696. It was latterly the National Sch. of St. Andrew's, Holborn. Figures of a boy and girl have disappeared since the Second World War, as also has a tablet commemorating distinguished residents in Hatton Garden, erected in 1936. On the house (No. 5) where Mazzini resided, there is a bas-relief.

In 1793 a man condemned to death for robbery in Hatton Garden, committed suicide in Newgate. The body, clothed and fettered, was extended on a plank on the top of an open cart, and the face covered with a white cloth. It was carried to the brow of Holborn Hill, opposite the end of Hatton Garden, and deposited in a deep pit, with a stake driven through the chest.

Northward lies the Italian quarter with its red brick ch. of St. Peter, Clerkenwell Rd. (1863). There is a picturesque street procession annually in July on the Festival of Our Lady of Mount Carmel.

Bloomsbury, which is in the bor. of Holborn, is treated separately.

Holborn Viaduct was constructed by the C.C. between 1863 and 1869. The demolition of the houses began in May 1863, but it was not until 1867 that the first stone was laid. It was formally opened by Q. Victoria on 6th Nov. 1869, the same day as the new Blackfriars Bridge. It is 1,400 ft. long and 80 ft. wide, including the iron bridge (107 ft.) which crosses Farringdon St. The total cost, including the new streets, was £2,100,000. On the bridge are pedestals, upon which are bronze statues representing, on the S. side Commerce and Agriculture, and on the N. side Science and Fine Art. On the fronts of houses were figures of four civic worthies—on the N., Sir Hugh Myddelton (see 'Water Supply') and Sir Wm. Walworth (see 'Companies'—Fishmongers'); on the S., Henry Fitz-Eylwin and Sir Thos. Gresham (see 'Royal Exchange'). The two on the N. were destroyed by bombs.

The bridge crosses the bed of the River Fleet (see 'Lost Rivers') where was Holborn Bridge.

Holland House dates from 1606, and was built by John Thorp. It is a stately piece of Jacobean architecture, though strangely enough Sir Walter Scott, apart from the 'air of deep seclusion which it spread around the domain,' could find nothing better to say of it than that 'it resembles many respectable matrons, who, having been absolutely ugly during youth, acquire by age the air of dignity.' It was built for Sir Walter Cope, purchaser of the manors into which the original manor of Kensington had been subdivided. The wings and arcades were added, and the interior decorations completed later, for the husband of his daughter and heiress, Sir Henry Rich, afterwards Ld. Kensington. He became E. of Holland; hence the name of the house. The first E. of Holland was a Royalist, and suffered execution in 1649, and after this General Fairfax entered into occupation of Holland House. At the Restoration it was given back to the Countess of Holland and her children, one of whom, the second E. of Holland, succeeded his cousin as the fifth E. of Warwick, in default of heirs in the elder branch of the family, and so the two coronets were united. The son of this second E. of Warwick and Holland left a widow, who in 1716 m. Joseph Addison.

Addison d. at Holland House, 1719. In 1721 his stepson, the fourth E., d., and was succeeded by his kinsman Edwd. Rich, with whom the title expired. Henry Fox, Paymaster of the Forces, bought Holland House in 1767, and the title was revived. At Holland House Chas. Jas. Fox spent his boyhood. Sir Geo. Trevelyan wrote:

'His earliest associations were connected with its lofty avenues, its trim gardens, its broad stretches of deep grass, its fantastic gables, its endless vista of boudoirs, libraries, and drawing-rooms.' ·

The second Ld. Holland, Fox's eldest brother, d. six months after their father, leaving a son less than a yr. old, whose guardianship devolved upon his famous uncle. Under the rule of this third Ld. Holland, Holland House became the chief *salon* of L. Byron. Wilberforce, P. Talleyrand, Sir James Mackintosh, and Ld. Macaulay were amongst the bevy of brilliant men to be met there. In 1857 a strip of the grounds of Holland House, on the N. side, was cut off and surrendered to the builder. In 1874, however, it was announced that the widow of the last Ld. Holland had sold the reversion of the property to the E. of Ilchester, the descendant of Henry Fox, first Ld. Holland. In his hands it remained until 1905, when it passed to his son, the sixth E. The house was in the occupation of the E. of Ilchester when it was badly bombed in 1940. The central block including the lib., was almost destroyed. In 1952 the L.C.C. purchased it and part is used as a Youth Hostel. There is a cosy arbour with a seat used by the poet Rogers when he was a frequent guest of the third Ld. Holland, with his host's inscription:

'Here Rogers sat, and here for ever dwell
With me those pleasures that he sang so well.'

There are elegant iron gates on the Kensington Rd. which bear the date 1871.

Holy Trinity Priory was founded in 1108 by Matilda, wife of Henry I, as a house of Augustinian canons. She gave to the Priory the gate of Aldgate, and the soke (a privileged area exempted from the jurisdiction of the City) belonging thereto. The soke of the English Knighten-guild, or Portsoken, was given to the Priory in 1125, and in consequence the Prior of Holy Trinity was presented as alderman of Portsoken Ward until the time of Henry VIII; he sat at Guildhall with the other aldermen and rode with them on state occasions. He was not, however, eligible for Ld.M.

'Only once,' says Chas. Pendrill, 'did this appointment of a non-elective Mayor arouse bad feeling in the City. This was in 1439, when the Common Council begged the Mayor and Aldermen to oppose the appointment of a new Prior on account of his dissolute life, not because he was to be a Prior, but because he would thereby become an Alderman. The protest came too late, and the new Prior, whose name was Sevenoak, was installed, and is often found afterwards taking part in civic business with his fellow Aldermen.'

In 1468 the K.'s marshal ventured to arrest a citizen between St. Katherine's Hosp. and London Bridge, an act which constituted violation of the City's liberty here. On a protest being addressed to the K., the marshal was compelled to bring his prisoner back to the exact spot where he had been arrested and there liberate him, in the presence of the Prior of Holy Trinity, representing the aldermen, one of the sheriffs, the chamberlain, and the clerk. It was sometimes called 'Christ Church Priory' often interchangeable with 'Holy Trinity.' Stow says the Priory comprised the site of several old pars., St. Mary Magdalene, St. Michael, St. Katherine, and Blessed Trinity, all united under the name of the Holy Cross or Holy Rood par., and that after the foundations of the Priory it was formed into the par. of Holy Trinity. The bull of Pope Innocent in 1137, confirming the foundation, mentions the ch. of St. Katherine, and the chapel of St. Michael, in the chyd. of the monastery. Matthew Paris records that two canons of Holy Trinity Priory were quarrelling about goats' wool—i.e. about nothing—when one drew a dagger and mortally wounded his fellow. He mutilated himself in several places to give the crime the appearance of an act of self-defence. The Priory was dissolved in 1531, and the site granted to Sir Thos. Audley. He pulled down the bdg., and erected a house on the site, afterwards called Duke's Place. There is a C.C. tablet in Mitre Sq.

Hospitals had their origin in monasteries and two L. hosps. survive from ancient monastic foundations. Apart from these institutions hosps. were unknown until the 18th century when, owing to the increasing population in the towns, the necessity of some public means of tending the sick became urgent, and more hosps. were opened.

The following are the oldest of the existing L. hospitals: they are all Teaching Hospitals and each has other associated hospitals within its group.

St. Bartholomew's was founded by Rahere at the same time as the priory, i.e. in 1123. (See 'City Churches; C'—St. Bartholomew the Great.) One of the canons, John Mirfield, produced a general treatise on medicine in 1380; Sir Norman Moore said of it:

'The picture is complete of the medical and surgical practice in St. Bartholomew's Hospital in the reign of Richard II.'

It was not very enlightened at a time when John of Gaddesden (1280–1361), court physician to Edward II, could advise in cases of smallpox that the patient should be wrapped in red and everything about him be of the same colour; and prescribe for stone a plaster of dung, headless crickets, and beetles rubbed over the affected parts.

The medieval St. Bartholomew's Hosp. was probably a very small one, with accommodation only for a few score patients. Wat Tyler, when mortally wounded by Walworth, was carried into the hosp., and it is said that the latter and his followers burst into the bdg., carried Tyler out, and beheaded him. It was at this time governed by a master, eight brothers, and four sisters, under the priory. It was repaired under the will of Whittington about 1423. There had been many previous benefactors, Thos. à Becket, Henry Fitz-Eylwin, first mayor of L., Longsword, E. of Salisbury and Henry III, who gave two oak trees from Windsor Forest to provide fuel. In 1539, the hosp. was surrendered, with the priory, to Henry VIII, but, through the influence of Sir Richd. Gresham, it was refounded in 1544. Henry VIII endowed it with 500 marks a yr., on condition that the citizens provided a similar amount,

bringing up the revenue to 1,000 marks, or £666 13s. 4d. The K.'s gift was more nominal than real, as some of the houses from which the revenue was to be derived were 'rotten ruinous,' and it was said they produced nothing more than was enough to maintain three or four harlots lying in childbed. The citizens had therefore to find four times as much money as they anticipated. These facts were set forth in *The Ordre of the Hospital of St. Bartholomewes, in West Smythfelde, in London*, published in 1552 by the governors. It appears that there were then seven grades of paid officers: (1) the hospitaller, (2) the renter clerk, (3) the butlers, (4) the porters, (5) the matron, (6) the sisters, (7) the beadles. There were also, says the *Ordre*—

'as in a kynde by themselves, three chirurgeons in the wages of the Hospitall, gevyng daily attendance upon the cures of the poore.'

The chirurgeons (surgeons) were charged—

'to the uttermost of their knowledge to help cure the diseases of the poor without favouring those with good friends: they are not to admit the incurables, so as to keep out those who are curable: when they dress any diseased person they are to advise him to sin no more and be thankful unto God: they are to receive no gift from anyone, and never to burden the house with any sick person for the curing of which person they have received any money.'

The sisters were also exhorted to ways of perfection:

'And so much as in you shall lie, ye shall avoyde and shonne the conversacion and company of all men.'

The first medical officer of St. Bartholomew's Hosp. was Thos. Vicary, Serjeant-Surgeon to Henry VIII. In Q. Elizabeth's reign Dr. Lopez (see 'Guildhall') was physician to the hosp. Dr. Harvey was physician from 1609 to 1643, and lectured at the hosp. on the circulation of the blood. Percivall Pott was surgeon there in the 18th century (see 'City Churches; C'—St. Mary Aldermary). He fell from his horse and broke his ankle in a peculiar way which is still called 'Pott's fracture.' Amongst his hearers when he lectured was John Hunter, destined to become a distinguished surgeon and anatomist. Dr. Abernethy was also on the staff of the hosp.

The gateway of the hosp. (it was not burnt in the G.F.) dates from 1702. In the pediment is a figure of Henry VIII (the only statue of that monarch in L.), and above it are figures personifying Lameness and Sickness. The hosp. was rebuilt 1730–60, the quadrangular structure being designed by Jas. Gibbs. The latter's work was gratuitous, and the cost of rebuilding was defrayed by public subscription. Wm. Hogarth, who was b. near the hosp., in 1736, presented two pictures, 'The Pool of Bethesda' and 'The Good Samaritan.' He took his models from the patients; and left instructions that the pictures should not be varnished, but this was done after his death. The coats of varnish were carefully removed in 1935 and the paintings (on large canvasses covering the staircase walls) seen once more in their original condition.

In the Great Hall is a painting of St. Bartholomew, and a number of portraits: Dr. Ratcliffe by Kneller; Percivall Pott by Reynolds; Abernethy by Sir Thos. Lawrence; Sir Jas. Paget by Millais; and Herkomer's portrait of Sir Sydney Waterlow, a treasurer who was the instigator of the first convalescent home. There is some stained glass in which Henry VIII appears. A laboratory was built by Geo. Dance, jun., in 1793. In 1881 the former Sch. of Medicine was replaced by a handsome structure of granite and Portland stone at a cost of £50,000, with a classical façade facing Giltspur St. The older part of the hosp. was rebuilt 1904–7, part of the adjoining site of Christ's Hosp. having been acquired at a cost of £255,325, but part of Gibbs's work still stands.

In the 1920s and 1930s new blocks were added and further rebuilding goes on.

ST. THOMAS'S HOSPITAL is the second oldest hosp. in L. It was founded early in the 13th century by the canons of St. Mary Overy's Priory (see 'Southwark Cathedral'), apparently from distress arising out of a great fire in Southwark, the date of which is given variously as 1207, 1212, and 1213. Probably, in the first instance, it was merely the assignment of a few cells in the priory. It was dedicated to St. Thomas the Martyr, otherwise Thos. à Becket. In 1228 a new hosp. was built on the E. side of the Borough High St. by Peter des Roches, Bp. of Winchester, and endowed by him with a yearly income of £343. To this institution was transferred the 'Almonry for indigent children and necessitous proselytes,' which up to that time had been under the charge of the abbots of Bermondsey. By the 15th century its administration was in the hands of a master and brethren, and it became a conventual establishment. It was surrendered to Henry VIII in 1538, the staff being then a master, six brethren, and three lay sisters. There were forty beds for poor infirm people, who also had victuals and firing supplied to them. The institution was suffered to decay, but in 1552, through a sermon by Bp. Ridley, the Hosp. was purchased by the City for £647 4s. 1d., and repaired and enlarged. In 1553 a royal charter was granted by Edward VI, the City authorities being made perpetual governors of the charity. There were admitted within four months of the purchase, '260 wounded soldiers, blind, maimed, sick and helpless objects,' under the charge of a clerk, hospitaller, and matron. 'These,' says Rendle, the historian of the hosp., 'were regarded as the most important members of the household, the surgeon taking rank after the shoemaker.' A physician was not added to the roll until 1566. During the reign of Q. Elizabeth unruly patients were disciplined with the stocks and whipping-post, and even nurses were occasionally punished with stripes. Patients not attending ch. on Sunday got no dinner. The contemporary prayer of the author of *Gammer Gurton's Needle* was, however, always answered:

'But belly God sende the good ale inoughe,
Whether hyt be newe or olde,'

for those who 'cannot eate but lytyll meate' for their 'stomacke ys not goode,' got a quart of ale for dinner and a pint for supper. At the beginning of the 17th century the hosp. had a ward for casuals, where wayfaring men might obtain a night's lodging. It just escaped the great Southwark fire of 1676, as a tablet over the entrance to the court room in the old bdg. recorded. The reign of William III (1689–1702) brought considerable structural alterations and improvements, and the addition of a third court. The old hosp., thus completed, contained 453 beds, and was built round three quadrangles, the red-brick front resting on stone pillars which provided a covered walk in each court and formed a pleasing architectural feature. The erection of the new London Bridge (1829-31) necessitated the demolition of the front quadrangle, and two new wings were subsequently added to make good the loss. In 1871 the hosp. was transferred to its present site on the Albert Embankment, the Southwark site having been acquired by the S. Eastern Railway Co., who paid £300,000 for land which was bought for £31 in 1507. The hosp. took with it the statue of Edward VI by Scheemakers, originally erected 'at the expense of Charles Joye Esquire' in 1739. He is described thereon as

'A most excellent Prince of exemplary piety, and wisdom above his years, the glory and ornament of his age, and most munificent Founder of this Hospital.'

This is between blocks 1 and 2. There is another statue of Edward VI on the terrace, facing the river. Its date and origin are unknown. It was brought from Southwark, as were also the figures of cripples at the main entrance. Amongst a number of busts are those of Drs. Mead and Cheselden, praised in one line by Pope.

The new bdg. was opened by Q. Victoria. The cost was half a million pounds, including £100,000 paid to the M.B.W. for the site. It consists of seven detached blocks, four stories high, 125 ft. apart. There is an annexe for private patients, known as St. Thomas' Home; opposite is the medical sch. The hosp. holds a great place in the history of nursing, for associated with it is the Nightingale Fund Training Sch. for Nurses, established with the national tribute subscribed in appreciation of the services rendered by Florence Nightingale during the Crimean War. It was the model for many similar institutions. Lady Riddell gave the hosp. £100,000 for the erection of a nurses' home and preliminary training sch. This was badly damaged by bombs.

Not surprisingly, Chas. Graves, the historian of the hosp., writing of the Second World War, said it seemed as if it had been singled out for destruction. Between 9th Sept. 1940 and 15th July 1944 there were ten attacks. Nevertheless an operating theatre was continually in use in the basement, and no other L. hosp. carried on operations continuously for the whole period. There were a few fatal casualties amongst the staff but none amongst patients.

Since the war a huge reconstruction scheme has been started which will completely alter not only the hospital but that whole section of the south bank.

GUY'S HOSPITAL was founded by Thos. Guy in 1721. He was a bookseller originally, and kept a shop in Lombard St. from 1668. He managed to conclude agreements with the university authorities, who had the monopoly for printing Bibles, and made money in this way. He made a large fortune in South Sea stock, and also by discounting seamen's tickets. He became M.P. for Tamworth, his mother's birthplace. When his fortune approached half a million pounds he became charitable. He built and furnished three wards in St. Thomas's Hosp., and gave annually to that institution. He endowed Christ's Hosp. with £400 p.a. In 1720 he decided to build the hosp. which bears his name. It cost him over £18,000, and he lived long enough to see it roofed. At his death in 1724 he left over £200,000 for its endowment. He was bd. in the chapel of the hosp., and his monument, the work of the elder Bacon, is said to have cost £1,000. The façade and much of the present bdg. date from 1773, and the sculpture thereon was the work of John Bacon. In two niches are emblematic figures—Aesculapius, the Greek god of medicine, and his daughter Hygieia, the goddess of health. The tympanum is ornamented with an emblematic relief. John Keats was in the medical sch. in 1816, and for ten yrs. from 1836 F. D. Maurice was chaplain. In 1949 a statue of Ld. Nuffield, a generous governor of the hosp., was unveiled in his presence.

Under the National Health Service Act Guy's Hosp., including York Clinic, Nuffield House, Evelina Hosp. for Sick Children and the Eleanor Wemyss Home, became a teaching hosp. group.

WESTMINSTER HOSPITAL was founded in 1720, when it was established in Petty France as the Westminster Dispensary. It was the first hosp. erected by public subscription, Mr. Henry Hoare being the chief promoter of the charity. In 1724 it was moved to Chapel St., and in 1734 to James St., where it remained until 1834, when it was transferred to a site opposite W.A. In 1936-7 it removed to Page St. Its address is now St. John's Gardens, S.W.1.

ST. GEORGE'S HOSPITAL (Hyde Park Corner) was begun in 1733 in Lanesborough House, the Westminster home of the peer of that name. John Hunter d. suddenly at the hosp. in 1793. He expected some acrimony at a meeting of the governors and, a sufferer from angina pectoris, he expressed to a friend a fear that his attendance might be fatal. The present bdgs. on the site of Ld. Lanesborough's house date from 1829 and were designed by Wm. Wilkins, the architect of the N.G.

LONDON HOSPITAL (Whitechapel Rd.)

The first student entered the hosp. in 1741, and the L. hosp. had the first complete medical sch. established in connection with a hosp. upon the model of the faculty of a university.

On 8th Sept. 1940, bombs fell on two nurses' homes and the laundry, causing very great damage. Later there were further direct hits from H.E. bombs and hundreds of incendiary bombs; a great number of houses belonging to the hosp. were destroyed. Its work, however, still continued, with the beds numbering about 360.

During 1941, on many occasions, the hosp. was without light, gas, water or lifts. In 1942 it suffered extensive damage from blast. There was hardly a complete window left.

The yr. 1943 was not much better. In 1944 the hosp. was hit by a flying bomb, which completely destroyed the kitchen in the nurses' home. The heavy equipment and boilers fell through the whole bdg. to the Steward's stores in the basement. There were, however, only two patients killed, these being carried away with the débris and buried in the basement.

THE MIDDLESEX HOSPITAL (Mortimer St.) was founded in 1745 in Great Windmill St. and removed to its present site in 1756. It was extended from time to time, and completely reconstructed 1925–36.

THE ROYAL FREE HOSPITAL (Gray's Inn Road) was founded by Dr. Wm. Marsden (1796–1867), who also founded the Brompton Cancer Hosp. There was, until the Blitz, a tablet to his memory in the ch. of St. Andrew, Holborn. It was entirely rebuilt between 1897 and 1900, and further additions made in 1916. The Sch. of Medicine for Women, founded in 1874, provides for the full training of women for the medical profession. One wing was destroyed by bombing.

CHARING CROSS HOSPITAL was built by Decimus Burton in 1831 and enlarged in 1904. The former Charing Cross Theatre, better known as Toole's Theatre, was acquired for its extension. This theatre was first a whisky store, and in 1848 became the chapel of the fathers of the Oratory of St. Philip Neri before they went to Brompton (see 'Oratory'). Here, in 1850, Newman delivered his *Lectures on Anglican Difficulties*. Thos. Huxley was trained at Charing Cross Hosp., and in the board room is a bust of him by Thos. Woolner.

Other teaching hospitals in L. are: King's College, Denmark Hill, S.E.5 (founded in Clare Market in 1839); Royal Dental, Leicester Square (founded in 1858); St. Mary's, Praed St.; and University College, Gower St. (founded 1833).

In all there are 91 hospitals in the Greater London area, with 73,387 staffed beds, 60,789 of which are occupied on an average day. The total out-patient attendances in 1966 was 8,771,845.

I

Inns in L. are now, with one exception, a reminiscence of the oldest inhabitants. Only a few of the most historic can be noticed here. The 'George' in Southwark might claim precedence as the one real survival, but this solitary remnant of a bygone age has remained more through its good fortune than its historic pre-eminence, so alphabetical order is preferred.

BELL (Carter Lane). Famous only for one thing. In the 'birthplace' mus. at Stratford-on-Avon there is a letter addressed (on 25th Oct., 1598) by Richard Quiney, to his 'lovinge countreyman Mr. Wm. Shackespere' asking for a loan of £30. It was written at the Bell, and a tablet (erected in 1899) records the fact.

BELL (Holborn). This was the last galleried inn in the City. The first reference is in 1538, and it was rebuilt about 1720, but its wooden gallery, with tiled roof, Dr. Philip Norman thought, dated from Charles II's reign. There was a narrow gateway with a ponderous gate including a grating closed by a sliding panel. This gave an opportunity of inspection, like the spy-hole of a prison, when the presence of a visitor had been announced by a rap on the lion-headed knocker. John Taylor referred to it in his *Carriers Cosmographie*, 1637: 'The Carriers of Wendover in Buckinghamshire do lodge at the Bell in Holborne.' Wm. Black thus introduces it into his *Strange Adventures of a Phaeton* (1872):

'Now from the quaint little yard, which is surrounded by frail and dilapidated galleries of wood that tell of the grandeur of other days, there starts a solitary omnibus, which daily whisks a few country people and their parcels to Uxbridge and Chalfont and Amersham and Wendover.'

It was demolished in 1898, and a Bell Tavern in Holborn marks the site. Some charming pictures will be found in Dr. Philip Norman's *London Vanished and Vanishing* (1905).

BELL (Bell Yard, Gracechurch St.). In the 16th century it was the property of Sir Andrew Judd, who was Ld.M. in 1550 (see 'City Churches; C'—St. Helen, Bishopsgate). In 1560 its landlady was carted round the streets for being a courtesan. Richd. Tarleton, the Eliza-

bethan comedian, acted there. It was burnt in the G.F. There is a C.C. tablet on the site.

BELL (Warwick Lane). This is famous for one thing. According to Bp. Burnet, Abp. Leighton used often to say that

'if he were to choose a place to die in, it should be an inn: it looking like a pilgrim's going home, to whom this world was but an inn, and who was weary of the noise and confusion in it. He added that the officious tenderness and care of friends was an entanglement to a dying man; and that the unconcerned attendance of those that could be procured in such a place would give less disturbance. And he obtained what he desired; for he died at the Bell Inn, in Warwick Lane' (1684).

BELLE SAUVAGE (Ludgate Hill). The first known reference is in 1453, when in a deed John Frensh confirmed to his mother Joan Frensh 'all that tenement or inn with its appurtenances called Savagesynn alias vocat "le Belle on the Hope" in the parish of St. Bridget in Fleet Street.' ('St. Bridget' is the correct name of 'St. Bride'; 'the Hope' may have implied a piece of enclosed land.) When the two names were first combined cannot be ascertained, but in 1529 it is the 'belle Savage.' It seems certain enough that this was a family name, as H. T. Riley discovered that in 1380 a Wm. Lawton was sentenced to the pillory for endeavouring to obtain, by means of a forged letter, 20s. from Wm. Savage in the same par. If, at a later date, it had the sign of a savage belle, this was probably a rebus on the original name. In 1554 Sir Thos. Wyatt, finding Ludgate closed in his face, according to Froude, ' sat down upon a bench outside the Belle Sauvage Yard. His followers scattered from him among the by-lanes and streets,' and soon after he surrendered. In 1568 John Craythorne gave the reversion of the inn to the Cutlers' Co. (in the modern yard, their arms, an elephant, supporting a castle, were carved in stone), on condition that two exhibitions to the university and certain sums to poor prisoners were paid by them out of the estate. (A portrait of Craythorne's wife still hangs in Cutlers' Hall). Tressilian and Wayland Smith put up there in Scott's *Kenilworth*. The yard of the inn was much resorted to by the strolling players in the early days of the theatre. According to Wm. Prynne, the Puritan, once the Devil himself appeared during a performance of Marlowe's *Dr. Faustus*. This may be the same story as was told by John Aubrey, who said that such an apparition during a play caused Edward Alleyn's remorse that led to the founding of the 'College of God's Gift' at Dulwich to appease the heavenly powers. It appears that some kind of a theatre was erected at the inn, for Richd. Raulidge, in *A Monster Lately found out and Discovered* (1628), wrote that 'soon after 1580 the authorities of the Corporation received permission for Queen Elizabeth and her Privy Council' to thrust the players out of the City and to pull down all playhouses, one on Ludgate Hill being included in the latter. In *The School of Abuse* (1579) in which he summarized the plot of *The Merchant of Venice* (see 'The Bull,' *infra*), Stephen Gosson wrote of

'the two prose books played at the Bell Savage, where you shall find never a word without wit, never a line without pith, never a letter placed in vain.'

Here Banks showed his famous horse (see 'St. Paul's Cathedral'). The inn seems particularly to have been patronized by fencers. Geo. Silver, in his *Paradoxes of Defence* (1599), relates how he and his brother once challenged two Italian fencers to a contest

'to be played at the Bell Savage upon the scaffold, when he that went in his fight faster back than he ought, should be in danger to break his neck off the scaffold.'

The American Princess Pocahontas stayed here in 1616–17 (see *London for Americans*, by Wm. Kent, 1950). Later, a painting of her served as a sign, for tokens of 1648 and 1672 show an Indian woman holding a bow and arrow. By Q. Anne's time, however, it was a savage man standing by a bell. Addison wrote on it in the *Spectator* in 1711:

'As for the Bell-Savage, which is the sign of a Savage Man standing by a Bell, I was formerly very much puzzled upon the Conceit of it, till I accidentally fell into the reading of an old Romance translated out of the French: which gives an Account of a very beautiful Woman who was found in a Wilderness,

and is called in the French la belle Sauvage; and is every where translated by our countrymen the Bell-Savage.'

Addison, like the host of the inn, knew nothing of its past history.

Parson Woodforde, the diarist, in 1786, had a bad time at the inn.

'*June* 24. We had a Coach and went with our Luggage to our old Inn the Bell Savage at Ludgate Hill where we supped and slept—and kept by the same People, Burton and his Wife. . . . *June* 25. We breakfasted, supped and slept again at the Belle Savage. Very much pestered and bit by the Buggs in the Night. . . . *June* 26. I was bit so terribly with Buggs again this Night that I got up at 4 o'clock this morning and took a long Walk by myself about the City till breakfast time. . . . *June* 27. I did not pull of my Cloaths last Night but sat up in a great Chair all night with my Feet on the bed and slept very well considering and not pestered with buggs. . . . *June* 28. We breakfasted again at the Bell Savage. I did not pull of my Cloaths last Night again but did as the Night before, and slept tolerably well.'

In Belle Sauvage Yard, in his obscure days, lived Grinling Gibbons. Dr. Rock, an 18th-century quack, lived here. Until railways commenced the inn was an important starting-place for coaches. It was demolished in 1873, and Messrs. Cassell's premises erected on the site. They were destroyed by incendiary bombs in 1941, when about a million books were lost.

THE BULL (Bishopsgate). Tarlton played there—somebody once throwing a pippin at him from the gallery—and from Gosson's *School of Abuse* we know that in 1579 *The Merchant of Venice* was performed in its yard. 'The Jew and Ptolone shown at the Bull: the one representing the greediness of worldly chusers, and bloody minds of usurers.' A play of *Henry V* was also performed there. In 1594 Anthony Bacon, the elder brother of Francis, came to lodge in Bishopsgate St. This fact disturbed his mother, who feared the corrupting influence of the plays to be seen close by. It was the L. quarters of Hobson, the Cambridge carrier, who compelled customers to hire the horse nearest the door and so handed down his name to posterity. He did it in this way more effectually than Milton in his sonnet *On the University Carrier*, wherein he wrote:

'Death was half glad when he had got
    him down;
For he had any time this ten years full
Dodged with him betwixt Cambridge
    and The Bull.'

The inn was burnt in the G.F., rebuilt, and demolished in 1866; 49–53 Bishopsgate is on the site.

BULL AND MOUTH (Aldersgate St.). The date of origin is uncertain. If, as is said, the name is a corruption of 'Boulogne Mouth,' from the harbour which Henry VIII captured in 1546, it was probably erected shortly after. It is, however, certain that there would be an inn of some importance close to Aldersgate, and this may have been a change of name. Another suggested derivation is 'Bowl and Mouth.' In the early days of Charles II the Quakers made it a meeting-place. The inn, burnt in the G.F., was rebuilt. In 1830 it was again rebuilt as the Queen's Hotel and this was demolished in 1887 for the extension of the Post Office bdgs. in St. Martin's le Grand. The two signs were then taken to the Guildhall Mus., where they still are. One on the front, facing St. Martin's le Grand, was a huge, grotesque face, in the mouth of which a bull is standing. It is surmounted by the arms of Christ's Hosp., the inn having been on its estate, and a bust of Edward VI. At the base is the inscription:

'Milo the Cretonian
An ox slew with his fist;
And ate it up at one meal,
Ye gods, what a glorious twist.'

The sign at the back entrance, in Angel St., was a well-carved bull and, below, a huge mouth with a double row of teeth. To this Dickens made a happy allusion in *The Haunted Man* (1848), regarding Mrs. Tetterby's baby:

'It was a peculiarity of this baby to be always cutting teeth. Whether they never came, or whether they came and went away again, is not in evidence; but it had certainly cut enough, on the showing of Mrs. Tetterby, to make a handsome dental provision for the sign of the "Bull and Mouth."'

There is a C.C. tablet on the site.

CROSS KEYS (Bell Yard, Gracechurch St.). Banks exhibited there his famous Marocco, the performing horse (see *supra*). Tarleton, playing at the neighbouring Bell Inn, went to see it and, according to the volume *Tarlton's Jests*:

'Banks perceiving, to make the people laugh, saies "Signior," to his horse, "go fetch me the veriest fool in the company." The jade comes immediately, and with his mouth draws Tarlton forth. Tarlton, with merry words, said nothing but "God a mercy, horse!" . . . Ever after it was a by-word through London, "God a mercy, horse!" and is to this day.'

It was burnt in the G.F. There is a C.C. tablet on the site.

CROSS KEYS (Wood St.) (both inns, it should be noted, were in the shadow of a ch. dedicated to the keeper of the keys of heaven). The crossed keys were the arms of the papal see, as in Milton's *Lycidas*:

'Two massy keys he bore of metals twain
(The golden opes, the iron shuts amain).'

It had a Dickensian association. Here (see 'Dullborough Town,' *Uncommercial Traveller*) the boy Dickens arrived from Chatham by coach in 1822, and here accordingly, in *Great Expectations*, Pip waited for Estella. It was demolished in 1865.

THE GEORGE (Southwark) alone retains the name of 'inn,' and thus properly proclaims its uniqueness. The original name was 'St. George and the Dragon,' and in 1935 both appeared in a handsome new sign. The first distinct reference is in 1554, when the George was the property of Humphrey Collett, who represented Southwark in Parliament. Stow's *Survey* (1598) refers to the inn, and in 1622 it was mentioned in a return as built of brick and timber. In 1634 the landlord was reported for allowing drinking during divine service. In 1637 John Taylor, the water-poet, mentioned the carriers who came from the various parts of Surrey and Sussex to lodge at the George. In 1655 appeared *Musarum Deliciae, or the Muses' Recreation, containing several select pieces of Sportive Wit*. The authors were Sir John Mennes and Rev. Jas. Smith. One poem is entitled *Upon a Surfeit caught by drinking evill Sack at the George Tavern at Southwark*. It was burnt in a great Southwark fire in 1676. In addition to several inns, some 600 houses were burned down. Rebuilding was doubtless completed as soon as possible, though business may have been 'carried on as usual' among the ruins, and therefore the present structure may be assumed to date, at latest, from 1677.

In the 18th century the George was the starting-place for many coaches and wagons. Austin Dobson suggested that Dr. Johnson, when he visited the country seat of his friend, Thrale, at Streatham, probably started either from the 'Golden Cross,' in the Strand, or from the George. If he accompanied Thrale from his brewery (now Barclay Perkins's, in Park St., Southwark) it is most likely he would have boarded the coach at the latter. Most of the coaches were bound for the S. and SE. coasts.

In 1785 the inn was conveyed to Lillie Smith Aynescombe, a merchant of Thames St. In 1809 Westerman Scholefield and his wife, Frances Scholefield, were host and hostess. After the former's death, his widow kept the George until she d., 1859. Guy's Hosp., which had acquired the freehold in 1849 for a sum of about £9,100, then granted a lease to Geo. Greenslade, and, after his death, to his executors. In 1874 the freehold was purchased by the Great Northern Railway Co. from Guy's Hosp. (which adjoins the site on the E.) for about £10,150. At the time of the purchase there were still three wings with galleries. They remained until 1889, when two were demolished, leaving the one happily still with us as a reminder of the common form of so many inn yards a century ago. The old entrance is now blocked up. It was too low for railway vans. In 1937 the North Eastern Railway Co. gave the inn to the National Trust.

Dickens only once alluded to it. In *Little Dorrit*, Maggy, speaking of Little Dorrit's brother, Tip, says that he goes into the George to write begging letters to Clennam.

The American novelist, the late F. Hopkinson Smith, wrote at some length of his visit to the George in 1912. E. V. Lucas has been a visitor (see *Loiterer's Harvest*, 1913), and H. V. Morton describes a night there in *The Nights of London* (1926).

GOLDEN CROSS (Charing Cross) as an inn probably commenced its history with the erection of the Eleanor Cross if not earlier. The carrier who, in 1 *Henry IV* (Act II, Sc. i), has to deliver 'a gammon of bacon and two razes of ginger at Charing Cross,' may have been calling there. In the 18th century it came into prominence for its exhibitions. In 1740 'the Great Rhinoceros or real Unicorn, that was taken in the Great Mogul's Dominions' was to be seen there for a shilling, whilst in 1742 a tacit compliment was paid to Swift by the exhibition of the Houyhnhnm, or the most beautiful Harlequin Mare, foal'd on the mountains in Wales, whose spots by far exceeded the Leopard.' In the same year there was shown:

'A Wonderfull Young Man, Aged 22, who never had the use of Hands, Arms, Legs, or Feet, 4 st. 2 lbs. in weight and 2 ft. long. . . . He writes with his mouth much better than others pretend to with their hands. . . . He has neither Stump nor any other instrument to perform with, and is justly esteemed the Wonder of the World. He does everything with his Mouth.'

It was a great coaching inn, and here Mr. Pickwick started his travels in 1827, in company with Mr. Jingle. The 'Commodore' coach, mentioned in the book, again started approximately from the site, with Dickensians appropriately attired, *en route* to Rochester on 30th Mar. 1936 in commemoration of the centenary of the publication of the *Pickwick Papers*. In the pictures of the inn the low archway (of which Jingle gave timely warning) in a bdg. with a castellated top is clearly seen. This stood about where is now the statue of Havelock, and was demolished in 1830. *David Copperfield*, in which it again figures, was written nearly twenty yrs. later, but it is manifestly the older inn which is still being referred to. The new Golden Cross was erected in 1832 on a site E. of the old one. There was in the latter an archway for coaches which remained until 1851. The Golden Cross was finally demolished in 1931.

KING'S HEAD (Borough High St.) is mentioned by Stow with the 'George' as one of the 'fair inns' of Southwark. Up to the time of the Reformation it was the 'Pope's Head,' and in 1588 it passed to the family of the Humbles, a well-known Southwark family (see 'Southwark Cathedral'). In 1647 it was owned by a Humble who was first Ld. Ward and ancestor of the Es. of Dudley. A farthing trade token had as obverse a bust of Henry VIII. It was burnt in the great Southwark fire of 1676, but in 1720 was reported as 'well built, handsome, and enjoying a good trade.' In 1879 a new public-house of the same name was erected and by 1885 the inn had entirely disappeared.

OXFORD ARMS (Warwick Lane) is first mentioned in 1673, the sign representing the coat of arms of the City of Oxford. In that year the *London Gazette* announced:

'These are to give notice that Edward Bartlet, Oxford-Carrier, hath removed his Inn in London from the Swan at Holborn Bridge to the Oxford Arms in Warwick Lane, where he did Inn before the Fire. His coaches and waggons going forth on their usual days, Mondays, Wednesdays, and Frydays. He hath also a hearse, and all things convenient to carry a Corps to any part of England.'

In the palmy days of coaching, just before the advent of railways, it was occupied by Edwd. Sherman, who carried on his chief coaching business at the 'Bull and Mouth.' After 1868 many of the rooms were let out in tenements, but the inn still did a good carriers' trade, carts leaving daily for Oxford and other places. It was closed in 1875 and pulled down the following year.

QUEEN'S HEAD (Southwark) was also mentioned by Stow. It was the 'Cross Keys' in 1558 (under Q. Mary), and no doubt the name was changed on Q. Elizabeth's accession. John Harvard, founder of the famous coll., inherited it from his mother. It escaped the Southwark fire of 1676. In 1691 it was mentioned in a tract called *The Last Search after Claret in Southwark, or a Visitation of the Vintners in the Mint* (the Southwark Mint is meant):

'To the Queen's-head we hastened, and found the House ring,
By Broom-men a singing old Simon the King;
Besides at the bar we perceived a poor Trooper
Was cursing his master and calling him Cooper.'

A writer in 1855 said:

'The Queen's Head has not changed much, the premises are very spacious— the north part, where the galleries still

remain, is now used by a hop merchant.' These galleries were latterly let out as tenements. For many years from 1848 the landlord was Robt. Willsher, a cousin of the famous Kent cricketer of the same name. The inn was finally closed in 1895, but the galleried portion remained until 1900. Part of the yard is now a railway depot.

SARACEN'S HEAD (Snow Hill) is said to have derived its name from Richard I. According to a story of John Lydgate, as he approached L. by Newgate in 1194, on his return from captivity in the Austrian castle, at an inn outside the gate he called for refreshment. He drank rather freely 'untille ye hedde of ye King did swimme ryghte royallie,' so that he went laying about him with an axe 'to the astoundment and discomfiture of ye courtiers.' A baron remarked: 'I wish His Majesty had ye hedde of a Saracen before him just now, for I trow he would play the deuce with it.' The K. paid the damage and gave permission for the inn to be called the 'Saracen's Head.' Lydgate also, in some *Verses of ye Kings of England,* said:

'Richard his son next by succession
First of that name—stronge hardy and able
Was crowned king called cuer de Lyon
With Saracens head served at his table.'

In 1522, on the occasion of the visit of the Emperor Charles V to L., accommodation was found for thirty men and forty horses. Stow referred to it as a 'fair and large inn.' In 1617 in *Fenner's Commonwealth* there is a reference to a sergeant 'with phisnomy much resembling the Saracen's Head without Newgate.' In 1661 Pepys helped to consume a barrel of oysters there. It was burnt in the G.F. and rebuilt. In 1770 Horatio Nelson (aged 12) stopped there one night when on the way to join a merchant ship sailing from L. to the W. Indies. It was a great coaching inn, and afterwards the proprietor christened his smartest coach the 'Lord Nelson.' It was introduced by Dickens in *Nicholas Nickleby* as the house of call of Squeers, and here Shaw, in part the prototype of the Yorkshire schoolmaster, collected his pupils. Dickens said:

'When you walk up the yard you will see the tower of St. Sepulchre's Church darting abruptly up into the sky.' This is an indication, apart from the C.C. tablet on Snow Hill Police Station that the hotel which was erected when the inn was pulled down in 1868—consequent on the construction of Holborn Viaduct— was not on the same site. The hotel ceased business in 1909, when the premises were acquired by Messrs. Ormiston & Glass. Their showroom was once the coffee-room of the hotel. Up to about 1925 a sign of the 'Saracen's Head' still hung outside. Dickens referred to the inn's

'portals guarded by two Saracen's heads and shoulders which it was once the pride and glory of the choicer spirits of the metropolis to pull down at night. . . . The inn itself, garnished with another Saracen's head, frowns upon you from the top of the yard.'

Referring to signs such as these, John Selden said:

'Do not undervalue an enemy by whom you have been worsted. When our countrymen came home from fight- ing with the Saracens, and were beaten by them, they pictured them with huge, big terrible faces (as you still see the signs of the "Saracen's Head" is), when in truth they were like other men. But this they did to save their own credits.'

Messrs. Ormiston and Glass placed over the entrance door to their premises a bust of Dickens, and below figures of Wackford Squeers and Nicholas Nickleby, with panels representing their departure from the Saracen's Head and the flogging of Squeers. This bdg. was destroyed in the Second World War.

There were other inns of the same name in the city; at Bishopsgate, Aldgate, and Fenchurch St., where there is a Saracen's Head Yard. Some panelling from the last inn is at the Guildhall.

TABARD (Southwark) is perhaps the best known of all the old London inns. Its history goes back to 1304, when the abbot and convent of Hyde, near Win- chester, purchased here from Wm. de Lategareshall two houses held of the Abp. of Canterbury. On this site the abbot built a house for himself and, it is believed, at the same time a hostelry for the convenience of travellers. In 1307 he obtained licence from the Bp. of Win- chester to build a chapel at or by the inn. In a later deed are the following words: 'The Abbot's lodgeinge was wyninge to

the backside of the inn called the Tabarde, and had a garden attached.' No doubt the abbot used it, as Stow suggested, on his occasional journeyings to London to attend the House of Lords. Another notice of the Tabard occurs in one of the Rolls of Parliament, dated 1381, where, in a list of people who had been connected with Wat Tyler's rebellion, there is the name of 'John Brewersman' staying at the 'Tabard.' This brings the history to Chaucer's time, and his introduction of it into the *Canterbury Tales* gave it world- wide fame:

'Byfel that in that seasoun on a day, In Southwerk at the Tabard as I lay, Ready to wenden on my pilgrimage To Caunterbury with ful devout corage, At night was come into that hostelrie Wel nyne and twenty in a compainye.'

Master Harry Bailly, mentioned by Chaucer, was a real personage. He repre- sented Southwark in a Parliament held in 1376. 'Jockey of Norfolk,' who died at Bosworth, fighting for Richard III, was a frequenter, and a volume on *The Manners and Household Expenses of England*, published by the Roxburghe Club, shows that he was there on 18th Apr. 1469. Dr. Philip Norman found a lease of the Tabard of pre-Reformation date. It enumerated the rooms, such as the 'Rose parlar,' the 'Crowne chamber,' the 'Keye chamber.' At the dissolution the Tabard was sur- rendered and granted by Henry VIII to Thos. and John Master. The sign of the Tabard (a sleeveless coat worn by heralds) was displayed until the end of the 16th century. In 1599 'Tabard' and 'Talbot' were both used. Talbot was a species of hunting dog. John Taylor, the water- poet, in 1637 mentions the 'Tabbard' as one of the inns where carriers from Lewes and other places stopped. It was burnt in the great Southwark fire of 1676 and rebuilt. In Urry's edition of Chaucer (1721) there is a view of the 'Tabardd' or 'Talbot' with the yard open to the street. The sign was suspended to the middle of a beam extending across the street, and supported by a timber post at each end. In 1763 it was removed as interfering with traffic. In a picture which appeared in the *Gentleman's Magazine* for 1812 it was Talbot Inn. A correspondent, appar- ently knowing nothing of the fire in 1676, said: 'The rooms still exist in which they [the Canterbury pilgrims] are stated to have been entertained. A well-painted sign by Mr. Blake represents Chaucer and his merry company setting out on their journey.' Edwd. Walfourd (*Londoniana*, Sept. 1879) described it in its last days:

'We entered the yard from the High Street under a wide square passage. On our right, with the words "The Talbot" written above the door, was what chiefly constituted the inn, a bar of no great dimensions, and adjoining a small room for drinking and smoking. Before us appeared the more ancient parts of the old "Tabard," but all in a state of great neglect. A very old-looking balustrade ran round the first story, and against this, in front of us, was the sign, which was so defaced and covered with dirt that its subject could hardly be distinguished. It represented the court-yard of the old inn, with a number of Canterbury Pilgrims preparing to start on their journey into Kent, and is said to have been painted by Blake. The figures of the pilgrims were copied from the celebrated print by Stothard. On the beam of the gateway facing the street was formerly inscribed, "This is the inn where Sir Jeffrey Chaucer and the nine-and-twenty pilgrims lay in their journey to Canterbury, anno 1383." This was painted out in 1831.'

It was demolished 1875–6, and a modern tavern alone remains to commemorate it. The yard alongside is still called Talbot Yard.

WHITE HART (Bishopsgate) is first heard of in 1480, but from its name it probably was in existence a century earlier. It had a sinister association with the neighbouring Bethlehem Hosp. (*q.v.*), for Peter, a rascally porter who was duly brought to book in 1383, filled it with verminous tramps who drank his beer. It was a great resort for the staff of the hosp. Rev. E. G. O'Donoghue, in his *Story of Bethlehem Hospital* (1914), gives illustrations of the tokens issued between 1658 and 1668 and of the White Hart Tavern which superseded the inn. There remains a court of that name.

WHITE HART (Southwark) was probably the largest of the transpontine inns. The sign, a common one, was the badge of Richard II, derived from his mother, Joan of Kent. In the summer of **1450 it was** Jack Cade's headquarters while he was striving to gain possession of L. Hall, in his *Chronicle*, says:

'The capitayn being advertised of the kynge's absence came first into Southwarke, and there lodged at the White Hart, prohibiting to all men murder, rape, or robbery; by which colour he allured to him the hartes of the common people.'

Here, according to the *Grey Friars' Chronicle*, 'Hawaydyne of sent Martyns was beheddyd.' In 2 *Henry VI*, Act IV, Sc. ii, Cade says: 'Hath my sword therefore broken through London gates, that you should leave me at the White Hart in Southwark?' When Cade was eventually slain in Kent his body was brought here to be identified by the landlord. In 1529 it is mentioned in connection with an interview with Thos. Cromwell. Like the 'George,' in 1637 the landlord was reported for allowing drinking during the hours of divine service. John Taylor, the water-poet, noting the number of inns and taverns of this name, said:

'Although these Harts doe never run away
They'll tire a man to hunt them every day;
The Game and Chase is good for Recreation,
But dangerous to mak 't an occupation.'

It was burnt in the Southwark fire of 1676 and rebuilt. In 1720 Strype said it was very large and one of the best inns in Southwark. Chas. Dickens in 1836 (*Pickwick Papers*, Chap. X) described it admirably in connection with the first meeting between Pickwick and Sam Weller. There is no reason for the belief that Dickens was then describing the 'George' under another name. In 1865–6 the S. side of the bdg. was replaced by a modern tavern, and the old galleries on the N. and E. side were let out in tenements. 'Here too,' said Dr. Philip Norman, 'every afternoon, might be seen a solitary omnibus which plied to Clapham, the last descendant of the old coaches.' The inn was pulled down in 1889 and the tavern closed in 1904. White Hart Yard alone remains as a reminder of its existence, save one of the balustrades which is preserved in the Dickens Mus. at Doughty St.

Institutes

BISHOPSGATE INSTITUTE. The Bishopsgate

Foundation Scheme was prepared by the Charity Commissioners under the City of L. Parochial Charities Act, 1883, and approved by Her Majesty in Council, on 23rd Feb. 1891. The Scheme consolidates the Charities of the par. of St. Botolph Without Bishopsgate and provides for the administration of the income to purposes beneficial to the inhabitants of the par. and the public generally.

The Bishopsgate Institute was erected and equipped under the above Scheme, and the foundation stone was laid on 13th May 1893, by the Rev. Wm. Rogers, then Chairman of the Governors, and the bdg. was opened by the E. of Rosebery, K.G., on 24th Nov. 1894.

It has a Reference Library, containing over 9,000 volumes, which is open free to all. A special feature is the collection of some 6,000 books on L. history and topography. It also includes the George Howell Library of books on economics, consisting of 4,138 volumes and 6,126 pamphlets on the early history of Trade Unionism and the Labour Movement; and the Geo. Jacob Holyoake Collection of 359 books and 424 pamphlets dealing with the early Co-operative Movement. The lending library is now a branch of the C. of L. Library Service, a public library system set up by the C.C. in 1966. There is a hall seating 450, and in the corridor is a fine collection of London topographical prints and water-colour drawings. The Institute is the headquarters of the London and Middlesex Archæological Soc. (*q.v.*).

CRIPPLEGATE INSTITUTE was built in pursuance of the provisions of a Scheme of the Charity Commissioners dated 23rd Feb. 1891, and is an educational and cultural centre serving the needs of persons residing, or employed, in the western half of the City. The foundation stone of the Institute was laid by the Duke of York (the late King George V) on 3rd July 1894, and it was opened for public use by the Ld.M. (Sir Walter Wilkin, K.C.M.G.) on 4th Nov. 1896.

The Lending Library is another of the C. of L. Library Service.

On the first floor the Governors have provided a Theatre, licensed by the Lord Chamberlain for the production of stage plays. This Theatre was entirely rebuilt in 1932, and is widely used by London's Amateur Dramatic and Operatic Societies. The Institute possesses large stocks of scenery and furniture which is also hired to the amateur societies in connection with their productions.

In addition to providing evening instruction in such subjects as Operatic Art, Dramatic Art, and Photography, the Institute is open during the day as a Secretarial Coll.

The first floor of the Institute is approached by a handsome and well-proportioned marble staircase. On this floor also is a handsome Board Room in which hang several Oil Paintings of Cripplegate celebrities, including Ald. Sir Matthew Wood and Sir Henry Knight, and Vicars, Rev. Fred. Blomberg, D.D. (1833–1847) and the Rev. Albert Barff (1888–1913). The wide corridors are adorned with marble busts of John Milton, Daniel Defoe, Oliver Cromwell, and John Bunyan, gifts of the late Mr. J. Passmore Edwards, sculptured by George Frampton, A.R.A.

The Income of the Cripplegate Foundation is derived from many numerous Cripplegate Charities which in 1877 were amalgamated under one administration. These Charities had their origin in numerous and comparatively small bequests established in Cripplegate for all sorts of purposes during the 16th, 17th and 18th centuries.

ST. BRIDE INSTITUTE was established under a scheme of the Charity Commissioners and provides a public swimming bath. The St. Bride Printing Library, a collection devoted to the history of the craft and based upon the collections of William Blades and of Talbot Baines Reed is part of the C. of L. Library Service as the lending library on the ground floor. The Institute also runs photographic, dramatic, and other sections, lecture courses, rambling, table-tennis, and other clubs.

The foundation stone was laid on 20th Nov. 1893 by Albert Edward, P. of Wales, and was opened exactly a year later by the Ld.M., Sir Joseph Renals.

There is a bust of Samuel Richardson, the novelist, and a printer of Salisbury Sq., by George Frampton, R.A., presented by J. Passmore Edwards (1901); and bas-reliefs of William Blades, City printer and bibliographer.

Islington, now part of the L. Bor. of Islington, was a met. bor., coterminous with the ancient par. of Islington, referred to in Domesday Book both as 'Isendone' and 'Iseldone,' which is conjectured to mean 'the lower town or fort,' to distinguish it from 'Tolentone,' the old name for the district on higher ground to the N., now part of the area known as Highbury. The English Place Name Soc., however, gives different derivations: 'Giseldine' (*c.* 1000)=Gisla's Hill; 'Tollandene' = Tolla's Hill.

At Highbury, originally a summer camp of the Romans, the priors of St. John of Jerusalem had a country house which in 1381 was destroyed by Jack Straw. The famous Highbury Barn tavern nearby takes its name from the priory barn. It was in the 13th century that part of Islington came into the hands of the two priories of St. John, Clerkenwell, and St. Bartholomew, Smithfield, and it was the property of the latter which later became known as Canonbury, the name it still bears. Other parts of the par. belonged to the Dean and Chapter of St. Paul's, and gave their name to a prebendal stall in the Cathedral choir. At the Reformation much of the land belonging to St. Bartholomew's was acquired by Sir John Spencer, some of it still being in the hands of his descendants, as represented by the present Marquis of Northampton.

Canonbury House, the borough's only ancient monument, was, according to John Stow, 'builded anew' by Prior Bolton, and his rebus, or punning mark, a bolt or arrow piercing a tun or barrel, may be seen in several places. Only the tower survives and this has been adopted to house the Tower theatre. Distinguished occupants of the bdg. include Sir John Spencer, Ld.M. 1594–5, Sir Francis Bacon, Oliver Goldsmith, John Newbery his publisher, and Ephraim Chambers the encyclopaedist.

The par. ch. is dedicated to St. Mary the Virgin. The 'old church' was the successor of one on the same site, and was over 300 yrs. old when demolished 1751; the present ch. was erected by Launcelot Dowbiggin, and was opened by Jas. Colebrook, lord of the manor (hence Colebrook Row), 1754. Destroyed in an air raid, with the exception of the tower, it has been rebuilt. Here was bd. Sir Richd. Cloudesley (his tomb is in the chyd.), Dame Alice Owen, 1613 (founder of date from 1557. Here was bd. Sir Richd. Cloudesley (his tomb is in the chyd.), Dame Alice Owen, 1613 (founder of Owen's Sch. and Almshouses; her portrait and death mask are in possession of the Brewers' Co.), Dr. Wm. Hawes, Richd. Earlom and John Thurston the engravers, John Nichols, F.S.A.; Geo. Wharton (son of Lord Wharton) and Jas. Steward (a godson of James I)—who, after a quarrel, fought a duel at Islington with sword and dagger, both being killed, and by the K.'s desire bd. in one grave. Two notable vicars were Dr. Strahan, the friend of Dr. Johnson, and Daniel Wilson, afterwards Bp. of Calcutta.

In the 19th century a number of new chs. were built in Islington, of which a few are worthy of mention. St. Mary, Holloway, 1815 (Wm. Wickings, architect); St. John, Holloway Rd., 1826, St. Paul, Balls Pond Rd., 1828, Holy Trinity, Cloudesley Sq., 1826, are three Gothic revival chs. by Sir Chas. Barry, the last named having an attractive E. window depicting a great benefactor to Islington, Sir Richd. Cloudesley.

Of the well-known inns, the Angel was never in Islington but in the neighbouring par. of Clerkenwell; the White Conduit House nearby had extensive pleasure gardens and a cricket ground where Thos. Lord (of 'Lord's') was groundsman, and the Rosemary Branch, near the Shoreditch boundary, adjoined the famous archery butts of Islington and Finsbury Common.

In the Essex Rd. was the Islington Cattle Market (1835), which occupied 15 acres. The former Caledonian or Met. Cattle Market was erected 1855 at a cost of £500,000, and originally covered 75 acres. The Clock Tower occupies the site of Copenhagen House, a famous 17th-century residence. Caledonian Rd. takes its name from the Caledonian Asylum, established 1815, for children of Scottish parents, now removed to Bushey. The Royal Agricultural Hall, between Upper St. and Liverpool Rd., was built 1861–2. Samuel Rhodes had a large farm on the site of the Angel Underground Stn.

Through Islington flows the New River. There is a statue of Sir Hugh Myddleton on Islington Green (1862). (See 'Water Supply'.) The Regent's Canal has a 900-ft. tunnel between White Conduit House and Colebrook Row.

J

Johnson House (17 Gough Sq., Fleet St.). In 1748 Samuel Johnson moved into this double-fronted and imposing house, probably built in the first yrs. of the 18th century. Maitland (1739) wrote of Gough Sq. as 'a place lately built with very handsome houses and well inhabited by persons of fashion.' Johnson hardly ranked amongst the latter, although he once prided himself upon his good breeding. Here, in 1749, he wrote his poem, *The Vanity of Human Wishes*. Here he produced *Irene* —only read, said Sir Leslie Stephen, 'by men in whom an abnormal sense of duty has been developed.' From its front door, a stout and heavily chained one, he departed arrayed in scarlet waistcoat, rich gold-laced hat, to see the first performance. It ran for nine nights at Drury Lane Theatre, thanks to his old friend Garrick. Here, from 1750, he brought out the *Rambler* on Tuesdays and Saturdays—price twopence. The circulation was about 500. It stopped on the death of Mrs. Johnson in 1752. She, strangely enough, was bd. in the par. ch. of Bromley (Kent). In the spacious garret Johnson compiled the *Dictionary*, having huge volumes hoisted on desks, like a counting-house. In these the words were written for his definitions with spaces for his five amanuenses to copy in the illustrative quotations. To this garret came Reynolds and Dr. Burney, where they found Johnson in company with five or six folios, a deal writing-desk, and a chair and a half.

'He never forgot its defects,' said Miss Reynolds, 'but would either hold it in his hand or place it with great composure against some support, taking no notice of its imperfections.'

The *Dictionary* was published in 1755, the price being four guineas, and Johnson's payment 1,500 guineas. As Johnson published *Rasselas* a few days after leaving Gough Sq. it is to be assumed that this also was written in this house.

A later occupant (he d. there) was Hugh Kelly, 'the poetical staymaker' (1739–77). For his play, *A Word to the Wise*, Johnson wrote a prologue; *False Delicacy* by some was claimed to be superior to Goldsmith's *She Stoops to Conquer*. There is a blank in the history of the house until Carlyle visited it about 1832—as mentioned in a footnote to his essay on Croker's edition of Boswell's *Life of Johnson*, published that yr.

'We ourselves, not without labour and risk, lately discovered Gough Square, between Fleet Street and Holborn (adjoining both to Bolt Court and Johnson's Court); and, on the second day of search, the very House there, wherein the English Dictionary was composed. It is the first or corner house on the right hand, as you enter through the arched way from the North-west. The actual occupant, an elderly, washed, decent-looking man, invited us to enter; and courteously undertook to be cicerone; though in his memory lay nothing but the foolishest jumble and hallucination. It is a stout old-fashioned, oak balustraded house. "I have spent many a pound and penny on it since then," said the worthy Landlord. "Here, you see, this Bedroom was the Doctor's study; that was the garden" (a plot of delved ground somewhat larger than a bed-quilt) "where he walked for exercise; these three garret Bedrooms (where his three copyists sat and wrote) were the place he kept his Pupils in. . . . I let it all in Lodgings, to respectable gentlemen; by the quarter, or the month; its all one to me."—"To me also," whispered the ghost of Samuel, as we went pensively our ways.'

About fifty yrs. later the house was marked by a Soc. of Arts tablet. At the beginning of the present century it was occupied by Messrs. Waller & Baines, a firm of printers. When the owner, Ld. Calthorpe, d. 1910, there was some danger of its demolition. Mr. Cecil (later Viscount) Harmsworth, to honour Johnson, purchased it, and had it fitted up as a Memorial House. That this would have pleased this 'permanent London object,' as Boswell once called Johnson, is evident from his remarks about Milton:

'I cannot but remark a kind of respect perhaps unconsciously paid to this great man by his biographers; every house in which he resided is historically mentioned, as if it were an injury to neglect naming any place that he honoured by his presence.'

In the 'Dictionary garret,' on 11th Dec. 1929, a dinner was held on the occasion of the house being handed over to a trust. There is none of Johnson's furniture in the house (there is little in existence), but the fittings have been chosen in harmony with the period. There are pictures of Johnson and his friends (from Burke and Reynolds to Mrs. Williams and Francis Barber), and a few of his personal belongings. The custodian could pass with honours any examination in Johnsoniana. The 'Dictionary garret' was badly damaged by bombs, but it was restored and reopened in May 1948. (See the booklet issued by the Trust and obtainable at the house.)

K

Keats House (Keats Grove, Hampstead). Keats first became a Hampstead resident in 1817. He was living then in a house in Well Walk with his brother Tom, who was in a decline with consumption. In this house (it was demolished in 1849 when the Wells Tavern was built) Tom died. Keats then went to live with his friend Brown at one of two houses called Wentworth Pl. in John St. Here he wrote the *Ode to a Nightingale, The Eve of St. Agnes,* and *Hyperion* (a portrait of Keats in the N.P.G.—by Joseph Severn—shows him in the sitting-room of the Hampstead house). In the summer of 1818 Brown and Keats were in Scotland together, the former having let his house to a widow named Brawne and her children, two girls and a boy. The eldest of the three was Fanny (christened at the parish ch. of St. John in 1800). With her Keats fell in love, almost at first sight. After Brown's return in the autumn the Brawnes moved, but only to the top of Downshire Hill, so there was no considerable distance between the lovers. Unfortunately failing health was the chief obstacle. 'There is death in that hand,' said Coleridge, when he shook it in Millfield Lane, Highgate, early in 1819. On 3rd Feb. 1820 Keats came from L. to Hampstead on the outside of a stage coach, caught a chill, and died little more than a year later. During that time he lodged for about three weeks at 25 College St., Westminster. It was, as Sir Sidney Colvin said—

'one of some sedately picturesque Queen Anne or early Georgian houses overlooking the Abbey gardens. No corner of the town could have been more fitted to soothe him with a sense of cathedral quietude resembling that which he had just left.'

His hope, however, of finding in College St. some abatement in the fever of his passion for Fanny was vain. After about three weeks he was back in Wentworth Pl., next door to her, for the Brawnes had returned to their old quarters in April 1819. In the summer of 1820 he went to lodge at 2 Wesleyan Pl., Kentish Town, and after that, for about seven weeks, he stayed with Leigh Hunt's family at 13 Mortimer St., in the same neighbourhood. He then returned to Wentworth Pl., and was under the care of Mrs. Brawne. He used to rest on a seat at the end of Well Walk. On 13th Sept. 1820 Keats left Wentworth Pl. for Italy, likening himself to a soldier walking up to a battery. He d. in Rome on 23rd Feb. 1821, and was bd. in the Protestant cemetery, where Shelley's ashes were also laid four yrs. later.

The Brawnes continued to reside at Wentworth Pl. until 1829, when Mrs. Brawne's dress caught on fire and she d. of burns. (Fanny Brawne m., and lived until 1865. She was bd. in Kensal Green Cemetery.) From 1828 to 1831 K.'s sister Fanny was living there. She had m. Valentino Llanos, a Spanish gentleman, and, returning to Spain, d. at Madrid at the age of 86. In 1838 Miss Chester, an actress, acquired the house. She added a long drawing-room in the garden, and made the two houses one. In 1868 the house became known as Lawn Bank. In 1896, on the suggestion of the Hampstead Antiquarian and Historical Soc., the Soc. of Arts placed a plaque above the front door. In 1920 the name reverted to Wentworth Pl. and at the same time John St. was first called Keats Grove. In the same year the house came into the market, and the Mayor of Hampstead made noble exertions for its preservation. A sum of £4,650 was raised, of which £2,534 came from U.S.A. The committee offered the property to the Hampstead B.C., to be maintained in perpetuity. The offer was accepted and the house was formally opened by Sir Arthur Quiller-Couch on 9th May 1925. The mus. with its lib., opened in 1931, has been built upon the site of the stables and out-buildings erected by Miss Chester and her successors. Here and in the house is a unique collection of Keats relics. There is Fanny Brawne's portrait and her engagement ring; a lock of Keats' hair; and his copy of Shakespeare. There is a number of letters: one (added in 1935) gives information to his sister Fanny on her approaching confirmation. Others include Fanny Brawne's letters to Fanny Keats. There is Thos. Hardy's poem on the house in his own handwriting. In 1935 there was presented the original of the bust of Keats (the work of Anne Whitney), a replica of which is in the par. ch.

There was some damage caused by flying bombs in the Second World War, but this was to the Chester drawing-room. Keats House was formally re-opened by John Masefield, Poet Laureate, on 27th Oct. 1945.

Kensal Green Cemetery (All Souls '). It is partly in the bor. of Kensington and partly in the bor. of Hammersmith. In 1830 the General Cemetery Co. was formed and in 1832 the cemetery was opened. At first it consisted of 50 acres; since it has been extended to 70 acres. The number of graves is about 50,000. Some of the most illustrious dead are buried here: Anne Scott (1833) and Charlotte Sophia Lockhart (1837) both daughters of Sir Walter Scott; Mary Scott Hogarth, Dickens' young sister-in-law (1837); W. M. Praed, poet (1839); Thos. Barnes, Editor of *The Times* (1841); Geo. Dyer, friend of Charles Lamb (1841); John Murray, publisher (1843); Thos. Hood (1845); Sydney Smith (1845); Chas. Kemble, younger brother of Mrs. Siddons (1854); Joseph Hume (1855); James Leigh Hunt (1859); W. M. Thackeray (1863); John Leech (1864); 'James' Barry—first woman doctor and army surgeon, who lived as a man (1865); Artemus Ward (1866); M. W. Balfe (1870); Shirley Brooks (1874); John Forster (1876); Geo. Cruikshank (1878); his remains were removed in the same yr. to St. P.'s Cath.; W. Harrison Ainsworth (1882); Anthony Trollope (1882); Wilkie Collins (1889); A. G. Steel, cricketer (1914); Dr. John Clifford (1923).

There are also royal personages: the D. of Sussex, sixth son of George III—bd. in a massive granite tomb opposite the chapel (1843); his sister, the Princess Sophia (1848); the D. of Cambridge (1904). In *Social Sketches*, by Mark Boyd, the reason for the interment of the D. of Sussex here is given:

'At the funeral of William IV there was so much delay and confusion, and so many questions of etiquette and precedence broke out, that the Duke remarked to a friend: "This is intolerable. Now, recollect what I say to you. If I should die before I return to Kensington"—he was then resident at the Palace—"see I am not buried at

Windsor, as I would not be buried there after this fashion for all the world." '

The Duke did not die before returning to Kensington, but his wishes as to interment were respected.

There is a memorial obelisk to Robt. Owen with a lengthy inscription, but he was bd. at Newtown, Montgomeryshire, his native place. Next to this obelisk is another known as the 'Reformers' Memorial,' bearing a number of distinguished names, e.g. Robt. Owen, Thos. Paine, W. K. Clifford, Henry Fawcett, Chas. Bradlaugh, Wm. Morris, John Ruskin, Herbert Spencer, Francis Newman, G. J. Holyoake, and Josephine Butler.

In the R.C. cemetery adjoining (wholly situated in the bor. of Hammersmith), which was opened in 1860, there are bd. Cardinal Wiseman (1865); Dr. St. George Mivart (1900); and two poets, Francis Thompson (1907) and Alice Meynell (1922). Dr. Mivart d. out of communion with his Ch. on account of writings which were held by Cardinal Vaughan to be heretical. His remains were removed from the Protestant cemetery by order of Abp. Bourne and the transfer was celebrated with a solemn requiem mass.

Kensington, now part of the L. Bor. of Kensington and Chelsea, was a met. bor., but distinguished as 'the Royal Borough' by grant of Edward VII in 1901. It gives its name to a suffragan bishopric in the diocese of L.

The bor. includes in addition (neglecting slight rectifications of the E. boundary) about half of Kensington Gardens (see 'Parks'), including Kensington Palace (*q.v.*)—formerly, despite their name, in Westminster—and also the former hamlet of Kensal New Town at NE., anciently S. half of a detached part of Chelsea. Kensington Gore, the Imperial Institute, the Albert Hall and Memorial, and the E. half of Kensington Gardens, are all in the City of Westminster.

The etymology of the name is uncertain. The Domesday form, 'Chenesitun,' seems to indicate connection with Chenesi, known as a personal name in Saxon times. The English Place Names Soc. gives derivation as 'Cynesige's farm.'

Kensington has long been a haunt of literary and artistic people, but its most famous bdg., Holland House (*q.v.*), damaged in the war, has been partially restored. One of the show places of Kensington is the house on the N. side of Holland Park Rd., where lived the artist, Ld. Leighton.

The picturesque old High St. has been swept away within the last generation. Kensington High St. is now shops; Ponting's drapery establishment covers the site of Scarsdale House.

Kensington is famous for its museums. The Natural History Mus., which stands in its own grounds N. of Cromwell Rd. Behind it, to the N., is the Science Mus., replacing some old sheds that housed the former 'South Kensington Museum,' and were known as the 'South Kensington boilers.' At the E. side of Exhibition Rd. stands the V. and A. Mus. The Mus. of Practical Geology stands in the NE. corner of the Natural History Mus. grounds. (See 'Museums.') The development of the district was a sequel to the Hyde Park Exhibition of 1851.

The par. ch. of Kensington (on the W. side of Church St.) is named St. Mary Abbot's, in commemoration of the connection with Abingdon Abbey. The old ch. had been many times altered, and was rebuilt, except for the tower, in 1696. Then in 1869 the present bdg. was begun from designs by Sir Gilbert Scott; it was not completed until 1881. It is a magnificent example of Victorian Gothic, and has a steeple 278 ft. high. The pulpit was retained from the old ch., as was a number of the monuments. In the N. porch is a damaged monument by Grinling Gibbons to Wm. Courten, friend of Sir Hans Sloane, 1702. In the additional chyd., NW. of the ch. was bd. the once popular novelist, Mrs. Elizabeth Inchbald (1821). The ch. was damaged by incendiary bombs during the Second World War.

A number of other chs. in Kensington are of considerable architectural interest. St. Augustine, Queen's Gate, by W. Butterfield, 1871, with an excellent modern reredos by Martin Travers; St. John, Holland Rd., a fine ch. by Jas. Brooks, 1889; Holy Trinity, Prince Consort Rd., by G. F. Bodley, 1904; and two early Gothic revival bdgs., St. Barnabas by Lewis Vulliamy 1827, and Holy Trinity, Brompton, by Prof. Donaldson, 1829.

Of the three notable R.C. churches in the bor. two, the Carmelite Ch. and Our Lady of Victories, were destroyed by bombs, but the Brompton Oratory by B. Gribble, 1884–97, was undamaged. There is also an attractive little Armenian Ch. of St. Sarkis (1922).

(See *The Intimate Charm of Kensington*, by Eric and Barbara Whelpton, 1949, and *The Royal Borough*, by Rachel Ferguson, 1950; *Kensington*, by W. Gaunt, 1958.)

Kensington Palace occupies the site of a house which was acquired in the reign of Charles I by Sir Heneage Finch, recorder of L. His son, the second Sir Heneage, Ld. Chancellor, was created E. of Nottingham, in 1681, and after him the mansion, which he is believed to have largely rebuilt, was styled Nottingham House. By his son, the second E. Nottingham House was in 1689 sold to William III for £18,000. The dryness of the air from the neighbouring gravel pits made the K. desire a change of residence from Whitehall. Wren at once set about the work of improvement, but in 1691, when some £60,000 had been spent, it was damaged by fire. The K. and Q. had a narrow escape from being burnt in their beds; they made a hasty flight, and witnessed the extinction of the flames by the Foot Guards. Some parts of the old Nottingham House still remain incorporated in the present bdg., to which Wm. Kent made additions in the reign of George I, including the cupola or cube room. A beautiful specimen of Wren's architecture which is very close to Kensington Palace is the Orangery. It was erected in 1704. It is of red brick and stands upon a platform of stone, the interior being embellished with the architect's favourite Corinthian pilasters. No authority seems to explain the origin of the name. It seems too elaborate for the purpose of growing fruit, and probably Q. Anne— 'who sometimes counsel took and sometimes tay'—took both here at times. Q. Mary d. in Kensington Palace in 1694, and so did her consort William III in 1702. His statue is outside (see 'Statues'). Q. Anne lived much in the Palace and here quarrelled with her friend the Duchess of Marlborough, known as her 'dear Mrs. Freeman.' The latter's feelings about the Q. when she was the dear departed were fickle, for when Voltaire visited her at Blenheim and asked her to lend him her manuscript memoirs, she declined, saying: 'Wait a bit: I'm reshaping the character of Queen Anne, since I've begun to like her again.' Q. Anne d. in Kensington Palace (1714). George I resided there for brief periods. George II's consort, Caroline of Anspach, was devoted to it. George III did not live there, having acquired Buckingham Palace. One of his sons, the D. of Kent, was living there when his daughter, the future Q. Victoria, was b. 1819. In the 'Cube' or 'Cupola' room (now open to the public) she was christened, and in the little bedroom near the nursery (also now open) the news of her accession was conveyed to her. The room in which she was born was marked with a brass plate on the occasion of her first Jubilee (1887), and in celebration of her eightieth birthday (1899) it was decided to restore the State apartments, as well as the Orangery, and throw them open to the public. Here are collected not only pictures which belonged to Kensington Palace, but some brought from Hampton Court and other royal palaces. There are seven pictures by Benjamin West, including the famous 'Death of General Wolfe.' There are pictures of old L. by Samuel Scott and others. In the Presence Chamber there is carving by Grinling Gibbons. There is a beautiful chimney-piece designed by Rysbrack, a curious clock with four distinct faces representing the four great empires Assyria, Persia, Greece, and Rome, and an old dial-hand, or pointer, actuated by an iron rod on the roof, which enabled William III to know which way the wind was blowing. Outside is a statue of Q. Victoria at the time of her accession, executed by H.R.H. Princess Louise in 1893. The latter resided at Kensington Palace for many yrs. She was the last surviving child of Q. Victoria and d. in 1939 at the age of 91. In 1940 two suites of apartments, including one of the state rooms was gutted.

Kensington Palace is now the home of the L.Mus., which is destined to move to the Barbican as part of the Mus of L.

King's College (Strand) was founded by royal charter in 1829 on Ch. of England lines, and the bdg., designed by Robt. Smirke, was erected on a plan which would complete the river front of Somerset House at its E. extremity in accordance with the original design of Sir Wm. Chambers. The bdg. was completed in 1834. It had first its Dept. of Liberal Education, which became known later as the 'Department of General Literature and Science.' There was soon added the Medical Dept., from which sprang King's College Hosp. In 1838 an Engineering Dept. was commenced, and in 1847 a separate Theological Dept. under the principalship of Dr. Jelf, with the object of preparing both graduates and non-graduates for holy orders. Of its earlier professors two became widely known, the Rev. F. D. Maurice, who was called upon to resign his professorship of ecclesiastical history in 1853 because of his looseness on the subject of eternal damnation, and the Rev. R. C. (afterwards Abp.) Trench. In 1856 evening classes were introduced; in 1861 an Oriental Section was formed; and in 1880 the Schs. of Practical Art commenced. Under the University of London Act, 1898, King's College is constituted a sch. of the university in all its faculties. The chapel was remodelled by Sir Geo. Gilbert Scott, the work being completed in 1881. It is a beautiful bdg.; included in the elaborate decorations are figures of St. Clement of Alexandria, St. Athanasius, St. Chrysostom, St. Basil, St. Ambrose, St. Augustine, St. Jerome, St. Gregory, Richard Hooker, Lancelot Andrewes, Jeremy Taylor, and John Pearson. There is a lib. containing over 70,000 volumes including a collection in memory of Dr. F. J. Furnivall and W. W. Skeat, and a mus. containing the valuable collection of mechanical models and philosophical instruments formed by George III at Kew, and presented to the coll. by Q. Victoria in 1842.

L

Lambeth, now part of the L. Bor. of Lambeth, was a met. bor., an area formerly in Surrey and extended along the S. bank of the Thames from just below the Waterloo Bridge. Its circumference is nearly 17 miles, and the least width—between Lambeth B. and Kennington Rd.—is half a mile. The name has been variously· written at different periods. It is first mentioned in a charter of Edward the Confessor (1062) as 'Lambe-hithe.' Most etymologists derive the name from *lam* (dirt or mud) and *hythe* (a haven).

It was a manor, possibly a royal one, in 1042, for K. Hardicnut d. there in that yr. in the midst of a wedding dinner. It was then part of the estate of Goda, wife successively to Walter, E. of Mantes, and Eustace, E. of Boulogne, who presented it to the ch. of Rochester, but reserved to herself the patronage of the ch. In Domesday Book it is registered as belonging to Goda. One of the holders of the see of Rochester in the reign of Henry II exchanged it for other lands with Baldwin, Abp. of Canterbury; and Hubert, one of his successors in the episcopate and Ld. High Chancellor in the reign of Richard I, resided there. It had an annual fair, from the time of K. John until 1754, when, having become riotous, it was abolished by request of Abp. Herring.

The par. ch., which abuts upon Lambeth Palace (*q.v.*), is dedicated to St. Mary. A ch. is mentioned in Domesday Book, and again in the time of William Rufus. There are differences of opinion as to the date of the ch. which succeeded this one; generally it has been assigned to the first half of the 15th century. It was many times altered and repaired, and in 1851–2 a thorough restoration, almost amounting to re-building, was carried out by P. C. Hardwick. All that remained of the old ch. were a few bosses, the nail-studded vestry door (16th century), and the 15th-century tower of the previous edifice. It is now a large and lofty Gothic bdg., consisting of a nave, a chancel, and two aisles. On the S. side are the Leigh or Pelham Chapel dating from 1552. Sir John Leigh was the son of the ld. of the manor of Stockwell, and it was restored in memory of the late Canon Pelham, who was rector of Lambeth, and also made a memorial of the First World War. The oldest monument is a tomb to Hugh Peyntwin (d. 1504). He was doctor of laws, an officer of the Abp.'s court under Morton, Dene, and Wareham. Opposite is the tomb of John Mompesson (d. 1524). He was a member of the household of Abp. Wareham. These tombs have been denuded of their brass. N. of the chancel, against the E. wall, is the brass of a lady representing Katherine, wife of Ld. William Howard, a son of Thos. D. of Norfolk. The inscription, and the remainder of the monument, have perished. The D. of Norfolk who—as E. of Surrey—commanded the English army at Flodden—added a chapel on the N. side in 1522, and many of his family were bd. there. On the N. wall near this chapel is the brass effigy of a man in armour. It is that of Thos. Clere, who d. 1545. He was a friend of the poetical E. of Surrey, who wrote his epitaph in English verse, but the tablet has disappeared. Cuthbert Tunstall, Bishop—first of L., and afterwards of Durham—was bd. here in 1559. He was beloved of Sir Thos. More, and accompanied him on an embassy to Flanders. He was mentioned in *Utopia*, and in More's epitaph which was in Chelsea Ch. before the bombing. There was also bd. in Lambeth Ch. Thirlby, the only Bp. of Westminster, who d. 1570. Both Tunstall and Thirlby were in the custody of Abp. Parker, by reason of their proclivity to Roman Catholicism. In the burial register the former was 'the popish-bishop.' A brass tablet commemorates them. In 1570 was also bd. the wife of Abp. Parker. In 1692 Elias Ashmole was laid to rest in the ch., and the place is marked by a large slab of blue marble at the E. end of the S. aisle. The epitaph states that his third wife was the daughter of Sir Wm. Dugdale, Garter King of Arms. He was the founder of the Ashmolean Mus. at Oxford. Five archbishops were bd. in the ch.; Bancroft (1610); Tenison (1715); Hutton (1758); Cornwallis (1783); Moore (1805).

The Pedlar window in the Pelham Chapel was destroyed in the war but has been replaced by a copy. Thereby hangs a tale of which there are various versions, discussed by G. L. Gomme, in his *Folk Lore as an Historical Science* (1908). One is that the original window (there was one in 1608, but that recently existing dated from 1703) was inserted in accordance with a stipulation that this should be done if the pedlar left to the par. an acre of ground which is called 'Pedlar's Acre' and forms part of the site of County Hall. Another version is that he insisted that he and his dog should be bd. in the churchyard. The fullest account relates that the pedlar sought shelter from a storm under the wall of the ch., where he was accosted by a priest who persuaded him to attend vespers. When the pedlar died many yrs. later, having prospered as a tradesman, he left his acre to the ch., with the prayer that 'God might prosper the land as he had prospered him.' The land did prosper. At the beginning of the 16th century it brought in 2*s*. 8*d*. per annum. Four centuries later the Lambeth B.C. were drawing from it £1,800 per annum, and the L.C.C. paid £81,000 for the site, the rector and churchwardens vainly entering into litigation with a view to obtaining part of the purchase price. John Timbs has, however, suggested that the window may be simply a rebus on the name 'Chapman.' In Swaffham Ch., Norfolk, the device of a pedlar and pack occurs several times, a John Chapman having been a great benefactor. The cover of the font (1851) has figures of angels. Two had to be replaced and they represent Abp. Davidson and his wife. In the SE. corner of the ch. is a baptistery; a memorial to Abp. Benson (d. 1896). This is a rare feature in an Anglican ch., and is for those who desire immersion in preference to sprinkling, as a prior step to confirmation. It has seldom been used. The wooden altar rails came from All Saints' Ch., Maidstone, and date from Laud's time. The altar piece was the work of Geo. Tinworth (1843–1913). It was damaged by bombs and has been removed.

The church has a fine collection of plate, including chalices of 1637 and 1638, a patten of 1639, and three flagons, all inscribed as given on Christmas Eve, 1664. The registers start in 1539.'Lambhith' is the spelling. The deaths from the plague of 1665 were: Sept. 171; Oct. 194; Nov. 134. In the baptismal register is the name of Arthur Sullivan (1842).

In the chyd. is a table monument of stone, the sides of which are adorned with bas-reliefs representing Egyptian and Grecian ruins, animals, trees, and shells. On the top is a slab of black marble bearing the names of John Tradescant (d. 1638), Jane Tradescant (d. 1634), John Tradescant (d. 1662), John Tradescant (d. 1652), and Hester Tradescant (d. 1678). Below are engraved the following lines:

'Know stranger, ere thou pass, beneath
    this stone
Lye John Tradescant, grandsire, father,
    son:
The last dy'd in his spring: the other two
Lived till they had travell'd Art and
    Nature through,
As by their choice collections may appear:
Of what is rare, in land, in sea, in air:
Whilst they (as Homer's Iliad in a nut)
A world of wonders in one closet shut:
These famous Antiquarians that had been
Both Gardiners to the Rose and Lily
    Queen
Transplanted now themselves, sleep here:
    and when
Angels shall with their trumpets waken
    men,
And fire shall purge the world, these
    hence shall rise
And change this Garden for a Paradise.'

The tomb, erected by the Hester Tradescant mentioned, was restored in 1773, and again in 1853. Tradescant House was in S. Lambeth, and had a mus., which was visited by Charles I and his Q., Abp. Laud, and John Evelyn. It was called 'Tradescant's Ark.' Allen (*History of London*, 1826) mentions the house as 'a plain building of brick with a garden in front with large iron gates.' It is doubtful if this was the original house. Tradescant Rd. now commemorates it. The younger Tradescant, who, like his father, had great botanical zeal and travelled much in search of new plants, bequeathed the collection to Elias Ashmole, who transferred it to the University of Oxford in 1682.

On the outside of the tower is a tablet recording that Bryan Turberville,

'late of St. James's Westminster, Gent., did by his last will and testament bearing date the 20th of October 1711, give and bequeath to this Parish of Lambeth One Hundred Pounds for ever to be laid out in a purchase and the interest thereof for the putting out yearly two poor boys apprentices.'

There is added:

'N.B. None to be put to Chimney-Sweepers, Watermen or Fishermen, and no Roman Catholic to enjoy any benefit thereof.'

Near the Tradescant tomb is a large one surmounted by an urn, and bearing a coat of arms. The inscription is:

'Sacred to the memory of William Bligh, Esquire, F.R.S., Vice-Admiral of the Blue, the celebrated Navigator who first transplanted the Bread Fruit Tree from Otaheite to the West Indies, bravely fought the battles of his country, and died beloved, respected and lamented, on the 7th day of December 1817, aged 64.'

His wife (d. 1812) is also commemorated. The verse is:

'Her spirit soar'd to Heav'n, the blest domain,
Where virtue only can its meed obtain,
All the great duties she performed thro' life,
Those of a child, a parent, and a wife.'

Bligh was the celebrated commander of the *Bounty*, who was turned adrift by his mutinous crew in 1789. A plaque is on the front of 100 Lambeth Road where Bligh established his home in 1794. In the porch there is a conspicuous monument to 'Robert Scott Esq.'; also a stone to:

'William Bacon of the Salt Office, London Gent., who was killed by Thunder and Lightning at his window, July the 12th 1787, aged thirty-four years.'

'By touch ethereal in a moment slain,
He felt the pow'r of death, but not the pain.
Swift as the lightning glanc'd his spirit flew
And bade this rough tempestuous world adieu.
Short was his passage to that peaceful shore
Where storms annoy, and dangers threat no more.'

Dr. Simon Forman was bd. (1611) without any memorial. He d. on a boat in the river. He was an alchemist and astrologer, who fled to Lambeth to escape trouble. He was a playgoer, and kept 'A Booke of Plaies and Notes thereon,' which furnishes some information about the Shakespeare dramas. He saw *Macbeth* at the Globe Theatre in 1610. In an extension of the chyd. in High St., Lambeth, there was bd. Peter Dollond, the optician, and Thos. Cooke, the translator of Hesiod, satirized by Pope:

'From these the world will judge of men and books,
Not from the Burnets, Oldmixons, and Cookes.'

A further burial ground was given to the par. by Abp. Tenison in 1705; it is now a park.

In her flight from England, Mary of Modena, second wife of James II, crossed by the Lambeth ferry. Macaulay says:

'She remained with her child cowering for shelter from the storm under the tower of Lambeth Church, and distracted by terror whenever the ostler approached her with his lantern. Two of her women attended her, one who gave suck to the Prince, and one whose office was to rock his cradle; but they could be of little use to their mistress, for both were foreigners, who could hardly speak the English language and who shuddered at the rigour of the English climate. The only consolatory circumstance was that the little boy was well and uttered not a single cry. At length the coach was ready. The fugitives reached Gravesend.'

The par. of Lambeth contains five manors: Lambeth, Kennington, Vauxhall, Stockwell, and Levehurst. The latter is not now known, but is probably sunk in the manor of Stockwell. The par. ch. of Kennington (from Saxon 'Kyning-tun'—town or place of the king) is St. Mark's. It stands on what was part of Kennington Common, where was the place of execution. Here many persons suffered as traitors after the battle of Culloden, 1745. The ch. was erected 1822–4. Kennington Common was the spot chosen by the Chartists for their great meeting in 1848.

Brixton has a large par. ch. dedicated to St. Matthew; it was erected in 1824. St. Luke's, Norwood (with Corinthian pillars and tower), dates from 1825. St. John's, Waterloo Rd., badly damaged by bombs, was erected in 1824. As the four mentioned were erected after 1815, they have been called 'Waterloo churches,' but they had been projected before the battle, and the Chancellor of the Exchequer said that 'the idea of appropriating churches to commemorate our triumphs did not appear to him to be one that could be entertained.' St. John's Ch. was restored and dedicated to the Festival of Britain.

Very close to the Camberwell border is the ch. of All Saints, Rosendale Rd., a fine Victorian Gothic bdg., by G. H. Fellowes Prynne.

There were two famous nonconformist churches: Christ Ch., Westminster Bridge Rd., opened in 1876, and Brixton Independent Ch., opened in 1870. The latter was sold to the Roman Catholics in 1950.

Kennington Oval is in the borough of Lambeth. It was opened in 1845. The pavilion dates from 1897, but the 'Surrey Tavern' was rebuilt in 1965. There are gates honouring the name of J. B. Hobbs. Blocks of flats surrounding the ground are named after famous cricketers.

(See *Living in Lambeth*, by Aileen D. Nash, 1950.)

Lambeth Palace probably originated in the manor house which was exchanged by the see of Rochester for other lands. It was convenient for both Bp. of Rochester and the primate, and so, on parting with it, the former built a residence close by, which remained the town-house of his successors until the end of the 16th century. Bps. of Rochester lodged in the so-called 'Lollards' Tower until the beginning of the 20th century. Abp. Boniface built the chapel between 1245 and 1270, and the crypt may at that date have been in existence some yrs. Not until the time of Abp. Reynolds (1313–28), when repairs were carried out for which the accounts remain, is there any certainty as to the different apartments of the palace. Then there was apparently an oratory or chapel in addition to the one mentioned, and Boniface had built a fine hall; there was also an almonry, and a *Magna Camera Domini*, or Great Chamber. During Reynolds's time the dole was instituted at the gate (the distribution of bread and meat continued until 1842, when under Abp. Howley a sum of £200 per annum was set aside to be given in weekly pensions). In 1381 the Wat Tyler rebels burned and destroyed books and charters, and drained the wine casks. Abp. Sudbury was beheaded on Tower

Hill. The second great builder of Lambeth Palace was Abp. Chichele, who held the primacy from 1414 to 1443, and who figures in the *Henry VI* plays. He built the Water Tower, wrongly called the Lollards' Tower, and repaired other parts of the bdg. Whilst Cardinal Morton was Abp. of C. and Ld. Chancellor (1486–1500) the present gateway was erected. On its N. side there is a leaden water-pipe which still bears on a square head the rebus of the builder, a tun with a letter M upon it. A petition survives amongst the chancery records of one of the labourers being attached for a vagabond. To show he was not he intimated that he 'had in his purse iijs vijd in monys which he had spared of your gracious wages'—his earnings whilst employed upon Morton's tower. The association of Lambeth Palace with Lollards is doubtful. Master Wm. Taylor appeared before Chichele in 1419, seeking release from a sentence of excommunication passed by Abp. Arundel fourteen yrs. before, and was absolved, and this presumably was his offence. He relapsed into his heresy, and in 1422 Chichele pronounced sentence of degradation, and handed over his victim to the secular arm and the fire. It is, however, not known that he was a prisoner at Lambeth Palace. The abps., as lords of the manor of Lambeth, had judicial powers over recalcitrant tenants, as well as ecclesiastic jurisdiction. In respect of the latter, Abp. Arundel (1396–1414) had before him for judgment a married chaplain from the dungeons within his manor of Lambeth. In the bare apartment in the upper part of Chicheles' tower there are still eight iron rings in the wainscot, and half sentences and letters cut with a knife. The names of Austin and John Worth are decipherable, but the Latin sentences are incomplete. The real Lollards' Tower was in St. P.'s Cath (*q.v.*). There was also a prison in Morton's Gateway. Friar Peto was imprisoned there as a result of a sermon before Henry VIII at Greenwich on the dangerous subject of his marriage with Anne Boleyn. John Aubrey says that the Gate-House and 'Lollards' Tower' were made prisons for the royalists. Dr. Guy Carleton, who was among them, escaped from the latter. A boat was ready below, but the cord was too short. He was obliged to drop to reach the ground, and in falling dislocated one of his legs. He was, however, safely conveyed to a place of concealment.

In 1534 Sir Thos. More was examined at Lambeth Palace, probably in the old Guard Room, by the Council, with Thos. Cromwell at their head. From there he went to W.A. for brief custody with the abbot, ere he departed for the T.L. Towards the close of Edward VI's reign Bp. Bonner was examined there by Cranmer, Ridley, and the Dean of St. Paul's. The swing of the pendulum brought Cardinal Pole there, to receive a deputation of the Ld.M. and aldermen. For long stored in the muniment chamber there were a chasuble, stole, and maniple of fine shot silk, together with a metal crucifix, a rosary, and a box, sealed, and inscribed to the effect that it contained relics of St. Bartholomew, part of the thigh-bone of St. Matthew, the skull of St. Apollonia, virgin and martyr, all duly approved and attested. The chasuble is still on view. With Parker as abp. (believed to be the original 'Nosey Parker' by reason of his inquisitiveness as to the conduct of the clergy), Q. Elizabeth visited Lambeth Palace. She spent a night or two there, and Dr. Pearce preached a sermon from a pulpit placed in the quadrangle, near the pump, whilst the Q. listened in the upper gallery. Parker, who d. 1570, was the only abp. to be bd. in the chapel. The most historical figure of a later era was Laud (1633-45). Dorothy Gardiner said:

'An accident, ill-omened, signalized his arrival at Lambeth: the over-laden ferry-boat, as it crossed with his servants and horses, sank to the bottom of the Thames, happily with the loss only of the Archbishop's coach.'

She adds:

'It is clear that Laud had a particular attachment to the old house and responded eagerly to the charm of his surroundings. The river so often traversed in his barge, flowing past the windows of chambers he himself had built, figures in his diary like a companion whose face is continually regarded for its changes of moods and expression. Now he records the low water in autumn, after "an extreme hot and faint October and November"; so low was it that vessels could scarce pass up and down; now on Twelfth Night,

the river freezes and, for the second time that century, continues stark and rigid for thirty days, the thaw at last bringing about a great inundation. A year after, in mid-November, "the greatest tide that hath been seen" floods gates, walks and cloisters at Lambeth; and on one occasion when Laud is returning home from the Star Chamber, "most extream tempest on the Thames" endangers his life at the landing-stairs.'

Before the construction of the Albert Embankment there was only a narrow road, affording room for one vehicle, between the palace and the river. A similar flood occurred in Jan. 1928. Laud's alterations at Lambeth Palace were brought against him at his trial; these included the provision of an altar-rail, and the reparation of a broken image of Christ in a stained glass window in the chapel, this being contrary to the statute of Edward VI against all images. In his diary he relates how, on the Eve of St. Simon and St. Jude, he went into his upstairs study to examine some manuscript he was about to send to Oxford.

'In that study hung my Picture, taken by the Life; and coming in I found it fallen upon the Face, and lying on the Floor, the String being broken by which it was hanged against the Wall. I am almost every day threatened with my Ruine in Parliament. God grant this to be no omen.'

The portrait now hangs in the new Guard Room. In Dec. of the same yr. he took farewell of the palace, being allowed to return under guard 'for a book or two to read in,' and to obtain the papers necessary for his defence.

During the Commonwealth some Dutch prisoners seem to have been confined at Lambeth Palace. Parker's tomb was broken open, the lead enclosing the body was plucked off and sold, and his bones bd. in a dung-hill in the palace yard. With the Restoration Juxon (the abp. who attended Charles I on the scaffold), returned. He brought Parker's remains back to the chapel, and they were bd. 'just above the Litany Deske, neere to the Steps ascending to the Altar.' At a later date Abp. Sancroft caused the words to be inscribed on a square of marble 'Corpus Matthaei Archiepiscopi tandem hic quiescit,' and in the ante-chapel he re-erected the former monument, adding a Latin epitaph 'graphically describing the tragedy of the rifled tomb.' Abp. Juxon rebuilt the Great Hall, which is 93 ft. long by 38 ft. wide and 50 ft. in height, at a cost of £10,500. It has a fine open hammer-beam roof, and now houses the greater part of the library (see 'Libraries').

Pepys came to the palace in 1669 to dine with Abp. Sheldon. He had a surprising experience:

'Most of the company gone, and I going, I heard by a gentleman of a sermon that was to be there; and so I staid to hear it, thinking it serious, till by and by the gentleman told me it was a mockery, by one Cornet Bolton, a very gentleman like-man, that behind a chair did pray and preach like a Presbyter Scot that ever I heard in my life, with all the possible imitation in grimaces and voice. And his text about the hanging up their harps upon the willows: and a serious, good sermon too, exclaiming against Bishops, and crying up of my good Lord Eglington, till it made us all burst; but I did wonder to have the Bishop at this time to make himself sport with things of this kind, but I perceive it was shown him as a rarity; and he took care to have the room-door shut, but there were about twenty gentlemen there, and myself, infinitely pleased with the novelty.'

In 1672 this same abp. married a boy of eight yrs., John Power, a grandson of the E. of Anglesey, to Katherine Fitzgerald, his cousin-german, a girl of about thirteen. 'They answered as well as those of greater age,' the bridegroom's father complacently recorded. Q. Mary visited Lambeth Palace in 1694, when Tillotson was primate. The bell-ringers received 5s. for their services. Peter the Great came about six yrs. later, to watch the ordination of an Anglican priest. He was greatly impressed by the library. He had never imagined there were so many printed volumes in the world.

The 18th century was fairly uneventful in the history of Lambeth Palace. In 1753 a tortoise owned by Abp. Laud d. at the age of 120 yrs. The shell is still exhibited. In 1780 about five hundred of the 'No Popery' rioters marched up from St. George's Fields. They knocked at the gates, threatened to return at night, and all day long paraded round the palace. A party of a hundred Guardsmen arrived, but the mob, notwithstanding, continued to demonstrate. The Abp. (Cornwallis) left the palace for a few days, and from 7th June to 11th Aug. two or three hundred soldiers were quartered there.

When Abp. Howley became primate in 1828 he made many alterations. In 1846 a groined roof was placed in the chapel in place of the previous flat one. The old guard room was rebuilt, but retained its original roof. It was so called from the soldiers, some of whom guarded the gate, who were lodged there. Here now hang a remarkable series of portraits of abps. Amongst the painters represented are Van Dyck (Laud); Sir Godfrey Kneller (Tillotson); Hogarth (Herring); Sir Joshua Reynolds (Secker). Howley swept away most of the residential part of the palace, replacing it with the present bdgs. in the Tudor style, from designs by Edwd. Blore. The cost was £60,000, and half of this was provided out of his own purse. In 1867 the first Lambeth Conference was held in the Great Hall. Four Colonial bps., unable to sleep without their pipes, had a four-wheeled cab posted at the palace door, and this they used as a smoking-room.

Lambeth Palace suffered by bombing in May 1941. The chapel was almost destroyed, and there disappeared the copy of the marble tomb of Abp. Tait in Canterbury Cath. The Great Hall was damaged, but restored. The top of Chichele's Tower was burnt away and considerable damage done to the residential part of the palace.

(See *Lambeth Palace* by J. Cave-Brown, M.A., 1883; *The Story of Lambeth Palace*, by Dorothy Gardiner, 1930; *Lambeth Palace*, by C. R. Dodwell, 1968.)

Leicester Square (N. of Trafalgar Sq., and in the city of Westminster) derives its name from Robt. Sidney, second E. of Leicester, who in 1631 obtained a licence to build a L. residence in what was termed Lammas land (it had to lie open for pasture after Lammas in every yr.), in the par. of St. Martin's in the Fields, NW. of the King's Mews (see 'Charing Cross'). The ground then laid out was afterwards called Leicester Fields, and ultimately became Leicester Sq. Leicester House was built on the N. side, but the land on the other three sides also belonged to the earl. He was ambassador in France 1636–41, and later was seldom in L., residing usually at Penshurst until his death in 1677. In 1642, however, he entertained the E. of Essex at a great supper here, when there was a plot (attributed to French papists), to poison him and his guests. The children of Charles I lived here during their father's imprisonment. Algernon Sidney, the ill-fated son of the 2nd E., was living here in 1649 and 1658. In Q. Anne's reign the house was let to the emperor's ambassador. George I quarrelled with his son, afterwards George II; and at that time (1718) Leicester House happened to be unlet. The latter therefore set up a court in rivalry to St. James's. There were b. there the D. of Cumberland (1721); Mary (1723), who m. the 'brute' P. of Hesse-Cassel; and Louisa (1724), who became Q. of Denmark. As George II whose statue was in the square for over a century (see 'Lost Monuments') had quarrelled with his father, so did his own son, Fredk., quarrel with him. Hence, from about 1741, Fredk. lived in Leicester House, which Pennant aptly called 'the pouting place of princes.' Here the children of the P.'s household acted Addison's *Cato*. Fredk. P. of Wales (father of George III) d. here in 1751— it has been said, on slender evidence, as the result of a blow from a cricket ball. The house stood some little way back from the sq., the frontage occupying nearly the western half of its breadth, and gardens behind running back as far as Lisle St. It was pulled down in 1791, and the site covered by the Empire Theatre in the eighteen-eighties. Adjoining on the W. and apparently connected with it, was Savile House, which in 1698 belonged to Ld. Carmarthen (son of the D. of Leeds), to whom William III confided the care of Peter the Great. The latter, however, was first lodged in Buckingham St., Strand. A little later P. Eugene, Marlborough's brother in arms, stayed there. It passed into the Savile family through marriage. On the accession of George III the new K. was proclaimed before Savile House, with an imposing ceremonial. In 1766 a resident was the D. of Cumberland. Sir Geo. Savile, a friend of Burke's, had introduced into Parliament the Bill which provoked the 'No Popery' riots. The house was

therefore pillaged; the railings were pulled down; and furniture, pictures, and books, burnt in the sq. The house was rebuilt at the beginning of the 19th century, and destroyed by fire in 1865.

Apart from Leicester House there was little building in Leicester Fields until after the Restoration. In 1678 it was first called Leicester Sq. Early residents were: Nathaniel Crewe, Bp. of Durham; the E. of Orrery in 1675; and the E. of Pembroke in 1680. Strype (1720) described it as

'a very handsome large square, enclosed with rails and graced on all sides with good built houses, well inhabited and resorted to by gentry.'

Sir Joshua Reynolds purchased a house on the W. side (built about 1700) in 1760; and in his studio there—a room some 20 ft. long by 16 ft. broad—almost up to his death in 1792, he painted the portraits which have made him famous. Here he dined with illustrious guests. A well-known picture (a copy is in Dr. Johnson's house in Gough Sq.) shows as his guests Boswell, Paoli, Goldsmith, Burke, Johnson, Thos. Warton (Prof. of Poetry), Dr. Burney, and David Garrick. It was at one of these dinners that Goldsmith tried to repeat a joke, and lost the point of it. Somebody had said that when peas were a poor colour they should be taken to Hammersmith, for that was the way to Turnham Green. Goldsmith rendered it 'make-em green.' The house was last in the occupation of Messrs. Puttick & Simpson, fine art dealers, established in 1794. Reynolds's studio had then gone, their sales-room being where it was situated. The room in which he died remained, and also the dining-room. There were Adam fireplaces, the upper part of the staircase was the original one; the lower part probably was altered during Reynolds's residence. The beautiful curve of the balustrade was probably due to the necessity for providing room for the hooped petticoats of the 18th century. According to Cunningham, Reynolds gave his servant £6 annually in wages, and offered him £100 a yr. for the door, i.e. gratuities others were accustomed to bestow. On the steps of the house he found the child that appears in his picture of 'Puck.' When the house was demolished in 1937 some of the fittings of the hall door, and the door of the room in which Reynolds died, went to the Abbey Folk Park, New Barnet. There is a L.C.C. tablet on the site. Wm. Hogarth's house has gone. He settled in Leicester Sq., on his marriage in 1733 to a daughter of Sir Jas. Thornhill. The latter disliked the match, but helped the young people to set up house on the E. side of Leicester Fields. Here Hogarth placed over the door a bust of Van Dyck, constructed out of pieces of cork and gilded over. The house therefore became known as 'The Golden Head.' Hogarth owned it until his death. He was taken ill at his country residence at Chiswick (which remains, and is a public gallery), and d. in about two hours after being brought from there to Leicester Sq. On the site of the house was afterwards the Sablonière Hotel (a resort of French, Italian, and German visitors), and later Abp. Tenison's Sch., since 1928 at Kennington Oval. Dr. John Hunter came to live at No. 29, and in 1785 built an addition in the rear of the house to accommodate his great collection, now in the Royal Coll. of Surgeons. In a house in St. Martin's St., on the S. side of Leicester Sq., lived Sir Isaac Newton, 1710–26. In 1774 Dr. Martin Burney occupied it, and his daughter, Fanny, announced the fact as follows:

'My father has bought a House in St. Martin's Street Leicester Fields,— an odious street—but well situated, and nearly in the centre of the town; and the house is a large and good one. It was built by Sir Isaac Newton.'

'His observatory' (she wrote later) 'is my favourite sitting place, when I can retire to read or write any of my private fancies or vagaries.'

It was a glazed turret, with a small fire-place and chimney and a cupboard. 'We show it to all our visitors,' Fanny wrote, 'as our principal Lyon.' In 1778, in a hurricane, the leaden roof and glazed sides were blown away, but Dr. Burney reconstructed it. There were some fine ceilings in the house. Dr. Johnson visited Dr. Burney here. The most memorable occasion was in 1778, when Mr. and Mrs. Greville came specially to meet the doctor and Mrs. Thrale. Greville was haughty and aloof, and Johnson did not conceal his resentment. Another visitor was Gabriel Piozzi. On the first meeting with him Mrs. Thrale mimicked his

pianoforte performance behind his back, but she eventually became his wife. Early in the 19th century, according to John Hollingshead, a wooden room was erected on the roof by a Frenchman, called 'Newton's Observatory,' and exhibited for money. It was eventually purchased and removed—it was said, to America. The house remained until 1913. An inscription is on the Westminster Public Library, which is on the site. In Orange St. (behind the National Gallery) Thos. Holcroft (stable boy, shoemaker, tutor, actor, author, whose autobiography was concluded by Hazlitt) was b. 1744. He was baptized in St. Martin's in the Fields Ch. In Orange St. is a small Congregational chapel, with the dates '1693, 1929' inscribed over the door. As Dickens's *Old Curiosity Shop* is supposed to have been a few yards from here—at the corner of Irving St. and Charing Cross Rd. (Castle St. in the time of the novelist), the earlier bdg. was identified with 'Little Bethel.' In its pulpit the Rev. Augustus Toplady preached in 1778 what he knew must be his last sermon, for he was stricken with consumption.

Leicester Sq. as it exists at present is largely due to a financial adventurer named Grant. E. V. Lucas perhaps did him too much credit—or discredit rather— in saying that he was 'the discoverer of those most susceptible and gullible of investors, the parson and widow.' His enterprise resembled Horatio Bottomley's. His real name was Gottheimer. He became M.P. for Kidderminster and owner of the *Echo*. Lawsuits resulted in bankruptcy, he sold his palace at Kensington, and d. forgotten at Bognor in 1899. He received a barony from the K. of Italy. Between 1872 and 1874 he spent some £28,000 in laying out Leicester Sq. An equestrian statue of George I was then removed. The gardens with busts of Reynolds, Hogarth, Hunter and Newton and a statue of Shakespeare are part of his scheme. Dickens (in *Bleak House*) admirably summarized the district as that curious region which is

'a centre of attraction to indifferent foreign hotels and indifferent foreigners, old china, gaming-houses, exhibitions, and a large medley of shabbiness and drinking out of sight.'

One of the curious exhibitions—in the pre-Grant era—was Wylde's Globe, which stood 1851–61. It was 60 ft. in diameter; and the world was figured in relief on the inside of the globe, and viewed from galleries at different elevations—an hourly explanatory lecture being given. The Leicester Square to which soldiers in the First World War sent kind regards in song was a Bohemian one. This aspect is dealt with under 'Music Halls.' It is not inappropriate to mention that birth-control specialities could be obtained at a very early date in this neighbourhood. Mrs. Philips in the closing yrs. of the 17th century announced that at 'No. 5 Orange Court near Leicester Fields' at the 'sign of the Golden Fan and Rising Sun' she sells 'implements of safety,' having had thirty-five yrs. experience of making and selling them.

(See *The Story of Leicester Square*, by John Hollingshead, 1892; *The Early History of Piccadilly, Leicester Square, and Soho*, by C. L. Kingsford, 1925.)

Lewisham (the first two syllables are either from leswe, a meadow, or from 'Liofs,' genitive of a personal name; ham means a dwelling; pronounce 'Lewis-ham,' not 'Lewi-sham') now a part of the L. bor. of Lewisham, was a met bor., consisting of the two old pars. of Lewisham and Lee, once in Kent, united into one civil par. of Lewisham since 1906.

The par. ch. is on the W. side of the long High St., a little to the E. of the Ravensbourne, which runs S. to N. through the par. Its chyd. borders that stream, on the other side of which is the long strip of the Ladywell Recreation Ground. Ladywell is the name of the region between High St. and Brockley: because, about 1472, a spring was discovered W. of the Ravensbourne near where Ladywell Station now is, and because its supposedly miraculous properties were attributed to St. Mary the Virgin, to whom the ch. was dedicated in A.D. 931. The old ch. was demolished, all but the tower, and the present one built in 1774–7. On the morning of 26th Dec. 1830 it was completely gutted by fire, through overheating for the Christmas service, and all the old par. registers were destroyed; they contained the entry of the baptism of Brian Duppa (1588–1682), Bp. of Winchester. There was immediate restoration, so far as that was possible. Another restoration took

place in 1881, and in 1882 the chancel was enlarged and the gallery, hiding the ancient arch in the tower, was removed. Among those bd. in ch. and chyd. were: Mrs. Margaret Colfe (wife of Abraham Colfe, to be mentioned later), 1643, she had a tablet in the ch.; and Thos. Dermody (1775–1802), Irish poet, pamphleteer, soldier, and debauchee, who d. in a wretched hovel at Perry Slough, near Sydenham.

The Almshouses founded by Abraham Colfe, Vicar, and administered by the Leathersellers' Co., dated 1664, were badly damaged by blast during the late war and have been demolished. Colfe in 1652 opened a free grammar sch. on Lewisham Hill in succession to a decayed foundation of his predecessor John Glyn 1569. The management of the sch. was left to the Leathersellers' Co. and it still flourishes.

Catford (ford of Ceatta, a personal name) is in the centre of the bor., S. of Lewisham proper—the village of Lewisham. The manor of Catford was anciently the property of the family of Abel. Anthony Beck, Bp. of Durham, d. seised of it in 1311.

Rushey Green, Hither Green, Southend Village, Bellingham and Downham, all have now practically lost their identity in the great housing estates built for the most part between the wars. St. John's, Southend, is a fine lofty ch. by Sir C. Nicholson 1928, containing memorials of the Forster family.

Lee (leah, a meadow) is perhaps the most interesting of the old villages now swallowed up in the modern bor. In High Rd. Lee is the little 17th-century chapel of the demolished Christopher Boone's Almshouses. It now survives as a reading room for the residents in the nearby Merchant Taylors' Almshouses. Boone was a man of antiquarian tastes, and friend of John Evelyn. In Old Rd. the Public Library occupies an interesting old house built in 1780.

The par. ch., dedicated to St. Margaret, stands in Lee Terrace, halfway up the hill towards Blackheath; it dates only from 1841, but contains some monuments from the older ch. which stood in the chyd. on the opposite side of the rd. Here may be seen the stump of the tower of the old ch., and among those here bd. are Edmund Halley and Nathanield Bliss, Astronomers Royal in the 18th century, Wm. Parsons, comedian (1795), and Robt. Cocking, 'who died on Burntash Field after descending in an experimental Parachute detached from the Great Nassau Balloon' (1837).

Libraries. Boswell said: 'In London I suppose we may find every book that should be found anywhere.' This, perhaps, was a little too much to ask, even of so great a city, but there can be no doubt that nowhere can so many be borrowed. The first lending library in L. that offered books beyond a very small circle (see also 'Books in London') was one founded by Abp. Tenison in 1684. It was open to persons resident in the ancient par. of St. Martin's in the Fields—i.e. in addition to the present par., St. James's, Westminster; St. Anne's, Soho; St. George's, Hanover Sq. It was not dispersed until 1861–2, when it was sold by public auction. The first library under the Act of 1850, known as the Ewart Act, authorizing their establishment was St. Margaret's and St. John the Evangelist's, Westminster, in 1856. This was located in Trevor Sq., Knightsbridge.

The following are brief accounts of what may be regarded as the great historical libraries of L.; there are of course many other great libraries including those of the Univ. of London (Senate House), Kings College (Strand), the Victoria and Albert Museum, the Science Museum, the Patent Office, the London School of Economics, the National Central Library and those of many Govt. departments.

THE BRITISH MUSEUM found the nucleus of its vast library in two great collections; those of Sir Robt. Bruce Cotton and Sir Hans Sloane. The former's was housed in his residence at Westminster, within the precinct of the old palace, and there he d. 1631. The site of the house is covered by the Houses of Parliament. R. Lapthorne, a visitor to Cotton House in 1692, said that it was

'of a great highth, but very narrow, as I remember, not full six feet in breadth, and not above 26 in length; the books placed on each side of a tolerable highth, so that a man of an indifferent stature may reach the highest. Over the books are the Roman Emperors, I mean their heads, in brass statues, which serve for standards in the Catalogue, to direct and find any particular book.'

The same nominal arrangement is retained to-day in the B.Mus., i.e. the presses in which the books are kept are named after Roman emperors: Augustus, Claudius, Vespasian, etc. Cotton House became dilapidated, and in 1727 a lease was taken of Essex House, Strand, for the purpose of housing more safely the books which were endangered by damp. In 1730 they were taken back to Westminster, and lodged in Ashburnham House, which still remains in Dean's Yard. In 1731 there was a serious fire at the latter, and the lib. came near to entire destruction. Here it remained until its transfer to the B.Mus. It was the Cotton trustees who, in 1750, petitioned for the foundation of a national library and mus. Sir Hans Sloane's collection was gathered first in his house in Great Russell St., and then moved to the manor house at Chelsea. His interests were more scientific than literary, but he loved books, and in 1753, when he d., it was found he had bequeathed his mus. and library to the nation. The former is dealt with elsewhere (see 'Museums'); the books supplied the second great source of supply to the Reading Room of the B.Mus. In 1757 a third collection was added. This was the Royal MSS., and the 'old' Royal Lib. of over 9,000 books.

The first Reading Room (opened 15th Jan. 1759) was a narrow dark apartment at the SW. angle of Montague House, with only two windows. Admission was by yearly ticket, always running from 1st Jan., whatever the date of issue. It was required that notice should be given the previous day of books and manuscripts required. The first Keeper of the Reading Room was Peter Templeman. The poet Gray was admitted in July 1759. He wrote:

'I often pass four hours in the day in the stillness and solitude of the reading-room, which is uninterrupted by anything but Dr. Stukeley the antiquary, who comes there to talk nonsense and coffee-house news.'

At this time admission was granted only to persons known either to the trustees or the staff, but in 1760 the powers were invested in the Principal Librarian, as they still are. Samuel Johnson obtained a ticket in 1761, though there is no record of his attendance. The first ladies to come were Lady Mary Carr and Lady Ann Monson on 1st Jan. 1762. Gibbon, who made great use of the Reading Room, was admitted in 1770, and Burke in 1771. John Wesley came on a visit in Dec. 1780. He noted, 'seven large apartments are filled with curious books,' and adds the characteristic remark: 'But what account will a man give to the Judge of quick and dead for a life spent in collecting these?' In 1799 Walter Scott was making researches, and in 1804 Chas. Lamb was admitted. Washington Irving described the Reading Room in 1815:

'I found myself in a spacious chamber, surrounded with great cases of venerable books. Above the cases were arranged a great number of black-looking portraits of ancient authors. About the room were placed long tables, with stands for reading and writing, at which sat many pale, studious personages poring intently over dusty volumes, rummaging among mouldy manuscripts, and taking copious notes of their contents. . . . Now and then one of these personages would write something on a small slip of paper, and ring a bell, whereupon a familiar would appear, take the paper in profound silence, glide out of the room, and return shortly loaded with ponderous tomes, upon which the other would fall tooth and nail with famished voracity.'

In 1818 there was bought for £13,500 the library of Dr. Chas. Burney. It included 13,000 printed editions and manuscripts of classical Greek and Latin authors, a collection of newspapers, and 329 volumes of cuttings, playbills etc.

The number of readers on the books was only about 750 in 1827. In 1830 Dickens's name appears as a reader. Dickens was not a bookman, and the B.Mus. was a ladder to climb by, not a love to be cherished. In 1831 Carlyle became a reader, and in 1832 Thackeray. About 1833 Edwd. FitzGerald took lodgings in Bloomsbury, to be near the B.Mus., and in the same yr. Wm. Cobbett, opposing a grant of £16,000 for its maintenance, said:

'He would ask of what use in the wide world was this British Museum, and to whom, to what class of persons, it was useful? It did a great deal of good to the majority of those who went to it, but to nobody else. . . . If the aristocracy wanted the Museum as a lounging place let them pay for it.'

Anthony Panizzi, at this time assistant librarian, said, however, before the Select Committee of the H. of C. in 1836 something that should have been after Cobbett's own heart:

'I want a poor student to have the same means of indulging his learned curiosity, of following his rational pursuits—of consulting the same authorities —of fathoming the most intricate inquiry—as the richest man in the kingdom, as far as books go.'

In 1837, amidst a certain amount of resentment by reason of his Italian birth, Panizzi was made Keeper of the Reading Room. He was a man of ability and enterprise. He advocated a grant of £10,000 a yr. to bring it up to the standard of the Royal Library in Paris, and the raising of the ordinary grant of £2,000 to £3,000. He also advocated an alphabetical catalogue. After many yrs. the Treasury granted £10,000 p.a. to remedy deficiencies and complete the library, and it was Panizzi's own design that was carried out in the present Reading Room which was opened in 1857. A new one was essential, as the old one was often overcrowded, and Thos. Carlyle complained that often he could not find a seat and that he had to sit on top of a ladder. The new room, offering accommodation for 458 readers, removed this difficulty, though perhaps the 'museum headache,' of which he also complained, could not entirely be eradicated by any architectural improvement. The dome of the Reading Room is 140 ft. in diameter, and was the largest in Europe, except that of the Pantheon at Rome, which is 2 ft. wider. When it was built it was meant to take the bulk of the library's collection of books. It is 106 ft. high, and the walls are covered, so far as the clerestory, with shelves accommodating 70,000 to 80,000 books. A bust of Panizzi is over the entrance. The total number of books now exceeds 4,000,000. In 1823 George IV was reported to have given the library of his father, George III, consisting of about 120,000 volumes, housed first at Kew, and afterwards at Kensington Palace and Buckingham Palace, to the nation. There was, in fact, a consideration in the form of an honorarium to His Majesty. A room was specially built for this S. of the Reading Room. Another 20,000 odd volumes came from the library of Thos. Grenville on his death in 1846. At Colindale, near Hendon, in 1905, a building was erected for storing newspapers; an extension was built in 1957.

The present opening hour of the Reading Room, 9 a.m., was fixed so long ago as 1836. The closing hour has varied. Prior to 1879 it was 7 p.m. only during the summer months, from 1879 to 1920 7 p.m. continuously. In the latter yr. it was reduced to 6 p.m. After the outbreak of the Second World War the closing hour was 5 p.m. and this has remained, although evening opening is being extended as staff becomes available. Scraps of paper were used to requisition books up to 1837, and the staff had to find the reference in the catalogue. In the yr. mentioned the printed form, suggested by Panizzi, was adopted. Up to 1838, when blotting-books were provided, sand was used for drying wet ink. The Reading Room (which now seats 400 readers) was redecorated in 1907, and it was then that the names were painted at the base of the dome: Chaucer; Caxton; Tindale; Spenser; Shakespeare; Bacon; Milton; Locke; Addison; Swift; Pope; Gibbon; Wordsworth; Scott; Byron; Carlyle; Macaulay; Tennyson; Browning. These were removed during spring cleaning in 1939.

The B.Mus. lib. lost about 150,000 volumes through bombing. The Reading Room was not in use for six years. At Colindale about 30,000 volumes of bound newspapers were destroyed. A scheme for much needed expansion of the library and a reconstruction of the entire B.Mus. site has received much publicity in the last few years but at the moment a political stalemate has been reached.

(See *The British Museum Library*, by Arundell Esdaile, 1946.)

THE GUILDHALL LIBRARY. The first mention is in 1425, when a separate structure was built for it on the S. side of the Guildhall Chapel. This was due to the generosity of Richd. Whittington and Wm. Bury, supported by John Carpenter, who left by his will such

'good or rare books [as] may seem necessary to the common library at Guildhall, for the profit of the students there, and those discoursing to the common people.'

It is referred to again in 1549 as

'a certen house nexte unto the sam Chapell apperteynyng called the Library, all waies res'ved for students to resorte unto.'

Stow records its fate:

'These bookes (as it is said) were in the raigne of Edward the 6 sent for by Edward, Duke of Sommerset, Lord Protector, with promise to be restored shortly: men laded from thence three Carriers with them, but never returned.'

There is one relic of this library at the Guildhall. It is a French 13th-century MS—a metrical version of the holy scriptures by Peter de Riga. An inscription on the back of the top fly-leaf and on the blank before the New Testament states: *hunc librum donavit magister Johannes Martil librarie communi Guyhalde civitatis Londonarium.*

Not until 1824 were steps taken by the C.C. to re-establish their library. It was then housed in rooms occupied by the Irish Soc.—in the E. wing of the front of the Guildhall. In 1869 the Court of Common Council resolved to erect a new library and mus.; they were opened in 1873. The total cost exceeded £100,000. The library measures 100 ft. long, 65 ft. wide, and 50 ft. in height. It has a beautiful roof with arched ribs, which are supported by the arms of the twelve great City cos. with the addition of those of the Leathersellers' and Broderers' and also the Royal and City arms. The large N. window of seven lights, divided by a transom, was the gift of some of the inhabitants of the Ward of Aldersgate.

No tickets are required, and books are more expeditiously supplied than at the B.Mus. When Bernard Kettle, a former librarian, retired, he recalled—

'the time when Francis Thompson was a constant visitor. He however got into such bad straits and was so poorly clad that it fell to my lot to have to perform the painful duty of asking him to forego his visits here. He always came in with two books in his pocket. One, I think, was Sophocles; and had I known that I was entertaining an "angel unawares" I should perhaps have been more reluctant to eject him.'

The library contains the most extensive collection in existence on the history and development of London, including printed books, prints, mss., drawings, maps, etc. Special collections include those of the Gardeners' Co. in horticulture, the Clockmakers' Co. on horology, the Cock collection on Sir Thomas More, and the playing card collection of the Makers of Playing Cards. The associated Art Gallery also contains many paintings relating to London history. The mss. collection includes the deposited archives of the Diocese and Archdeaconry of London, the city Parish Churches and most of the City Companies.

A new Guildhall Library is being built as part of the Guildhall Reconstruction Scheme (see 'Guildhall'). A new City Business Library has replaced the Commercial Reference Room (founded as a service to business men as long ago as 1879). The old Guildhall Library will become the Council Chamber of the C.C. Lending Libraries were also established in the City, under the auspices of the C.C., in 1966.

LAMBETH PALACE LIBRARY contains about 42,000 volumes and 1,300 volumes of manuscript. It owes its foundation to Abp. Cranmer, the next and larger contributor being Abp. Whitgift (1583–1604); whilst Bancroft (d. 1610) bequeathed hundreds of books and pamphlets—

'for ye service of God and his church, of the kings and commonwealth of the Realm and particularly of the archbishops.'

It was therefore opened for public use, and James I thereupon borrowed a number of books, which were never returned. Abp. Laud added to the library. During the Commonwealth there was a danger of its being dispersed. John Selden, however, who made much use of it, exerted his influence, and it was given by Parliament to the University of Cambridge. There it was separately catalogued, and at the Restoration reclaimed by Abp. Juxon to be housed in the hall, which he rebuilt in 1663. Considerable additions were made by Abps. Sheldon (1677), and Sancroft (1678–90). The latter catalogued the books and collections of manuscripts with his own hands, and with the assistance of his accomplished librarian rearranged the whole library. Abps. Tenison (1694–1715) and Secker (1758–68) left about 1,000 volumes each, and the library benefited by a large portion of Abp. Tait's collection when he d. 1882. It also received 100 volumes from the Soc. of Lincoln's Inn, and the Swedish collection of Wordsworth,

Bp. of Salisbury. Most abps. have left some books to the library. Sumner (1848–62), left only two, the subjects being butterflies and gout. An interesting exhibit was a cookery-book of the wife of Abp. Tenison.

In the Second World War about 8,000 volumes were damaged, but perhaps half not beyond repair; these included some incunabula. Nearly 150 of the spacious book-shelves, dating from 1829, were destroyed by fire.

LONDON LIBRARY, found in 1841, was first at 49 Pall Mall. Thos. Carlyle was largely influential in its formation, a meeting held at the Freemasons' Tavern in 1840, in which Milman, John Forster, Bulwer (Lytton), Gladstone, and Jas. Spedding participated, being due to his efforts. Later Dickens, Thackeray, and Macaulay gave their support. In 1843 a reading room was provided for members, and in 1845 larger premises were required. These were found in Beauchamp House, St. James's Sq. Carlyle made great use of it. He was guilty of the bad habit of marking even borrowed books, sometimes drawing asses' ears at the end of a purple passage. The library was rebuilt 1896–8, and there was a further extension in 1913. Starting with 3,000 volumes, it now numbers more than 500,000, of which 10,000 are for reference. It has a number of incunabula, and is particularly rich in works of foreign literature and on art.

About 10,000 volumes were lost through bombing.

SION COLLEGE LIBRARY was founded under the will of Dr. Thos. White, who d. 1624. He was a prebendary of St. Paul's, and vicar of St. Dunstan's in the West (see 'City Churches; C'). He was founder of the White Professorship of Moral Philosophy at Oxford. The foundation in 1632 took the form of a guild for the clergy of L. and the suburbs, with an almshouse for ten poor men, and as many poor women, and to this a library was added by Dr. John Simpson, rector of St. Olave's, Hart St. The books were first housed in a long room added to the coll. at the expense of the latter. This first bdg. was on the site of Elsing Spital in L. Wall (see 'City Churches; B'—St. Alphage, London Wall). Under an Act of 1884 the almshouses were abolished, but the number of pensioners was increased. This part of the foundation is now under separate management. In 1886 the coll. (which had been burnt in the G.F. and rebuilt) was removed to the present bdg. on the Victoria Embankment. It was designed by Sir Arthur Blomfield and the site acquired from the C.C. for £31,000. The coll. still consists of incumbents of City and suburban pars., but access to the library is granted to others. Before the Second World War it contained about 200,000 volumes. It is naturally largely theological, but aims at adding the principal books in most other departments of literature. In 1682 it acquired about 1,000 volumes from the first E. of Berkeley, being about half of the library of his uncle, Sir Robt. Cooke. In 1705 Dr. John Lawson willed to the coll. his fine collection of upwards of 1,000 volumes; in 1713 Compton, Bp. of L., bequeathed his important collection of theological books. The coll. also came into possession of a number of books which had been stored at the house of the Jesuits at Clerkenwell, and were found during the alleged Popish plots, and has a collection of theological pamphlets (comprising 357 volumes), collected by Edmund Gibson, Bp. of L. in the 18th century. There is also in the library a fragment of a copy of the Gospels in Greek, dating from about 1050; a York Breviary of about 1330; Wycliffe's version of the Old Testament (c. 1420); a 15th-century copy of four of the *Canterbury Tales*; a Processional executed in 1480 by the Brigittine Nuns of Syon near Isleworth; a copy (wanting 16 folios) of the *Recuyell of the Historyes of Troye*, 1475; and John Lydgate's translation of Guillaume Deguilleville's *Pylgremage of the Soule*, 1483.

About 6,000 volumes were destroyed by bombs. The treasures mentioned had been removed for safety.

The library has an open-timbered hammer-beamed roof. In a stained-glass window at the S. end were figures of St. Augustine, St. Olave, Caxton, St. Martin, Bp. Mellitus, Abp. Laud, Shakespeare, Chaucer, Edmund Spenser, and Thos. White, the founder. It was badly damaged.

Dr. Williams's Library was founded under the will of Dr. Daniel Williams, who d. 1716. He bequeathed about 10,000 volumes, including the lib. of Dr. Wm. Bates, which he had purchased in

1699. It was opened in Red Cross St., Cripplegate, in 1720. At first its use was restricted to dissenters. A clause in Dr. Williams's will provided for the elimination of useless books that should never be in a public library. A first edition of Butler's *Hudibras*, included in Thos. Rowe's donation of 1737, was therefore discarded. R. A. Rye wrote:

'Butler's caustic satire must indeed have proved an embarrassing possession for a "Dissenters' Library," and the wonder is not so much that it was turned out but that it ever found its way in.'

By 1841 the preface to the catalogue said the library was 'open without distinction to all persons of all classes and parties.' The library contains about thirty 15th-century books. It has also the manuscript collection bequeathed to the library by Walter Wilson, author of *History and Antiquities of Dissenting Churches and Meeting Houses in London, Westminster, and Southwark* (1814). The library also possesses the whole of the lengthy diary of Crabb Robinson, from which selections have been published. It received 2,500 volumes from G. H. Lewes's collection. By 1865 the library numbered 22,000 volumes. In that yr. it was removed to 8 Queen St., Bloomsbury, and eight yrs. later it was transferred to Grafton St. In 1890 it went to its present home in Gordon Sq., occupying premises formerly used by Manchester Coll. before its removal to Oxford. The reading room of the library was previously the reading room of the coll. The lecture hall was previously the dining hall of the coll. It is adorned with frescoes, including forty-seven full-length representations of worthies, mostly in the realm of literature.

(See *The Libraries of London*, by R. Irwin and R. Staveley, 2nd ed. 1961.)

Lincoln's Inn derives its name from Henry Lacy, E. of Lincoln. His arms have been those of the inn for three centuries. The E.'s town house was on a different site, i.e. at the NE. corner of Shoe Lane. This property, part of the manor of Holbourne, he purchased from the Black Friars in 1286; he d. in the house in 1311. He was a royal justice and a trusted minister, and it is evident a considerable amount of legal business was transacted in his house. This continued after his death. It is thought by one writer that this was the beginning of the Soc. of Lincoln's Inn. W. P. Baildon, F.S.A., however, thought that de Lacy established his company of lawyers in Thavies Inn (*q.v.*), properly Davy's or David's Inn, opposite his own house. Wherever the first Soc. of Lincoln's Inn was located, the second occupied a site between Holborn and the Chapel of the Rolls (see 'Public Record Office'). This property was acquired in 1334 by Thos. de Lincoln, the K.'s serjeant. Three yrs. earlier he had acquired other property to the E., and in 1332 a garden to the SE. These three properties formed the inn subsequently known as 'Lyncolnesynne.' There is a reference to its being in ruins at the beginning of the 15th century, and this probably caused the removal of the soc. to the Bp. of Chichester's mansion W. of Chancellor's (Chancery) Lane. This occurred between 1415 and 1422. The 'Black Books,' as the records of Lincoln's Inn are called, commence in the latter yr. At the head of the Soc. were the masters of the bench, next in order were the utter barristers, and lastly the clerks or students. The benchers were those utter barristers who had performed the duties of reading.

None of the existing bdgs. date back to that period. The first hall of the inn probably occupied the site of the Bp.'s hall, and was demolished about 1489. The hall was used in common. In 1427 17*s*. 8½*d*. was paid for three table-cloths. Probably these were for the benchers: the juniors sat at uncovered tables, using bread as trenchers, and knives, but no forks. This was the hall in which John Fortescue sat as one of the governors 1424–5. In 1442 he became Chief Justice of the King's Bench, and continued to dine in hall when in town. He retained his office until 1460, and was present at the battle of Towton in 1461. At the battle of Tewkesbury in 1471 he was taken prisoner. He is said to have lived to be ninety. His portrait hangs in the present hall. The second hall was erected 1489–91. Entrance was through a wooden portal at the N. end, beyond which were two wooden screens. Over these was erected, in 1565, 'a stronge and fayre' gallery, and in 1578 the hall was furnished with the bench table on the dais. In the centre was the open hearth beneath the louvre. The windows at the E. end were glazed in 1454, and in 1552 fines of 12*d*. each were imposed on three young members for breaking them whilst playing ball in the hall. There was renovation of the hall in 1625, and 1657.

Hogarth, at the suggestion of Ld. Mansfield, painted his picture of 'Paul preaching before Felix.' This painting, which still hangs in the hall, was not unjustly referred to by Leigh Hunt as Hogarth's 'celebrated failure.' 'It seems hard upon a great man,' he said, 'to exhibit a specimen of what he could not do.' There was restoration in 1806. In 1819 the hall was lengthened, and in 1824 two more bar messes were added. To meals members were then summoned by a horn blown in all the courts. This hall was used by the Court of Chancery from about 1737, and is therefore the one frequently referred to by Dickens in *Bleak House*. *The Microcosm of London* includes an interesting picture (drawn by Pugin, with figures by Rowlandson), showing the Ld. Chancellor sitting at the S. end: before him are two rows of bewigged counsel, and in the rear a large stove out of harmony with the oriel window, the panelling of the walls and the roof. In 1819 a court of the Vice-Chancellor (a title now abolished) was built at the NW. angle of the hall, and in 1841 another was erected E. of the hall. Both courts were demolished in 1883. Early in the present century Mr. Justice Bucknill sat in the hall when the Royal Courts of Justice were crowded out. Between 1926 and 1928 the hall was rebuilt. It was possible to utilize some of the old stones and a little of the brickwork. The panelling was renewed with old oak, and the old 'loover' or 'lanthron' (renewed after a great wind in 1551) was reinstated. The carved stone corbels having been hacked away, they were replaced by heraldic shields displaying the royal arms as borne by Henry VII and George V (recording the sovereigns when the hall was built and repaired). The roof-tiling is modern, but reproduces a few of the old tiles that were found. The oak floor of the dais was made from the ancient material used for repairing the roof woodwork. The main floor is laid with west-country tiles after the pattern mentioned in a 14th-cenutry manuscript.

In 1518 the gateway to Chancery Lane was built. The coats of arms above are:

to the left that of Henry Lacy, E. of Lincoln (the fact that they are here is some confirmation of the belief that he was the founder of the inn); in the centre the arms of Henry VIII with the date 1518 below; on the right that of Sir Thos. Lovell. He fought at Bosworth for Henry VII in 1485, was M.P. for Northampton and Speaker of the H. of C. He was a benefactor of the inn. The great oak door dates from 1564; the postern on the N. side of the gate is of 19th-century construction; the windows, save one, are modern 'improvements.'

The members of Lincoln's Inn for two centuries utilized the chapels of Our Lady and St. Richard, which had been part of the Bp. of Chichester's palace. In 1620–3 a new chapel was erected after the plans and under the personal supervision of Inigo Jones. The opening sermon —on 22nd May 1623—was delivered by Dr. Donne, Dean of St. Paul's, and later preacher to the Soc. The chapel was so crowded that several people were nearly crushed to death. In 1685 Wren was consulted and carried out repairs. Further repairs were necessary at the end of the 18th century, and a sum of about £7,000 expended. In 1820 an organ was installed in the gallery at the W. end. The chapel was originally 60 ft. in length, 40 ft. in width, and 44 ft. in height. In 1883 an extension at the W. end was carried out under the direction of Ld. Grimthorpe. The W. end was extended, and a fourth window added on either side. Two sculptured heads on the exterior, of the Bp. of Chichester and Q. Victoria, date from this time. The armorial bearings in the W. window, with the exception of the royal arms of James I, were transferred to the first window on the S. The coats of arms in this window, with the exception of those of a few of the benchers of later date, are those of the readers, commencing with Thos. Spencer (1586), and ending with those of Jas. Stedman, the last of the readers, who read in the autumn of 1677. He afterwards became treasurer of the inn. The E. window contains the arms of the treasurers from 1680 to 1862. Those on the N. and S. were filled by figures of the prophets and apostles, and were executed by Bernard and Abraham van Linge, the Flemish artists, in 1623–6. One on the S. side shows Lincoln's Inn when it was still somewhat rural in its setting. The W. window contains the arms of readers, and continues those of the treasurers from 1863. There is only one monument and that is in the vestibule. It is in memory of Spencer Perceval, the Prime Minister, who was murdered in the H. of C. in 1812. (He was bd. at Charlton.) Scott expressed surprise at the dearth of monuments in his journal (1828):

'A very handsome place of worship; it is upstairs, which seems extraordinary, and the place beneath forms cloisters in which the ancient Benchers of the Society of Lincoln's Inn are interred. . . . There was only one monument in the chapel, a handsome tablet to the memory of Perceval. The circumstance that it was the only monument in the chapel of a society which had produced so many men of talents and distinction was striking—it was a tribute due to the suddenness of his strange catastrophe.'

Christenings rarely take place. When they do, in the absence of a font a silver gilt cup, given to G. F. Watts for his work in the hall and returned by his widow, or a silver rose-bowl, the gift, in 1925, of Ld. Justice Lawrence, are used.

The open undercroft is a unique feature of Lincoln's Inn Chapel. This was intended as a place for students and barristers 'to walk and talk and confer for their learnings.' It was used like the Round of the Temple. Butler refers to it in *Hudibras*:

'Or wait for customers between
The pillared rows of Lincoln's Inn.'

Here, in 1663, Pepys went to 'walk under the Chapel of agreement.' In the pre-umbrella era—English weather was no better than now in the 'good old times'—it was a very convenient rendezvous. It was also used as a burial ground. Here lie, amongst others, Alexander Brome, Cavalier poet (d. 1666); John Thurloe, Cromwell's Secretary of State (d. 1668); and Wm. Prynne (d. 1669), who was imprisoned in the T.L., had his ears cropped, and was fined for publishing his *Histrio-Mastix: the Players Scourge or Actors Tragedie* (1663); Sir John Anstruther, Chief Justice of Bengal (d. 1811). Of these the only one whose tombstone remains is Thurloe—with a Latin inscription.

The old hall became too small for requirements, and a new hall, W. of the old one, and built from the designs of Philip Hardwick, R.A., was opened in 1845, Q. Victoria and the P. Consort being present. The architect's initials are in the diaper-work on the S. front, and in an ornamental niche, above the apex of the S. gable, is a statue of Q. Victoria. The gable rises between large square towers of three storeys in height, and with a great window below presents an impressive exterior. The new gateway to Lincoln's Inn Fields dates from the same time. The hall beyond the towers is 120 ft. in length, 45 ft. in width, and 62 ft. in height, and consists of six bays, including the oriel formed by buttresses. There is an octagonal louvre, crowned by a weather vane. The upper portion of the N. wall is covered by G. F. Watts's 'Justice; a Hemicycle of Law-givers.' The fresco was undertaken without any promised payment except for materials, in 1854, but on completion in 1860 the inn gave him 500 sovereigns in a Russian leather purse, placed in a silver-gilt cup. There are thirty-three figures, including symbolical ones of Justice, Mercy, and Religion. Moses, Sesostris, Zoroaster, Pythagoras, Confucius, Lycurgus, Minos, Draco, Solon, Numa Pompilius, Servius Tullius, Mohammed, Charlemagne, Attila, Ina of Northumberland, Alfred, Edward I, the Es. of Pembroke and Salisbury, and Stephen Langton, Abp. of C., are represented. Several of the figures are portraits of Watts's contemporaries: Minos is Tennyson; Justinian is said to be Sir Wm. Harcourt; Ina is Holman Hunt. On the panelling round the walls are painted the arms of the treasurers, preachers, and others who have attained high office in the State. There is a number of portraits, including those of the first E. of Shaftesbury, and Sir John Fortescue. The window in the W. bay contains the arms of George V and P. Albert Victor, both benchers. There are also busts of Inigo Jones, Wm. Pitt, Ld. Denman, Ld. Lyndhurst. and Chas. Butler, K.C. In the council chamber are portraits of George V by Sargent; Roundell Palmer, Ld. Selborne (Ld. Chancellor 1872 and 1880), by G. F. Watts; Ld. Haldane, by Fiddes Watt; and H. H. Asquith, E. of Oxford, by Sir Wm. Orpen. There is a deed chest which was presented to the Soc. by Thos.

Haydon, treasurer 1548; a case containing an interesting collection of objects found on the site, including a Greek statuette in bronze, and some specimens of green-glazed ale jugs. The library, dating from 1497, 130 ft. long, has some treasured volumes, e.g. Prynne's *Records*, for which £335 was paid in 1849; *The Book of Common Prayer and Administration of the Sacraments* (1634). Bound up with it is *The Whole Book of Psalmes*, by Thos. Sternhold, John Hopkins, and others, published in 1632. The black morocco cover is embellished with eight half-length figures of the apostles; whilst the clasps have small full-length figures of the four evangelists. On each side are the arms of Henry Lacey, E. of Lincoln.

The centenary of the opening of the Great Hall and Library was celebrated in 1945 by a party which was attended by Q. Mary, as one of the benchers. The Queen planted a walnut tree in the garden.

The chambers erected on the N. side of the gateway were earlier in date than those on the S. side. They were built in 1536, enlarged about thirty yrs. later, and rebuilt in 1607, and the whole block reconstructed in 1872. At present, therefore, the chambers on the S. side attract far more interest. They were probably built about the yr. 1562. At No. 24 lived John Thurloe, already mentioned, from 1646-59. A piquant story is related of his residence there. Cromwell came to confer with his secretary on the subject of a plot to decoy Charles and his brothers, the Ds. of York and Gloucester, from Bruges to England, and to assassinate them on arrival. During the discussion Cromwell observed that Thurloe's clerk, Samuel Morland, was in the room apparently asleep. Cromwell, fearing that this conversation had been overheard, drew his dagger, and was proposing summarily to dispatch him. Thurloe, however, begged for his life, as he was confident that he was asleep, and to prove it passed a candle close in front of his face. The clerk was, in fact, awake, and conveyed the intelligence to Charles, so that he evaded the trap. Charles II subsequently rewarded Morland with a knighthood. From 1659-68 Thurloe lived in Dial Court—in chambers now demolished. Here, in the reign of William III, a large mass of papers was discovered hidden in a false ceiling in one of the garrets. A clergyman, temporarily occupying the rooms during the long vacation, made the discovery. Apparently he was allowed to retain them, for subsequently he sold them to Ld. Somers, who had them bound in sixty-seven volumes. A selection was published in 1742 by Dr. Birch, a well-known antiquary. There is a tablet recording Thurloe's residence in Chancery Lane—a few yds. S. of the gatehouse. In Chancery Lane, according to Fuller, Ben Jonson was found by a bencher laying bricks. In Gatehouse Court, N. of the gateway, Wm. Murray, afterwards Ld. Mansfield, first studied law; while at No. 2 another great lawyer, Ld. Campbell, occupied chambers. Among modern occupants in this part of Old Sq. was Thos. Hughes, the author of *Tom Brown's Schooldays.*

At 1 New Sq. Arthur Murphy, dramatist and biographer of Dr. Johnson, lived from about 1757 to 1780. At No. 2 Sir Samuel Romilly resided before he went to No. 6. Of No. 11, Sir John Scott, afterwards Ld. Eldon, took a lease in 1794. Stone Bdgs. were erected about 1775. There Wm. Pitt occupied a set of chambers when he was treasurer of the inn in 1794. Both New Square and Stone Buildings sustained considerable damage during the Second World War.

Distinguished members of Lincoln's Inn not previously mentioned have been Sir Thos. More, admitted in 1496, when 18 yrs. of age; Robt. Harley, E. of Oxford (1701); David Garrick (1737); Ld. Erskine (1775); W. E. Gladstone (1833); Chas. Kingsley (1839); Wilkie Collins (1846); Ld. Morley (bencher 1891); H. H. Asquith (called to bar 1876).

(See *Gray's Inn and Lincoln's Inn,* by H. L. Bellot, 1925; *Some Account of the Old Hall of Lincoln's Inn,* by Sir John Simpson, 1928; *The Romance of Lincoln's Inn,* by E. Beresford Chancellor 1933; *Short History of Lincoln's Inn,* by Sir Gerald Hurst, 1946; *Lincoln's Inn, its History and Traditions,* by Sir Wm. Ball, 1947; *The Origin of Lincoln's Inn,* by Sir Ronald Roxbrugh, 1963.)

Lincoln's Inn Fields take their name from the Inn of Chancery. They represent what, in 1592, were known as Cup Field and Purse Field; another small area on the S. (bounded by Portugal St., Carey St., and Serle St.) was known as Fickett's Field. These were open spaces for the citizens to walk and take the air. A petition of the inhabitants of the neighbourhood during the time of the Commonwealth, stated that Fickett's Field 'was a common walking and sporting place for the citizens of London' in 1376. A portion of the ground was known as 'Campum Templariorum' (field of the Templars), and was probably used by them as a jousting ground. This explains the proximity of a forge, for which a quit-rent is still paid (see 'Customs'). It was not until the later yrs. of Q. Elizabeth that the fields began to be built upon, and Agas's map (*c.* 1562) shows only about three houses in a position approximating to the present Sardinia St. Between there and Holborn is another row, on the N. side, of about three houses. Lincoln's Inn Fields were occasionally used for executions, and here in 1586 Anthony Babington and some of his confederates suffered the extreme penalty in its most diabolical form. Froude wrote:

'They were hanged but for a moment, according to the letter of the sentence, taken down whilst the susceptibility of agony was unimpaired, and cut in pieces afterwards with due precautions for the protraction of the pain.'

Q. Elizabeth, apparently horrified at the report of this agony, forbade its repetition, and the rest of the victims were hanged until they were dead. There is perhaps some allusion to a scene like this in the cry of Shakespeare's Macbeth: 'As they had seen me with these hangman's hands.' The execution probably took place here for a particular reason. Babington was a Catholic, implicated in plots in favour of Mary Q. of Scots, and in Lincoln's Inn Fields had been found a wax figure of Elizabeth pierced with pins, a means whereby witchcraft then was supposed to contrive the death of a person so represented. This was probably held to be an intimation that here the conspirators had met, and so the place of punishment was made to fit the crime. At a later period it was the secret resort of Catholics. In Little Turnstile, at the NW. corner, is the Ship Tavern. There is outside the following inscription:

'This tavern was established in the year 1549. During the proscription of the Roman Catholic religion it was used as a shelter for Priests, and Services were held here secretly. The neighbourhood was once notorious for the gambling houses of Whetstone Park. Famous visitors have been Richard Penderell who aided King Charles's escape, Bayford, shoemaker and antiquarian, the woman Chevalier d'Eon who lived as a man, and Smeaton, builder of the first Eddystone Lighthouse. It was a centre of Freemasonry and a Lodge with the number 234 was consecrated here by the Grand Master the Earl of Antrim in 1786.'

There were four different ways to approach the ancient tavern—the present one is modern despite the inscription—Holborn, Gate St., Whetstone Park, or Lincoln's Inn Fields. Leopold Wagner wrote:

'The worshippers called for a mug of ale at the bar and at once passed into the parlour. If, as sometimes happened, the waiter stationed at the door gave a warning sign, the priest sought a convenient hiding-place upstairs, and nothing more incriminating than drinking, smoking and talking declared itself to the emissaries of the State when they looked in.'

The embassy referred to was lodged in two houses where is now Sardinia St. The chapel was erected in 1648. In 1688 it was in possession of the Franciscans and, stirred by James II's ill-timed attempts to impose Roman Catholicism, the mob attacked it, and made a fire in the Fields of crucifixes and other idolatrous objects. A silver medallion was struck to commemorate this event, and, says Beresford Chancellor,

'the wrath of heaven is depicted by lightnings, although whether aimed at the Franciscans or their depredators, seems a little uncertain.'

The Franciscans were naturally obliged to depart after this episode, and the mansion remained untenanted until the beginning of the 18th century, when it was taken as the Portuguese embassy. The exact date of the Sardinian embassy's occupation is unknown; it was some time prior to 1729. The house was greatly damaged by fire in 1759. It was attacked again during the 'No Popery' riots of 1780, as Dickens mentions in the early part of *Barnaby Rudge*. Books, benches, and other appurtenances of the chapel were brought out and burnt. In 1737 there was

baptized in the chapel Joseph Nollekens, the sculptor (whose life was so delightfully written by John Thos. Smith); and in 1793 there were m. there Fanny Burney (a favourite of Dr. Johnson's and the author of *Evelina*) and General D'Arblay. Dr. Arne, who in 1748 was living in Great Queen St., was organist here for a time. About the middle of the 19th century the chapel passed out of the hands of the Sardinian ambassador, although until 1858 it remained under the patronage of the K. of Sardinia. It became vested in the chaplains and vicars apostolic. In 1853 the name of the Sardinian Chapel was changed to 'St. Anselm's, Duke Street,' and in 1861 it became known as 'the Church of St. Anselm and St. Cecilia.' The original name of the st. was inscribed on an archway, 'Duke Streete 1648'; in 1878, the name was changed to Sardinia St. The chapel remained until 1909, when, together with the old archway, it was demolished. A new Roman Catholic Ch. on the E. side of Kingsway was similarly dedicated. It contains a few of the fittings from the older building.

By the time of the erection of the chapel in 1648 Lincoln's Inn Fields had been to some extent laid out. A commission was given to Inigo Jones, then royal surveyor-general, to draw up a plan of the area, with a view to frustrating the designs of those who (in the words of a petition lodged with the Privy Council by the Soc. of Lincoln's Inn),

'doe goe about to erect buildings in a field neere unto them called Lincoln's Inn Fielde, with an intent to convert the whole feild into new buildings contrary to His Majestie's Proclamacion.'

By 1641 nearly all the S. and W. sides of the Fields had been covered with houses. The only house now remaining which is believed to have been of Inigo Jones's architecture is Lindsey House (Nos. 59 and 60). The Civil War interrupted the scheme, which was never completed by Inigo Jones, who d. 1652.

In 1683 another execution took place here, as recorded on a tablet in the centre of the shelter in the gardens. Ld. Wm. Russell met his end for alleged complicity in the Rye House Plot. His last days, and his wife's noble but vain efforts to obtain a reprieve, have been related with feeling and art by Leigh Hunt in *The*

Town. The D. of York (afterwards James II), with a horrible refinement of cruelty, at first proposed that he should be executed outside his own residence— Southampton House, Bloomsbury Sq. After execution the body was taken to Lindsey House, where the head was sewn on, after which it was taken to Southampton House, prior to burial at Chenies (Bucks.).

The land here appears to have been unenclosed, except by a few posts and rails, up to about 1735, and according to the *Trivia* of John Gay (1716) was a place of considerable danger.

'Where Lincoln's Inn wide space is rail'd around,
Cross not with vent'rous step; there oft is found
The lurking thief, who while the daylight shone,
Made the walls echo with his begging tone:
That crutch which late compassion mov'd, shall wound
Thy bleeding head and fell thee to the ground.'

A preamble to an Act of 1735 stated that the sq. had 'become a receptacle for rubbish dirt nastiness of all sorts,' and that

'many wicked and disorderly persons have frequented and met together therein, using unlawful sports and games, and drawing in and enticing young persons into gaming, idleness and other vicious courses; and vagabonds, common beggars and other disorderly persons resort therein, where many robberies, assaults, outrages and enormities have been and continually are committed.'

It was reported too, that owing to the roughness of the ground, the Master of the Rolls had, when riding on horseback, received such hurt that he was still lame. The Act was to enable the residents to enclose the Fields, and they were laid out with grass and gravel walks, and enclosed with an iron palisade upon a stone plinth. In the centre was a large basin filled with water. This was a source of much anxiety to the twenty-one trustees who had been elected by the householders, and in 1790 it was filled up. In the early part of the 19th century the garden was arranged largely on the present plan. In 1876 there was a movement to throw it open to the public, and in 1880, with this in view, the D. of Westminster headed a deputation to the M.B.W. In 1891 the trustees were approached by the Public Gardens Association, represented by the E. of Meath, but with no result. In 1894 the trustees agreed to surrender their rights, and to lease the garden to the L.C.C. for $661\frac{1}{2}$ yrs. (the remainder of the 900 yrs. lease granted originally to the benchers of Lincoln's Inn) for the sum of £12,000, and a nominal rent of £1 p.a. Since then it has been open to the public.

A few of the important houses demand attention. Lindsey House, already mentioned, was once said to have been erected for Robt. Bertie, E. of Lindsey, but the investigations of the L.C.C. Survey Committee have shown that this was an error. It was built—in 1640—by Sir David Cunningham. It originally possessed a fine entrance gate flanked by six brick piers; of the latter only two remain. In 1652 it was in the possession of the Hon. Chas. Rich, son of the E. of Warwick. Lady Warwick wrote an autobiography in which various references to the house include the fact that her eldest son d. of smallpox here in 1664. It then passed into the hands of one of L.'s eccentrics, the Marquess of Winchester, afterwards D. of Bolton. In 1703 it was in the occupation of Robt. Bertie, 4th E. of Lindsey, from whom its later name was derived. About 1752 it was divided into two, and in No. 59 Spencer Perceval lived from 1791 to 1808.

Newcastle House, at the corner of Great Queen St., was originally known as Powis House, having been erected in 1685 by Wm. Herbert, E. of Powis. Before the new residence was actually finished the owner, a Roman Catholic, had followed James II into exile, and his new house was threatened by the rioters who attacked the Sardinian Chapel. The Lds. Commissioners of the Treasury proposed to occupy it as an official residence, and Sir Christopher Wren surveyed it for that purpose. Having been renovated in accordance with his recommendations, it was occupied by Ld. Somers in 1697, the yr. in which he was appointed Ld. Chancellor. In 1700 he was dismissed from the office, and succeeded by Sir Nathan Wright. In 1705 the house was restored to the Marquess of Powis, who sold it to John Holles, D. of Newcastle, the price being £7,500. The offices of the Great Seal had been transferred to 51 and 52 Lincoln's Inn Fields, but as the new owner had been appointed Ld. Keeper of the Privy Seal, he determined to make Newcastle House, as it was then called, his private residence. In 1711, on his death, it became the abode of his nephew and successor, Thos. Pelham-Holles, afterwards D. of Newcastle. The new owner employed Sir John Vanbrugh to reconstruct it. Amongst Vanbrugh's work were two arcades, one of which—on the N. side—remains. The double staircase was of a slightly later date. The D., who became Prime Minister, in 1753, was a great Whig, with rather a small brain, according to most of his contemporaries.

If the D. did not adorn his office, he did adorn his house. It was said that one of his guests here gave the death-blow to the custom of bestowing on all domestics vails or tips. On one occasion they were all lined up in his hall to receive gratuities from parting guests. Sir Timothy Waldo gave the cook five shillings. 'I don't take silver, sir,' said that gentleman. 'Don't you indeed?' replied Sir Timothy, pocketing the money, 'and I don't give gold.' A frequent caller was Sir Thos. Robinson. If his Grace were denied him, he would ask permission to enter the hall and look at the clock or play with the monkey, in the hope of intercepting the D. on his way out. The servants wearied of his importunity, and so the formula used to be, when Sir Thos. called: 'Sir, his Grace has gone out, the clock has stopped, and the monkey is dead.' The D. of Newcastle d. in 1768, and in 1771 the house was sold by the widow to a banker. One of the subsequent occupiers was the Soc. for the Promotion of Christian Knowledge, who purchased the freehold in 1825. The Soc., after being here for about half a century, was followed by Messrs. Ingram Harrison & Co., solicitors. On their failure, after a period of vacancy, it was taken by Sir Wm. Farrer. In 1930 certain defects were found, necessitating rebuilding, and the owner, Mr. H. L. Farrer, decided to rebuild on the lines of the original mansion, of which an engraving exists. So the present structure, designed by Sir Edwin Lutyens, represents, with certain inevitable modifications, the house which the E. of Powis had begun, and which the D. of Newcastle completed. Before these changes were carried out, the old house had on its façade the arms of various notable people who had occupied it. As E. Beresford Chancellor said:

'The place, in spite of rebuilding remains a splendid example of a noble residence of the late seventeenth and early eighteenth centuries, and recalls perhaps better than anything else in Lincoln's Inn Fields, the day when the quality lived there, and it was as fashionable as Grosvenor Square was to become later.'

Nos. 57 and 58 represent what was once one house, erected by Sir Edwd. Bellingham in 1640. The original house on the site was that of Pepys's master, Ld. Sandwich. He occupied it in 1664, paying £250 p.a. rent. Pepys called it 'a fine house but deadly dear.' A later resident, Chas. Tate, who became Ld Chancellor, rebuilt it. It was divided in 1795, and No. 58 from 1834 to 1856 was the residence of John Forster, the friend and biographer of Dickens, who introduced it into *Bleak House*, as the residence of Mr. Tulkinghorn. There was in one room a painted ceiling, with a figure whose finger seemed to point down at the lawyer's corpse when he had been murdered. Here it was, as shown in Maclise's drawing, that in 1844 Dickens read the manuscript of *The Chimes* to a group of literary gentlemen, including Thos. Carlyle.

In the gardens of Lincoln's Inn Fields on the N. side, is a memorial to Mrs Ramsay MacDonald. It represents a group of happy children, with Mrs. MacDonald in their midst, and the inscription reads:

'She was the daughter of John and Margaret Gladstone. She was born in Kensington in 1870, was married to J. Ramsay MacDonald in 1896, and lived with him at 3 Lincoln's Inn Fields. Here her children were born and here she died in 1911. She brought joy to those with whom and for whom she lived and worked. Her heart went out in fellowship to her fellow women and in love to the children of the people whom she served as a citizen and helped as a sister. She quickened faith and zeal in others by her life and took no rest from doing good.'

It was erected in Dec. 1914. The sculptor was Mr. Richd. R. Goulden.

On the S. side there is a memorial to the second Viscount Hambleden (1865–1928), 'head of the firm of W. H. Smith & Son,' whose premises are in Portugal St.

The N. side is called Canada Row, in honour of the Canadian Air Force whose headquarters were there. There is a memorial tablet, close to a maple tree planted by Alderman W. E. Mullen, Mayor of Holborn in 1945.

The Royal Coll. of Surgeons and Soane Mus. are dealt with separately.

(See *Lincoln's Inn Fields*, by C. W. Heckethorn, 1896; *L.C.C. Survey Committee*, Vol. 3, 1912; *Romance of Lincoln's Inn Fields*, by Beresford Chancellor, 1933.)

Lloyd's (Corporation of). Marine insurance, which in some form or another had been known on the Continent since the Middle Ages, was first practised in this country in the 16th century, and merchants, bankers, and others who undertook such risks became known as 'underwriters' because they wrote their names one under the other as they assumed responsibility for their own proportion of an insurance venture. After the Royal Exchange was destroyed in the G.F. various groups of citizens who had met there daily had to find other meeting-places and by 1687 those interested in shipping and in marine insurance were frequenting the Coffee House of Edward Lloyd in Tower Street.

Newspapers, save for a few occasional news-sheets, did not exist. Coffee houses were centres of news and gossip, and Lloyd employed a number of 'runners' who collected news of all kinds—especially concerning ships and shipping. When such information reached the Coffee House it was read to the customers by a boy called the 'kidney' from a 'pulpit' from which ships and gear were also auctioned. Steele in the *Tatler* (1712) describes the scene. The last vessel to be sold by auction at Lloyd's was the *Great Eastern* in 1881.

From these beginnings have developed the two phases of the institution which is called 'Lloyd's.' Underwriters, frequenting a coffee house to meet their clients and transact their business, laid the foundation of a great Insurance Bourse or Exchange which affords no parallel in any other Country. The collection of maritime news has also developed, and Lloyd's to-day is the world's centre of marine information where the movements of every vessel under every flag in the world is daily (and nightly) recorded.

Lloyd moved to Lombard St. at the corner of Abchurch Lane (a C.C. tablet marks the site). He d. in 1712 and was succeeded by his son-in-law. He was bd. in the Ch. of St. Mary Woolnoth (see 'City Churches'—C) where a tablet to his memory has been placed by the Corporation of Lloyd's. In 1696 he had circulated a small news-sheet called *Lloyd's News*, which owing to the inclusion of some prohibited Parliamentary news was suppressed in the following year. It was revived as *Lloyd's List*, but in another form, in 1734, and has been published continuously for 216 years and is thus one of the oldest newspapers in this country.

In 1720, the year of the South Sea Bubble, the first marine insurance companies (the London and the Royal Exchange) were granted a Royal Charter which gave them, jointly and severally, the monopoly of Marine Insurance for a century. But although other companies and even partnerships were forbidden to act, individuals ('private insurers') were allowed under the Charter to continue, and thus the background of individualism was established under which Lloyd's has developed.

Throughout the 18th century there was no real organization, but the Coffee House became something of an informal Club, the only official being the Master, who managed the Coffee House, arranged for auction sales of ships and gear, collected subscriptions, was responsible for the publication of *Lloyd's List*, kept the Book of Arrivals and Losses, and established correspondents in home and foreign ports.

In 1760 the first printed *Register of Ships* was issued. In 1769 there was a division in the Coffee House. Some of the younger and less responsible underwriters embarked upon hazardous and speculative schemes and the majority of the leading underwriters, brokers, and merchants transferred their meeting place to Pope's Head Alley in Cornhill as

'New Lloyd's Coffee House.' Gradually the Lombard St. establishment declined, and passed out of existence, when the word 'New' was dropped.

In 1771 Lloyd's became a formal organization, but without a standing Committee or Chairman. Committees were appointed for specific purposes and various underwriters took the Chair at General Meetings. The first Minute Book dates from this year.

In 1774, largely through the initiative of John Julius Angerstein (the 'Father of Lloyd's'), underwriters took a suite of rooms on the first floor of the Royal Exchange. The Refreshment Room, in which auctions were also held, became known as the 'Captain's Room,' and business was carried on in the 'Subscribers' Room'—the complete suite being known as 'Lloyd's Coffee House within the Royal Exchange.'

In 1800, all subscribers to Lloyd's, who were now limited to merchants, bankers, underwriters, and brokers, had to be elected by ballot. In 1802 underwriters assisted Henry Greathead, the inventor of the lifeboat, to perfect and patent his invention, and subscribed a sum during the following years to place 26 lifeboats around the coast. In 1824 the National Lifeboat Association was founded, and underwriters still subscribe annually to maintain one of the lifeboats of the Association.

In 1808 Lloyd's Patriotic Fund was inaugurated, and during its history large sums have been raised for patriotic and philanthropic purposes—mainly in connection with the sea. In 1804, Earl Camden, Secretary at War, declining to 'enter into epistolatory communications with waiters at Lloyd's Coffee House,' the Assistant Master, John Bennett Jun., was appointed to be the first Secretary. He remained in office until his death in 1834.

Lloyd's agency system was set up in 1811, the first agent being appointed at Falmouth. There are now Lloyd's agents in all parts of the world, and from them come at all hours of the day and night news of the movements and fortunes of every vessel throughout the world. In 1811, a Deed of Trust was drawn up and remained in force until the passing of Lloyd's Act in 1871.

In 1838 the second Royal Exchange was destroyed by fire, and underwriters met at various places; finally, at South Sea House until the completion of the new Exchange in 1844, when they moved back into the present bdg. In 1840 the title of 'Coffee House' was finally dropped, but the Post Office continued to use it until the end of 1918.

In 1852 the first Lloyd's signal station was erected at Deal, and in 1870 the system of cash deposits by all underwriters as security for policies signed in their names, was made compulsory.

In 1871 Lloyd's Act passed into law, and Lloyd's now became a legal entity— the Corporation of Lloyd's. During the decade following 1880 the non-marine market came into existence, and now all forms of insurance (except life and one or two other forms of indemnity) are underwritten at Lloyd's.

Business at Lloyd's having increased rapidly after the First World War, accommodation in the Royal Exchange became more and more inadequate and the Corporation acquired a site in Leadenhall St. formerly covered by the East India House (*q.v.*), and built thereon a new Underwriting Room and offices, the architect being the late Sir Edwin Cooper. During the short period of time which elapsed since its opening in 1925, these premises became insufficient and a further new building on an area between Lime St. and Billiter St. was built.

Amongst the treasures of Lloyd's are a number of old documents, including a policy dated 20th Jan. 1680–1, underwritten at the Coffee House and believed to be the oldest existing original policy effected in this country. The policy insured the *Golden Fleece* on a voyage from Lisbon to Venice, the rate being 4%. The wording remained unaltered until 1779 when, with a few slight alterations, it was adopted as the standard wording and has so remained until the present day. There is also a policy insuring a cargo of slaves, dated 1794; a marine policy underwritten at Marseilles during the French Revolution; and a contingency policy agreeing to pay if Napoleon Bonaparte 'ceased to exist or be taken prisoner' before a specified date in 1813.

The unique collection of Nelson relics includes a number of Nelson's personal possessions; some articles of silver plate which formed part of a dinner service presented to the Admiral after one of his victories by underwriters at Lloyd's; his Collar of the Order of the Bath, a number of letters written by him (one of them before he lost his right arm at Teneriffe); and the logbook of the *Euryalus*, one of the smaller supporting vessels at Trafalgar which contains what is believed to be the only record of Nelson's immortal signal written whilst the battle was actually in progress.

The *Lutine* Bell was salved from the wreck of the *Lutine*, a French ship captured and taken into the British Navy. It was carrying a cargo of specie (all of which was insured at Lloyd's) and was sunk off Terschelling in Holland in 1799. A salvage expedition between 1857 and 1861 resulted in the recovery of about a quarter of the cargo and other relics included the bell, rudder and a gun. The bell hangs in the Rostrum in the middle of the Underwriting Room and is rung when important announcements are made. When news of a vessel posted as 'overdue' comes to hand it is rung, once for a loss and twice for an arrival.

There are now 6,000 underwriter members who are grouped in around 300 syndicates. Business with the insuring public must be transacted through the medium of brokers, who are the only authorised intermediaries between underwriters and the public. The Coffee House tradition still survives, as underwriters sit to do business in 'boxes' similar to those in a 17th-century Coffee House and the uniformed attendants are called 'waiters.' (See *Lloyds of London*, by D. E. W. Gibb, 1957.)

London Clubs. The clubbable disposition is very old, though evidence is vague regarding its manifestations before the latter part of the 16th century. There is trace of one known as *Le Court de Bone Compagnie* in the reign of Henry IV (*c.* 1400). Of this club the medieval poet Occleve left a description. Late in the 16th century there is a suggestion of a club at the Mermaid Tavern, called the Bread St. or the Friday St. Club; there were entrances to that hostelry from both turnings. This is said to have been founded by Sir Walter Raleigh. There is no evidence that Shakespeare ever went there. If he had, Francis Beaumont would hardly have addressed his famous lines to Ben Jonson. Ben Jonson founded an Apollo Club at the Devil in Fleet St. (See 'Taverns.')

Nothing is heard of these clubs when the Puritans gained power. Probably they were suppressed with the theatres.

It is odd that so unstimulating a beverage as coffee seems to have warmed the heart of man and made him more clubbable. Bernard Darwin, in his book, *British Clubs*, begins with 'a mysterious Cretan undergraduate who used to have coffee in his rooms at Balliol. He was expelled from the University, not on this ground, in 1648, but he had sown the seed.' Pepys in 1660 records three visits to a 'Coffee Club,' in Westminster. This, no doubt, was purely social. Its real name was the Rota Club, and it was founded in 1659 by Jas. Harrington, author of *The Commonwealth of Oceana*. Political clubs were soon to follow. In 1675 came the Green Ribbon Club. Of this Dr. G. M. Trevelyan wrote:

'That Club occupied the King's Head Tavern at the west side of Chancery Lane End, opposite to Inner Temple; it was named after the new party colours that had succeeded to "Presbyterian true blue." Before the Club was founded in 1675 no party in England ever had a local habitation, beyond such as was afforded by the private hospitality of individual chiefs. Certainly no party ever before showed such organising power as the Green Ribbon men. When a display of force was needed, Southwark and Wapping were called out by the Club, like the Faubourg St. Antoine by the Jacobins. Although in the streets of London the mob might only massacre priests in effigy, the work of the Green Ribbon was no child's play, and resembled that of the Jacobin Club in many of its functions'

The King's Head Tavern was on the E. side of Chancery Lane. There is a C.C. plaque.

With a king over the water—or about to go—a Sealed Knot Club was founded in 1688. About 1700 Jacob Tonson, publisher, founded the Kit-Cat Club, to which reference is made under the heading 'National Portrait Gallery.' It met at Shire Lane, Temple Bar. There was a 'Scriblerius' Club which was started by Swift in 1711—during his residence at

Chelsea, and seems to have been the first literary fraternity. John Gay, Alexander Pope, and Dr. Arbuthnot were members. The last was physician to Q. Anne, and the meetings took place in his rooms at St. James's Palace. The quarrels between Robt. Harley, E. of Oxford and Viscount Bolingbroke brought it to an end. In 1710 the October Club was founded by 150 staunch Tories who met at the 'Bell,' King St., Westminster. According to Justin McCarthy (*A History of the Four Georges and William IV*, 1905), their object was 'to drink October ale, under Dahl's portrait of Queen Anne, and to trouble with their fierce uncompromising Jacobitism the fluctuating purposes of Harley and the crafty counsels of St. John.'

Justin McCarthy rightly doubted the existence of the Calves' Head Club. Whilst after the Restoration groups here and there favoured the usurpation, as royalists had called it, it is doubtful if there was any real organization. In a book attributed to Ned Ward there is a picture of such a Club at dinner. On the wall is an axe. On the table is a calf's head, supposed to be symbolical of the Stuart adherents; there is a boar's head, said to symbolise voracity, and a pike to represent tyranny. One of Tom Brown's *Letters from the Dead to the Living* (1702) is 'An Answer by the Calves Head Club to Ludlow the Regicide.' Both Ned Ward and Tom Brown mixed up fact and fiction in a desire to be above all things facetious, and this is not evidence. Moreover some of the clubs referred to in the former's *Secret History of Clubs* are obviously as chimerical as some mentioned by Addison in the *Spectator*. The following appeared in the *Gentleman's Magazine* for Feb. 1735, under date 30th Jan.:

'Some young noblemen and gentlemen met at a house in Suffolk Street calling themselves the Calves' Head Club; dres'd up a calf's head in a napkin and after some huzzas threw it into a bonfire, and dipt napkins in their red wine and waved them out at window. The mob had strong beer given them and for a time holloo'd as well as the best; but taking disgust at some healths proposed grew so outrageous that they broke all the windows and forced themselves into the House, but the Guards being sent for prevented further mischief.'

It appears from a letter quoted by John Timbs that there were no grounds for suspecting anything in the way of a Club meeting, or in fact any allusion to the execution of Charles I. This is the last heard of this dubious club.

WHITE'S CLUB (St. James's St.). It was founded in 1693. It began in a chocolate house, which was on the W. side of St. James's St., and its name is derived from a steward there. In this regard it is similar to Lloyd's Corporation, where the founder was a man of small importance. White carried on his business until death in 1711. His widow then continued, and Mrs. White's Chocolate House in St. James's St. became an agency for the distribution of tickets for the varied amusements of the aristocracy. Richd. Steele was a frequenter, and some issues of *The Tatler* were inscribed from there. John Gay mentioned it in *Trivia*, and Pope, in *The Dunciad*, referred to 'Familiar White.'

On the death of Mrs. White one John Arthur became proprietor. The premises were burned down in 1733, and during rebuilding there was resort to Gaunt's Coffee House. In 1736 the new structure was available and, as a Club, White's dates from then. It was intimated that the Chocolate House was not open to all and sundry, and a subscription of a guinea was imposed. There was blackballing of candidates, and in 1752 Horace Walpole wrote to his friend Sir Horace Mann mentioning one who had only six white balls out of twelve, although he had been promised eight.

Its members were notorious for gambling, and in 1748, when a Gaming Act was passed, Walpole suggested that the Club would 'put up an escutcheon for the death of play.' In 1755, in one night, one member lost £32,000, though he recovered the greater part of it. 'The citizens,' wrote Walpole, 'put on their double channeled pumps and trudge to St. James's Street in expectation of seeing judgment executed on White's—angels with flaming swords, and Devils flying away with dice boxes.' In 1755 the Club moved to its present premises (at the NE. end of St. James' St.)—the 'Great House' as it was called. It was once the residence of the Countess of Northumberland. In 1775 the subscription was raised to ten guineas, and the membership restricted to 151. Under new rules of 1797, the regulation Club dinner was 10s. 6d., and there were hot suppers at 8s. It was further ordained that 'every member who plays at Chess, Draughts, or Backgammon, do pay one shilling each time of playing by daylight and half a crown each by candlelight.' Although White's Club was very select, by 1800 the membership was raised to 450.

In 1811 the front of the Club-house was altered there being installed the fine bow window. In 1814 White's gave a ball at Burlington House to the Emperor of Russia, the K. of Prussia, and the allied sovereigns then in England. Covers were laid for 2,400, and the cost was £9,849. On 6th July there was a dinner in honour of the D. of Wellington, and this cost £2,480. Richd. Bush, the American minister to Gt. Britain, was in L. in 1818. He wrote: 'Let me here relate what I heard of one of the clubs—White's —a great Tory Club in St. James's. Somebody spoke of the lights kept burning there all night. "Yes," said a member, "they have not been out I should think since the reign of Charles II."' If the member had said William III he might have been right. In 1850 the façade of the Club-house was remodelled, and four bas-reliefs representing the four seasons were erected. Gaming proceeded until well into the Victorian era, as the still existing betting book shows. On 17th July, 1856, is the following entry:

'Mr. F. Cavendish bets Mr. H. Brownrigg 2-1 that he does not kill a blue bottle fly before he goes to bed. . . .

'W. Frederick Cavendish. -

'Henry M. Brownrigg, recd. H.B.'

It is extraordinary that a ban on tobacco was maintained until 1845. when it was permissible to smoke cigars only in the special room assigned for such practices. In 1866 some of the young members wished to be permitted to smoke in the drawing-room. This decadent departure from prescribed rules was bitterly opposed by the elder members. The non-smokers prevailed, greatly to the annoyance of Albert Edward, P. of Wales, who expressed his displeasure at this ban on tobacco. For this reason he supported the foundation of the Marlborough Club, in 1869.

THE SUBLIME SOCIETY OF BEEFSTEAKS was founded in 1735, and met at the George and Vulture, destined to greater fame a century after as the residence of Samuel Pickwick. The founder was John Rich, producer of Gay's *Beggars' Opera* and proprietor of Covent Garden Theatre. Amongst the 24 members with which the Club started there were Sir John Thornhill and his son-in-law, Wm. Hogarth. Rule 4 was: 'That beef-steaks shall be the only meat for dinner and the broiling begin at two of the clock on each day of meeting, and the table cloth be removed at half an hour after three.' The members at first wore brass buttons impressed with a gridiron and the motto 'Beef and Liberty.' Amongst its members were Frederick, P. of Wales, and John Wilkes. One member, Chas. Morris, wrote a song which commenced:

'Like Briton's island lies our steak,
   A sea of gravy bounds it;
Shalots, confus'dly scattered, make
   The rockwork that surrounds it.'

The Club ceased to exist in 1867, and the property was sold at Christie's two yrs. later. A gridiron—not the original one— brought £5 15s. There was also sold a bust of Wilkes and portraits of Churchill and Garrick. At the time of the Club's dissolution the Duke of Leinster had been a member for 45 yrs. In 1876 a Beef Steak Club was formed. Its headquarters were at Toole's Theatre. Its small membership consisted of men in political, literary, and theatrical circles.

BOODLE'S (St. James's St.). It was founded in 1763 (presumably by a now unknown Boodle), and originally was the *Savoir Vivre*. The first Club-house was built in 1765. Gibbon was a member, and dated letters from Boodle's in 1772 and 1774. The premises were much altered, 1821-4, when a reading room was added. It was much favoured by men of rank, and the celebrated caricaturist, Gillray, drew a picture called 'A standing dish at Boodles'. It represented Sir Frank Standish sitting at one of the windows of the Club. It was said that anyone uttering the words 'Where's Sir John?' in the Club-house would immediately find himself surrounded by a crowd of members.

BROOKS' CLUB (St. James's St.). It was founded in Pall Mall in 1764 by 27 noblemen and gentlemen, including the D. of Roxburgh, the D. of Portland, the

D. of Richmond, the D. of Grafton, and the E. of Strathmore. It was, to begin with, a gaming house, first farmed by Wm. Almack, a wine merchant, later to be associated with the famous assembly rooms in King St., St. James's. In 1778 a move was made to the present premises, and from then it was known as Brooks'. In 1779 the subscription was eight guineas; in 1791 it was raised to ten guineas, with an entrance fee of five guineas. In 1828 the subscription became eleven guineas. The high subscription seems to have been too much for some of the members, for in 1809 it was reported that the arrears amounted to £10,000.

Like White's, it was a great place for gambling. Fox, according to Croker, once staked '£5,000 on a single card at faro and he talked of £7,000 lost and won in one night.' Appropriately with these nocturnal diversions, members were elected between 11 p.m. and 1 a.m. One black ball excluded, and Sheridan was thus excluded three times by Geo. Selwyn. On the fourth occasion he was successful through a ruse of George P. of Wales (afterwards George IV) who held Selwyn in conversation whilst the voting was proceeding. Sir Philip Francis, reputed author of the *Letters of Junius*, was a member of Brooks'. He had done great deeds with the dice in Calcutta where he had an official appointment. He is said there to have won £30,000. Garrick, Burke, Pitt and Gibbon were members. Wm. Wilberforce, the future philanthropist, in his salad days was a man about town, and a member of Brooks' and other clubs. Seeing him engaged in faro, with Selwyn in the bank, a friend said, 'Why, Wilberforce, is that you?' Selwyn resented the interference, and turned to him and said in his most expressive tone, 'Oh, sir, don't interrupt. Mr. Wilberforce could not be better employed.' John Campbell (afterwards Ld. Campbell) thought it a great privilege to belong. In 1822 he wrote to his father:

'To belong to it is a feather in my cap. Indeed since we lost our estates in the County of Angus I am inclined to think that my election at Brooks' is the greatest distinction our house has met with. The Club consists of the first men of rank and talent in England.'

Radicals were not very welcome, and Palmerston was not elected until 1830.

(See *Memorials of Brooks' from 1764 to the Close of the Nineteenth Century*, 1907.)

THE LITERARY CLUB. It was founded by Sir Joshua Reynolds and Samuel Johnson in 1764. It met first at the Turk's Head, Gerrard St., Soho, every Monday at seven. In 1772 the night was changed to Friday. When the Turk's Head was converted into a private residence, the Club moved to Prince's in Sackville St., then to Le Telier's in Dover St. At the time Boswell published his *Life of Johnson* (1792) it was at Parsloe's, St. James's St. Amongst the original members were Edmund Burke, Oliver Goldsmith, and Johnson's executor and biographer, Sir John Hawkins. Later came Garrick, Gibbon, Sheridan, and Boswell. The Club, as sometimes it was called, has never ceased to be. Its venue is not divulged.

UNITED SERVICE CLUB (Pall Mall). It was founded in 1815, the yr. of Waterloo, and commenced with a meeting at the Thatched House Tavern three weeks before the battle. This was attended by representatives of the P. Regent, the D. of York, the D. of Kent, and the D. of Cambridge, as well as 51 officers. The meeting had been convened by Ld. Lynedoch, who in a memorandum said:

'It must materially contribute to the comfort and respectability of officers of every rank to have a place to meet where they can enjoy intercourse with economy, where they can cultivate acquaintances formed on service, and where officers of different ranks can have frequent opportunities of knowing each other, where a good collection of books and maps will always be ready for the use of members, and where officers may meet in the most creditable manner, and on moderate terms.'

The subscription was fixed at 20 gns., the membership at 1,200, and by 26th Oct. 483 had joined. The Club's first premises were at 23 Albemarle St. As the Navy Club evinced a strong desire to be admitted, it was amalgamated and the present title adopted. In 1819 a move was made to Charles St. In 1826 John Nash was appointed architect of a new bdg. in Pall Mall, and in 1828 this was completed. One of the features of the Club is a colossal bust of the D. of Wellington. There is also a number of pictures including portraits of Ld. Nelson and William IV, and Clarkson Stanfield's 'Battle of Trafalgar,' framed in wood from the *Victory*.

TRAVELLERS' CLUB (Pall Mall). It was founded in 1819 by Ld. Castlereagh. The present Club-house was built by Sir Chas. Barry in 1832. A rule which remains is that members must have travelled out of L. at least five hundred miles in a straight line. Theodore Hook, who was given to rhyming about clubs, wrote:

'The travellers are in Pall Mall and
    smoke cigars so cosily
And dream they climb the highest Alps
    or roam the plains of Moselai,
The world for them has nothing new,
    they have explored all parts of it,
And now they are club-footed!—and
    they sit and look at charts of it.'

It is remarkable for the distinction of some who have been blackballed. They include Thackeray, Ld. Randolph Churchill, and Cecil Rhodes.

The ATHENÆUM (Pall Mall). It was founded in 1824. The prime mover was John Wilson Croker, M.P., to-day known best as the victim of a venomous attack by Ld. Macaulay on his edition of Boswell's *Life of Johnson*, published in 1831. Croker was supported by Sir Humphrey Davy, President of the Royal Soc., and Michael Faraday, who became the Club's first secretary. Its object was the association of individuals known for their scientific or literary attainments, artists of eminence, and patrons of literature and art. Princes of the blood royal, Cabinet ministers, and bishops were also welcomed. Actors were at first discouraged, but later a few were admitted, such as Kemble, Macready, Sir Squire Bancroft and Sir Henry Irving. The membership was first limited to 500, 400 of whom were to be nominated by the Committee and 100 elected by ballot. Election to the Club soon became so sought after that the figure was gradually increased to 1,200, and to-day—including all classes of members—it stands at about 1,400.

At first its home was at 12 Waterloo Place. In 1828, after the destruction of Carlton House, part of its site was acquired. The architect of the Club-house was Decimus Burton, and, in accordance with the classical devotion of many of its members, the Greek style was to be followed. There was therefore to be a frieze. According to Ralph Nevill, the members wanted an ice-house (an ancient substitute for a refrigerator), but Croker got his way. Hence the epigram:

'I'm John William Croker,
    I do as I please;
They ask for an ice-house,
    I'll give them a frieze.'

The Club-house was opened in Feb. 1830. The eight pillars in the entrance hall were copied from the Temple of the Winds at Athens. The portico is surmounted by a figure of the Pallas Athene, and on the grand staircase is a reproduction in gilt of the Apollo Belvidere. About seventy yrs. ago, in order to meet the modern demand at clubs for members' bedrooms the top storey was reconstructed and recessed, thus slightly modifying the exterior appearance of Burton's original club-house.

Early in its career the Committee of the Athenæum decided that the Club must have a good library, and an annual sum is allocated for purchasing books of permanent value. The collection is especially rich in classics, history, topography, belles lettres, dictionaries, works of reference, and other indispensable tools for literary workers. The 'silence' room, dedicated solely to the use of students, is rarely unoccupied, and its cloistered atmosphere is preserved inviolate as neither smoking, refreshments, nor conversation are here permitted. During the last fifty yrs. or so the Athenæum has also acquired, by gift or purchase, works of art in the form of pictures, prints, and rare volumes, including a few *incunabula*.

A list of members of the Athenæum would comprise more eminent men than any other club could boast. The following are some of the names: Sidney Smith; Isaac D'Israeli; Rowland Hill; Wilkie Collins; Rev. F. D. Maurice; J. L. Motley; Benjamin Disraeli; Thomas Carlyle; Chas. Dickens; W. M. Thackeray; Sir Francis Galton; John Ruskin; John Stuart Mill; Sir Chas. Barry; Daniel Maclise; Prof. John Tyndall; Ld. John Russell; Thos. H. Huxley; J. A. Froude; W. P. Frith; Anthony Trollope; W. E. H. Lecky; Wm. Holman Hunt; R. H. Hutton; J. R. Green; Walter Bagehot; Cardinal Manning; Lord Rutherford; Sir J. J. Thomson; Andrew Lang; E. A.

Freeman; Sir Walter Besant; Frederic Harrison; Austin Dobson; Robert Louis Stevenson; Herbert Spencer; Ld. Snell.

It is not surprising that Theodore Hook, a Club member, wrote:

'There first the Athenæum Club, so wise
    there is not a man of it
That has not sense enough for six (in
    fact that is the plan of it).
The very waiters answer "Yes" with
    eloquence Socratical,
And always place the knives and forks in
    order mathematical.'

One original, 1824, member, Lettsom Elliott, survived till 1898.

There are busts of Milton (a bequest of Trollope), Pope, Johnson, and Croker.

A treasure of the Athenæum is a chair from Dickens's chalet at Gads Hill. This was bought at the sale of Dickens's property, and was presumably the one in which he wrote the last pages of the unfinished *Edwin Drood*.

An incident at the Athenæum in which Dickens and Thackeray were concerned is referred to under the Garrick Club.

Owing to its distinctive character and the varied interests of its members the Athenæum has a world-wide reputation, and visitors from abroad who occupy in their countries a similar position in the learned world to that represented by the Club's own members are eligible for honorary temporary membership during residence in England. Ambassadors from foreign countries and High Commissioners and Governors in the British Commonwealth and Empire are also admitted to membership. This privilege is highly valued, and the list of honorary members is nearly always full. The relations between the Athenæum and the scientific, literary, and professional classes in U.S.A. have always been singularly happy, and exchanges of hospitality have been constant ever since the foundation of the Club.

(See *History of the Athenæum*, 1824–1925, by Humphry Ward, 1926.)

GARRICK CLUB (Garrick St.). It was founded in 1831. Its objects were to combine patrons of the drama, the formation of a theatrical library and the collection of works on costume. Its first Club-house was in King St., Covent Garden. In 1855 the Club was entertained to dinner at the Mansion House by Ld.M.

Moon, one of its members. In 1864 it removed to a new bdg. erected in the recently constructed Garrick St.—so called from Garrick's residence in the neighbouring Southampton St., which is commemorated by a tablet. The Club possesses the remarkable collection of theatrical portraits made by Chas. Matthews. There are some good pictures such as Harlow's 'Mrs. Siddons as Lady Macbeth'; 'Garrick as Richard III' by the elder Morland; 'Samuel Phelps as Wolsey,' by Forbes Robertson; 'Sir Henry Irving' by Millais. There is also a bust supposed to represent Shakespeare which was found bricked up in a wall near the old Lincoln's Inn Theatre—'The Duke's' of Pepys's Diary. It is said to have adorned the proscenium. It came into possession of Richd. Owen, the naturalist, and he sold it to the D. of Devonshire. In 1851 the D. presented it to the Garrick Club. A treasured possession is the chair in which Sir Henry Irving d. at Bradford (1905).

Perhaps the best-known incident connected with it occurred in 1858. This was the quarrel between Thackeray and Dickens, which arose out of an injudicious article in *Town Topics*, written by Edmund Yates, and criticizing Thackeray. The information contained in this article could only have been gathered from club conversations, and Thackeray, rightly incensed, complained to the Garrick Club committee about the matter. It was Dickens's defence of Yates that led to the estrangement between the two great novelists—which has been described as 'a battle of giants, with Tom Thumb between them.' Yates was forced to resign from the club in consequence, and the break in the two writers' friendship was not healed until 1863, when they met by chance in the hall of the Athenaeum Club, spontaneously shook hands, and made up their senseless quarrel. Three weeks later Dickens stood round the grave of Thackeray in Kensal Green Cemetery.

The CARLTON CLUB (St. James's St.) was founded by the D. of Wellington in 1832. Its first premises were in Charles St. In the same yr. it removed to Ld. Kensington's house in Carlton Gardens, and in 1836 Sir Robt. Smirke built in Pall Mall a new Club-house of Grecian design. In 1854 the original club house was pulled down, and a new wing and centre added. The bdg. was a copy of Sansovino's Library of St. Mark in Venice. There was somewhat rapid decay owing to the unsuitability of the Caen stone to the L. atmosphere. In 1923 therefore it was refaced with Portland stone at a cost of £60,000, one half of which was defrayed by Sir Mallaby Deeley. To celebrate the completion of the work, the men who had been employed on the contract were entertained to a dinner by the members of the Carlton Club. There is a number of portraits of well-known statesmen: Lord North, the E. of Chatham, Ld. Castlereagh, Sir Robt. Peel, Ld. Salisbury (by Sir Hugh Herkomer), and Ld. Balfour (by Sargent). The bdg. was reduced to ruins by German bombs in 1941. The portraits survived.

There is a JUNIOR CARLTON CLUB in Pall Mall. It was founded in 1868. It has a beautiful library. There are portraits of Q. Victoria, Edward VII, when P. of Wales, Ld. Beaconsfield, Ld. Derby, and the D. of Wellington.

The REFORM CLUB (Pall Mall) was founded in 1832, as a rival to the Carlton Club. The prime mover was Edwd. Ellice, prominently associated with the Hudson's Bay Co. It first met at 21 Gt. George St., but after a few yrs. went to Gwydyr House, Whitehall. From there it went to the present site in Pall Mall, and there in 1840 was completed a fine bdg., designed by Sir Chas. Barry. It is in the Italian style, and resembles the Farnese Palace at Rome, designed by Michelangelo. There is a large square hall, covered with glass.

It was also famous for its cook, Alexis Soyer, a Frenchman who came to England as *chef* to the D. of Cambridge, son of George III. He was so useful in his art that at the time of an Irish famine he was sent to Ireland by the Govt. to assist the natives to make the best of what little food they had.

The Library of the Reform Club contains more than 70,000 volumes. There are portraits of Bright, Palmerston, Gladstone, etc. There is also a bust of the latter.

ARMY AND NAVY CLUB (Pall Mall). It was founded in 1838, and originally established as the Army Club. At the request of the D. of Wellington naval officers were admitted, and the name was altered. Through Capt. Wm. Duff of the

23rd Royal Fusiliers it was given the name of 'Rag and Famish,' this officer having had occasion to complain of the meagre refreshments when, late one night, he came in to supper. According to Nevill, 'this tickled the fancy of the members, and a Club button bearing the nickname and a starving man gnawing a bone was designed and for a time worn by many members in evening dress!' The original premises were at the corner of King St. and St. James Sq., in a house that had previously been Ld. Castlereagh's. Between 1848 and 1851 the present premises were erected on the model of Sansovino's Palazzo Corner Della la Grande on the Grand Canal at Venice.

SAVAGE CLUB (37 King St., W.C.2) was founded in 1857. It has no connection with savages as ordinarily understood. It does not either commemorate Johnson's friend Richd. Savage, but Henry of that ilk who seems also to have been of the fraternity of Grub St. He was found dead from starvation in Covent Garden Market. According to Stephen Fiske, one of its members:

'The fearful contrast between this poor waif and the masses of the best fed surrounding him—starving in the midst of plenty—touched every heart and fired the imagination of the Bohemian. "We must have a Savage Club," they cried, "to immortalise this terrible incident of London life." '

This account of the origin of the name—it is not the only one—almost sounds as if a charitable institution was to be launched. It was not that, although early members were needy adventurers in streets of ink.

The first premises were in Henrietta St., Covent Garden. In 1874 there was a move to Evans' Hotel, Covent Garden. Whilst here the Savage Club was entertained to dinner at the Mansion House by Francis Wyatt Truscott, Ld.M. in 1880. In 1881 the Club moved to the Savoy Hotel. Albert Edwd. P. of Wales was a member, and in 1882, to commemorate the 25th anniversary of the founding, he presided over a dinner held at Willis's Rooms, King St., Covent Garden. Others present were (Sir) Arthur Sullivan and Sir Fredk. Leighton. Until his succession George V was a member, and in 1909 he attended a dinner at the Hotel Cecil. Other members include J. L. Toole, G. A. Sala, Sir Squire Bancroft, 'Tom' Robertson,

M

G. A. Henty, Sir John Gilbert, Sir Arthur Sullivan, Ld. Kitchener and Ld. Roberts. A great feature has always been the Saturday night dinner.

In 1890 the Savage Club removed to Adelphi Terrace. Its destruction compelled migration, to Carlton House Terrace, in 1936, and after the war, to King St.

St. James's Club (Piccadilly). It was founded in 1857, the promoter being the Marquis d'Azeglio and others. The object was to provide a meeting place for secretaries and attachés after balls and parties. In its early days it was in Bennett St. and Grafton St. It then succeeded to the premises of the short-lived Coventry Club which had occupied a house built by Wm. Kent for Sir Hugh Hunlock and bought for £10,000 by the Marquis of Coventry in 1764. Until 1889 the Club had neither pictures nor engravings. Then there were additions to the bdg. and prints were presented by various embassies and legations. A feature of the bdg. is a magnificent ceiling in the dining room; it was painted by Angelica Kauffmann.

National Liberal Club (Whitehall Place). It was inaugurated at a meeting at the Westminster Palace Hotel in Nov. 1882. The objects were:

'To provide a central, convenient, and inexpensive Club in London for Liberals throughout the kingdom at which they may obtain every comfort and club advantage and where they may meet in friendly intercourse and interchange information and views.'

Temporary premises were acquired in Trafalgar Sq. An inaugural banquet was held at the Royal Aquarium in 1883. Ld. Glanville presided. The President, W. E. Gladstone and about 2,000 members were present. In 1887 the present premises, designed by Sir Alfred Waterhouse, R.A., were opened. The Club's large library was inaugurated by W. E. Gladstone in 1888. It now includes his own huge collection of 31,000 volumes and 33,000 pamphlets.

The Royal Toxophilite Soc. was founded in 1781. There is some uncertainty as to the original place used for archery, but in the early part of the 19th century it was proceeding on a ground behind Gower St., and carried on its business in Gt. Russell St. From about 1822 to 1833 the grounds were in Bays-

water—approximately where Sussex Sq. now is. From 1833 to about 1923 there was a part of Regent's Park used by the Club. They then removed to the disused burial ground of St. George, Hanover Sq., Bayswater Rd. For some yrs. the ground has been in Albion Mews, Hyde Park, W.2.

There are two literary clubs that should be mentioned. The Authors' Club was founded in 1891, largely through the efforts of Sir Walter Besant. There was a reconstruction when premises were taken in Whitehall Court in 1908. At the first dinner there Sir F. C. Gould was the guest of the evening, and Chas. Garvice was in the chair. Amongst those subsequently entertained were Sir Geo. Trevelyan, Mark Twain, Rudyard Kipling, Conan Doyle, Augustine Birrell, and Emile Zola. The P.E.N. was founded in 1921 by C. A. Dawson Scott, English poet and novelist. 'Its aim is to promote and maintain friendship and intellectual co-operation between men of letters in all countries in the interests of literature, freedom of expression and international goodwill. It is not concerned with State or party politics, and must not be used to serve their interests.' The first President was John Galsworthy (1921–33).

(See *Club Life of London*, by John Timbs; *London Clubs: their History and Treasures*, by Ralph H. Nevill, 1911; *British Clubs*, by Bernard Darwin, 1943; *The Clubs of Augustan England*, by R. J. Allen, 1967.)

London County Council. The London County Council was the local authority under the Local Govt. Act, 1888, and L. Govt. Act, 1939, for the Administrative County of L. It consisted of 150 members, of whom 129 were called councillors, and 21 aldermen.

The L.C.C.'s powers and duties may be grouped as follows:

(1) Those transferred in 1888 from the M.B.W. as central authority for main drainage, for street improvements, and the construction or purchase of tramways, for the fire brigade, for housing the poor, for supervising the laying out of streets and construction of bdgs., and for the provision and maintenance of parks and open spaces. The powers and duties in respect of tramways were transferred to the L. Passenger Transport Board by an Act of 1933.

(2) The administrative business transferred also by the Act of 1888 from the justices, such as the licensing of houses and other places for music, dancing, or such places, the provision and maintenance of mental hosps. and reformatory and industrial schs., duties with regard to county bridges, the appointment, etc., of coroners, and the carrying out of duties under the Weights and Measures Acts.

(3) Powers and duties mainly transferred from the L. Sch. Board in 1903, coupled with additional powers relating to education.

(4) Powers directly conferred by Parliament at various times in regard to a number of matters prior to the passing of the Local Govt. Act, 1929. The chief of these were the working of tramways (although the L.C.C. could own, it was not permitted to work tramways until after the passage of the L. County Tramways Act, 1896), the protection of children, the licensing of cinematograph halls, employment agencies, massage establishments, motor cars, etc., the provision of ambulances, museums, and small-holdings and allotments, town planning, and various health services, including arrangements for the diagnosis and prevention of tuberculosis.

(5) Powers transferred on 1st Apr. 1930, from the late Poor Law authorities, viz., the twenty-five boards of guardians, the Met. Asylums Board, the four boards of sch. district managers and the Central (Unemployed) body. This transfer considerably enlarged the scope of some of the previously existing services of the L.C.C., e.g. the public health, mental hosps., education, and ambulance services, but the chief effect was to make the L.C.C. responsible for the consideration of applications for relief, and for the provision of all forms of assistance, including the provision of hosps. and of treatment for the sick. The L.C.C. also became the central hosp. authority for L. for infectious diseases. Many of the Council's duties in matters of health and relief of the poor have now been transferred to the National Health Service and the National Assistance Board.

The area of jurisdiction of the L.C.C. was called the Administrative County of London. This title goes back to 1888, the year in which the Local Govt. Act, which

created county councils, was enacted. As an area of jurisdiction it goes back to 1855, in which year the M.B.W. was created by the Metropolis Management Act, which established also the met. vestries and district boards as the primary local authorities. No change whatever was made in this area between 1855 and 1888, nor between 1888 and 1899, when the L. Govt. Act which created the met. bor. councils was passed. By the latter Act of 1899, however, three relatively large alterations were made. Penge and the area known as Clerkenwell Detached were removed from the county, and the area known as South Hornsey was added to the county. Further, in 1903 and 1907 respectively, small adjustments of boundary were made (1) in the neighbourhood of Mitcham and Wandsworth, and (2) in the neighbourhood of Tottenham and Hackney, under orders of the Local Govt. Board confirmed by Parliament.

The following are a few key facts and dates in the history of the L.C.C.:

1889. Meeting of the first L.C.C., under the chairmanship of first, the E. of Rosebery, and then Sir John Lubbock, afterwards Ld. Avebury.

John Burns was a member of this first L.C.C.

1892–1908. Works Dept. run by the L.C.C.

1903. Abolition of the Sch. Board for L., and transfer of its powers to the L.C.C.

1905–7. Thames steamboat service run by the L.C.C.

1922. Opening of New County Hall by K. George V.

1929. Abolition of the Met. Asylums Board, the Boards of Guardians, and the Central (Unemployed) body, and transfer of their powers to the L.C.C.

1933. Creation of the L. Passenger Transport Board, and transfer of the tramways powers of the L.C.C. thereto.

From 1st April 1965 a completely new plan for London government came into operation (see 'Greater London Council').

London Guides. The history of L. guides has not yet been written, but doubtless they have an antiquity greater than many of its bdgs. It is known from two sources that W.A. had its guides in Elizabethan times. Sir John Davies, in one of his

Epigrams (*c.* 1594), wrote:

'Amongst the poets Dacus numbered is,
    Yet could he never make an English
    rhyme,
But some prose speeches I have heard of
    his,
    Which have been spoken many a
    hundred time;

He first taught him that keeps the
    monuments
At Westminster his formal tale to say.'

John Donne, afterwards Dean of St.
Paul's, is evidently referring to Dacus's
pupil in one of his satires (*c.* 1597):

'He, like to a high-stretched lute-string,
    squeak'd, "O sir,
'Tis sweet to talk of kings." "At West-
    minster,"
Said I, "the man that keeps the abbey
    tombs,
And for his price doth with whoever
    comes
Of all our Harrys and our Edwards talk,
From king to king, and all their kin can
    walk." '

In *The Puisne's Walke about London,* a
Harleian MS., probably of Charles I's
time, are these stanzas:

'To see the Tombes was my desire,
    And then to Westminster I went:
I gave one twopence for his hyre,
    'Twas the best twopence y^t e'er I
    spent.
"Here lyes," quoth hee, "King Henry the
    Third."
" 'Tis false," said I, "hee speaks not a
    word.
"And here is King Richard ye Seacond
    inter'd;
And here is good King Edward's sword.
' "And this," quoth he, "is Jacob's stone,
    This very stone here under ye chaire." '

Peacham's tract, *The Worth of a Penny*
(1667), says:

    'For a penny you may hear a most
eloquent oration upon our English
Kings and Queens, if keeping your
hands off, you will seriously listen to
David Owen, who keeps the monuments in Westminster.'

Much is heard too of the guides who
showed the waxworks. In *The Citizen of
the World,* Goldsmith's Chinese philosopher is thus addressed:

    ' "And pray observe this cap: this is

General Monk's cap." "Very strange
indeed, very strange, that a general
should have a cap also! Pray, friend,
what might this cap have cost originally?" "That, sir," says he, "I don't
know, but this cap is all the wages I
have had for my trouble." "A very
small recompense, truly," said I. "Not
so very small," replied he, "for every
gentleman puts some money into it,
and I spend the money." '

Andreas Riem, a German, visiting L. in
1798, after being chased by the guide
from monument to monument, saw him
snatch General Monk's cap from his head
and hold it out for tips. The same cap is
referred to in *The Ingoldsby Legends*:

'I thought on Naseby, Marston Moor, and
    Worcester's crowning fight,
When on mine ear a sound there fell, it
    filled me with affright,
As thus in low, unearthly tones, I heard
    a voice begin:
"This here's the cap of Gen'ral Monk!
    Sir please put summat in." '

Part of the figure of the general, but
not the cap, is now in the abbey mus.
The same writer, referring to the inscription on Wren's grave in the crypt of
St. P.'s Cath—'*Si monumentum requiris,
circumspice*'—said:

'Which an erudite verger translated to me,
    If you ask for his monument, Sir-come-
    spy-see!'

This may be matched by the self-
appointed guide referred to by Mrs.
M. V. Hughes, who explained that the
oil-paintings of Moses and Aaron in the
ch. of All Hallows London Wall, were
'portraits of two rectors of this parish,
now passed away,' and the one who
pointed out Dr. Johnson's back garden
at the house in Gough Sq., and said that
was where he bd. his wife so that she
could be near him.

The British Travel Association now
accredits guides who can be contacted at
the Guild of Guide Lecturers, Mount Royal
Hotel, Bryanston St., W.1.

London Societies. THE LONDON AND
MIDDLESEX ARCHAEOLOGICAL SOC. owes
its inception largely to the Rev. Thos.
Hugo, M.A., F.S.A., for some yrs. vicar of
St. Botolph's, Bishopsgate, a gentleman of
considerable reputation as an antiquary.
At his instigation, in 1855, a group of eight

enthusiasts formed a provisional committee which met at the headquarters of the Surrey Archaeological Soc. In Dec. the inaugural meeting was held in the Throne Room at Crosby Hall, and a motion: 'That a society be denominated the London and Middlesex Archaeological Society be now established' was carried unanimously. The objects (*inter alia*) were:

'To collect, record and publish, the best information on the ancient arts and monuments of the Cities of London and Westminster, and of the County of Middlesex, including primæval antiquities; architecture—ecclesiastical, civil, and military.'

The first transactions were published in 1856. Amongst the useful work of the soc. has been the appointment of a committee to consider means for the preservation of the Chapter House of W.A.; obtaining a grant of £200 from the C.C. towards the restoration of the Ch. of St. Bartholomew the Great (1866); and the presentation of a successful memorial against a proposal for the demolition of Charterhouse (1885).

The soc. annually arranges a memorial service for John Stow at the Ch. of St. Andrew Undershaft, and in 1950, in conjunction with the Pepys Club, it revived a similar service for the diarist at the temporary Ch. of St. Olave, Hart St.

THE LONDON SOCIETY was founded in 1912, and its aim is to stimulate a wider concern for the beauty of the capital city, the preservation of its charms, and the careful consideration of its development.

LONDON TOPOGRAPHICAL SOCIETY was founded for the publication of material illustrating the history and topography of the City of L. from the earliest times to the present day. It reproduces maps, views and plans, publishes documents and data of every description.

LONDON EXPLORERS CLUB. This caters for the more plebeian L. lover (the subscription was 2s. 6d. until 1950 and is now only 3s. 6d.). It was founded in 1930 by Wm. Margrie, who has taken live coals from many altars in his time, and has managed to keep this one alight. His voluminous works include a study of an L.C.C. sch.—*Rosemary Street* and booklets: *Mighty London*, *London's Fairylands* (the parks), *The Romance of Morley College*, *The Camberwell Jubilee 1900–1950*, etc. Over three hundred different places have been visited. There has been a number of topographical races.

LONDON APPRECIATION SOCIETY was founded in 1932 by H. L. Bryant Peers, F.R.G.S. One of its objects is to enable Londoners to visit places of historic and topical interest under the direction of competent guides and lecturers. Many parts of L. have their own flourishing antiquarian and local history societies, many doing most useful work.

London Stone (Cannon St.) is believed to be the most ancient relic of L. now in the streets. Stow said it was mentioned in a gospel book given by K. Athelstan (895–940) to Christ Ch., Canterbury. Camden, the Elizabethan antiquary, thought it was the millarium or stone from which the Romans measured distances. Sir Jas. Frazer (*Golden Bough*) quotes the Danish historian, Saxo Grammaticus, as saying that

'the ancients when they were to choose a king were wont to stand on stones planted in the ground, and to proclaim their votes, in order to foreshadow from the steadfastness of the stones that the deed would be lasting.'

This, coupled with Stow's allusion, suggests a Saxon origin, like the stone at Kingston. Henry Fitz-Eylwin, L.'s first mayor, is described as of London Stone. This was probably an indication of the proximity of his house thereto. John Lydgate, in *London Lickpenny*, refers to it as 'Canwick Street.' It figures in 2 *Henry VI*, Act IV. Sc. vii:

'*Enter Jack Cade and the rest, and strikes his staffe on London stone.*

Cade. Now is Mortimer lord of this city. And here, sitting upon London-stone, I charge and command that of the city's cost, the pissing-conduit run nothing but claret wine this first year of our reign.'

The above is an excerpt from the First Folio. 'London. Cannon Street,' in modern editions, is an editorial gloss. The incident is lifted from Holinshed, the only change being that in his history Cade strikes the stone with a sword. This act may have been symbolical of the fact that the rebel had got to the very centre of the city. Sir Laurence Gomme mentioned that at Bovey Tracey in Devonshire it was the practice of the mayor, after election, to ride round the cross and strike it with his staff. A minor Elizabethan play carries on the idea of its symbolical significance:

'Set up this bill at London Stone. Let it be done solemnly with drum and trumpet and look you advance my colour on the top of the steeple right over against it.'—*Pasquill and Marfarius*, 1589.

The steeple was presumably St. Swithun's. Stow says the stone was

'fixed in the ground very deep, fastened with bars of iron, and otherwise so strongly set, that if carts do run against it through negligence, the wheels be broken, and the stone itself unshaken.'

It was then on the S. side of Cannon St., and was still there when Strype mentioned it (1720):

'It is now for the preservation of it, cased over with a new stone, handsomely wrought, cut hollow underneath, so as the old stone may be seen, the new one being over it, to shelter and defend the old venerable one.'

In 1742 it was removed to the N. side of Cannon St., and in 1798 again removed, as an obstruction. It would have been destroyed but for the intervention of a local antiquary, Mr. Thos. Maiden, a printer of Sherborne Lane. It was then placed in the wall of St. Swithun's Ch., and in 1869 a grille was added, with an inscription above composed by the L. and Middlesex Archaeological Soc. It consists of oolite stone, such as was used by the Romans in their bdgs. Dryden mentions it in his fable of the *Cock and the Fox*:

'The bees in arms
Drive headlong from their waxen cells in swarms.
Jack Straw at London Stone, with all his rout,
Struck not the City with so loud a shout.'

Jack Straw was one of Wat Tyler's lieutenants, and Dryden was evidently a little hazy about his history. Wm. Blake in *Jerusalem* (*c.* 1804) has the couplet:

'They groaned aloud on London Stone, They groaned aloud on Tyburn's brook.'

Since the Ch. of St. Swithun, destroyed in the bombing, has been demolished, the stone is now fixed behind a grille on the wall of a bank on the N. side of Cannon St.

London Transport.

BOATS. In the L.Mus. there is a dug-out canoe, made from the trunk of a large oak tree, hollowed out by stone or bronze tools. It was found in the channel of the Thames between Kew and Mortlake, and must have been made at a time when even Father Thames appears young in retrospect. It might be described as a Transport Board primitive and undivided. It was probably a ferry-boat, and how many, one wonders, did it carry of those passengers who, thousands of yrs. back, were ferried over the river Styx. Others have been found at Shepperton, Hampton Court, and between Tottenham and Walthamstow. The last is in the B.Mus. The Roman galley found on the site of County Hall was not fit for a passenger service. The man-power it demanded hardly made an economic fare possible. Passenger boats amongst the ancient Britons seem to have taken the form of coracles, small oval rowing boats made of skins stretched on wicker-work; they are still used on the Towy at Carmarthen, and the Tevi in Cardiganshire. Transport by water did not make rapid strides, and there seems little, if any, difference between the Roman galley referred to, and those in which the Normans are depicting as invading these islands in the famous Bayeux tapestry.

HORSES. The horse was, of course, the principal means of travel in the Middle Ages. The horse-fair at Smithfield (*q.v.*), and the attention Fitzstephen, writing about 1172, gave to it, shows how important the creature was. It used to be said that the wings of Pegasus in the Temple were formerly two men, and this joint possession of one animal indicated the real poverty of the 'Poor Fellow-soldiers of Christ' of the 'Temple of Solomon.' This is probably a myth, but certainly to be horseless was to be a poverty-stricken man.

CARRIAGES. Those in higher circles fared better. There were for them carriages fit for a modern Ld.M. The famous Luttrell Psalter (see 'Museums') shows one most elaborately carved, with small windows, through which ladies behold the world very much as animals in medieval drawings survey the progress of the Flood from Noah's Ark. It is not surprising that these were bequeathed by will from generation to generation. Jusserand (*English Wayfaring Life in the Middle Ages*) mentions one that was worth 1,600 oxen. There were also litters, two horses carrying these: one before and one behind. They had a sort of hood, in which were large openings to provide some kind of a view. Whatever the disadvantages of these conveyances, they almost invariably had most spirited horses. Frequently they are depicted as behaving in shafts as more modern horses in a circus. They paw the air in a mood of vigorous rampancy, as though they scented the Derby as a far-off event to which their creation moved, even as the horses in the Bible smelt the battle from afar. For the middle classes there were literally dog-carts. In a B.Mus. manuscript a team of three is shown in single file, a driver blowing a horn, whether to stimulate the animals or to warn pedestrians, does not appear. Remarkable to relate, in a picture at the Guildhall of the Mansion House in 1750, dogs are drawing small carts.

COACHES were not introduced into England until the middle of the 16th century. The first was made by Walter Rippon for the E. of Rutland (1555): in 1564 he also made one for Q. Elizabeth. The idea came from the Continent, the name being derived from Kocs in Hungary, where they were first made in the 15th century. The only protection from bad weather was curtains: the seating was as in a modern coach, but there was a boot at the side. Q. Elizabeth used hers when, in 1588, she went to St. P.'s Cath. to return thanks for the defeat of the Spanish Armada, and it is said that this was the first time it was seen in public. They speedily multiplied, and Stow (1598) said

'the use of coaches brought out of Germany is taken up and made so common as there is neither distinction of time nor difference of persons observed: for the world runs on wheels with many whose parents were glad to go on foot.'

Fynes Moryson (1617) said:

'Sixty or seventy years ago coaches were very rare in England, but at this day pride is so far increased, as there be few gentlemen of any account who have not their coaches, so as the streets of London are almost stopped up with them.'

John Taylor, the water-poet, inveighed against them. His trade was in danger. He did not complain against those that

'belong to persons of wealth or quality, but only against the caterpillar swarm of hirelings. They have ruined my poore trade whereof I am a member.'

He estimated that 'this infernal swarm of trade spoilers carry five hundred and sixty fares daily from us.' The hired coaches were called 'Hackney Hell Carts.' The implied stigma was in the second word; the first has given rise to so much dispute, but seems to have derived from *haquenée*, Old French for an ambling horse or nag. In 1634 Capt. Bailey, who had served under Raleigh in Guiana, established a hackney coach stand at the Maypole, outside St. Mary le Strand Ch. In 1636 a broadsheet was published giving, in the form of a dialogue, a

'contest between Coach and Sedan, pleasantly disputing for Place and Precedence, the Brewer's Cart being Moderator.'

SEDAN CHAIRS were first used in England by the D. of Buckingham in 1623, according to Timbs. In a well-known print of the visit to L. in 1638 of Marie de Medici, the mother of Charles I's consort, one is shown with a horse back and front; usually, however, men were in the shafts; The progress must have been slower, but the comfort was greater. Von Uffenbach, a visitor from Frankfort, in 1710 complained that the hackney coaches jolted most terribly. They remained in use until early in the 19th century, and Dickens made capital use of one in the famous episode at Bath in *Pickwick Papers*. They were, before there was any adequate street lighting, attended by a boy or a footman carring a large link (torch).

The link extinguishers remain to-day in many places in L., e.g. Gwydyr House, Whitehall; Berkeley Sq.; Amen Court; Adelphi. Gay in *Trivia* indicated the dangers of those who

'Box'd within the chair, contemn the street.
And trust their safety to another's feet.
    .   .   .   .
The drunken chairman in the kennel spurns,
The glasses shatter, and his charge o'erturns.'

Dr. Johnson, in a letter purporting to be sent to his *Idler* by a chairman, indicates the risks the carrier ran, as well as the carried:

'Sir,

'There is in this town a species of oppression which the law has not hitherto redressed.

'I am a chairman. You know, Sir, we come when we are called and are expected to carry all who require our assistance. It is common for men of the most unwieldy corpulence to crowd themselves into a chair, and demand to be carried for a shilling as far as any airy young lady whom we scarcely feel upon our poles. Surely we ought to be paid like all other mortals, in proportion to our labour. Engines should be fixed in proper places to weigh chairs as they weigh waggons; and those whom ease and plenty have made unable to carry themselves, should give part of their superfluities to those who carry them.'

Did the worthy doctor himself have an altercation with the chairman over the vexed question of whether he should be charged by the pound weight? If so, there may have been a pleasing philosophical match such as that in which Mr. Pickwick (in whom some writers have found Johnsonian traits) engaged with the cabman at the 'Golden Cross.' Johnson, however, was generous, and probably a tip was given in some proportion to his avoirdupois.

The view from the chairs was certainly limited, but they had movable tops, so that the occupant who wished to descry the horizon could do so by appearing suddenly upwards like a jack-in-the-box. They had one advantage in respect of which no modern conveyance can compare, they took the passenger not merely to his home, but into it. De Quincey said in his *Autobiography*:

'Nine-tenths at least of the colds and catarrhs, those initial stages of all pulmonary complaints (the capital scourge of England), are caught in the transit between the door of a carriage and the genial atmosphere of the drawing-room. By a sedan-chair all this danger was evaded; your two chairmen marched right into the hall: the hall door was closed; and not until then was the roof and the door of your chair opened: the translation was from one room to

another.'

Almost in identical terms Mrs. Gaskell (*Wives and Daughters*) praised the sedan chair, but—a woman—she found an additional advantage in increased decorum:

'Miss Browning had decided to keep to the more comfortable custom of the Sedan chair, which, as she said to Miss Piper, one of her visitors, came into the parlour, and got full of the warm air and nipped you up and carried you tight and cosy into another warm room where you could walk out without having to show your legs by going up or down steps.'

Swift, in his *City Shower*, gives an idea of the din caused by a heavy shower of rain:

'Box'd in a chair, the beau impatient sits,
While spouts run clattering o'er the roof by fits,
And ever and anon with frightful din,
The leather sounds; he trembles from within.'

Sedan chairs never appear to have been made for two. The man-power then required could not be obtained, or made effective for such a weight. This must have prejudiced them as rivals to the hackney carriages, yet they remained in use a very long time, and not many yrs. separates the last chair from the first train. It is said that the place where they were last seen was Church Row, Hampstead, where Austin Dobson once lived. If so, it is appropriate, as one of his most delightful poems was *The Old Sedan Chair* (1884).

THE STAGE COACH began in England about 1640, though before that long broadwheeled wagons travelled between towns with goods and passengers, and these were called 'stages.' Six are known to have been plying in 1675, but they were seasonal; they ran from spring to Nov. They were not numerous until the 18th century. Outside passengers sat in a basket between the hind wheels, or sat on the roof. This is shown in Hogarth's picture, 'The Country Inn Yard, or the Stage Coach.' They were often called 'machines.' No doubt in a journey by coach there was a spice of adventure lacking in travelling by the modern railway train. To travel hopefully was not so certainly to arrive, and advertisements announced that the guards were 'fully armed.'

OMNIBUSES. It is possible to be most precise as to the date of their birth into the vehicular world. The following elegant paragraph appeared in the *Morning Post* of 7th July 1829:

'Saturday the new vehicle, called the Omnibus, commenced running from Paddington to the City, and excited considerable notice, both from the novel form of the carriage, and the elegance with which it is fitted out. It is capable of accommodating 16 or 18 persons, all inside, and we apprehend it would be almost impossible to make it overturn, owing to the great width of the carriage. It was drawn by three beautiful bays abreast, after the French fashion. The Omnibus is a handsome machine, in the shape of a van, with windows on each side and one at the end. The width the horses occupy will render the vehicle rather inconvenient to be turned or driven through some of the streets of London.'

One Geo. Shillibeer was the pioneer who launched the vehicle upon L. streets. He had been a coachbuilder who had set up business in Paris, and been commissioned to build some omnibuses of novel design. Thinking that an enterprise that was profitable in Paris might pay here, he started his bus, which ran between Paddington and the Bank, via Marylebone Rd., Somers Town, and the City Rd., the Paddington terminus being the 'Yorkshire Stingo,' a tavern still to be found at the Lisson Grove end of Marylebone Rd. It was an artistic vehicle which appears to have worn a wreath of roses on its highly decorated sides. Four services were provided in each direction daily, the fare being 1s. all the way, and 6d. for the stages between Islington and Paddington or the Bank. These early vehicles catered more for the amusement of passengers than does any public vehicle to-day. Shillibeer's omnibus had been preceded by Miles's coach which, about twenty-five yrs. before, plied also between Paddington and the City. The fares were 2s. and 3s. (the former presumably for outside and the latter for inside passengers), and this included such an amenity—the journey took more than three hours somehow, so some diversion was desirable —as the hearing of tales and tunes on the fiddle from Miles's boy! Originally Shillibeer provided books and newspapers for his passengers. They, however, travelled beyond the termini of the buses either through lapse of memory or lapse of morals, so Mr. Shillibeer quickly abandoned his attempts to ensure that he who rides can read.

Then the prestige of the personnel of the staff was at first carefully guarded. Mr. Shillibeer assured possible patrons that 'a person of great respectability attended his Vehicle as Conductor,' and in a picture of his omnibus still extant a gentleman is seen opening the back door of the vehicle and ushering a lady in with as much decorum as if it were a private pew rather than a public conveyance that she was entering. Nothing is heard of tickets in those days. Punches were not introduced until 1873.

Luggage was then carried on top. Passengers were promoted in 1850. Male ones only, of course. The Victorians could not contemplate female legs in an exalted position, and indeed the ascent was precipitous and not without hazard. In 1855 the Compagnie Générale des Omnibus de Londres, subsequently renamed the London General Omnibus Co., was established in Paris with a Franco-British directorate, and offices in both capitals. In 1881 its most serious competitor, the London Road Car Co., appeared. It introduced the 'garden' or transverse seat on the upper deck and more convenient stairways. In 1897 the first motor omnibus was licensed—it was on the Charing Cross to Victoria route. The last 'General' horse bus ran on 25th Oct. 1911, but another company ran one over Waterloo Bridge so late as 1916.

'A halfpenny fare was charged on this vehicle, which was known to users as the "Flea Box," the latter possibly because of its having dirty looking red velvet cushions.'

In 1925 the first buses with covered tops were put in service.

CABS. The 'cabriolet de place,' invented about 1660 by Nicolas Sauvage, was introduced into L. from Paris in 1823. Besides the driver they could carry two passengers inside. They stood for hire in Portland St., and were painted yellow. In 1832 they were limited to twelve in number, but as their popularity increased this limit was removed. There are facetious references to these in Dickens's *Sketches by Boz*. The cabriolet, in its turn, was supplanted by a new kind of cab, invented by Mr. Boulnois. In this vehicle the occupants faced one another, and the driver sat on top. This led, in 1834, to Joseph Aloysius Hansom taking out a patent for 'a vehicle for conveying loads, etc.' The cab which bore his name for about seventy yrs. differed in construction from time to time. It was a popular mode of conveyance among those whose purse did not restrict them to public vehicles. It was lightly constructed, and having regard to its speed Dr. Johnson might in the 19th century have substituted it for the post-chaise, a ride in which— with a pretty woman as companion—he envisaged as the acme of human pleasure. In 1886 there were 7,020 hansom cabs in L., and 3,997 four-wheelers. In the first decade of the 20th century they were almost entirely superseded by taxi-cabs.

A hansom was on exhibition in the L.Mus. In 1937 there were three plying for hire. One was used for a wedding at Caxton Hall in 1937. In 1941 the driver of one was killed in the Blitz. In 1942 the last driver died at the age of 83. In 1946 Tom Robinson was still driving a four-wheeler cab from Victoria Station.

TRAINS. The first railway in L. was sanctioned by Parliament in 1833, and was to run between L.B. and Greenwich, by means of a viaduct four miles long. The first brick was laid on 4th Apr. 1834, and a yr. later 400 arches had been built. On 8th Feb., Londoners had their first train journey, from Spa Rd., Bermondsey, to Deptford. The first week the receipts amounted to £17; they rose to £31 the second week. There was a gravelled footway alongside the line, and before the trains started to run foot passengers were allowed to use it by payment of a toll. The straight track saved about 1¼ miles' walk. On 14th Dec., 1836 the Ld.M. opened the railway from L.B. to Deptford. There were five engines. Trains ran every quarter of an hour from 8 a.m. to 10 p.m. (11 p.m. on Sundays). During the first week the railway started from the L. terminus it was used by 20,000 people. On Christmas Eve 1838 a temporary station was opened at Greenwich. By that time three million passengers had travelled uninjured. In 1840 a permanent station was opened at

Greenwich. The arches had been fitted up for houses, but found few tenants owing to the noise of the trains. Moreover, they were not allowed to have coal fires lest the smoke obscured the view of the engine drivers.

Trains having once come, however, the public could return no more to stage-coaches. L. Bridge Station was not long alone in its glory. In 1838 Euston Station was opened. Next in date, of present termini, was Waterloo (erected in 1848 and rebuilt between 1900 and 1921). Its centenary in 1948 was duly celebrated by an exhibition and a handsome brochure. The original terminus of the London and South-Western Railway was Nine Elms. King's Cross Station dates from 1852, and Paddington from the same yr. From 1838 until that date the terminus of the Great Western Railway had been Bishop's Rd. St. Pancras Station was completed in 1870 (its clock came from the Great Exhibition of 1851.) Of the other L. stations on the old South-Eastern Railway Charing Cross Station was opened in 1864, and Cannon St. in 1866.

The first Met. Railway was opened in 1863, from Bishop's Rd., Paddington, to Farringdon St. The number of passengers on the first day was 30,000, and in the course of the first yr. 9,500,000. The carriages were open trucks, and a well-known picture shows a number of gentlemen enjoying the first journey and waving top hats. In 1868 the first section of the District Railway between High St., Kensington, and Gloucester Rd., was opened. In 1869 the first tube railway in the world was to be seen in L. This was a cable car running in a subway between the T.L. and Bermondsey. Since the opening of Tower B. the tunnel has been used for carrying hydraulic mains beneath the Thames. In 1884 the Inner Circle Railway was completed. In 1890 the first section of the City and South London Railway was opened—from K. William St. to Stockwell. In 1900 the Central Railway was opened between Shepherd's Bush and the Bank. The fare being at first uniform for any distance it was known as the 'Twopenny Tube.' It was followed by the Great Northern and City (1904), and the Bakerloo—Baker St. to Lambeth N. to begin with (1906).

STEAMBOATS. During the centuries previously reviewed from a transport aspect, the Thames at one time was used for the same purpose as much as the road. It has steadily declined in favour. As travel became faster on land there was a tendency to become impatient of the slowness of the water-way. Some idea of what the activity was at one time on the river will be obtained by reference to articles on the Watermen's Co. (see 'Companies; A') and 'The Thames' in this volume. There was no real passenger service on the Thames until 1815, when Mr. Geo. Dodd bought a steamboat at Glasgow, fitted it up, brought it to L., and organized pleasure trips on the river. In 1831 steamers were running daily through the season from the City to Richmond, and from the St. Katherine Docks to various seaside resorts. Later a halfpenny steamer plied between the Adelphi Pier and L.B. In 1847, when it was on the point of leaving the former, it blew up, causing six deaths and a large number of injuries. The River Thames Steam Navigation Co. (1872–87) and its successor, the Thames Steamboat Co. (1887–1902), ran services of boats with a moderate amount of success. In Milford Lane, Strand—at its junction with Tweezers Alley—can still be seen part of an inscription directing to the steamboats. The L.C.C. took over the boats of the latter. This service was inaugurated in 1905, the P. of Wales, afterwards George V, embarking on one at Westminster Pier. The boats, about thirty in number, were named after celebrated Londoners. The service was unfortunately not sufficiently remunerative, and was discontinued after a few yrs. In 1924 the 'Edmund Ironside' was seen on the Tigris River. The name was still visible on the stern, but it had been renamed 'Azizieh' (Home of Aziz), and the skipper wore white robes and a turban.

In 1948 a water bus service began and this now plies regularly in season between Greenwich, Westminster, Kew and even Windsor.

TRAMCARS. According to Prof. Weekley the word 'tram' goes back to 1555. He quotes a will 'To the amendinge of the highwaye or tram, from the west ende of Bridgegait, in Barnard Castle 20s.' The name is not, therefore, derived from Jas. Outram, an engineer, who in 1776 laid down a light railway at the D. of Norfolk's colliery at Sheffield. Passenger tramways

were first seen in America in 1832 between New York and Harlem. The first in England was at Birkenhead, laid down by Francis Train in 1860. In L. they made their debut that yr., through the instigation of the same gentleman. It is remarkable that where trams were first seen in L. they are not now to be found. The first line was from Marble Arch, along Bayswater Rd., to Paddington. The following yr. another line was permitted to be laid along Victoria St. to Pimlico. The lines were, however, raised above the ground, and were therefore such an intolerable nuisance that, after a few months' experiment, their removal was ordered. But the suppression of the trams was only temporary; their eventual success was as inevitable as the train's. In 1870 the first regular tram service was inaugurated by the opening of a line between Brixton Station and Kennington Gate, and a week later E. London followed suit with a line between Whitechapel Ch. and Bow Ch. After a few years' use in a few places of cable trams, notably up 'Brixton Hill, in 1905 electric trams appeared, the P. of Wales (George V) rode in the first one from Westminster B. Trams have cut poor figures in literature. They came too late for Dickens, and they made but rare appearances in Gissing. H. G. Wells referred to them in terms of praise as land gondolas, and in *Riceyman Steps* Arnold Bennett wrote of 'a hell of noise and dust and dirt, with the County of London tramcars.' The fastidious Bennett did not ride in them, or he would laconically have said 'L.C.C.' Under the London Passenger Transport Board (see 'London Transport Board') the tramcar was destined to disappear before the trolley bus, the first of which ran in L. in 1935. From 1st Oct. 1950 many trams were scrapped, and for the first time buses ran along the whole length of the Victoria Embankment.

(See *Locomotion in Victorian London*, by G. A. Seckon, 1938, and *Travel in England*, by Thos. Burke, 1946.)

The London Transport Board. The L. Passenger Transport Board was incorporated by Act of Parliament on 13th Apr. 1933, to take over and merge the railway undertakings of the Metropolitan Railway, the Metropolitan District Railway, the L. Electric Railway (which itself comprised the former Great Northern, Piccadilly and Brompton Railway, the Charing Cross, Euston and Hampstead Railway and the Baker Street and Waterloo Railway), the City and South L. Railway, and the other Central L. Railway; the whole of the tramway undertakings in the L. area, the L. General Omnibus Co. Ltd. and practically all the bus and coach undertakings working regular services wholly within the L. Passenger Transport Area. It commenced operation on 1st July 1933.

On 1st Jan. 1948, the London Transport Executive (commonly called 'London Transport'), as agents of the British Transport Commission, constituted under the Transport Act, 1947, assumed the obligation, in conjunction with the Railway Executive, of providing an efficient, adequate, economical, and properly integrated system of passenger transport both by road and by rail in the L. Passenger Transport Area.

Following an announcement in 1967 from the Govt. and the G.L.C. it is expected that from 1969 (or thereabouts), L. Transport will cease to be a nationalized undertaking and the L. Transport Board will become responsible to the G.L.C.

The L. Transport area runs from N. of Stevenage to Horsham and from W. of Amersham to E. of Gravesend, an area of 65 by 50 miles. The population of this area in 1967 was 10,217,000 of which 3,119,000 (30 per cent) were in Inner L., 4,762,000 (47 per cent) were in Outer L. and 2,336,000 (23 per cent) were in the Outer Country Area. It is estimated that the population served in 1981 will be 10,650,000.

The traffic on the services in 1967 was:

	Passengers carried (million)	Passenger miles paid for (million)	Car miles (million)
Central buses .	1,760	3,711	227
Country buses .	195	497	39
Coaches .	24	243	21
Railways. .	661	3,045	198
Total .	2,640	7,496	485

More than 9,000 car parking spaces are available at L. Transport stations and the number is rapidly increasing. Automatic trains, manned only by a single 'train operator' are being introduced, as is automatic ticket issue and control. A new Underground line, the Victoria Line, was

opened in 1969, while extensions planned are for the Aldwych branch to Waterloo, the Fleet line from Stanmore to Surrey Docks, and the extension of the Piccadilly line to Heathrow Airport.

The problems involved in serving central L. can be seen from the figures of a one-day census of road traffic entering central L. during the morning peak period (7 a.m. to 10 a.m.):

	Vehicles	Passengers
L.T. buses and coaches .	4,400	172,000
Private cars . . .	69,700	98,100
Motor cycles and scooters .	8,500	9,000
Pedal cycles . . .	3,700	3,700
Total . . .	86,300	282,800

Between 1957 and 1967 the number of road vehicles entering central L. during the morning peak rose by 15,000 (21 per cent) but the number of people who travelled by road decreased by nearly 64,000 (18 per cent). (All figures from L.T.B. Annual Report 1967.)

The Head Office of L. Transport is at 55 Broadway, Westminster, S.W.1, over St. James Park Station. This striking bdg. has been a well-known landmark since its erection in 1929, and possesses exterior sculptures symbolical of Day and Night by Jacob Epstein. There is also a medallion of Ld. Ashfield. The design is cruciform, and the bdg. covers an area of 31,000 sq. feet.

Lost Monuments. The most historic is the statue of Charles II from the Stocks Market. This was erected in 1672 through the loyalty of Sir Robt. Vyner, who was Ld.M. in 1674. The statue had really been designed to represent Sobieski, K. of Poland, trampling down a Turk, and there are two versions of how Vyner acquired it: one that he found it boxed up on Tower Wharf, awaiting exportation; the other that he first heard of it at Leghorn, and bought it for a song. At any rate the gentleman who called Charles II back to have 't'other bottle' (see *Spectator*, 20th Aug. 1712) had the head of the Polish monarch altered to represent Charles II, but left the supposititious Cromwell underneath the horse with a turban on his head.

There is a piquant passage about it in Defoe's *A Tour thro' the Whole Island of Great Britain* (1727):

'They tell us a merry story of this statue, how true it may be, let those testify who saw it, if any such witnesses remain, viz. That a certain famous Court lady, I do not say it was the Duchess of Portsmouth, being brought to bed of a son late in the night, the next morning this glorious equestrian statue had a pillion handsomely placed on it behind the body of the king, with a paper pinned to the trapping of the pillion, with words at length, "Gone for a midwife." '

The statue was removed in 1738 in clearing the site for the Mansion House (*q.v.*). It had attracted more attention from waggish versifiers than any L. statue has ever done. The most amusing of these efforts was: *A Dialogue Between two Horses—the one bearing Charles I at Charing Cross, the other Charles II at the Stocks Market*. 'The Last Dying Speech and Confession' of the latter was given as follows:

'Ye whimsical people of London's fair town,
Who one year put up what the next year you pull down;
Full sixty-one years have I stood in this place,
And never till now met with any disgrace.
What affront to crowned heads could you offer more bare
Than to pull down a king to make room for a Mayor?
'The great Sobieski, on horse with long tail
I first represented when set up for sale;
A Turk, as you see, was placed under my feet,
To prove o'er the Sultan my triumph complete.
'When the King was restored, you then, in a trice,
Called me Charles the Second, and, by way of device,
Said the old whiskered Turk had Oliver's face—
Though you know, to be conquered, he ne'er felt the disgrace.
'As the market is moved, I'm obliged to retreat:
I could stay there no longer with nothing to eat:
Now the herbs and the greens are all carried away,
I must trot unto those who will find me in hay.'

Until 1779 the statue lay about in a builder's yard, and then the Common Council presented it to a descendant of Vyner's, who set it up at Gautby Park, Lincolnshire.

The original statue of Q. Anne which was outside St. P.'s Cath. (see 'Statues') is in the garden of a convent at Holmhurst St. Mary, near St. Leonards. A statue of Charles II, which was in Soho Sq., and was the work of the Danish sculptor, Caius Gabriel Cibber, went to Grim's Dyke, Harrow (Sir Wm. Gilbert's estate) in 1876. It was returned to Soho Sq. in 1938. Still another statue of Charles II has travelled—not surprisingly, for his merits have not worn well. It stood outside the old Southwark Town Hall erected in 1686, and demolished in 1793. His Majesty was rejected as an ornament for the new bdg., and was bought by a few local worthies. They set him up on a hollow pedestal of brick, whose interior they turned into a watch-box. The statue survived the disappearance of the latter, and later was found in a field near Hayes in Middlesex. It was purchased by some Kensington dealer, and when he proceeded to remove it he was surprised to find a solemn crowd and a watchful lawyer in attendance. There was a local legend that underneath a treasure of gold lay hidden. The present whereabouts of the statue, seen by Wilfrid Whitten in Kensington in 1915, is unknown. The statue of George I, which stood in the centre of Leicester Sq., was removed in 1872 and sold for £16. It is believed to have been broken up.

A statue of George III, set up in Berkeley Sq. in 1760, was removed in 1827, and its whereabouts are unknown.

The large statue of George IV, was erected at King's Cross in 1833 and taken down in 1842, was probably destroyed.

William IV's statue, which was placed at the E. end of King William St. in 1844, was removed to Greenwich Park in 1935.

A statue of Sir Robt. Peel, erected in Cheapside in 1855, was removed in 1935.

The D. of Wellington has suffered most from removals. In 1887 the colossal statue at Hyde Park Corner was removed to Fox Hills, Aldershot. Another statue, set up on Tower Green in 1841, was removed to Woolwich.

Lost Rivers. L. possesses many streams

which are usually referred to as 'lost' rivers, though perhaps some could more correctly be described as 'hidden,' as they still exist, flowing in unromantic pipes instead of as open streams, as formerly. A river can sometimes be diverted, but it is a very hard thing to lose it altogether.

The following are the chief 'lost' rivers in the metropolis:

FLEET. The name is from Anglo-Saxon —*fléot*—a creek or inlet. 'Fleet,' 'Northfleet,' 'Purfleet,' and 'Ebbsfleet' are names similarly derived. It had two distinct sources: the W. arm from Hampstead ponds; the E. from Highgate ponds. These two arms formed a junction at Hawley Rd., a little above the Regent's Canal. Keeping a nearly due southerly direction it followed the windings of Pancras Rd., and flowed towards Battle Bridge. It then passed between Bagnigge Wells Rd. (King's Cross Rd. now) and Gray's Inn Rd., and where is now Mount Pleasant Post Office it made an almost right-angled turn towards Clerkenwell Green. Its course then lay beneath Ray St. until it reached Farringdon Rd., and thence it proceeded with few bendings to Holborn Bridge, where it ran between high banks, which gradually fell away until it reached the Thames at a spot a little to the W. of Blackfriars Bridge. Its width at the mouth is estimated at one time to have been 600 ft.

In 1200 K. John granted to the Knights Templars a place 'upon the Flete' near Castle Baynard to construct a tide mill. In 1307 Henry Lacy, E. of Lincoln (see 'Lincoln's Inn'), complained that this mill farther up the stream lessened the width and depth of water under Holeburne Bridge and Fleet Bridge. The E.'s petition refers to the time when ten or twelve 'navies' (ships) with merchandise 'were wont to come to Flete Bridge, and some of them to Holeburne Bridge.' The result of the petition was that the creek was cleaned, and the mills removed. It was soon, however, choked with filth again, and a commission was shortly afterwards appointed to arrange for its cleansing. In 1355 inquiry was made as to the state of the ditch surrounding the Fleet Prison (see 'Prisons'), and the jurors said it ought to be 10 ft. broad, and have sufficient water to float a vessel freighted with a tun of wine. It was found that the course of the water

was so obstructed that it no longer surrounded the prison. In 1502 it was cleared from the Thames to Holborn, and once more made navigable thus far for barges laden with fish and fuel. The names of Seacoal Lane and Newcastle St. recall the latter cargoes. Between 1668 and 1673, under the supervision of Wren, the Fleet river was canalized over a length of about 2,100 ft. to Holborn Bridge. Wharfs on both sides were 35 ft. in breadth. This, however, did not appear to benefit trade, and in 1732 it was found choked with mud. Gay, in *Trivia* (1716) had referred to

'Where Fleet Ditch with muddy current flows.'

Pope's reference to the Fleet river in the *Dunciad* (1728) suggests that there was no improvement since Ben Jonson—in one of his epigrams—described 'Fleet lane furies' (the lane still leads off Farringdon St.) as throwing into it

'. . . grease, and hair of measled hogs,
The heads, houghs, entrails, and the hides of dogs.'

Pope made Dulness descend

'To where Fleet Ditch with disemboguing streams
Rolls the large tribute of dead dogs to Thames,
The king of dykes! than whom no sluice of mud
With deeper sable blots the silver flood.'

The patriotic Ld. Chesterfield, seeking a derisive comparison for the Seine, said they had a river in L. like it, and called it the Fleet Ditch. In 1737 the river was covered in so far as Fleet Bridge, and thereafter there remained a small filthy dock. In 1763 a man slipped in and was suffocated by the mud. A Bromley barber was found one morning stuck in with feet in air. He had been frozen to death. In 1765 the rest of the stagnant stream was covered in. In 1835 a man making a new sewer slipped in, and was carried into the Fleet ditch, and

'owing to its having been swollen by the heavy shower, floated along as far as the mouth at Blackfriars, where his body was found, covered with the filth of the sewer.'

In 1840 a Mr. Anthony Crosby accomplished the hazardous feat of exploring the stream. The tide rose so fast that he had to fly, and was somewhat wet and very exhausted when he arrived at Holborn Bridge. In 1919 there was a proposal for a subway under Ludgate Circus, but it was said to be impracticable by reason of the flow of the water from the Fleet River. It is still possible to walk up the bed of the river to Hampstead, but it is permissible only to officials of the G.L.C.

There were three bridges over the Fleet river, a name only borne by the stream S. of Holborn Bridge. N. of there it was known variously as the Hole Burne, the River of Wells, and Turnmill Brook. Holborn Bridge was where the viaduct is now. Wren rebuilt it, and the name of Wm. Hooker, Ld.M. 1673–4, was cut on the coping of the E. approach. In 1840, during the opening of a sewer at Holborn Hill, an arch of the old bridge, about 20 ft. span, was disinterred. The mayor's name and the date were still visible. The next was called the Middle Bridge. It was at Fleet Lane, and the arch was high enough to permit the passage of ships beneath. Next in order was Fleet Bridge, which was where is now Ludgate Circus. Stow described it as a stone bridge, coped on both sides, with iron pikes, with stone lanthorns on the S. side. It had either been built or repaired by John Wells (Ld.M.) in 1431, and on the coping Wells, 'imbraced by angels,' was engraved. This bridge was burnt in the G.F. A new bridge was built, and Strype says it had sides breast high, and the City arms engraved thereon. Ned Ward (1699) says that on the bridge were nuts, gingerbread, oranges, and oysters piled up in movable shops that ran upon wheels, attended by ill-looking fellows, some with but one eye, and others without noses. Over against these stood a parcel of trugmoldies, in straw hats and flat caps, selling stockings and furmity, night-caps, and plum puddings. There was a coffee house—the 'Rainbow' —on the bridge in 1751. It was demolished in 1765, when the river was finally covered in. At the same time Bridewell Bridge (about where is now Bridewell Pl.) was removed. It was of stone, and against the back gate of the prison (see 'Prisons'). In addition to Newcastle St., Fleet Lane, and Seacoal Lane, Turnagain Lane (off Farringdon St.) has reference to the

Fleet river making it a cul-de-sac. It was 'Wendageynes lane' *c.* 1293, and was probably in Wm. Tyndale's mind when, in a sermon in 1531 he referred to 'a turnagaine lane which they cannot goe through.' There was an old proverb that 'he must take him a house in Turn-again Lane.' It is first found mentioned by its present name in 1601.

WALBROOK. The derivation of the name has been much discussed. The earliest form, H. A. Harben says, is 'Walebroc' (1114–30), and his conclusion, therein confirming J. R. Green, is that it had nothing to do with its flowing beneath the wall of L., but came from the Anglo-Saxon *wealh,* meaning a stranger, and was the brook of the strangers, perhaps so called by the Saxon settlers. The name 'Wales' has the same source. Harben suggests that the strangers may have been the Britons; equally plausibly J. R. Green thought that it was from the fact that on its navigable channel the trade of the foreigner was brought up from the Thames to the very heart of the 'chepe' or market at the port or hythe commemorated in Barge Yard, fixed by tradition in modern Bucklersbury. In 1871, when Q. Victoria St. was being constructed, a barge was there found embedded in the mud with the calcined remains of a load of corn still in it. There was the same difficulty in keeping the Walbrook clean, as there was in the case of the Fleet River. In 1288 it was ordained that the watercourse of the Walbrook should be made free from dung and other nuisances. It had already at this time been partially covered in, and in 1374 the moor of Finsbury was leased to a brewer for seven yrs., without rent, but upon the understanding that he would keep the said moor well and properly, and have the watercourse of the Walbrook cleansed for the whole of the term. In 1383, however, this lease having apparently expired, it was ordered to be kept clean under supervision of aldermen of the wards through which it passed. In 1415 the canalization of the Walbrook commenced; here again it anticipated the Fleet river, which was so treated after the G.F. In 1463 the inhabitants were ordered to vault it over, and pave, each to be responsible for that part opposite his own house or land so far as the middle of the stream, and any refusing to obey were threatened that their land would be forfeited, and given to others who were willing to execute the work. The bridges over the Walbrook were at Blomfield St., at Bucklersbury, and at Cloak Lane, which in Stow's time was Horseshoe Bridge St. According to the same writer at Dowgate, where the Walbrook entered the Thames, a fatality occurred in 1574.

'In the afternoon there fell a storm of rain where through the channels suddenly arose, and ran with such a swift course towards the common shores, that a lad of 18 years old minding to have leapt over the channel near unto the said conduit, was taken with the stream, and carried from thence towards the Thames with such a violence, that no man with staves or otherwise could stay him, till he came against a cart wheel that stood in the said watergate, before which time he was drowned and stark dead.'

In 1803, Sir Richd. Phillips, author of a history of L., saw the Walbrook 'still trickling among the foundations of the new buildings at the Bank.' It now seems to be not merely a buried river, but one that is dead. It is sometimes said that it can be seen trickling into the Thames about where is Cannon St. Railway Bridge, but there is now no outlet to the river. What has been mistaken for the Walbrook is a sewer.

THE WESTBOURNE rose near Jack Straw's Castle Tavern at Hampstead, whence it flowed across the Finchley Rd., after which it turned S. to Kilburn High Rd., and from this reason was also sometimes known as the Kilbourne. It proceeded to the Uxbridge Rd., where it was formerly known as Baynard's Water (from which comes the name 'Bayswater') after a former landowner in this district. It still runs overground for a space, for the Serpentine in Hyde Park is but the Westbourne river widened out into a lake. At Sloane Sq. tube station the Westbourne is 'seen' every day by thousands who do not recognize it, for it flows through a huge iron conduit 15 ft. above the platform and finally joins the Thames near Chelsea Bridge. Old chronicles tell of the Westbourne as late as the early 19th century, overflowing its banks, and the inhabitants round Knightsbridge being forced to take to boats till the floods subsided.

THE TYBOURNE was a little river that rose in two sources: one from the Old Shepherd's Well by Fitzjohn's Av., NW., and the second near the Old Belsize House at Hampstead. The two streams met at Avenue Rd., and formed one river as they flowed S. across Marylebone Rd. and High St., then down Marylebone Lane, formerly a small riverside pathway on the left bank of the stream, which accounts for the crookedness of that thoroughfare. It then crossed Oxford St., by Stratford Place (the Street Ford), and on to Brick St. The former name of this was Engine St., which indicates the existence of some sort of water-wheel in bygone times. The stream continued on across Piccadilly into the Green Park, and passed the site of Buckingham Palace. At this point the river divided into three parts before it joined the Thames: one followed mainly the direction of Vauxhall Bridge Rd.; the second fed the lake in St. James's Park; the third ran through what were formerly the gardens of W.A., where it worked the mill built by the monks.

South London has several hidden rivers.

THE EFFRA is the best known, and can still be seen above ground for about a quarter of a mile in Dulwich village, near which it rises in the woods towards Norwood. It once flowed alongside Croxted Lane (now Croxted Rd.), and past Brockwell Park. It now enters a conduit at Dulwich village, which leads it through Brixton, Stockwell, and Kennington, where it once ran through the meadows that now form the Oval Cricket Ground, and so on to the Thames at Vauxhall Bridge.

THE NECKINGER once flowed through the Bermondsey Marshes, across the Old Kent Rd., at a spot known as St. Thomas-a-Watering, where the Canterbury Pilgrims first halted, as mentioned by Chaucer in *The Canterbury Tales*. Later on it flowed by 'Jacob's Island,' a spot of evil reputation, made familiar by Chas. Dickens in *Oliver Twist*.

THE FALCON BROOK rose near Nightingale Lane at Balham, and flowed across Battersea Fields to the Thames; the tramlines down Falcon Rd. followed the course of this little river, for the road above it was at one time its bankpath.

THE TYGRIS. Traces of the stream which bore this curious name were discovered a little while ago near the 'Elephant and Castle.' Possibly, however, it was not really a river at all, but the remains of the canal cut by Canute to get the Danish ships above the heavily defended London Bridge. Up to a hundred years ago several traces of it were visible in Lambeth Marshes, but all have now disappeared, except by accidental exposure during building excavations.

It will be easily seen how these little rivers affected the nomenclature of L., and gave their names to many well-known streets, such as Fleet St., Holborn; Westbourne Grove; Kilburn Rd.; Walbrook; and dozens of others which all tend to remind us of the important part these 'lost' rivers played in the daily life of medieval L.

(See *Springs, Streams, and Spas of London*, by A. S. Foord, 1910, and 'The Fleet and Its Neighbourhood in Early and Medieval Times,' by Marjorie B. Honeybourne, *London Topographical Record*, No. xix, 1947; *The Lost Rivers of London*, by N. J. Barton, 1962.)

Ludgate was probably one of the Roman gates, though probably later in date than Newgate, which had a name that belied its history. It may have been erected when the original Roman city was extended westwards. It has been suggested that 'Ludgate' is a Celtic survival, Lud being a Celtic god of water-worship. Remains of a temple to this deity have been found at Lydney in Gloucestershire, where there were small plaques of bronze representing him. Possibly the fine head of a river-god in the B.Mus. was supposed to be a representation of Lud. The statement of Geoffrey of Monmouth that the gate was built by K. Lud in 66 B.C. cannot be accepted. K. Lud seems to have been a mythical personage, though what purports to be his head is carved on the K. Lud Tavern at Ludgate Circus. The first mention is 'Lutgata' (1100–35). It may have been derived from the personal name 'Luda' or 'Lude', or from Old English hlidgeat or hlydgeat (a postern). It was repaired in 1260, and beautified with images of K. Lud and his two sons— on the E. side. Over it was Ludgate Prison (*q.v.*). In the reign of Edward VI the citizens, in their zeal against idolatry,

smote off the heads of K. Lud and his two sons. Q. Mary had them replaced. In 1554 a strong force was thrown into Ludgate to thwart the advance of Sir Thos. Wyatt and his followers. On being refused admission by Ld. Wm. Howard, he sat down despondent outside the Belle Sauvage Inn (*q.v.*). In 1586 the gate, having become 'sore decayed,' was pulled down. It was newly built with fresh images of K. Lud and his sons on the E. side, and a statue of Q. Elizabeth on the W. side. The gate was not much damaged in the G.F. In 1760 it was pulled down, and the materials sold. The statue of Q. Elizabeth is now in Fleet St. (see 'City Churches;' C'—St. Dunstan in the West). The figures of K. Lud and his two sons, according to Thornbury (*Old and New London*) were assigned to the par. bone-house. The Marquis of Hertford, however, purchased them, together with the old clock, and took them to his villa in Regent's Park. They returned, with the clock, in 1935, and are in the entrance doorway to St. Dunstan's Sch. At the coronation in 1911 an inscription was displayed outside the K. Lud Tavern: 'King Lud welcomes George V.'

Ludgate Circus was constructed between 1864 and 1875. On the S. side, until its removal in 1950, was an obelisk that was erected in 1775 as a lamp standard by order of the C.C. It bore the inscription, after the date, 'The Right Honorable John Wilkes, Lord Mayor.' It had come to be regarded as a memorial to Wilkes, as he was Alderman of the Ward of Farringdon Without, in which the Circus is. It was not intended as such. The obelisk (also removed) on the N. side is in memory of Robt. Waithman (see 'City Churches; C'—St. Bride). NW. of the Circus is a tablet with a bas-relief inscribed as follows:

Edgar Wallace
Reporter
Born London 1875
Died Hollywood 1932
Founder member of the Company of
Newspaper Makers
He knew wealth and poverty
yet he had walked with kings and kept his bearing, and his talents he gave lavishly to authorship but to Fleet Street he gave his heart.

Ludgate Hill, at its W. end, was originally called 'Fletestrete,' the same name being used for the thoroughfare right up to the gate. E. to St. Paul's Chyd. it was Ludgate St. or, earlier (1359) Bowyer Row. It is mentioned as Ludgate Hill first in the time of Q. Elizabeth. It was widened in 1864, when Ludgate Circus was formed; again in 1893.

John Evelyn lived at the 'Hawk and Pheasant' on Ludgate Hill 1658–9. The L. Coffee House was on the N. side. It was opened in 1731 by Jas. Ashley. Here, in the early part of the 18th century, book auctions were held. It was later a resort of Americans, and also a meeting-place of a scientific club of which Dr. Priestley was president, and Dr. Price, Benjamin Franklin and other scientists were members. The grandfather of John Leech was landlord for some years, and was succeeded by his son, the father of the artist. Here Arthur Clennam, in *Little Dorrit*, sat one Sunday evening maddened by the jangling of ch. bells. The ground floor has been rebuilt, but the upper part of the premises (No. 42) remain unchanged. At No. 45 Wm. Hone had a shop, and here published his *Every-Day Book* and his *Year Book*. In the shop window, about 1817, Hone displayed an etching by Cruikshank of an imitation bank note. There was the £ sign made by a noose, a number of manacles, and eleven criminals hanging, the note being signed: 'For the Govr. and Compa of the Bank of England, J. Ketch.' This was Cruikshank's protest against the number of executions for forging £1 bank notes. It caused a great sensation, and the crowds gathered in such numbers that the Ld.M. had to send for such police as the City could then provide to disperse the crowd. The bank directors held a meeting, and they decided to issue no more of the notes. (The etching is reproduced in *Bygone Punishments*, by Wm. Andrews, 1890.)

M

Main Drainage is an unsavoury subject, vital to the health of L. It was entirely ignored as a public concern until recent times; once everyman was his own sanitary authority. The Thames, for this reason, was little better than an open sewer. There had been commissioners of drains and sewers for particular undertakings since the beginning of the 14th century, and in 1667 there were set up by the Court of Common Council Commissioners of Sewers, a permanent body for the whole City. Outside it was left to the chance interest of the par. In 1843 the Poor Law Commissioners found the state of L. sewerage so bad that they went out of their way to call attention to the need for remedial legislation. Local sewers discharged into the Thames, and at low tide the mud stank. Parliament, itself affected by the foul state of the river, readily took the matter up. Cesspools were completely abolished in 1847, about 30,000 being removed in six years. In 1850 the C.C. appointed a sanitary inspector at a salary of £150 p.a. The M.B.W. came into existence in 1855 largely to improve matters. It constructed great subterranean rivers to take sewage outside L.—in the N. to Barking; in the S. to Crossness. When, however, those districts came to be built over, and complaints of the pollution of the river became general, a royal commission was appointed. The gist of the report, issued two years later, was that sewage should not be discharged into the river in its crude state. Out of this report came the elaborate plant and machinery at Barking and Crossness. At both places sewage is treated, the effluent discharging into the Thames, the sludge being taken down the river by the G.L.C.'s steamers and deposited in the sea. The G.L.C. is responsible for the main sewers, but the L. Bors. for the local sewers, which total a mileage of over 2,000.

It is remarkable that main drainage has been the subject of verse. Samuel Carter, a Victorian poet—said to have suggested Samuel Pecksniff to Dickens—wrote:

'Magnificent, too, is the system of drains,
Exceeding the far-spoken wonders of old:
So lengthened and vast in its branches
    and chains,
That labyrinths pass like a tale that is
    told:
The sewers gigantic, like multiplied veins,
Beneath the whole city their windings
    unfold,
Disgorging the source of plagues, scourges
    and pains,
Which visit those cities to cleanliness cold.
Well did the ancient proverb lay down
    this important text,
That cleanliness for human weal to
    godliness is next.'

Mansion House was the first official home of the Lord Mayors. Prior to its erection they held their mayoralty in their own houses. Sir Geo. Barne (1587) received people 'over against the George in Lombard-street.' Some Lord Mayors, living in rooms over their places of business, hired a house for the year of office. One was hired in Old Jewry, another—afterwards the Windmill Inn—in Lothbury. No doubt sometimes they made the honour patent by some kind of inscription. In the G.Mus. there is a stone, carved: 'Sir Peter Proby Lord Mayor 1623,' which was outside his house in Gower's Walk, Whitechapel. Williamson's Hotel, Bow Lane, was wrongly called the 'Old Mansion House,' and the same name was once given to a mansion in Cheapside. (No. 73) occupied by Sir Wm. Turner (Ld.M. 1668-9).

In 1670, a Mansion House was contemplated, but only in 1728 did the C.C. appoint a committee to select a proper site, procure plans, and provide the funds. One source of the latter was the fines received from persons who refused, on conscientious or other grounds, to serve the office of sheriff, which by 1736 amounted to £20,700. After the inspection of many sites, in 1735 the committee decided on the Stocks Market (see 'Markets'); part of the site was also that of the chyd. of St. Mary Woolchurch Haw (see 'City Churches; A'). The architect chosen was Geo. Dance, the elder. He produced a stately bdg., erected upon piles between 1739 and 1752. Sidney Perks, historian of the Mansion House, described it as 'sedate, severe, churchy, and dignified, a kind of Hallelujah Chorus in stone.' It cost more than £70,000.

It had two curious excrescences called the 'Noah's Ark' and 'Mare's Nest.' The former was removed in 1795; the latter in 1842. The first Ld.M. to go into residence was Sir Crisp Gascoigne (1753).

The principal apartment is the dining-room; it accommodates nearly 400 guests, and is known as the Egyptian Hall. In 1868 the two windows were filled with stained glass; the four compartments depicting the signing of Magna Carta; Q. Elizabeth's procession from the City to Westminster; the death of Wat Tyler; procession of Edward VI. After the Great Exhibition of 1851 a number of marble statues by eminent sculptors were placed round the hall. The two most imposing are 'Caractacus,' by J. H. Foley, R.A., and 'Sardanapalus,' by H. Weekes, R.A. In the Old Ballroom, one of the most beautiful apartments, there is an ornate representation in plaster of the mythological legend of Leda and the Swan. In the Victorian era it caught the eye of 'Mrs. Grundy,' and was boarded up for a year! In the saloon (it was open to the sky before 1793, when a roof was erected) are four pieces of tapestry.

In 1930 over £60,000 were spent on repairs, during the course of which the Ld.M., Sir Wm. Phene Neal, lived at the Hotel Metropole in Northumberland Avenue.

One Ld.M. (Nottage—in 1885) has died at the Mansion House, and one Lady Mayoress—Lady Pryke (1925). There have been several marriages. Two Lady Mayoresses (Miss White and Miss Pryke) were m. at St. P.'s Cath.; and, daughters of Ld.M. Knight, Ld.M. Davies, and Ld.M. Samuel were m. from the Mansion House. There have been two births: Augusta Perchard Winter, grand-daughter of the Ld.M. (1805) and a grandson of Ld.M. Cotton (1876). In 1919 a granddaughter of the Ld.M. (Ld. Marshall) was christened in his official residence.

There are busts of Q. Victoria, Edward VII, George V, and Edward VIII when P. of Wales. Amongst the plate are a silver tankard, given by Sir Bevis Bulmer in 1593; a small cup, given by Mr. Secondary Christopher in 1662; and the Oliver cup, given by the City to Alderman Oliver in 1772 for joining in the release of a freeman who had been illegally arrested by order of the H.C. Most of the other plate consists

of loving-cups, salvers, rose-water dishes, snuff-boxes, etc. There is also a pearl sword, presented to the City by Q. Elizabeth. It is the custom for each Ld.M. to add to the collection.

The justice room is one of the smallest police-courts. There are several cells below.

The railings were removed from the front of the Mansion House in 1886.

The Mansion House sustained some damage in the Second World War, but, after the bombing of the Guildhall, the Ld.M.'s Banquet was held in the Egyptian Hall. On one occasion Sir Geo. Wilkinson, then Ld.M., returning home after inspection of the City Fire-Fighting Services, found the Mansion House without windows, with doors shattered, ceilings down, and no lights. His dinner was served in the entrance hall by the light of hurricane lamps.

(See *History of the Mansion House*, by Sydney Perks, 1922; *The Mansion House*, by Lady Knill, 1937; *My Lord Mayor*, by Wm. Kent, 1948.)

Markets.

BILLINGSGATE MARKET. Geoffrey of Monmouth (c. 1100–54), as Stow says, derived the name from the supposed fact that

'Belin a King of the Britons, about 400 years before Christ's nativity builded this gate, and named it Belings-gate after his own calling: and that when he was dead his body being burned, the ashes in a vessel of brass were set upon a high pinnacle of stone over the same gate.'

Stow was almost certainly right in suggesting that it was a later Beling or Biling who gave it its name. It was probably one of the two gates in the river wall of the old Roman city which Fitzstephen said had been washed away, the other being Dow-gate. It was a port or quay from the earliest times, for in the Laws of K. Ethel-red (979) provision was made for the payment of tolls and customs by vessels arriving at 'Billingsgate.' In 1279 it was provided that all vessels should be moored at night either at Queenhithe or Billings-gate, and not elsewhere. At that time there was a dock at Billingsgate, as still at Queenhithe (*q.v.*). The Customs of Billingsgate in Edward III.'s time fixed the tolls that the several vessels were to pay according to their size, and the dues on various cargoes of coal and corn. It was then, like Queenhithe, primarily a corn market. In 1559 an Act was passed restricting the nature of goods sold, and a statute of 1699 made it a free and open market for fish. There was at times a resentment at this monopoly, and on the rebuilding of Hungerford Market, the *Gentleman's Magazine*, in 1832, said:

'It may now, however, be anticipated with confidence that this propinquity to water-carriage will make the situation particularly convenient for the sale of fish, and the removal of London Bridge will allow the vessels to come up, which was before impracticable. Thus an effectual remedy will be provided against the monopoly of that article which has been too long tolerated at Billingsgate.'

This hope was not realized, and a previous effort of the same kind in 1749—to establish a fish market at Westminster—had been frustrated. Between 1848 and 1853 the dock was filled up, and the market sheds were rebuilt by J. R. Bunning, the City architect. In 1874 the market was further enlarged. In 1908 there was a proposal to remove the market to Shadwell, but both the railway cos. and the fishing industry were opposed to it. During the past fifty yrs. some £350,000 has been expended on enlarging and improving Billingsgate Market, where annually about 200,000 tons of fish are handled. Opposite the market, at the corner of St. Mary at Hill, is a dispensary, with a few beds for accidents in the market.

'Billingsgate' as a synonym for ribald and abusive talk is very old. In *The Chronicle History of King Leir*, undoubtedly the source of the Shakespeare tragedy, the Messenger says, in reply to Goneril's recommendation of his 'good tongue': 'And as bad a tongue, if it be set on, as any oyster-wife at Billingsgate hath.' Addison, in the *Spectator* (1711), referred to the 'Debates which frequently arise among the Ladies of the British Fishery,' and, in 1712, said: 'Our Satyr is nothing but ribaldry and Billingsgate.' Tom Brown (1700) refers to the same thing, but found some bargees surpassed Billingsgate 'in stupendous obscenity, nitrous verbosity, and malicious scurrility.' Ned

Ward (1699) 'turn'd into the Crowd of Thumb-Ring'd Flat Caps, from the age of Seven to Seventy, who sat Snarling and Grunting at one another, over their Sprats and Whitings like a pack of Domestic Dogs over the Cook-Maids kindness, or a parcel of hungry Sows at a trough of Hogwash.'

BOROUGH MARKET was established by virtue of a royal charter granted by Edward VI, and in 1671 Charles II enacted that the market should continue to be held in that locality. In 1756 it was ordained that this market should no longer be held in the High St., the carts, stalls, and stands having become a nuisance to the carriages and cattle passing along it. In an Act of 1757, the area for a new market was defined. It included a piece of ground called the Triangle, and some bdgs. and courts adjoining, as well as a portion of the houses, ground, and bdgs. known as Rochester Yard, which formerly belonged to the Bp. of Rochester. This site formed the nucleus of the 'New' or Borough Market. It was rebuilt and greatly enlarged when the extension of the South-Eastern Railway to Cannon St. and Charing Cross was constructed. The area S. of Southwark Cath. is now nearly three acres in extent. The management of the market—for fruit and vegetables—is vested in trustees, including churchwardens and bor. councillors.

CALEDONIAN MARKET, between York Rd. and Caledonian Rd., covered about fifty acres. It was built on what used to be Copenhagen Fields, a site bought by the C.C. in 1852, covering 15 acres. The market was completed at a cost of about £500,000 and opened by the P. Consort in 1855. The cattle market, which could accommodate 42,000 sheep and 7,000 cattle at a time, besides thousands of calves and pigs, was held on Mondays and Thursdays, and the general market on Tuesdays and Fridays. Almost anything could be bought—from pins to bullocks. Despite much agitation the C.C. declined to allow the market to be re-opened after the Second World War. What is reckoned as a continuation is held every Friday in Bermondsey Sq., Tower Bridge Rd.

COVENT GARDEN MARKET started in an informal way, vendors of fruit and vegetables from the villages around using the centre of the sq. made by the arcade or piazza of Inigo Jones (see 'Westminster') for the display of their produce, simply because it was a convenient open space. In 1632 the E. of Bedford began to build sheds, and in 1671 market rights were acquired by the E. of Bedford in a charter granted by Charles II. In 1710, as appears from a print, it was still only an affair of stalls and sheds. There was a tendency to make it something of a fair, and Steele, in the *Spectator* (1712), mentions that 'People of Quality hastened to assemble at a Puppet-Show on the other Side of the Garden,' while the bells of St. Paul's Ch. were tolling, whilst another writer refers to the sale of medical herbs, snails, parrots, and love-birds. It continued to grow, and in 1830 the nucleus of the present bdgs. was erected by the sixth D. of Bedford from designs by Chas. Fowler. At the SE. corner of the quadrangle, stretching down to Tavistock St., the bdg. known as the English Flower Market was erected by the ninth D. of Bedford. The French Flower Market was erected in 1903. The market rights remained with the D. of Bedford up to 1910, when he sold them to a company. The market is open daily at 6 a.m., but the regular market days are Tuesdays, Thursdays, and Saturdays.

LEADENHALL MARKET has a long history. In 1357 poultry was ordered to be sold there. Whittington acquired the market and manorial rights in 1411, and through him they passed to the C.C., which has held them ever since. A granary was erected in 1446. It was used for the weighing and sale of cloth and wool, and in 1488 it was ordained that the assay of leather should be held there. The butchers had stalls there in 1595. In 1622 it was enacted that all cutlery was to be sold at Leadenhall, and nowhere else in the City; apparently shops and warehouses had been built for the purpose. It developed into a great meat market, and in 1662 the Spanish ambassador, after a visit, told Charles II that he believed more meat was sold there than in the whole of Spain. Leadenhall Market was destroyed by the G.F., and Strype (1720) described it, when rebuilt, as a very large bdg. of freestone, wholly converted into a market, with three courts: the Beef Market at the NE. corner of

Gracechurch St., properly Leadenhall; the Green Yard, with shops in the middle and on the S. and W. sides; and the Herb Market, also with stalls. The market house was at the E. end, inhabited by fishmongers, etc., and in the passages into the markets were poulterers, fishmongers, etc. Under the Act for the Improvement of Leadenhall Market, 1879–80, the old bdgs. were demolished, and the first stone of the new market, with an area of about 26,900 sq. ft., was laid in 1881, the principal entrance being in Gracechurch St. It has two small spires with birds as weather vanes. To-day there is partly a wholesale, and partly a retail, trade in poultry, fish, and miscellaneous provisions.

LONDON CENTRAL MARKETS (SMITHFIELD). A market was established in Smithfield in 1614 for the sale of livestock. There had been from the 12th century an annual market for livestock in connection with St. Bartholomew's Fair (*q.v.*). The removal of the cattle market did not take place until 1855. Then the trade was transferred to the Caledonian Market (*supra*), and in 1860 an Act was obtained for erecting market bdgs. on the site of Smithfield. The completion of these bdgs. in 1869 enabled the C.C. to abolish Newgate Market, which had become a serious obstruction to traffic. From time to time additions were made to the Central Markets, which now cover over eight acres, and have involved a capital expenditure of about £2,000,000. Although primarily a wholesale market for the sale of dead meat, poultry and provisions are also dealt in, and there is a section devoted to the sale, wholesale and retail, of fish and vegetables. Under the main bdg. there is an extensive railway goods depot. There are fifteen miles of meat-hanging rails, capable of hanging 60,000 sides of beef, approximately 9,000 tons. In 1964 the Ld. M. opened the new Poultry Market of Smithfield to replace one destroyed by fire in 1958.

SPITALFIELDS MARKET (for fruit and vegetables) received a charter from Charles II in 1682, granted to John Balch and his heirs. The freehold was purchased by the C.C. in 1902, and subsequently leasehold interests were acquired. Provision was made for an expenditure of £2,000,000, and as a result, instead of a straggling street market, there are thoroughly up-to-date bdgs., covering an area of about five acres, with floor space available for trade purposes over eight acres. Overseas products have been added to those home-grown, and approximately 1,500 tons are handled daily.

Mention should be made of five markets no longer existing.

CLARE MARKET came into existence in 1657. Howell refers to it as 'a new market called Clare Market; there is there a street and palace of the same name, built by the Earl of Clare who lives there in a princely manner, having a house, a street and a market both for flesh and fish, all bearing his name.'

The market, authorized by an Act of 1657, was on Tuesdays, Thursdays, and Saturdays. The market was never a large one, but Cunningham says that, so late as 1850, from 350 to 400 sheep, and from 50 to 200 oxen were slaughtered there. There was also a yard where the Jews did their slaughtering in accordance with their religious laws. The last vestiges of Clare Market disappeared during the Aldwych - Kingsway improvement (1900–5).

COLUMBIA MARKET, situated between Hackney and Bethnal Green Rds., was built by Baroness Burdett-Coutts, under the powers given by the Bethnal Green Market and Approaches Act, 1866. Opened in 1869, it was a philanthropic enterprise, and was intended as a general market to relieve the narrow and crowded streets of their stalls. It was not a success, probably because many of the street traders begrudged the expense and girded at the restraints. It was afterwards used as a fish market, but this project was also a failure. The C.C. took control for a short time, but, as it could not be made self-supporting, it was returned to the baroness in 1874. The bdg., which can claim some architectural beauty, cost £200,000.

FLEET MARKET, for meat and vegetables, occupied the centre of the whole length of what is now known as Farringdon St. It followed the removal of the Stocks Market (see *infra*) for the erection of the Mansion House. The Fleet River was covered over for the purpose so far as Ludgate Circus. It consisted of two lines of shops, one storey high, with a covered walk between them, provided with skylights. It was closed in 1829.

HUNGERFORD MARKET was erected on the gardens of Hungerford House, the residence of Sir Edwd. Hungerford, in 1680. On the N. side of the market was a bust of the knight who probably hoped by its means to retrieve his fortunes. It never really prospered, perhaps because of the proximity of Covent Garden Market. In 1815 it almost came to an end, but in 1831 it was rebuilt, when it became a meat, fish, vegetable, and fruit market. In 1862, when Charing Cross railway station was constructed, the market disappeared. Its site was W. of Villiers St.

NEWGATE MARKET was in Newgate St. before the G.F. Increasing in size and importance after the G.F., it was removed from the par. of St. Nicholas Shambles to the S. side of Newgate St. The market was closed on the construction of the Central Meat Market at Smithfield in 1869. Paternoster Sq. is on the site.

SHADWELL FISH MARKET, opened in 1885, covered 4½ acres, and was 1½ miles E. of Billingsgate; it was closed during the First World War.

STOCKS MARKET. First mentioned 10 Edward I (*c.* 1282) as a place adjoining the wall of the chyd. of St. Mary Woolchurch, erected for the sale of flesh and fish. It was ordained that the rent arising from the stalls should go to the maintenance of London Bridge. It was so called from the City stocks being there. The market was rebuilt in 1410. After the G.F. it was enlarged. It was then also called 'Woolchurch Market.' Fruit, roots, and herbs were sold there in place of flesh and fish. It was removed about 1739 for the erection of the Mansion House (*q.v.*).

Marlborough House (Pall Mall) was erected in 1709–10 by Wren for the great D. of Marlborough, on land leased to the duchess through the good offices of Ld. Godolphin. It was built of small red bricks, and, according to one writer, the thrifty D. had them brought over from Holland, during his campaign, in the transports which plied between that country and Deptford. The walls were covered with pictures depicting the battles in which the D. had been engaged. He spent his last yrs. at Marlborough House, where, after his death at Windsor (1722), his body lay in state before burial in W.A., from whence it was removed twenty-four yrs. later to Blenheim. The duchess d. in the house, 1744. The third D. added another storey, and it remained in the family until 1817, when it passed to the Crown, and was allotted to the Princess Charlotte and her husband P. Leopold, afterwards K. of the Belgians. The princess died before it was ready for her occupation, but her husband lived there till 1831. In 1837 it was settled by Act of Parliament upon Q. Adelaide as a dowager house, and occupied by her until her death (1849). In 1850 it was settled upon the P. of Wales, but for some yrs. was used for a picture gallery. In 1861 it was remodelled for the P.'s occupation, and in 1863, on his marriage, he took possession. From that time, at the instance of Princess, afterwards Q., Alexandra, a Danish service was held on Sunday afternoons in the chapel —built in 1628 by Charles I for his Q., Henrietta Maria. It remained the L. house of the P. of Wales until he ascended the throne in 1901, and there in 1865 his son, the future George V, was b. The latter took up residence there when his father became K., and during her widowhood Q. Alexandra occupied Marlborough House. There is a memorial to her on the W. side of the house, fronting the road cut through the grounds of St. James's Palace after the fire there in 1809. In the gardens (the house and grounds cover four acres) are four tiny tombstones to the memory of Muff, Joss, and Tiny, three favourite dogs, and Benny, a pet rabbit; they were erected by Q. Alexandra. Edward VIII had no affection for it when P. of Wales, and preferred to reside at York House, St. James's. It has now little resemblance to the bdg. designed by Wren, a third storey being added at the end of the 18th century and an attic storey in the 19th century.

Metropolitan Board of Works. It was constituted under the Metropolis Local Management Act, 1855, the members being exclusively elected by the vestries. L. was thus provided for the first time with a central administration. The Board was, however, at its inception mainly a drainage authority (there had previously been seven commissions acting); otherwise it was to be the servants of the vestries. It had annually to report on the

work done. Many improvements were carried to a successful conclusion by the M.B.W. e.g. the construction of the two embankments (see 'Thames'), Queen Victoria St., and Northumberland Ave. Its powers were increased by Parliament from time to time, and in the course of its brief career it cleared 42 acres, affecting 22,900 persons, at a cost of £1,325,000. The M.B.W. came to an end by the provisions of the Local Government Act of 1888, which in part was provoked by charges of corruption so grave as to justify the appointment of a royal commission to deal with them. Under that Act the London County Council (q.v.) came into being.

Metropolitan Police. In 1784 Wm. Pitt introduced a Bill into the H. of C. for policing the streets of L., but City merchants saw in it plans for tyranny and espionage, and it was withdrawn. Similar suggestions were scouted until (Sir) Robt. Peel became Home Secretary in 1822. He appointed a committee to report on 'the state of the police,' and on means of obtaining for the metropolis as perfect a system of police as was consistent with the character of a free country. This commission was alarmed by possible restriction of freedom of action by a police force. Peel, however, continually pressed, and another committee of inquiry in 1828 was more favourable, but in consequence of opposition the City of L. was excluded and the Metropolitan Police came into existence under the Metropolitan Police Act, 1829. There were then ten police offices: Bow St.; Queen St.; Marlborough St.; Hatton Garden; Worship St.; Whitechapel; Shadwell; Union Hall (now Tower Bridge); the Marine Police Office (opened at 259 Wapping New Stairs in 1789); and 4 Whitehall Pl. The Metropolitan Police District, as planned in 1829, had a radius varying from four to seven miles from Charing Cross. The new police, having been paraded in the grounds of the Foundling Hosp., on 26th Sept. 1829, made their first appearance in the L. streets on 29th Sept. By 1st June 1830, the force consisted of 17 superintendents, 68 inspectors, 323 sergeants, and 2,906 constables, totalling 3,314 of all ranks. It was distributed, according to discretion as to numbers, in seventeen divisions for the districts of Whitehall, Westminster, St. James's, Marylebone, Holborn, Covent Garden, Finsbury, Whitechapel, Stepney, Lambeth, Southwark, Islington, Camberwell, Greenwich, Hampstead, Kensington, and Wandsworth. Great care was taken in selecting the members of the force, and between 1830 and 1838 there were nearly 5,000 dismissals, and more than 6,000 'voluntary' resignations. By 1833, out of a total strength of 3,389 of all ranks in the force, there were only 562 men who were recruits in 1829. In 1832, in refutation of the charge that the new police was merely a disguised military force, statistics were published which showed there were 135 who had been butchers, 109 bakers, 198 shoemakers, 51 tailors, 402 soldiers, 1,151 labourers, 205 servants, 141 carpenters, 75 bricklayers, 20 turners, 55 blacksmiths, 151 clerks, 141 shopkeepers, 141 superior mechanics, 46 plumbers and painters, 101 sailors, 51 weavers, and 8 stonemasons. The Act having been fathered by Peel, the new force became known as 'Peelers' and 'Bobbies.' The former sobriquet died out; the latter remains. The wages of the constables to begin with were 19s. a week; sergeants received 22s. 6d.; and sub-divisional inspectors £100 p.a.

There was at first remarkable hostility to the new force. On the occasion of a royal procession in 1830 a placard displayed read:

'Liberty or Death! Englishmen! Britons!! and Honest Men!!! The time has at length arrived. All London meets on Tuesday. Come Armed. We assure you from ocular demonstration that 6000 cutlasses have been removed from the Tower, for the use of Peel's Bloody Gang. Remember the Cursed Speech from the Throne!! These damned Police are now to be armed. Englishmen, will you put up with this?' This animosity of extremists could hardly avail against the speedy recognition of the far greater security of property that resulted from the institution of the Metropolitan Police. The loss to the public in small thefts, burglaries, and highway robberies, estimated at £990,000 annually, fell to less than £20,000 within the first three yrs. of the existence of the new police. The constables carried a rattle, and were armed with a staff or baton marked 'Police Officer.' The rattle,

carried in a coat-tail pocket, was replaced by the whistle about 1860, and was really, as Alwyn Solmes points out, 'the last link with the Charlies.' The uniform was less comfortable and attractive than now. Ex-Chief Inspector Cavanagh, in his *Reminiscences* (1893) said:

'I had to put on a swallow-tail coat, and a rabbit-skin high top hat, covered with leather, weighing eighteen ounces; a pair of Wellington boots, the leather of which must have been at least a sixteenth of an inch thick, and a belt of about four inches broad, with a great brass buckle some six inches deep.'

In 1833 the police were called out for the first time to disperse an armed mob, assembled for a meeting in Coldbath Fields. Victory rested with the force, but three were stabbed, and one killed by a dagger. At the inquest on the latter, a verdict of 'justifiable homicide' was returned. The Crown then took the case to the Court of King's Bench, and the verdict was quashed. A select committee was appointed to make exhaustive inquiry, and the police were almost entirely exonerated. The Chartist agitation of 1848 gave the Metropolitan Police little unusual activity, though in fear of possibilities 170,000 special constables were sworn. By this time the Metropolitan Police district had been extended to fifteen miles from Charing Cross; the Houses of Parliament, London Docks, Woolwich and Deptford Dockyards, Woolwich Arsenal and Greenwich, and the T.L. had all been embraced. By 1852 the force had increased to 5,626. In 1855 a Hyde Park demonstration against a Sunday Trading Bill (see 'Parks') led to the police charging the crowd. There were forty-nine police casualties and seventy-two arrests. This led to another commission, and a reserved approval of the conduct of the Metropolitan Police, three constables being proceeded against, and several dismissed. The Metropolitan Police also came under some censure in 1867, by reason of the plot to blow up the Middlesex House of Detention at Clerkenwell, for the purpose of releasing certain Fenians. The prison wall was blown down, houses were damaged, four people were killed, and eight others died of injuries. This raised serious questions as to whether, with proper police vigilance, the catastrophe could not have been prevented. The onus, however, had really been upon the Commissioner, Sir Richd. Mayne, who had received a warning of what was being planned, and his resignation followed. In 1872 there was the first police strike, limited to 180 men and 3 stations: 179 were suspended and later 69 of these men were dismissed, but the majority of them were ultimately reinstated. In 1887 occurred the famous 'Black Sunday,' when, the use of Trafalgar Sq. being forbidden for a meeting, an attempt was made by the crowd to break through the police cordon. The sq. was cleared and two sustained fatal injuries. Wm. Morris, who was in the vicinity, wrote verses on one of them named Linnell, and delivered an address at his grave in Bow cemetery. In 1890 there was another police strike, the Life Guards being called out to disperse the crowd of sympathizers gathered round Bow St. police station. The strikers were summarily dismissed, but there followed the Police Act, providing increase of pay and new pension privileges. In 1907 Peel House, Regency St., Westminster, was opened for the education of police recruits. There was another strike in 1919, and this led to the resignation of the Commissioner, Sir Edwd. Henry, and the appointment of Sir Nevil Macready. In May 1926 came the General Strike, and the fund raised by *The Times* as an expression of the appreciation of the public for the conduct of the police reached a total of nearly a quarter of a million pounds. This fund is administered as a National Trust for the benefit of the police as a whole. In 1931, when Ld. Trenchard was Commissioner, a redistribution of the force was made. The title of Commissioner dates from 1839; previously there had been two heads, called justices. The strength of the Metropolitan Police is now about 19,000 (including 500 women); the City Police (still separately administered) numbers about 750 (including 20 women). During the Second World War there were 1,900 cases of damage to police bdgs.; 124 of these were serious. Only one H.E. bomb fell on Scotland Yard, but the damage cost over £22,000 to repair. 208 police officers were killed in air raids. They are commemorated in a register exhibited at W.A.

(See *The English Policeman*, by Alwyn Solmes, 1935; and *The Rise of Scotland Yard*

by D. G. Browne, 1956.)

Minories takes its name from the community of the 'Sorores Minores' (in English the 'Minoresses'), which was established just outside the walls of the City in 1293, largely through the influence of Edmund, E. of Lancaster, and his wife. It belonged to the second Order of St. Francis. In papal bulls and royal patents it was generally described as consisting of 'the Abbess and Sisters Minoresses of the Order of St. Clare of the grace of the Blessed Mary the Virgin.' In the beginning, the community seems to have observed some of the Franciscan scorn of wealth and love of charity. One relic of the pristine purity of the early yrs. is a service-book, probably of late 15th-century date, consisting of two treatises and a commentary on the ninety-first Psalm. At the top of the page on the fly-leaf at the end of the book is written:

'Dame Elyzabeth horwode Abbas of ye Menoresse off London to her gostle comforthe bowgth thys boke hyt to Remayne to the use off ye Systers of ye sayde Place to pray for ye geuer and ffor ye sowles off hyr ffader and her moder Thomas horwode & beatryxe & ye sowle of mayster Robert Allerton.'

At the bottom of the page in another handwriting (probably early 16th century) are the words: 'thys bok lengyth to ye abbessy.' Later, asceticism gave way to creature comforts, and piety became a trade, gifts being conditional upon prayers —for the easy passage of souls through purgatory. The wealth of the abbey was enhanced by advowsons, and in 1341 Edward III, 'at the request of Isabella Queen of England our dearest Mother, also of our beloved cousin and our faithful Lancaster Earl of Derby,' granted a patent enabling the abbess and sisters to acquire land up to the value of £30 p.a. Moreover, the sisters were allowed individual funds. In 1399 property was increased by an 'alien' priory—a cell attached to the abbey of St. Mary Mountbury in Normandy; a result of the war with France. Amongst those bd. in the abbey were the Lady Isabel of Gloucester; Katharine Ingham, the Countess of Dunbar; and the Lady Elizabeth de le Pole. There was also bd. the heart of Edmund, E. of Lancaster (his body was bd. in W.A., *q.v.*).

In 1519 Henry VIII paid to Sir Wm. Holgill the sum of £200 for some rebuilding, and probably part of this money was spent upon a new infirmary. In 1538 the abbey, so familiar to John Stow, was surrendered to the K. In 1539 it was granted to the see of Bath and Wells in exchange for the episcopal residence near Temple Bar. In 1548 it came into the hands of the Crown by another exchange, and in 1553 it passed, by patent, to Henry Grey, D. of Suffolk, father of Lady Jane Grey (see 'City Churches; B'—Holy Trinity, Minories). A few weeks later, by licence of alienation, the K. gave power to the D., on payment of 60s. 8d. to himself, to alienate the property of Ld. Thos. Gray, Ld. John Gray, Geo. Medley, Esq., and John Harryngton, Esq. The first two were the D.'s younger brothers, Medley was a half-brother. The two former were concerned in the Wyatt rebellion (1554), and in consequence of their attainder (Ld. Thos. Gray was executed) their estates were forfeited to the Crown. Q. Elizabeth, however, in 1559, granted to Ld. John Gray 'the late monastery of the Minoress.' He, however, soon sold it to the Marquis of Winchester, and in 1563 the latter resold it to the Crown. Then followed its conversion into storehouses and workshops for the Ordnance Dept.; it was also assigned for the residence of lieutenant-generals. A considerable part of the abbey bdgs. remained until they were destroyed by fire in 1797.

The name Minories seems to have been given to the st. at the end of the 16th or beginning of the 17th century. Stow mentions the st. without naming it; it is named in Ryther's map, 1608. G. H. Cunningham says that Ld. Cobham, who falsely accused Sir Walter Raleigh of a share in his plot, d. of starvation here in the garret of his laundress's house, and that Isaac Watts lived in the st. in 1702. Inside the shop of Messrs. Norrie & Wilson (No. 123), until the Second World War, was the 'Little Wooden Midshipman,' which in *Dombey and Son* was outside Sol Gills's shop. In Dickens's time it was in Leadenhall St. It is now in the Dickens House (*q.v.*).

Mint, the Royal, was in the T.L. until 1811, when it was transferred to a bdg. on Little Tower Hill, designed by John Johnson, surveyor of the county of Essex,

and completed by Sir Robt. Smirke, who was responsible for the entrances. The bdg. cost more than a quarter of a million pounds, and is on the site of a Cistercian Abbey (see 'Eastminster'). It was enlarged in 1881–2.

Monument was erected to commemorate the G.F., in accordance with an Act of 1667 for rebuilding the City of L. One section provided as follows:

'And the better to preserve the memory of this dreadful Visitation, Be it further enacted, That a Columne or Pillar of Brase or Stone be erected on or as neere unto the place where the said Fire soe unhappily began as conveniently may be, in perpetuall Remembrance thereof, with such Inscription thereon, as hereafter by the Maior and Court of Aldermen in that behalfe be directed.'

The construction was assigned to Wren, but from the recently published diaries of Robt. Hooke, the City surveyor, it appears that it is his design which is represented by the column now so familiar to Londoners. Wren's idea was that there should be sculptured flames of gilt bronze issuing from the loopholes of the shafts, and a phoenix on the summit rising from her ashes, also of gilt bronze. This was found unsuitable, and there was then designed a fluted column, surmounted by a statue of Charles II, 15 ft. high. The statue, however, proved to be too costly, and the present vase of flames was eventually adopted. Defoe quaintly describes the Monument as 'built in the form of a candle,' the top making a 'handsome gilt flame like that of a candle.' It is constructed of Portland stone, and is 202 ft. high, this, according to the inscription, being the distance to the house in Pudding Lane where the G.F. broke out. The bas-relief on the W. side was the work of Caius Gabriel Cibber (both he and his son Colley Cibber were bd. in the Danish Ch. in Wellclose Sq.). The official description of this is as follows:

'The design is allegorical, and displays a female figure representing the City of London, sitting on ruins in a languishing condition, her head hanging down, her hair dishevelled, and her left hand lying carelessly upon her sword. Behind is Time, with his wings and bald head, gradually raising her up. Another female figure by her side gently touches her with one hand, and, with a winged sceptre in the other, points upwards to two goddesses sitting in the clouds, one with a cornucopia, denoting Plenty, the other having a palm branch in her left hand, signifying Peace. At her feet is a bee-hive denoting Industry, by which the greatest difficulties can be surmounted. Underneath the figure of London, in the midst of the ruins, is a dragon supporting a shield bearing the arms of the City of London. Over her head are shown houses burning, and flames breaking out through the windows. Behind Time is a group of citizens raising their hands in encouragement.

'Opposite these figures is a pavement of stone raised with three or four steps, on which stands King Charles II in a Roman costume, with a baton in his right hand, and a laurel wreath on his head, coming towards the City of London, and commanding three of his attendants to descend to her relief. The first represents Science, with a winged head and a circle of naked boys dancing on it, and in her hand a figure of Nature, with her numerous breasts ready to give assistance to all. The second is Architecture holding in the right hand a plan, and in the left a square and compasses. The third figure is Liberty, waving a cap in the air.

'Behind the King stands his brother, the Duke of York, holding in one hand a garland to crown the rising city, and in the other an uplifted sword for her defence. The two figures behind are Justice with a coronet, and Fortitude with a reined lion. Above these figures are represented houses in building, and labourers at work. Lastly, underneath the stone pavement on which the King stands, is a figure of Envy gnawing a heart and emitting pestiferous fumes from her envenomed mouth.'

The inscriptions on the Monument are translated as follows:

NORTH SIDE

'In the year of Christ 1666, on the 2nd of September at a distance eastward from this place of 202 feet, which is the height of this column, a fire broke out in the dead of night, which, the wind blowing, devoured even distant buildings, and rushed devastating through every quarter with astonishing swiftness and noise. It consumed 89 churches, gates, the Guildhall, public edifices, hospitals, schools, libraries, a great number of blocks of buildings, 13,200 houses, 400 streets. Of the 26 wards, it utterly destroyed 15 and left 8 mutilated and half burnt. The ashes of the city, covering as many as 436 acres, extended on one side from the Tower along the bank of the Thames to the church of the Templars, on the other side from the north-east gate along the walls to the head of Fleet-ditch. Merciless to the wealth and estates of the citizens, it was harmless to their lives, so as throughout to remind us of the final destruction of the world by fire. The havoc was swift. A little space of time saw the same city most prosperous and no longer in being. On the third day, when it had now altogether vanquished all human counsel and resource, at the bidding, as we may well believe, of Heaven, the fatal fire stayed its course and everywhere died out.'

SOUTH SIDE

'Charles the Second, son of Charles the Martyr, King of Great Britain, France, and Ireland, Defender of the Faith, a most gracious prince, commiserating the deplorable state of things, whilst the ruins were yet smoking, provided for the comfort of his citizens, and the ornament of his city; remitted their taxes, and referred the petitions of the magistrates and inhabitants of London to the Parliament; who immediately passed an Act, that public works should be restored to greater beauty, with public money, to be raised by an imposition on coals; that churches, and the cathedral of St. Paul's, should be re-built from their foundations, with all magnificence; that the bridges, gates, and prisons should be new made, the sewers cleansed, the streets made straight and regular, such as were steep levelled, and those too narrow made wider, markets and shambles removed to separate places. They also enacted, that every house should be built with party-walls, and all raised by an equal height in front, and that all house walls should be strengthened with stone or brick; and that no man should delay building beyond the space of seven years. Furthermore, he procured an Act to settle beforehand the suits which should arise respecting boundaries, he also established an annual service of intercession, and caused this column to be erected as a perpetual memorial to posterity. Haste is seen everywhere, London rises again, whether with greater speed or greater magnificence is doubtful, three short years complete that which was considered the work of an age.'

EAST SIDE

'Begun, Sir Richard Ford, knt., being Lord Mayor of London, in the year 1671; carried higher in the Mayoralties of Sir George Waterman, knt., Sir Robert Hanson, knt., Sir William Hooker, knt., Sir Robert Viner, knt., and Sir Joseph Sheldon, knt.; and finished in the Mayoralty of Sir Thomas Davies, in the year of the Lord 1677.'

In 1681, in consequence of the machinations of Titus Oates, the Court of Aldermen ordered an addition to the inscription. It was in English and read as follows:

'This pillar was set up in perpetual remembrance of that most dreadful burning of this Protestant city, begun and carryed on by yᵉ treachery & malice of yᵉ Popish faction in yᵉ beginning of Septembʳ in yᵉ year of ovr Lord 1665, in order for carrying on their horrid plott for extirpating the Protestant and old English liberty, and introducing Popery and slavery'.

Soon after James II's accession in 1685 this was obliterated. In 1689, with William III on the throne, it was reinstated. This caused Pope's well-known lines in *Moral Essays*:

'Where London's column, pointing at the skies,
  Like a tall bully, lifts the head and lies.'

This inscription was finally removed in 1830.

There was a suicide from the Monument in 1788, two in 1810, two in 1839 (one a boy of 15), and one in 1842. After the last tragedy it was temporarily closed, and the gallery at the summit, reached by 345 black marble steps, was enclosed with an iron cage.

Moorfields, in the Middle Ages, was a great marsh on the N. side of L., stretching from Bishopsgate to Cripplegate, and from London Wall to Finsbury Sq. It was caused originally by the blocking of the Walbrook, consequent upon the erection of the Roman wall over the stream. Fitzstephen (*c.* 1183) indicates this place as where the youth of L. skated in hard weather, and a Ld.M.'s record of 1301 mentions that City officials inspected it in a boat. In 1411 it was drained. The drainage was unsuccessful, and for the next 100 yrs. the citizens seem to have used the facility of access provided by Moorgate to carry out their rubbish and throw it into the marsh. In 1511 and 1527 further drainage schemes were carried out, and what had been, in Stow's words, 'waste and unprofitable ground,' became a place where archery and other sports were practised. In 1606, instead of a drainage scheme, there was one to raise the level of the ground 3 or 4 ft. by piling up dry rubbish upon it. It was then laid out with trees and walks and benches, and became the first public park in L. Here, after the G.F., came the homeless poor, 'some under tents,' said Evelyn, 'some under miserable huts and hovels; many without a rag or any necessary utensils, bed or board, who from delicateness, riches and easy accommodations in stately and well furnished houses, were now reduced to extremest poverty and misery.'

Pepys, in 1664, described a fray here between the butchers and weavers,

'between whom there hath ever been an old competition for mastery. . . . So first the butchers knocked down all the weavers that had green or blue aprons, till they were fain to pull them off and put them in their breeches. At last the butchers were fain to pull off their sleeves, that they might not be known, and were soundly beaten out of the field, and some deeply wounded and bruised; till at last the weavers went out tryumphing, calling £100 for a butcher.'

In 1730 the S. part of Moorfields called the 'Quarters,' had fallen into disrepair, and the dry rubbish had sunk irregularly. This part was therefore raised another 3 ft., chiefly with broken bricks, and laid out again. Under an Act of 1812 the 'Quarters' were built upon, and became Finsbury Circus. In the Mus. at Guildhall there is a remarkable collection of objects found in Moorfields—jettons (reckoning pennies), candlesticks, compasses, shears, buckles, and pewter spoons, as well as some skates of bone, such as are referred to by Fitz-stephen.

Moorgate took its name from the moor to which it led. It was not one of the original City gates. The marshy nature of the ground, and the fen to which Fitz-stephen referred in this quarter of L., would have made a gate at one time superfluous (see 'Moorfields'). It is described in Henry IV's reign (1411–12) as a postern in the N. wall between the gates of Bishopsgate and Cripplegate. In 1415 it was enacted by ordinance that the postern should be pulled down, and a new and larger one built to the westward of it, with a gate to be shut at night and other fitting times. Stow says it was rebuilt (by Wm. Hampton, Ld.M.) in 1472, and improved in 1511. It was pulled down in 1672, and a new gate of stone erected. It was condemned with the other gates in 1761, and the materials sold for £166. It was finally demolished in 1762, and the stones repurchased by the C.C., to be used with the stones of the other gates, to support the starlings of the newly widened centre arch of London Bridge.

Museums are comparatively modern as national institutions, and are derived from private collections. Some churches, in the Middle Ages, had something of the aspect of museums. Stow mentions the exhibition of the shankbone of a giant in St. Mary Aldermanbury, and in St. Lawrence Jewry 'the tooth of some monstrous fish as I take it. A shanke bone of 25 inches long, of a man as is said, but might be of an Oliphant.' In the 18th century 'Don Saltero' at Chelsea had a remarkable coffee-house collection. He first appears to have been at the corner of Lawrence St., and later on the W. side of Danvers St.; about 1717 he went to what is now 18 Cheyne Walk. The coffee house was visited by Steele; it was satirically described by him in No. 34 of the *Tatler* (1709). There was a catalogue, and the following were some of the items:

'A piece of Queen Catherine's skin.' 'The Pope's candle with which he curses the heretics.' 'A painted ribbon

from Jerusalem with which our Saviour was tied to the pillar when scourged.' 'Manna from Canaan.' 'Instruments for scratching the Chinese ladies' backs.' 'Mary Queen of Scots' pincushion.' 'A piece of nun's skin.' 'A necklace made of Job's tears.' 'Queen Elizabeth's strawberry dish.' 'A pair of nun's stockings.' 'A starved cat found between the walls of Westminster Abbey when repairing.' 'Queen Elizabeth's chambermaid's hat.'

The last item, no doubt, suggested Steele's remark:

'He shows you a straw hat, which I know to be made by Madge Peskad, within three miles of Bedford; and tells you "It is Pontius Pilate's Wife's chambermaid's sister's hat." '

Steele was quite right in saying:

'He is descended in a right line, not from John Tradescant [see 'Lambeth'] as he himself asserts, but from that memorable companion of the Knight of Mancha.'

The father of Thos. Pennant, historian of London, met Richd. Cromwell at Don Saltero's coffee-house, 'a little and very neat old man with a most placid countenance, the effect of his innocent and unambitious life.' The Don had other pursuits besides the exhibition of his 'Knackatory.'

'Through various Employs I've past
     A Scraper, Vertuos' Projector,
Tooth Drawer, Trimmer, and at last
     I'm now a Gimcrack Whim Collector.'

He d. 1728, but the coffee-house was carried on by his daughter Mrs. Hall and her husband. Smollett, who went to live in Chelsea in 1753, became a patron and benefactor, and when Peregrine Pickle visited Rotterdam, and the cheesemonger begged them to compare his collection with that of Mynheer Sloane, the painter exclaimed in patriotic disgust:

'By the Lard! they are not to be named of a day; and as for that matter, I would not give one corner of Saltero's coffee-house at Chelsea for all the trash he hath shown.'

In 1799 the lease of Don Saltero's Coffee House was sold, with all the curiosities; and in 1867 a private residence was built on the site. A photograph, taken before the demolition, is in Reginald Blunt's book *In Cheyne Walk and Thereabout.*

Von Uffenbach, who came to L. from Frankfort in 1710, went several times to a mus. kept by one Campe, who lived at Charing Cross. He had 'two fairly large rooms full of antiques, and an extremely elegant cabinet of coins.' He saw a very large Indian crab, a collection of idols, including 'Moloch the God of the Ammonits to sacrifice Children to him,' and a piece of a thorn bush, on which was written, 'Jerusalem thorn the like as our Saviour was crowned with.' He also noticed a great quantity of ancient musical instruments, and the head of Cromwell. He saw, too, some life-size **wax** figures, such as:

'Cleopatra lying on her couch clasping the asp to her bosom. Opposite was a quite incomparable representation of her maid weeping. Her eyes were all swollen, as if she had been crying them out, and tears were coursing down her cheeks, whilse she wrung her hands most piteously.'

There was Rosamond kneeling before Q. Eleanor, who was offering her rival the dagger or the poisoned cup. There was also 'Queen Anne, well made but flattered.'

Pennant praised the mus. of the Royal Soc. at Gresham Coll., 'consisting of natural and artificial curiosities,' and said that it fell into neglect when the soc. went to Crane Court, when his friend Daines Barrington undertook the restoration. From 1736 to 1772 in Fleet St. (No. 197) was Rackstraw's Mus. It occupied a picturesque old house, erected before the G.F., which stood four doors W. of Chancery Lane. There were anatomical models, and that was why 'a proper person attends the ladies.' There were also bones of beasts and fishes, and figures of Bamford, the giant, and Coan, the Norfolk dwarf. Bamford was 7 ft. 4 in. in height, and was bd. in St. Dunstan's in the West Ch. in 1768. A tempting offer of £200 was made for his body for dissection. There was also the skeleton of a whale more than 70 ft. long. The admission fee was so high as half a crown. Another mus. was Sir Ashton Lever's, which was first at his family seat at Allington. He removed it to L. in 1775, and opened it to the public in Leicester House, Leicester Sq. The exhibition was not very successful, and,

for want of public patronage, Sir Ashton Lever in 1790 was obliged to dispose of the mus. by public lottery. It fell to the lot of Mr. Parkinson, who housed it in a bdg. called the Rotunda at the corner of Blackfriars Rd. and Stamford St. 'This Admired Assemblage of the Productions of Nature and Art,' including 'a variety of Specimens of the most rare and beautiful Birds from Guayana, in South America', could be seen for half a crown. Again the public did not roll up in sufficient numbers, and the collection was dispersed in 1806 by a public auction which lasted forty days. A further mus. was Bullock's, which was at the Egyptian Hall, Piccadilly, and was erected in 1812 to house the collection made by Mr. Wm. Bullock during thirty years' travel in Central America. The mus. of Sir Ashton Lever, and one at Lichfield, contributed to the collection, which consisted mostly of objects of natural interest, though it had Napoleon's travelling carriage—before it went to Madame Tussaud's; and the 'living skeleton'—a man 5 ft. 7½ in. in height who weighed only 77¾ lb. The Siamese Twins also were shown here in 1829, and in 1844 'Tom Thumb.' The date of its closure (it was sometimes known as the London Mus.) cannot be ascertained. In 1874 Maskelyne and Cooke commenced their conjuring exhibitions in the same place.

BRITISH MUSEUM. All the above private museums were bound to be eclipsed by the national one at Bloomsbury, which was opened in Montagu House (erected in 1691) in 1759. The foundation of the B.Mus. was in the collections of Sir John Cotton, Robt. Harley, first E. of Oxford, and his son Edwd., the second E., and Sir Hans Sloane. Cotton's—consisting of books and manuscripts—was presented to the nation by his grandson, Sir John Cotton, in 1700; Sir Robt. Harley's manuscripts were purchased for £10,000, a very moderate sum, in 1753; Sir Hans Sloane's, which, in addition to books and manuscripts, included prints, medals, coins, antiquities, precious stones, and natural history specimens, was purchased for £20,000. Sir Hans Sloane stipulated in his will that they should be offered to the nation for this sum, very much less than the cost entailed in collecting them. Parliament, in 1753, passed

'An Act for the Purchase of the Museum or Collection of Sir Hans

Sloane, and of the Harleian Collection of Manuscripts, and for providing one General Repository for the better Reception and more convenient Use of the said Collections, and of the Cottonian Library and of the additions thereto.'

The Act established a body of trustees, headed by the Abp. of C., and they were to provide funds by authorizing a public lottery, in which there should be 100,000 shares at £3 each. £200,000 was to be set aside for prizes, and £100,000 applied to the purposes set forth in the title of the Act. At this time there was nothing like the freedom now enjoyed by the visitor. Until 1820 formal application had to be made in advance for admission, and only five parties of fifteen were admitted on visiting days, which were Mondays, Wednesdays, and Fridays. The names of all those composing the parties were entered in a book, and guides allotted to conduct them through the bdg. Thos. Gray, the poet, was a visitor in the yr. it was opened. From time to time Montagu House was enlarged, but in 1823, when the King's Lib. was presented by George IV, it was found necessary to begin the construction of a new bdg. Sir Robt. Smirke was appointed architect. He first built the present King's Lib., and, the work being carried out by instalments, it was not until 1845 that the four sides of the present mus. had been completed, and the last remnant of Montagu House had disappeared. The portico was finished in 1847, and the reading room in 1857 (see 'Libraries'). In 1883-6 the natural history collections were removed to a separate bdg. in Cromwell Rd. In 1884, under a bequest made by Mr. Wm. White, accruing on the death of his widow, who had survived him fifty-six yrs., a new gallery was built on the W. side for the Mausoleum marbles, and a wing (named after the donor) on the E. side for the Prints and Drawings Dept. In 1914 there was erected on the N. the wing known as King Edward VII's galleries. On the W. side there has been erected a new gallery for the Elgin Marbles; the gift of Ld. Duveen.

The contents of the B.Mus. can only briefly be summarized. There are: Graeco-Roman Rooms. A room of archaic Greek sculpture; an Ephesus Room (sculpture from the Temple of Diana, mentioned by St. Paul); Elgin Room, containing the marbles from the Parthenon—the temple of the virgin goddess Athena at Athens, built between 447 and 433 B.C. Phigaleian Room (frieze from the temple of Apollo at Phigaleia, in Arcadia, late 5th century B.C.). Mausoleum Room, which contains remains of the tomb of Mausolus, a p. of Caria in Asia Minor, who d. 353 B.C. Egyptian Gallery. Here is the famous Rosetta stone. This is inscribed with a decree in two forms of Egyptian writing, viz. the priests' writing, or hieroglyphic, and the people's writing, or demotic, and also in Greek, 195 B.C. It was found at Rosetta in Egypt in 1798, and brought to England in 1801. It gave the clue, through Greek, to the reading of the Egyptian. Assyrian Sculpture Gallery. Smaller Greek and Roman Antiquities. Gallery of Roman Britain (see 'Roman Remains'). Smaller Egyptian and Near Eastern Antiquities (including mummies). Ceramic, Glass, and Medieval Collections. Ethnographical Gallery. Asiatic Saloon. Indian Religions Room. Early Christian Room. Coin Room (coins from 7th century B.C.). Manuscript Saloon, the oldest—in Greek—being on papyrus from 3rd century B.C. King's Library. The wall cases contain the books collected by George III. Here are also Oriental manuscripts and some very early specimens of Chinese printing. Specimens of the earliest books printed on the Continent and in England (Gutenberg Bible, Caxton, etc.). Exhibition of bookbindings; English Bibles; early maps; music; early editions of famous English books, e.g. Shakespeare, *Paradise Lost*, *Pilgrim's Progress*, etc.). Here is also the Tapling collection of postage-stamps.

BRITISH MUSEUM (NATURAL HISTORY) was designed by Alfred Waterhouse, R.A., erected in Cromwell Rd., 1873-80, and opened in 1881 to relieve the rapidly increasing congestion in the old bdg. at Bloomsbury. The removal of the dept. of zoology (which then included entomology), was begun in 1882 and completed in 1886. There are a bird gallery; a fish gallery; an insect gallery; a reptile gallery; a whale hall; geological galleries.

GEFFRYE MUSEUM (Kingsland Rd.) was opened in 1914 in a bdg. erected as almshouses about 1715 under the will of Sir Robt. Geffrye, who d. in 1704. He was a Master of the Ironmongers' Co. and

19 Portobello Road street market

20 Marble Arch fountains

21 Chester Terrace, Regent's Park

22 Devereux Arms, Essex Street

23 Wyndham Place, St Marylebone, at night

24 St Paul's Cathedral

25 King's Bench Walk

26 St Paul's from Waterloo Bridge

Ld.M. in 1685. His statue is over the main door, leading into what was once a tiny chapel.

The exhibits illustrate the history of furnishing and are mainly furniture and household utensils. There are a number of carefully furnished 'period rooms' running up to modern times as well as a Georgian Street.

GUILDHALL MUSEUM. Before the Second World War it was in the spacious 15th century crypt, and the collection of L. exhibits was worthy of comparison with those in the L. Mus. These two museums are to be merged in a 'Museum of London' on the Barbican site. Meanwhile Guildhall Museum occupies premises in Gillett House, London Wall.

HOME OFFICE INDUSTRIAL MUSEUM (Horseferry Rd.), now the Industrial Health and Safety Centre, was opened in 1927. The exhibits deal with safety appliances in factories; the principal industrial diseases and methods of preventing these, by (*inter alia*) efficient lighting, heating, and ventilation; and welfare work—ambulances, rest-rooms, canteens.

IMPERIAL WAR MUSEUM (Geraldine Mary Harmsworth Park, Lambeth Rd.) was founded by the War Cabinet in 1917, and established by Act of Parliament in 1920, as a memorial of the effort and sacrifices made by the men and women of the empire during the First World War (1914–18), and to provide a record and a place for the study of that period. Until 1935 it was in Imperial Institute Rd., S. Kensington. It was then transferred to the vacated premises of Bethlehem Hosp. (*q.v.*). The collection includes paintings and drawings divided about evenly between the two wars. There are guns, other implements of warfare, models of ambulances, hospital trains, etc., and personal relics of famous military leaders. The Mus. sustained some damage in the Second World War.

LONDON MUSEUM. It is housed in Kensington Palace but was until 1939 in Lancaster House, St. James' Park, a bdg. erected as a residence for Fredk., D. of York, son of George III. The D.'s column points to the skies not far away (see 'Statues'). The architect was Benjamin Wyatt. It was unfinished at the D.'s death, and completed by Barry as the town house of the Dukes of Sutherland. It is said that when Q. Victoria visited the D. there, she was so impressed that she remarked: 'I have come from my house to your palace.' The lease of the house was purchased in 1913 by the late Ld. Leverhulme, and presented to the nation to house the collection previously exhibited at Kensington Palace. Originally called 'York House,' and subsequently renamed 'Stafford House,' in 1913 it became known as 'Lancaster House.'

The Mus. is rich in L. history from Roman to present times. Apart from furniture and other exhibits there are many L. paintings and such association items as a silk shirt worn by Charles I on the scaffold and the Tangye collection of Cromwellian relics. The mus. is destined to be joined to the Guildhall Mus. and become 'The Museum of London.'

MUSEUM OF PRACTICAL GEOLOGY (Exhibition Rd., S. Kensington) is the headquarters of the Geological Survey which was started in 1835. Its first headquarters were at Craig's Court, Charing Cross. In 1851, the year of the Great Exhibition, the joint Geological Mus. and Survey offices were handsomely housed in Jermyn St., Piccadilly. The collection outgrew the accommodation, and in 1933 the present handsome bdg. was erected. The purpose of the mus. is to illustrate (*a*) the work of the Geological Survey; (*b*) the general principles of geological science; (*c*) economic geology and mineralogy. There are wonderful specimens of stalagmite, and crystals; specimens of wood opals in which silica has taken the place of wood, preserving the markings meticulously. There are remarkable photographs and reconstructions of scenery.

NATIONAL MARITIME MUSEUM. It was established by Act of Parliament in 1934. It is housed in the bdgs. vacated in 1933 by the Royal Hosp. Sch. It includes also the Queen's House, a beautiful bdg. erected by Inigo Jones for Anne of Denmark, consort of James I, and subsequently completed for Henrietta Maria, Charles I's Q. The principal rooms here are the Great Hall, where the body of Admiral Robt. Blake lay in state before burial in W.A. (1657), and the Q.'s bedroom and parlour. Some of the ceilings are finely moulded. There are portraits, battle pieces, and models illustrating the history of the Navy from the time of Henry VIII. There are Nelson relics, including his pigtail, given to the nation by his daughter Horatia.

SCIENCE MUSEUM (Exhibition Rd., S. Kensington) was first proposed by the P. Consort after the Great Exhibition of 1851, and in 1857 collections illustrating foods, animal products, etc., were on show in S. Kensington. The collection of scientific instruments was first formed in 1874. In 1876 there was a special loan collection of scientific apparatus from various countries, and a large number of the exhibits were acquired by the mus. Subsequently many additions were made, including in 1884 the collection of machinery formed by the Commissioners of Patents, in 1900 the Maudslay collection of machine tools and marine engine models, and in 1903 the Bennet Woodcroft collection of engine models and portraits. Until 1899 the science and engineering collections, together with the art collections, formed the S. Kensington Mus., but in that year the name was changed to the Victoria and Albert Mus., which included both collections until 1909. The collections were then separated; the art collections remained in the Victoria and Albert Mus., and the science and engineering collections were rehoused and formed the Science Mus.

SOANE MUSEUM (Lincoln's Inn Fields) is due to the enthusiasm and enterprise of Sir John Soane (1753–1837). He was b. at Gorham, near Reading. As a youth he attracted the notice of Jas. Peacock, of the Guildhall, chief assistant to Geo. Dance, R.A., the City architect. He thus came to L. in 1768, and became the most brilliant pupil of the architect of old Newgate Prison. About 1770, by a friendly arrangement, he passed to the office of Henry Holland Junr., son of Henry Holland, sen., a well-known builder who had worked for Robt. Adam and other distinguished architects. Soane was thus brought early in life into the circle of the leading architects of his day. In 1771 he entered the schs. of the Royal Academy, and won the silver medal for his measured drawing of the Banqueting House, Whitehall, when he was only 19, and four yrs. later (1776), a travelling studentship for his design for 'A Triumphal Bridge.' He went to Rome to pursue his studies; also to Sicily, Malta, and Athens. He returned to L. in 1780, and in 1788, against numerous competitors, he won the position

of architect to the Bank of England, a responsible post he held for forty-five yrs. His first house and office, on his return from the Continent, was in Margaret St., from which locality he moved to Scotland Yard. In 1792 he moved into Lincoln's Inn Fields, building a house (No. 12) on the N. side, then known as Holborn Row. This house was adorned with casts brought with him from Italy, as well as furnished with valuable books and objects of art. This was the beginning of a valuable collection. In 1808 he took over from his friends at No. 13 the back premises of that house, and erected the dome or first part of the mus., which was then entered from No. 12. In 1812 he arranged to exchange houses, and at once rebuilt No. 13, still retaining the back premises of No. 12. In 1824 he rebuilt No. 14, thus creating the 'Picture Room' (Hogarth Room), and the 'Monks' Parlour,' etc., while letting off separately the house in front on a lease. At the same time he added a story to No. 13—the present attic floor. The mus. then consisted of one entire house, No. 13, and the back bdgs. of Nos. 12 and 14. In 1815 Mrs. Soane d. (she lay in state in the library). In 1824 Soane held a three-day reception in honour of the acquisition of the Seti I sarcophagus (found in 1817, and believed to be at least 3,000 yrs. old). Soane was knighted in 1831; and in 1833, on his retirement from the post of architect to the Bank of England, he obtained a private Act of Parliament for the preservation of his collection 'for the promotion of the study of Architecture and the Fine Arts.' The Act also provided that free admission to the house should be given at least two days in every week throughout the months of Apr., May, and June, and at such other times in the same or any months as the trustees should direct. Sir John also desired that the whole construction and arrangement of his house and mus. should remain as he left it at the time of his death; in 1835 he wrote and illustrated his *Description of the House* as a record of this. In 1837 Sir John d. there. His bust by Sir Francis Chantrey, R.A., is on view. In addition to the sarcophagus, the most treasured exhibit, there is a large number of Hogarth originals; a first folio of Shakespeare and first editions of *Paradise Lost* and *Robinson Crusoe*; a watch given to Sir Christopher

Wren by Q. Anne; and a jewel of Charles I, captured at Naseby.

VICTORIA AND ALBERT MUSEUM (Cromwell Rd., S. Kensington) is the national mus. of industrial art, and includes a large reference library. In 1837 a sch. of design was instituted at Somerset House under the auspices of the Board of Trade. The movement spread, and other schs. were instituted, not only in L., but in Birmingham, Manchester, and other large towns. The Great Exhibition of 1851 gave it an impetus, and from its contents a selection was made of art objects which formed the Mus. of Ornamental Art inaugurated at Marlborough House in 1852. Five yrs. later the collection was moved to S. Kensington, and a bdg. known as the South Kensington Mus. was opened in 1857 by Q. Victoria and the P. Consort. The bdgs. were gradually completed between 1860 and 1884, the decorative ornament being executed mainly by students of the Art Training Sch. (now the Royal Coll. of Art). In 1899 the foundation stone of the extension was laid by Q. Victoria, by whose command the bdg. was renamed the V. & A. Mus. The new bdgs. (the Cromwell Rd. frontage is 720 ft. long) were completed ten yrs. later, and were opened by Edward VII in 1909. On the exterior of the bdg. is a series of statues: Chas. Barry, Wm. Chambers, Wren, Inigo Jones, John Thorpe, Wm. of Wykeham, Millais, Leighton, Watts, Constable, Q. Alexandra, Q. Victoria, P. Consort, Edward VII, Cosway, Romney, Gainsborough, Reynolds, Hogarth, Alfred Stevens, Foley, Chantrey, Flaxman, John Bacon, Grinling Gibbons, Wm. Morris, Roger Payne, Wedgwood, Chippendale, Tompion, Geo. Heriot, Huntingdon Shaw, Caxton, Torel, St. Dunstan. There are ten depts.: architecture and sculpture, ceramics, engraving, illustration and design, lib. and book production, metal-work, paintings, textiles, woodwork, India Mus., and a circulation dept. The last-mentioned has objects available for loan to provincial museums, local schs., etc., and also lantern slides.

The following exhibits have a L. interest. A model in plaster of the bust of Alderman Boydell in St. Margaret, Lothbury Ch. (see 'City Churches; C'); Roubiliac's bust of Jonathan Tyers (see 'Vauxhall'); a panel said to have come from Merchant Taylors' Hall; terracotta sketch and drawing by Roubiliac for the monument of John, D. of Argyll, in W.A.; 'The Stoning of Stephen,' a carving in lime and lancewood by Grinling Gibbons; Roubiliac's bust of Hogarth; Caius Gabriel Cibber's 'Piper and Dog', a bust of Inigo Jones, said to have been on a water-gate near the Savoy—probably that of York House (q.v.); cast of Nollekens's bust of Dr. Johnson, now in W.A. Chantrey considered it his best bust, but Johnson did not like the manner in which his head had been loaded with hair. According to 'Rainy Day' Smith, the sculptor insisted upon this as making Johnson look more like an ancient poet, the hair being modelled from 'the flowing locks of a sturdy Irish beggar, who, after he had sat an hour, refused to take a shilling, stating that he could have made more by begging.' Here also is a terracotta sketch for Beckford's monument in the Guildhall (q.v.); a statuette of Matthew Prior by Roubiliac; a preliminary sketch of the Garrick monument of Shakespeare in the B.Mus., also the work of Roubiliac; a model for the figure of Lady Rebecca Atkins (d. 1711) on the monument of Sir Richd. Atkins in St. Paul's Ch., Clapham (see 'Wandsworth'); sketch model in terra-cotta by Rysbrack for Sir Isaac Newton's monument in W.A. In other parts of the mus. there are a state coach of George III (c. 1760-70); a state carriage of the Marquis of Lansdowne (1863-6); panelled rooms from Clifford's Inn, 27 Hatton Garden, 5 George St., Westminster, and Norfolk House, St. James Sq. There are also a pinewood doorway from Queenhithe; a beautifully carved cravat in wood by Grinling Gibbons; the front of Sir Paul Pindar's house from Bishopsgate; the front of Birch's shop from Cornhill; the front of a house at Enfield in which Keats received part of his education. The mus. also has the Great Bed of Ware. Its dimension are 11 ft. 1 in by 10 ft. 8 in. It is mentioned in *Twelfth Night*; Sir Toby Belch's advice to Sir Andrew Aguecheek, when the plot is being concocted against Malvolio, is: 'As many lies as will lie in the sheet of paper, although the sheet were big enough for the bed of Ware.' There is a reference to the bed, about the same time, in the poetical itinerary of a German p. Ben Jonson alludes to it in *The Silent*

Woman (1609). In 1725 César De Saussure, who came to L. from Lausanne, wrote: 'Ware is a pretty village three miles from Hertford. Here I was shown Og's bedstead, which is of iron, and enormously wide and high, and to get into it you must climb a flight of stairs. I was told that a few days ago twelve butchers, with their wives, came from London, and made up a party to sleep in this bed; twelve of them slept at the head and twelve at the foot.'

As the bed is made of finely carved wood, and is not particularly high, the description is inaccurate, but there can be no doubt that this bed is described, as a similar incident was recorded by another visitor, as mentioned in the official account of it. Byron referred to it in *Don Juan* (canto vi):

'Most wise men, with *one* moderate woman wed,
  Will scarcely find philosophy for more;
And all (except Mahometans) forbear
To make the nuptial couch a "Bed of Ware." '

There is also an allusion in Dickens. When De Saussure saw the bed it was in the Crown Inn, Ware; in 1764, it was removed to the 'Saracen's Head' there; and when acquired by the mus. in 1933 it had been for about fifty yrs. in the grounds of Rye House, Hoddesdon. The mus. sustained some damage during the Second World War, as a result of which there has been some re-arrangement.

BETHNAL GREEN MUS. is a branch of the V. and A. Mus. It was opened by Albert Edward P. of Wales and Princess Alexandra in 1872. The Museum's iron structure was part of the temporary bdg. erected in 1857 for the S. Kensington (now V. & A.) Mus. When a permanent bdg. at S. Kensington was well advanced, this section of its first home was dismantled and removed to Bethnal Green, where it was re-erected and encased in brick, with a slate roof. Since the destruction by fire of the Crystal Palace, Bethnal Green Mus. is the most important surviving example of the type of iron and glass construction employed by Sir Joseph Paxton for the Great Exhibition of 1851.

The Mus. includes paintings by Turner, Clarkson Stanfield, Landseer, Peter de Wint, David Cox, David Wilkie, C. R. Leslie, etc. There is also a good collection of porcelain, pottery, boots and shoes (of English and foreign manufacture), and Spitalfields silks. It is particularly attractive to children by reason of some large dolls' houses and model shops.

WALLACE COLLECTION is in Hertford House, Manchester Sq. In the last yrs. of Q. Anne there was a project for laying out a Queen Anne Sq. with a ch. in the centre. The death of the Q. changed the proposal, and the D. of Manchester bought the plot on the N. side and built the house in 1776–88. On the death of the D. the house was bought for the Spanish ambassador, commemorated in the adjacent Spanish Place, with its Roman Catholic Chapel, once that of the Embassy. The French Embassy succeeded, and Talleyrand and Guizot were possibly among the occupants of the house. In the days of the Regency it was acquired by the second Marquess of Hertford, one of the Prince's friends. The third Marquess—Thackeray's Ld. Steyne—commenced a collection of pictures and other works of art, and it was greatly increased by the fourth Marquess, who lived in Paris the life of an elegant recluse. He specialized in 18th-century French paintings, sculpture, and furniture. When Ld. Hertford d. he had been an absentee from his English estates for nearly thirty yrs. The collection remained in France until the siege of Paris, and the destructive mood of the Commune, led Sir Richd. Wallace, Ld. Hertford's son, to transfer it to a place of greater safety. In 1872 it was installed in the Bethnal Green Mus.; in 1875 it was transferred to Hertford House. Lady Wallace, who d. 1897, bequeathed it to the nation, on the condition that the Govt. provided for it a mus. in a central part of L. and maintained it as a separate collection. The former condition was fulfilled by the purchase from Sir John Murray Scott, Sir Richd. and Lady Wallace's heir, of Hertford House, and its adaptation to the purposes of a mus., which was opened in 1900. The whole cost to public funds was about £80,000. The collection was the finest gift ever made to the British nation, and is computed to be worth from four to five million pounds. The objects of art include a collection of Sèvres porcelain, only equalled by those in Windsor Castle and Buckingham Palace, and a wonderful collection of French furniture of the 17th and 18th centuries, said to be unrivalled even in France. There are also many pictures of great value and beauty, e.g. Boucher's 'Marquise de Pompadour,' Hals's 'Laughing Cavalier,' and Watteau's 'The Music Lesson.'

A small but interesting collection is in the Cuming Mus., Walworth Rd.; it is in one of the Southwark B.C.'s libraries. The founder was Richd. Cuming, who first had his treasures in his house in Dean's Row, now 196 Walworth Rd. He left them to his son, Henry Syer Cuming, who, on his death in 1902, bequeathed them to the library. There are 15,000 exhibits. They include several of Dickensian interest. There is the pump of the Marshalsea Prison, mentioned in *Little Dorrit*; the brazen dog's head in a pot which the boy Dickens used to pass on his walk between the blacking factory at Hungerford Stairs and his attic in Lant St., Southwark; and the gravestones of the Mannings (see 'Prisons'—Horsemonger Lane).

The Horniman Mus. (London Rd., Forest Hill), opened by the L.C.C. in 1901, has a large exhibition of old musical instruments, exhibits illustrating man and his tools, and a natural history collection.

There is also a number of private museums. See 'Surgeons, Royal College of'; 'Physicians, Royal College of.' There is a mus. of crime at the headquarters of the Metropolitan Police and a Jewish mus. in Woburn House, Woburn Place.

Music Hall and Pantomime.

MUSIC HALL. Music hall is hardly a fitting title for the L. theatres in which variety programmes are presented, but it is a reminder of those early yrs. when many taverns set aside a room for public entertainment of a musical and vocal character. It was from those taverns directly that the variety profession developed although there were many years of cradling.

In the early 18th century, when Patents were granted to the Theatre Royal, Drury Lane, and the Covent Garden Theatre, many actors adopted a less exacting form of art to live and these were the fathers of the variety profession as we know it to-day. The legitimate theatre being closed to the majority of them, because of

their numbers and the monopoly given to the two theatres mentioned, actors took to the country appearing at fairs in miscellaneous programmes of diversified items. When more settled conditions came about many of these strollers returned to the re-opened permanent theatres, but others continued with their booth entertainments. There followed music houses situated in pleasure gardens, such as the Spring Gardens at Charing Cross, and the Mulberry Gardens in the vicinity of the present Buckingham Palace. Later, Vauxhall Gardens and lesser known rendezvous similar to St. Helena Gardens, Bermondsey, met the demand for light entertainment and when such places had closed variety had been accepted, and commanded a large public following.

In the early 1800s. the Cider Cellars in Maiden Lane, and the Coal Hole, in Fountain Court, Strand, were catering for men about town who required tavern amusement. Both resorts were limned by Thackeray under the name of 'Caves of Harmony' in *The Newcomes*, and it was at the Coal Hole (and the Antelope in Whitehall) that Edmund Kean, when in his thirties, debauched and depraved, made his last public appearances. At these resorts such commendable artistes as G. W. Ross, Sam Hall, and Jenny Hill, made frequent attendance as performers.

The first music hall above ground was Evan's Supper Rooms in Covent Garden. These rooms boasted a stage and the 'Late Joys' entertainment then presented has been revived at the Player's Theatre in Villiers St., Strand, being televised early in 1950; this theatre is the old Gatti's Music Hall the auditorium being one of the arches beneath Charing Cross Station. The first variety star who appeared at Evan's was Jenny Hill, the 'Vital Spark.' In 1829 the Rotunda Assembly Rooms in Blackfriars were opened, being conducted until 1870; here Sloman made an appearance in a career which lasted for 50 years terminating at Gatti's in 1870 in the year of his death. The Caves of Harmony, a similar place of entertainment in St. Martin's Lane, opened in 1830.

In 1850 no L. tavern was complete without its Concert Room and Chairman; the Grecian Saloon in the City Road even provided a stage suitable for ballet and here Sim Reeves first came to fame. Scarcely less known were the old Mogul (afterwards the Middlesex and since demolished with the Winter Gardens Theatre on the site); Weston's in Holborn; The White Lion in Edgware Rd.; the Canterbury in Westminster Bridge Rd. (later to have a music hall as a development); and the Grapes (or Surrey) in Blackfriars Rd.; the last-named was the first to adopt the title Music Hall. The later Surrey Music Hall (sometime a theatre for transpontine production and pantomime) was derelict for many yrs. and was demolished in 1930, the site having been purchased for an extension of the near-by Eye Hospital. Other scenes of evening entertainment in the 1850s were Vauxhall Gardens; Cremorne Gardens, Chelsea, Eagle Tavern (afterwards Lusby's Music Hall); and the Temple of Harmony at Whitechapel. Stars of those early days were Sam Cowell, the Great Mackney (the *lion comique*), Geo. Leybourne (the singer of 'Champagne Charlie'), and The Great Vance ('The Chickaleary Cove').

The first boom came upon the music halls in 1860 when Weston's (later the Royal, more recently the Holborn Empire, erected in 1857) was followed by the bdg. of the South London Palace (1860); Bedford (1861); Deacon's (1861); London Pavilion (1861); Oxford Music Hall (1861); Collins', Islington Green (1862); Standard, now the Victoria Palace (1863); Metropolitan, Edgware Rd. (1864); and Gatti's, Westminster Bridge Rd. (1865). Contemporary with these important new halls was the lesser Sebrights where the alliterative and wordy bills of Geo. Belmont anticipated the American method of extravagant circus phrasing. Minor music halls included The Star, Bermondsey; The Montpelier, Walworth; and many others. In 1852 Chas. Morton, who was to make music hall history and revive the halls again in 1880, built the Canterbury Music Hall attracting a W. end public with his gallery of oil paintings and his excellent programmes; an innovation at this hall was the installation of the first sliding roof in L.

The second boom, as stated, came in 1880 when Chas. Morton, leaving the Canterbury, crossed the river and applied his genius to the resuscitation of (in turn) the Tivoli and the Palace and followed these successes at the Alhambra and the Empire. The decade which followed his entry into the W. end included the greatest years of the halls. During that period Dan Leno, Marie Lloyd, Vesta Tilley, Albert Chevalier, Eugene Stratton, 'Little Tich' (Harry Relph), G. H. Chirgwin, Arthur Roberts (a 'recruit' from musical comedy), and perhaps fifty others, scarcely less eminent in their profession, were in their prime; not all were stars in their billing in L., but all commanded the premier position when in the provinces. Ballet flourished at the Alhambra and at the Empire, where Adeline Genee became reigning queen.

With the turn of the century the variety theatre began to attract a wider public. Family entertainment which had previously been confined to the Moore and Burgess Minstrels, the German Reed's Entertainments, Maskelyne and Cooke's mysteries at the Egyptian Hall, and the annual Christmas pantomimes, broadened to include music hall artistes acceptable to mixed audiences which included children. The opening of the L. Hippodrome (1900) with its circus arena and large tank for aquatic spectacle, and Oswald Stoll's Coliseum (1904) with its great auditorium and revolving stage, were refining influences on both performers and audiences. Musical items became increasingly popular and great stage players like Sarah Bernhardt, Ellen Terry, Geo. Alexander, Irene Vanbrugh, and Martin Harvey, were booked to appear. Mascagni and Leoncavallo came over to conduct their operas. Fashionable society was attracted to the Palace to see such stars as Maud Allen and Gaby Delys. The glory of the Chairman, that picturesque personality who had seen the halls emerge from obscurity to respectability and success, had long since waned but it was not until 1902 that the last of his line took his last bow, although between the Great Wars a revival of old-time variety at the Garrick Theatre gave him a fleeting public revival since renewed at the Player's Theatre.

Currently with the cinema boom just prior to the 1914–19 War, many L. music halls changed their programmes to full length touring revues, and during that War revue and spectacle displaced variety at the Alhambra, Hippodrome, Palace, Pavilion, and Empire but the decline of the music hall as the home of variety was most marked in the 1920s.

To-day the W. End is often without a true music-hall programme.

L. is without any minor music halls; many of those small and larger halls of the past, in which flowered artistes later to be acclaimed the stars of variety when the boom came, are now cinemas or are used for other purposes, and others were destroyed or damaged by bombing during the 1939–45 War. Such halls include Shoreditch Olympia (bombed and demolished); Kilburn Empire (cinema); Holloway Empire (bombed); Camden Town Hippodrome (used as a studio); Rotherhithe Hippodrome (bombed); Forester's (cinema); Montpelier (cinema); Star (cinema); Euston (cinema); Islington Empire (cinema); Barnard's, Woolwich (cinema); Holborn Empire (bombed); Gatti's, Westminster Bridge Rd., at which Sir Harry Lauder made his first L. appearance in 1900 (bombed, and demolished in 1950); South London Palace (bombed); Mile End Empire (cinema); Imperial (Canning Town), formerly the Royal Albert Music Hall at which George Formby Senr. made his first L. appearance in 1902 (demolished); Empire, Shoreditch (war damaged); Woolwich Hippodrome (war damaged); Putney Hippodrome (cinema); The Variety Theatre, Pitfield St. (cinema); and The Canterbury (bombed and demolished). Dan Leno made his first L. appearance at the Forester's in 1883. Again, many L. music halls were, between the two Wars, demolished, super-cinemas being erected on the sites, to give way in turn to Bingo.

Although nostalgic reference is made in various books to many of the past L. music halls, it is the Empire, Leicester Sq., which has maintained place in the recollection of the Victorian man-about-town. Opened in 1887 it was, until the First World War, perhaps the best-known and most discussed L. centre of light entertainment in the world. Music hall programmes and ballet, with its famous promenade, attracted habitues who looked upon it as a Club. In 1894 the L.C.C. insisted on a partition being erected between the circle-bar and the auditorium and this led to a small riot, the barrier being removed and its wreckage taken in triumph round Trafalgar Sq.; one of the active participants in this gesture was stated to be Mr. Winston Churchill. The Empire was the scene of one of Mrs. Ormiston Chant's protests against the sale of liquor when mirrors in the famous bar were smashed as a demonstration of her distaste of vinous and other consolations of the frequenters. In its last years revues and musical comedies were attractions at the Empire; *Round the Town Again* was presented and *Lilac Domino* started a run of 747 performances in 1918. The last show to be given was *Lady be Good* after which the hall was demolished and a Cinema erected on the site.

The Alhambra, on the opposite side of Leicester Sq. (with an entrance in Charing Cross Rd. also), although with a long history as a theatre, became a music hall; in 1936 it was decided to demolish it and the Odeon Cinema was erected on the site. The original Alhambra was built in 1854 and opened with the name of the Panopticon of Science and Art. It was an establishment designed to provide a popular demonstration of scientific and technical achievements. It contained amongst other things an artesian well, a diving apparatus, and an organ; the last-named was later taken to St. P.'s Cath. This entertainment lasted only three years, but in 1858 the bdg. was re-opened by E. T. Smith, and re-named the Alhambra from its Moorish style of architecture. Circus entertainments, panoramas, gymnastics were shown here; Blondin was amongst those who appeared. In 1860 a stage was built and regular music hall entertainment was provided. After 1871, when the lessee, John Baum, took out a theatrical licence, the Alhambra became the home of ballet in England. The ballets were excellently produced and the company was the best to be found. Amongst many successes, mention must be made of Alfred Moul's ballet, *Victoria and Merry England*, the music for which was written by Sullivan. In 1882 the theatre was burnt down, rebuilt, and reopened a year later as a theatre with a revival of Burnand's *Black Eyed Susan*. This was not a success, and in 1884 the Alhambra reverted to a music hall. Ballet was revived for a time by Alfred Moul, but later the revues produced at the Alhambra became famous, Lee White playing in *Keep Smiling* (1913), and Connie Ediss in *Not Likely* (1914). During the 1914–18 War, the Alhambra was the home of the *Bing Boy* productions to which Geo.

Robey, Violet Loraine, and Alfred Lester contributed so much. After that war the Alhambra presented variety interspersed with visits of the Russian Ballet.

Each year a 'Royal Command' performance (actually it is a submitted programme) is given by the members of the variety profession; this is in aid of the Music Hall Artistes Benevolent Institution and is held at one of the most important L. music halls.

PANTOMIME. It is accepted that pantomime—the Harlequinade with Clown, Columbine, Pantoloon, etc.—made its first appearance in England at the Lincoln's Inn Theatre in 1717. The production was *Harlequin Sorcerer*, an adaptation from the Italian presented by John Rich and it found immediate favour. An earlier Pantomime, *The Tavern Bilkers*, based on Roman tradition, had been sponsored by John Weaver at the Theatre Royal, Drury Lane, in 1702, but as a new form of entertainment it was still-born.

With little modification, the Harlequinade held its place until Grimaldi the elder built up the part of Clown to such a marked degree that his son, the famous Joe (see Life, edited by Charles Dickens), created Pantomime almost as we know it to-day. His first appearance in this form of entertainment was a leading part in *Mother Goose* at the Theatre Royal, Drury Lane, in 1806, since which date almost every theatre in L. has staged pantomime at some time or another whilst practically every well-known music hall artiste and many actors and actresses of the legitimate theatre have appeared in L. productions. It is because variety artistes are, normally, imported into the L. theatre at Pantomime season, that pantomime is included in this section.

The Harlequinade, because of the development of the later form of Pantomime, had almost disappeared from L. theatres at the beginning of this century. Whimsical Walker—clown at the Theatre Royal, Dury Lane, for twenty-five years —was the last of his stage race when he d. in 1934 at the age of 84; nearly two decades had then passed since his last appearance in the final harlequinade— which in a truncated form had always followed the pantomime—at the Theatre Royal, Drury Lane.

Notable L. pantomime theatres were:

Surrey (first appearance of Dan Leno in pantomime); the Britannia, Hoxton; Theatre Royal, Drury Lane; Lyceum; Princess; Sadler's Wells; Olympic; Grecian; and the Standard. Famous clowns were the two Grimaldis, Harry Flexmore, and George Lupino, whilst James Barnes was a notable pantaloon and John Rich, James Bryne, Jack Bologna and Tom Ellar were Harlequins whose names appear frequently in old Pantomime records.

Contemporary Pantomime is given at a few W. end theatres and at almost all suburban theatres during the season, which runs from four to six weeks with an exceptional longer run of up to eight weeks. The production often depends upon *décor*, choreography and vocalizing of popular songs for its appeal. The onetime elaborate transformation scenes are rarely employed whilst rhyming 'books' have been discontinued. Experiment in subject has not been apparent for many years, and during the last two decades some six of the more popular stories, although differing slightly in treatment, have re-appeared each season.

Music in London. In St. Dunstan's in the West Ch. there is a memorial tablet inscribed with a line of Milton—

'Such sweet compulsion doth in music lie.' This is most manifest in L., for in England, more than in most countries, musical activity has centred in the metropolis. L. is full of memories of the music-making of nearly four centuries.

Of our great Elizabethan sch. of composers, nearly all lived and worked, and many d., in L. Thos. Tallis (?1510–85), whose preces and responses are still in daily use in the English Ch., was organist of Waltham Abbey and later of the Chapel Royal. He is bd. in Greenwich Ch., where a memorial window was destroyed in the blitz. Wm. Byrd (?1538–1623), generally accounted the greatest of the group, was joint organist with Tallis of the Chapel Royal (bd. at Stondon Massey, near Ongar). Thos Morley (?1557–1604), madrigalist, was also a Londoner, a gentleman of the Chapel Royal, and for a time organist of St. P.'s Cath. Little is known of his life, and even the date of his death is uncertain. John Dowland (?1563–1626) was a native of Westminster, and had a continental reputation as lutanist and song-writer. John Bull

(?1563–1628) also had a European reputation as a keyboard composer and virtuoso. He was first professor of music at Gresham Coll. and, owing to his deficiencies in Latin, the first to lecture in English. Thos. Weelkes (1575–1623), madrigalist, though he lived at Winchester and Chichester, d. on a visit to L. and is bd. in St. Bride's, Fleet St. (see 'City Churches —C'). On the other hand, Orlando Gibbons (1583–1625), gentleman of the Chapel Royal and organist of W.A., d. on a visit to Canterbury and is bd. in the cathedral. The black marble bust in the N. aisle of W.A. is copied from the Canterbury monument. Henry Lawes (1595–1662), friend of Milton and composer of the original music to *Comus*, is bd. somewhere in the abbey cloisters. Our greatest composer, Henry Purcell (?1658–95), was b. in the abbey precincts and served it in turn as chorister, copyist, and organist. He lies in the N. choir aisle, and near him is his master, John Blow (1648–1708). In the N. aisle, or the cloisters, are bd. the series of organists who served the abbey faithfully in their generation, from Wm. Croft (?1677–1727) to Sir John Fredk. Bridge (1844–1924); also a musical historian, Sir John Hawkins, executor and biographer of Dr. Johnson (1719–89); and two foreign musicians, Johann Peter Salomon (1745–1815), and Muzio Clementi, the 'father of the pianoforte' (1752–1832). Of later composers, Wm. Sterndale Bennett (1816–75) and Sir Chas. Stanford (1852–1924) lie in the N. aisle; and there are monuments to Michael Wm. Balfe, of *Bohemian Girl* fame, and to another musical historian, Chas. Burney (1726–1814). The former was bd. at Kensal Green and the latter at Chelsea (*q.v.*). Handel (1685–1759) lies in the S. transept with the poets.

Thos. Arne (1710–78), best remembered by his Shakespeare songs and his *Rule, Britannia!* was b. in King St., Covent Garden, and is bd. in the chyd. of St. Paul's nearby. There is a tablet in the ch. John Playford, a Londoner, set up the first regular music-publishing business in 1650, near the Temple Ch., and during the Commonwealth period alone issued thirty-four collections of vocal and instrumental music, including three editions of *The English Dancing Master.* Thos. Britton, a working coal-merchant, established the first public concerts in a loft over his shop in Aylesbury St., Clerkenwell, in 1678. These were attended by music-lovers of all ranks of society, and the leading musicians of the day, including Handel, took part in them. Britton d. in 1714 and was bd. in St. James's Ch., Clerkenwell.

L. has always been hospitable to foreign musicians. Handel first visited L. in 1710, and returned two years later to become the dominant figure of L.'s artistic life for nearly half a century. He lived first at Burlington House, Piccadilly, then at Canons, near Edgware, and finally, for thirty-four years, at 25, Brook St., where a tablet marks the house. Although Bach never came to L., his youngest son Johann Christian made amends by settling here in 1762, and later opening the Hanover Sq. Rooms, which remained the principal concert hall for nearly a century. He d. in 1782 and was bd. in old St. Pancras chyd.

Mozart stayed in Frith St., Soho, in 1764, when touring as an infant prodigy, and there composed his first, or 'London' Symphony at the age of 8. Haydn came to L. on Salomon's invitation in 1791, where he lodged at 18 Gt. Pulteney St. Here he stayed eighteen months and wrote six of the 'Salomon' Symphonies. He came again in 1794 and lodged at 1 Bury St. Here he wrote the last five of the 'Salomon' Symphonies. They are among his most mature works; the one known as the 'London' Symphony was his 104th and last. Mendelssohn visited L. several times and remained for a generation the musical idol of the English people; Weber came in 1826—to produce *Oberon*, and to die. He d. at 103 Great Portland St., and was bd. in the R.C. chapel in East St., Finsbury Circus, whence his remains were removed to Dresden in 1844. Chopin stayed at 48 Dover St. in 1848, and there on one occasion played all night to a gathering of Polish exiles. Berlioz, Liszt, and Wagner visited L. in turn, and, though Beethoven did not, his ninth Symphony belongs to L., having been commissioned by the Philharmonic Soc., who also sent him a gift of £100 during his last illness. Vauxhall Gardens (*q.v.*) played an important part in L.'s musical life in the 18th century.

Concerts continued to be held at the Hanover Sq. Rooms until the middle of the 19th century, when St. James's Hall (on the site now occupied by the Piccadilly Hotel) was built. For over forty yrs. this was the principal home of orchestral, choral, and chamber music, and its Monday and Saturday 'pops.' were a feature of L.'s musical life, Joachim being leader of the quartet. What these concerts did for chamber music, the Crystal Palace concerts, under August Manns, did for orchestral music during the same period. The triennial Handel festivals at the Crystal Palace continued until the First World War.

The Queen's Hall, Langham Place, built in 1894, was the centre of L.'s music until its destruction by enemy action in 1941. Its Promenade Concerts, held nightly from August to October were a notable feature of L.'s musical life for 45 years, and almost throughout were under the conductorship of the late Sir Henry Wood, to whom there is a memorial window in St. Sepulchre's Ch. (*q.v.*). These concerts were latterly organized by the B.B.C., and on the destruction of the Queen's Hall were transferred—in common with most other large-scale choral or orchestral concerts— to the Albert Hall, with its much greater seating capacity but less perfect acoustics. The remarkable growth in L.'s musical public in recent years, however, has created audiences which fully utilize the extra capacity. The Royal Festival Hall and the Queen Elizabeth Hall on South Bank bear witness to this. Sacred choral works are given periodically at St. P.'s Cath., W.A., Southwark Cath., St. Michael's, Cornhill, and other chs.; while masses and motets of the polyphonic period are the special feature of the services at Westminster Cath. Lunch-hour recitals are held at several City and W. End Chs., Bishopsgate Institute and occasionally in Guildhall.

The Aeolian Hall, New Bond St., and the Wigmore Hall, Wigmore St., are mainly used for chamber music and solo recitals.

Opera is associated in the Londoner's mind with Covent Garden, but though there has been a theatre there since 1732, it was not until 1847 that it was entirely devoted to opera, under the management of Fredk. Gye, who, when the theatre was burnt down in 1856, rebuilt it at his own expense, and continued to direct its fortunes for twenty yrs. His statue,

found in a dilapidated condition in an antique shop, has been restored at the V. & A. Mus., and again set up in Covent Garden Theatre. Another brilliant period in its history was the management of Sir Augustus Harris from 1888 to 1896. (See 'Theatres'.)

English light opera is inseparably associated with the names of Gilbert and Sullivan. Both were b. in L., the former at 17 Southampton St., Strand, and the latter at 8 Bolwell St., Lambeth. Sullivan lived for some yrs. at 58 Victoria St., dying there in 1900. There is an L.C.C. tablet on the house. He is bd. in St. P.'s Cath. There is a monument to him in the Embankment Gardens, and a memorial, with medallion, to Gilbert on the Embankment wall at Charing Cross. These are not far from the Savoy Theatre, where most of the operas were produced.

Paradoxically, the English Folk Dance and Song Soc., which exists to conserve and revive the old music and dances of rural England, has its headquarters in L. (Cecil Sharp House, Regent's Park).

The Royal Soc. of Musicians was founded in 1738, and granted a charter by George III in 1789. Handel, who was amongst the founders, composed concertos for its benefit, and at his death bequeathed it a legacy of £1,000. The soc. possesses some interesting memorials of music, these including a list of the 'Four and Twenty Fiddlers of King Charles II's Band; their names and emoluments.' This is in the handwriting of Thos. Purcell, who styles himself 'Master of the Musick and Chief and Leader of the Four and Twenty Fiddlers. 15 May 1674.' The collection of portraits includes a life-size painting by Gainsborough of George III, and a painting of Henry Purcell by Closterman. The soc. has done beneficent work for aged and infirm musicians, so much as £9,000 being spent in one yr. in their behalf. In 1931 the soc. left Lisle St., Leicester Sq., the bdg. being condemned as unsafe, and moved to new quarters in Stratford Place, Oxford St.

L. has several great national schs. of music. The Royal Academy of Music was founded in 1822 and its present premises at York Gate, Marylebone, were opened in 1912. The Royal Coll. of Music is of later growth, having been founded in 1883, and moved to its present bdgs. in Prince

Consort Rd., in 1890. Sir Chas. Stanford was professor of composition there for forty yrs. The Coll. houses the Donaldson Mus., an interesting collection of musical instruments of various periods.

Trinity Coll. of Music, Mandeville Place, was founded in 1875 as a centre for Anglican Ch. music, but early became a general musical coll. The Guildhall Sch. of Music and Drama, John Carpenter St., and the London Coll. of Music, Gt. Marl-borough St. also award their own qualifications. All these colleges give periodic students' concerts to which the public are admitted free of charge.

Old musical instruments can be seen at Horniman Mus., Dulwich. The collection made by the late Major Benton Fletcher is at 3 Cheyne Walk, Chelsea.

There is a City Music Soc., founded in 1943. Concerts are given at Bishopsgate Inst.

N

National Gallery was erected 1832–8 on the site of the King's Mews (see 'Charing Cross'), and cost £96,000. The mean little cupolas, resembling pepper-boxes, led to its being referred to as the 'National Cruetstand.' The architect was restricted by conditions imposed upon him. He was not to impede the view of the portico of St. Martin's Ch.; he was not to infringe upon the barrack space in the rear, and the columns of Carlton House (*q.v.*) were to be worked into the composition, which was also to embrace a dome, cupolas, and porticoes. The idea of a N.G. was first mooted in 1824, when the Angerstein collection of thirty-eight pictures was purchased. When the gallery was opened only six rooms were devoted to the national collection, the remainder being used by the Royal Academy of Arts, formally located at Somerset House (*q.v.*). In 1869, when the Royal Academy was removed to Burlington House, the N.G. was enlarged, and became worthy of its title. In addition to British, French, Dutch, Italian, and Spanish schools are represented. (See 'Art in London.').

National Portrait Gallery (St. Martin's Place) was the gift to the nation of Mr. W. H. Alexander of Shipton, Andover, who, in 1889, undertook to devote a sum of £80,000 to this object. The total cost was £96,000 the balance being provided by the Govt. The architect was Mr. Ewan Christian; after his death the work was supervised by Mr. J. H. Christian. It was completed in 1895, and the gallery was opened in 1896. The national collection of portraits was founded by an Act of Parliament in 1856, and first housed at 29 Gt. George St., Westminster, until 1869, when it was removed to S. Kensington. In 1885 it was transferred to the Bethnal Green Mus., where it remained until the new bdg. was ready.

The oldest portraits are on the top floor. Here is probably the earliest, Margaret Beaufort, Countess of Richmond and Derby, and mother of Henry VII. It was painted on a panel about 1485. Others almost as old are Elizabeth of York, consort of Henry VII, who d. in 1502 and one of Henry VII about 1505. In the N.P.G. are the famous Kit-Cat portraits. These were painted during the yrs. 1700 to 1720 by Sir Godfrey Kneller for Jacob Tonson, a famous publisher. The portraits took their strange name from a Kit-Cat Club that met first at a tavern near Temple Bar, kept by Christopher Cat. It was famous for its mutton pies, known as 'Kit-Cats,' and from these the Club took its name. In 1703 Jacob Tonson, who was one of the members, bought a house at Barn Elms, near Putney, where he set aside a special room for the Club's meetings. To fit this room the portraits had to be of special dimensions, 36 × 28 inches, and this has remained since as a stock size known as the 'Kit-Cat.' Amongst the subjects are Wm. Congreve, Sir John Vanbrugh, Sir Richd. Steele, Joseph Addison, and Tonson.

Newgate was one of the gates of Roman L.—probably the chief W. gate and across Watling St. In 1285 it is mentioned as 'Chamberlain's Gate,' and it is known from Domesday Book that Wm. the Chamberlain had a vineyard at 'Holeburn.' It is probable therefore that he was responsible for its re-erection. If so, it must have had a different name before, and this may have been Westgate. The gaol (see 'Prisons') is mentioned in Henry II's reign (*c.* 1188); Harben suggests that the gate may have been so called after the necessary rebuilding following a fire in 1137. It was again rebuilt with the prison, under a bequest of Whittington's (*c.* 1423). It was repaired in 1555–6 and 1630. It was damaged in the G.F., and rebuilt in 1672 in a stronger and more convenient way, with a postern for foot passengers. On the E. side were three stone statues, Justice, Mercy, and Truth; on the W., Liberty, Peace, Plenty, and Concord. Four of the figures ornamented part of the front of old Newgate Prison. In its last days, on its summit, was a machine for air, invented by Dr. Hales, which is mentioned by Hayley in his *Ode to Howard*. It was part of the necessary ventilation of the prison, which included apartments over the gateway. The gate was demolished in 1777; it was the last to disappear. In 1874–5 traces of the old Roman gate were found. It appeared to have been 31 ft. wide. In 1903 an arched subway was discovered at right angles to the road. There is a C.C. tablet in Newgate St., on the N. wall of the Central Criminal Court.

O

Old Bailey. The origin of the name is somewhat obscure. Stow thought it derived from the Court of the Chamberlain of the City, and as Newgate (*q.v.*) was once called Chamberlain's Gate, this may be correct. Weekley, however, says: 'The Old Bailey (*Vetus Ballium*) was the ballium of the City wall between Ludgate and Newgate, the word' bailly in Middle English, being enclosure. 'In ballio' is a reference to it in 1241–8; 'The Baillie' appears *c.* 1289. Strype refers to the Great and Little Old Bailey. The latter was the name at the N. end which was widened towards the close of the 18th century by the removal of a row of old tenements which stood in the middle, and divided Old Bailey into two narrow passages.

Here, outside the debtors' door of Newgate Prison (about where is now the entrance to the Central Criminal Court), public executions took place. The first were on 9th Dec. 1783 when ten malefactors were hanged by Edwd. Dennis. He was the hangman who figures in Barnaby Rudge, and for his share in the 'No Popery' riots he had been threatened with execution. The drop was introduced when the scene of execution was changed from Tyburn. Twenty men were hanged in one morning in 1785. 'Before going out,' said a newspaper report, 'the unhappy criminals kissed each other in the quadrangle, then marched on solemnly, two and two, singing a funeral hymn.' In 1789 a woman was burned after first undergoing strangulation—for coining. This was the last occasion of such a punishment being inflicted in England. On 23rd Feb., 1807 when Owen Haggerty, John Holloway and Elizabeth Godfrey were hanged, a cart gave way. Through concussion and suffocation, caused by the pressure of the people, 28 were killed and 15 injured. In 1824 Henry Fauntleroy, a banker, was hanged for forgery. In the L. Mus. a picture shews him being manacled on the morning of his execution. The last public execution took place on 26th May, 1868; a young Fenian, Michael Barrett, was the victim of Wm. Calcraft, the executioner. He had tried to blow up the Middlesex House of Detention (see 'Prisons'). A correspondent of the *Sunday Times* recalled his 'knifeboard' bus

stopping at the end of Old Bailey on this occasion. 'There was the gallows before us, with the poor wretch hanging by the neck.' A correspondent of *John o' London's Weekly* wrote:

'I was born in Newgate Street, opposite the corner of Old Bailey. . . . I remember that our blinds, by order of my father, were pulled down until nine o'clock, when the murderers' bodies were cut down. One Monday I went to lift the corner of the blind; my mother took my hand and led me away, saying "Not yet, sonnie." It was before I was three years old.'

'The Hon. Mr. Sucklethumbkin's Story' (*Ingoldsby Legends*) presents a vivid view of the scene on these occasions. Rev. R. H. Barham, the author of the *Ingoldsby Legends*, lived in Amen Court, close to the Old Bailey. He said that from his windows he had a fine view of a hanging wood!

The 'Magpie and Stump' was opposite the place of execution. Rebuilt since Barham's time, it was, for no known reason, renamed the 'King of Denmark.' Now it has reverted to the more historic sign. Huge crowds assembled on these occasions. In 1864, when Franz Müller (he committed a murder in a train) was hanged, it was estimated that 50,000 people were packed into the Old Bailey and Smithfield. Barrels of beer were brought, and vendors of ginger-beer and other refreshments plied their trade amongst the waiting crowd, who sang such ditties as:

'Oh my!
Think I 've got to die.'

Jas. Payn (editor of the *Cornhill Magazine* from 1882 to 1896, and a popular novelist) had in earlier days, with some friends, paid twenty guineas for a window to witness an execution—presumably at the 'Magpie and Stump.'

Old Bailey is full of criminal associations. In 1830 the pillory was set up there for the last time; the victim was Jas. Bossy, convicted of perjury, the only offence for which it had not been abolished in 1815. In 1837 the pillory was abolished for all offences.

It has a few other less sinister associations. Wm. Camden, the antiquary, was b. here. In Green Arbour Court (at the

N. end) Oliver Goldsmith was living in 1759. In Old Bailey lived Wm. Hone when he published his three political parodies on the Catechism, the Litany, and the Creed, for which he was three times tried and acquitted at Guildhall. (See 'Central Criminal Court.')

Oratory (Brompton Rd.) is that of St. Philip Neri, an order composed of secular priests living voluntarily in a community, but not bound by religious vows; it was introduced into England by Newman in 1847. A temporary ch. was erected in 1854, and succeeded by the present bdg. in 1884. The outer dome and the façade were not completed until 1897. There are beautiful twin Corinthian pilasters of Devonshire marble to carry the entablature. The choir stalls are of Italian walnut, exquisitely carved and inlaid with ivory, and, like the inlaid floor of the sanctuary, they were the gift of Anne, Dowager Duchess of Argyll. The high altar is of statuary marble, enriched with gilt ornamentation; the baldachino is copied from that in the shrine of St. Anthony at Padua; the picture behind it is by Father Philipin de Rivière of the L. Oratory; the two seven-branched lamps are an imitation of those on the Arch of Titus, which were copied from the lamps in the Temple of Jerusalem. The side chapels have some fine mosaic and carving. The dome has a height to the summit of the cross of 200 ft., and the nave is only exceeded in width by those of Westminster Cath. and York Minster. There are statues of great size, in Carrara marble, of the twelve Apostles. They were carved by Mazotti, and stood for 200 years in Siena Cath. before they were acquired by the Oratorian Fathers. Facing the Brompton Rd., on the W. side of the ch., is a statue of Cardinal Newman by Chavalliaud (1896).

Oxford Street was in 16th-century plans of L. 'The Waye from Uxbridge.' C. L. Kingsford admirably surveyed its early history here related. In the Act for St. Anne's, Soho, in 1678 it is called simply 'the King's highway or great road'; in 1682 'the Road to Oxford' is shown as beginning at St. Giles's Pound, which was at the S. end of Tottenham Court Rd. In the rate-book of St. Anne's, Soho, for 1691 it is the Acton Rd. In the map

(1707) in Hatton's *New View of London* it is 'the Road to Oxford.' Hatton, however, did not include the Oxford Rd. in the list of streets in his text. He there defines the Tyburn Rd. as 'between St. Giles's Pound east, and the lane leading to the gallows west, 350 yards.' This point would be nearly to Berwick St., which was about the limit of building when Hatton wrote. Beyond that there was but a country road, leading to the gallows, and Strype (1720) still applied the name Tyburn Rd. to the eastern portion. The present name had, however, already come into use, for at the corner of Rathbone St. there is a tablet with the inscription 'Rathbone Place in Oxford Street, 1718.' Rocque's map of 1746 extends Oxford St. so far W. as New Bond St., beyond which point it is called the Tyburn Rd.

On the N. side there were only a few houses farther W. than Tottenham Court Rd. in 1707, but Rathbone Pl. (now Rathbone St.) was built in 1718. Rocque's map shows a network of sts. on both sides of Oxford St. and Tyburn Rd., open country being reached only with the 'Tyburn Turnpike' and the gallows. Cavendish Sq. and neighbouring sts. were built on the estate which came to Edwd. Harley, afterwards second E. of Oxford, by his marriage in 1713 to Henrietta Cavendish-Holles, daughter and heiress to the D. of Newcastle. Their only child Margaret m. Wm. Bentinck, second D. of Portland. To these two marriages the sq. (designed in 1717–18 and delayed through the South Sea Bubble crisis) and neighbouring sts. owe their names. The district attracted the aristocracy, and one suspects that this was not unconnected with the removal of public executions from Tyburn to Newgate in 1783. They can hardly have relished all the riff-raff of L. so frequently passing their doors; this was less edifying than a modern socialistic demonstration proceeding to Hyde Park.

This, however, would make it an appropriate venue for a boxing ring, and in 1743 John Broughton opened a new amphitheatre opposite Poland St., on the site of a sch. of arms instituted by Jas. Figg in 1720. At No. 173 was the Pantheon, opened in 1772, and referred to by Horace Walpole as 'a winter Ranelagh.' The latter was most enthusiastic:

'The ceilings, even of the passages, are the most beautiful stuccos in the best taste of the grotesque. The ceilings of the ballrooms, and the panels painted like Raphael's loggia in the Vatican. A dome like the Pantheon glazed. It is to cost fifty thousand pounds.'

At a masquerade a little later Walpole was present, and this moved him to call it 'the most beautiful building in England. . . . All the friezes and niches were edged with alternate lamps of green and purple glass, that shed a most heathen light, and the dome was illuminated by a heaven of oiled paper well painted with gods and goddesses.'

Dr. Johnson went with Boswell, in the yr. it was opened, and compared it unfavourably with Ranelagh. It provoked the following characteristic dialogue:

'I said there was not half a guinea's worth of pleasure in seeing this place. Johnson: "But, Sir, there is half a guinea's worth of inferiority to other people in not having seen it." Boswell: "I doubt, Sir, whether there are many happy people here." Johnson: "Yes, Sir, there are many happy people here. There are many people here who are watching hundreds, and who think hundreds are watching them." '

Gibbon frequented the Pantheon; Goldsmith and Fanny Burney also. Evelina there met Ld. Orville. Mrs. Hardcastle (*She Stoops to Conquer*) thought a knowledge of it essential to manners. Masquerades for years were the principal entertainments, but there were other diversions. Lunardi's balloon was suspended from a ceiling in 1785, and when the Haymarket Theatre was burnt in 1789, it was sought to introduce music equal to that which had been provided there. In 1792 the

Pantheon was also burnt out, giving Turner the subject for an early picture, 'The Pantheon the Morning after the Fire,' in which he shows the ruins draped in great masses of ice. A second Pantheon was built, and concerts and masquerades again carried on. It had little success, and they were discontinued in 1810, Messrs. Gedge and Bonner then taking it at £1,000 p.a. as the headquarters of their 'National Institution for improving the manufactures of the United Kingdom, and arts connected therewith, etc.' After the issue of a magnificent prospectus, the scheme of a colossal exhibition of these manufactures was abandoned, and Col. Greville came on the scene and opened it as a Pantheon Theatre in 1812 for Italian burlettas and ballets. This was a failure, and in 1813 another attempt was made to establish it as a regular opera house. No proper licence had been obtained, and it was compulsorily closed. In the same year it was again opened—for ballets and pantomimes at popular prices. Still one more failure was recorded, and in 1814 it was put up to auction under a distraint for rent which had remained unpaid for three years. It was closed for a number of yrs., and in 1834 reconstructed by Sidney Smirke at a cost of £30,000 and opened as a bazaar. It had some success until, in 1867, it passed into the hands of W. & A. Gilbey, Ltd., wine merchants, whose business headquarters it remained until 1936, when they sold it. The pillared entrance then remained, but now everything has gone and a branch of Marks and Spencer Ltd. occupies the site (171–181).

Modern Oxford St. is not the resort of the historical student but of those bent upon shopping.

P

Paddington, now part of the City of Westminster, was a met bor. and par. in the NW. of L. The name is personal in origin and means 'the farm of Padda.'

The nucleus of Paddington is Paddington Green, on the Harrow Rd. which leads W. from that part of the ancient Watling St. which is called Edgware Rd., more than a quarter of a mile NW. of Tyburn Tree site by the Marble Arch.

Bayswater is now a name vaguely applied to most of that portion of the bor. lying S. of the G.W.R. It took its title from 'Baynard's Watering,' mentioned in a grant of land in Paddington in 1653, which by 1720, in a terrier of the Dean and Chapter of Westminster, had become 'Bear's Watering.' It was the spot where the Westbourne reached the Uxbridge Rd. (now Bayswater Rd.) and comprised the site of the street called Lancaster Gate, S. of Craven Hill. This latter district took its name from a 17th-century owner, the first Ld. Craven. The Baynard of the Watering may possibly have been the builder of the original Baynard's Castle in the City (*q.v.*), as he held lands in Ossulston Hundred, but Loftie believed it to have been called after a later bearer of the name. Most of the present Bayswater district, and that corner of it between the Edgware and Bayswater Rds. sometimes referred to as Tyburnia, was developed in the ten yrs. 1839–49. At the beginning of the 19th century there had been hereabouts the Bayswater Tea Gardens, occupying the site of an earlier physic garden owned by the notorious 'Sir' John Hill, an apothecary who turned quack and unsuccessful playwright, and got for himself a Swedish knighthood. Of him Garrick wrote:

'For physic and farces, his equal there scarce is;
His farces are physic, his physic a farce is.'

The Bayswater reservoirs on both sides of Praed St. were made to supply Kensington Palace. The conduit a little to the N. of Craven Hill belonged to the City of L., and supplied the Bond St. area, which is C.C. property.

Maida Vale takes its name from a town in Calabria where Sir John Stuart defeated the French in 1806.

A chapel was built in Paddington before 1222, and the first par. ch. seems to have been dedicated to St. Catherine. It stood on the Green, and was demolished in 1678. The second Ch. was dedicated to St. James, and had a bell turret at the W. end, crowned with a small spire. Wm. Hogarth and Jane Thornhill were m. here in 1729, and there was a curious annual custom of throwing bread from the steeple to be scrambled for. The present ch. was built from designs by John Plaw, and consecrated in 1791. It is a quaint bdg., cruciform in plan, and has been little altered. It contains a tablet to Sarah Siddons, 1831 (her statue may be seen nearby on the Green and her tomb in the chyd.), and one to Nollekens the sculptor, 1823. Other notable graves are those of B. R. Haydon, the painter of gigantic historical canvases who committed suicide at 14 Burwood Place (1846); Wm. Collins, R.A. (1847); Sarah Disraeli, the statesman's favourite sister; and Harriet, the unhappy first wife of P. B. Shelley, who drowned herself in the Serpentine after he had deserted her (1816).

St. Mary's ceased to be the par. ch. in 1845, being supplanted by St. James', Sussex Gardens, built in 1843 but practically rebuilt in 1882 on a larger scale, Street being the architect. Another notable ch., also by Street, is St. Mary Magdalene, 1873, and there are two by that fine architect J. L. Pearson—the Catholic Apostolic Ch. in Maida Hill W., and St. Augustine's, Kilburn, notable for its tall spire, by many considered its finest ch. Of other churches in the bor., mention must be made of Holy Trinity, Bishop's Rd., 1846, by Thos. Cundy; Christ Ch., Lancaster Gate, by Francis, 1855; the R.C. Ch. of St. Mary of the Angels, 1857, with additions by J. F. Bentley; the Greek Orthodox Ch. of St. Sophia, Moscow Rd., 1895, by J. O. Scott; the Westbourne Pk. Baptist Chapel, scene of the ministrations of Dr. John Clifford, 1877–1915.

Panyer Alley (Paternoster Row) is first mentioned in 1442 as 'yᵉ Panyer Ale' at a time when there was a tavern of that name. This was probably the 'Panyer on the hoope' in the par. of St. Michael le Querne, and mentioned 1535–6. Here was the corn market; H. T. Riley thought that in the 15th century it was a place where bakers' boys stood with their baskets or panyers. The waiter who at Middle Temple Hall still blows the horn to summon the members to dinner is called the panyer man, recalling the time when the waiters went to Westminster to fetch the bread. Until 1940 here was the sculptured figure of a boy sitting on a basket. Strype thought it was a basket of fruit, but it was probably intended for a bread basket. The inscription reads:

'When ye have sought the City round
Yet still this is the highest ground
August the 27 1688.'

It is not quite correct. Panyer Alley is 58 ft. above sea-level, and Cornhill 60 ft. The house against which the stone stood was demolished in 1892. The new premises were altered in 1908, to suit the requirements of Farrow's Bank, which acquired them; policemen then guarded the stone day and night to protect it from damage. Mr. Thos. Farrow had a glass case placed over it, and the bank issued a pamphlet concerning its history. The concluding paragraph is pathetic:

'The Boy of Panyer Alley has watched with unchanging mien the ever-increasing prosperity of the City whose crown he adorns. May he see the same success attend the efforts of the Bank with whose future years he is inseparably connected, and by whom he is protected.'

The boy (he remained long after the bank had gone) is the property of the Vintners' Co., and during the construction of the new St. Paul's Station was kept in their hall. He was ceremonially reinstalled in 1939, under the auspices of the London Passenger Transport Board. During the Second World War he was removed but has been replaced on the wall of the new Paternoster precinct near to St. Paul's tube station.

Parks. The five great L. parks are Green Park, Hyde Park, Kensington Gardens, Regent's Park, and St. James's Park. These parks began their histories as royal preserves, they were given to, not made for, the people.

GREEN PARK (53 acres) seems to have derived its name from the green grass

that 'grew all round.' It is really part of St. James's Park, and, in 1767, when George III reduced it to enlarge the gardens of old Buckingham House, it was occasionally called 'Upper St. James's Park.' In 1731 a duel was fought there between Mr. Pultneney, afterwards E. of Bath, and John Ld. Hervey. After each of the combatants had been slightly wounded they were parted. Another duel was fought in 1771 between Viscount Ligonier and Count Vittoria Alfieri. Benjamin Franklin here made the experiment of smoothing, i.e. stilling the water by pouring oil upon it on a windy day, on the large piece of water at the head of the Green Park. It was much improved by Ld. Duncannon, when Chief Commissioner of Woods and Forests during the Grey and Melbourne administration (1830–41). At the NE. end was a large reservoir or canal; it was filled up in 1856. On the N. side of Green Park, and facing Piccadilly, there are fine wrought-iron gates which recently bore the following inscription:

'These gates were probably made by Warren about 1735 and originally stood at Lord Heathfield's house at Turnham Green. They were acquired by the Duke of Devonshire in 1837 and erected at his Chiswick house, the Devonshire arms replacing those of Lord Egmont who occupied Heathfield House from 1765 to 1771. In 1898 they were removed to Devonshire House, Piccadilly, and in 1921 they were purchased out of the Queen Victoria Memorial Fund by the Commissioners of His Majesty's Works and Public Buildings and re-erected on this site.'

The gates near the Q. Victoria Memorial and the pillars of Portland stone at the entrances from The Mall and Birdcage Walk were part of the contribution from the Dominions and Dependencies to commemorate the reign of Q. Victoria.

Another gate, at Hyde Park corner, as the inscription records, was the gift of the first Baron Michelham in 1912, as a memorial to Edward VII. Surmounting the arch is the bronze Quadriga, symbolizing Peace alighting on the Chariot of War. It was designed by Capt. Adrian Jones.

HYDE PARK (360 acres) was in Saxon times the manor of Eia—from which later the name 'Hyde' was derived. On a pedestal supporting a vase at the E. end of the Serpentine is the following inscription:

'A supply of water by conduit from this spot was granted to the Abbey of Westminster with the Manor of Hyde by King Edward the Confessor. The Manor was resumed by the Crown in 1736, but the springs as a head and original fountain of water were preserved to the Abbey by the Charter of Queen Elizabeth in 1560.'

It appears first to have been enclosed by the abbot and convent of Westminster. In the reign of Henry VIII (1536) it passed into the possession of the Crown. By 1637 it had become a public park; it was then used for horse-racing. In 1652 the Commonwealth Govt. sold it into private hands, and Evelyn records that 'every coach was made to pay a shilling, and a horse sixpence, by the sordid fellow who had purchased it.' It must have seemed an avenging Nemesis that led to Cromwell's accident when he was driving in a coach. Carlyle wrote:

'The horses, beautiful animals, tasting of the whip, became unruly; galloped would not be checked, but took to plunging; plunged the postillion down; plunged or shook his Highness down, dragging him by the foot for some time so that "a pistol went off in his pocket," to the amazement of men. Whereupon? Whereupon—his Highness got up again, little the worse; was let blood; and went about his affairs much as usual!'

At the Restoration in 1660, the contract of sale was cancelled, and Hyde Park once more became a favourite rendezvous of fashion, as well as a convenient place for military reviews. It was then enclosed by a brick wall, which stood until 1726. In 1730 the *élite* played cricket in the park, the players including the Ds. of Devonshire and Richmond and the E. of Albemarle. In the same yr. the Serpentine lake was formed by order of Q. Caroline (consort of George II), from the flow of the river Westbourne (see 'Lost Rivers'). In 1749 Horace Walpole was robbed in Hyde Park by the famous highwayman McLean. In 1768—for the last time—there was royal hunting there; Christian VII of Denmark joined his brother-in-law George III in hunting,

but only a single buck was allowed to be shot. In 1769 the *Public Advertiser* informed its readers that Gen. Paoli (of Corsica),

'accompanied by James Boswell Esq., took an airing in Hyde Park in his coach. His Excellency came out and took a walk by the Serpentine River and through Kensington Gardens with which he seemed very much pleased.'

The elder Pitt, the E. of Chatham, was the first· to call the park 'the lungs of London.' It was a great place for duels. The most notable was between Ld. Mohun and the 4th D. of Hamilton in 1712 when both combatants were killed. This encounter is immortalised in Thackeray's *Henry Esmond*. In the 18th century there were many robberies and a bell was rung at intervals to mobilize people who were about to cross it *en route* to town. In 1784 the Serpentine was frozen, and the E. of Carlisle, Benjamin West, and Dr. Hewitt danced minuets on the ice. In 1803 two respectable tradesmen aged 73 and 62 engaged in a race over a course of 100 yds. In honour of a single cossack—Russia having, it was held, saved Europe from Napoleon—so many as 100,000 people are said to have assembled in the park in 1813. In 1814, for the first time since 1357—when John of France was brought prisoner after the battle of Poitiers—a French K. was in L. Louis XVIII went to Hyde Park attended by an imposing cavalcade, and was accompanied by the P. Regent. In the same yr., by way of a centenary celebration of the accession of the House of Hanover to the British throne, a miniature battle of Trafalgar was staged on the Serpentine. In 1818 a band of Canadian Indians, each in wardress and bearing a tomahawk, attracted a huge crowd. In 1825 the brick wall in Park Lane, and between Hyde Park Corner and Kensington, was taken down and replaced by iron railings. In the same yr. a son of Henry Hunt, a notorious Radical, drove a four-in-hand over the frozen Serpentine.

In the Victorian era it became the greatest resort of popular orators. In July 1855 it was proposed to hold a huge open-air meeting there to protest against a Sunday Trading Bill. Sir Richd. Mayne, Commissioner of Police, opposed it, and no meeting was held. On 14th Oct. 1855 a carpenter addressed a meeting there, and, finding no interference, repeated the performance on the following Sunday. He then congratulated his audience on again exercising their own recognized privilege of meeting in 'their own park.' On 28th Oct., 4th, 11th, and 18th Nov. there were further meetings, riotous in character; on the last date there was a strong force of police in attendance to disperse the crowd. There were no further meetings until 1859. In that yr. one was held to present an address to the Emperor Napoleon, sympathizing with him in the course he had taken respecting Italy. In 1862, at meetings in support of Garibaldi, there was some blood shed. In 1866 a monster meeting was to be held in Hyde Park, organized by the Reform League. Sir Richd. Mayne prohibited it. On being denied admission, the demonstrators tore down hundreds of yds. of iron railings, and swarmed into the park. The serious riot that followed led eventually to a more conciliatory attitude towards the right of meeting which was persistently claimed, and in 1872 the Commissioner of Works definitely assigned a certain spot 150 yds. from the 'Reformer's Tree'—the place where meetings of the Reform League had been held—for such assemblies. From that time 'Orator's Corner' has been one of L.'s attractions. Here 'every splintered fraction of a sect' finds utterance; and G. K. Chesterton, wishing to indicate the sorrows of a really limited monarchy, pointed out that our sovereigns alone were not allowed to do a little tub-thumping in Hyde Park. A fascinating book on this subject is *A Hyde Park Orator*, by Bonar Thompson (1934). For many yrs. the author earned his living by exuberant and cynical verbosity, making an average of £2 10s. per week in summer and £1 15s. in winter, despite the fact that, owing to regulations, contributions can be received only outside the gates. He suggests as his epitaph: 'The collection was not enough.' Other books are *Around the Marble Arch*, by F. W. Batchelor (1944), and *A Saint in Hyde Park*, by E. A. Siderman (1950). The 'saint' was Father Vincent McNabb of St. Dominic's Priory. This book has had a well-merited popularity.

The Great Exhibition was an idea expounded by the P. Consort to the Royal Soc. of Arts (*q.v.*), of which he was President, in 1849. In 1850 a commission was appointed, and, despite protests against what was regarded in some quarters as a profanation of the park, Jos. Paxton erected his palace of glass and iron in the autumn and winter of 1850-1. The exhibition—'of the works of all nations'—was opened on 1st May 1851 by Q. Victoria, who was accompanied by the P. Consort and other members of the royal family. Ld. Playfair described a curious incident that occurred whilst the *Hallelujah Chorus* was being sung:

'A Chinaman, dressed in magnificent robes, suddenly emerged from the crowd and prostrated himself before the throne. Who he was nobody knew. He might possibly be the Emperor of China himself who had come secretly to the ceremony, but it was certain that he was not in the programme of the procession, and we who were in charge of the ceremony did not know where to place his Celestial Highness. The Lord Chamberlain was equally perplexed, and asked the Queen and the Prince Consort for instructions. We were then told that there must be no mistake as to his rank, and that it would be best to place him between the Archbishop of Canterbury and the Duke of Wellington. In this dignified position he marched through the building, to the delight and amazement of all beholders.'

The next day it was ascertained that this illustrious Chinaman was the keeper of a Chinese junk which was lying in the Thames for inspection at 1s. a head. The exhibition was opened for 114 days, and closed on 11th Oct., 1851. According to *Fireside Facts from the Great Exhibition* (1851), it was visited by 6,201,856 persons, who consumed, amongst other edibles, 311,731 lb. of Bath buns and 460,657 lb. of plain buns. The admission fees amounted to £506,100. Mrs. Carlyle went, and did not think much of it.

'Oh how tired I was! Not that it was not really a very beautiful sight—especially at the entrance; the three large trees built in because the people objected to their being cut down, a crystal fountain, and a large blue canopy gives one a momentary impression of a Bazaar in the Arabian Nights Entertainments; and such a lot of things of different kinds and of well dressed people—for the tickets were still 5/-—was rather imposing for a few minutes; but when you come to look at the wares in detail there was nothing really worth looking at—at least that one could not have seen samples of in the shops. . . . And the fatigue of even the most cursory survey was indescribable, and to tell you the God's truth I would not have given the pleasure of reading a good Fairy Tale for all the pleasure to be got from that "Fairy Scene"!'

The Crystal Palace, as it was called, was taken down during the year 1852 and re-erected at Sydenham. It was there again opened by Q. Victoria in 1854. For many years there was outside the George Canning Tavern in Effra Rd., Brixton, a piece of statuary said to have dropped from a lorry *en route* from Hyde Park to Sydenham. The Crystal Palace there was burned down on 28th Nov., 1936. For a capital description of a day there in the eighteen-eighties, see Geo. Gissing's *The Nether World* (Chap. XII, 'Io Saturnalia').

There still remains the Royal Commission for the exhibition of 1851. They are landlords of 87 acres in S. Kensington, on which stand the V. & A. Mus., Imperial Coll. of Science and Technology, Royal Coll. of Art, Royal Coll. of Music and Albert Hall. They also award science scholarships.

The Albert Memorial occupies a site a little W. of that of the Great Exhibition. It was completed in 1872, and then inspected by Q. Victoria, but not actually unveiled until 1876. The structure is crowned by a lofty spire of rich tabernacle work in gilt and enamelled metal, and is terminated by a cross rising to a height of 180 ft. Beneath the canopy is a figure of the P. Consort in gun-metal. He is holding a book in his hand. It is not the Bible, as many suppose, but a copy of the catalogue of the Great Exhibition. (There were four volumes of this work; it is not known which one the P. is perusing.) The steps, 200 ft. in length, are of granite from Penryn in Cornwall. The eight bronze statues at the angles of the structure represent the greater sciences: Astronomy, Chemistry, Geology, Geometry, Rhetoric, Medicine, Philosophy, Physiology. The four statues in the great niches of the spire represent the four greater Christian virtues: Faith, Hope, Charity, and Humility. The four statues at the angles of these niches typify the four greater moral virtues: Fortitude, Prudence, Justice, and Temperance. The four lower groups include an animal surrounded by a group of figures. Europe is represented by a bull, Asia by an elephant, Africa by a camel, America by a bison. The four upper groups represent the industrial arts of Agriculture, Manufacture, Commerce, and Engineering. Round the podium are 169 portrait-figures of men who have excelled in the arts of poetry, music, painting, architecture, and sculpture.

The Dogs' Cemetery at the Victoria Gate is due to the D. of Cambridge. In 1880, when ranger of the park, he obtained permission for his wife to bury a pet dog there. Other burials followed, with his sanction, with the result that between that time and 1915 about 300 small tombstones were erected, all—except a few to the memory of cats and birds—commemorating canine losses. No new graves are now made, but old ones are occasionally opened. Thus one inscription reads:

'My Wee Pet Monte
6.3.17.
My Sweet Baby Quita
11.2.1936.
Also Darling
Tsing
9.5.15.'

Amongst the names of other dogs are 'Dear Pepys,' 'Little Lord Quex,' and 'My Little Dorrit.' One grave bears a quotation from Shakespeare, slightly altered:

'After life's fitful slumber he sleeps well.'

A feature of the park which has attracted little admiration is Westmacott's Achilles statue, set up in 1822. It was cast from cannon captured in the Peninsular War, and represents the gratitude of the ladies of England to the D. of Wellington 'and his brave companions in arms.' Leigh Hunt remarked:

'The figure seems to be manifesting the most furious intentions of self-defence against the hero whose abode it is looking at.'

The monument was copied in part from one of the Dioscuri on the Monte Cavallo at Rome. Equally criticized has been the memorial, in a bird sanctuary, to the memory of W. H. Hudson. It was the work of Epstein in 1925, and represents Rima, a semi-human embodiment of the spirit of the forest in *Green Mansions* (1904). H. J. Massingham (*London Scene*, 1933) criticizes it at some length. He says: 'The large eagle-like bird in the sculpture must be a portrait statue of old Hudson himself. When I used to go and see him at St. Luke's Road, Bayswater, and go out to lunch with him at Whiteley's, it was like taking one of the hunched eagles at the Zoo out of his cage for an airing.'

The chief entrances to Hyde Park are as follows. At Hyde Park Corner, a handsome gateway with three arches connected by an Ionic screen, erected 1828 by Decimus Burton, and embellished with friezes imitated from the Elgin Marbles in the B. Mus. The Cumberland Gate was first known as the Tyburn Gate until its name was changed as a compliment to the 'hero of Culloden.' Here stands the Marble Arch, first erected in 1827, in front of Buckingham Palace. It was the work of John Nash, and is said to have been modelled upon the Arch of Constantine at Rome. The reliefs on the N. side are by Westmacott; on the S. by Baily. The statue of George IV, now in Trafalgar Sq. (see 'Statues'), was to have been placed on top. The arch was removed to its present site in 1851. It is no longer an entrance to anywhere, as in 1908 it was islanded. Other entrances to Hyde Park are Prince's Gate, near the Albert Memorial (these handsome iron gates were purchased from the Great Exhibition of 1851); and Victoria Gate at the NW. extremity.

Rotten Row, usually called 'The Row,' is a fashionable resort for horse and carriage exercise. It runs from Apsley Gate to Kensington Gardens. The origin of the name is unknown.

KENSINGTON GARDENS, adjoining Hyde Park, consist of 275 acres. They are mostly in the City of Westminster, but a small part W. of the Broad Walk is in the royal bor. of Kensington. When William III acquired Kensington Palace (*q.v.*), the gardens, which did not exceed 26 acres, were laid out with the formality then in vogue. They were extended by Q. Anne, and, later, by Q. Caroline (consort of George II). At first a private preserve of the royal family, the gardens were then, when the Court was at Richmond, thrown open on Saturdays to such of the public as could appear in full dress. In the early years of the 19th

century they were accessible to the general public from spring to autumn, and it was at this time that Shelley was to be seen sailing paper boats on the Round Pond. One story is that sometimes he used bank-notes for his small craft! In the early Victorian era they were described as being open 'all the year round, to all respectably dressed persons, from sunrise to sunset.'

Features of the gardens are Queen Anne's Orangery, erected 1704–5 from a design of Sir Christopher Wren's, a beautiful structure which the Q. loved to visit; and the modern sunk garden with a lily-pond. The latter was opened to the public in 1909 by order of Edward VII. Here are three antiquated leaden tanks, now used as fountains. There is a statue of Edward Jenner, who, in 1798, introduced vaccination; it was first erected in Trafalgar Sq. in 1858 and removed in 1862. Speke, the discoverer of the source of the Nile in 1858, is commemorated by a polished red granite obelisk erected in 1866. 'Physical Energy,' by G. F. Watts, is a replica of the central portion of the Rhodes Memorial on the slope of Table Mountain, Cape Town; Peter Pan.

REGENT'S PARK (410 acres) was formed out of the pasture lands known as Marylebone Park Fields. In 1811, when the lease, held of the Crown by the D. of Portland, fell in, the Crown procured the passage of an Act of Parliament, and appointed a commission to lay out a park, and let the adjoining land on building leases. At one time it was the intention of the P. Regent to have a palace built in the north-eastern part, Regent St. being a connecting-link between it and Carlton House. The laying-out was begun in 1812, and the park (470 acres) thrown open in 1838. In the winter of 1866–7, the large lake was the scene of a disaster. Whilst it was crowded with skaters a large tract of ice gave way, and over 200 of the skaters were immersed, nearly forty being drowned. At the SE. corner formerly stood the Colosseum, a vast circular edifice with a glazed cupola and a massive portico. It was used for exhibitions and panoramas, but after a time it went out of fashion as a place of public recreation. In 1875 it was demolished, and houses erected on the site. Running through the park from N. to S. is the Broad Walk. There is also the Inner

Circle, lined with fine chestnut trees, and the road surrounding it, called the Outer Circle. A summer feature of the park is the open-air performance of Shakespeare plays. In the northern part are the Zoological Soc.'s Gardens (*q.v.*), and close to these is the Regent's Canal (see 'Canals'). There is a number of fine terraces, designed by John Nash and Decimus Burton, and damaged by bombs. On the E. are Cambridge, Chester, and Cumberland Terraces; on the W. Cornwall Terrace, Sussex Pl., and Hanover Terrace. Several of the houses in the Inner Circle were erected for people in favour at Court, such as Mrs. Fitzherbert, and Sir Herbert Taylor, private secretary to George IV. St. Dunstan's Villa, erected by Decimus Burton for the Marquis of Hertford (Thackeray's Marquis of Steyne), was on the W. side. There, from 1831 until 1935, were the clock and figures of K. Lud and his sons now in Fleet St. (see 'City Churches; C'—St. Dunstan in the West; and 'Ludgate').

ST. JAMES'S PARK (93 acres including roads; 52 inside railings) was first formed and enclosed by Henry VIII; it was land taken from the Abbot of Westminster. It remained somewhat desolate until the reign of James I, who took a great interest in it, and established a menagerie. It was replanted and generally improved by Charles II, who employed Le Nôtre, a leading French landscape gardener. He made a canal from a chain of pools, and a decoy, where ducks and wild-fowl resorted. Rosamund's Pond, an oblong pool, lay at the SW. end of the canal. The origin of the name is unknown; Rosamund's land is mentioned so early as 1531. A pheasant walk was formed where Marlborough House now stands. Two oak trees, planted by Charles II from acorns brought from Boscobel, survived until a storm blew them down in 1833. Birdcage Walk takes its name from the K.'s aviary in St. James's Park. Storey's Gate is named after Edwd. Storey, who lived there and was keeper of the aviary for Charles II. The Mall, like Pall Mall, recalls a game which resembled croquet. A writer in 1621 wrote:

'A paille mall is a wooden hammer set to the end of a long staff to strike a boule with, at which game noblemen and gentlemen in France doe play

much.'

In 1770 Rosamund's Pond was filled up. In 1779 a gentleman was killed in a duel in the park. It was made particularly attractive on the occasion of the visit of the allied sovereigns in 1814 to celebrate the temporary peace. A temporary bridge, surmounted by a Chinese pagoda, was then designed by John Nash. A model of the park at this time is in the L. Mus. In 1825 the bridge was removed, the park was finally laid out, and the canal converted into a piece of ornamental water under the superintendence of Nash. The present bridge dates from 1857. Since that date the park has changed little and 'Duck Island' is still famous for its fowl, as in the time of Charles II. On the E. side the penguins attract much attention.

In the Greater London area there are a total of 215 parks, covering 44,458 acres.

Paternoster Row. In 1312 it was 'Paternosterstrete.' About 1339 the form 'Pater Noster Rowe' occurs. Richd. Russell, who was dwelling there in 1375, was described as a 'paternosterer'—a turner of beads, and from this occupation Stow derived the name, though he also mentions the

'text writers that dwelled there, who wrote and solde all sortes of Bookes then in use, namely A.B.C. with the Pater Noster, Ave, Creed, Graces, etc.'

This no doubt explains the names of the neighbouring Ave Maria Lane and Creed Lane. Stow also says that the houses were first built in 1282 by Henry Walles, Mayor, and that the rents went to the maintenance of L.B. In Elizabethan times it was famous for its taverns, the most popular of which was the 'Castle,' kept by Dick Tarlton, the famous clown. On the site was afterwards Dolly's Chop House, demolished in 1883. In Pepys's time it was famous for mercers and dealers in silks. The diarist several times went there on shopping bent. In 1660 there he bought 'some green watered moyre for a morning wastecoats.' In 1662 his wife—

'by my lady's advice, desires a new petticoat of the new silk striped stuff, very pretty. So I went to Paternoster Row presently, and bought her one, with Mr. Creed's help, a very fine rich one, the best I did see there.'

Apparently Mrs. Pepys's assistance was not required.

It was not until the beginning of the 18th century that Paternoster Row became the resort of booksellers, then succeeding Little Britain in that respect. In 1719 *Robinson Crusoe* was published by Wm. Taylor, whose premises were at the W. end. Largely through the profits that accrued from Defoe's masterpiece, Taylor was able to acquire the premises next to his. He d. in 1724, and left as executor John Osborne, a bookseller of Lombard St., who had as apprentice Thos. Longman, a member of a family of Bristol soapmakers. The latter m. his master's daughter, and in 1724 bought Taylor's business and made his father-in-law a partner. This firm, now Longmans Green & Co. Ltd., was on the same site when, on 29th Dec. 1940, almost the whole of Paternoster Row was destroyed. There were then 26 other publishers in the Row, and the loss of books from their stocks, and the far greater stock of Simpkin Marshall Ltd., the greatest book distributors in the world, amounted to about four million volumes.

There were literary associations of Paternoster Row, apart from publishing. Thos. Chatterton and Oliver Goldsmith frequented the Chapter House Coffee Tavern. Here, too, in 1777, Dr. Johnson discussed with the booksellers the terms for his *Lives of the Poets*. In 1842 Charlotte and Emily Brontë stayed at the tavern, and in 1848 Charlotte and Anne Brontë. It was a favourite resort of clergymen, and well known to the Rev. Patrick Brontë. The Chapter Coffee House was demolished in 1858, and a set of the first edition of the Brontë novels bound in wood from the beams. It was replaced by a tavern that was destroyed by bombs. The area has now been rebuilt as the Paternoster project, part of a setting designed to frame St. Paul's.

Physicians, Royal College of, now in St. Andrews Place, Regents Park, was formerly in Pall Mall East. The college was founded by Thos. Linacre, physician to Henry VII, Henry VIII, Edward VI, and Q. Mary. It first met in Linacre's house in Knightrider St. in 1518, and he held the office of president for seven yrs. He d. 1524 and bequeathed the house to the coll. Dissections were permitted by Q. Elizabeth in 1564, and in 1583 a spacious anatomical theatre was built adjoining Linacre's house. In 1614 the coll. removed to a house near Amen Corner, and here the famous Dr. Wm. Harvey gave his lectures on the circulation of the blood. A physic garden was planted and an anatomical theatre erected. Harvey built a mus. and lib. at his own expense in 1653 and, then nearly 80, relinquished his office of professor of anatomy and surgery. This bdg. was destroyed by the G.F., and only 112 folio volumes were saved. A piece of ground was then purchased on the W. side of Warwick Lane, and a new bdg. commenced in 1674, and completed in 1689. It was built upon the site of the E. of Warwick's mansion. It had an octagonal domed entrance-porch, 40 ft. in diameter, of which Garth wrote in *The Dispensary*:

'A golden globe, plac'd high with artful skill,
Seems, to the distant sight, a gilded pill.'

Below this was a statue of Sir John Cutler, rich but miserly. He expressed a wish to contribute liberally to the cost of the new bdg. In 1680 the coll., grateful for favours promised though then unrealized, voted statues to Charles II and Sir John, and nine yrs. afterwards borrowed money from him to discharge debts to the builder. Cutler d. (his funeral cost £7,000), and in 1699 his executors made a demand on the coll. for £7,000, including a sum promised but never forthcoming. The indignant coll. threw down £2,000, which the executors accepted in full settlement, and they erased the inscription which had been engraved upon the statue:

'Omnis Cutleri cedat labor Amphitheatro.'

The statues of Cutler and of Charles II are now at the Guildhall.

Sir Hans Sloane was elected president of the Royal College in 1719. In 1825 the coll. quitted the Warwick Lane site (the Cutlers' Hall now occupies it) for a bdg. in Pall Mall East, designed by Sir Robt. Smirke. It was erected on the site of the King's Mews (see 'Charing Cross'), acquired largely through the influence of Sir Henry Halford.

The coll. has a large number of treasures. The lib. contains between 40,000 and

50,000 volumes, and some of the most treasured tomes were those formerly possessed by the Marquis of Dorchester, whose whole library, then one of the finest in England, was presented to the coll. in 1687. It included the Wilton Abbey Psalter (c. 1250), and a copy of the first book printed in English—Caxton's *Recuyell of the Historyes of Troy* (1474). There is also an early manuscript of Chaucer's *Canterbury Tales*; a Nuremberg Latin Bible (1475); the first English translation of Homer (1488); and what is probably the first book on dancing—*L'Art et instruction de bien danser* (1496). In all there are about 130 books printed before 1501. The library also contains the report of the post-mortem examination of Dr. Johnson. The coll. owns about 130 portraits. Three are by Sir Thos. Lawrence—Edwd. Jenner (1749–1823), Sir Henry Halford (1766–1844), and Matthew Baillie (1761–1823); one by Thos. Gainsborough — Richd. Warren; and one by Sir Joshua Reynolds—Wm. Pitcairn. There is a second portrait of Matthew Baillie by Hoppner, and another fine painting by the same artist is of David Pitcairn (1749–1809). There is a portrait of Wm. Harvey by Cornelius Jansen, and of Sir Hans Sloane by Murray; of Sir Edmund King (1629–1709) by Lely; and of the president, Sir Norman Moore, by Russell. There is a portrait also of Sir Thos. Browne. Another treasure is a silver caduceus made by order of Dr. Caius, carried by the president on official occasions; and a silver-gilt mace of the time of Charles II, presented to the coll. by Dr. John Lawson, although he was not a fellow. There is also a gold-headed cane, which was owned successively by five physicians, all of whose arms are engraved upon it: Dr. Radcliffe, Dr. Mead, Dr. Askew, Dr. Wm. Pitcairn, and Dr. Matthew Baillie.

(See *A History of the Royal College of Physicians of London*, by Sir George Clark, 2 vols., 1964–6.)

Piccadilly. Piccadilly is a piquant name in L. nomenclature, first met in the Middlesex county records for the yr. ended 23rd Mar. 1623, where there is a reference to 'William Cable, yeoman, dwelling near Pickadilly Hall.' In Apr. 1623, in the account of the overseers of St. Martin in the Fields, a reference is made to Robt. Baker having left to the par. £2 10s. and 10s. for bread for the poor. He is described as of 'Pickadilly Hall.' Thos. Blount, in his *Glossographia* (1656) wrote:

'A Pickadil is that round hem, or the several divisions set together about the skirt of a garment or other thing; also a kind of stiff collar, made in fashion of a band.'

Robt. Baker, the original builder of 'Pickadilly Hall,' had been a tailor, and his residence seems to have had a nickname derisively attached to it to illustrate one of the means whereby he came by his wealth. Scott refers to 'a hot piccadilloeneedle' in *Kenilworth*. The name extended from one house to several, and in 1624 'Pickadilly Hall' is given definitely as the name of divers houses and messuages. In the record of Lammas payments for 1623–4 it is 'for land near the Windmill builded upon and lately called Pickadilly'; in 1627–8 it is land 'usually called Pickadillie.' In the 1633 edition of Gerard's *Herbal* it is said 'the small wild buglosse grows upon the drie ditch bankes about Pickadilla.' There was an ordinary and gaming-house of the same name; and Blount, already cited, after defining 'pickadil' as given, suggested that 'it took denomination because it was then the utmost *skirt* house of the suburbs that way.'

By 1651 there were eleven houses in Piccadilly. In 1631 there is a reference to John Blundstone, a Roman Catholic priest, being 'much at Piccadilly Hall, at the Countess of Shrewsbury's.' There was also a tavern 'of the Signe of the Crowne,' which was the house on a site where is now the corner of Coventry St. Other taverns were 'the Feathers,' and 'the Hornes.' In 1664 the E. of Clarendon obtained a grant of land; and of his use of it Pepys reports on 20th Feb. 1665, when he rode with Sir J. Mennes—

'into the beginning of my Lord Chancellor's new house near St. James's; which common people have already called Dunkirke-house from their opinion of his having a good bribe for the selling of that town. And very noble I believe it will be.'

In 1666 Pepys pronounced it—

'the finest pile I ever did see in my life, and will be a glorious house.'

A little later he went—

'to the top of it, and there is there the noblest prospect that ever I saw in my life, Greenwich being nothing to it.' This house 'without hyperboles,' wrote Evelyn, 'the best contrived, most useful, graceful and magnificent house in England'—contributed to Clarendon's downfall. Evelyn paid a farewell visit on 9th Dec. 1667 and found the gouty Clarendon sitting in his wheel-chair to see the gates set up towards the N. and the fields. After Clarendon's exile, the house was let for a time to the D. of Ormonde, who was residing there in 1670. His heirs sold it to Christopher Monk, second D. of Albemarle, for £25,000, half of what it had cost. In 1682 it was sold again, and in 1683 Evelyn surveyed 'the sad demolition of Clarendon House.' He says 'it fell to certain rich bankers and mechanics, who gave for it and the ground about it £35,000; they design a new town as it were, and a most magnificent piazza.' The prime mover in this building speculation was Sir Thos. Bond who had lent money to Charles II when in exile. He gave his name to the principal st. that was planned on the site of Clarendon House and Albemarle St.—'a street of excellent quality' said Hatton (1708)—was named after the D. mentioned.

The famous fountain in Piccadilly Circus is a memorial to Ld. Shaftesbury, the philanthropic nobleman who d. in 1885, and whose name is commemorated by Shaftesbury Avenue. It was the work of Sir Alfred Gilbert (1893). No reference was made to it as Eros at the time of the unveiling, nor in the L.C.C. *Return of Outdoor Memorials* (1910). A feeling of impropriety in associating it with a puritanical peer was expressed by the correspondent of a Sunday paper in 1947.

'Kindly allow me to protest against the proposed return of that erotic statue of Eros to Piccadilly Circus. The nymphs and fauns who flit about there may welcome their old pagan god, but I am sure that respectable people want to have nothing to do with him.'

The description at the time of unveiling, was that 'the fountain is purely symbolical and is illustrative of Christian charity.' Another writer said: 'The figure is not intended for a Mercury or a Ganymede, or any other classical personage. It is charity flying swift as an arrow to help.'

However, Sir Seymour Hicks relates that when he, with Irving and Toole, was shown the memorial before unveiling, Gilbert said 'I have called it Eros.'

The graceful figure is said to be the largest in aluminium in the world, was removed to the Embankment Gardens in 1923 for alterations in Piccadilly Circus. It returned in 1929. During the Second World War it was at Egham (Surrey). It was reinstated with all due ceremony, arranged by the L.C.C., on 30th June 1947. Two of the flower-sellers, Mrs. Emma Baker and her daughter Mrs. Bruce, had respectively been there for 57 and 39 yrs.

On the site of the Criterion Restaurant in Piccadilly Circus was until 1852 the 'White Bear,' a galleried inn. The name is perpetuated by a public house on the site.

The Piccadilly Hotel (21) is on the site of St. James's Hall, which stood there 1858–1905. There Dickens gave his last reading in 1870.

Albany Chambers take their name from Frederick, D. of York and Albany, second son of George III. The D. disposed of his house here to Alexander Copland, a builder, by whom in 1803 it was converted into chambers. Ld. Brougham lived here from 1806 to 1808, when studying for the Bar. Ld. Byron lived in 2A in 1814-5, and Jackson, the pugilist, used to come here to give him boxing lessons. It was from here that he went to be m. to Miss Millbanke. Here he wrote the *Ode to Napoleon. Lara*, published in 1814, was probably composed here. Gladstone was a resident from the time he left his rooms in Jermyn St. in 1833 until he was m. in 1839, and Macaulay from 1841 to 1856. He hoped to lead, he said,

'during some years, a sort of life peculiarly suited to my taste, college life at the West-end of London. I have an entrance hall, two sitting rooms, a bedroom, a kitchen, cellars, and two rooms for servants,—all for ninety guineas a year; and this in a situation which no younger son of a Duke need be ashamed to put on his card.'

His nephew and biographer, Sir Geo. Trevelyan, called the Albany

'that luxurious cloister, whose inviolable tranquillity affords so agreeable a relief from the road and flood of the Piccadilly traffic.'

Here Macaulay wrote the first volumes of his *History of England*, the essays on Bacon, Hastings, and Addison; and from here sent to the press his *Lays of Ancient Rome*. Amongst recent residents have been Lewis Waller, Arthur Bourchier, Henry Arthur Jones, Sir Squire Bancroft, Clifford Bax, and J. B. Priestley.

Burlington House was originally built by Sir John Denham for Richd. Boyle, E. of Burlington 1665–8. The E. is said to have chosen the site because he was determined to have no bdg. beyond him. There were bdgs. farther W., and what he had in mind, C. L. Kingsford suggested, was

'the open ground on the north side, in reference to which Strype writes "the spacious garden behind faces the fields and from thence receives a fresh and wholesome air." '

The first house, a plain bdg. of red brick, was remodelled in 1717, under the direction of the third E. of Burlington, who was himself an architect of some distinction, and particularly devoted to classical forms. Gay, a frequent visitor, said of it:

'Beauty within: without proportion reigns';

but a malicious wit, said to be Hervey, described it as

'Possessed of one great hall of state, Without a room to sleep or eat.'

Wm. Kent lived here for some time and d. here in 1749. Handel lived here for four yrs. The D. of Portland, Prime Minister of the Coalition Govt. of 1783, lived in Burlington House. It had a fine gateway which appears in Hogarth's plate 'Masquerades and Operas.' The house had been left to the Cavendishes on the death of the third E. of Burlington in 1753. In 1811 it was tenanted by the E. of Harrington, and later it became the rallying place of the Whigs. At Burlington House were exhibited the Elgin Marbles on their first arrival in England in 1816. In 1854 the Govt. bought the property, and between 1868 and 1874 new wings were erected. The annual exhibitions of the Royal Academy are held here. Also there are housed the Geological Soc., the Chemical Soc., the Royal Soc., the Soc. of Antiquaries, the Royal Astronomical Soc., the Linnean Soc., the L. Mathematical Soc., the British Association for the Advancement of Science. There is a statue of Sir Joshua Reynolds in the courtyard.

Burlington Arcade a little to the W. of the House is a famous resort of shoppers.

In Albemarle St. are the offices of the famous publishers, John Murray; also the offices of the National Book League.

The original White Horse Cellar was on the S. side. Here came Sir Joshua Reynolds, when he arrived from Plymouth in 1740. It was the starting-place for coaches for the W., and Hazlitt said:

'The finest sight in the metropolis is that of the mail-coaches setting off from Piccadilly. . . . Some persons think the sublimest object in nature is a ship launched on the bottom of the ocean; but give me for my private satisfaction, the mail coaches that pour down Piccadilly of an evening, tear up the pavement, and devour the way before them to the land's end.'

Berkeley Hotel is on the site of St. James's Hotel where Dickens stayed in 1869. At 11 Bolton St. Fanny Burney lived for some yrs. from 1818. There is a L.C.C. plaque on the house. On its W. corner is Bath House, the residence of Lady Harriet Baring, about whose relations with Carlyle his wife had misgivings. She was 'one new female in whom he takes a vast pleasure.' Carlyle was frequently there in the 1840s. The name was derived from Wm. Pulteney, E. of Bath, the great opponent of Sir Robt. Walpole, who lived in a previous house on the site (demolished 1821) entirely alone. At the E. corner of Half Moon St.—the bdg. has been bombed—Fanny Burney lived after she left Bolton St.

Piccadilly is the most club-ridden of all L. thoroughfares. The Naval and Military Club is located at No. 94, in a house which was the residence of the D. of Cambridge, seventh son of George III, from about 1829 till his death in 1850. Q. Victoria visited him, and on leaving was struck by Robt. Pate with a small cane which slightly wounded her forehead. Ld. Palmerston lived here from about 1854 until his death in 1865. At No. 95 is the American Club. At 100 are the Royal Societies Club; the Public Schools Club; the St. James's Club. At 119 the Royal Aero Club of the United Kingdom; at 127 the Cavalry Club; at 128 the Royal Air Force Club.

At 145 George VI was residing at the time of his accession (11th Dec. 1936). The house was badly damaged by bombs.

Apsley House was originally built from designs by the brothers Adam in 1771–8 as a red-brick mansion for Ld. Chancellor Apsley, second E. Bathurst. In 1808 the lease came into the possession of the Marquess Wellesley. In 1816 his brother, the D. of Wellington, began to reside in the house; in 1820 he purchased the lease. The house was faced with stone, and enlarged by the Wyatts (Benjamin and Philip) in 1828; in 1830 the Crown sold its interest to the D. for £9,350. Further alterations were made in 1853. In the W. gallery the Waterloo banquet was held annually during the D.'s lifetime; his study is still preserved intact. The house—sometimes called No. 1 London—contains a good collection of pictures, and many relics of the Napoleonic era. It is open to the public.

On the S. side of Piccadilly is the Ritz Hotel and—a few yds. W. of the St. James's Ch. (see 'Westminster') is the imposing bdg. erected in 1882 by the Royal Institute of Painters in Water Colours, founded in 1831. On the façade are medallions of Sandby, Cozens, Girtin, Turner, D. Cox, De Wint, Geo. Barrett, W. H. Hunt. Here also are the headquarters of the Royal Institute of Oil Painters, Pastel Socy., Socy. of Miniaturists, Soc. of Graphic Arts, the Soc. of Women Artists, the National Soc. of Painters, Sculptors, Engravers, Potters.

Pickering Place, a cul-de-sac off the E. side of St. James's St., derives its name from Wm. Pickering, founder of a coffee business in adjoining premises, now occupied by Berry Bros., wine merchants. There is a curious collection of spirit flasks, made of earthenware, in all imaginable shapes and designs, and a collection of bottles, many of the early 17th century. There are also huge scales in which celebrated customers have been weighed; these include all the sons of George III, Byron, Beau Brummell, Louis Philippe, and Chas. Lamb. An oak-lined passage leads to a small sq. paved with flagstones. On the wall in the passage is a plaque recording that the house was the official residence of the representative of the Republic of Texas to the Court

of St. James in 1845. There is also a sundial of a rather unusual pattern, bearing the inscription: 'William Pickering Fundator 1710 Geo. B. Harvey Memorator 1919.' Secluded from the st., it was a favourite place for duels, and it is said that the last in L. was fought here.

Plaques. Throughout L. the visitor will see round blue plaques fixed to the walls of houses, recording facts about famous people who lived there in the past. Other plaques commemorate famous buildings which once stood on the site. For the City they are recorded in the Corporation's *Commemorative plaques in the City of London*, and for the rest of the metropolis in the G.L.C.'s *Commemorative tablets on houses of historical interest*.

Although many hundreds of famous men and women are thus brought to memory, such is the richness of L. history that only a fraction can be so commemorated: few indeed are the great figures in English history who have no L. association. In some areas the very richness makes it difficult to record; in the City particularly a single site can have Roman, 16th-century political, and 19th-century literary interest.

Poplar, now part of the L. Bor. of Tower Hamlets, was a met. bor. and par. in the E. of L., taking its name from the trees which once flourished there. Poplar proper was originally a hamlet in Stepney par., being made into a separate par. in 1817.

Most of the area of the original par. is in the Isle of Dogs, formerly known as Stebunhethe, or Stepney, Marsh. It was a swampy peninsula used mainly for grazing, and for centuries uninhabited, and the origin of its name is uncertain. Some attribute it to there having been kennels hereabouts for the royal hounds when the Court was at Greenwich. Others maintain that 'dogs' is a corruption of 'ducks.' Millwall, its western side, was Marshwall until the bdg. there of seven windmills early in the 18th century. Attempts had been made to embank the land as early as the reign of Edward II, and in 1324 there is mention of a great flood which breached the banks. On the island was the little chapel of St. Mary in Stepney Marsh, long since demolished and its site covered by the Millwall Docks.

A foot-tunnel connects the southern extremity of the isle with Greenwich, and from the Island Gardens can be had what is perhaps the finest view of Greenwich Hosp.

Blackwall is the NE. corner of the isle, and is first heard of in 1377 in connection with embanking the river. In 1612 the E. India Co. purchased land at Blackwall for a dock, later leased to Henry Johnson under whom it became a noted ship-building yard. He was grandson to Peter Pett of Deptford (*q.v.*), and is mentioned on several occasions in Pepys' diary. Another famous Blackwall shipbuilder was Richd. Green (d. 1863) whose statue is in the E. India Dock Rd. and whose name is perpetuated in the repairing co. of R. and H. Green and Silley Weir Ltd. He owned a fleet of fast sailing ships used in the India trade.

The oldest ch. in Poplar par. is that which stands S. of the Recreation Ground in the E. India Dock Rd. and is now known as St. Matthias'. Built in 1654 on ground given by the E. India Co. near to their Almshouses (now gone), it was originally a small brick bdg. with an aisled nave, a chancel, and a wooden turret at the W. end. It was reconstructed in 1776, and completely altered externally in 1867 by S. S. Teulon when it became a par. ch. Up to this time it had been served by a chaplain appointed by the E. India Co.; their coat-of-arms may be seen carved on the nave roof. In the ch. are tablets to Geo. Steevens (d. 1800), with a bust of Shakespeare of whose works he was a commentator (a monument by Flaxman); Robt. Ainsworth (d. 1743), compiler of a Latin dictionary; Geo. Green (d. 1863) shipbuilder; J. N. Perry (d. 1810) founder of the Commercial Dock ; and Sir John Gayer (see 'City Churches—C'; St. Katherine Cree). Ld.M. and a Governor of the E. India Co., whose arms were in the E. window of the first chapel.

A furlong E. of the Recreation Ground is the par. ch. of All Saints, consecrated in 1823 and designed by Chas. Hollis. Built in the classical style of the period, of which it is a good example, it has a lofty W. portico and a graceful steeple, but was badly damaged by blast from a rocket which fell only 20 yds. from its W. end.

St. Saviour's Ch., Northumberland St., was the ch. of Father Dolling from 1898–1902. St. Edmund's R.C. Ch. in Ferry Rd., Millwall, is an imposing bdg., and there is a Danish Lutheran Ch. in King St., erected 1873 as a successor to an older foundation in Wellclose Sq. It contains oak statues of Moses, St. John the Baptist, St. Peter and St. Paul, by the famous carver Caius Gabriel Cibber, and a modern tablet to his memory; from the roof hangs a fine model of a ship. Damaged by a bomb in 1917, it came unscathed through the recent raids.

The various docks established in Poplar are: W. India Docks, 1802, extending across the neck of the Isle of Dogs and almost making it an island in reality; the E. India Docks, incorporating Perry's Commercial Dock, 1806; Millwall Docks, 1864. The Blackwall Tunnel under the Thames to Greenwich Marshes was made 1892–7 under the direction of Sir Alex. Binnie. It was modernized after the Second World War and a second, parallel, tunnel was opened in 1967. During the recent war Poplar was one of the worst bombed areas of L.

Bromley St. Leonard's, or Bromley-by-Bow, was Braembelege in 1000 and Brambeley in 1128, probably meaning a clearing among the brambles. The second part of its name is from a convent of Benedictine nuns established here, according to one authority, in K. Edgar's time, but by others dated only to the Conqueror's reign. Of the convent no trace remains, and the ch., dedicated to St. Mary the Virgin, was almost entirely rebuilt by Wm. Railton, 1842, with additions 1874. It contains an interesting collection of monuments from the older ch. On the floor of the tower is a Purbeck marble slab with indent of a brass to John de Bohun and his wife (1336). Wm. (d. 1625) and Jane Ferrers have portrait busts on their monument in the N. aisle with the inscription 'Live well, and dye never, Dye well, and live ever.' Below is depicted a sleeping infant. On the S. wall is a beautiful monument with kneeling figures of Sir John Jacob (d. 1629) and his wife. In addition there is a large and finely carved tablet to Sir Wm. Benson (d. 1712) Ld. of the Manor; another, with full length figures of angels under a canopy supported on twisted columns, to Sir John Roberts (d. 1692); and a white marble memorial to Sir Richd. Munden (d. 1680), a sea captain and taker of St. Helena. The old reredos (17th century) of carved wood is now in St. Andrew's, Gurley St.

Bromley's famous palace which stood at the NW. corner of St. Leonard's St. was pulled down in 1893. It was built in 1606, probably from designs by John Thorpe, and its wonderful panelled room is preserved in the V. & A. Mus.

Stratford le Bow or Stratford atte Bow was once a chapelry of Stepney, but made a separate par. 1719. It derives its name from the ford where the Roman street or rd. to Colchester crossed the Lea, and from the bow-shaped bridge over that river built by Matilda, Q. of Henry I. This bridge, with alterations, stood until 1835. Chaucer in the *Prologue to the Canterbury Tales* speaks slightingly of the Prioress's French as being 'after the scole of Stratford atte Bowe' rather than Parisian. Newcourt's *Repertorium* gives 1311 as the date of the foundation of the chapel 'on the King's highway,' where, right in the middle of it, the ch. of St. Mary still stands. It was very badly damaged by bombs. The lower part of the tower, which remains, is 15th century, but the upper storeys dated from an 1829 rebuilding. In the nave was a brass of 1551 to Mrs. Grace Amcott, and a monument to the founder of a local sch., Miss Prisca Coborn, d. 1701, and her daughter Alice, d. 1689.

Old Ford is the most northerly part of the bor. Through it, by way of Old Ford Rd. from Bethnal Green, ran the rd. from L. to Colchester before Bow Bridge was built, and it was here that Q. Matilda on a pilgrimage to 'Our Ladye of Berkynge' got the wetting that induced her to build Bow Bridge. At Old Ford there used to be a bdg. popularly known as K. John's Palace. The district has yielded many Roman remains. In olden times bread was supplied to L. by the bakers of Bow (there is a Bakers' Alley S. of the ch.) until the reign of Henry VIII; and for some time from the reign of Edward III Bow was a slaughtering-place of the L. butchers.

Population of London. Many estimates have been made of the population of L. prior to the earliest census figures of 1801 but the accuracy of many of them is very questionable. The matter is complicated by the fact that the estimate can refer to

the City within the walls, the whole city or to L. as a whole, which in later periods can be taken to include not only Westminster, Southwark and parts of Middlesex but also the Tower hamlets. In *British Mediaeval Population*, J. C. Russell quotes the following:

Poll tax of 1377	.		35,000
Henry VIII's reign			50,000
1553	.	.	86,000
1563	.	.	93,276
1582	.	.	120,000
1593	.	.	138,000 or 152,000

Other estimates are given below together with their authorities:

1557   185,000. Population of L. estimated by Venetian Ambassador (State Papers Venetian, 1556–7, p. 1045).

1631   130,280 men, women and children within City and liberties. Certified by the Ld. M. to Privy Council (cited in E. Lipson's *Economic History of England*, 1943–49, vol. 2, p. 249).

1695   69,581 within City walls; 53,508 in the City without the walls (Jones, P. E. and Judges, A. V., 'London population in late 17th century,' *Econ. Hist. Rev.*, vol. 6, pp. 45–63).

1700   139,300 in City (within and without the walls) and 69,000 in liberties. (Brett-James, N. G., *Growth of Stuart London*, 1935, p. 512).

1750   87,000 within City walls; 57,000 in City without the walls (George, M. D., *London life in the 18th century*, 1925, p. 329).

From 1801 the official census figures *for the City* are:

1801	78,000 within City walls;
.	56,300 in City without the walls
1811	57,700 within City walls;
	68,000 in City without the walls
1851	128,000 total population of City
1861	112,000 total population of City
1871	75,000 total population of City
1901	27,000 total population of City
1931	11,000
1961	4,600

The only conclusion to be drawn from these figures is that there was little change in the City's resident population between 1695 and 1851, but a steady decline commenced around, or before, 1861.

As people moved out of the central area in search of more spacious surroundings and as the suburbs grew the total population naturally increased: today the total population of the Greater L. area is around

7,913,600 (with 2,700,000 households and 2,480,000 dwellings); but the L. Transport area holds 10,217,000 people of whom 3,119,000 (30 per cent) were in Inner L., 4,762,000 (47 per cent) were in Outer L. and 2,336,000 (23 per cent) were in the Outer country area. Within a radius of 40–45 miles from Charing Cross there were in 1961 12,453,372 people, three quarters of a million more than ten years earlier. Obviously the growth of the metropolis goes on.

Of the total population of L. in 1966, the following is a breakdown by age groups:

	(thousand)	(thousand)	(thousand)
0– 4 years	.	638·8	
5–14 years	.	951·4	
15–24 years	.	1,187·1	
25–44 years	.	2,028·1	
45–64 years	.	2,107·8	
65–74 years	.	630·1	
75 + years	.	370·3	
		7,913·6	

and by sex:

male	.	.	3,778·9 thousand
female	.	.	4,134·7 thousand
			7,913·6 thousand

It is not possible to say how many foreigners' there are in the Greater L. area but the number of overseas-born residents is:

place of birth

Ireland	.	.	.	287,530 (3·8 per cent)
Asia	.	.	.	117,840 (1·5 per cent)
Caribbean	.	.	.	152,330 (2·0 per cent)
Africa	.	.	.	43,120 (0·6 per cent)
Mediterranean	.	.	.	57,140 (0·7 per cent)
Elsewhere	.	.	.	40,850 (0·5 per cent)

The area of Greater L. is 394,487·6 acres (616·4 square miles) and there are 7,844 miles of road within it, the average density of population being 20·1 per acre.

The number employed in the Greater L. area is 4,695,500 made up as follows:

Agriculture and fishing	.	.	6,300
Mining etc.	.	.	6,000
Food, drink, and tobacco	.	.	150,100
Chemicals etc.	.	.	99,900
Metal manufacture	.	.	30,200
Engineering and electrical goods	.	.	457,400
Shipbuilding, marine eng'n'g.	.	10,100
Vehicles	.	.	.	86,900
Metal goods	.	.	.	81,500
Textiles	.	.	.	19,700

Leather etc.	.	.	.	16,700
Clothing and footwear	.	.	113,800
Bricks, pottery, glass etc.	.	.	34,300
Timber, furniture etc.	.	.	71,200
Paper, printing and publishing	.	188,500
Other manufacturing industries	70,800
Construction	.	.	.	297,900
Gas, electricity and water	.	.	85,200
Transport etc.	.	.	.	447,800
Distribution	.	.	.	716,100
Insurance, banks and finance	.	274,600
Professional services	.	.	481,300
Miscellaneous	.	.	.	607,400
Public administration	.	.	339,100
Not stated	.	.	.	2,600

The number of retail and service trade establishments is:

	Full-time	Staff Part-time	
Grocery and provisions	13,134	46,048	18,852
Other food retailers	19,332	63,112	19,384
Confectioners, tobacconists, newsagents	12,277	21,453	22,852
Clothing and footwear shops	14,511	55,102	19,987
Household goods	13,146	42,341	9,729
Other non-food retailers	11,102	35,276	11,219
General stores	569	55,412	18,910
Hairdressers	6,237	25,704	3,449
Boot and shoe repairs	2,079	3,769	827
Total	92,387	348,217	125,209

excluding gas and electric showrooms.

To accommodate their vehicles there are:

Parking meters	.	.	16,121
		Local authority	Private
Car park spaces (off street)	.	38,886	40,676

(Source of 1966 statistics: *Annual Abstract of Greater London Statistics*, G.L.C.)

Port of London Authority. It is a modern organization, having come into existence on 31st Mar. 1909. Prior to its inception there was no central body responsible for the administration of the port. The docks were run by private enterprise, and the river came under the jurisdiction of the Thames Conservancy (see 'Thames'). The docks cos. were in keen competition with one another, and neither they nor the Thames Conservancy had adequate funds to provide the necessary accommodation for the larger type of ships then being built. Conditions in the port were far from satisfactory, and in 1900 Parliament appointed a royal commission to enquire into this state of affairs. The outcome of its report was the Port of London Act (1908), which brought into being the P.L.A. to take over and administer as one unit, the docks and the tidal portion of the River Thames.

The authority consists of 28 members, ten of whom are appointed as follows: Admiralty, one, Min. of Transport, two, G.L.C., four, C.C. two and Trinity House one. Eighteen members are elected: the payers of rates and charges (which include ship owners and merchants), wharfingers, and owners of river craft elect 18 members. The members may, if they wish, elect a chairman and a vice-chairman from outside their number. The members hold office for three yrs. and receive no payment for their services.

The capital of the P.L.A. (approximately £54,000,000) is in the form of Port Stock, bearing fixed rates of interest. The authority derives its revenue from dues and charges for the accommodation provided for shipping and for warehousing and other services rendered. The authority receives no Govt. or municipal subsidy.

While the authority is the controlling body of the Port of L., it has no monopoly, for there is a large number of privately owned wharves on the riverside in competition with the docks. In addition to owning the docks, the P.L.A. provides storage accommodation for 1,000,000 tons of merchandise and performs such trade operations as may be required of it, such as weighing, sorting, sampling, etc. On the river its duties include all matters relating to navigation, dredging, the location and removal of wrecks, the prevention of pollution, and the registration of craft employed exclusively within the port.

In addition to the P.L.A. there are other bodies responsible for certain services within the port, viz. H.M. Customs; the Port and City of L. Health Authority; Trinity House, who license pilots and light and buoy the Thames; and the Thames division of the Metropolitan Police.

In 1966 the port handled 47·3 million tons of imports, 9·6 million tons of exports and 2·1 million tons of transhipments. The total tonnage of shipping was 91·619 million tons, 19·2 per cent of the U.K.

total.

Prince Henry's Room (17 Fleet St.). Its history begins with 1610, when E. of Inner Temple Lane an inn called the 'Hand' was being rebuilt. Therefore a blatant signboard which, before the L.C.C. acquired the premises, announced that it was 'formerly the Palace of Henry VIII and Cardinal Wolsey' was erroneous. In 1610 the chambers over the gateway were sold to Wm. Blake, the proprietor of the eastern portion, and his tavern, the 'Prince's Arms,' extended over the gateway. In 1665 the premises were called the 'Fountain,' M. Angiers advertising that his remedies for stopping the Plague were to be had at the sign of the Fountain, Inner Temple Gate. In 1795 the front part was taken by Mrs. Clark, who had for some time shown, on the opposite side of Fleet St. the well-known 'Mrs. Salmon's Wax-works.' The *Morning Herald* in 1795 announced the removal of the figures—

> 'to the very spacious and handsome apartments at the corner of Inner Temple Gate, which was once the Palace of Henry Prince of Wales, the eldest son of King James the First, and they are now the residence of many a royal guest.'

The wax-works remained until about 1816 (they went to Water Lane, now Whitefriars St., and were melted down in 1831), and it appears that, during this time, the tavern business was still carried on in the back part of the premises.

Any connection with P. Henry, James I's eldest son (created P. of Wales in 1610), is dubious. It is known that the council chamber of the Duchy of Cornwall was, at this time, situated in Fleet St., but its exact site is unknown. This, and the ornamental initials on the ceiling (see *infra*), are the sole facts upon which any connection is based.

When the L.C.C. became interested, Prince Henry's Room was a barber's shop. By its General Powers Act of 1898, the L.C.C. had acquired authority to purchase places of architectural and historical interest, and, in 1900 it decided to acquire the freehold of the premises—the price was £27,000—to rebuild the back portion, and to restore the front. The C.C. gave its consent to the upper storey projecting, provided the ground floor was put back to the level of the surrounding bdgs., and, more-over, contributed £2,500 towards the cost. At the time of the L.C.C.'s acquisition, the façade, above the ground storey, was a false or screen front, constructed of timber and glass, comparatively modern in date, and this completely masked the ancient work. To it had been affixed eight of the carved oak panels belonging to the original front.

'Some twenty inches behind the screen, however, remained the original early 17th century, half timbered front, which though shorn of its bay windows, and otherwise mutilated, contained the essential features intact. . . . It was found that the work was in almost perfect preservation. . . . This false front was taken down . . . and the façade, as now visible, is as nearly as could be ascertained by analysis of the work, and by comparison with prints, contemporaneous with the building, a reinstatement of what was erected in 1611; the only exception being the ground storey, which, including the archway to Inner Temple Lane, has been set back about 5 feet as necessitated by the widening of Fleet Street.' 'The great treasure of the house is the plaster ceiling. It is believed to be unique in design, and is one of the best of the remaining Jacobean enriched plaster ceilings. In the middle of the design occur the Prince of Wales Feathers, accompanied by the letters P.H. and enclosed in a star-shaped border. At the Victoria and Albert Museum the ceiling was cleaned, straightened and strengthened, and afterwards refixed.' The panelling of the W. side of the room is probably original, that on the other side is of 18th-century date, as also is the staircase leading to the floor above.

Prince Henry's Room is open to the public free of charge from 1.45 p.m. to 5 p.m.

Prisons are not now patent to all of L.'s citizens, as once they were. Where there were once a number of gaols in the City, not one remains, and no bor. so contiguous as Southwark, where they abounded, has now what Micawber delicately called a 'place of incarceration.' Prisons, too, have lost some of their piquancy. The old ones cut a figure in history. A respectable

dictionary of national biography could be compiled from their inmates. In modern days a 'good old George' Lansbury—in Brixton—may contrast with a bad old Bottomley—in Maidstone Gaol—but gener-ally public men expect to finish their career without experiencing the nearest approach to monastic life now offered apart from the religious world.

It is convenient, for the reasons given, to divide prisons of the past from prisons of the present, and justifiable to be more liberal in space in the case of the former. PRISONS OF THE PAST

Bridewell. See separate article.

Cold Bath Fields. The name was derived from a well of cold water, discovered in 1697, on the W. side of Clerkenwell. The prison was erected in 1794. It became notorious for its severity. In 1799 Gilbert Wakefield, the classical scholar, expressed a morbid horror of it; Coleridge (*The Devil's Thoughts*, 1799) wrote:

'As he went through Cold-Bath Fields he saw
  A solitary cell,
And the Devil was pleased, for it gave him a hint
For improving his prisons in Hell.'

John Hunt was a prisoner 1813-15. He was, as proprietor of the *Examiner*, involved with his brother, James Leigh, in the latter's attack upon the Prince Regent, who was characterized as a 'violator of his word, a libertine over head and ears in debt and disgrace.' John Townsend, the most celebrated 'Bow Street Runner,' was later made governor, and he some-what improved the conditions of the prisoners. When Hepworth Dixon wrote (1850), they numbered from 1,200 to 1,400; he favourably compared their health with that of prisoners in Newgate, Millbank, and Pentonville. He noted that 'some of the men . . . bear stars upon their arms: these are marks of good conduct, of great value to the wearer when in gaol, and entitling him to a certain allowance on discharge, varying according to circumstances from five shillings to a pound. These allowances are often the salvation of offenders.' He regretted, however, 'the wheel and oakum room' as the worst features. In Samuel Butler's *The Way of All Flesh* (1903), Ernest Pontifex is confined in Cold Bath Fields, and there is a reference to the 'dingy crowded lane called Eyre Street Hill,' which remains. In 1850 the female prisoners were removed to Tothill Fields Prison. In 1885 W. T. Stead was a prisoner as a result of his campaign for the exposure of vice in the *Pall Mall Gazette*. On the anniversary of his conviction he used to attire himself in the convict's garb, which he was allowed to retain, and drive into the city. Cold Bath Fields Prison was demolished in 1889. Coldbath Sq. commemorates it to-day.

Clerkenwell House of Detention. A prison —known as the Clerkenwell Bridewell— was erected in 1615 on a site NE. of the present Clerkenwell Close. Many Popish priests were imprisoned there, and Pepys mentions an attack upon it by L. apprentices in 1668. Jack Sheppard and his mistress, Edgeworth Bess, were prisoners here in 1724. They managed to escape by filing their fetters and the window bars. Smollett's 'Humphry Clinker' (1771) was a prisoner here. In 1774–5 the prison was rebuilt. In 1780 the 'No Popery' rioters attacked the 'New Prison,' as it was called, and released the inmates (see *Barnaby Rudge*, Chap. LXVI). In 1818 it was rebuilt on a larger scale. There was further rebuilding in 1818 and 1845–6. It then became known as the House of Detention, and was for those awaiting trial. On 13th Dec. 1867 a Fenian, with a view to releasing some of his comrades, placed a barrel of gunpowder against the northern wall. The explosion which followed shattered the row of houses opposite, and blew a great hole in the prison wall. Six persons were killed and fifty injured. One of the latter, who was blinded, could be seen begging in Aldersgate St. in the first decade of the present century. A tablet recording the casualties is in the ch. of St. James, Clerkenwell. The prison was closed in 1877. The Hugh Myddelton Sch. stands upon the site.

Clink is first referred to by Stow—'in old time for such as should brabble, frey, or break the peace on the said Bank, or in the brothel-houses.' It belonged to the liberty of the Bp. of Winchester, whose palace was adjacent. John Bradford and Bp. Hooper, the martyrs, were prisoners in 1555. Massinger is said to have been a prisoner. Later it became in part a debtors' prison. Selden mentions it in his *Table Talk* in this connection. In 1745 it was so decayed that a dwelling-house on Bankside was substituted. It was burnt down by the 'No Popery' rioters in 1780, and never rebuilt. Clink St. commemorates it: it is ironical that centuries after its disappearance the name has become a generic term for prisons.

Fleet. It was first mentioned in 1197, and was on an island formed by ditches and the river from which its name derived. The water became stagnant, and the contamination from such foul environs caused a commission to sit in St. Bride's Ch. in 1356. Moreover, L. butchers were allowed to clean their carcasses in the vicinity of the prison, the water from the river being so handy. In 1355 the ditches were completely choked with sewage, and an epidemic raged amongst the prisoners. In Henry VIII's reign Thos. Cromwell was petitioned to ameliorate these pestilential conditions. In 1593 a petition was addressed to Ld. Burghley stating that 'the place is a congregation of unwholesome smells of the town.'

There was a number of distinguished prisoners in the Fleet Prison in the Tudor and Stuart periods: E. of Surrey, the sonneteer (1543); Thos. Nash, for his play *The Isle of Dogs* (1597); Wm. Herbert, E. of Pembroke, one of 'the incomparable paire' to whom the First Folio of Shakespeare was dedicated (1601); John Donne, afterwards Dean of St. P.'s Cath., for marrying without his father-in-law's consent (1601); Jas. Howell, author of *Familiar Letters* (1643–51). It was burned in the G.F.

In the 18th century it became notorious for its hastily improvised weddings. Touts paraded the adjacent streets, offering a nuptial knot on the lowest terms and the briefest acquaintance of the parties concerned. Thomas Pennant (1790) related his youthful experience:

'I have often been tempted by the question, "Sir will you be pleased to walk in and be married?" Along this most lawless space was hung up the frequent sign of a male and female hand conjoined, with "Marriages performed within," written beneath. A dirty fellow invited you in. The parson was seen walking before his shop; a squalid, profligate figure, clad in a tattered plaid night-gown, with a fiery face, and ready to couple you for a dram of gin or roll of tobacco.'

2,954 marriages occurred in four months; 173 in one day. One parson made £57 in one month from fees. (See Besant's *Chaplain of the Fleet* and Lecky's *History of England in the Eighteenth Century*, vol. ii.) These marriages were abolished by Ld. Hardwicke's Act (1753); therefore Dickens was guilty of an anachronism in introducing them into *Barnaby Rudge*.

John Howard visited the Fleet Prison in 1774. He reported that it was clean, but ill-managed. Some improvement had, however, taken place in the latter respect since 1726, when it was found that the warden had farmed the fees so profitably that his office was sold for £5,000. Howard found there 243 prisoners, mostly debtors; their wives and children, also there, numbered 475. The prison was burned by the 'No Popery' rioters. It was restored, and in the prison in 1797 d. Mrs. Cornelys of Soho (*q.v.*). Dickens introduced it into *Pickwick*; Jingle, Sam Weller, Mrs. Bardell, and the hero himself were all confined within its walls. Aleph, of the *City Press*, writing in 1863, recalled the—

'lofty, dreary-looking wall of the Prison, the sole entrance being through a wretched sort of lattice door, defended by a barrier.'

He also mentioned, as did Dickens, the heavily barred but unglazed window, at which, during the whole day, miserable prisoners stood, repeating the monotonous chant: 'Pray remember us poor debtors.' Thackeray's Barry Lyndon and Capt. Shandon found themselves in the Fleet Prison. The prison was closed in 1842; one of its then seventy prisoners had been there twenty-eight yrs. It was demolished in 1844. The Memorial Hall, Farringdon St., is on the site, and bears a C.C. plaque.

Gate House (Westminster). Stow wrote:
'The Gatehouse is so called of two gates, the one out of College Court towards the north, on the east side whereof was the Bishop of London's prison for clerks convict; and the other gate, adjoining to the first, but towards the west, is a gaol or prison for offenders, thither committed. Walter Warfield, cellarer to the monastery, caused both these gates, with the appurtenances, to be built in the reign of Edward III.'

The office of Keeper of the Gate House was in the gift of the dean and chapter of W.A. Sir Walter Raleigh spent his last night there, before execution in Old Palace Yard (1618). Sir John Eliot, prior to transfer to the T.L., was there in 1627. John Selden was a prisoner in 1630. In the Gate House Prison Richd. Lovelace (1642) composed his poem *To Althea, from Prison*, which contains the lines:

'Stone walls do not a prison make,
Nor iron bars a cage.'

Lilly, the astrologer, was a prisoner just after the Restoration. Sir Jeffery Hudson came there in 1679 on a charge of complicity in a Popish plot. Scott was in error in saying that he d. in the Gate House Prison. Samuel Pepys was imprisoned there for three weeks in 1690: in Evelyn's words, 'on suspicion of being affected to King James.' Jeremy Collier was there in 1692, on a similar suspicion. In 1727 Johnson's friend Savage was committed to it for the murder of Mr. Sinclair at Robinson's Coffee House, Charing Cross, but was at once transferred to Newgate. H. B. Wheatley says:

'It was the custom at the Gate House, as at other prisons, to have an alms-box at the prison door to receive the offerings of the benevolent for the benefit of the prisoners; and when a Westminster boy was found playing with money during school hours, the rule was to send him "under a trusty guard" to put it into the prisoners' box at the Gate House door.'

Dr. Johnson was in some measure responsible for its removal. In an essay on the *Coronation of King George III, or Reasons offering against confining the Procession to the usual track* (1761) he wrote:

'Part of my scheme supposes the demolition of the Gate House, a building so offensive that, without any occasional reason, it ought to be pulled down, for it disgraces the present magnificence of the capital, and is a continual nuisance to neighbours and passengers.'

The Gate House was ordered to be pulled down by the dean and chapter of W.A. in 1776. A wall was still standing in 1836. In his *Memorials of Westminster Abbey*—in which is a picture of the Gate House—Dean Stanley says one of the arches remained in a house which in 1839 was celebrated as formerly a residence of Edmund Burke. Its site was N. of Dean's Yard—about the position of the Crimea statue to Westminster scholars.

Horsemonger Lane. The lane took its

name from 'Horsemonger lande' in possession of St. Thomas's Hosp., then in Southwark, in 1536. The jail was erected at the suggestion of John Howard, from the designs of Geo. Gwilt, under provisions of an Act passed in 1791, and was completed in 1798. The bdg. consisted of a quadrangle of three storeys. Three of the sides were appropriated to criminals, the fourth to debtors. Provision was made for 400 prisoners, the wall enclosing an area of about 3½ acres. Col. Despard, on a charge of treasonable conspiracy, was hanged there in 1803. The hurdle on which he was drawn to the place of execution was long preserved. Leigh Hunt (see *supra*) was a prisoner from 1813 to 1815. In 1849 Dickens attended here the execution of Mr. and Mrs. Manning, who had murdered their lodger (their models are at Madame Tussaud's). He wrote a strong letter to *The Times* on the appalling scenes he had witnessed, in which he said:

'I do not believe that any community can prosper where such a scene of horror as was enacted this morning outside Horsemonger Lane gaol is permitted at the very doors of good citizens, and is passed by unknown or forgotten.'

The name of the thoroughfare was changed from Horsemonger Lane to Union Rd. in 1865. In 1879 the prison was demolished. In 1884 a pleasure garden on the site was opened by Mrs. Gladstone. In 1930, in the Weights and Measures Office of the L.C.C., which adjoined the garden, the gravestones of Mr. and Mrs. Manning were found. They are now in the Cuming Mus. (see 'Museums'). The neighbourhood has not altogether changed since Dickens's time. There are old houses with long front gardens on the N. side of Harper Rd., as the former Union Rd. is now called. It is said that the occupants once made more than the amount of their annual rent by letting windows to view executions.

King's Bench (Southwark) was first mentioned in connection with the Wat Tyler rebellion in 1381. It was then on the E. side of Borough High St. John Bradford a martyr (see 'Smithfield'), was a prisoner in 1554. Richd. Baxter was there in 1670, under the Act of Uniformity. His wife accompanied him and, he wrote in his *Autobiography*,

'we kept house as contentedly as at home, though in a narrower room, and I had the sight of more of my friends in a day than I had at home in half a year.'

His chamber was over the gate,

'which was knocked and opened with noise of prisoners just under me almost every night. I had little hope of sleeping but by day.'

John Rushworth, clerk of H. of C., whose *Collections* were much used by Carlyle in his *Cromwell*, d. a prisoner, in 1690. The second King's Bench was erected in 1758, on a site SW. of the first one—at the corner of the present Borough Rd. and Borough High St. Here Smollett was a prisoner in 1759 for libelling Admiral Knowles in the *Critical Review*. John Wilkes was a prisoner from 1768 to 1770. On the meeting of Parliament after his first election, a mob assembled outside the prison to escort him to the House. It refused to disperse and was fired upon, and several of Wilkes's supporters were killed or injured. About 1790 Leigh Hunt's father was a prisoner for debt. Wm. Combe was a prisoner for many years, and here wrote *Dr. Syntax's Three Tours*. In 1815 Ld. Cochrane, guilty of Stock Exchange frauds, made his escape. He, however, was rearrested and returned to the prison. That ill-fated artist B. R. Haydon was here four times between 1823 and 1837 and here he painted 'The Mock Election.' In *David Copperfield* it is the 'place of incarceration in civil process' in which Micawber is confined.

It was a large bdg., consisting of 224 rooms. There was a courtyard about 120 yds. long, including a taproom, a wine-room, and a market comprising a chandler's shop, butcher's stall, and surgery. Probably it was these amenities that made Allen say (*History of London*, 1828) that 'it was the most desirable place of incarceration for debtors in England.' Moreover, it was possible to get leave of absence for a day by payment of a fee of 4s. 2d.; for a second day there was a reduction to 3s. 10d. For a large payment a nominal prisoner was allowed the privilege of living in what was called the liberties or rules of the King's Bench Prison. At one time about three square miles, latterly this area included about a dozen sts. round the prison. The manager of the Surrey Theatre in the Blackfriars Rd. was at one time nominally a prisoner of the King's Bench, and once, when Ld. Ellenborough was asked to extend the liberties for the convenience of a prisoner, he replied that they already extended to the E. Indies! Latterly the King's Bench was a military prison. It was demolished in 1880. A wall outside Queen's Bdgs., Borough Rd., and the doors of the water-closets at the latter—with their spy-holes—may be remains of the prison.

Ludgate was a prison constructed over the gate in the reign of Richard II (1377–99). It was appropriated to the freemen of the City and to clergymen committed for 'debts, trespasses, accounts and contempts.' It was too small for the purpose and in 1443, at the expense of Dame Agnes Forster, widow of Stephen Forster (Ld.M. 1454), it was enlarged. H. B. Wheatley says:

> 'A chapel was built, leads erected to walk upon, and lodging and water found for each person, without a fee to the keeper.'

Maitland relates that Sir Stephen in younger days had been a prisoner. He was begging at the grate when a rich widow who was passing asked how much would release him. He said 'Twenty pounds.' She paid it, and took him into her service, and his industry and fidelity so won her admiration that a marriage was arranged. Many complaints of the prison, the insufficiency of food, and the extortions of the officials got into print. It was burnt in the G.F. and rebuilt with the gate. Steele (*Spectator*, 4th June 1711) mentioned

> 'a voice bawling for charity. . . . Coming near to the Grate, the prisoner called me by my name, and desired I would throw something into the box: I was out of countenance for him and did as he bid me, by putting in half a crown.'

When Ludgate was demolished in 1760 the prisoners were removed temporarily to the London Workhouse in Bishopsgate St.

Marshalsea. This Southwark gaol, like the King's Bench, was attacked by the Wat Tyler rebels in 1381, and then first emerges into history. It was on a site between the present Newcomen St. and Mermaid Court. Here, in 1557, Gratwick, one of the Protestant martyrs, was confined. After trial by Gardiner, Bp. of Winchester, probably in St. Saviour's Ch. (see 'Southwark Cathedral'), he was

burned in St. George's Fields. When Elizabeth succeeded her sister Mary, Bonner, Bp. of L., was brought to the Marshalsea Prison. He d. there in 1569, and, according to Stow, was bd. in St. George's Chyd. It is mentioned in *Henry VIII*, Act v, Sc. iii. In 1601 Christopher Brook was a prisoner for giving Ann More in marriage to Dr. Donne, unknown to her father (see *supra*—Fleet Prison). Geo. Wither, the poet, was here in 1613 as a prisoner for debt, and wrote during that time his *Shepherd's Hunting*. In 1629 Sir John Eliot was transferred there from T.L. In the B.Mus. is a poem entitled *Hell in Epitome, or a Description of the M—sh—sea*, and published by an unknown author who had been a prisoner there in 1738. The prison is described in dark colours as:

> '. . . an old pile most dreadful to the view,
> Dismal as wormwood or repenting rue.
> Thither the graduates in sin resort
> And take degrees becoming Satan's court,
> There are instructed in the Paths of Vice,
> There sell good Linen, there they purchase Lice.'

The prison is mentioned in Smollett's *Roderick Random* (1748). Late in the 18th century it was removed to a site N. of St. George's Ch., and in 1811, when the Govt. purchased the White Lion—the old county jail which stood on an adjacent site, and had been superseded by the one in Horsemonger Lane (see *supra*)—a new Marshalsea Prison was erected. A picture sometimes published—e.g. in Beresford Chancellor's *The London of Charles Dickens*—is of the earlier Marshalsea Prison. There is no contemporary picture of the last Marshalsea Prison, which would have gone into oblivion but for Dickens. His father was a prisoner for debt there in 1824, but only for three months (the records of arrest and discharge are in the Public Record Office). Dickens therefore naturally introduced it into *Pickwick* ('The Old Man's Tale about the Queer Client'), and lengthily into *Little Dorrit*. It was much smaller than the King's Bench. Nield, in his *State of Prisons in England, Scotland, and Wales* (1812) says that it consisted of about sixty rooms, the average size of which was $10\frac{1}{2}$ ft. by $8\frac{1}{2}$ ft. The debtors' court measured 177 ft. by 56 ft., including the area occupied by the debtors' prison. The Marshalsea Prison was closed at the same time as the Fleet—1842. There were then only three prisoners; they were transferred to the neighbouring King's Bench. Much of it remained when Messrs. Harding & Sons took over the bdg. in 1887, and changed it into a factory. The Marshalsea Press (in Angel Pl.—called by Dickens Angel Court in the preface to *Little Dorrit*) also occupies part of the bdg. Some of the doors of the prison rooms have been adapted for interior windows. In Angel Pl., too, is a high blank wall, which undoubtedly was part of the Marshalsea Prison. A glass roof in St. George's Chyd. covers part of its small recreation ground, and on an adjacent wall are two commemorative tablets. The draper's shop, 211 Borough High St., is built on the courtyard of the turnkey's house which remains behind it; and from one of its back windows can be seen a row of spikes which were on the wall of the prison. Marshalsea Rd., on the W. side of Borough High St., commemorates the prison, but is misleading as to its site.

Millbank, originally known as the Penitentiary, was built in accordance with Jeremy Bentham's *The Panopticon or Inspection House* (1791). In 1794 the Treasury and Bentham entered into a contract whereby the latter was to erect a prison for 1,000 convicts, with chapel and other necessary bdgs., for £19,000. The ground was acquired (E. of where later Vauxhall B. appeared), but the undertaking did not proceed, and eventually the Govt. decided to erect the prison on its own account, but on a larger scale than at first proposed. The bdg. was erected between 1813 and 1816. There was one entrance—facing the Thames. The corridors were three miles in length, and Hepworth Dixon said it was the largest English prison. In 1843 it was changed into an ordinary prison and the inmates thereafter were there only for a few months, prior to being transferred to Pentonville, Reading, Wakefield, or Parkhurst. They numbered about 1,550, and between 4,000 and 5,000 prisoners passed through annually. It was made a military prison in 1870; closed in 1890; demolished in 1903. The Tate Gallery (*q.v.*) is on the site.

Newgate was first over the gate, as was the prison at Ludgate (*q.v.*). It was certainly in existence in 1189, being referred to in a Pipe Roll of that date. In 1241, according to Stow, on the Jews of Norwich circumcising a Christian child, L. Jews were fined 20,000 marks with the alternative of imprisonment at Newgate. It was a prison for the county of Middlesex as well as for the City of L., and it was in charge of the sheriffs of L. and Middlesex, who appointed the keeper, or jailer. It acquired an evil reputation early in the 14th century. In 1334 an official inquiry was made. It was found that

'prisoners detained on minor charges were cast into deep dungeons, and there associated with the worst criminals. All were alike threatened, many tortured, till they yielded to the keeper's extortions, or consented to turn approvers and swear away the lives of innocent men. These poor prisoners were dependent upon the charity and good will of the benevolent for food and raiment' (Major Griffiths).

In 1381 Newgate Prison was much damaged by Wat Tyler's followers. In 1414 the keeper and sixty-four of his charges d. of prison plague. Some rebuilding became necessary; in 1423 this was undertaken by the executors of Richd. Whittington, not under a specific provision of his will, but possibly, as Dr. Reginald Sharpe suggested, in fulfilment of a privately expressed wish. Newgate Prison was damaged but not destroyed in the G.F. In 1670 Claude Duval, the famous, and sometimes gallant, highwayman, was a prisoner. Defoe was a prisoner (1702–3) for his *The Shortest Way with the Dissenters*. In 1721 in the prison was the last case of the ordeal of *peine forte et dure*. Two highwaymen, Spiggot and Cross, taken at the Black Horse Inn in Broadway, Westminster, refused to plead, with a view to saving their property for their relations. When Cross was being laid down his courage faltered, and he begged to be allowed to plead 'not guilty.' Spiggot persisted and was laid on his back, with his legs and hands extended at full length, and weights placed on his body. When 4 cwt. had been put upon his breast, he also begged to plead 'not guilty.' In 1723 Jack Sheppard and Edgeworth Bess escaped from the prison by means of a rope made of blankets and sheets. In 1724 the former was again in

Newgate Prison. He left it—for Tyburn— the same yr. In 1777 Dr. Dodd (editor of *The Beauties of Shakespeare*) was a prisoner, prior to execution for forgery. He was exhibited for money, as Jack Sheppard had been, for two hours before his execution, the charge being 1s. (see 'Tyburn').

In 1770 rebuilding commenced, and in the process Newgate (*q.v.*), still part of the prison, was demolished (1777). The new bdg. was not complete when attacked by the 'No Popery' rioters (1780). Geo. Crabbe, the poet, in his journal, vividly recorded this attack:

'I went close to it, and never saw anything so dreadful. The prison was a remarkably strong building; but, determined to force it, they broke the gates with crows and other instruments. . . . They broke the roof, tore away the rafters, and having got ladders descended. Not Orpheus himself had more courage or better luck. Flames all around them. . . . The prisoners escaped. I stood and saw about twelve women and eight men ascend from their confinement to the open air, and they were conducted through the street in their chains. Three of these were to be hanged on Friday.'

The havoc wrought was soon repaired, and by 1783 the new Newgate Prison, designed by Geo. Dance the younger, was completed. Appropriately, Ld. Geo. Gordon, then a convert to the Jewish faith, was the first distinguished prisoner. He published a pamphlet professing to be a petition from the prisoners in Newgate, which was held to be a libel. Consequently he was a prisoner from 1787 to 1793, when he died. (For Ld. Geo. Gordon and the 'No Popery' riots see Dickens's *Barnaby Rudge*, Rochester edition, with topographical notes.) Major Griffiths said the façade of the new bdg. was a marvel of strength and solidity. Hepworth Dixon wrote:

'Of all the London prisons, except the Tower, it alone has an imposing aspect. . . . The solid masses of its granite walls, strong enough to resist artillery, unbroken by door or casement—save those low and narrow slits in the centre, iron-bound and mounted as they are— frown down upon the great arteries of London, as the Bastille formerly did upon the Rue St. Antoine.'

Inside it was dark, ill-ventilated, and incommodious. In 1813, on the debtors' side, which was built for 100, no less than 340 prisoners were lodged, and in the female felons' ward, designed for sixty, 120 victims were crowded. There was no restraint, no discipline, and drink was freely sold; prisoners had every opportunity of intercourse, and the officials of extortion and oppression. In 1873 a parliamentary enquiry was ordered. It was reported that on the debtors' side, built for a hundred, 340 prisoners were housed. About this time Mrs. Fry began her visits. The task of reform, however, was slow and difficult. In 1850 Col. (afterwards Sir Joshua) Jebb declared before a Select Committee on Prison Discipline, that he considered Newgate from its defective construction, one of the worst prisons in England. There was not room enough for all its requirements, and only the relief afforded in 1852 by the erection of Holloway Prison (see *infra*) improved the conditions. It was then used only for the custody of prisoners committed for trial at the Old Bailey, and for those awaiting execution, which then took place outside the Debtors' Door (see 'Old Bailey'). The interior was remodelled (1857) on the separate cell system. In 1861–2 a new block was built for the use of female prisoners. In 1880 it ceased to be used as a prison except during the sittings of the Central Criminal Court. In 1902 Newgate Prison was demolished, and the Central Criminal Court (*q.v.*) erected on the site. An interesting auction sale followed the demolition. A gate, weighing over 1,800 lb., of iron-bound oak and riveted lattice construction, was purchased and taken to Buffalo, U.S.A., where it still is. This is probably the one referred to in Chap. LII of *Oliver Twist*. A similar one is in the L.Mus. In St. Sepulchre's Ch., Newgate (see 'City Churches; C') there are some plates from Newgate Prison and a charred beam, probably a relic of the 'No Popery' riots.

Tothill Fields was on the site of Westminster Cath. It was erected in 1618 (when Hepworth Dixon wrote in 1850, a stone bearing that date remained). It was repaired or enlarged in 1655, the date given by Wheatley and others for its erection. The enlargement may have been for the confinement of Scotch prisoners taken after the battle of Worcester. Trumbull, an American artist, was a prisoner in 1780 (see *London for Americans*). It was enlarged in 1788. This—the Westminster Bridewell—was the one depicted in Hogarth's 'The Rake's Progress' (see 'Bridewell'). In 1834 it was closed, and a new Tothill Fields Prison erected in Francis St. Here some of the Chartists, including Ernest Jones, were confined. This prison was demolished in 1885, and Westminster Cath. stands on the site.

Wellclose Square (or *Neptune Street*) was a small prison, connected with the high court of the liberties of the Tower. It was originally for debtors; afterwards for prisoners awaiting trial. There is said to have been an underground passage from the prison to the T.L. and the docks. A number of prisoners in the Peninsular campaign were brought here, and these account for the foreign names cut on the walls of the fearsome-looking cell which was in the L.Mus. A portion of it became a public-house, the cells being used for storage purposes. At the time the cell was acquired by the mus. it was part of a lodging-house.

Whitecross Street. This was erected 1813–15. It was entirely for debtors, and accommodated 400. It was a large, gloomy bdg., and was demolished in 1870, the prisoners being transferred to Holloway.

EXISTING PRISONS

Brixton. It was erected in 1820 as a house of correction for Surrey, and furnished about four years later with the first of the treadmills. In 1853 it was purchased by the Government, and restricted to female convicts. In 1882 it became a military prison. In 1898 it was returned to the Prison Commissioners. Extensive alterations followed, and in 1902 it became the trial and remand prison for the whole of the L. area. It is now used for male offenders only; those whose sentences do not exceed six months, and civil prisoners.

Holloway. The erection was commenced in 1848; it was completed in 1852 at a cost of £91,547. It was described at the time as 'a noble bdg. of the castellated style for accommodation of some 350 prisoners, the battlements and lofty tower being reminiscent of some noble castle of the olden feudal times.' It was under the jurisdiction and control of the common council of the C.C. It was first used mainly for the incarceration of debtors and first-class misdemeanants, and as a place of detention for persons awaiting trial. Dr. Jameson and his fellow-raiders served their term of imprisonment here in 1896. In 1903 it was restricted to female offenders.

Pentonville was erected 1840–2, on the separate and silent system. It was called 'a model prison,' and was the one satirically treated by Dickens in the closing pages of *David Copperfield*. It occupies an area of 6¾ acres. It has a curtain wall with massive posterns in front, where stands a large entrance gateway whose arches are filled with portcullis-work, whilst from the main bdg. rises an Italian clock-tower. From the central corridor within radiate four wings, constructed after the fashion of spokes to a half-wheel, and one long central hall leading to the central point.

Here, in 1888, John Burns and Cunninghame Graham were confined for six weeks, a sequel to 'Bloody Sunday' in Trafalgar Sq. In 1916 Sir Roger Casement was hanged at Pentonville Prison for high treason.

Wandsworth was erected in 1851. Its historian said:

'It has nothing to recommend it to the eye, having none of the fine gloomy solemnity of Newgate, nor any of the castellated grandeur of the City Prison at Holloway, nor does it possess any feature about it that will bear comparison with the noble portcullis gateway at Pentonville. . . . The central mass rising behind the stunted gateway is heavy to clumsiness, and the whole aspect of the structure uncommanding as a Methodist Chapel.'

It is divided into two distinct parts; a central hall with five radiating halls and a central hall with three radiating halls. There are a tinsmith's shop, a shoemaker's shop, a tailor's shop, and a mailbag shop. There is an attractive chapel.

Wormwood Scrubs was designed by Sir Edmund du Cane, the famous chairman of the Prison Commission, after whom is named the road that skirts it on the S. It was built entirely by convict labour, and proceeded by instalments until 1890, when it was completed. It has an imposing gateway, and on the two flanking towers are medallions of Mrs. Fry and John Howard. It accommodates about twelve hundred prisoners but the average number of inmates at present is just under eleven hundred, both men and boys. The men are 'star' class prisoners serving medium and long sentences: the boys are mostly bound for Borstal and are only in the prison for a short period. There is also a surgical and psychiatric centre and a pre-release hostel. There are a particularly fine chapel, and lib. A large number of classes are conducted in a variety of subjects.

(See also 'Bridewell,' 'Compters.')

(See *The Fleet, its River, Prison, and Marriages*, by John Ashton, 1889; *The Fleet and its Neighbourhood in Early and Medieval Times*, by Marjorie B. Honeybourne (London Topographical Record. Vol. XIX, 1947); *The Chronicles of Newgate*, by Arthur Griffiths, 1902; *The Old Bailey and Newgate*, by Chas. Gordon, 1902; *The London Prisons*, by Hepworth Dixon, 1850; *London Prisons Today and Yesterday*, by Albert Crew, 1933. For Dickensian prisons, see *London for Dickens Lovers*, by W. Kent, 1935. See also *The History of Newgate and the Old Bailey, a Survey of the Fleet, the Marshalsea and other jails*, by W. E. Hooper, 1935.)

Public Record Office. It stands on the site of a bdg. known originally as the Chapel of the House of the Converts. This was founded by Henry III in 1232 for the reception of Jews who had embraced the Christian faith, a course usually dictated by expediency rather than conviction. After the expulsion of the Jews from England the office became a sinecure; it was usually given to the Clerk of Chancery whose duty it was to keep the rolls and other records of that department of the Govt. In 1377 Edward III definitely assigned the House of the Converts to the Keeper of the Rolls of Chancery and his successors. All the early Keepers of the Rolls were ecclesiastics, but in the reign of Henry VIII the office became tenable only by a lawyer. The actual custody of the records of Chancery was, moreover, delegated to others. The chapel then became attached to his official residence, and, not only a place of worship for him and his family, but for the masters, clerks, and registrars of the Court of Chancery; also a repository of records, and a meeting-

place for the discharge or the foreclosure of mortgages. The preacher was practically a domestic chaplain, though occasionally special sermons were preached to large congregations. Pennant says that the chapel was rebuilt by Inigo Jones in 1617. It was possibly damaged in the G.F. It was largely rebuilt 1717–24, and further alterations were made about 1784. Galleries and presses were from time to time put up within for the accommodation of the records of the Chancery, the seats for the congregation being made in the form of lockers. Soon after the completion of the first block of the adjacent Public Record Office in 1856, most of the documents stored in the Rolls Chapel were transferred thither. The interior was thereupon entirely remodelled, and a new ceiling of lath and plaster was put up, in imitation of late Gothic vaulting. In 1895 the crumbling walls of the chapel were pulled down. There is no medieval work now left in what was once a chapel, but fragments of a fine chancel arch of the 13th century were discovered during the demolition of the E. wall, and were put together and affixed to a neighbouring wall. There are three tombs left: (1) Dr. John Yong, Master of the Rolls and Dean of York (d. 1516). This has a terra-cotta effigy, and was the work of Torrigiani (see 'Westminster Abbey'). (2) Richd. Alington of Lincoln's Inn (d. 1561), mainly of alabaster. (3) Edward, Ld. Bruce of Kinloss, Master of the Rolls (d. 1611). This is mainly of alabaster. There are four detached figures kneeling on cushions. One was a daughter, who, having been born on Christmas Day, was named Christian. She was m. in the Rolls Chapel to Wm. Cavendish, afterwards E. of Devonshire, in 1608, being then 'a pretty red-headed wench of less than thirteen.' The E. and W. windows contain heraldic glass commemorative of Keepers or Masters of the Rolls from the latter part of the reign of Edward III. Another window contains the arms of four eminent persons who occupied the office of preacher at the chapel: Edward Stillingfleet, afterwards Bp. of Worcester; Gilbert Burnet, afterwards Bp. of Salisbury; Francis Atterbury, afterwards Bp. of Rochester; and Joseph Butler, afterwards Bp. of Durham, and author of the famous *Analogy of Religion*. Other heraldic glass represents P. Henry, eldest son of

James I, and George I. The oldest exhibit in the mus. is the Domesday Book. There is a remarkably interesting collection of letters: from Catherine of Aragon to Wolsey; from Anne Boleyn to Gardiner, afterwards Bp. of Winchester; from Wolsey—'poor heavy wrechyd prest'—to Henry VIII, daily crying 'for grace, mercy, remissyon and pardon'; from John Knox to Sir Wm. Cecil; and another from the same writer to Mary Q. of Scots. A letter from the E. of Essex to Q. Elizabeth says:

'Hast paper, to thatt happy presence whence only unhappy I am banished. Kiss that fayre correcting hand which layes new plasters to my lighter hurtes, butt to my greatest woond applyeth nothing. Say thou cummest from shaming, languishing, despayring S.X.'

There are letters from Ben Jonson, Sir Walter Raleigh, Dryden, and Defoe, and the famous one to Ld. Monteagle which led to the discovery of the Gunpowder Plot. There is also a memorandum from Sir Thos. More and a deposition of Shakespeare's. There is a petition of John Milton; and a memorial from Sir Christopher Wren. There is also exhibited the earliest known specimen of English printing—an indulgence by John, Abbot of Abingdon, a papal nuncio, and commissary in England. This must have been printed soon after Caxton's arrival in England in the summer of 1476.

Of interest to Americans is a letter of Geo. Washington to his 'great and good friend' George III, dated 25th Aug. 1795. There is also exhibited 'The Olive Branch Petition' to George III from the representatives of twelve of the states expressing how they 'ardently desire a restoration of the former harmony between Great Britain and her colonies.' It is dated 1775.

Q

Queenhithe is first mentioned in a charter of Alfred the Great of 899, granting land near 'Aetheredes hyd' to Abp. Plegmund, and to Werflid, Bp. of Worcester. In early times it was a port equal in importance to Billingsgate. In the 12th century it was in possession of Q. Adelaide of Louvain, wife of Henry I, and she mentioned it in a charter granted by her to the ch. of Reading. About 1246 it was leased by Richd., E. of Cornwall, to the mayor and citizens of L. at a fee farm rent of £50 by the name of Queenhithe, and the gift was confirmed by the king. *Liber Albus*, the City's 'White Book', sets out the regulations. Corn was to be landed at Queenhithe only, and fish for foreign parts. It declined in importance; being above L.B. was a disadvantage. The harbour still remains in Upper Thames St.

Queen Victoria Street came into existence as the result of an Act of 1863, promoted by the M.B.W. It was not until Oct., 1869 that the eastern extremity, from the Mansion House to Cannon St., was opened. The section from St. Andrew's Hill westwards to Blackfriars Bridge was opened in Jan. 1871; the section from St. Andrew's Hill to Bennett's Hill in May of the same year; and the final portion from Bennett's Hill eastwards in the following Nov. The piecemeal completion was due to delay in the construction of the Met. District Railway, which runs beneath it

from St. Andrew's Hill to the Mansion House Station. During the excavations a fine specimen of Roman tessellated pavement was discovered (see 'Roman Remains'). Nearly one-half of the houses in Bucklersbury had to be cleared away—thus this thoroughfare is intersected by Queen Victoria St.—and almost the whole of Size Lane. Another effect was that one City par.—St. Mary Mounthaw (see 'City Churches; A') was reduced to six shops.

In addition to the chs. of St. Benet, Paul's Wharf, St. Andrew by the Wardrobe, St. Nicholas Cole Abbey, St. Mary Aldermary (see 'City Churches; C'), and the Coll. of Arms (*q.v.*), the offices of the British and Foreign Bible Soc. are here. This soc. started with a public meeting at the L. Tavern in Bishopsgate St. in 1804. The present bdg., which dates from 1868, is a little to the E. of its predecessor, which stood in what was then known as Earl St., and now forms part of Upper Thames St. Nearly opposite, almost entirely destroyed in the Second World War but now rebuilt, are the headquarters of the Salvation Army. W. of the British and Foreign Bible Soc.'s premises are the offices of *The Times* (1874). They extend to Printing House Sq., which takes its name from the office of the King's printer. Here was printed the first *London Gazette* (1666); and here on 1st Jan. 1785, there was published *The Daily Universal Register*. Its name was changed to *The Times* on 1st Jan. 1788.

R

Ranelagh (now included in the grounds of the Royal Hosp., Chelsea), was a famous pleasure resort which, in its day, rivalled the claims of Vauxhall Gardens (*q.v.*). The name originated with Ld. Ranelagh, Paymaster-General to the Army in the reign of Charles II, to whom the 'merry monarch' granted the land at a nominal rental of £5. The magnificent gardens which the former planted were purchased eventually by Sir Thos. Robinson, who opened them in 1742, having erected the rotunda in the previous yr. The interior of this interesting structure was guarded by four portals of classical design, and the amphitheatre measured 185 ft. in diameter. Upon entering, the visitor must have been at once attracted by the vast central fire-place, the double row of gaily painted and gilded boxes, the circle of pendent chandeliers that shed light upon many a gallant in powdered wig, flowered waist-coat, knee-breeches, and buckled shoes and many a fair lady in bright-hued hoop-petticoat and elaborate head-dress.

Ranelagh has numbered among its guests many eminent men of letters. Ld. Chesterfield became so attached to it that he ordered all his letters to be directed there. Goldsmith forgot his wretched lodgings as he watched the 'fêtes, frolics, fire-works, and fashionable frivolity' of this place, while even the sober Dr. Johnson confessed that his visits here gave 'expansion and gay sensation to the mind.' Laurence Sterne found the gardens a welcome change from the quietude of his Yorkshire parsonage; Tobias Smollett strolled hither from his house in Lawrence St.; Fielding sought 'local colour' for scenes in his *Amelia*. Horace Walpole, however, preferred Vauxhall 'for the garden is pleasanter and one goes by water.'

Towards the end of the 18th century the fortunes of Ranelagh declined: the gardens were closed in 1803, and the once splendid rotunda was demolished in 1805, the materials being soon afterwards sold for firewood, while nettles and weeds crept over the grounds where nobility and commonalty had 'jostled each other' in the motley swarm.' The gardens were finally acquired by the hosp., so that to-day we may saunter in fancy with the beaux, belles, and *literati* of the 18th century.

For more than forty yrs. this part of the Royal Hosp. grounds has been in May the scene of the Royal Horticultural Soc.'s display, usually known as the Chelsea Flower Show.

(See *Invitation to Ranelagh*, by Mollie Sands, 1946.)

Restaurants in L. tend to become more uniform and less historic. There are still, however, a number of restaurants which were opened towards the end of last century and which are now almost synonymous with the name of L. when the food question arises.

BIRCH'S was established on Cornhill in the reign of George I by a Mr. Horton, and bought from him by Samuel Birch (Ld.M., 1814–5). Birch's was famous for its turtle soup, which it supplied for the Ld.M.'s banquet. Birch d. 1840, having four yrs. before disposed of the business to Messrs. Ring and Brymer. The old shop front, dating from about 1790, was taken to the V. & A. Mus. in 1927, a replica being placed in Old Broad St. when Messrs. Ring and Brymer removed there in that yr. In 1937 there was another move to Angel Court, near the Bank.

CAFÉ ROYAL was originally a tiny cafe in Glasshouse St., just behind Regent St., which was opened by Daniel Nicholas Thevenon and his wife, Celestine. He was b. at Chomplost, Burgundy, in 1833, and at the age of 21 m. his cousin. It was through the failure of his shop in Paris that he and his wife decided to try their fortune in L., where they arrived, with practically no money, in 1863. The café prospered, and they gradually extended it, acquiring adjacent property until eventually they took premises in Regent St. itself. The Café Royal gradually gained a wide reputation for its marvellous French cooking and wines, and became the favourite resort of the Arts. In 1897 Daniel Nichols (he had taken this English form of name since first opening the café) d., and the business was carried on by his wife until her death at the beginning of the First World War. The present bdg. replaces that of the original Café Royal, which was demolished when the Regent St. Quadrant was rebuilt, but the new bdg. retains many relics of the old—in the red velvet benches and decorations—though much of it is reconstructed on more modern lines.

GEORGE AND VULTURE is approached by St. Michael's Alley, Cornhill, or Castle Court, Birchin Lane. It was mentioned as the 'George' by Stow (1598). It is probable that the addition was made to its name on the ground of its possessing some kind of an aviary. It was burnt in 1748, and rebuilt. Its fame is entirely Dickensian. Here were the headquarters of Mr. Pickwick after he abandoned the insidious Mrs. Bardell. An inn when Dickens wrote, it has not been used for residential purposes since 1860. There is a small figure of Pickwick, carved in wood, on the stairs, a few illustrations from the novels on the walls, and photographs of the City Pickwick Club. It was announced in Feb., 1951, that the tavern was to be demolished for an extension of Deacon's Bank, but it is now to be preserved in some form. There was a delightful article in *The Times*.

OLD WATLING, in Watling St., is of a date immediately after the G.F. It has a conspicuous notice displayed: 'Every customer taking Alcoholic Liquor at this Counter must first be supplied with Food.' Such is the requirement laid down in the licence.

PAGANI'S (Gt. Portland St.) originated in a little coffee shop kept by a certain Mario Pagani, in 1871. It became a happy rendezvous for Italians, particularly those with musical taste. Says Edwd. Cecil, in his Jubilee Souvenir:

'They dropped into the habit of signing their names, sketching their friends, scribbling some bars of melody they had found in the music floating through this happy contentment, on the grey distempered walls, now preserved under glass panels.'

These inscriptions, now numbering hundreds (the first is dated 1874), are the feature of the now very much enlarged restaurant. Amongst the names are Sarah Bernhardt, Caruso, H. G. Wells, Arthur Roberts, Lily Langtry, Maeterlinck, Tschaikovsky, T. P. O'Connor, Geo. Robey, Sir Henry Irving, Melba, Paderewski, Mrs. Patrick Campbell, Dr. Jameson, Tod Sloan. G. R. Sims was a regular diner, and left a signed portrait.

It suffered from bombing but the inscribed walls survived.

'PIMM'S.' The original 'Pimm's' was founded by a Kentish farmer's boy, who came to L. more than 120 yrs. ago. The business gradually extended, and Pimm's became the owners of Pimms in the Poultry, the 'King's Head' in Threadneedle St., 'Ye Olde Dr. Butler's Head' in Mason's Av. (a restaurant founded in 1616 as a tavern or ale-house by Wm. Butler), the 'Red House' in Bishopsgate, and another 'Pimm's' in the Old Bailey. The firm has now given up its restaurants and concentrates on its 'cups'; the first of these—Pimms No. 1 Cup, still based on a secret recipe—is famous all over the world.

RULE's in Maiden Lane was established in 1798, and Leopold Wagner rather surprisingly calls it—

'the earliest rendezvous for superior intelligences of which we possess any record.

'Before the Athenaeum Club came into being in 1824,' he adds, 'and the Garrick Club in 1831, the votaries of Literature, Art and the Drama had no place to meet save at Rule's.'

It was patronized regularly by Sir Henry Irving, John L. Toole, and Wm. Terriss, and amongst the literary brotherhood at Rule's Sir Walter Besant and Jas. Rice planned their joint novel, *The Golden Butterfly*. Francis Burnand, editor of *Punch*, and later a knight, once wrote of it: 'To get anything indifferent here would be the exception, not the rule.' A great feature is its collection of theatrical portraits, and exhibits relating to the stage.

SCOTT'S (Coventry St., near Piccadilly Circus), the famous 'home' of lobsters and oysters, was known in Dickens's day, when it was an oyster shop. Towards the end of last century and the beginning of this, Scott's was known all over the country as the haunt of sporting and stage figures, and it has always been connected with Boat Race nights. The buffet on the ground floor is for snacks, behind is a grill-room and restaurant, while on the first floor are more restaurant rooms. The first impression of hurried meals is dissipated as one passes through to the rooms where more leisurely eating is encouraged.

SIMPSON'S, Bird-in-Hand Court, Cheapside, where the famous 'fish ordinary' followed by a cheese guessing competition had been an institution since about 1870—was entirely destroyed by bombs.

Mention must be made of the Criterion, Piccadilly Circus; and the Holborn Restaurant at the corner of Kingsway.

There is a number of hotels which specialize in the attraction of non-residents to the famous restaurants.

THE CARLTON, opened in 1899, gained a wide reputation for its excellent food, a reputation which it still holds. It is here that the famous chef, Escoffier, worked for a number of yrs., many of the famous head chefs in the world's best hotels being trained by him. When the hotel was opened restaurant life was becoming a recognized thing and it is here that King Edward VII as P. of Wales was often to be found on Sunday evenings. Dancing was not usual in those days in restaurants, but after dinner the people would retire to the Palm Court for coffee, and listen to the orchestra. The restaurant now has a dancing space in the centre, and it is still a favourite with stage and aristocracy, and much frequented by Americans visiting L.

CLARIDGE's, situated in Brook St., was opened over 100 yrs. ago by a Frenchman, but shortly after was bought by Mr. Claridge. It started as two quite modest houses, but was gradually extended, until it was finally rebuilt between 1894 and 1898.

THE RITZ (Piccadilly), a luxury hotel, built on the site of Walsingham House at the beginning of the present century, and though many more modern hotels have since been built it still holds a firm place as the recognized haunt of well-known people. The bdg. is decorated and furnished in the style of Louis XVI and the restaurant windows open on to Green Park, giving a magnificent view.

THE SAVOY, built on the site previously occupied by the Savoy Palace (q.v.) which ran down to the river. A gilt figure of Peter of Savoy is over the entrance of the hotel, which was opened in 1889. The restaurant now contains also four smaller rooms, named after the Savoy Operas: *Patience, Pinafore, Iolanthe*, and *Princess Ida*. The grill-room is a special feature of the Savoy.

Roman Remains. The Romans occupied L. for nearly four centuries (A.D. 43 to c. 430). Antiquarian opinion now holds that the town wall was erected at about the middle of the 2nd century. It enclosed an area of about 330 acres; the circuit was a little more than two miles. Much of the wall that remained was swept away by the Commissioner of Sewers in 1766, but there is still a considerable number of fragments to be seen. A small portion is visible at the T.L.—behind the ruin of the Wardrobe Tower, and to the N. of the Tower on the opposite side of Tower Hill an impressive piece can be seen. There is also a fine piece in the courtyard behind Midland House, 8–10 Coopers' Row. Immediately south of this is more of the wall in the basement of the Toc H Club, Trinity Sq.; nearby have been found parts of the tomb of Gaius Julius Alpinus Classicianus, with an inscription in Latin, translated as follows:

'In memory of Gaius Julius Alpinus Classicianus of the Fabian tribe . . . procurator of the province of Britain, his unhappy wife Julia Pacata, daughter of Julius Indus, set this up.'

The first part was found in 1852, and the rest in 1935. The stone had evidently been used to build or repair the bastion in this place. The following is from *London Wall through the Centuries*, by W. G. Bell, F. Cottrill, and Chas. Spon (1937):

'This Julius Classicianus was indeed a procurator, in charge of the Imperial revenues in the province of Britain. Moreover he is actually mentioned by the historian Tacitus as having been appointed to that post at the time of Queen Boudicca's rebellion, for which event his predecessor's mismanagement had been partly responsible. He was at variance with the military governor, Suetonius, on whose activities he was intended to act as a check. The confidence of the Imperial authorities in him does not seem to have been misplaced, as he considered the interests of the people of the province who had formerly had cause to bear ill will towards the Roman officials. His father-in-law, Julius Indus, is also mentioned by Tacitus; he belonged to the Gaulish tribe of the Treveri, and remaining loyal to the Romans, helped to suppress a revolt of his countrymen in the year A.D. 21.'

Both parts of the memorial stone are in the B. Mus. In a car park behind Tower

House is a reproduction on the site where they were found together with a 'Roman' statue which is in fact two sections from separate 18th-century garden ornaments brought from Southampton within recent years. In 1905 a section about 40 ft. long was exposed during work on the site of 18–20 Jewry St. and 1 Crutched Friars. The Skinners' Co., ground landlords, took steps to have this preserved, and it was built into the basement of Roman Wall House, where it can still be seen. In 1889 a long strip was revealed running parallel with and towards the centre of Duke St. It was about 120 yds. in length. Various portions were found in Bevis Marks in 1880, 1884, and 1923. A bastion was discovered in Camomile St. in 1876, and some of the rough material—fragments of a monument—are in the Guildhall Mus. In 1905 a small portion was uncovered N. of the chyd. of All Hallows London Wall (see 'City Churches; C'). Another piece is the N. boundary of the chyd. of St. Alphage, London Wall visible from the upper pedestrian way N. of London Wall. In 1822 part of another angle-bastion, and a considerable length of wall, were exposed during excavations on the site of the Castle and Falcon Hotel in Aldersgate St. Another part, with a hollow angle-bastion, is underneath the General Post Office yard in Giltspur St. It is here 7½ ft. thick. A small section exposed during work on the premises of the Oxford University Press in Warwick Sq. has been preserved. Most remaining parts of the wall above the present level are medieval work. Roman L. is about 18 ft. below the present surface. In 1910, in excavating the site of County Hall, there was discovered the remains of a Roman boat, 38 ft. in length. There were also coins dating from 268 to 296, when the usurper Allectus was in power. The boat is in the L. Mus.

In 1962 a portion of another Roman boat was found in the Thames mud at Blackfriars and it is believed that this was one of the barges bringing stone from the Maidstone area for making the wall, which sank while being unloaded.

The Second World War provided unprecedented opportunities for excavation and there was created a Roman and Medieval Excavation Council, with W. F. Grimes, M.A., F.S.A., of the L. Mus., as Director of the Excavations. The principal result of their work has

been to prove the existence of a hitherto unknown fort in the Cripplegate area—in the NW. corner of the wall. Its southern wall was traced for over 400 ft. to a point E. of Wood St. The town wall had been incorporated into it. The dimensions of the fort have been estimated at 230 by 250 yds. or 11 acres. The decade A.D. 70 to 80 is assigned to its construction; the inner town wall is dated by a coin embedded in the mortar which puts it beyond the yr. A.D. 140. The fort therefore followed the rebellion of Boudicca, but preceded the town wall. It can be visited by the public, at the West gate on London Wall, between 12.30 and 2 p.m. on weekdays.

In Walbrook a timber-lined well was excavated. At a depth of about 8 ft. an iron bucket-handle and a complete Roman boot, with sole strengthened and decorated with bronze studs, was found. There were also a wooden knife handle, a spindle whorl, and a fine bronze coin of Postumus, an army leader who established a provincial 'empire' from A.D. 259 to 269, during the nominal reign of Gallienus, and whose authority was acknowledged by the legions in Britain as well as those in Gaul and Spain. In the same place there were discovered a writing tablet, some Roman leather shoes, a 'strigil' (a toilet article made for the purpose of wiping off perspiration after a hot bath); a bronze fibula with chain of early second century; a Roman sandal; a head in mica-dusted pottery. Here also was found a piece of hewn stone which was probably a bollard to which boats were tied at a time when the Walbrook was navigable. In Gutter Lane, Cheapside, remains of what seemed to be wooden huts or shacks, possibly of the 1st century, were found. They were of wattle and daub. Close by was found a complete Roman mortarium bowl of the 1st century, a vase of the same period with some broken pottery. In Billiter Sq. there was discovered a Roman lamp, believed to be of 2nd-century date. It is in the form of half a pear, with two small holes in the flat side for the wick and the oil container.

In Southwark much has been done. In King's Head Yard there was found early British pottery, remains of a three-roomed timber house of about A.D. 150, and a Roman jar of the second century.

In Newcomen St. a Roman pavement of the first century was unearthed. There is always at the Guildhall Mus. an exhibition of the latest finds.

Previously there had been several fine specimens of Roman mosaic paving. The largest was found during the construction of Q. Victoria St. (*q.v.*), at its E. end, near the Mansion House. It is in the Guildhall east crypt. There are further specimens at the B. Mus. The Guildhall Mus. has a good collection of monumental stones, e.g. one found in 1806 on Ludgate Hill, erected to 'a most devoted wife,' and another found in 1837 at L. Wall, opposite Finsbury Circus, to the memory of another wife. There is also here a sarcophagus found at Clapton in 1867. In the centre is a medallion with a bas-relief of the deceased. There are further stone coffins—found in Fleet Lane and Bishopsgate St. There are tombstones also at the B. Mus. and L. Mus. (See 'Children's Memorials.')

In the Chapter House of W.A. is a sarcophagus which was found in the green on the N. side in 1869. It bears a cross which may have been added in Saxon times, and the inscription is translated:

'In memory of Valerius Amandus, made by Valerius Superventor and Valerius Marcellus for their father.'

The most spectacular of all discoveries was made in 1954; that of the Temple of Mithras in Queen Victoria St. While investigating the course of the Walbrook stream in Roman times, Prof. Grimes made the discovery which caught public imagination and attracted huge crowds to the site. Many of the finds were presented to the Guildhall Mus.; although the site has been built on (offices of the Legal and General Assurance Co.), the ground plan was rebuilt in nearby Temple Court and is open to the public. In the L. Mus. is the fine marble head of a river-god, found 20 ft. down in the bed of the Walbrook. Here also is a jug, found in Southwark, bearing the inscription 'Londini ad fanum Isidis' ('At the shrine of Isis in London'). This is the only find which bears the name of L. In the Guildhall Mus. there is a mutilated statue of the Deae Matres; statuettes of Demeter, Mercury, Apollo, and Mars. In the B. Mus. is the head of the Emperor Hadrian, found in the Thames near L.B. in 1834. It was possibly

part of a large statue used for Emperor worship. In Guildhall Mus. there is a bronze arm of heroic size, discovered in 1884 at Seething Lane, during work on the Inner Circle railway. Various articles with the Christian symbol Chi Ro are in the Guildhall Mus. and B. Mus.

Further excavations continue in the City. The site of the Coliseum near Gracechurch and the Roman Bath under the old Coal Exchange in Lower Thames St. are still being investigated. The old City has not yet yielded all its secrets.

Any general reader interested in the subject is recommended to read *The Roman City of London*, by Ralph Merrifield (1965); a more detailed work is *The Excavation of Roman and mediaeval London*, by W. F. Grimes (1968).

Royal Courts of Justice (for centuries housed in the Palace of Westminster, *q.v.*), now stand on a site of about 5½ acres, N. of the Strand and Fleet St. In 1868 designs for the bdg. were exhibited, but not until 1874 was a commencement made with the work. The architect was G. E. Street. He d. before the work was completed, and (Sir) Arthur Blomfield assisted his son thereafter. In 1882 the Courts were opened by Q. Victoria. There is a painting of the scene in the central hall, including twenty-nine judges. The last survivor was Ld. Linley; he was last also of the serjeants-at-law. He d. in 1921. The contract for the bdg. was for a sum of £700,000, and together with the site, the cost was £1,250,000 sterling. The estimated number of bricks used was 35,000,000, and every brick made was of an approved size—10 in. by 5 in. by 2½ in. The central hall is 238 ft. long, 48 ft. wide, and 82 ft. high, and is entered by a fine Gothic archway. Over its apex is a statue of Christ. On the W. side of him is K. Solomon; on the E. Alfred the Great (Moses faces Carey St.). The windows of the hall are emblazoned with the escutcheons of many Ld. Chancellors. It is singularly bare. There is a statue of Ld. Russell of Killowen by Thos. Brock. Ld. Russell was leading counsel for Parnell and the Irish members before the Parnell Commission; and in these walls performed one of the greatest feats of advocacy which modern times have furnished. He once spoke for six days.

There is a statue of the famous Wm. Blackstone. He became a judge in 1770. Ld. Stowell said he was the only man who acknowledged and lamented a bad temper. There is also Armstead's statue of G. E. Street, the plinth of which is a bas-relief showing the bdg. in course of construction. In 1918 the hall was a dormitory for 600 sailors of the United States Grand Fleet who visited L. just after the First World War ended. Here, during that War, wounded soldiers were entertained, and legal gentlemen drilled. There are twenty-three courts (four date from 1911) grouped round three sides of the great hall, and all at a higher level. In the Admiralty Court there always hangs a silver oar in front of the judge's desk when the court is sitting. The hall on the second floor, from which the Masters' rooms open, is colloquially called the 'Bear Garden.' The name is of immemorial antiquity, and probably was satirically used by some ancient who had been to a bear-pit, and thought the noise of competing attorneys comparable with it. There are cells in the basement for prisoners in attendance on the Court of Criminal Appeal. The Central Criminal Court (*q.v.*) is not here but further E. in the City. Despite the very heavy bombing of this part of L. during the Second World War (St. Clement Danes, almost outside the Courts, was bombed several times) the main building was not damaged. There was some damage however to adjacent parts. (See also 'Customs').

Royal Exchange was first instituted by Sir Thos. Gresham, and was modelled after the Bourse at Antwerp. It was completed by the end of 1568, and opened then for L. merchants. Q. Elizabeth visited it in Jan. 1571; thereafter it was called 'Royal.' It was a long bdg. opening on to Cornhill, with a ground floor and good courtyard for the merchants, and above the piazza the 'pawn' with its hundred shops. In a tower was a bell, which summoned the merchants daily at noon and six in the evening. Both this tower, and a lofty Corinthian column on the N. side, were surmounted by a grasshopper, Gresham's crest. There were grasshoppers in stone elsewhere, for the same reason. In niches above the ambulatory were statues of English monarchs from Edward the Confessor to

Q. Elizabeth, and near the N. end of the W. piazza stood a statue of Gresham. It appears to have been shoddily built, for the inquest book of the ward of Cornhill in 1581 records that it was reported to be 'dangerous for those which walk under, part being broken and like to fall down.' In 1624 the clock was complained of for 'the worst kept of any clocke.' To the royal statues mentioned were added James I, Charles I, and Charles II. The first Royal Exchange was burnt in the G.F., but Gresham's statue survived.

The second structure was designed by Edwd. Jerman, the City surveyor, and completed in 1670. It was similar in plan to the first, with a quadrangle and piazzas supporting 'pawns.' In niches above the piazzas were statues of monarchs looking down into the open courtyard, in the centre of which was a statue of Charles II by Grinling Gibbons. The design was classical; the principal entrance on Cornhill was by a lofty archway, flanked on each side by two Corinthian columns, and surmounted by an imposing clock tower. The cost of the bdg. was £58,962, in addition to a sum of £7,017 expended in acquiring additional lands. In 1767 a petition was presented to Parliament stating that it was so much decayed as to threaten its total demolition, unless speedily and effectively repaired. Thousands of pounds were spent upon it, and in 1821 the tower of the Cornhill front was rebuilt. In 1838 the second Royal Exchange was burnt down. Oddly enough, the eight bells before they fell chimed out *Life let us cherish* and *There's nae luck aboot the house*. Of the statues, Gresham's again survived.

In 1842 the foundation stone of the third Royal Exchange was laid by the P. Consort. A glass bottle, containing coins, and a tablet, with a long Latin inscription, were duly deposited, with all ceremony, in the appropriate places. It was opened by Q. Victoria in 1844. The cost was £168,534, and £223,700 had been expended in enlarging the site and improving the approaches. This had involved the demolition of the ch. of St. Benet Fink (see 'City Churches; B'), and of the French Protestant Ch., the widening of Cornhill, and the removal of Freeman's Court, a place where Defoe, in fact, and Messrs. Dodson & Fogg, in fiction, had carried on business. The most imposing feature of the new bdg. was the portico, consisting of eight Corinthian columns. On the frieze is inscribed: 'Anno Elizabethae R. XIII Conditum Anno Victoriae R. VIII Restauratum,' the second Exchange being ignored. In the spacious tympanum is an allegorical representation of commerce. It was the work of Richd. Westmacott, and was executed some yrs. later. The figures are seventeen in number, and, except for two, they are modelled entire and detached; that in the centre is 10 ft. high, and the others 7 ft. On the right of the former stand the Ld.M., an alderman, and a common councillor in their robes. Amongst the other figures are a Hindu, a Mohammedan, a Greek, a Turk, a Persian, and a Negro. The motto, 'The earth is the Lord's and the fullness thereof,' was selected by Dean Milman. The Gresham grasshopper surmounts a small cupola at the E. end. It is 8 ft. long and of beaten copper, so may be the original one. In niches flanking the N. entrance—that from Threadneedle St.—are statues of Hugh Myddelton (see 'Water Supply'), and Whittington. Behnes's statue of Gresham is in a niche in the front of the clock tower. The beautiful courtyard inside was open to the sky until 1883. In that yr. Chas. Barry, son of the architect of the Houses of Parliament, constructed a graceful roof of glass and stone. It is paved with Turkey stones arranged in patterns. These survived from the former bdg.

In the SE. corner is the statue of Charles II. It was erected in 1842, as successor to the one by Grinling Gibbons. In the NW. corner is a statue of Q. Elizabeth, this and a statue of P. Consort were erected in 1844. Q. Victoria's statue is in the centre. It was the work of Hamo Thornycroft (1896), and replaces an earlier one which had suffered by exposure to the weather at a time when there was no roof. There is a bust of Abraham Lincoln, of heroic size. Statues of Charles I, Charles II, and Sir Thos. Gresham, which were on the previous bdgs., are now in niches in the upper hall of the Central Criminal Court.

In 1895 Ld. Leighton presented to the Royal Exchange his canvas The Phoenicians trading with the Early Briton on the Coast of Cornwall. This was the first of the frescoes, and the others are: Alfred the Great repairing the Walls of the City; William the Conqueror granting the Charter to the City; William II building the T.L.; Woman's Work in the Great War; K. John signing Magna Carta; K. George V and Q. Mary visiting the battle districts in France, 1917; National Peace Service on the steps of St. P.'s Cath.; Henry Picard entertaining the Ks. of England, France, Scotland, Denmark, and Cyprus (see 'Companies'— Vintners'); Destruction of the Second Royal Exchange; Richd. Whittington dispensing his charities; Philip the Good presenting the Charter to the Merchant Adventurers; Trained Bands marching to support Edward IV at Barnet; Blocking of Zeebrugge Waterway; Reconciliation of Merchant Taylors' and Skinners' Co. by the Ld.M., 1484; Crown offered to Richard III at Baynard's Castle; Foundation of St. Paul's Sch.; Q. Elizabeth opening the first Royal Exchange; Charles I demanding the Five Members at the Guildhall; the Great Fire; The Foundation of the Bank of England; Nelson leaving Portsmouth, 1803; Opening of the third Royal Exchange by Q. Victoria; Modern Commerce. The date of Q. Elizabeth's opening is given as 1570. This is the 'old style' date.

So far as its original purpose is concerned the Royal Exchange is simply a relic. After the First World War, for a time on two days in the week (Tuesdays and Thursdays) brokers used to assemble for about an hour to transact business in foreign bills, but that ceased in 1921. Lloyd's departed in 1928; then the Royal Exchange came into sole possession of the Royal Exchange Assurance Corporation. Now the courtyard is mainly for the sightseer, and for City clerks to while away the lunch hour.

S

St. James's Palace, which abuts upon the Mall, stands upon the site of a hosp. for 'maidens that were leprous' founded about, and perhaps before, the time of the Norman Conquest. It was dedicated to St. James the Less, Bp. of Jerusalem. Henry VIII took possession of it, giving in exchange lands in Suffolk. He rebuilt it as a palace, 1532-3. Of his bdg. there remains only the picturesque brick gateway facing St. James's St. (the clock has replaced one removed to Hampton Court by William IV), the Presence Chamber or Tapestry Room—which still bears the initials of Henry and Anne Boleyn, the Chapel Royal, and the Guard Room, Edward VI, Elizabeth and Mary lived here from time to time, and it was the birthplace of Charles II (1630); James II (1633); Q. Mary II (1662); Q. Anne (1664); P. James Edward, the 'Old Pretender,' son of James II (1688); and George IV (1762). Here d. Q. Mary (1558) and P. Henry, eldest son of James I (1612). Here Charles I spent his last night (1649). He is said to have slept in the Guard Room, and on one of the windows was found scratched 'William Rutherford God bless Ki.' Sir Cecil Harcourt Smith (*Daily Telegraph.* 2nd Jan., 1936) said:

'It is not difficult to picture the circumstances. William Rutherford, who may have been in attendance on the King, having inscribed his name, felt the desire, which must have been in many minds at the time, to add an expression of loyalty to his Master. We may suppose that he intended to write "King Charles," but before his task was completed he was interrupted probably by one of the Roundhead Guards, and not allowed to finish the self imposed task.'

In 1935 there was found another inscription scratched on glass—this time in the Throne Room:

'Thos Smith broke his rist and fell in the Garden throw this window May 30th 1767.'

What so nondescript a person was doing in the Throne Room was not vouchsafed to the 20th century discoverer of his marks to know.

Anne Hyde, first wife of James II, d. at St. James's Palace (1671). Here d. also Q. Caroline, consort of George II. George II lived on here and his grandson, George III, resided occasionally in the palace, though he was more often at Buckingham Palace.

In the Chapel Royal many marriages have taken place. Princess Mary, daughter of Charles I to P. of Orange (1641); Princess Mary, daughter of James II, to Wm., P. of Orange (1677); Princess Anne to P. George of Denmark (1683); George III to Princess Charlotte (1761); George P. of Wales, afterwards George IV, to Caroline of Brunswick (1795); Q. Victoria to P. Albert (1840); their eldest daughter, Princess Royal to the then Crown P. of Prussia (1858); D. of York, afterwards George V, to Princess Mary of Teck (1893); A noteworthy marriage outside the royal family was that of Sir Christopher Wren to his second wife, Jane Fitzwilliam (1676).

In 1809 the E. wing was destroyed by fire. In recent times the W. wing, known as York House, was the residence of Edward VIII when P. of Wales. In Friary Court, at the E. angle of the palace, the guard is changed at 10.30 a.m. when the K. is not in residence at Buckingham Palace; overlooking the court is the balcony from which proclamation is made on the death of the monarch. The Ambassadors' Court is on the S. Levees are held in the Throne Room where, until 1865, Q. Victoria held her drawing-rooms. In the Presence Chamber is much of Wm. Morris's work, executed in 1881—silk damask and hand-painted ceilings. In various rooms there are paintings of sovereigns from Henry VIII to Q. Victoria. The Ld. Chamberlain's Dept. is in the palace, and here also, if required, is found official accommodation for holders of such sinecure offices as Poet Laureate and Keeper of the King's Swans

St. James's Palace suffered some damage in the Second World War, but the older parts were not affected. The window inscriptions were destroyed.

St. Katharine's Royal Chapel, Regent's Park, is a little-known bdg. of considerable interest. Its history starts in 1148 when Matilda of Boulogne, wife of K. Stephen, whose figure in stone will be found near the present edifice, founded a hosp. in E. Smithfield, for the repose of the souls of her son Baldwin and her daughter Matilda, and for maintenance of a master and several poor brothers and sisters. In 1273 Eleanor, widow of Henry III, dissolved the old foundation, and refounded it, in honour of the same saint, for a master, three brethren, chaplains, three sisters, ten bedeswomen, and six poor scholars. Another great benefactor of the hosp. was Q. Philippa of Hainault, Edward III's consort. She rebuilt the chapel in 1340, founded a chantry, and gave houses in Kent and Herts. to the charity, and lands worth £10 p.a. for an additional chaplain. Henry V confirmed the annual grant of Q. Philippa's for the endowment of the chantries of St. Fabian and St. Sebastian; his son, Henry VI, was also a benefactor. In 1445 Thos. de Bekington, afterwards Bp. of Bath and Wells, master of the hosp., obtained a charter of privileges, to help the revenue. By this charter the precincts were declared free from all jurisdiction, civil or ecclesiastical, except that of the Ld. Chancellor, and they had a special spiritual and temporal court. To help the funds, an annual fair was to be held on Tower Hill to last twenty-one days. Henry VIII and Catherine of Aragon founded in the chapel the guild of St. Barbara, which was governed by a master and three wardens, and included on its roll Cardinal Wolsey, the Ds. of Norfolk and Buckingham, and the Es. of Shrewsbury and Northumberland. In 1526 the K. confirmed the liberties of the foundation, and surprisingly it escaped the general dissolution. In the reign of Q. Elizabeth, however, Dr. Thos. Wilson, her secretary, having become the master, surrendered the charter of Henry VI, and obtained a new one from which was omitted any reference to the liberty of the fair on Tower Hill. He endeavoured to secure all the hosp. estates, but the parishioners, tried beyond endurance, appealed to Sir Wm. Cecil, afterwards Ld. Burghley, and Wilson was restrained. In 1672 a fire destroyed a hundred houses in the precincts; another fire during a great storm in 1734 destroyed thirty bdgs. During the 'No Popery' riots (1780) a Protestant mob, headed by Macdonald, a lame soldier, and two women—one white and one a negress— armed with swords, were about to demolish the ch., as a relic of Popish times,

when the gentlemen of the L. Association arrived and prevented them. The three leaders in the attack were hanged on a temporary gallows on Tower Hill.

In 1825 the ch. was pulled down to make way for the St. Katharine Docks. In 1828 a new chapel was erected in Regent's Park. It is a Gothic bdg. similar in character to King's Coll., Cambridge, and was designed by Ambrose Poynter. The cost was defrayed out of the money awarded as compensation for the removal of the old hosp. There was carving from the stalls which came from the old chapel. One of the most remarkable features was the altar tomb of John Holland, D. of Exeter (d. 1447), who fought in the wars of Henry VI in France. He was High Admiral and Constable of the T.L. He left the chapel a beryl cup, garnished with gold and precious stones, and a gold chalice and eleven silver candlesticks, etc., for priests of his chantry chapel. Upon the tomb lie effigies of the D. and his first and third wives. It is handsomely carved with figures of men and animals, and only Henry VII's tomb in W.A. can equal it. The pulpit is a curious one. It is well carved with various ecclesiastical bdgs. One resembles the medieval St. P.'s Cath., but according to Nichols's *Bibliotheca Topographica Britannica* (1782) it represents various views of the Hosp. Round the sides of the pulpit is the inscription: 'Ezra the scribe stood upon a pulpit of wood, which he had made for the preachin''—Neh. viii. 4 (in the Authorized Version it reads, 'which they had made for the purpose'). It was given by Sir Julius Cæsar (see 'City Churches; C'— St. Helen's, Bishopsgate).

The chapel is a 'royal peculiar' in the possession of the Queens of England.

In 1950 it was dismantled preparatory to its being used for worship by the Danish community in L. Some of the fittings have been taken to the Royal Foundation of St. Katherine, Butcher Row, Ratcliff, E. This is near the site of the original hosp., and part of the donations of the English Queens now serves the comfort of old age pensioners in the latter institution. The tomb of the E. of Holland will be placed in the chapel of St. Peter ad Vincula in the T.L., as he was Constable there.

St. Marylebone was a met. bor. and

ancient par. and since 1965 has been part of the C. of Westminster.

The first par. ch. was dedicated to St. John. It was built probably by Aubrey de Vere, second E. of Oxford, in the 12th century 'in a lonely place,' near the highway (i.e. to Uxbridge—the modern Oxford St.). Lysons says 'on or near the site of the present court-house'; that is at the foot of Marylebone Lane. In 1400 Bp. Braybrooke granted a licence to remove it because of the frequent robberies to which it was subjected. The next ch. was built ¼ mile to the N., and came to stand on the W. side of High St. when that was made. It would seem that, on this change of site, the dedication was changed to St. Mary. It was on the same (E.) bank of Tyburn stream, on somewhat higher ground: it came to be known as 'St. Mary at Bourne'—this in time became Mary le Bone,' a name that was preferred to Tyburn for obvious reasons. Here Francis Bacon m. Alice Barnham in 1606. The ch. stood until 1740: its interior was depicted by Hogarth in the marriage scene in the *Rake's Progress*. The ch. built on this site became only a chapel in 1817; in 1949 it was demolished and in 1951 the site was laid out as a garden of rest and a commemorative plaque reminds us of the past. On the floor was a stone to the memory of Humphrey Wanley (1672–1726), antiquary and librarian to the E. of Oxford. There were monuments to Giuseppe Baretti (1719–89), author of Italian and Spanish dictionaries, friend of Dr. Johnson and Burke; and Jas. Gibbs (1682–1754) architect. The register records the burials of the following: Johann Van de Banck (c. 1694–1739), painter of many royal portraits and illustrator of *Don Quixote*; Edmund Hoyle, writer on card games (1672–1769); John Michael Rysbrack (c. 1693–1770), sculptor; Jas. Ferguson (1710–76), astronomer; Allan Ramsay (1713–84), painter; Chas. Wesley (1707–88), hymn writer, brother of John Wesley (there is a memorial in the chyd.); Francis Wheatley, R.A. (1747–1801), bd. in cemetery, Paddington St.; Geo. Stubbs (1724–1806), animal painter and anatomist. Two notable baptisms are recorded: Byron, 1788; Horatia, daughter of Nelson and Lady Hamilton, 1803. R. B. Sheridan was m. in the ch. to Elizabeth Lindley in 1773.

The present par. ch. fronting Marylebone Rd. and backing on the old chyd. was built in 1817. The architect was Thos. Hardwick. The Corinthian portico was an afterthought, designed when it had been decided to make the newly-erected ch. parochial. The altar-piece, representing the nativity, is by Benjamin West. There is a double gallery. Bd. in the ch. are Richard Cosway, R.A. (1742–1821); Jas. Northcote, R.A. (1746–1831). Robt. Browning was here m. to Elizabeth Barrett in 1846. In 1950 a part of the ch. was arranged as a Browning Chapel; there is a bronze plaque of the poet, once exhibited at the Royal Academy; his study table is the altar; his chair the priest's chair.

In 1733 a cemetery was opened S. of Paddington St. which leads W. out of High St. It is a triangular ground, now laid out as a pleasure garden. Bd. here were Joseph Bonomi the elder (1739–1808), architect; several Stuarts descended from Charles II, the last one 1807; Geo. Canning the elder (1771). In 1833 this graveyard was said to contain 80,000 bodies. In the nearby workhouse in 1793, d. Lieut. John McCulloch, aged 77; who, when a prisoner of the French in Quebec, formed a plan for the taking of that city which plan was that successfully pursued by Gen. Wolfe, to whom it was communicated on McCulloch's release by exchange.

In Marylebone Rd. is Holy Trinity Ch. by Sir John Soane (1828), where Florence Nightingale used to worship. St. Cyprian's, Clarence Gate, is a fine modern ch. by J. N. Comper (1902).

In Lisson Grove stands the Ch. of Our Lady by J. J. Scoles (1836), one of the earliest R.C. Churches to be erected in L. Near the Marble Arch, until it was wrecked by a bomb, was the Tyburn Convent of the Sacred Heart. The altar was shaped to resemble gallows, and it was the terminus of an annual procession from Newgate St. in memory of Catholic martyrs.

Close to the NW. of Regent's Park is St. John's Wood, really such in Elizabethan times for in it the Babington conspirators (See 'Lincoln's Inn Fields') were captured in 1586. It was once the property of the Knights Hospitallers of St. John of Jerusalem. St. John's Wood Ch., at the NE. end of St. John's Wood Rd., near the park, was built by Thos. Hardwick in the Ionic style, in two storeys with square windows. It was badly damaged in a raid, but has been repaired. There are a great many monuments in it, including a splendid one to Sarah Capel by Chantrey (1822). In a vault below is bd. Elizabeth, wife of Benjamin West, the American-born President of the Royal Academy. Among the many persons who have had monuments of one kind or another in the surrounding cemetery are: Joanna Southcott, the religious fanatic, bd. in 1814. There is a stone over her grave, and another stone, with a long inscription, a few yards away. (See *English Messiahs*, by Ronald Matthews, 1936, and *London Worthies*, by Wm. Kent, 1939.) Here also were bd. two artists: John Jackson (1831) and J. S. Cotman (1842).

To some St. John's Wood is a synonym for a cricket ground. Thos. Lord's first pitch was on the site of Dorset Sq., a little E. of the Marylebone railway terminus. In 1810 the site was changed to the N. bank of the canal NE. of Grove Rd.—where the Central Electric power station is now. In 1812 the present site was adopted, and the first match was M.C.C. v. Hertfordshire on 9th May 1814. The principal features of the ground are the pavilion (1890) where is the Commonwealth Cricket Memorial which houses a gallery, museum and library of cricket mementoes, opened in 1953; the grand-stand with its figure of Father Time removing bails from a wicket; and the memorial gates to W. G. Grace who d. in 1915.

In the bor.—at 1 Devonshire Terrace, Marylebone Rd.—Chas. Dickens resided after leaving Doughty St. in 1839. He remained until 1850. In this house—it has undergone considerable alteration since—Dickens wrote *The Old Curiosity Shop, Barnaby Rudge, American Notes, Martin Chuzzlewit, The Christmas Carol, The Chimes, The Cricket on the Hearth, Dombey and Son* and *David Copperfield*. Here, in 1849, his last surviving son, Henry Fielding Dickens, was born.

In the bor.—in 1884 at 17 Osnaburgh St., Regent's Park—the Fabian Soc. came to birth.

St. Pancras was a met. bor. (since 1965 part of the L. bor. of Camden) and an ancient par. deriving its name from the saint to whom it is dedicated—Pancratius, a youth who suffered martyrdom in Rome, *c.* 304. (At the extreme W. end—Gloucester Gate, Regent's Park—there is a sculptured representation of St. Pancras.) The par. has been known as St. Pancras since about the 9th century; but, according to Goldsmith's *Citizen of the World*, it was pronounced 'Pancridge' in the 18th century. From Domesday survey, and from a survey of St. Pancras in 1251, it is deduced there were four ancient prebendal manors held by the clergy of St. Paul's: Pancras, the land near the Ch.; Cantelowes or Kentistoune in the N. (said by Moll, as quoted by Samuel Palmer in *History of St. Pancras*, 1870, to derive its name from the family of Cantilupe); Tothill or Totenhall, whose centre was at the 'Adam and Eve' corner of Hampstead Rd. and Euston Rd.; and Ruggemere, supposed to have been the SE. corner, containing the sites of Bagnigge Wells and the Foundling Hosp.

Although there is a legend that the ch. of St. Pancras was the first erected in the county of Middlesex, the first recorded mention of one here is 1183 when one Fulcherius was made vicar at an annual stipend of 2s. The present 'old' ch. was probably built about 1350, of stone and flint. In 1593 John Norden described it as 'utterly forsaken, old and weather-beaten.' Jonathan Wild m. his third wife in the ch., Joseph Grimaldi his second in 1801. In 1847–8 it was practically rebuilt, losing all exterior marks of antiquity. The old square tower, which for some time had a bell-shaped roof instead of the original short spire, was removed in order to lengthen the nave, a new tower being erected on the S. side. The W. end was given a porch of Norman design, and a wheel window in the gable above. The remains of the old monuments were placed as nearly as possible in their original positions, and include an altar-tomb of Purbeck marble with a canopy forming an elliptical arch ornamented with quatrefoils that once had small brasses at the back. There is a memorial, with palette and pencil to Samuel Cooper, the miniature painter, d. 1672. St. Pancras is shown in a stained glass window on the N. side.

The chyd., which is the scene of the mock funeral and attempted body-snatching in the *Tale of Two Cities*, Bk. II,

Chap. XIV, was enlarged 1793 by the addition of a large piece of ground to the SE. The whole area is now laid out as a garden. In the ch. or chyd. have been bd. Jonathan Wild, 1725—his body was disinterred and is now in the Royal Coll. of Surgeons (*q.v.*); Jeremy Collier, non-juring bp., and castigator of the stage, 1726; Ned Ward, author of *The London Spy*, 1731; a son of Bach's, 1782 (see 'Music in London'); Wm. Woollett, landscape and historical engraver, 1785; Mary Wollstonecraft Godwin, 1797—the body has been removed to Bournemouth; John Walker, lexicographer, 1807; Pasquale Paoli, the Corsican patriot, 1807 (removed 1889); the Chevalier d'Eon, 1810; Jas. Peller Malcolm, topographer and engraver, 1815; and the family of Cecil Rhodes. It was long a favourite burial place for Roman Catholics, and the ch. is said to have been the last par. ch. in England where the bell was rung for mass. In 1803 a large piece of ground adjoining the chyd. on the N. was appropriated to a cemetery for the par. of St. Giles in the Fields; in it were bd. John Flaxman, sculptor (1826), and Sir John Soane (1837).

The new par. ch. of St. Pancras was built 1819–22, in imitation of the Erechtheum at Athens, by Wm. Inwood on the S. side of the New Rd. (now Euston Rd.), cut in 1756. The steeple is modelled on the Temple of the Winds, built by Pericles. The W. front has a fine portico of six columns. Towards the E. end are lateral porticoes, supported by caryatides not generally admired. Inside, above the Communion table, are some verd-antique scagliola marble columns, copied from the Temple of Minerva. The pulpit and reading-desk are made of wood from the Fairlop Oak, blown down 1820.

A chapel is said to have been erected at Kentish Town in the reign of Henry III by Walter and Thomas de Cantilupe, but the first record of the present ch. dates only from 1553. Rebuilt by Wyatt in 1783, and again almost entirely by Hakewill in 1845, it became the par. ch. of St. John the Evangelist in 1868. In 1948 a memorial garden in memory of those killed in air raids was opened by Q. Mary.

The ch. of Camden Town is All Saints', Camden St., built 1824. It is now used by the Greek Orthodox Ch. The ch. of Somers Town, which grew up after 1790, is St. Mary's, Seymour St., built in 1813. In Clarendon Sq. is St. Aloysius, built 1808, a plain little bdg., but one of the earliest R.C. churches remaining in L. St. Thomas's, Agar Town Ch. was built in 1863. Agar was a barrister who bought the manor in 1810. A recent vicar, Rev. R. Conyers Morrell, M.A., wrote *The Story of Agar Town* (1935).

S. of Parliament Hill Fields is the region of Gospel Oak. A gospel oak was a tree on a boundary line, where the gospel of the day was read during the beating of the bounds. This particular oak was at the W. end of the district, and as near as may be on the spot where Southampton Rd. crosses the railway. All Hallows Ch. by Brooks has some good modern stained glass, and an altar table from a demolished city ch. St. Dominic's Priory, Haverstock Hill (see 'Blackfriars') is a most impressive structure by C. A. Buckler (1863–83).

St. Saviour's Hospital in Osnaburgh St. has a chapel containing some magnificent 17th-century wood carving from a Bavarian monastery.

In 1811 Wm. Huntington, the notorious 'Sinner saved,' opened a chapel on the E. side of Grays Inn Rd. In 1846 it was taken over by the Established Ch.

On the E. side of Hampstead Rd. is St. James's. Ch., built 1793. In the chyd. were bd. Ld. Geo. Gordon (1793) and Geo. Morland (1804), but there are no memorials.

The original Whitefields Tabernacle was built for Geo. Whitefield in 1756. The bdg. opened in 1899, and associated with the ministry of the Rev. C. Silvester Horne, was destroyed by one of the last rockets in 1944. A basement hall bears the name of Toplady, the hymn-writer who was bd. in the previous bdg. (1778) (see 'Leicester Square').

In the bor. of St. Pancras are three great railway termini. Euston Station was built 1837; it was designed by Philip Hardwick, and had the most imposing of all station frontages until the splendid Great Hall, the vast Doric Arch and the Euston Hotel were all swept away in the modernization of the 1960s. King's Cross dates from 1852. The name derived from a neighbouring statue of George IV, erected in 1833 and removed in 1842. The clock on King's Cross Station came from the Great Exhibition of 1851. St. Pancras Station was completed in 1870 by Sir Gilbert Scott.

(See *St. Pancras Through the Centuries*, 1935, and various issues of *St. Pancras Journal*.)

St. Paul's Cathedral. The premier Protestant ch. stands in the heart of the City, and almost at its highest point—on the summit of Ludgate Hill. It is the third cath. on the site. The first was a Saxon edifice (*c.* 604); the second was Norman to begin with, and afterwards had Early English additions, the bdg. being under construction from 1087 until about 1285, a period that denotes long periods of inactivity. The third is the present Cath., the work of Sir Christopher Wren (1675–1710).

There have been traditions of a Christian temple on the site in the 2nd century. K. Lucius (see 'City Churches; C':—St. Peter's, Cornhill) is said to have obtained two missionaries from Rome who founded a metropolitan see. Dean Milman, however, consigned Lucius and the missionaries to the 'dim region of Christian mythology.' Milman was more hospitably inclined to the suggestion that a shrine of Diana had stood there. Two images of the goddess, acclaimed by the mob when St. Paul was at Ephesus, have been found near the site. One, only 2½ in. in height, mentioned by Wren, was found between the Deanery and Blackfriars. Its present whereabouts is unknown. In 1830, when the foundation of Goldsmiths' Hall (see 'Companies') were being excavated, a stone altar with the image of the goddess was found. In a list of bps. inscribed upon the S. wall of the choir of the present cath. is Restitutus. He was present at the Council of Arles (314). Where there was a bp. there must have been a ch. It is possible the ch. was St. Peter's Cornhill, but it might have been on Ludgate Hill.

The Saxon Cathedral. History commences with the reference of the Venerable Bede to L. as the metropolis of Kent, and the conversion of K. Ethelbert 'by the preaching of Mellitus'; as a result Ethelbert built the church of St. Paul.' These events, in Bede's *Ecclesiastical History*, are under date 604. Of this first ch. nothing is known.

The *Anglo-Saxon Chronicle* records that in 961 'the monastery of St. Paul's wa burnt,' and in the same yr. restored, but there is no record of monks. In 1087 the cath. was destroyed in a general confla gration.

Maurice, a Norman bp. commenced to rebuild. Fresh ground was secured and houses demolished for the enlargemen of ch. and chyd. 'Barges,' wrote J. R. Green, 'came up the river with stone from Caen for the great arches that moved the popular wonder.' An earthquake in 1089, a destructive storm two yrs. later, and a fire in 1136, impeded the work, but it moved Wm. of Malmesbury (d. 1143) to write:

'It is worthy of being numbered amongst the most famous of buildings: such the extent of the crypt and of such capacity the upper structure that it seemed sufficient to contain a multitude of people.'

After the fire, which devastated an area extending from L.B. to beyond the River Fleet, restoration was again resorted to, and there then appeared in their final form those massive columns familiar in the engravings of Wenceslaus Hollar, published in Sir Wm. Dugdale's *History of St. Paul's Cathedral* (1658). In the middle of the 13th century a new choir was in course of construction. When completed it had twelve bays, as also the nave. In the choir there were clustered pillars, pointed arches, and, above these, an arcade with, still higher, a row of windows with geometrical tracery. The choir screen was comparatively low; it had a Gothic doorway in the centre, and four niches for statuary on either side. A much longer vista was presented than in the present cath., and it culminated in the rose window at the E. end. Absolon, in Chaucer's *Miller's Tale*, had 'Powles window corven on his shoes,' the leather work being cut after the same design There were transepts and, in one of the aisles, was held the consistory court.

Up to 1256 there was a ch. of St Faith at the E. end of the Cath. It was then demolished, and the parishioner were allotted the crypt for their ch. On a pump near the NE. corner of St. P.' Chyd. was an inscription 'Erected by St Faith's parish 1819.' The parishioner were at one time bd. in the crypt, but the vault was closed in 1853. A few are bd in the chyd. In 1312 the choir of the cath. was paved with marble. In 1315 the old steeple, having become dilapidated, was taken down and a new one of wood, covered with lead, erected. The cross (15 ft. 6 in. in height) was above 'a pomel and ball well gilt,' which was 9 ft. 1 in. in circumference. It was large enough to contain ten bushels of corn. At a later date there was surmounting it an eagle as a weather vane.

A wall had been placed round the cath. about 1109. In 1285 it was greatly strengthened by order of Edward I because—

> 'by the lurking of thieves and other bad people in the night time within the precincts of the churchyard, divers adulteries, homicides, and fornications had been committed therein.'

The area leading from the present St. P.'s Chyd. to Paternoster Row, represents the position of the gates and posterns. They were closed at night. The wall enclosed a variety of bdgs. The chapter house was on the SW. corner. It had a diameter of nearly 40 ft., supported by massive buttresses, and some bases of the pillars which survived the chapter house was on the SW. corner. It had a diameter of nearly 40 ft., supported by massive buttresses, and some bases of the pillars which survived the G.F. are in the present chyd. They were discovered in 1878. Hollar's engraving shows the tracery to have been of Perpendicular Gothic. To the W. of the chapter house was the small ch. of St. Gregory by St. Paul's (see 'City Churches; A'). Thos. Fuller quaintly said that 'St. Paul's was indeed a mother church, for it had one child in its arms (St. Gregory's) and another in its bosom (St. Faith's).'

On the N. side, near the W. end, was Pardon Ch. Haugh, where there were many important burials. Here was a chapel founded by Gilbert, father of Thos. à Becket, and rebuilt by Dean More in Henry V's time. On the walls of the cloister was portrayed 'The Dance of Death,' a series of symbolical paintings, with verses translated from the French by John Lydgate. A fine copy is on exhibition in the lib. of Lambeth Palace. Death, personified by a skeleton, appears in succession holding the hand of an emperor, a cardinal, a k., a patriarch, a constable, an abp., for

'To this complexion we must come at last.'

On the E. side of this cloister was a library built by Walter Sheryngton in the time of Henry VIII. He was Chancellor of the Duchy of Lancaster, as well as a residentiary canon. In 1458 Sheryngton also built a chapel adjacent to the library; it was demolished by the D. of Somerset in 1547.

A little farther E. was the Coll. of Minor Canons, from which 'Canon Alley' derives its name. Still more eastward was the 'Charnel Chapel,' containing a few monuments. This also was pulled down by the D. of Somerset, and the material used for the construction of his palace in the Strand. The bones from the vaults beneath were conveyed to Finsbury fields, and are said to have numbered 1,000 cartloads (see 'Bunhill Fields').

Paul's Cross. This was at the NE. angle. First mentioned in 1194, it was, for at least four and a half centuries L.'s great public pulpit. Carlyle called it 'the Times newspaper of the Middle Ages.' It was that rather than the Hyde Park, for only utterances that were officially sanctioned could be heard there. There papal bulls were read. In 1441 Roger Bolingbroke, a necromancer, was exposed with all his instruments during sermon. He was afterwards drawn, hanged, and quartered (see 2 *Henry VI*, Act 1, Sc. ii). In 1449 Thos. Kemp, Bp. of L., rebuilt the pulpit and cross (damaged by a 'tempest of lightning' in 1302) in a more splendid style. In 1469 there was read at the Cross a papal bull pronouncing a curse upon shoemakers who made their shoes with peaks of more than 2 in. These shoes (specimens can be seen in the L.Mus.) made kneeling for prayer a difficulty and so, in medieval art, the devil is usually so shod. In 1483 Dr. Shaw preached, advocating the claims to the throne of Richd. D. of Gloucester, an event referred to in the play of *Richard III* and Sir Thos. More's history of that monarch. Richd. came from Baynard's Castle (*q.v.*), and proposed to arrive just at the moment when his mouthpiece was casting doubts upon the legitimacy of the young ps., the children of Edward IV. There was, however, delay, perhaps traffic congestion even then in the City, and when the K. came the psychological moment had passed, and the hoped-for acclamation was not forthcoming.

The Reformation brought the 'drum

ecclesiastic' to a loud beating. In 1521 John Fisher, Bp. of Rochester, preached against Martin Luther by command of Pope Leo X. Cardinal Wolsey was present, and four doctors of divinity held a cloth of gold over his head. (The occasion has been the subject of a picture by J. Seymour Lucas.) In 1530 Wolsey was there also, when three copies of Tyndale's version of the New Testament were burnt. Bp. Fisher again preached. In 1533 Henry VIII ordered that all who preached at Paul's Cross should deny the supremacy of the Pope. In 1534 'Remembrances' were sent by 'Thomas Crumwell' for the Council to the Bp. of L. to order the preachers not to pray for the Pope at the cross, and also to the Ld.M. and nobles they should commonly assert that the Pope is only the Bp. of Rome. In 1534 Elizabeth Barton, 'the Holy Maid of Kent,' and her associates did penance before execution at Tyburn for her 'revelations' against Henry VIII's divorce. Her indiscretion helped to bring Sir Thos. More to the block. In 1538 Latimer preached there, and in the same yr. the Bp. of Rochester exposed the machinery of the Rood of Grace from Boxley Abbey in Kent before it was broken in pieces. It had been ingeniously constructed so that the figure seemed to nod and open and shut its eyes. In 1548, with Edward VI on the throne, Latimer preached there his famous *Sermon on the Ploughers*. In 1549 the maypole was taken from the ch. of St. Andrew Undershaft (see 'City Churches; C') as the result of a sermon preached there by the parson of St. Katharine Cree Ch. Here, in 1552, Ridley, Bp. of L., proclaimed before the Ld.M. the value of the new Book of Common Prayer used for the first time that day. In 1554 the swing of the pendulum in favour of Roman Catholicism revealed itself at Paul's Cross. Dr. Pendleton preached, and exhibited a cat made to resemble a priest with a wafer, which had been taken from a gallows in Cheapside, and a gun was fired at him as he denounced the blasphemy.

In 1601 the preacher was ordered to decry the E. of Essex as a hypocrite and a papist, and as one in league with the Pope and the K. of Spain. A few weeks after the accession of James I in 1603, a Mr. Hemmings of Trinity Coll., preached,

and was 'very severe on women'. Some of this severity appears to have been justified when, in 1617, Lady Markham appeared at the cross clad in a white sheet for marrying one of her servants in her husband's lifetime. She was also fined £1,000.

A diptych in the possession of the Soc. of Antiquaries somewhat crudely depicts a service at Paul's Cross, at which Dr. King, Bp. of L. is preaching. The occasion represented was the visit of James I in 1620 for the purpose of inaugurating the repair of the cath. Dr. Sparrow Simpson thought it was executed so early as 1616, at the instigation of Henry Farley, in anticipation of a royal visit which was long delayed. The pulpit appears as an octagonal structure, surmounted by a large and elegant cross. It is surrounded by a brick wall, made in 1595. An hour glass stands at the preacher's right hand. James I is sitting in a projecting bay of an upper gallery, evidently erected for the occasion. Below sit the Ld.M., aldermen and judges. The audience sit closely packed on forms; horses are being led away, and a dog whipped—presumably to keep it quiet. Pigeons fly in excellent formation round the tower. They can be associated with the cath. earlier than this. The Chronicle of the Grey Friars says that in 1550 'one man fell down in Powles church and brake his neck for kecheynge of pegyns.' In 1643 Paul's Cross was taken down by order of the Long Parliament. Its foundations were discovered by F. C. Penrose, the Cath. surveyor, in 1879 where there are now stones octagonally arranged at the E. end of the chyd. In 1910, under the will of Mr. H. C. Richards, M.P., a beautiful cross, in the Italian Renaissance style, was erected a few yds. away. It is surmounted by a statue of St. Paul. Strangely it has never been used for preaching.

At the extreme E. end of the cath. was the Bell Tower. It had a spire of wood, covered with lead. The bell in Saxon times had called the citizens of L. to the folkmoot held there. On the summit was a figure of St. Paul. This is clearly shown in the graffito of the medieval cath. scratched on the wall of Ashwell Ch. (Herts.) reproduced in earlier editions of this book. The rose window is also shown. On the walls of the same ch. there are inscriptions relating to the Black Death of 1349. Probably these were the work of one man—a visitor to L. drawing upon his recollection of its most famous bdg. The bells, four in number according to Dugdale, were won by Sir Miles Partridge from Henry VIII by one cast of the dice, and then removed by the winner. (Sir Miles was hanged on Tower Hill in 1552.) The two western towers of the cath. were used as prisons, and the SW. one was the real Lollards' Tower (see 'Lambeth Palace'). Foxe's *Acts and Monuments*—familiarly known as the Book of Martyrs—includes a woodcut which purports to represent its interior. Apparently it contained stocks. The palace of the Bp. of L. was on the NW. this volume. The rose window is also shown. On the walls of the same ch. there are inscriptions relating to the Black Death of 1349. Probably these were the work of one man—a visitor to L. drawing upon his recollection of its most famous bdg. The bells, four in number according to Dugdale, were won by Sir Miles Partridge from Henry VIII by one cast of the dice, and then removed by the winner. (Sir Miles was hanged on Tower Hill in 1552.) The two western towers of the cath. were used as prisons, and the SW. one was the real Lollards' Tower (see 'Lambeth Palace'). Foxe's *Acts and Monuments*—familiarly known as the Book of Martyrs—includes a woodcut which purports to represent its interior. Apparently it contained stocks. The palace of the Bp. of L. was on the NW. side of the cath. The hall was a gloomy prison-like apartment, scantily furnished, and was used for the incarceration of 'malignants,' as the royalists were called by the parliamentary forces in the Civil War. L. House Yard commemorates its position.

Size and Staff. The total length was 585 ft. Breadth, including aisles, 104 ft. Height of nave interior, 93 ft. Height of choir interior, 101½ ft. Height of Lady Chapel interior, 98½ ft. Height of tower, 285 ft. Height of spire, 208 ft. The staff at one time consisted of the dean, 4 archdeacons, treasurer, precentor, chancellor, 30 greater canons, 12 minor canons, 50 chaplains or chantry priests, and 30 vicars, in addition to boy choristers. There were also bedesmen and various poor folk to ration, and in 1286 there were brewed 67,894 gallons of beer; there were also required 175 quarters

of barley, the same amount of wheat, and 720 quarters of oats. Paul's Bakehouse Court, now gone, marked the site of the ovens. In the early part of the 14th century there were no fewer than 111 obits annually celebrated at St. P.'s Cath.

There was a Lady Chapel with the altar of the Blessed Virgin. There were also chapels of St. Dunstan (endowed by the Grocers' Co.—he was their patron saint), St. George, the Holy Ghost, the Holy Trinity, St. James, St. John the Baptist, St. Margaret, St. Paul; there was also Bp. Kemp's chantry; and (in the crypt) Jesus Chapel, and chapels of St. Anne, St. Radegund, and St. Sebastian.

Tombs. The principal were: St. Erkenwald (d. 693); he was the Bp. of L. sometimes associated with the building of Bishopsgate. Eustace de Fauconbridge (d. 1228); he became Bp. of L. in 1221. Sir John Beauchamp (d. 1360); he was Admiral of the Fleet, Constable of T.L., and Ld. Warden of the Cinque Ports. John of Gaunt, 'time-honoured Lancaster' (d. 1399). Robert Braybroke (d. 1404). He was made Bp. of L. by papal bull in 1380, and his term of office was marked by endeavours to stop the profane uses of the cath. His monument was in the Lady Chapel; there was an effigy, fully equipped with vestments and crosier, lying under a canopy. It was referred to by Pepys after the G.F., Nov. 12 1666:

'He fell down in his tomb out of the great church into St. Fayth's this late fire, and is here seen, his skeleton with the flesh on, but all tough and dry like a spongy dry leather or touchwood all upon his bones. His head turned aside. A great man in his time and Lord Chancellor and now exposed to be handled and derided by some though admired for its duration by others.'

Dean Colet (d. 1519). (See 'Schools.') Sir Philip Sidney (d. 1586). As there was a funeral train of 700 mourners, including the Ld.M., the City trained bands, and representatives from the seven united provinces of the Netherlands, it is surprising that he had no better memorial than a tablet of wood. Sir Christopher Hatton (d. 1591) had a sumptuous tomb; Stow says that its proximity to those of Sidney and Walsingham elicited from a 'merry poet' the lines:

'Philip and Francis have no tombe,
For great Christopher takes all the roome.'

John Donne (d. 1631). This was the only one to escape the G.F. in its entirety. It now stands in the S. choir aisle. The famous dean (still celebrated for prose and poetry) is shown in a shroud with his feet resting on an urn. The strange flight of fancy which dictated the form of this memorial is explained in a passage from Walton's biography of his friend:

'A monument being resolved upon, Dr. Donne sent for a Carver to make for him in wood a figure of an Urn, giving him directions for the compass and height of it; and to bring with it a board of the just height of his body. These being got, then without delay a choice Painter was got to be in readiness to draw his picture, which was taken as followeth.—Several charcoal fires being first made in his large study, he brought with him into that place his winding-sheet in his hand, and having put off all his clothes, had this sheet put on him, and so tied with knots at his head and feet and his hands so placed as dead bodies are usually fitted, to be shrowded or put into their coffin, or grave. Upon this Urn he thus stood, with his eyes shut, and with so much of the sheet turned aside as might show his lean, pale and death-like face, which was purposely turned towards the East, from whence he expected the second coming of our Saviour Jesus. In this posture he was drawn at his just height; and when the picture was fully finished, he caused it to be set up by his bedside, where it continued and became his hourly object till his death, and was then given to his dearest friend and executor Dr. Henry King, then chief Residentiary of St. Paul's, who caused him to be thus carved in one entire piece of white marble, as it now stands in that Church.'

It was the work of Nicholas Stone, and his price was £120. Walton was enthusiastic about the work, speaking of it as 'as lively a representation as marble can express.' Sir Henry Wotton, he reported, thought that it 'seems to breathe faintly and posterity shall look upon it as an artificial miracle.' The Latin epitaph was also desired by Donne.

Desecration of the Cathedral. By this time all the Cath.'s relics had disappeared under the Protestant Reformation. These included 'a piece of the true cross, stones from the Holy Sepulchre, and the Mount of Ascension; some hair of Mary Magdalene; some blood of St. Paul; a bone of St. Lawrence; a tooth of St Vincent. The circular tonsure plate—a piece of copper 3 in. in diameter—is still preserved in the B.Mus. On the concave side is engraved a somewhat attenuated lion rampant.

Despite the presence of tombs, shrines and holy relics, impregnating the fane with the odour of departed sanctity, as it was literally pervaded by the use of incense, the cath., to the modern mind would seem to have been given up to the world and the flesh—if not the devil. In Paul's Cross was not the Hyde Park of the Middle Ages, St. P.'s Cath. was its equivalent. As with the chs. now, human gregariousness, more than divine worship, made it a bait to draw some odd fish. It cannot be said, however, that everything profane was illicit. The carved foot of Algar, first prebendary of Islington, rested at the base of a pillar, and became the standard measure, cited in deeds of contract in land. Moreover from 1275 to the time of Q. Elizabeth it was the custom for the canons, attired in their vestments, and adorned with chaplets of flowers, solemnly to receive at the chancel steps the offering of a buck and its doe as the equivalent of a rent for 22 acres in Essex. The buck's horns were then carried round the cath. on the point of a spear to the accompaniment of a great noise from horn-blowers. This so shocked a later writer that he called it 'a weil-nigh incredible story.'

Then there was the extraordinary ceremony of the 'Boy Bishop', suggesting in its childishness the Victorian game of playing chapels. On Holy Innocents Day the boy even preached a sermon. In 1263 rules were drawn up for the regulation of the function, and Dean Colet, when he founded St. Paul's Sch., expressly ordered that all the scholars should attend the sermon 'with the maisters and surveyors of the scole,' and that each scholar should offer a penny to the juvenile prelate. Some of the sermons—no doubt composed by elders—were published. Cranmer forbade the proceedings; Q. Mary restored them; they were finally abolished by Q.

Elizabeth. In 1569 the first State lottery was drawn at the W. door of St. P.'s Cath. There were 40,000 lots at 10s. each; the prizes were plate, and the proceeds were to be applied towards repairing the havens of the kingdom. In 1586, for a similar purpose, Stow says, 'a house of timber and board' was erected.

It is impossible to say when this desecration of the cath. began. Bp. Braybroke referred to those who—

'expose their wares as it were in a public market, buy and sell without reverence for the holy place. Others too by the instigation of the Devil do not scruple with stones and arrows to bring down birds, pigeons and jackdaws which nestle in the walls and crevices of the building; others play at ball and at other unseemly games, both within and without the church, breaking the beautiful and costly painted windows to the amazement of the spectators.'

The bp. threatened further offenders with excommunication. In 1411 a proclamation was made against wrestling within the sanctuary, the penalty being a fine and forty days' imprisonment. These secular encroachments were not restricted to recreation. In 1487 there is a reference to a receipt for forty mares paid in the ch. 'at le Rode [rood] by the north door.' In 1530 a deed of settlement concludes:

'for which marriage the earl of Shrewsbury is to pay £200 on the day of St. Nicholas next at the font in St. Paul's Cathedral, London.'

Shakespeare, Dekker, and Ben Jonson amongst writers, and Bps. Bancroft, Corbet, and Earle amongst ecclesiastics, testified to the desecration. The dinnerless Elizabethan announced, not that he would dine on air pie, but with D. Humphrey. (The tomb of Sir John Beauchamp was mistakenly referred to as that of the 'good' d., whose tomb is at St. Albans Abbey.) The phrase is found so late as Dickens's *Martin Chuzzlewit* (Chap. I). In June 1561, a not uncommon vagary of an English summer brought a thunderstorm, and the lightning struck the steeple of the cath., which was of wood, covered with lead. For four hours the fire burned; the bells were melted, and the stones fell. The lead, wrapt in flames, fell down and the fire ran along the nave and transepts, causing the roof to fall in. This was naturally regarded by some Jeremiahs as a judgment from Heaven. Pilkington, Bp. of Durham, prophesied worse things than smoking ruins if more righteous men were not found in Sodom. He referred to 'the south alley [aisle] for popery and usury and the north for simony, and the horse fair in the midst for all kinds of bargains, meetings, brawlings, murders, conspiracies, and the font for ordinary payments of money.'

Steeple. It is very surprising that the spire of the cath. was never rebuilt. It was probably hoped that some City magnate would provide funds by gift or bequest. In Catholic times such an oblation would have been held to purchase eternal felicity but, as Prof. Tawney has shown, Protestantism was more plutocratic in its passions. The old steeple, higher than Salisbury's is now, was L.'s great landmark and a wonder of the medieval world. In the first English comedy, *Ralph Roister Doister*, Truepenny says:

'Yet I look as far beyond the people
As one may see out of the toppe of Paul's steeple.'

In 1547, on the occasion of Edward VI's procession, from T.L. to Westminster, a man came down a rope from the battlements of the steeple, 'as if he had been an arrow out of a bow,' and then kissed his majesty. Bankes, a vintner in Cheapside, had a horse which danced in silver shoes, and in 1600 it climbed to the top of the tower of St. P.'s Cath. to the delight, said Dekker, 'of a number of asses who brayed below.' There is an allusion to the horse in *Love's Labour Lost* (Act 1, Sc. ii). In 1630 Sir Thos. Gardiner, Recorder of L., in a petition to Charles I, said:

'My youngest daughter . . . without my consent or knowledge, shee mounted upp to Topp of Powles, the nearer to Heaven, for to shewe God there howe wise she was in her Actions, and there she was married unto Sir Henry Maynewaringe, and yet she was not there taken up into heaven, but came down again upon Earth, here further to trouble mee before . . . although the greate Care and Charge I had in breeding her upp did not deserve such disbedience.'

Seventeenth-century Restoration. The extraordinary indifference to the religious aspect of the cath. was happily not equalled by entire unconcern for its material welfare. As a result of Dr. King's sermon before James I, his 'princely heart was moved with such compassion to this decayed fabric,' that a royal commission was appointed to carry out repairs. Amongst its members were Bacon and Inigo Jones. This commission moved, as have others, at the snail's pace of Shakespeare's schoolboy, and on the death of James I (1625), matters had come to a standstill. Laud persuaded Charles I to appoint a new one. A handsome sum was then collected, the most munificent contributor being Sir Paul Pindar (see 'City Churches; C'—St. Botolph, Bishopsgate). He is said to have spent more than £4,000. The exterior of the nave and W. side of the two transepts were cased throughout, and some repairs executed at the E. end. Inside the choir screen was repaired and adorned. Inigo Jones (c. 1637) erected a classical portico at the W. end, statues of James I and Charles I being prominently displayed on its roof. In 1643 Inigo Jones ceased to act as surveyor, and in the period of the Civil War 'horses stamped in the Canons' stalls,' as Carlyle said; whilst Hugh Peters and other Puritan divines declaimed in the crypt and side chapels. The money collected for the repairs was seized by the Parliament, and mean shops were erected in Inigo Jones's portico. The tombs were used as tables for idle amusements, and the game of nine-pins was played in the cath. Puritan profanation, however, hardly exceeded what had gone before, and Dryden's lines had a more general application than he conceived when he wrote of the G.F. of 1666:

'The daring flames peeped in, and saw from far
The awful beauties of the sacred quire:
But, since it was profaned by civil war,
Heaven thought it fit to have it purged by fire.'

At that time repairs had been recommenced, some £3,600 having been spent in three yrs. A few days before the fire broke out John Evelyn and (Sir) Christopher Wren, both members of the new commission, had been inspecting the cath. Evelyn reported that:

'We had in mind to build it with a noble cupola, a form of church building not at the time known in England but of wonderful grace.'

The Great Fire. Evelyn's *Diary* affords a terse and vivid account of what the G.F. wrought:

'I was infinitely concerned to find that goodly church, St. Paul's now a sad ruin and that beautiful portico (for structure comparable to any in Europe . . .) now rent in pieces, flakes of large stone split asunder and nothing remaining entire but the inscription in the architrave showing by whom it was built, which had not one letter of it defaced. It was astonishing to see what immense stones the heat had in a moment calcined, so that all the ornaments, columns, friezes, capitals and projections of massy Portland stone flew off even to the very roof, where a sheet of lead covering a great space (no less than 6 acres by measure) was totally melted.'

Wren's Cathedral. The cath. was not entirely destroyed (some 200 ft. of the tower remained), and restoration was at first considered. This project was abandoned, and in 1668, by royal warrant to the commissioners, clearing and excavation began. A committee of eight was appointed, in addition to the Dean and Chapter; a record of the proceedings of both the pre- and the post-Fire Commissions may be seen in Guildhall Library. In the same yr. Wren produced his first design. It was in the form of a Greek cross, and Corinthian pillars—Wren's favourite— predominated. The architect had to make modifications, and it was not until 1675, the site having been cleared the previous yr., that Charles II issued his warrant to the commissioners approving of the second design because it was 'very artificial, proper and useful.' Wren did not entirely adhere to this plan. In drawings now preserved at All Souls' Coll., Oxford, there is, surmounting the dome, a spire resembling that of St. Bride's Ch. There were to have been two clocks on the W. front; the blank space for one remains. The two chapels at the W. end are said to have been introduced at the request of James, D. of York, who anticipated restoration of Roman Catholicism.

The first stone was laid on 21st June, 1675 at the SE. corner of the choir. By 1685 the walls of the choir were finished, with the N. and S. portico, and the piers of the dome placed in position to the same height. When fixing the centre of the dome, Wren ordered a labourer to find a stone as a mark. He brought a broken fragment of an old gravestone on which was inscribed the Latin word *Resurgam.* From Thos. Fuller's *History of the Worthies of England* (1662) it appears that this was the epitaph of Dr. John King, who d. in 1621. Hence the carving of the Phoenix—the symbol of resurrection over the south portico. It was the work of Caius Gabriel Cibber. In 1697 the choir was ready, and a special service was held there to mark the Treaty of Ryswick. William III was not present, but civic representatives attended in full state to hear a sermon by Compton, Bp. of L. A monogram of William and Mary, encircled by a wreath, is underneath the centre window of the apse in the chyd. Early in 1699 the NW. chapel was opened for daily morning service, the nave not being completed. Not until 1710 was the dome completed. Wren was 78, and did not hazard the ascent. His son Christopher placed the last stone on the summit of the lantern. To commemorate the sovereign in whose reign the bdg. was completed there was placed at the W. end a statue of Q. Anne by Francis Bird (see 'Statues'). Bird was also responsible for the sculptured representation of the conversion of St. Paul in the pediment of the W. front. The statues of St. Paul and the four evangelists are not in the round. St. Peter is accompanied by a cock.

Cost and Dimensions. The cost of the new cath. was about £850,000, and was defrayed by a duty on sea-borne coal of 1s. 6d. per chaldron, and subscriptions. It is 513 ft. in length; 123 ft. in breadth in the nave, and 179 ft. at the W. front with the chapels. The height is: 182 ft. to the stone gallery; 281 ft. to the upper gallery at the summit of the dome; 365 ft. to the summit of the cross.

Wren's Memorials. In 1718, in his eighty-sixth yr., Wren was supplanted by Benson, who was responsible for a flight of steps at the W. front, which have now disappeared. Wren annually visited the cath. to sit even in decrepitude, beholding the consummation of his conception; no doubt, despite all his disappointments, he thought it was good. He was the first to be bd. in the new cath (1723). His grave is a plain black marble slab in the crypt. On the wall is the original of the famous inscription: 'Lector, si monumentum requiris, circumspice' (Reader, if you seek his monument, look around you). His second wife, Jane Coghill, his daughter Jane, and other relatives also lie here. In 1924 a tablet to the memory of Wren was unveiled in the gallery over the N. aisle, where Wren's own model and the original design are preserved. It was an American tribute, taking the form of a bronze plaque displaying the golden-rod, the American national emblem, and oak leaves entwined. The inscription reads:

'In recognition of the inspiration and enduring influence on American architecture of the work of Sir Christopher Wren this tablet is inscribed by the Architectural League of New York.'

Wren was assisted by Tijou, a French-man who was a skilled craftsman in iron, and by the magnificent carving of Grinling Gibbons, particularly manifest in the organ case and choir stalls. There are thirty-one of the latter; some are additions by F. C. Penrose, the cath. surveyor. Each has the name of the prebend attached, and on fifteen on either side Latin inscriptions of the headings of the Psalter divided into thirty parts in accordance with a medieval provision for the whole of the latter being recited monthly. Some of the prebends have L. names, e.g. Islington, Hoxton, St. Pancras; whilst one, Consumpta per Mare, indicates an estate of long ago swallowed up by the sea, probably in Suffolk. The cath. chapter still draws a small income from one prebendal estate— Tillingham in Essex. This is probably the oldest ecclesiastical estate in England. It is believed to date from the seventh century. The gates, both at the W. end of the aisles and in the doorways of the reredos arch, are part of Tijou's work, restored and replaced as occasion arose. The marble pulpit is modern (1879).

Chapels. The apse now forms a separate chapel, and is called the Jesus Chapel. Here is a monument of Canon Liddon. The chapel at the SW. is now dedicated to the Order of St. Michael and St. George, instituted in 1818 to honour men distinguished in colonial affairs. It has a beautiful oak screen. Here is a statuette of Rev. H. H. Montgomery, Bp. of Tasmania, and father of Field-Marshal Viscount Montgomery. The NW. chapel, corresponding to this, is St. Dunstan's. Here, at the E. end, are the first mosaics done by Richmond in the cath. These led to his being given the work of decorating the choir and aisles. Opposite, at the W. end, is another mosaic by Salviati, portraying the Holy Women at the Sepulchre, given in memory of Archdeacon Hale. There is a window to Dean Mansel; and a chandelier, dated 1778, formerly in the ch. of St. Mildred, Poultry. Next to this chapel is All Souls' Chapel, where is the Kitchener memorial.

Interior Decoration was first carried out between 1715 and 1721. Sir Jas. Thornhill painted the lower dome with eight scenes in the life of St. Paul. In 1773 Sir Joshua Reynolds and others put forward a suggestion for further decoration, but the project was opposed, possibly as savouring of Romanism.

In 1861 came the first stained glass window. In 1864 the mosaics under the dome were commenced. G. F. Watts was responsible for St. Matthew and St. John; A. Brittan for St. Mark—modelled from John Burns—and St. Luke; Alfred Stevens for Isaiah, Jeremiah, Daniel, and Elijah. In 1888 the new reredos was unveiled. There was further wall painting—in sanctuary, choir aisles, and quarter domes—completed by 1896. Three famous pictures are exhibited: 'The Light of the World,' by Holman Hunt, an enlarged replica of that at Keble Coll., Oxford; 'Time, Death and Judgment' and 'Peace and Goodwill,' by G. F. Watts.

In 1837 the nave and choir were opened freely for public inspection. Canon Sydney Smith, surprisingly for such a radical, anticipated dire results from the rabble of L. Happily his gloomy predictions were not fulfilled. In 1858 the old arrangements were altered by the removal of the choir screen with a view to attracting larger audiences on Sunday.

Monuments. There was none until John Howard's was erected at the entrance to the choir in 1795. It was the work of John Bacon, R.A. Howard's fine zeal for prison reform is indicated by his being shown on the pedestal trampling on fetters and relieving prisoners. The long epitaph says:

'In every part of the civilised world which he traversed to reduce the sum of human misery, from the throne to the dungeon, his name was mentioned with respect, gratitude and admiration.' This is the monument that Lamb wanted to spit upon. He unhappily got into his head the idea that solitary confinement for 'blue-coat boys' was a 'sprout of Holy Howard's brain.' Howard advocated it for prisoners as an advance on the herding together in a small compartment of men in a state of filth and degradation. Bacon was also responsible for the next statue—that of Dr. Johnson (1796). Strangely the date of Johnson's funeral is given as 13th Jan. 1785 when it was on 20th Dec. 1784. Johnson is in classical costume, and his sturdy limbs, so nakedly displayed, have suggested that he was represented as a retired gladiator meditating upon a wasted life, or as going down to bathe at Brighhelmstone—our Brighton. Oliver Wendell Holmes wrote:

'Poor Dr. Johnson, sitting in semi-nude exposure, looked to me as unhappy as our own half naked Washington at the national capital. The Judas of Matthew Arnold's poem would have cast his cloak over those marble shoulders, if he had found himself in St. Paul's and earned another respite.'

The third was Flaxman's—of Sir Joshua Reynolds. He is shown draped in the robes of a Doctor of Law; in his right hand are his discourses to the Royal Academy; beneath the left hand is a medallion of his master, Michelangelo. A later imposing monument to an artist is Ld. Leighton's.

The largest is to the D. of Wellington. This was the work of Alfred Stevens (1858). The horse was not hoisted to the top until 1912, there having been much discussion as to the propriety of admitting the figure of an animal into a sacred bdg. The other principal monuments are Sir John Moore; Sir Ralph Abercrombie; Vice-Admiral Ld. Collingwood; Ld. Nelson; Viscount Melbourne; Major-General Gordon; Ld. Roberts, Dean Milman (his *Annals of St. Paul's Cathedral*, published in 1869, the yr. after his death is a fascinating and informing account of the Cath.'s history); Bp. Creighton; Abp. Temple; Ld. Roberts. The most original monument is Viscount Melbourne's. It is a representation of the gate of death in black marble, with angels in white marble. It was designed by Marochetti. Melbourne, Q. Victoria's first prime minister, was bd. at Hatfield.

In 1820 a new ball and cross, designed

by C. R. Cockerell, the Cath. surveyor, replaced the old one, erected in 1708. According to *Real Life in London* (1821):
'The intrepid aeronauts cheered the admiring multitude far beneath and, seated in the clouds like the deities of Mount Olympus, drank to the prosperity of their friends in the nether region.'
On completion a small luncheon party was held in the new ball. In 1874 the railings were removed from the W. front. Some of them found their way to Toronto (see *Walks in London*, by Wm. Kent). Their course is now marked by a row of granite posts.

Crypt. In the crypt the memorials are less conventional, and sometimes unexpected. At the E. end is the Chapel of St. Christopher—a compliment to the architect—with a tablet recording thirty-five distinguished burials in the pre-Fire bdg. Those of most interest are the following: Sebba, K. of the East Saxons, 677; Ethelbert, K. of the English, 1016; Henry de Lacy, E. of Lincoln, 1311 (see 'Lincoln's Inn'); Hamo de Chigwelle (six times Ld.M.), 1328; Sir John Poultney (four times Ld.M.), 14th century; John of Gaunt, D. of Lancaster, 14th century; Walter de Sheryngton, 15th century (see *supra*); Wm. Lily, first master of St. P.'s Sch., 1522; Thos. Linacre, founder of Coll. of Physicians (*q.v.*), 1524; Nicholas Bacon, Ld. Keeper of the Great Seal and father of the essayist, 1579; Sir Philip Sidney, 1586; Sir Francis Walsingham (see *supra*), 1590; Sir Christopher Hatton (see *supra*), 1591; Sir Anthony Van Dyck, 1641. The mutilated figure of Bacon is still preserved in the chapel of St. Faith, together with the figures also damaged, of Brian Walton, Thos. Heneage and wife, Wm. Hewitt, Wm. Cockayne, and John Wolley and his wife. The figure of Wolley's wife at the W. end of the chapel is but little damaged. There is also a fine marble wall-tablet, bearing a bust, in memory of Van Dyck.

There is one monument recording the death in 1680 of a person long lost to fame—John Martin. It represents him and his wife on their knees, facing each other, over a pile of nine various-sized books, while each is perusing an open book; below are two children in swaddling-clothes.
Apart from Sir Christopher Wren, whose

grave has already been mentioned, a number of other architects are bd. in the crypt: Robt. Mylne, architectural superintendent of the cath. from 1762 to 1811. His 'magnificent bridge'—Blackfriars—is referred to on the epitaph. Geo. Dance the younger (1741–1825). F. C. Penrose (1817–1903). He was for forty-five yrs. surveyor of the cath., 'architect, antiquary and astronomer.' There is a memorial to Sir Edwin Lutyens, bd. elsewhere. It shows the Cenotaph. Musicians whose graves are in the crypt are Sir Arthur Sullivan, (d. 1900), and Sir Chas. Parry (d. 1918). Amongst sculptors is Sir Edwin Landseer, also an artist (there is a slab on the floor, and a wall-tablet—showing a coffin partly covered by a pall and a dog). There are memorials of Sir Hamo Thornycroft (1850–1925); Sir Geo. Frampton (1860–1928); and Sir Alfred Gilbert (1854–1934). These show Peter Pan and Eros. They were bd. elsewhere. Artists are well represented. There is a slab marking the place of interment of Sir Joshua Reynolds. A contemporary of his to whom there is a monument is Jas. Barry, 1741–1806 (see 'Society of Arts'). The epitaph on the latter refers to his 'strong native powers of mind added to intellectual riches (the only riches he ever heeded or possessed).' The artist-poet, Wm. Blake, is represented by a medallion on a wall-tablet inscribed with the famous lines:

'To see a World in a grain of sand,
    And a Heaven in a wild flower,
Hold Infinity in the palm of your hand,
    And Eternity in an hour.'

It was the work of Henry Poole in 1927. There are also tablets to John Constable (bd. at Hampstead, 1837), and Wilson Steer (bd. elsewhere 1942). Geo. Cruikshank was first bd. in Kensal Green Cemetery, and in the same yr. removed here. The inscription is remarkable for precision. It informs the reader that he was b. at
'No.   Duke Street, St. George's, Bloomsbury, London on Sept. 27, 1792. Died at 263 Hampstead Road on Feb. 1, 1878, aged 86 years.'
There are some memorial lines by his wife dated 9th Feb. 1880.
There is a mural tablet to Holman Hunt, and slabs on the floor to Turner, to Sir John Millais, and to Baron Leighton. Sir John Goss, 34 yrs. organist to

the cath., is commemorated by a mural tablet bearing as epitaph the opening bars of the anthem he composed for the D. of Wellington's funeral. A few literary men are represented, all bd. elsewhere. There is a tablet to the Rev. R. H. Barham, author of the *Ingoldsby Legends*: '18 years rector of the united parishes of St. Gregory's and St. Mary Magdalene's, and later of St. Augustine's and St. Faith's.'

There are mural tablets to Ld. Lytton, novelist and poet; Chas. Reade, novelist; and Sir Walter Besant. The last is rightly described as 'Historian of London.' The medallion was the work of Sir Geo. Frampton. There are busts of W. E. Henley, by Rodin, and Geo. Washington, and close to the latter a tablet and wings commemorating the first American airman to die in the Second World War. There is a tablet to Geo. Smith, the publisher, founder, and proprietor of the *Dictionary of National Biography*. There is also a mural tablet to Sir W. H. Russell (1820–1907) described in the epitaph as 'the greatest of war correspondents.' The tablet to Florence Nightingale (bd. elsewhere) shows her with a wounded soldier. There is a memorial to Chas. Booth, sociologist; and a bust near the grave of Sir Geo. Williams who founded the Y.M.C.A. in St. P.'s Chyd. A remarkably fine brass shows Ld.M. Geo. Swan Nottage in full mayoral robes. He d. in 1885 during his yr. of office and thus was entitled to burial in the cath. Amongst the many inscriptions to soldiers the most sensational is Sir Henry Wilson's— 'Murdered outside his home, 36 Eaton Place, June 22nd, 1922.' In the SE. of the crypt is an inscription indicating that the ch. of St. Faith is E. thereof. There are huge tombs of Nelson and Wellington, and the funeral car of the latter, which weighed 18 tons, is at the W. end. Recent memorials are to E. Jellicoe; Lawrence of Arabia; Rev. Wilson Carlile, founder of the Church Army; and Baron Keyes (1872–1945); he was 'Chief of Combined Operations,' also his son Col. Geoffrey Keyes. There is a tablet in memory of 173 men and women of all nations who were in the Air Transport Auxiliary. There is also a model of the pre-Fire cath.

Other interesting features of the Cath. are the huge font—the work of Bird (1720); the Whispering Gallery, the library, and the small spiral staircase at the SW. corner of the nave.

Twentieth Century Restoration. The foundations of St. P.'s Cath are only 4½ ft. below the level of the floor of the crypt, and Canon Alexander said the security of the eight pillars had 'been struggling to hold up like giants the enormous weight of the dome above them.' They became affected by the impingement of sewers and railways, and the increasing vibration of modern traffic. In 1913, therefore, some work was undertaken, but discontinued by reason of the First World War. In 1925 a commission reported, and advocated grouting (i.e. pumping in liquid cement at a high pressure, to fill up the interstices between the rubble) in preference to the more expensive alternative of reconstructing the piers entirely. This was closely followed by a bombshell in the form of a 'dangerous structure' notice served upon the Dean and Chapter.

Considerable sensation was caused by a report on the instability of the bdg. and the eastern part of the cath. was closed for five yrs. while the necessary work to save the dome from collapse was carried out. A national fund provided about £250,000 for the purpose. Canon Alexander recalled how in 1913 a letter came from New South Wales, telling him that the dying wish of a little girl had been that her father would send 5s. to the Cath. It had evidently become in her mind the focal centre of L. life, and therefore of the home country.

In 1933 there was an exhibition in commemoration of the tercentenary of Sir Christopher Wren's birth. There were displayed portraits, busts, statuettes, models, and plans of the great architect; and other relics relating to him. A recent discovery was an advertisement found in 1928 during the restoration work in the hip timbers. It announced that—

'a dwarf 2' 8" in height and aged 49, the mother of two children, sings and dances incomparably. She is carried in a box to any gentleman's house for what they may be pleased to give her.' This lady was to be seen in L. in 1700, and it looks as if some workmen had accidentally left the bill there.

Deanery. A deanery was first erected by Ralph de Diceto in 1182. Little is heard of its history, but it is known to have been used for Royalist prisoners during the Commonwealth. It was completely rebuilt much earlier than the cath., viz. in 1670, Bancroft being the first dean to occupy it. It is a very capacious bdg., in Dean's Court (SW. of the cath.). The front door, which probably was carved by Grinling Gibbons, opens on to a hall large enough for diocesan meetings.

Chapter House (*c.* 1712). Ruined in the bombing, this has been rebuilt and is on the N. side of the cath., a plain red-brick bdg. It has served many purposes. At one time it was the meeting-place of the Convocation of Canterbury. Later it was let to a bank and the City Livery Club.

Amen Court is the residence of some of the canons. At No. 1 Canon Alexander, who did so much for the restoration of the cath., d. in Jan, 1949, after forty yrs.' residence there. Next door there had resided, more than a hundred yrs. before., Canon Sydney Smith and Rev. R. H. Barham, author of *The Ingoldsby Legends*. In Amen Court is a piece of the old City wall. St. P.'s Cath. was beset by German bombs but it survived almost intact. Truly did a writer in *The Times* say, in reference to the awful Sunday night of 29th Dec. 1940:

'No one will ever forget their emotions on the night when London was burning, and the dome seemed to ride the sea of fire like a great ship, lifting above smoke and flame the inviolate ensign of the golden cross.'

On 12th Sept. 1940 a heavy delayed-action bomb buried itself 27 ft. in the ground near the SW. tower. It made a crater 100 ft. wide. On 10th Oct., 1940, a bomb penetrated the roof of the choir and destroyed the modern high altar. On 16th Apr. 1941, a bomb fell on the N. transept, pierced the saucer dome, and exploded inside the cath. Almost all the stained glass was destroyed, as also the portico inside the N. door, on which was inscribed Wren's famous epitaph.

At the E. end of the Cath., there is an American Memorial Chapel, with a marble lectern bearing a book, in which are inscribed the names of the 28,000 American soldiers and airmen who lost their lives whilst serving in Gt. Britain or in operations based on this island.

(See *Annals of St. Paul's Cathedral* by Dean Milman, 1869; *The Three Cathedrals Dedicated to St. Paul in London* by Wm.

Longman, F.S.A., 1873; *Chapters in the History of Old St. Paul's*, 1881; *Gleanings from Old St. Paul's*, 1889; and *St. Paul's Cathedral and Old City Life*, 1894—by Dr. W. Sparrow Simpson; *St. Paul's Cathedral* by Rev. A. Dimock, 1900; *St. Paul's Cathedral* by Geo. Clinch, 1906; *St. Paul's Cathedral* by Canon Sinclair, 1913; *St. Paul's Cathedral* by S. A. Warner, 1926; *St. Paul's in Wartime* by Dr. W. R. Matthews, 1946.)

Savoy Chapel derives its name from Peter of Savoy, seventh son of Thos., Count of Savoy, who came to England in 1241 and gave his name to the manor which was bestowed on him by Henry III, who had m. his niece, Eleanor of Provence. Land lying between the river and the st. called 'La Straunde,' and extending from the present-day Adelphi to the Temple was conferred upon him in 1246. Peter left his house here on becoming Count of Savoy in 1263: in 1265 it was assigned as a residence for Eleanor of Castile, wife of P. Edwd., afterwards Edward I. In 1272, on the succession of her husband to the throne, she removed to the Palace of Westminster, and in 1276 the Savoy came into possession of Edmund, a young brother of the King's. Edmund's son, Thos., succeeded his father in 1296. He became involved in the wars between certain of the nobles and Piers Gaveston, the favourite of Edward II. He secured the execution of Gaveston, and with the turn of fortune, was himself executed in 1322. After a brief occupancy by Edward II's eldest son, afterwards Edward III, the Savoy came into the hands of Edmund's brother, Henry, E. of Lancaster, in 1326. He d. 1345, and was succeeded by his son Henry, E. of Derby, who was high in favour with Edward III. In 1351 he was created first D. of Lancaster, and the K. extended to his duchy all the powers and privileges of a palatinate. From this time the Savoy became the headquarters of the great Duchy Palatine of Lancaster. The office of the chancery still stands in the precinct near the chapel.

Here in 1351 came John, K. of France, made prisoner by the Black P. at the battle of Poictiers. He was released in 1360, but the vast ransom demanded, 3,000,000 golden crowns, could not be raised amongst his subjects, so he returned to England, was again lodged in the

Savoy, and d. there 1364. D. Henry d.
three yrs. before, and was succeeded by
two daughters. Matilda d. childless,
leaving her sister Blanche, wife of John
of Gaunt, E. of Richmond, sole heiress
to the vast estates of the House of Lancaster, including the manor and palace
of the Savoy.

Chaucer was 'our good friend' to John
of Gaunt, and from the revenues of the
Savoy the latter granted him a pension
of £10 p.a. It is possible that Chaucer
was m. in the chapel of the D.'s palace.
In 1381 the Wat Tyler rebels attacked it,
and practically destroyed the bdgs. John
of Gaunt fled to the Bp. of Ely's palace,
and d. there (see 'Ely Place'). On the
succession of Henry IV in 1399, one of
his first acts was to annex the manor of
the Savoy, with all the estates of the
House of Lancaster, to the Crown; at
the same time declaring them to be a
separate inheritance, distinct from that
of the sovereign. It is under this charter
that the manor of the Savoy has ever
since remained a royal possession. The
National Anthem as sung in the chapel
of the Savoy preserves this distinction.
The first lines run:

'God save our Lord the King,
Long live our noble Duke,
God save our King.'

For 100 yrs. thereafter the manor was
administered by a succession of stewards
and bailiffs. There are records of fines
inflicted for the escape of a prisoner, and
(1401) of the expenditure of 11s. 6d. for the
repair of stocks, ducking stool, and pillory.

Henry VII, who d. 1509, bequeathed
10,000 marks for the restoration of the
ruined palace of the Savoy, and for its
endowment as a hosp. for 100 'pouer,
nedie people,' who were to be visited in
their 'siknesses, refresshed with mete and
drinke, and if nede be with clothe, and
also buried if thei fortune to die.' The
King dedicated his hosp. 'to the honour
of Our Saviour, the Blessed Virgin and
St. John the Baptist.' A little later the
chapel of the Savoy was erected. The
orientation was N. to S., and this suggests
that it stands upon the site of a previous
consecrated bdg. In 1522 Gavin Douglas,
Bp. of Dunkeld, who d. of plague at the
house of his friend, Ld. Dacre, in the par.
of St. Clement Danes, was bd. in the
chapel at his own request. He was a poet

and strangely enough, shared a grave
with another prelate, Thos Halsey, Bp. of
Leighlin in Ireland, also a plague victim.
There is a memorial brass to both prelates in the chancel. The pious intentions
of Henry VII were at one time faithfully
carried out, and it is recorded that so
many as 8,339 poor or sick persons were
relieved in one yr. Mismanagement, however, brought suspicion upon the hosp.,
and in 1553 it was surrendered to Edward
VI. He made over the endowments,
estates, and even the furniture to the new
hosp. at Bridewell (q.v.). The chapel was,
however, allowed to retain a bell, a
chalice, and other accessories for religious
services. Q. Mary refounded the hosp.,
but under Elizabeth it declined again.
The mastership, nevertheless, was much
in request, for holders of the office
trafficked in the apartments of the Savoy
with the various nobles, whose mansions
lined the Strand. From 1547, when the
D. of Somerset demolished the ch. of
St. Mary (see 'Strand'), the chapel of the
Savoy was used by the parishioners. In
this way it became erroneously known at
times as 'St. Mary le Savoy.' Amongst
the ministers who then officiated was
Thos. Fuller, ch. historian, and author
of the *Worthies of England*. He began his
ministry in 1641, but in 1643 joined the
King's forces, and was absent until 1660,
when he was restored and appointed a
royal chaplain by Charles II. Pepys
records hearing him on several occasions.
In 1667 Geo. Wither, the poet, was bd.
in the chapel. In 1685 a sch., conducted
by Jesuits, was established in the precinct
by James II. It ceased with the King's
abdication in 1688. In William III's
reign it became a disreputable quarter,
ill-doers claiming there the rights of
sanctuary, also cherished in Whitefriars.
The result was that in 1702 the hosp.
was dissolved, the rents confiscated to
the Crown, and a receiver appointed to
administer the estates. The chapel remained. Various religious bodies met in
the precinct, and a French Huguenot
chapel was founded by Charles II, whilst
in 1723 George I granted a warrant for
a German Lutheran ch. In 1731 the
chaplain of the hosp. was John Wilkinson,
and when the Marriage Act of 1753 put
an end to the marriages at the Fleet
Prison this gentleman, on the ground that
the Savoy was extra-parochial, tied the

nuptial knots on terms as advantageous as the Fleet parsons had offered. In 1755 he m. as many as 1,190 couples. He was eventually apprehended and sentenced to fourteen yrs.' transportation, but d. at Plymouth in 1757. During the period of his incumbency an event occurred in the history of the Savoy which has a poignancy in distinct contrast to the conduct of the matrimonial huckster. Dr. Archibald Cameron was a Scot who had been with the rebel army of the 'Young Pretender' at Culloden. Like Nurse Cavell in modern times, he succoured indifferently friend and foe. He fled to the Low Countries, but imprudently returned, and was identified and betrayed. The entry in the burial register of the chapel reads:

'1754. June. Drawn on a sledge from the Tower and executed at Tyburn for high treason on Thursday 7th and buried as above in the Chancel vault. 'Vault fee not paid.'

A stained glass memorial window was destroyed in the Second World War.

Many of the bdgs. of the Savoy disappeared during the construction of Waterloo Bridge, 1815–17. In the latter yr. the French Huguenot chapel was destroyed. The German Lutheran ch. remained until 1877 when, an approach to the Victoria Embankment being made, it was necessary to remove it. The chapel was repaired by George I in 1720, and again by George III in 1775 and 1786. George IV carried out extensive restorations in 1826 and 1830, as recorded by a tablet on the exterior W. wall. Q. Victoria was responsible for a restoration in 1843; and after a disastrous fire in 1864, which destroyed the roof and nearly all the monuments and interior fittings, she ordered a complete and careful restoration which was carried out by Sidney Smirke. Her Majesty also added the new vestry in 1877, and in 1883 a sch. for choristers, adjacent to the chapel, which is now demolished. The ceiling of the chapel is of great beauty. It is of wood, and consists of a series of eighty-eight ribbed quatrefoil panels, within which are emblazoned at intervals the shields of various royal personages associated with the manor and chapel. These are: K. John of France; Henry III; Edmund, first E. of Lancaster; Henry, third E. of Lancaster; Henry, first D. of Lancaster; John of Gaunt,

second D. of Lancaster; Henry IV; Henry VI; Edward IV; Henry VII; Henry VIII; Q. Victoria and P. Consort. A stained glass window (over the reredos) commemorating P. Consort, was damaged in the Second World War. Another window is in memory of Richd. D'Oyley Carte, associated with the Gilbert and Sullivan operas, and depicts a procession of angelic musicians, with a quotation from Psalm lxviii: 'The singers go before, the minstrels follow after.' On 12th May 1935 a window in commemoration of the Jubilee of George V was unveiled by the donor, Viscount Davidson, then Chancellor of the Duchy of Lancaster. It represents the armorial insignia of eleven Ks., Qs., Ps., and nobles, who have in some special way beautified, restored, or dignified the chapel. The carved oak pulpit had a half-hour glass. It was incorporated in the candelabra, and was given by Q. Victoria in 1877 in place of an earlier one lost in the fire. The bronze lectern commemorated Lawrence Irving and his wife, who perished in the sinking of the *Empress of Ireland* in 1919. Within the sanctuary, resting on stone corbels set in the walls on either side, are two small kneeling figures. They are fragments of 16th-century monuments, destroyed by the Fire. The one on the right represents Alicia Steward, daughter of Simon Steward of Kingeth in Suffolk (d. 1573); the left-hand figure is that of Nicola Moray, wife of Sir Robt. Douglas (d. 1612). There is a restored double sedilia and an ancient piscina. The latter was discovered after the fire had destroyed a monument which concealed it. The reredos screen exhibits beautiful carved stonework, and extends over the whole width of the chapel. A painting of the Madonna—it has been loaned to the N.G.—is in the reredos. It was in the master's lodging at the dissolution of the hosp. in 1702. It disappeared, and was traced to Hereford and returned to the chapel in 1876. A wall-tablet in memory of a young actor, H. V. Esmond, shows him in bas-relief with a cigarette in his fingers, an unusual feature of a monument. In the vestry there are the verger's silver-topped staff, dated 1792; a handsome service-book presented by George III in 1777; and the registers, which date from 1685. Over the steps by which the chapel is entered there is a small stone which reads: 'Thomas

Britton died November 12th 1839, aged 101 years.' Britton's age, like Methuselah's, as Sir Thos. Browne said, is his only chronicle.

There is a pleasing allusion to the Savoy Chapel in *All the Year Round*, which Rev. W. J. Loftie ascribed to Dickens. The style is not his, and the former did not notice that the article was written in 1877, seven yrs. after the novelist's death. It is worth quoting, however:

'At early morn there is not a quoin in the old Chapel wall, not a mullion in its blinking windows, not a cartouche or a cantilever, but stands forth sharp and clear in its proper light, shade and reflection, as in a Venetian photograph. You shall see the rugosities of the stone as through an opera glass. You shall count the strands in the cordage of the rigging of the great hay-boats floating up and down the river. This early morning beautifies and enriches everything, so does the summer sun glorify the hoary old Precinct when Aurora touches it with her finger tips. . . . So run the sands of Life through this quaint hour-glass. So glides the Life away in the old Precinct. At its base, a river runs for all the world: at its summit is the brawling raging Strand; on either side are the gloomy Adelphi Arches, the Bridge of Sighs, that men call Waterloo. But the Precinct troubles itself little with the noise and tumult, and sleeps well through life without its fiftul fever.'

In 1937 George VI ordained the title 'The King's Chapel of the Savoy' and appointed it to the use of the Royal Victorian Order. For this purpose the interior was completely re-fitted. Stalls for the royal family now occupy the S. end, where the old Willis organ formerly stood—a Hammond electronic organ being installed in its stead. Bronze and enamelled armorial stall-plates of the Knights of the Order now form a series along the newly oak-panelled walls. A new Robing-room was built at the S. end of the garth. The royal family presented new silver altar plate, which during the war was preserved in the cath. of St. John the Divine in New York. On 22nd Oct. 1946, the K. and Q. attended the chapel to confirm the new arrangements. On this occasion an anthem entitled 'England' was a paraphrase of the speech of John of Gaunt in Shakespeare's *Richard II* (see Ely Place.). In 1949 the K., as

Sovereign of the Order, unveiled a War Memorial to Members of the Order. During the Second World War the Chapel was damaged by enemy action six times, but although some of the original windows have been lost, the main fabric remains intact.

(See *Memorials of the Savoy*, by Rev. W. J. Loftie, 1878; and *The Savoy, Manor, Hospital, Chapel*, by Sir Robert Somerville, 1960.)

Schools

CHRIST'S HOSPITAL was founded by Edward VI in 1553, eleven days before his death, as a home for orphans or other poor children. The number received at the outset was 380, and John Howes's contemporaneous account says:

'Many of them, being taken from the dunghill, when they came to swete and cleane keping and to a pure dyett, dyed downe righte.'

Within a few months it became a sch. instead of a mere home for foundlings, and the staff consisted of a grammar master and his usher, a writing master, a music master, two elementary teachers, and a matron to look after the 'maydenchildren.' In the 17th century a curious use of the scholars was to send them out as mutes for funerals, and between 1622 and 1648 1,000 funerals were so served. This was, of course, a source of income. The G.F. wrought havoc with the bdgs. They were in part rebuilt by Wren. In 1685 James II went to the sch. and in the hall at Horsham is Verrio's picture of the K. receiving the mathematical scholars, Samuel Pepys being in attendance. In 1694, for the first time, about a dozen scholars were selected for drawing tickets at public lotteries. In 1775 a boy was found to have been bribed in the interest of a ticket-holder. The boy was expelled, and precautions taken against a repetition of the incident, but no suggestion of the impropriety of using schoolboys for the purpose was made.

Christ's Hosp. is mostly famous to-day for its association with three men of letters: Coleridge, Lamb, and Leigh Hunt.

Coleridge went there in 1781. He wrote of his experience there mostly in *Biographia Literaria* (all his writings upon the subject appear in *Christ's Hospital*, edited by R. Brimley Johnson, 1896). Although Coleridge was under the severe Rev. Jas. Boyer, his praise of that pedagogue was unstinted.

Lamb went in 1782 (see *Recollections of Christ's Hospital* and *Christ's Hospital Five and Thirty Years ago*).

Lamb recalled

'our stately suppings in public, when the well-lighted hall, and the confluence of well-dressed company who came to see us, made the whole look more like a concert or assembly, than a scene of a plain bread and cheese collation; the annual orations upon St. Matthew's Day . . . the doleful tune of the burial anthem chanted in the solemn cloisters upon the seldom-occurring funeral of some schoolfellow; the festivities at Christmas, when the richest of us would club our stock to have a gaudy day, sitting round the fire, replenished to the height with logs . . . the carol sung by night at that time of the year, which, when a young boy, I have often lain awake to hear.'

At the latter part of the last century an old gentleman used to stop all the Christ's Hosp. boys he met and present them with a shilling 'in memory of Charles Lamb.' Some boys used to run round the corner and meet the old gentleman a second time. Since 1875 a Lamb medal has been given for English essays. Leigh Hunt went to the sch. in 1791.

The hall was rebuilt 1825–9 by John Shaw. There hung the hosp.'s most celebrated picture—the great canvas once attributed to Holbein, showing Edward VI granting the charter of incorporation. In the hall were the suppings in public to which Lamb referred. They took place on four Thursday evenings in Lent. The ceremony commenced by the steward rapping a table three times with a hammer. The first was for taking places, the second for silence, the third was the signal for a Grecian to read the evening lesson from the pulpit. The boys used also to attend the Spital Sermon in Christ Ch. (see 'Customs'). The well-known costume dates from the founding of the sch., and there is a manuscript note of John Howes that in 1553, when Q. Mary entered the City, she slighted the governors and boys who had assembled on a stage without Aldgate, the reason was that 'shee did not lyke the blewe boyes.' It was not the colour Her Majesty was criticizing, but doubtless a foundation which had supplanted a monastery. Up to 1865 there

used to be worn under the blue coat in winter, and in earlier times in summer, a long yellow smock. In the middle of the 19th century caps were discarded.

The sch. was removed to Hcrsham in 1902, and the old bdgs. in L. were demolished. A wing of the General Post Office and an extension of St. Bartholomew's Hosp. stand on the site. The cloisters and some other features of the Newgate St. bdg. have been incorporated in the new sch., including the statue of Edward VI, which looked down upon Christ Ch. Passage, where it was placed in 1682 by Alderman Sir Robt. Clayton, one of the benefactors in respect of the rebuilding after the G.F. Scholars still come to L., 21st Sept., on St. Matthew's Day. In addition to a preparatory sch., which was at Hertford from 1683 to 1902, when it also removed to Horsham, there is a Christ's Hosp. for Girls at Hertford.

(See also 'City Churches; D')—Christ Church, Newgate.)

CITY OF LONDON SCHOOL was founded in 1837, and really owes its origin to John Carpenter. Funds left by the latter, who was 'common clerk' of the C.C. in the days of Whittington, so accumulated that there was sufficient money nearly four hundred yrs. after his death to build a sch. It was first in Milk St., Cheapside. Its object was to supply a useful and liberal education for the sons of the professional, commercial, and trading classes. In 1882 it was transferred to Victoria Embankment, the bdg. there, in the style of the French Renascence, being erected at a cost of about £100,000. There are statues on the façade of Bacon, Shakespeare, Milton, and Newton, besides allegorical figures of the Arts and Sciences. The great hall has a handsome open-timbered roof. One of the stained-glass windows represents Shakespeare with Milton and Spenser. Among distinguished old boys may be mentioned: Sir J. R. Seeley; the Rev. E. A. Abbott, D.D., afterwards head master; Ld. Ritchie, once Chancellor of the Exchequer; and H. H. Asquith, afterwards E. of Oxford and Asquith. The street on the W. side of the sch. bears the name of the founder.

MERCERS' SCHOOL. (See 'Companies'—Mercers'.)

MERCHANT TAYLORS' SCHOOL was originally founded in Suffolk Lane in

1561. It remained in that narrow st. beside the Thames until the G.F., when it was burnt. It was rebuilt, and continued on the same site until 1875, when it was removed to the handsome Gothic bdgs. erected on the site of Charterhouse Sch., from designs by E. I'Anson, an old boy. It is essentially a day sch., and numbers some 500 boys. Amongst men whom it has educated are a number of prelates, including Abp. Juxon, Lancelot Andrewes, and Bp. Matthew Wren (Sir Christopher's uncle); Thos. Lodge and Jas. Shirley, the dramatists; Bulstrode Whitelocke, the man who gave Crómwell so much trouble; Daniel Neale and Edmund Calamy, the Nonconformists; the great Ld. Clive; the elder and the younger Chas. Mathews; and Samuel Birch, the Egyptologist. The Sch. left Charterhouse for Sandy Lodge, near Rickmansworth, in 1933.

St. Paul's School was founded (in St. P.'s Chyd.) by John Colet (he was a son of a Ld.M., and a famous dean of St. P.'s) in 1510, for 153 boys. The number was dictated by that of the miraculous draught of fishes. This is odd to the modern mind, but probably Colet felt some limit must be fixed, and this was as good as any other. Colet provided three masters: a 'high-master' who was to receive £35 p.a. (equal to about £400 in modern money) and a house; a 'surmaster,' with £18 and a house, and a chaplain who was to sing mass in the sch. chapel, and 'pray for the children to prosper in good life and in good literature to the honour of God and our Lord Jesus Christ.' The Chaplain was to hold no benefice, but to give all his time to the sch., teaching 'the Catechism and instruction of the Articles of the Faith and the X commandments in English.' He was to be lodged in the sch., and have £8 a yr. and a livery gown. The masters were to have no permanence, but to be re-appointed annually by the governors, and only so long as they did their work well. The first 'high-master' was Wm. Lily, a contemporary of Colet at Magdalen Coll., Oxford. He retained his office until his death in 1522. The government of the sch. was vested in the Mercers' Co., and to the latter Colet, between 1511 and 1514, transferred a great part of his father's property, both in Buckinghamshire and L. Its value, in

modern money, amounted to more than £80,000. The original bdgs. consisted of a schoolroom divided into two parts by a curtain, a small chapel, and houses for the 'high-master' and 'surmaster.' On the front of the bdgs. Colet put the inscription:

'Schola Catechizationis puerorum in Christi Opt. Max. fide et bonis literis Anno Verbi incarnati MDX.'

In the schoolroom, over the master's chair, he placed an image of the 'Child Jesus' (to whom the sch. was dedicated) in the attitude of teaching, with the motto 'Hear ye Him.' John Leland, Wm. Camden, John Milton, and Samuel Pepys went to the pre-Fire sch., of which no picture remains. In the sch. that was rebuilt after the G.F., the D. of Marlborough and John Strype were educated. It was rebuilt in 1823, and there Benjamin Jowett was amongst the scholars. In 1884 the sch. was removed to Hammersmith, where a bdg. was erected from the designs of Alfred Waterhouse. In the grounds is a statue of Dean Colet designed by W. Hamo Thornycroft, and unveiled in 1902. The best known of modern pupils was the late G. K. Chesterton.

Sir John Cass Foundation School and Technical Institute are due to the generosity of Sir John Cass (1661–1718). He was the son of an architect of the Admiralty, and became alderman of the ward of Portsoken, and M.P. for the City in 1710. In 1712 he became a sheriff, and in the same yr. was Master of the Carpenters' Co. He was greatly interested in the children of his ward, and in 1710 established the sch. that bears his name, for which he built a school-house at the corner of Houndsditch, on the W. side of the present par. ch. of St. Botolph, where there is a memorial window. There is a story that, whilst signing the deeds, he burst a blood vessel whereby the quill pen was stained red. For this reason the girls of the school wear a red quill in their berets.

In 1760, on the demolition of Aldgate, and improvements contingent thereon, a new site had to be found, and a large and roomy house was acquired. It had formerly been a Quaker boarding sch., and was well adapted for the purpose. The sch. continued here until 1869, when it was removed to premises in Jewry St. Owing to increased revenues from trust estates, the Charity Commissioners prepared a new scheme which was approved by Q. Victoria in 1895. This made provision for the establishment and maintenance of an institution to be called 'The Sir John Cass Technical Institute.' The sch. in Jewry St. was demolished in 1898, and a new sch. and institute bdg. was erected on the site in 1902. In 1908 the sch. was transferred to new premises from Duke St. to Mitre St., surrounding the old disused chyd. of St. James's, Duke's Place, after which the bdg. in Jewry St. became wholly devoted to the work of technical education. A new wing was opened by the E. of Athlone in 1934. The building was damaged in the war but rebuilt; three additional floors were added in 1955. In 1950 the name became the Sir John Cass College.

WESTMINSTER SCHOOL has a history that goes back to the latter part of the 14th century. In 1371 the 'master of the boys of the Subalmonry' received 13s. 4d. p.a., together with a 'gown and two shillings for fur to adorn it.' In 1385 a new official appears in the rolls entitled 'Magister scolarium.' 'He and his nine boys,' says Lawrence Tanner, 'are clearly differentiated from the boys of the Sub-almonry and from the choir boys who are not mentioned until 1480.' The school-house seems to have been in the almonry, and to have occupied a site roughly corresponding to the angle formed by the modern Victoria and Tothill Sts. After the dissolution, when W.A. became the centre for a short time of a bishopric, Henry VIII added to the foundation two masters to teach forty grammar scholars, and John Adams, the first known head master, was appointed in 1540. Q. Elizabeth, however, is always regarded as the founder of the sch. (or St. Peter's Coll.) as it is at present. The number of boys on the foundation was to be forty, as before; they were to be chosen by preference from among the choristers or from the sons of the chapter tenants. Provision was also made for some eighty other boys, oppidans, and there was to be right of election annually from among the Q.'s or resident scholars to three studentships at Christ Ch., Oxford, and the same number of scholarships at Trinity Coll., Cambridge. This arrangement continued down to 1874, when the studentships and scholarships at the universities were thrown open to the

whole sch.

The most famous of early head masters was Nicholas Udall. He was the author of the first English comedy, *Ralph Roister Doister*, and Prof. J. W. Hales thought that Udall, who became head master about 1553, probably wrote it for the boys. Wm. Camden, the famous antiquary, was head master 1593–9. Probably the best-known head master was Dr. Busby, who held office from 1638 to 1695. His flogging propensities have perpetuated his memory more than the library which, as his will said, was 'built and fitted by me at my own great coste and charges.' This room had an elaborately modelled and beautifully domed ceiling, and may have been designed by Inigo Jones. The book-cases there (destroyed in the Blitz) were made to Busby's order, and in his will he directed that 'a great part' of his books should be placed in the library, as he had 'for some time intended' they should be. Others of interest, have survived, as those left to the sch. by Mildred, Lady Burghley, the wife of Elizabeth's great minister. There are a first edition of Milton's *Lycidas*; books printed by Wynkyn de Worde; a work of Erasmus, with the arms of Henry VIII and Catherine of Aragon stamped on the side; and books with the autographs of Roger Ascham, John Locke, John Evelyn, and others. The sch. was originally part of the dormitory of the monks. The lower part of the walls, some of the windows, and also the vaults underneath (the undercroft) date from 1090–1100. After the great fire of 1298, which devastated the monastic bdgs., later tracery was introduced into some of the Norman windows. This tracery remains untouched in the window at the NE. corner of the sch., which was bricked up until 1862, when it was opened out by Sir Gilbert Scott. The fine hammer-beam roof dated probably from the latter part of the 16th century. In 1814 the walls of the sch. were in a ruinous condition, and were rebuilt with brick. At the same time the ugly side windows were inserted by Wyatt, the architect to W.A. From about 1602 to 1884 practically the whole sch. was taught in the one large apartment. The upper sch. was divided from the lower sch. by a curtain which hung from a bar over which the pancake was thrown on Shrove Tuesday (see 'Customs').

The head master presided above the curtain; the under master below it. The forms were first placed against the walls, with the masters facing them, but in 1852 the forms were rearranged in semicircles, with the master in the middle, with his back to the wall. At the N. end of the sch. was an apse or 'nitch' 7 ft. broad, which was probably built during the Commonwealth. It became usual to speak of the form taught in front of it as the form taught in the 'Shell,' and ultimately of the 'Shell' form. This name has been adopted by many of the more modern public schs., e.g. Harrow, Marlborough, Charterhouse, Wellington, and can usually be traced to a head master who was an 'old boy' of the sch. In 1881 the sch. exercised a right conferred by an Act of 1868, and purchased Ashburnham House for £4,000. This bdg. derived its name from the Ashburnham family, Wm. Ashburnham, whose brother Jack was the faithful friend and companion of Charles I, having been granted a lease in 1662. It is believed to have been designed by Inigo Jones, and contains a fine staircase and reception rooms. In 1730 it had been leased to the Crown to house the K.'s and Cottonian libs. (see 'Libraries'); there was a serious fire in 1731. Ashburnham House (used by the Churchill Club during the Second World War) is now used to provide rooms for the boarders, for class-rooms, and for the sch. lib. The dormitory, designed by the E. of Burlington, dates from 1730, and here the Latin play (the acting of one formed part of the ordinances of Q. Elizabeth) was performed at Christmas.

The sch. gateway dates from 1734. On it is carved the names of boys but none of the most distinguished. The most famous Westminster scholars have been Ben Jonson (who was under Camden), Cowley, Dryden (his name was shown cut on a form—a certain early Victorian, A. Slade, added his name, and had to do 500 lines for each letter), Geo. Herbert, Nathaniel Lee, John Locke, Sir Christopher Wren, Matthew Prior, Nicholas Rowe, Chas. Churchill, Wm. Cowper, Robt. Southey, Augustus Toplady, Edwd. Gibbon, and Warren Hastings. The arms of some of these were on the panelling of the sch. There s a bust of Busby, unveiled in 1895. The head master's chair is traditionally said to have been given to Busby by Charles II. This remains.

The bombs that—for the most part—missed W.A. fell on the sch. The hall (with the names on the walls and the coats of arms) as also the dormitory, were burnt out, whilst Dr. Busby's library was badly damaged but considerable rebuilding has taken place. What Dean Stanley called the 'star chamber door'—it cam₍ from the Palace of Westminster and was of Tudor date—was destroyed. There also went the form inscribed with Dryden's name. Among the debris was found a photograph of young Ribbentrop, admitted above the usual age as a hopeful act of courtesy to his father. The old beam over which was thrown the pancake survived. In the ruins it was rigged up once more on 5th Mar. 1946 for the pancake 'greaze,' and on this occasion, instead of a guinea, the winner received a golden sovereign, worth nearly twice as much (see 'Customs').

The Churchill Club gave its library to the sch. after the war.

(See *Westminster School*, by Reginald Airy, 1902; *Westminster School*, by L. E. Tanner, 1923; *Westminster School: A History*, by J. D. Carleton, 1965.)

Scotland Yard is said to preserve the name of an old palace where, in Saxon times and later, the Kings of Scotland resided when they came to L. to do homage to the Kings of England for Cumberland, Huntingdon, and other fiefs held by them as vassals of the English crown. Margaret, sister of Henry VIII, was the last sovereign to use the palace. No longer required after the union of the crowns by James I, it was dismantled and converted into offices. Milton had lodgings in Scotland Yard during his secretaryship to Cromwell, and other residents were Inigo Jones (1650) and Sir John Denham, who d. there, 1668. Here (the address was sometimes 4 Whitehall Place) an additional police office was set up in 1829, and this became the headquarters of the new Met. Police (*q.v.*).

When the police removed from this site the new premises designed (1891) by Mr. Norman Shaw, R.A., in what has been termed 'the Scottish baronial style,' were called New Scotland Yard. (A medallion of the architect is on the E.

side.) The site was an irregular polygon of land, close to Westminster Bridge, of which the greater part had been reclaimed from the river through the construction of the Victoria Embankment. At first it was proposed to build an opera house there. The foundation stone was laid in 1875, and remains of it still exist in the cellars of Scotland Yard. This scheme failed for lack of funds, and the ground was then purchased by a syndicate, which commenced the construction of a combination of offices and residential flats. That also failed, and then the Govt. took possession.

New Scotland Yard is built of granite, quarried by convicts in Dartmoor.

In 1967 the Met. Police moved to Broadway, Westminster premises consisting of a 20-storey tower block and 2 other blocks; it has $1\frac{1}{2}$ miles of corridor, 13 lifts and 4,240 windows. New Scotland Yard is to be used for the staffs of various Govt. depts.

(See *The Story of Scotland Yard*, by Sir Ronald Howe, 1965.)

Serjeants' Inn (Fleet St.) takes its name from a legal title now extinct. The Order of the Coif was a select and distinguished one, and for centuries no one could be made a judge either of K.'s Bench or of Common Pleas who was not a member of the Order, which numbered about forty. It is impossible to ascertain with any certainty when the serjeants first occupied a house in Fleet St. There is a reference to 'le Sergeauntes Inne' *c.* 1544, but there is ground for believing that some were residing there previously. At the date mentioned it was the property of the dean and chapter of York. It was, said Stow, 'so called for that divers judges and serjeants at the law keep a commons, and are lodged there in term time. It was burnt in the G.F., and, according to Strype (1720), rebuilt in 'a more fair, substantial and uniform manner.' Luttrell records his being made a serjeant, and tells how he invited the judges and the Ld. Keeper 'to a noble dinner at Sergeants Inn in Fleet Street' (1701). In 1758 the inn gave up the Fleet St. premises and removed to Chancery Lane. Here there was another Serjeants' Inn, but not properly an inn of court. The hall here was erected by Ld. Keeper North, whose residence in Chancery Lane communicated by a door into the garden of the inn. In 1837–8 much rebuilding took place under the direction of Sir Robt. Smirke. The hall, however, was left untouched, and was fitted up as a court for Exchequer Equity sittings. Later it was used as a dining-room for the serjeants and the common-law judges. In another apartment, according to Timbs, there was one of the finest collections of legal portraits in L., among them one of Sir Edwd. Coke by Cornelius Janssen. Coke was living in Serjeants' Inn at the time of the inquiries into the murder of Sir Thos. Overbury (1616). The Judicature Act of 1873 dispensed with the necessity for a judge to have been a serjeant-at-law; the soc. was dissolved in 1876, and the inn sold by auction in 1877, and pulled down. The purchaser was Mr. Serjeant Cox, who transferred the stained glass, the illuminated arms of the judges, the furniture, the plate, and the crested dinner-service to his residence at Mill Hill. The twenty-six portraits were transferred to the N.P.G. The proceeds, £57,100, were divided amongst the surviving serjeants, a procedure that caused much comment. There is a C.C. plaque on the E. side of Chancery Lane.

Some stained glass from Serjeants' Inn Hall has, since 1926, been in the Law Soc.'s Hall in Chancery Lane.

The thoroughfare known as Serjeants' Inn—it leads to Mitre Court by way of the old Ram Alley of Alsatia (see 'Whitefriars') has lost much of its interest through its almost complete destruction by bombs. There has disappeared the house, bearing date 1669, in which Ld. Erskine, the famous advocate, once lived; also the house referred to by Lamb in his essay *Old Benchers of the Inner Temple*; and the one occupied by J. T. Delane, editor of *The Times*, from 1841–77. It is said of him that he saw more sunrises than any other man of his day.

Seven Dials. The significance of the name is epitomized in a sentence in Evelyn's Diary, under date 5th Oct. 1694: 'I went to see the buildings near St. Giles's, where seven streets make a star from a Doric pillar placed in the middle of a circular area.' This enterprise was due to a speculative builder, Thos. Neale, and the land was known as 'Cock and Pye Fields' from an inn of that name which appears to have been at the NW. corner of Long Acre. The sts. as planned by Neale were St. Andrews St., Earl St., White Lion St., and Queen St. In 1708, when Hatton published his *New View of London*, only those four sts. had been made. Strype (1720) wrote:

'Cock and Pye Fields, which was made use of for a laystall for the soil of the streets, but of late built into seven handsome streets with a dial placed in the midst.'

Gay had referred to it in *Trivia*:

'Where fam'd Saint Giles's ancient limits
    spread,
An inrail'd column rears its lofty head.
Here to sev'n streets sev'n dials count the
    day,
And from each other catch the circling
    ray.'

Notwithstanding there seems reason to doubt if there were more than six dials. In 1773 a rumour spread that the base of the pillar concealed treasure. It was therefore taken down for a search. The stones were purchased by a stonemason, and removed to a place called Sayes Court, near Chertsey. In 1822 the column was set up on Weybridge Green, and surmounted with a ducal coronet, as a memorial to the Duchess of York, who had d. at Oatlands in 1820. One of the dials according to Clinch—who included an excellent picture of the column in his *Bloomsbury and St. Giles*—was used as a stepping-stone at the Ship Inn at Weybridge. It is now outside the Weybridge Mus.

Dickens describes Seven Dials, as it was in his early days, in *Sketches by Boz*.

'The gordian knot was all very well in its way, so was the maze of Hampton Court: so is the maze of Beulah Spa; . . . but what involution can compare with those of Seven Dials? Where is there such another maze of streets, courts, lanes and Irishmen?'

It was the synonym of poverty, as later in *Iolanthe*:

'Hearts just as pure and fair
    May beat in Belgrave Square,
As in the lowly air
    Of Seven Dials.'

The character of the neighbourhood was greatly improved by the cutting of Charing Cross Rd., and there is none of the rowdyism indicated in the Cruikshank illustration to Dickens' sketch.

Shepherd Market is in Mayfair, S. of Curzon St., and can be approached by way of White Horse St., Piccadilly. It was formed *c.* 1735, and was so-called after Edwd. Shepherd, an architect, who d. 1747. G. H. Cunningham says the 'King's Arms' is—

'the descendant of the "Three Jolly Butchers," where Woodward, the comedian and harlequin, made his first appearance in connection with the festivities of the old May Fair, which used to be held in the region occupied by this and the neighbouring streets.'

Until recently this area of small shops had the atmosphere of a small country town but to-day there is little left of its old-world charm.

For an account of life here during the Second World War see *A Village in Piccadilly*, by Robt. Henrey (1943).

Shoreditch, now part of the L. Bor. of Hackney, was a met bor. and par. It received its name neither from Jane Shore nor from the Shorditch family that were once its lords. The oldest forms of the name are Soredich (1148) and Schoredich (1236), and 'shore' or 'sor' may refer to the ditch or sewer then existing on the boundary of Shoreditch and Hackney.

Haggerston and Hoxton (often referred to as Hoggesden) are both names of doubtful origin: Holywell takes its name from a well near Curtain Rd. first mentioned in 1104, a Benedictine nunnery of St. John Baptist being built there in the 12th century.

The par. ch. of St. Leonard is in the High St., near to the E. boundary of the bor. A ch. dating from the 13th century or possibly earlier stood here until 1736, when the present one was erected from designs by Geo. Dance, Senr. The body of the ch. is plain, but at the W. end is a Doric portico and a graceful steeple. Opened in 1740, it was restored by Sir A. Blomfield toward the end of last century, and badly damaged by a flying bomb in 1944. The famous peal of 12 bells (now 13, Haberdashers' Co. added the 13th) is to be rededicated. Three of Keats' brothers, Geo., Tom and Edwd., were baptized here in 1801, and Chas. Bradlaugh in 1833. The fine E. window no longer exists, but there is a remarkable monument in stone which shows two vigorous figures of Death pulling down the Tree of Life. The Latin inscription records that the deceased, Elizabeth Benson (d. 1710), was the daughter of a notable philosopher, and sprang from the ancient Ks. of Pannonia (Hungary) and from Kentish knights, and that 'Death with heavy foot stole on her and the threads of her life were not spent to the full but snapped.' Yet she was in her 90th yr.! In 1913 there was placed in the ch. a memorial to the three Burbages (Jas., Cuthbert, and Richd.), R. Tarlton, Gabriel Spencer (killed by Ben Jonson in a duel), and Will Sly—all actors bd. in the precincts—and Will Somers, Henry VIII's Jester. In the chyd. the par. stocks and whipping-post are preserved.

Thos. Fairchild, who d. in 1728, and was a member of the Gardeners' Co., bequeathed a sum of money to the ch. for the annual preaching of a sermon on these subjects: 'The Wonderful Works of God in the Creation' or on 'The Certainty of the Resurrection of the Dead, Proved by the Certain Changes of the Animal and Vegetable Creation.' This was regularly preached up to the outbreak of the Second World War.

There are three good Victorian Gothic churches by Jas. Brooks, which merit attention : St. Columba, Haggerston (1868), with stained glass windows of modern design, one representing a boy playing cricket with lamp-post for wicket: St. Chad, Nichols Sq.—a quaint little backwater off the Hackney Rd. (1869): and St. Michael, Mark St. (1866), now closed but can still be visited. In St. Augustine's, Yorkton St., are seven sacrament windows and seven windows showing scenes in the life of the par. St. John the Baptist, Pitfield St., is a classical bdg. of 1826. There are two R.C. Chs., St. Mary's, Eldon St., Moorfields (1903), successor to an older ch., 200 yds. S.E. of the corner of Finsbury Circus, and St. Monica's Priory, Hoxton Sq., designed by Pugin.

Shoreditch occupies the proud position of being the first par. in England to have a theatre. It stood a few yds. from the site of Curtain Rd. schs., and a tablet on Nos. 86–88 marks the site. The L. Music Hall, High St., was founded 1893. The

Eagle Public House in City Rd. used to be the Grecian Theatre. At 73 Hoxton St. was Pollock's famous shop where toy theatres were sold. R. L. Stevenson visited it and mentioned it in his essay 'Penny Plain and Twopence Coloured'. (*Memories and Portraits*).

In the Kingsland Rd. is the interesting little Geffrye Mus. of the G.L.C. (see 'Museums').

There runs E. from St. John's Rd., Hoxton, to the SE. of St. John's Ch. a narrow lane called Pimlico Walk; a reminder that the original Pimlico district was in Hoxton and not in Westminster. In *Newes from Hogsden*, 1598, there is an allusion 'Hey for old Ben Pimlico's nut browne.' In a drollery of 1609 called *Pimlyco or Runne Redcap. 'Tis a mad world at Hogsdon*, Pimlico means a brand of ale or beer surpassing a brand called Eyebright, and Ben Jonson in *The Alchemist*, 1610, speaks of 'a second Hogsden, in days of Pimlico and Eyebright.' The Britannia Theatre (1858) at the E. end of Pimlico Walk is now demolished but in the garden are two pillars; this was said to be the site of a tavern called the Pimlico, attached to which were Pimlico Gardens.

Smithfield is a large area, about three acres in extent, to the NW. of the City adjoining the ch. and hosp. of St. Bartholomew the Great. In the time of Stephen (1135–54) it was 'Smethefelde.' In 1358, it was 'Westsmythefelde'—in distinction from East Smithfield—I.E. of the T.L. Fitzstephen, writing about 1180, said:

'In the suburb outside one of the gates there is a smooth field both in fact and in name . . . where there is a much frequented show of fine horses for sale.'

He then proceeds to a vivid description of their graceful movements, and of the thrill of a horse race there. In his time much of it was marsh, one of the dry places being used for a gallows (see 'Tyburn'). It was a place resorted to for jousts, and its spaciousness made it very convenient for Bartholomew Fair (*q.v.*).

The fact, too, that it afforded accomodation for so large a number, probably led to the stake being erected here. There were cruel executions here before Mary's time. In 1530 John Roose, a cook, was boiled to death for having thrown poison into gruel made for the household of

Fisher, Bp. of Rochester, where seventeen were poisoned and two died. In 1541 a woman was boiled for poisoning her mistress and some others. In 1537 Father Forest was to suffer there a cruel death at the hands of his fellow Christians. He was the prior of the Observants' Convent at Greenwich, and had been confessor to Q. Catherine. The figure of an ancient Welsh saint which had been venerated in a chapel at Llandderfel, in N. Wales, was made fuel for his burning, and he was suspended in a cradle of chains from a gallows erected over the stake. Latimer preached the sermon on this occasion. In 1546 Anne Askew and three companions suffered there, in the presence of Wriothesley, the Ld. Chancellor, the D. of Norfolk, the E. of Bedford, and the Ld.M.—seated on a bench outside St. Bartholomew's Ch. In 1550 a friend of Anne's suffered in the same place. The event is calmly recorded in the diary of Edward VI:

'Joan Bocher, otherwise called Joan of Kent, was burnt for holding that Christ was not incarnate of the Virgin Mary, being condemned the year before, but kept in hope of conversion—the 30th April, the Bishop of London and the Bishop of Ely were to persuade her, but she withstood them and reviled the preacher that preached at her death.'

It is said that Edward was reluctant, and yielded to the persuasions of Cranmer, also burned in the following reign, but there is no confirmation in this cold entry. Under Mary, forty-three suffered at Smithfield—seven in one day, 27th June 1558. The first here and in England was John Rogers, vicar of St. Sepulchre's Ch., in sight of which he d. (1554). He left a wife and five children, with whom he declined to have a parting interview. There is a tablet on the wall of St. Bartholomew's Hosp. commemorating the martyrdoms, but naming only three of the martyrs: John Bradford, John Rogers, and John Philpot. The first two were condemned at the same time in the ch. of St. Saviour's, now Southwark Cath. (q.v.). Philpot was tried in the Bp. of L.'s house (see 'St. Paul's Cathedral'). The last to suffer at Smithfield for religion was Bartholomew Legate in 1611. He was condemned as a 'blasphemous heretic,' having Arian leanings, and his sentence was pronounced by King, Bp. of L.

In 1849, when excavations were being made for a sewer 3 ft. below the surface, a little to the W. of the gateway of St. Bartholomew's Ch., there were found unhewn stones, covered with ashes and human bones, charred and partially consumed, some of which were carried away as relics. With them were strong oak posts in a charred condition, a staple and ring. The tablet was therefore placed near the spot. The inscription refers to the ch. of the English Martyrs, St. John St., Clerkenwell. There are panels on that bdg., representing martyrdoms, and on projecting buttresses statues of martyrs. In 1873 a fountain was erected in the centre of Smithfield. There is, near the martyrs' tablet, a tablet to the memory of William Wallace, the Scots hero.

Smithfield is associated with fire in more than one way. At the corner of Cock Lane (q.v.) and Giltspur St. is a gilded boy. This was supposed to commemorate the place where the G.F. stopped. It is difficult to understand what is meant by this, as it extended much farther W.—touching the fringe of the Temple. The boy was formerly on the Fortune of War Tavern, now demolished, and it is said—there is no very reliable testimony—an inscription under the figure ran: 'This boy is in memory put up for the late Fire of London occasioned by the sin of Gluttony, 1666.' In J. T. Smith's print of 1791 the figure had wings, but these have disappeared. (See also 'Hospitals' and 'Markets.')

Society of Arts (John Adam St., Adelphi) owes its inception to Wm. Shipley, a drawing-master of Northampton, and brother of Jonathan Shipley, Bp. of St. Asaph, and friend of Benjamin Franklin. Its full title was: 'The Society for the Encouragement of Arts, Manufactures, and Commerce.' It was first established at a meeting held in 1754 at Rawthmell's Coffee House in Henrietta St., Covent Garden, and its first president was Viscount Folkestone. Its early meeting-places were Crane Court, Fleet St.; Craig's Court, Charing Cross; rooms opposite the New Exchange; and (1759) Beaufort Bdgs., Savoy. In 1771 the brothers Adam entered into an agreement with the Soc. for the erection of a bdg. in the Adelphi. The first stone was laid by Ld. Romney on 28th Mar.

1772, and the bdg. opened in 1774. During the first fifty yrs. of its existence the Soc. was occupied principally in making awards for discoveries and inventions. In the Great Room Jas. Barry, R.A., painted a series of pictures on the walls. Barry was an eccentric individual with a terrible temper, and he ceased to exhibit at the Royal Academy in 1776 in disgust at the bad reception accorded to his 'Death of General Wolfe,' in which all the figures were represented as nude. He had an ambition to paint great mural pictures. He lived meagrely—on tea, porridge, and milk mainly—during the execution of the work. Later the Soc. voted him their gold medal, and sums of 50 guineas and 200 guineas; they also threw open the room for exhibition for his benefit, and by this he gained £503 2s. The general title of the pictures was 'Human Culture,' and, according to Barry's own description, they were—

'to illustrate one great maxim or moral truth, viz. that the obtaining of happiness, as well individual as public, depends upon cultivating the human faculties.'

The first picture is the story of Orpheus; the second a Harvest Home, or Thanksgiving to Ceres and Bacchus; the third the Victors of Olympia; the fourth Navigation, or the Triumph of the Thames; the fifth the Distribution of the Premiums in the Soc. of Arts; and the sixth Elysium, or the State of Final Retribution. Barry introduced portraits of a number of celebrities, living and dead, including Wm. Penn, Mrs. Elizabeth Montagu, Sir Geo. Savile, Arthur Young, Bp. Hurd, Soame Jenyns, Edmund Burke, Dr. Johnson, and Dr. Burney. Barry d. in 1806, and his body lay in state in the Great Room before burial in St. P.'s Cath. Johnson thought highly of Barry.

Many of the specialized institutions of science and industry originated in the Soc. of Arts, and as they grew in proportion became socs. on their own. Meetings were held for the discussion of scientific discoveries, so bringing recognition and attention from the general public to many discoveries which might otherwise not have been widely known.

There are sections of the Soc. covering all subjects, including mechanics and manufactures, and minerals and chemistry. In 1869 an Indian section was

formed and in 1879 this became the Foreign and Colonial section. The section helped to promote in this country a wider knowledge of subjects relating to the empire.

The Dept. of Fine Arts has been instrumental in assisting many eminent artists in the early stages of their careers, among them being such men as Romney, Nollekens, Bewick, Landseer, Turner, and Millais. It was also through the efforts of the soc. that the Royal Coll. of Music was founded. The soc. was instrumental in establishing the international exhibitions, the first of which was that held in 1851.

There is also a large educational section with an organized system of local examinations, commenced in 1854. It was through the efforts of the soc. that the need for technical education was realized and efforts made to provide for this branch of education.

There is an Albert Medal, founded in honour of the P. Consort, who became president in 1843, awarded annually to some eminent man who has distinguished himself by promoting arts, manufactures, or commerce. The first award was to Sir Rowland Hill in 1864. In 1847 the soc. was incorporated by royal charter and in 1908 Edward VII granted permission to add 'Royal' to the name of the soc. Another useful work of the Soc. has been to commemorate houses outside the City associated with famous men by marking them with a tablet. Thirty-four were so adorned before they handed over the duty to the L.C.C. in 1902.

Soho. One of the oddest names in L.'s nomenclature, is first heard of in 1632, when it appears as 'So Ho' in the ratebooks of St. Martin in the Fields. It seems to be derived from a cry used to draw hounds off; Machyn mentions—

'a good cry for a mylle, and after the hondys kylled the fox at the end of sent Gylle and theyr was a grett cry at the deth.'

A Dog and Duck Tavern in Frith St. commemorates the old hunting association.

In 1634 there is a reference to a water course from a place called 'So Howe,' and in 1636 mention of tenements at the brick-kilns near 'Sohoe.' As would be assumed from the last allusion, the dwellings were those of the poorer classes.

Soho Sq. was originally called King's Sq., after Gregory King: he was a herald; also an engraver and surveyor, and as such was employed by Ogilby on his map of L. and book of roads. It was built in 1681; and the first house of importance therein was Monmouth House, built on land conveyed to the D. by Richd. Fryth, whose name is commemorated by Frith St. The house is said to have been designed by Wren. The tale, accepted by Pennant and others, that the use of 'So Ho' as a watchword at the Battle of Sedgemoor led to the district being so called, is untenable. It was sold in 1693, and eventually came into possession of Ld. Bateman (d. 1744), whose son let it to the Comte de Guerchy. It was pulled down in 1775. During demolition, J. T. Smith visited it with Nollekens, and described the gate entrance as massive ironwork, supported by stone piers; within the gates there was a spacious courtyard; there were eight rooms on the ground-floor which were richly decorated. Anthony Carlisle, a surgeon, lived at No. 12 Soho St.; to his house, before Carlisle was knighted, was brought Jas. Barry the artist (see 'Society of Arts'), when stricken with illness. No. 31, in 1824, was the home of Chas. Kemble the great actor. Sir Joseph Banks lived at No. 32 from 1777: he was naturalist, botanist, and president of the Royal Soc.; he voyaged with Capt. Cook in the *Endeavour*, and gave Botany Bay its name from the number of unknown plants he discovered; he was one of Dr. Johnson's pall-bearers. Nos. 31 and 32 were demolished early in 1937. Wm. Beckford, Ld.M. in 1762 and 1769 (see 'Guildhall'), lived in a house at the corner of Greek St., now St. Barnabas' House of Charity. St. Patrick's Roman Catholic Ch., at the corner of Sutton Row, is on the site of Carlisle House, built by the E. of Carlisle about 1692; in 1760 it was purchased by Mrs. Cornelys, who held a series of dances and masquerades here which were not patronized by really 'nice people'; these entertainments lost their popularity; and, after the bankruptcy of Mrs. Cornelys in 1788, the house was pulled down with the exception of the ball-room—which in 1792 was transformed by Father O'Leary into a mission chapel; and it was so used until 1893, when the present ch. was

opened. A tablet in the porch records that it is the oldest mission in England dedicated to St. Patrick. In the ch. is a shrine containing a relic of Oliver Plunket (see 'Bloomsbury'); it was carved out of the old oak beams of Father O'Leary's chapel, and there is a mural tablet in the latter's memory in the ante-chapel. A feature of the ch. at night is the illuminated cross on its summit. Two famous publishing firms are in Soho Sq., A. & C. Black and W. & R. Chambers. The former purchased Scott's copyrights in 1851, and the latter are noted for their encyclopaedias and reference works. On the N. side is the French Protestant Ch., formerly in St. Martin's le Grand and Threadneedle St. On it there is a plaque, erected in 1950, to commemorate the 400th anniversary of the granting of the charter to Protestant refugees in 1550. In the centre of Soho Sq. is a statue of Charles II (see 'Statues').

Soho has a number of literary associations. Dryden d. in Gerrard St. It was in the square that De Quincey sat down on a doorstep and was befriended by Ann, a st.-walker. He said he never passed the spot without recalling the incident with a pang of grief. In 1802 he was living at 61 Greek St. (a tablet marks the house). In 1803 Douglas Jerrold was b. in this st. Wm. Hazlitt d. at No. 6 Frith St. (marked by an L.C.C. tablet) in 1830, having moved from Bouverie St. His last words are reported to have been: 'Well, I've had a happy life.' His death was caused by gastric weakness, said to have been due to drinking injudicious quantities of tea. A large 18th-century house in Carlisle St. which was generally accepted as Dr. Manette's in *A Tale of Two Cities* (Manette St. is off Greek St.) was destroyed in the Blitz. At the Hercules' Pillars Tavern, in Greek St. (where there is an old archway) Francis Thompson was often to be seen in 1896. Shaftesbury Av., which extends NE. into Holborn bor. and SW. into St. James's, was cut diagonally through the par. in 1886.

The par. ch. of St. Anne was built in 1686; the tower dates from 1802. The par. of Soho was taken out of St. Martin's in the Fields in 1678, and the dedication was in honour of Anne, Princess of Denmark—afterwards Q. The baptismal registers include the names of two children of George II and five children of Fredk.,

P. of Wales, b. at Leicester House (see 'Leicester Square'). John Horne—afterwards known as Horne Tooke—was baptized here in 1736; and Theodore, K. of Corsica, was bd. here. He accepted the crown in 1736, but was driven out in a few months, and after two more attempts to gain his kingdom settled in England in 1749. While here he was arrested and imprisoned for debt, but obtained his liberty by surrendering to his creditors all his effects, which consisted chiefly of his claim to the kingdom. After his release he obtained lodgings with a tailor in Great Chapel St., where shortly afterwards he d. He was saved from a pauper's grave by John Wright, an oilman of Compton St., who said that he was willing, *for once*, to pay the funeral expenses of a King. There is a tablet with a sculptured crown on the W. wall of the tower. The inscription is as follows:

Near this place is interred
The King of Corsica
Who died in this parish
Dec. 12th MDCCLVI
Immediately after leaving
The King's Bench Prison
By the benefit of the Act of Insolvency
In consequence of which
He registered his Kingdom of Corsica
For the use of his creditors.

The grave, great teacher, to a level brings,
Heroes and beggars, galley slaves and kings,
Fate pour'd its lessons on his living head,
Bestow'd a kingdom and denied him bread.

The lines were written by Horace Walpole. The ch. was badly bombed but is to be rebuilt soon.

There is in the chyd. a headstone to the memory of Hazlitt, who was bd. there. The original inscription was a very lengthy one, written by R. H. Horne. It has been replaced by the present one:

'On the northern side of this ground lie the remains of William Hazlitt, painter, critic, essayist.

Born at Maidstone April 10, 1778.
Died in Soho. September 18, 1830.
Restored by his grandson.
February 1901.'

Wardour St., for many people, epitomizes Soho. Leigh Hunt heard Lamb expatiate on its pleasures, and recall a treasure hunt:

'Rummaging over the contents of an old stall in an alley leading from Wardour Street to Soho Square yesterday, I lit upon a ragged duodecimo, which had been the strange delight of my infancy. . . . The price demanded was sixpence, which the owner (a little square duodecimo of a character himself) enforced with the assurance that his own mother should not have it for a farthing less.'

Wardour St. now stands for films more than for faked furniture. An interesting tavern is the 'Intrepid Fox' at the corner of Peter St.; it owes its name to Sam House, a landlord who was a great admirer of Chas. Jas. Fox. There was free beer there for Foxites at the Westminster election in 1784; and the Duchess of Devonshire, who aided the cause by free kisses, is also said to have taken her share of free liquor. Fox and 'Sam' are shown in bas-relief on the modern tavern.

John Galsworthy, who had many a meal in this neighbourhood, said:

'Of all the quarters in the sheer adventurous amalgam called London, Soho is perhaps the least suited to the Forsyte spirit. Untidy, full of Greeks, Ishmaelites, cats, Italians, tomatoes, restaurants, organs, coloured stuffs, queer names, people looking out of upper windows, it dwells remote from the British Body Politic.'

Much of the foreign appearance is due to the influx of French refugees after the revocation of the Edict of Nantes in 1685. They settled in this part of L., and later their numbers were increased by others of their countrymen fleeing from the French Revolution. Greek St. is particularly foreign in its aspect. There was at one time a colony of Greeks located where was until 1934 ch. of St. Mary the Virgin, Charing Cross Rd. Inside the ch.—on the W. wall of the nave—was a stone with a Greek inscription from the old bdg. stating that the ch. was built for the Greeks in 1677.

(See *The Romance of Soho*, by E. Beresford Chancellor, 1931; *Soho*, by Simon Dewes, 1952.)

Somerset House (Strand) has an interest that lies almost entirely in its past; the present structure houses clerks, the previous palace lodged Queens. It takes its name from the uncle and first protector of the young Edward VI, Edwd. Seymour, D. of Somerset. At the height of his ambition he coveted a palace for himself. For this purpose he demolished the ch. of St. Mary le Strand; the episcopal house of the Bp. of Lichfield and Coventry, known as Chester's Inn; the episcopal house of the Bp. of Llandaff; an inn of Chancery—and a number of tenements. The D. made a collection of stone—from the cloisters and charnel house of St. P.'s Cath. and from the priory of St. John's, Clerkenwell; he would, it is said, have collected more from St. Margaret's Ch., Westminster, but with clubs and bended bows its parishioners menaced the D.'s workmen, and they had to retreat. John Knox bitterly said that the D. was fonder of watching masons than of hearing sermons, and enthusiastically he spent upwards of £10,000 in contemporary currency upon the bdg. At the time of his execution (1552) it was still incomplete. It was then forfeited to the Crown, and assigned as a residence for Princess Elizabeth. In 1554 apartments were prepared for one of her suitors, Philibert of Savoy, though it is not certain that he occupied them. As Queen, however, she was seldom there, preferring Whitehall. She showed some favour towards the family of the D. who had erected it, and bestowed upon his son the Protector's earlier title of E. of Hertford, with the right to occupy Somerset House as a residence. The palace, however, remained in the hands of the Crown, and relatives and dependants of the Q. lodged there. Some meetings of the Privy Council were held here in Elizabeth's time—in 1589, 1593, and 1595. At the first it is known the Q. was present. James I assigned the palace to his Q., Anne of Denmark, and it was renamed Denmark House in her honour. In 1626 Charles I settled it for life on his Q., Henrietta Maria. During the Commonwealth it was a residence for Ld. Gen. Fairfax, and the headquarters of the army. The chapel, which Inigo Jones had built, provided a pulpit for the Boanerges of Puritanism. Amongst these was a woman, described as an—

'audacious virago, a feminine tub-preacher, who last Sunday held forth for almost two hours in the late Queen's Mass Chapel at Somerset House Strand, and has done so there and elsewhere

several times. She claps her Bible and thumps the pulpit cushions with almost as much confidence (I should have said impudence) as honest Hugh Peters himself.'

The sculpture and pictures (including examples of the work of Titian, Michelangelo, Holbein, and Van Dyck) were sold, and also the beds, including one of French satin valued at about £1,000. Inigo Jones had apartments in Somerset House, and here he d. in 1652. In 1658 the body of Oliver Cromwell lay in state there, with a richly attired effigy above, as was customary on the burial of Ks. (see 'Westminster Abbey'). Geo. Fox was greatly aggrieved, and found 'the Lord highly offended' at all this show, whilst Ludlow recorded that the people showed their disapprobation by throwing dirt in the night on the escutcheon over the great gate of the house. The funeral, the cost of which amounted to £28,000, did not take place until eleven weeks after Cromwell's death at Whitehall. On the Restoration Charles I's widow, Henrietta Maria, returned to reside at Somerset House. There in 1662 Pepys saw her and the new Q., Catherine of Braganza, when the chapel was again fitted up for Roman Catholic worship.

There in 1678 was brought the body of Sir Edmund Berry Godfrey, found in a ditch on Primrose Hill. Titus Oates accused Catherine of Braganza of a deeply-laid plot concocted in her palace against the K., and one Bedloe deposed to interviews in the gallery of the chapel between the Q. and some French priests. Search was made in Somerset House, and a number of priests found. According to one confession, Godfrey had been murdered in the courtyard of the house, and then carried in a sedan-chair to Primrose Hill. Two Roman Catholic priests were hanged at Tyburn, and Somerset House was nicknamed 'Godfrey Hall.' In the walls of a passage under the quadrangle of the present Somerset House are tombstones of five people who lived there in the 17th century. The stones came from the chapel.

On the death of Charles II in 1685 Catherine of Braganza removed from Whitehall to Somerset House. She lived there in great privacy during the short reign of James II. William III was at first friendly towards her, but he suspected 'caballings against his government' at her residence and requested that she should leave town and reside at either Windsor or Audley End. The Q. replied spiritedly that—

'her earnest desire was to quit his territories altogether for Portugal, if he would but have ships appointed for the voyage; as it was she did not intend to go out of her house, which was her own by treaty.'

William thereupon begged her not to think of moving. During his absence in Ireland, however, some unpleasantness occurred between Catherine and Mary, on the ground of the omission of a prayer for the success of the Irish campaign from the service in the Savoy Chapel (under Catherine's jurisdiction and used by the Protestants of her household). This intensified Catherine's desire to depart, and she left for Portugal in 1692. Somerset House then became a haven of refuge for faded nobility. In Q. Anne's reign the chapel which Henrietta Maria had had built was divested of its Roman character and given over to the Established Ch. A register was kept of the baptisms, marriages, and burials which took place in the chapel between 1714 and 1775. The numbers are respectively 36, about 450, and 14. It is said that about 1713 the 'Old Pretender' was secreted there. In 1749 it was the scene of a highly fashionable subscription masquerade at which George II and Augusta, Princess of Wales, were present. In 1764 the Hereditary P. of Brunswick-Luneburg lodged at Somerset House, while engaged in negotiating his marriage with Augusta, daughter of George III. In 1771 the State apartments were granted to the newly constituted Royal Academy for the accommodation of its schs. of design, and an illustration to J. T. Smith's *Book for a Rainy Day* is of 'R.A.s reflecting on the True Line of Beauty at the Life Academy, Somerset House,' a number of artists being depicted drawing a nude female form. The first official dinner of the academy was held there in 1771, but the annual exhibition continued until 1780 in the academy's rooms in Pall Mall. A description of the first Somerset House in its last days is in Noorthouck's *History of London* (1773). He said:

'It was so far neglected as to be permitted to fall to ruin in some of the back

parts. . . . The front in the Strand is adorned with columns and other decorations, which are much defaced by time and the smoak of the City, the principal ornament having mouldered away.'

The last housekeeper was Mrs. Charlotte Lennox, Dr. Johnson's friend (see 'Taverns').

The architect of the second Somerset House was Wm. Chambers. It was commenced in 1775, and completed in 1790, but even then some elaborate decorative work remained to be done. Over the windows on the Strand front are medallions of George III, Q. Charlotte, and the P. of Wales, afterwards George IV (see also 'Statues'). The arches here have keystones representing Ocean, Thames, Humber, Mersey, Medway, Tweed, Tyne, Severn, Dee. They were the work of Joseph Wilton and Agostino Carlini. The idea of representing rivers by heads was more original than artistic, and identification is difficult. Of the four figures fronting the attic towards the Strand, the two at the extremities are the work of Giuseppe Ceracchi, the two in the centre being due to Carlini. The corresponding figures on the courtyard side are by Wilton, who also executed the busts of Sir Isaac Newton and Michelangelo in the vestibule. The armorial decorations surmounting the attic, on both the Strand and the interior fronts, are by John Bacon. Nollekens is said to have carved five masks after drawings by Cipriani; these are the keystones to the arches on the courtyard side of the vestibule. There are grotesques flanking the main doorways on three sides of the quadrangle, symbolical of the business that was first transacted in the bdg. The designs were probably Cipriani's, and the execution Wilton's or Carlini's.

The Royal Academy was at the new Somerset House from 1780 to 1838, and held here its annual exhibitions in some fine upper rooms. In 1792 the body of Sir Joshua Reynolds lay in state at Somerset House, and the funeral of Benjamin West took place from there in 1820. The Royal Soc. and the Soc. of Antiquaries met there; both moved to Burlington House in 1856. Amongst Govt. departments housed there were the Navy Pay Office and the Navy Office. In the former was the father of Chas. Dickens; Trollope was possibly referring to the latter in describing the 'office of the Commissioners of Internal Navigation' in *The Three Clerks* (1858).

'Somerset House is a nest of public offices, which are held to be of less fashionable repute than those situated in the neighbourhood of Downing Street, but are not so decidedly plebeian as the Custom House, Excise, and Post Office.'

The higher officials in Somerset House still work in handsome rooms, with beautifully moulded ceilings painted by Cipriani and Benjamin West. The terrace has lost some of its attractiveness since the construction of the Victoria Embankment. On that terrace Herbert Spencer used to have intimate discussions with Geo. Eliot, then working in the Strand for John Chapman (see 'Strand').

This terrace was opened to the public on Sundays and, being one of the finest promenades in L., many people used it. As there was for many yrs. a Navy mus. in connection with the many Admiralty departments, Somerset House was then much more attractive than it is now, when it is given up to the Board of Inland Revenue, the Registrar General, and the Probate Registry. Certificates of births, deaths, and marriages can also be obtained at Somerset House, these having been compulsorily registered since 1st July 1837. A W. wing was added to Somerset House in 1852–6. The river front was damaged in the Second World War. The arches here, before the construction of the Victoria Embankment, were water gates.

(See *Somerset House, Past and Present*, by Raymond Needham and Alexander Webster, 1905; and *Somerset House*, by L. M. Bates, 1967.)

South Bank. Despite a long correspondence in *The Times* as to the propriety of changing the name—one suggestion was that Q. Elizabeth should be honoured as Q. Victoria and P. Consort had been in naming the Embankments—it remains the same though indeed the expression was little in use before it was selected as the site of the Festival of Britain in 1951.

Owing to the marshy nature of the soil, there had not been a great deal of building here in the 18th century, and in some pictures it had quite a rural aspect. In 1789 a shot tower was erected. It was 200 ft. high. This first shot tower has long disappeared; a second one, erected in 1826, remains. The building is hollow with a circular staircase winding to the top of the tower against the outside wall. At the top of the tower is a floor with a square hole cut out of it; on this floor the lead was melted and poured into a sieve over the hole. The separate drops of lead thus formed fell through the hole down to a water tank on the ground floor. Each piece of shot therefore had time during the fall to cool and harden by the time it fell into the tank before reaching the water.

Also in Belvedere Rd. was a factory for the manufacture of Coade stone. The exact composition of this product remains unknown. It had good weathering qualities, and the material was used for outdoor monuments and ornamentation. The lion on the Lion Brewery had inscribed on one of its paws 'W. F. W. Coades May 24th 1837.' Figures of a school boy and girl in the chyd. of St. Botolph, Bishopsgate, are of this material. Other examples are the 29 vases (designed by Sir Wm. Chambers) on the parapet of Somerset House, coats of arms and decorative features on the Admiralty and at Trinity House, the caryatids at the Bank of England, and the tomb of Capt. Bligh of the Bounty in the chyd. of St. Mary's, Lambeth.

There was one imposing house left in Belvedere Rd. It was built about 1818; this is the date that was on a lead water pipe on the bdg., together with the initials J.C.P. They probably stood for Jas. Courthope Peache. He and his father Clement bought much of the land in this area which was known as Float Mead. Peache was a member of the Turnpike Trust, and a Freeman of the City. About 1870 his heirs leased wharves and premises in Belvedere Rd. to such firms as John Aird, contractors, and the Burnham Brick Co., and the family's connections with the area was thus severed.

The Lion Brewery has always been associated with a famous crime. In 1872 Dr. W. C. Minor, who had been a surgeon in the American Civil War, and—on a visit to this country—was staying at 41 Tenison St., shot a stoker, an employee of the Brewery, in Belvedere Rd. At the trial, at the Kingston assizes, he was defended by Sir Edwd. Clarke. He was found guilty but insane. From Broadmoor criminal lunatic asylum, where he was confined, he contributed between five and eight thousand quotations to Sir James Murray's famous *Oxford English Dictionary*, and his name will be found amongst the acknowledged assistants in the Preface to that great work. He was still living (in U.S.A.) in 1915, and in *The Springfield Sunday Republican* for 25th July 1915 there was an article on him. By way of illustration there was a picture of Belvedere Rd. and the Lion Brewery, showing a lion above the entrance gate and the shot tower in the background.

The second lion—closer to the river and higher up—and with tail poised, has aroused a great deal of interest. Emile Zola was attached to it. Recalling his visit to L. in 1893 he said:

'When I went to the window of my room I noticed the mist parting—one mass of vapour ascending skyward, while the other still hovered over the river, and, in the rent between, I espied a lion poised in mid air. It amused me vastly; and I called to my wife, saying to her, 'Come and see, here's the British Lion waiting to bid us good-day. We went to the end of the Bridge and thence espied the Lion which surmounts the brewery of that name.'

Londoners were interested in its fate, and so was K. George VI. It was removed, but is to be reinstated in the Festival grounds. While being cleaned a bottle sealed with a William IV farthing and containing a message was found in its stomach. It is 13 ft. in length, and 8 ft. high.

In the process of making a site for the Festival of Britain sixty men used 93,000 tons of demolition material to build the river wall which is 1,691 ft. long. The necessary granite was brought from Pelastine Quarry, near Penryn, Cornwall. So loose is the clay upon which L. is built that in some places the men had to dig down to a depth of 64 ft. to lay the foundations. At times their pickaxes reached within 12 ft. of the top of the Bakerloo Tube tunnel which passes under the river. In the course of excavations, a skeleton was found near Howley Terrace. It was 12 ft. below ground level, and in two ft. of mud. It is believed to have been two hundred yrs. old. Its legs were sprawled in odd directions, which seemed to indi-

cate a violent end. The bones were handed to the police. The Dome of Discovery was the largest unsupported dome in the world. It was 365 ft. in diameter, and the apex was 97 ft. from the ground. It was covered with a huge sheet of aluminium. The job involved the use of 960,000 bricks, 230 standards of timber, 3,960 tons of steel, and 150,000 sq. ft. of glass. The Festival Hall, which was built for the occasion, has been developed by the G.L.C. into a cultural centre by the addition of the Queen Elizabeth Hall and the Purcell Room which offer regular concerts under the heading 'Music on the South Bank'. The recently opened Hayward Gallery has brought exhibitions of art into this area of modern architecture just across the river from the City.

Southwark, now part of the L. Bor. of Southwark, formerly a met. bor. south of the Thames, was also the name of an ancient bor. with very different boundaries composed of the pars. of St. George the Martyr, St. Margaret, St. Mary Magdalen, St. Thomas, and St. Olave. After the dissolution of the monasteries St. Margaret's and St. Mary Magdalen's were amalgamated and called St. Saviour's par., out of which Christ Ch. was taken in 1670. The name Southwark—fifty yrs. ago called Southwork, has reference to the ancient defences of the City of L.

Southwark Cath. is the subject of a separate article. The R.C. Cath. is on the NE. side of St. George's Rd., between Lambeth Rd. and Westminster Bridge Rd. It is dedicated to St. George, and was built as a par. ch., 1841–8, by the elder Pugin. It became the cath. of the new diocese in 1850. It is Gothic: outwardly a very plain bdg. of very dark brick; within its length and its clustered columns and wide windows give it a stately appearance. It was badly damaged in a raid, but it was patched up, and in Sept. 1950, to celebrate the centenary of the R.C. hierarchy in England, a special service was held. It was attended by Cardinal Griffin, as papal legate, and his throne was on the spot where Cardinal Wiseman, his predecessor as Abp. of Westminster, was enthroned in 1850. There were also six visiting cardinals from Lyons, Malines, New York, Toronto,

Cologne and Berlin.

St. George the Martyr Ch., Borough High St., was granted to the Bermondsey monks in 1122 by Thos. de Arderne and his son of the same name; it had a tower 98 ft. high; and eight bells by **Abraham Rudhall**, 1718. In 1639 it was repaired and beautified. In it was m. in 1653 General Geo. Monk, afterwards D. of Albermarle; and here was bd. Edward Cocker (1675). Dr. Johnson took a copy of Cocker's *Arithmetic* on his tour to the Hebrides, and tipped the maid with it! The phrase 'according to Cocker' derives from him. Another probable burial here was Bonner, Bp. of L. in Q. Mary's time. He d. in the Marshalsea Prison—not then adjoining the ch.—in 1569.

The present ch., known to Dickensians as 'Little Dorrit's,' was built 1734-6. A new E. window (1951) has a figure of her; there were extensive repairs in 1808. Besides Rudhall's bells, it has a sanctus bell by T. Lester. Most of the ch. is brick; its square tower over the W. door, with an octagonal upper storey (containing a clock) below the steeple, is very conspicuous.

St. Margaret's Ch., part of which was turned into an assize court and prison when its par. became part of St. Saviour's in 1541, had totally disappeared after the great Southwark fire in 1676. On its site, to the S. of which was a wide space called St. Margaret's Hill, a town hall was built 1686, rebuilt 1793: it remained in use as such, and as the office of the High Bailiff, until 1859, when that officer removed to the City.

The more northerly par., swallowed up in St. Saviour's, was St. Mary Magdalen's, whose parishioners used as ch. the chapel, so dedicated, about 1239, on the S. side of St. Mary Overy's Ch., the pre-Reformation name of the present Southwark Cath. Their chapel was pulled down in 1822, in the course of somewhat unnecessary demolitions preparatory to the rebuilding of London Bridge.

The par. of Christ Ch., roughly approximating the area of Paris Garden, was formed 1670, in accordance with a bequest by John Marshall, 1627. The new ch., opened 1671, was built on ground provided by Wm. Angel, then in possession of the manor. It was badly built; and it was replaced in 1741 by the present ch., now bounded on the E. by Blackfriars Rd.—originally a plain quadrangular

bdg. of brick, with stone quoins and window dressings. It had been enlarged and altered at different times, was burnt out in an air-raid, but has been rebuilt.

Newington is a par. in the Brixton hundred, in the angle between the roads from London Bridge into Kent. In Domesday Book it was 'Waleorde, farm of Wale, or, some say, farm of the serfs.' Wherever the first par. ch. stood, a St. Mary's Ch. stood for centuries on a site half-way along the W. side of Newington Butts, where is now a clock tower. An old ch. on the site was replaced by a new one in 1721; there was almost entire rebuilding in 1793, and there was extensive restoration in 1810. It was demolished in 1876, on the completion of its successor in Kennington Park Rd. The latter ch. is now a ruin. Amongst those bd. in the old ch. and chyd. were: Thos. Middleton, dramatist and City chronologer (1627); Geo. Powell, K. of the Gipsies (1704); and W. Davy, serjeant-at-law and humorist (1780).

In Trinity Sq. is Holy Trinity Ch. (1824) and off Walworth Rd. is St. Peter's, another classical ch. by Sir John Soane (1823). Behind Kennington Park is St. Agnes Ch. It replaces that built by G. G. Scott, and destroyed in the war.

The Metropolitan Tabernacle of the Baptists is in Newington Butts. It was built for Rev. Chas. Haddon Spurgeon (1834-92), a native of Kelvedon, Essex. He began his L. ministry at New Park St. Chapel, near Bankside in 1854. (Until the Blitz the bdg., transformed into factory, survived.) After a short spell of preaching in the Surrey Music Hall, Walworth Rd., Spurgeon commenced at the Tabernacle in 1860. It was burnt out in 1898, rebuilt and re-opened in 1900. It was reduced to a ruin by German bombs, but has been rebuilt.

Once, in 1898, Southwark had a street lamp which supplied boiling water, cocoa, and tea on the penny-in-the slot system. There was at the same time a hot-water street lamp in Clerkenwell, of which there was a picture in *The Radio Times* for 12th Jan., 1951.

(See *Southwark Story*, by F. M. G. Evans, 1955.)

Southwark Cathedral (on the Surrey side of the Thames and SW. of L.B.) in the course of its history has had three names: (1) St. Mary Overie Ch.; (2) St. Saviour's Ch.; (3) Southwark Cath.

(1) St. Mary Overie Ch. The first part of the dedication was to the Virgin. The second part means 'of the ferry,' 'over the river' or, possibly, 'of the bank or shore.' Roman tesserae found on the site, and now in the pavement at the entrance to the S. choir aisle, suggest the possibility of a Roman temple on the site. Stow says the ch. had a beginning long before the Conquest, and was first 'a house of sisters founded by a maiden named Mary.' He adds that she left to this nunnery the 'oversight and profits of a cross ferry . . . over the Thames, there kept before any bridge was built.' A story of this lady is one of the most piquant in L. lore. Her father, the ferry-keeper before her, was miserly, and thought that, if he feigned death, a grief-stricken household would eat little and save much. Instead there was rejoicing. He burst in upon the merriment, like Daniel Quilp upon his wife, and a boat-man, believing he was a ghost, assailed him with an oar, and really killed him. The lady then sent for her lover; he fell from his horse and was killed, whereupon in grief she founded a nunnery and entered it. This nunnery was dissolved in 852, and St. Swithun, Bp. of Winchester, established a coll. of secular priests. In 1106 this coll. was dissolved, and the ch. refounded for canons regular by two Norman knights, Wm. Pont de la Arch and Wm. Dauncey. The canons (of the Order of St. Augustine) built a ch. in the Norman style. In 1207 it was almost entirely destroyed by fire, and a Gothic edifice took its place. At this time a ch. of St. Mary Magdalene Overie was erected between the walls of the choir and the S. transept, for the use of the parishioners. In the reign of Richard II there was another fire, involving repairs, and then, as well as in the reign of Henry IV, Perpendicular Gothic features were introduced by Cardinal Beaufort, Bp. of Winchester. He is said to have restored the S. transept at his own expense, and is there commemorated to-day by a sculptured representation of his hat and coat of arms, affixed to a pier by the door. In 1469 the stone roof of the nave fell in, and a new roof was built of wood. In 1540 the priory was surrendered to Henry

VIII.

(2) St. Saviour's Church. By an Act of 1540 the priory ch., St. Mary Magdalene's, and a third ch. in the immediate vicinity dedicated to St. Margaret, were united into a single par., under the title of St. Saviour's. In some of Visscher's views, however, more than seventy yrs. later, the pre-Reformation title remained. It can also still be found at the dock W. of the cath., where probably provisions were landed for the canons. St. Margaret's Ch., which stood on ground afterwards occupied by the old Southwark town hall was secularized and used as a Sessions Court, a Court of Admiralty, and a prison. A relic of the ch. survives in the shape of a monumental slab to Aleyn Ferthing, five times M.P. for Southwark about the middle of the 14th century. It was discovered in 1833 during excavations on the site of the old ch., and placed in the Lady Chapel. From 1540 the priory ch. and rectory were leased to the parishioners by the Crown at a rental of about £50 p.a. till 1614, when the ch. was purchased from James I for the sum of £800. The Lady Chapel had been in a sorry condition. Stow says it

> 'was leased and let out and the House of God made a bakehouse. . . . In this place they had their ovens . . . in that their kneading trough, in another (I have heard) a hog's grouth, for the words that were given me were these: "This place have I known a hog-stie, in another a storehouse to store up their hoarded meal, and in all of it something of this sordid kind and condition." '

In the reign of Q. Mary the Lady Chapel was turned to a sinister if not a sacrilegious use. A commission appointed by the Cardinal Legate sat there for the trial of certain preachers and heretics. It was presided over by Bps. Gardiner of Winchester and Bonner of L. The trials ended in the condemnation of the Rev. Lawrence Saunders, rector of All Hallows, Bread St.; Rev. John Bradford, prebendary of St. P.'s Cath.; Rev. John Rogers, vicar of St. Sepulchre's, Newgate; Rev. Rowland Taylor, rector of Hadleigh (Suffolk); the Rt. Rev. Robt. Ferrar, Bp. of St. David's; the Rt. Rev. John Hooper, Bp. of Gloucester; and Rev. John Philpot, prebendary of Winchester. All of these suffered martyrdom at the stake. A figure of Hooper is in a window of the Lady Chapel, and a figure of Rogers is in the reredos. From 1618 to 1626 Dr. Lancelot Andrewes was Bp. of Winchester (he d. in the neighbouring Winchester Palace). His tomb, twice moved, is a most ornate one. His head, bearing an academic cap, rests upon a cushion, and the right hand holds a book—probably intended for the famous *Manual of Devotion*. The canopy is modern. In his time there were galleries across the N. and S. transepts, and a screen and gallery in place of the old rood loft between the nave and choir. Closed and rented pews were introduced, and evidently carefully allotted according to rank The churchwardens, addressing the Bp. of Winchester in 1639, said:

'We assure your Lordship that a Pew wherein one Mrs. Ware sits, and pleads to be placed, is, and always hath been, a Pew for Women of a far better rank and quality than she, and for such whose husbands pay far greater duty than hers, and hath always been reserved for some of the chiefest Women dwelling on the Borough side of the said Parish and never any of the Bankside were placed there.'

(An account of the 'quality' of the Bankside will be found under that head.) In 1680 the candelabrum of thirty lights was given by Dorothy Applebee. In 1703 a new altar-piece, in the Corinthian style, was erected in front of the beautiful screen of Bp. Fox, dating from about 1520. In 1821–2 the choir was restored by Gwilt when St. Mary Magdalene's Ch. was demolished. The nave was so neglected that it remained without a roof from 1830 to 1839. The walls were then pulled down, and an unworthy edifice erected on the site. In 1877 Southwark was transferred from the diocese of Winchester to that of Rochester. In 1889 Thorold, Bp. of Rochester, appealed for funds to rebuild the nave. The architect was Sir Arthur Blomfield, whose work, completed in 1897, harmonised beautifully with the Early English choir (*c*. 1220) and the later Gothic transepts. In 1907 the chapel of St. John the Divine, on the N. side was restored in memory of John Harvard (b. in Borough High St., and baptized in the ch. in 1607). It had a stained glass window (with some Elizabethan glass included) which was designed by the American artist John Le Farge, and displayed the arms of Emmanuel Coll., Cambridge, where Harvard was educated, and of Harvard University. The window was almost entirely destroyed in the Second World War, but restored in U.S.A. and again formally unveiled in 1949. In this chapel is also a tablet commemorating the work of the Pilgrim Trust. There is a carved shell—representing the old pilgrims' badge.

(3) SOUTHWARK CATHEDRAL. In 1905 the diocese of Rochester was divided, and the ch. of St. Saviour became Southwark Cath. In 1905–12 the reredos was filled with the figures of men associated with its history. Previously its bareness, by one visitor to the cath., was associated with the 'depredations of Cromwell.' The figures are as follows, commencing from the top and proceeding N .to S.: Bp. Thorold; St. Olave; Wm. of Wykeham; Cardinal Beaufort; St. Paul; Christ; St. Augustine of Hippo; Bp. Giffard; Prior Aldgood; St. Justus of Rochester; Bp. Talbot; Prebendary Rogers; St. Swithun; St. Thomas of Canterbury; St. Margaret of Antioch; St. Peter; the Virgin Mary; St. John; St. Mary Magdalene; John Gower; Bp. Peter de Roche; Dr. Randall Davidson; the twelve apostles; angels holding the arms of Canterbury, Winchester, Rochester, and Southwark; Henry I; Bp. Lancelot Andrewes; Bp. Fox; Edward VII. The last visited the ch. in 1897 to commemorate the completion of the restoration and again in 1905 when it was made a cath. (For brief accounts of these personages, see *The Story of Southwark Cathedral*, by Canon T. P. Stevens.)

There is a number of interesting monuments. The oldest is John Gower's on the N. side of the nave. He d. in 1409 and was bd. in the chapel of St. John the Baptist, where he had founded a chantry. The poet is represented lying on his back, with his hands clasped, and his head resting upon the three volumes upon which his fame depends: *Speculum Meditantis* (beholding yourself in a glass), *Vox Clamanti* (voice of one that crieth), and *Confessio Amantis* (confession of a lover). He is dressed in a long dark habit, buttoned down to the feet, after the manner of an English gentleman of the time. There is a garland of roses round his head, and at his feet a lion couchant. The SS. collar adorns the neck, with a pendent jewel on which a swan is en-graved—the device of Richard II. At one time, at the back, were three painted figures of Charity, Mercy, and Pity. They were obliterated in 1748, when a large sum was spent on 'embellishment.' The cornice at the top is modern. The inscription is translated:

'Here lieth J. Gower Armiger [a title by patent], celebrated English poet, also a noted benefactor to this sacred edifice, who lived in the reigns of Edward III, Richard II, and Henry IV.' A semi-nude figure commemorates Wm. Emerson, who 'lived and died an honest man.' Ralph Waldo Emerson saw this in 1872; it may have been an ancestor. The Latin inscription is 'remember you must die.' On the N. side of the choir is the monument of Richd. Humble (d. 1616). He is shown kneeling at a small altar with his two wives behind, his sons and daughters being represented in bas relief. The inscription has been attributed to Beaumont and Quarles:

'Like to the damask rose you see,
Or like the blossom on the tree,
Or like the dainty flower of May,
Or like the morning of the day,
Or like the sun or like the shade,
Or like the gourd which Jonas had,
Even so is man whose thread is spun,
Drawn out and cut and so is done.
The rose withers, the blossom blasteth,
The flower fades, the morning hasteth,
The sun sets, the shadows flies,
The gourd consumes, and man he dies.'

Another interesting monument is John Trehearne's. He was a servant to Q. Elizabeth and 'Gentleman Porter' to James I. Trehearne and his wife are represented in a kneeling posture with their family in bas-relief below. The inscription says that if his royal master had had his way he would have retained his services rather than that Trehearne should have gone aloft. There is a large mural monument to Wm. Austin (d. 1633) of which Strype has given a lengthy description. The Bingham monument (1625) exhibits a half-length coloured effigy of the deceased, in gown and ruff. He was saddler to Q. Elizabeth, and the arms of the City of L. and the Saddlers' Co. are shown. There is also the 'Bene-field' monument (1615). In the choir are cut the names of Edmund Shakespeare,

brother of Wm. (d. 1607), John Fletcher (d. 1625), Philip Massinger (d. 1640)—all bd. here. There is a monument to Thos. Lockyer, a quack doctor. There is the fine Offley Chest—of Elizabethan date (see 'Epitaphs').

The most recent monument is that of Talbot, first diocesan bp. (1905–11). There is a recumbent bronze figure, and the whole work vies with Bp. Andrewes's tomb for beauty. There is also a figure, finely carved in oak, of a mailed knight, possibly a Templar. The sword is drawn 5 or 6 in. from the scabbard. In reciting the creed every morning a Templar half drew his sword and then put it back in token of his willingness to defend the faith. There is also a stone effigy of an emaciated woman, associated by some with Mary of the Ferry, whose story has been related.

On the N. side, inside a door leading to the vestry, are the jambs of the Norman entrance to the cloister. The archway was demolished c. 1840. There is also a holy water stoup.

A great feature of the Cath. was the stained glass windows. On the S. side, starting in 1897, was a series commemorating dramatists and an actor associated with Bankside: Shakspere; Francis Beaumont; John Fletcher; Philip Massinger; Edwd. Alleyn, Warden of the K.'s bears and founder of the Coll. of God's Gift, Dulwich. These were all destroyed in the Second World War. On this side the memorial to Shakespeare—unveiled by Sir Sidney Lee in 1912—remains. The figure is of alabaster, and the face resembles that of Edwd. de Vere, the 17th E. of Oxford. In the background are shown L.B., with heads over the S. gate, St. Saviour's Ch., as the Cath. then was, Winchester House, and the Globe Theatre. The brief history given beside the monument of Shakespeare's association with Southwark is unfounded in any known facts, and the L.C.C. Survey volume on Southwark intimates that there is no evidence of his residence in the neighbourhood. Certainly in view of the known residence in the City (see p. 86), he could not have lived in Southwark so long as is claimed. As to this being Shakespeare's ch., R. M. Wingent, in his excellent book *The Borough and the Borough Hospitals*, 1913, says: 'There is little evidence to show that the majority of these old players were acquainted with the inside of a church to any extent. In Shakespeare's case particularly it would be idle to follow his biographers in their surmises and conjectures; few of them venture on assertions that are not qualified by doubtless.' One such purple passage, highly imaginative, can be found in Arthur Mee's *London*, touching the funeral of Edmund Shakspeare. On the N. side there are windows in memory of Samuel Johnson—by reason of his friendship with the brewer of Park St., Henry Thrale; Oliver Goldsmith—as a physician on Bankside; John Bunyan—mistakenly said to have preached much at a chapel in Zoar St. which was not opened until the yr. of his death; Alexander Cruden—of Biblical Concordance fame—because he was bd. in a dissenting cemetery near the Ch.; Geoffrey Chaucer in respect of the Canterbury pilgrims starting from the Tabard Inn. Dr. Sacheverell—he was chaplain of St. Saviour's, 1705-9. All these windows have been damaged, but have since been restored. Another window—in the Lady Chapel—commemorates three Anglican martyrs, Thos. à Becket, Abp. Laud, and Charles I. There are also windows commemorating St. Augustine (d. 430), St. Paulinus (d. 644), and St. Swithun (d. 862).

There are some Norman arches in the Harvard Chapel. The Lady Chapel (*c.* 1228) is a beautiful specimen of early Gothic architecture. Here, in 1854, took place the proceedings annulling the marriage of John Ruskin and his wife. Ruskin was not present. There is Early English arcading near the SW. door. In the S. choir aisle are some of the wooden bosses removed in 1830 from the roof where they had been since 1469. The subjects include the pelican feeding her young with her blood; a woman with a swollen face; a K. with a long beard; a man with a twisted tongue. It is suggested that the last two were moralizations upon the evils of vanity and lying. There is also the Devil swallowing Judas Iscariot—who seems to be wearing a priestly robe. In the NW. corner of the ch. there is a case containing relics of the Roman occupation and of bombing in the First World War.

The tower dates from *c.* 1520; the height is 129 ft., exclusive of the crocketed pinnacles designed by Gwilt, the cath.

architect, in 1818. There are twelve bells unsurpassed for purity of tone; their aggregate weight is 215 cwt.

In 1937 a new constitution was set up under the title of the 'Cathedral and Collegiate Church of St. Saviour and St. Mary Overie', Southwark, the incumbent becoming provost and head of the chapter.

In 1948 a garden on the S. side of the Cath. was opened by Q. Mary.

(See *Southwark Cathedral*, by George Worley, 1905; *Southwark Cathedral*, by Canon Thompson, 1910; *The Story of Southwark Cathedral*, by Canon T. P. Stevens, 1929; *The Story of Southwark Cathedral*, by Canon Monroe, 1934.)

Squares. By some visitors to L. it is loved for its squares, as Bath for its crescents. The shape is of no account; what attracts is the oasis in the midst of stone mansions and what Ruskin called brick boxes. There are within the county about 437 grass enclosures of various sizes that help to kindle in the citizen a desire for green fields, as the bird in Cheapside did for Wordsworth's Susan. Some are in the E., e.g. Arbour Sq., off Commercial Rd., E., and Beaumont Sq., near Mile End Rd., but in the general mind squares stand for the 'West End.'

BEDFORD SQUARE (Bloomsbury) was formed between 1775 and 1780. The sq. was part of the Bedford estate, and was constructed immediately to the N. of the ample gardens attached to the D. of Bedford's house, which was demolished in 1800. It was very select; no errand boys were allowed. Goods must be delivered in person. The central gardens, where there are some fine plane trees, were originally maintained by those who held bdg. leases from the ground landlord; it was not until 1874, when these leases expired, that the supervision of the sq. was taken over by the Bedford Estate. The tenants were then allowed the use of the garden during the D. of Bedford's pleasure. Amongst the residents have been: No. 6-6A, Ld. Loughborough (it was his official residence as Ld. Chancellor, 1787-96), and (1804-15) Ld. Eldon; No. 22, Sir Johnston Forbes Robertson; No. 25, B. W. Procter ('Barry Cornwall'); No. 44, Rt. Hon. H. H. Asquith, afterwards E. of Oxford; No. 53, Seymour Hicks.

The most exciting resident was Ld. Eldon. In 1815 an anti-Corn Law demonstration suspended a noose outside his house, tore up the railings and smashed the windows. Military assistance was summoned.

BELGRAVE SQUARE was built in 1825, on what was known as the Five Fields, a part of Ebury Farm which came into the Grosvenor family in the 17th century through the marriage of Mary Davies, daughter and heiress of the owner, to Sir Thos. Grosvenor, ancestor of the Ds. of Westminster. E. Grosvenor was formerly Viscount Belgrave. It is perhaps the most aristocratic of L. squares, and W. S. Gilbert regarded it as a synonym for high life (see 'Seven Dials'). Amongst the dukes and earls who mostly figure in the long list of residents given by G. H. Cunningham are Henry Labouchere (1854) and Sir Henry Campbell-Bannerman. The latter formed his ministry there in 1906. The sq. is the centre of the district known as Belgravia (q.v.).

BERKELEY SQUARE (Mayfair) is named after Berkeley House, erected about the middle of the 17th century for Ld. John Berkeley of Stratton, with gardens extending back to and covering the area of the sq. The sq. was laid out in 1698. There was an equestrian statue of George III, erected by Princess Amelia in 1766; it was removed in 1827. There is a long list of distinguished residents: No. 6, Wm. Pitt, E. of Chatham; No. 10, Colin Campbell (Ld. Clyde); No. 11, formerly No. 40, Horace Walpole; No. 13, the fourth Marquess of Hertford; No. 16, Lady Randolph Churchill; No. 20, Colley Cibber; No. 21, Ld. Brougham; No. 25, Chas. Jas. Fox; No. 45, Ld. Clive (he committed suicide here in 1774); No. 48, E. Grey. On the S. side was until 1934 Lansdowne House, built 1762-7 for John, E. of Bute, when prime minister, by Robt. Adam. Here Dr. Johnson called in 1762 to thank his lordship for his pension. Berkeley Sq. is a most dignified sq., with some of L.'s finest plane trees. The garden is open to the public.

BLOOMSBURY SQUARE was originally made about 1665, and was first known as Southampton Sq.—from the builder, Thos. Wriothesley, E. of Southampton, whose title is still commemorated by Southampton Row. His house was on the N. side of the Sq., and there he was visited by Evelyn in 1665, who said he was building 'a noble square or piazza, a little towne.' Later it passed into the hands of the Bedford family, and was called Bedford House. Pepys referred to the making of the sq. as 'a very great and noble work.' Richd. Baxter was living in the sq. when his wife d. in 1681. Sir Richd. Steele was a resident 1712-15. Philip Stanhope, second E. of Chesterfield, Ld. Chamberlain to Charles II's Q., lived at No. 45, 1681-1713; he was the friend of Dryden. His son and grandson also lived here. The house is marked by a tablet.

Sir Hans Sloane resided in the sq. from 1696 to 1742, and crowded the house with those treasures which provided much material for the new B. Mus. Mark Akenside, the poet, was a practising physician in Bloomsbury Sq. from 1749 to 1759. Ld. Mansfield was occupying a house in the NE. corner at the time of the 'No Popery' riots of 1780. Outside his house a huge fire was made into which plate, money, furniture, books, and manuscripts were thrown. No attempts were made to destroy the contents of his wine cellars which served to intoxicate some of the mob. As Ld. Chief Justice it was Ld. Mansfield's lot to preside at the trial of Ld. Geo. Gordon; but his impartiality was such that the latter's friends were not perturbed. At No. 6 Isaac D'Israeli lived 1818-29, coming here with Benjamin from King's, now Theobalds Rd. Some of the later volumes of *Curiosities of Literature* were written in this house, which is marked by a tablet. Herbert Spencer lived at No. 29, from 1863 to 1865, when engaged on his *Principles of Biology*.

The statue of Chas. Jas. Fox (1816) was the work of Sir Richd. Westmacott.

BRUNSWICK SQUARE (Bloomsbury) was laid out under an Act of 1794, when besides the various duties of paving, lighting, washing, and repairing the footways around the sqs., the special commissioners were empowered to lay out and enclose with iron or other rails the middle of the sqs. in such manner as they thought fit, and were to remove all encroachments, obstructions, nuisances, and annoyances, and were also given power to levy rates upon the inhabitants. John Leech and 'Barry Cornwall' have resided there, and it was a favourite walk of Ld. Macaulay's when his family was living in Gt. Ormond St.

BRYANSTON SQUARE (St. Marylebone) was built at the beginning of the 19th century. It is so called from Bryanston, near Blandford, Dorset, the seat of Ld. Portman, the ground landlord. At. No 6 Joseph Hume, M.P., d. 1855.

CAVENDISH SQUARE. It was laid out in 1717, Jas. Brydges, D. of Chandos, began building on the N. side. At No. 32 lived Geo. Romney from 1775–97 and did his best work. Lady Hamilton sat for him here. He executed fourteen portraits of her.

CHESTER SQUARE (Pimlico) was built in 1840. Its name is due to the fact that the D. of Westminster's principal seat is Eaton Hall, near Chester. Matthew Arnold resided there for some yrs. He left in 1867.

'We are fairly driven out of Chester Square, partly by the number of our children, partly by the necessity of a better school for boys.'

Mary Wollstonecraft Shelley, the widow of the poet, d. at No. 24 in 1851. J. St. Loe Strachey, for many yrs. editor and proprietor of the *Spectator*, lived at No. 76 in 1926.

EDWARDES SQUARE (Kensington), which dates from the Napoleonic era, owes its designation to the family name of Ld. Kensington. Leigh Hunt lived at No. 32 from 1840–51, and there wrote *The Old Court Suburb*.

FITZROY SQUARE (Euston Rd.). Fitzroy was the family name of the Ds. of Grafton, owners of the manor of Tottenham Court. In 1790 the S. and E. sides were built by Robt. and Jas. Adam; it was not until 1828 that the other two sides were completed. Sir Chas. Eastlake, President of the Royal Academy, d. at No. 7 in 1865. Ford Madox Brown d. at No. 37 in 1893. In 1890 Bernard Shaw was living at No. 29, and in the sq. is said to have danced in the early hours of the morning with a policeman. Hesketh Pearson, however, was incredulous of the story, calling it 'a tissue of lies.' Wm. Archer lived at No. 27 in 1924.

GOLDEN SQUARE. It was built between 1688 and 1700. In 1753 Van Nost's statue of George II was placed in the centre. The K. is crowned with laurel, and attired in Roman dress. In the left hand he holds a lizard—for what reason is undiscoverable. The sq. has been almost entirely rebuilt. Henry St. John Ld.

Bolingbroke lived here, and in 1714 on the death of Q. Anne left his residence in the dress of a servant to escape to the Continent. Wm. Windham was born in the sq. in 1750. Angelica Kauffman was another resident (1767), as was also Cardinal Wiseman (1850). Golden Sq. was the residence of Ralph Nickleby. Dickens describes it in Chapter II of the novel.

'It is one of the squares that have been; a quarter of the town that has gone down in the world, and taken to letting lodgings. Many of its first and second floors are let, furnished, to single gentlemen; and it takes boarders besides. . . . It is the region of song and soke. Street bands are on their mettle in Golden Square; and itinerant glee singers quaver involuntarily as they raise their voices within its boundaries.'

GROSVENOR SQUARE was built in 1695. G. H. Cunningham says that it was the last public place in L. to be lighted with gas, oil lamps being preferred. The last of these remained until 1842. There has been a remarkable number of distinguished residents. Ld. Chesterfield lived here from 1733 to 1750, and here Samuel Johnson was repulsed from his door, as he complained in the celebrated letter written seven yrs. later (1755). Henry Thrale, Johnson's friend, d. in the Sq. in 1781. Ld. Rockingham lived there for many yrs., and d. there in 1782. Wm. Beckford, owner of Fonthill Abbey, and author of *Vathek*, was another resident. In 1800, when Sir Wm. and Lady Hamilton came to L., Beckford lent them his house as their residence; and when Nelson returned to England in the same yr. after the Battle of the Nile, he was a frequent visitor here. John Wilkes d. in the Sq. in 1797. Ld. Lytton had been living here for five yrs. when he d. at Torquay in 1873.

This quarter has had American associations. From 1785 to 1788 John Adams, Minister to Great Britain and later second President of U.S.A., lived in a house at the corner of Duke St. and Brook St.; at No. 6 Walter Hines Page, Ambassador of U.S.A., 1913–18, lived. The present American Embassy is an unmistakable feature of the square. In the centre is a statue of Franklin Delano Roosevelt (see 'Statues').

GORDON SQ. (St. Pancras) was built in the eighteen-twenties. It was named after

Lady Georgiana Gordon, second wife of the 6th D. of Bedford. In the SW. corner is the Catholic Apostolic Ch., built 1851–4. Close by is University Hall (with frescoes of Chas. and Mary Lamb and their contemporaries), and in the same bdg. is housed Dr. Williams' Library (see 'Libraries'). At No. 35 Dr. Jas. Martineau d., after about 25 yrs.' residence. At No. 51 Lytton Strachey was living in 1924.

HANOVER SQUARE (SW. of Oxford Circus). It was built 1716–20, and named after the new dynasty. In the centre is Chantrey's bronze statue of Wm. Pitt, erected 1831. The Hanover Rooms were at the NW. corner of Hanover St. They were built in 1775, and there in 1791 and 1792, and again three yrs. later, Haydn conducted his twelve grand symphonies. In 1796 John Braham made his *debut* here as a tenor. From 1833 to 1866 the concerts of the Philharmonic Soc. were held in the rooms. In 1874 the bdg. was altered at the cost of £25,000, and reopened as the Circle of the Nations; afterwards as the Hanover Sq. Club. The bdg. was demolished in 1900. Another structure was Harewood House, built by Robt. Adam for the D. of Roxburghe, but afterwards the town house of the E. of Harewood. Late in the 19th century it came into possession of the Royal Agricultural Soc. of England. They sold it in 1905, and it was pulled down in 1908. Well known residents include Admiral Ld. Rodney (1784–92); Percival Pott, surgeon (1777–88); Talleyrand (1835). (For St. George's Ch., see 'Westminster City.')

KENSINGTON SQUARE. It was built in 1698. In a house in the SE. corner Mazarin lived in 1692, and Talleyrand in 1792. At No. 18 John Stuart Mill lived from 1837–51. At No. 41 Sir Edwd. Burne-Jones resided from 1865–8; at No. 14 J. R. Green from 1879–83.

MECKLENBURG SQUARE (Bloomsbury) was laid out under the same Act as Brunswick Sq. (see *supra*). Henry Thos. Buckle, author of the *History of Civilization in England*, was living there in 1830. At No. 46 Geo. Augustus Sala lived in 1881–2.

PORTMAN SQUARE (Baker St.) was built in 1764-84. It was a scheme of John Elwes the miser. It was called after Wm. Henry Portman, of Orchard-Port-

man in Somersetshire (d. 1796), the proprietor of an estate in Marylebone of about 270 acres. In Espriella's letters (1807) Southey described the sq. as 'on the outskirts of the town, and approached on one side by a road unlit, unpaved, and inaccessible by carriages.' Montagu House (NW. corner) was designed by Jas. ('Athenian') Stuart, and completed in 1782 for Mrs. Elizabeth Montagu the 'blue-stocking,' author of *An Essay on the Writings and Genius of Shakespeare*. General Paoli, the Corsican patriot, lived in the sq. about 1786.

QUEEN SQUARE (Bloomsbury). It was laid out in the reign of Q. Anne, but the statue in the centre is Q. Charlotte, consort of George III. In 1728 the Bps. of Carlisle, Chester, and Chichester had their town houses in this sq. In 1772 Dr. Burney was living here when he was visited by Capt. Cook. His son James, afterwards Admiral Burney, a friend of Lamb, then accompanied Capt. Cook on his second journey. At No. 12—marked by a tablet—lived Rev. F. D. Maurice from 1846–56. On the site of No. 26 was the residence and workshops of Wm. Morris from 1865–81. R. L. Stevenson wrote of Queen Sq. as 'a little enclosure of tall trees and comely old brick houses, easy enough to see into over a railing at one end, but not very easy to enter for all that.'

RED LION SQUARE (Holborn). It was built in 1698 by Nicholas Barbon, son of Praise God Barbon, on the Red Lion Fields. At No. 17 D. G. Rossetti, Wm. Morris and Edwd. Burne-Jones lived between 1856 and 1859. The house is marked by a tablet. Hanway House commemorates the site of the residence of the philanthropist who was the first male to carry an umbrella in L. sts. He d. here in 1786. Haydon, the ill-fated artist, was living here in 1838. In the NE. corner is Conway Hall. The garden in summer has been used for children's concerts.

RUSSELL SQUARE (Bloomsbury) was built in 1804, and so called after the Russells, Es. and Ds. of Bedford. Each side is about 670 ft. in length. On the S. side is a statue of Francis, D. of Bedford (hero of Burke's *Letter to a Noble Lord*, 1796) by Sir Richd. Westmacott, R.A. At No. 5 (now the site of Hotel Russell) F. D. Maurice lived 1856–62. At No. 13 Sir Geo.

Williams, founder of the Y.M.C.A., lived for over twenty-five yrs. At No. 21 Sir Samuel Romilly d. by his own hand (1818). At No. 56 Mary Russell Mitford lived in 1836. At No. 65 (site now of the Imperial Hotel) Sir Thos. Lawrence d. 1830.

ST. JAMES'S SQUARE. It owes its origin to a speculation of Henry Jermyn, E. of St. Albans, who leased 45 acres of St. James's Fields in 1662, and purchased the property outright a few yrs. later. He began to build about 1664, and ten yrs. later there were residents of an exclusive character. The centre was neglected for a considerable period, and it was not until 1727 that it was properly paved. At No. 10—known as Norfolk House—Wm. Pitt, E. of Chatham, lived from 1759–62. Edward Stanley, afterwards E. of Derby and three times Prime Minister, was resident from 1837 to 1854, and W. E. Gladstone, during the parliamentary session of 1890. The old link extinguishers remain.

Robt. Walpole lived in the sq. between 1732 and 1735. Another resident was the 4th E. of Chesterfield, author of the famous Letters: he was b. in the sq. in 1694. Two future Abps. of C. lived here: Tait from 1857 to 1868, and Frederick Temple from 1886 to 1896 when he became primate.

In the SE. corner is another Norfolk House; the name is derived from the E. of St. Albans' house once in the sq. On this is an inscription stating that the bdg. from 24th June to 8th Nov. 1942 was the headquarters of the First Allied Force under General Eisenhower.

TAVISTOCK SQUARE (Bloomsbury) was built in the early yrs. of the 19th century. It was called after the second title of the Ds. of Bedford, the ground landlords. The British Medical Association's premises cover the site of a house in which Dickens lived 1851–60. There he wrote *Bleak House*, *Hard Times*, and *Little Dorrit*. Its garden remains at the rear of the Mary Ward Settlement. The garden in the sq. is now open to the public.

(See *History of the Squares of London*, by E. Beresford Chancellor, 1907.)

Staple Inn. It has a name the derivation of which is open to considerable doubt. It is possibly connected with a post, bar or pillar, and it was suggested that the present Holborn Bars—denoting the boundary between the City and the bor. of Camden (late Holborn)—are sufficient explanation. The Oxford English Dictionary gives this derivation, and also from an old French word *estaple*, an emporium or mart, in this case for wool. In 1375 the Soc. of the Merchants of the Staple (incorporated in 1319) removed from Westminster 'to a place called Staple Inn in Holborn.' Apparently however, they were only there about three yrs., although this brief period has left its mark behind. There is a representation of a wool-pack in the wrought iron gate at the back of the garden; there was one in stained glass in the destroyed hall. There is one on the modern pump (1937) in the forecourt.

In Edward I's time it was ordered that law students of character should be brought from the provinces and placed in proximity to the courts at Westminster, and it would appear that by 1415, perhaps earlier, it had become an Inn of Chancery. It was purchased by the Benchers of Gray's Inn in 1529. In Q. Elizabeth's reign there were 145 students in term and 69 out. Stow referred to it, saying 'The same of late is for a great part thereof fair built and not a little augmented.'

Amongst the inns of court it was inconspicuous and not notable in history. In the 18th century it fell into disuse as a legal sch., and in 1761 it was reported as—

'taken up by attorneys, solicitors, and clerks who have separate chambers and their diet at a very easy rate in an hall together, where they are obliged to appear in grave, long robes, and black round knit caps.'

In 1811 Staple Inn regained its independence, and was no longer under the control of Gray's Inn. In 1854 there was a Royal Commission on Inns of Court and Chancery. It decided that the funds of Staple Inn could not be applied to the study of the law, having passed to private owners, and in other instances they were heavily in debt, whilst they had not in any case been able to find such a special appropriation of the funds as to fix upon the inns a legal liability to expend any money for the benefit and advancement of the legal profession. This was a decision that was most welcome to the eight ancients and twelve juniors then comprising the 'Honourable Society of Staple Inn.' In 1884 they sold the inn to a firm of auctioneers, and from them in 1886 the Govt. bought the southern portion for an extension of the Patent Office. The northern part, including the hall and the Tudor houses, was sold to the Prudential Assurance Co. for £68,000. The Co. had the houses restored by Alfred Waterhouse, and they added a charming garden on the S. side. The hall had a fine hammer-beam roof, and some stained glass. It was leased to the Soc. of Actuaries who added a statuette of Napier, the inventor of logarithms. The hall was destroyed by a flying bomb in Sept. 1944.

In chambers in Staple Inn, not identified, Samuel Johnson was living in 1759, at the time he published *Rasselas*. Another resident was Isaac Reed. He lived in Staple Inn for 37 yrs., and was the author of a *History of the English Stage*, and editor of the first variorum edition of Shakespeare. Dickens happily introduced Staple Inn into *Edwin Drood*, his incomplete novel, as the residence of Mr. Grewgious. The chambers mentioned remained until 1944, with the inscription 'P.J.T. 1747' over their portal. The initials meant Principal John Thompson, President of the Inn for that yr.

Nathaniel Hawthorne, too, found Staple Inn when 'he went astray in Holborn,' and wrote delightfully of it:

'The windows were open; it was a lovely summer, afternoon, and I had a sense that bees were humming in the Court, though this may have been suggested by my fancy, because the sound would have been so well suited to the scene. There was not a quieter spot in England than this, and it was very strange to have drifted into it so suddenly out of the bustle and rumble of Holborn; and to lose all this repose as suddenly on passing through the arch of the outer court. In all the hundreds of years since London was built it has not been able to sweep its roaring tide over that little island of quiet.'

With regard to the Tudor shops, the following inscription is under the archway: 'Original building erected 1545–1589 by Vincent Enghame and another. The rear elevation was cased in brick 1826. The front, after various alterations, was restored to its original design in 1886.

The entire building was reconstructed in 1937, the old front being retained.'

(See *Staple Inn*, by T. Cato Worsfold, 1903; and *Staple Inn, Customs House, Wool Court, and Inn of Chancery*, by E. Williams, 1906.)

Statues and Other Outdoor Memorials. At the time of the Wembley Exhibition, where a statue of the P. of Wales in butter was exhibited, Bernard Shaw expressed a wish that many L. statues were of the same material so that they might melt away in the summer sun. There is an abundance, and a complete census would demand unwarrantable space. In this selection monarchy must take precedence.

BOADICEA; more correctly Boudicca. Victoria Embankment, by Westminster Bridge (1902). She is with her two daughters, in a chariot with scythed wheels. The sculptor was Thos. Thornycroft. It was presented by Sir John Isaac Thornycroft. On the pedestal are Cowper's lines:

'Regions Cæsar never knew
Thy posterity shall sway.'

ALFRED THE GREAT. Until 1822 there was, outside Westminster Hall, a statue which was supposed to be his. It was one of those concealed by two coffee-houses. When they were demolished this one was removed to Trinity Sq., Southwark, then being laid out. It is still there. The K., who is more than life-size, has lost both hands. It is supposed that one held a sword, and the other a book, suggestive of his military prowess and love of learning. The statue probably dates from 1395. If so, it is easily the oldest outdoor statue in L. There is also a statue of Alfred on the Royal Courts of Justice.

RICHARD I. Old Palace Yard. The sculptor was Baron Marochetti. It is a bronze equestrian statue of the plaster model shown at the Great Exhibition of 1851, and was erected in 1860. The cost was over £3,000; this was defrayed by public subscription. The pedestal, which cost £1,650, was provided by Parliament. The bas-relief represents the attack on the gates of Jerusalem in the Crusades, and the archer who shot Richard being brought before him on his death-bed. (A cat is shown, sitting under a chair.) The K. asked that his life should be spared, but he was flayed alive. During the Second World War blast from a bomb bent the K.'s sword. A suggestion was made that it should be left and a plaque inscribed as follows: 'A battered brand may be a token that we were bent but never broken.' The sword was, however, duly straightened.

Bp. Lightfoot expressed his amazement that Edward I was ignored in L.'s statuary, and that—

'here under the very shadow of the Parliament Houses, the shrine of the legislature which he matured, and of the Old Hall of Westminster, the seat of the judicature which he had created, was instead the first Richard—a man of sinewy arm and bull-dog courage, who cared nothing for laws or judicature or constitution, or any of these things— a hero of romance, a ruffian in real life, a bad son, a bad husband, a bad man, a worse king, who bestowed upon England nothing but a contemptuous neglect and a heavy debt.'

Figures of Edward I (with Edward VII) are outside the National Provincial Bank, 114 High Holborn. They date from 1902.

There are figures of Henry III and Edward I over the archway of the Public Record Office. They date from 1856.

HENRY VIII. It is remarkable that there is a great gap after Richard I, and the next monarch whose effigy in stone is visible outside a bdg. is Henry VIII, who straddles over the gateway of St. Bartholomew's Hosp. This was erected, with the gateway, in 1702, and commemorates the monarch's 'generosity' in returning to the citizens the hosp. he had taken from them.

EDWARD VI. There are two statues at St. Thomas's Hosp., one (bronze) was the work of Scheemakers (1737); the other is of Portland stone, and its origin is unknown. His head is carved over the door to Bridewell Hosp. (q.v.). The date is about 1805. There are statues of Edward VI, Elizabeth I, and Charles I, all by Nicholas Stone on the stairs of Guildhall Library.

QUEEN ELIZABETH. It is the oldest outdoor statue in L. with the possible exception of Alfred. It is in the chyd. of St. Dunstan's in the West, Fleet St., and was originally on Ludgate, where it was placed when the gate was rebuilt in 1586. Referring to the G.F., Evelyn noted in his diary (7th Sept. 1666) that it 'continued with but little detriment.' On the destruction of Ludgate it was given by the City to Sir Francis Gosling, alderman of the ward of Farringdon Without, who in the yr. 1766 caused it to be placed on the exterior of the ch. The Q. holds the sceptre in one hand, and the orb in the other, and wears the side panniers and farthingale and stiff collar. In the niche on Ludgate the Q. faced W. On old St. Dunstan's Ch. she faced E., and now she faces S. (See also 'Royal Exchange.')

CHARLES I is at Charing Cross, and this statue comes next to Q. Elizabeth's in order of antiquity. It is the work of Le Sueur, a Huguenot sculptor, who arrived in England in 1628, and lived in Drury Lane and Bartholomew Close. It was apparently ordered by Ld. Weston, afterwards E. of Portland. The statue was cast in 1633 (the date, in addition to the sculptor's name, is on the left forefoot of the horse). It was first placed on a plot of ground in King St., Covent Garden, close to the site whereon St. Paul's Ch. was then being built. It was first intended to erect it in a garden at Roehampton, but it does not appear that it was erected at all during the lifetime of the K.; it seems to have remained in the chyd. of St. Paul's. In 1642, on the outbreak of the Civil War, it was concealed in the crypt of the ch. In 1650 the Council of State instructed Mr. Sergeant

'to make enquiry after the statue of the late king in Covent Garden, being cast in brass, and to report in whose custody it now is.'

No report appears to have been forthcoming. In 1655 a Council of State gave a definite order to Gen. Desborrow 'to state the matter of fact touching a statue in the churchyard of Covent Garden and to report.' It was then brought to light again. It was seized by Cromwell's representatives and sold 'for the rate of old brass, by the pound rate' to John Rivett, a brazier who lived at the Dial near Holborn Conduit, in St. Sepulchre's par. Rivett had orders to break it up, but, with a keen eye to business, he sold 'knife-handles, candlesticks, nut-crackers, bodkins, thimbles, spoons, and patty-pans' which he pretended to have made from the material of the statue, which in fact was still intact.

'These mementoes,' says D. G.

Denoon, 'were eagerly bought by those persons of Royalist sympathies as a relic of their martyred king, and at the same time the Puritans were eager to secure the pieces of metal-work as evidence of Cromwell's triumph. By such inglorious means was the equestrian monument of the ill-fated king presumed to have met its end.'

Le Sueur had left England in 1642, but Rivett is also believed to have been a Huguenot, and may have been acting in the sculptor's interest in thus concealing his work. At the Restoration the E. of Portland (successor to Le Sueur's patron) claimed that the statue was his property, but only after petition and legal pressure was Rivett induced to part with it. The E. d. 1663, and the statue had not then been set up anywhere. It was not until 1675 that it was bought from his widow for £1,600, and then became the property of Charles II. In a Treasury minute book of 1675 is recorded: 'April 19—The effigy of the old King to be brought to Charing Cross and a place made for it.' Andrew Marvell wrote describing 'the Busyness of Parliament last sitting,' and mentioned that 'for more pageantry the old King's statue on horseback of brass was bought and to be set up at Charing Cross . . . but does not yet see the light.' The pedestal was the work of Joshua Marshall, the K.'s mason. The design followed was one of Wren's. The statue was set up late in 1675 (on the site of the old Charing Cross), and there is an inaccurate engraving of it by Hollar. There was a story that the horse had no girth, and that the omission caused the suicide of the sculptor. The girth is plainly seen in old engravings. The statue became a great L. landmark. Amongst L.'s cries were:

'I cry my matches at Charing Cross,
Where sits a black man on a black horse.'

In 1719 a model was made of the statue with a view to a similar one in Dublin. In 1769 six globe lamps were fixed round it for the safety of carriages. In 1825, according to the *Sunday Times*, it was proposed to erect 'Cleopatra's Needle' (*q.v.*) on the site. In 1844, when Q. Victoria visited the City in state to open the new Royal Exchange, seats were erected round the pedestal. The sword and the 'George' decoration were then stolen. These were never returned, but the missing sword was later replaced by one reputed to have been of the original period. In 1853 a second cast was made by Signor Brucciani for the Sculpture Court at the Crystal Palace. In 1860 iron railings round the statue were removed. In 1867 during the fire at His Majesty's Theatre a newspaper reporter climbed the pedestal, and grasped the sword, which broke off in his hand; having dropped to the ground it was seized by a bystander, who presumably carried it away as a souvenir. In 1917 at a cost of approximately £400 the statue was protected by layers of sandbags, a wooden framework, and a casing of corrugated iron. After the First World War some necessary repairs were executed, there having been fractures in the foreleg, and a danger of the horse's tail dropping off. In 1927 a copper plate inscribed with a brief account of the monument was placed on the E. side. During the Second World War it was at Ld. Rosebery's estate at Mentmore (Bucks.). It returned in 1947, when a new sword was placed by the K.'s side (see 'Customs'). The statue has been the subject of a poem by Lionel Johnson.

(See paper by D. G. Denoon in *Transactions of the London and Middlesex Archaeological Society*, new series, vol. vi, pt. 3, 1931.)

CHARLES II. There is a statue at Chelsea Hosp., said to have been erected in 1692. It was the work of Grinling Gibbons, and was presented by Tobias Rustat. There is also one in Soho Sq. This was the work of Caius Gabriel Cibber (*c.* 1681). In its present position until 1876, it was then taken to Grims Dyke, Harrow Weald, the estate of Sir W. S. Gilbert. It returned to Soho Sq. in 1938.

JAMES II. There is a statue representing him in Roman costume, in Trafalgar Sq., outside the N.G. This also was the work of Grinling Gibbons, and the gift of Rustat. It was first erected in 1688, behind the banqueting hall of Whitehall Palace; in 1897 it was removed to the garden of Gwydyr House; in 1903 it was taken to St. James's Park; in 1948 it was erected on its present site.

WILLIAM III. There is a bronze equestrian statue in St. James's Sq. He also is represented in Roman costume. It was erected under the will of Samuel Travers

(d. 1724), who bequeathed

'sufficient money to purchase and erect in St. James's square an equestrian statue in brass to the glorious memory of my master King William the Third.'

The pedestal had been erected by 1732, but nothing more was done until 1806, when Travers's money was found in the list of unclaimed dividends. The statue, the work of John Bacon junior, was erected in 1808. There is another statue in the grounds of Kensington Palace. It is of bronze, and double life-size. The sculptor was Herr Bancke. It was erected in 1907, and, as the inscription says: 'Presented by William II, German Emperor and King of Prussia, to King Edward VII, for the British Nation.'

QUEEN ANNE. The statue outside St. P.'s Cath. is a copy of the original, the work of Francis Bird, and erected 1712. It became dilapidated, and in 1885 was acquired by Augustus Hare, who conveyed it on lorries to his park of 'Holmhurst,' near St. Leonards. It is still there, in the grounds of what is now a convent sch. The Q. is standing, crowned in a robe of state, and bearing sceptre and orb. Around the pedestal are four female figures in sitting attitude, representing England, France, Ireland, and N. America. In 1710 'Four Indian Sachems or Kings' came to the court of Q. Anne, offering assistance against the French in Canada, and the fourth figure was perhaps introduced in compliment to them. The statue's position, having regard to the Q.'s brandy-loving proclivities, was commented upon:

'Brandy Nan, Brandy Nan, you're left in the lurch,
With your face to the gin-shop, your back to the church.'

The present statue dates from 1886. Another statue is in Q. Anne's Gate (see 'Westminster'). It is believed to have been erected early in the 18th century by Wm. Paterson, the founder of the Bank of England, who was the builder of the houses there. The Q. is attired in the costume of the Order of the Garter.

GEORGE I. His only statue is on the tower of the ch. of St. George's, Bloomsbury (see 'Holborn').

GEORGE II. There are two statues. (1) In Golden Sq. It is of Portland Stone, repaired with cement and lead, on a Portland stone base. The K. is represented in Roman costume, and for some inexplicable reason he seems to be grasping a lizard. The sculptor was Van Nost. It was erected 1753. (2) At Greenwich Hosp. A statue of marble on a pedestal of the same material. Again the K. is represented in Roman costume. The sculptor was J. M. Rysbrack, and it was erected in 1735.

GEORGE III. There is a bronze equestrian statue in Cockspur St. The K. is represented in cocked hat and pigtail on a favourite charger. It was unveiled in 1836. There is another statue in the quadrangle of Somerset House. It is a bronze statuary group upon a stone pedestal. A colossal figure of Neptune or Father Thames, reclines with arm on an urn; at his back is a cornucopia, and behind, on a higher place, the K. in Roman garb, leaning on a rudder with a lion couchant on one side and a prow of a Roman vessel on the other. The sculptor was John Bacon. Q. Charlotte was no admirer of this effort. 'Why did you make so frightful a figure?' she inquired. 'Art,' said Bacon, bowing, 'cannot always effect what is ever within the reach of Nature—the union of beauty and majesty.' Q. Charlotte's statue is in Queen Sq., Bloomsbury.

GEORGE IV. In Trafalgar Sq. A bronze equestrian statue, by Sir Francis Chantrey. The K. is represented bare-headed, in semi-classical dress, and strangely has no stirrups. The statue was intended for the Marble Arch. The K. ordered it, and paid one-third of the cost. As he did not live to see its completion (it was not erected until 1843) after repeated applications a parliamentary grant was obtained for the balance of the money.

WILLIAM IV. Greenwich Park (1844). S., 15 ft. high, of Foggin Tor granite. In K. William St. until 1935.

QUEEN VICTORIA. (1) In Kensington Gardens (1893). The work of Princess Louise. The Q. is represented as at the time of her accession, when she was residing in the palace. The statue is of white Carrara marble, and the Q. is seated, crowned, and holding the sceptre. The inscription says it was the gift of 'her loyal Kensington subjects . . . to commemorate fifty years of her reign.' (2) On Victoria Embankment, by Blackfriars B. (1896). Bronze statue, 9 ft. high, of the Q. in mature life, with crown, orb, and sceptre. Presented by Sir A. S. Haslam. (3) Royal Military Academy, Woolwich (1904). The Q. is represented standing, attired in State robes, with crown, sceptre, and orb. On the pedestal, of polished granite, are panels showing incidents connected with the Royal Artillery and Royal Engineers in her reign. (4) In front of Buckingham Palace The memorial, including a statue, was designed by Sir Thos. Brock, and unveiled by George V in 1911. The height of the memorial is 82 ft., the statue of Q. Victoria being 13 ft. The groups alongside represent Justice and Truth, and facing Buckingham Palace is a group of Motherhood. The whole is surmounted by a winged figure of Victory, this figure being poised on a sphere supported by figures of Courage and Constancy. At the base is a marble basin with fountains. (See also 'Royal Exchange.')

There are four statues of the P. Consort. The best known is in Holborn Circus (1874), where the P., in the uniform of a field-marshal, is shown raising his hat. It has been described therefore as the most polite statue in L., as it is said that field-marshals never so act, at any rate on horseback. The second is at the entrance to Albert Hall (1863). It was first placed in the gardens of the Royal Horticultural Soc.; removed to present site in 1899. The third is on the Albert Memorial (see 'Parks'—Hyde). The fourth is in the grounds of the Licensed Victuallers' Asylum, Asylum Rd., Old Kent Rd. (1864).

EDWARD VII. Tooting Broadway (1911); Euston Rd., outside the offices of the Hearts of Oak Benefit Soc. (1918); Waterloo Pl. (1921).

GEORGE V. Abingdon St., Westminster (1947).

OLIVER CROMWELL. Old Palace Yard. In 1895 a statue was proposed by the Liberal Govt., and a vote of £500 asked. The Irish were hostile, and asked: 'Did the peace Liberals honour Cromwell as the great soldier; was it the jingo in international policy, or the founder of the big navy, or the destroyer of the House of Commons?' The vote was withdrawn. In 1899, however, an anonymous donor —it transpired to be Ld. Rosebery— offered a statue. The latter unveiled it with a typical oration in which he praised Cromwell as a great practical mystic,

symbolized by the sword and the Bible included in the statue, which was the work of Hamo Thornycroft. The spurs are turned the wrong way.

The statues of Ks. are not the most exalted in L. Apart from Nelson's (see 'Trafalgar Square') there is that of Fredk., D. of York, on Carlton House Terrace. It is 13½ ft. high, at the summit of a Tuscan column of granite, 124 ft. high. The erection of the column was begun in 1831, and finished in 1834. It was said to be erected by the voluntary contributions of the army; in fact a day's pay was stopped of all ranks, from drummer-boys to colonels. It had attracted the wits, as the D. was not particularly distinguished as Commander-in-Chief. He was the 'good old Duke of York,' who led his men up a hill and then led them down again. He left heavy debts, and the spike projecting from his head was said to be for the purpose of filing his bills. There is a staircase and up to the late 1880s the column could be ascended by visitors.

There are many statues to literary worthies. Shakespeare is near the site of St. Mary Aldermanbury (see 'City Churches; C'), and in Leicester Sq. The latter, erected in 1874, is an imitation of Scheemaker's statue in W.A., and was due to Baron Grant. Milton was outside the ch. of St. Giles, Cripplegate (see 'City Churches; C'), but owing to bombing he is at present under the tower of the ch. Bunyan is outside the Baptist Ch. House in Southampton Row. Dr. Johnson is at the E. end of the ch. of St. Clement Danes, Strand. The statue is not a particularly good one. It was the work of Percy Fitzgerald (1910). A Lamb memorial which was at Christ Ch., Newgate (see 'City Churches' D'), is temporarily removed (see 'Temple'). Byron is represented by a statue in bronze in Hamilton Gardens (1880)—said by his friend Trelawny to bear no resemblance to him. Carlyle is in Chelsea Embankment Gardens (1882). This is a particularly fine piece of work. The statue of Burns (1884), in the Victoria Embankment Gardens, ranks next in excellence. The sculptor was Sir John Steell. The poet is attired in the rustic dress of a Scotch peasant, and is seated on the broken stump of a tree, near the foot of the figure is a broken ploughshare. On the granite pedestal is inscribed a passage from the dedication of the second edition of his poems. At 39 Cornhill is a tablet commemorating the birthplace of Thos. Gray in 1716. On the doorway of the Cornhill Insurance Co. (No. 32) there is a representation of the meeting of Thackeray with Charlotte and Anne Brontë in the publishing office of Smith Elder & Co. There is a medallion of Chas. Dickens on the Red Lion Tavern, Parliament St., commemorating an incident in its predecessor in the novelist's boyhood (see Forster's *Life of Chas. Dickens*, chap. 2). There is a medallion of Sir Walter Besant on the Victoria Embankment, a replica of one in St. P.'s Cath. For Bacon, see 'Gray's Inn,' for Edgar Wallace, see 'Ludgate Circus.'

John Stuart Mill is the only religious 'heretic' honoured by a L. statue. The admirable figure—eager and alert—was well represented by T. Woolner in the Victoria Embankment Gardens in 1878.

Journalists are represented by W. T. Stead, on Victoria Embankment (facing Norfolk St., where the offices of the *Review of Reviews* were) (1920); and in Fleet St. by Ld. Northcliffe (see 'City Churches; C' —St. Dunstan in the West); and T. P. O'Connor (1936).

Political worthies are well represented. Chas. Jas. Fox is in Bloomsbury Sq. and Wm. Pitt in Hanover Sq. (see 'Squares'). There are five statues in Parliament Sq.: (1) Geo. Canning. It was first erected in Palace Yard in 1832, and removed to Parliament Sq. in 1867. (2) Viscount Palmerston (1869). (3) E. of Derby (1874). On the pedestal is an accurate representation of the H. C. before the fire of of 1834 (see Hardy's *Dynasts*, Act 1, Sc. iii). (4) Sir Robt. Peel (1876). (5) Benjamin Disraeli, E. of Beaconsfield (1883). On 19th Apr., his birthday, the statue is adorned by primroses, said to have been his favourite flowers. Sir Robert Peel is also represented in Postman's Park (see 'City Churches: C'—St. Botolph, Aldersgate).

W. E. Gladstone. (1) In Bow Road, W. end of Bow Chyd. (1882). (2) The Strand, at junction of eastern end of Aldwych (1905). It is a bronze statue. Gladstone is shown erect, dressed in the robes of Chancellor of the Exchequer. At the foot of the statue are four groups representing Brotherhood, Education, Aspiration, and Courage. On panels between the groups are decorated escutcheons bearing the arms of some of the counties and bors. which Gladstone represented in Parliament. It was the work of Hamo Thornycroft, and was unveiled by Ld. Morley.

Richd. Cobden is in High St., Camden Town (1868). Sir Rowland Hill is in K. Edward St., opposite the General Post Office. It was first erected by the Royal Exchange in 1882, removed in 1920, and installed in its present position in 1923. W. E. Forster was placed in Victoria Embankment Gardens, opposite the offices of the L. Sch. Board, in 1890. Henry Fawcett, the blind Postmaster-General, is commemorated in Victoria Embankment Gardens and Vauxhall Park. Ld. Curzon is in Carlton House Terrace (1931). Wm. Booth is on the N. side of Mile End Rd. and J. R. Green in East India Dock Rd.

Social workers are represented by Geo. Peabody (see *infra*); Lady Henry Somerset is in Victoria Embankment Gardens (1897); Quintin Hogg, in Langham Pl. (1906); Sir Wilfrid Lawson, in Victoria Embankment Gardens (1909); Samuel Plimsoll, on Victoria Embankment (1929).

Religion has its memorials. (1) Wm. Tyndale, in the Victoria Embankment Gardens. He is represented with his right hand laid on an open copy of the New Testament, resting on a primitive printing press, copies from one in the Plantin Mus., Antwerp. This statue was the work of Sir Edgar Boehm (1884). (2) Robt. Raikes, in the Victoria Embankment Gardens, erected by contributions from teachers and scholars of Sunday Schs. in Great Britain (1880). (3) John Wesley, in front of City Rd. Chapel (1891).

Explorers are honoured by four statues: (1) Sir John Franklin in Waterloo Pl. (1866). The bas-relief shows the position of ships at the time of Franklin's death, and his funeral. (2) Capt. Cook, at St. James's Park, near Admiralty Arch (1914). (3) Capt. Scott, Waterloo Place (1912). (4) Sir Ernest Shackleton, wall of the Royal Geographical Soc. bdg., Kensington Gore (1932).

The stage is represented by Sir Henry Irving's statue in Charing Cross Rd. (behind the N.P.G.) (1910). There are memorials to W. S. Gilbert and Sir Arthur Sullivan on the Victoria Embankment. For an actress see *infra*.

Statues of military men abound. They are the most conventional, and arouse least interest. Gen. Wolfe is in Greenwich Park (1930); Robt. Clive is in K. Charles St. (the statue was first, 1912, in the gardens of Gwydyr House, Whitehall, and was removed to its present site in 1916); the D. of Wellington is (1) at the Royal Exchange (1844), (2) at Woolwich Arsenal (this statue was first at T.L., 1848–63), (3) at Hyde Park Corner. In Trafalgar Sq.: Sir Chas. Napier (1856) and Sir Henry Havelock (1861). Colin Campbell, Ld. Clyde, in Waterloo Place (1867), Gen. Gordon's (1888) has been removed and has been re-erected in the gardens between the new Govt. offices in Whitehall and the river; D. of Cambridge (1907), Whitehall. On Horse Guards Parade are Viscount Wolseley (1920), E. Roberts (1924), and Viscount Kitchener (1926). Marshal Foch is at Grosvenor Gardens (1930). E. Haig (1937), Whitehall. For admirals Nelson, Jellicoe and Beatty, see 'Trafalgar Sq.'

There are four notable statues of women: (1) Sarah Siddons at Paddington Green (1897). (2) Florence Nightingale, Waterloo Pl. (1915). (3) Emmeline Pankhurst, Victoria Tower Gardens, Westminster (1930): this is an excellent piece of work, unveiled by Ld. Baldwin. The leader of the women's suffrage movement is posed most naturally as when addressing a public meeting. (4) Nurse Cavell, in St. Martin's Pl., is the best known. It was unveiled by Q. Alexandra in 1920. In 1924 the words 'Patriotism is not enough' were added by the Labour Govt. The figure is an admirable one, but the background is unsightly.

AMERICAN MEMORIALS. There are statues of four American citizens.

1. GEO. PEABODY. Threadneedle St. It was erected in his lifetime (1869), and unveiled by Albert Edwd. P. of W., to commemorate his great beneficence in providing funds for working men's dwellings of which 29 blocks still remain.

2. ABRAHAM LINCOLN. Parliament Sq. The statue in Parliament Sq. was unveiled by the D. of Connaught in 1920. It is a copy of Saint-Gaudens' marble statue in Lincoln Park, Chicago.

3. GEO. WASHINGTON. Trafalgar Sq.— outside N.G. This is a copy of a statue made by Houdon. It was unveiled by Miss Judith Brewer, daughter of the Chairman of the Virginia Commission, in 1921.

4. FRANKLIN DELANO ROOSEVELT. Grosvenor Sq. Unveiled by Mrs. Roosevelt on 12th Apr. 1948, in the presence of George VI, Q. Elizabeth, the Rt. Hon. Winston Churchill, and the Rt. Hon. C. R. Attlee. (See *London for Americans*.)

In 1921 *John o' London's Weekly* arranged a competition for L.'s best statue. Peter Pan, in Kensington Gardens (the work of Sir Geo. Frampton in 1912), was an easy first. Richard I was second. Peter Pan is also in the crypt of St. P.'s Cath. (*q.v.*).

Oddities in L.'s statuary are the umbrella and hat which Sir Wm. Waterlow holds in Waterloo Park (a replica is in front of the City of Westminster Sch., Palace St.); the football held by a boy in Quintin Hogg's statue (see *supra*); the prominent spectacles in the medallion of Sir Walter Besant.

There are statues and other sculptured memorials on public bdgs. such as Home Office, Whitehall, the N.P.G., Victoria and Albert Mus., City of London Sch., Burlington House, Houses of Parliament, Institute of Civil Engineers.

(See L.C.C.'s *Return of Outdoor Memorials in London*, 1910; and *The Outdoor Monuments of London*, by C. S. Cooper, 1928.)

Stepney, now part of the L. Bor. of Tower Hamlets, was a met. bor. but was also the name of an ancient par. of even greater extent which included Bethnal Green and parts of Poplar; also, at a very early date, Shoreditch and Hackney.

The name occurs in the 11th century as Stibenheall, and in the 13th century as Stebenhythe—possibly 'timber haven,' but more probably the hythe or landing place of Stybba.

When the population began to swarm outside the City on the E., beyond the purview of the C.C., the district was policed by the Lieutenant of the T.L. which is not in the City but occupies the SW. corner of this bor. Hence the villages that grew up got the name of the Tower Hamlets, the name at one time of a parliamentary division. The hamlet which grew up along the riverside was Ratcliff (believed to mean red cliff), a district adjoining the W. side of the Regent's Canal and Dock, now part of the electoral division of Limehouse.

The mother ch. of Stepney, at the N. end of Ratcliff and near the centre of the bor., is dedicated to St. Dunstan (Bp. of

L., 959–61). It lies in its old chyd., to the E. of the High St. of Stepney, about half-way between the ancient thoroughfare of Mile End Rd. and the Commercial Rd. (made 1803), which branches off that thoroughfare at Whitechapel. It dates nominally from the 14th century; but it has been often restored and altered. After a restoration, rebuilding of the organ, removal of galleries, and other improvements, in 1897, the roof, organ, altar, and vestries were destroyed by fire in 1901. Another restoration was completed, and celebrated by a re-opening in 1902, by the Suffragan Bp. of Stepney (bishopric created 1895). The peal of ten bells includes one given in 1386 to the priory of Holy Trinity, Aldgate (*q.v.*), and sold to St. Dunstan's in 1540. In a wall of the tower there is what purports to be a stone from the wall of Carthage, with a 17th-century rhyming inscription. Till 1544 the rectory was a sinecure; there was an active vicar appointed by the rector; and vicars continued to officiate at a much later period. Richd. Pace, secretary of state, ambassador and vicar, was bd. here in 1532. Another vicar was John Colet, founder of St. Paul's Sch. (*q.v.*). His father, Sir Henry Colet (Ld.M., 1486 and 1495) was bd. in the ch. So was Sir Thos. Spert, founder of Trinity House. Innumerable master-mariners were bd. in the chyd.—among them Admiral Sir John Leake (1656–1720), the reliever of Londonderry. Stephen Segrave, afterwards Abp. of Armagh, was rector early in the 14th century as was, in the 15th, Richard Foxe, afterwards Bp. of Winchester, and founder of Corpus Christi Coll., Oxford. There is another ch., which also has a chyd., at the S. end of the same hamlet, near Regent's Canal Dock—St. James Ratcliff, Butcher Row. It was erected in 1837, and burnt in the Second World War. The Rectory is an 18th-century bdg. with interesting wall paintings. It is now the headquarters of the ancient St. Katherine's foundation, which has recently returned here from its 19th-century home in Regent's Park. In Plumbers Row, Feldgate St., is the Whitechapel Church Bell Foundry dating from 1570.

In Mile End Old Town is what is left of the People's Palace, after subtraction of the E. London or Q. Mary Coll. premises and the fire of 1931. The People's Palace was the outcome of Sir Walter Besant's novel, *All Sorts and Conditions of Men* (1882). At the W. end of Mile End Rd. are the ruins of the picturesque almshouses of Trinity House, called Trinity Hosp. (1695). The oldest Anglican ch. is St. Peter's, Cephas St. (1838). There are eight other churches, including St. Rhystyd's Welsh Ch., Longfellow Rd.

Whitechapel (possibly named from the whitewash covering its primitive chapel) was the first part of the original Stepney par. to become separate (1329). The par. ch. is called St. Mary Matfelon. 'Matfelon' is derived from an old French word *matfellon* meaning knapweed. Knapweed looks somewhat like a thistle; a thistle is like a teasel; and a teasel appears on the arms of the Co. of Fullers, who once had a trade colony in Whitechapel. Herein is a possible derivation, but it may have been a personal name. The ch. stands on the SE. side of Whitechapel High St.—part of the ancient thoroughfare mentioned under Ratcliff. The old ch. was restored 1633; rebuilt as a brick ch. early in the 18th century; rebuilt again 1875–8; destroyed by fire 1880; and rebuilt soon afterwards. It was completely wrecked by bombs in 1940 and the site cleared. The register of burials includes Richd. Brandon. The entry in 1649, a few months after the execution of Charles I, states that he is believed to have cut off the King's head. St. Philip's, Stepney Way, is a beautiful modern Gothic ch.

The ch. of St. Jude, Commercial St., was demolished 1925—it was famous as the ch. of Canon S. A. Barnett, the first warden of Toynbee Hall adjoining. This was a university settlement established in 1883, in memory of Arnold Toynbee. There is a memorial tablet to Canon Barnett in W.A. There was, in the ch., a copy of G. F. Watts' picture 'Time and Death' which was presented to Canon Barnett and his wife in 1884, expressing gratitude for their action in opening a free picture gallery in Whitechapel. For some inexplicable reason, on the demolition of the ch., the picture was placed on a wall at the corner of Endell St. and Broad St., St. Giles, which has since been absorbed in High Holborn. The art gallery referred to is on the N. side of High St., Whitechapel. The gallery was opened in 1900, Chas. Aitken, afterwards director of the Tate Gallery, being the first director.

Shadwell (formerly 'Chadwell,' conjectured to be from a spring dedicated to St. Chad) is a small par., by the riverside, between Ratcliff and Wapping, was separated from Stepney par. in 1670. The ch., dedicated to St. Paul, was built 1656. The patronage is with the dean of St. P.'s. Joseph Butler, as dean, nominated as rector, 1741, his nephew of the same name. He liked the place so little that he preached his first sermon from the text 'Woe is me that I sojourn in Mesech,' etc. (Psalm cxx. 5)—nevertheless he seems still to have been there when Lysons wrote in 1795. The old ch., demolished 1817, was replaced by the present one in 1821. It is on the S. side of The Highway, a continuation of old 'Ratcliff Highway.' In K. Edward VII Memorial Park there is a tablet commemorating Sir Hugh Willoughby, Martin Frobisher, and others who sailed from here to explore the northern seas.

Wapping. The books are silent as to the meaning of the name. There is an old English word 'wap' that means to knock or thump, and this was the centre of the shipping trades. Wapping-on-the-Wose, Stow calls it, for it was subject to inundations. It was separated from the mother par. in 1694. Johnson urged Boswell to visit Wapping. When he did, it did not come up to expectations. The par. ch. of St. John-at-Wapping is on the E. side of Scandrett St. (formerly Church St.). It was founded as a chapel-of-ease in 1617, and rebuilt in 1756 by Joel Johnson. It was almost destroyed, but for the tower, in an air-raid. It possesses plate given by the first D. of Marlborough. The old rectory adjoins. Rev. Francis Willis, M.D. (1718–1807), who attended George III in his first attack of insanity, was rector here. There is a R.C. Ch. of St. Patrick (1880).

St. George's-in-the-East is a par. formed out of Stepney in 1729. The ch., facing W. on Cannon Street Rd. was designed by Nicholas Hawksmoor (1715). It is a large bdg. of Portland stone, with something like a little castle instead of a steeple on top of its stout, square tower. It was burnt out in 1941. A temporary ch. has been erected inside the ruin. In 1886 the chyd. was converted into a

public garden. One corner contains the remains of the victims of the Ratcliff-Highway murders of 1811: the murderer committed suicide, and was bd., with a stake through him, at the top of Cannon Street Rd., where Commercial Rd. crosses. Of the four other Anglican churches in the par., the best known is St. Peter's, L. Docks (1866), off Old Gravel Lane.

Spitalfields takes its name from a hosp. or spital (see 'Customs,' regarding Spital sermons). It was the immigration centre of the Huguenots that came to England on the revocation of the Edict of Nantes: they established the silk-weaving industry which has become extinct within living memory. The par. ch. dedicated to Christ, is on the E. side of Commercial St.; it was designed by Nicholas Hawksmoor and completed in 1729. It has a fine interior and a tower and steeple 234 ft. high. The Great Synagogue in Brick Lane was once a Huguenot Chapel (1743).

Limehouse, made a separate par. 1730, is the most easterly part of the bor. There used to be lime-kilns here, and on 19th Oct. 1661 Pepys went 'by coach to Captain Marshe's, at Limehouse, to a house that hath been their ancestors' for this 250 years, close by the lime-house which gives the name to the place.' The par. ch., St. Anne's, stands in its large chyd. on the S. side and at the E. end of Commercial Rd. It also was by Nicholas Hawksmoor (1730). The clock is the highest ch. clock in L. The whole of its oak interior, and the clock and bells, were destroyed by fire in 1850. The restoration cost £13,000. There is a mythical notion that all children b. at sea are registered in Limehouse par. St. Peter's Ch., Garford St., near the Thames, was opened 1885.

Stock Exchange. The function of providing capital for new enterprises, both Government and private, and the issue of stocks and shares for this purpose, began as long ago as the 17th century. At first in the Royal Exchange (q.v.), the brokers later moved to the nearby coffee-houses. The first Stock Exchange building was erected in 1773 at the corner of Threadneedle Street and Sweetings Alley; the present building was begun in 1801 but almost entirely reconstructed in 1854 by

Thomas Allason. Brokers and jobbers only can buy and sell on 'The Floor' and the scene can be viewed from the Visitors' Gallery (8 Throgmorton St.) free of charge from 10 a.m. to 3.15 p.m., Monday to Friday. A free film show is also arranged.

A new Stock Exchange is now in course of erection and the towers, which will be 350 ft. high, are already dominating the skyline. The brokers (agents for clients) and the jobbers (dealers in specific securities) now number about 3,400. Around 9,000 securities are quoted daily and valued at over £75 thousand million.

Stoke Newington, now part of the L. Bor. of Hackney, was a met. bor., containing but 863 acres; little more than 612 acres were contained in the ancient par. of 'Stoke Neweton' of 'Neweton Canonicorum' or 'Newington-Stoke'—it was 'Neutone' in Domesday, wherein it was said that here the canons of St. Paul's had two hides. 'Stoke' is usually held to mean 'a wood,' and no doubt the place was originally a clearing in the Middlesex forest.

The ancient ch. of St. Mary, Stoke Newington, much altered from time to time, still stands in its chyd. on the N. side of Church St., E. of Clissold Park—though it ceased to be the par. ch. in 1858. Its successor was then built on the site of the old wooden rectory, directly opposite. It was formerly a small Gothic structure, built of hewn stone, flint and pebbles. In 1563 it was repaired—or 'rather new builded', by Wm. Patten, who was the first recorded lessee of the manor. His initials are to be seen above the South door and his arms on the adjacent entrance. In 1702 it was repaired after a great storm. It was enlarged in 1723, and again repaired in 1770. In 1826-9 Chas. Barry carried out restoration. The chapel known as Q. Elizabeth's is on the S. side of the ch., separated by stone pillars and arches from the nave. The E. window of the nave was filled with fragments of stained glass: formerly it contained the arms of Q. Elizabeth and several Bible scenes. The N. window used to contain the Drapers' arms; the S. those of the City of L. The N. extension of the ch. is separated from the nave by pillars loftier than those of the chapel. On the S. side of the chancel is the monument of John Dudley (or Duddelye) and his wife and only child—he in armour.

Bd. in or about the ch. are Lady Abney; Elizabeth Abney; Jas. Brown (1709-88; oriental traveller, and originator of Kent's L. Directory; see 'Directories'); Mrs. Barbauld, and her brother, Dr. Aikin; the sister of Wm. Wilberforce, Jas. Stephen, fellow worker with Wilberforce; and Alderman Pickett (who tried to improve the E. end of the Strand). Lysons' statement, copied by Walford, that Bridget, Oliver Cromwell's daughter, who m. General Fleetwood, lies bd. here is erroneous—she was bd. at St. Anne's Blackfriars in 1662. The par. registers go back to 1559. The ch. was badly damaged by bombs.

The new ch., in the French decorated style, was designed by Sir Geo. Gilbert Scott and consecrated in 1858. It was not completed until 1890, when Scott's son finished the spire (about 250 ft. high)—understood to be a reduced facsimile of Salisbury Cath. This, and the tower beneath, are much inferior to the body of the ch. It has been badly damaged by bombs but well restored. The ch. of St. Olave, Woodberry Down (1894) has a carved pulpit and font from the city ch. of St. Olave Jewry.

An important congregational ch. is Abney Ch. in Church St., opposite the disused gates of Abney Park. It was built in 1838, but had predecessors in the neighbourhood from 1662. This was also damaged but restored with extensions.

Nearly all the historical associations of Stoke Newington cluster round Church St. Hereby lived General Fleetwood; Daniel Defoe—who wrote *Robinson Crusoe* in a house situated at the NE. corner of Defoe Road; Hannah Snell, female soldier; Mrs. Barbauld; Dr. John Aikin; and Thos. Day, author of *Sandford and Merton*. Edgar Allan Poe attended sch. here 1817-20. He described the school house in *William Wilson*. (See *London for Americans*.)

Abney Park, since 1840 a cemetery, whose only entrance is from High St., contains thirty acres. Isaac Watts, who had been educated under Thos. Rowe at Newington Green, was tutor in 1696 to the son of Sir John Hartopp. In 1712 Watts began to reside with Sir Thos. and Lady Abney at Theobalds; and after Sir Thos.'s death (1722), Watts continued to be Lady Abney's guest, removing with her to Abney Park in 1735. He d. there in

1748. A favourite seat of Watts, on a slight elevation in the NE. is marked by his statue. Among those bd. here are Jas. Braidwood, hero of Tooley St. fire, 1861; Catherine Booth 1890; Rev. Christopher Newman Hall, minister of Christ Ch., Westminster Bridge Rd., 1902; Wm. Booth, founder of the Salvation Army, 1912.

Strand means the verge of the river; and in the *Anglo-Saxon Chronicle*, under date 1052, in a reference to the war between E. Godwin and the force of Edward the Confessor, it says: 'The land-force meanwhile came above [the bridge] and arrayed themselves by the strand.' At this date probably the bank of the Thames is meant, and not any road. So late as 1315 the footway between Temple Bar and Westminster was reported as so bad that the feet of horses and of rich and poor men alike received considerable damage, particularly in rainy seasons, while the footway was interrupted by thickets and bushes. An order was made for a tax on the inhabitants to pay for the upkeep of the road, and the Ld.M. and sheriffs were made overseers of the work. In 1353 there seems to have been no improvement; the road was almost impassable; and Edward III gave orders for a tax to be levied on certain commodities, in order to secure funds for the proper repair of the roadway. He issued a further edict that those whose houses abutted on the st. should keep in repair such part of it as lay before their premises. In this document the roadway is described as being 'profunda et lutosa' (deep and muddy) owing to the constant traffic to and from the market at Westminster, and the pavement so broken as to be a source of danger both to pedestrians and to carriages. It is doubtful if anything effectual was done, for the matter was raised again in 1359 and 1361, and it does not appear that the Strand was properly paved before the time of Richard II. In his reign tolls were granted for this purpose, the extent of such paving being from Temple Bar to the Savoy. In 1446 similar measures were taken, while in 1532 an Act was passed for 'sufficiently paving, at the charge of the owners of the lands, the street way between Charing Cross and Strand Cross'—the latter was at the W. end of

St. Mary-le-Strand Ch. It was described as being 'full of pits and sloughs, very perilous and noisome,' and an entry in the Parliament Rolls says, 'so deep and miry as to be almost impassable.'

THE STRAND HOUSES: S. SIDE

Notwithstanding this suggestion that the Strand was not a very desirable place of residence, from a very early period it attracted great magnates. Chas. Pendrill, on the authority of an anonymous chronicler, says that, so early as 1099, Ralph Flambard, Bp. of Durham (see 'Tower of London') was residing there. In 1238 *Durham House* is mentioned in connection with penance imposed upon the abbot and canons of Oseney and the masters of the Oxford colls. for an insult to Cardinal-deacon Otto, legate of Pope Gregory IX to Henry III. They had to walk with bare feet and hands, and naked to the waist, through the sts. of L. from St. P.'s Cath. to Durham House, where they humbly sued the legate for pardon. Matthew Paris refers again to Durham House in 1258, and calls it a 'noble palace.' It is said to have been rebuilt by Antony Bek, Bp. of Durham in the latter part of the 13th century. Richd. de Bury (see 'Books in London'), the great mediaeval bibliophile, occupied it at intervals between 1333 and 1345. Thos. Hatfield, who succeeded him in the bishopric, seems to have added to the bdg. In 1536 Henry VIII turned out Tunstall, then bp., giving him in exchange part of the manor of Coldharbour in Upper Thames St. Before this, the K. had been in possession of the episcopal residence. In 1529 he twice attended service in the chapel here; and about the same time he allocated the house as a residence for Anne Boleyn, and her father, Thos., E. of Wiltshire. Here stayed Thos. Cranmer as the E.'s guest. In 1540 a great feast was held here for Henry VIII and Anne of Cleves; followed, a few days later, by a similar feast to the Ld.M. and aldermen. It had then been leased to Wm. Forth or Ford. Later P. Edward was resident here, and on his accession (1547) he gave Durham House to his sister Elizabeth; but, owing largely to the intrigues of Sir Thos. Seymour, brother of the Protector Somerset, it does not appear that she resided here. On Mary's accession Dudley, D. of Northumberland, was residing here; and on 21st May of that yr.

(1553) in the chapel Lady Jane Grey had been m. to his son, Ld. Guildford Dudley. Q. Mary returned the house to Tunstall, though it is not on record that he took up residence again. When Elizabeth came to the throne, it became a residence for ambassadors, and consequently a place for plotting; and, in 1563, when it was in the occupation of Alvaro de Quadra, Bp. of Aquila and representative of Philip II of Spain, Machyn records:

'The second day of February called Candlemas day there was certain men went to Durham Place and to St. Mary Spital to hear mass, and there was certain of them carried by the guard and other men to the counter [compter] and other places.'

In 1566 the E. of Leicester was living here, and Q. Elizabeth dined with him. It is also said that at first she granted it to Sir Henry Sidney, and that his son Philip spent a yr. of his boyhood here. A tenant in 1572 was Walter Devereux, first E. of Essex, and father of Q. Elizabeth's favourite. In 1584 Q. Elizabeth leased part of it to Sir Walter Raleigh: he occupied the upper part, and had the use of the stables and outhouses fronting the Strand; the lower part was reserved for Sir Edwd. Darcy.

Here, it is said, when tobacco smoke was issuing from Raleigh's mouth, his servant threw over his head a tankard of ale, thinking he was on fire and needed an extinguisher. On James I's accession, Raleigh got notice to quit; Toby Matthew, then Bp. of Durham, regaining possession for the bishopric. Raleigh was indignant about it. He declared that he had spent £2,000 on the place, that 'the poorest artificer hath a quarter's warning given him by his landlord,' and that he had laid in provision for his household of forty persons and nearly twenty horses.

'Now to cast out my hay and oats in the streets at an hour's warning and to remove my family and stuff in fourteen days after, is such a severe expulsion as hath not been offered to any man before this day.'

He had to go: and evidently Lady Raleigh was not so sorry; for she called it 'a rotten house.' Durham House remained until the Restoration, being occupied by the bp. until 1640; when, with the exception of the E. of Salisbury's part, it was leased to Philip Herbert, E. of Pembroke. Only the name 'Durham House Street' now recalls it.

In 1607–8 the gate-house and adjoining bdgs. passed into the hands of the E. of Salisbury, who had the design of building an emporium for trade on the site. The first stone of what was to be called 'Britain's Burse' or the 'New Exchange' was laid in 1608. It included an arcade of shops with sleeping quarters above. It was opened in 1609; James I and his Q., the D. of York (afterwards Charles I), and the Princess Elizabeth, being in attendance. Later, Pepys shopped there, buying ribands, gloves, linen, lace, bandstrings, shoe strings, garters, stockings, and more rarely books. It is said a sensation was caused in 1688 by Frances Jennings —once a Court beauty, and Duchess of Tyrconnel; wife of Richd. Talbot, Ld. Deputy of Ireland under James II— sitting there, in a white mask, as a sempstress. The story may be apocryphal, but it was dramatized by Douglas Jerrold under the name of *The White Milliner* at Covent Garden Theatre in 1840. Hatton's *New View of London* (1708) says there were then about 150 shops, about 76 being those of milliners and mercers. The New Exchange ceased to be profitable early in the 18th century, and in 1737 it was pulled down. Houses built on the courtyard of the old palace became known as Durham Yard, and David Garrick was living there about 1740— according to Samuel Foote with three quarts of vinegar in the cellar so that he could call himself a wine merchant! Durham House Yard became part of the site of the Adelphi (*q.v.*).

E. of the Adelphi at one time was *Salisbury* (sometimes called Cecil) *House.* Q. Elizabeth attended the house-warming in 1602, three months before her death. It was hardly complete then. Sir Robt. Cecil, who became Ld. Salisbury, d. in 1612; and his son, the second E., divided the mansion into two residences, which became known as Great and Little Salisbury House—residing himself in the former. In 1673 Little Salisbury House was demolished, and the other house survived only a few yrs. longer.

Next came *Worcester House*, on the site of a house that had belonged to the Bps. of Carlisle, but had come into the possession of the Crown, which bestowed it on the first E. of Bedford. A grant of land on the N. side of the Strand was made to the Russells in 1552, and there they moved. The old house was then sold to the third E. of Worcester, who made it his L. residence. During the Civil War a guard was set over Worcester House by order of Parliament, the E. being one of the K.'s partisans. After the death of Charles I it became the depôt for the security of the treasure seized by Parliament, and was also used for parliamentary committees who fitted it up for the reception of the Scotch Commissioners. Subsequently it was sold to the E. of Salisbury; but in 1659 by Act of Parliament it passed into the hands of Margaret, Countess of Worcester, during the life of Edwd., Marquess of Worcester. After the Restoration Ld. Worcester was able to return to his own house, and he offered it rent-free to Ld. Clarendon, who did not accept the generous offer, but rented it for six yrs. In this house, in 1660, between eleven and two at night, Jas., D. of York, m. Anne Hyde. After Clarendon's departure, Worcester House does not appear to have been used by its owners, but to have been given over to important functions: such as the installation of the D. of Ormond as Chancellor of Oxford University in 1669, and of the D. of Monmouth as Chancellor of Cambridge University in 1674. Finally the place was pulled down by the first D. of Beaufort, from whom Beaufort Bdgs. (replaced by Savoy Court) derived its name. A smaller house erected on the site was destroyed in 1695.

The D. of Somerset, when erecting *Somerset House* (*q.v.*), destroyed three bps.' inns. The most westerly was the Bp. of Worcester's, which has a bare mention in Stow. Next was the Bp. of Chester's, 'first builded,' says Stow, 'by Walter Langton Bishoppe of Chester, treasurer of England in the raigne of Edward the first.' The Bp. of Llandaff, he says, secured the site for his house, which was next in order, of Thos. E. of Lancaster.

Arundel House was in the Middle Ages the inn or town house of the Bp. of Bath. Stow wrote of it as having been 'lately new built, for a great part thereof, by the Lord Thomas Seymour, admiral.' On the latter's execution in 1549 the twelfth E. of Arundel purchased the place. The house appears to have retained its original name for a time, for Machyn, on 9th Aug. 1553, refers to the Bp. of Winchester going on that day 'with my lord of Arundell to denir at Bayth plasse,' while, on 21st Oct. 1557, he records the death of 'my lade the countes of Arundell at Bathe place in sant Clement parryche.' The E. d. 1580, and after his grandson and successor d. abroad in 1595, his son being then only nine yrs. of age, Arundell House was granted for a time, in 1603, to Thos. Howard, E. of Nottingham, Ld. High Admiral of the Fleet against the Armada. By an arrangement with the K., however, Ld. Nottingham gave up possession of the place in 1607, and it was restored to Thos. Howard, who had been reinstated in his titles of E. of Arundel and Surrey in 1603. They had been lost by reason of the execution of his grandfather, the fourth D. of Norfolk, in 1562 for intriguing with Mary Q. of Scots. This E. was a patron of the arts. Painters and engravers were given lodgings in Arundel House. Van Dyck worked here, once painting Evelyn. Hollar made etchings of the house, and one shows what appears to have been a rather elegant chapel. Hollar also made some of his engravings of L. from its roof. Here, as Evelyn records, was to be heard fine music; here also could be seen the famous Arundel marbles. 'The very marbles are become vocal and cry you for pity and that you should even breathe life into them,' wrote Evelyn to the E. This was the E. who, in 1635, invited Old Parr to L.; he d. in the E.'s house. The E. d. 1646. Later Pepys was here often. In 1661 he saw—

'some fine flowers in his garden, and all the fine statues in the gallery, which I formerly had seen, and is a brave sight, and thence to a blind dark cellar, where we had two bottles of good ale.'

In 1666 the Royal Soc. began to meet here, the library of Thos., E. of Arundel, on Evelyn's advice having been presented to it. It was Evelyn too who persuaded this E. to present the marbles to Oxford in 1667. Here, in 1668, Pepys 'did try the use of the Otacousticon, which was only a great glasse bottle, broke at the bottom, putting the neck to my eare, and there I did plainly hear the dashing of the oares of the boats in the Thames to Arundell gallery window, which, without it, I could not in the least do.'

The E. d. in 1677, and was succeeded by his brother who, in the following yr., caused the mansion to be taken down, and sts. to be made on the site. It was not until about 1690 that the whole of the site, now represented by Howard, Norfolk, Arundel, and Surrey Sts., was covered.

Essex House, when it first emerges into history, was occupied by a house or inn of the Bp. of Exeter. The land appears to have been leased from the Knights of St. John of Jerusalem, who acquired what was known as the Outer Temple after the eviction of the Knights Templars. It is probable that the bp. who built it was Walter Stapleton, for when, in 1326, he was murdered by a mob in Cheapside, his body was dragged to 'his house without Temple Bar,' and bd. beneath a heap of rubbish in the garden. In the reign of Henry VI a great hall was added by Bp. Lacy. It is next heard of in the reign of Henry VIII, having then fallen into his hands. He gave it to Sir Wm. Paget, who was a secretary of state, and who subsequently helped the Protector Somerset to set aside the provisions of Henry's will. It was known as Paget House, and Sir Wm., afterwards Ld. Paget, considerably enlarged it. On his death in 1563 Robt. Dudley, E. of Leicester, obtained possession, and practically rebuilt the house. Edmund Spenser, at this time, was a frequent visitor, and in his *Prothalamion* wrote:

'Next whereunto there standes a stately place,
Where oft I gayned giftes and goodly grace
Of that great Lord, which therein wont to dwell.'

At Leicester's death in 1588 the house passed to Robt. Devereux, second E. of Essex, whose mother (after the death of the first E. of Essex) had m., as his second wife, the E. of Leicester. The name was again changed to Essex House.

Now it became a storm centre. Agnes Strickland said it

'became the headquarters of the disaffected and desperate. The earl courted the Puritans, and encouraged them to hold conventicles and preach seditious sermons to political congregations under the shadow of his roof.'

Here on 8th Feb. 1601 he collected 300 of his partisans; when—having failed to rouse the City—he took boat at Queenhithe and returned, to find the house invested on every side, cannon being placed on the tower of St. Clement Danes Ch. The writer just cited wrote:

'Sore vexed with the tears and incessant shrieks of the ladies, he after several parleys from the leads of his mansion with the assailing force below, surrendered his sword to the Lord Admiral about ten o'clock at night.'

On the execution of Essex the same yr., his widow, the only daughter of Walsingham, continued to reside at Essex House. In 1613 the Elector Palatine, who came to England to marry the Princess Elizabeth, was lodged there. When the third E. of Essex attained his majority he resided there, and in consequence of the loose behaviour of his two wives, it was alluded to in Cavalier songs as 'Cuckold's Hall.' In 1639 the E. leased half the house to the E. of Hertford, on the payment of a premium of £1,100. The former (b. at Essex House in 1591) became commander of the parliamentary forces and, after the battle of Newbury (1643), received there the congratulations of the H.C., the Ld.M., and aldermen. He d. there in 1646, and Pepys, who called it a 'large but ugly house,' went to see the body lying in state. The fourth E. of Southampton was living at Essex House in 1660, and the Ld. Keeper, Sir Orlando Bridgman, in 1669, when Charles II visited him there. About 1680 the property was purchased by Nicholas Barbon. He demolished most of the house, leaving only the pillars and cornice of the watergate, which probably dated from about the time of the Restoration, and parts of the premises near the Strand. In one of these (where Essex Hall stood until it was destroyed by bombs) from 1727 to 1730 was housed the famous Cotton Lib. (see 'Libraries'). This remaining portion was demolished in 1777. The remains of the water-gate were damaged by bombs in the Second World War, and all but a small part near the ground has been demolished.

Northumberland House was the last of all the great Strand mansions to be demolished. It was erected early in the reign of James I, being completed by 1605, on the site of the Hosp. of St. Mary Rouncevall (see 'Charing Cross'). The builder was Henry Howard, E. of North-ampton. The house consisted of three sides of a square, with extensive gardens stretching down to the river. The front was 162 ft. long, and on the coping on the Strand front was a border of capital letters. (At the funeral of Q. Anne of Denmark in 1619 a young man in the crowd was killed by the letter 'S,' which had been pushed off by spectators on the roof.) Towers with turrets were at the four corners. In 1614 Ld. Northampton d., and left Northampton House, as it was then called, to his nephew, Thos. Howard, first E. of Suffolk; who changed the name to Suffolk House, and completed it by the addition of a river façade. Suffolk d. in 1626, and was succeeded by his son Theophilus, whose second daughter Elizabeth m. in 1642 Algernon Percy, tenth D. of Northumberland. On the death of the second Ld. Suffolk in 1646, his successor, the third E. being childless, made over the property to his brother-in-law, the D. of Northumber-land, and the place received its final name after that title. Here Monk con-ferred with the D., and planned the Restoration. The latter rebuilt the river front from designs said to be those of Inigo Jones. In 1688 he d., and was succeeded in the title and estates by his son Jocelyn. The latter enjoyed his property for two yrs. only, and with his death the direct line of the Percys ended. Northumberland House and the other family estates descended to his daughter, Elizabeth Percy. She had been m. to the E. of Ogle when twelve yrs. of age, and on his death to Thos. Thynne of Longleat, who was murdered in 1682 (see 'West-minster Abbey'). She had never lived with either of her husbands; and in the same yr. as the second was murdered, and before she was seventeen, she m. the third, the sixth D. of Somerset. She and the D. lived at Northumberland House until her death in 1722. The D., who again m. (Lady Charlotte Finch), d. 1748, and was succeeded by an elderly son; who, in 1749, was made E. of Nor-thumberland. He d. without male issue; and the property went to Sir Hugh Smithson, who had m. his only daughter, and who in 1766 was created D. of Northumberland. Dr. Percy, afterwards Bp. of Dromore, had apartments in the house, and was here visited by Goldsmith.

In 1780, after many improvements and additions had been made, the st. façade was wholly destroyed by fire and Dr. Percy nearly lost his fine library. Fortun-ately a handsome ballroom, added by Robt. Adam in 1774, escaped. There were, in addition to magnificent rooms, some fine pictures. In 1851, during the Great Exhibition, the public was ad-mitted by ticket to view the house at the rate of 10,000 a week. In 1866 the M.B.W. suggested a new st. through the site of Northumberland House and its grounds. The D., however, strenuously opposed a proposal to destroy the last of the Strand palaces. In 1873 it was learned that the then D. was willing to sell, and an agreement was made and ratified by Parliament, under which the Board acquired the property upon pay-ment of £500,000. It also obtained powers to construct a new st. The materials of the house were sold by auction, the lots consisting of 3,000,000 bricks, the grand marble staircase, the elaborate ornamentation of the various apartments and corridors, and lead to the weight of 400 tons. The sale realized but £6,500. Of this sum the great staircase —subsequently removed to 49 Prince's Gate—brought £360. Some of the pic-tures had been removed to Alnwick Castle, Northumberland; others to the ducal town residence at 2 Grosvenor Pl. The dignified lion, so prominent a feature of the Strand façade, was taken to Syon House, Isleworth, where it can still be seen: it was cast in lead in 1752. At the same place is the D.'s coach, made c. 1820, and also adorned with a lion. Northumberland Av. was opened in Mar. 1876. It is 950 ft. long and 84 ft. wide. The Strand portion of the site of Northum-berland House is marked by the bdg. that was till recently the Grand Hotel, the opening of which in 1880 was attended by the Ld.M. Amongst the bdgs. in this thoroughfare are the Constitutional Club, and the Royal Commonwealth Soc.

THE STRAND HOUSES: N. SIDE

There were several important houses on the N. side of the Strand. *Wimbledon House* was erected towards the close of the 16th century by Sir Edwd. Cecil, the third son of the first E. of Exeter, who was created Viscount Wimbledon in 1625 and d. 1638. It is said to have been designed by Inigo Jones, and Strype called it 'very handsome.' It was partly destroyed in 1620, and entirely demolished in 1782. It appears to have occupied the NE. corner of the present Wellington St. Next, in a westerly direction, was *Exeter House*. The latter was its final name; it was previously known as Burghley and Cecil House. It was built in the time of Edward VI, and granted by Q. Elizabeth to Sir Wm. Cecil, who, in Stow's phrase, 'beautifully increased it.' John Norden (1592) described it:

'A verie fayre house raysed with brickes, proportionablelie adorned with four turrets placed at the four quarters of the howse; within it is curioslye beautified with rare devises, and especially the oratory, placed in an angle of the great chamber.'

In 1561 Q. Elizabeth visited Burghley here. On another occasion she found her minister suffering from gout. She made him sit in her presence, remarking: 'My Lord, we make use of you not for the badness of your legs, but for the goodness of your head.' It is said too that in this house the Q. had once to stoop on going through a doorway, and she exclaimed to the servant who was conducting her: 'For your master's sake I will stoop, but not for the King of Spain.' Ld. Burghley d. in 1598, and was succeeded by his son, Thos. Cecil, who was created E. of Exeter in 1605. The name was then changed to Exeter House. In 1617 James I and his Q. were entertained, and at the end of his reign the Spanish ambassador extraordinary was resident for a short time. After the Restoration, its chapel was fitted up as a place of worship for Charles I's widow, Henrietta Maria. Later, the second E. of Shaftesbury rented the house; and here was b. his son, the third E., and author of the *Characteristics*, in 1671. In 1676 Ld. Shaftesbury left to take up residence at Thanet House, Aldersgate St. Soon afterwards Exeter House was pulled down, and sts. and bdgs. arose on the site.

Exeter Change was erected soon after the demolition of the house, for on its architrave was the inscription 'Exeter Change 1676.' This was similar to the 'New Exchange,' farther W., and there were shops for 'Semsters, Milenners, Hosiers, &c.' according to Strype. Many of the shops in his time were untenanted. In 1732 the body of John Gay laid in state here, and in 1772 the body of Ld.

Baltimore. About 1773 it began to be used as a menagerie; and Malcolm, describing it in 1807, said:

'The building covered with daubings of monsters and wild beasts, and exhibiting parts of vast Corinthian pillars, has a strange grotesque appearance, not a little heightened by the antique habit of Pidcock's sham yeoman of the guard, stationed to invite spectators to the dens of lions, tigers, elephants, ouran-outangs, and a long et cetera of animals, rare and interesting to the people of England.'

Byron sometimes came here to see the animals fed, and discovered a hippopotamus 'like Lord Liverpool,' and a sloth with 'the very voice and manner of my valet.' In 1829 Exeter 'Change, which projected into the roadway, was demolished in a Strand improvement. In 1855 the second Marquess of Exeter sold the whole of his property at this spot for £50,000.

Exeter Hall was erected in 1831, and became the great centre for 'May meetings,' which commenced sometimes in Apr., and continued until June. It was a synonym for religious dissent. Macaulay once referred to the 'bray of Exeter Hall.' Later it became the headquarters of the Young Men's Christian Association. It was demolished in 1907. Its site is now covered by the Strand Palace Hotel.

Bedford House was erected about 1552, a little W. of the modern Southampton St. The E. of Bedford moved there from Bedford House (later Worcester House) on the S. side of the Strand. Bacon was living there 1622–3. It continued to be the town residence of the Es. and Ds. of Bedford until 1700. The second D., who then succeeded to the title, continued to live with his mother, Lady Rachel Russell, in Southampton House, Bloomsbury; and then the house in the Strand was given up, and shortly afterwards demolished.

THE CROSS AND MAYPOLE. Over against the Bp. of Chester's house, Stow says, was the stone cross where in 1294 and other times the justices itinerant sat. In 1242 it was mentioned in the Calendar of Patent Rolls:

'The Common pleas of the county of Middlesex are summoned to be at the Stone Cross of la Strand, on Tuesday after the octaves of the Purification, before those whom the King shall appoint to be justices.'

It is possible this rallying place dated from the Danish occupation of this quarter, the Scandinavian custom being that the community had their thingstead, where the town moot was held, in the open air. It is not known when this cross was demolished. Upon or near its site, the famous maypole in the Strand was probably erected in Elizabethan days. It was destroyed by the Puritans in 1644, and there is a lengthy account of a reinstatement in 1661; it took four hours, and there was a musical accompaniment.

It is said to have been put up at the instance of John Clarges, the blacksmith, in rejoicing at the marriage of his daughter Anne with the D. of Albemarle. It was 134 ft. high; and in 1672, according to Aubrey, a violent gale broke off a portion of it. In 1713 it was found to have become decayed in the ground and was removed. Another was erected, which had two gilt balls and a vane on the summit. In 1717 this also was removed; and Sir Isaac Newton, then living near Leicester Fields, bought it from the parishioners, and sent it as a present to his friend the Rev. Mr. Pound at Wanstead, where it was erected in the park for the support of a telescope, 125 ft. in length.

ST. MARY-LE-STRAND CHURCH. In 1222 a 'Church of the Innocents' existed —on the S. side of the Strand. Its name had expanded by Stow's time into 'the Nativity of Our Lady, and the Innocents'; and he adds that some call it, 'by means of a brotherhood kept there, St. Ursula at the Strand.' He says that the ch., whose designation had settled down into 'St. Mary's,' and all the adjacent bdgs. were demolished by the D. of Somerset for his new house in 1549. Beresford Chancellor questioned the reason for demolition; pointing out that Wyngaerde depicts the old ch. on practically the same site as the present one, and asking why the ch. that then existed interfered more with the first Somerset House than its successor does with the Somerset House of to-day. He overlooked the fact that an uninterrupted view is an advantage to a palace and matters little in a Govt. office. In 1564 Bp. Grindal arranged for the parishioners to worship at the chapel of the Savoy, which is in consequence sometimes called St. Mary-le-

Savoy, though dedicated to St. John the Baptist. This arrangement continued until 1724, when the new ch. of St. Mary-le-Strand—erected between 1714 and 1717—was consecrated. Pope refers to it in some lines in the *Dunciad*:

'Amid that area wide they took their stand,
Where the tall maypole once o'erlooked the Strand,
But now (so Anne and piety ordain)
A church collects the saints of Drury Lane.'

It was one of the fifty new chs. that were ordered to be erected under the Act of Q. Anne, who died in the yr. it began to be built. The ch., built of Portland stone, was designed by Jas. Gibbs. The graceful steeple was not part of the original design. It was proposed to have a small campanile for a bell at the W. end, and 80 ft. W. of this a statue of Q. Anne on a column 250 ft. high. Gibbs' design for this was approved, but on the death of the Q. he was ordered to erect a steeple in place of the campanile. The ch. is not remarkable for either its architecture or its history. In the latter regard, however, one incident, if not very well authenticated, is piquant enough. According to Hume, here Chas. Edwd., the Young Pretender, formally renounced the Roman Catholic faith as a measure of political expediency. Beresford Chancellor thought it more likely that this formality took place at St. James's, Piccadilly, but gave no reason for the suggestion. If the P. was residing in Essex St. in 1750, as has been said, he would surely choose the most convenient ch. Hughson (*Walks through London*) mentions that when the heralds came to the Strand in 1802 to make the proclamation for the Peace of Amiens one of the urns from the roof fell, killing three men and injuring a woman. In this ch., on 13th June 1809, John Dickens m. Elizabeth Barrow. The father of Chas. Dickens was at the time a clerk in the Navy Pay Office at Somerset House. There is a tablet to Jas. Bindley, a well-known book-collector (d. 1818), and Joseph Cradock (d. 1826) is also bd. in the vaults—he was a friend of Johnson's and Goldsmith's, and author of *Literary and Miscellaneous Memoirs*.

ST. CLEMENT DANES CHURCH has a history which antedates that of the other island ch. By reason of the manner of St. Clement's martyrdom (see 'City Churches; C'—St. Clement, Eastcheap) an anchor is the weather-vane of the present ch.; an anchor figured elsewhere externally and internally, and also outside the 'Anchorage'—as the vicarage is called—in St. Clement's Passage. St. Clement was a patron saint of seamen, for an obvious reason; and this lends colour to the suggestion that the first ch. on the site was one specially allocated to the Danes. Fleetwood, recorder to Ld. Burghley, who may have had some authority, now vanished, said that, when the Danes were driven out of England, those who had m. English women were ordered by the K. (Alfred the Great) to dwell between the Isle of Thorney (Westminster) and Caer Lud (Ludgate), and that there they erected a place of devotion, which was afterwards consecrated and called 'Ecclesia Clementis Danorum.' According to Maitland (1739), during the massacre of the Danes in the reign of Ethelred, many fled to St. Clement Danes Ch. for sanctuary, but were butchered on the very steps of the altar. Roger of Wendover (d. 1237) and 'Matthew of Westminster' both record an incident which probably relates to the ch. In 1040 when Hardicanute came to the throne he caused the body of his half-brother Harold to be taken out of its grave in W.A., and thrown into the Thames. The body was shortly afterwards found by a fisherman and 'buried by the Danes in their burying ground in London' (Roger of Wendover). A st. near the ch. in the 13th century was called 'Dencheman's Street.' In 1846 Christian VIII of Denmark sent Prof. Worsaae to England to report on Danish memorials, and he was convinced that a colony of Danes once inhabited this spot. A rune stone in Denmark records of three men: 'They lie in London.'

The first ch. was probably a small wooden structure similar to that at Greenstead, near Ongar, in Essex. It is believed to have been rebuilt of stone about 1025, and the round arches of the tower with large square stones may be a remnant of this bdg. There is not much history attached to this second ch. There were some distinguished parishioners; and the S. gallery, it is said, was decorated

with the arms of the D. of Norfolk, the E. of Arundel, and the E. of Salisbury. The E. of Essex was also a parishioner. Two sons of Ld. Burghley were baptized: in 1561 Wm. Cecil, who d. young; and, in 1563, Robt. Cecil, who lived to occupy his father's office of Ld. Treasurer, and was created E. of Salisbury. (In 1929 the present Ld. and Lady Burghley were m. at the present ch.) Another baptism was Florence, daughter of Edmund Spenser, 1587. The wife of Dr. Donne was bd. here in 1617; and her husband preached a sermon that, according to Izaak Walton, 'did so work upon the affections of his hearers, as melted and moulded them into a companionable sadness.' Pepys was there in 1661, but the minister, Mr. Alsopp, did not come up to expectations. In 1667 Pepys went to a tavern in the chyd., where he met Dean Wilkins, Dr. Whistler, Dr. Floyd, 'and other brave men.' In 1680 the ch. was rebuilt. The superintending architect was Edwd. Pierce; but the plans were Wren's, and a tablet which was in the N. gallery commemorated the latter's gratuitous assistance. Evelyn came in 1684, and said it was 'a pretty built and contrived Church.' No doubt he was impressed by the elaborate ceiling and the fine woodcarving. The upper part of the steeple is due to Jas. Gibbs by whom it was built in 1719. In 1685 Thos. Otway, the dramatist, was bd. here; he d. in great poverty, hiding from his creditors, and his death is said to have been caused through too hastily swallowing a piece of bread which charity had supplied. In 1692 Nathaniel Lee, another dramatist, was bd. here. He is best known by the *Rival Queens* and *Alexander*. In 1725 a sensation was caused by an altar-piece in the ch., the removal of which, after four yrs., was ordered by Dr. Gibson, Bp. of L. The figures were said to be the Young Pretender's wife and children. Hogarth, who made a facsimile, denied this, as also that it was 'St. Cecilia as the Connoisseurs think,' and stated it was 'a choir of angels singing in consort.' It was taken to the coffee room of the 'Crown and Anchor' (see 'Taverns'), and afterwards to the vestry-room over the old almshouses in the chyd. In 1803 it was transferred to the new vestry-room on the N. side of the chyd. In 1896 it was in the vestry hall, Clare Market; whence, in 1900, it was restored to the ch., where, until the Second World War, it hung over the staircase leading to the S. gallery. An interesting tombstone, also in the ch., was Joe Miller's. He was bd. in what was described as that 'pestiferous Churchyard in Clare Market'—in 1738. In 1853 the site of the burial-ground was acquired for the erection of King's College Hosp. Miller's tombstone was preserved for many yrs. in the basement of the hosp. When the hosp. was removed to Denmark Hill in 1913 the stone was removed to the ch. Miller, b. in Clare Market in 1684, was an actor at Drury Lane Theatre. He was illiterate, and m. a literate woman so that she could read his parts to him. 'That's an old Joe Miller,' was the usual remark to make upon a stale joke, and he was the putative father of many he never made. When Scrooge, in Dickens's *Christmas Carol*, proposes to send the fat turkey to Bob Cratchit, he says it will be as good as a Joe Miller.

Dr. Johnson regularly attended the ch. It was not his par. ch. This was at one time St. Bride's, at another St. Dunstan's in the W. He commenced to attend because Mrs. Elizabeth Carter induced him to go to hear a nephew of hers who was preaching there. It does not appear that subsequently Johnson went for the preaching. Dr. Thos. Campbell, whose diary of a visit to England contains so much interesting information about Johnson, said (9th Apr. 1775):

'Went to St. Clement's to hear Mr. Borrows, so cried up by Lord Dartrey, preach, but I was wofully disappointed; his matter is cold, his manner hot, his voice weak, and his action affected.'

As neither Boswell nor Johnson praised the vicar's preaching it may be assumed that they too did not share his lorship's enthusiasm.

There was the following inscription in the N. gallery:

'In this pew and beside this pillar for many years attended divine service the celebrated Dr. Samuel Johnson, the philosopher, the poet, the great lexicographer, the profound moralist and chief writer of his time. Born 1709, died 1784. In remembrance and honour of noble faculties nobly employed some inhabitants of the parish of St. Clement Danes have placed this slight memorial. A.D. 1851.'

It was composed by Dr. Stephen Croly (see 'City Churches; C'—St. Stephen, Walbrook). There was behind it (it was installed in 1909—the bi-centenary yr.) a memorial window to Johnson showing him in company with Burke, Mrs. Carter, Garrick, Boswell, and Goldsmith. Mrs. Carter was one of the 'blue-stockings' of her day. Johnson's physician, Dr. Brocklesby, was bd. here in 1797.

The ch. has been only an 'island' since 1810, when a number of houses on the N. side were removed, including Butcher Row, where Johnson met his friend Edwards. A portico on the S. side remained until about 1863.

The Danish associations of the ch. were still maintained until its ruination. The Danish flag, the Danebrog, hung in the chancel. It was presented by Sir F. J. Hansel, formerly Danish Consul. The legend is that the original flag fell from heaven on a summer's day, during a battle in 1219, when Valdemar was fighting on a crusade in Esthonia. The seven hundreth anniversary of the supposed event was commemorated in 1919; and Mrs. Pennington Bickford, as a token of gratitude for the decoration of the ch., was presented with a choice piece of porcelain by the committee of the Danish Ch. in L. The first person to be bd. in the ch. after the rebuilding in 1682 was Nicholas Byer, a Dane. In 1920 the K. and Q. of Denmark accompanied by Q. Alexandra visited the ch.

It was also the ch. of the Old Devonians, and there was annually an Anzac Day service, the ch. being near Australia House.

This ch. claims to be the one associated with oranges and lemons in the nursery rhyme. The same claim has been made for St. Clement's, Eastcheap. There may be no historical basis in either case; the necessity for finding a rhyme for 'Clemens' may have suggested the association. Frank Lockwood, however, in his *Law and Lawyers of Pickwick* (a lecture delivered in 1893), gave some reason for the Strand ch. being the one referred to:

'I once lived myself in Clement's Inn, and heard the chimes go, too; and I remember one day I sat in my little room very near the sky . . . and as I sat there a knock came at the door, and the head of the porter of Clement's

Inn presented itself to me. It was the first of January, and he gravely gave me an orange and a lemon. He had a basketful on his arm. I asked for some explanation. The only information forthcoming was that from time immemorial every tenant on New Year's Day was presented with an orange and a lemon, and that . . . every tenant was expected to give half-a-crown to the porter. Further inquiries from the steward gave me this explanation, that in old days when the river was not used merely as a sewer, the fruit was brought up in barges below the bridge and carried by porters through the Inn to Clare Market. Toll was at first charged, and this toll was divided among the tenants whose convenience was interfered with; hence the old lines beginning: "Oranges and lemons, said the bells of St. Clement's." '

In 1920 the Rev. W. Pennington Bickford began an annual children's service, held at the end of Mar., to commemorate the association of the rhyme. The tune was afterwards played upon the bells, whilst there was given to each of the children, on leaving, an orange and a lemon.

The ch. was several times bombed and reduced to a ruin. For 14 years it was derelict and in 1955 rebuilding began. In 1958 it was re-consecrated as the church of the Royal Air Force. Inside are commemorated all the squadrons of the R.A.F. and there is a memorial to the Air Forces of the Commonwealth. The statues of Johnson and Gladstone remain (see 'Statues').

St. Clement's Well is specifically mentioned by Fitzstephen (c. 1175) as one of those visited by scholars and youth of the City when they go out to take the air in the summer evenings. With regard to its position, Stow says, in referring to Clement's Inn (q.v.), it was 'so called because it standeth near St. Clement's Church, but nearer to the faire fountain called Clement's Well.' Its position may now be located as W. of the Law Courts, opposite the last doorway in the bdg. before ascending the steps. As to its condition, Stow said:

'It is yet faire and curbed square with hard stone, and is always kept clean for common use. It is always full and never wanteth water.'

Maitland (1739) wrote:

'The well is now covered, and a pump placed therein on the east side of Clement's Inn and lower end of St. Clement's Lane.'

The Times of 1st May 18-₊ said:

'Another relic of Old London has lately passed away; the holy well of St. Clement, on the north of St. Clement Danes Church, has been filled in and covered over with earth and rubble, in order to form a part of the foundation of the Law Courts of the future.'

On the NE. side of St. Clement Danes Ch. is the following inscription on the railings:

'The Well underneath
191 feet deep and containing 150 feet of water, was sunk and this Pump erected at the expense of the Parish of St. Clement Danes.

'Wm. Robinson ⎫ Churchwardens,
H. Essex ⎬ 1807.'

It is possible that this was the Holywell from which the now vanished st. derived its name. It is, however, open to serious doubt whether the holy well referred to by Fitzstephen was here at all. It is more likely, as A. S. Foord thought, that the one at Shoreditch was referred to. This would have been no farther, for a country evening's walk from the City, than the one in the Strand. Holy Well may therefore have been an alternative name for Clement's Well. A correspondent of the *Morning Herald* in 1899, however, mentioned an old well which was between 274 Strand and Holywell St.

The derivation of the names of the sts. off the Strand are in most cases obvious from the history given. Immediately E. of the Adelphi is Ivy B. Lane, blocked up at the Strand end, but now opening at the river and into Savoy Court. It is shown in Agas's plan (c. 1588), in Norden's (1593) and in Rocque's (1745). It was once the dividing line between the Duchy of Lancaster and the City of Westminster: it took its name from the bridge or pier which once existed at the riverside end. The name 'Ulebrig' mentioned in 1222 may apply to it. Down this lane James, D. of York, afterwards James II, escaped in 1648 to take boat from the pier. In the 1840s from that pier a steamer took passengers to L.B. for a halfpenny (see 'London Transport'). In Exeter St. (made about 1677) Johnson lived in his early days in L. Southampton St. is said to have been so called after Lady Rachel

Russell, daughter of Thos. Wriothesley, E. of Southampton. Mrs. Oldfield, the actress, lived there in 1712. At 27 Garrick lived from 1749 (the yr. of his marriage) till 1772 (the house remains and is marked by a tablet). Dr. Lemprière, whose *Classical Dictionary* was a godsend to Keats, was another resident—in 1824. Surrey St. derives from the E. of Surrey, a member of the Howard family. Evelyn lived there in 1696. Congreve lived there for some yrs., and was visited by Voltaire. The poet and dramatist is said to have resented Voltaire's interest in him as a man of letters, and desired to be visited simply as a gentleman. The French writer is said to have replied that on that basis he should not have regarded him as worth visiting at all. In this st. Congreve d. 1729, and Geo. Sale, the translator of the Koran, 1736. Milford Lane, where there was probably once one of the many small streams that crossed the Strand, was the boundary between the property of the E. of Essex and the E. of Arundel: in the 17th century it was a hiding-place for debtors. Sir Richd. Baker, author of the *Chronicle* that Sir Roger de Coverley loved, lived here from 1632 to 1639. Out of this lane runs Tweezer's Alley, which perhaps derives its name from the blacksmith's tongs: a forge there—which had existed since 1852, when 186 Strand came into possession of the forge's final proprietors, W. H. Smith & Sons, the wholesale newsagents—was closed so recently as 1932. All their vehicles being automobiles, it was no longer required. There still remains part of a direction to the steamboats. There was a pier at the end of Strand Lane, called 'Strand Bridge.' Steele, in the *Spectator* (1712) refers to 'Ten Sail of Apricock Boats' landing there. In Strand Lane is the Watch House of St. Clement Danes par. and the so-called Roman Bath. The latter became the property of the Rev. W. Pennington Bickford, rector of St. Clement Danes Ch. Its discovery was very late in L. history, and one of the earliest allusions is in *David Copperfield* (Chaps. XXXV and XXXVI). Arthur Mee says it was used by Geo. Borrow as well as Chas. Dickens. It is not surprising that it has now been decided that the bath—at present in charge of the G.L.C.—was of 17th-century origin.

Devereux Court takes its name from the Es. of Essex. A bust of the E. (son of Q. Elizabeth's favourite), who commanded the Parly. forces at the battle of Edgehill (1642) is high up on the wall of what was once the Grecian Coffee House. It bears the inscription: 'This is Devereux Court, 1676.' The coffee-house mentioned was so called from a Greek named Constantine who kept it. In 1665 he advertised his Turkish coffee berry, chocolate, sherbet, and tea, and his willingness to instruct any one in the preparation of such beverages. Steele mentions it in the *Tatler*, and Addison in No. 1 of the *Spectator* says: 'My face is likewise very well known at the Grecian.' Sir Isaac Newton used to visit it after the meetings of the Royal Soc. Ralph Thoresby the diarist (1658–1725) tells of his meeting Sir Hans Sloane at the Grecian. Goldsmith mentions it. Mrs. Sarah Mapp, the bone-setter, made her headquarters here. Dr. King, rich in 18th-century anecdotage, relates that here one man ran another through the body over a quarrel arising out of a dispute about a Greek accent. The Grecian closed its doors in 1843, and Beresford Chancellor writes as though it was then entirely rebuilt. The upper part of the premises are certainly older than the lower part, and may date from an 18th-century rebuilding. Messrs. Twining's tea firm is close by. The founder of the firm was Thos. Twining; who, in 1706, in this court, opened what was sometimes styled Tom's Coffee House, and sometimes Twining's Coffee House. In 1667, when Pepys found his wife 'making of Tee, a drink which Mr. Pelling the Potticary tells her is good for her cold and defluxions' it was from £6 to £10 per lb. When Thos. Twining began to sell it (i.e. by 1710), it was about 20s. a lb. One member of the Twining family, a contemporary of Dr. Johnson's, was an M.A., and his portrait is in the Johnson House in Gough Sq. Theodore Hook wrote wittily of Twining's:

'It seems in some cases kind Nature hath planned
That names with their callings agree,
For Twining the tea-man that lives in the Strand
Would be whining deprived of his "T." '

The back part of the premises have been badly damaged by bombs. All the old ledgers, including those containing the accounts of Sir Christopher Wren, have survived.

The Strand has many literary associations. In Fountain Court, now entirely modernized, Wm. Blake d. (1827). At No. 186 (corner of Arundel St.) were the premises of Messrs. Chapman & Hall, where Dickens purchased the number of the *Old Monthly Magazine*, which contained his first literary effort. Here *Pickwick Papers*, and many of his subsequent books, were published by Messrs. Chapman & Hall. At No. 142 were the office of the *Westminster Review*, and the premises of John Chapman, a publisher, its proprietor and editor. Among his assistants were Wm. Hale White ('Mark Rutherford') and Marian Evans ('George Eliot'). Here the latter met Herbert Spencer (see 'Somerset House'). Geo. Eliot was resident on the premises between 1851 and 1853. The ground-floor has been reconstructed as Slater's Restaurant. This is on the site of the Turk's Head Coffee House, where Boswell and Johnson sometimes dined.

The Strand, widened in recent yrs., has vastly improved since Disraeli called it the finest thoroughfare in Europe. What it has gained in modern convenience it has lost in historic interest.

(See *The Annals of the Strand*, by E. Beresford Chancellor, 1912; and *The Strand District*, by Besant and Mitton, 1902.)

Surgeons, Royal College of (Lincoln's Fields), was founded in 1745 when the Surgeons left the Barber Surgeons' Co. (see 'Companies; A'—Barbers'). Their first hall was in the Old Bailey, where, in accordance with the Act of 1752, the bodies of murderers were taken for dissection. In 1760 the body of E. Ferrers (see 'Tyburn') was brought there, this being part of the sentence, one that caused his lordship to cry out 'God forbid!' until, collecting himself, he added 'God's will be done.' It was here that Goldsmith presented himself for examination as a surgeon's mate, and failed to qualify. In 1803 a curious experiment was made of galvanizing an executed criminal. The excitability of the human frame under this treatment was fully proved. The legs, thighs, and arms were set in motion and, according to a version of the experi-

ment in Chas. Knight's *London*, one of the limbs struck an officer of the Coll. of Surgeons, who d. of the shock. This hall was certainly most conveniently situated in 1783 when executions took place at the Old Bailey instead of Tyburn. In 1800, however, the coll. removed to the S. side of Lincoln's Inn Fields, a charter of incorporation being granted in the same yr. The hall was almost entirely rebuilt by Sir Chas. Barry in 1835-7, when the stone front was extended from 84 to 108 ft. The interior contains a mus., a theatre, and a lib. The mus. (with John Hunter's collection, purchased from his widow for £15,000 by the Govt., and presented to the coll.) was erected in 1836. Additions were made in the 1880s and the laboratories were reconstructed in 1936-7. Amongst the exhibits in the theatre, in addition to a large collection of specimens of morbid anatomy, are the skeletons of Chas. Byrne, the Irish giant (he was 8 ft. high, and d. in 1783, aged 22) and of Jonathan Wild. The mus. suffered badly from bombing in 1941: most of the college was destroyed and many mus. exhibits lost. In rebuilding the opportunity was taken to extend the premises; the building of the Nuffield College of Surgical Sciences added to its strength and the existence of the H.Q. of the Imperial Cancer Research Fund makes this part of Lincoln's Inn Fields the centre of these branches of medical science.

The coll. grants licentiate and fellowship diplomas, and a special licentiateship in dental surgery. (See *The History of the Royal College of Surgeons of England*, by Sir Zachary Cope, 1959.)

Synagogues. At the outbreak of the Second World War there were two in the City of L. The older was the Spanish and Portuguese Synagogue in Bevis Marks. It was the successor of a previous one in Creechurch Lane which was the first to be opened after the Jews were allowed to return to England by Cromwell in 1657. (There is a C.C. plaque on the site.) The synagogue in Bevis Marks was opened in 1701. It is almost a copy of the synagogue in Amsterdam which also survived the Second World War. Some of the candlesticks were brought from there. In 1738 the roof had to be reconstructed; otherwise it has been little altered, and has the original fittings. The report of the Royal Commission on Ancient Monuments in 1928 recommended it as most worthy of preservation. The doorway of the W. front has a key block inscribed A.M. 5461–1701. The birth of Benjamin Disraeli in 1804 is recorded in the synagogue register.

The Great Synagogue in Duke's Place, Aldgate, was opened in 1722. It was rebuilt in 1790. It was visited in 1809 by three sons of George III—the Ds. of Cumberland, Cambridge and Sussex. This inspired a cartoon by Rowlandson. It was regarded as the Cathedral of L. Jewry. It had a bright interior, a fine old candelabra (though fitted with electric light), whilst there were two flags of the Jewish Battalion of the Royal Fusiliers who fought in Palestine in the First World War. There was a fine 18th century painting of Moses and Aaron. The bdg. and all its contents were destroyed in the Second World War.

Tate Gallery is on the N. side of the river, and between Vauxhall and Lambeth Bridges. It is on the site of Millbank Prison (see 'Prisons'). The gallery had its origin in the offer to the nation of (Sir) Henry Tate, the sugar refiner, of a series of fifty-seven paintings, subject to the proviso that they should not be under the control either of the N.G. or of the S. Kensington Mus. authorities. This stipulation led to some delay in acceptance of the offer, and the difficulty was solved when the donor anonymously offered the sum of £80,000 for the erection of a gallery on a site to be provided by the Govt. After some delay, owing to disagreement about the appropriate site, work was commenced in 1893 (the architect was Mr. Sidney R. J. Smith, F.R.I.B.A.), and the gallery was opened by the, P. of Wales (afterwards Edward VII) in 1897. In 1899 the donor generously enlarged the bdg. In 1908 there was a further addition, due to Sir Joseph Duveen. This was to provide accommodation for the Turner Collection, for which there was insufficient room at the N.G. Thirty yrs. later he added a new Sculpture Gallery. Another artist well represented at the Tate Gallery is Wm. Blake. The gallery has a Corinthian portico, supporting a figure of Britannia. The galleries are built round a handsome central hall; they are spacious and well lighted. Amongst the statuary is a bust of Sir Henry Tate.

Taverns of L. are now usually called 'pubs' and there are more than 7,000 of them: only a few can be mentioned here. Their names tend to become more respectable. No new one is now called the 'Devil' although there is a 'Printer's Devil' in Fleet St.; there is now no sign of 'The Good Woman,' showing (as in Hogarth's 'Noon') a woman without a head; or the 'Baptist's Head' (shown in the same picture)—the saint's head lying on a dish. These signs reflect history and change in taste. 'Garrick's Heads' are not now to be found, and no tavern has the sign, as one did in Long Acre, of 'Kemble's Head.' Goldsmith, in the *Bee* essay 'On the Instability of Worldly Grandeur' (1759), says:

'An alehouse keeper near Islington, who had long lived at the sign of the French King, upon the commencement of the last war pulled down his old sign, and put up that of the Queen of Hungary. Under the influence of her red face and golden sceptre, he continued to sell ale till she was no longer the favourite of his customers; he changed her therefore, some time ago, for the King of Prussia, who may probably be changed in turn, for the next great man that shall be set up for vulgar admiration.'

An illustration of Goldsmith's remark (the tavern referred to was opposite Sadler's Wells Theatre) was seen during the First World War, when the sign the 'King of Prussia' was painted out on a tavern in Leather Lane; it could still be faintly detected when the armistice came. At the Guildhall Mus. there is a good collection of tavern signs. (See *The History of Signboards*, by Larwood and Hotten, revised 1951.)

PAST TAVERNS

Barley Mow (Salisbury Sq.) was at the time of the Hanoverian succession (1714) known as Read's Coffee House. The Whigs used various taverns and coffee-houses to form clubs. The members used mugs decorated with pictures of K. George and his ministers, and these clubs were found in such places as St. John's Lane, Long Acre, and the 'Magpie and Stump,' Old Bailey. The opposing party did the same, and Leopold Wagner thinks the phrase about an 'ugly mug' was first coined in this way, the Old Pretender's head probably appearing on some of them. There was a serious affray at Read's Coffee House in 1716. It is unknown at what date the coffee-house became the Barley Mow Tavern. It had no subsequent history except that for long it was the home of the Cogers (*q.v.*). It was demolished in 1936, and the tavern erected on the site named *The Cogers*. The sign erroneously shows Dr. Johnson smoking a pipe.

Boar's Head (Eastcheap). The earliest known record is in the reign of Richard II (1377–99), when Walter Mordon, stockfishmonger, left all his tenement called the 'Boreshedde in Eastchepe' (worth £4 a yr.) to the sustenance of a chaplain to pray for his soul for ever (in the chapel in St.

Michael's Ch., Crooked Lane). In the Suppression Roll, in Edward VI's reign, Mordon's bequest (being for 'superstitious' uses) is mentioned, the house being referred to as 'all that Tavern called the Bores Head in the tenure of Joan Broke, widow.' 'It is further described,' says Dr. Kenneth Rogers (in his admirable monograph on *The Boar's Head*), ' "with its cellars, solars and other appurtenances in East Cheape," in the Certificate of Chantries 2 Edw. VI—1548-9, as having been leased in 32 Henry VIII (1541) to William Broke, and to be then held by Johanna Broke, widow.'

This tenancy is confirmed by a passage in Larwood and Hotten's *History of Signboards*:

'On the removal of a mound of rubbish at Whitechapel, brought there after the great fire, a carved boxwood bas relief boar's head was found, set in a circular frame formed by two boars' tusks, mounted and united with silver. An inscription to the following effect was pricked in the back "Wm. Brook, Landlord of the Bore's Hedde, Estchape, 1566." This object, formerly in the possession of Mr. Stamford, the celebrated publisher, was sold at Christie and Manson's, on January 27, 1855, and was bought by Mr. Halliwell.'

According to Dr. Philip Norman it afterwards went into the possession of Baroness Burdett Coutts, and was shown at a Tudor Exhibition about 1890. Dr. Rogers found the entry of burial of a Wm. Brooke in the registers of St. Michael's, Crooked Lane, in 1543, and assumed that the date on the sign should have been given as 1536. The Boar's Head was one of the forty taverns permitted to continue their trade by the Act of 7 Edward VI shortly before the young K.'s death in 1553. In 1588 the inn was kept by Thos. Wright, a native of Shrewsbury; and Dr. Rogers found entries of the baptisms and burials of his children in the registers of St. Michael's Ch. In 1597 John Hodgson or Hodgkin was landlord. The Boar's Head is not mentioned by name in any of the Shakespeare plays. It was first introduced by Theobald in his edition of Shakespeare (1733). In the old play, *The Famous Victories of Henry the Fifth*, which doubtless provided the groundwork for the Shakespearian plays relating to the same period, 'the old Taverne in Eastchepe' is twice alluded to

as a place of resort for 'the young Prince with a very disordered Company.' In 1 *Henry IV* Falstaff says: 'You shall find me in Eastcheap' (Act 1, Sc. ii), and the P. says: 'Meet me to-morrow night in Eastcheap, there I'll sup.' In 2 *Henry IV* there is a tacit allusion to the Boar's Head: 'Doth the old boar feed in the old frank?' asks P. Hal. Bardolph replies: 'At the old place, my lord, in Eastcheap.'

Whilst, however, plays were performed at the Boar's Head in Aldgate, notably by the E. of Oxford's co., there is no evidence of their being performed in Eastcheap. There is in existence a farthing token of the Boar's Head. Obverse—'The Bore's Head Tavern,' a boar's head with a lemon in mouth. Reverse—'In Great Eastcheap—I.I.B.' The issuers were John and Jane Boyce, and the dates therefore between 1649 and 1657. The other has: Obverse—'John Sapcott At ye Boreshed,' a boar's head with lemon in mouth. Reverse—'Taverne in Great Eastcheap— His 1d I.E.S.' Penny tokens are rare, and this was probably issued after the G.F. John Sapcott joined the Vintners' Co. in 1667.

After the G.F., the tavern was rebuilt, and a carved stone bas-relief of a boar's head, with the initials 'I.T.' and the date 1668, was placed above one of the first-floor windows. Dr. Rogers was unable to find any landlord whose initials these could have been, and concluded they were those of John Thorneycroft. It appeared that he paid for sites in Friday St., Wood St., and Eastcheap. Maitland mentions that the inscription on the sign informed the passer-by that 'This is the chief tavern in London.' It was the custom in the 18th century to hold an annual Shakespeare banquet at the Boar's Head. At the last, in 1784, Pitt and Wilberforce were present. From a reference in Boswell's *Johnson* it would appear that a Shakespeare Club assembled there, for Boswell mentioned it to the doctor, and said that all the members assumed Shakespeare's characters. 'Don't be of it, sir,' said the latter. 'Now that you have a name, you must be careful to avoid many things not bad in themselves, but which will lessen your character.' Goldsmith wrote very pleasantly of the tavern in his *Reverie at the Boar's Head* (1760).

He gives some idea of the apartment in which he sat, but he had forgotten the G.F. and supposed it went back to Tudor times:

'The oak floor also conspired to throw my reflections back into antiquity: the oak floor, the Gothic windows, and the ponderous chimney-piece, had long withstood the tooth of time.'

Thos. Pennant, in *Some Account of London* (1790), wrote:

'The site is now covered with modern houses, but in the front of one is still preserved the memory of the sign, the Boar's Head, cut in stone.'

In 1818 Washington Irving came. He wrote:

'I sought, in vain, for the ancient abode of Dame Quickly. The only relic of it is a boar's head, carved in relief in stone, which formerly served as the sign, but at present is built in the parting line of two houses, which stand on the site of the renowned old tavern. . . . Adjoining the church, in a small cemetery, immediately under the back window of what was once the Boar's Head, stands the tombstone of Robert Preston, whilom drawer at the tavern.'

The ch. was St. Michael's, Crooked Lane (see 'City Churches; B'). The tombstone is now in a small yard at the back of the ch. of St. Magnus the Martyr (see 'Epitaphs'). A water-colour painting of the Boar's Head in the possession of Dr. Rogers shows the sign as referred to by Washington Irving. The two shops are a hair and perfumery manufactory, and a hatmaker's. On their demolition the sign went to the Guildhall, where it still is. The site was, approximately, that of the statue of William IV, removed in 1934. The Boar's Head was on the S. side of Eastcheap, which up to the time of the construction of L.B. included a part of the E. end of what is now Cannon St.

Crown and Anchor (Strand) was at the E. corner of Arundel St., and took part of its sign from the anchor of St. Clement. The Academy of Music was inaugurated here in 1710, and Strype referred to it as 'a large and curious house with good rooms, and other conveniences fit for entertainment.' Here the rejected altar-piece from St. Clement Danes Ch. was brought (see 'Strand'). Dr. Johnson came on several occasions. In 1768 he quarrelled with Dr. Percy about Dr. Mounsey of Chelsea Coll.; there were also present Robertson, the historian, and Dr. Hugh

Blair. In 1776 he was there with Sir Joshua Reynolds. It was here that the latter defended wine-drinking, as it enlivened the mind, provoking Johnson to the retort: 'I have heard none of those drunken—nay, drunken is a coarse word—none of those *vinous* flights.' In 1790 it was rebuilt, and then contained one splendid room 84 ft. by 35 ft. In 1798 a great banquet was given there to Chas. Jas. Fox, on his birthday, when the D. of Norfolk was in the chair. It was a rallying-point for the Westminster electors, and resounded to the oratory of Sheridan, O'Connell, and Cobbett. At a great Whig dinner in 1795 was given the famous toast of 'The Liberty of the Press.' In 1845 Douglas Jerrold instituted the Whittington Club here. In the club-room hung a picture of Whittington listening to Bow Bells, presented by the president. In 1854 the tavern was burnt down, and the picture with it. The Whittington Club moved to 37 Arundel St., where a club-house was erected in 1858.

Devil (Fleet St.) had originally the sign of 'The Devil and St. Dunstan.'

'The signboard,' says W. G. Bell, 'was painted with a vigorous representation of St. Dunstan, the patron of the goldsmith's art, and his sable majesty leering over his shoulder, tempting him from his labour at the forge.'

A token in the Beaufoy collection at the Guildhall shows the two at closer quarters, the saint tweaking the devil by the nose with his pincers, and this seems to have been the original pictorial sign. Referring to the ch. of St. Dunstan, Stepney, Pennant says it

'was originally called "Ecclesia omnium Sanctorum," but was afterwards styled that of St. Dunstan; for the whole body of saints was obliged to give way to him who had the courage to take the devil himself by the nose.'

In this case the devil ousted the saint, for his name came to be dropped. The tavern is mentioned in an interlude, *Jacke Jugeler*, in 1563. Ben Jonson made it a great place for convivial meetings, and founded the Apollo Club there. The twenty-four rules which he drew up in Latin are still preserved in the partners' room in Child's Bank; they are in gilt letters on a board. Some of them are excellent, e.g.:

'12. Let the contests be rather of books than of wine;

13. Let the company be neither noisy nor mute;

14. Let none of things serious, much less of divine,
    When belly and heart's full, profanely dispute.'

In 1624 John Chamberlain sent to Sir Dudley Carleton certain convivial laws of Ben Jonson's,

> 'made for a fair room or chamber lately built at the tavern or sign of the Devil and St. Dunstan's by Temple Bar; they be reasonably good, and not improper for such a place.'

Jonson mentions the Devil in his *Staple of News*. Of *The Devil is an Asse* he said it was written 'when I and my boys drank bad wine at the Devil.' There are memoranda at Dulwich Coll. referring to it:

> 'Mem. The first speech in my Catilina, spoken by Sylla's Ghost, was writ after I parted with my friend at the Devil Tavern.
>
> 'Mem. Upon the 20th May, the King (Heaven reward him!) sent me £100. At that time I often went to the Devil, and before I had spent forty of it I wrote my Alchymist.'

Rowley's comedy, *A Match at Midnight* (1633), mentions it:

> '*Bloodhound.* As you come by Temple Bar, make a step to th' Devil.
>
> *Tim.* To the Devil, father?
>
> *Sim.* My master means the sign of the Devil; and he cannot hurt you, fool. There's a saint holds him by the nose.'

Dr. Johnson patronized the Devil. There in 1751 he went to an entertainment to celebrate the publication of Mrs. Lennox's first novel. George II once visited the Devil. It was part of a plot against Heidegger, master of the revels, reputed to be the ugliest man of his day. A bust, now in the Soane Mus., assists the belief. The rather long story is interestingly related in W. G. Bell's *Fleet Street in Seven Centuries*. The Devil was demolished in 1788 when Child's Bank was enlarged. In addition to the rules mentioned, the bank also treasures a bust of Apollo which stood in Jonson's clubroom.

Goose and Gridiron. This tavern was in St. P.'s Chyd., near to London House Yard. Here, from about 1695, was a Lodge of Freemasons of which Sir Christopher Wren was elected Grand Master. He presented this Lodge with three beautifully carved mahogany candlesticks, and the trowel and mallet which he used in laying the first stone of the Cath. The odd sign has been said to derive from the 'Swan and Harp' which, satirised by customers as the 'Goose and Gridiron,' led the landlord to make a change. Sir Walter Besant, however, mentioned that there was a 'Swan and Harp' in Cheapside, and it seems much more likely that one landlord was making a satirical hit at another than that the witticism of customers should induce mine host of the tavern in St. P.'s Chyd. to change his sign. The tavern was demolished about 1898. The sign is at the Guildhall Mus.

Half Moon (Aldersgate St.—where is now Half Moon Court). This was a resort of Ben Jonson's. Finding it closed once, he went to the Sun Tavern in Long Lane, and then wrote:

> 'Since the Half Moon is so unkind,
>   To make me go about,
> The Sun my money now shall have,
>   And the moon shall go without.'

Half Moon (Bedford St.) was a tavern much patronized by Pepys, who once refers to it as 'in the street over against the Exchange'—meaning the New Exchange (see 'Strand'). It is mentioned also by Ned Ward in his *London Spy*; he passes it on his way to Covent Garden.

Half Moon (Cheapside) was mentioned in 1682 by Elias Ashmole, who resided there, at a dinner of the freemasons. In 1745 the following advertisement appeared in the *Gentleman's Magazine*:

> 'Half-Moon Tavern, Cheapside, April 13. His Royal Highness the Duke of Cumberland having restored peace to Britain, by the ever-memorable Battle of Culloden, fought on the 16th of April 1745, the *choice spirits* have agreed to celebrate that day annually by a GRAND JUBILEE in the MOON, of which the Stars are hereby acquainted and summoned to shine with their brightest Lustre by six o'clock on Thursday next in the Evening.'

At the Guildhall Mus. there is the sign of a H.M. dated 1690; it is said to have come from another tavern of that name in High St., Aldgate.

Mermaid (Bread St.) is one of the mystifications of L. topography. Much praised in literature, it has been described by nobody, neither is there any contemporary picture of it. There is a reference in 1464. The steward of Sir John Howard ('Jockey of Norfolk') wrote:

'Paid for wyn at the Mermayd in Bred Stret for my mastyr and Syr Nicholas Latimer xd. ob.'

It is remarkable, too, that it was not rebuilt after the G.F., and that no tablet records its site. It stood between Bread St. and Friday St., and it would appear from Ben Jonson's allusions to 'Bread Street Mermaid,' that there was no frontage to Cheapside. Ben Jonson referring to a trip up the River Fleet, said:

'At Bread Street's Mermaid having dined and merry,
Proposed to go to Holborn in a wherry.'

And again:

'A pure cup of rich Canary wine
Which is the Mermaid's now but shall be mine.'

Beaumont exclaimed:

'What things have we seen
Done at the Mermaid!'

All that remains of the name is the new Mermaid Theatre.

Mitre (Fleet St.) was probably a medieval tavern. The first known reference is in 1603, when complaint was made, in connection with the adjacent 'Alsatia'—

'that there is a door leading out of Ram Alley to the tenement of tavern called the Miter in Fleet-streete, by means whereof such persons as do frequent the house upon search made after them are conveyed out that way.'

In a comedy entitled *Ram Alley, or Merrie Tricks* (1611) is another reference:

'Meet me straight
At the Mitre door in Fleete Street.'

In 1640, in the tavern, Lilly, the astrologer, met Will Poole, another astrologer. Pepys was there twice in 1660, and mentions a music room. It was not entirely destroyed in the G.F., but was 'very much demolished and decaied in severall parts, and the Balcony was on fire, and was pulled downe.' Dr. Johnson seems to have frequented the Mitre more than any other tavern, and Boswell refers to its 'orthodox high-church sound.' This perhaps helped him to remember the name

better than the 'Cheshire Cheese.' Here Johnson dined with the pretty Methodists, and dandled them on his knees, solely with a view to their conversion! (It was the strange subject of a picture by D. G. Rossetti). Here he made the famous retort to the Scot about the high road to England being the best prospect to him. The Mitre closed its doors as a tavern in 1788; Macklin then re-opened it as the Poets' Gallery. It was lastly Saunders's auction room, and was finally demolished for the enlargement of Hoare's Bank, in 1829. Chamberlain Clark, who d. 1831, aged 92, was the last survivor of the Johnsonian period. There is a C.C. tablet on the site of the Mitre, 37 Fleet St. The Mitre Tavern, in Mitre Court, was once known as Joe's Coffee House, and took the same name when the original Mitre disappeared. It was much altered in 1865. Beresford Chancellor said:

'So determined were its proprietors to connect Dr. Johnson with it, that his "corner" was preserved with due reverence, and a copy of Nollekens' well-known bust of the Doctor given an honoured place.'

It is now called 'The Clachan.'

Mitre (Wood St.) is mentioned by Ben Jonson in *Every Man in his Humour* and *Bartholomew Fair*. It was a resort of Pepys in 1660—'a house of the greatest note in London,' he calls it, and he was there 'very merry and had a very good dinner.' The landlord d. at Islington, of the Plague, in 1665.

Poulter's Arms (Freeman's Court, Cheapside), claimed by some to be the oldest licensed inn in the City, was destroyed by bombs.

Ship and Shovel (Great Maze Pond) was near Guy's Hosp. The name is said to be a deterioration of the 'Sir Cloudesley Shovel,' but Larwood and Hotten thought it was more likely an allusion to the 'shovels used in taking out ballast, coal, corn (when in bulk) and various other cargoes.' The tavern has been destroyed by bombs, but a table that bears the names of eminent medical men, carved by them when students at Guys' Hosp., is preserved there.

Thatched House. This was in St. James's St., on the site of the present Conservative Club. Its history probably went back to Tudor times, but it came into notice first in the days of Swift, who wrote to Stella in 1711 of 'having entertained our society at the Thatched House Tavern.' Later it added a large room often used for public meetings. From about 1799 the Dilettanti Soc. met there. It was concerned with classical antiquities—the art and sculpture of Greece and Rome. For a time the Literary Club, of which Dr. Johnson was a foundation member, met at this Tavern.

Here, on 20th Aug., 1791, Thos. Paine read a paper entitled *An Address and Declaration of the Friends of Universal Peace and Liberty.* It was unanimously adopted and plans made for a wide circulation. W. E. Woodward (*Tom Paine: America's Godfather*) said:

'The address did not attack the King or the English form of government. It was essentially a plea for doing away with abuses of one kind or another, and it urged a more liberal policy in handling problems concerning the welfare of the people.'

The tavern was demolished in 1843, and another erected close by. This remained until 1865 when the premises of the Thatched House Club were erected on the site.

Three Cranes (Vintry) derived its name, says Stow, from 'three strong cranes of timber placed on the Vintry wharf, by the Thames side, to crane up wines there.' These cranes are represented in Visscher's view of L. (1616). Here there was a landing-place where, according to Foxe, the D. of Somerset disembarked on his way to the T.L. in 1552. It figured in Ben Jonson's plays. In *Bartholomew Fair* (1614) it is the first of a trinity of taverns; the others are the 'Mitre' and 'Mermaid.' In *The Devil is an Asse* is an indication of the whereabouts of the most famous of the taverns of this name (there were at various times Three Cranes taverns in the Poultry, Old Bailey, Savoy, etc.):

'Shoot the Bridge, child, to the Cranes in the Vintry,
And see there the gimblets how they make their entry.'

At this tavern Charles II and Ld. Wilmot had agreed to meet if they found their way to L. after the battle of Worcester. Pepys (23rd Jan. 1662) went there and
'in such a narrow dogg-hole we were crammed . . . that it made me loathe

my company and victuals; and a sorry poor dinner it was too.'

It must have been burnt in the G.F.; it is not known if it was rebuilt.

EXISTING TAVERNS

Cheshire Cheese (Wine Office Court, Fleet St.) was erected soon after the G.F., and has extensive vaults anterior to that date. From the Johnsonian aspect it is not canonical. No contemporary biographer of Johnson mentions it. It can hardly, therefore, have been a favourite resort of Johnson's, though, having regard to its proximity to his many residences in the neighbourhood, it is difficult to believe he was never there. Cyrus Redding (*Fifty Years' Recollections, Literary and Personal,* 1858) mentioned that he went to live in Gough Sq. in 1806 and often dined there. He met individuals who had met Johnson and his friends there. Cyrus Jay (*The Law—What I have Seen, Heard, and Known,* 1868) had met 'very old gentlemen who remembered Dr. Johnson nightly at the Cheshire Cheese.' He was said to have preferred it to the 'Mitre' or the 'Essex Head' when he lived in Gough Sq., Johnson's Court, and Bolt Court, because 'nothing but a hurricane would have induced him to cross Fleet Street.' It is, however, not claimed that the rather small arm-chair belonged originally to the C.C. It came from the Mitre Tavern. In what is called Dr. Johnson's Corner there is a copy of one of Reynolds's portraits and underneath the inscription:

'The Favourite Seat of
DR. SAMUEL JOHNSON
Born September 18, 1709. Died
December 13, 1784.

'In him a noble understanding and a masterly intellect were united to great independence of character and unfailing goodness of heart, which won the admiration of his own age, and remain as recommendations to the reverence of posterity.
' "No, sir! there is nothing which has yet been contrived by man, by which so much happiness has been produced as by a good tavern." '

The well-worn step of the Cheshire Cheese is now protected by an iron guard. The great feature of the tavern was its pudding. It ranged usually from 50 lb. to 80 lb. in weight; was composed of a light crust in a huge basin; and there were—

'entombed therein, beef-steaks, kidneys, oysters, larks, mushrooms, and wondrous spices and gravies, the secret of which is only known to the compounder.'

It took from sixteen to twenty hours to boil, and it was said that 'the smell on a windy day has been known to reach as far as the Stock Exchange'! Dr. Johnson never knew the pudding, though Harry Bartlett, a youthful essayist of St. Clement Danes Sch. imagined him going to the Cheshire Cheese with Goldsmith and ordering—

'two portions of Ye Pudding rather greedily, remarking after consumption "Ah, so much the better for that!" '

Galsworthy introduced the pudding into the *Forsyte Saga*. Soames and Winifred partake of it. The pudding season opened on the first Monday in Oct., when some distinguished visitor presided, and made the first cut.

The Cheshire Cheese may be the one Dickens had in mind when in *A Tale of Two Cities* (1859) Carton takes Darnay 'down Ludgate Hill to Fleet Street, and so up a covered way into a Tavern.' The entrance to the Cheshire Cheese is through a covered way.

(See *The Book of the Cheese*.)

Amongst several other taverns of the same name, there is a Cheshire Cheese Tavern in Milford Lane, Strand, which displays the figure of Dr. Johnson on its sign, but there is no justification for this.

Cock (Fleet St.) was originally the 'Cock and Bottle.' One of its tokens, dated 1655, is still in existence. On the obverse are the words: 'The Cock Ale House,' with a figure of a cock in the centre; and on the reverse: 'At Temple Barr, 1655.' In 1665 the *Weekly Intelligencer* announced:

'The master . . . hath dismissed his servants, and shut up his house, for this Long Vacation, intended (God willing) to return at Michaelmas next, so that all persons whosoever who have any accompts with the said master, or farthings belonging to the said house, are desire to repair thither before the 8th of this instant July, and they shall receive satisfaction.'

This was at the time of the Plague. Pepys came at times, notably on 13th Apr. 1668:

'By water to the Temple, and thence to the Cock Alehouse, and drank and eat a lobster, and sang, and mighty merry.'

A pint moved Tennyson to verse about it. In *Will Waterproof's Lyrical Monologue, made at the Cock*, he wrote:

'O plump head-waiter at the Cock,
To which I most resort,
How goes the time? 'Tis five o'clock.
Go fetch a pint of port.'

It is said that when the head-waiter's attention was drawn to the lines, he could 'not remember the gent.' Until 1887 the Cock was on the N. side of Fleet St., where is now the Law Courts branch of the Bank of England. The sign now displayed is a modern one; its predecessor, dating from the end of the 17th century, is inside.

Dirty Dick's (Bishopsgate) commemorates a strange story of 18th-century date. The hero was not a Dick, but a Nathaniel, and his surname was Bentley. His father was a man of wealth who is said to have given money for a ch. bell in the City to be rung on every anniversary of his birth until his death, which occurred in 1761. He left the whole of his property to his son, who became a dandy, and dressed in the height of fashion. He had a love affair, and was engaged to be m. to a young lady to whom he was greatly attached. He arranged a banquet to celebrate the engagement, and on the day appointed received news of her death. He ordered the dining-room to be shut up, and resolved that it should never again be opened during his lifetime. He then lived a solitary life, and paid a man to attend to his shop, although he always removed and replaced the shutters with his own hands. He went about unkempt, washed seldom, and mended his own clothes. He d. at Musselburgh in Scotland in 1809, and then the upper part of the premises, locked up for about forty yrs., was investigated. To quote a poem which appeared in *Household Words* in 1852 under the title *The Dirty Old Man*:

'The guests for whose joyance that table
was spread,
May now enter as ghosts, for they're
every one dead.
'Through a chink in the shutter dim
lights come and go,
The seats are in order, the dishes a-row;
But the luncheon was wealth to the rat
and the mouse,

Whose descendants have long left the dirty old house.

'Cup and platter are masked in thick layers of dust,
The flowers fallen to powder, the wine swath's in crust.
A nosegay was laid before one special chair,
And the faded blue ribbon that bound it is there.'

Amidst the cobwebs and the dirt and dust there are said to have been found skeletons of rats and mice such as are to be seen in the vaults of the present tavern. There is, however, reason to believe that Bentley's hardware business was in Leadenhall St., and that the landlord of the tavern in Bishopsgate, whose family in 1893 had been in possession for 150 yrs., bought up the contents of the room at the beginning of the 19th century, as an attraction for his house, thereafter called 'Dirty Dick's Tavern.' This is confirmed by the fact that the tavern is said to have originated in 1745. Obviously the small mus. in the vaults has received accessions since Dick's day. The skeleton of a small alligator was not found in his rooms! The story is referred to in an old and one-time popular song, *The King of the Cannibal Islands*:

'His palace was like Dirty Dick's—
'Twas built of mud for want of bricks!'

Eagle (City Rd.) is most famous for another popular song, traced back to 1779:

'Up and down the City Road,
In and out the "Eagle,"
That's the way the money goes,
Pop goes the weasel.'

In short, you must then pawn your watch, as Mr. Micawber, who lived in Windsor Terrace, a few yards from the Eagle, would have said. It is surprising Dickens never took Micawber, particularly as 'Miss J'mima Ivins' (*Sketches by Boz*) went when—

'there were walks beautifully gravelled and planted—and the refreshment-boxes, painted and ornamented like so many snuff-boxes—and the variegated lamps shedding their rich light upon the company's heads—and the place for dancing ready chalked for the company's feet.'

This was the time when the Grecian Theatre occupied the first floor. Two

vocalists who made great hits here were Harry Howell and Robt. Glindon. The latter was the author of two most popular songs, *Biddy the Basket Woman* and *The Literary Dustman*. Marie Lloyd made her first professional appearance here in 1885 under the name of Bella Delmere and sang two songs, *My Soldier Laddie* and *Time is Flying*. She was billed as Marie Lloyd when she reappeared at the same place later in the yr. The modern Eagle has lost all its old interest. (See 'Music Halls.')

Feathers (Upper Ground). This is on the site of Cuper's Gardens, a place of entertainment of dubious character which was opened in 1691. They took the name from Boydell Cuper, gardener to the E. of Arundel. In contrast to the more westerly pleasaunces, they were regarded as resorts of riff-raff. Horace Walpole reported in 1746 that Lds. Bath and Sandys there had their pockets picked. The gardens were about 800 ft. long by 200 ft. wide, and extended southwards nearly to St. John's Ch. Johnson was once passing with Langton, Beauclerk, and Lady Sidney Beauclerk, and suggested they should go in. The last replied that 'an old man should not put such notions into young men's heads.' They were closed in 1759 as a public resort, but remained for long after. The tavern was opened in 1817, on the second anniversary of the battle of Waterloo. The peculiarity of the Feathers before the Second World War, was that there was one public house built on the top of another, as there was a complete set of bars in the Waterloo Bridge Rd. Now there is only the lower tavern.

The *Grapes* at Limehouse and the *Prospect of Whitby* at Wapping are riverside taverns with balconies overhanging the water. Both are of considerable age. The claim has been made for each that it is the original of the 'Six Jolly Fellowship Porters' of Dickens's *Our Mutual Friend*. This distinction, however, rightly belongs to the now demolished *Two Brewers*, which until about fifty yrs. ago stood at the top of Duke Shore Stairs in Narrow St., Limehouse. (See article by G. F. Young, *Dickensian*, Spring, 1935.)

The odd name of *The Prospect of Whitby* has given rise to much conjecture. It was nothing but a guess that it had relation to the Yorkshire town. On an engraving by Wenceslaus Hollar (exhibited at the B. Mus. in 1950) there was the following endorsement: 'Prospect of Whitby by Tangier where the stone for mould is fetsh'd and the workmen doe quarter.' Hollar went on the Moroccan mission in 1669. One of the workmen may, on his return to England, have taken a tavern and given it the name of his foreign quarters.

The *Railway Tavern* in West India Dock Rd. remains, but all Charlie Brown's treasures have gone—some to 'The Roundabout,' Woodford. Many other L. pubs of historical interest can be traced in *London Pubs*, by Alan Reeve-Jones (1962), and *Guide to London Pubs*, by Martin Green and Tony White (1968). More serious readers should consult *London Inns and Taverns*, by Leopold Wagner (1924) and the same author's *More London Inns and Taverns* (1925).

Temple is not a Jewish quarter of L., but its name is linked directly with Solomon's Temple. In 1099 Hugh de Payens, a knight of Burgundy who had distinguished himself at the capture of Jerusalem, induced companions to undertake with him the task of guarding the main roads leading to the 'Holy City' for the protection of pilgrims. They were enrolled as regular canons by the Patriarch of Jerusalem, and took the vows of perpetual chastity, obedience, and self-denial. They occupied a palace which was formerly part of a bdg. erected by the Emperor Justinian, and partly of a mosque built by the Caliph Omar upon the site of Solomon's Temple; hence the latter part of the title of the order: *Pauperes Commilitones Christi et Templi Salomenio* (Poor fellow-soldiers of Christ of the Temple of Solomon). Under the patronage of St. Bernard the order was reconstituted in 1128. Pope Honorius II gave the members, as their distinctive dress, a white mantle symbolical of purity and innocence. Pope Eugenius III added the red cross as an emblem of the dedication of the order to the Christian faith. Thenceforth the order spread rapidly; rights and privileges were lavished upon it, and in 1162 Pope Alexander III rendered it immune from all jurisdiction other than that of the Holy See. At the head was the Grand Master of the Temple, resident at the Temple of Jerusalem until its capture by Saladin in 1187, when the

headquarters were transferred to Acre. There were three orders: knights, priests, and serving brethren. The first must have been knighted by an earthly potentate.

The date of the establishment in England is unknown, but Richd. de Hastings (a friend of Becket's) is known to have been English master of the Temple in 1135. Their first house was in Chancery Lane; they were probably there in the early yrs. of the 12th century. A round ch. existed on the site until Q. Elizabeth's reign; the foundations were discovered in 1904 upon the site of the London and County Bank. This was known as 'The Old Temple.' In 1830, during some excavations in the present ch., a portion of a round shrine was discovered. On it were three mail-clad figures carved in high relief, supposed to be Roman soldiers watching the body of Christ. The costume was early 12th century. The relic was therefore of earlier date than the present ch., and was probably brought by the Templars from the first ch. in Chancery Lane. About 1160 the Knights Templars acquired new quarters on the banks of the Thames, and these became known as 'The New Temple.' A round ch. was the common form for those of the Knights Templars. There are round chs. to-day at Ludlow, Cambridge, Northampton, and Little Maplestead. They were thus designed in imitation of the Ch. of the Holy Sepulchre in Jerusalem. In 1185 the Round Ch. in the new Temple was erected, and dedicated to the Virgin Mary by Heraclius, Patriarch of the Ch. of the Holy Resurrection in Jerusalem, in the presence of Henry II and his court. (It was not until 1926 that another patriarch visited the Ch. This was Patriarch Damianos, who came with the Patriarch of Alexandria and other distinguished prelates of the Eastern Ch.) On Ascension Day 1240 a second dedication took place before Henry III and his barons, and it is generally accepted that at this time the rectangular chancel was added. There was, however, a chancel or choir attached to the Round prior to 1240; it was some 50 ft. in length; and the foundations still exist under the present bdg. By some it is considered to date from Saxon times.

The Knights Templars, when no crusade called, lived a monastic life. They took vows of perpetual chastity, obedience, and self-denial. In the words of a Commendation of St. Bernard:

'Never an idle word or a useless deed, or immoderate laughter, or a murmur, even if only whispered, is allowed to go unpunished. Draughts and dice they detest. Hunting they hold in abomination and take no pleasure in the absurd pastime of hawking. Soothsayers, jesters and story tellers, ribald song and stage plays, they eschew as insane follies. They cut close their hair, knowing as the apostle says that it is a shame for a man to have long hair. They never dress gaily and wash but seldom. Shaggy by reason of their uncombed hair, they are also begrimed with dust and swarthy from the weight of their armour and the heat of the sun.'

They were ordered:

'To make known wants that could not be expressed by signs in gentle, soft, and private way.

'Two to live together so that one might watch the other.'

No one must read or dispatch letters without consent of the Master, who might peruse the correspondence.

'Every Templar to shun feminine kisses, whether from widow, virgin, mother, sister, aunt or any other woman.'

The last prohibition is as comprehensive as any modern Temple conveyancer could desire. There was, until the Blitz, in the NW. corner of the choir, a cell built in the thickness of the wall—4 ft. by 2ft. 9 in. —and approached by a round-headed doorway. 'In this miserable cell,' wrote Addison (1842–3), the historian of the Temple—

'were confined the refractory and disobedient brethren of the Temple, and those who were injoined severe penance and solitary confinement. Its dark secrets have long since been buried in the tomb, but one sad tale of misery and horror connected with it has been brought to light.'

This was the case of Walter le Bacheler, Grand Preceptor of Ireland (the date is unknown—it was divulged during the Templars' trial in 1312). He was imprisoned here in chains for disobedience to the Master of the Temple, and d. from the severity of confinement in a cell too small to allow him to lie down. His body was carried in the early morning to the old chyd. between the ch. and the hall.

In the cell two small windows admitted light and air, one looking eastward into the choir, so that the prisoner might see the altar and hear the offices carried on there.

The order was suspected of Gnostic and Manichaean heresies, and its wealth excited the envy of medieval monarchs. Edward I suppressed it in England, and with the aid of the Pope it was dissolved by the Council of Vienne in 1312. Upon the dissolution all the property was assigned to the Knights Hospitallers, but not more than one-twentieth reached their hands. In England, immediately upon the eviction of the Templars, they were allowed to take possession of the consecrated portions—roughly what is now known as the Inner Temple. This was more than they required for their own uses, and in 1326—or perhaps much earlier—thirteen houses, built by Roger Blom, formerly nuncius or messenger of the Templars, N. of the ch., were let to a body of lawyers. The unconsecrated places, consisting of a hall, four chambers, a garden, a stable, and a chamber outside the Great Gate, were apparently let to another body of lawyers about 1356. These places correspond approximately with what is known as the Middle Temple.

It is now generally held that the socs. of the Inner and Middle Temple have always been distinct. The first mention of Middle Temple as a distinct soc. occurs in a will dated 1404. In the *Paston Letters* several references to the Inner Temple appear so early as 1440. Here, then, for about six centuries, men 'of lawe expert and curious,' as Chaucer says of the masters of his 'gentil maunciple of a temple,' have carried on their practice. The crests of the two socs. have provoked much discussion. The original banner of the Knights Templars was made of two pieces of woollen stuff, one black, the other white, with the red cross of the order in the midst. It was called Le Beauseant (originally spelt 'Bauceant'), which signified in Old French a piebald horse. Possibly from this sprang the Pegasus, the horse with two wings, the present badge of the Inner Temple. The seal is two men on one horse. A common suggestion is that this was an emblem of poverty. More probably it was symbolic of the succour given by the knights to wounded pilgrims. A second seal was the

Agnus Dei (Lamb of God) with the flag, but this was only adopted at a much later date, its first known use being in 1241. This was appropriately adopted by members of the Middle Temple as the badge of their soc.

The Temple is private property—belonging to the Socs. of the Inner and Middle Temple. Hence it can be closed, except to residents. Its privileges are carefully guarded. From time to time the City claimed jurisdiction over it, and Pepys relates that in 1668 when Sir Wm. Turner (Ld.M.) was invited by Christopher Goodfellowe to his Readers' Feast in the Inner Temple Hall, he came—

'endeavouring to carry his sword up. The students did pull it down and forced him to stay all day in a private Councillor's chambers until the Reader himself could get the young gentlemen to dismiss, and then the Lord Mayor did retreat out of the Temple by stealth with his sword up.'

The City appealed to Charles II to decide whether the Temple was within the City, but the K., unwilling to offend either party, gave no decision, and the matter rose again on the occasion of a serious fire in the Temple in 1679. Not until 11th Oct. 1939, when Major Sir Frank Bowater inspected Troops in the Temple, was another Ld.M. seen there.

Another matter of dispute, the boundary between the Inner Temple and the Middle Temple, was decided by a Deed of Partition dated 2nd Nov. 1734.

The G.F. caused considerable damage. As Ld. Clarendon wrote:

'There was scarce a man to whom those lodgings appertained who was in town; so that whatsoever there was there, their money books and papers, besides the evidences of many men's estates deposited in their hands were all burnt or lost to a very great value.'

The whole of King's Bench Walk, the Master's House, and most of the bdgs. E. of the Inner Temple Hall were destroyed. The flames licked the E. end of the ch., and set light to the roof of the Inner Temple Hall. Later the fire broke out in Fig Tree Court, and this was partially blown up in order to save the hall. James, D. of York, exerted himself in this work of salvation.

The Temple had several subsequent fires of its own. In 1677 much of King's Bench Walk was destroyed. In 1679 another fire burnt down the chapel of St. Anne, which was at the SW. corner of the ch. Seven large flagstones indicate its site. In it were kept the judicial records and writs. In 1683 there was another fire S. of King's Bench Walk, and in 1704 still another destroyed about half of Brick Court as it was then.

In the Second World War, starting with 24th Sept. 1940, the Temple suffered a succession of grievous blows from the air, and on 15th Oct. and 8th Dec. 1940 land-mines wrought great havoc. On the latter date there was left a crater 40 ft. wide and 18 ft. deep. In Mar. 1941 about fifty incendiaries fell; two were on the Middle Temple Hall, and two on the Ch., whilst fires were started in New Court, Essex Court, Pump Court, and on Lamb Bdg. On the night of 10th May 1941, when there was the last serious raid on the centre of L., the Master's House and the Cloisters were destroyed. The Middle Temple, which had started the Second World War with 285 sets of chambers, had by then only 173.

The damage caused to the various parts will be noted in the course of this survey of the Temple.

TEMPLE CHURCH. An inscription on the inside of the entrance door—a copy of one removed in 1695—stated that on 10th Feb. 1185 it was dedicated in honour of the Blessed Mary by the Lord Heraclius by the Grace of God the Patriarch of the Ch. of the Holy Sepulchre (Jerusalem), who had granted an indulgence of sixty days to those seeking it. The roof was supported by clustered columns of highly polished Purbeck marble, with richly moulded capitals. Some of these were erected during one of several restorations—by Wren, 1681–3, and Robt. Smirke, 1828. The doorway is a fine specimen of later Norman or Transitional work. It has been restored at times, but is still composed chiefly of the original Caen stone. The sculptured capitals reveal signs of Saracenic influence to which the Knights Templars, as Crusaders, were susceptible. There is an intermixture of foliage, lozenges, and tooth-moulding, terminating in capitals of half-length statues. The figures on the N. side are supposed to represent Henry II with three Templars, to whom he is presenting the charter of their foundation, and on

27 Tower Bridge

28 Armour in the Tower

29 Nelson's Column

30 Trafalgar Square

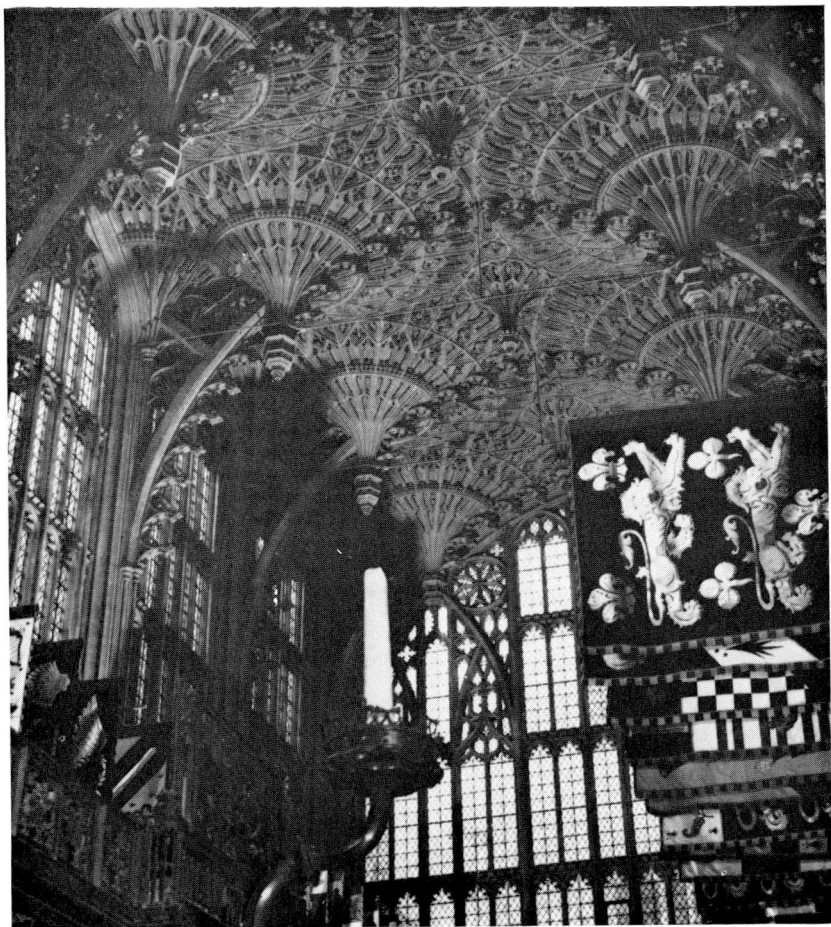

31 Henry VII's Chapel, Westminster Abbey

32 The River Thames and the Houses of Parliament

33 Whitehall from St James's Park

34 The Palace of Westminster

35 Whitehall; the Horse Guards

the S. side the Patriarch Heraclius, with three attendant clergy. The porch is a survival of the ancient cloisters which, rebuilt by Wren, were so badly damaged by bombs that they have been demolished. A conical roof—also bombed out of existence—dated only from 1840; previously there had been a flat castellated one. The pavement of the ch. was then lowered about 16 in. and at that time a number of gravestones were removed to the N. chyd.

Effigies. These attracted most attention. It used persistently to be said that the crossed legs were an indication that the deceased represented had been to a crusade, and that the point of the crossing was an indication of the number of crusades in which he had participated. Geo. Worley characterized the latter as 'an interesting superstition.' The crossed legs are not always found in those of known crusaders, and they are found sometimes when it is known that the deceased could not have been on a crusade. It was probably due to a general idea of representing repose and perhaps making the sign of the cross in death, as arms are sometimes crossed upon the breast. The effigies were repaired and painted at the beginning of the 18th century, and were somewhat mutilated before 1840, when they were restored. In some cases fragments were missing, and there was need for conjecture. Composition had to be introduced where the original parts had gone beyond recall. The effigies have been many times moved, and the places of burial were quite unknown. They all lie with their heads to the E. Sir Walter Scott, at a funeral, once noticed that the deceased was not so lying, but remarked, as he had been a wrong-headed fellow in life it did not much matter which way he lay in death! The Knights Templars, however, would have attached considerable importance to this. Of the nine effigies, two probably dated from the 12th century, and seven from the 13th century. None of them were Knights Templars, as the latter, bd. in the habit of their order (a long white mantle with the red cross over the left breast), had it represented on the tombs. Sir Geoffrey de Magnaville (E. of Essex and Constable of the T.L., d. 1144), Wm. Mareschal the elder (E. of Pembroke, d. 1219), Wm. Mareschal the younger (d.

1231), Gilbert Mareschal (E. of Pembroke, brother of Wm. the younger, d. 1241), Robt. de Ros (d. 1227), had been identified with five of the figures. They have all been badly damaged by bombs.

There have survived (through bricking up) the monument to Edmund Plowden, Treasurer of the Middle Temple during the rebuilding of the Hall. He d. in 1584. Plowden Bdgs. in Middle Temple Lane are named after him. He is represented in a long black close fitting gown, lying upon his back with his hand joined across his breast. There also remains the monument of Richd. Martin, Recorder of L. (d. 1615). He wears a flowing scarlet robe, and is kneeling on an embroidered and tasselled cushion, before a small desk or *prie dieu* with an open book in his left hand while his face is turned upwards in an attitude of prayer. The curious carved heads, some dating from restorations, remain in the round nave.

The monuments of Richd. Hooker (d. 1600) and John Selden (d. 1651), both bd. in the Ch. have been destroyed, as also a monument of Goldsmith which was in the triforium. There has survived the fine effigy of a bp. The recumbent figure is represented in the full episcopal vestments. The right hand is raised in the act of benediction, and the left holds a crosier, with richly ornamented crook, turned towards the body. It is believed to represent Sylvester de Everden, who became Bp. of Carlisle in 1247, and was sometime chancellor. He was killed by a fall from a horse in 1255, and bd. in the Temple Ch. In 1810 the coffin was opened. It measured 10 ft. in length by 3 ft. in height, with a semicircular cavity for the head. There were some broken pieces of a crosier, fragments of vestments, and a skeleton, with a leaden envelope, at the feet of which lay the bones of an infant, apparently only a few months old. Mrs. Arundell Esdaile (*Temple Church Monuments*) thinks they were the remains of Henry III's infant son. The K. had desired to take the Cross, and finally to lie in the Temple Ch. That could not be, and so he gave the body of his infant son to the ch.

The ch. was lighted by large wax candles until 1886. The Templars having been exempted by papal bull from episcopal jurisdiction, the Master is appointed by the joint socs. without

R

induction. It is, in fact, a 'royal peculiar,' having letters patent from the Crown.

In 1933 D. B. Somervell, K.C., Conservative M.P. for Crewe, was m. in the 'Round.' Dr. Carpenter, Master of the Temple, said that it might reasonably be conjectured that this was the first wedding there since the erection of the choir in 1240. There have been many weddings in the choir (including Sir Christopher Wren's; he m. his first wife here in 1669). In 1684 they numbered 69. Now they are few. Burials ceased in 1853.

The Temple Ch. was reduced to a ruin on 10th May 1941 but has been largely reconstructed. About five feet below the choir there were discovered the remains (including a beautifully carved capital) of a bdg. probably dating from the 12th century. This is believed to be on the site of the Chapel of St. Anne, which was removed in 1827.

Graveyard. There was once a graveyard both N. and S. of the ch. On the N. are the slabs brought from the ch. in 1840. The long, low stone inscribed with the name of Oliver Goldsmith is simply a memorial; the exact place of burial in the Temple chyd. is unknown, but it was probably hereabouts. It was placed there in 1860. Thos. Carlyle stood reverently by it in 1879. The bewigged gentlemen represented by effigies are John Hiccock (d. 1726) and Samuel Mead (d. 1733). Inside the rails are six stone coffins, discovered in 1861, when the chambers and vestry which stood against the NW. wall of the ch. were taken down. They are at the level at which they were found, and in the same position—feet towards the E. Each coffin is a single massive stone, hollowed out for the reception of the corpse. On the S. side, within the rails, are a few gravestones.

BRICK COURT. Its name is said to derive from its being the first structure of brick in the Temple. It suffered badly from fires in 1679 and 1703, and in the Second World War was almost entirely destroyed but has been rebuilt. Here, at No. 2, Oliver Goldsmith lived from 1767 until his death in 1774. He furnished his chambers 'with mahogany sofas, card tables, and bookcases, with curtains, mirrors, and Wilton carpets.' Here he was visited by Johnson and Reynolds. Here he gave supper parties to young people, and they played blind-man's buff amongst other games. It is said that Wm. Blackstone, who occupied the chambers below, used to send up requests for less noise, when he was engaged upon his *Commentaries on the Laws of England.* Here Goldsmith wrote *She Stoops to Conquer* and part of *The Deserted Village.* In 1906 a tablet, designed by Percy Fitzgerald, was placed on the chambers, which had some history subsequent to Goldsmith. In 1794 a Miss Brodrick shot her lover Mr. Eddington, who had deserted her. W. M. Praed, the poet, had chambers here about 1830, and Thackeray from 1853-9.

CROWN OFFICE ROW. The Clerk of the Crown had his office here until 1621, when he removed to 2 King's Bench Walk, from whence it was removed to the Royal Courts of Justice on their completion in 1882. Here Chas. Lamb was born, and a tablet bore the following inscription:

'Charles Lamb
was born in these chambers
10 February 1775
"Cheerful Crown Office Row (place of my kindly engendure) . . . a man would give something to have been born in such places." '

The chambers have been destroyed, but have been rebuilt. Here, too, Thackeray had chambers from 1848 (when he was called to the Bar) to 1857.

DR. JOHNSON'S BUILDINGS (Inner Temple Lane). They date from 1857, and are so-called by reason of the fact that in chambers on the site Johnson resided from 1760 to 1765. Here he was living when, in Davies' bookshop in Russell St., Covent Garden, he first met Boswell, who described the apartments as 'very airy, and commanding a view of St. Paul's and many a brick roof.' Whilst living here—in 1763—Johnson was awarded his pension. When the chambers were demolished in 1857, *The Times* said that the staircase, wainscoting, banisters, and carved wood over the doorway would be preserved in perpetuity by the benchers, but this was not done.

At No. 4 Inner Temple Lane Lamb lived from 1809-17. His back windows overlooked Hare Court. To Manning he wrote:

'Our place of final destination—I don't mean the grave . . . looks out upon a gloomy churchyard-like court, called Hare Court, with three trees and a pump in it.'

The court is shown in a water-colour in the Crace Collection (B. Mus.), with the pump on the W. side. It still conveys the same gloomy impression, but the pump has gone. The trees there are not those Lamb saw. Of the pump, Lamb said, in another letter to Manning, 'the water is excellent cold with brandy, and not very insipid without.' Samuel Garth (1699) wrote:

'Sooner shall glow worms vie with Titan's beams
Or Hare Court pump with Aganippe's streams.'

It was here that the Lambs discovered 'four untenanted unowned rooms,' through the cries of a cat which led them to force a lock. One of these Mary fitted up as a study for her brother. The cat lived with them for a time, for they felt, in gratitude, bound to keep it.

ESSEX COURT. Evelyn, in 1640, had—'a handsome apartment just over against the Hall Court but four payre of stayers high w'ch gave us the advantage of the fairer prospect.' This was Essex Court. In 1677 the W. side was rebuilt, as recorded in the inscription over the archway. The bdgs. on the N. were pulled down and rebuilt in 1883, when a new passage through what is now known as the Outer Temple was constructed.

FIG COURT, which took its name from a fig tree, first mentioned in 1525, has been wiped out by bombs. In the court lived Edwd. Thurlow, afterwards Ld. Chancellor. He and Cowper were friends, being both pupils of Mr. Chapman, an eminent solicitor of Lincoln's Inn. Here also Cowper came in 1759, and made his three attempts at suicide, partly because of his nervousness at the prospect of an examination for the post of Clerk of the Journals of the House of Lords.

FOUNTAIN COURT. The original fountain was constructed in 1681, when Wm. Whitelock was treasurer. There was then an iron palisade around it, and this remained until Lamb's time. Hatton (1708) refers to the fountain as 'forcing its stream to a vast and almost incredible altitude.' Lamb speaks of its water,

'which I have made to rise and fall, how many times! to the astoundment of the young urchins, my contemporaries, who,

not being able to guess at its recondite machinery, were almost tempted to hail the wondrous work as magic!'

Dickens introduced it into *Barnaby Rudge*, *Martin Chuzzlewit* and *Great Expectations*. Ruth Pinch and John Westlock did their courting in the Temple, and 'merrily the Temple fountain sparkled in the sun.'

GARDEN COURT. S. of Fountain Court, occupied the site of what was once the Benchers' Garden. Upon the purchase of a portion of Essex House from Dr. Barbon (son of 'Praise God' Barbon) in 1676, chambers were erected on a portion of the new ground abutting on the garden, and these became known as Nos. 3 and 4 Garden Court. In 1830 the old bdgs. were demolished. Their successors in turn disappeared in 1883, to be replaced by the present ones, which admirably harmonize with the surroundings. At No. 2 Rufus Daniel Isaacs, called to the Bar by Middle Temple in 1887, commenced his practice which led finally to his becoming Attorney-General and Ld. Chief Justice.

GATEWAYS. Inner Temple dates from 1610 (see 'Prince Henry's Room'). Middle Temple, rebuilt by Wren in 1684; the date is over the arch. The E. entrance is Whitefriars—opening on to Tudor St. The W. entrance is from Devereux Court. The gate here was constructed in 1676. There is also another N. entrance at Mitre Court Bdgs., and S. entrances from the Victoria Embankment at Middle Temple Lane and at the foot of the steps from Essex St.

GOLDSMITH BUILDING has no association with the poet beyond proximity to the grave, and dates from 1861. It replaced a row of timber-framed houses, probably erected in 1608.

HARE COURT. Named after Master Nicholas Hare, a bencher, and nephew of Sir Nicholas Hare, Master of the Rolls under Q. Mary (he d. in Chancery Lane and was bd. in the Temple Ch.). The former rebuilt the S. side of Hare Court. The W. and S. sides were swept away by fire in 1679, and there has been much rebuilding since. The infamous Judge Jeffreys—a member of Inner Temple—was in chambers here (c. 1668) at No. 3—corresponding with the present No. 2. They remained until the beginning of the 20th century. The back windows of Lamb's rooms in Inner Temple Lane overlooked

Hare Court (see *supra*). Daines Barrington, a friend of Lamb's (he was bd. in the Temple Ch. and a memorial stone was once in the triforium), mentioned the pump as unlike most of the others, since it never failed in summer, and was consequently most patronized by the inhabitants of the Temple.

INNER TEMPLE GARDENS. Up to 1528 the gardens were not protected from the river. In that yr. a wall was built. It was here in 1430, according to tradition, that occurred the scene, immortalized by Shakespeare, which is said to have been the starting-point of the Wars of the Roses. The gardens were for centuries famous for their red and white roses, the old Provence, the Cabbage, and the Maiden's Blush. The sundial, now opposite Crown Office Row was purchased in 1707, and in 1730 the great gate, a beautiful specimen of wrought-iron work, was erected. It bears, in addition to the device of the winged horse, the arms of Gray's Inn.

In the part of the garden near King's Bench Walk there is a kneeling black figure supporting a sundial. This was brought from Clement's Inn about 1905. It is said to have been presented by Ld. Clare who bought it in Italy in about 1700.

In 1930 a memorial to Lamb was placed in the centre of the garden. It is a stone figure of a pretty boy clasping a book, on the open pages of which are words from the essay *Old Benchers of the Inner Temple*: 'Lawyers were children once.' The idea was due to the master of the garden; the execution to Miss Margaret Wrightson.

INNER TEMPLE HALL. The Inner Temple undoubtedly succeeded to the ancient hall of the Knights Templars, which was built or restored in the reign of Edward III. *The Tragedie of Gorboduc* was performed in this hall. It was the work of Thos. Norton and Thos. Sackville, afterwards Ld. Buckhurst. It is regarded as the first English tragedy. The hall, small and inadequate, was demolished in 1866, and in its place Sidney Smirke erected the fine Gothic bdg. which was reduced to a ruin by German bombs. It was rebuilt in 1955 in a Georgian style. On the E. end of the wall was Sir Jas. Thornhill's painting of Pegasus, surrounded by Neptune and the Muses springing from Mount Helicon. It was painted in 1709.

This was destroyed by the bombs, as also statues of Knights Hospitallers and Knights Templars by Armstead (1875). Portraits of Wm. III, Q. Mary, George II, Q. Caroline, Sir Matthew Hale and Sir Simon Harcourt, were badly damaged, but there has survived a portrait of Sir Edmund Coke. There also remain the wooden fee bowl in which were some coins of Corinth (*c.* 300 B.C.), with the emblem of the winged horse on the reverse, and some illuminated drawings of the courts at the time of Henry VII, presented by Ld. Darling.

INNER TEMPLE LANE. (See 'Dr. Johnson's Buildings,' *supra*.)

INNER TEMPLE LIBRARY (1882). It was destroyed, except for the Reading Room. About half of its 70,000 volumes were lost but it was rebuilt in 1958 and the books replaced.

KING'S BENCH WALK takes its name from the King's Bench Office which was burnt down in 1677 and never rebuilt. With most of the other bdgs. in the walk it had been destroyed in the G.F. No. 4 was rebuilt in 1678, as the stone tablet over the door shows; No. 5 in 1694. At the latter the celebrated Ld. Mansfield occupied the chambers referred to by Colley Cibber in a parody of Pope:

'Persuasion tips his tongue whene'er he talks,
And he has chambers in the King's Bench Walks.'

Here Mansfield was pestered by Sarah, Duchess of Marlborough, who sent him a retaining fee of 1,000 guineas, all but five of which were returned. Joseph Jekyll, one of Lamb's 'Old Benchers,' was in occupation from 1793 to 1810. At No. 12 lived, in 1850, Samuel Warren, Q.C., author of *Ten Thousand a Year*, which had an enormous sale. At No. 13, the Rt. Hon. W. C. Gully, thrice Speaker of the H.C., had chambers.

On the N. side of King's Bench Walk there is a tablet commemorating the Alienation Office once here.

LAMB BUILDING. It was a beautiful house, S. of the Temple Ch. It was so called by reason of the *Agnus Dei* over the entrance. All that remains is a flight of stone steps. Here Sir Wm. Jones lived after his call to the bar by the Middle Temple in 1774. He became an Indian judge; his statue is in St. P.'s Cath. A fellow lodger was Thos. Day, author of *Sandford and Merton*, a charming eccentric. (See *The Exemplary Mr. Day*, by Sir S. H. Scott.)

MASTER'S HOUSE. This was another beautiful bdg. which has been entirely destroyed. It was erected in 1764, and the ground floor consisted of one spacious room. The title Master for the preacher at the Temple Ch. derives from the Knights Templars (see *supra*).

MIDDLE TEMPLE GARDENS. They are neither so old nor so extensive as those of the Inner Temple. They have increased in extent by the construction of the Victoria Embankment in 1865. The pedestal sun-dial on the S. terrace was erected in 1719. These gardens are partly within the par. of St. Clement Danes, and a choirboy was gently bumped on a par. mark here on the occasion of the beating of the bounds.

MIDDLE TEMPLE HALL. Erected 1562–72 under the treasureship of Plowden, and opened in 1576 by Q. Elizabeth in person. Repairs were necessary in 1699 and in 1745, and in 1758 the exterior was 'improved' by a casing of stone, and its original red-brick character destroyed. The entrance tower, which replaced a tower with semicircular steps, dates from 1832. The hammer-beam roof, erected in 1574, is the best of the period in England. The hall is 100 ft. in length, 40 ft. in breadth, while from the floor to the spring of the louvre is 50 ft. The walls are wainscoted up to the window-sills, and the arms and names of the readers and treasurers are painted upon the panelling, commencing with Richd. Swain, reader in 1597. In the two bay windows at the W. end are some fine examples of heraldry, etc., dating back to 1540, probably a relic of the old hall. Plowden's arms are in the middle of the top lights, with the date 1573. There are some examples of punning heraldry. James Whalley's arms (1770) carry three whales' heads; John Delagent's (1774), a fountain playing into a basin; Robt. Scarr Sowler's (1871), three shore soles.

The table on which the plate is displayed on Grand Nights is believed to have been presented by Q. Elizabeth, and to have been made from oak from Windsor Forest. It is 29 ft. 4 in. in length. In the middle of the hall, below the dais, is a serving-table (a 'cupboard') reputed to have been made from Drake's ship, the *Golden*

Hinde. Drake is claimed as a member by both Inner Temple and Middle Temple. There is a portrait of Charles I, either a replica of the picture at Windsor Castle or a copy by Henry Stone, who d. 1653. The portrait of Charles II is Kneller's. Other portraits are Q. Elizabeth, James II (as D. of York), William III, Anne (specially painted for the inn by Thos. Murray), and George I. From the floor of the minstrel gallery is suspended a handsome brass lantern, said to be as old as the hall. The glass lights bear the arms of Elizabeth, Raleigh, Drake, and two crests of the Knights Templars. In the S. bay is a wine-cooler dated 1612, the lid of which was made from the timber from the old Temple 'Bridge' (see *infra*).

A very interesting entry regarding Middle Temple Hall is in the diary of John Manningham, a barrister, discovered at the B. Mus. in 1828. Under date 2nd Feb. 1602, he wrote:

'At our feast wee had a play called "Twelve Night or What you Will," much like the Commedy of Errores, or Menechmi in Plautus, but most like and neere to that in Italian called Inganni. A good practice in it to make the Steward beleeve his Lady widowe was in love with him, by counterfeyting a letter as from his Lady in generall termes, telling him what shee liked best in him, and prescribing his gesture in smiling, his appairaile, &c., and then when he came to practise, making him beleeve they took him to be mad.'

The suggestion that Q. Elizabeth was present is unfounded. Manningham would hardly have omitted to mention it. Neither is there any justification for saying that it was the first performance.

The hall was refloored in 1730, and under the boards were found 100 pairs of small dice. The louvre is a restoration dating from about 1831, prior to which an open fire had been in the centre of the hall. The ancient hearth was still in use in 1812. The electric light comes from groups of flambeaux, placed on the wall in ancient fashion in 1902. During the installation in 1894, a box was found concealed in a recess of the wall near the roof, containing a skeleton in a perfect state of preservation. From its appearance it was surmised that it must have been hidden for upwards of 200 yrs. The beautifully carved doors of the hall screen are of a later date than the screen. In 1609 some junior members of the soc. resented an order forbidding Christmas festivities, made in consequence of licentious conduct, and forcibly took possession. Various penalties were meted out, and doors made at a cost of £60 14s. The smith's bill included the iron *fleur de luce* spikes meant to discourage the climber.

In the benchers' chambers are a pair of ancient carved doors, and portraits of: Sir Walter Raleigh; Edwd. Hyde, E. of Clarendon; Fredk., P. of Wales, father of George III; and Francis North, Baron Guildford.

Another treasure of the Middle Temple is one of the first pair of globes known to have been made in England. They bear date 1592, and were paid for by Wm. Sanderson, the merchant who helped to finance Raleigh.

On 15th Oct. 1940 the Middle Temple Hall was badly damaged. A huge piece of masonry was hurled through the east gable of the Hall, smashing the minstrels' gallery and burying the fine oak screen beneath a mass of rubble. Part of the Clock Tower was demolished, as also the window in the N. bay. Much of the panelling adorned with the Readers' Arms was torn from the wall. Happily the hammer-beam roof remained intact, and the damage to the screen and panelling was not of a serious character. The two famous tables and all the portraits mentioned above survived.

The carved oak screen was restored. The eastern gable wall was rebuilt with a new E. window to take some of the original stained glass. Above the window a stone panel was built in the wall with a magnificent Lamb and Flag badge carved in relief. The inscription is as follows:

'E.T.R. Denud Surrexit Domus. AS. MCMXLIX. Vivat Crescat Floreat.

'(the house which was destroyed is raised up; may it live, thrive and flourish)'.

The bust of Edmund Plowden, referred to above, survives.

MIDDLE TEMPLE LANE. It probably existed in 1330, when there was an order that the gates of the New Temple should be kept open so that the K.'s justices, clerks, and others who wished to go by water to Westminster might pass through to Temple Stairs. On the E. of the gatehouse is a quaint bdg. occupied by short-

hand writers. Formerly known as the Old Post House, it was used as a post office from the days of George I until the institution of the penny post. Here, in the 18th century, were published some well-known works including Nicholas Rowe's edition of Shakespeare (1709). Rowe was a member of the Middle Temple. No. 1 was rebuilt in 1693. Nos. 2 and 3 are thought to have been rebuilt after the fire of 1679. Elias Ashmole, friend of Evelyn and founder of Ashmolean Mus. at Oxford, had chambers in Middle Temple Lane, between Pump Court and Elm Court—which has entirely disappeared through bombing. They were broken into by soldiers in pretence of searching for Charles II. The imposing bdg. at the S. end of Middle Temple Lane dates from 1878, and was designed by Sir Chas. Barry. The archway beneath gives access to the Victoria Embankment. It has been suggested that if Temple Bar returned to L., it might be re-erected here.

MIDDLE TEMPLE LIBRARY. This Gothic structure, SW. of the Hall, was designed by H. R. Abraham. It was opened in 1861 by the P. of Wales, and contained about 70,000 volumes. About 50,000 books were thrown off the shelves by bombs in Dec. 1940, and 8,000 damaged. The only one beyond repair was replaced.

MITRE COURT BUILDINGS, at the N. end of King's Bench Walk, are on the site of old Fuller's Rents, where Sir Edwd. Coke had chambers in the early days of Q. Elizabeth. Chas Lamb resided here from 1800 to 1808. The present bdgs., which have sustained some bomb damage, date from 1830.

NEW COURT is the latest court added to the Temple. It was formerly part of Essex House garden, the land being purchased from Dr. Nicholas Barbon. It consists of one bdg., erected in 1676 from designs by Wren.

NIBLETT HALL. This is approached from the NE. corner of King's Bench Walk. It was erected under the provisions of the will of Wm. Chas. Niblett, a barrister of Singapore, who d. in 1920.

PAPER BUILDINGS. The chambers on this site were first known as Heyward's Bdgs., after their first tenant in 1610, who had for his fellow John Selden. They were known as Paper Buildings half a century later. They were referred to by

Lamb in his essay *The Old Benchers*:

'Who has removed those frescoes of the Virtues, which Italianized the end of the Paper Buildings,—my first hint of allegory!'

In a painting of 1741 they are faintly discernible. Dickens, in *Barnaby Rudge*, described them as a 'row of goodly tenements, shaded by ancient trees, and looking at the back upon the Temple Gardens.' In the broad, old-fashioned window-seat sat Sir John Chester, whose chambers were here. A fire in 1838 destroyed these old bdgs., and responsibility appeared to rest between John Campbell (afterwards Ld. Chief Justice) and John Maule, a judge. It is said that after a convivial evening the latter got confused as to the uses of a chamber-pot and a candle, and put the latter under the bed! Later residents here were Sir Frank Lockwood (author of *The Law and Lawyers of Pickwick*—see 'Strand') (No. 2), H. H. Asquith, afterwards Ld. of Oxford and Asquith (No. 1), Sir H. F. Dickens, K.C., common serjeant (No. 2). In Paper Bdgs. also lived H. H. L. Bellot, author of a charming book on the Temple.

PLOWDEN BUILDINGS. Named after the Elizabethan treasurer. Before the construction of the Embankment only Nos. 1, 2, and 3 existed. In 1849 the S. front was rebuilt and the W. front repaired. The E. front was refaced in 1906.

PUMP COURT. One of the oldest courts. The E. end is bounded by the cloisters. It was here the fire of 1679 broke out. Henry Fielding was here about 1737, and Cowper until 1759, when he went to Fig Tree Court. Blackstone was here about 1766. The South side of the Court was rebuilt after war damage.

SUNDIALS. There were six in the Temple at the outbreak of the Second World War; only three remain. (1) Back of 1 Essex Court (opposite Middle Temple Hall); motto: 'Discite justiciam moniti' ('Learn ye justice, ye who are now being instructed'). (2) Pump Court. Erected 1686; motto: 'Shadows we are and like shadows depart.' (3) In Middle Temple Gardens (see *supra*).

TANFIELD COURT (badly bombed) derives its name from Sir Lawrence Tanfield, a judge of the time of James I, who presided over the Court of Exchequer. Here, in 1733, a cruel murder took place. A charwoman, Sarah Malcolm,

strangled an old lady, Mrs. Duncomb, and cut the throat of her little maid, Annie Price. Malcolm's portrait was painted by Hogarth (see 'Tyburn').

TEMPLE STAIRS. This is often called Temple Bridge, but a pier is meant (see 'Bridges'). The first was probably built by the Knights Templars; it was restored by Edward III in 1331. Subsequently the K. ordered the Templars to repair the bridge, so that those who were attending Parliament might not be inconvenienced. Here in 1441 Eleanor Cobham, Duchess of Gloucester, landed clad in a white sheet, and carrying a taper, in the course of her appointed penance which compelled her thus to walk through Fleet St. to St. P.'s Cath. She and others were accused of acts of witchcraft against Henry VI. In 1541 there was a conference between the two socs. relating to its repair. In 1584 Q. Elizabeth subscribed towards the cost of this. In 1620 a new bridge and stairs were ordered to be built. In 1683, during the Great Frost, it was the terminus of the coaches plying on the frozen river from Westminster. In 1703 the bridge was again repaired. In the *Spectator* (1712) Sir Roger de Coverley goes to the Temple Stairs. The present Victoria Embankment has Temple Stairs which are about 100 yds. S. of the old ones. They are adorned with the crests of both socs.

The Temple before the Second World War was the most charming spot in L., combining as it did antiquarian interest with a rural quietude. These were never better described than by Dickens in *Barnaby Rudge*:

'There are still worse places than the Temple, on a sultry day, for basking in the sun, or resting idly in the shade. There is yet a drowsiness in its courts, and a dreamy dulness in its trees and gardens; those who pace its lanes and squares may yet hear the echoes of their footsteps on the sounding stones, and read upon its gates in passing from the tumult of the Strand or Fleet Street, "Who enters here leaves noise behind." There is still the plash of falling water in fair Fountain Court, and there are yet nooks and corners where dun-haunted students may look down from their dusty garrets, on a vagrant ray of sunlight patching the shade of the tall houses, and seldom troubled to reflect

a passing stranger's form.'
(See *The Temple Church and Chapel of St. Ann*, by T. H. Baylis, 1893; *The Church of the Knights Templars in London*, by Geo. Worley, 1907; *The Middle Temple*, by G. S. Godwin, 1954.)

Temple Bar. When the first bar was erected it is impossible to say. In 1293, in a patent roll, is a reference to the 'Bar of the New Temple, London.' There is a similar allusion in 1301. In 1315, in another patent roll, there is reference to a dangerous and muddy track which led from Westminster, through 'Charynge' and St. Clement's, to Temple Bar, which required repair. In 1351 Wm. de Mourden made a bequest to chs., friars, hosps., and 'to the poor prisoners of Newgate, and the prison of Templebarre, and the prison of Fleete.' A similar bequest was made by Adam de la Pole in 1358. This indicates that it was used for a prison, as were other of the gates, e.g. Newgate and Ludgate, and was not simply an affair of posts and rails. It was thrown down by Wat Tyler (1381). In 1502 there is the first definite reference to it as a gateway, in connection with some popular ferment, apparently connected with the acclamation of a league made between Henry VII and the K. of the Romans. In 1503 the hearse of Henry VII's Q., Elizabeth of York, halted at Temple Bar on its way from the T.L. to W.A., and the abbots of Bermondsey and Westminster blessed the body. In 1533 it was 'newly painted and repaired' for the coronation of Anne Boleyn, and thereon 'stood divers singing men and children.' In 1547 it was painted and supplied with new battlements for the coronation procession of Edward VI. In 1554 new gates were made and assigned to the custody of the City. This was on the occasion of the marriage of Q. Mary with Philip of Spain, when they were received at the bar with a Latin oration. At this time Temple Bar was probably as shown in Hollar's engraving. It appears to have been almost as high as the top of the bdgs. at present on the S. side of the Strand and Fleet St. There was a centre arch with two side arches. The roof was sloping, with gables, and between the three openings for traffic stood two columns with plain pedestals, and there was another column at each end. James I (like his predecessor Elizabeth),

Charles I, Cromwell, and Charles II, all had the gate opened for them. During his restoration of St. P.'s Cath. between 1632 and 1642 Inigo Jones had been invited to design a new arch. He completed a plan, but it was not carried out. The G.F. stopped a little to the E. of Temple Bar, but in 1669 it was decided to remove it, and by 1672 the new bar, designed by Wren, was erected at a cost of £1,397 10s., including the four effigies, the work of John Bushnell. These were of James I and his Q. (on the City side), and Charles I and Charles II (on the Westminster side). In 1684, in the words of W. G. Bell, 'the Rye House Plot brought the first trophy to the Golgotha at Wren's Temple Bar.' This was in the shape of the forequarter of Sir Thos. Armstrong. It was placed there after being boiled in pitch at Newgate. The head was placed over Westminster Hall, and the rest of the body was sent for exposure to Stafford, Sir Thos.'s constituency in Parliament. In 1696 (10th Apr.) Evelyn wrote:

'The quarters of Sir William Perkins and Sir John Friend, lately executed on the plot, with Perkins's head, were set up at Temple Bar, a dismal sight, which many pitied. I think there never was such at Temple Bar till now, except once in the time of King Charles II, namely of Sir Thomas Armstrong.'

With regard to such heads, there is a familiar piece of dialogue between Johnson and Goldsmith. They had been together in W.A., and in Poets' Corner, Johnson said to Goldsmith, in Latin: 'Perhaps some day our names may mingle with these'—a possibility that saw fulfilment. Their walk was continued to Temple Bar, and there, pointing up at the heads, Goldsmith said: 'Perhaps some day our names may mingle with *these*.' The heads mentioned were probably those of the Scotch lds., executed after the failure of the Young Pretender's rebellion with the battle of Culloden in 1745. Horace Walpole said that at one time you could hire for a halfpenny a spy-glass to see them better. The last was blown down in 1772, and it is said that the head of Ld. Lovat (see 'Tower of London'), placed there in 1747, was kept for some yrs. in the upper story of Temple Bar, then occupied by Child's Bank, which paid £25 p.a. to the City for its use. Remarkable to relate, not until 1753 was it ordered by the C.C. that the posterns for foot passengers should be kept open all night. In 1787 the Common Council discussed its proposed removal, but by one vote it remained for nearly 100 yrs. more. New gates, oak-panelled, and surmounted by festoons of fruit and flowers, were erected for the funeral of Ld. Nelson in 1806. In 1830 there was a Reform Bill riot at Temple Bar. In 1863 it was magnificently decorated when L. welcomed Princess Alexandra, consort of the future Edward VII. In Feb. 1872 Temple Bar was for the last time washed, cleaned, and decorated, in order that Q. Victoria and the P. of Wales might pass under it on their way to St. P.'s Cath. to attend the thanksgiving service which followed the P.'s recovery from typhoid fever.

In 1853 there had been a cry for the Bar's removal in the newspapers, but it was not until 1878 that what G. A. Sala called 'the grimy, ramshackle, obstructive old Temple Bar with its Golgotha memories' was demolished. For long it lay about in pieces in a yard in Farringdon Rd. It was then given to Sir Henry Bruce Meux, who paid all the expenses of removal to his estate at Theobald's Park, near Waltham Cross. There it is accessible, but unfortunately more than a mile's walk from any public vehicle. In 1921 an attempt was made to return it to L. This proposal was resisted by Sir Henry's son on the grounds that its removal to its present site had been at great expense to his father, and also because there were fewer historic relics in that neighbourhood than in L. On 22nd Sept. 1935 the Ld.M., Sir Stephen Killik, passed through Temple Bar to be the guest of Alderman Sir Geo. and Lady Collins who were the owners of Theobald's Park. He was the first Ld.M. to do so since its demolition.

At the Guildhall there is a silver model of old Temple Bar in the form of an inkstand. It is used on such occasions as the election of sheriffs.

At Temple Bar, on state occasions, the Ld.M. gives up his sword of state to the sovereign, who is graciously pleased to return it. When there was a gate, it was formally closed on the approach of the sovereign, and the herald knocked thrice upon it before it was opened. This was a token of the rights of the C.C. as against the sovereign. The ceremony is said to have commenced in 1588, when Q. Elizabeth went to St. P.'s Cath. to return thanks for the defeat of the Spanish Armada.

(See *Memorials of Temple Bar*, by T. C. Noble, 1870; *Temple Bar tapestry*, by Simon Dewes, 1948.)

Thames. The classical story of L.'s river is in Jas. Howell's *Londinopolis; An Historical Discourse or Perlustration of the City of London* (1657). James I is said to have been refused a loan by the City, whereupon in high dudgeon the K. threatened to remove his Court to Windsor.

'The Lord Mayor calmly heard all, and at last answered: "Your Majesty hath power to do what you please, and your City of London will obey accordingly; but she humbly desires that when your Majesty shall remove your Court, you would please to leave the Thames behind you." '

Perhaps Howell's story is a variant of one of Stow's:

'When as on a time it was told an alderman of London by a courtier that Queen Mary, in her displeasure against London, had appointed to remove the Parliament to Oxford, this plain man demanded whether she meant also to divert the river of Thames from London or no? And when the gentleman had answered "No," "Then," quoth the alderman, "by God's grace we shall do well enough at London whatsoever become of the parliament." '

The moral is an excellent one in either case.

The Thames has varied in depth and breadth.

'Geological evidence,' writes Gordon Home, 'reveals considerable change in the level of high tide in the Lower Thames Valley at a period not very much earlier than the Roman occupation of Britain. Evidence has been obtained which proves that high-water mark at London at that period was in the neighbourhood of 12 feet lower than at present.'

At Tilbury remains of Romano-British huts, with ovens and Roman pottery, have been discovered at a level which would submerge them by 16 ft. at high water. At Brentford were also found the remains of similar huts below low-tide level. The river was then, and probably in Saxon times broader and shallower. More than once an intrepid venturer has forded the Thames at Westminster. Spenser wrote of 'silver streaming Themmes.' Morris, in *The Earthly Paradise*, visualized—in Chaucer's day—

'London, small, and white, and clean;
The clear Thames, bordered by its gardens green.'

Sir John Denham, in lines admired by Johnson, wrote:

'O, could I flow like thee, and make thy stream
My great example, as it is my theme!
Though deep, yet clear; though gentle, yet not dull;
Strong without rage; without o'erflowing full.'

Poets are not historians, and in 1598, only forty-four yrs. before *Cooper's Hill* was published, Hentzner, a German traveller, had noted that the citizens washed their clothes in the river, and its odour was on the garments. In the H.C., in 1858, a speaker said:

'They had built on the banks of the Thames a magnificent palace for the legislature, but how could they direct the attention of any foreigner to it, when he would be welcomed by a stench which was overpowering? When he was a young man Thames salmon were celebrated. The salmon, wiser than members of Parliament, had avoided the pollution, and he was informed that cartloads of fish were taken out of the Thames which had died in consequence of the state of the river.'

In the same yr. a correspondent of *The Times* said:

'I am one of those unfortunate lawyers who "hug the festering shore," and festering it is indeed, with a vengeance. The stench in the Temple to-day is sickening and nauseous in the extreme; we are enveloped in the foul miasma, which spreads on either side of this repository of the filth of nigh three millions of human beings, and day and night every breath of air which we draw for the sustenance of life is tainted with its poisonous exhalations.'

A proper system of drainage (see 'Main Drainage') has put an end to this.

The Thames was once much more used than it is now. John Norden, in 1594, stated that 40,000 persons were maintained by the river alone. The figure was probably exaggerated, and he included barge and lightermen, stevedores, porters, watermen, fishermen, boat-builders, mastmakers, and makers of all kinds of gear. Still, the number so employed was undoubtedly very considerable. At this time there were about 2,000 wherries on the river, and a tilt-boat plied between L. and Gravesend. This remarkable business on the Thames naturally provoked John Taylor, the 'Water Poet,' to a remonstrance when coaches became popular. In *The World runs on Wheels* (c. 1623) he wrote:

'I do not inveigh against any coaches that belong to persons of worth or quality, but only against the caterpillar swarm of hirelings. They have undone my poor trade, whereof I am a member; and though I look for no reformation, yet I expect the benefit of an old proverb, "Give the losers leave to speak." . . . This infernal swarm of trade-spillers have so overrun the land that we can get no living upon the water; for I dare truly affirm that every day in any term, especially if the Court be at Whitehall, they do rob us of our livings, and carry five hundred sixty fares daily from us.'

So late as 1822 9,000 watermen earned their livelihood by working on the river. L., apart from the annual University boat-race from Putney to Mortlake and the annual race for Doggett's Coat and Badge (see 'Customs'), has now little reason for watching the river. Pepys found much public and private pleasure on the Thames. The Ld. Mayor's Show made it part of its route until 1855, and the gaily coloured barges of the City Cos. provided a most attractive spectacle. Q. Elizabeth's body was brought by water from Richmond to Whitehall in 1603; Ld. Nelson's from Greenwich to the same place in 1806, Sir Winston Churchill was accorded a similar honour in 1964. There are in the summer months, boats daily plying between Westminster and Greenwich, for Kew, Richmond, and Hampton Court; the City Festival has recently revived pageantry on the river.

The frosts also once provided for the Londoner most welcome diversions on the

Thames. In 1281 it was possible for both men and horses to cross between Lambeth and Westminster. In 1410 there was another frost. In 1434 the Thames froze below L.B. to Gravesend, so that the merchandise which came to the mouth of the river was carried to L. by land. In 1505, and again in 1516, the river was frozen over. In 1564 a football match was played on the ice. In 1608 the ice was so solid that booths for business and pleasure were set up. In 1683 whole sts. of shops were erected, including a printing office which Charles II visited. Bull-baiting, horse-racing, and coach-races took place, and carriages, instead of ferries, carried passengers from West-minster to the City. Evelyn (9th Jan. 1684) mentions walking from Westminster to Lambeth to dine with the Abp. of C. This frost was the subject of one of Hollar's numerous engravings. In 1698 a coach and six drove from Westminster to L.B., and a fair was held on the ice. In 1739 shoals of ice floated down the Thames, presenting a range of hills of ice and snow. In 1811 two men were able to walk on the ice from Battersea Bridge to Hungerford Stairs. The last great Thames ice-fair was held in 1813–14. When the great thaw came the ice cracked so quickly that it floated away with the booths, printing-presses, and swings, and the people with them. The removal of old L.B. caused a freer flow of water, and there has rarely been ice on the river since.

EMBANKMENTS. It is probable that the Romans built some kind of embankment. The river wall mentioned by Fitzstephen had no doubt as its objective the restrain-ing of the tides. There are many records of floods in medieval and Tudor L. The plans drawn up for the rebuilding of L. after the G.F. by Wren and Evelyn included an embankment. Neither of these plans, however, was put into execu-tion. Napoleon, contemplating invasion, contemplated their construction. The Victoria Embankment was constructed between 1864 and 1870. It was opened in state in the latter yr. by the P. of Wales. The Albert Embankment, on the S. side of the river, was constructed be-tween 1866 and 1869. It was opened in the latter yr. by Sir John Thwaites, chairman of the M.B.W. The Board's engineer, Sir Joseph Bazalgette, was responsible for

both embankments. In 1901 he was commemorated by a mural monument on the wall of the Victoria Embankment, opposite Northumberland Av. In 1906 tramcars first travelled along the Victoria Embankment, but not until 1950 did buses transverse its whole length. The Chelsea Embankment was opened in 1874, and extends for about a mile from the Royal Hosp. to Battersea Bridge.

TUNNELS. The Thames Tunnel was opened in 1843; it took twenty yrs. to complete. The engineer was M. I. Brunel. It was not a financial success, and was sold to the E. London Railway, and now forms part of the electrified line between Whitechapel and New Cross. The Black-wall Tunnel was opened in 1897; it is nearly a mile and a quarter in length, and 24½ ft. in diameter. A second parallel tunnel, the new Blackwall Tunnel, was opened in August 1967. In 1902 a Green-wich Footway Tunnel provided a means of communication between the Isle of Dogs and Greenwich. In 1908 the Rotherhithe Tunnel—communicating with Shadwell on the N. bank—was opened by the P. of Wales. There is also a tunnel for pedestrians at Woolwich (1912).

THE THAMES CONSERVANCY was ap-pointed in 1857 to look after all matters concerning the river, including fishing, locks, navigation, and the purity and flow of the water. In 1909 its work below Teddington lock in Middlesex was taken over by the Port of L. Authority (q.v.), and the work of the Thames Conservancy is now confined to the river above that point up to Cricklade. The conservators number twenty-eight, and are appointed by the various local authorities through whose areas the river flows.

The Thames Police preceded the Metropolitan Police. The originator was Dr. Patrick Colquhoun, a native of Dumbarton, who, in 1796, published a treatise On the Police of the Metropolis. He planned a Thames Police Force, at the request of some West Indian merchants. This body undertook loading and unload-ing of ships at the Docks, and they were paid by the owners of the cargoes. They used long-oared gigs, and were armed with cutlasses and blunderbusses. This led to a great reduction in thefts, and the innovation was so welcomed that the force was taken over by the Government. By an act of 1800, a River Police Office, with three Justices assigned to it, was authorised. This remained separate from the Metropolitan Police Force when it was started in 1829, being under the direct control of the Magistrates of the Thames Police Office. Within ten yrs., however, this force—mainly recruited from ex-sailors and watermen—was amalgamated with the Metropolitan Police. Colquhoun d. in 1820, and was bd. in St. Margaret's ch., Westminster. At the W. End there is a tablet with a long inscription. It says that 'He originated' gratuitously and carried into effect the Marine Police by which . . . the morals of the river labourer materially improved.'

(See *Let's All Go on the Thames*, by Wm. Kent, 1950; *London's river*, by Geoffrey S. Fletcher, 1966; *The Thames*, by A. P. Herbert 1966.)

Thavies Inn was correctly 'Davy's' or 'David's' Inn. The owner, John Davey, an attorney, by his will in 1398, left his lands and tenements in Holborn to Alice his wife, with remainder to John Osborn and Emma his wife, testator's daughter, in tail; with remainder in trust for the maintenance of a chantry in St. Mary's Chapel in the ch. of St. Andrew. John Davey was a chancery clerk and receiver for the K. for the counties of Caermarthen and Cardigan, and a man of great prominence in Holborn from 1350 to 1397. He has been confused with a John Davy, or Thavy, an armourer who had a house in the par. of St. Andrew, and who d. in 1348. The latter was commemorated by a stained glass window in St. Andrew's Ch. David's Inn was purchased by Lincoln's Inn in 1550. Little is known of its history. Some writers think that a small company of lawyers that settled down in Davey's Inn really originated the Soc. of Lincoln's Inn.

The thoroughfare, a cul-de-sac off St. Andrew's Hill, Holborn, was much curtailed by the construction of Holborn Viaduct. It is familiar to Dickensians as the place of residence of Mrs. Jellyby of Borioboola Gha fame. Up to the beginning of the Second World War, whilst the archway mentioned by Dickens had long since gone, it was still 'a narrow street of high houses, like an oblong cistern to hold the fog.' It is now—what little remains—rebuilt. The railings in which it is supposed Mrs. Jellyby's baby's

head got fixed—one enthusiastic Dickensian forty yrs. ago maintained that these were the only railings that would accommodate such a thing, a great tribute to Dickens' powers of observation—have been replaced by new ones.

Theatres in England had their origin in L. The chs. and chyds., in which the miracle and morality plays were performed, were followed by the inn yards. The 'Bull' in Bishopsgate and the 'Belle Sauvage' on Ludgate Hill (see 'Inns') were particularly the resort of the players. Probably, in designing the first theatres, the promoters were influenced by classical example in having them exposed to the sky, as such performances had hitherto been customary in the open. The galleries of the first theatres had considerable resemblance to the galleries of the inns. PAST THEATRES.

It is best to deal with these in chronological order.

The Theatre. This, the first th., was built at Shoreditch late in 1576 or early in 1577, through the enterprise of Jas. Burbage. He acquired the lease for 21 yrs. of a small strip of land, formerly in possession of Holywell Priory, and close to the rd. leading from Bishopsgate to Shoreditch Ch. The theatre was probably constructed of wood and thatch, and the diameter was about 60 ft. It is known from *Gosson's School of Abuse* (1579), that *The Blacksmith's Daughter, Catiline's Conspiracy* (not Ben Jonson's play but an earlier one on the same subject), *Cæsar and Pompey*, and *The Plays of Fabii* were performed there. Lodge, in *Wit's Miserie and the World's Madness* (1596), mentions one who
'looks as pale as the wizard of the ghost which cried so miserably at the theatre like an oister wife, "Hamlet, revenge." '
It is probable, therefore, that *Hamlet* in its abbreviated quarto form was first performed there. A reference in the *Black Book* (1604) to 'one of my divells in Dr. Faustus, when the old Theatre crackt and frighted the audience,' proves that Marlowe's *Faustus* was produced on its stage. In 1597, Jas. Burbage d., and in 1598 the theatre was taken down, and the materials used to build the Globe on Bankside. The site of the Theatre is near the junction of Great Eastern St.

and Curtain Rd., and a tablet on the wall of Nos. 86 and 88 in the latter thoroughfare was unveiled in 1920 by Miss Lilian Braithwaite. It was placed there by the L.C.C. and the inscription is as follows:

'The site of this building forms part of what was once the precinct of the Priory of St. John the Baptist, Holywell. Within a few yards stood from 1577 to 1598 the first London building specially devoted to the performance of plays, and known as "The Theatre." '

Blackfriars was constructed out of the rooms in the priory of the Blackfriars (*q.v.*). The first playhouse of that name was opened early in 1577, only a few months after the first theatre. The promoter was Nicholas Farrant, producer for the boy-players of the Chapel Royal at Windsor. There were let to him—

'six upper chambers, loft lodgings or rooms lying together within the precincts of the late dissolved house or priory of the Blackfriars otherwise called the Friars Preachers.'

Until 1584 plays were performed here by cos. of boys from the Chapel Royal at Windsor, the Chapel Royal at Whitehall, and sometimes from the choir of St. P.'s Cath. In 1584, with Q. Elizabeth present, there was produced for the first time Lyly's play, *Alexander and Campaspe.* In 1584 the landlord, Sir Wm. More, regained possession of the rooms, and reconverted them into tenements. The second Blackfriars theatre was the work of Jas. Burbage (see *supra*). He acquired, in 1596, what was called the Parliament Chamber of the priory, one of Henry VIII's Parliaments having sat therein. It had the advantage of being accessible by a special staircase which made it independent of the rest of the bdg. Included in the purchase was the friar's parlour, the hall adjoining, and the Duchy Chamber. The parlour and the hall Burbage converted into the theatre, the dimensions of which were 66 ft. by 46 ft. This theatre had a roof and included two galleries. It was usually called a private theatre, whether by reason of its roofing or some exclusive admission is not quite clear. It seems more probable that the term was used in contrast to the performances of the boys (referred to by Hamlet—Act 2, Sc. ii), as soon after Burbage acquired the premises, he was

forbidden to use them as 'a public playhouse.' in 1604, however, the 'Children of the Queen's Revels,' as they were then officially titled, gave offence by acting Samuel Daniel's *Philotas*, which related to the Earl of Essex, and a greater enormity was the production in 1605 of *Eastward Hoe*, a comedy in which Marston, Chapman, and Jonson, collaborated. It ridiculed the Scots in general, and James I's creation of knights. The playhouse was closed for a time, and the children were denied the patronage of James I's Q., their title being thenceforth 'Children of the Revels' or 'Children of Blackfriars.' In 1606 the children were again playing, but in 1608 further resentment was aroused by the production of Chapman's *Conspiracy and Tragedy of Charles, Duke of Byron*, the French ambassador being offended, and this led to the retirement of these 'young eyases' from the stage. Rd. Burbage, a son of Jas., and the great tragedian of his time, then took over the building for the use of the 'King's Men,' and it was operated as a playhouse by a syndicate of seven equal shareholders, including Rd. and Cuthbert Burbage, Wm. Shakspere, John Heminge, Henry Condell, and Wm. Sly. It became the winter house of the co., the Globe being preferred in summer. Probably most of the Shakespearian plays were performed at the Blackfriars Theatre. The title-page of the quarto edition of *Othello*, published in 1622, mentions its performance there. The theatre was closed in 1642, and was pulled down in 1655.

The Curtain was erected in 1577, less than a yr. after the first theatre, and about 200 yds. from it. It derived its name from the estate upon which it was erected, also formerly part of the priory of Holywell. Naturally, it was supposed to have some connection with The Theatre, and Aubrey referred to it as the 'green Curtain playhouse,' and, according to Malone, 'the original sign was the painting of a curtain striped.' John Marston, in *The Scourge of Villainy* (1598), refers to 'Courtain plaudities' being given to *Romeo and Juliet*. Jonson's *Every Man in his Humour* was first performed here, and enthusiastically received, in 1598. No detailed history of the time is available. In the early days of Charles I it was apparently being used only by prize-fighters. The last reference was, in 1627, to 'the common shoare near the Curtain playhouse.' This is a pun on Shoreditch.

Newington Butts appears to have been in existence in 1580. In 1594, in the course of ten days, such plays as *The Jew of Malta, Titus Andronicus, The Taming of the Shrew,* and *Hamlet* were performed there. In *A Woman is a Weathercock,* printed in 1612, but written earlier, one of the actors exclaims of an atrocious pun: 'O Newington conceit!' The playhouse was therefore probably held in low esteem like some transpontine theatres of later date. It seems to have been demolished by the close of the 16th century.

Rose. This was the first of the Bankside theatres and was erected by Philip Henslowe in 1587. From Henslowe's *Diary,* preserved at Dulwich Coll., it is known that the exterior was of lath and plaster, and that it had a thatched roof. It appears to have been circular in shape. In 1592 *Harey the vj.,* Henslowe recorded, was played there. Other plays performed at the Rose were Greene's *Friar Bacon and Friar Bungay, The Spanish Tragedy, The Jew of Malta,* by Marlowe, and *Orlando Furioso.* The last play was acted there in about 1603, and in the Sewer Records of 25th Apr. 1606 it is referred to 'as the late playhouse.' It is not recorded whether it was demolished or converted into tenements. Rose Alley commemorates its name.

Swan, the second theatre to appear on the Bankside, was built about 1595. The Swan was the sign of one of the brothels thereabouts, and probably the new theatre borrowed the name. In 1596 Wm. Gardener, a justice of the peace, desired to pluck down (as Elizabethan phraseology ran) the Swan, and this led to bitter recriminations between him and the players. Gardener had married a daughter of Sir Thomas Lucy of Charlotte Park in Warwickshire, and the suggestion therefore of Leslie Hotson (*Shakespeare versus Shallow,* 1931) is that the justice in *The Merry Wives of Windsor* was a satire on Gardener, not Sir Thomas Lucy, as commonly supposed. Hotson found that Gardener had presented the church of St. Mary Magdalene, Bermondsey, with a communion cup, and that his arms which were engraved thereon quartered the three luces, which were those of his father-in-law (see 'Bermondsey'). The

Swan survived Gardener's attacks. It is believed to have been the largest of the Elizabethan theatres, and is the only one of which there is a contemporary drawing. This was the result of a visit to L. made by a Dutch traveller named Johannes de Witt, priest of St. Mary's in Utrecht in 1596. He communicated a description to his friend Arend van Burchell, who recorded it as 'supported by wooden columns painted in such excellent imitation of marble that it is able to deceive even the most cunning.' He also made a crude drawing from the description, and both lay unnoticed in Utrecht until 1888. The play represented is believed to be *Twelfth Night;* the figure crossing the stage looks like the cross-gartered Malvolio. It is the only Elizabethan theatre of which there is a playbill extant. This is in the possession of the Soc. of Antiquaries. It is a most artistic production, and can hardly have been exhibited on Bankside. The play announced was *England's Joy.* The programme was to embrace the coronation of Q. Elizabeth, and the victory over the Armada. It concluded:

'And so with music, both with voice and instruments, she is taken up into heaven; when presently appears a throne of blessed souls; and beneath, under the stage set forth with strange fire-works, diverse black and damned souls, wonderfully described in their several torments.'

After the money had been collected for this show, the producer showed his victims 'a fair pair of heels.' The members of the audience then

'revenged themselves upon the hangings, chairs, stools, walls, and whatsoever came in their way, very outrageously, and made great spoil.'

It was at the Swan that Nash's *Isle of Dogs* was presented in 1597. This led to the imprisonment of Gabriel Spencer, an actor, and Ben Jonson. After 1598 the Swan was of little importance, and *England's Joy,* mentioned above (1602), was an example of the kind of variety entertainment that was offered. In 1611 Henslowe established the 'Lady Elizabeth's Men' there for about two yrs.; afterwards the Swan was occupied by 'Prince Charlie's Men.' Between 1615 and 1621 it seems to have been disused, and after a few performances in the latter yr. it ceased its association with drama. In *Holland's Leaguer* (1632), a pamphlet celebrating one of the most notorious houses of ill-fame on the Bank-side, there is a reference to it as 'now fallen to decay, and like a dying Swanne, hanging down her head, seemed to sing her own dirge.' The theatre is shown in Merian's view of L. (1638), but not in Hollar's (1647); probably it was demo-lished between those yrs.

Globe. The best remembered of all the early theatres, was built on Bankside early in 1599 with the materials of the first playhouse at Shoreditch. It was regarded as a fine bdg., for it was used as a model for the Fortune, and Ben Jonson, in *Every Man out of his Humour*, produced soon after its opening, says of one of his characters:

'A well timbered fellow! he would have
    made a good column
an he had been thought on when the
    house was abuilding.'

It was polygonal externally, and circular internally. The frame was of timber, and the roof of thatch. In front of the main door was suspended a sign of Hercules, bearing the globe upon his shoulders, under which was written, says Malone, the old motto: *Totus mundus agit histrionem.* Both of these features have corresponding passages in Shakespeare. Hamlet asks: 'do the boys carry it away?' (a reference to the boy actors at the Blackfriars Theatre). Rosencrantz replies: 'Ay, that they do, my Lord; Hercules and his load too.' The Latin motto is recalled in the passage in *As You Like It* which commences: 'All the world's a stage.' In the Prologue to *Henry V* there is probably a reference to the Globe:

'. . . can this cockpit hold
The vasty fields of France? or may we
    cram
Within this wooden O the very casques
That did affright the air at Agincourt?'

Probably most of the Shakespeare plays were performed at the Globe. *Richard II* was played on the eve of the E. of Essex's rebellion in 1601; and from Simon Forman's *Booke of Plaies* (see 'Lambeth') it appears that he saw at the Globe, *Macbeth* in 1610 and *The Winter's Tale* in 1611. In 1613 the theatre was burnt down in a few hours during a performance of a play called *All is True*; this appears to have been the Shakespearian *Henry VIII*. There were no fatalities, but Sir Henry Wotton said in a letter that—

'one Man had his Breeches set on fire, that would perhaps have broyled him if he had not, with the benefit of a provident wit, put it out with Bottle-Ale.'

The Globe was rebuilt, and probably more handsomely, for John Taylor, the waterman's poet, wrote:

'As gold is better that's in fire tried,
So is the Bankside Globe that late was
    burn'd,'

whilst Ben Jonson, who was present at the fire, referred to the new building as 'the glory of the Bank.' The Globe was closed by the Puritans in 1642, and demolished in 1644.

There has been considerable contro-versy as to the exact position of the Globe Theatre, but the discovery in the Guildhall of a map of Southwark made in 1618 (reproduced in the L.C.C. survey volume on Bankside, 1950) shows it to have been on the S. side of the present Park St., but a little to the W. of the tablet.

Fortune was in Golden Lane ('Golding Lane' in Elizabethan times), and was built in 1600 for Edwd. Alleyn and Philip Henslowe. The Globe was made the model for this new bdg., the specifica-tion for which is still preserved at Dulwich Coll. The theatre was burnt down in 1621, according to John Chamberlain, in a letter to Sir Dudley Carleton, 'in two hours, and all their apparel and play-books lost, whereby these poor companions are quite undone.' It was rebuilt, and, said Edmund Howes (who continued Stow's *Survey*), it was 'farre fairer' than the old playhouse. It is known from Heywood's *English Traveller* (1633) that a sign was prominently displayed:

'. . . A statue in the forefront of your house
For ever like the picture of Dame Fortune
Before the Fortune Playhouse.'

In 1642 the Fortune should have been closed by ordinance of the Long Parlia-ment, which was intended to suppress all stage-plays; the actors, however, con-tinued their performances, with a result reported in the *Weekly Account*, 27th Sept.–4th Oct. 1643:

'The players' misfortune at the Fortune in Golding Lane, their players' clothes being seized upon in the time of a play by authority from the Parliament.'

This doubtless led to the closing of the theatre. When the ordinance prohibiting plays expired in Jan. 1648, the actors, promptly reopened the Fortune, and Kingdom's *Weekly 'Intelligencer* stated that on 27th Jan. 120 coaches were crowded about the bdg. This unhealthy craving for the things of the world was too much for the Puritans, and a more stringent ordinance, penalizing spectators as well as actors, put an end finally to performances at the Fortune. In the same year it was sacked by soldiers, as was the Phœnix and the Salisbury Court theatres. In 1650 parishioners of St. Giles', Cripplegate, asked to be allowed to use the place as a house of worship, but permission was refused. In 1656 the bdg. was reported as being incapable of repair, and 'in great danger of falling, to the hazard of passengers' lives.' In 1661 it was advertised to be let 'with the ground thereto belonging' and in that yr. the materials of the bdg. were sold. In the records of Dulwich Coll. for 4th Mar. 1662, it is stated it had been 'totally demolished.' Fortune St. between Whitecross St. and Golden Lane commemorates the theatre.

Red Bull was erected about 1605 in the par. of St. James', Clerkenwell (the S. end of the present Woodbridge St. was once called Red Bull Yard). It took its name from the estate upon which it was erected. There is no pictorial representation. Wright's *Historia Histrionica* (1699) says that it was large and partly open to the weather, and that—

'before its door was displayed a sign on which was painted a red bull; hence the playhouse is sometimes referred to simply as at the sign of the Red Bull.'

It was patronized mostly 'by the meaner sort of people.' Suppressed, with the other theatres in 1648, it was the first L. th. to reopen in 1659, and the authorities interfered. In 1660, however, it had resumed its full activities, and in 1661 Pepys was there:

'The play, which is called *All's Lost by Lust*, poorly done; and with so much

disorder, among others, that in the musique-room, the boy that was to sing a song not singing it right, his master fell about his ears, and beat him so that it put the whole house in an uproar.'

The actors did not stay long at the Red Bull. They had sometimes acted at Gibbon's Tennis Court in Clare Market, which they had fitted up as a theatre, and when Drury Lane was opened in 1663, Clerkenwell was abandoned. Davenant's *The Play-house to be Let* (1663) has the lines:

'Tell 'em the Red Bull stands empty for fencers;
There are no tenants in it but old spiders.'

Hope. This was the name given to the Bear Pit on Bankside when, having been rebuilt in 1613, it was sometimes used for plays. Ben Jonson's *Bartholomew Fair*, first acted there in 1614, refers to the malodorous neighbourhood:

'And though the Fair be not kept in the same region that some here perhaps would have it, yet think that therein the author hath observed a special decorum, the place being as dirty as Smithfield, and as stinking every whit.'

In 1632 a pamphlet entitled *Holland's Leaguer* says, 'wild beasts and gladiators did most possess it,' and this apparently was the chief use of the bdg. down to 1642, when animal-baiting was prohibited by Parliament. In 1647 the Hope was sold, and the bdg. converted into tenements. At the Restoration it was again fitted up as an amphitheatre for bear- and bull-baiting, and Pepys and Evelyn went there. The last reference is in 1682. The date of demolition is not known.

Cockpit was originally used at Whitehall Palace for cock-fighting; later it was adapted for drama. In 1604 masques and revels were held there, and the rolls of the expenses of P. Henry (1610–11) show that plays were performed on a number of occasions. About 1633 it was reconstructed, and the opening of 'The New Theatre at Whitehall' was celebrated by a speech written by Th. Heywood. Inigo Jones designed the bdg. and his original sketches are at Worcester Coll., Oxford. From these sketches it appears that the theatre was 58 ft. by 36 ft. Amongst a number of plays performed in 1638 were *The Merry Wives of Windsor* and *The Mery Divell of Edmonton.* Pepys visited the theatre in 1662, seeing *The Cardinal, The Scornful Lady,* and *The Valiant Cid.* On the second occasion he 'saw the King, Queen, Duke of Monmouth, his son, and my Lady Castlemaine, and all the fine ladies.' It is impossible to state the date or cause of the end of the theatre. It appears to have become part of the Privy Council offices at the end of the 17th century (see 'Cockpits').

Whitefriars had its beginning in the refectory of the priory of Whitefriars (*q.v.*), about 1605. The prime mover in its institution was Michael Drayton, who secured a patent from James I for a co. of child actors to be known as 'The Children of His Majesty's Revels.' The theatre is believed to have been about 85 ft. by 35 ft. It was about where is now Bouverie St.

In 1608 a new management assumed charge of the troupe, but the acting continued to be done by boys. After the closure of the Blackfriars Theatre through the performance of *Byron,* the children from that theatre came to Whitefriars, and amongst them was Nathaniel Field, who took the leading part in Jonson's comedy, *Epicœne.* The Whitefriars Theatre seems to have come to the end of a brief career about 1614.

Salisbury Court was built in 1629, SW. of what was then Salisbury Court, and is now called Salisbury Sqr. The co. called 'Prince Charlie's Men' (the prince was now two years old!) were acting there in 1632, and Lovelace's now lost comedy was staged. The theatre came under the general ban of 1642, but furtive attempts were made to keep it open. There is a story that so late as 1647 Beaumont and Fletcher's *A King and No King* was being performed when the sheriffs interrupted, and took 'Tim Reade the Fool' into custody. There was certainly, in that yr., a complaint that plays were still being acted, and the justices ordered speedy suppression. The Salisbury Court Theatre was pulled down in 1648. In 1660 a new one was erected, probably a wooden structure. Pepys, of course, went. In 1661 he saw there, amongst other plays, *The Scornful Lady* and '*Tis Pity She's a Whore.* Of the latter he wrote:

'A simple play, and ill acted, only it was my fortune to sit by a most pretty and ingenious lady, which pleased me much.'

The theatre was burnt down in the G.F. and was not rebuilt. There is a C.C. plaque in Salisbury Sq.

Duke's was in Portugal St. and was the converted Gibbons Tennis Court. It was opened as a theatre by Sir Wm. Davenant in 1661 with his own play *The Siege of Rhodes.* For one of the songs therein, 'Beauty Retire,' Pepys composed music. His portrait in the N.P.G. shows him holding it. Charles II was present; the company consisted of survivors of the old pre-Restoration actors. The first stage appearance of Nell Gwyn took place here in 1665. The theatre was a successful venture, and with Betterton as a star, it is stated that *Love in a Tub* brought a profit of £1,000 in the first month of its performance. Duke's was the first theatre in which scenery was regularly introduced, and Killigrew and Davenant enjoyed a Patent allowing women in female roles for the first time in England. *Othello* was presented on 8th Dec. 1660, when Mrs. Bugles was probably Desdemona. Because of the Plague and the G.F. the theatre was closed from 1666 to 1672, and in the latter yr. it was leased to Killigrew and the King's Co. on the loss of Drury Lane Theatre through fire. At the reconstruction of the Drury Lane Theatre in 1674, Killigrew and his players returned to theirs. Duke's then reverted to its former use as a tennis court, and apparently so continued until 1695, when it was re-opened as the New Theatre, with Congreve's *Love for Love,* the cast including Betterton, Mrs. Barry, Mrs. Bracegirdle and Thos. Doggett; William III was present on that occasion. In 1704 complaints were made that the theatre constituted a public nuisance, and Betterton thereupon assigned his lease to Vanbrugh. The new lessee, however, found it too small, and erected a new playhouse in Haymarket. Duke's was again abandoned as a theatre, and so remained until 1714, when Christopher Rich took it, and began to erect a new theatre. He d. before it was completed. His son, John, carried on the work and opened the theatre in 1715 with Farquhar's *The Recruiting Officer.* His ever-memorable success came much later with Gay's *The Beggar's Opera.*

Performed first on 29th Jan. 1728, it had the then phenomenal run of 61 nights. It was aptly said that it made Gay rich and Rich gay; when this opera was revived some 200 yrs. later at the King's, Hammersmith, it ran for 1,463 performances. Duke's was the first to stage English pantomime. From 1717 to 1760, John Rich was in competition here, and later at Covent Garden, with Drury Lane yet all his pantomime productions were successful; these included *Harlequin Sorcerer* (1717) and *Necromancer, or Harlequin Executed* (1723), and it is recorded that his takings for pantomime were double those of Drury Lane. In 1732 he had Covent Garden Theatre built; to this he transferred his undoubted ability as a producer; the playhouse in Portugal St. was then closed. In 1745 the bdg. was fitted up as a temporary barracks because of the scare caused by the 'Young Pretender.' It was used for at least eleven yrs. by the military and, later, became an auction room and warehouse for china. In 1848, when it was necessary to enlarge the Royal College of Surgeons (*q.v.*), the premises were acquired for that purpose and were demolished.

Dorset Gardens was designed by Wren, and opened in 1671 with Dryden's *Sir Martin Mar-all*. It was so called from having been erected on the site of the gardens of Dorset House—the L. residence of the Es. of Dorset, which was not rebuilt after the G.F. There is an allusion to its situation in Wycherley's *Gentleman Dancing-master*:

'Where punk and visor dare not rant and tear,
To put us out, since Bridewell is so near.'

In 1682 Otway's *Venice Preserved* was performed and Mrs. Aphra Behn (see 'Westminster Abbey') had many of her plays produced here. In that yr. the co. joined the K.'s servants at Drury Lane, and thereafter the theatre was only occasionally used for theatrical purposes. In 1689 it was renamed the Queen's Theatre, after William III's consort. In 1699 a strong man was performing here, and other attractions were fencing and wrestling. Allusion is made to the first in Farquhar's *Constant Couple* (1700):

'Ah, friends! Poor Dorset Gardens house is gone,

Quite lost to us; and for some strange misdeeds,
That strong man, Samson, pull'd it o'er our heads.'

The bdg. was demolished in 1709, and the site used for a woodyard, then the New River Co.'s offices and, after a long interval, for the City Gasworks. The City of L. Sch. was built on the land in 1882.

Astley's, in Westminster Bridge Rd. was erected in 1774 by Philip Astley, a light horseman in Gen. Elliott's regiment, said to have been the handsomest man in England. Originally it was an open area, but was afterwards covered and divided into pits, boxes, and gallery. In 1786 it was refitted and called 'The Royal Grove,' and in 1792 'The Royal Saloon or Astley's Amphitheatre.' In 1794 it was destroyed by fire and it was burned again in 1803. Old Philip Astley (d. 1814) and his son, the latter an extraordinarily skilful equestrian, carried on for a few yrs. The management was then taken over by W. Davis, who made a great hit with *The Blood-red Knight* (by which he made over £10,000) and *Waterloo*. Davis was succeeded by Andrew Ducrow, and his dislike of patter was conveyed in the familiar phrase: 'Cut the cackle and come to the 'osses.' This Astley's, the one so delightfully described by Dickens in connection with the visit of the Nubble family in the *Old Curiosity Shop* (Chap. XXXIX), was burned down in 1841; Ducrow lost his reason because of his losses and d. soon afterwards. The theatre was again rebuilt in 1842 by Wm. Batty, who presented such spectacles as *The Battle of the Alma*, *The Chase*, and *The Chinese War*, but horsemanship was discontinued in 1862 and then it was remodelled by Dion Boucicoult and renamed the Th. Royal, Westminster. Grimaldi was often engaged here as clown, and in 1864 Adah Menken played Mazeppa to crowded houses. Dickens devoted one of his *Sketches by Boz* to Astley's, and Thackeray mentions it in *The Newcomes*. In 1873 the theatre was taken over by 'Lord' George Sanger and renamed Sangers. It was demolished in 1896.

Reference may be made to two of the many lesser known theatres that have had their day and ceased to be.

1. *Royalty, Spitalfields*. Situated in Well-

close Sq. it opened in 1787, when Braham first appeared on the stage as *Cupid*. It was burnt down in 1826, but it was rebuilt in seven months for John Palmer the actor. It reopened on 25th Feb. 1828 as the Royal Brunswick Theatre. A few days later, during a rehearsal of *Guy Mannering*, the roof collapsed ten people being killed and several seriously injured; it was demolished in that yr.

2. *City of London*. It is the only theatre that was in the City. (There is a stage for amateurs at Cripplegate Inst. (*q.v.*) and now there is the Mermaid.) It stood on the W. side of Norton Folgate. It was built in 1837 by Geo. Honey an actor. When the extension of the G.E. Rly. from Shoreditch to Liverpool St. was made the theatre was closed as the new line passed through part of the stage and the auditorium. The remainder of the bdg. was then used as a public hall, but modern offices now occupy the site. *The Cricket on the Hearth* was produced here in 1846.

EXISTING THEATRES.

Adelphi (Strand). The first theatre on the site was opened in 1806 as the Sans Pariel but soon changed its name, a great claim then being made for the brilliance of the gas chandelier. The bdg. was improved in 1821 and enlarged in 1827; later it was known as the New Century but returned to the name Adelphi in 1930. In 1844, a few months after publication, a dramatic version of Dickens' *Christmas Carol* was produced here; it figured in a bill which included *Antony and Cleopatra Married and Settled* which was 'greeted with roars of laughter.' The theatre was completely rebuilt in 1858 and opened on Boxing night of the same year. On 16th Dec. 1897 Wm. Terriss was stabbed outside his personal entrance to the theatre, by another actor who was found, on his trial, to be insane. The longest run was *Bless the Bride* (812 perfs.; 1947).

Aldwych. Built for Sir Seymour Hicks, the actor, this theatre opened on 23rd Dec. 1905 with *Bluebell in Fairyland*. The longest run was *Watch on the Rhine* (673 perfs.; 1942).

Ambassadors (West St., Shaftesbury Ave.). This small theatre opened on 5th June 1913 with *Panthea*. *Escape* (Galsworthy) was very successful here in 1926. It is peculiarly suitable for intimate revue and a *Sweet and Low* series ran successfully

for a long period (870 perfs.; 1944). The theatre reopened on 19th Oct. 1939 after the outbreak of War, with *The Gate Revue*. Here Agatha Christie's play *The Mousetrap* has been running since 1953.

Apollo (Shaftesbury Ave.). Opened on 21st Feb. 1901 with a failure, an American play, *The Belle of Bohemia*. *Kitty Gray*, a musical play, was perhaps its first success, although Sir Martin Harvey had played earlier in *A Cigarette Maker's Romance* and *The Only Way*. *The Follies* in 1908 and 1910 ran for 500 perfs. on each production, while the revue *Going Up* proved equally successful in 1918. Notable successes have been: *Tilly of Bloomsbury* (1919); *Housemaster* (662 perfs.; 1936); *Follow My Leader*; *Flare Path* (670 perfs.; 1942); *Private Lives* (revived: 716 perfs.; 1944).

Cambridge (Earlham St., St. Martin's Lane). Opened in 1930 with Beatrice Lillie in *Masquerade*. *Ace of Clubs* (Coward) was produced here on 7th July 1950, and in that yr. the theatre changed hands for a figure stated to be about £250,000.

Comedy (Panton St., Haymarket). This theatre, costing £20,000, was opened on 15th Oct. 1881 under the management of Alex. Henderson. The first production was an English version titled *Lord Mascott* of Audran's comic opera *La Mascotte*. Although only a small theatre (it then seated 1,000 against the present reduced number), several celebrated actors and actresses made it famous among them being Beerbohm Tree (*With the Red Lamp* in 1887 as his first managerial production), Chas. Hawtrey, Marion Terry, Penley (in *Falka*), Winifred Emery, Violet Cameron, Cyril Maude, Forbes-Robertson, Maxine Elliott, and Marie Tempest, who made her L. debut here on 30th May 1885 in *Boccaccio*. Barrie's *Professor's Love Story* was produced here in 1894. Winifred Emery was particularly successful in Sydney Grundy's *The New Woman*, and Pinero's *The Benefit of the Doubt*. In 1902 when the fortunes of the theatre were not at their highest, Lewis Waller produced *Monsieur Beaucaire*, a play of which little was expected, but which roused the enthusiasm of L. audiences, and ran for 430 perfs. Later productions which were especially successful were: *Man of Destiny* (1901); *Raffles* (1906); *Peg o' my Heart* (710 perfs.; 1914); *Shell Out* (1915); *Bubbly* (1917); *Tails Up*

(1918); *Three Wise Fools* (1918); *The Romantic Age* (1920); *The Silent House* (420 perfs.; 1927); *Hi-Diddle-Diddle* (1934); and *Someone at the Door* (transferred from the New Theatre in 1935). The theatre reopened on 27th Sept. 1939 after the outbreak of War. Productions since have included *The Bare Idea* (1940); *New Faces* (revue—1940), and *On Monday Next*, a comedy which was an outstanding success in 1949; *Worm's Eye View*, which transferred from Whitehall theatre on 3rd June, 1950, ran for eight years.

Court. This theatre, a reconstructed chapel, was opened on 16th Apr. 1870 under the name of the New Chelsea Theatre. It was renamed the Belgravia, but not until it was rebuilt by a new lessee, Miss Marie Litton, and reopened in Jan. 1871, with W. S. Gilbert's *Randall's Thumb*, did it become prominent as the Royal Court Theatre. Gilbert's satire *The Wicked World* was played here, and later the theatre was known for the successes scored by several plays especially *The Happy Land* (1873) and *Trelawney of the Wells* (1898). In 1875 John Hare had taken it over, and he presented the Kendal's co. for five yrs. There was a change of management in 1885, and a subsequent outstanding success was *The Magistrate* in that yr. In 1838 the management again changed, opening with *Mamma* by Sydney Grundy. It was famous for the Vedrenne-Barker productions of Shaw's plays, 1904-5. A phenomenal success was gained here in 1924 by Eden Phillpott's *The Farmer's Wife*, which ran for 1,329 perfs., while the theatre is also to be remembered for the work of Sir Barry Jackson who produced Shaw's *Back to Methuselah* here in 1923 with Laurence Olivier. This theatre, which was damaged in the Second World War, is now conducted as The Royal Court Theatre.

Covent Garden (Royal Opera House). Opened on 7th Dec. 1732 by John Rich, the famous harlequin with *The Way of the World*. Peg Woffington made her début at the original theatre, and nearly all the stars of the 18th century were seen on its stage. It was almost entirely rebuilt and reopened in 1792. In 1803 John Philip Kemble purchased a sixth part of the patent, and he brought with him his brother Chas. and his sister Mrs. Siddons from Drury Lane. In 1806 he engaged Joe Grimaldi (who had recently left Drury Lane) and this actor opened as Orson (in *Valentine and Orson*) in Oct. of that yr., and was an instantaneous success in his new *métier*. In the early hours of 20th Sept. 1808, after the performance of *Pizarro*, the whole theatre and much adjacent property was burned to the ground. A new theatre was built (the architect being Smirke who was then 27 yrs. old) and opened on 18th Sept. 1809 with *Macbeth* and *The Quaker*. Kemble had increased the prices and as a consequence the O.P. (old prices) riots took place; the rioters attended the theatre for some nights, chanting a parody, 'This is the House that Jack (Kemble) built. These are the boxes, let to the great, that visit the house that Jack built,' etc. etc. On Dec. 15th energetic action was taken by Kemble, who reduced the prices and in other ways accommodated the rioters. In 1812 Mrs. Siddons retired; in 1817 Kemble followed. The fortunes of the theatre declined, and in 1829, the rates being in arrear, the theatre was seized by the parochial authorities. It was rescued by public subscription. In 1833, the yr. in which Edmund Kean appeared for the last time at Covent Garden Theatre it was united with Drury Lane, under the management of Alfred Bunn. In 1837 Macready (who had made his first L. appearance here in 1816) took it over, and inaugurated an historic Shakespeare revival, which, however, was not financially successful. In 1843, Macready having retired, it was leased for two yrs. to the Anti-Corn Law League. In 1847, having undergone considerable alteration, it was reconstructed as the Royal Italian Opera House. In 1856 it was again burned down. In 1857 Fredk. Gye obtained from the D. of Bedford a lease for an extended site, and a new opera house in its present form by E. M. Barry was opened on 15th May 1858 with *The Huguenots*. This theatre has since been the headquarters of grand opera when such has been given in L., and has been the scene of great promenade concerts. Amongst the famous singers who have been heard there there may be mentioned Patti, Alboni, Albani, Tetrazzini, and Sammarco. Notable productions listed are: *She Stoops to Conquer* (first performance; 1775); *The Rivals* (1775); *The Country Squire* (1837); *The Lady of*

Lyons (1838); *Richelieu* (1839). For two years (1925-7) international operatic seasons were presented; in 1928 Russian Ballet was given. In 1941 the theatre was converted into a Dance Hall. Since the last War its ballet and operatic activities have been resumed.

Criterion (Piccadilly Circus). This theatre is built on the site of the old St. James's Market, and was opened on 23rd ·Mar. 1874 in conjunction with Messrs. Spiers and Pond's new hotel. The first production was J. H. Byron's *An American Lady*, followed by a period of opera bouffe. In 1877 Alex. Henderson produced a series of three-act farces, which were a novelty at that time; chief amongst them was *Pink Dominoes*, which ran for 555 perfs. In 1883 the theatre was reconstructed and enlarged, electric light being installed, and it reopened in Apr. 1884. Sir Chas. Wyndham succeeded Henderson, and aided by an excellent co. continued the tradition of brilliant comedy, presenting *The Liars* in 1897. In 1899 Sir Chas. left the Criterion for his own theatre, Wyndham's, but he maintained his connection. The theatre was remodelled in 1903, reopening on 10th Feb. with *A Clean Slate*. The longest run was *A Little Bit of Fluff* (1915); it ran for 1,241 perfs.

Drury Lane (*Theatre Royal*). Though this theatre extends to the thoroughfare by which it is called, it has its front on Catherine St. and its colonnade in Russell St. There was an earlier theatre actually in Drury Lane. Originally a cockpit, the theatre was erected in 1617, and was sometimes called the Cockpit and sometimes the Phœnix Theatre. There Pepys took his wife to see a French comedy in 1661. The first theatre on the present site was erected in 1663, Charles II having granted a patent for a new one. It was known as the Theatre Royal, and opened by Killigrew and his co., called 'King's Servants,' who had previously been at Gibbon's Tennis Court in Clare Market. This was the theatre so much patronized by Pepys:

'*3rd Apr. 1665.* All the pleasure of the play was, the King and my· Lady Castlemayne were there; and pretty witty Nell, at the King's house, and the younger Marshall sat next us; which pleased me mightily.'

A fire destroyed this first house (1672),

and it was rebuilt by Wren in 1674. In 1682 the 'Duke's Servants,' under Davenant, hitherto at Lincoln's Inn Theatre, joined Killigrew, and both cos. played together at Drury Lane. There was a secession under Betterton to Lincoln's Inn Fields in 1694, and in 1707 the theatre was closed, by order of the Ld. Chamberlain, in consequence of the violent quarrels between the proprietors and actors. In 1714 a life patent was granted to Sir Richd. Steele, which five yrs. afterwards was revoked. In 1747 Lacey and Garrick entered into partnership, the latter reviving the performance of Shakespeare's plays. The prologue was written by Samuel Johnson. In 1775 Mrs. Siddons made her first appearance as Portia in *The Merchant of Venice*. In 1780 during the Gordon Riots, a 'No Popery' mob made a great disturbance, and did considerable damage to the theatre. The objects of their fury were the 'papists and Frenchmen,' whom Garrick engaged to dance in a grand spectacular piece entitled *The Chinese Festival*. George III who was present, it is said, found more amusement than cause for alarm. In 1784 Kemble made his first L. appearance here as Hamlet; in 1788 he became manager. The theatre was pulled down in 1791, rebuilt by Hy. Holland, and reopened by Sheridan in 1794. For some yrs. after the principal attractions were the gifted Kemble family—John and Chas., and their sister, Mrs. Siddons. The prosperity of the theatre was seriously affected by their withdrawal in 1803. The theatre was again burnt down in 1809, and the new bdg. was designed by Wyatt (who was then 26 yrs. old); he introduced a domed rotunda with grand staircases and this feature is the only interior parts of a Georgian theatre in L. now. The new theatre was opened on 10th Oct. 1812 with *Hamlet*, with a prologue by Ld. Byron. The committee's advertisement for this prologue gave rise to the *Rejected Addresses* of J. and H. Smith. The Doric portico in Catherine St. was not added until some yrs. later. In 1822 the proscenium was remodelled by Saml. Beazley, and the colonnade in Russell St. was added in 1831. Grimaldi took his leave of the stage here in 1828; he had made his first appearance at Sadler's Wells on 26th Apr. 1781. Other famous names associated with this theatre are Macready and Phelps. One of the ablest managers of more recent yrs. was Sir Augustus Harris. After his death in 1896 a mural statue was erected by public subscription beside the portico in Catherine St. The theatre was remodelled in 1922, until which yr. Wyatt's exterior had existed and reopened on 20th Apr. 1922 with *Decameron Nights*. Successes since have included *Rose Marie* (851 perfs.; 1926); *Dancing Years* (1,799 perfs.; 1939).

The 'Baddeley Cake,' provided by an amount left by a comedian of 'His Majesty's Servants' (1603), is cut upon the stage, after the performance, on Twelfth Night.

Drury Lane Theatre is the *locus* of an authenticated 'haunt.' Said to have been seen by hundreds of persons at different times the spectre, in 18th-century costume, emerges from the wall at the left of the circle and traversing the rear of the seating, enters the opposite wall of the auditorium. Its appearances are frequent but not cyclic; it normally favours matinées of successful productions. Its *corpus*, together with a dagger, was discovered 103 yrs. ago in a sealed room within the wall from which it walks. It is three-dimensional but not opaque, and becomes imperceptible when approached. The purpose of its perambulations can not be ascertained, for it does not react in any way to endeavours to communicate.

Duchess (Aldwych). Opened 25th Nov. 1929 with *Tunnel Trench*. Subsequent successes were: *Rose without a Thorn* (1932); *Night Must Fall* (400 perfs.; 1935); *Playboy of the Western World* (1939); *Ballet Rambert* (1939). It opened a further short season on 15th Mar. 1940. Other plays were *Beyond Compère* (1940); *Blithe Spirit* (1944); *Linden Tree* (1947).

Duke of York's (St. Martin's Lane). It was originally called the Trafalgar Sq. Theatre and opened on 10th Sept. 1892 with a comic opera *The Wedding Eve*. The name of the theatre was changed in 1895. Several notable plays have been staged here, including Barrie's *The Admirable Crichton*, which ended a run of 330 perfs. in Aug. 1903. Others were *Alice Sit by the Fire* (1905); *Strife* (1909); *Justice* (1910); *The Madras House* (1910); and *Romance* (1,040 perfs.; 1915).

Everyman (Holly Bush Vale, Hampstead.) Opened by Norman Macdermott on 15th Sept. 1920 with *Bonds of Interest*, this small theatre presented many good plays such as *Tragedy of Nan* (Masefield); *Mary Stuart* (Drinkwater); Galsworthy's *The Foundations*; Zangwill's *Melting Pot* and Arnold Bennett's *The Honeymoon* in its first few months. Productions since have included *Vortex* on a trial run and a series of Ibsen's plays. It was experimental to a marked degree, but is now used as a cinema.

Fortune (Drury Lane). Opened on 8th Nov. 1924 with *The Sinners*. Other productions have been *Plough and the Stars* (1926); *On Approval* (1927); *Silver Box* (1931); *Fly Away Peter* (1947); *The Paragon* (1948); *How I Wonder* (1950). This theatre reopened in Apr. 1949 after a long closure.

Garrick (Charing Cross Rd.) was opened by Sir John Hare in Apr. 1889 with Pinero's *The Profligate*. Grundy's *Pair of Spectacles* followed in 1890, and Pinero's *Lady Bountiful* and Robertson's *School* in 1891, with the reappearance of the Bancrofts in *Diplomacy* on 12th Jan. 1893 after an absence of eight yrs. from the stage. *San Toy* reached 768 perfs. in 1909. Some of the most successful productions since the turn of the century have been *Where the Rainbow Ends* (1911); *The Double Mystery* (1914); *Tiger's Cub* (1916). A very notable performance of *Cyrano de Bergerac* was given in 1919 with Robt. Loraine in the name part. *Love on the Dole*, ran for 385 perfs. in 1935.

Globe (Shaftesbury Ave.) was opened in Dec. 1868 with H. J. Byron's comedy, *Cyril's Success*. Under successive managements every kind of dramatic entertainment, from tragedy to farce, was produced. Pinero wrote a comedietta produced there in 1877, and in the following yr. were seen J. L. Toole's *Trying a Magistrate*, and another play by H. J. Byron, *A Fool and his Money*. In the early eighties Jerome K. Jerome, Sydney Grundy, and Robt. Buchanan had productions running there. In 1885 Chas. Hawtrey played in *The Private Secretary*, transferred from the Prince's; Penley took the part of the curate, and the play, although previously a' failure, was at the Globe an outstanding success. In 1897 Sir John Hare took possession of the theatre, and during his tenancy as many as twelve different plays by well-known authors were produced. *The Three Musketeers* was given in 1898, and the following yr. Pinero's *Gay Lord Quex*, in which Hare scored a success in the title role, was staged. In 1902 the old bdg. was condemned, but was rebuilt and opened again, on 27th Dec. 1906 with *The Beauty of Bath*. Successful plays were *Our Betters* (Maugham; 548 perfs.; 1923), and *While the Sun Shines* (1,154 perfs.; 1943). The theatre reopened on 26th Dec. 1939 after the outbreak of war with *The Importance of Being Earnest* and a revue, *Tuppence Coloured*, was successful later. Other productions were *They Came to a City* (1943); and *The Lady's not for Burning* (1949).

Haymarket was built by John Potter at a cost of £1,500 in 1720, and became known as 'The Little Theatre in the Haymarket,' by way of distinction from the larger house on the other side of the street (i.e. His Majesty's). In 1734 it was occupied by 'The Great Mogul's Co.' which produced some of Fielding's satires. In 1730 Fielding produced there *The Tragedy of Tragedies, or Tom Thumb the Great*; Fielding became manager in 1734, and with Colley and Theo. Cibber fought the Patent monopolies. The *Historical Register*, performed at the Haymarket in 1736, so bitingly portrayed Sir Robt. Walpole that it led to the passing of the Act whereby the Ld. Chamberlain's licence has to be obtained before a play can be publicly produced. In 1747 Samuel Foote became manager, and under his régime, in 1767, it became a Theatre Royal. In 1776 Foote sold the Haymarket to Colman the elder, who continued to manage it till 1794. In the latter yr. at a command performance before George III and his consort, fifteen people were trampled to death and twenty seriously injured (see 'City Churches; C'—St. Benet, Paul's Wharf). In 1820, the younger Colman having sold his interest, the theatre was demolished. A new theatre, erected a little N. of the old one, was opened in 1821 with Sheridan's *Rivals*. The last stage appearance of Mr. and Mrs. Chas. Kean was at this theatre on 29th Aug. 1859, whilst Ellen Terry's *début* in L. took place here in 1863. A reconstruction was carried out in 1880, when the theatre was taken by Sir Squire and Lady Bancroft, and the Haymarket then became the one L. theatre without a Pit; it was opened with a revival of *Money*.

During the first six months Mr. Squire Bancroft—as he then was—cleared £5,000 with later profits on *The School for Scandal* of £10,000. The Bancrofts' last appearance was made at this theatre—with the second act of *Our's* on 12th May 1896. H. Beerholm Tree had the management from 1887 to 1896. At the beginning of 1905, when after redecoration, it was reopened by Cyril Maude, the pit was restored, but the exteriors in Haymarket and Suffolk St. are those of the 1879 theatre. Plays listed include *The Red Lamp* (1887); *Ideal Husband* (1893); *Woman of No Importance* (1893); *Little Minister* (1893); *Bunty Pulls the Strings* (1911); *Man with a Load of Mischief* (1925); and Shakespeare's plays with John Geilgud.

His (now *Her*) *Majesty's* (Haymarket). The first bdg. on the Haymarket site was built by Sir John Vanbrugh, with whom Congreve was associated in management, and was opened in 1705 with Dryden's *Indian Emperor*. The acoustic properties were defective, and in 1708 it became an opera house. From 1711 to 1738 it was under the management of John J. Heidegger (see 'Taverns'—Devil). In 1789 it was destroyed by fire, and rebuilt by the Polish architect Novssielsky. The second theatre lasted from 1791 to 1867, when it was burnt down. The first production of *Lohengrin* was at this theatre in 1880. Again rebuilt, the theatre remained open until 1892, when, the lease having expired, it was demolished and the whole island site reconstructed by Nash and Repton. The theatre had been put to various uses; Moody and Sankey revival meetings, Wagner's operas, and French plays with Sarah Bernhardt in the cast. In 1897 the fourth theatre was opened on 28th Apr. with Sir Beerholm Tree as proprietor and manager, the production being *The Seats of the Mighty*. There were, under his direction, many remarkable Shakespearian productions and spectacular dramas, lavishly staged; the most successful play was *Chu Chin Chow* (2,238 perfs.; 1916).

London Coliseum (Charing Cross). Opened with variety on 24th Dec. 1904; as a theatre 8th Apr. 1931 with *White Horse Inn* (651 perfs.). Various types of entertainment have been presented here, including ballet and musical plays and pantomime, but a phenomenal success was *Annie Get Your Gun*, which completed a run of 1,304 perfs. on 29th Apr. 1950. At one time, when it was conducted as a music hall, four perfs. a day were given, two complete cos. being engaged with alternating appearances. It was the policy pursued at this theatre which lifted variety to the level of family entertainment, suggestiveness and *double entendres* being rigorously barred; the use of even a small d. on the stage gave the management power to terminate an artiste's contract. The Coliseum had the first revolving stage in London (see 'Music Hall and Pantomime'). After being used as a cinema for a period, from 23rd May 1968 the Coliseum became the permanent home of the Sadler's Wells Opera Co.

London Hippodrome (Cranbourn St.). Opened 15th Jan. 1900 after a postponement of some days with *Giddy Ostend*, Circus and Variety. In 1901 Annette Kellerman gave aquatic performances in a newly installed tank of water, whilst 'looping the loop' in a motor car and on a bicycle was presented; the last by a one-legged cyclist. Later a water-chute was installed, and Hagenbeck's Polar Bears entertained. Louis de Rougement appeared here harnessing and riding an outsize turtle. The most successful revue production has been *Joy Bells* (723 perfs.; 1919); *Hullo Ragtime*, an American revue, opened here in 1912, and the claim has since been made that it introduced syncopation into Great Britain. Now used as a 'Theatre Restaurant' with stage performances.

Lyric (Shaftesbury Av.). Opened on 17th Dec. 1888 with the success *Dorothy*, in which Marie Tempest and Hayden Coffin both distinguished themselves. Comic opera continued to draw the public to this theatre with *Floradora* reaching 455 perfs. in 1899; there followed religious plays, such as *The Sign of the Cross*, in which Wilson Barrett was a striking success. Later Forbes-Robertson and Mrs. Patrick Campbell produced *Macbeth*, while in 1912 *The Girl in the Taxi* and in 1918 *The Purple Mask* ran for 385 and 365 perfs. respectively. Other successful productions have been *Lilac Time* (626 perfs.; 1922); *Victoria Regina* (1937); *The Flashing Stream* (1938); *Murder in the Cathedral* (1947); *Edward my Son* (1947); whilst in 1949–50 *The Beaux' Stratagem* ran for 532 perfs., a record for a classical play.

New (St. Martin's Lane). Opened by Sir Chas. Wyndham on 12th Mar. 1903 with a revival of *Rosemary*. Later *The Light that Failed*, with Forbes-Robertson, was transferred from the Lyric and a translation from Sudermann, *The Joy of Living*, followed, in which Mrs. Patrick Campbell acted. A. A. Milne's *Mr. Pim Passes By* (1920), Shaw's *St. Joan* (1924), *Young Woodley* (produced by the 300 Club in 1928), and *The Constant Nymph* by Margaret Kennedy, were first presented in this theatre, while John Gielgud proved a distinguished success with *Richard of Bordeaux* (1933), *Noah* (1935) and *Romeo and Juliet* (136 perfs., the longest run on record, in 1935–6). During the Second World War the theatre was the home of the Sadler's Wells Ballet Co. and here have since been presented many Shakespearian plays and other revivals by the 'Old Vic' company; such included *King Lear* (with Laurence Olivier); and *Cyrano de Bergerac* (with Ralph Richardson). Plays presented by other managements included *Giaconda Smile* (1948), and *The Cocktail Party* (1950).

'Old Vic' (Waterloo Rd.). Opened in 1818 as the Coburg Theatre. The name was assumed by way of compliment to the husband of the Princess Leopold of Saxe-Coburg. Edmund Kean was among the early actors to appear. In 1833, after redecoration, it was reopened as the Victoria, in honour of the future queen. One of the first celebrities to appear there was Paganini, the violinist. Usually the theatre was given up to sanguinary melodrama. Chas Mathews wrote:

'The lower orders rush there in mobs, and in shirtsleeves, frantically drink ginger-beer, munch apples, crack nuts, call the actors by their Christian names, and throw them orange peel and apples by way of bouquets.'

It offered, however, a more refined and intellectual entertainment under the management of Miss Emma Cons. In 1912 Princess Christian was present at a performance of *Tannhäuser*, and during the interval she received purses on the stage to the amount of £200. In the same year Miss Cons died, at the age of 74. There was a bas-relief of her in the theatre. Her niece Miss Lilian Bayliss, assumed the post of lessee and manager. In 1918 Q. Mary, with Princess Mary, was present at the performance to celebrate the 'Old Vic's 100th birthday,' on which occasion Ellen Terry, Matheson Lang, Russell and Dame Sybil Thorndike appeared. Princess Mary was also present in 1923 at a performance to celebrate the tercentenary of the publication of the First Folio of Shakespeare. In 1924 the enlargement, consequent upon structural alterations required by the L.C.C., was completed. Thanks to a generous gift of £30,000 from Sir Geo. Dance, the 'Old Vic' was able to increase its accommodation by acquiring the space vacated by Morley Coll. which was transferred to Westminster Bridge Rd. A few original productions have taken place at this theatre, e.g., Halcott Glover's *Wat Tyler*, *Arthur*, by Laurence Binyon, and *Britain's Daughter*, by Gordon Bottomley. Just prior to the Second World War, Bernard Shaw's plays were occasionally given, notably *Major Barbara*. Although seasons of grand opera and productions of *Peer Gynt* were presented, the 'Old Vic' was primarily the home of Shakespeare, and the late Sir Ben Greet manfully held the stage amidst the disasters of the First World War, including an air raid when bombs were dropping round the theatre. In the Second World War the theatre was so damaged by enemy action that it had to be closed. Towards the end of 1949 the stage portion of the theatre was patched up sufficiently to allow it to be used for rehearsals and for the training of members of the 'Old Vic' school of acting and on 4th Nov. 1950 the theatre, after being remodelled, reopened with a series of Shakespearian plays, Jonson's *Bartholomew Fair*, etc., the first being *Twelfth Night*. Ernest Milton was prominent here in leading Shakespearian roles, and a full list of others would include almost every actor and actress who has taken leading parts in Shakespearian plays at W. End theatres. In October 1963 the 'Old Vic' became the home of the National Theatre.

Palace (Shaftesbury Av.). Opened as the Royal English Opera House on 31st Jan. 1891 with *Ivanhoe*. Notable productions have been *Bunty Pulls the Strings* (1911); *Co-optimists, 2nd Edit.* (207 perfs.; 1924), *No, No, Nanette* (665 perfs.; 1925); *Carissima* (1948). During its yrs. as a variety theatre, Gabys Delys and Sir Harry Lauder were very successful here.

Phœnix (Charing Cross Rd.). Opened on 24th Sept. 1930 with *Private Lives*

which ran for 101 perfs. *Tonight at Eight* was produced here in 1936. More recent productions included *Love for Love* (1943); *Relapse* (1948); *The Browning Version* (1948); *Death of a Salesman* (with Paul Muni; 1949).

Piccadilly. Opened on 27th Apr. 1928 with *Blue Eyes*. Successful plays since have included *A Sleeping Clergyman* (Bridie; 1933); *George and Margaret* (1939); *The Corn is Green* (which resumed its run on the reopening of the theatre on 19th Dec. 1939 after the outbreak of the last war). *Blithe Spirit* (1,997 perfs.; 1941); *Macbeth* (with John Gielgud; 1942); *Panama Hattie* (1944).

Playhouse (Charing Cross). Opened on 28th Jan. 1907 with *Toddles*. This theatre was originally The Avenue. Outstanding productions listed include *The Flag Lieutenant* (1,381 perfs.; 1908); *White Cargo* (821 perfs.; 1924); two Somerset Maugham plays, *The Letter* (1927–8), and *The Secret Flame* (1929); *Mr. Bolfry* (1944); *Lady from Edinburgh* (1945). In the autumn of 1950 the theatre was acquired by the B.B.C.

Prince of Wales (Coventry St.). Originally called the Prince's, it is notable for being the first theatre at which an Ibsen play was produced in England; this was a free adaptation of *A Doll's House*, called *Breaking the Butterfly*, in Mar. 1884. The theatre had opened on 18th Jan. with a revival of Gilbert's *Palace of Truth*, with Beerholm Tree. Tree also acted in *The Private Secretary* (785 perfs.); this had been produced at Cambridge (1883), and then at Oxford and Chas. Hawtrey is reputed to have made £10,000 by it. In 1897 *La Poupée* reached 576 perfs. In 1899 Mrs. Patrick Campbell and Forbes-Robertson presented a Japanese play, called *The Moonlight Blossom*. Subsequent plays were distinguished by the acting of Chas. Hawtrey and Marie Tempest. *A Gaiety Girl* (1893), *Miss Hook of Holland* (1907), *Fair and Warmer* (1918), all ran for over 400 perfs., whilst *Yes Uncle* (1917), touched 626 perfs. In 1932 *I Lived with You* was a conspicuous success. The original theatre was the first in L. at which a Safety Curtain was installed. It was rebuilt, and renamed the Prince of Wales in 1937, opening with *Les Folies des Paris de Londres*.

Prince's. See *Shaftesbury*.
Royal Court. See *Court*.

Sadler's Wells (Rosebery Av.). This theatre took its name from the medicinal springs in the grounds of the Music House belonging to Thos. Sadler; these were discovered in 1683. In 1699 the theatre on the site was called 'Miles's Music House,' and a later proprietor was Rosoman (builder of Rosoman St.), who, in 1765, pulled down the old wooden structure and erected a theatre. In 1781 Grimaldi (the son) made his first appearance there. In 1807, in a panic raised by a cry of 'Fire!' 18 persons were killed and several others seriously injured. Water dramas and equestrian performances were in vogue from 1804 to 1844. In the latter yr. Samuel Phelps became manager. Between 1844 and 1862 he produced more than 30 Shakespearean plays, *Hamlet* achieving a run of 400 nights. After Phelps' retirement, Sadler's Wells never had the prestige it once enjoyed, and when it closed in 1916 it was a cinema. A committee under the chairmanship of the D. of Devonshire succeeded in obtaining enough money to build a new theatre, £14,200 coming from the Carnegie United Kingdom Trust, and £2,000 from the Finsbury B.C. The new theatre was opened on 14th Jan. 1931 with a performance of *Twelfth Night*. It became the 'Old Vic' of North London, presenting Shakespeare, opera and ballet. Gilbert and Sullivan productions and *Peer Gynt* have also been staged. The first English performance of Verdi's *Simone Boccanegra* was presented here in 1950. Since 1968, when the Sadler's Wells Opera Co. moved to the Coliseum, the theatre has been devoted to visiting opera and ballet companies, many from overseas.

St. Martin's (West St., Shaftesbury Av.). Opened 23rd Nov. 1910 with *Houp La.* Notable plays listed include *The Skin Game* (1920); *Bill of Divorcement* (1921–2); *Shall we Join the Ladies?* (1922–3); all of which ran for more than a year.

Saville (Shaftesbury Av.). Opened 8th Oct. 1931 with *For the Love of Mike.* Notable plays listed include *Over She Goes* (248 perfs.; 1936); *Fine and Dandy* (1942); *Junior Miss* (1943); *Bob's your Uncle* (1948); and *Belinda Fair* (1949).

Savoy (Strand). This theatre in the Strand was built by Richd. D'Oyly Carte to house the operas by Gilbert and Sullivan which he was producing in partnership with them; finance was provided by the profits of these produced at the Opera Comique where D'Oyly Carte had been acting manager. The theatre was opened on 10th Oct. 1881 with *Patience*, which had been running at the Opera Comique since April. *Iolanthe* followed in 1882, and *Princess Ida* in 1884. Sir Squire Bancroft who listed the first production dates of the Gilbert and Sullivan operas here gave these as *Pinafore*, 12th Nov. 1887 (120 perfs.); *Pirates of Penzance*, 17th Mar. 1888 (80 perfs.); *Patience*, 10th Oct. 1881 (448 perfs.); *Iolanthe*, 25th Nov. 1882 (398 perfs.); *Princess Ida*, 5th Jan. 1884 (246 perfs.); *Mikado*, 14th Mar. 1885 (672 perfs.); *Ruddigore*, 22nd Jan. 1887 (288 perfs.); *The Yeoman of the Guard*, 3rd Oct. 1888 (423 perfs.); and *The Gondoliers*, 7th Dec. 1889 (554 perfs.); between the première of *Pirates of Penzance* and 31st Dec. 1909, there were twenty revivals of the operas, the performances of these revivals totalling 1,993. With the opening night of *The Mikado* at the Savoy on 14th Mar. 1885, Gilbert and Sullivan operas entered upon their most uproariously popular phase. Ever since its building the Savoy has retained its association with them. It was, at the time of its opening, one of the most attractive houses in L. for the decorations, and electric lighting marked a great advance in theatre construction. The settings of the operas were beautifully staged, and the co. which included Geo. Grossmith, Richd. Temple, Rutland Barrington, and others, was an excellent one. *The Mikado* was revived in 1888, 1895, 1896, and 1908. *Ruddigore* and *The Gondoliers* were produced in 1887; *The Yeoman of the Guard* in 1888. It has been stated that the quarrel which developed between Gilbert and Sullivan during the run of *The Gondoliers* (1890) was because of their differing views upon a new carpet for the theatre. In 1892 Sullivan wrote the music to Sydney Grundy's libretto, *Haddon Hall*, but later again collaborated with Gilbert in *Utopia Limited* (1893) and *The Grand Duke* (1896). Pinero, Comyns Carr, and Ivan Caryll also wrote for the Savoy, and there were frequent revivals of operas. The theatre was closed in 1903 for a short time, following the production of *The Princess of Kensington*. Gilbert's last opera, *Fallen Fairies*, for which Edwd. German wrote the music, was produced here in 1909. During the First World War the most successful productions were a revival of Barrie's *The Professor's Love Story* which ran for 235 perfs. in 1916 and *Nothing But the Truth* which reached 578 perfs. in 1918. Between the two wars the Savoy, in addition to being the home of the Gilbert and Sullivan operas, was the scene of a number of successful plays, chief among them being *Paddy the Next Best Thing*, which had its first night on 5th Apr. 1920 and scored an unusual success with 867 perfs., and the war-play *Journey's End* which ran for 594 perfs. in 1929–30. John Van Druten's play, *Young Woodley*, with Frank Lawton in the name-part, reached 429 perfs. in 1928.

Shaftesbury (Princes Circus). The former Prince's Theatre, opened in 1911, reopened under the new name in March, 1963.

Strand (Aldwych). This theatre is on the site of Punch's Playhouse which was also known as The New Strand Theatre. The present theatre was built in 1905, and was opened as The Waldorf on 22nd May 1905 with *Il Maestro de Capella*. Among the well-known people who have appeared at this theatre, or the earlier one which staged many of Douglas Jerrold's early plays, were Rayner, the comedian, Mrs. Waylett, the singer, Rogers, the female impersonater, and it was here that in 1884 the Daly co. made their first L. appearance. Notable plays listed include *A Chinese Honeymoon* (1,074 perfs.; 1901); and *Arsenic and Old Lace* (1,337; 1942). The theatre reopened on 26th Dec. 1939 after the outbreak of war with *Spotted Dick* which had been produced here on 23rd July 1938.

Vaudeville (Strand). Built in 1870, it was first under the management of three celebrated actors of the day—H. J. Montague, David James, and Thos. Thorne, stated to have been known as 'The Jew, The Gent., and The Gentile.' The first productions, on 16th Apr. 1870 were Halliday's *Love and Money* and *Don Carlos*, but the theatre's reputation was made later in the yr. by Albery's comedy, *The Two Roses*, in which Henry Irving took the part of Digby Grant. Another notable success was *Our Boys*, which ran for four yrs. from 16th Jan. 1875. In the eighties a revival of *The School for Scandal*, ran for 400 nights.

Of then contemporary plays, H. A. Jones' *Saints and Sinners* (1885) created a sensation. It was at this theatre that Ibsen's *Hedda Gabler* and *Rosmersholme* were first acted in England, in 1891. In the same yr. the theatre was redecorated (and the façade extended) reopening on 31st Jan. with *Woodborrow Farm*. In 1892 Messrs. Gatti became the lessees. *Our Boys* was revived, and later Seymour Hicks and Ellaline Terriss brought success to the theatre in *Sweet and Twenty*, *The Catch of the Season*, and other plays. In recent yrs. straight plays, such as *The Breadwinner*, have succeeded here, and also other types of entertainment such as the revival of the *Co-optimists* in 1929, and Charlot's *Char-à-Banc* in 1935. *No Medals* (940 perfs.) was produced here in 1944.

Westminster (Palace St.). This theatre was Charlotte Chapel, which was converted into a cinema. It was opened as a theatre on 7th Oct. 1931, with Bridie's *Anatomist*. During the following eight yrs. more than twenty plays were staged, and these included *Six Characters in Search of an Author*, *Children in Uniform*, *Jonah and the Whale*, *The Moon in The Yellow River*, *King Lear*, *Alien Corn*, *Hamlet*, *Waste*, *Mourning Becomes Electra*. In 1938 The London Mask Theatre was established here when *Troilus and Cressida* was presented in modern dress; following this, *Dangerous Corner* etc., were presented. During the Second World War the theatre came under the direction of Donald Wolfit and Robt. Atkins; in 1944 Robt. Donat was lessee, and the plays given included *Ideal Husband*, *It Depends What you Mean*, *Yellow Sands*, and *The Cure for Love*. In 1946 three plays were staged and then the theatre was taken over by the Oxford Group for the staging of non-commercial Moral-Rearmament plays. The theatre was reopened as a commercial one on 2nd Nov. 1948 with *The Anatomist* (Alastair Sim as Dr. Knox), and later (in July 1949) Flora Robson appeared in *Black Chiffon*; both plays were very successful. The theatre is without boxes, has two floors only, and is very well appointed.

Whitehall (Trafalgar Sq.). Opened Sept. 1930, with *The Way to Treat a Woman*. *Anthony and Anna* ran for 789 perfs. here (1935), but this run, and that of almost every other play produced in L., was outstripped by *Worm's Eye View*. This comedy opened on Nov. 1944 at The Grand Theatre, Wolverhampton, attracted commercial backing, was next played at Norwich in Apr. 1945; and commenced its run at the Whitehall in Dec. 1945. It was transferred to the Comedy Theatre on 26th June 1950, having reached 1,822 consecutive perfs. When the Whitehall Theatre opened it was proposed that the telegraphic address should be 'Red Tape,' but the Postmaster-General refused.

Wyndham's (Charing Cross Rd.). Opened on 16th Nov. 1899 with a revival of *David Garrick*, in which Sir Chas. Wyndham played the title role. It produced £4,000 on the one night for Boer War soldier's wives and families. *The Liars* by H. A. Jones, and *Cyrano de Bergerac* were also revived, but *Mrs. Dane's Defence* was a more distinguished success in 1900, with Wyndham and Lena Ashwell. *Little Mary* (Barrie) was first produced here in 1903, and *Dear Brutus* in 1917; the latter ran for 365 perfs. and was revived in 1922, when it ran for 258 perfs. Plays of the type of *Bulldog Drummond* (1921), Edgar Wallace's *The Ringer* (1926), and *The Calendar* (1929), have also done well at this theatre, while *Clive of India* (1934) and *Sweet Aloes* (1934-5) have been conspicuous successes, with 409 and 431 perfs. respectively.

More recently opened theatres include the Mermaid in Puddle Dock (the only theatre in the city), Palladium, Queen's, and Victoria Palace. (See *The Theatres of London*, by R. Mander, 1963.)

Tower Hill, apart from the T.L. which overshadows it, has an historical interest. The Crooked Billet Tavern, it is said, once possessed a secret tunnel leading to the Tower. The level area is E. London's Hyde Park so far as oratory is concerned. It was the scene of huge mass meetings during the famous dock strike of 1889. In Pepys's time it seems to have been used for labour demonstrations:

'Thence home, and upon Tower Hill saw about 3 or 400 seamen get together; and one, standing upon a pile of bricks made his sign, with his handkercher, upon his stick, and called all the rest to him, and several shouts they gave. This made me afeard; so I got home as fast as I could' (19th Dec. 1666).

The kiosk near the entrance to the T.L.

marks one end of the first tube railway in L. In 1869, at this point, a tunnel was made under the Thames 7 ft. in diameter and 1,340 ft. in length. It cost from £18,000 to £20,000. In 1870 a cable-operated carriage, seating fourteen persons, worked by steam-engines, ran through it. Fares were 2d. first class and 1d. second class. It lasted only a few months, as apparently it did not work satisfactorily. The carriages, lifts, and accessories were taken away, and it then became a halfpenny subway for pedestrians. A million people used the subway every yr. until the opening of Tower B. (1894) made it unnecessary, and it was closed to the public. Later it was bought by the L. Hydraulic Power Co., for the purpose of conducting its water mains under the river, and there are now also two pipes of the Metropolitan Water Board (see *Under London*, by F. L. Stevens, 1939). The present brick kiosk took the place of a wooden one in 1926. Close by is the Tower Pier, where the Port of L. Authority trips start. The Tower Hill Improvement Committee, which is doing admirable work, has laid out the river beach as a children's playground, as it is at Greenwich. The foreshore—Crown land —by permission of George V was in 1935 dedicated in perpetuity for the use of the children of L. The 'Czar's Head,' in Great Tower St., was a modern tavern, which, by its name, continued the tradition of a previous inn having been frequented by Peter the Great of Russia. The E. end of Lower Thames St. was for centuries known as Petty Wales, a name which occurs frequently in documents concerning land from the 13th to the 18th century. Stow says that here was a palace of the Welsh ps., until Wales lost its independence at the end of the 13th century.

Near the huge premises of the Port of L. Authority (*q.v.*) is a war memorial to 12,000 of the merchant navy and fishing fleets. It easily surpasses any other memorial in L. for the number of named inscribed. In the enclosure W. of this, marked by low encircling rails, is the site of the scaffold (see 'Tower of London').

(See *Round about Tower Hill*, by Chas. Spon, 1934.)

Tower of London. A Roman origin has

sometimes been assumed. Fitzstephen, writing of L. about 1180, did not introduce Julius Cæsar, but he seems to imply that this was his belief, in the reference to the—

'Palatine Citadel, exceeding great and strong, whose walls and bailey rise from very deep foundations, their mortar being mixed with the blood of beasts.'

This was, no doubt, an allusion to gladiatorial shows. The Shakespeare plays give the idea support, notably in *Richard III*, where P. Edward (nominally Edward V) remarks to Buckingham:

'I do not like the Tower of any place. Did Julius Cæsar build that place, my lord?'

to which Buckingham replies:

'He did my gracious lord, begin that place; Which, since, succeeding ages have re-edified,'

and he adds it is 'upon record.' In *Richard II* it is 'Julius Cæsar's ill erected tower.' Stow, however, mentioning the tradition, expresses scepticism:

'Cæsar remained not here so long, nor had he any such matter, but only to dispatch a conquest of this barbarous country, and to proceed to greater matters. Neither do the Roman writers make mention of any such buildings created by him here.'

A writer so erudite as Thos. Gray referred to 'Ye towers of Julius,' and nearly twenty yrs. after Gray's death, Thos. Pennant (1790) mentioned a bdg. called 'Cæsar's Chapel.'

The tradition may have been founded on the fact that the T.L. was in relation to the Roman wall something like a padlock on a chain. The proximity of the wall and the existence of bastions at the SE. angle suggested the site. It was not broken down for its erection, for nearly eight acres of the T. stands outside it, and the bdgs. are in the bor. of Stepney. According to A. W. Clapham and W. H. Godfrey (*Some Famous Buildings and Their Story*):

'The Norman builders determined to incorporate a portion of it in the defences of the castle. . . . The medieval building known as the Wardrobe Tower, of which a portion still remains, has been proved to stand on the base

of a Roman bastion. The line of the still existing city wall between Aldgate and Tower Ditch, when produced southwards, exactly strikes this point, and a portion of its base adjoining the tower has been uncovered.'

WHITE TOWER. Here, then, just within the wall, Wm. the Conqueror, about 1078, began to build the great keep known as the White Tower. It is said to have been so called because it was first of white Caen stone, but it may well be, as suggested by E. O. Gordon (*Prehistoric London, its Mounds and Circles*, 1914), that it derived its name from the Bryn Gwyn, or White Hill, upon which it was erected, 'white being a Celtic synonym for "holy".' Gundulf has always been regarded as the architect, but this priest, who designed the keep of Rochester Castle, seems only to have supervised the work. It is impossible to say how long a period was taken by its erection. No doubt it was finished long before Gundulf's death in 1108. Its walls vary from 15 ft. at the bottom to 11 ft. at the top. The original entrance was probably at what is now first floor level, where on the S. wall are the remains of an important arch. A few only of the small Norman window openings remain. Wren has been blamed for the removal of the others, but as they are shown on a plan of 1721, at which date Wren was nearly ninety, he was probably innocent.

In the White Tower was confined Ralph Flambard, Bp. of Durham, the first on record of the T.'s many prisoners. On the death of his patron, Wm. Rufus in 1100, he was placed here for a considerable time. He attempted to escape, crozier in hand, through a window 65 ft. above the ground, and fell. He was picked up unhurt, and lived for many yrs. after. Griffin, son of Llewellyn, P. of Wales, attempted to imitate Flambard. The rope, however, parted before he reached the ground, and when he was found by the guards next morning his neck was broken. About 1296 John Baliol, K. of the Scots was a prisoner; and P. Chas. of Orleans, father of Louis XII, who having been made prisoner at Agincourt, was confined here from 1415 for twelve yrs. By that time the sum of 300,000 crowns had been raised for his ransom. He was a poet, and whiled away his time by composing poems. A richly illuminated manuscript,

Poesies de Charles duc d'Orleans, which was given to Elizabeth of York by her consort Henry VII on their wedding day, is now in the B. Mus. It contains the well-known illumination representing the D. in his prison, with L.B. in the background, and the chapel dedicated to St. Thomas clearly depicted.

In the council chamber on the top floor some notable events in English history have been enacted. In 1399 came Richard II to the T.:

'To whose flint bosom my condemned lord
Is doom'd a prisoner by proud Bolingbroke.'

as his Q. says in Shakespeare's play. He there resigned the crown to Bolingbroke, as described by Froissart.

In this same council chamber Act 3, Sc. iv of *Richard III* had its stage in history. Here, after asking for strawberries from the Bp. of Ely's gardens (see 'Ely Place'), the D. of Gloucester ordered Hastings's instant execution for alleged treasonable plots against him. A rough timber log was found close to the White Tower, and this served as a block. Of course, when the T. was occupied as a residence, this, and other adjacent apartments, were more inviting than they are now. Arras and tapestry hung upon the walls; rushes, and at a later date, carpets were places upon the floor.

In the round turret, at the NE. of the White Tower, Flamsteed, the first Astronomer Royal (he was appointed by Charles II), had his observatory till the time when Greenwich was ready for use.

The White Tower includes St. John's Chapel, one of the most perfect specimens of Norman architecture in this country. It is 55 ft. 6 in. long by 31 ft. wide, and has a nave and aisles of four bays, and an apse opening by five arches to an ambulatory. The arches are plainer than those of St. Bartholomew's Ch., which is about fifty yrs. later, and there is no billet moulding. Some capitals have a T-shaped figure found only at this early date. There is a clerestory, lighted by a second tier of windows; its gallery is a continuation of the wall passages of the second floor.

Henry III, in 1240, gave particular directions for repairing and ornamenting this chapel. In 1381, Simon Sudbury, Abp. of C. was kneeling before its altar

when he was seized by Wat Tyler's rebels, and dragged out to Tower Hill and beheaded. His head is preserved at the Ch. of St. Gregory, Sudbury. Here, probably, Richard II's body rested for a night in 1400 after his murder in Pontefract Castle. Sir Thos. Brackenbury was at prayer before the altar in 1483 when he received Richard III's order to put his nephews, the young princes, to death. Here lay in state the body of Elizabeth of York, the consort of Henry VII, in 1503, with 500 tapers and candlesticks round her bier. She died in the T. in childbirth. Here Q. Mary caused a requiem mass to be celebrated for her brother, Edward VI, at the same time that his funeral was taking place, according to Protestant rites, in W.A. Here also, in 1554, she was betrothed to Philip of Spain, Count Egmont being proxy. In the same year, Ld. Guildford Dudley, husband of Lady Jane Grey, in view of his wife, who must have been saddened by the spectacle, entered the chapel to publicly proclaim his apostasy from the Protestant faith and to participate in a mass. This did not save him. The installation of the Knights of the Bath took place here, and on his accession in 1399 Henry IV created 46. In this chapel they kept their all-night vigil—watching their armour and praying. Any canonicals belonging to the chapel, such as rich vestments and laces of Venice and Flanders, were dispersed by Cromwell, and in the reign of Charles II it became a storehouse for State records.

The stained glass came from Horace Walpole's collection at Strawberry Hill. Some of the events depicted, according to Maj.-Gen. Sir George Younghusband, are crude in execution. One—

'represents the Roman soldier, dressed in English armour, awaking with horror and surprise to notice that the sepulchre, represented by a stone box with the lid half off, is empty. Another (near the entrance) depicts Joshua, with one hand on the sun and the other on the moon, holding them still till he has completed the slaying of the Amalekites.'

The records were removed to the Chapel of the Rolls in 1857 (see 'Public Record Office').

On the main floor of the White Tower is a stone crypt. It is below St. John's Chapel. The block exhibited was specially made for the execution of the Scotch lords. Cuts from the axe are visible. The headsman's axe is of earlier date. A few instruments of torture are exhibited here, such as the thumbscrews, the scavenger's daughter, by which the victim was crushed (readers of Scott will remember these implements being employed by the Duke of Lauderdale in *Old Mortality*), a spiked collar, and bilboes for securing captives by the feet. There is also a large gibbet. This was not usually a prison, but some of the followers of Sir Thos. Wyatt were thrust into it in 1553. There are inscriptions on the wall of this date. 'He that endureth to the ende shall be savd. M. 10 R. Rudston. Dar. Kent Anno 1553.' Another is: 'Be feithful unto thy deth, and I wil give the a crowne of life. T. Fane. 1554.' There is also: 'T. Culpeper of Darford.' The place was originally much darker than now. The window made in the thickness of the wall is modern.

The dungeons of the keep are level with the ground on the S. side, and sunk only a few feet on the N. side. There are now three chambers. One of these has been christened 'Little Ease.' It may have been used as a cell, and Guy Fawkes is the prisoner with whom it is traditionally associated. There is a heavy oak door, and spikes on which a wicket once swung on the other side. In 1278 Jews to the number of 600 were thrust into these dungeons, accused of clipping and defacing the K.'s coin. Probably many of them perished here. Edward I's wars in Scotland and Wales brought many prisoners here, and it is here, it is said, that the sub-prior of W.A. and some of his monks were confined as accomplices to the robbery of the royal treasury in 1303 (see 'Westminster Abbey'). Here, too, the rack was kept, and men were 'by tortyre tryed,' as two of the inscriptions say, by the truly dim religious light of a lantern, and in that mental darkness which, as Shakespeare said, was ignorance. In one of the dungeons (now called 'The Cannon Room') is the well. It dates from the 12th century, and is 40 ft. deep. When cleaned out in 1910, the wooden frame on which its stones were built was found in place at the bottom.

It was in William Rufus's reign that a wall was built round the T., for which purpose, wrote Henry of Huntingdon, 'the country was heavily burthened by taxes without end.' The moat probably dates from the erection of the W.T. In Richard I's time (1189–99) Wm. Longchamp, Bp. of Ely, who was then Constable of the T., deepened the channel fully 10 ft. In Edward III's time bathing in the T. moat was punished by death. The difficulty of keeping the moat sufficiently clean induced the D. of Wellington, when Constable of the T.—in 1843—to order it to be drained. During floods in Jan. 1928 it was filled again.

The T.L. has on several occasions been subject to mild attacks. In 1141, when the Empress Matilda arrived in L., the inhabitants rose in revolt and attacked it because Geoffrey de Magnaville (see 'Temple'), who was Constable, had been persuaded to espouse her cause. The Q. was compelled to flee, and then the Constable transferred his allegiance to the consort of Stephen, who arrived soon after. Ld. Scales, in 1460, had to defend the T., as a Lancastrian, against the E. of Warwick and his Yorkist forces. Stone shot found in the moat in 1843 are attributed to this engagement. In 1554 Sir John Gage, the Constable, fired cannon balls across the river at Sir Thos. Wyatt's troops, who were encamped in Bermondsey. There was an attack by German aircraft during the First World War. The result was the breaking of a small window at the entrance to the Wakefield Tower, and the death of a pigeon.

The flagpole erected on the White Tower in 1890, having been seriously affected by dry rot, it was taken down. In 1948 Mr. Prentice Bluedel, a lumber merchant of Vancouver, presented, on behalf of the Boy Scouts of British Columbia, a flagpole made from a Douglas pine. The tree, 185 ft. in height was reduced to 85 ft. and erected in June 1948 on the White Tower.

The remaining towers will be dealt with in alphabetical order.

BEAUCHAMP TOWER dates from Edward I's time. It derives its name from its most distinguished prisoner, Thos. Beauchamp, third E. of Warwick, who was attainted under Richard II in 1397, but restored to liberty and honour under Henry IV in 1399. There are ninety-one inscriptions on its walls; some have been brought from other places. The earliest is No. 89 (in a passage opposite the entrance): 'Thomas Talbot 1462.' The two best pieces of carving are Nos. 14 and 66. The former was done by John Dudley, son of the D. of Northumberland, and a brother of the husband of Lady Jane Grey. He has left the family cognizance, the lion and bear, and ragged staff, underneath which is his name, the whole being surrounded by a border consisting of oak sprigs, roses, geraniums, and honeysuckles, emblematical of the Christian names of his four brothers, as appears from an inscription added. No. 66 is the carving of a bell with the letter 'A' above, to represent Thos. Abel. He was a learned gentleman who was for a time domestic chaplain to Catherine of Aragon. He incurred the displeasure of Henry VIII by advocating her cause during the divorce proceedings. Later he further offended by denying the K.'s supremacy. He was executed in 1540. There is also an inscription (13) by Philip Howard, son of Thos. Howard, D. of Norfolk (see 'Charterhouse'):

'The more suffering for Christ in this world, the more glory with Christ in the next. Thou hast crowned him with honour and glory, O Lord! In memory everlasting He will be just. Arundell, June 22nd, 1587.'

He died in the T.L. in 1595, having been a prisoner ten years, and was bd. in the chapel of St. Peter. The large window in the Beauchamp Tower was the work of Salvin, an architect who carried out restoration work when the D. of Wellington was Constable (1826–51). Therefore this gloomy apartment, approached by a narrow and dangerous stair, was still darker when used as a prison.

BELL TOWER dates from Richard I's time (c. 1190). The curfew which once summoned the Knights of the Bath to their all-night vigil, still sounds nightly to warn late strollers to depart before the gates are closed. It is dated 1651. Sir (now also St.) Thomas More, and St. John Fisher were confined in the Bell Tower in 1534–5 before execution. There is here an inscription commencing: 'By torture straung my trouth was tried,' possibly the work of Thomas Miagh, a Catholic martyr, as there is a similar one with his name attached, and the date 1581, in the Beauchamp Tower. Here, in 1561 and 1563 were born two children

to Lady Catherine Seymour (Lady Jane Grey's sister). As Q. Elizabeth had forbidden her husband Ld. Hertford, access to her, she was angry about it. Lady Arabella Stuart died here, crazy and broken-hearted, in 1615. The D. of Monmouth was a prisoner for two nights in 1685, before execution on Tower Hill. John Thirlwall, charged with treason for corresponding with the French Revolutionists, and Thomas Hardy (see 'Bunhill Fields') were prisoners for four months in 1794. Strangely enough, Thirlwall described his prison as 'large, airy and pleasant.'

BLOODY TOWER dates from the reigns of Edward III and Richard II. It was originally called the Garden Tower, as its upper storey opens on to that part of the parade ground which was formerly the Constable's garden. The present name can be traced back to so early a date as 1597, and was probably due to the belief that it was the scene of the murder of the two young princes, Edward V and his brother, the Duke of York, in 1483. At any rate, in 1674, excavations at the foot of a staircase in the T. disclosed the bones of two young boys. Charles II believed them to be the royal remains, and they were interred in Westminster Abbey (see 'Children's Memorials'). Ridley, Latimer and Cranmer (all burned at Oxford, the first two in 1554 and the last in 1555), were prisoners here for a short time in 1553. Henry Percy, E. of Northumberland, committed suicide in the Bloody Tower. Placed there for plotting with the Guises to set Mary Stuart on the throne, he anticipated his fate by putting three bullets into his breast. Here, in 1613, Sir Thos. Overbury was poisoned. He had been imprisoned in consequence of the intrigues of Lady Frances Howard, whose match with Robt. Carr, E. of Somerset, the K.'s favourite, he had boldly discountenanced. Both the E. and the lady, who became his wife, found themselves in the same place two years later, and Somerset remained there for seven yrs., i.e. until 1622. Sir Walter Raleigh spent most of his thirteen yrs.' imprisonment in the Bloody Tower. He wrote his *History of the World* here, and a copy of it is preserved in a glass case. Here his son, Carew, was b. It was also the prison of Sir John Eliot, a martyr for constitutional liberty. He was removed finally to another room, where he died in 1632. Charles I when his relatives asked for his body, wrote across the petition, 'Let Sir John Eliot be buried in the church of that parish where he died,' so he was laid in the chapel of St. Peter ad Vincula. There followed into the Bloody Tower John Felton, the murderer of the D. of Buckingham. Crowds gathered to see him take exercise on 'Raleigh's walk.' From 1641 Abp. Laud was a prisoner in the same place. It was probably through the window over the arch that he held out his hands in blessing as Strafford passed to execution (1641). Laud left the Bloody Tower for execution in 1645. In 1652 Edward Somerset, Marquess of Worcester, Earl of Glamorgan, whilst a prisoner of war, discovered from the boiling of a kettle the principle of the steam engine, but nothing came of it. To the Bloody Tower, in 1688, came the infamous Judge Jeffreys. Here he died, aged 41, in 1689. The last prisoner of note was Thistlewood, one of the Cato St. conspirators (1820).

CEREMONY OF THE KEYS. The portcullis at the Bloody Tower is the only entrance into the inner ward of the T.L., and so it is that here nightly is held this ancient ceremony. A sergeant and four privates are assigned for this duty, one carrying a lantern. The barrier gate, the Middle Tower, and the Byward Tower are closed and locked in turn, and at each of these places the escort presents arms. The party then return to the main guard, and immediately they pass into the arch of the Bloody Tower the sentry challenges them with: 'Halt! Who comes there?' The answer is given by the chief warder: 'The keys.' 'Whose keys?' the sentry demands. 'Queen Elizabeth's keys.' 'Advance Queen Elizabeth's keys: all's well,' is the reply. The escort then proceeds to the main guard, and guard and escort then present arms in honour of the keys. The chief warder then steps two paces in front of the escort, and, removing his hat of Tudor fashion, calls: 'God preserve Queen Elizabeth.' Guard and escort then answer loudly: 'Amen.' The keys are thereupon carried to the Queen's House for delivery to the resident governor, with whom they remain for the night.

'Once,' says Mr. W. G. Bell, 'there was a change. Queen Victoria died about seven o'clock on a January night,

and in the pressure of so many State matters to be settled immediately, the new Sovereign, Albert Edward, had not decided what name he should bear upon the English Throne. The Tower was locked as usual, and on the Chief Warder's return with the escort answer was given to the sentry's challenge "The King's keys." '

The password of the T. is known only to the K. and the Constable, but the former, every quarter, communicates it in a signed document to the Ld.M.

BOWYER TOWER was built in the reign of Edward I, and derives its name from the fact that formerly it was the lodging of the royal bow-maker. It was either here, or in the Bloody Tower, that Geo., D. of Clarence, was drowned in a butt of malmsey wine in 1478. He was said to have been found with his head hanging over the edge of the butt; he may have drunk himself to death.

BRICK TOWER dates from the reign of Edward IV or Richard III. It was Sir Walter Raleigh's prison in 1592, when he was guilty of seducing Elizabeth Throckmorton, one of Elizabeth's maids of honour. Ld. Grey de Wilton spent nine yrs. here for his share in the 'Main' and 'Bye' conspiracies to place Arabella Stuart on the throne. Raleigh spent here his last few weeks in the T. He was removed here from the Wardrobe Tower, 'which,' said Sir Thos. Wilson, Keeper of the State Paper Office, who was his custodian, 'though it seems nearer Heaven, yet is there no means of escape from thence for him to any place but Hell.' Raleigh was transferred from here to the Gate House, Westminster (see 'Prisons'). Sir Wm. Coventry, at one time Secretary to the Navy Office, and therefore figuring much in Pepys's diary, was a prisoner here for challenging the D. of Buckingham to a duel. Here Pepys visited him on 9th Mar. 1669:

'Up, and to the Tower; and there find Sir W. Coventry alone, writing down his Journal, which, he tells me, he now keeps of the material things; upon which I told him, and he is the only man I ever told it to, I think, that I kept it most strictly these eight or ten years; and I am sorry almost that I told it him, it not being necessary, nor may be convenient, to have it known.'

s

BROAD ARROW TOWER may have been so named from the use of the arrow as a defence of the T. Another suggestion is that it was due to the T. having been used for the dispatch of official letters and orders, the broad arrow having for centuries been a Govt. mark. There are many inscriptions on the walls, mostly cut in the reigns of Q. Mary and Q. Elizabeth. One, 'John Daniell, 1556,' was done by a man who was both hanged and beheaded on Tower Hill. His crime was that of attempting to rob the exchequer.

BYWARD TOWER dates from Edward I's reign (1272–1307). Here the pass- or by-word had to be given. This was the first tower on the island, i.e. the one created by the moat. Here the youthful Edward VI, in 1547, was met on the drawbridge by the Abp. of C., the Ld. Chancellor, and numerous noble men, who conducted him to the state apartments, where it was then customary for a new sovereign to reside until the date of his coronation. The portcullis is no longer used, but the oak door is locked nightly, in the course of the ceremony of the keys. This tower includes two interesting chambers, on either side of the centre archway. The one on the right, 15 ft. square, is believed once to have been used as a chapel, and it still has its original loophole window and stone fireplace. It is now assigned for the use of the Yeomen Warders, better known as Beefeaters. Brunt, one of the Cato St. conspirators, was imprisoned here in 1820.

CRADLE TOWER was named after a cradle or slip by means of which boats were slung from the moat, through the arch beneath, to the roadway which runs inside the outer defences. Father Gerard managed to escape from this tower, about 1586, by means of a long thin string with a leaden weight attached. It was thrown to some friends, who caught it and attached a stout rope. This the priest pulled in and made fast to a turret of the tower, and so worked his way down and was received into a boat.

DEVEREUX TOWER, like the Salt Tower, was at one time known as Julius Cæsar's Tower, though it is believed to date only from Richard II's time. Later it was 'Robin the Devyl's Tower,' though it is impossible to say who Robin was. It may well have been, as R. C. Davey suggested, that Wm. the Conqueror's son, known as Robert the Devil, was confined here. Another prisoner, in 1601, was Robt. Devereux, E. of Essex. Q. Elizabeth's favourite; its modern name is derived from him. It consists of two storeys, with walls 11 ft. thick, and includes an ancient kitchen with a vaulted ceiling, beneath which is a dungeon. This tower at one time contained a number of secret passages, one of which led eastward to the Flint Tower, and another to the vaults under St. Peter's Chapel. It also possesses a winding stair-case, leading to two gruesome cells con-structed in the thickness of the wall.

FLINT TOWER was anciently considered the most dreadful of the prisons, and was suggestively nicknamed 'Lytle Helle.' In 1796, however, that old tower was demolished and the present one erected in its place.

LANTHORN TOWER was originally built by Henry III (1216–72) and was at one time richly embellished with tapestries, Catherine of Aragon, Katharine Parr, and Q. Mary having worked upon them. In Henry VIII's time the King's bed-chamber and privy closet were here. The upper storey was destroyed in a fire in 1788. The tower was, however, com-pletely restored, and now outwardly well represents the original bdg.

MARTIN TOWER dates from Henry III's reign. The identity of Martin has not been discovered. In 1644 the regalia were removed to the basement, and here in 1671 Colonel Blood stole the Crown Jewels. He was captured, and for a time imprisoned in the White Tower, probably in one of the dungeons. He was com-manded to attend before Charles II a few days later at Whitehall. He was thereupon set free, and his Irish estates, which had been forfeited and were worth £500 a year, were restored to him.

MIDDLE TOWER—of Edward I's date, if not earlier—was so called as being, when the Lion Tower existed, midway between it and the Byward Tower. The finely carved royal arms over the arch are Hanoverian. Originally, a drawbridge stood before the Middle Tower, but all trace has disappeared. In front of this tower Q. Elizabeth, on returning to the place where five yrs. before she had been a prisoner, alighted from her horse to return thanks. In 1760 E. Ferrers was a prisoner here prior to his execution for the murder of his bailiff, Johnson (see 'Tyburn'). In 1820 John Wilson, one of the Cato St. conspirators, was here for a time.

SALT TOWER is believed to be nearly as old as the White Tower. The origin of the name is unknown. Probably it was used to house that commodity at a time when it was stored in large quantities to preserve meat in winter for the garrison. Its former name, for a reason that is obscure, but may confirm its antiquity, was Julius Cæsar's Tower. It has a number of inscriptions. Amongst these is the figure for casting horoscopes accompanying which are the words: 'Hew Draper of Brystow made this spheer the 30 daye of Maye anno 1561.' He was sent to the T. on an accusation of witchcraft, against Lady St. Lo, better known as Bess of Hardwick, and her husband Sir Wm. St. Lo. Other inscriptions were cut by priests in Elizabeth's reign. A pierced heart, hand, and foot, occur in different places on the wall, signifying the five wounds of Christ. A remarkably plain one is Henry Walpole's. A Jesuit father, he spent a yr. here before being taken to York and hanged, in 1594, at the age of 35. (His full story is told by Walter G. Bell in *London Rediscovered*.) The name of Michael Moody recalls a plot to murder Q. Elizabeth. He was a prisoner in Newgate for debt, and the small sum was to be paid to secure his release on his undertaking, in Froude's words,

'to poison the Queen's saddle, or introduce a bag of powder under her bed, or something else equally chimerical.'

He was betrayed to Walsingham.

ST. THOMAS'S TOWER, on the other side of Water Lane, as it is called, is over Traitors' Gate. It was erected by Henry III, and so called in honour of St. Thos. à Becket, and contained a chapel dedicated both to him and Edward the Confessor. Some of the old timbering of this tower was removed by Henry VIII in 1532, and in 1866 a complete restoration, under the direction of the architect Salvin, took place. With the exception of parts of the interior rooms, and a piscina of the chapel, little of the original bdg. remains. An old subterranean passage connects St. Thomas's Tower with the Wakefield Tower. The Keeper of the Crown Jewels now resides in this tower

and the Crown Jewels are kept in it. It was probably here, in 1591, that Sir Walter Raleigh m. Elizabeth Throckmorton, one of Q. Elizabeth's maids of honour, who was already with child. In St. Thomas's Tower Sir Wm. Seymour, mentioned above, was a prisoner in 1611, and from here he escaped dressed in a carter's smock-frock and a rough wig, a cart full of faggots being driven up to the top of the steps of Traitors' Gate. In 1614 Ld. Grey d. in the tower after eleven yrs.' imprisonment. He had been condemned to death in 1603 for his share in a plot to place Arabella Stuart on the throne, and reprieved at the last minute.

WAKEFIELD TOWER also dates from Edward I's reign. In 1360 the records of the kingdom, previously kept in the White Tower, were removed here. Its name was probably derived from Wm. de Wakefield, King's Clerk, appointed to hold custody of the Exchange in the T. in 1344. Here, in 1460, prisoners taken by the victorious Lancastrians at the battle of Wakefield were confined (some authorities derive the name from this fact). Probably some were drowned, for the dungeons could be flooded and then emptied by a mechanical device. In 1471, in this tower, Henry VI was murdered. According to Fabyan's *Chronicles*, he was 'strikked with a dagger by the hands of Richard of Gloster' in a little oratory there. Annually three lilies are placed on the spot, on the anniversary of the K.'s death (see 'Customs'). A piscina and sedilia are still there.

WELL TOWER has not one of the three ancient wells near it. Possibly, therefore, Maj.-Gen. Younghusband suggests, it was named after some well-known personage who lived there. It has also been used as a prison, and an inscription reads: 'As for the vicious such they are as is the heedles flye.'

THE LIEUTENANT'S LODGINGS, now called the QUEEN'S HOUSE, has sheltered many famous prisoners. It was built by Henry VIII, and, unhappily, stucco conceals its original features, save on the western face. In a little room on the top storey Anne Boleyn is said to have spent the last night of her life. It is 14 ft. square, the walls being panelled to the low ceiling with dark oak. Here, too, was formerly the council chamber, and in it Robt. Cecil and the Council of State examined Guy

Fawkes, who 'would give no account of himself save that his name was Johnson, and other fictions.' He had to be racked before he would make the confession which was signed by his shaking hand. There is a very large tablet, with a contemporary and highly coloured portrait in relief of James I, accompanying a florid Latin inscription recalling the dedicatory words of the Authorized Version of the Bible. It commences:

'James the Great King of Great Britain, most renowned for piety, justice, prudence, learning, courage, clemency, and the other Royal virtues; of the Christian faith, of the public safety, of universal peace, the champion, a cherisher, an author, most keen-sighted, most noble, most auspicious.'

It concludes:

'The names of the conspirators to the everlasting Infamy of themselves and the eternal detestation of so great savagery.'

Then follows a long list. This was the work of Sir William Waad ('that beast Waad' Raleigh called him), who evidently knew that his royal master liked the butter laid on thickly.

A small chamber adjoining the council room was the scene of the most thrilling escape made from the T.L. In 1716, Ld. Nithsdale was to have been executed, with the E. of Derwentwater and Viscount Kenmure, who were confined here, for his part in the Scottish rising. On the eve of his execution Lady Nithsdale took with her, when she visited her husband, a younger lady, Miss Hilton. The latter shed a garment and departed. Another lady, Mrs. Mills, did the same, and then took an affectionate farewell. A few minutes after Ld. Nithsdale, disguised in female attire, with a wig like Mrs. Mill's, and weeping into a large handkerchief held to his face, was led sorrowfully forth by Lady Nithsdale, and handed over to the maid whom they met at the door. Lady Nithsdale then returned to her husband's room, and carried on a conversation with herself, imitating her husband's voice. On the way downstairs she met a servant going with lights to his lordship's room, but she told him he was at prayers, and must not be disturbed. In the sequel her husband escaped to the Continent, where he lived until 1744. One of Ld. Nithsdale's com-panions, Ld. Tullibardine, died in the Lieutenant's lodgings before he was tried. A full account of the adventure was given in a letter from Lady Nithsdale to a sister, Abbess of the Augustine nuns at Bruges. It is printed in Hepworth Dixon's *The London Prisons*. It is also the subject of a play by Clifford Bax, *The Immortal Lady*. She survived her husband by five yrs.

Adjoining the Queen's House is the Gentleman Jailer's House. It is of red brick, and of late 17th-century date. It stands on the site of a previous house of the same name, wherein Lady Jane Grey was a prisoner. From one of its windows she looked out to see the headless body of her husband, covered with a sheet, being trundled on a handcart on its way to burial in St. Peter's Chapel. 'A sight to hir no less than deathe,' wrote John Stow. 'It was not wilful cruelty,' said Froude. 'The officer in command had forgotten that the ordinary road led past her window.'

Four prisoners who cannot be located to any particular quarter of the T.L., should be mentioned. Francis Bacon, then Viscount St. Alban, was here for a week in 1621. In 1668–9 Wm. Penn was there for publishing his book, *Sandy Foundation Shaken*, in which he attacked the doctrine of the trinity, without a licence. In 1763 John Wilkes was confined for a week on the charge arising out of No. 45 of the *North Briton*. He was released because the Ld. Chief Justice declared his imprisonment was illegal. Sir Roger Casement was a prisoner for a short time in 1916, prior to his transfer to Brixton gaol.

TRAITORS' GATE was the common entrance to the Tower by water, and it was convenient when prisoners were tried at Westminster Hall.

'To the water side I must conduct your grace,'

says Sir Thomas Lovell (see 'Lincoln's Inn') in *Henry VIII*. He was addressing Edwd. D. of Buckingham, who passed under this arch in 1521 prior to his execution. Others who have found it a watery way to dusty death have been Bp. Fisher and Sir Thos. More (1534), Q. Anne Boleyn (1536), Cromwell, E. of Essex (1540), Q. Katharine Howard

(1542), Lady Jane Grey (1554), the E. of Essex (1601), James, D. of Monmouth (1685). One who did not die was the Princess Elizabeth (1554). She sat down on the wet steps, vowed her innocence, and refused to budge a step further until she was promised her liberty. Only after a long parley in the rain could the Lieutenant persuade her to take up more comfortable quarters.

PLACE OF EXECUTION. This was a few yds. from the Gentleman Jailer's House. Here six notable prisoners were beheaded, five of them women: Q. Anne Boleyn (1536). She was executed by the sword of an executioner brought from Calais. Margaret, Countess of Salisbury (1541). She was the last of the old Angevin or Plantagenet family, and was 71 yrs. of age. She declined to lay her head on the block, and was pursued round the scaffold by the executioner until she was hacked to death by his axe. The third was Jane, the Viscountess Rochford, in 1542. She was regarded as an abettor of Q. Katharine Howard, Henry VIII's fourth wife, who was executed at the same time. The Q., who was brought from Syon House, Isleworth (what is said to have been her prison still remains), actually had the block brought to her room. In the presence of the executioner, she knelt and placed her head in the appropriate place, declaring, as she rose to her feet, that she 'could go through the ordeal with grace and propriety.' Lady Jane Grey was the fifth, in 1554. The last was Robt. Devereux, E. of Essex. Elizabeth met his last request—for a private death. 'The acclamation of the people might have been a temptation unto him,' he said, 'all popularity and trust in man was vain.' Possibly Elizabeth the more readily complied as there was still some fear of a popular rising in his favour. As it was, it got bruited abroad that it had taken three strokes of the axe to complete the execution, and the executioner when he left the T. was threatened by the crowd.

Most executions took place on Tower Hill. The scaffold was about 5 ft. high. It was made of rough planks, with railing surrounding it, draped in black. Wooden steps gave access at one end, and of these, not stoutly made, as needed for so brief a use, Sir Thos. More made fun: 'See me safely up, for my coming down I can shift for myself.' The scaffold was littered with straw, and by the block was a basket half filled with sawdust to receive the head. The first recorded execution here was Sir Simon Burley in 1388. Others who suffered were Dudley, Henry VII's minister (1510), Edwd., D. of Buckingham (1521), Fisher, Bp. of Rochester, and Sir Thos. More (1535), Thos. Cromwell, E. of Essex (1540), the E. of Surrey (1547), D. of Somerset (1552), D. of Northumberland (1553), Sir Thos. Wyatt and Ld. Guildford Dudley, the D. of Suffolk (1554) —see 'City Churches; B'—Holy Trinity, Minories—the D. of Norfolk (1572), the E. of Strafford (1641), Abp. Laud (1645), Sir John Fenwick (1697), the last to be executed under a Bill of Attainder, E. of Kilmarnock and Ld. Balmerino (1746), and Ld. Lovat (1747). In 1780 two women were hanged for complicity in the 'No Popery' riots. The site of the scaffold is now a grassy enclosure for perambulating nursemaids. Here are four plaques bearing the names of 27 famous persons put to death on the site. A centre stone commemorates more than 125 who were known to have died here.

CHAPEL OF ST. PETER AD VINCULA. Nobody has more eloquently acclaimed its unrivalled pathos than Macaulay, and here there is no ground for the charge of strained rhetoric that can sometimes be made against him:

'In truth there is no sadder spot on the earth than that little cemetery. Death is there associated, not, as in Westminster Abbey and Saint Paul's, with genius and virtue, and with public veneration and with imperishable renown; not, as in our humblest churches and churchyards, with everything that is most endearing in social and domestic charities; but with whatever is darkest in human nature and in human destiny,. with the savage triumph of implacable enemies, with the inconstancy, the ingratitude, the cowardice of friends, with all the miseries of fallen greatness and of blighted fame. Thither have been carried, through successive ages, by the rude hands of gaolers, without one mourner following, the bleeding relics of men who had been the captains of armies, the leaders of parties, the oracles of senates, and the ornaments of courts.' When the path of glory had led to a premature grave there was sometimes an unnecessary ignominy. The body of Bp.

Fisher was stripped by the executioner, and left naked to the common gaze until night fell, and two of the watch raised the mangled corpse upon their halberds to carry it to burial. Anne Boleyn's body was thrown into a common chest of elm that had been made to put arrows in. On a memorial tablet near the entrance door will be found a 'List of Remarkable Persons Buried in this Chapel'; it is as follows: Gerald Fitzgerald, Earl of Kildare, 1534; John Fisher, Bishop of Rochester, 1535; Sir Thomas More, 1535; George Boleyn, Viscount Rochford, 1536; Queen Anne Boleyn, 1536; Thomas Cromwell, Earl of Essex, 1540; Margaret of Clarence, Countess of Salisbury, 1541; Queen Katharine Howard, 1542; Jane, Countess Rochford, 1542; Thomas, Lord Seymour of Sudeley, 1549; Edward Seymour, Duke of Somerset, 1552; Sir Ralph Vane, 1552; Sir Thomas Arundell; John Dudley, Duke of Northumberland, 1553; Lord Guildford Dudley, 1554; Lady Jane Grey, 1554; Henry Grey, Duke of Suffolk, 1554; Thomas Howard, Duke of Norfolk, 1572; Sir John Perrott, 1592; Philip, Earl of Arundel, 1595; Robert Devereux, Earl of Essex, 1601; Sir Thomas Overbury, 1613; Thomas, Lord Grey of Wilton, 1614; Sir John Eliot, 1632; William, Viscount Strafford, 1680; Arthur, Earl of Essex, 1683; James, Duke of Monmouth, 1685; George, Lord Jeffreys, 1689; John Rotier, 1703; Edward, Lord Griffin, 1710; William, Marquis of Tullibardine, 1746; Lord Balmerino, 1746; Simon, Lord Fraser of Lovat, 1747. All of these save Perrott, Philip, Earl of Arundel, Overbury, Lord Grey, Sir John Eliot, Arthur, Earl of Essex (he was found with his throat cut), John Rotier, and Lord Griffin died by the executioner's axe. (Rotier was mineralist at the Mint, then in the Tower, and designed the picture of Britannia still on our pennies.) Some of the headsman's victims were buried elsewhere. Lady Arabella Stuart, who d. in the T. in 1615, was bd. in the Stuart vault in W.A. Sir Walter Raleigh was bd. in St. Margaret's Ch. (see 'Westminster'). Wentworth, E. of Strafford was bd. (1641) at Wentworth Woodhouse (Yorks.). For Abp. Laud see 'City Churches; C'—All Hallows, Barking. For Sir Thomas More see 'Chelsea.' Philip, E. of Arundel's remains were removed to Arundel in 1624, and Judge Jeffrey's

to St. Mary Aldermanbury Ch. (see 'City Churches; D') in 1693. Sir Gervase Helwyss (1613)—the only Lieutenant to be executed—is not mentioned. He was convicted of complicity in the plot to poison Sir Thos. Overbury, and was sentenced to be drawn, hanged and quartered at Tyburn. His plea that the execution should be carried out in a place less associated with picaresque personalities was granted, and he suffered on Tower Hill in 1613. A remarkable entry in the burial register in 1587 is as follows:

'Mr. William Foxley, buried 4 May. He slept fourteen daies and fifteen nights, and lived after forty-one years. Potmaker in the Mint.'

Stow refers to this and says he— ·

'could not be wakened with pricking, cramping, or otherwise burning whatsoever, till the first day of term, which was 14 days and 15 nights.'

The physicians, learned men, even Henry VIII himself, inquired into matter, but could find no reason for this prolonged slumber.

After all this sad parade of the court of the king of terrors, it should be mentioned that there have been a few children of the Tower baptized in its chapel, and entered in the baptismal register, which commences in 1587. Amongst these were the two children of Lady Catherine Seymour (see *supra*). Sir Walter Raleigh's son Carew was b. during his father's first imprisonment in the T., and probably also baptized in the chapel. The marriage register commenced in 1586, but contains no names of importance. Probably all the bridegrooms and some of the brides were on the staff of or connected with the T. In a few cases children of Yeoman Warders have been married in the chapel.

Particular attention was drawn to the bdg. in 1871 when it was proposed to bury Sir John Fox Burgoyne, the Constable of the Tower, in the chapel. During the construction of his grave in the chancel it was apparent that older bones had been disturbed. It was found that in some instances interments were barely 2 ft. below the surface, and in no distance was the depth greater than 5 or 6 ft. The remains were therefore removed to the crypt, on the N. side of the chapel. In some cases coffins were found intact.

Where there were none, the remains were enclosed in boxes with suitable inscriptions. What were undoubtedly the bones of Anne Boleyn were found in the place where she is known to have been bd. Within the altar rails inscribed tablets now indicate where Anne Boleyn, Katharine Howard, the D. of Northumberland, the D. of Somerset, and the D. of Monmouth are bd. Lady Jane Grey and Ld. Guildford Dudley are said to rest near the foot of the Blount monument, but it was considered unsafe to verify this lest the monument should be damaged. The names of those whose interments were not thus verified, but are known to be bd. before the altar, are recorded on a stone on the floor just outside the altar railings. During these investigations the coffin plates of three of the Scotch nobility executed in 1746–7 were found—E. of Kilmarnock, Ld. Balmerino, and Ld. Lovat. They are now displayed on the W. wall. There was once a burial ground outside and here the male accomplices of Anne Boleyn were bd.

The dedication of this chapel is unusual. There is another at Cudworth in Warwickshire. 'Ad Vincula'—in chains—refers to the apostle's miraculous release from his first imprisonment in Jerusalem. On 1st Aug. each yr., at the ch. of S. Pietro in Vincoli in Rome the chains are shown. A chapel so dedicated is known to have been in existence in the T. in John's reign, but the present bdg. was erected by Edward I—1305–6. In its present state it is largely the work of Henry VIII. The fine chestnut roof dates from the latter part of his reign. The arches and the windows, except that over the W. entrance, are of the same period. Of the two altars the chief was dedicated to St. Peter. The other, in the N. aisle, was in honour of the Virgin, and there is a hagioscope cut through the wall. The view through it is now blocked by the Blount monument. Sir Richd. and Sir Michael Blount both held office for Q. Elizabeth as Lieutenants of the T. Philip Howard, E. of Arundel, reproved the latter's brutality upon his deathbed, saying to him:

'When a prisoner come hither to this Tower, he bringeth sorrow with him; then do not add affliction to affliction. Your commission is only to keep with safety, not to kill with severity.'

Sir Richd. and Sir Michael, 'according to tradition,' says Maj.-Gen. Sir Geo. Younghusband, 'conceived the quaint conceit of placing their skulls in niches in the alabaster frieze which forms the monument. One of these skulls is still in place, and was not long ago taken down and verified as a genuine skull. The other was lost or mislaid, and has in some previous century been replaced by a plaster replica.' A daughter, Lyster Blount, was also interred here, a tablet recording it ending with the words: 'Here they all lye to expect ye coming of our sweet Saviour Jesus. Amen, Amen.' There is also a fine sarcophagus erected in 1522 by Sir Richd. Cholmondeley, Lieutenant of the T. He and his wife intended to occupy it and blanks are left for the dates of death. Sir Richd. d. elsewhere in 1544, and neither he nor his wife was bd. here. During the restoration of 1876 the tomb, which bears upon it their recumbent figures in alabaster, was opened. It was found to contain nothing but the fragments of a font of Edward III's time. This was repaired and now stands at the SW. corner of the chapel. An old stone on the S. wall is inscribed as follows:

'Here lieth ye body of Talbot Edwards gentn late Keeper of his Mats Regalia who dyed ye 30 of September 1674. Aged 80 yeares and 9 moneths.'

This was the Keeper of the Regalia when Col. Blood made his attempt to steal the Crown Jewels.

The T. has had its amenities in times past, though they pale into insignificance against its harsh asperities. Up to the time of Charles II it was the practice of English sovereigns to spend the night before the coronation within its fastness. Perhaps it was then discontinued because the royal apartments had been demolished. They stood between the White Tower and the river. Probably in the great hall Anne Boleyn was tried in 1536. Either here or in the Lieutenant's Lodgings were Q. Elizabeth's apartments. Cromwell is said to have been responsible for their demolition. Some of the Plantagenets resided there at times, but there are no traditions of feasting as at other royal palaces. There were, too, taverns within the outer wall. There was the 'King's Head,' and an iron bar which bore its sign still projects from the Bell Tower. A similar sign was the 'Cold-Harbour,' near the Byward Tower. One tavern, the 'Gold Chain' remained until 1843.

The most cheery association of the T. was for many centuries its menagerie. It came into existence in the reign of Henry III. A present of three leopards (symbolic of the English king's coat of arms), sent him in 1235 by the Emperor Frederick II, made a beginning. In the same yr. the collection was increased by the addition of a white bear, for the maintenance of which the Privy Purse allowed 4d. a day. Two orders relating to it still exist. One of these reveals that it was sent from Norway, and directs that there should be procured 'one muzzle and one iron chain, to hold that bear without the water.' There was also to be 'one long and strong cord to hold him when fishing in the River Thames.' Evidently, therefore, the animal was encouraged to catch its own food. In 1255 Henry III was presented with an elephant by King Louis of France, and it was commanded that a house 40 ft. long by 20 ft. deep should be built for it. Edward III added to the collection in the T., a lion, a lioness, a leopard, and two wild cats. In 1436 it was recorded that 'there deyde all the lyons that were in the Tour of London, the which was nought sen in no mannys tyme before out of mynde.' In Elizabeth's reign Paul Hentzner, the German traveller, gave a list of the animals kept in the Lion Tower. He mentions 'three lionesses,' a large lion called Edward VI from his having been born in his reign, a 'tyger,' a 'lynx,' a wolf excessively old—a very scarce animal in England,' a porcupine, and an eagle.

'All these creatures are kept in a remote place, fitted up for the purpose with wooden lattices at the Queen's expense.'

James I had no liking for the T., but would be induced to go to see bear-baitings and similar 'sports.' In 1604 he and the entire court visited the Lion Tower to see the edifying spectacle of a combat between a lion and a lioness and a live cock. In 1609 he was there again with his Q. and P. Henry to witness a fight between a bear which, having killed a child, was 'doomed to punish-ment,' and a lion. Several lions were brought out, but they, one and all, on

seeing the bear, turned tail and hid in their cages. Finally, to please the K., the bear was baited to death with dogs. In 1682 two lions were brought from Tunis in Barbary—one called Charles and the other Catherine. Nicholas Luttrell noted an accident in 1686:

'A woman that lokt after the lions at the Tower putting her hand to near the old one he caught hold of it and grip'd it so hard that it was forc'd to be cut off to prevent gangrene, but she died of it in a little time.'

By the 18th century the number of lions had increased to eleven, five being the gifts of the Emperor of Morocco to Q. Anne and one a gift from the consul of Algiers. In 1775 George III was pre-sented with another from Senegal. In a guide to the T.L. of 1792 the animals come first. It appears from this book that an ostrich had lately died, revealing eighty nails hidden in its stomach. There were also some monkeys, two black bears from N. America, a hyena from the E. Indies, two racoons, and an eagle. There were in addition to lions, lionesses, leopards, etc. At one time it was a hoax to persuade the country cousin that the lions were annually washed, and that the operation was one worth witnessing. Probably loafers round the entrances to the T. sold the tickets for the exhibition, which Mr. W. G. Bell reproduces in one of his two books on the T. In this case there was a double hoax, for the year is 1856, twenty-one years after all the animals had been removed; the date, too, is 1st April! In the last days of the collection the following notice appeared in the *Sunday Times* in 1827:

'Few objects are calculated to throw a greater lustre on our national charac-ter, in an emulative point of view, than the splendid specimens of savage nature which the resources of Govern-ment have succeeded in collecting. Birds, beasts, reptiles, in endless variety, press on the spectator's view, and lead him through a labyrinth of wonderment superior to any ever before exhibited.'

The collection was taken to Regent's Park in 1835, and this led to the removal of the Lion Tower, which stood where is now the ticket office. Now a feature of the T. is the ravens—maintained by the Office of Works. In 1946 in the T. an

American homing pigeon was presented with the Dickin Medal for gallantry. It took place here because the exploit was associated with the 56th London Division during the allied campaign in Italy.

The exhibits in the T. attract less attention than the bdg. itself, save for the instruments of torture mentioned. On the first floor of the White Tower there are models of the T. in 1842, 1882, and 1890, and a model of the White Tower as it was in 1597. Also here are two wooden figures of 'Gin' and 'Beer' which once stood over the buttery and pantry of Greenwich Palace. There is a very large collection of armour; that of Henry VIII attracts most attention.

The first Yeoman Warder who can be traced by name is John O'London, who lived in the 14th century. The word 'beefeaters' is quite unjustified. They have no connection, except in respect of uniform, with the yeomen who in times past served the buffet at St. James's Palace, and became known as Buffetiers.

The T.L. is now under the control of three officers, the Constable, the Lieutenant, and the Major and Resident Governor. The Lieutenant has had his private residence outside since about 1689. Long before that the Constable had given up residing within; his office is now a nominal one.

In the First World War eleven spies were shot in the miniature rifle range beside the Martin Tower. They were bd. in Brixton Prison.

From 25th Apr. to 15th May 1916, Sir Roger Casement was a prisoner in the T. He was hanged at Pentonville Prison on 3rd Aug. 1916.

In the Second World War, 15 H.E. bombs fell on and in the precincts of the T., and three flying bombs burst beside it. The N. bastion (1848) was hit twice; a canteen which housed the main guard was burnt out; a portion of the hospital block was destroyed; some residences were demolished and others wrecked. Although there were 1,227 alerts sounded in the vicinity, no damage was caused to the ancient parts of the T., though two bombs missed the White Tower by seven yds. There were five killed, including a Yeoman Warder.

In Aug. 1939, the Crown Jewels were removed to an unknown destination, and by instalments the armour was taken away. The T. was used for prisoners of war. These included Herr Gerlach, German Consul in Iceland, who was confined in the K.'s house in 1940 for $3\frac{1}{2}$ months, and Herr Rudolf Hess, deputy Führer, who was there for four days. His signature is exhibited in the Beauchamp Tower. One spy was shot in the T.

(See *The Tower from Within*, by Sir Geo. John Younghusband, 1918; *The Tower of London*, by W. G. Bell, 1935; *St. Peter's Chapel in the Tower of London*, by Doyne C. Bell, 1877; *His Majesty's Tower of London*, by Col. E. H. Carkeet-James, Resident Governor and Major, 1950; *The Tower*, by J. E. N. Hearsey, 1960.)

Trafalgar Square, as the name implies, is one of L.'s modern improvements. The neighbourhood in medieval times is described under 'Charing Cross.' In Agas's map part of the site is covered by the King's Mews and St. Martin's Lane, though on the W. side it appears fairly open. In Rocque's map (1746) the sts. seem quite congested. The area was laid out as a war memorial between 1829 and 1841, and there then disappeared some squalid courts in a vicinity known as 'Porridge Island,' because of the cheap cookshops thereabouts; it was introduced by Mrs. Thrale into a bantering conversation with Dr. Johnson. Part of St. Martin's Lane went too; previously it joined the N. side of the Strand, and to-day there is a reminder of this in the curious fact that its first number is 28. The Nelson column was very slowly erected. It was begun in 1840, but the figure of Nelson was not hoisted to the top until 4th and 5th Nov. 1843—it was a piecemeal performance.

The panels were not fixed until 1849–52, and not until 1867 did the lions appear. It is a Corinthian column of granite. The capital is of bronze cast from cannon recovered from the wreck of the *Royal George*. The stone statue is 17 ft. high; it weighs 16 tons. The distance from the pavement to the top of Nelson's hat is 184 ft. Nelson is represented in full-dress uniform; a capstan has been introduced. On the sides of the pedestal are four bronze bas-reliefs, cast from the metal of captured French cannon, and representing incidents in the battles of St. Vincent,

Aboukir, Copenhagen, and Trafalgar. It was designed by W. Railton; E. H. Bailey was the sculptor of the statue, and Sir Edwin Landseer of the lions. The total cost was £50,000, of which £20,000 was raised by subscription, and the remainder voted by Parliament. On the N. side of the sq. there are busts of Admirals Jellicoe, Beatty and Cunningham. The capacious lamp standard at the SE. corner of the sq. is a conning-tower for the police. The small cell within has a telephone in direct communication with Scotland Yard, and the slits like arrow-holes in medieval castles enable a look-out to be kept without the observers being under observation. On the E. side are the offices of the S. African Govt., who acquired Morley's Hotel in 1921 and erected the present handsome structure 1931–2. On the W. side are the Canadian Govt. offices; and close by is Norway House, formally opened by K. Haakon in 1911.

Spring Gardens, at the SW. corner of the sq., are first heard of about 1610. The name was that of a pleasance which, as part of St. James's Park, was at first probably a royal resort. Hentzner, the German visitor, in 1598, described a garden in which was a—

'jet d'eau, with a sundial, at which, while strangers are looking, a quantity of water forced by a wheel, which the gardener turns at a distance, through a number of little pipes, plentifully sprinkles those that are standing round.'

A little later it appears the public were admitted. In 1629 a bowling-green was constructed in the gardens for Charles I with turf brought from Blackheath, and a new garden house erected for the K. to rest in. In 1634 it was temporarily closed, having apparently been ill-used by the public, and a new Spring Garden opened behind the Mews (see 'Charing Cross'). This does not appear to have been a success, and the old Spring Garden was reopened. Evelyn was there in 1649. Cromwell closed it in 1654, but it was open again before his death, for in May 1658 Evelyn 'collationed' there. In a work entitled *A Character of England*, published in 1659, and attributed to Evelyn, there is a pleasing account of the gardens. The writer refers to

'the solemness of the grove, the warbling of the birds . . . the thickets of the gardens seem to be contrived to all

advantages of gallantry.'

Pepys does not seem to have gone, although he went a number of times to the new Spring Garden at 'Foxhall', whose attractions seem to have caused those of the one at Charing Cross to fade away. The garden at Vauxhall was the predecessor of the famous Vauxhall Gardens (*q.v.*).

In excavating the foundations of the National Provincial (formerly Drummond's) Bank at the corner of Spring Gardens, a number of remains of pre-historic animals were found (see *The Making of London*, by Sir Laurence Gomme, 1911).

In Spring Gardens was the first County Hall of the L.C.C. It was erected in 1860 for the M.B.W. Some depts. of the L.C.C. remained in this bdg., which, during the Second World War, was occupied by the Canadian Beaver Club. The old council chamber was badly damaged by bombs.

The Admiralty Arch across The Mall was erected in 1910.

(See 'National Gallery' and 'Statues and Other Memorials.')

Trinity House is believed to have originated early in the 15th century, in a fraternity of pilots, seamen, and mariners at what was known as Deptford Strond. Harben says the house they occupied was pulled down in 1787. The next meeting-place was at Ratcliff, and the date when this was first occupied is not ascertainable. In 1514 Henry VIII bestowed upon the fraternity, then one with some centuries of history behind it, a charter with the title of 'The Brotherhood of the Most Glorious and Undivided Trinity of Deptford-Stronde.' The charter gave the brotherhood charge of all sea marks, and made it advisory to the navy. Later it acquired some measure of control over the Deptford Dockyard, and of naval stores on the banks of the Thames. During the religious troubles of Edward VI's reign an attack was ingeniously avoided by a change in the title, and it has since been known as the Corporation of Trinity House on Deptford Strand. The work of the corporation suffered from lack of income, and in Q. Elizabeth's reign, through the efforts of Ld. Howard of Effingham, a steady revenue was assigned to it from Thames ballast dues. In Charles I's time Trinity House was given the task of organizing against piracy at sea, and of keeping the 'fairway' clear of wrecks and obstructions. As a corporation it was suppressed by the Commonwealth, and maintained as a Govt. dept. The rights and privileges of Trinity House were also assailed in the reign of Charles II, who, to fill his always needy purse, granted patents to individuals to erect lighthouses, and extract by other means profits out of shipping. At that time Trinity House was in Water Lane (Great Tower St.), but there was an additional office at Ratcliff. The Water Lane premises were burnt in the G.F. and rebuilt in 1671. A second fire burned this new bdg. in 1714. The bdg. on Tower Hill was built 1793–5 by Samuel Wyatt. The bdg. was burnt out in the Second World War, and the contents destroyed.

In 1836 the Corporation of Trinity House was given complete control of all English lighthouses (it built its first in 1680). At present it consists of a Master, a Deputy Master, who is a practical seaman, and nine Elder Brethren. In addition there are a number of Honorary Elder Brethren, who have no voice in the control. The Younger Brethren number 200, the necessary qualification being captain's rank in the merchant service, or lieutenant's rank in the Royal Navy. They are elected by the Elder Brethren. In addition to lighthouses, Trinity House has complete control over all lightships in British waters and a number of buoys. It also maintains steam cutters at Dungeness, and the Sunk to put pilots on board all ships coming into Gravesend. It works in close association with the Navy, particularly with the hydrographic department.

Tussaud's Exhibition. Madame Tussaud was the daughter of a Swiss clergyman, and at the age of 6 was adopted by an uncle who practised in Paris the fashionable art of clay-modelling, for which she early revealed a remarkable aptitude. She passed through the horrors of the French Revolution and arrived in England in 1802, bringing models of the heads of many of its victims. She seems first to have shown her exhibits in Fleet St. and the Lowther Arcade in the Strand. Afterwards she was at the old Lyceum Theatre in the Strand, before she went on tour in England, Scotland, and Ireland. It was not until 1833 that the exhibition had a permanent L. home. Then, after

a short period in Assembly Rooms attached to the Green Man Hotel at Blackheath, it was removed to the Assembly Rooms adjoining the Royal L. Bazaar in the Gray's Inn Rd. In 1835 it removed to Baker St. Madame Tussaud d. 1850 at about 90 yrs. of age. In 1884 the collection, then consisting of more than 400 figures, was removed to the premises in Marylebone Rd. which were burned down in 1925. A new bdg., including a cinema and restaurant, was constructed. In the fire many of the most valuable treasures perished, including Napoleon's carriage, some relics of Newgate Gaol, and a doorway from Horsemonger Lane Jail (see 'Prisons'). There still remain, however, the cell which Ld. Geo. Gordon, leader of the 'No Popery' (1780) rioters, occupied in Newgate; and there are figures of Mr. and Mrs. Manning (see 'Prisons'—Horsemonger Lane) also in the 'Chamber of Horrors.' Once Chas. Dickens was there, but only as a victim of the guillotine. A discarded figure of the novelist, lying head downwards, was not recognized by visitors! Cardinal Wolsey's figure holds an orange in his hand, as does the cardinal in a picture at the Guildhall Art Gallery. This is explained in the *Life of Wolsey* by his gentleman-usher, Geo. Cavendish; describing his pompous and ceremonious walks abroad, he says he went

'holding in his hand a very fair orange, whereof the meat or substance within was taken out, and filled up again with the part of a sponge, wherein was vinegar, and other confections against the pestilent airs; to the which he most commonly smelt unto, passing among the press, or else when he was pestered with many suitors.'

As the label on the cardinal makes no reference to this habit, it is to be feared that very few understand it, and probably some suppose that the cardinal habitually ate oranges in public! The Exhibition has been extended and shows new 'celebrities' as they achieve fame; associated with it is a nearby Planetarium.

Tyburn has a history in singular contrast to the derivation of the name (see 'Lost Rivers'). The place of execution W. of L.—to 'go west' in Elizabethan literature meant to end life there—was used so long ago as 1196. In that yr. Fitzosbert, otherwise 'Longbeard,' a rebel against Richard I's govt. who commanded a large following, according to Ralph de Diceto, a contemporary chronicler, had 'his hands bound behind him, his feet tied with long cords,' and was 'drawn by means of a horse through the midst of the city to the gallows near Tyburn.' Another contemporary writer, Gervase of Canterbury, does not mention Tyburn, but refers to 'the Elms.' A place of execution at Smithfield was so called, and Stow states that this was where Fitzosbert suffered. In face, however, of the definite statement of Ralph de Diceto, Stow cannot be accepted on this point. Moreover, the gallows at Tyburn were specifically at an early date called the 'King's gallows,' probably because they were used for political offenders, and Fitzosbert would be regarded as such. In 1220 there was an order from Henry III to the sheriff of Middlesex to cause two good gibbets to be made in the place where the gallows was formerly erected, viz. at the Elms, and this was probably Tyburn. In 1222, Constantine Fitz-Athulf, leader of a riot in L., to obviate a popular tumult was taken by water to the place of execution. This, therefore, cannot have been Smithfield. Probably he was landed at Westminster, or the Horseferry, both convenient for Tyburn. In 1305 Wm. Wallace was dragged there for a barbarous execution. Roger Mortimer, E. of March, was executed there in 1330. In 1388 Sir Robt. Tresilian, and Sir Nicholas Brembre (Ld.M. 1377 and 1378, and from 1383 to 1385) were hanged at Tyburn. There is an interesting allusion to it in *Piers the Plowman*. In the B and C texts of the poem (the former dates from about 1377) the advantages of learning in procuring 'benefit of clergy' are alluded to as follows:

'Wel may the barne blisse that hym to boke sette;
That lyuyne after letterure saved hym lyf and soule!
Dominus par hereditatis mee is a meri verset,
That has take fro Tybourne twenti strong theves;
There lewed theves ben lolled up loke how thei be saved!'

In 1447 an extraordinary thing happened. Five men were sentenced to execution in connection with the mysterious death of the 'good Duke Humphrey.' They had been cut down alive, stripped, and marked for dismemberment, when a reprieve arrived. The hangman was entitled to the clothes of his victims. He refused to part with them, and the reprieved gentlemen, nudists willy-nilly, walked naked back to the City. Perkin Warbeck was hanged at Tyburn in 1496, Elizabeth Barton, the 'Holy Maid of Kent,' in 1534, the Carthusians (see 'Charterhouse') in 1535. In 1594 Dr. Lopez, a Jewish physician, accused of an attempt to poison Q. Elizabeth, was executed here. In 1660 the bodies of Cromwell, Ireton, and Bradshaw were hanged from angles of the gallows until sunset. They were then taken down and beheaded, the heads being placed on Westminster Hall. Claude Duval perished here in 1670, and in 1681 Oliver Plunket. He was Abp. of Armagh, and was accused of engaging with the French in a plot to murder all the Protestants. He has been canonized recently. In 1717 a most piquant incident occurred *en route*. Wm. Marvell, the executioner, was arrested for debt. The bailiff who had served the writ intimated his willingness to wait until the latter had done his day's work, but the mob would not have it, they pounced upon Marvell and mauled him so badly that he lost consciousness. The grim procession restarted, and at Tyburn a bricklayer volunteered to be deputy-hangman. The mob, however, fell upon him also, and nearly beat him to death. Eventually the three criminals were taken back to Newgate, and the sentence was commuted to one of penal servitude. In 1724 Jack Sheppard was executed at Tyburn, and in 1725 Fielding's 'Jonathan Wild the Great.' The great novelist's account of his end is delicious:

'We must not, however, omit one circumstance, as it serves to show the most admirable conservation of character in our hero to his last moment, which was that, whilst the ordinary [the chaplain] was busy in his ejaculations, Wild, in the midst of the shower of stones, etc. which played upon him, applied his hands to the person's pocket, and emptied it of his bottle-screw, which he carried out of the world in his hand. The ordinary being now descended from the cart, Wild had just opportunity to cast his eyes around the crowd, and to give them a hearty curse, when immediately the horses moved on, and with universal applause our hero swung out of this world.'

It was at this time that condemned prisoners had taken to the strange habit of making the last journey in a shroud. Whether there was a melodramatic motive in this, or a fervent desire of the unrighteous to rob the executioner of his perquisites in the form of their clothes, it is impossible to say. In one of the *Newgate Calendars* there is a picture of Stephen Gardiner in a dainty shroud that looks like a lady's night-dress, receiving the final attentions of 'Jack Ketch.' (The latter was the actual name of the executioner from 1663 to 1686.) In 1726 Catherine Hayes (the subject of a story by Thackeray) was to be half hanged and then burned alive for murdering her husband. The faggots, however, were prematurely ignited, and she was slowly roasted. When E. Ferrers was executed in 1760 for murdering his steward, he was brought from the T.L. in a landau drawn by six horses. He was dressed in a light suit, embroidered with silver, said to have been worn on the occasion of his wedding. Behind it was a hearse with six horses. The journey took 2¾ hours. It was said that in deference to his rank the E. would be hanged in a silken cord, but this was not forthcoming. His body was taken to the Surgeons' Hall for dissection. In 1777 the execution of Dr. Dodd, for whom Dr. Johnson vainly endeavoured to obtain a reprieve, drew the largest crowd ever known to Tyburn. There were rumours that he would be resuscitated with the connivance of the hangman, Dennis, a notable figure in *Barnaby Rudge*. He was to be taken for treatment to the house of an undertaker in Goodge St., Tottenham Court Rd. He was left hanging too long. In 1779, when the Rev. Jas. Hackman was executed for shooting Miss Martha Ray, the mistress of Ld. Sandwich, Jas. Boswell accompanied the murderer in the prison coach. He was attired in a decent suit of black that he kept for such occasions. He took Sir Joshua Reynolds to Tyburn on one occasion and received from him a letter of thanks.

'I am convinced,' the latter wrote, 'it is a vulgar error in the opinion that it is so terrible a spectacle, or that it in any way implies a hardness of heart or cruelty of disposition.'

Dennis's last famous victim was Wm. Ryland, the engraver, hanged for forgery on 29th Aug. 1783. On 7th Nov. 1783 the last Tyburn execution—that of John Austin—took place.

There has been considerable discussion as to the exact site of the gallows. It has, however, been established that from 1571 to 1759 the triangular form permanently stood near where is now Marble Arch, and opposite the mouth of Edgware Rd. In the latter yr. the permanent structure was removed, its site being taken by the turnpike gates. (A correspondent of *John o' London's Weekly*, in 1921, mentioned that he had been shown these gates, in a good state of preservation, at the 'Welsh Harp,' Hendon. They were removed in 1829.) For executions thereafter moving gallows were used, and there are various places suggested for the site of this, i.e. 49 Connaught Sq., and a house on the N. side of Upper Bryanston St., a few doors from Edgware Rd. There, below the level of the st., according to a writer in *Notes and Queries* in 1873, was a massive brickwork pillar, in the centre of which was a large socket, 'evidently for one of the pillars of the old gallows.' Another place mentioned was Connaught Place, and a correspondent of *The Times* in 1860 called attention to the discovery there of human bones which might have been those of the hangman's victims. The corner of Upper Seymour St. was a spot also favoured. It is said that the last gallows was chopped up and used for stands for beer-barrels in a tavern in Adam St. West, now Seymour Pl.

A bronze tablet was affixed to the railings of Hyde Park by the Office of Works, bearing the following inscription:

'TYBURN TREE

The triangular stone in the roadway sixty-nine feet north of this point indicates the site of the ancient gallows known as Tyburn Tree, which was demolished in 1759.'

The site is now covered by a large traffic island with fountains which retains the name of 'Tyburn Way.'

In Tyburn Convent in the Bayswater Rd., about 100 yds. from the Tyburn tablet, until bombing in the Second World War, the altar was designed in the form of 'the triple tree.'

Tyburn was not the sole place of execution before the 18th century. Up to then it appears to have been favoured only for prisoners of some importance. The Elms at Smithfield, already mentioned, was a common place. A few executions took place at St. Giles's in the Fields. Sir John Oldcastle in 1417 suffered there because it was the place where he had assembled his followers. In 1586 some of the Babington conspirators (see 'Lincoln's Inn Fields') were executed there. It was never a regular place of execution. At the Bowl Tavern at St. Giles's in the Fields the criminal had a final drink. Leopold Wagner says that to more gentlemanly sufferers sherry was given instead at the 'George and Blue Boar,' 285 High Holborn, now a railway goods yard. Swift says:

'Clever Tom Clinch, when the rabble was bawling,
Rode stately through Holborn to die of his calling.
He stopt at the George for a bottle of sack
And promised to pay for it when he came back.'

Sometimes the place of punishment was planned to suit the crime. Stow saw a prisoner 'executed upon the pavement of my doore, where I then kept house,' i.e. within Aldgate. In 1619 Sepcoats Mullingay was hanged 'over against the King's Head Taverne in Fleete Street.' In 1661 Venner, the leader of the Fifth Monarchy insurrection, and Hodgkins, were hanged and quartered in Coleman St., and two others implicated at the end of Wood St. The murderers of Thos. Thynne (see 'Westminster Abbey') were executed in Pall Mall in 1682. In 1733 Sarah Malcolm (see 'Temple') was executed at the Fleet St. end of Mitre Court. In 1761 Theodore Gardelle, the French miniature painter, who murdered his landlady in Leicester Sq., was hanged in Haymarket.

(See L.C.C. pamphlet; *Tyburn Tree; its History and Annals*, by Alfd. Marks, 1908; *The Hangmen of England*, by Horace Bleakley, 1929; *The road to Tyburn*, by A. K. Hibbert, 1957.)

U

University College (Gower St.) was founded in 1826 through the efforts of Ld. Brougham, Thos. Campbell, the poet, Jeremy Bentham and others (see 'University of London'). The object was to provide a literary and scientific education to students of all denominations at a small cost. The foundation stone was laid by the D. of Sussex in 1827, and the bdg. —designed by Wm. Wilkins—opened in 1828. It was first called the University of L., but a few yrs. after the foundation, when the present University of L. was founded, the name was changed. In 1900 when the University of L. was reorganized and became a teaching, as well as an examining body, University Coll. was affiliated to it as one of its schs.

The library contained over 500,000 books and pamphlets, of which about 70,000 were lost during the Second World War. Its principal exhibit was the skeleton of Jeremy Bentham who d. in 1832. Under his will the body was dissected, and the bones wired together so that the skeleton was complete. He sits in a chair he used in life; in the attitude in which he sat when engaged in thought; and in one of his own suits and hats. The face was modelled from a portrait, and the skull, in a small case at the bottom of the larger one, was found stowed away in the packing of the body. Bentham's idea was that in this way he should appear still to be presiding over meetings of the council of the coll. Nowadays, however, his posthumous presence is not desired, and he remains in his cabinet. The skeleton was removed to Stanstead Bury (Herts.) during the Second World War. There were then destroyed a statue of Sir Thos. Browne, and a bronze portrait plaque of Mrs. Craigie ('John Oliver Hobbes'), unveiled by Viscount Curzon in 1908. She was a student 1889–92. It was erected by public subscription, and out of the same fund an English literature scholarship named after that writer was created.

University of London. The first public pronouncement of a proposed L. University was in a letter in *The Times* of 9th Feb. 1825. It was an open letter from Thos. Campbell, the poet, to Ld. Brough-

am. The latter, in the same yr. vainly introduced into the H.C. a measure for the purpose of providing university education at an incorporated college in L. for those who could not proceed to the ancient universities. Nothing daunted by this failure, an appeal by Campbell and his associates was so successful that a sum of £160,000 was raised by subscribers who made a Deed of Settlement and became 'Proprietors of the University of London.' Land had been acquired in Gower St., and in 1827 the foundation of a new bdg., to be known as University Coll., was laid by the D. of Sussex. In 1831, on a site in the Strand presented by the Govt., King's Coll. (*q.v.*) was opened.

At first the application of 'London University' for incorporation and degree-giving powers met with bitter opposition. It was not until 1836 that a Charter was obtained from William IV. The first Chairman of the Senate was the E. of Burlington, afterwards the D. of Devonshire. The Senate was required to hold examinations for degrees once at least in every yr. Before 1858 only students of affiliated cols. were allowed to take the examinations. After 1878 women were also allowed to take degree examinations, L. being the first university to recognize them. Another innovation was that in awarding degrees in the faculty of arts the English language was to be considered as a necessary branch of study in addition to Greek and Latin. In 1859 special provision was made for including English Philology and Literature in the examinations for degrees and honours in the Arts. L. University also founded for the first time in England a faculty of Science, and in 1860 began to hold examinations for the degrees of bachelor and doctor in that faculty. The First Doctor of Science was admitted in 1862, and the first Doctor of Literature in 1868. Degrees of Surgery were instituted in 1863, and in Music in 1877.

The first premises were in Somerset House. In 1853 the University was removed to what was described as a 'miserable garret in Marlborough House.' This was only temporary accommodation, and in 1855 a move was made to Burlington House. In 1870 a new bdg., which was erected for the University at Burlington Gardens (now occupied by the Civil

Service Commission), was opened by Q. Victoria, and this was used until 1900. In that yr. an arrangement was made with the Govt. by which these premises were vacated, and the University was given the use of those portions of the Imperial Institute at S. Kensington which it occupied as headquarters until 1936. It had long been felt that the University should have its headquarters in a bdg. of its own, and in 1927 the Senate, with a gift of £400,000 from the Rockefeller Foundation and the grant of £125,000 from the Treasury, were enabled to purchase a site in Bloomsbury, near the B. Mus. The architect chosen was Chas. Holden, F.R.I.B.A., and on 26th June 1933 George V laid the foundation stone. Grants to cover the costs of the bdg. had been sent from all quarters—in addition to the Treasury, from county councils of L. and the home counties, C.C., City Livery Cos., business houses, etc. Considerable progress had been made in the erection of the bdg. when the Second World War came, and by then the Institute of Education, the School of Slavonic and East European studies, and the Institute of Historical Research were housed in the new bdg. It was then taken over by the Govt. for the Ministry of Education. The official headquarters of L. University were then removed to the Royal Holloway Coll., Egham, and later to Richmond Coll. The only departments remaining at Bloomsbury were the Library and the Maintenance Department.

After the war bdg. work was completed.

There are 14 Institutes (including the Warburg Inst., and the Courtauld Inst. of Art) and 18 Schools (including Bedford, Birkbeck, King's and Queen Mary Colleges, and the Imperial College). There are also Medical Schools (including St. Bartholomew's, St. Thomas's, Guy's and Westminster Hospitals), Training Colleges and Veterinary Colleges. University extension and tutorial classes have been a feature since 1902, and courses are held at a number of L. centres, where full-time and part-time studies over a number of yrs. are encouraged. These courses are not primarily for those taking degrees, but diplomas are granted to full-time students. In 1838 there were only 23 candidates for matriculation; in 1850, 299; now there are 3,978 full-time staff, 24,990 full-time and 8,850 part-time students. Of the full-time students, 20,368 came from the U.K., 2,568 from the Commonwealth, and 2,054 from other countries.

The Library dates from 1838 when a gift of books was made. It now contains more than 500,000 books. There are some special collections, e.g. Goldsmiths' Co.'s Library of Economic Literature (about 56,000 books and pamphlets); Grote Library (5,000 volumes, mostly Greek and Latin classics); Durning Lawrence Library. Part of the room in which it is housed has been reproduced to resemble the library of the donor at 13 Carlton House Terrace. It includes a copy of the first four folios of the Shakespeare plays, a collection of incunabula, early Bibles, many of Defoe's works in original editions, and most of the works published touching the Baconian theory of Shakespeare authorship. There is also the Austin Dobson Collection. This was presented by his son Alban T. A. Dobson in 1945. It includes the original manuscripts of Austin Dobson's poems, and every edition of his works in their original bindings.

Amongst manuscripts the library owns a MS. life of the Black Prince, a metrical chronicle dating from the end of the 14th century; the original agreement made in Calais between the envoys of Henry V and the D. of Burgundy, redressing infringements of the truce with Flandera; a signed dispatch in Arabic sent by Gen. Gordon from Khartoum on 22nd June 1884, and received on 23rd Aug.

V

Vauxhall Gardens were in the par. of Lambeth (*q.v.*). In 1728 Jonathan Tyers (whose son Thos. was one of Johnson's many biographers) took a lease of the old 'Spring Gardens' for thirty yrs. He embarked upon reconstruction and improvement, and opened in 1732 with a 'ridotto alfresco,' at which the P. of Wales was present. The admission was one guinea, the hours 9 p.m. to 4 a.m. Attractions increased; Hogarth painted pictures—one was said to be Henry VIII and Anne Boleyn, but was recognized for Fredk., P. of Wales, and his mistress; Cheere produced leaden statuary. Later came Roubiliac with a statue of Handel; it is said also one of Milton. An orchestra in the Gothic style appeared in 1758. There were a pavilion, tree-lined walks, and a semicircular arcade; at night hundreds of small lamps. The novels of Richardson, Fielding, and Smollett introduce it as a resort of gaiety which every Londoner periodically visited, and every country cousin felt he must 'do.' Fanny Burney's Evelina (1778) has to confess after some days in L. that she has not been, and is informed: 'Why, you have seen nothing of London yet.' She goes, and is properly pleased:

'The trees, the numerous lights, and the company in the circle round the orchestra make a most brilliant and gay appearance. . . . There was a concert; in the course of which a hautbois concerto was so charmingly played, that I could have thought myself upon enchanted ground, had I had spirits more gentle to associate with. The hautbois in the open air is heavenly.'

The Victorian writers, in their generation, took their heroes and heroines there. One of Dickens's *Sketches by Boz* is on the subject of 'Vauxhall Gardens by Day,' and Amelia Sedley and Becky Sharp were accompanied there by Geo. Osborne and Joseph Sedley in *Vanity Fair*, whilst Pendennis also went to saunter in the dark walks, look at 'the devices of the lamps,' and consult the fortune-teller. In the 19th century rope-dancing and balloons became attractions. It deteriorated, and became too much the resort of rowdies. Gas-lamps were substituted for the old oil ones, but it was a gleam of 18th-century pleasure destined to fade away, and on 25th July 1859 it was finally closed, the firework display concluding with the pathetic device of 'Farewell for Ever.' An interesting reminiscence of Vauxhall Gardens in their last days is in the *Recollections and Experiences* of Edmund Yates, the friend of Dickens. He quoted one Hayward who had been a visitor:

'One night about 1850 the elder Miss Berry, aged 85, Horace Walpole's flame, asked me to escort her there, and she suddenly on entering the Gardens, looked at my white tie and she said to me, "The last time I was here I came with Beau Brummell who wore a white necktie for the first time and it attracted much notice, and there rose an inquiry whether Beau Brummell had taken orders." '

Now it is remembered by the names of a few sts. in Lambeth—'Marble Hall Lane,' a cul-de-sac N. of Vauxhall Bridge, which was probably where boats landed with visitors for the gardens; Tyers St.; and Italian Walk. St. Peter's Ch., Upper Kennington Lane, is also on its site. Vauxhall Park is no part of the old gardens, nor is it on the site, though there, in 1922, a pageant was held by night, and the park lighted up by lamps, in an effort to recall the past of that far more celebrated pleasance. Its real successor was the Crystal Palace (see 'Hyde Park').

W

Wandsworth, now part of the L. Bor. of Wandsworth (although the eastern section is now in the L. Bor. of Lambeth), was the largest met. bor. (9,193 acres) and embraced the ancient pars. of Clapham, Putney, Streatham, Tooting, and Wandsworth.

That Wandsworth was settled so far back as the Palaeolithic Age is evident from the discovery at St. Anne's Hill, some sixty yrs. ago, of pear-shaped flint implements which are now in the B. Mus. The generally accepted meaning of the place-name is Wendel's farm. It is thrice mentioned in Domesday-book, but it was during the Middle Ages that craftsmen and traders discovered the valuable properties of the waters of the river Wandle. The City records of 1376 tell of an historic dispute between the 'fullers' and 'hurers' (fur-cap makers) regarding the use of this stream, and of the expulsion of the latter body after trial at Guildhall.

The par. ch. is All Saints', Wandsworth High St.; it is an ancient foundation though the present bdg. is in the main 18th century, with a modern chancel. The list of vicars begins with John de Panorino (1243) and certain of the memorials within the ch. are of singular interest. The oldest is a monumental brass, now affixed to the N. wall. It commemorates a knight named Nicholas, who is depicted in plate armour of the 15th century. The head is missing and the inscription mutilated, but the date of his death, 1420, and the words 'Servens Regis Henrice' conjure up visions of 'the warlike Harry' and the field of Agincourt. Nearby is the excellently preserved effigy of a benefactress Susanna Powel (d. 1630) 'daughter of Thomas Hayward of Wandsw^th yeomen of ye Guard unto King Henry ye 8 to King Edward ye 6 to Queen Mary & to Queen Elizabeth, and wife unto John Powel of Wandsworth, gent., who was servant to Queen Elizabeth and King James.' Her husband, the above mentioned John, d. 1611, as is recorded on a brass in the floor. Another fine monument perpetuates the memory of Henry Smyth, Alderman of L., d. 1627, who is shewn kneeling before an open Bible, a skull in his hands—emblems of immortality and mortality. He was a benefactor to many Surrey towns and villages, and to his birthplace Wandsworth; he also bequeathed 'one thousand (pounds) to buy lands for perpetuity to redeeme poor captives and prisoners from ye Turkish Tyranie.'

With the coming of the Huguenots new industries, such as dyeing, hatmaking, silk and calico printing, were introduced into Wandsworth. At the top of East Hill is the little Huguenot Burial Ground of Mount Nod, where amid the graves a memorial has been erected to those heroic exiles. Surmounted by the lilies of France and the standard of England is the inscription, 'Here rest many Huguenots who on the Revocation of the Edict of Nantes in 1685 left their native land for conscience' sake and found in Wandsworth freedom to worship God after their own manner. They established important industries and added to the credit and prosperity of the town of their adoption.' Below are inscribed the names of 30 notable Huguenot families.

A bridge spans the Wandle where anciently was only a ford. First built in 1602, it was reconstructed in 1757 and again in 1820 and in modern times. In the High St. is an old Friends' Meeting House, dating from 1697 but rebuilt 1778; and on St. Anne's Hill stands the ch. of that name, built by Smirke in 1823 in the classical style of the period.

Emanuel Sch. was founded under the will of Lady Anne Dacre in 1595, and stood originally in Westminster. It was incorporated under a Royal Charter of Q. Elizabeth dated 1601 as Emanuel Hosp., a charitable foundation for the maintenance of 20 poor aged men and women and 20 children, in Tothill Fields. In 1623 it was placed under the management of the Ld.M. and Aldermen of the City of L., and 200 yrs. later the number of children had risen to 68. Under the Endowed Schs. Act, the boys of several of the small charity schs. of Westminster were combined together at Emanuel Sch., which moved to its present home at Wandsworth in 1882. In the Chapel may be seen the original Jacobean pulpit, and an altar table, communion rails, and paintings of Moses and Aaron, from the demolished City Ch. of St. Benet Fink.

Putney also derives its name from a former inhabitant, and is Putta's hythe or quay.

The par. ch. of St. Mary stands by the river-side at the southern end of Putney Bridge. Its earliest record dates from 1302, but the present ch. was almost entirely rebuilt by E. Lapidge in 1836, only the 15th century tower being left. The glory of the place is Bp. West's Chapel, originally in the SE. corner of the ch. but taken down in 1836 and re-erected at the NE. corner. It is a little gem of Tudor architecture, and has a beautiful vaulted roof with armorial bosses. It also contains two interesting brasses representing John Welbeck (1477) and his wife Agnes (1478). Nicholas West, to whom the chapel stands as a memorial, was b. at Putney, the son of a baker. He was educated at King's Coll., Cambridge, where, it would seem, his conduct was not above reproach, but on reaching man's estate he grew wiser, attracted the attention of Henry VIII, and became successively Dean of Windsor (1510) and Bp. of Ely (1515). He d. 1533. Still better known is the scheming figure of Thos. Cromwell, the 'Hammer of the Monks.' He was b. in a cottage near Point Pleasant, the son of a man who seems to have followed a variety of trades, owning a fulling mill and being also a brewer, innkeeper, blacksmith, and shearer. His son Thos., too, found occupation as a common soldier, a clerk, wool merchant, and moneylender, before becoming the man of business to Wolsey, and, after his master's fall, Vicar-General and Chancellor. He was subsequently made Baron Cromwell and E. of Essex, but his recommendation of Anne of Cleves proved his undoing, and he d. by the axe in 1540.

Putney figured prominently in the Civil Wars, and in the summer of 1647 Oliver Cromwell made it the headquarters of the parliamentary army. Not many of its old houses now remain, but in one still standing in the High St. Leigh Hunt resided for a while. Algernon Chas. Swinburne lived with Theodore Watts-Dunton at The Limes, 11 Putney Hill (there is a tablet), and in a house called Lime Grove which once stood thereabouts Gibbon the historian was b. in 1727. George Eliot lived in Wimbledon Park Rd. in 1859–60; a tablet marks the house.

Clapham is an ancient village, the name of which probably signifies the homestead on the hill, standing on high ground overlooking the river.

The original par. ch. of Holy Trinity was finally cleared away in 1814, and occupied the site of the present St. Paul's Ch., built in the yr. of Waterloo. In the latter bdg. may still be seen some of the memorials from the old ch., including the finely executed marble effigies of Sir Richd. and Lady Rebecca Atkins and their three children. These lay hidden for many yrs. in the family vault, until in 1886 they were rediscovered by a local antiquary, J. W. Grover. In the vestry is a monument with a medallion portrait of Wm. Hewer, Treasurer for Tangier and a Commissioner of the Navy. He was a friend of Pepys, who d. at his house on the N. side of Clapham Common in 1703. Hewer, whose association with Clapham extended over 30 yrs., was a generous benefactor and rebuilt the N. aisle of the old ch. The oldest memorial is a small brass recording the death of Wm. Tableer in 1401.

The present par. ch. of Holy Trinity (consecrated in 1776), pleasantly situated on the Common, also exhibits features of considerable interest, but was badly damaged by blast from a rocket which fell close by. Within it largely retains the 18th-century appearance, though a new chancel was added in 1903. There are memorials to the saintly and scholarly rector John Venn (d. 1813), to John Jebb (d. 1833), 'the learned, the wise, the good' Bp. of Limerick, and to John Gillies (d. 1836), 'Historiographer to his Majesty for Scotland.' But what perhaps will most attract the visitor is the tablet on the outside of the S. wall of the ch. to the memory of—'The Clapham Sect, who in the latter part of the XVIIIth and early part of the XIXth centuries laboured so abundantly for the increase of National Righteousness and the Conversion of the Heathen and rested not until the curse of slavery was swept away from all parts of the British Dominions.' There follow the names of ten prominent members of the sect, which include those of Zachary Macaulay (father of Ld. Macaulay), Henry and John Thornton, Henry and John Venn, and Wm. Wilberforce. They are also commemorated in the new E. windows recently placed in the ch. (1950).

Clapham can still show a number of fine old houses, notably the row on the North Side dated 1720, and those in

Old Town, NE. of the ch. Here too is the parochial sch., many times rebuilt but founded in 1648. Notable residents include Ld. Macaulay at 5 The Pavement; J. F. Bentley, the architect of Westminster Cath., at 43 Old Town (a tablet was erected on the house in 1950); Sir Chas. Barry, the great Victorian architect; Samuel Pepys; Henry Cavendish the scientist; and Mrs. Cook, the widow of the famous circumnavigator. The R.C. Ch. in Clapham Park Rd. was built by Wardell in 1850, with later additions by J. F. Bentley, and has a fine spire.

Streatham is a name of doubtful origin, perhaps meaning 'the settlement by the road.'

Its ch., dedicated to St. Leonard, is of considerable antiquity, but was almost entirely rebuilt in 1831. The earliest recorded rector is Robt. Rothomago (1230), and the brass memorial remains of another, Wm. Mowfurth (d. 1513). Other interesting memorials are the mutilated effigy of Sir John Ward; the tablet, much adorned with heraldry, to Edmund Tylney (d. 1610) (see 'Clerkenwell'); the finely carved monument to John Howland (d. 1686); and the series of tablets commemorating the Thrale family, the inscription on Henry Thrale's having been composed by Dr. Johnson. There is also a 15th-century font, and a fine Jacobean pulpit.

Opposite the par. ch. is the R.C. Ch. of the English Martyrs (1896). Christ Ch. is an interesting bdg. in the Venetian style by Wild (1841), and in Streatham Vale is a modern ch. of the Holy Redeemer, erected in 1931 from designs of Martin Travers, in memory of the Clapham Sect.

The attractions of 17th-century Streatham were enhanced by the discovery in 1637 of a spring of mineral water said to possess valuable medicinal qualities. Streatham thereupon became quite a fashionable spa, and a Well House was erected to accommodate visitors. The original well was in what is now a delightful public park called the Rookery. Other wells were discovered subsequently, and the pump house erected over one of these in 1792 may still be seen in Valley Rd.

Streatham Place enjoyed an interesting literary association with Dr. Johnson, who here had an apartment set aside for him in the villa residence of Mr. and Mrs. Thrale, where he almost became one of the family. A summer house from the garden, in which Johnson is said to have written part of the *Lives of the Poets*, is now at Knockholt (Kent). The house—commemorated by Thrale Rd.—was demolished in 1863. Three mahogany doors preserved in St. Clement Danes' Ch. were destroyed when the latter was bombed.

Balham, once in Streatham par., has its links with nonconformity, for John Wesley so frequently visited his friend, Geo. Wolff, that he became a familiar figure here, while the Rev. C. H. Spurgeon lived in Nightingale Lane.

Tooting is in all probability another place-name personal in origin, and may indicate the home of the people of Tota. The addition of Bec to the name of that part of the district known as Upper Tooting recalls its ancient connection with the famous Abbey of Bec in Normandy, a connection severed in the reign of Henry V.

Like so many of the chs. in the bor., St. Nicholas Tooting was rebuilt entirely in 1832, on a site a little to the E. of the medieval ch. The present bdg. contains a few of the old monuments, but none of special note. In Brudenell Rd. is the fine modern Gothic ch. of All Saints, designed by Temple Moore (1906), and in the main rd., by Trinity Rd. Station, is an attractive R.C. Ch. of St. Anselm (1931), with a statue of the saint on its outer wall.

Tooting's most distinguished resident was Thos. Hardy, who lived at 1 Arundel Terrace, now renumbered as 172 Trinity Rd., where there is a tablet. On the S. side of this rd. David Lloyd George resided in his early days. His house is also marked. The alleged connection of Daniel Defoe with Tooting is unsupported by any evidence.

Wandsworth has a Mohammedan mosque in Gressenhall Rd., Southfields, built 1928. New and dignified municipal bdgs. were completed in 1937 in the High St., and on the opposite side of the rd. is the impressive red-brick Technical Coll.

Wardrobe, The, was a house in Blackfriars, built by Sir John Beauchamp (d. 1359). His executors sold it to Edward III, and it was subsequently converted into the office of the Master of the Wardrobe.

'There were kept in this place,' wrote Fuller, 'the ancient clothes of our English Kings, which they wore on great festivals; so that this Wardrobe was in effect a Library for Antiquaries, therein to read the mode and fashions of garments in all ages.'

From here, in 1604, Wm. Shakspeare of Stratford-on-Avon received 4½ yds. of scarlet cloth for a dress on the occasion of the state entry of James I into L. The Wardrobe was burnt in the G.F. With the death in 1709 of Ralph, D. of Montague, who was Master of the Wardrobe, the office was abolished. Strype (1720) said the gardens of the Wardrobe had been 'converted into a large and square court with good houses and called Wardrobe Court.' The court remains, opening out of Carter Lane, and the houses on the W. side probably date from Strype's time.

On the S. elevation of No. 1 Wardrobe Place there is a stone shield the charge of which has a rounded base and tapering stem, making it somewhat to resemble a battle axe. This was discussed in a paper by L. B. Ellis, M.A., in the *Transactions of the London and Middlesex Archaeological Soc.*, New Series, Part III (1947), but no solution could be found.

Water Supply. Prior to the establishment of the Metropolitan Water Board, the history of L.'s organized water supply divides itself into two overlapping periods, namely, the City conduit and the private water undertaking periods.

The conduit period began in the latter half of the 13th century, when the first conduit bringing water from the Tyburn (in the neighbourhood of what is now Stratford Place, Oxford St.), to a fountain head in Cheapside was completed. The conduits were controlled by the City, some being erected by the C.C. and others by wealthy citizens. Water from the conduit heads was generally distributed to houses by water bearers, a large body of men and women who in early Tudor times formed a guild (the 'Brotherhood of Saint Cristofer of the Waterbearers') and had their own hall in Bishopsgate St. Certain houses, however, were supplied by small lead pipes called 'quills' from the conduit pipe itself. The importance of the conduits declined in the 17th century, with the growth of private water undertakings supplying houses direct, and they disappeared from the City in the first half of the 18th century.

The period of private water undertakings begins in 1581, with a grant of a 500 yrs. lease by the C.C. to Peter Morris, a Dutchman, of the first arch of old L.B., to enable him to erect therein a water wheel harnessed to pumps. The subsequent 300 yrs. saw the rise of a number of separate undertakings, and the final emergence during the latter part of the 19th century of the following eight large water cos. serving the Metropolis:

1. THE NEW RIVER Co. (inc. 1619). The New River was constructed by Sir Hugh Myddelton in 1609–13 with financial assistance from K. James I. Sir Hugh (1561–1631) was a banker and jeweller who devoted much of his time and money to engineering projects and was created a baronet on account of his achievements in 1622, the first engineer to be thus honoured. The 'river' or channel, about forty miles long when constructed, brought water from the springs of Chadwell and Amwell near Ware in Herts. to a reservoir in the par. of Clerkenwell (the site of the head offices of the Metropolitan Water Board), whence it was distributed to houses in the City by wooden pipes. It was considerably shortened in the middle of the last century, and now terminates at the Board's Stoke Newington works. Its present length is 24 miles. The New River is no longer a source of supply, but receives water from the River Lee, from Chadwell Spring (when flowing) and from a number of wells along its course.

In the course of its long history, the Co. acquired a number of smaller undertakings including the L.B. Waterworks (see above) in 1822, which then occupied five arches of the old bridge on the N. side and one on the S. The York Bdgs. Waterworks (estd. 1675) was acquired by the Co. in 1818. This undertaking, the site of whose works now forms part of Charing Cross Station, was the first to apply steam power for raising water. Thos. Savery about 1712 and Thos. Newcomen in 1726 each installed one of their early machines here but they were not a success owing to the high cost of fuel.

2. THE CHELSEA WATERWORKS Co.

(est. 1723) originally possessed works consisting of canals stretching from the site of Victoria Station to the Thames at Chelsea. This Co. was the first in L. to adopt slow sand filtration for purifying water (1829)—the precursor of the process now universally adopted.

3. THE LAMBETH WATERWORKS CO. (est. 1785). The original works were situated at Belvedere Rd., on part of the site occupied by the Festival of Britain, 1951, where the Thames water was abstracted. In 1852 the Co. opened a new intake at Surbiton and was thus the first of the Thames supplied cos. to take its water from above the tideway (i.e. Teddington Weir).

4. THE WEST MIDDLESEX CO. (estd. 1806) set up works at Hammersmith. It was the first of the cos. to make use of cast iron pipes (1807).

5. THE EAST LONDON WATERWORKS CO. (estd. 1807). This Co.'s principal works were originally constructed at Old Ford on the River Lee, where, in Dec. 1838, the first Cornish mining engine adapted for waterworks was started and proved a great success.

6. THE KENT WATERWORKS CO. (estd. 1809) bought up an older undertaking on the River Ravensbourne at Deptford, previously acquired by John Smeaton and which had been furnished by him with a water wheel. From 1861 onwards this Co. obtained all its water from deep wells.

7. THE GRAND JUNCTION WATERWORKS CO. (estd. 1811) was an offshoot of the Grand Junction Canal Co. Its first engineer was John Rennie, under whose direction an attempt was made to use stone pipes on a large scale for the distribution of water. The experiment was a failure, and the Co. turned to cast iron pipes (1812). Part of its works were erected on the site now occupied by the Royal Hosp. at Chelsea.

8. THE SOUTHWARK AND VAUXHALL WATER CO. (estd. 1845). This Co. was an amalgamation of two older cos., the Southwark Co., originating in the latter half of the 18th century and incorporated in 1834, and the South London Water Co. (estd. 1805 and renamed the Vauxhall Co. in 1834). The amalgamated works were originally situated at Battersea, on the site now occupied by the Battersea Power Station of the British Electricity

Authority.

The Metropolis Water Act, 1852, obliged all the Metropolitan water cos. to filter river-derived water and prohibited them from drawing water from the tideway. This resulted in the water cos. establishing works at Hampton and Surbiton in 1855–6 and later at Molesey.

The Metropolitan Water Board came into existence in 1903, consequent upon the Metropolis Water Act, 1902. It is composed of 88 members, six of whom are appointed by the G.L.C. and one each by the county councils of Essex, Hertfordshire, Kent and Surrey, the C.C., all the new London boroughs in addition to the Thames Conservancy and the Lee Conservancy Catchment Board. The offices are at Rosebery Avenue, on the site of the original New River Head Basin. The bdg. was erected in 1920. Laboratories were added in 1938. The area of supply covers about 540 sq. miles and extends from Ware on the N. to Sevenoaks on the S., and from Sunbury on the W. to Southfleet on the E. The resident population is about 6½ million persons—nearly one sixth of the total for England and Wales.

The water for L. is obtained from the River Thames, the River Lee, and from wells and springs mainly in the Lee Valley and in Kent. Of these, the Thames yields about two-thirds and each of the other sources about one-sixth, of the total.

During the year 1966 the average daily supply was 381 million gallons—enough to fill four tanks each the size of Trafalgar Sq. (2½ acres) and the height of Nelson's Column (167 ft.). Large storage reservoirs are necessary to ensure the supply when the natural sources are inadequate; the chief of these are situated at Littleton, Staines, Walton and Molesey (Thames) and at Chingford (Lee). The Littleton (Queen Mary) reservoir is the largest artificial one in the world. When full it contains 6,679,000,000 gallons of water. The area is 707 acres or about the combined size of Hyde Park, Kensington Gardens and St. James's Park. The total acreage of the reservoirs is 2,950, and the total capacity 29,952 million gallons. All river water is filtered and purified, for which extensive plant and buildings are needed. Since all L.'s water has to be pumped a wide variety of machinery is necessary, broadly in three groups. Firstly, for pumping river water into or out of storage reservoirs; secondly, for delivering filtered water into supply (this group is the largest); thirdly, for raising water from below ground to the surface and for forcing it into supply.

The purity of the water is controlled from laboratories at New River Head, in three sections, viz.: biological, bacteriological and chemical. Examinations are based on samples collected from all points of the system.

The capital invested in the Board's undertaking at 31st Mar. 1967 was £68,799,355, while the estimate of expenditure on revenue account for the year 1966-7 is £18,794,478. To raise its income the Board levy a domestic water rate calculated on the net annual value of the premises supplied, and a scale of charges for metered supplies.

Watling Street (from St. P.'s Chyd. to Queen St.). The earliest form of the name of this thoroughfare is 'Aphelingestrate,' 1213, and the form 'Athelyngestrate' occurs 1272-3. Leland (1506-52) called it 'Atheling or Noble Street,' and *aethel* in Anglo-Saxon = noble. 'Athel' or 'Aethel' was a common personal name, and the 'W,' as Harben suggested, may have been inserted through a copyist's error which has perpetuated itself. The Roman Watling St. from Dover seems first to have crossed the Thames at Westminster and, after the construction of London Bridge, at the point where it was constructed—about 100 ft. E. of the present one. A branch westwards, through the centre of the Roman city, would connect it with the line of the st. along the present Edgware Rd., and the remains of a Roman road, with a substratum of chalk and a pavement of flint, have been found at the E. end of Watling St. and in Budge Row at a depth of 20 ft. Mr. C. E. Vulliamy (*The Archaeology of Middlesex and London*) says:

'There is indirect evidence for a highway passing through the town wall at Ludgate, following the line of Fleet Street and crossing the north side of Trafalgar Square. Before the erection of St. Paul's Cathedral the present Watling Street may have been connected with Ludgate Hill.'

Chaucer says in *The House of Fame* that some men called 'the Milky Wey' 'Watlynge strete.' This suggests the importance of the thoroughfare, as the Way stretches across the sky as Watling St. stretches across England.

The Shunamite's House, an inn fitted for the accommodation of preachers who travelled a distance to preach at St. P.'s Cath., was in Watling St. Walton relates how Richd. Hooker got his wife through the match-making propensity of the wife of the landlord, John Churchman.

Westminster, now the City of Westminster, was a met. bor. in the sense that it obtained incorporation as one by statute, and not by charter. However, in its first yr., 1900, it received a charter as a city in recognition of its ancient status, for although it had never before had a mayor it had been the residence of all the monarchs of England for nearly 900 yrs., and from 1540-50 the see of a bp. In 1966 the Mayor was granted the title 'Lord Mayor.'

The met. bor. and city had an area of about 4 sq. miles (the present City is more than 8 sq. miles) and was formed by uniting the following areas: the pars. of St. Margaret, St. John the Evangelist, St. George Hanover Sq., St. James, St. Martin, St. Anne Soho, St. Paul, Covent Garden, St. John the Baptist Savoy, St. Mary le Strand, and St. Clement Danes, with the Liberty of the Rolls (see 'Public Record Office') and the close of the Collegiate Ch. of St. Peter, i.e. W.A. (*q.v.*).

The nucleus of the ancient city was W.A., and the K.'s Palace between it and the river. The custom of affording sanctuary to fugitives from the law in and near the Abbey precincts resulted in the herding together there of a most undesirable population. Broad and Little Sanctuary still exist as street names, and the Westminster rookery, crossed by the unsalubrious Thieving Lane, extended from the present Parliament Sq. as far as Christ Ch. Yard. It was almost entirely swept away on the formation of Victoria St. in 1851. N. of it was an area occupied by French refugees and known as Petty France. Q. Anne's Gate contains a charming statue of that Q. and a number of 18th-century houses with finely carved porches. Cockpit Steps, leading down into Birdcage Walk, recalls the neighbourhood of a once popular entertainment (see 'Cockpits').

The main st. of old Westminster was King St. (plates on the Govt. bdgs. at the corner of Gt. George St. indicate its width) which led to the wide space fronting the palace of Whitehall (*q.v.*). King St. became a back st. when Parliament St. was made parallel to it in the reign of George II: shortened at the S. end when Parliament Sq. was made a century later, it entirely disappeared when Parliament St. was widened and new Govt. offices were erected on the W. side early in the 20th century. (See 'Whitehall.')

W. of Parliament Sq., recently replanned, is the Middlesex Guildhall, the meeting place of the County Council of Middlesex until its abolition in 1965. It was rebuilt in the Gothic style in 1913. Before there were any County Councils there stood here the Westminster Guildhall, which was the sessions-house of the City and Liberties of Westminster; it had occupied various sites, this site being that of the old Sanctuary of St. Peter.

The name of Tothill St. is venerable with age. H. B. Wheatley wrote:

'The origin in this instance appears to be that given in an ancient lease which particularizes a close called the Toothill, otherwise the Beacon Field. The Toot Hill was the highest ground in a locality, which would be used as a post of observation, for the erection of a beacon or a stronghold. Thus in the second book of Samuel, v. 7, where the authorized version has "Nevertheless David took the stronghold of Zion," Wycliffe renders it "Forsooth David toke the tote hill Syon," and in v. 9, "So David dwelt in the fort and called it the City of David," Wycliffe has "David dwelt in the tote hill." '

At the corner of Tothill St. is the Wesleyan Central Hall, 1912, on the site of the old Westminster Aquarium and adjoining Imperial Theatre.

SW. of the Middlesex Guildhall was from 1832 Westminster Hosp., now rebuilt in Page St. Within living memory a row of houses E. of the greensward by Poets' Corner and numbered in Abingdon St. were removed. Abingdon St., leading S. to Millbank, used to be called with frank medieval descriptiveness, Dirty Lane. Barton St. and Cowley St., old fashioned quiet sts. close to the S. of the Abbey,

are said to have been built by the actor, Barton Booth. Just beyond the line of College St. was the mill ditch stream that turned the Abbot's mill.

The par. of St. Margaret's S. and W. boundary, as settled in 1728 when St. John's par. was carved out of it, began at the river near the SE. corner of the Houses of Parliament, turned down Abingdon St., ran W. along College St., and irregularly to Artillery Pl.; thence SW. to the top of Willow Walk (now Warwick St.), and thence N. alongside St. George's par. to Buckingham Gate, where it joined the N. boundary. The par. therefore includes the Westminster Roman Catholic Cath. (*q.v.*). A good deal of the western part was rural till well into the 18th century, in which Elliot's 'Stag' Brewery (now Watney's) was established at the end of Brewer St.

Before there was a separate par. ch. in Westminster, the abbey was used as one. It is said that Edward the Confessor founded the ch. on the N. side of the abbey, dedicated to St. Margaret of Antioch, but this is open to doubt, and it probably dates from the 12th century. It was rebuilt by the wool-merchants in the reign of Edward I. In 1614 it began to be used as the ch. of the H.C., whose members disliked the abbey ceremonies. In 1735 the ch., in the course of repairs, was deprived of nearly all external ornaments; the tower being cased, and mostly rebuilt. Demolition of the houses in St. Margaret St., that had hemmed in the ch. E. and N., began about 1806: the apse of the chancel was then replaced by a square end. In 1876 was begun a restoration, which included the removal of all galleries: it was complete by 1882, when the monuments were rearranged. The W. porch dates from 1891. In 1905 the E. wall was moved eastward 6 ft. The interior, being removed from the insistency of comparison with the dimensions of the abbey, is more impressive—well lighted from sides and clerestory, as well as from each end. The roof is panelled, and slightly curved. Twelve clustered columns divide the nave from the wide aisles. The great E. window was made by order of Ferdinand and Isabella of Spain as a present to Henry VII for his chapel in the abbey; but Henry d. before it was finished; and it was set up in the private chapel of the Abbot of

Waltham, at New Hall, Essex—where Gen. Monk, coming into possession, saved it from demolition. At the Restoration it was set up again; but the chapel fell into decay, and the window went to the private chapel of a Mr. Conyers of Copt Hall, in the same county, whose son, in 1758, sold it to the Restoration Committee of St. Margaret's for 400 guineas. It represents the Crucifixion, but in so odd a manner that even good churchmen took offence at it. The three central lights are occupied by three crosses: with, below, spectators in 16th-century costumes; and, above, an angel on Christ's right bearing away the soul of the penitent thief, and a devil on Christ's left bearing away the impenitent soul. Upper lights are occupied by more angels: while, on the penitent's right-hand side, the figure of St. George stands over P. Arthur (the P. of Wales whose marriage is here commemorated); and, on the impenitent's left-hand, the figure of St. Catherine (with her emblematic wheel which has given its name to a firework) stands above Arthur's bride—Catherine of Aragon, afterwards Q. of Henry VIII. The window was removed for safety during the First World War and again in 1939.

The W. window was erected in 1882 by American subscribers: it contains figures of Q. Elizabeth, P. Henry, Sir Walter Raleigh, and Sir Humphrey Gilbert—Raleigh's body (his head was preserved by his widow) was bd. in the chancel, 1618, on the day of his execution in Old Palace Yard, close to the E. end of the ch., where is a tablet.

There is a tablet in memory of Wm. Caxton, the first English printer, who was bd. here (1491). A stained glass window to his memory was destroyed by bombs and in its place is a window in memory of Capt. Fitzroy, lately speaker of the H. of C., whose ashes were bd. in the chancel, where there is a tablet. In 1888 a window was put up on the N. side to the memory of Admiral Robt. Blake—whose body, ejected from its grave in the abbey, was thrown into a pit in St. Margaret's chyd., 1661.

Near the E. end of the S. wall is the tomb of Mary, Lady Dudley (d. 1600), made of alabaster, with a painted effigy. Other monuments are to: Blanche Parry (d. 1589), an old maid who was a great benefactor of the poor of Westminster;

Thos. Arneway (d. 1603), who left money to establish young men in business; and Cornelius Van Dun (c. 1483–1577), a yeoman of the guard, who established almshouses (now gone) in Petty France and neighbouring St. Ermin Hill. (For a child's monument, see 'Epitaphs.') The par. register records the marriage of John Milton and 'Katherin' Woodcocke, 1656. This accounts for the stained glass window in memory of Milton, unveiled by Matthew Arnold in 1888. It was damaged by bombs in the Second World War. Other notables m. here were: Edmund Waller (1631), Samuel Pepys (1655), and Thos. Campbell (1803).

In the middle of the 19th century, St. Margaret's chyd. was a nuisance to the neighbourhood. After a report in 1850, fresh ground for burials was obtained near the Fulham Rd. There had existed from c. 1640 another burial-ground, around Broadway Chapel—a chapel-of-ease succeeded in 1843 by Christ Ch. on the N. side of Victoria St.: in this chyd. are bd.: Sir Wm. Waller, parliamentary general (1668), and Margaret Batten (1739), her reputed age was 136. Broadway used to be the scene of a haymarket and a stopping-place for stagecoaches. Nearby in Caxton St. is the little red-brick bdg. of the Westminster Bluecoat Sch., 1709.

There is a detached portion of St. Margaret's par., beyond that of St. George, Hanover Sq.: it was called the Hamlet of Knightsbridge; it takes in Hyde Park W. of the Serpentine—it used to take in so much of Kensington Gardens as was not in Paddington; but the W. part, including the palace, is now in Kensington (q.v.). Moreover, it is only the part W. of Albert Gate that is in St. Margaret's: the E. part was in St. Martin's and is now in St. George's. St. Margaret's detached includes the Albert Memorial (see 'Parks'), the Albert Hall (q.v.), the Imperial Institute and Hyde Park, or Knightsbridge Barracks, established 1795. Albert Gate is beside the site of the stone bridge over the Westbourne that gave Knightsbridge its name at least as early as Edward I. In 1849 was built the ch. of All Saints, Ennismore Gardens, by Vulliamy in the Italian basilica style. Here W. R. Inge was vicar 1904–11.

In 1728 was consecrated the ch. in Smith Sq. of the new par. of St. John the Evangelist that had been carved out of

St. Margaret's. Designed by Thos. Archer, after it had been begun in 1716, a tendency to sink into the swampy soil was observed in its foundations, and the architect conceived the device of four equal towers at the corners to ensure that any sinking should be uniform. The ch. was burnt out in 1742 and again during an air-raid in the Second World War. It has been rebuilt and was reconsecrated in 1968. The poet, Chas. Churchill, was curate here from 1758–63, when his unedifying behaviour brought an end to his clerical career.

In Gt. Smith St. are the Colonial Office and Church House (1940). In the latter at times the H. of C. and the House of Lords met after the bombs had fallen on the Houses of Parliament. The Lords met in the Convocation Hall; the Commons in Hoare Memorial Hall. On the panelled wall of the latter there is an inscription which was unveiled by the Rt. Hon. Winston Churchill. It is as follows:

'This Hall of Church House
Was as occasion required during the years
1940, 1941 and 1944
The Chamber of the House of Commons
Within its Walls
The Prime Minister, Winston Churchill,
In the darkest days of the War,
Spoke to the Commons and to the
Nation
The words here recorded.

Millbank was once the name of what is now Grosvenor Rd.: the narrow and crooked thoroughfare that preceded it was Millbank St.—now called Millbank—which looked very primitive and picturesque when viewed from the S. with the Victoria Tower rising over it. When the change was made in this century, the Victoria Tower Garden was lengthened, taking in the site of old wooden wharves as far as Lambeth Bridge. The garden contains Rodin's sculptured group, the 'Burghers of Calais' (1895), and a statue of Mrs. Pankhurst (see 'Statues'). Since 1932 much rebuilding has been going on in and about the N. end of Grosvenor Rd. Before the wholesale rebuilding had taken place, the river, in Jan. 1928, flooded the basements of the area between Horseferry and Vauxhall Bridge Rds., drowning people and rendering many families homeless. Between Regency St. and Grosvenor Rd. was Millbank Penitentiary (see 'Prisons').

On its site are the Alexandra Military Hosp., the Tate Gallery (q.v.), and Millbank Barracks. The W. boundary of St. John's par. was that outflow of the Tyburn stream called King's Scholars' Pond Sewer: from St. Margaret's boundary at Willow Walk, down Tachbrook St. The par. takes in Rochester Row, and, NE. of that, Greycoat Pl.—where stands the Greycoat Hosp., founded 1698 to provide education for poor children. The façade still presents an old-fashioned appearance, with its clock-turret and arms of Q. Anne, but it was gutted in the Blitz. On the NW. side of Rochester Row are the United Almshouses: a modern bdg., commemorating several benefactors, including Emery Hill, whose foundation dates from 1677. Opposite the almshouses is the Gothic ch. of St. Stephen, erected from the designs of Benjamin Ferrey by Miss (afterwards Baroness) Burdett-Coutts, 1847–9: it has painted glass by Willement. Between Rochester Row and Horseferry Rd. is Vincent Sq., with the headquarters of the Royal Horticultural Soc. on its N. side, and in the centre the playing fields of Westminster Sch. St. Martin's in the Fields, the ch. of the par. lying N. of old Westminster City, competes with St. Margaret's for priority of foundation. It was separated from the latter in 1222, attaining parochial status in 1536. The present ch. by Gibbs was finished in 1726, and has a fine Corinthian portico reached by a large flight of steps. On the pediment are the royal arms and a Latin inscription commemorating George I, who was a churchwarden there. Behind the portico rises a sq. tower containing the bells; above that is the clock, and above that an octagonal steeple rising to 185 ft. from the ground. The interior is very fine in the 18th-century manner, and the ceiling has some elaborate plasterwork ornamentation. At the W. end of the nave is a bust of Gibbs by Rysbrach, and his model of the ch. stands in the porch. In the vaults, now cleared and in use for various purposes, are many memorials from the older bdg. (see 'Epitaphs'), an old whipping post, and a memorial to a very popular vicar, Canon Sheppard. In the old ch. have been bd. Nell Gwynne (1687), and G. Farquhar the playwright (1707). The churchwarden's accounts record that Sir Nicholas Bacon was bd.

here (1579), but Weever's *Funeral Monuments* says St. P.'s Cath. His son Francis was baptised in the old ch. (1561). In the present ch. have been bd. the sculptor, J. F. Roubiliac (1762); and Thos. Chippendale (1779). The par. as formed in the reign of Henry VIII had its W. boundary at about the same line as that of St. George's, Hanover Sq. to-day—that is, on the borders of Kensington and Chelsea; while eastward, its area took in the Strand to the W. border of the Savoy and the district N. of that as far E. as Drury Lane.

Many famous bdgs. in the par. are separately noticed, such as the N.G., N.P.G., St. James's Palace, L. Mus. (see 'Museums'), part of Buckingham Palace, and the Admiralty (see 'Whitehall'), as are Trafalgar Sq. (*q.v.*), St. Martin's St. (see 'Leicester Sq.'), Carlton House Terrace (see 'Carlton House'), and the Adelphi. The par. of St. Anne, Soho, was formed in 1678 and is noticed under 'Soho.'

St. Paul's, Covent Garden, was first erected in 1633 by Inigo Jones for the E. of Bedford. In 1645 it became the par. ch. of the then newly developed district. 'The handsomest barn in England,' according to a remark imputed to its architect, it was burnt down in 1795, and reconstructed in identical style by T. Hardwick. In its chyd. were bd. many actors and literary men of the 17th and 18th centuries, but they have no memorials. Wm. Wycherley (1716), Samuel Butler, author of *Hudibras* (1680), Sir Peter Lely (1680), Grinling Gibbons (1721), and Chas Macklin (1797), lie there. There is a tablet in memory of the last, a famous comedian. It gives his age as 107, whereas the coffin plate records that it was 97! In the ch. there is a casket, in an ornamental niche containing the ashes of Ellen Terry (1928). The first scene in Bernard Shaw's *Pygmalion* is in the Covent Garden portico of this ch.

The district takes its name from the convent garden of Westminster, and passed to the Russells in 1553. Opposite the handsome great portico at the E. end of the ch. used to be erected the hustings for the Westminster elections; here was the centre of the struggle between Chas. Jas. Fox and Sir Cecil Wray in 1784, when the poll lasted forty days.

In Bow. St., opposite the Covent Garden

Theatre (see 'Theatres'), are the famous police station and court. It was established at Nos. 33-34 in 1748, and destroyed by the Gordon Rioters in 1780. There Henry Fielding lived, and is said to have written part of *Tom Jones*. Rebuilt on the same site, the court was moved in 1825 across the st. a little S. of the theatre. In 1881 the present bdg. was opened on the E. side, next to Broad Court. In Broad Court there is a tablet commemorating the residence of seven famous men in Bow St. Henry Fielding; Sir John Fielding; Grinling Gibbons; Chas. Macklin; John Radcliffe (physician); Chas. Sackville; E. of Dorset; and Wm. Wycherley. Maiden Lane is a back way parallel to the Strand, and there J. M. W. Turner was b. at 26 in 1775. On the site of a laboratory established 1680 by Godfrey & Cooke, and famous for experiments made there by Robt. Boyle, now stands the R.C. Ch. of Corpus Christi.

Wellington St. was made as an approach to Waterloo Bridge in 1829–30, and on the E. side was the office of *Household Words* when Dickens edited it.

St. Clement Danes Ch. is dealt with under 'Strand.' Within the par. are the Royal Courts of Justice (*q.v.*), and the part of Aldwych covering the site of Wych St. and Holywell St. (otherwise Booksellers' Row). A small detached portion of St. Clement Danes' par. is W. of the Savoy, between Savoy Hill and the backs of the houses on the E. side of Carting Lane.

Savoy Precinct is a very small area lying S. of the Strand between Lancaster Place (the approach to Waterloo Bridge) and the E. side of Savoy Hill. For the palace that used to stand here see 'Savoy Chapel.'

St. Mary-le-Strand Ch. is dealt with under 'Strand.' The par. is small and includes Somerset House and three theatres, the Lyceum, the Gaiety, and the Aldwych.

St. James's Ch., Piccadilly, was built by Wren in 1680 at the expense of Henry Jermyn, E. of St. Albans, and the par. was taken out of St. Martin in the Fields in 1685. Evelyn went to see it on 16th Dec. 1684, and said it was:

'elegantly built. The altar was especially adorned, the white marble enclosure curiously and richly carved, the flowers and garlands about the walls by Mr.

Gibbons in wood; a pelican with her young at her breast, just over the altar in the carved compartment and border environing the purple velvet fringed with I.H.S. richly embroidered.'

This is one of the only three L. chs. in which it is definitely known that Grinling Gibbons personally carried out the work. He was also responsible for the beautiful white marble font here, representing Adam and Eve and the Tree of Life. The ch. was seriously damaged in 1940 by a bomb which fell on the rectory house (killing the verger and his wife). It has now been restored, and in 1946 Q. Mary opened a Garden of Remembrance in the N. Chyd. to commemorate the courage and fortitude of Londoners during the Second World War. Amongst those bd. in the ch. are Chas. Cotton, friend of Izaak Walton (d. 1687); Dr. Thos. Sydenham (d. 1689); Jacob Huysmans the painter (d. 1696); Tom D'Urfey the dramatist (d. 1723); Wm. van de Velde the painter (d. 1707); Dr. Arbuthnot (d. 1770); Jas. Dodsley, bookseller (d. 1797); and Jas. Gillray, the caricaturist (d. 1815).

The par. has its centre in Piccadilly (*q.v.*). It extends N. to Oxford St., is separated on the E. from Soho by Wardour St. roadway, and from St. Martin's par. by the Haymarket roadway: it takes in Pall Mall on the S. (with the front only of St. James's Palace): the W. boundary comes down Regent St. past Conduit St.: then it goes SW., but stops short of Bond St., strikes Piccadilly just W. of the Burlington Arcade, goes W., turns a little way down St. James's St., and then takes in all the houses fronting the Green Park, from Park Place to Cleveland Row. The part E. of Regent St. is similar in character to Soho. It includes Golden Sq., almost all recently rebuilt except for the R.C. Ch. of the Assumption re-erected in 1788 after its destruction in the Gordon riots. It was then the Bavarian minister's chapel. Berwick St. is used as a street market: it was formerly 'a haunt of artists of little note.' In Poland St. lived the musician Chas. Burney and his novelist daughter Fanny. Gt. Windmill St. is named after a windmill that stood there (N. of the part of Shaftesbury Avenue that is in St. James's par.) in the time of Charles II. At its S. end stood the Piccadilly Hall mentioned under 'Piccadilly': it was a gambling-house in the 17th century.

Regent St. was laid out by John Nash in 1813, as part of a great scheme for a rd. from Carlton House to Regent's Park. It was nearly complete by 1820, but has now been entirely rebuilt. N. of Piccadilly Circus, where Regent St. turns W. and curves round to the N.—a part known as the Quadrant—Nash made a colonnade on both sides, a very effective feature which however darkened the shop fronts and was removed 1848. Regent St. Polytechnic is in Marylebone. Near the Oxford Circus end, on the E., Foubert's Pl. commemorates a riding-academy kept on this spot in the time of Charles II by a Frenchman named Foubert. Lower down, the ch. of St. Thomas, in Chapel Court, replaces Abp. Tenison's chapel, opened 1702 as a chapel-of-ease to St. James's. Lower Regent Street leads on to the area of Clubs and to the magnificent Carlton House Terrace by way of Waterloo place which contains a Crimea memorial and other monuments (see 'Statues').

St. George's, Hanover Square—or, as it now is officially, St. George's, Westminster—was a par. carved out of St. Martin's-in-the-Fields in 1725. (The name is now also applied to the western of the two present parl. divisions of Westminster, and in this sense it includes the detached part of St. Margaret's par. lying W. of St. George's par.). Hanover Sq. itself, at the NE. extremity of the par., was built 1716–20. The ch., situate E. of George St., S. of the sq., was built 1722–4 by John James (d. 1746). It seems to be crowded by the adjacent houses, and as it were pushed out by them toward the roadway: its portico projects over the pavement of narrow George St., quite spoiling the view of the sq. from Conduit St. There is oddly a pair of black dogs seeming to guard it. In line with the st.'s frontage is its tower, continued above the clock to a belfry and a small dome. Early in the 19th century, this ch. gained a reputation as the only place where persons of fashion and quality could be m. (see Samuel Butler's *Way of All Flesh* for marital meditations in the sq.), and the reputation lingers with it still. Over the altar is a painting of the Last Supper, attributed to Sir Jas. Thornhill: over that is a painted window, said to be 16th-century, but brought here 1841, showing 'the genealogy of Our Lord, according to his human nature.' The par., which consists mainly of the area of the old manor of Eia, is bisected, by Piccadilly and Knightsbridge, into a N. region containing Mayfair and Hyde Park, E. of the Serpentine, and a S. region, or Pimlico. Mayfair consists of at most half the built-up part of the N. region; i.e. the S. half of it, bounded on the N., say, by Mount St. and Bourdon St. The site of the old May Fair is Shepherd Market (*q.v.*), S. of Curzon St.: there, from the time of James II it is said (but the beginning is uncertain), a fair was held annually—the first fortnight in May appears to have been the usual time—being finally abolished in 1760. Mayfair marriages, without banns or licences, were solemnized at Mayfair (or Curzon) Chapel, Curzon St., by the Rev. Alexander Keith, from 1730 till 1743—when he was sent to prison. There he continued to marry persons by means of a deputy in a house near the chapel. The chapel occupied the island-site between E. Chapel St. and W. Chapel St., and was pulled down in 1879. Crewe House, Curzon St., residence of the Marquess of Crewe, was formerly Wharncliffe House, erected about 1735. Madame Vestris lived in Curzon St.; E. of Beaconsfield d., 1881, in No. 19. Edwd. Jenner lived at 14 Hertford St. In Chesterfield St. lived Beau Brummell. John Wilkes (d. 1797) and his daughter (d. 1804) are bd. in Grosvenor Chapel, S. Audley St. In Farm St. is the Jesuit Ch. of the Immaculate Conception which celebrated its centenary in 1949. Park Lane, the W. boundary of Mayfair, overlooking Hyde Park, has been largely transformed from a place of aristocratic residence to a place of flats and shops: Grosvenor House and its gardens, opposite Grosvenor Gate, once the residence of Ds. of Westminster, are gone. At what is now No. 29 in the lane, Benjamin Disraeli lived thirty-three yrs. For Marble Arch, see 'Parks.' In N. Audley St., in St. Mark's Ch., founded 1828, Sir Hudson Lowe, of St. Helena fame (d. 1844), is bd. In Green St. d. (1845) Sydney Smith. Brook St. to some extent maintains its traditions as a quarter of fashionable physicians. The glories of Berkeley Sq., lying away SE. of Grosvenor Sq., have been greatly dimmed by the passing of Lansdowne House on the S. side: the sq. was built 1698 by John, Ld. Berkeley. At 45 on its W. side lived

Ld. Clive, founder of the Indian Empire. In Charles St. is a public-house with the sign of the Running Footman—an echo of the past. In Albemarle St. is the Royal Institution, a scientific body founded by Count Rumford. Bond St. is in two portions, Old and New—the latter is the longer; the former is the part adjoining Piccadilly. By 1700 Old Bond St., and New Bond St. to Clifford St., were complete. The whole thoroughfare early acquired a reputation as the place of fashionable shops. The N. part of the Pimlico half of St. George's is Belgravia, covering a once-notorious area called the Five Fields, haunted by footpads well into the 19th century. It was laid out for the second E. of Grosvenor, who became Marquess of Westminster, and to whom the manor of Ebury (part of, Eia) had descended from Mary Davies of Ebury Farm (d. 1730), who m. Sir Thos. Grosvenor, third baronet, 1677. James I had sold the manor of Ebury 1623 to a predecessor in title of Mary Davies. Belgravia's N. extremity is St. George's Hosp. at Hyde Park Corner. Southward from the E. side of the hosp. runs Grosvenor Place, bounded on the E. by the back wall of Buckingham Palace grounds. At the cross-roads where this wall turns the corner into Little Grosvenor Place, a suicide was bd. 1823—the last to be bd. at cross-roads in the old fashion. On the E. side of Wilton Place is the ch. of St. Paul, Knightsbridge, built by Thos. Cundy the younger 1843—a Gothic edifice with ritualistic traditions associated with Wm. Jas. Early Bennett (1804–86). On the outer wall is a memorial to the 52 brave women of the F.A.N.Y. who lost their lives 1939–45, 13 of them as secret agents in Occupied Europe. Lowndes Sq., Lowndes St., Chesham St., Eaton Place, and Eaton Terrace, mark Belgravia's W. boundary. Eaton Sq. was designed and built by the Cubitts in 1827: it is named after Eaton Hall, Cheshire, the principal seat of the Grosvenor family. It is bisected by the King's Rd., running into Chelsea. At its NE. end is St. Peter's Ch., built 1824–6 by Henry Hakewill, nearly all burnt 1837, and rebuilt in same style by Gerrard. At 92 lived Admiral Codrington, hero of Navarino (d. 1851). At 13 Eccleston St. lived Chantrey the sculptor. The ancient way to Chelsea was along the line of Ebury

St.; which, with Pimlico Rd., may be taken to mark the line between Belgravia and less-aristocratic Pimlico proper. Ebury St. gets its name from Ebury Farm, whose bdgs. were on the Ebury Sq. and Avery Farm Row sites, SE. of Ebury St. The manor of Ebury, which Mary Davies brought to the Grosvenors, had a detached piece at the N. of Eia Manor, where Davies St. keeps up Mary's memory. Buckingham Palace Rd., and the part of Buckingham Gate in line with it, mark the old road from the Mulberry Garden (see 'Buckingham Palace') to Ebury Farm. Buckingham Palace Rd. contains the library and baths instituted when St. George's was a separate administrative area: also the Ch. of St. Philip, erected 1887–90 and now given over to the Russian Orthodox Ch. In St. Barnabas St., S. of the Pimlico Rd., stands the handsome ch. of St. Barnabas built by Cundy in Early English style and completed 1850. It won great fame as a ritualistic centre in its early days, and was the object of hostile demonstrations. It has a 170 ft. tower and spire with a peal of ten bells.

Most of Pimlico proper lies E. of Victoria Station and is officially known as Victoria Ward. Pimlico was a transplanted title originating in a popular pleasure resort at Hoxton, and later applied to a garden of similar type attached to Jenny Whim's tavern, the last traces of which have now been obliterated by the railway. Crossing Ebury Bridge eastward, on the left, Willow Walk (Warwick St.) led toward the old City of Westminster: while, on the right, Turpentine Lane (still extant, and preserving its name at the back of the houses on the W. side of Westmoreland St.) led to the white lead mills on the river bank where Grosvenor Rd. now extends. The region E. of this was chiefly market-gardens, known as 'Neat Houses'—the common E. Anglian name for a cowhouse. In the reign of Edward III the manor house (for the whole of Eia) was called La Neyte: it was perhaps a cattle-dépôt, was retained by Henry VIII, and was a common place of entertainment by the time of Q. Elizabeth; later visited by Pepys, its exact site is not known. The Neat House estate is now the ecclesiastical par. of St. Gabriel's, Warwick Sq., whose ch. was erected by Thos. Cundy the younger.

The whole district was developed by the Cubitts after 1834, and long rejoiced in the name 'S. Belgravia.' Its streets, whose houses were built in imitation of the 'Belgravian' style, are full of acute and obtuse angles, making its geography difficult for the stranger. By the river, between St. George's Sq. and Claverton St., stood from 1868 the Army Clothing Dépôt, recently replaced by flats. Near by, and almost continuous with the long garden of St. George's Sq., is Pimlico Garden, where there used to be a steam-boat pier. St. Saviour's Ch. was built by Cundy, architect to the Grosvenor estate. The ch. and schs. of St. James the Less (1862), an ornate bdg. in Garden St., near Vauxhall Bridge Rd., were designed by Street. Holy Trinity, close by the bridge, is an early work of J. L. Pearson. Since the destruction of The Second World War, the City of Westminster includes what is probably L.'s longest court—Brydges Pl. connecting St. Martin's Lane with Bedford Bury. It has also one of the quaintest—Goodwin's Court, St. Martin's Lane.

For Westminster Sch. see 'Schools.' Westminster City Sch., now in Palace St., was founded 1633. The City of Westminster contains more than 30 theatres. One, the Westminster in Palace St. (then Charlotte St.), was a chapel in the 19th century, and the scene of the ministrations of the notorious Robt. Crawford Dillon from 1829 to 1840.

Westminster Abbey has as its official title 'the Collegiate Church of St. Peter Westminster.' There are legends of a Temple of Apollo on the site. This is a pleasing pendant to the suggestion of a temple to Diana having once been on the site of St. P.'s Cath. (*q.v.*). Milman, as dean of the latter, was naturally more credulous in the case of the cath., and he had some archaeological evidence in the altar to Diana discovered near its site.

'The Dean of Westminster,' he wrote, 'must produce an image of Apollo as like that of the Belvedere as this to the Diana of the Louvre, before he can fairly compete with us for the antiquity of heathen worship.'

The further suggestion that the temple of Apollo was destroyed by an earthquake adds a dramatic, and therefore highly contestable, sequel to the old monks' tale.

The absence of any reference to W.A. in the *Ecclesiastical History* of Bede is significant in considering the story that the foundation was due (*c.* 616) to Sebert, K. of E. Saxons, whose tomb is still shown in the ambulatory, and has been exhibited somewhere since Edward the Confessor's bdg. was completed. There are also in the paving of the Chapter House designs representing salmon. This relates to the tradition that on the eve of the consecration of Sebert's abbey, St. Peter himself appeared to consecrate his own ch., and that, after enjoining the ferryman who had conveyed him across the river to inform Mellitus, Bp. of L., of the 'celestial splendours' and angelic choir he had seen, he concluded:

'For yourself go out into the river; you will catch a plentiful supply of fish, whereof the larger part shall be salmon. This I have granted on two conditions —first, that you never fish again on Sundays: secondly, that you pay a tithe of them to the Abbey of Westminster.'

Dean Stanley said:

'So late as 1382, one of the Thames fishermen took his place beside the Prior, and brought in a salmon for St. Peter. It was carried in state through the middle of the Refectory. The Prior and the whole fraternity rose as it passed up to the high table, and then the fisherman received ale and bread from the cellarer in return for the fish's tail.'

With the 8th century, the historian who has faltered previously can tread more firmly. There still exists a charter of K. Offa of Mercia, dated 785, granting and confirming lands and privileges to the ch. of St. Peter 'at Thorney, in the terrible place.' Thorney was an island formed by the Long Ditch and effluents from the Tyburn (see 'Lost Rivers'). It is estimated as having been 470 yds. long and 370 yds. broad. It may have been a jungle for wild ox or red deer—the bones of both were found below the foundations of the Victoria Tower of the Palace of Westminster (*q.v.*), i.e. the Houses of Parliament, and the tusk of a wild boar was found at a great depth below the refectory floor of W.A. Probably, however, it was regarded as a desirable site by reason of several springs to supply drinking water, and of the fish then to be caught in the river.

St. Dunstan is said to have restored the monastery, and also to have obtained a further charter. The latter is dated 951, and purports to have been granted by K. Edgar. It is of doubtful authenticity. At any rate, Dunstan, Abp. of C. from 960 to 988, brought twelve Benedictine monks from Glastonbury to the Abbey. W.A. received the manor of Hampstead from K. Ethelred in 986, and other lands were granted to it by one Leofwinc in 998. Harold I was first bd. at W.A. in 1040, but by Hardicanute's orders his body was dug up and thrown into a neighbouring ditch (see 'Strand—St. Clement Danes Ch.').

Edward the Confessor (1042–66) was really the founder of W.A. Before he ascended the throne, he vowed to make a pilgrimage to the tomb of the Apostle Peter at Rome. His Great Council discountenanced the proposal when he became K. and a deputation was sent to Pope Leo IX to persuade him to release the K. from his vow. Consent was given on condition that Edward would found or restore a monastery to St. Peter; the K. was willing; he came to live at Westminster, where he rebuilt the old palace and, *c.* 1050, began also to rebuild W.A. on a site E. of the previous bdg. In his time little more than the choir was completed, and this, says Chas. Hiatt, 'was joined by a porch, or *atrium*, to the old church, which thus became the nave of the new structure.' In the abbey ch. itself there is now nothing to be seen above-ground of Edward's work. In 1866 small fragments consisting of wall-footings and bases of piers were discovered by Sir Gilbert Scott beneath the floor of the sanctuary. They were left *in situ*. In 1930, beneath the floor of the Nave, further remains were uncovered. These showed that the Ch. was practically the same length as the later and present Ch. (See *Archaeologia*, Vol. LXXXIII.) The new ch. was dedicated on 28th Dec. 1065; on 6th Jan. 1066 Edward the Confessor was bd. in the new bdg. The Bayeux Tapestry depicts the funeral of the K.; his bier is being conveyed towards a ch. with a tower and round Norman arches. William I was crowned in W.A. on Christmas Day 1066. Every sovereign since, except the nominal Edward V and Edward VIII, has been crowned here.

Henry III was the second royal builder of W.A. In 1220 he laid the foundation of the Lady Chapel, thus inaugurating his work. 'A devout Prince,' according to Holinshed; 'a very pious King,' to Fuller, he was naturally interested in the shrine of the most pious of the Saxon monarchs, Edward the Confessor. Two months after his accession he saw the body of Becket—St. Thos. of Canterbury—placed in a new tomb in its cath., and probably then, as Lawrence Tanner suggests, he conceived the idea of a more splendid shrine for the only K. hitherto bd. in W.A. It is surprising that Henry should have decided to pull down a great Norman ch. with hardly more than a century of yrs. behind it, but a reference in a papal bull of 1245 to its being 'consumed with excessive age' may indicate that some structural defects had been revealed that made rebuilding to some extent a matter of necessity. In 1245 Edward the Confessor's bdg. was pulled down so far W. as the nave. The new bdg. was commenced at the E. end, as was the custom with medieval builders. By 1254 the work had proceeded so far as the central crossing, and the transepts, the N. front, the rose windows, and parts of the cloister and chapter house had been completed. The architects were Master Henry, Master John of Gloucester, and Master Robert of Beverley.

Meanwhile, in 1247, W.A. received its most sacred and valuable relic. K. Edgar had given some of the stones with which Stephen was stoned, some bones of the Holy Innocents, and a tooth of the Magi. Edward the Confessor had presented a girdle dropped by the Virgin to convince St. Thomas of her assumption. (It was used for averting the perils of childbirth, and was often employed for that purpose by Q. Philippa, but Dean Stanley pointed out that it is also shown in the Vatopédi Convent of Mount Athos.) Henry I's consort, Q. Matilda, gave a large part of the hair of Mary Magdalene. These were, however, of trifling value in comparison with the Holy Blood which was sent to Henry III by the Knights Templars and Hospitallers, and was first brought to St. P.'s Cath. The phial was carried with the utmost solemnity to W.A. by the K. himself, who had spent the night before in prayer and fasting. At that time there was added to the reliquary a stone believed to show the footprint of the ascending Christ, and a tooth of St. Athanasius.

It was not until 1269 that the choir and the bay beyond was completed, and in that yr. the body of Edward the Confessor was 'translated' from before the altar and placed in a shrine in the chapel named after him. It was composed of gold and mosaic work; its beauty is difficult to realize by those who see it now in its discoloured and defaced condition. In the same yr. the mosaic pavement (still in front of the high altar and in Edward's Chapel) was brought from Rome by Abbot Ware. In 1272 Henry III d. When the Templars were so munificent in their gifts the K. had thought of making their ch. his place of sepulture. His affection for W.A. had, however, grown with the yrs., and so he became the first K. since Edward the Confessor to find a resting-place there. Edward I, then in the Holy Land, brought home with him the precious marbles, the slabs of porphyry, with which the tomb now to be seen was built nine yrs. later. It was not until 1291 that the body of Henry III was removed there from its first grave before the high altar—a place vacated by Edward the Confessor's bones on the direction of Henry himself. Henry's heart, having been promised there in his earlier yrs., was deposited with the ashes of his kindred in the abbey of Fontevrault.

While his successor, Edward I, was fighting in Scotland in 1303 there occurred a sensational event in the history of the abbey. The treasury, which is believed to have been kept in the crypt of the Chapter House, was robbed. This apartment has thick walls and a huge central pillar, in which are cavities where the precious metal may have been kept. Matthew of Westminster wrote with a desire to exculpate the ecclesiastics, but it is difficult to believe that the crime could have been so successful without their connivance, although the instigating villain was, without doubt, Richd. de Podlicote, keeper of the neighbouring palace, who obtained access through a window of the Chapter House. Part of the valuables was said to be hid in a crop of hemp specially grown in the graveyard of St. Margaret's Ch., which surrounded the bdg. Some of it was found in the

Thames; some hidden behind tombstones in St. Margaret's Chyd.; and some so far distant as Kentish Town. The abbot and forty-eight monks were taken to the T.L., and a long trial took place. They were all released, and Podlicote alone was hanged, no doubt greatly to the satisfaction of the Church. Human skin found in the middle of the 19th century under the iron cramps of a door near the treasury may have been his, placed there to terrorize similar criminals, though most writers are inclined to associate this with the Danes.

In 1378 occurred a remarkable example of the tenacity with which the right of sanctuary was guarded in the Middle Ages. Two prisoners in the T.L., placed there at the instigation of John of Gaunt, escaped and took sanctuary in W.A. They were pursued by the Constable of the Tower and Sir Ralph Ferrers, and 50 armed men. In the words of Dean Stanley:

'It was the moment of the celebration of High Mass. The Deacon had just reached the words of the Gospel of the day, "If the goodman of the house had known what time the thief would appear," when the clash of arms was heard, and the pursuers regardless of time or place, burst in upon the service. Shackle escaped but Hawle was intercepted. Twice he fled round the Choir, his enemies hacking at him as he ran, and at length, pierced with twelve wounds, sank dead in front of the Prior's Stall, that is at the north side of the entrance to the Choir. His servant and one of the monks fell with him. He was regarded as a martyr to the injured rights of the Abbey and obtained the honour (at that time unusual) of burial within its walls. A brass effigy and long epitaph marked till within the last century the stone where he lay, and another inscription was on the stone where he fell. The Abbey was shut up for four months and Parliament was suspended, lest its assembly should be polluted by sitting within the desecrated precincts.'

Richard II was the third royal builder. He was responsible for a most elaborate porch. He was the only sovereign (as such) to be m. in W.A. (1382).

Henry VII was the fourth great royal builder. His interest was a dynastic rather than a devout one. To provide a noble tomb for his uncle, the previous Lancastrian K., when the Wars of the Roses had ceased, and he had healed the breach by marrying a daughter of the House of York, was to seal in stone what had been done in war and by love. He proposed, therefore, to translate the 'bodie and reliques' of Henry VI from Windsor to Westminster. He applied to Pope Julius II for the canonization of Henry VI, who was called 'The Holy King.' He was already venerated as a saint, and a statue was put up in York Minster. Miracles, the indispensable attestation of sanctity, were reported to have been manifested at his tomb. The papal court granted the request, but the price proposed was prohibitive to the parsimonious K., so Henry's body remained at Windsor, though the Pope had granted a licence for its removal and the Abbey had paid a large sum towards the expenses.

With the abandonment of the idea of a shrine for Henry VI, there emerged in Henry VII's mind a still more pious idea, the erection of a ch. in honour of the Virgin Mary—

'in whom,' he said afterwards in his will, 'hath ever been my most singular trust and confidence . . . and by whom I have hitherto in all myne adversities ever had my special comforte and relief.'

On 24th Jan. 1503 the abbot, John Islip, laid the first stone. About a month after Henry VII's Q., Elizabeth of York, d. in the T.L. Her body was temporarily bd. in a side chapel, pending the completion of the new Lady Chapel. In 1509 the K.'s mother, Margaret Beaufort, d. at the abbot's house. In due course a tomb as fine as her son's appeared; the portrait effigy of Margaret in old age is considered to be Torrigiano's masterpiece. It was not until about 1519 that Henry VII's Chapel was finished. It was called by John Leland 'orbis miraculum' or 'wonder of the world.' There are fine bronze gates of superb design leading to an architect's earthly paradise. The doors display the York and Lancaster roses; the lions of England; the French fleurs-de-lis; the Beaufort portcullis, surmounted by a crown with the words 'Altera Securitas'; the letters 'H R' crowned, and connected by a chain; a badge of a crown in a bush (an allusion to Henry's coronation at

T

Bosworth); the dragon of Cadwallader; the root of daisies (an allusion to his mother's name Margaret); the greyhound of the Nevilles; and the falcon of Edward II. These symbolized Henry's ancestry and his various titles to the Crown. The chapel beyond presents 'God's plenty' of beauty. J. P. Malcolm (1807) drew a vivid picture of it as it must have been before the Reformation:

'Then the windows were filled with painted glass, and the light which streamed through them was tinged with a warm glow of colours which brightened the brilliancy of the gold and silver utensils of the various altars and the embroidered vestments of the priests, at the same time touching one pendant of the roof with purple, another with crimson, and a third with yellow. The burning tapers waving with every current of air, varied the strong shadows on the exquisite statues above them, and showed their features in every lineament. In the centre stood the vast cross of gold, the statue of the Virgin, and the high altar. Behind it the polished brazen screen, and within it the tomb and altar, glowing with the light of tapers. The sculptured walls and exquisite, minutely carved roof, bounded this unparalleled view, and, thanks to the skill of its architect, still enchants us, though all the accompaniments are buried in irretrievable ruin.'

This architect was probably Robt. Vertue, one of Henry VII's master masons, whose relative, Wm. Vertue, vaulted St. George's Chapel, Windsor, in 1505. The eulogy of the Englishman, Malcolm, finds a fitting pendant in the praise of an American, Washington Irving:

'The very walls are wrought into universal ornament, encrusted with tracery and scooped into niches, crowded with statues of saints and martyrs. Stone seems, by the cunning labour of the chisel, to have been robbed of its weight and density, suspended aloft, as if by magic, and the fretted roof achieved with the wonderful minuteness and airy security of a cobweb.'

Sir Gilbert Scott considered the chapel presented generally the richest specimen of Tudor architecture, and in particular of fan-tracery vaulting, peculiarly English.

One of the varied incidents represented in the stained glass was that of Henry's coronation at Bosworth Field by Ld. Stanley, with the crown of Richard III found under a hawthorn bush. The stalls added to the dignity of the chapel. Originally they occupied only three bays, the eastern bays on either side being divided from the body of the chapel by a stone screen. Additional seats were provided when the Order of the Bath (founded by Richard II) was reconstituted by George I in 1725. The banner of each knight hangs over his stall, on the back of which is a copper plate emblazoned with his arms. The lower row of stalls is occupied by the esquires, whose arms are affixed in similar fashion. The use of the chapel for installations lapsed in 1812, and was revived by George V in 1913. In the lower stalls are the subsellae adorned with curious sculptures. There are scriptural subjects like 'The Judgment of Solomon,' some satirical of monastic life; and others of domestic interest such as a husband receiving chastisement from his wife (the more Rabelaisian of the two devoted to this theme is illustrated in *Churches, with a Story*, by Geo. Long). One, showing simply foliage, is of 13th-century date. The black-and-white marble pavement of the chapel was presented by Dr. Henry Killigrew, prebendary of W.A. (d. 1700). His gift is commemorated by a brass tablet in the floor.

In 1509 Henry VII d. and was bd. in the incomplete chapel beside his Q. The monument was the work of Pietro Torrigiano, and took twenty yrs. to complete, the Italian living meanwhile within the precincts of the abbey. The tomb itself is of black marble, and its sides are divided into panels by bronze pilasters, ornamented with Henry VII's emblems, the roses and the portcullis. The panels are filled with bas-reliefs, representing the Virgin and Child; the Archangel Michael trampling on Satan; St. John the Baptist and St. John the Evangelist; St. George of England; St. Anthony of Padua; St. Christopher and St. Vincent (the K.'s two patron saints); the Magdalene and St. Barbara and St. Anne. Torrigiano received £1,500 for his work. The figures of the K. and his consort are most lifelike.

'His face,' said Pennant, 'resembles all his portraits. I have seen a model of a still stronger likeness in possession of Mr. Walpole, a bust in stone taken from his face immediately after his death. A stronger reluctance to quit the possessions of this world can never be expressed on the countenance of the most griping mortal.'

The tomb was enclosed within a grate of brass. This was begun in the K.'s lifetime, and seems to have been the work of Thos. Ducheman. Torrigiano also completed in 1522 'an aulter and various images' to stand within the screen. This was destroyed during the Civil War. A small altar was erected by Dean Stanley. This was re-constructed in 1935, retaining portions of the 16th-century original.

Islip (b. at Islip in Oxfordship 1464) was abbot from 1500 to 1532. He was the last of the great abbots, and during his term of office the nave was finished. It was then paved with stone, and, the W. window being filled with glass in 1517, W.A. was completed.

The dissolution of the monastery at Westminster was effected on 16th Jan. 1540. The abbot was converted into a dean; for the monks twelve prebendaries were substituted. Over the head of the newly constituted body was placed a prelate entitled Bp. of Westminster, whose diocese extended over the whole of Middlesex, with the exception of Fulham. In 1550, however, Thirlby, Westminster's only bp., resigned and the diocese was reunited to the see of L. In 1550, under Edward VI, the Communion Service was substituted for the Mass; in 1553, under Q. Mary, the Roman ritual was restored; in 1556 the monastic rule was revived, and John Feckenham, who brought with him fourteen monks, was appointed abbot. In 1560, under Q. Elizabeth, the monastery was again suppressed, and W.A. established as a collegiate ch., as it still remains.

The various features of W.A. will be considered in alphabetical order.

ABBOT'S PEW. This is a wooden balcony in the nave; it was built by Abbot Islip, and communicated with a private chapel in the abbot's house (now the deanery).

CANDELABRA. There are two—at the E. end of the nave. They are the work of Benno Elkan, a German refugee who came here in 1933. They display Bible characters.

CHAPELS. Apart from Edward the Confessor's and Henry VII's, there are: St. Faith; St. Benedict; St. Edmund; St. Nicholas; St. Paul; St. John the Baptist; Islip; St. John the Evangelist; St. Michael, St. Martin, and All Saints; St. Andrew; St. George's (the Warriors' Chapel); Pyx (in Cloisters); R.A.F. Chapel; Henry V's Chantry. The most interesting are:

ISLIP CHAPEL is the only chantry chapel erected at other than royal command. On the front of the chapel the abbot's name appears twice in large letters. There are also two rebuses—an eye and a tree with a man slipping off it; and an eye and a tree with a hand plucking a slip or twig. Here is a window, executed by Mr. Hugh Easton in 1948 as a thank offering for the deliverance of W.A. and St. Margaret's Ch. from the perils of the last war and in remembrance of John Islip, sometime Abbot, and of Paul de Labilliere, sometime Dean.

The chapel was opened by Q. Elizabeth in 1950, and is dedicated to 'the lasting honour of all the men and women from the United Kingdom and all parts of the British Commonwealth and Empire who gave their lives in the Second World War 1939-45, whilst caring for the sick and wounded.' There are 3,076 names in a roll of honour in a casket.

PYX CHAPEL (E. Cloister) has a heavy oak doorway, with six locks. It is a vaulted chamber, built between 1040 and 1100, and formed part of the early monastic bdgs. The only stone altar left at W.A. *in situ* is here; there is also a 13th-century piscina. At one time, possibly after the robbery referred to (see *supra*), it was used as the monastic treasury. In this chamber was afterwards kept the 'pyx' or box containing the standard pieces of gold and silver, and here annually took place the trial of the pyx—the testing of the current gold and silver coinage—which now takes place in the Mint.

HENRY V'S CHANTRY is at the E. end of Edward the Confessor's Chapel. It was constructed in accordance with his will that—

'over his body be made a high place to be ascended by steps at one end of his tomb, and descended in like manner at the other end, in which place the relics were to be placed and the altar founded.'

There are sculptured representations of

scenes in Henry V's life, including his coronation—the only one represented in any way in W.A. The tomb of his consort, Katharine of Valois, is now here (see *infra*).

CHAPTER HOUSE. The largest in England except that of Lincoln, it was built on the crypt of Edward the Confessor's Chapter House by Henry III in 1250. It is octagonal, and measures 58 ft. in diameter. The mouldings of the outer arch are decorated with ten small figures on either side, in niches formed by foliage, the stem of which springs from the lowest figure—possibly Jesse. The tympanum has the remains of a statue of the Virgin and Child, with angels on either side. The original pavement which is much worn still remains. Below it lie Abbot Edwin, the Confessor's adviser; Hugolin, chamberlain and treasurer to the Confessor; and Sulcardus, a monk, who wrote the first history of the abbey. (For Roman coffin see 'Roman Remains.')

The Chapter House was used originally as the place of assembly for the monks. In Edward I's reign, when the Lords and Commons were separated, the latter held their sittings here, and continued to do so until 1547. In 1554 it was used as a record office. The records continually multiplied, and in 1740 the groined roof was removed, and an upper storey inserted. In 1865 the records were moved to the Chapel of the Rolls (see 'Public Record Office') and a restoration under Sir Gilbert Scott was undertaken. The roof was rebuilt and the windows restored after the pattern of one still remaining. Later they were filled with stained glass as a memorial to Dean Stanley. These were destroyed in the war and have since been reglazed. The tiled pavement of 1268 still remains. It is pictorially engraved with scenes and patterns, such as Edward the Confessor giving his ring to St. John the Evangelist, Henry III on his throne, and Q. Eleanor of Provence with a hawk, etc. The wall paintings were skilfully cleaned by Office of Works experts in 1931. Those on the E. wall (i.e. facing the doorway) are of mid-14th-century date, and perhaps also those in the third arch of the SE. wall. The subject was the Last Judgment or Christ in Majesty. The rest—late 15th-century—represent scenes from the Revelation of St. John. In the lowest compartment of each arch was a picture of an animal, and a 'Reynder,' a 'Ro,' a 'Wyld

Asse,' 'Tame Asse,' 'Dromedary,' and 'Kameyl,' can still be traced. The beautiful figures above the inner doorway represent the Virgin and the Angel of the Annunciation. They were taken to the Exhibition of British Art at Burlington House in 1934. The Chapter House sustained damage in the Second World War and was closed until 1951.

THE CHAPTER LIBRARY is approached by a staircase from the E. cloister. It was fitted up by Dean Williams (1620–44), who gave many valuable books and MSS. Much of his manuscripts were destroyed by fire in 1694.

CLOISTERS.

East Walk. The bays between the Abbey Ch. and the Chapter House were built 1245–50; the rest belong to the middle of the 14th century. The first bay was probably where the great bookcase stood. There are no shafts running down here. The door S. of the Chapter House leads to the Muniment Room.

Mrs. Aphra Behn (1640–89) is bd. here —the only feminine imaginative writer in W.A. One of her best stories is *Oroonoko*.

Tom Brown was bd. here; also *Jane Lister* (see 'Children's Memorials'). There is a stone over the grave of *Rev H. F. Westlake* (1879–1925). He was Assistant-Keeper of the Muniments, and wrote a number of volumes on W.A., and one on St. Margaret's Ch.

South Walk (c. 1350, but practically rebuilt in 1838).

The large blue stone called 'Long Meg' was traditionally supposed to cover the remains of a female giantess who lived in Henry VIII's reign, but more probably marks the resting place of twenty-six monks who d. in 'the Black Death.' Seven of the abbots lie in this cloister.

Vitalis (1082). His name was erroneously inscribed on Laurence's tombstone. *Gilbert Crispin* (d. 1117). A worn slab of black marble, and the oldest sculptured effigy in W.A. It was moved beneath the bench in the 18th century to preserve it. *Herbert* (d. 1136). *Sir Gervase de Blois* (deposed c. 1157, d. 1160). He was a natural son of K. Stephen, and a man of doubtful character. *Abbot Laurence* (d. 1173), a favourite of Henry II and the Empress Maud, who was successful in obtaining the long-promised canonization of Edward the Confessor in 1161. He was granted the favour of wearing the mitre, ring, and gloves by Pope Alexander III, but d. before they arrived. *Walter of Winchester* (d. 1190) was granted the additional privilege of the dalmatic, tunic, and sandals, but was inhibited from wearing the mitre on account of the disgraceful quarrel for precedence between the two abps. (see *infra*). *William Postard* (d. 1201), the first abbot to wear the mitre. *William de Humez* (d. 1222). He collected large sums of money for the building of the new Lady Chapel, but d. two yrs. after Henry III had laid the foundation stone. There is a slab with a worn effigy in full vestments. Here also are bd. four nephews of John Wesley; their father was a master at Westminster Sch. and *Ephraim Chambers* (1686–1740), author and originator of the first English encyclopaedia. In the Latin epitaph now in the *North Walk* he describes himself as a man whose name was—

'familiar to many, himself known to few; one who walked betwixt light and shade, neither erudite nor ignorant, who passed his life in devotion to letters.'

Here are the monks' towel aumbries, and doorways which led to the refectory.

Near Dean's Yard is the monument to Capt. Cornewall (1699–1742), killed in a naval battle with the French off Toulon. The action is represented in bas-relief. This monument was brought from the nave in 1932.

WEST WALK (*c.* 1350).

John Broughton (1705–89), the most famous pugilist of his day. Henry Fielding expressed a wish that he would put fist to paper in a treatise on pugilism. His arms were the models for Rysbrack's statue of Hercules. It is said it was proposed to describe him as 'Champion of all England,' but the Dean objected, and the blank remains after his name on the slab. Strangely a contemporary account says he was bd. in Lambeth par. ch., but there is no doubt he lies here.

William Woollett (1735–85). The most celebrated English engraver of his time. His best-known work was of 'West's Death of General Wolfe' (1776), now in Kensington Palace, which so pleased George III that he gave him the title of 'Historical Engraver to His Majesty.' He was bd. in the old chyd. of St. Pancras (*q.v.*). It is said that the monument was placed here by reason of an inscription crudely chalked or cut there:

'Here Woollett lies, expecting to be saved He graved well, but is not well engraved.'

NORTH WALK (*c.* 1350). The stonework was refaced, and window tracery renewed in the late 19th century by Sir Gilbert Scott.

Dr. William King. He was a Westminster schoolboy, and became a miscellaneous writer.

Sir John Hawkins (1719–89). One of the original members of Dr. Johnson's club and wrote a biography of him; he also published an edition of Izaak Walton's *Compleat Angler.*

Samuel Foote (1720–77) was bd. by torchlight. He was a witty comedian— 'the dog was so very comical, Sir, he was irresistible,' said Dr. Johnson.

General John Burgoyne (1722–92). Commander-in-chief of the British forces, he was forced to surrender to Gates, the American general, early in the War of American Independence, and returned in disgrace. He figures in Bernard Shaw's *The Devil's Disciple.*

For Wm. Laurence see 'Epitaphs.'

In the walk at the W. end are holes in the stone bench, said to have been made by the monks in playing marble games. They may have been made by Westminster schoolboys who, in the 18th century, played football in the cloisters. From here the remaining wall of the refectory is visible; the rest of the bdg. was demolished in the middle of the 16th century.

THE LITTLE CLOISTERS (S. out of E. cloister) stand upon the site of the monks' infirmary, one large room with smaller rooms around for the sick, infirm and aged monks. There is a small Norman window on the N. side, and in the E. wall a beautiful 14th-century doorway, which used to lead into the ancient chapel of St. Catherine. A few arches of it also remain in an adjacent garden.

In this chapel occurred the incident so quaintly described by Fuller in his *Church History.*

'A synod was called at Westminster, the pope's legate being present thereat; on whose right sat Richard, Archbishop, as in his proper place; when in springs Roger of York, and finding Canterbury so seated fairly sits him down on Canterbury's lap (a baby too big to be dandled thereon); yea, Canterbury's servants dandled this lap-child with a witness, who plucked him thence, and buffeted him to purpose.'

The northern primate accused the Bp. of Ely of throwing him down and trampling upon him. He rushed into the Abbey Ch., where he found Henry II hearing mass, showed his torn cope, and denounced his brethren of Canterbury and Ely. The K. laughed at him, and the dispute was finally settled by the Abp. of C. receiving the title of 'Primate of all England,' and the Abp. of York the inferior title of 'Primate of England.'

The monks were not bd. in the cloister garth, except possibly in very early days. Their cemetery was at the SE. end of the abbey, near where is now the George V statue.

CORONATION CHAIR. It was made, *c.* 1297, by order of Edward I to enclose the stone of Scone. This stone, according to legend, was originally the pillow of Jacob at Bethel, and after wanderings, only equalled by the most peripatetic of the patriarchs, it reached Scone about A.D. 850, where it was enclosed in a wooden chair. From Malcolm IV's coronation to that of John Baliol all the Scottish Ks. were crowned here. It is said that Edward I was crowned K. of Scotland on the sacred stone of Scone after he had defeated Baliol at Dunbar in 1296. He certainly carried off the stone and the Scottish regalia, and placed them near the Confessor's shrine in 1297. Attempts have been made to regain the stone, and Edward III consented to restore it. The regalia were allowed to depart, but the Londoners, it is said, would not allow the stone to 'depart from themselves.'

So recently as 1924 a Bill for its removal was introduced by Mr. David Kirkwood, M.P., in the H.C., but in vain.

The chair is of oak. Now worn and colourless, originally it was covered with gilt gesso work, wrought into patterns. On the back was the figure of a K. enthroned, with his feet on a lion. This probably was intended to represent Edward the Confessor. Edward II and all succeeding sovereigns, except the nominal Edward V, and the abdicated Edward VIII, have been crowned on this chair. It was bd. under the Islip Chapel during The Second World War. In the early morning of Christmas Day, 1950, it was removed by Scottish Nationalists and secreted in Scotland but

was found and restored to its old place.

Cromwell sat in it—in Westminster Hall, not W.A.—when he was appointed Ld. Protector in 1657. In the 18th century visitors, by tipping a guide, could sit in it. In the 19th century various names were cut on the chair, amongst them that of one Abbot, who boasted that he had slept all one night there, 5th July 1800, and Ld. de Ros, who as a Westminster Schoolboy, spent a night in W.A. In June 1914 some damage was caused to the woodwork and to the stone mullions at the back of the chair by a bomb placed there by a suffragette.

In the First World War the chair was placed in the crypt of the Chapter House. For a second time the chair was removed from W.A. in 1940. It was bd. and a plan shewing where was deposited with the late Mackenzie King, Prime Minister of Canada. The smaller chair that was made for Q. Mary II (1689) is in the library.

Close by are the sword and shield of Edward III, which were, it is said, carried before the K. in France. The sword is 7 ft. long, and weighs 18 lb.

JERUSALEM CHAMBER, approached by the Jericho Parlour, was probably so called from tapestry representations of the history of Jerusalem which formerly adorned it. Henry IV d. here (as described in the *Chronicles* of Fabyan, and in Shakespeare (*Henry IV*, Part II, Act IV, Sc. iv). The death of the K. is represented in a carved panel over the fireplace. Addison, Newton, and Congreve lay in state here. In 1643 the Assembly of Divines met in this room; as also the compilers of the Revised Version of the Bible from 1871 to 1881.

PULPITS. The one in use is of late 17th-century date. The pulpit now in the nave is said to have been occupied by Cranmer when preaching before Edward VI.

SANCTUARY. The altar and reredos were erected in 1867, after a design by Sir Gilbert Scott. The sculptured figures are by H. H. Armstead. The mosaic representing the Last Supper is by Salviati. In front of the altar are bd. Abbots Ware, Wenlock, Kydyngton, and Henley. The first-named brought the mosaic and porphyry of the pavement from Rome in 1268; also the material for the paving of the Chapter House. On the S. side is the tomb of Anne of Cleves. It was not finished. The initials A.C. are on it. She turned Roman Catholic, and d. at Chelsea in 1557, during Mary's reign.

SANCTUARY. The rights of sanctuary became seriously impaired with the growth of Protestantism. They were much abused, as is indicated by a passage in Sir Thos. More's *History of Richard III* (*c.* 1513), though he advocated reform, not abolition. An Act of 1540 set up seven cities of refuge, among which Westminster was one. There was, however, no longer to be protection for offenders accused of murder, robbery, and certain other heinous felonies. The criminal lost these privileges under Edward VI, but they were restored by Mary, and in 1556 Machyn saw a procession of

'sanctuary men with cross keys upon their garments,' including 'a boy that killed a big boy that sold papers and printed books, with hurling of a stone, and hit him under the ear in Westminster Hall.'

Westminster, in the reign of Elizabeth, was still the resort of debtors, and Dean Williams said that, if the privilege was entirely abolished, the value of house property would decline! All legal rights of sanctuary were abolished in 1623, but they lingered illegally for another century (see 'Whitefriars'). The thoroughfares Broad Sanctuary and Little Sanctuary mark the site of the Sanctuary Towers of W.A., which, according to Maitland, may have dated from Edward III's reign. They were finally demolished in 1775.

(See *Transactions of the London and Middlesex Archæological Society*, New Series, Vol. VI, Part iii.)

TOMBS AND MONUMENTS.

'Think how many royal bones
Sleep within these heaps of stones:
Here they lie, had realms and land,
Who now want strength to stir their hands:
Where from their pulpits seal'd with dust,
They preach, "In greatness is no trust."
Here's an acre, sown indeed
With the richest, royall'st seed
That the earth did e'er such in,
Since the first man died for sin.'

Francis Beaumont's lines were written when few had been bd. in W.A. who had not been on the throne or lived in its shadow. Those of lower degree had, in

death, come near to them at an early date, but with no monumental distinction to mark the fact. The earliest, according to Dean Stanley, was Hugolin, the chamberlain of Edward the Confessor. Later came the body of Geoffrey de Mandeville, who fought for William the Conqueror at Hastings. In 1072 Egelric, Bp. of Durham, who as a prisoner in W.A., by prayer and fasting acquired the reputation of an anchorite, was bd. there. Trussel, Speaker of the H.C. in the reigns of Edward II and Edward III, was bd. there in 1364. Walter Leycester, serjeant-at-arms, was bd. in the N. transept, at the foot of the great crucifix, in 1391. Chaucer's body was there interred in 1400 (see *infra*). Now the collection of mortal men represented is as various in its human interest as any wax-work show, like Madame Tussaud's. W.A. encompasses humanity more completely even than Shakespeare's plays. Dean Stanley expressed his astonishment at the motley throng of the dead within its walls.

'Unequal and uncertain is the commemoration of our celebrated men. It is this which renders the interment or notice within our walls a dubious honour, and makes the Abbey, after all, but an imperfect and an irregular monument of greatness. . . . The exclusiveness of Churchmen has allowed the entrance of the Nonconformist Watts, of the Roman Catholic Dryden, Couraeer, the foreign latitudinarian, Ephraim Chambers, the sceptic of the humbler, and Sheffield the sceptic of the higher ranks, were buried with all respect and honour by the "college of priests" at Westminster. . . . If Byron was turned from our doors, many a one as questionable as Byron has been admitted. Close above the monument of the devoted Granville Sharpe is the monument of the epicurean St. Evremonde. Close beneath the tablet of the blameless Wharton, lies the licentious Congreve.'

Dean Stanley rightly added:

'But it is this also that gives to it that perfectly natural character of which any artificial collection is entirely destitute.'

Since Stanley wrote, inevitably with the march of time, more heretics have had to be admitted. The agnostic Chas.

Darwin found here a grave (1882); there is a bust of the sceptical Matthew Arnold —bd. at Laleham; the ashes of Thos. Hardy, author of that grim poem 'The Funeral of God' were interred here, minus the heart which was bd. at the 'Wessex' Stinsford (1928). In 1936 W.A. received the remains of Ld. Allenby; he paid his subscription to the Rationalist Press Association a few weeks before his death. The ashes of Sidney and Beatrice Webb were brought from Passfield Corner and bd. in the nave in 1948. They were completely secularistic in outlook, more so than Bernard Shaw, whose ashes were not received in the national shrine by reason of his request that there should be no religious ceremonial.

The following are the royal burials: Edward the Confessor (1066); Henry III (1272); Edward I (1307); Q. Eleanor (1290); Edward III (1377); Q. Phillipa (1369); Richard II (d. 1400; first bd. at Abbot's Langley in Herts., re-bd. in W.A. 1413); Anne of Bohemia (1394); Henry V (1422); Katharine of Valois— after the death of Henry she m. Owen Tudor (see 'Bermondsey')—(1437); Henry VII (1509); Elizabeth of York (1503); Anne of Cleves (1557); Edward VI (1553); Q. Mary I (1558); Mary Q. of Scots (first bd. at Peterborough Cath. 1587; rebd. in W.A. 1612); Q. Elizabeth (1603); James I (1625); Anne of Denmark (1619); Elizabeth, Q. of Bohemia, daughter of James I and mother of P. Rupert (1662); Anne Hyde, first wife of James II (1671); Charles II (1685); Q. Mary II (1694); William III (1702); P. George of Denmark (1708); Q. Anne (1714); George II (1760); Q. Caroline (1737).

The royal tombs (they were but graves after the interment of Mary Q. of Scots) have at times been molested. Soon after James II's coronation, one of the choristers noticed a hole in the tomb of Edward the Confessor, and abstracted a golden cross and chain. He brought them to the dean, and he to the K., and a bounty of £50 was paid. The lucky finder saw the saint's head 'solid and firm, the upper and lower jaws full of teeth, a list of gold round the temples,' and 'all his bones and much dust in the coffin.' James had the old coffin enclosed in one strongly clamped with iron, and this remains to-day. A Westminster schoolboy removed Richard II's jawbone in 1776; it was restored

by his descendants in 1906. Whilst the tombs have been shorn of some of their adornments, the effigies of the Ks. and Qs. are almost unimpaired except that of Henry V. The head, sceptre, and other regalia, all of silver, and the plates of silver gilt which covered the body were stolen in 1546. It was not the work of 'some Whig,' as Addison's Sir Roger de Coverley suggested. The body of Henry's Q.—Katharine of Valois—was also ill-fated. It was removed when Henry VII pulled down the old Lady Chapel, and ultimately placed above ground in an open coffin of loose boards near Henry V's tomb. There it remained for over 200 yrs., and Pepys (23rd Feb. 1669)—

'did see by particular favour the body of Queen Catherine of Valois; and I had the upper part of her body in my hands, and I did kiss her mouth, reflecting upon it that I did kiss a queen, and that this was my birthday, thirty-six years old, that I did first kiss a queen.'

In the 18th century the bones were still 'firmly united, and thinly cloth'd with flesh, like scrapings of tanned leather.' In 1776 the Q.'s body was hidden from sight beneath the Villiers monument in the chapel of St. Nicholas. In 1878 it was removed by Dean Stanley to a place beneath the ancient altar slab in the Chantry Chapel of Henry V.

Oliver Cromwell was first bd. in Henry VII's Chapel (1658). His body, together with the bodies of Ireton, Bradshaw, and Admiral Blake, was disinterred at the Restoration (1660). The bodies of all except Blake were dragged to Tyburn, where they were hanged and decapitated, the heads being afterwards exposed on Westminster Hall.

Three of the finest tombs are those in the Sanctuary—on the N. side: Aveline of Lancaster (d. *c.* 1273); Edmund Crouchback, her husband (d. 1296); Aymer de Valence, E. of Pembroke (d. 1323). Notable graves of the nobility are as follows: Frances Grey, Duchess of Suffolk, mother of Lady Jane Grey (1559); Henry, P. of Wales (1612) (see 'Prince Henry's Room'); Lady Arabella Stuart (1615) (see 'Tower of London'); Edwd. Montagu, first E. of Sandwich, 'my Lord' of *Pepys's Diary* (1672); P. Rupert (1682); Sarah, Duchess of Somerset (1692); Sir Geo. Savile, Marquess of Halifax, Ld. Keeper of the Privy Seal in the reigns of Charles II, James II, and William III; known as 'the Trimmer' (1695).

The graves and monuments of the men of fame and renown in W.A. may be divided into categories (m. indicates a monument as well as grave):

Actors and Actresses Ann Oldfield (1730); Hannah Pritchard (1768); David Garrick (1779), m ; Sir Henry Irving (1905); There are monuments to Sarah Siddons (d. 1831) and John Kemble, her brother (d. 1823), both bd. elsewhere.

Admirals. The two most celebrated are Robt. Blake (1657). He was first bd. in W.A. but his body was disinterred in 1660, and laid in St. Margaret's Chyd. Admiral Sir Cloudesley Shovel (1707). He was wrecked off the Scilly Isles, and his dead body was found and buried on one of the islands by some fishermen. The remains were discovered, brought to L. and reinterred in the Abbey two months after the shipwreck. Thirty yrs. later a fisherman's wife confessed on her deathbed that she had found the Admiral lying unconscious on the rocks, and had put an end to his life for the sake of a valuable emerald ring upon his finger. This ring she had secreted ever since; it was sent by the clergyman who received her confession to Shovel's old friend, the E. of Berkeley. The Admiral is absurdly dressed, as Addison said, 'as a beau, in a long periwig and reposing himself upon velvet cushions under a canopy of state.' Horace Walpole said: '*Bird* bestowed busts and bas-reliefs on those he decorated, but Sir Cloudesley Shovel's and other monuments by him made men of taste dread such honours.' This criticism of Bird was quite undeserved; recent research has proved that the celebrated Grinling Gibbons was the sculptor of this monument, on the base of which is a representation of the shipwreck.

Antiquaries. Wm. Camden (d. 1623), m.; Sir Henry Spelmann (1641).

Architects. Robt. Adam (1792); Sir Wm. Chambers (1796); Jas. Wyatt (1813); Sir Chas. Barry (1860); Sir Geo. Gilbert Scott (1878); G. E. Street (1881); J. L. Pearson (1897).

Divines. Dr. Isaac Barrow (1677); Dr. South (1716) m. There is a modern tablet commemorating Wm. Tyndale, martyred

in Belgium (1536) and monuments to Isaac Watts (bd. in Bunhill Fields, 1748) and John Wesley (bd. at City Rd. Chapel, 1791).

Explorers. David Livingstone (d. in Africa, 1873; bd. in W.A. 1874). There is a monument of Sir John Franklin, who d. in the Arctic regions in 1847.

Historians and Prose Writers. Dr. Samuel Johnson (1784). His bust, by Nollekens, was placed in Poets' Corner in 1939. Ld. Macaulay (1859), m.; Geo. Grote (1871), m.; Connop Thirlwall, Bp. of St. David's (1875).

Novelists. Chas. Dickens (1870); Ld. Lytton (1873); Thos. Hardy (1928); Rudyard Kipling (1936). There is a bust of Sir Walter Scott, bd. at Dryburgh Abbey in 1832, and of Thackeray, bd. at Kensal Green. In 1939 a tablet was erected in Poets' Corner commemorating Charlotte, Emily and Anne Brontë.

Painter. Sir Godfrey Kneller (1646–1723) is the only painter commemorated in W.A., and he despised a grave there. His dying words to Pope were: 'My God, I will not be buried in Westminster. . . . They do bury fools there.' He was bd. in the grounds of his house at Whitton (Middx.). The monument, for which Kneller left £300, was intended for a place in Twickenham Ch., but the spot selected was already occupied by Pope's tablet to his father, and, after a long altercation between Pope and Kneller's widow, it was placed in W.A.

Poets and Dramatists. Chaucer (1400). It was made in 1555. Edmund Spenser (1599), m.; Francis Beaumont (1616); Michael Drayton (1631), m.; Sir Wm. Davenant (1668); Abraham Cowley (1667), m.; Sir John Denham (1669); Nicholas Rowe (1719), m. in the triforium; Joseph Addison (1719), m.; John Dryden (1700), m.; Matthew Prior (1721), m.; Wm. Congreve (1729), m.; John Gay (1732), m. in triforium; R. B. Sheridan (1816); Thos. Campbell (1844), m.; Robt. Browning (1889); Ld. Tennyson (1892), m. There are the following monuments of poets and dramatists bd. elsewhere: Shakespeare. This memorial was designed by Wm. Kent, and executed by Scheemakers in 1740. There are medallions of Q. Elizabeth, Henry V, and Richard III, and on the scroll some misquoted lines from *The Tempest*. Samuel Butler; John Milton; Jas. Thomson; Thos. Gray; Oliver Goldsmith; Robt. Burns; Robt. Southey; S. T. Coleridge; Wm. Wordsworth; Chas. Kingsley; H. W. Longfellow; Matthew Arnold, and Adam Lindsay Gordon, the Australian poet, are all represented by monuments. The notable absentees are Keats, Byron and Shelley.

Schoolmasters. Dr. Busby of Westminster Sch. (1695), m.; Thos. Arnold, commemorated by a bust; he was bd. at Rugby, 1842.

Scientists. Sir Isaac Newton (1727), m.; Sir J. F. Herschel (1871); Sir Chas. Lyell (1875); Chas. Darwin (1882), m.; Baron Kelvin (1907); there is a window to his memory (see *infra*). There is a monument to Jas. Watt (bd. near Birmingham, 1819).

Soldiers. The principal one is Ld. Clive, who d. by his own hand (1774). He was Governor of Bengal. The memorial was erected in 1919.

Statesmen. Ld. Chancellor Clarendon (1674); Ld. Chatham (1778), m.; Wm. Pitt (1806), m.; Chas. Jas. Fox (1806), m.; Geo. Canning (1827), m.; Spencer Perceval (1812), Viscount Castlereagh (1822), m.; Wm. Wilberforce (1833), m.; Sir Robt. Peel (1850), m. (bd. at Drayton); Viscount Palmerston (1865), m.; W. E. Gladstone (1898), m.; Andrew Bonar Law (1923); Neville Chamberlain (1940). There is a statue of the E. of Beaconsfield (bd. at Hughenden in 1881). Marquis of Salisbury (bd. at Hatfield in 1903) has a marble monument, erected by Parliament in 1909. There is a recumbent effigy in bronze. There are busts of H. Campbell-Bannerman (d. 1908) (the face has a pleasant smile—rare in sculpture), and of Joseph Chamberlain, d. 1914. They were bd. respectively at Meigle (Perthshire) and Birmingham. There is a tablet in memory of H. H. Asquith, E. of Oxford and Asquith, bd. at Sutton Courtenay (Berks.).

A few other monuments of special interest but not easily classifiable may be mentioned.

Jonas Hanway (d. 1786) has a large one, but he was bd. at Hanwell. He was a benevolent man, and founded the Marine Soc. His attack on tea-drinking was defended by Dr. Johnson. He was the first *man* regularly to carry an umbrella in L. sts. He was jeered at by the coachmen and chairmen, who saw their livelihood threatened by this practice. There

is a monument to Wm. Wilberforce (d. 1833) and to the E. of Shaftesbury (d. 1885). His monument was the work of Sir Edgar Boehm. There is also a memorial to Canon Barnett (d. 1915).

On the tablet to the scholarly Isaac Casaubon (d. 1614) are the initials 'I.W.' These are believed to be those of Izaak Walton.

Lady Elizabeth Russell. This monument, in the Chapel of St. Edmund, has made a remarkable number of appearances in literature. She was a daughter of Ld. Russell, and Dean Stanley called her 'the child of Westminster,' as she was b. in the precincts, christened and bd. in W.A. She became a maid of honour to Q. Elizabeth, her godmother, and d. of consumption in 1601, at the age of 26. She is represented as pointing with her index finger to a skull at her feet (the emblem of mortality). This gave rise to a 'vulgar error' that she d. from pricking her finger with a needle. Henry Keepe (see *infra*) started it in 1683, though he did not commit himself to the theory. Tom Brown (*Amusements Serious and Comical*, 1700), in describing a visit to W.A., refers to the lady who had the odd fate of dying by pricking her forefinger with a needle. Von Uffenbach, a visitor from Frankfort in 1710, improved on this:

> 'Pricking her finger with a pin, bled to death. She is portrayed holding her finger towards the ground with the blood dripping from it.'

The story is also referred to by Addison, Richardson, Johnson, Goldsmith and Dickens. The last had her in Mrs. Jarley's wax-work show and—for the first time—she is said to have been sewing on Sunday!

Thos. Thynne (1648–82). He was called, by reason of his wealth, 'Tom of Ten Thousand.' His assassination in Pall Mall—is shown on the monument in the S. Choir aisle. The instigator was Count Konigsmarck, who thereby hoped to obtain the hand of Thynne's bride, the heiress of the Percy family. She, however, refused his suit and m. the D. of Somerset (see 'Strand'—Northumberland House).

Spencer Perceval. The only Prime Minister to be murdered has a monument on the N. side of the nave. He is shown falling after being shot in the H.C. in 1812. Below is a recumbent figure.

Major André. He was shot as a spy in

the American War of Independence (1780). His body was brought from America in 1820. The monument on the S. side of the nave shows him, on the way to execution, pleading with Washington for a soldier's death, but the incident is not verified by history.

Dr. John Hunter. The body of this famous surgeon was first bd. in the crypt of St. Martin-in-the-Fields Ch. (1793). In 1859 it was sought by Frank Buckland and found, when he had nearly reached, after a fortnight's work, the last of two thousand coffins, and re-interred in the nave of W.A.

Carola (d. 1674) and *Ann* (d. 1680), the two wives of Sir Samuel Morland, are commemorated (nave, S. aisle) by an inscription in English, Hebrew, Greek, Ethiopic—'as if,' said Tom Brown, 'by the multiplicity of the figures they would express the volubility of the sex.'

Lady Elizabeth Nightingale (d. 1731) (Chapel of St. Michael, St. Martin, and All Saints). She was the daughter of E. Ferrers, and wife of Mr. Gascoigne Nightingale, both bd. in the N. aisle. The white marble monument was erected by her son in 1761. Death is starting from beneath and aiming his dart at Lady Elizabeth shrinking into her husband's arms. John Wesley admired it, but it has been the subject of much criticism. Horace Walpole said it was 'more theatric than sepulchral.' Allan Cunningham praised the figures, but objected to the conception.

In Poets' Corner is bd. Old Parr (d. 1635). His only title to this distinction was the alleged age of 152 yrs. cut on the stone in the pavement. This is generally now regarded as quite unproven. He d. at the E. of Arundel's house (see 'Strand').

An interesting burial is that of 'Spot' Ward, so called on account of a birthmark on one side of his face. His fame was made as a doctor when George II was suffering from an injury to the thumb. Ward requested permission to examine the affected part, and gave it so sudden a wrench that the K. cursed him and kicked his shins. Ward bore the indignity patiently, and asked His Majesty to move his thumb. The K. found he was able to do so easily, and that the pain had gone. Ward received a vote of thanks from the H.C. He generously opened a hospital for the poor in Pimlico. His private patients included Ld. Chesterfield, Gib-

bon, and Fielding. In his will (he d. 1761) he expressed a desire to be bd. in front of the altar. Remarkably successful in pushing his way to the front in life, he was not permitted to be quite so forward in death, so he was bd. in Poets' Corner. For his statue, see 'Society of Arts.'

For musicians, see 'Music in London.'

All burials now in W.A. are subsequent to cremation. Apart from the Unknown Warrior, the last body bd. was Baroness Burdett-Coutts (near the W. door) in 1907.

NORTH FRONT. It has often been called 'Solomon's Porch,' a name which, according to Sir Gilbert Scott, was originally applied to a large porch here, erected in Richard II's reign. It had become very dilapidated in Wren's time, and in his word 'much encumbered with private tenements, which obscure and smoke the fabric, not without danger of firing it.' Wren endeavoured to patch it up. In 1884 the N. front was entirely remodelled by J. L. Pearson, partly from the plans of Sir Gilbert Scott.

The figures are as follows:

Upper Tier of Corbels from E. to W., beginning NE. Corner.

Latin and Greek Learning: (1) The Venerable Bede; (2) Theodore, the Greek Abp. of C. The Primitive Ch.: (3) St. Alban, martyr; (4) St. Aidan, first Celtic missionary to England. Roman Christianity: (5) St. Augustine, first Abp. of C.; (6) Paulinus, first Abp. of York. Monastic Institutions: (7) St. Benedict, founder of Benedictine Order; (8) St. Dunstan, statesman and reformer, Abp. of C. Missions and Martyrdoms: (9) St. Boniface, the English apostle to Germany; (10) St. Edmund the Martyr, K. of E. Anglia. Medieval Learning and Science (SW. Corner): (11) Roger Bacon; (12) Robt. Grosseteste, Bp. of Lincoln, holding Magna Carta.

Lower Tier of Corbels are all connected with the history of the abbey, while those above are connected with the history of the Universal Ch.

From NE. to SW. Corner as above: (1) Monastic History, Matthew of Westminster, chronicler; (2) Printing, Wm. Caxton. Early Abbots: (3) Wulsinus, traditional abbot; (4) Edwin, first abbot of the Confessor's foundation. Royal Benefactors and their Qs.: (5) and (6) Richard II and Anne of Bohemia; (7) and (8) Henry V and Katharine of Valois. Abbots who were Benefactors to the

Structure: (9) Ware holding his *Consuetudines*, a manuscript containing the rules of the monastery; (10) Litlington, builder of part of the cloisters. Deans of the New Foundation: (11) Goodman, second dean of Elizabeth's collegiate foundation, holding the new statues; (12) Williams, Ld. Keeper, founder of the present chapter lib.

Over the Side Doorways, on each side of the windows, are four other abbots, all special benefactors to the monastery.

(1) Laurence holds the papal bull which granted the mitre, ring, and gloves to the Westminster abbots. He also procured the canonization of the Confessor from Rome; (2) Langham, the only abbot who became a cardinal and Abp. of C. He left large sums of money to the fabric, which were spent on the bdg. by Litlington; (3) Esteney, builder of the W. window; (4) Islip, beneath whose rule the chapel of Henry VII was built; he also completed the W. end of the nave as far as the towers.

In the Triple Doorway.

Christ enthroned in Majesty, blessing the Church and the World. Below, the Apostles, St. Paul substituted for St. Matthias. In the panel a procession illustrative of those who have done faithful service to God and to man. *Upon the E.*: Music, Painting, Sculpture, Architecture, Letters, Poetry, History, Philosophy—led by the Church. Two Benedictine monks, an abbot, an abp. *Upon the W.*: Three royal builders of the abbey head the procession—Edward the Confessor, Henry III, Richard II; followed by Law, Justice, Wisdom, typifying Legislation. A crusader and a knight representing War. Then Navigation, Astronomy, Physics, and Engineering, complete the series. On the centre corbel below, the Virgin holds the Crowned Christ in her arms.

THE UNKNOWN WARRIOR was bd. in the nave on 11th Nov. 1920, the second anniversary of the Armistice. George V and Edwd. P. of Wales (afterwards Edward VIII) were present, also Rt. Hon. Lloyd George, then Prime Minister, Rt. Hon. H. H. Asquith, and many members of Parliament followed the coffin. There were also present: Q. Mary, Q. Alexandra, the Q. of Spain, and the Q. of Norway. The grave was not closed until 18th Nov.; in the meanwhile thousands of mourners brought their floral tributes. The silver sand of Thorney surrounded the coffin,

and upon it was heaped the earth which had been brought from France in 100 sacks. Upon the coffin, beside an ancient sword presented by George V, was a plate engraved with the simple inscription: 'A British Warrior who died in the Great War 1914–18.' In 1921 the medal presented by Congress was placed beside the K.'s wreath by Gen. Pershing, the Commander-in-Chief of the Army of the U.S.A.. and afterwards raised to its present position in the column close by. On 11th Nov. 1921, the third anniversary of the Armistice, the permanent gravestone, of black Belgian marble from a quarry near Namur, was unveiled at a commemoration service which was attended by Field-Marshal Ld. Haig; Sir Henry Jackson, Admiral of the Fleet; and Sir J. M. Salmond, Air-Marshal, representing the Army, Navy, and Air Forces, and the Ypres Union Jack was carried in procession to the high altar, and afterwards hung in the nave. The inscription is shown below.

X ✕ THE LORD KNOWETH THEM THAT ARE HIS ✕ X

✕ BENEATH THIS STONE RESTS THE BODY ✕

OF A BRITISH WARRIOR

UNKNOWN BY NAME OR RANK
BROUGHT FROM FRANCE TO LIE AMONG
THE MOST ILLUSTRIOUS OF THE LAND
AND BURIED HERE ON ARMISTICE DAY
11 NOV: 1920, IN THE PRESENCE OF

HIS MAJESTY KING GEORGE V

HIS MINISTERS OF STATE
THE CHIEFS OF HIS FORCES
AND A VAST CONCOURSE OF THE NATION

THUS ARE COMMEMORATED THE MANY
MULTITUDES WHO DURING THE GREAT
WAR OF 1914–18 GAVE THE MOST THAT
MAN CAN GIVE LIFE ITSELF

FOR GOD

FOR KING AND COUNTRY
FOR LOVED ONES HOME AND EMPIRE
FOR THE SACRED CAUSE OF JUSTICE AND
THE FREEDOM OF THE WORLD

THEY BURIED HIM AMONG THE KINGS BECAUSE
HE HAD DONE GOOD TOWARD GOD AND TOWARD
HIS HOUSE

✕ ✕ IN CHRIST SHALL ALL BE MADE ALIVE ✕ ✕

Left border (bottom to top): GREATER LOVE HATH NO MAN THAN THIS

Right border (top to bottom): DYING AND BEHOLD WE LIVE UNKNOWN AND YET WELL KNOWN

THE WAX EFFIGIES were in a chamber

above the Islip Chapel, which has now been made a nurses' memorial chapel but are now in the museum in the undercroft. These are reminiscent of a remote period when, on the death of a famous man, his effigy, dressed as he himself in life, was placed over his coffin. James I was the last to have one. He had two—one was set up in state at Denmark (Somerset) House, and the other at W.A. Such an effigy is to be seen in a drawing of the funeral of Q. Elizabeth (attributed to Camden, and published in vol. ii of *The Progresses and Public Processions of Queen Elizabeth*, by John Nichols, F.S.A., 1788). Dryden referred to 'open presses where you could see them all in a row'—figures of Edward I and Q. Eleanor, Edward III and Q. Philippa, Henry V and Q. Katharine, Henry VII and Q. Elizabeth of York, James I and Q. Anne of Denmark, and Henry P. of Wales. Some of these have since been identified and are on show.

The effigy of *Queen Elizabeth* is a restoration by the chapter in 1760, and the face is probably from a mask taken after death, and possibly the original one. It is not likely that the Q. would have approved of it. Another effigy is *Charles II*. There is no evidence that it was carried at his funeral, which, Evelyn says, was unceremonious, and took place at night. It must, however, have been made very shortly after, for in June 1686 Philip Packer, paymaster of the works, was allowed £18 10s. 'for a press for the late King's effigies,' and Lawrence Tanner thinks the glass-fronted cupboard in which it now stands is probably the one referred to. The effigy is 6 ft. 2 in. in height, and the costume, with the exception of the wig which is known to have been renewed in 1729, is contemporary with it. It is dressed in the mantle and surcoat of the Order of the Garter. The effigies of *William III* and *Mary* are in one large case: William is propped up on a footstool to bring him nearer to his wife's height. *Queen Anne* has a pale face and homely look. She wears brocaded silk robes, and her hair is loose on her shoulders. *Frances, Duchess of Richmond* (d. 1702), is dressed in the robes she wore at the coronation of Q. Anne. By her side is a parrot, which is said to have lived with her for over forty yrs., and to have survived her only a few days. She sat for the figure of Britannia

on the coins. She left orders for the effigy. *Edmund Sheffield*, last *D. of Buckingham*, who d. in Rome in 1735 aged 19. He was bd. in Henry VII's Chapel and his effigy lies on a bier in the centre of the chapel. *Catherine, Duchess of Buckingham* (d. 1743). Mother of the young D. of Buckingham mentioned above. She is dressed in the robes she wore at George II's coronation. This effigy was made to her own approval, and was carried at the funeral, probably the last so used. Beside her is her three-year-old son, the Marquess of Normanby. *Earl of Chatham*. This figure was made in 1771, and is probably the one which was modelled by an American, and seen by Horace Walpole at an exhibition in Cockspur St. in 1773. *Lord Nelson*. This is said to have been taken from a smaller figure for which he sat; the clothes, except the coat, are those he actually wore. Maclise borrowed the hat to paint 'The Death of Nelson,' and found the eye-patch still attached to the inner lining, and the stamp which the makers were obliged to put in to show that the hat tax had been paid was in the crown.

WESTERN TOWERS. In the opening yrs. of the 18th century Wren made drawings for the completion of these stunted towers. The work was commenced in 1713, Staunton being master mason. In 1723 Wren d., and control passed to his pupil, Nicholas Hawksmoor. On the latter's death his place was probably taken by John James. The work was finished in 1740. There is very little medieval work left in any part of the Western Towers now, and not much externally in any part of W.A.

WINDOWS. There is an abundance of stained glass in W.A. The E. window is 'a strange medley of ancient and modern glass.' Some pieces of 'pot metal' remain, and there are fragments of 13th-, 14th-, and 15th-century glass. The central figures of St. Edward, holding out the ring to his patron saint, St. John the Evangelist, who is in pilgrim's dress, date from about 1490, with the exception of the K.'s head, which is later. The rose window in the N. transept was remodelled and had new glass inserted in 1722. Eleven apostles, 7 ft. high, are represented—they were from designs of Sir Jas. Thornhill. In the late 19th century the tracery of this window was remodelled. The rose and wheel window in the S. transept is the largest of this type; the stonework outside was entirely remodelled under Sir Gilbert Scott in 1849–50; the present glass dates from 1902. The subject is the Preparation of the World for Christ. Included in the many figures are a number of secular worthies: Plato, Aristotle, Aeschylus, and Seneca. At the W. end of the nave the figures in the 15th-century windows, N. and S., are supposed to represent Edward III and the Black Prince. The figures in the large window between these two small ones represent various Old Testament characters. There are also represented here the arms of George II (in the centre), K. Sebert, Q. Elizabeth, Dean Wilcocks, and the Coll. of Westminster. In the nave memorial windows to modern celebrities represent Edward III and Abp. Langham (Sir Benjamin Baker's), Richard II (Baron Strathcona's), and Henry V, with Whittington and his cat (Baron Kelvin's). There is a memorial window to Bunyan in the W. aisle of the N. transept; to Geo. Herbert and Wm. Cowper on the S. side, near the baptistry. The lancet windows below the North Rose window were replaced in 1958 to represent the Six Acts of Mercy.

The architectural attractions of W.A. are mentioned under 'Architecture in London.' Mention may be made of the beautiful censing angels in the S. transept —recently cleaned (there is a capital illustration in the book by L. E. Tanner), and of the paintings there revealed by the removal of the large monuments in Poets' Corner.

DIMENSIONS.

Interior. Length of nave, 166 ft.; breadth of nave and aisles, 71 ft. 9 in.; height of nave, 101 ft. 8 in. Length of choir, 155 ft. 9 in.; extreme breadth 38 ft. 4 in.; height, 101 ft. 2 in. Extreme length from N. to S. of the transepts and choir, 203 ft. 2 in. Length of each transept, 82 ft. 5 in. Entire breadth, including aisles, 84 ft. 8 in. Length from the W. doors to the piers of Henry VII's Chapel, 403 ft. Extreme length, including Henry VII's chapel, 511 ft. 6 in.

Exterior. Length, 423 ft. 6 in. Extreme length, including Henry VII's Chapel, 530 ft. Height of nave and transept roofs, 138 ft. 3 in.

On the night of 10th May 1941, a bomb pierced the Lantern (*c.* 1830) above the crossing of Choir and transepts. The roof timbers were burnt, and the pulpit partly destroyed. Damage was caused to the stonework of Henry VII's Chapel. There was entirely destroyed the memorial window to Chaucer over his tomb. The Deanery and three houses in the Little Cloister were burnt out. The Dean, Dr. de Labilliere, and his wife, lost everything except the clothes they wore. The Dean said he was probably the only one in Christendom without Bible or Prayer Book.

Henry VII's Chapel was restored, and re-opened in 1949.

The post-war additions, apart from Islip Chapel, are as follows: memorial to Ld. Baden-Powell, stone tablet, S. of the Unknown Warrior's grave (1947). Battle of Britain Memorial Chapel. It is at the E. end of Henry VII's Chapel, and was opened by George VI in 1947. The window replaces stained glass shattered on 10th May 1941, and a hole in the stone-work, just under the window in the N. corner, has been allowed to remain, filled in with a few sq. inches of plain glass. The window shows the badges of the 63 fighter squadrons that took part in the Battle of Britain, and the flags of the countries they represented. There is a carved walnut altar, altar cross, rails, candelabra, and candlesticks of silver, and on a lectern outside the chapel is a roll of honour, splendidly illuminated and bound. A page is turned over each day.

In 1948 a tablet in memory of President Roosevelt (on the S. side of the W. door) was unveiled by the Rt. Hon. C. R. Attlee, M.P., Prime Minister, and the Rt. Hon. Winston Churchill, M.P.

In 1949 there were placed in W.A. four volumes containing the names of the 60,000 civilians killed by enemy action in the United Kingdom. One volume is displayed close to the Roosevelt tablet. A light is kept burning day and night, and each day a new page is turned by the Dean's verger.

In 1949 there was installed a lectern in carved walnut. It was the gift of the Baptist Missionary Soc., to commemorate the life and work of Wm. Carey, the missionary and Bible translator. There was also placed in the nave, at the E. end, a register of the members of the L. police force who lost their lives in the

Second World War.

The Rt. Hon. Winston Churchill unveiled in the W. walk of the cloisters a memorial to the Commandos, the airborne forces, and submarine officers. There is a figure of each.

In 1950 the Upper Islip Chapel was made a memorial to nurses.

There was, in Latin, a list of monuments in W.A., compiled by Wm. Camden in 1598. The first guide in English had a Latin title: *Monumenta Westmonasteriensia.* It was the work of Henry Keepe—'of the Inner Temple, Gent.', and was published in 1683. It is fairly comprehensive but strangely omits Chaucer's tomb.

(See *Memorials of Westminster Abbey*, by Dean Stanley, 1876; *The Story of Westminster Abbey*, by Lawrence Tanner, 1932; *A House of Kings*, by E. F. Carpenter, 1966; *The Westminster Abbey Guide*, 32nd edition, 1953.)

Westminster (Roman Catholic) Cathedral

stands on the site of Tothill Fields Prison (see 'Prisons'); it was vacant when in 1883 it was bought by Cardinal Manning. Herbert Vaughan, third Abp. of Westminster, soon after his election to the see in 1892, began the bdg. The architect was J. F. Bentley. The first stone was laid in 1895; the foundations were completed in 1896; and the fabric of the bdg. early in 1903. Neither architect nor bp. lived to see the completion of their work. Bentley d. suddenly in 1902, when 50 ft. of the campanile had still to be erected. The cardinal d. a few months later, and the first public religious service held in the Cath. was the requiem of its founder. The type of architecture is Early Christian Byzantine. It was chosen as being less costly than Gothic, as providing ample space for ceremonial occasions, and also it enabled rapid execution. The columns are of dark green marble, hewn from a forgotten quarry from which in 563 Justinian drew the marbles for the great basilica of St. Sophia in Constantinople. Twelve and a half million hand-made bricks were used in construction. The bricks of the interior were left rough and unpointed to afford a satisfactory surface for the adherence of the marble and mosaic; this work is gradually being carried out, beginning with the chapels. The total expenditure to June 1933 was £401,684. This sum included the cost of purchase of the island site, the erection of the Cath., and its decoration, of the Abp.'s house and other bdgs. The total length of the interior is 322 ft., width 149 ft. (It is the widest nave in L.) The height of the campanile is 283 ft., and there is a passenger lift. There have been several suicides from the top. In 1925 a woman threw herself and her three children down. As a result the Cath. authorities withheld any further permission to ascend the tower until high railings had been erected round the balcony. On either side of the entrance are sculptured medallions containing demifigures of twelve Abps. of C., with dates when they assumed the office: St. Augustine, 597; St. Laurentius, 604; St. Mellitus, 619; St. Justus, 624; St. Honorius, 627; St. Theodore, 668; St. Dunstan, 960; St. Elphege, 1005; St. Anselm, 1093; St. Thomas, 1162; St. Edmund, 1234; St. Boniface, 1254. There are also medallions of four great doctors of the Ch.: St. Augustine of Hippo, 430; Pope St. Gregory, 604; St. Francis of Sales, 1622; St. Alphonsus Liguori, 1787; and figures of St. Peter, the key-bearer, and St. Edward the Confessor, to whom the Cath. tower is dedicated, bearing in his arms the model of W.A., which he founded.

The following are the chapels: Holy Souls; St. George and the English Martyrs (in a shrine here lies the body of John Southworth, a secular priest in Westminster. In 1654 he was hanged and quartered at Tyburn. He was bd. at Douai, and the coffin was discovered during excavations in 1927); St. Joseph; St. Thomas of Canterbury; also the Vaughan Chantry (a recumbent effigy of the cardinal faces the altar, and in accordance with Roman custom the cardinal's red hat hangs over the altar, where it will remain till it falls into decay); Blessed Sacrament; The Sacred Heart and St. Michael; Lady Chapel; St. Paul the Apostle; St. Andrew and the Saints of Scotland; St. Patrick and the Saints of Ireland; St. Gregory and St. Augustine. The high altar is a solid twelve-ton block of Cornish granite, uncarved and undecorated, save for the five small crosses cut on its upper surface. It is only to be seen on Maundy Thursday and Good Friday. The baldachino or canopy over the altar is supported on columns of yellow marble from Verona. The vault-ing is inlaid with mosaics of gold decora-ted with lapis lazuli or mother-of-pearl. The metropolitan throne of the Abp. is modelled on the papal chair in the Lateran. The great rood is 30 ft. long. There is a copy of the famous statue of St. Peter at Rome, representing the apostle with the keys, and a statue of John the Baptist, a replica in block tin of one by the Danish sculptor Thor-waldsen.

In the crypt is a curious chair. An inscription gives its history:

'This venerable relic served the pur-pose of the first Metropolitan Throne of Westminster; its lower part consists of an ancient faldstool used during penal times by the Vicars-Apostolic of the London district. The back part is the door of a saint's room—believed to be that of St. Philip Neri, brought from Rome by Cardinal Wiseman. The chair was first used at the old Pro-Cathedral of St. Mary's, Moorfields, and thereafter remained until the opening of this present church, at the Pro-Cathedral, Our Lady of Victories, Kensington.'

Here are the bodies of Cardinal Wiseman (d. 1865); and Cardinal Manning (d. 1892). Both were re-interred in the Cath. in 1907. There is a bronze effigy of Manning, and his cardinal's hat is here. There are four relic chambers. Amongst their most interesting contents are parts of the shroud of Edward the Confessor; mitre of St. Thomas à Becket; a piece of the hair shirt of Sir Thos. More; a portion of the body of Oliver Plunket, the last English martyr—see 'Holborn' (there is a picture of him in the S. aisle of the Cath.); and a book which belonged to Q. Mary Tudor entitled 'The Ceremonies used in the time of K. Henry VII for the Healing of them that be Diseased with the King's Evil.'

A recent addition is an altar in the Baptistery commemorating R.C. Canadian Airmen who fell in the Second World War. It was consecrated by Cardinal Griffin on 11th Oct., 1948.

Westminster, Palace of. The man in the street knows only the Houses of Parlia-ment, but they are historically a very young child, of a very old parent. The Palace of Westminster, their official title,

was in existence before the Norman Conquest, and there Edward the Confessor, who seems to have rebuilt it, d. 1066. A small part of it is crudely shown in the famous Bayeux tapestry. It was added to by William the Conqueror; his successor was responsible for further additions, among which was the great hall. This was finished in 1097, and William Rufus held his Christmas there in 1099. Accord-ing to some of the chroniclers, he said it was but a bedroom to the great palace he proposed. He was killed a yr. later. In 1163 Thomas à Becket, then Chancellor, superintended further repairs, for, accord-ing to Stow, 'it was ready to have fallen down.' It was the scene of the coronation of young P. Henry in his father's lifetime (1170). On New Year's Day 1236, Henry III is said to have feasted 6,000 poor people, when 30,000 meat dishes were laid on the table. In 1236 wherries were rowed in the hall, owing to the over-flowing of the Thames. In 1265 it was the scene of a Parliament summoned by Simon de Montfort. In 1299 there was a great fire in the palace, and the damage wrought led to a restoration by Richard II in the style of architecture of his day. He provided the magnificent hammer-beam roof, carved into the similitude of angels, and bearing his badge, the white hart. The hall is 238 ft. long, 67½ ft. broad, and 90 ft. high.

Whilst it was continually used for ban-quets (it was the usual practice for the sovereign, if in L., to spend Christmas here), it was from the very earliest days utilized as a court of law. Wm. Wallace was tried here in 1305. Strangely enough, another captive, K. John of France, was entertained royally in the same place. In 1520 the D. of Buckingham was on trial in the hall, and in 1535 Sir Thos. More. Others were the D. of Somerset (1551), the D. of Northumberland (1553), the D. of Suffolk, father of Lady Jane Grey (1554), the E. of Essex (1601), Guy Fawkes and his confederates (1606), the E. of Strafford (1640), Charles I (1649), the Seven Bishops (1688), and Warren Hastings, whose trial lasted seven yrs. (1788–95), and provided Macaulay with a subject for one of his finest essays. The hall was not restricted to state trials; when not in use for festive occasions, it was divided amongst a number of courts: Common Pleas, King's Bench, Ld. Chancellor's, Master of the Rolls, etc. The courts were divided from one another only by a low partition, and any vacant space was occupied by shops. Law and other books were sold at some of these, but in the 18th century it was also possible to purchase pictures, jellies, sweetmeats, toys, millinery, coffee, ale, etc. The courts were not removed to the Strand until 1882, and this strange association of bench and counter must have continued well into the 19th century, as in 1923 a correspondent of *John o' London's Weekly* recalled 'two fruit and sweetstalls in Westminster Hall' when as a schoolboy he went there to play marbles and other games. Foreigners expressed surprise at this. Von Uffenbach in 1710 said:

'The three Courts of Judicature are quite open excepting that in front there are enclosed seats for the barristers. One is allowed to listen to everything, but anyone who does not understand English gabble very well can hear little, being disturbed by the tumult of those who walk up and down and by the fact that there are stalls on both sides where books and all kinds of wares are sold.'

Of recent events in the Palace of Westminster—apart from politics, which is not the concern of this volume—the following may be mentioned: In 1898 the body of W. E. Gladstone lay in state in Westminster Hall, on a spot now marked by a brass tablet. It was estimated that in two days nearly 300,000 people passed through the hall. Another tablet indicates the place where the body of Edward VII lay in state in 1910. In thirty-two hours 532,000 people were admitted. In 1930 the victims of the airship *R.101* lay in state in the hall, and in 1936 the body of George V. In Westminster Hall there are nine statues (in recesses) believed to be of 14th-century date. They probably come from the N. façade, from where also came the statue supposed to be Alfred the Great (see 'Statues').

The chapel of the Palace was dedicated to St. Stephen, probably because it was first erected by the K. of the same name (1135–54). It was rebuilt by Edward I after a fire in 1298; and again rebuilt by Edward III about 1364. From 1547, when the H.C. left the chapter house, until 1834, when the palace was burned down, this was their meeting-place. The practice of members bowing when

passing in front of the Speaker's chair, has sometimes been attributed to an altar which was in the chapel; others have traced it still farther back—to an image of the Virgin which was in the chapter house of W.A. The chapel of St. Mary Undercroft, which still remains, was completed in 1327. It is 90 ft. by 26 ft., and consists of five vaulted bays with a fine groined roof, having four carved bosses at the intersection of the ribs, representing various subjects: St. Stephen being stoned; St. John being pushed into a cauldron of boiling oil; St. Katherine on the wheel; and St. Lawrence on the gridiron. It is remarkable, too, for a circular mural decoration, representing Judas Iscariot with silver coins over his head. The chapel was very carefully restored after the fire of 1834, and the walls and roof were regilded and redecorated. In the course of the work the remains of Wm. Lyndwoode, Bp. of St. David's and Keeper of the Privy Seal to Henry VI, were found. He founded a chantry in the upper chapel of St. Stephen, and d. 1446. At the W. end of this chapel is the flight of stairs where in 1910 Miss Emily Davison concealed herself for forty-eight hours to escape the census. This was the suffragette who eventually was killed by throwing herself in front of a horse at the 'Derby.' Occasionally members of Parliament are married here, or bring their children for christening. In 1924 the question was raised as to whether an M.P. who was not an Anglican could have his child christened in the chapel. The law officers of the Crown decided that no ecclesiastical jurisdiction existed in respect of the crypt chapel, and that it was solely under the control of the Ld. Great Chamberlain. The adjacent cloisters were rebuilt at the expense of Dr. John Chambers, the last dean of St. Stephen's, before its suppression in 1547. They were built 1526–9; the fan vaulting is of similar beauty to that of Henry VII's chapel in W.A. There are elaborately carved bosses with Tudor roses, portcullises, fleurs-de-lis, and pomegranates.

Two other chambers merit special mention. In the Painted Chamber the House of Lords held its sittings. It was so called from a series of mural pictures, representing the Wars of the Maccabees, and incidents in Edward the Confessor's life. These were revealed in 1800, when tapestry and wainscoting were removed to increase the accommodation. It was used for conferences between the two houses, and possibly in a room hereabouts, Edward the Confessor d. The House of Lords met in a bdg. which ran at right angles with St. Stephen's Chapel, and was variously known as the Court of Requests, and the White Hall. The latter name passed to the new palace of Henry VIII (see 'Whitehall'). The Star Chamber, a name of sinister import, stood parallel with the river on the E. side of New Palace Yard. Its name originated with the Jewish starrs, or bonds, at a time when they were kept there by the early Plantagenets. There is no reason to doubt that it had a star-spangled ceiling, but this was a typical example of ornamentation being designed to suit a name that arose from a different association. The fittings of this chamber, after the fire, were transferred to Leasowe Castle, Birkenhead, the seat of Sir Edwd. Cust, one of the commissioners for rebuilding, and by his grandson presented to George V. They are now at Windsor Castle. After the abolition of the court that took its name from the chamber in 1641, it fell into disuse, and later the tallies, notched sticks once used for keeping the exchequer accounts, were stored there. It was these tallies (specimens of which can be seen at the Public Record Office Mus.), that caused, in 1834, the fire in which the greater part of the palace disappeared. They were stuffed into a stove in the House of Lords, the fire was stoked too much, the panelling caught fire, and the whole bdg. was soon aflame. The cause of the conflagration gave Dickens—in a speech at Drury Lane Theatre in 1855— an admirable point with which to adorn a satirical invective against the Govt. He suggested that the 'worn-out, worm-eaten, rotten old bits of wood' might have been given to the poor of Westminster, but they 'never had been useful, and official routine required that they never should be.' Dickens might have found, too, a barb for his anti-circumlocutory arrows, had he known of another incident. Sir Francis Palgrave, keeper of the records in the chapter house, wanted to remove them when the flames threatened to cross the narrow gulf that separated the palace from W.A. The Dean of Westminster decided he could not do so

without permission of the Lds. Commissioners of H.M. Treasury. Fortunately this official caution did not receive its reward, and the fire was stayed. There remained, when it had burnt out, the chapel of St. Mary, part of the cloisters, and Westminster Hall.

There was much discussion as to the new bdg. William IV offered Buckingham Palace, and the Green Park was considered as a site. There was, however, great objection to leaving the river side, and the D. of Wellington expressed the view that the Houses of Parliament ought to be so situated that they could not entirely be surrounded by a mob. He regarded the Thames as a wall of defence—for conservatism. As in 1941, the H.C. sat in the House of Lords chamber (temporarily patched up) and the Lords used the Painted Chamber, already referred to. Not until 1837 was a start made with the new bdgs., the architect of which was Chas. Barry. A commencement was then made on the river wall. It was 1840 before the superstructure was started, and not until 1847 was the House of Lords ready for occupation. It was 1850 before the H.C. had a trial sitting, and not until 1852 was the new palace opened by Q. Victoria, who then conferred a knighthood upon the architect. It was not completed until 1857. The Victoria Tower—336 ft. high—was erected in 1860. The Clock Tower is 316 ft. high. It stands almost on the site of the clock tower of the old palace, which had a great bell given by William III to the Dean of St. P.'s Cath. This was recast to make its present great bell. It was known as 'Westminster Tom.' 'Big Ben' takes its name from Sir Benjamin Hall, Commissioner of Works in 1858, when the clock was made by Messrs. Dent. It was installed in 1859. It is reached by 374 steps. The dials are 23 ft. in diameter, the figures 2 ft. long, and the minute spaces 1 ft. square; the minute hands (of copper) are 14 ft. long, and weigh about 2 cwt.; the hour hands are 9 ft. long and weigh much heavier; the pendulum is 13 ft. long, beating two seconds. The first blow on the bell, which weighs 13½ tons, indicates the hour. A light is kept burning in the clock tower while the House is sitting. G. J. Holyoake claimed the merit of this idea; it originated in 1893. Adjoining the first floor of the Clock Tower is the room in which refractory members of Parliament are confined. The last prisoner there was Chas. Bradlaugh in 1880. The detention ends with the session, if not sooner terminated by the House.

The E. or river front of the P. is about 940 ft. long, including the terrace, which is 680 ft. long and 33 ft. wide. The material was magnesian limestone from Yorkshire. The whole front is highly decorated, having the arms of the Ks. and Qs. of England, from William the Conqueror to Q. Victoria, along the principal floor, and many statues, the uppermost being one of Q. Victoria. There are four floors, and eleven open courtyards. The following is a brief account of the principal apartments, omitting the destroyed H.C.:

HOUSE OF LORDS. The most ornate of all. The throne is beneath an ornamented canopy, and on the right is the chair occupied by the P. of Wales. The 'Woolsack' (the seat of the Ld. Chancellor) is stuffed with hair. The stained-glass windows which had figures of all the sovereigns and their consorts from William I to William IV, and also some Scotch Ks. and Qs. have been destroyed by bombs. In niches between the windows are effigies of the barons who were deputed to obtain Magna Carta from K. John. The galleries are available for peeresses, ambassadors, and other distinguished persons. There are frescoes representing: (1) Edward III conferring the Order of the Garter on the Black Prince; (2) Baptism of St. Ethelbert; (3) P. Henry acknowledging the authority of Judge Gascoigne; (4) The Spirit of Justice; (5) The Spirit of Religion; (6) The Spirit of Chivalry. The first and third were the work of Maclise.

ST. STEPHEN'S HALL stands upon the site of St. Stephen's Chapel, and corresponds with its ground plan. Here there are statues of: Richard I and his consort, K. John, Q. Matilda, Henry II, Q. Eleanor, William I, Q. Maud, William II, Henry I, his consort Q. Matilda, and Stephen. There are also statues of the following statesmen: Ld. Clarendon, Hampden, Ld. Falkland, Selden, Ld. Somers, Sir Robt. Walpole, Ld. Mansfield, Ld. Chatham, Fox, Pitt, Grattan, Burke. There is a tablet indicating the position of the partition between the H.C. and the lobby in the old bdg. Bellingham, who shot Perceval (see 'Westminster Abbey'),

stood on the spot now covered by the statue of Burke.

THE KING'S ROBING ROOM has a chair of state, beneath a handsome canopy of carved oak, and fresco paintings by W. Dyce, R.A., illustrative of the legends of K. Arthur. Here the House of Lords sat from 1941 to 1950, after giving up their chamber to H.C.

THE ROYAL GALLERY, 110 ft. long, is most distinguished by two huge paintings; 'The Meeting of Wellington and Blücher,' and 'The Death of Nelson.' Both were the work of D. Maclise, R.A., and were completed respectively in 1863 and 1865. In the window above the latter is still a small hole made by a piece of German shrapnel during the war. There are also statues of Alfred the Great, William I, Richard I, Edward III, Henry V, Elizabeth, William III, and Q. Anne.

THE PRINCES' CHAMBER has a massive statue group of Q. Victoria, and a number of bas-reliefs illustrating historic events in the Tudor period, commencing with the visit of the Emperor Charles V to Henry VIII in 1522. There is also a series of Tudor portraits, commencing with Henry VII and his Q., Elizabeth of York.

The Peers' Lib. has a panelled ceiling, and is lined with oak bookshelves. Here is kept the original warrant for the death of Charles I. The Commons' Lib. is also finely designed. On the walls are portraits of many distinguished statesmen. The Central Hall is a vast apartment, 60 ft. in diameter, octagonal in plan, and stone vaulted. There is a number of statues of monarchs, from Isabella, K. John's consort, to Richard III. There are also statues of E. Russell, E. of Iddesleigh, E. Granville, and W. E. Gladstone. Other statues of statesmen are Sir Wm. Harcourt, Joseph Chamberlain, and John Bright. The most recent addition is a statue of the E. of Oxford and Asquith, unveiled by Rt. Hon. Winston Churchill in 1950. There is also a bust of Cromwell, attributed to the Italian sculptor Bernini, who was a contemporary. It is an excellent piece of work, showing 'warts and all.' It was presented by Mr. Chas. Wertheimer, the celebrated art collector. On the pedestal are sculptured the royal arms. In the H.C. lobby there are frescoes, executed in 1910, representing incidents in Tudor history; and in the Commons corridor frescoes of Stuart history.

On 8th May 1941 a vote of confidence in the Govt. was carried by 477 to 3. On 9th May there was a short sitting of the H.C. On the night of 10th–11th May it was practically destroyed. At the same time the roof of Westminster Hall was pierced by bombs, and some damage caused to the interior, as also to the cloisters. The face of 'Big Ben' was blackened and scarred, and the apparatus that broadcasts the time put out of action, but the clock continued without interruption to tell the time.

After a few weeks the H.C. met in the Hoare Memorial Hall, on the first floor of Church House, Westminster. The House of Lords was then given up to the Commons, although for a short time, in 1944, a return was made to the Church House, where later a memorial tablet was erected.

On 26th May 1948 Mr. Speaker Clifton Brown laid the foundation stone of the new H.C. It is higher than the old one, and above its ceiling and below its floors there are rooms for the officers of the House, for ministers, and for secretaries. The new bdg. is Gothic in design, and the walls are covered with English oak: 'treated to give a mellow but pleasant colour.' The seats, in deference to a tradition said to have originated in the days of Cardinal Wolsey, are coloured green, and made of hide. The Speaker's Chair is a reproduction of the old one. The floor has precisely the same dimensions as that of the old House, 68 ft. by 25½ ft., but the galleries have been increased in size, and in the new Chamber it will be possible to seat 939 persons of whom 437 will be members. It is strange that once more the accommodation is so strictly limited, the number of Members of Parliament being now 624. It is less even than in the previous bdg. The Chamber is approached by the Churchill Arch, constructed from damaged stones from the old bdg. placed there, in the words of Hilary St. George Saunders, Librarian of the H.C., 'as a memorial of a night of fire and fury and of the triumph of a great Prime Minister who led his country through peril to victory.'

Every Dominion and Colony of the British Empire made a contribution to the new House, and the following is a complete list.

Aden: One Member's writing table.
Australia: The Speaker's Chair.

Bahamas: Minister's writing table and chair.
Barbados: Minister's writing table and chair.
Basutoland: Two silver-gilt ashtrays.
Bechuanaland Protectorate: One silver ashtray.
Bermuda: Two silver triple inkstands.
British Guiana: Four silver triple inkstands.
British Honduras: Minister's writing table and chair in Mayflower.
Canada: Table of the House in Canadian oak.
Ceylon: Serjeant-at-Arm's Chair.
Cyprus: One member's writing table.
Falkland Islands: One silver ashtray.
Fiji: One silver inkstand.
Gambia: Two silver ashtrays.
Gibraltar: Two table lamps.
Gold Coast: Minister's writing table and chair.
Hong Kong: One silver-gilt triple inkstand.
India: One entrance door to new chamber.
Isle of Man: One silver inkstand and two silver ashtrays for Prime Minister's Conference Room.
Jamaica: Bar of House.
Kenya: Minister's table and chair.
Leeward Islands: Six table lamps.
Malta: Three silver ashtrays.
Mauritius: Minister's table and chair.
Newfoundland: Six single chairs for Prime Minister's Conference Room.
New Zealand: Two dispatch boxes.
Nigeria: Furniture for one Division Lobby.
North Borneo: One table and five chairs for Interview Room.
Northern Ireland: Three chamber clocks.
Northern Rhodesia: Two pairs of brackets for the Mace.
Nyasaland: One silver triple inkstand and one silver ashtray.
Pakistan: One entrance door to new Chamber.
St. Helena: Chairman's chair for Prime Minister's Conference Room.
Seychelles: Minister's writing table and chair.
Sierra Leone: Minister's writing table and chair.
Singapore: One table and five chairs for Interview Room.
South Africa: Three chairs for Clerks' Table in the New Chamber.

Southern Rhodesia: Two silver-gilt ink-stands for Chamber.

Swaziland: One silver-gilt ashtray.

Tanganyika: One table and five chairs for Interview Room.

Trinidad: Minister's writing table and chair.

Uganda: Furniture for one Division Lobby.

Windward Islands: Granada, Dominica, and St. Lucia, each one silver inkstand; St. Vincent, one silver ashtray.

Zanzibar: One silver ashtray.

States of Jersey: One minister's writing table and chair and one silver-gilt inkstand.

Repairs have been carried out to Westminster Hall. The oak for the restoration came from Ld. Courthope's Wadhurst estate which supplied the original timber in Richard II's reign.

In 1948, during excavations for a new boiler house for the Houses of Parliament, a ninth-century sword was found: it was 30 ft. below the present surface, beneath what was formerly the bed of the Thames. It is 2 ft. 9½ in. long, the double-edged blade measuring 2 ft. 6 in. Part of the decoration is an ivy leaf scroll, similar to that on a sword found in Fetter Lane some yrs. ago.

(See *Parliament House,* by Maurice Hastings, 1950; *Westminster Hall,* by H. A. St. G. Saunders, 1951.)

Whitefriars. There is no certainty about the origin of the Friars of the Blessed Virgin of Mount Carmel, known as the White Friars from the colour of their mantle. It is said that in 1121, Almeric, Bp. of Antioch and Legate of Rome, brought them together from dens and caves where they had lived an ascetic life, and laid the foundation of their convent on Mount Carmel. Berthold, a Calabrian monk and crusader, is, however, regarded as the founder of the order. Their rule, which was chiefly that of St. Basil, is said to have been given them by Albert, Patriarch of Jerusalem, *c.* 1205, and to have been confirmed by Pope Honorius III in 1224. They were driven out of Palestine by the Saracens *c.* 1238, and then sought refuge in Europe. Their first houses in England were at Hulne in Northumberland, and Aylesford in Kent. At the latter place they held their first European chapter in 1245. Meanwhile, in 1241 Sir Richd.

Grey founded a house of Carmelites between Fleet St. and the Thames on land given by Henry III. Here arose a large priory which, with its garden, extended to the Thames. In width it covered all the area between the modern Serjeants' Inn and Whitefriars St. There was a large ch., to which additions were made in 1350. On the N., towards Fleet St., was the friars' cemetery; on the S. the guest hall, the cloister, the frater, and the prior's house (these domestic apartments were always on the S. side, so that the ch. protected the brothers from the N. winds). Like the Temple, the priory was sometimes regarded as being a good bank; but in 1307 faith in the security of a Carmelite priory was affronted when robbers broke into the bdg. with the aid and connivance of one Friar Judas (the name was probably a punishment to fit the crime), and carried away 40 lb. of silver stored there by a certain knight.

'They bound in an atrocious way,' says the old chronicler, 'the hands of the prior and of several of the friars, and one they killed and then took their departure. Judas also went away with them, but soon afterwards he had a halter put round his neck and was hanged.'

An incident of 1290 throws light on the abominable foulness of the L. air. The Carmelites complained to Edward I of the putrid exhalations arising from the Fleet river as overpowering their incense and causing death, but twenty yrs. later it seems to have been quite unaltered. The Fleet must have been about 100 yds. from the nearest point of the priory. There was further rebuilding of the ch., the Carmelites winning more and more land from the K., in the reigns of Richard II and Henry IV. Stow says that Robt. Marshall (Mascall), Bp. of Hereford, himself a Carmelite, built the choir, presbytery, the tall steeple, and many other parts, and was bd. in the ch. in 1416. In 1477 Sir John Paston, who had fought in the French wars, directed that he should be bd. in the Whitefriars Ch. He d. in 1479, and judging from a letter written by his brother to his mother (among the Paston letters in the B. Mus.), this was regretted:

'The more pity is if it pleased God, that my brother is buried in the White Fryers at London, which I thought would not have been; for I supposed that he would have been buried at Bromholme' [a priory in Norfolk].

In 1883, said W. G. Bell:

'On the removal of some old buildings in Bouverie Street, the north wall of No. 29 was found to be a massive structure of fourteenth or fifteenth century date, about 35 feet in height, built of chalk and rag-stone, with quoins of Godstone stone. The wall returned at right angles, and a small arched vault contained an interment.'

The late Sir A. W. Clapham, who drew a conjectural plan of the priory—reproduced in Bell's *Fleet Street in Seven Centuries* —pointed out that the interment occupied the exact spot where Sir John Paston directed that he should be bd., and the remains may have been his. Stow gives a long list of worthies who were bd. here, and it is introduced into the play of *Richard III*. Henry VI has been murdered:

'*Gloucester:* Sirs, take up the corse.
Gentleman: Towards Chertsey, noble lord?
Gloucester: No, to Whitefriars; there attend my coming.'

Holinshed, however, says the corpse was taken from St. P.'s Cath., where 'the same in presence of the beholders did bleed' to Blackfriars. The order was dissolved in 1538, and by 1545 the ch. was destroyed. Much of the priory remained to give shelter to outlaws called Alsatians, referred to by Scott in *The Fortunes of Nigel*. The G.F. swept it away, but a vault was left. It was rediscovered in 1867, but forgotten. In 1895 a Mr. Henry Lumley had instructions to sell the property. Investigations took him into a cellar which extended under Britton's Court, Whitefriars St. It had been used for the storage of coal and wood. A family named Hurrell occupied the house as a dwelling. They had been there for about ninety yrs., but were incurious. On closer examination it proved to be a 14th-century vault, measuring 12 ft. 3 in. on each side.

'Blocks of hard chalk,' said W. G. Bell, 'form the walls, and they have preserved through all the centuries their original whiteness. They glisten in the candlelight. Eight moulded ribs, of a dark stone, stretch across like a spider's web, meeting in a carved rose in the centre. The roof forms a dome, the ribs rising from the same springing level all around. Into the south-east side a corner of a dwelling house projects, for which purpose one of the ribs has been cut away and another shortened. This is the only mutilation the little chamber has undergone, save that a coal shaft has been cut through the 14th-century chalk, closed by a Victorian iron plate in the pavement. It is a typically English touch.'

There is an ancient doorway in the W. wall that was the original entrance to the vault, which is 2 ft. 6 in. below pavement level and was believed by Clapham to have been the undercroft of the prior's lodging. A tablet is in Britton's Court—on the bdg. which gives access to the vault.

Whitehall, to most Londoners merely the name of one of two thoroughfares leading from the Houses of Parliament to Trafalgar Sq., has a great historical lineage. It commences with Hubert de Burgh, Ld. Chief Justice of England, in the reign of Henry III. About 1240 he built himself a 'fayre house' on land he had either bought or leased from the abbot of Westminster, on the E. side of the road leading from the palace of Westminster to the village of Charing (see 'Charing Cross'). He d. 1243 at his manor of Banstead, and, says Matthew Paris:

'His venerable body was carried with respect to London, to be interred in the house of the brothers of the Preachers, on whom in his lifetime he had bestowed many gifts, and among other things his noble palace at Westminster, and which afterwards the Archbishop of York purchased.'

The preachers referred to were the 'Black Friars' (see 'Blackfriars'), then in Holborn, who sold de Burgh's palace to Walter de Grey, Abp. of York. The latter d. in 1255, and left it to the see of York. Edward I and Q. Eleanor stayed there twice, and there is a record of a Parliament meeting there in 1360. It was known from the middle of the 13th century as York House. When Wolsey came into possession, as Abp. of York, in 1514, he largely rebuilt it, providing a chapel and a fine hall. Wolsey's palace was in Tudor style, and apparently covered about twenty-three acres. Its N. extremity was about where is now the junction of Northumberland Av. with the Strand; its S. limit where is now Downing St. On the fall of Wolsey it passed to Henry VIII, as mentioned in the Shakespeare play:

> '*First Gent.* Sir,
> You must no more call it York-place;
> that 's past;
> For, since the cardinal fell that title's lost:
> 'Tis now the King's, and call'd White-hall.'

The name now used for the first time of this palace was derived from a chamber in Westminster Palace (*q.v.*). Henry VIII was responsible for its two great gateways. One was called King's Gate, and was erected across what was probably then called King St., at the N. end—near where is now Downing St.; the other, known as Holbein Gate, was about where is now Derby House. It has usually been said that both gates were designed by Hans Holbein the younger, probably about 1536, when he was assigned apartments in W. Palace, but there is no evidence of his connection with either. Henry VIII, who, according to Stow, added fair tennis courts, bowling alleys, and a cockpit, d. in the palace in 1547. Little was done to improve it in the reigns of Edward VI and Q. Mary. Q. Elizabeth resided there at times, and found it convenient to entertain some of her suitors, notably John, D. of Finland. Hentzner was there in 1598, and said it was a 'truly royal structure,' but added it was furnished in a peculiar fashion. In the hall of the palace some of the Shakespeare plays were performed, in the reign of James I. In 1604–5 *The Moor of Venis, The Merry Wives of Winsor, Mesur for Mesur, The plaie of Errors, Loves Labours Lost, Henry the Fift, The Martchant of Venis,* were all in the Revels Account. Under the heading, 'The poets which mayd the plaies' is 'Shaxberd.' These are on exhibition at the Record Office Mus.

Q. Elizabeth had erected what Stow called 'the old rotten slight-builded Banqueting House'—a shed James I is said to have called it. At any rate that monarch desired a better, and in 1607 he had one built, 'very strong and stately.' The K. was not very pleased with his architect, he complained that 'he could scarce see by reason of certain pillars which are set up before the windows.' He was probably therefore not altogether displeased when a fire removed it from his sight in 1619. Inigo Jones was then commissioned to build a new banqueting house, and the bdg. now so familiar to Londoners, was completed in 1622. It used to be said that Inigo Jones designed a grand new palace, and that the project was never carried out because of the Civil War, although twenty yrs. elapsed between the completion of the banqueting house and the outbreak of hostilities. J. A. Gotch, M.A., in his work on Inigo Jones (1928), has shown that the plans at Worcester Coll., Oxford, of a palace with a frontage to the Thames of 1,152 ft., were those of John Webb, a pupil, and that the work accomplished by Jones was all he was asked to execute. The hall is 110 ft. long, 55 ft. broad, and 55 ft. high. Its dignity and proportion have been highly praised. When Horace Walpole said it 'was so complete in itself that it stands a model of the most pure and beautiful taste,' he was only confirming as an Englishman, the verdict of foreign judges. Charles I commissioned Paul Rubens to paint the ceiling, and intended, it is said, to instruct Van Dyck to adorn the walls. Rubens carried his work to a successful conclusion. The sketches were made in Antwerp, but the painting was executed in England in 1630–5. He was paid £3,000 for his work, and awarded also a knighthood. The subject is the apotheosis of James I, and that monarch is being assisted by a cherub towards the crown and orb that await him. It is reminiscent of a passage from Scott. He refers to—

> 'those ancient monuments on which a small cherub, singularly inadequate to the task, is often represented as hoisting upward towards the empyrean the fleshly bulk of some ponderous tenant of the tomb, whose disproportioned weight bids fair to render ineffectual the benevolent and spirited exertions of its fluttering guide and assistant.'

James I's death brought all the flattery that the K. had so loved in life.

> 'The Angells carrying up our blessed King
> Did still with Musique his sweet Requiem
> sing.'

wrote a poet, whilst John Chamberlain

said in a letter:

'The King's funeral sermon is come forth, wherein the Lord Keeper has shown a great deal of wit and learning in comparing King James to King Solomon in all his actions saving his vices.'

The small boys—genii—which are on the other sections of the ceiling measure over 9 ft. The ceiling, of which there is a small reproduction on the W. wall of the bdg., has been several times cleaned. In 1906–7 it was taken down and restored at the Science and Art Department of S. Kensington Mus. It was removed during the Second World War, and, after some sections had been exhibited at the Chancery in Kensington Gardens in Dec. 1950, it was reinstated in 1951.

On 30th Jan. 1649, after spending his last night in St. James's Palace, Charles I was executed, in accordance with the Warrant, now in the library of the House of Lords, 'in the open street before Whitehall.' The exact place of execution has given rise to much controversy.

W. G. Bell said the tablet on the bdg. was no guide. When it arrived no instructions had been received as to where it was to be placed, so—solely for aesthetic reasons—it was installed in the centre. Canon Shepherd thought that the K. passed through the banqueting hall by way of a gallery which then existed, and through an aperture in the N. wall to an annexe which is shown on that side in old engravings, and from there on to the scaffold. Sir Wm. Bull, in 1889, conversed with a builder's foreman who had been engaged in repairing the windows. He had removed the second window from the N., and in the interstices behind the woodwork, found sawdust which he believed had been left by workmen who had removed it for the execution. The other matter of controversy is as to whether the K. knelt or lay full length across the block. Both questions can be left unanswered.

In 1654 Cromwell moved from the Cockpit close by to the palace. Mrs. Cromwell appears to have been an efficient and astute housewife. In the latter regard she had little confidence in the industry of her staff, and engaged—

'a surveyor to make in her room some little labyrinths and trap-stairs by which she might at all times unseen, pass to and fro, and come unaware upon her servants and keep them vigilant and honest in the discharge thereof.'

Here she prepared 'open table' for the officers of the army. Cromwell d. in Whitehall Palace on 3rd Sept. 1658. Charles II's reign seems to have marked the hey-day of the palace's history. Much is known of it from the pages of Samuel Pepys and John Evelyn. Into the great stone gallery anybody who was decently dressed could press their way to see the K. pass to and from the State apartments. In the privy gardens of the palace Pepys 'saw the finest smocks and linen petticoats of my Lady Castlemaine —it did me good to look upon them.' In these gardens was a famous sundial, erected in 1668 by Father Hall. It called forth, not surprisingly, some satirical lines from the industrious Andrew Marvell:

'This place for a dial was too insecure,
    Since a guard and a garden could not it defend;
For so near to the Court they will never endure
    Any witness to show how their time they mis-spend.'

Marvell is probably referring to the damage caused to it by the infamous Earl of Rochester. Bowman, an actor, and vocalist of his time, had been singing in the palace Shirley's lines commencing: 'The glories of our blood and state,' when in a drunken fit Rochester flung his arms about it, saying:

'Sceptre and crown
Must tumble down
And so must thou,'

and then flung it down. Von Uffenbach, in 1710, reported that

'a special description is published in quarto. It is made of stone and was once very fine, but now, like the garden, has gone to ruin.'

Pepys reports that in the tennis court, the site of which is covered by the Treasury, a Quaker dropped an oath, and Charles II lost 4½ lb. in weight through a strenuous game. Evelyn was perturbed by the thoughtless frivolity and looseness of the life of the palace. With the death of Charles II there the palace went into eclipse. James II lived in it, but so soon were his days numbered that he never settled down. He erected the weathercock still on its N. end in order to watch the direction of the wind, and thereby anticipate the course of William of Orange. When the 'Protestant wind' came he prepared for flight. Down the back stairs of the palace his wife went, crossing the Thames at Lambeth (q.v.). He followed a few days later. When William III. arrived in L. there was some talk of rebuilding the palace, and Wren was consulted. Nothing came of it: William III did not like Whitehall, and so was not disposed to incur expense upon it. In 1698 a great fire broke out, and the entire palace, with the exception of the banqueting house and a few adjoining bdgs., was destroyed. There seems to have been no idea of rebuilding. The site was leased out to various aristocrats. Montagu House was erected about 1719 on part of the old privy garden granted on a thirty-one yrs.' lease by George I. Dover House, on the W. side of the road, stands on the site of the tilt-yard of the palace. It was erected on ground leased to Viscount Falmouth in 1717. It derives its name from Ld. Dover, who took it in 1830.

Upon the succession of George I in 1714, the banqueting hall, which had been used as a chapel in 1699, was properly fitted up for worship. The K. presented some handsome gold plate, and attended himself. A result of this change was that more light was required. Hitherto only the centre window on the E. side had been opened, and so late as 1761 the third and fifth were still built up. It was apparently not until 1830, when the hall was restored by Sir John Soane, that all the windows on the W. side were opened. (The ground-floor windows were opened first for the United Service Institution about 1890.) Occasionally ordinations were held in the chapel, although it appears never to have been consecrated. William IV and Q. Adelaide attended in state after the restoration referred to, and the P. of Wales (Edward VII) was there soon after his marriage in 1863. Here the distribution of Maundy money took place. In 1891 the bdg. was handed over to the Royal United Service Institution by Q. Victoria, on condition that there should be no material interference with the architecture, exterior or interior, and that the ceiling should be specially and care-

fully maintained. Their collection (see 'Museums'), installed from that date, includes some relics connected with the history of the bdg. There is a fine black bust of James I, representing that monarch as far more imposing than the pens of historians make him; it was the work of Le Sueur. There are also relics of the Civil War, an old print of the execution of Charles I, and a model of the palace of Whitehall. The bust of Charles I which is over the entrance to the United Service Mus., dates from about 1815; the sculptor is unknown.

Parliament St. is of modern construction. The old thoroughfare, part of which remained until about 1900, was King St.—being the road of Ks. to the palace of W., or for coronation or burial in W.A. (see 'Westminster'). The E. side ran through the site of the Cenotaph, and when this was in course of erection, excavation for the base revealed a complete kitchen with a grate, belonging to Govt. offices once on the site. A view in 1807 shows the offices with King St. on the W. and Parliament St. on the E. Parliament St. was cut through part of the old privy garden of the palace about 1732. In 1723 the King's Gate had been removed. The Holbein Gate remained until 1759. A proposal to re-erect it in Windsor Park was not carried out. Some of the busts—of Roman emperors——were, however, placed on a keeper's lodge at Virginia Water. The Admiralty stands upon the site of Wallingford House. Here Geo. Villiers, D. of Buckingham, was b. 1627, and from the roof Abp. Ussher witnessed the execution of Charles I. The present bdg. was erected 1722–6; and in 1760, in Horace Walpole's phrase, 'was deservedly veiled by Mr. Adam's handsome screen.' Here the body of Nelson lay in state in 1806 after coming from Greenwich. There is a number of interesting portraits, including one of Samuel Pepys. The Horse Guards bdg. was completed in 1753 from designs by Wm. Kent. It derives its name from the four regiments of cavalry raised by Charles II in 1660 for the protection of the royal person. Tom Brown shows his Indian visitor the Horse Guards. The guard is the 'Queen's Life Guard,' and is changed daily at 11 a.m. (10 a.m. on Sundays) from the regiment at Hyde Park barracks.

In W. are statues of the eighth D. of

Devonshire, the D. of Cambridge, and E. Haig.

The Cenotaph was erected in 1920, designed in place of a temporary memorial erected for the peace celebrations in July 1919. It was designed by Sir Edwin Lutyens, A.R.A., who recognized that the soldiers it commemorated were of all creeds and none, by omitting any religious symbol.

Whitehall is the synonym of Govt. At the S. end, on the W. side, are the offices of the Ministry of Health—formerly the Local Govt. Board, built in stages between 1900 and 1915. In the arch over King Charles St. John Burns is represented as Vulcan; in 1908 when it was opened he was President of the Local Govt. Board. It is a good likeness of him at the age of fifty. On the N. side of Downing St. (wherein is the Foreign Office) are the Treasury, Home Office and Privy Council Office. The Treasury bdg. was erected 1846–7 from the designs of (Sir) Chas. Barry; of the rest of the block the architect was Sir Gilbert Scott. On the E. side—between Whitehall Place and Horse Guards Av.—is the War Office.

The Old Ship, the Clarence, the Shades, the Silver Cross Taverns, and the Whitehall Restaurant, being within the 'verge' of the Palace of Whitehall, are licensed by the Board of Green Cloth, which meets at Buckingham Palace.

In 1938 Whitehall Gardens disappeared. The houses in which Sir Robt. Peel had lived (from 1824 until his death in 1850) and Benjamin Disraeli (from 1873–5) were demolished. New Government offices now cover the site.

Gwydyr House derived its name from Ld. Gwydyr; it was erected in 1770, there is a link extinguisher outside. 8 Richmond Terrace dates from 1824. It is on the site of a house built by the D. of Richmond early in the 18th century.

A relic of the old palace still remaining at the time of this demolition was Cardinal Wolsey's wine cellar (it had been used, up to 1840 for the storage of records). His arms were in the spandrels of a door. Late in 1948 the cellar was removed from its original position, and early in 1949, by a remarkable feat of engineering, it was lowered 20 ft. so that it was on the original site, though at a lower level. The whole of the structure, which measured 70 ft. by 30 ft., weighed 800 tons.

It is now in the basement of the 10-storey office block which houses the Board of Trade and the Air Ministry.

(See *Old Royal Palace of Whitehall*, by Edgar Sheppard, 1902; *Old Whitehall*, by Austin Brereton, 1912; *Whitehall Through the Centuries*, by G. S. Dugdale, 1950; *Bridge, church and palace in old London*, by J. E. N. Hearsey, 1961; *Triumph of peace* (Banqueting house), by P. Palme, 1966.)

Woolwich (pronounced 'Wool-idge'), now part of the L. Bor. of Greenwich, was a met. bor. forming the E. extremity of L. County. It consisted of the three pars. of Woolwich, Plumstead, and Eltham; all formerly in Kent, although two small portions of Woolwich par. lie N. of the Thames—the only instance of a met. bor. being on both sides of that river. In 1965 the areas north of the river became part of the L. Bor. of Newham.

The name is given in Domesday as 'Hulviz'—probably only a Norman attempt to catch the pronunciation of 'Wulewic,' one of the earliest Saxon forms—but its derivation is uncertain.

The par. of Woolwich slopes up southward to a considerable height, the W. ascent of Shooter's Hill; but the old town was close to the river and alongside it, where its most primitive part now stands. There are traces of Roman occupation in the hollow and on the heights.

The old ch. is dedicated to St. Mary Magdalene, and stands on the top of a small precipice overlooking the old dockyard and the river. Early in the 18th century it was discovered that its foundations had been imperilled by the digging of ballast from the river face of the hill, and in 1733 a new ch. was erected further back. A view dated 1739 shows the two chs. standing side by side. The new one is a brick bdg. with (at the W. end) a sq. tower on which, before the days of the electric telegraph, a semaphore apparatus stood. The interior of the ch. still has its galleries on three sides, but a new chancel was added in 1885. The organ dates from 1750, and was built chiefly out of a bequest by Mrs. Anne Withers: in the NE. Chapel is a memorial to Daniel Wiseman (d. 1739), who gave money towards rebuilding the ch. In the chyd. are bd. Andrew Schalch, a German and master-founder at the Warren from 1716, when guns began to be cast there, until his death in 1776; Henry Maudslay (d. 1831), a great engineer who began his career in the Arsenal; and Tom Cribb (d. 1848), the pugilist, whose tomb is surmounted by a large lion. Burials ceased in 1855. It claims to be the first church in the country to have a restaurant and coffee bar within its walls.

Woolwich village began with bdgs. between dockyard and arsenal sites, on chalk soil in the neighbourhood of Bell Watergate; a place that retained an ancient appearance until the end of last century—an inn, the 'Bell,' stood there from the 17th century till within living memory. What raised Woolwich from a fishing-village was the establishment of the dock-yard opposite the ch. Henry VIII bought two parcels of land in the manor, called Boughton Docks; and the *Harry Grace de Dieu* (or *à Dieu*), afterwards called the *Great Harry*, launched 1514, was built in Woolwich Dockyard. Pepys visited Wool-wich on many occasions. In June 1667 ships were sunk in the river at Woolwich to keep off the Dutch. Ships for the navy continued to be built here until the inven-tion of the ironclad and the enlargement of vessels rendered the place inconvenient: it was closed as a dockyard in 1869; and, while retaining its name, it became a mere annexe, chiefly for stores, of the arsenal. Its closing caused great distress and wholesale emigration. Part of the site was sold in 1926.

According to Vincent, the institution now known as the Arsenal has a history going back as far as the dockyard's. Sir Martin Bowes, *temp.* Henry VIII, owned 'the Tower in Woolwich': which Vincent held to be one of the look-out posts placed along the Thames for the protection of Greenwich Palace, and the same as that popularly called P. Rupert's Tower, demolished in Aug. 1786; which stood beside the house (afterwards the pattern-room of the Royal Laboratory) wherein was founded, 1741, the Royal Military Academy, at the W. end of the arsenal. Charles II in 1667 wrote to P. Rupert as to certain works and batteries at or near Woolwich for better security of the river against the Dutch fleet, and a sixty-gun battery was built at Woolwich that yr. The oldest plan of the Royal Warren (no doubt a great place for rabbits once), dated 1701, shows a parapet along the river-front thereof, pierced with forty

embrasures; and in the rear of this parapet is 'Prince Rupert's Walk.' In 1805 the Warren was, by royal com-mand, renamed the Royal Arsenal. The town of Woolwich developed eastward, taking in Plumstead; and the sq. in front of the arsenal's main gate, E. of Warren Lane, superseded, by dint of traders' persistence in spite of authority, the old market-place in the High St. It was named Beresford Sq. (after Viscount Beresford, 1768–1854, master-general of ordnance) when the new main gateway was built there, 1828–30.

The Royal Arsenal area, within the walls, which were raised from 8 ft. to the present height of 20 ft. in 1804, is 350 acres. For generations the place was a great centre for the manufacture and testing of arms. Much of the site has been developed now for housing.

On the W. of the sq., Holy Trinity Ch. was built 1833: Beresford St., on the site of the Ropewalk, before 1843. The Garrison Ch. of St. George, in the Italian Gothic style, E. of the parade in front of the barracks, was first opened 1863. It was damaged in a raid and since demol-ished. Gen. Chas. Geo. Gordon was b. 1833 at 1 Kemp Terrace, corner of Jackson St., Woolwich Common: the house still stands. The Royal Military Academy, popularly called 'the Shop,' erected 1801 from the designs of Sir Jeffry Wyatville, is at the SE. corner of W. Common. This activity has been transferred to Sandhurst.

By N. Woolwich was understood the town that has grown up partly in the smaller or W. piece of Woolwich N. of the Thames, and which is now in Newham. Its history is slight. It had a tile house in the 14th century. There was apparently no dwelling on the spot in the 18th century—unless Devil's House or Duval's House, which is said to have stood till 1860, was within the area. Bdgs. multi-plied when the railway came in 1846; while the main town of Woolwich was successfully opposing the introduction of a railway, which it did not admit until 1849. The other and larger part of Woolwich, N. of the Thames, also now in Newham, consists of the place called Gallions and part of the gas-works district of Beckton. At the W. extremity of this piece, on the riverside, is Barge House Rd.; named from an old Barge House Tavern, which had a smuggling reputation. It was off Gallions Point that the great river-steamer 'Princess Alice' was rammed by the 'Bywell Castle' in 1878, and about 600 lives were lost.

Plumstead was in 1851 only a hamlet, but is now an integral part of the ever-growing suburban L. The NW. part of the par. between Vicarage Rd., formerly Dead Man's Lane, and the boundary of Woolwich par. which straggles S. from just E. of Beresford Sq. to the Eltham boundary at Shooter's Hill, was the part most rapidly built in last century: it is called Burrage Town. Burrage is a corruption, through Burwash, of Burgh-ersh. Bartholomew, 3rd Baron de Burghersh, fought at Crécy, having at one time owned the estate.

The present par. ch. of Plumstead is St. Margaret's, a handsome sq. towered Gothic bdg. of 1853 at the SE. corner of Vicarage Rd. The ancient ch. of Plum-stead (the par. ch. till 1853) is that of St. Nicholas on the low flat land N. of the long High St. and W. of Church Manor-way. The ancient ways leading down to the marshes are all called manor-ways: there is Griffin Manor-way near the station, and Harrow Manor-way at Abbey Wood. The ch. was seriously damaged by enemy action during the Second World War and has been de-molished; the churchyard is now St. Nicholas Gardens.

Abbey Wood, partly farm land as late as the nineteen-twenties, is now a built-up area. The Abbey referred to is Lesnes Abbey, the remains of which, though very fragmentary, have been excavated and laid out as a public garden in Abbey Rd.

Eltham is notable chiefly for its royal palace. Henry III is known to have kept Christmas there in 1270. Parliaments were held there in 1329 and 1375 by Edward III, who also gave a splendid entertainment at Eltham to K. John of France in 1365. Richard II, Henry IV, Henry V, Henry VI, and Edward IV, all kept Christmas there, but Henry VIII preferred Greenwich. Q. Elizabeth and K. James I visited the palace, but after that it ceased to be a royal residence and

gradually fell into ruin. It got the name of King John's Palace through confusion with P. John, son of Edward II, b. here in 1316 and called John of Eltham. Of the palace there remain only the great hall (1479), the bridge, and a few of the houses of the outer court beyond the still existing moat.

Eltham High St. is continuous with the road coming E. from Lee Green, Lewis-ham, by way of Eltham Green. Near its W. end is the par. ch., dedicated to St. John the Baptist, and dating only from 1875: it was built on the ancient ch. site by Sir Arthur Blomfield in Early English style. The chyd. contains the grave of Thos. Doggett, founder of Doggett's Coat and Badge boat-race, d. 1721 (see 'Customs'). The house called Well Hall, N. of the railway line through Bexley to Dartford, was successor to the residence of Wm. and Margaret Roper, respectively biographer and daughter of Sir Thos. More: its grounds have been acquired for public purposes by the bor. council, together with a fine old barn dated 1568, beside the remnants of a moat. At the eastern end of Eltham High St. is Avery Hill Park, the 'nursery' of flowers for the L. parks, with its hot-houses. Eltham Lodge, a fine house built 1665 for a Ld. M. of L., Sir John Shaw, is now the club house of the Royal Black-heath Golf Club (1608).

Shooter's Hill (446 ft. above sea level) on the Dover Rd. from L., lying between Plumstead and Eltham, is famous in story—mostly in connection with highway robbery; from which some think the name is derived, but it may have come from archery practice. In 1739 the course of the road was somewhat altered, to avoid the worst of the ascent and descent. To the S., between Eltham Common and Castle Wood, may be seen 'Severndroog Castle'—a triangular tower, erected 1784 by the widow of Sir Wm. James in honour of her husband, who had distin-guished himself against pirates in the Indian seas, especially in the capture of the fortress of Severndroog on the coast of Malabar in 1775.

Y

York House was originally Suffolk Place. It stood between Charing Cross and the Thames and is known to have been in existence and in possession of the D. of Suffolk in 1539; the date of erection cannot be ascertained. In the reign of Q. Mary, Heath, Abp. of York, acquired it, and apparently, although it then derived its second name, he was the only holder of that see to occupy it. From 1561 to 1606 it was leased to the Crown, and became the official residence of the Ld. Keepers of the Great Seal. This office was held by Sir Nicholas, father of Francis Bacon, and here the latter was b. in 1561. Bacon had a great affection for the house. On his disgrace the D. of Buckingham, who had coveted it, managed to get a Bill through Parliament in 1624 providing for its transfer. He intended, with the help of Inigo Jones, to erect a splendid palace in its place. All that was done, however, was to pull down the existing mansion and on its site to erect a large temporary structure for the D.'s art collections and for his lavish entertainments. In 1628 the D. was murdered. In 1645 Parliament ordered all 'the superstitious pictures' to be sold. York House was presented to Fairfax, and fell into neglect. In 1661 the Spanish ambassador rented it; two yrs. later the Russian ambassador was there. Pepys visited York House on 6th June 1663:

> 'That that pleased me best, was the remains of the noble soul of the late Duke of Buckingham appearing in this house, in every place, in the door-cases and the windows.'

In 1672 the property was sold by the second Duke of Buckingham, a condition in the deed of sale imposing upon the purchasers the necessity of calling the sts.

erected upon the site after the vendor's name. Accordingly there were George Court, Villiers St., Duke St., Of Alley, Buckingham St. All these names except Duke St. still remain, although in the case of the least important word it was for long dropped. Now a court off Buckingham St. has on its name-plate: 'York Place, formerly known as Of Alley.'

The water-gate of York House still stands in the Victoria Embankment Gardens, and is an impressive illustration of the amount of ground recovered from the river by the construction of the Victoria Embankment. It was erected in 1626 by Nicholas Stone from the designs of Inigo Jones. Stone's *Account book of Workes* (in the lib. of Sir John Soane's Mus. (see 'Museums') refers to it, and says of Stone:

> 'Ye right hand lion hee did, fronting ye Thames. Mr. Kearne, a Jarman, his brother by marrying, did ye Shee lion.'

The gate was excellent in design and the stone was material collected for the repair of St. P.'s Cath. The arms of the Villiers family appear on the side facing the river, and on the reverse side is their motto: 'Fidei Coticula Crux' ('The Cross is the Touchstone of Faith').

An 18th-century engraving suggests that the gate and the adjacent terrace were a resort of courting couples. Now, as the gate is always closed, it serves no utilitarian purpose. It was neglected, and in 1823 it was found necessary to carry out thorough repairs. To defray the cost of £300 a rate was levied on the occupants of York Bdgs. Thirteen yrs later complaint was made that the gate was almost smothered in river mud. It is now in the care of the G.L.C.

Z

Zoological Gardens. They are the headquarters of the Zoological Soc., which was founded in 1826, Sir Stamford Raffles being the prime mover in its institution, with the assistance of Sir Humphrey Davy. The former became the first president of the soc. The first headquarters of the soc. was in Bruton St., with a meeting-room, mus., dissecting-room, and offices, but in 1836 the soc. moved to larger premises in Leicester Sq., and again in 1843 to Hanover Sq. The soc., which was granted a royal charter in 1829, has no aid from public funds, but is supported partly from the entrance fees to the Zoological Gardens and partly from the Fellows' subscriptions.

Almost immediately on the formation of the soc. grounds were obtained in Regent's Park, and the lay-out planned by Decimus Burton (1827). The Zoological Gardens were first opened to the public on 27th Apr. 1828, much of the design differing, however, from that originally planned by Burton, who, in 1830, was officially appointed the architect, with the sole direction of all future bdgs. in the Gardens. In 1830 the collections of animals that were housed in the T.L. and at Windsor Castle were taken to Regent's Park.

In 1848–50 a Reptile House was erected; in 1864 a Monkey House. In 1905 a Sea-lions' Pond was constructed. It contains 100,000 gallons of water. In 1913 the Insect House was built, with the aid of £15,000 from Sir J. K. Caird, Bart. In 1910 the offices were removed from Hanover Sq. to Regent's Park. In 1914 the Mappin Terraces were opened, through the generosity of J. Newson Mappin of Mappin and Webb Ltd. In 1924–5 the Chimpanzee House was built. (The first chimpanzee baby was b. in Regent's Park in Feb. 1935.) In 1924, at a cost of £55,000, a new Aquarium was completed. In 1924–5 Monkey Hill was built, and in 1927 it was followed by a new Monkey House. In the same yr. a new Reptile House was erected. The Parrot House and Diving Birds' House were originally built as the refreshment rooms, but on completion of new rooms for the latter purpose, the old refreshment rooms were converted for the use of these birds. The Penguin Pond was designed in 1934, and the Ant Enclosure in 1935.

In 1957 the Zoo Hospital was built at a cost of more than £60,000; an Elephant and Rhinoceros Pavilion was opened in 1965. The Penguin Pool is a centre of attraction as is the Children's Zoo. A tunnel leads to a section beside the Regents Canal, which has a landing stage there. Bridges across the Canal give access to other parts of the Zoo.

The Park Paddock was taken over from the grounds of Regent's Park, a condition being that the animals should be visible to the public in the Park. Thus there is a portion which is a free Zoo.

At the outbreak of the Second World War the dangerous snakes were destroyed. The elephants had been sent to Whipsnade because their house was under reconstruction. There were no casualties among any of the livestock, although H.E. bombs, hundreds of incendiaries, a few oil-bombs and one flying bomb fell in the Zoological Gardens. The only bdg. completely destroyed by direct hits were two refreshment bars and the Zebra House. The Camel House (one of Decimus Burton's bdgs.) and Aquarium received direct hits which caused considerable damage, but did not completely destroy them. Fire bombs badly damaged the roof of the restaurant, and other bdgs. Almost every pane of glass in the Zoo was broken once or twice, in some cases several times. The two big tunnels were converted into very fine air-raid shelters and in spite of day-raids etc. there were always visitors to the Gardens which were never closed. During the first ten yrs. of the Zoological Soc.'s existence the average number of visitors annually was 200,100. Now the average is about 2,000,000. But the yr. 1950 was a record, the aggregate number of visitors being 3,013,571. This was largely due to the attraction of Brumas, a baby polar bear, born on 27th Nov., 1949.

There is an annual stocktaking. The value of an African rhinoceros is £2,000; gorillas and elephants £1,500. Tigers are worth about £600; lions only £100. A Mississippi alligator is valued at £150. At the other extreme of size and price are white mice, valued at 1s. 6d. On 1st Jan., 1951, there were in the gardens 839 mammals; 1,919 birds; 750 reptiles and amphibians; 3,109 inhabitants of the aquarium; a total of 6,617.

Whipsnade Zoo, in Beds. (opened in 1931), is an extension of the L. Zoo, where more space is allowed to enable the animals to lead a life in more natural surroundings than is possible in the area of Regent's Park.

INDEX

INDEX